Managerial Accounting

Ninth edition
Global edition

Ronald W. Hilton
Cornell University

David E. Platt
University of Texas at Austin

McGraw-Hill Irwin

MANAGERIAL ACCOUNTING: CREATING VALUE IN A GLOBAL BUSINESS
ENVIRONMENT GLOBAL EDITION

Published by McGraw-Hill/Irwin, a business unit of The McGraw-Hill Companies, Inc., 1221 Avenue of the
Americas, New York, NY, 10020. Copyright © 2011, 2009, 2008, 2005, 2002, 1999, 1997, 1994, 1991 by The
McGraw-Hill Companies, Inc. All rights reserved. No part of this publication may be reproduced or distributed
in any form or by any means, or stored in a database or retrieval system, without the prior written consent of
The McGraw-Hill Companies, Inc., including, but not limited to, in any network or other electronic storage or
transmission, or broadcast for distance learning.

Some ancillaries, including electronic and print components, may not be available to customers outside the United
States.

This book is printed on acid-free paper.

1 2 3 4 5 6 7 8 9 0 CTPS/CTPS 1 0 9 8 7 6 5 4 3 2 1

ISBN 978-0-07-122086-6
MHID 0-07-122086-0

PRAISE FOR HILTON *MANAGERIAL ACCOUNTING*

"In addition to discussing manufacturing industries the text also emphasizes managerial accounting for service industries and not-for-profits."—**Mike Metzcar, Indiana Wesleyan University**

"I would describe it as the Cadillac of core management accounting textbooks."—**Bill Wempe, Texas Christian University**

"This is an excellent text—well balanced, well organized, and up to date with current topics, including service industries and state-of-the-art manufacturing environments. I highly recommend it also for the excellent examples and illustrations through focus companies and contrasting companies."—**John C. Anderson, San Diego State University**

"I've been using this text since its second edition, and it gets better each year with continuous improvement."—**Steve G. Green, United States Air Force Academy**

"Well written with good explanations of the 'why' and 'how'"—**Christa Morgan, Georgia Perimeter College**

"Major strength is how it relates managerial accounting to the general management function and reveals the managerial accountant as an important member of the management team."—**Linda C. Bowen, University of North Carolina–Chapel Hill**

"Better coverage of service businesses."—**Chiaho Chang, Montclair State University**

"Makes a sincere effort to focus on service-based businesses." **Waqar Ghani, Saint Joseph's University**

"The book goes beyond covering the basics and organizes and integrates contemporary topics nicely." —**Harrison McCraw, State University of West Georgia**

"Well written, well organized and excellent end of chapter problems."—**Kathleen Sevigny, Boston College**

"The technology supplements and instructor resources are top-notch and very appropriate for our students."—**Marilyn Okleshen, Minnesota State University–Mankato**

"The book is very thorough, well written, and still remains student-friendly. The supplements are outstanding."—**Ben Baker, Davidson College**

"A solid, well-written, user-friendly book; can't go wrong with it!"—**Rochelle Greenberg, Florida State University**

AND NOW, AFTER EIGHT EDITIONS AS A MARKET LEADER, THE HILTON TRADITION OF MANAGERIAL ACCOUNTING INNOVATION AND EXCELLENCE CONTINUES WITH THE FIRST VERSION SPECIFICALLY ADAPTED FOR STUDENTS AROUND THE WORLD.

HILTON & PLATT

MANAGERIAL ACCOUNTING: CREATING VALUE IN A GLOBAL BUSINESS ENVIRONMENT

ABOUT THE AUTHORS

Ronald W. Hilton is a professor of accounting at Cornell University. With bachelor's and master's degrees in accounting from The Pennsylvania State University, he received his PhD from The Ohio State University.

A Cornell faculty member since 1977, Professor Hilton also has taught accounting at Ohio State and the University of Florida, where he held the position of Walter J. Matherly Professor of Accounting. Prior to pursuing his doctoral studies, Hilton worked for Peat, Marwick, Mitchell and Company and served as an officer in the United States Air Force.

Professor Hilton is a member of the Institute of Management Accountants and has been active in the American Accounting Association. With wide-ranging research interests, he has published articles in many journals, including the *Journal of Accounting Research, The Accounting Review, Management Science, Decision Sciences,* the *Journal of Economic Behavior and Organization, Contemporary Accounting Research,* and the *Journal of Mathematical Psychology.* His current research interests focus on contemporary cost management systems and international issues in managerial accounting. In recent years, he has toured manufacturing facilities and consulted with practicing managerial accountants in North America, Europe, Asia, and Australia.

David E. Platt is a senior lecturer in the Department of Accounting and director of the Center for International Business Education and Research (CIBER) in the McCombs School of Business at the University of Texas at Austin. He received his PhD from Cornell University, where he studied under Ron Hilton, and he also holds degrees from the Wharton School at the University of Pennsylvania and from Syracuse University. At the University of Texas, Dr. Platt teaches accounting to MBA and executive MBA students in the United States and Mexico and taught for several years in the BBA and MPA programs as well. He also consults with companies such as Dell and M.D. Anderson Cancer Center and has been a frequent visiting lecturer at the University of Paris.

Dr. Platt served for three years as co-chair of the Partnership in International Management (PIM), a consortium of 56 top graduate business schools worldwide, and he also is a past president of the Association for International Business Education and Research. Before earning his PhD, Dr. Platt worked for Raymond Corporation, Procter & Gamble, and PricewaterhouseCoopers, where he began his career as a CPA.

WHY A GLOBAL EDITION? AN INTERVIEW WITH PROFESSORS RON HILTON AND DAVID PLATT

Why did you decide to create a Global Edition of Hilton Managerial Accounting?

Ron: Business is global, and so is business education. Students all over the world are studying managerial accounting, and many teachers outside of the United States are using my textbook. So I asked David to help me do a verison of the book that would speak a little more directly to non-U.S. students.

David: I have been using Ron's book in my managerial accounting classes at Texas for years. And during the last decade I have been directing our Center for International Business Education and Research and have had the opportunity to teach students in Mexico, France, China, South Africa, and the U.K. So when Ron asked me to work on this project, I was delighted. What a great fit!

So what did you do to create the Global Edition?

David: Well, of course, the managerial accounting content was solid to begin with, since we started with Hilton *Managerial Accounting,* 9th Edition. So the adaptation was more about helping students from around the world connect with the text. As we all know, there is an emotional aspect to learning, and by helping the text to speak more directly to students outside of the U.S., we can help their learning process.

Ron: No one sets out to write a book for the whole world! When I wrote the first edition of this textbook 20 years ago, I had no idea how successful it would become and I was largely writing for my home market in the U.S. And while the book has become more global in scope over the years, it still had a bit of a bias toward U.S. companies, examples, and scenarios. David helped to fix that.

Can you give us an example?

Ron: Sure. One of the most popular features of the book is that each chapter is built around a focus company and a contrast company. These companies provide the context and examples for that chapter's topic. Only two of the focus and contrast companies in the regular book are set outside of the U.S.

David: Ron is selling himself a bit short, because the scenarios for some of the U.S.-based companies involve decisions made all over the world. But again, our goal was to create a text where as many of the world's students as possible would feel welcome and feel connected to the text, so setting most of the focus and contrast companies outside of the U.S. for the Global Edition was one way to help accomplish that.

What other changes did you make?

David: There were many of them. Individually small changes that add up to a text with a different feel. For example, in the opening chapter, we changed the company used to illustrate the application and scope of management accounting from Disney to HSBC. Now, The Walt Disney Company is, in fact, a very global company and brand, but it is strongly identified with the U.S. and about three-quarters of its revenues are earned in the U.S. So we changed the focus company to HSBC Holdings plc. HSBC styles itself "The World's Local Bank," and its history is part of the history of global commerce. It was created to facilitate business between Europe and Asia (as the "Hongkong and Shanghai Banking Corporation"). It then moved its headquarters to London in preparation for Hong Kong's return to China and grew in the U.S. and Europe, and now seems to be once again feeling the gravitational tug of China and the rest of Asia.

Ron: Other changes include references to IFRS where appropriate, a bit more discussion of the international tax aspects of transfer pricing, and replacing many of the U.S. companies and organizations that are cited in the text by companies based all over the world. We also changed quite a few of the "Management Accounting Practice" and "In Their Own Words" feature boxes to reflect a more global mix of companies. Finally, we changed photos to more international settings and changed most measures to the metric system. We even changed some references to the "World Series" (baseball) to the "World Cup." And we called it football, not soccer!

Any compromises?

Ron: We went around a bit on the currency issue. On one hand, with focus companies located all over the world it only seemed logical to use the currency that would be native to that company and country. On the other hand, the focus companies change every chapter and we were concerned that changing currencies every chapter could be quite confusing for the students. In the end, McGraw-Hill/Irwin polled their worldwide sales force, who felt strongly that we should stick with one currency and that the currency most familiar to students other than their own is the U.S. dollar. So that is what we did, and although it was a compromise, we think we made the right decision in the end.

Are you satisfied with the result?

David: We are proud of what we have accomplished with this edition. We are confident that students around the world will feel included in this text, perhaps for the first time in any managerial accounting textbook. That said, this is a first step, and we look forward to improving future Global Editions and to hearing suggestions from the book's users, both professors and students, about other ways that we can make the book speak to their needs.

Ron: But overall, yes, we think this is a great textbook, the best one on the market for managerial accouting students worldwide. We couldn't be happier with it!

FEATURES OF HILTON *MANAGERIAL ACCOUNTING* THAT ARE INCORPORATED INTO THE HILTON & PLATT *GLOBAL EDITION*

Relevant.

Focus Companies provide a powerful strategy for fostering learning, and Hilton's integration of Focus Companies throughout the text is unmatched by any other managerial accounting book. Each chapter introduces important managerial accounting topics within the context of a realistic company. Students see the immediate impact of managerial accounting decisions on companies and gain exposure to different types of organizations.

Balanced.

Hilton's *Managerial Accounting* offers the most balanced coverage of manufacturing and service companies. Hilton recognizes that students will be working in a great variety of business environments and will benefit from exposure to diverse types of companies. A wide variety of examples from retail, service, manufacturing, and nonprofit organizations are included.

Contemporary.

Hilton continues to be the leader in presenting the most contemporary coverage of managerial accounting topics. The traditional tools of managerial accounting such as product costing and budgeting have been updated with current approaches. Emerging topics such as environmental cost management and The Sarbanes-Oxley Act are covered.

Flexible.

Managerial Accounting is written in a modular format allowing topics to be covered in the order you want. For example, Chapter 8 covers absorption and variable costing. Many instructors like to cover this topic early in the course. So, Chapter 8 is written so that it can be assigned right after Chapter 3. A table showing the text's flexibility is in the Instructor's Resource Manual.

"It is a well-written book with numerous well-selected cases, allowing students to see the contemporary business operations and practices in the real world."
—Dennis Hwang,
Bloomsburg University

"The company story acts as a hook to get students interested in the chapter material."
—Michele Matherly,
University of North Carolina at Charlotte

"I like the mix of company types."
—Barbara Durham,
University of Central Florida

"Balanced, time-proven approach to managerial accounting."
—Michael Flores,
Wichita State University

"Illustrates service companies not just manufacturing firms."
—William Eichenauer,
Northwest State Community College

"Perhaps what sets Hilton apart from the competition is its recognition that the world consists of more than manufacturing firms and that managerial accounting plays a significant role in service and not-for-profit organizations."
—Lanny Solomon,
University of Missouri–Kansas City

"The Hilton text is very current with managerial accounting topics (bar codes, RFID, mass customization, ABC outsourcing, decision making)."
—Maggie Houston,
Wright State University

HOW DOES HILTON & PLATT 9e *GLOBAL EDITION* HELP STUDENTS LEARN MANAGERIAL ACCOUNTING IN THE CONTEXT OF BUSINESS?

WORLDWIDE FOCUS COMPANIES

Students need to see the relevance of managerial accounting information in order to actively engage in learning the material. By using Focus Companies to illustrate concepts, Hilton and Platt help students see the significance of the material and become excited about the content. Locating those companies around the world helps students experience the diversity of global business and feel a connection to the global business environment.

Whenever the Focus Company is presented in the chapter, its logo is shown so the student sees its application to the text topic.

> *"I like the 'Focus on the Company' at the beginning of each chapter and this type of boxed info throughout each chapter".*
> —Anna Cianci,
> Drexel University

CONTRAST COMPANIES

A Contrast Company is also introduced in each chapter. In most cases these highlight a company in an industry different from that of the Focus Company, but one located in the same country. This feature allows even greater emphasis on service-industry firms and other nonmanufacturing environments.

FOCUS COMPANY >>>

MANAGERIAL ACCOUNTANTS play a critical role in the operation and control of organizations worldwide. Whether operating within one country or across geopolitical boundaries, they help their employers to define and achieve the organization's goals. To help us understand the role of the managerial accountant, this chapter's focus company is HSBC Holdings plc. This banking and financial services company is a giant in the industry, with offices in 88 countries throughout the Asia-Pacific region, Africa, the Americas, Europe, and the Middle East. Founded as The Hong Kong and Shanghai Banking Corporation Limited in 1865 to serve the growing trade between China and Europe, HSBC operates through an international network of companies to offer e-commerce, investment and financial services, and commercial and private banking. Using HSBC as an illustration, we will introduce the field of managerial accounting. We will explore how managerial accountants work in partnership with managers to add value to the organization. The major themes of managerial accounting also are introduced, and we will return to them throughout the book.

Each chapter is built around a focus company, in which the chapter's key points are illustrated. This chapter's focus is on HSBC Holdings plc. The focus companies in subsequent chapters are not real companies, but they are realistic scenarios built on actual company practices. Whenever the focus company is discussed in the chapter, the company logo appears in the margin.

36

1
The Changing Role of Managerial Accounting in a Global Business Environment

IN CONTRAST >>>

In contrast to the financial services setting of HSBC, we will turn our attention to LVMH Group. This major luxury goods manufacturer and retailer has over 2,400 stores around the world, selling products under 60 brands including Louis Vuitton handbags, Christian Dior perfume, and TAG Heuer watches. We will explore LVMH's value chain, which is the set of linked, value-creating activities, ranging from securing basic raw materials and energy to the ultimate delivery of products and services. As a retailer, LVMH focuses on design, marketing, distribution, and sales. Production of most of its product lines is contracted out to manufacturers throughout the world.

Each chapter also includes a contrast company. In most cases, the contrast company will present a key chapter topic in an industry that is different from that of the focus company. In this chapter, the focus company (HSBC) is a financial services company, whereas the contrast company (LVMH) is a luxury goods retailer.

... financial goals in the *future*.

Many companies, in all types of industries, have developed a balanced scorecard to help management and employees achieve success on the company's key long-term goals. Among the many service-industry firms that have developed a balanced scorecard are Bank of Tokyo-Mitsubishi, Citicorp, JPMorganChase, BMW Financial Services, Saatchi & Saatchi Worldwide, Nationwide Mutual Insurance, and Disney. Retailers, too, have made use of the balanced scorecard. Among them are The Gap and IKEA.

Among the well-known manufacturers making use of the balanced-scorecard concept are Apple Computer, Caterpillar, Cisco Systems, Ricoh, Eli Lilly, ExxonMobil, General Motors, Microsoft, Motorola, and Phillips Electronics. Finally, governmental units have benefited from a balanced scorecard, among them the City of Brisbane (Australia), NASA, the U.S. Department of Energy, and the Ontario (Canada) Ministry of Health.

We will come back to the balanced scorecard in Chapter 10.

> *"The content provides a thorough discussion of applicable concepts and practical applications relevant to managerial accounting. It has excellent illustrations and examples throughout the chapters."*
> —Mike Metzcar,
> Indiana Wesleyan University

Professional Organizations

"You've got to know how to talk to people, express yourself. And that's oral and written. You also have to be able to understand a lot of different areas, not necessarily just accounting. You've got to understand the business itself." (1k)

Qwest

To keep up with new developments in their field, managerial accountants often [belong] to one or more professional organizations. The two largest of these are the Insti[tute of] Management Accountants (IMA) and the Chartered Institute of Management A[ccoun]tants (CIMA). The IMA, which has over 60,000 members and is based in the [United] States, publishes two journals, entitled *Management Accounting Quarterly* and *St[rategic] Finance*. CIMA, which is based in Europe and has offices throughout Asia, pu[blishes] educational e-journals for its 172,000 members. Both organizations have published research studies on managerial accounting topics. Other professional organizati[ons in] which managerial accountants hold membership include the Financial Executives In[ternational]

[13]James Vicini, "Top Court Hears Appeal by Enron's Skilling," *Reuters*, March 1, 2010; and Allan Sloan, "[Laying] Enron to Rest," *Newsweek*, 147, no. 23 (June 5, 2006), pp. 25–30.

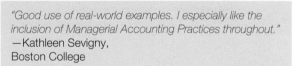

AIRLINES KEEP A CLOSE EYE ON BREAK-EVEN LOAD FACTORS

Some airlines disclose their systemwide break-even load factors in their annual reports. The Emirates Group, for example, listed its break-even load factor as 64.4 percent in a recent annual report. Utilization of that load capacity is critical to the financial success of an airline. When Indian budget carrier SpiceJet Ltd. announced that they would break even in 2009, they said "It (the break-even) will be backed by our business plan, which primarily includes higher utilization of our capacity."[1]

Load factors can be improved either by attracting more business or by reducing the capacity available and its related costs. Air France-KLM responded to the economic recession with a " . . . sharp reduction in cargo capacity and a rationalization of existing cargo assets [that] should bring the cargo division back to break-even during the 2011–2012 financial year . . . and the airline will reduce its passenger capacity by a further 2% for the coming winter season." Simultaneously, the airline attacked the problem through cost reduction: "The airline said it will pursue its cost-cutting efforts in an effort to return to break[-even] . . .

Management Accounting Practice

Air France-KLM, Emirates Airways, and SpiceJet

> *"Good use of real-world examples. I especially like the inclusion of Managerial Accounting Practices throughout."*
> —Kathleen Sevigny,
> Boston College

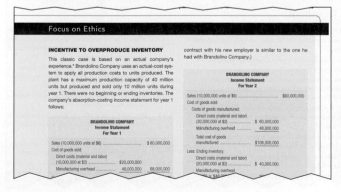

Focus on Ethics

INCENTIVE TO OVERPRODUCE INVENTORY

This classic case is based on an actual company's experience.* Brandolino Company uses an actual-cost system to apply all production costs to units produced. The plant has a maximum production capacity of 40 million units but produced and sold only 10 million units during year 1. There were no beginning or ending inventories. The company's absorption-costing income statement for year 1 follows:

BRANDOLINO COMPANY
Income Statement
For Year 1

Sales (10,000,000 units at $6)		$60,000,000
Cost of goods sold:		
Direct costs (material and labor)		
(10,000,000 at $2)	$20,000,000	
Manufacturing overhead	48,000,000	68,000,000

contract with his new employer is similar to the one he had with Brandolino Company.)

BRANDOLINO COMPANY
Income Statement
For Year 2

Sales (10,000,000 units at $6)		$60,000,000
Cost of goods sold:		
Costs of goods manufactured:		
Direct costs (material and labor)		
(30,000,000 at $2)	$ 60,000,000	
Manufacturing overhead	48,000,000	
Total cost of goods		
manufactured	$108,000,000	
Less: Ending inventory		
Direct costs (material and labor)		
(20,000,000 at $2)	$ 40,000,000	
Manufacturing overhead		

Real-World Examples

The Hilton and Platt *Global Edition* text provides a variety of thought-provoking, real-world examples to focus students on managerial accounting as an essential part of the management process. Featured organizations come from around the globe and include Samsung, Ford, IKEA, Emirates Airline, Haier, BHP Billiton, Embraer, and many others. These companies are highlighted in blue in the text.

In Their Own Words

Quotes from both practicing managers and managerial accountants are included in the margins throughout the text. These actual quotes show how the field of management accounting is changing, emphasize how the concepts are actually used, and demonstrate that management accountants are key players in most companies' management teams.

Management Accounting Practice

The managerial accounting practices of well-known, real-world organizations are highlighted in these boxes. They stimulate student interest and provide a springboard for classroom discussion.

Focus on Ethics

This feature is included in most chapters. Focus on Ethics poses an ethical dilemma, then asks tough questions that underscore the importance of ethical management. Some of these are based on real-world incidents while others are fictional but based on well-established anecdotal evidence.

HOW CAN MY STUDENTS USE HILTON AND PLATT 9e *GLOBAL EDITION* TO MASTER THE CONCEPTS OF MANAGERIAL ACCOUNTING?

End-of-Chapter Assignment Material   Each chapter includes an extensive selection of assignment material, including Review Questions, Exercises, Problems, and Cases. Our problem and case material conforms to AECC, AACSB, EQUIS, and AMBA recommendations and facilitates class discussions and projects, interactive learning, and internationalization.

Review Problems present both a problem and a complete solution, allowing students to review the entire problem-solving process.

Key Terms are bolded in the text and repeated at the end of the chapter with page references. The book also includes a complete Glossary of Key Terms.

Review Questions, Exercises, Problems, and Cases are comprehensive in covering the points in the chapter. They exhibit a wide range of difficulty, and the Solutions Manual provides guidance for the instructor on the time required for each problem. Numerous adapted CMA and CPA problems are included.

> "Homework assignments are varied in terms of types (writing, calculations, analysis, research, ethics, internet research) and degree of difficulty."
> —Leslie Fletcher,
> Georgia Southern University

Review Problems on Cost Classifications

Problem 1

Several costs incurred by Myrtle Beach Golf Equipment, Inc. are indicate which of the following classifications best describe the c tion may apply to the same cost item. For example, a cost may product cost.

Cost Classifications

a. Variable
b. Fixed
c. Period

Key Terms

For each term's definition refer to the indicated page, or turn to the glossary at the end of the text.

activity base, 89	departmental overhead centers, 104	plantwide overhead rate, 104	service departments, 104
actual costing, 102		predetermined overhead rate, 90	source document, 88
actual manufacturing overhead, 96	departmental overhead rate, 104	process-costing system, 86	supply chain, 88
applied manufacturing overhead, 95	job-cost record, 86	product-costing system, 82	throughput time, 103
bill of materials, 88	job-order costing, 85	proration, 98	time record, 89
cost distribution (sometimes called cost allocation), 104	material requisition form, 87	schedule of cost of goods manufactured, 99	two-stage cost allocation, 104
cost of goods manufactured, 99	normal costing, 100	schedule of cost of goods sold, 99	underapplied overhead, 97
cycle time, 103	overapplied overhead, 97	service department cost allocation, 104	volume-based cost driver, 89
	overhead application (or absorption), 89		

Review Questions

3–1. List and explain four purposes of product costing.

3–2. Explain the difference between job-order and process costing.

3–3. How is the concept of product costing applied in service industry firms?

3–4. What are the purposes of the following documents: (*a*) material requisition form, (*b*) labor time record, and (*c*) job-cost record.

3–5. Why is manufacturing overhead applied to products when product costs are used in making pricing decisions?

3–6. Explain the benefits of using a predetermined overhead rate instead of an actual overhead rate.

3–7. Describe one advantage and one disadvantage of prorating overapplied or underapplied overhead.

3–8. Describe an important cost-benefit issue involving

3–13. Define each of the following terms, and explain relationship among them: (*a*) overhead cost dist tion, (*b*) service department cost allocation, and (*c*) overhead application.

3–14. Describe how job-order costing concepts are use professional service firms, such as law practices consulting firms.

3–15. What is meant by the term *cost driver*? What is *volume-based cost driver?*

3–16. Describe the flow of costs through a product-co system. What special accounts are involved, and are they used?

3–17. Give an example of how a hospital, such as the Clinic, might use job-order costing concepts.

3–18. Why are some manufacturing firms switching fr direct-labor hours to machine hours or throughp as the for ove applic

EXCEL SPREADSHEETS

Spreadsheet applications are essential to contemporary accounting practice. Students must recognize the power of spreadsheets and know how accounting data are presented in them. Excel applications are discussed where appropriate in the text.

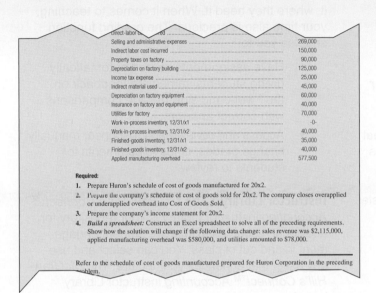

Direct-labor	
Selling and administrative expenses	269,000
Indirect labor cost incurred	150,000
Property taxes on factory	90,000
Depreciation on factory building	125,000
Income tax expense	25,000
Indirect material used	45,000
Depreciation on factory equipment	60,000
Insurance on factory and equipment	40,000
Utilities for factory	70,000
Work-in-process inventory, 12/31/x1	-0-
Work-in-process inventory, 12/31/x2	40,000
Finished-goods inventory, 12/31/x1	35,000
Finished-goods inventory, 12/31/x2	40,000
Applied manufacturing overhead	577,500

Required:

1. Prepare Huron's schedule of cost of goods manufactured for 20x2.
2. Prepare the company's schedule of cost of goods sold for 20x2. The company closes overapplied or underapplied overhead into Cost of Goods Sold.
3. Prepare the company's income statement for 20x2.
4. *Build a spreadsheet:* Construct an Excel spreadsheet to solve all of the preceding requirements. Show how the solution will change if the following data change: sales revenue was $2,115,000, applied manufacturing overhead was $580,000, and utilities amounted to $78,000.

Refer to the schedule of cost of goods manufactured prepared for Huron Corporation in the preceding problem.

Several exercises and problems in each chapter include an optional requirement for students to **Build a Spreadsheet** to develop the solution.

> *"Use of spreadsheets [is a strength]."*
> —Ralph Greenberg,
> Temple University

Icons identify key business areas in the Problems and Cases in each chapter:

Ethical Issues

Group Work

Internet Research

Business Communication

HOW CAN TECHNOLOGY HELP

 MCGRAW-HILL CONNECT ACCOUNTING

Less Managing. More Teaching. Greater Learning.

McGraw-Hill's Connect™ Accounting is an online assignment and assessment solution that connects students with the tools and resources they'll need to achieve success.

McGraw-Hill's Connect™ Accounting helps prepare students for their future by enabling faster learning, more efficient studying, and greater retention of knowledge.

McGraw-Hill's Connect™ Accounting features

McGraw-Hill's Connect™ Accounting offers a number of powerful tools and features to make managing assignments easier, so faculty can spend more time teaching. With *McGraw-Hill's Connect™ Accounting,* students can engage with their coursework anytime and anywhere, making the learning process more accessible and efficient. *McGraw-Hill's Connect™ Accounting* offers you the features described below.

Simple assignment management With *McGraw-Hill's Connect™ Accounting,* creating assignments is easier than ever. The assignment management function enables you to:

- Create and deliver assignments easily with algorithmic end-of-chapter questions and test bank items.
- Streamline lesson planning, student progress reporting, and assignment grading to make classroom management more efficient than ever.
- Go paperless with the eBook and online submission and grading of student assignments.

Smart grading When it comes to studying, time is precious. *McGraw-Hill's Connect™ Accounting* helps students learn more efficiently by providing feedback and practice material when they need

it, where they need it. When it comes to teaching, your time also is precious. The grading function enables you to:

- Have assignments scored automatically, giving students immediate feedback on their work and side-by-side comparisons with correct answers.
- Access and review each response; manually change grades, or leave comments for students to review.

Instructor Library The *McGraw-Hill's Connect™ Accounting* Instructor Library is your repository for additional resources to improve student engagement in and out of class. You can select and use any asset that enhances your lecture. The *McGraw-Hill's Connect™ Accounting* Instructor Library includes:

- eBook
- Instructor PowerPoint® Presentations (updated for the Global Edition)
- Instructor's Manual
- Solutions Manual (updated for the Global Edition)
- Test Bank
- Excel Spreadsheet Solutions
- Managerial Accounting Videos
- Text Exhibits
- Supplementary Chapter Solutions

Student progress tracking *McGraw-Hill's Connect™ Accounting* keeps instructors informed about how each student, section, and class is performing, allowing for more productive use of lecture and office hours. The progress-tracking function enables you to:

- View scored work immediately and track individual or group performance with assignment and grade reports.
- Access an instant view of student or class performance relative to learning objectives.
- Collect data and generate reports required by many accreditation organizations, such as AACSB and AICPA.

IMPROVE STUDENT SUCCESS?

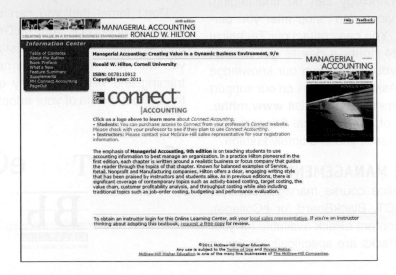

McGraw-Hill's Connect™ Plus Accounting

McGraw-Hill reinvents the textbook learning experience for the modern student with *McGraw-Hill's Connect™ Plus Accounting*. A seamless integration of an eBook and *McGraw-Hill's Connect™ Accounting*, *McGraw-Hill's Connect™ Plus Accounting* provides all of the *McGraw-Hill's Connect™ Accounting* features plus the following:

- An integrated eBook, allowing for anytime, anywhere access to the textbook.
- Dynamic links between the problems or questions you assign to your students and the location in the eBook where that problem or question is covered.
- A powerful search function to pinpoint and connect key concepts in a snap.

In short, *McGraw-Hill's Connect™ Accounting* offers you and your students powerful tools and features that optimize your time and energies, enabling you to focus on course content, teaching, and student learning. *McGraw-Hill's Connect™ Accounting* also offers a wealth of content resources for both instructors and students. This state-of-the-art, thoroughly tested system supports you in preparing students for the world that awaits.

For more information about *McGraw-Hill's Connect™ Accounting*, go to **www.mcgrawhillconnect .com,** or contact your local McGraw-Hill sales representative.

ONLINE LEARNING CENTER (OLC)

We offer an Online Learning Center (OLC) that follows *Managerial Accounting* chapter by chapter. It doesn't require any building or maintenance on your part. It's ready to go the moment you and your students type in the URL: **www.mhhe.com/ hilton9e.**

As students study and learn from *Managerial Accounting,* they can visit the Student Edition of the OLC to work with a multitude of helpful tools:

- Interactive Chapter Quizzes
- PowerPoint® Presentations
- Narrated PowerPoint® Presentations
- Supplementary Chapters
- Managerial Accounting Videos
- Excel Templates
- Spreadsheet Guide
- Company Websites

MCGRAW-HILL CUSTOMER CARE CONTACT INFORMATION

At McGraw-Hill, we understand that getting the most from new technology can be challenging. That's why our services don't stop after you purchase our products. You can contact our Technical Support Analysts 24 hours a day to get product training online. Or you can search our knowledge bank of Frequently Asked Questions on our support website. For Customer Support, visit **www.mhhe. com/support.** One of our Technical Support Analysts will be able to assist you in a timely fashion.

ONLINE COURSE MANAGEMENT

No matter what online course management system you use (WebCT, BlackBoard, or eCollege), we have a course content ePack available for your course. Our new ePacks are specifically designed to make it easy for students to navigate and access content online. They are easier than ever to install on the latest version of the course management system available today.

Don't forget that you can count on the highest level of service from McGraw-Hill. Our online course management specialists are ready to assist you with your online course needs. They provide training and will answer any questions you have throughout the life of your adoption.

SUPPLEMENTS FOR INSTRUCTORS

INSTRUCTOR'S MANUAL

This comprehensive manual includes step-by-step, explicit instructions on how the text can be used to implement alternative teaching methods. It also provides guidance for instructors who use the traditional lecture method. The guide includes lesson plans and demonstration problems with student work papers, as well as solutions.

SOLUTIONS MANUAL

Prepared by the authors and updated for the Global Edition, the manual contains complete solutions to all the text's end-of-chapter review questions, exercises, problems, and cases.

POWERPOINT PRESENTATIONS

These can serve as interactive class discussions and have been updated for the Global Edition.

TEST BANK

This test bank in Word™ format contains multiple-choice questions, essay questions, and short problems. Each test item is coded for level of difficulty learning objective AACSB, AICPA and Bloom's.

COMPUTERIZED TEST BANK

This test bank utilizes McGraw-Hill's EZ Test software to quickly create customized exams. This user-friendly program allows instructors to sort questions by format, edit existing questions, or add new ones. It also can scramble questions for multiple versions of the same test. The test bank is available via the Instructor OLC and at the Instructor Library and **Eztestonline.com.**

MANAGERIAL ACCOUNTING VIDEO LIBRARY

These short videos, developed by Dallas County Community College, help facilitate classroom discussion.

ASSURANCE OF LEARNING READY

Many educational institutions today are focused on the notion of *assurance of learning,* an important element of some accreditation standards. *Managerial Accounting* 9e Global Edition is designed specifically to support your assurance of learning initiatives with a simple, yet powerful, solution. Each test bank question for *Managerial Accounting* maps to specific chapter learning objectives listed in the text, as well as other outcomes such as AACSB. You can use our test bank software, EZ Test, or *McGraw-Hill's Connect*™ *Accounting* to easily query for learning objectives and outcomes that directly relate to those of your course. You can then use the reporting features of EZ Test or *McGraw-Hill's Connect*™ *Accounting* to aggregate student results making the collection and presentation of assurance of learning data simple and easy.

AACSB STATEMENT

The McGraw-Hill Companies is a proud corporate member of AACSB International. Understanding the importance and value of AACSB accreditation, *Managerial Accounting* 9e Global Edition recognizes the curricula guidelines detailed in the AACSB standards for business accreditation by connecting selected questions in the test bank to the six general knowledge and skill guidelines in the AACSB standards.

The statements contained in *Managerial Accounting* 9e Global Edition are provided only as a guide for the users of this textbook. The AACSB leaves content coverage and assessment within the purview of individual schools, the mis-

sion of the school, and the faculty. *Managerial Accounting* 9e Global Edition and the teaching package make no claim of any specific AACSB qualification or evaluation, we have within *Managerial Accounting* 9e Global Edition labeled selected questions according to the six general knowledge and skills areas.

SUPPLEMENTS FOR STUDENTS

MCGRAW-HILL'S CONNECT™ PLUS ACCOUNTING

This integrates all of the text's multimedia resources. Students can obtain state-of-the-art study aids, including an online version of the text.

> *"The book is very thorough, well-written, and still remains student-friendly. The supplements are outstanding."*
> —Ben Baker,
> Davidson College

MCGRAW-HILL'S CONNECT™ ACCOUNTING

This Web-based software duplicates problem structures directly from the end-of-chapter material in the textbook. It uses algorithms to provide a limitless supply of self-graded practice for students. It shows students where they made errors. All applicable Exercises and Problems are available with *McGraw-Hill's Connect™ Accounting*.

NARRATED POWERPOINT PRESENTATIONS
(Available on the Online Learning Center)
These PowerPoint slides cover key chapter topics in an audio-narrated presentation to help students learn.

> *"The technology supplements and instructor resources are top notch, and very appropriate for our students."*
> —Marilyn Okleshen,
> Minnesota State University–Mankato

> *"There is an excellent set of pertinent videos online which are related to the chapters. The videos bring the student into the workplace."*
> —Mike Metzcar,
> Indiana Wesleyan University

STUDY GUIDE
ISBN-10: 007317564   **ISBN-13: 9780077317560**
This proactive guide incorporates many of the accounting skills essential to student success. Each chapter contains a review and explanation of the chapter's learning objectives, as well as multiple-choice problems and short exercises.

ONLINE LEARNING CENTER (OLC)
www.mhhe.com/hilton 9e
See page 15 for details.

> *""It has good content and great supporting materials, especially for students who must miss class from time to time, and want to study on their own."*
> —Roy Regel,
> University of Montana at Missoula

> *"It provides good support in the way of solution manual, test bank and PowerPoints."*
> —Maggie Houston,
> Wright State University

ACKNOWLEDGMENTS

This Global Edition would not exist without Hilton, *Managerial Accounting*, 9e. Accordingly, we would like to express our appreciation to the many people who have provided assistance in the development of that textbook over many years and nine editions. The professors who have provided reviews are listed below.

Our gratitude also goes to the thousands of managerial accounting students we have had the privilege to teach over many years. Their enthusiasm, comments, and questions have challenged us to clarify our thinking about many topics in managerial accounting.

HILTON, *MANAGERIAL ACCOUNTING*, NINTH EDITION REVIEWERS

Phillip Blanchard, *The University of Arizona*
Linda Brown, *St. Ambrose University*
Russell Calk, *New Mexico State University*
Chiaho Chang, *Montclair State University*
Anna Cianci, *Drexel University*
Deb Cosgrove, *University of Nebraska at Lincoln*

William Eichenauer, *Northwest State Community College*
Amanda Farmer, *University of Georgia*
Leslie Fletcher, *Georgia Southern University*
Waqar Ghani, *Saint Joseph's University*
Marybeth Govan, *Sinclair Community College*
Ralph Greenberg, *Temple University*
Rochelle Greenberg, *Florida State University*
Maggie Houston, *Wright State University*
Dennis Hwang, *Bloomsburg University*

Mike Metzcar, *Indiana Wesleyan University*
Christa Morgan, *Georgia Perimeter College*
David Platt, *University of Texas at Austin*
Karl Putnam, *University of Texas at El Paso*
Casey Rowe, *Purdue University, West Lafayette*
Kathleen Sevigny, *Boston College*

PAST EDITION REVIEWERS

John C. Anderson, *San Diego State University*
Jeffrey Archambault, *Marshall University*
Florence Atiase, *University of Texas at Austin*
Rowland Atiase, *University of Texas at Austin*
Ben Baker, *Davidson College*
K. R. Balachandran, *Stern School of Business, New York University*
Frederick Bardo, *Shippensburg University*
Joseph Beams, *University of New Orleans*
Michael Blue, *Bloomsburg University*
Linda Bowen, *University of North Carolina*
Richard Brody, *University of New Haven*
Wayne Bremser, *Villanova University*
Richard Campbell, *University of Rio Grande*
Gyan Chandra, *Miami University*
Marilyn Ciolino, *Delgado Community College*
Paul Copley, *James Madison University*
Maureen Crane, *California State University, Fresno*
Stephen Dempsey, *University of Vermont*
Patricia Derrick, *George Washington University*
Martha Doran, *San Diego State University*
Allan Drebin, *Northwestern University*
Barbara Durham, *University of Central Florida*
James Emig, *Villanova University*
Robert Eskew, *Purdue University*
Andrew Felo, *Pennsylvania State University at Great Valley*

Michael Flores, *Wichita State University*
Kimberly Frank, *University of Nevada at Las Vegas*
Alan Friedberg, *Florida Atlantic University*
Steve G. Green, *United States Air Force Academy*
Edward Goodhart, *Shippensburg University*
Denise Guithues Amrhein, *Saint Louis University*
Sueann Hely, *West Kentucky Community & Technical College*
Susan B. Hughes, *University of Vermont*
Paul Juras, *Wake Forest University*
Sherrie Koechling, *Lincoln University*
Stacey Konesky, *Kent State University*
Christy Larkin, *Bacone College*
James Lasseter, Jr. *University of South Florida*
Angelo Luciano, *Columbia College*
Lois Mahoney, *Eastern Michigan University*
Ana Marques, *University of Texas at Austin*
Scott Martens, *University of Minnesota*
Maureen Mascha, *Marquette University*
Michele Matherly, *University of North Carolina at Charlotte*
Harrison McCraw, *State University of West Georgia*
Sanjay Mehrotra, *Northwestern University*
Jamshed Mistry, *Worcester Polytechnic Institute*
Hamid Mohammadi, *St. Xavier University*

Cynthia Nye, *Bellevue University*
Marilyn Okleshen, *Minnesota State University*
Mohamed Onsi, *Syracuse University*
Samuel Phillips, *Shenandoah University*
Thomas H. Ramsey, *Wake Forest University*
Frederick Rankin, *Washington University*
Roy Regel, *University of Montana at Missoula*
Laura Rickett, *Kent State University*
Don Samelson, *Colorado State University*
Angela Sandberg, *Jacksonville State University*
Rebecca Sawyer, *University of North Carolina at Wilmington*
Pamela Schwer, *St. Xavier University*
Thomas Selling, *Thunderbird, the Garvin School of International Management*
Lanny Solomon, *University of Missouri at Kansas City*
Lynda Thoman, *Purdue University*
Wendy Tietz, *Kent State University*
Ralph Tower, *Wake Forest University*
Mark Turner, *Stephen F. Austin State University*
Michael Tyler, *Barry University*
Bill Wempe, *Texas Christian University*
James Williamson, *San Diego State University*
Priscilla Wisner, *Thunderbird, the Garvin School of International Management*
Richard Young, *Ohio State University*

We want to thank *Ilene Persoff* and *Beth Woods* for their thorough checking of the text and solutions manual for accuracy and completeness.

The supplements are a great deal of work to prepare. We appreciate the efforts of those who developed them, since these valuable aids make teaching the course easier for everyone who uses the text. *Leslie Fletcher of Georgia Southern University* prepared the Test Bank. *Anna Cianci of Drexel University* prepared the Instructor's Manual. *Suzanne Gradisher of University of Akron* prepared the PowerPoint slides. *Douglas deVidal of the University of Texas at Austin* wrote the Study Guide. *Linda Schain of Hofstra University* prepared the Excel Spreadsheet templates and solutions. *Julia Shapland of University of Illinois at Urbana-Champaign* authored the online quizzes. We thank *Rochelle Greenberg of Florida State University* for her thorough accuracy checking of the Test Bank, Quizzes, and PowerPoints, and *LuAnn Bean of Florida Institute of Technology* for accuracy checking the Instructor's Manual.

We acknowledge the Institute of Management Accountants for permission to use problems from Certified Management Accountant (CMA) examinations. We also acknowledge the American Institute of Certified Public Accountants for permission to use problems from the Uniform CPA Examinations, Questions, and Unofficial Answers. We are indebted to *Professors Roland Minch, Michael Maher, and David Solomons* for allowing the use of their case materials in the text. The sources for the actual company information in Chapters 1 and 2 regarding HSBC Holdings plc, LVMH Group, AirAsia Group, Caterpillar Inc., and Wal-Mart Stores, Inc. are the companies' Web sites and published annual reports.

Finally, we wish to express our gratitude to the fine people at McGraw-Hill/Irwin who so professionally guided this book through the publication process. In particular, we wish to acknowledge *Donna Dillon, Tim Vertovec, Stewart Mattson, Craig Leonard, Lori Koetters, Michelle Gardner, Joanne Mennemeier, Allison Souter, Kathleen Klehr, Katie Jones, Christine Vaughan, Laurie Entringer, Jeremy Cheshareck, Michael McCormick, Joyce Chapetto,* and *Greg Bates.*

Ronald W. Hilton
David E. Platt

Brief Contents

Contents

Note: Entries printed in blue denote topics that emphasize contemporary issues in managerial accounting and cost management.

3 Product Costing and Cost Accumulation in a Batch Production Environment **115**

**6 Activity Analysis, Cost Behavior, and
Cost Estimation 267**

7 Cost-Volume-Profit Analysis 309

11 Flexible Budgeting and the Management of Overhead and Support Activity Costs *493*

12 Responsibility Accounting, Quality Control, and Environmental Cost Management *539*

13   Investment Centers and Transfer Pricing   **581**

Managerial Accounting

MANAGERIAL ACCOUNTANTS play a critical role in the operation and control of organizations worldwide. Whether operating within one country or across geopolitical boundaries, they help their employers to define and achieve the organization's goals. To help us understand the role of the managerial accountant, this chapter's focus company is HSBC Holdings plc. This banking and financial services company is a giant in the industry, with offices in 88 countries throughout the Asia-Pacific region, Africa, the Americas, Europe, and the Middle East. Founded as The Hong Kong and Shanghai Banking Corporation Limited in 1865 to serve the growing trade between China and Europe, HSBC operates through an international network of companies to offer e-commerce, investment and financial services, and commercial and private banking. Using HSBC as an illustration, we will introduce the field of managerial accounting. We will explore how managerial accountants work in partnership with managers to add value to the organization. The major themes of managerial accounting also are introduced, and we will return to them throughout the book.

HSBC

Each chapter is built around a focus company, in which the chapter's key points are illustrated. This chapter's focus is on HSBC Holdings plc. The focus companies in subsequent chapters are not real companies, but they are realistic scenarios built on actual company practices. Whenever the focus company is discussed in the chapter, the company logo appears in the margin.

1

The Changing Role of Managerial Accounting in a Global Business Environment

In contrast to the financial services setting of HSBC, we will turn our attention to LVMH Group. This major luxury goods manufacturer and retailer has over 2,400 stores around the world, selling products under 60 brands including Louis Vuitton handbags, Christian Dior perfume, and TAG Heuer watches. We will explore LVMH's value chain, which is the set of linked, value-creating activities, ranging from securing basic raw materials and energy to the ultimate delivery of products and services. As a retailer, LVMH focuses on design, marketing, distribution, and sales. Production of most of its product lines is contracted out to manufacturers throughout the world.

HSBC

Each chapter also includes a contrast company. In most cases, the contrast company will present a key chapter topic in an industry that is different from that of the focus company. In this chapter, the focus company (HSBC) is a financial services company, whereas the contrast company (LVMH) is a luxury goods retailer.

1 Define managerial accounting and describe its role in the management process.

2 Explain four fundamental management processes that help organizations attain their goals.

Learning Objectives highlight the key topics to be covered in the chapter. They are repeated in the margin of the text where they are discussed. Also, each end-of-chapter assignment lists its learning objectives in the margin.

3 List and describe five objectives of managerial accounting activity.

4 Explain the major differences between managerial and financial accounting.

5 Explain where managerial accountants are located in a global organization, in terms of formal structure, deployment in cross-functional teams, and physical location.

6 Describe the roles of an organization's chief financial officer (CFO) or controller/comptroller, treasurer, and internal auditor.

7 Briefly describe some of the major contemporary themes in managerial accounting.

8 Understand and explain the concepts of strategic cost management and the value chain.

9 Understand the ethical responsibilities of a managerial accountant.

10 Discuss the professional organizations, certification process, and ethical standards in the field of managerial accounting.

Many different kinds of organizations affect our daily lives. Manufacturers, retailers, service industry firms, agribusiness companies, nonprofit organizations, and government agencies provide us with a vast array of goods and services. All of these organizations have two things in common. First, every organization has a set of *goals* or objectives. An airline, such as Quantas or South African Airways, might specify profitability and customer service as its goals. The Hong Kong Police Force's goals would include public safety and security coupled with cost minimization. Second, in pursuing an organization's goals, managers need *information*. The information needs of management range across financial, production, marketing, legal, and environmental issues. Generally, the larger the organization is, the greater is management's need for information.

Learning Objective 1

Define managerial accounting and describe its role in the management process.

Managerial accounting is the process of identifying, measuring, analyzing, interpreting, and communicating information in pursuit of an organization's goals. Managerial accounting is an integral part of the management process, and managerial accountants are important strategic partners in an organization's domestic and international management teams.

In this chapter, we will explore the role of managerial accounting within the overall management process. In the remaining chapters, we will expand our study by exploring the many concepts and tools used in managerial accounting.

Managerial Accounting: A Business Partnership with Management

The role of managerial accounting is very different now than it was years ago. In the past, managerial accountants operated in a strictly staff capacity, usually physically separated from the managers for whom they provided reports and information. Now, managerial accountants serve as internal business consultants, working side-by-side in cross-functional teams with managers from all areas of the organization. Rather than isolate managerial accountants in a separate accounting department, companies now tend to locate them in the operating departments where they are working with other managers to make decisions and resolve operational problems. Managerial accountants take on leadership roles on their teams and are sought out for the valuable information they provide. The role of the accountant in leading-edge companies "has been transformed from number cruncher and financial historian to being business partner and trusted advisor."[2]

An organization's management team, on which managerial accountants play an integral role, seeks to create value for the organization by managing resources, activities, and people to achieve the organization's goals effectively.

> "We are looked upon as business advisors, more than just accountants, and that has a lot to do with the additional analysis and the forward-looking goals we are setting." (1a)[1]
> **Caterpillar**

Managing Resources, Activities, and People

The owners, directors, or trustees of an organization set its goals, often with the help of management. For example, HSBC Holdings plc's goals are set by its board of directors, who are elected by the company's shareholders. The overall goal of HSBC, according to its Investor Relations Web site, may be expressed as a commitment to building its banking and financial products businesses through profitable investment in fast-growing emerging markets, with a focus on international connectivity.[3]

In pursuing its goals, an organization acquires *resources*, hires *people*, and then engages in an organized set of *activities*. It is up to the management team to make the best use of the organization's resources, activities, and people in achieving the organization's goals. The day-to-day work of the management team comprises four activities:

- Decision making
- Planning
- Directing operational activities
- Controlling

HSBC

> **Learning Objective 2**
>
> Explain four fundamental management processes that help organizations attain their goals.

Decision Making

Several years ago, HSBC's board of directors decided that one of the company's growth objectives should be to concentrate on expansion in fast-growing emerging economies. It was not immediately clear, however, what would be the best way to accomplish that goal. Would it be best to expand in the relatively strong economies of the so-called BRIC nations (Brazil, Russia, India, China)? Or should HSBC perhaps build on its historical strength in Asia and target the fast-growing economies in that region, such as Vietnam and Indonesia? Should the company target large companies or consider microfinance to help promote sustainable entrepreneurship in the economies? And what about the challenges and opportunities of Islamic

---

[1] *In Their Own Words* Throughout the text, you will find these quotes from both practicing managers and managerial accountants. Collectively they portray the important role managerial accounting plays in today's dynamic business environment. The references for these quotes appear at the end of the text, beginning on page 820. The references are organized by chapter; thus reference, (1a) relates to the first quote in Chapter 1, and so forth.

[2] Gary Siegel, "The Image of Corporate Accountants," *Strategic Finance* 82, no. 2 (August 2000), p. 71.

[3] HSBC Holdings plc, which is discussed in this chapter, is, of course, a real company. However, the subsequent focus organizations around which chapters are built are not real organizations. They are, however, realistic settings in which to discuss business and managerial accounting issues. In most cases, they are based on real organizations. Similarly, each chapter includes a discussion of a contrast company. Some of these contrast companies, such as luxury goods retailer LVMH Group in this chapter, are real companies. Others, however, are fictitious companies that are based on real organizations. These realistic illustrations and scenarios are intended to help students connect the business and managerial accounting issues discussed in this book to everyday life.

finance, serving the growing populations of Islamic nations by designing financial products consistent with sharia law's prohibition of interest charges? How would each of these alternative courses of action mesh with the company's other goals such as focusing on international connectivity and maintaining profitability and appropriate shareholder returns? HSBC's top management team had to *make a decision* about the best way to expand the company's emerging market operations, which entailed *choosing among the available alternatives.*

Planning

HSBC's top management team decided to expand the company's operations in Indonesia and in 2009 acquired almost 90% ownership in Bank Ekonomi. In an Indonesian release announcing the acquisition, HSBC noted that Indonesia is that world's fourth most populous country and cited its growth prospects, observing that Indonesia's GDP is forecast to grow 4.5% in 2010 despite the global recession.

The aquisition would be followed by a detailed planning phase. How would the new Indonesian operation be integrated with existing HSBC operations in the region? What financial products and services would be appropriate? How many employees would be needed at the various branches and how would the management structure be organized? What level of sovereign debt risk would be appropriate and what lending policies would be in effect? What would be the role of Islamic finance products in this, the largest Muslim population in the world? Finally, how much would it cost to operate the Indonesian operation and how much revenue could be generated to offset those costs and return a reasonable profit? The HSBC management team had to plan for running the Indonesian operation, which meant *developing a detailed financial and operational description of anticipated operations.*

Directing Operational Activities

Once the acquisition's transition period is complete, HSBC's Indonesia operations would need to be operated in a smooth and profitable manner. How many tellers (cashiers) should be on duty on a Monday morning? How much currency, and which ones, should be ordered each day? How much cash will be needed to meet the payroll, pay the utility bills, and buy security services next month? All of these questions fall under the general heading of *directing operational activities,* which means *running the organization on a day-to-day basis.*

Controlling

By this time, HSBC's post-acquisition Indonesian operations have been operating for more than a full business cycle (a full year). Are the company's goals for the operation being accomplished? More specifically, have HSBC's Indonesian operations adhered to the plans developed by management for achieving these goals? In seeking to answer these questions, management is engaged in *control,* which means *ensuring that the organization operates in the intended manner and achieves its goals.*

> "The accounting people are expected to do things that are much more strategic and much more forward looking than [they] have been expected to do in the past." (1b)
>
> **Caterpillar**

In Their Own Words
These quotes are from practicing managers or managerial accountants. The quotes show how various managerial accounting concepts are actually used and that management accountants are key players in most companies.

How Managerial Accounting Adds Value to the Organization

Managers need information for all of the managerial activities described in the preceding section. That information comes from a variety of sources, including economists, financial experts, marketing and production personnel, and the organization's managerial accounting system.

Objectives of Managerial Accounting Activity

Learning Objective 3

List and describe five objectives of managerial accounting activity.

Managerial accountants add value to an organization by pursuing five major objectives:

1. Providing information for decision making and planning, and proactively participating as part of the management team in the decision-making and planning processes.

2. Assisting managers in directing and controlling domestic and international operational activities.

3. Motivating managers and other employees toward the organization's goals.

4. Measuring the performance of activities, subunits, managers, and other employees within the organization.

5. Assessing the organization's competitive position, and working with other managers to ensure the organization's long-run competitiveness in its industry.

Managerial accounting analysis is considered so crucial in managing an enterprise that in most cases managerial accountants are integral members of the management team. Far from playing a passive role as information providers, managerial accountants take a proactive role in both the strategic and day-to-day decisions that confront an enterprise.

Although much of the information provided by the managerial accounting system is financial, there is a strong trend toward the presentation of substantial nonfinancial data as well. Managerial accountants supply all kinds of information to management and act as strategic business partners in support of management's role in decision making and managing the organization's activities. As we will see in subsequent chapters, contemporary managerial accounting systems are focusing more and more on the activities that occur on all levels of the organization. Measuring, managing, and continually improving operational activities are critical to an organization's success.

To illustrate the objectives of managerial accounting activity, let us continue with the example of HSBC's Indonesia operations.

> "In five years [we will become] even more strategic. Really understanding the ins and outs of all the organizations, and really trying to be visionary—understanding what is happening to our business." (1c)
> **Hewlett-Packard**

Providing Information for Decision Making and Planning, and Proactively Participating as Part of the Management Team in the Decision-Making and Planning Processes

For virtually all major decisions, HSBC's management team would rely largely on managerial accounting information. For example, the *decision* to acquire Bank Ekonomi would be influenced heavily by estimates of the costs of integrating the acquisition with existing HSBC operations in the Asia-Pacific region and operating the branches after the acquisition. The HSBC managers also would rely on managerial accounting data in formulating plans for the bank's lending operations. Prominent in those *plans* would be a budget detailing the projected revenues and costs of providing and servicing loans.

While HSBC's top management contemplated its decision about the Indonesian acquisition, the company's managerial accountants could not simply gather information and then sit on the sidelines. The managerial accountants were key participants in the management team as decisions were made and plans formulated for the bank's operations.

Assisting Managers in Directing and Controlling Operational Activities

Directing and controlling day-to-day operations require a variety of data about the process of providing financial services. For example, in *directing* operational activities, the bank's management team would need data about customer visit patterns in order to make sure appropriate staffing was provided in the bank branches. In *controlling* operations, management would compare actual costs incurred with those specified in the budget.

> "What we're seeing is less transactional and more decision support type of work. More analytical, more . . . option analysis. Looking at the whole spectrum of options in helping management make decisions." (1d)
> **Boeing**

Managerial accounting information often assists management through its **attention-directing function.** Managerial accounting reports rarely solve a decision problem. However, managerial accounting information often directs managers' attention to an issue that requires their skills. To illustrate, suppose HSBC's main Indonesia branch in Jakarta incurred electricity costs that significantly exceeded the budget. This fact does not explain why the budget was exceeded, nor does it tell management what action to take, but it does direct management's attention to the situation. Suppose that upon further investigation, the accounting records reveal that the local electric rates have increased substantially. This information will help management in framing the decision problem. Should steps be taken to conserve electricity? Should the branch's hours be curtailed? Perhaps management should consider switching to a lower-cost method of air conditioning.

Motivating Managers and Other Employees Toward the Organization's Goals

Organizations have goals. However, organizations comprise people who have goals of their own. The goals of individuals are diverse, and they do not always match those of the organization. A key purpose of managerial accounting is to motivate managers and other employees to direct their efforts toward achieving the organization's goals. One means of achieving this purpose is through budgeting. In establishing a budget for HSBC's Indonesia operations, top management indicates how resources are to be allocated and what activities are to be emphasized. When actual operations do not conform to the budget, the bank's managers will be asked to explain the reasons for the deviation.

One way in which employees can be motivated toward the organization's goals is through *empowerment*. Employee **empowerment** is the concept of encouraging and authorizing workers to take the initiative to improve operations, reduce costs, and improve product quality and customer service. At HSBC, for example, bank employees are routinely asked for suggestions about ways to improve service to their customers

Measuring the Performance of Activities, Subunits, Managers, and Other Employees Within the Organization

One means of motivating people toward the organization's goals is to measure their performance in achieving those goals. Such measurements then can be used as the basis for rewarding performance through positive feedback, promotions, and pay raises. For example, most large corporations compensate their executives, in part, on the basis of the profit achieved by the subunits they manage. In other companies, executives are rewarded on the basis of operational measures, such as product quality, sales, or on-time delivery. At HSBC, for example, management could be rewarded, in part, on the basis of growth in the number of new small-business customers.

In addition to measuring the performance of people, the managerial accounting system measures the performance of an organization's subunits, such as divisions, product lines, geographical territories, and departments. These measurements help the subunits' managers obtain the highest possible performance level in their units. Such measurements also help top management decide whether a particular subunit is a viable economic investment. For example, it may turn out that a particular financial product is too costly for HSBC to offer in the Indonesian market, despite the efforts of a skilled management team.

Assessing the Organization's Competitive Position, and Working with Other Managers to Ensure the Organization's Long-Run Competitiveness in Its Industry

The modern business environment changes very rapidly. These changes are reflected in global competition, rapidly advancing technology, and improved communication systems, such as the Internet. The activities that make an enterprise successful today may no longer be sufficient next year. A crucial role of managerial accounting is to continually assess how an organization stacks up against the competition, with an eye toward continuously improving. Among the questions asked in assessing an organization's competitive position are the following:

- How well is the organization doing in its internal operations and business processes?
- How well is the organization doing in the eyes of its customers? Are their needs being served as well as possible?
- How well is the organization doing from the standpoint of innovation, learning, and continuously improving operations? Is the organization a trendsetter that

> "You want to be on the team. You want to be the business consultant. You want to be thought of as a value-adding department versus just someone who closes the books." (1e)
>
> **Qwest**

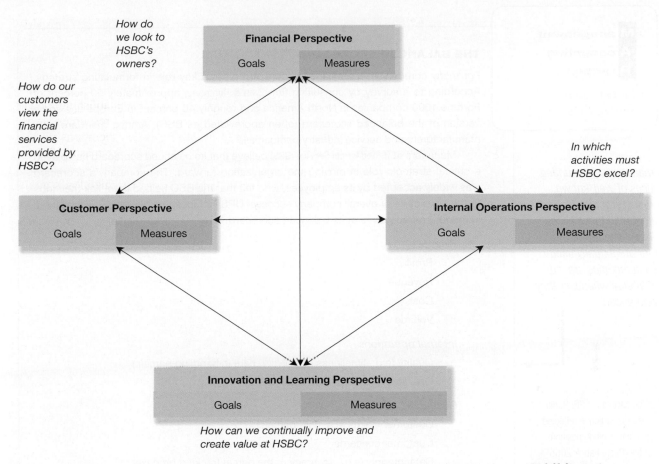

How do we look to HSBC's owners?

How do our customers view the financial services provided by HSBC?

In which activities must HSBC excel?

Financial Perspective
Goals   Measures

Customer Perspective
Goals   Measures

Internal Operations Perspective
Goals   Measures

Innovation and Learning Perspective
Goals   Measures

How can we continually improve and create value at HSBC?

Exhibit 1–1
Hypothetical Balanced Scorecard for HSBC

embraces new products, new services, and new technology? Or is it falling behind?

- How well is the organization doing financially? Is the enterprise viable as a continuing entity?

The Balanced Scorecard

The questions listed in the preceding section are so important for any organization's management to address that they have been organized into a management framework called the *balanced scorecard,* which is depicted in Exhibit 1–1 for HSBC.[4] The **balanced scorecard** is a model of business performance evaluation that balances measures of financial performance, internal operations, innovation and learning, and customer satisfaction.

If an organization is to remain viable in a changing and ever more competitive business environment, its managers need to continually ask the questions emphasized in the balanced scorecard. HSBC is no exception. Its management team must be concerned with the cost effectiveness of the company's business processes as well as its financial products and services. Management must continually monitor the needs of its customers and assess their level of satisfaction with the products and services provided. The company's

---

[4]The balanced scorecard concept was developed by Robert S. Kaplan and David D. Norton. See Robert S. Kaplan and David D. Norton, *The Strategy-Focused Organization: How Balanced Scorecard Companies Thrive in the New Business Environment* (Boston: Harvard Business School Press, 2001).

Management
Accounting
Practice

United Parcel
Service (UPS)

The managerial accounting practices of well-known, real-world organizations are highlighted in these boxes. You'll see how topics in the chapter are actually used. Actual companies are indicated in blue whenever they are referenced.

"The success of SRI Radio Systems, which is reflected in a high ranking position in the 'Beste Fabrik 2005' (Best factory of 2005) awards, is due in part to our BSC [balanced scorecard] solution. With this system we can keep an eye out for ways to constantly optimize changes to the process."

**SRI Radio Systems
(division of Siemens)
Germany**

THE BALANCED SCORECARD

For many companies, the balanced scorecard plays a key role in formulating strategy. According to a survey by consulting firm Bain & Company, approximately 50 percent of Fortune 1000 companies in North America and roughly 40 percent in Europe use some version of the balanced scorecard (often abbreviated as BSC). Among them are both manufacturers and service industry companies.[5]

Managers at United Parcel Service (UPS) believe that its balanced scorecard has played a critical strategic role in moving the organization forward. The company's scorecard was widely accepted by its employees, who felt that the BSC helped them link their jobs to the big picture of overall company success. UPS includes the following key measures in the four perspectives of its balanced scorecard.[6]

Financial
Profit
Revenue
Cost
Volume

Internal operations
Quality (e.g., timeliness of delivery, care in handling parcels)
Operations (i.e., operational efficiency)

Customer
Customer claims (e.g., lost parcels)
Customer concerns
Data integrity (e.g., accuracy of the parcel tracking process)

Learning & growth*
Employee injuries
Employee retention
Employee relation index

*Referred to as people *in the UPS scorecard.*

overall financial strength also must be prominent in management's thinking. Finally, are the company's financial products and services "keeping up with the times" in terms of culture and technology? Are the company's employees providing the innovation that is critical to the company's future success?

We will hold off on an extensive discussion of the balanced scorecard until Chapter 10. However, let's briefly consider the goals and measures that HSBC's top management might consider for the balanced scorecard depicted in Exhibit 1–1. According to the company's Web site, HSBC's "strategy is focused on delivering superior growth and earnings

---

[5]Raef Lawson, William Stratton, and Toby Hatch, "Scorecarding Goes Global," *Strategic Finance* 87, no. 9 (March 2006), pp. 35–41; and Thomas Wunder, "New Strategy Alignment in Multinational Corporations," *Strategic Finance* 87, no. 5 (November 2005), pp. 35–41.

[6]Robert S. Kaplan and David D. Norton, *The Strategy-Focused Organization*: *How Balanced Scorecard Companies Thrive in the New Business Environment* (Boston: Harvard Business School Press, 2001); and Bruce Stanley, "UPS Battles Traffic Jams to Gain Ground in India," *The Wall Street Journal,* January 25, 2008, p. B1.

over time" by investing "primarily in fast-growing markets." So HSBC's *financial perspective* would include such measures as revenue growth, earnings, earnings per share, and cash flow.

Now the question is, for HSBC to achieve its *financial goals* in *the future,* what does the company need to be doing *now* in the balanced scorecard's *other three perspectives?* For its *customer perspective,* HSBC might use surveys to access customer satisfaction with its financial services and products, as well as collect more objective data such as the number of visitors per day at its branches and market share in key global markets. For the *learning and growth perspective,* HSBC could focus on new branches opened, employee retention, and introduction of new financial products. For its *internal operations perspective,* HSBC could focus on measures such as operating expense per employee, percent of revenues from emerging markets, implementation of key technology goals, security failures, and so forth. The key point of the balanced scorecard concept is that by focusing on measures of performance *now* in these three key perspectives, HSBC can achieve its financial goals in the *future.*

Many companies, in all types of industries, have developed a balanced scorecard to help management and employees achieve success on the company's key long-term goals. Among the many service-industry firms that have developed a balanced scorecard are Bank of Tokyo-Mitsubishi, Citicorp, JPMorganChase, BMW Financial Services, Saatchi & Saatchi Worldwide, Nationwide Mutual Insurance, and Disney. Retailers, too, have made use of the balanced scorecard. Among them are The Gap and IKEA.

Among the well-known manufacturers making use of the balanced-scorecard concept are Apple Computer, Caterpillar, Cisco Systems, Ricoh, Eli Lilly, ExxonMobil, General Motors, Microsoft, Motorola, and Phillips Electronics. Finally, governmental units have benefited from a balanced scorecard, among them the City of Brisbane (Australia), NASA, the U.S. Department of Energy, and the Ontario (Canada) Ministry of Health.

We will come back to the balanced scorecard in Chapter 10.

Managerial versus Financial Accounting

Take another look at the major objectives of managerial accounting activity. Notice that the focus in each of these objectives is on *managers.* Thus, the focus of *managerial accounting* is on the needs of managers *within* the organization, rather than interested parties outside the organization.

Financial accounting is the use of accounting information for reporting to parties outside the organization. The annual report distributed by McDonald's Corporation or Lloyd's of London to its investors is an example of the output from a financial accounting system. Users of financial accounting information include current and prospective stockholders, lenders, investment analysts, unions, consumer groups, and government agencies.

There are many similarities between managerial accounting information and financial accounting information because they both draw upon data from an organization's basic *accounting system.* This is the system of procedures, personnel, and computers used to accumulate and store financial data in the organization. One part of the overall accounting system is the **cost accounting system,** which accumulates cost data for use in both managerial and financial accounting. For example, production cost data typically are used in helping managers set prices, which is a managerial accounting use. However, production cost data also are used to value inventory on a manufacturer's balance sheet, which is a financial accounting use.

Exhibit 1–2 depicts the relationships among an organization's basic accounting system, cost accounting system, managerial accounting, and financial accounting. Although similarities do exist between managerial and financial accounting, the differences are even greater. Exhibit 1–3 lists the most important differences.

Learning Objective 4

Explain the major differences between managerial and financial accounting.

Exhibit 1–2
Managerial Accounting,
Financial Accounting, and
Cost Accounting

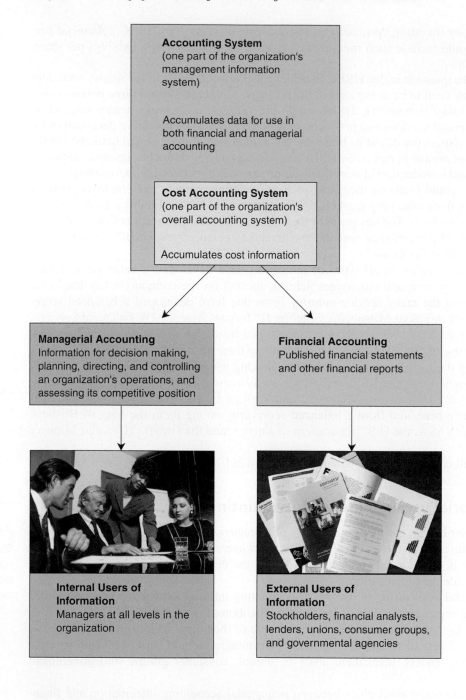

Accounting System
(one part of the organization's management information system)

Accumulates data for use in both financial and managerial accounting

Cost Accounting System
(one part of the organization's overall accounting system)

Accumulates cost information

Managerial Accounting
Information for decision making, planning, directing, and controlling an organization's operations, and assessing its competitive position

Financial Accounting
Published financial statements and other financial reports

Internal Users of Information
Managers at all levels in the organization

External Users of Information
Stockholders, financial analysts, lenders, unions, consumer groups, and governmental agencies

> "[We are] a partner with all of the other functions in the business here. We are an equal partner with our product groups, with the engineering and manufacturing cohorts in making sure this business is a success." (1g)
>
> **Caterpillar**

Managerial Accounting in Different Types of Organizations

All organizations need information, whether they are profit-seeking or nonprofit enterprises and regardless of the activities they pursue. As a result, managerial accounting information is vital in all organizations. Ford, United Colors of Benneton, Emirates Airlines, Hong Kong and Shanghai Hotels, Zurich Financial Services, American Express, Cornell University, Doctors Without Borders, MD Anderson Cancer Center, the City of Los Angeles, and the United Nations all have managerial accountants who provide information to management. Moreover, the five basic purposes of managerial accounting activity are relevant in each of these organizations.

	Managerial Accounting	**Financial Accounting**
Users of Information	Managers, *within the organization.*	Interested parties, *outside the organization.*
Regulation	*Not required* and *unregulated*, since it is intended only for management.	*Required* and must conform to International Financial Reporting Standards (IFRS) or Generally Accepted Accounting Principles (GAAP). *Regulated* internationally by the International Accounting Standards Board and in the U.S by the Financial Accounting Standards Board.
Source of Data	The organization's *basic accounting system, plus various other sources,* such as rates of defective products manufactured, physical quantities of material and labor used in production, occupancy rates in hotels and hospitals, and average take-off delays in airlines.	Almost exclusively drawn from the organization's *basic accounting system,* which accumulates financial information.
Nature of Reports and Procedures	*Reports often focus on subunits* within the organization, such as departments, divisions, geographical regions, or product lines. Based on a combination of historical data, estimates, and projections of future events.	*Reports focus on the enterprise in its entirety.* Based almost exclusively on historical transaction data.

Exhibit 1–3
Differences between Managerial and Financial Accounting.

Where Are Managerial Accountants Located in an Organization?

This question can be interpreted in three different ways:

- Where are managerial accountants *located in an organization chart?*
- How are managerial accountants *deployed?*
- In what *physical location* do managerial accountants actually do their work?

Take a look at Exhibit 1–4, which portrays the organization and deployment of managerial accountants in HSBC.

> **Learning Objective 5**
>
> Explain where managerial accountants are located in an organization, in terms of formal organization, deployment in cross-functional teams, and physical location.

Organization Chart

First, let's focus on panel A of the exhibit, which depicts HSBC's organization structure.[7] Notice that the company's top management group consists of the board of directors, chairman of the board, and group chief executive officer (CEO).

Line and Staff Positions

The other positions in HSBC's organization chart are of two types: line positions and staff positions. Managers in **line positions** are *directly* involved in the provision of goods or services. For example, HSBC's line positions include the presidents responsible for personal financial services, commercial banking, and insurance. Also in line positions would be the thousands of managers in the various operating units of the divisions shown in the organization chart. For example, the general manager of HSBC's retail banking operations in Tokyo, the manager of trust operations in New York, and the vice president in charge of the HSBC branches in Sydney, would all be in line positions.

> "[Management accountants] need to be strongly partnered with the line management. They need to be proactive. They need to have a broad sense of business. It's not strictly accounting. It's looking at the full spectrum and range of business." (1h)
>
> **Boeing**

---

[7]The information for the organization chart is adapted in highly simplified form from a structure chart and various press releases on the HSBC Web site.

A. Organization Chart for HSBC Holdings plc

Exhibit 1–4

Managerial Accountants in HSBC Holdings plc

Managers in **staff positions** supervise activities that support HSBC's overall mission, but they are only *indirectly* involved in operational activities. HSBC's staff positions include the legal counsel, the executive VP for technology, and the chief financial officer (CFO), among others.

CFO or Controller

In many organizations, the designation given to the top managerial *and* financial accountant is the **chief financial officer (CFO).** In other organizations, this individual is called the **controller** or **comptroller**.

The CFO or controller usually is responsible for supervising the personnel in the accounting department and for preparing the information and reports used in both managerial and financial accounting. As the organization's chief managerial accountant,

B. Deployment of Managerial Accountants in Cross-Functional Management Teams

Hypothetical Planning Team for HSBC's Indonesian Operations

Marketing Manager, *HSBC Financial Services*	Country Manager, *HSBC Indonesia*	Development Manager, *HSBC Amanah**	Managerial Accountants, *HSBC Asia-Pacific*

* HSBC Amanah is the global Islamic financial services division of HSBC.

Hypothetical Planning Team for New Branch Locations of HSBC Indonesia

Operations Manager, *HSBC Asia-Pacific*	Security Manager, *HSBC Asia-Pacific*	General Manager, *HSBC Indonesia*	Human Resources Manager, *HSBC Indonesia*	Managerial Accountants, *HSBC Asia-Pacific and Indonesia*

Hypothetical Decision-Making Team for a New Line of Islamic Financial Products to Be Offered in Indonesia

Marketing Personnel, *HSBC Indonesia*	Product Manager, *HSBC Amanah*	Branch Manager, *HSBC Indonesia, Jakarta Region*	Relationships Manager, *HSBC Private Banking*	Managerial Accountants, *HSBC Indonesia and Amanah*

Hypothetical Decision-Making Team for a Data Center to Be Built in Bangalore, India

Intellectual Property Manager, *HSBC Asia-Pacific*	General Manager, *HSBC India*	Operations Manager, *HSBC Technology*	Staff Lawyers, *HSBC Asia-Pacific*	Managerial Accountants, *HSBC Asia-Pacific and India*

the CFO or controller often interprets accounting information for line managers and participates as an integral member of the management team. Most controllers are involved in planning and decision making at all levels and across all functional areas of the enterprise. This broad role has enabled many managerial accountants to rise to the top of their organizations. Former accountants have served as top executives in such companies as General Motors, Singer, General Electric, and Fruehauf.

In addition to the CFO or controller for the entire corporation, most companies, including HSBC, have divisional controllers. Thus, HSBC's detailed organization chart would show a controller for HSBC Indonesia, HSBC Asia-Pacific, HSBC Amanah, and so forth.

Treasurer The **treasurer** typically is responsible for raising capital and safeguarding the organization's assets. In addition, the treasurer is responsible for the organization's assets, the management of its investments, its credit policy, and its insurance coverage.

Internal Auditor Most large corporations and many governmental agencies have an internal auditor. An organization's **internal auditor** is responsible for reviewing the accounting procedures, records, and reports in both the controller's and the treasurer's areas of responsibility. The auditor then expresses an opinion to top management regarding the effectiveness of the organization's accounting system. In some organizations, the internal auditor's role is much more extensive than this and can include a broad performance evaluation of middle and lower management.

Cross-Functional Deployment

On a formal organization chart, accountants generally are in a staff capacity, as explained in the preceding section. However, managerial accountants are increasingly being *deployed* in cross-functional management teams. Managerial accountants work with executives from top management, marketing and sales personnel, design engineers, operations managers, legal experts, quality-control personnel, and virtually every other specialized type of employee in an organization. Managerial teams are formed to make decisions, engage in planning exercises, or address operational problems from many perspectives. Since financial and other managerial accounting issues often are critically important in addressing business problems, managerial accountants routinely play a major role in these cross-functional teams. Panel B of Exhibit 1–4 depicts several plausible cross-functional teams formed to address a variety of hypothetical business problems at HSBC. Notice that each of these teams pulls together individuals from a variety of specialties, such as marketing, operations, general management, customer relations, and the general counsel's office (legal issues). Given HSBC's business finance talent is almost always present in these cross-functional teams; moreover, managerial accountants play an important role as well.

> "Most of the people . . . are decentralized and actually are co-located with the people that they support. That's our approach and we're moving more and more toward that and less and less toward a central group that provides information." (1i)
>
> **Boeing**

Physical Location

Finally, where do managerial accountants actually do their work? The answer is "just about everywhere." As the global nature of HSBC's business would suggest, managerial accountants are not sequestered in some remote corner of the business. To the contrary, they are located in every part of an enterprise, from corporate headquarters to the locations where goods and services are being produced. At HSBC, for example, managerial accountants would be present in India when a customer service outsourcing arrangement is being finalized, in Paris when a new marketing campaign is planned, and in New York when a new credit card line is being developed.

Major Themes in Managerial Accounting

Learning Objective 7

Briefly describe some of the major contemporary themes in managerial accounting.

Several major themes influence virtually all aspects of managerial accounting. We will briefly introduce these themes now, and they will be apparent throughout the text.

Information and Incentives

The need for information is the driving force behind managerial accounting. However, managerial accounting information often serves two functions: a *decision-facilitating* function and a *decision-influencing* function. Information usually is supplied to a decision maker to assist that manager in choosing an alternative. Often, that information is also intended to influence the manager's decision.

To illustrate, let us consider HSBC's annual budget. Although the budget is prepared under the direction of the CFO, it must be approved by the Chairman of the Board and the Group CEO and, ultimately, by the Board of Directors. As part of the budget approval process, the CEO and the board of directors will make important decisions that determine how the company's resources will be allocated. Throughout the year, the decisions of management will be facilitated by the information contained in the budget. Management decisions also will be influenced by the budget, since at year-end actual expenditures will be compared with the budgeted amounts. Explanations will then be requested for any significant deviations.

Behavioral Issues

The reactions of both individuals and groups to managerial accounting information will significantly affect the course of events in an organization. How will the general manager of HSBC's Indonesia branch react to a budget? How will data regarding the cost of providing financial services affect the way the branch's management prices those services?

Managerial accounting information is vital in all types of organizations. Managerial accountants act as strategic business partners in support of management's roles in decision making and directing operational activities. Pictured here are a manufacturer, a service-industry firm, a retailer, and a nonprofit city firefighting service. How would managerial accounting be important in each of these organizations?

How much detail should be included in the quarterly accounting reports to the general manager? If too much detail is provided, will the manager be overloaded with information and distracted from the main points?

All of these questions involve the behavioral tendencies of people and their cognitive limitations in using information. The better a managerial accountant's understanding of human behavior is, the more effective he or she will be as a provider of information.

Costs and Benefits

Information is a commodity, much like wheat or corn. Like other goods, information can be produced, purchased, and consumed. It can be of high or low quality, timely or late, appropriate for its intended use or utterly irrelevant. As is true of all goods and services, information entails both costs and benefits. The costs of providing managerial accounting information to the managers in HSBC's Indonesia branch include the cost of compensation for the branch's controller and Accounting Department personnel, the cost of purchasing and operating computers, and the cost of the time spent by the information users to read, understand, and utilize the information. The benefits include improved decisions, more effective planning, greater efficiency of operations at lower costs, and better direction and control of operations.

Thus, there are both costs and benefits associated with managerial accounting information. The desirability of any particular managerial accounting technique or information must be determined in light of its costs and benefits. We will reinforce this cost-benefit trade-off throughout the text by pointing out areas where managerial accounting information could be improved, but only at too great a cost.

Management of Capacity and Capacity Costs

A key objective of managerial accounting information is the management of an organization's capacity and the costs of providing that capacity. By **capacity** we mean the upper limit on the amount of goods or services that an organization can produce in a specified period of time. For example, how many iPads can Apple manufacture in a month? Or how many people can the tellers at HSBC Indonesia's Jakarta main branch effectively accommodate in a day? Or how many cell phone calls or text messages can your cell phone company process in an hour?

There are various concepts of an organization's capacity. *Theoretical capacity* refers to the upper limit on production of goods or services if everything works perfectly. (This means that no employees miss time for illness, no machines break down, there are no unexpected interruptions such as power outages or severe storms, and so forth.) Most management accountants believe that a more useful concept of capacity is **practical capacity,** which allows for normal occurrences such as machine downtime and employee fatigue or illness.

Important questions for the managerial accounting system to address are: (1) What is an organization's practical capacity? (2) What are the costs of the resources supplied to provide that capacity? and (3) How have those resources been used?

To explore these issues, let's focus on a familiar scenario, the pizza business. Suppose you have taken a job at the nearby college pizza shop making pizzas. (You know, the one just down the street where you go with your friends after an exam to celebrate, or before studying for the exam to fortify yourself, or when you should be studying for the exam, because, well, eating pizza is more fun than studying.) You work the 8:00 to 10:00 PM shift three evenings a week, Monday, Wednesday, and Friday. In addition to the obvious fringe benefit of getting the occasional free slice of pizza with your favorite toppings, you receive a wage of $8 an hour. So each evening that you work, you make $16.

After some training and a little experience, you can make a pizza, on average, in about five minutes. This includes picking up a premeasured lump of pizza dough, patting it out, twirling it ostentatiously over your head a few times, putting it down, covering it with pizza sauce, applying the cheese and other toppings, and tossing it in the oven. (The difference in time to apply the toppings on a plain cheese pizza or one with "the works" is negligible.) Also, the five-minute average time required per pizza allows for occasional mistakes, fatigue, cell-phone calls, and other normal events. You have one 20-minute break during your two-hour shift, so on a busy evening, you could make as many as 20 pies (100 minutes available ÷ the average 5 minutes per pizza).

So, using the terminology discussed above, the cost of the labor *resources supplied* for your two-hour shift is $16, and the *practical capacity* of that two-hour shift is 20 pizzas made.

Now suppose that during the first week of October, you experience very different levels of demand on your three evening shifts. Monday night football causes a steady demand for pizzas, and you make 20 pies that evening. Wednesday evening is pretty slow, and you make just 10 pies. Friday evening, which is normally very busy, is unusually slow because of a rally held that evening before the next day's big match against your school's arch rival. You make just one pie.

Now we must calculate the cost of your labor for a pizza during each of your three shifts. One fairly simple answer is to divide your labor cost per shift by the number of pizzas you made in each shift, as follows:

Shift	Labor Cost	Pizzas Made	Cost per Pizza
Monday	$16.00	20	$ .80
Wednesday	16.00	10	1.60
Friday	16.00	1	16.00

Let's stop and think about this. Does this analysis make any sense? Most accountants and managers would argue that it does not make much sense to say that Monday's pizzas cost $.80 each for your labor, Wednesday's cost $1.60 each, and the one you made Friday cost $16.00! This result highlights the problem of confusing the cost of a resource *supplied* with the cost of a resource *used*. The cost of your labor resource *supplied* during each shift was $16.00, but the cost of your labor resource *used* varied from shift to shift due to widely diffcrent demand levels.

Many cost managers would argue that the cost of your labor resource *used* should be computed as shown in column (c) of the following table. Moreover, the cost of your labor resource used *per pizza* is a constant $.80 per pizza, regardless of demand, as calculated in column (d). Finally, the cost of your labor resource *unused* (i.e., the cost of unused capacity) is calculated in column (e).

To best understand the table, start with column (a) and work across.

(a) Shift	(b) Cost of Labor Resource Supplied (2 hours × $8.00 per hour)	(c) Cost of Labor Resource Used [$16.00 × (pizzas made ÷ pizzas in practical capacity)]	(d) Cost of Labor Resource Used per Pizza [cost of labor resource used ÷ pizzas made]	(e) Cost of Labor Resource Unused (i.e., cost of unused capacity) [$16.00 − cost of labor resource used]
Monday	$16.00	$16.00 [$16 × (20 ÷ 20)]	$.80 ($16.00 ÷ 20)	$ .00
Wednesday	16.00	8.00 [$16 × (10 ÷ 20)]	.80 ($8.00 ÷ 10)	8.00
Friday	16.00	.80 [$16 × (1 ÷ 20)]	.80 ($.80 ÷ 1)	15.20

The moral of the story is that it is very important to distinguish between the cost of resources supplied [column (b) above], the cost of resources used [column (c) above], and the cost of resources unused [column (e) above], which is the same as the cost of unused capacity. An important task for any management team is to understand and manage the cost of capacity.[8]

Evolution and Adaptation in Managerial Accounting

Learning Objective 7

Briefly describe some of the major contemporary themes in managerial accounting.

Compared to financial accounting, managerial accounting is a young discipline. As a result, managerial accounting concepts and tools are still evolving as new ways are found to provide information that assists management. Moreover, the business environment is changing rapidly. For managerial accounting to be as useful a tool in the future as it has been in the recent past, managerial accounting information must be adapted to reflect those changes. Several changes in the business environment that are especially pertinent to managerial accounting are discussed briefly here. The effect of these changes on various topics in managerial accounting will be explored in subsequent chapters.

E-Business   E-commerce, e-business, e-tailing! Our ever-expanding e-vocabulary is testimony to the rapid electronic transformation of the business environment. Many of us have gone online to order a book from Amazon.com, an airline reservation from expedia.com, or possibly a computer from dell.com. We are all aware of the many dot-com companies that populate the electronic-retailing landscape. We're also aware that these companies appear and often disappear at an alarming pace. Nevertheless, the electronic revolution in the marketplace is here to stay.

Perhaps what we're less aware of, though, is the depth of the e-commerce impact throughout the spectrum of the business environment. Just as we can order books, CDs, or clothing online in *consumer-to-business* e-commerce channels, businesses can order raw materials and supplies using *business-to-business* networks. *Supply-chain management,* which encompasses the coordination of order generation, order taking, order fulfillment, and distribution of products and services, is increasingly an electronic, online process. *E-commerce* may be defined as buying and selling over digital media.[9] E-business is a broader concept. In addition to encompassing e-commerce, *e-business* includes the business processes that form the engine for modern business.

Managerial accountants are rapidly moving toward *e-accounting* themselves by harnessing the power of online communications to streamline the procedures of managerial accounting. For example, *e-budgeting* is now used by hundreds of companies to quickly and effectively transmit the information needed to construct a budget from far-flung business units around the globe.

E-business is here to stay, and it will affect our lives and our jobs in ways we can't even imagine today.

---

[8]This is, of course, a very simple illustration, because it focuses on a single resource, i.e., the cost of one employee's labor. Even a business as simple as a pizza shop involves many resources, such as pizza ingredients, multiple employees, buildings and equipment, and advertising. Imagine how much more complicated capacity issues are for a major airline or a large manufacturer. Nevertheless, by exploring the concepts of capacity and the cost of capacity in a very simple scenario, you should have an initial understanding of this critical issue. For a current article about managing capacity, see D. Welch and I. Rowley, "Risky Business at Nissan," *BusinessWeek,* November 2, 2009, p. 34.

[9]Ravi Kalakota and Andrew B. Whinston, *Electronic Commerce: A Manager's Guide* (Reading, MA: Addison-Wesley, 1997), p. 287; and Ravi Kalakota and Marcia Robinson, *e-Business: Road Map for Success* (Reading, MA: Addison-Wesley, 1999), p. 4.

Service versus Manufacturing Firms The service sector occupies a growing role in the U.S. economy. Moreover, several key service industries have been deregulated by the government. The telecommunications, financial services, and airline industries are among them. As more and more companies provide financial, medical, communication, transportation, consulting, and hospitality services, managerial accounting techniques must be adapted to meet the needs of managers in those industries. The key difference between service and manufacturing firms is that most services are consumed as they are produced. Most services cannot be inventoried like manufactured goods. Service organizations also tend to be more labor-intensive than manufacturing firms. Many of the techniques developed for measuring costs and performance in manufacturing companies have been adapted successfully to service industry firms. Throughout the text, you will notice that roughly two-thirds of the illustrations of managerial accounting techniques involve service industry firms and non-profit organizations.

Global Competition "It's a small world!" Although this cliché has been around a long time, it concisely sums up today's business environment. Today the marketplace is truly a global one. A firm in Tokyo is just as likely to be in competition with a company from China, Germany, or Korea as from across town. Intense international competition is forcing companies to strive for excellence in product quality and service more than ever before.

Moreover, international economic arrangements and potential trade agreements are constantly in the news, as national economies become more and more intertwined. Organizations such as the European Union (EU), the Association of Southeast Asian Nations (ASEAN) and the World Trade Organization (WTO), as well as international agreements like the North American Free Trade Agreement (NAFTA) and Mercosur/Mercosul, all have the potential to dramatically change international commerce.

A *multinational* company is an organization that has operational subunits, such as manufacturing plants or sales facilities, in two or more countries. Multinational firms face several challenges that do not confront domestic companies. Political systems, accounting rules for external reporting, legal systems, and cultural norms vary widely among countries. Managers of multinationals must be aware of these differences to successfully carry out operations across international boundaries. Income tax systems differ among countries also. In planning international operations, managers of multinationals must take into account the different tax laws and rates in the countries where they do business.

Monetary systems also differ among countries, and multinationals must continually monitor the fluctuating values of foreign currencies. The price at which one country's currency can be converted into that of another country is called an *exchange rate*. For example, on the day this paragraph is being written, it takes $.9199 in U.S. dollars to buy one Australian dollar. The exchange rate can fluctuate daily as various forces shape the world economy. As a result of these fluctuating exchange rates, managers of multinationals face challenges as they sign contracts, buy and sell goods, and conduct business operations in many countries.

Cross-Functional Teams In years past, managers tended to stick to their own turf. Production managers focused on how best to manufacture a product or produce a service. Marketing managers concentrated on selling the product or service. Design engineers often emphasized engineering elegance rather than designing a product for manufacturability. Managerial accountants provided information for decision making, planning, control, and performance evaluation.

Management
Accounting
Practice

Walmart
Harrah's Casino,
Continental Airlines,
and MoMA

THE INTERNET AS A LIFELINE

In a tough economic environment, the Internet can be a lifeline. "Companies in a sales squeeze are looking to the Net as a tool for cutting costs, generating new revenue streams, trimming inventories, and serving customers and employees more efficiently." Here are some examples of how companies are using the Web to their advantage.

Walmart

Walmart has recently made a major foray into the realm of online sales. "Customers who buy some of the more than 1.5 million products on Walmart.com can have them shipped free to a local Walmart, where new service desks at the front of some stores make it easier for customers to retrieve their stuff." Walmart is even experimenting with drive-through windows for merchandise pickup. *The payoff:* Walmart is now one of the top e-commerce sites in terms of traffic.

Harrah's Casino

"For years, casino operator Harrah's has had a database of customers it woos with cheap hotel rooms. Harrah's linked the database to its Web site, allowing customers to go online and book rooms at discount prices based on their past spending habits." *The payoff:* After the terrorist attacks of September 11, 2001, occupancy at Harrah's flagship Las Vegas hotel fell by 25 percent. "The chain sent e-mails with bargain offers, filling 4,000 rooms that otherwise would have stayed empty and bringing the hotel back to near-100 percent occupancy by September 30."[10]

Continental Airlines

The airline adopted a project to "analyze data on the fly to improve customer care. One online system alerts the company when planes arrive late and assesses passenger needs—delaying departures on other flights or sending carts to make connections easier. *The payoff:* After ranking last in the industry for customer satisfaction, Continental climbed into the top tier—ahead of American, United, and USAirways."

Museum of Modern Art (MoMA)

This New York City art museum undertook a $425 million rebuilding project, and "the museum's management pumped up the use of technology to cater better to visitors. *The payoff:* New services include podcast audio tours, on demand printing of tickets," Internet-based viewing of programming and displays, and an online store.[11]

Today a cross-functional approach has replaced this narrow managerial perspective. Cross-functional managerial teams bring together production and operations managers, marketing managers, purchasing and material-handling specialists, design engineers, quality management personnel, and managerial accountants to focus their varied expertise and experience on virtually all management issues. If products are to be designed and manufactured with the customers' needs in mind, a cross-functional approach is crucial. Marketing managers have the best feel for customer needs, and production managers are

---

[10]The information and quotations for Walmart are from M. Bustillo and G. A. Fowler, *The Wall Street Journal,* December 15, 2009, p. B1. The information and quotations for Harrah's Casino in this inset are from David Rocks, "The Net as a Lifeline," *BusinessWeek,* October 29, 2001.

[11]The information and quotations for Continental Airlines and MoMA are from "Websmart 50—Pacesetters: Customer Service," *BusinessWeek,* November 21, 2005, p. 85.

up on the latest in manufacturing technology. Design engineers know how to build the functionality into a product that customers demand, and purchasing managers can acquire the materials, parts, and services necessary to get the job done. Managerial accounting information is the glue that holds the cross-functional team together. The managerial accountant designs an information system and provides data ranging across all aspects of the organization's internal operations and external environment. Then the managerial accountant works as an integral member of the cross-functional team, interpreting information and analyzing the implications of decision alternatives. Working together, the cross-functional team creates value for the organization by meeting the customer's needs in the most effective manner possible.

Product Life Cycles and Diversity One impact of highly automated manufacturing systems has been to enable manufacturers to produce an ever-more diverse set of products. Moreover, the rate at which technology is changing means that the life cycles of most products are becoming shorter. In the computer industry, for example, product models are used only a few years before they are replaced by more powerful versions. To be competitive, manufacturers must keep up with the rapidly changing marketplace. Managers must have timely information about production costs and other product characteristics in order to respond quickly and effectively to the competition.

Information and Communication Technology We are all confronted with the breakneck pace of technological change. Just as we learn how to get the most out of our personal computers or to set up our cell phones, they are replaced by new and better models. It would be hard to overestimate the impact of technological innovation on the business environment. Although large mainframe computers still perform certain kinds of tasks, businesses now make heavy use of personal computers. In most offices, virtually every employee has a personal computer for such tasks as word processing, data analysis, report generation, presentation preparation, and communication. These PCs are usually linked together in a network that enables employees to electronically transfer files and reports, share data, and communicate via e-mail. Often called an *intranet,* these networked PCs are invaluable tools in the era of crossfunctional management teams. Moreover, these intranets are not confined to the walls of a building, as the World Wide Web or *Internet* allows computer-to-computer interface anywhere in the world.

Managerial accounting analyses that in years past would have to be scheduled on a mainframe computer are now done on PCs using a variety of software products. Spreadsheet programs, such as EXCEL®, are in wide use for data analysis.[12] Software packages specifically designed for accounting applications are also widely available. Many businesses are adopting integrated business software packages that handle a broad range of computing needs, such as customer and supplier databases, personnel and payroll functions, production scheduling and management, inventory records, and financial and managerial accounting functions. Among the integrated software packages in wide use are SAP, which stands for Systems Applications and Products in Data Processing, and Oracle. Managerial accountants often play significant roles in selecting software for their organizations or designing in-house software to meet the organization's unique needs.

> "The pace of change in technology is becoming much faster, and accounting and finance people are very heavy users of technology, more so than a lot of the other functions." (1j)
> **Hewlett-Packard**

Just-in-Time Inventory Management In traditional manufacturing settings, inventories of raw materials and parts, partially completed components, and finished goods were kept as a buffer against the possibility of running out of a needed item. However, large buffer inventories consume valuable resources and generate hidden costs. Consequently, many companies have completely changed their approach to production and inventory management. These manufacturers have adopted a strategy for controlling the flow of manufacturing in a multistage production process. In a **just-in-time (JIT) production system,** raw materials and parts are purchased or produced just in time to be

---

[12]EXCEL® is a registered trademark of Microsoft Corporation.

| Demand for raw materials and parts is signaled when there is a need in stage I for more inputs. | Demand for production activity in stage I is signaled when there is a need in stage II for more inputs. | Demand for production activity in stage II is signaled when there is a need in stage III for more inputs. | Demand for finished goods is signaled when sales activity warrants more finished units. This triggers manufacturing activity in the final stage of production (stage III). |

⟶ Denotes flow of materials, parts, partially finished goods, and finished goods.
◄ ─ Denotes a signal that more goods are needed at the next stage of production

Exhibit 1–5
Just-in-Time (JIT) Production and Inventory Management System

used at each stage of the production process. This approach to inventory and production management brings considerable cost savings from reduced inventory levels.

The key to the JIT system is the "pull" approach to controlling manufacturing. To visualize this approach, look at Exhibit 1–5, which displays a simple diagram of a multistage production process. The flow of manufacturing activity is depicted by the solid arrows running across the page from one stage of production to the next. However, the signal that triggers more production activity in each stage comes from the *next* stage of production. These signals, depicted by the dashed-line arrows, run from right to left. We begin with sales at the right-hand side of the exhibit. When sales activity warrants more production of finished goods, the goods are "pulled" from production stage III by sending a signal that more goods are needed. Similarly, when production employees in stage III need more inputs, they send a signal back to stage II. This triggers production activity in stage II. Working our way back to the beginning of the process, purchases of raw materials and parts are triggered by a signal that they are needed in stage I. This pull system of production management, which characterizes the JIT approach, results in a smooth flow of production and significantly reduced inventory levels. The result is considerable cost savings for the manufacturer.

Total Quality Management   One implication of a just-in-time inventory philosophy is the need to emphasize product quality. If a component is to be produced just in time for the next production stage, it must be "just right" for its intended purpose. One flawed component can shut down the entire production line, entailing considerable cost. Therefore, managerial accountants have become involved increasingly in monitoring product quality and measuring the costs of maintaining quality. This information helps companies maintain programs of **total quality management,** or **TQM.** This refers to the broad set of management and control processes designed to focus the entire organization and all of its employees on providing products or services that do the best possible job of satisfying the customer.

Continuous Improvement   Global competition is forcing companies to continuously improve their operations. **Continuous improvement** is the constant effort to eliminate waste, reduce response time, simplify the design of both products and processes, and improve quality and customer service. One compelling reason for the need for continuous improvement is the *price down/cost down* concept. This refers to the tendency of prices to fall over the life cycle of a newly introduced product. Think, for example, about the prices of laptop computers, personal listening devices, and high-definition televisions. When each of these products was first introduced, prices were quite high. However, as manufacturers gained experience in producing them, prices fell and the products became accessible to a much wider customer pool. However, if prices are to fall over time, manufacturers must continually reduce costs as well.

One widely used approach to cost reduction is **kaizen costing,** which is the process of cost reduction during the manufacturing phase of an existing product. The Japanese word *kaizen* refers to continual and gradual improvement through small betterment activities rather than large or radical improvement made through innovation or large investments in technology. The idea is simple. Improvement is the goal and responsibility of every worker, from the CEO to the manual laborers, in every activity, every day, all the time! Through the small but continual efforts of everyone, significant reductions in costs can be attained over time.

Cost Management Systems

The explosion in technology we are experiencing, coupled with increasing worldwide competition, is forcing managers to produce high-quality goods and services, provide outstanding customer service, and do so at the lowest possible cost. These demands are placing ever-greater requirements on the information provided by managerial accounting systems. Many companies have moved away from a historical cost accounting perspective and toward a proactive *cost management* perspective. A **cost management system** is a management planning and control system with the following objectives.

- Measure the cost of the resources consumed in performing the organization's significant *activities*.
- Identify and eliminate **non-value-added costs.** These are the costs of *activities* that can be eliminated with no deterioration of product quality, performance, or perceived value.
- Determine the efficiency and effectiveness of all major *activities* performed in the enterprise.
- Identify and evaluate new *activities* that can improve the future performance of the organization.

Notice the emphasis of a cost management system on the organization's activities. This emphasis, sometimes called **activity accounting,** is crucial to the goal of producing quality goods and services at the lowest possible cost. In keeping with the focus on activities, managerial accountants have developed a system for determining the cost of producing goods or services called **activity-based costing (ABC).** In an ABC system, the costs of the organization's significant activities are accumulated and then assigned to goods or services in accordance with how the activities are used in the production of those goods and services. An ABC system helps management understand the causal linkages between activities and costs.

Using an activity-based costing system to improve the operations of an organization is called **activity-based management,** or **ABM.** We will have considerably more to say about activity-based costing, activity-based management, and the role of cost management systems throughout the text.

Strategic Cost Management and the Value Chain

How are the goods and services that we all consume created? Usually many activities are involved in securing basic raw materials and turning them into valuable products or services. The set of linked, value-creating activities, ranging from securing basic raw materials and energy to the ultimate delivery of products and services, is called the **value chain.** Although there may be only one organization involved in a particular value chain, usually there are many.

At the MD Anderson Cancer Center in Houston, for example, the value chain would include not only the hospital but also the suppliers of pharmaceutical products and medical supplies, the manufacturers of diagnostic equipment, the private-practice physicians whose patients use MD Anderson, and the ambulance services that transport patients to the hospital.

> **Learning Objective 8**
>
> Understand and explain the concepts of strategic cost management and the value chain.

LVMH

The value chain for HSBC would include *upstream* contributions such as loan underwriting, facility construction and maintenance, financial product design, central bank regulation, and risk management. Once the financial product or service is available, the *downstream* contributions include advertising personnel; TV, radio, and print media; and branch personnel, brokers, and financial advisors.

The major steps in the value chain for LVMH Group. are depicted in Exhibit 1–6. LVMH is a major luxury goods retailer with over 2400 stores worldwide. As Exhibit 1–6 shows, major steps in the LVMH value chain include the following:

- Securing raw material, energy, and other resources.
- Research and development.
- Product design.
- Production.
- Marketing.
- Distribution and sales.

What is the role of LVMH in this value chain? As the company describes it,

> We continue to invest selectively in key performance drivers. Firstly, we are developing our production capacity in order to support our growth... Enhancing the quality of our distribution networks is also a priority... Finally, an array of innovations and substantial marketing efforts will be directed towards the most profitable projects in our business lines.
>
> (Letter to Shareholders, July 2010)

LVMH designs its products, manufactures some and outsources the production of others, markets the products, distributes them to retail stores where they are sold, and provides customer service. LVMH even owns many of the retail outlets for its products.

In order for any organization to most effectively achieve its goals, it is important for its managers to understand the *entire* value chain in which their organization participates. This understanding can help managers ask, and answer, important questions about their organization's strategy. Should the company concentrate on only a narrow link in the value chain, such as design or retailing? Or should it expand its operational scope to include securing the raw materials or manufacturing the product? Are there opportunities to form beneficial linkages with suppliers, which come earlier in the value chain? Or with customers?

Exhibit 1–6
Manufacturer's Value Chain

LVMH's value chain consists of a myriad of activities, from securing raw materials through distribution and sales.

LVMH

Securing raw materials, energy, and other resources

Research and development

Product design

Production

Marketing

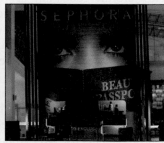
Distribution and sales

These questions involve fundamental, strategic issues about how an organization can best meet its goals. Although many factors affect such decisions, one important factor concerns the costs incurred in creating value in each link in the value chain. In order for a company to achieve a sustainable competitive advantage, it must either (1) perform one or more activities in the value chain at the same quality level as its competitors, but at a lower cost, or (2) perform its value chain activities at a higher quality level than its competitors, but at no greater cost. Understanding the value chain, and the factors that cause costs to be incurred in each activity in the value chain, is a crucial step in the development of a firm's strategy. These cost-causing factors are called **cost drivers,** and we will have much more to say about them throughout the text. The overall recognition of the importance of cost relationships among the activities in the value chain, and the process of managing those cost relationships to the firm's advantage, is called **strategic cost management.** Issues in strategic cost management will arise in a variety of contexts as we pursue our study of managerial accounting.

Theory of Constraints   Along with a value-chain analysis, managers should carefully examine the chain of linked activities with a view toward identifying the constraints that prevent their organization from reaching a higher level of achievement. Sometimes called the **theory of constraints,** this approach seeks to find the most cost-effective ways to alleviate an organization's most limiting constraints. When binding constraints are relaxed, the organization can reach a higher level of goal attainment. For example, suppose a delay occurred in the design process for LVMH's spring line of Louis Vuitton handbags because too few designers were assigned to the project. This could result in a delay in contracting for the manufacturing of the summer line, which could ultimately delay the delivery of the products to Louis Vuitton's many retail outlets. In this context, the design process is a *bottleneck operation,* meaning that it slows down the progress of LVMH's products through the retailer's value chain. By assigning even one or two more designers to the Louis Vuitton handbag line, the delay could perhaps have been avoided.

The Ethical Climate of Business and the Role of the Accountant

Who among us is not shocked and dismayed by the seemingly endless stream of corporate scandals that we have experienced over the past decade? Most recent among these was the near total collapse of the U.S. and world banking and financial systems. And the headlines keep on coming. Many of the cases involve mismanagement, some are characterized by alleged ethical lapses, and in some instances there is alleged criminal behavior. Who is to blame? According to most observers, there is plenty of blame to go around: greedy corporate executives, managers who make overreaching business deals, lack of oversight by various companies' boards of directors (particularly the boards' audit committees), substandard work by external auditors, lack of sufficient probing by Wall Street analysts and the financial press, and some accountants who have been all too willing to push the envelope on aggressive accounting to (or beyond) the edge. Billions of dollars have been lost in employee retirement funds, several state and national investment portfolios, and the private investment accounts of the public. It will no doubt take many years to sort out the mess. Companies have gone bankrupt; fortunes have been lost; careers have been ruined; and more of the same is yet to come. Several financial executives have filed guilty pleas on felony charges. Others have been convicted by juries. Some are serving time in prison. Some observers have wondered if the confidence of the investing public can ever be regained.

One important lesson from these scandals is that not only is unethical behavior in business wrong in a moral sense, but it also can be disastrous from the standpoint of the economy. We cannot have businesspeople lying, stealing, perpetrating frauds, and making up accounting rules as they go without seriously disrupting business. Thus, ethical behavior by businesspeople in general, and accountants in particular, is not a luxury or a discretionary "good thing to do." It is an absolute necessity to the smooth functioning of the economy.

> **Learning Objective 9**
>
> Understand the ethical responsibilities of a managerial accountant.

Sorting out the details of the major scandals mentioned above would require a book (or books) in itself and would take us well beyond the subject matter of this text. Most of the purely accounting issues in these cases involve financial accounting (external reporting) rather than managerial accounting (internal reporting). In most companies, however, many of the same individuals are involved in both types of accounting. In the notorious Enron case, for example, investigators allege that a massive fraud was perpetrated on the investing public by creating so-called related parties with names like Raptor for the sole purpose of hiding debt and overstating earnings. Yet the same alleged fraud must have been perpetrated on many at Enron itself. Surely not all of the company's thousands of employees knew of these accounting schemes. So ultimately, what may have been largely financial (external) accounting misstatements almost certainly resulted in misstated managerial (internal) accounting reports as well.[13]

The chaos in corporate governance and accounting spawned a movement for reform. The U.S. Congress passed the Sarbanes-Oxley Act in 2002, which, among other things, requires publicly held companies whose shares are traded in the United States to establish, assess, and regularly report on their internal controls over financial reporting. Similar legislation was adopted around the world, including the Financial Instruments and Exchange Law in Japan, CLERP 9 in Australia, and the LCF in France. Appendix I covers the Sarbanes-Oxley Act and related legislation, and their implications for managerial accounting. (Appendix I, on pages 800 through 806, can be assigned now.)

For many in the accounting profession, the scandals have served as a wake-up call to concentrate more on ethical issues in practicing and teaching accounting.[14] To this end, a significant *ethical issue in managerial accounting* will be addressed at the end of most chapters. The goal of these *Focus on Ethics* pieces is to raise the consciousness of students that legitimate ethical issues do arise in the daily practice of managerial accounting. In the last section of this chapter, we will turn our attention to managerial accounting as a profession. In the context of that discussion, the *Focus on Ethics* piece for this chapter will be a summary of the Institute of Management Accountants' *Statement of Ethical Professional Practice.*

Managerial Accounting as a Career

Learning Objective 10

Discuss the professional organizations, certification process, and ethical standards in the field of managerial accounting.

Managerial accountants serve a crucial function in virtually any enterprise. As the providers of information, they are often in touch with the heartbeat of the organization. In most businesses, managerial accountants interact frequently with sales personnel, finance specialists, production people, and managers at all levels. To perform their duties effectively, managerial accountants must be knowledgeable not only in accounting but in the other major business disciplines as well. Moreover, strong oral and written communication skills are becoming increasingly important for success as a managerial accountant.

Professional Organizations

"You've got to know how to talk to people, express yourself. And that's oral and written. You also have to be able to understand a lot of different areas, not necessarily just accounting. You've got to understand the business itself." (1k)

Qwest

To keep up with new developments in their field, managerial accountants often belong to one or more professional organizations. The two largest of these are the Institute of Management Accountants (IMA) and the Chartered Institute of Management Accountants (CIMA). The IMA, which has over 60,000 members and is based in the United States, publishes two journals, entitled *Management Accounting Quarterly* and *Strategic Finance*. CIMA, which is based in Europe and has offices throughout Asia, publishes educational e-journals for its 172,000 members. Both organizations have published many research studies on managerial accounting topics. Other professional organizations in which managerial accountants hold membership include the Financial Executives Institute,

---

[13]James Vicini, "Top Court Hears Appeal by Enron's Skilling," *Reuters,* March 1, 2010; and Allan Sloan, "Laying Enron to Rest," *Newsweek,* 147, no. 23 (June 5, 2006), pp. 25–30.

[14]Joann Lublin and Kara Scannell, "Critics See Some Good from Sarbanes-Oxley," *The Wall Street Journal,* July 30, 2007, p. B1; and John Hodowanitz and Steven A. Solieri, "Guarding the Guardians," *Strategic Finance* 87, no. 2 (August 2005), pp. 47–53.

the Institute of Internal Auditors, and various national and international organizations for certified or chartered public accountants.

The primary professional association for managerial accountants in Canada is Certified Management Accountants of Canada and Australia's organization is the Institute of Chartered Accountants in Australia. In all, over 75 countries have professional organizations for their practicing accountants.

Professional Certification

In keeping with the importance of their role and the specialized knowledge they must have, managerial accountants can earn a professional certification. In the United States, the IMA administers the Certified Management Accountant (CMA) program. The requirements for becoming a **Certified Management Accountant** include meeting specified educational requirements and passing the CMA examination. CIMA focuses on managerial accounting competency via a series of 10 professional qualification exams as well as specialized certifications in areas such as company direction and Islamic finance.[15] Many countries also have professional certification programs for their managerial accountants.

Professional Ethics

As professionals, managerial accountants have an obligation to themselves, their colleagues, and their organizations to adhere to high standards of ethical conduct. In recognition of this obligation, the IMA has developed the ethical standards below for its members, who are practitioners of managerial accounting and financial management.[16] Note: *Various problems and cases at the end of each chapter in this text include ethical issues to be resolved. In addressing those issues, readers will need to refer to these ethical standards.* For even further discussion of professional ethics in accounting, CIMA has produced an extensive, 81-page document addressing managerial accountant ethics that is available from its Web site.

Focus on Ethics *These scenarios discuss ethical issues and underscore the importance of ethical behavior in mangerial accounting.*

---

[15]For information about the CMA program, write to the Institute of Management Accountants, 10 Paragon Drive, Montvale, NJ 07645-1718, or visit their Web site at imanet.org. For information about the CIMA programs, see their Web site at cimaglobal.com.

[16]In 2005, the Institute of Management Accountants (IMA) revised its *Statement of Ethical Professional Practice.* See Curtis C. Verschoor, "Do the Right Thing," *Strategic Finance* 87, no. 5 (November 2005), pp. 42–46.

Focus on Ethics

IMA STATEMENT OF ETHICAL PROFESSIONAL PRACTICE

Members of IMA shall behave ethically. A commitment to ethical professional practice includes overarching principles that express our values and standards that guide our conduct.

Principles

IMA's overarching ethical principles include: Honesty, Fairness, Objectivity, and Responsibility. Members shall act in accordance with these principles and shall encourage others within their organizations to adhere to them.

Standards

A member's failure to comply with the following standards may result in disciplinary action.

Competence

Each member has a responsibility to:

1. Maintain an appropriate level of professional expertise by continually developing knowledge and skills.

2. Perform professional duties in accordance with relevant laws, regulations, and technical standards.

3. Provide decision support information and recommendations that are accurate, clear, concise, and timely.

4. Recognize and communicate professional limitations or other constraints that would preclude responsible judgment or successful performance of an activity.

Confidentiality

Each member has a responsibility to:

1. Keep information confidential except when disclosure is authorized or legally required.
2. Inform all relevant parties regarding appropriate use of confidential information. Monitor subordinates' activities to ensure compliance.
3. Refrain from using confidential information for unethical or illegal advantage.

Integrity

Each member has a responsibility to:

1. Mitigate actual conflicts of interest. Regularly communicate with business associates to avoid apparent conflicts of interest. Advise all parties of any potential conflicts.

2. Refrain from engaging in any conduct that would prejudice carrying out duties ethically.
3. Abstain from engaging in or supporting any activity that might discredit the profession.

Credibility

Each member has a responsibility to:

1. Communicate information fairly and objectively.
2. Disclose all relevant information that could reasonably be expected to influence an intended user's understanding of the reports, analyses, or recommendations.
3. Disclose delays or deficiencies in information, timeliness, processing, or internal controls in conformance with organization policy and/or applicable law.

Chapter Summary

Each chapter's summary is built around the learning objectives, which appear at the beginning of the chapter.

LO1 Define managerial accounting and describe its role in the management process. Managerial accounting is the process of identifying, measuring, analyzing, interpreting, and communicating information in pursuit of an organization's goals. Managerial accounting is an integral part of the management process, and managerial accountants are important strategic partners in an organization's management team.

LO2 Explain four fundamental management processes that help organizations attain their goals. In pursuing its goals, an organization acquires resources, hires employees, and then engages in an organized set of activities. It is up to the management team to make the best use of the organization's resources, employees, and activities in achieving the organization's goals. The four fundamental management processes are decision making, planning, directing operational activities, and controlling.

LO3 List and describe five objectives of managerial accounting activity. Five objectives of managerial accounting activity are (1) providing information for decision making and planning, and proactively participating as part of the management team in the decision-making and planning processes; (2) assisting managers in directing and controlling operations; (3) motivating managers and other employees to achieve the organization's goals; (4) measuring the performance of activities, subunits, managers, and other employees within the organization; and (5) assessing the organization's competitive position and working with other managers to ensure the organization's long-run competitiveness in its industry.

LO4 Explain the major differences between managerial and financial accounting. The users of managerial accounting information are managers inside the organization. Managerial accounting information is not mandatory, is unregulated, and draws on data from the basic accounting system as well as other data sources. The users of financial accounting information are interested parties outside the organization. Financial accounting information is required, is regulated, and is based almost entirely on historical transaction data.

LO5 Explain where managerial accountants are located in an organization, in terms of formal organization, deployment in cross-functional teams, and physical location. Managerial accountants occupy staff positions in an organization chart. They are deployed as members of cross-functional teams, which address a variety of managerial decisions. Managerial accountants are physically located throughout an enterprise alongside the managers with whom they work closely.

LO6 Describe the roles of an organization's chief financial officer (CFO) or controller, treasurer, and internal auditor. The organization's top managerial and financial accountant is called the chief financial officer or controller. The treasurer is responsible for raising capital and safeguarding the organization's assets. An organization's internal auditor is responsible for reviewing the accounting procedures, records, and reports and sometimes makes a broad performance evaluation of management.

LO7 Briefly describe some of the major contemporary themes in managerial accounting. Some major themes in managerial accounting include its role in providing information and incentives, the behavioral implications of managerial accounting information, the management of capacity and capacity costs, the evolution and adaptation of the field, and the role of cost management systems. In managing capacity, it is important to distinguish between the cost of resources supplied, the cost of resources used, and the cost of resources unused (i.e., the cost of unused capacity).

LO8 Understand and explain the concepts of strategic cost management and the value chain. The value chain is the set of linked, value-creating activities, ranging from securing basic raw materials and energy to the ultimate delivery of products and services. Understanding the value chain is a crucial step in the development of an organization's strategy. Managing the cost relationships in the value chain to the organization's advantage is called strategic cost management.

LO9 Understand the ethical responsibilities of a managerial accountant. Managerial accountants are expected to display a commitment to ethical professional practice characterized by the overarching principles of honesty, fairness, objectivity, and responsibility.

LO10 Discuss the professional organizations, certification process, and ethical standards in the field of managerial accounting. As professionals, managerial accountants must successfully complete a certification process and may enjoy the benefits of membership in one or more professional organizations, such as the Institute of Management Accountants (IMA). They are expected to adhere to the ethical standards of competence, confidentiality, integrity, and credibility.

Key Terms

For each term's definition refer to the indicated page, or turn to the glossary at the end of the text.

activity accounting, 59	chief financial officer (CFO), 48	empowerment, 42	practical capacity, 52
activity-based costing (ABC), 59	continuous improvement, 58	financial accounting, 45	staff positions, 48
activity-based management (ABM), 59	controller (or comptroller), 48	internal auditor, 49	strategic cost management, 61
attention-directing function, 41	cost accounting system, 45	just-in-time (JIT) production system, 57	theory of constraints, 61
balanced scorecard, 43	cost driver, 61	kaizen costing, 59	total quality management (TQM), 58
capacity, 52	cost management system, 59	line positions, 47	treasurer, 49
Certified Management Accountant (CMA), 63		managerial accounting, 38	value chain, 59
		non-value-added costs, 59	

Review Questions

1–1. According to some estimates, the volume of electronic commerce transactions exceeds $3 trillion. Business-to-business transactions account for almost half of this amount. What changes do you believe are in store for managerial accounting as a result of the explosion in e-commerce?

1–2. List two plausible goals for each of these organizations: Amazon.com, American Red Cross, General Motors, Walmart, the City of Seattle, and Hertz.

1–3. List and define the four basic management activities.

1–4. Give examples of each of the four primary management activities in the context of a national fast-food chain such as Burger King.

1–5. Give examples of how each of the objectives of managerial accounting activity would be important in an airline company such as American Airlines.

1–6. List and describe four important differences between managerial and financial accounting.

1–7. Distinguish between cost accounting and managerial accounting.

1–8. Distinguish between line and staff positions. Give two examples of each in a university setting.

1–9. Distinguish between the following two accounting positions: controller and treasurer.

1–10. How could your college or university use the concepts in the balanced scorecard? List two possible performance measures that would be relevant to a college or university, for each of the balanced scorecard's four areas.

1–11. What does the following statement by a managerial accountant at Caterpillar imply about where in the organization the managerial accountants are located?

"[We] are a partner with all of the other functions in the business here." (Reference 1g at end of text.)

1–12. What is meant by the following statement? "Managerial accounting often serves an attention-directing role."

1–13. What is the chief difference between manufacturing and service industry firms?

1–14. Explain the following terms: practical capacity, cost of resources supplied, cost of resources used, and cost of resources unused.

1–15. Explain the difference between e-business and e-commerce.

1–16. Define and explain the significance of the term *CMA*.

1–17. Briefly explain what is meant by each of the following ethical standards for managerial accountants: competence, confidentiality, integrity, and credibility.

1–18. What is meant by the term *non-value-added costs?*

1–19. Managerial accounting is an important part of any enterprise's management information system. Name two other information systems that supply information to management.

1–20. Can managerial accounting play an important role in a nonprofit organization? Explain your answer.

1–21. A large manufacturer of electronic machinery stated the following as one of its goals: "The company should become the low-cost producer in its industry." How can managerial accounting help the company achieve this goal?

1–22. What do you think it means to be a professional? In your view, are managerial accountants professionals?

1–23. Name several activities in the value chain of (*a*) a manufacturer of cotton shirts and (*b*) an airline.

1–24. Define the term *strategic cost management.*

Exercises

All applicable Exercises are available with McGraw-Hill's *Connect Accounting*™.

■ **Exercise 1–25**
Managerial Accounting and Decision Making
(LO 2, 3)

Give an example of managerial accounting information that could help a manager make each of the following decisions.

1. The president of Europcar is deciding whether to add luxury cars to the rental car fleet.
2. The production manager in a Saab plant is deciding whether to have routine maintenance performed on a machine weekly or biweekly.
3. The manager of a Carrefour store is deciding how many security personnel to employ for the purpose of reducing shoplifting.
4. The City of Houston board of representatives is deciding whether to build an addition onto one of the county libraries.

■ **Exercise 1–26**
Objectives of Managerial Accounting Activity
(LO 3, 4)

For each of the following activities, explain which of the objectives of managerial accounting activity is involved. In some cases, several objectives may be involved.

1. Developing a bonus reward system for the managers of the various offices of the AAA (American Automobile Association) Travel Agency.
2. Comparing the actual and planned cost of a consulting engagement completed by an engineering firm such as Allied Engineering.
3. Determining the cost of manufacturing a tennis racket by Wilson Sporting Goods.
4. Measuring the cost of the inventory of compact disc players on hand in a Best Buy store.
5. Estimating the annual operating cost of a newly proposed Wachovia branch bank.
6. Measuring the following costs incurred during one month in a Hyatt Regency hotel:
   a. Wages of table-service personnel.
   b. Property taxes.
7. Comparing a Sheraton Hotel's room rate structure, occupancy rate, and restaurant patronage with industry averages.

■ **Exercise 1–27**
Contributions of Managerial Accounting; Use of Internet
(LO 1, 3, 5)

This logo indicates use of the Internet.

Use the Internet to access the Web site for one of the following companies, or any other company of your choosing.

American Airlines	www.americanair.com
Coca-Cola	www.cocacola.com
Deere and Company	www.deere.com
IBM	www.ibm.com
Sears	www.sears.com

Required: Find the management discussion and analysis portion of the firm's most recent online annual report. Then briefly discuss how managerial accounting can contribute to the company's financial goals.

Use the Internet to access the Web site for one of the following companies, or any other company of your choosing.

This logo indicates group work.

Avis Rent-a-Car	www.avis.com
Expedia.com	www.expedia.com
Holland America Cruise Lines	www.hollandamerica.com
Levi Strauss & Company	www.levistrauss.com
Nokia	www.nokia.com
Regal Cinemas	www.regalcinemas.com

Required: After perusing the company's Web site, work as a group to list several key activities you believe would be in the company's value chain.

Problems

All applicable Problems are available with McGraw-Hill's *Connect Accounting*™.

David Garza recently retired at age 48, courtesy of a very healthy stock market and numerous stock options he had been granted while president of tiendas.com, an Internet start-up company. He soon moved to Valparaíso, Chile, to follow his dream of living by the sea. Garza, always the entrepreneur, began a sporting-goods store shortly after relocating. The single store soon grew to a chain of four outlets throughout the state. As Garza put it, "I can't believe how fast we've expanded. It's basically uncontrolled growth—growth that has occurred in spite of what we've done."

Although business has been profitable, the chain did have its share of problems. Store traffic was somewhat seasonal, with a slowdown occurring as winter approached. Garza therefore added ski equipment and accessories to his product line. The need to finance required inventories, which seemed to be bulging, left cash balances at very low levels, occasionally giving rise to short-term bank loans.

Part of Garza's operation focused on canoe building and white-water rafting trips. Reports from the company's financial accounting system seemed to indicate that these operations were losing money because of increasing costs, although Garza could not be sure. "The traditional income statement is not too useful in assessing the problem," he noted. "Also, my gut feeling is that we are not dealing with the best suppliers in terms of quality of goods, delivery reliability, and prices." Additional complications were caused by an increasingly competitive marketplace, with many former customers now buying merchandise and booking river excursions via the Internet, through catalogs received in the mail, or through businesses that advertised heavily in outdoor magazines.

Garza's background is marketing, and he appeared somewhat puzzled on how to proceed. The company's chief financial officer (CFO) would be an obvious asset in terms of addressing these problems. Unfortunately, she knew her numbers but lacked key knowledge of general business operations. The same could be said for other executives who managed somewhat in "silos," becoming experts in a narrow facet of the company but, in general, lacking a big-picture outlook for the firm.

The pen logo indicates a verbal written response.

Required:
1. Explain how the CFO and managerial accounting could assist Garza in addressing the company's problems.
2. Would a cross-functional team be useful here? Briefly discuss.
3. Does e-commerce appear to be a viable option for the firm? Explain, citing the difference between business-to-consumer and business-to-business channels. Which of the two channels, if any, would you recommend? Why?

Susan Lopez, a consultant with Deloitte & Young, has just begun an engagement at Four Corners Airlines, which is based in Santa Fe, New Mexico. The company has fallen on hard times of late despite record profits for the rest of the airline industry. Management is somewhat set in its ways and could probably use some "new blood," as the most recent hire to the firm's executive team was 12 years ago.

In Lopez's first meeting with the team, the airline's chief executive officer commented that "all that mattered in this industry were load factors—the percentage of seats sold on scheduled flights. If load factors were adequate, everything else would take care of itself." Lopez noted that while this measure was important, other, broader facets of operation were significant as well. She asked if any of the management team had heard of the balanced scorecard, and received dead silence as a response.

Based on her experiences with other engagements, including two that involved airlines, Lopez was convinced that the balanced scorecard could provide benefits in helping to solve the airline's woes. After a presentation about the philosophy of the balanced scorecard, Four Corners Airlines' management team accepted her idea, feeling that a shift in operating philosophy was needed for survival.

Required:

1. What is a balanced scorecard, and what are its typical key elements?

2. Lopez wants to assemble a committee to prepare the airline's balanced scorecard. List several of the company's functional areas (e.g., marketing) that should be represented on the committee.

3. Identify a number of measures to evaluate the key elements that you specified in requirement 1. Measures would include items such as load factors, number of passenger complaints, percentage of on-time arrivals, and so forth.

4. Do you see any problems with management's prior focus on only one measure (i.e., load factor)? Briefly explain.

■ **Problem 1–31**
Quality Control; Ethical Behavior
(LO 6, 7, 9, 10)

The balance logo identifies an ethical issue.

AccuSound Corporation manufactures printed circuits for stereo amplifiers. A common product defect is a "drift" caused by failure to maintain precise heat levels during the production process. Rejects from the 100 percent testing program can be reworked to acceptable levels if the defect is drift. However, in a recent analysis of customer complaints, Marie Allen, the assistant controller, and the quality control engineer determined that normal rework does not bring the circuits up to standard. Sampling showed that about half of the reworked circuits will fail after extended amplifier operation. The incidence of failure in the reworked circuits is projected to be about 15 percent over five years.

Unfortunately, there is no way to determine which reworked circuits will fail, because testing will not detect the problem. The rework process could be changed to correct the problem, but the cost-benefit analysis for the suggested change indicates that it is not economically feasible. AccuSound's marketing analyst has indicated that this problem will have a significant impact on the company's reputation and customer satisfaction. Consequently, the board of directors would interpret this problem as having serious negative implications for the company's profitability.

Allen included the circuit failure and rework problem in her report prepared for the upcoming quarterly meeting of the board of directors. Due to the potential adverse economic impact, Allen followed a long-standing practice of highlighting this information. After reviewing the reports to be presented, the plant manager and his staff complained to the controller that he should control his people better. "We can't upset the board with this kind of material. Tell Allen to tone that down. Maybe we can get it by the board in this meeting and have some time to work on it. People who buy those cheap systems and play them that loud shouldn't expect them to last forever."

The controller called Allen into his office and said, "Marie, you'll have to bury this one. The probable failure of reworks can be mentioned briefly in the oral presentation, but it should not be mentioned or highlighted in the advance material mailed to the board."

Allen feels strongly that the board will be misinformed on a potentially serious loss of income if she follows the controller's orders. Allen discussed the problem with the quality control engineer, who simply remarked, "That's your problem, Marie."

Required:

1. Discuss the ethical considerations that Marie Allen should recognize in deciding how to proceed.

2. Explain what ethical responsibilities should be accepted by (*a*) the controller, (*b*) the quality control engineer, and (*c*) the plant manager.

3. What should Marie Allen do? Explain your answer.

(CMA, adapted)

■ **Problem 1–32**
Role of the Divisional Controller; Retailer
(LO 4, 6, 9, 10)

Urban Elite Apparel designs women's apparel and sells it through retail outlets across the country. All of the company's clothing lines are manufactured by contract manufacturers around the world. A division manager is responsible for each of the company's retail divisions. Each division's controller, assigned by the corporate controller's office, manages the division's accounting system and provides analysis of financial information for the division manager. The division manager evaluates the performance of the division controller and makes recommendations for salary increases and promotions. However, the final responsibility for promotion evaluation and salary increases rests with the corporate controller.

Each of Urban Elite Apparel's divisions is responsible for product design, sales, pricing, operating expenses, and profit. However, corporate management exercises tight control over divisional financial operations. For example, all capital expenditure above a modest amount must be approved by corporate management. The method of financial reporting from the division to corporate headquarters provides further evidence of the degree of financial control. The division manager and the division controller submit to corporate headquarters separate and independent commentary on the financial results of the division. Corporate management states that the division controller is there to provide an independent view of the division's operations, not as a spy.

Required:

1. Discuss the arrangements for line and staff reporting in Urban Elite Apparel.

2. The division manager for Urban Elite Apparel has a "dual reporting" responsibility. The controller is responsible both to the division manager, who makes recommendations on salary and promotion, *and* to the corporate controller, who has the final say in such matters.

   a. Identify and discuss the factors that make the division controller's role difficult in this type of situation.

   b. Discuss the effect of the dual reporting relationship on the motivation of the division controller.

(CMA, adapted)

Case

Progressive Applications Corporation, a developer and distributor of business applications software, has been in business for five years. The company's main products include programs used for list management, billing, and accounting for the mail order shopping business. Progressive's sales have increased steadily to the current level of $75 million per year. The company has 300 employees.

Andrea Nolan joined Progressive approximately one year ago as accounting manager. Nolan's duties include supervision of the company's accounting operations and preparation of the company's financial statements. No one has noticed that in the past six months Progressive's sales have ceased to rise and have actually declined in the two most recent months. This unexpected downturn has resulted in cash shortages. Compounding these problems, Progressive has had to delay the introduction of a new product line due to delays in documentation preparation.

Progressive contracts most of its printing requirements to Web Graphic Inc., a small company owned by Rob Borman. Borman has dedicated a major portion of his printing capacity to Progressive's requirements because Progressive's contracts represent approximately 60 percent of Web Graphic's business. Nolan has known Borman for many years; as a matter of fact, she learned of Progressive's need for an accounting manager through Borman.

While preparing Progressive's most recent financial statements, Nolan became concerned about the company's ability to maintain steady payments to its suppliers; she estimated that payments to all vendors, normally made within 30 days, could exceed 65 days. Nolan is particularly concerned about payments to Web Graphic; she knows that Progressive had recently placed a large order with Web Graphic for the printing of the new product documentation, and she knows that Web Graphic will soon be placing an order for the special paper required for Progressive's documentation. Nolan is considering telling Borman about Progressive's cash problems; however, she is aware that a delay in the printing of the documentation would jeopardize Progressive's new product.

Required:

1. Describe Nolan's ethical responsibilities in this situation.

2. Independent of your answer to requirement (1), assume that Nolan learns that Borman of Web Graphic has decided to postpone the special paper order required for Progressive's printing job; Nolan believes Borman must have heard rumors about Progressive's financial problems from some other source because she has not talked to Borman. Should Nolan tell the appropriate Progressive officials that Borman has postponed the paper order? Explain your answer.

3. Independent of your answers to the first two requirements, assume that Borman has decided to postpone the special paper order because he has learned of Progressive's financial problems from some source other than Nolan. In addition, Nolan realizes that Jim Grason, Progressive's purchasing manager, knows of her friendship with Borman. Now Nolan is concerned that Grason may suspect she told Borman of Progressive's financial problems when Grason finds out Borman has postponed the order. Describe the steps that Nolan should take to resolve this situation.

(CMA, adapted)

■ **Case 1–33**
Disclosure of Confidential Information; Ethics; Software Developer
(LO 1, 3, 6, 9, 10)

THIS CHAPTER'S FOCUS COMPANY is the Comet Computer Company, which produces consumer electronics in its Guangzhou, China, plant.

Most of the company's computer sales are made online via business-to-consumer ("B2C") internet technology using its Web site, cometcomp.com. This manufacturer is a mass customizer, which means that its computer products combine many standard electronic components in different ways to produce custom-made computers to customer order. In this chapter, we will explore the many different issues involved in understanding the costs of running this or any business.

2 Basic Cost Management Concepts and Accounting for Mass Customization Operations

In contrast to the manufacturing setting of the Comet Computer Company, we explore the cost issues covered in the chapter in the **MİDAS** context of Midas, Inc. One of the world's largest automotive service companies, Midas has more than 2,400 company-owned or franchised automotive service locations on five continents. Midas' management, like that of any other company, must understand its costs in order to be successful in a competitive business environment.

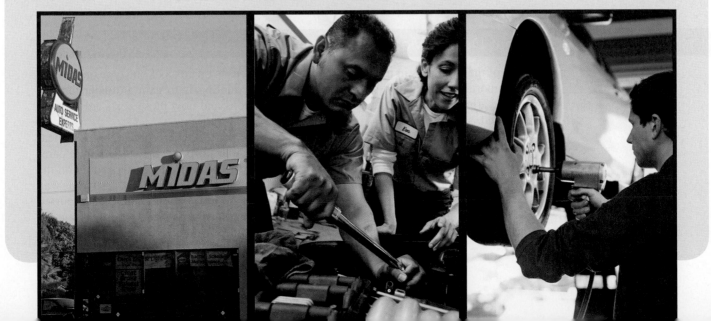

1 Explain what is meant by the word *cost*.

2 Distinguish among product costs, period costs, and expenses.

3 Describe the role of costs in published financial statements.

4 List five types of manufacturing operations and describe mass customization.

5 Give examples of three types of manufacturing costs.

6 Prepare a schedule of cost of goods manufactured, a schedule of cost of goods sold, and an income statement for a manufacturer.

7 Understand the importance of identifying an organization's cost drivers.

8 Describe the behavior of variable and fixed costs, in total and on a per-unit basis.

9 Distinguish among direct, indirect, controllable, and uncontrollable costs.

10 Define and give examples of an opportunity cost, an out-of-pocket cost, a sunk cost, a differential cost, a marginal cost, and an average cost.

The process of management worldwide involves formulating strategy, planning, control, decision making, and directing operational activities. Managers can perform each of these functions more effectively with managerial accounting information. Much of this information focuses on the costs incurred in the organization. For example, in *formulating its overall strategy,* AirAsia's management team considered the cost savings that result from being a low-cost, no-frills airline. In *planning* AirAsia's routes and flight schedules, managers must consider aircraft fuel costs, salaries of flight crews, and airport landing fees. *Controlling* the costs of manufacturing heavy equipment requires that Caterpillar's managerial accountants carefully measure and manage production costs. In *making decisions* about locating a new store, Walmart managers need information about the cost of building, maintaining, equipping, and staffing the store. Finally, to *direct operational activities,* managers in all three of these companies need information about the cost of salaries, utilities, security, and a host of other goods and services.

What Do We Mean by a Cost?

Learning Objective 1

Explain what is meant by the word *cost*.

Each of the examples in the preceding paragraph focuses on costs of one type or another. An important first step in studying managerial accounting is to gain an understanding of the various types of costs incurred by organizations and how those costs are actively managed.

At the most basic level, a **cost** may be defined as the sacrifice made, usually measured by the resources given up, to achieve a particular purpose. If we look more carefully, though, we find that the word *cost* can have different meanings depending on the context in which it is used. Cost data that are classified and recorded in a particular way for one purpose may be inappropriate for another use. For example, the costs incurred in producing gasoline last year are important in measuring ExxonMobil's income for the year. However, those costs may not be useful in planning the company's refinery operations for the next year if the cost of oil has changed significantly or if the methods of producing gasoline have improved.

The important point is that different cost concepts and classifications are used for different purposes. Understanding these concepts and classifications enables the managerial accountant to provide appropriate cost data to the managers who need it. The purpose of this chapter is to enable the users of this textbook to gain a firm grasp of the cost terminology used in managerial accounting, which will be used throughout the book.

Product Costs, Period Costs, and Expenses

An important issue in both managerial and financial accounting is the timing with which the costs of acquiring assets or services are recognized as expenses. An **expense** is defined as the cost incurred when an asset is used up or sold for the purpose of generating revenue. The terms *product cost* and *period cost* are used to describe the timing with which various expenses are recognized.

A **product cost** is a cost assigned to goods that were either purchased or manufactured for resale. The product cost is used to value the inventory of manufactured goods or merchandise until the goods are sold. In the period of the sale, the product costs are recognized as an expense called **cost of goods sold.** The product cost of merchandise inventory acquired by a retailer or wholesaler for resale consists of the purchase cost of the inventory plus any shipping charges. The product cost of manufactured inventory includes all of the costs incurred in its manufacture. For example, the labor cost of a production employee at Foxconn Technologies Group is included as a product cost of the iPads that it assembles for Apple. Exhibit 2–1 illustrates the relationship between product costs and cost-of-goods-sold expense.

> "We are expected to say, 'Here are the costs, and this is why the costs are what they are, and this is how they compare to other things, and here are some suggestions where we could possibly improve.'" (2a)
> **Caterpillar**

Learning Objective 2

Distinguish among product costs, period costs, and expenses.

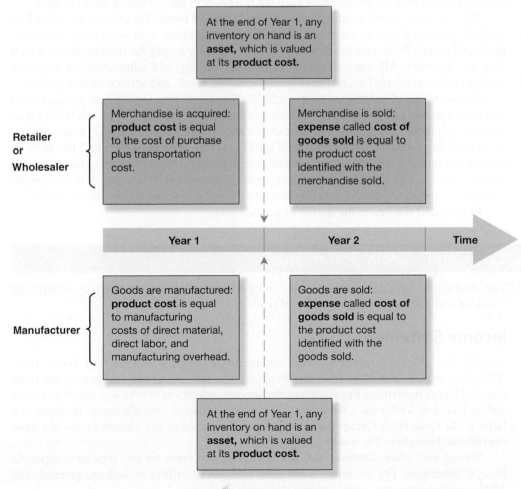

Exhibit 2–1
Product Costs and Cost of Goods Sold

Exhibit 2–2
Period Costs

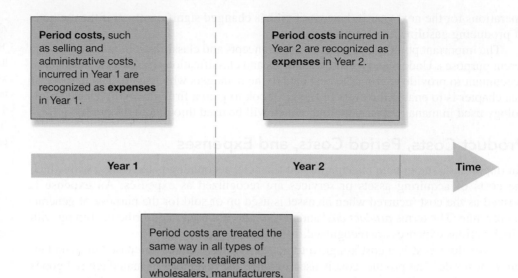

Another term for product cost is **inventoriable cost,** since a product cost is stored as the cost of inventory until the goods are sold. In addition to retailers, wholesalers, and manufacturers, the concept of product cost is relevant to other producers of inventoriable goods. Agricultural firms, lumber companies, and mining firms are examples of nonmanufacturers that produce inventoriable goods. Apples, timber, coal, and other such goods are inventoried at their product cost until the time period during which they are sold.

All costs that are not product costs are called **period costs.** These costs are identified with the period of time in which they are incurred rather than with units of purchased or produced goods. Period costs are recognized as expenses during the time period in which they are incurred. All research and development, selling, and administrative costs are treated as period costs. This is true in manufacturing, retail, and service industry firms.

Research and development costs include all costs of developing new products and services. The costs of running laboratories, building prototypes of new products, and testing new products are all classified as research and development (or R&D) costs. *Selling costs* include salaries, commissions, and travel costs of sales personnel and the costs of advertising and promotion. *Administrative costs* refer to all costs of running the organization as a whole. The salaries of top-management personnel and the costs of the corporate accounting, legal, and public relations activities are examples of administrative costs.

Exhibit 2–2 illustrates the nature of period costs.

Costs on Financial Statements

Learning Objective 3

Describe the role of costs in published financial statements.

The distinction between product costs and period costs is emphasized by examining financial statements from three different types of firms.

Income Statement

Exhibit 2–3 displays recent income statements, in highly summarized form, from AirAsia Group, Caterpillar, Inc., and Walmart Stores, Inc. These companies are from three different industries. Representing the service industry is AirAsia, a major low-cost airline based in Malaysia. Caterpillar is a heavy equipment manufacturer. Walmart is a large retail firm. Both Caterpillar and Walmart are based in the United States but have operations throughout the world.

Selling and administrative costs are always period costs on any type of company's income statement. For example, Caterpillar lists $3.19 billion of selling, general, and administrative expenses on its income statement in Exhibit 2–3.

For Caterpillar, the costs of manufactured inventory are product costs. All costs incurred in manufacturing finished products are stored in inventory until the time period when the products are sold. Then the product costs of the inventory sold become cost of goods sold, an expense on the income statement.

AIRASIA GROUP
Statement of Income for a Recent Year
(converted from Malaysian Ringgits to US Dollars, in thousands)

Operating revenue:	
Passenger seat sales	$ 674,554
Aircraft lease income	101,066
Travel and tour operations	19,199
Fees, baggage, freight, other	193,627
Total operating revenue	$ 988,447
Less: Operating expenses:	
Salaries, wages, and benefits	$ 96,545
Fuel	292,724
Maintenance materials and repairs	129,541
Aircraft lease expenses	33,838
Travel and tour expenses	16,887
Depreciation and amortization	141,234
Other operating expenses	22,000
Total operating expenses	$ 732,770
Operating income	$ 255,676
Other expenses (income):	
Interest expense	$ 118,305
Interest income	(26,662)
Other (gains) losses, net	(32,302)
Total other expenses (income)	$ 59,341
Income before income taxes	$ 196,335
Provision for income taxes	36,605
Net income	$ 159,730

CATERPILLAR, INC.
Statement of Income for a Recent Year

Sales revenue	$ 36,339,000
Less: Cost of goods sold	26,036,000
Gross profit	$ 10,303,000
Less: Operating costs:	
Selling, general, and administrative expenses	$ 3,190,000
Research and development expenses	1,084,000
Depreciation	1,477,000
Total operating costs	$ 4,552,000
Operating income	$ 4,552,000
Add: Nonoperating income	450,000
Less: Nonoperating expenses	1,028,000
Income before taxes	$ 3,974,000
Provision for income taxes	(1,120,000)
Net income	$ 2,854,000

(continues)

Value measured by product costs →

Exhibit 2–3
Income Statements from Three Different Industries (all figures in thousands of dollars)

CATERPILLAR®

Exhibit 2–3
(concluded)

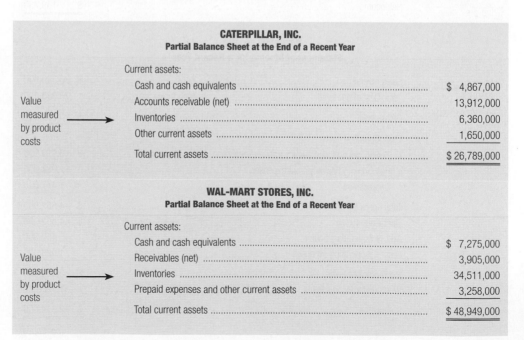

WAL-MART STORES, INC. Statement of Income for a Recent Year	
Sales revenue	$ 405,607,000
Less: Cost of goods sold	306,158,000
Gross profit	$ 99,449,000
Less: Selling, general, and administrative expenses	76,651,000
Operating income	$ 22,798,000
Less: Interest expense	1,900,000
Income before income taxes	$ 20,898,000
Provision for income taxes	(7,145,000)
Minority interest and income from discontinued operations	(353,000)
Net income	$ 13,400,000

(Value measured by product costs → Sales revenue, Less: Cost of goods sold)

Product costs for Walmart include all costs of acquiring merchandise inventory for resale. These product costs are stored in inventory until the time period during which the merchandise is sold. Then these costs become cost of goods sold.

There are no inventoried product costs at AirAsia. Although this firm does engage in the production of air transportation services, its service output is consumed as soon as it is produced. Service industry firms, such as Saudi Telecom, JPMorganChase, Sheraton Hotels, China Life Insurance, and McDonalds, generally refer to the costs of producing services as **operating expenses.** Operating expenses are treated as period costs and are expensed during the period in which they are incurred. AirAsia includes costs such as employee wages, aviation fuel, and aircraft maintenance in operating expenses for the period.

> "What we should become is a business partner who helps people understand what the financials are saying." (2b)
>
> Qwest

Balance Sheet

Since retailers, wholesalers, and manufacturers sell inventoriable products, their balance sheets are also affected by product costs. Exhibit 2–4 displays the current-assets section from recent balance sheets of Caterpillar and Walmart. Included in the current-assets section of each of these balance sheets is inventory. Manufacturers, such as Caterpillar,

Exhibit 2–4
Partial Balance Sheets for a Manufacturer and a Retailer (all figures in thousands of dollars)

CATERPILLAR, INC. Partial Balance Sheet at the End of a Recent Year	
Current assets:	
Cash and cash equivalents	$ 4,867,000
Accounts receivable (net)	13,912,000
Inventories	6,360,000
Other current assets	1,650,000
Total current assets	$ 26,789,000

(Value measured by product costs → Inventories)

WAL-MART STORES, INC. Partial Balance Sheet at the End of a Recent Year	
Current assets:	
Cash and cash equivalents	$ 7,275,000
Receivables (net)	3,905,000
Inventories	34,511,000
Prepaid expenses and other current assets	3,258,000
Total current assets	$ 48,949,000

(Value measured by product costs → Inventories)

have three types of inventory. **Raw-material** inventory includes all materials before they are placed into production. **Work-in-process** inventory refers to manufactured products that are only partially completed at the date when the balance sheet is prepared. **Finished-goods** inventory refers to manufactured goods that are complete and ready for sale. The values of the work-in-process and finished-goods inventories are measured by their product costs.

On the Walmart balance sheet, the cost of acquiring merchandise is listed as the value of the merchandise inventories.

> "Now the accountants are not only the interpreters. They drive management toward the proper response to what the numbers are telling us." (2c)
> **ITT Automotive**

Manufacturing Operations and Manufacturing Costs

Although there are tens of thousands of manufacturing firms, their basic production processes can be classified into five generic types. The nature of the manufacturing process can affect the manufacturing costs incurred. Therefore, the management team is in a better position to manage these costs if the relationship of the production process to the types of costs incurred is understood. Exhibit 2–5 defines and describes the five generic manufacturing processes.[1]

We will study the role of managerial accounting and cost management in four of these manufacturing processes. This chapter will focus on a mass customization operation, similar

> **Learning Objective 4**
>
> List five types of manufacturing operations and describe mass customization.

---

[1]The exhibit is based on the well-known and widely used Hayes-Wheelwright production process matrix, with the exception of mass customization, which postdates the Hayes-Wheelwright formulation. See Robert H. Hayes and Steven C. Wheelwright, *Restoring Our Competitive Edge* (New York: John Wiley and Sons, 1984), p. 209.

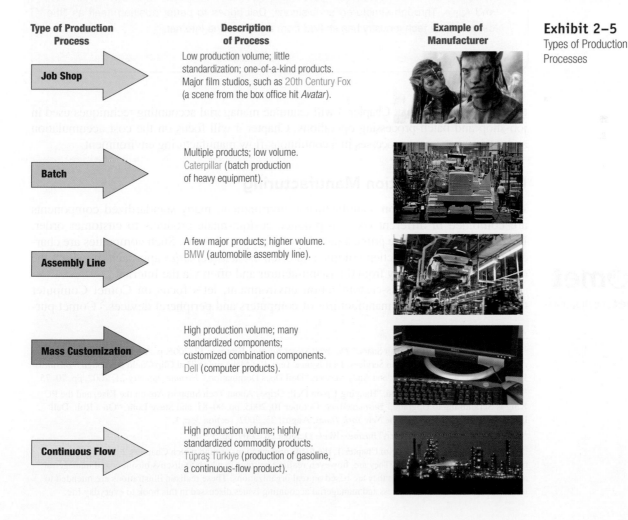

Type of Production Process	Description of Process	Example of Manufacturer
Job Shop	Low production volume; little standardization; one-of-a-kind products. Major film studios, such as 20th Century Fox (a scene from the box office hit *Avatar*).	
Batch	Multiple products; low volume. Caterpillar (batch production of heavy equipment).	
Assembly Line	A few major products; higher volume. BMW (automobile assembly line).	
Mass Customization	High production volume; many standardized components; customized combination components. Dell (computer products).	
Continuous Flow	High production volume; highly standardized commodity products. Tüpraş Türkiye (production of gasoline, a continuous-flow product).	

Exhibit 2–5
Types of Production Processes

MASS CUSTOMIZATION

"There is no better way to make, sell, and deliver PCs than the way Dell Inc. does it, and nobody executes that model better than Dell." The company's machines are made to order and delivered directly to customers, who get the exact machines they want cheaper than they can get them from Dell's competition. "Dell has some 24 facilities in and around Austin and employs more than 18,000 local workers. Michael Dell, the company's restless founder, is constantly looking for ways to improve the company's operations."[2] In one year alone, Dell cut $1 billion out of its costs—half from manufacturing—and Dell executives vowed to cut another $1 billion.

At the Topfer Manufacturing Center in Austin, workers "scuttle about in the 200,000-square-foot plant like ants on a hot plate. Gathered in cramped six-person 'cells,' they assemble computers from batches of parts that arrive via a computer-directed conveyor system overhead. If a worker encounters a problem, that batch can instantly be shifted to another cell, avoiding the stoppages that plague conventional assembly lines. Dell is constantly tinkering with factory layout and product design to move computers through at a higher velocity."

In spite of the ups and downs of the computer technology industry, most observers believe that Dell's business model will continue to be successful. However, the company has acknowledged that it needs to upgrade its tech support services in order to better serve its customers.[3]

Recently, Michael Dell has charted a change in course for Dell, by seeking to acquire companies that can help Dell compete more effectively with rivals Hewlett-Packard, Lenovo, and Apple. Through structured acquisitions, Dell hopes to better position itself as "the center of the tech industry has shifted from the PC to the Internet."[4]

to that used by Dell Inc. Chapter 3 will examine managerial accounting techniques used in job-shop and batch-processing operations. Chapter 4 will focus on the cost accumulation and cost management processes in a continuous-flow manufacturing environment.

Mass-Customization Manufacturing

In a **mass-customization** manufacturing environment, many standardized components are combined in different ways to produce custom-made products to customer order. Dell Inc. and Lenovo are prime examples of mass customizers. Such companies are characterized by high production volume and often use a *direct-sales* approach, in which the consumer orders directly from the manufacturer and often via the Internet.

To illustrate a mass-customization environment, let's focus on Comet Computer Corporation, a Chinese manufacturer of computers and peripheral devices.[5] Comet pur-

[2]Thaddeus Herrick, "Dell's Profit Soars," *The Wall Street Journal,* February 17, 2006, p. A3; Louise Lee and Spencer Ante, "Can the PC King Excel in Services: Dell Is on a Tear, But Maintaining That Clip Could Be Tough," *Business-Week,* May 30, 2005, pp. 70–73; and Andy Serwer, "Dell Does Domination," *Fortune,* January 21, 2002, pp. 70–75.

[3]Louise Lee and Emily Thornton, "Hanging Up on Dell: Gripes About Tech Support Are on the Rise, and the PC King is Scrambling to Upgrade," *BusinessWeek,* October 10, 2005, pp. 80–81; and Steve Lohr, "On a Roll, Dell Enters Uncharted Territory," *The New York Times,* August 25, 2002; section 3, p. 1.

[4]Cliff Edwards, "Dell's Do-Over," *BusinessWeek,* October 26, 2009, pp. 37–40.

[5]As mentioned at the beginning of Chapter 1, the focus organizations around which Chapters 2 through 17 are built are not real organizations. They are, however, realistic settings in which to discuss business and managerial accounting issues. In most cases they are based on real organizations. These realistic illustrations are intended to help students connect the business and managerial accounting issues discussed in this book to everyday life.

chases computer parts such as motherboards, computer chips, and power supplies and then assembles these parts into customized personal computers to customer specifications. A finished computer is then packaged with the monitor, keyboard, printer, and cables ordered by the customer, all of which are purchased by Comet.

The direct-sales model, which was popularized by Dell Inc. is used. Ninety percent of Comet's orders are placed on the company's Web site, cometcomp.com, and 10 percent are taken on an a toll-free phone number. No sales are made through retail channels.

Comet's production process is triggered when a customer places an order, either on the company's Web site, cometcomp.com, or on its toll-free phone line. The customer specifies every aspect of the desired computer system, including the type of processor and amount of memory in the hard drive, the size of the monitor and type of printer, and finally any preinstalled software. Either a Web or a phone sales representative transmits the order electronically to the appropriate production cell module.[6] A production cell module, or *mod,* is responsible for manufacturing a particular product line, such as a desktop computer, laptop, or server. When the order is received in the appropriate mod, the assembly process begins. Memory and processor chips are installed in the motherboard, which is then mounted on the chassis. Then such components as the DVD drive, hard drive, and power supply are placed into the chassis. After all of the components are chassis-mounted, the computer's hood (cover) is installed, and the finished unit moves to a test and inspection mod. After the unit checks out for reliability, it goes to the software installation mod, where the software ordered by the customer is preinstalled. From the software mod, the unit goes to the shipping mod, where it is boxed and prepared for shipping. Comet strives to ship every customer order within six days.

Before we discuss Comet's production process further, let's turn our attention to the types of manufacturing costs incurred by Comet and other manufacturers.

> "[Management accountants] will be more analytical . . . and more of a partner with the operational side of the business." (2d)
> **ITT Automotive**

Manufacturing Costs

To assist managers in planning, decision making, and cost management, managerial accountants classify costs by the functional area of the organization to which costs relate. Some examples of functional areas are manufacturing, marketing, administration, and research and development. Manufacturing costs are further classified into the following three categories: direct material, direct labor, and manufacturing overhead.

> **Learning Objective 5**
>
> Give examples of three types of manufacturing costs.

Direct Material   Raw material that is consumed in the manufacturing process, is physically incorporated in the finished product, and can be traced to products relatively easily is called **direct material.** Examples include the sheet metal in a Subaru automobile and the semiconductors in a Comet computer.

Some students are confused by the seemingly interchangeable use of the terms *raw material* and *direct material.* However, there is a difference in the meaning of these terms. *Before* material is entered into the production process, it is called *raw* material. *After* it enters production, it becomes *direct* material.

Direct Labor   The cost of salaries, wages, and fringe benefits for personnel who work directly on the manufactured products is classified as **direct-labor cost.** Examples include the wages of personnel who assemble Comet computers and who operate the equipment in a Royal Dutch Shell refinery.

The cost of fringe benefits for direct-labor personnel, such as employer-paid health-insurance premiums and the employer's pension contributions, also should be classified as direct-labor costs.

---

[6]The description of the manufacturing process is based on that used by Dell Inc.

Manufacturing Overhead
All other costs of manufacturing are classified as **manufacturing overhead,** which includes three types of costs: indirect material, indirect labor, and other manufacturing costs.

Indirect Material
The cost of materials that are required for the production process but do not become an integral part of the finished product are classified as **indirect material** costs. An example is the cost of drill bits used in a metal-fabrication department at Ford Motor Company. The drill bits wear out and are discarded, but they do not become part of the product. Materials that do become an integral part of the finished product but are insignificant in cost are also often classified as indirect material. Materials such as glue or paint may be so inexpensive that it is not worth tracing their costs to specific products as direct materials.

Indirect Labor
The costs of personnel who do not work directly on the product, but whose services are necessary for the manufacturing process, are classified as **indirect labor.** Such personnel include production department supervisors, custodial employees, and security guards.

Other Manufacturing Costs
All other manufacturing costs that are neither material nor labor costs are classified as manufacturing overhead. These costs include depreciation of plant and equipment, property taxes, insurance, and utilities such as electricity, as well as the costs of operating service departments. **Service departments** or **support departments** are those that do not work directly on manufacturing products but are necessary for the manufacturing process to occur. Examples include equipment-maintenance departments and computer-aided-design (CAD) departments. In some manufacturing firms, departments are referred to as *work centers.*

Other manufacturing overhead costs include overtime premiums and the cost of idle time. An **overtime premium** is the extra compensation paid to an employee who works beyond the time normally scheduled. Suppose a technician who assembles Comet computers earns $16 per hour. The technician works 48 hours during a week instead of the scheduled time of 40 hours. The overtime pay scale is time and a half, or 150 percent of the regular wage. The technician's compensation for the week is classified as follows:

Direct-labor cost ($16 × 48)	$768
Overhead (overtime premium: ½ × $16 × 8)	64
Total compensation paid	$832

Only the *extra* compensation of $8 per hour is classified as overtime premium. The regular wage of $16 per hour is treated as direct labor, even for the eight overtime hours.

Idle time is time that is not spent productively by an employee due to such events as equipment breakdowns or new setups of production runs. Such idle time is an unavoidable feature of most manufacturing processes. The cost of an employee's idle time is classified as overhead so that it may be spread across all production jobs, rather than being associated with a particular production job. Suppose that during one 40-hour shift, a machine breakdown resulted in idle time of 1½ hours and a power failure idled workers for an additional ½ hour. If an employee earns $14 per hour, the employee's wages for the week will be classified as follows:

Direct-labor cost ($14 × 38)	$532
Overhead (idle time: $14 × 2)	28
Total compensation paid	$560

> "If you just simply have [an employee] performing an [assembly] operation, that's direct labor. But when you put in a robot to do the job, which we're all doing, then you've got to have an engineer to make sure the [robot] is programmed right. So now it becomes indirect labor." (2e)
>
> **Chrysler**

Overtime premiums and the cost of idle time should be classified as manufacturing overhead, rather than associated with a particular production job, because the particular job on which idle time or overtime may occur tends to be selected at random. Suppose several production jobs are scheduled during an eight-hour shift, and the last job remains unfinished at the end of the shift. The overtime to finish the last job is necessitated by all of the jobs scheduled during the shift, not just the last one. Similarly, if a power failure occurs during one of several production jobs, the idle time that results is not due to the job that happens to be in process at the time. The power failure is a random event, and the resulting cost should be treated as a cost of all of the department's production.

To summarize, manufacturing costs include direct material, direct labor, and manufacturing overhead. Direct labor and overhead are often called **conversion costs,** since they are the costs of "converting" raw material into finished products. Direct material and direct labor are often referred to as **prime costs.**

Manufacturing Cost Flows

Direct material, direct labor, and manufacturing overhead are the three types of production costs incurred by manufacturers. These costs are product costs because they are stored in inventory until the time period when the manufacturer's products are sold. Manufacturers have product-costing systems to keep track of the flow of these costs from the time production begins until finished products are sold. This flow of manufacturing costs is depicted in Exhibit 2–6. As direct material is consumed in production, its cost is added to work-in-process inventory. Similarly, the costs of direct labor and manufacturing overhead are accumulated in work in process.

When products are finished, their costs are transferred from work-in-process inventory to finished-goods inventory. The total cost of direct material, direct labor, and manufacturing overhead transferred from work-in-process inventory to finished-goods inventory is called the **cost of goods manufactured.** The costs then are stored in finished goods until the time period when the products are sold. At that time, the product costs are transferred from finished goods to cost of goods sold, which is an expense of the period when the sale is made. Exhibit 2–6 concentrates on the conceptual basis of a product-costing system. The detailed procedures and accounts used to keep track of product costs are covered in Chapters 3 and 4.

Manufacturers generally prepare a **schedule of cost of goods manufactured** and a **schedule of cost of goods sold** to summarize the flow of manufacturing costs during an accounting period. These schedules are intended for internal use by management and are

> "In my mind, cost accountants are going to be business analysts." (2f)
> **Boeing**

Learning Objective 6

Prepare a schedule of cost of goods manufactured, a schedule of cost of goods sold, and an income statement for a manufacturer.

Exhibit 2–6
Flow of Manufacturing Costs

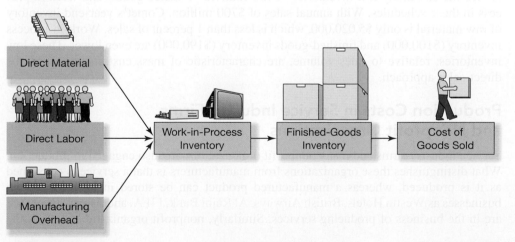

Product costs . . .   . . . are stored in inventory . . .   . . . until the products are sold.

Exhibit 2–7
Manufacturing Cost
Schedules

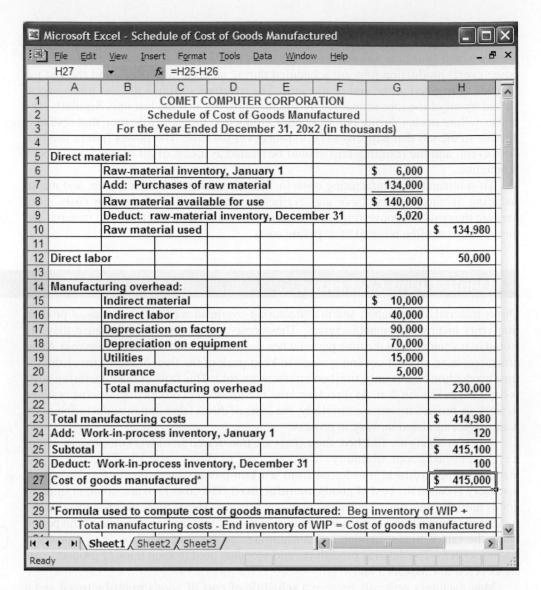

	A	B	C	D	E	F	G	H
1			COMET COMPUTER CORPORATION					
2			Schedule of Cost of Goods Manufactured					
3			For the Year Ended December 31, 20x2 (in thousands)					
4								
5	Direct material:							
6		Raw-material inventory, January 1					$ 6,000	
7		Add: Purchases of raw material					134,000	
8		Raw material available for use					$ 140,000	
9		Deduct: raw-material inventory, December 31					5,020	
10		Raw material used						$ 134,980
11								
12	Direct labor							50,000
13								
14	Manufacturing overhead:							
15		Indirect material					$ 10,000	
16		Indirect labor					40,000	
17		Depreciation on factory					90,000	
18		Depreciation on equipment					70,000	
19		Utilities					15,000	
20		Insurance					5,000	
21		Total manufacturing overhead						230,000
22								
23	Total manufacturing costs							$ 414,980
24	Add: Work-in-process inventory, January 1							120
25	Subtotal							$ 415,100
26	Deduct: Work-in-process inventory, December 31							100
27	Cost of goods manufactured*							$ 415,000
28								
29	*Formula used to compute cost of goods manufactured: Beg inventory of WIP +							
30	Total manufacturing costs - End inventory of WIP = Cost of goods manufactured							

H27   =H25-H26

generally not made available to the public. The Excel spreadsheets in Exhibit 2–7 show these two schedules along with an income statement for Comet Computer Corporation.[7] Notice the extremely low inventories of raw material, finished goods, and work in process in these schedules. With annual sales of $700 million, Comet's year-end inventory of raw material is only $5,020,000, which is less than 1 percent of sales. Work-in-process inventory ($100,000) and finished-goods inventory ($190,000) are even lower. These low inventories, relative to sales volume, are characteristic of mass customizers using the direct-sales approach.

Production Costs in Service Industry Firms and Nonprofit Organizations

Service industry firms and many nonprofit organizations are also engaged in production. What distinguishes these organizations from manufacturers is that a service is consumed as it is produced, whereas a manufactured product can be stored in inventory. Such businesses as Westin Hotels, British Airways, Al Rajhi Bank, FIFA, and Allianz Insurance are in the business of producing services. Similarly, nonprofit organizations such as the

---

[7]Some numerical displays in the text will be presented as Excel spreadsheets, since this tool is widely used in business.

Exhibit 2–7
(concluded)

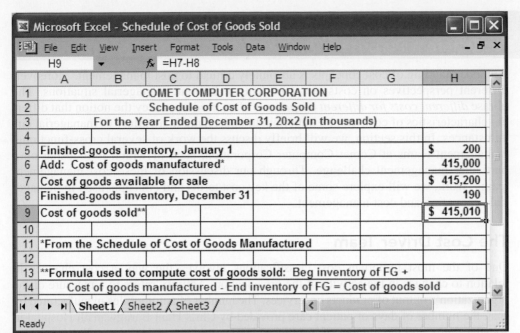

Microsoft Excel - Schedule of Cost of Goods Sold

File Edit View Insert Format Tools Data Window Help

H9   *fx* =H7-H8

	A	B	C	D	E	F	G	H
1	COMET COMPUTER CORPORATION							
2	Schedule of Cost of Goods Sold							
3	For the Year Ended December 31, 20x2 (in thousands)							
4								
5	Finished-goods inventory, January 1							$ 200
6	Add: Cost of goods manufactured*							415,000
7	Cost of goods available for sale							$ 415,200
8	Finished-goods inventory, December 31							190
9	Cost of goods sold**							$ 415,010
10								
11	*From the Schedule of Cost of Goods Manufactured							
12								
13	**Formula used to compute cost of goods sold: Beg inventory of FG +							
14	Cost of goods manufactured - End inventory of FG = Cost of goods sold							

Sheet1 / Sheet2 / Sheet3 /

Ready

Microsoft Excel - Income Statement

File Edit View Insert Format Tools Data Window Help

H11   *fx* =H9-H10

	A	B	C	D	E	F	G	H
1	COMET COMPUTER CORPORATION							
2	Income Statement							
3	For the Year Ended December 31, 20x2 (in thousands)							
4								
5	Sales revenue							$ 700,000
6	Less: Cost of goods sold*							415,010
7	Gross margin							$ 284,990
8	Selling and administrative expenses							174,490
9	Income before taxes							$ 110,500
10	Income tax expense							30,000
11	Net Income							$ 80,500
12								
13	*From the Schedule of Cost of Goods Sold							

Sheet1 / Sheet2 / Sheet3 /

Ready

International Federation of Red Cross and Red Crescent Societies and the Guggenheim Museum also are engaged in service production. While less commonly observed in service firms, the same cost classifications used in manufacturing companies can be applied. For example, Air France produces air transportation services. Direct material includes such costs as jet fuel, aircraft parts, and food and beverages. Direct labor includes the salaries of the flight crew and the wages of aircraft-maintenance personnel. Overhead costs include depreciation of baggage-handling equipment, insurance, and airport landing fees.

The process of recording and classifying costs is important in service industry firms and nonprofit organizations for the same reasons as in manufacturing firms. Cost analysis is used in pricing banking and insurance services, locating travel and car-rental agencies, setting enrollment targets in universities, and determining cost reimbursements in hospitals. As such organizations occupy an ever-growing role in our economy, applying managerial accounting to their activities will take on ever-greater importance.

Basic Cost Management Concepts: Different Costs for Different Purposes

An understanding of cost concepts is absolutely critical to cost management. Moreover, different perspectives on costs are important in different managerial situations. The phrase *different costs for different purposes* is often used to convey the notion that different characteristics of costs can be important to understand in a variety of managerial circumstances. In this section, we will briefly discuss the work of several cross-functional management teams at Comet Computer Corporation, each of which is focusing on a particular management challenge. Through our discussion of these cost management teams' work, we will explore some of the key cost terms and concepts used in managerial accounting and cost management.

The Cost Driver Team

One of the most important cost classifications involves the way a cost changes in relation to changes in the activity of the organization. **Activity** refers to a measure of the organization's output of products or services. The number of automobiles manufactured by Fiat, the number of days of patient care provided by Chris Hani Baragwanath Hospital in Johannesburg, and the number of insurance claims settled by Allstate are all measures of activity. The activities that cause costs to be incurred are also called *cost drivers*.

Cost drivers in the airline industry are complex. The capacity of an airplane and its passenger load drive costs, but so do a variety of other factors related to the airline's operations.

One of Comet Computer Corporation's cost management teams was formed to examine the various costs incurred by Comet. The team consisted of an engineer, a production manager, a purchasing manager, and a managerial accountant. After identifying the various costs incurred by Comet, the team was charged to go on to identify the cost drivers upon which various types of costs depend.[8] A **cost driver** is a characteristic of an activity or event that causes costs to be incurred by that activity or event. In most organizations, different types of costs respond to widely differing cost drivers. For example, in a manufacturing firm, the cost of assembly labor would be driven by the quantity of products manufactured as well as the number of parts in each product. In contrast, the cost of machine setup labor would be driven by the number of production runs. The cost of material-handling labor would be driven by material-related factors such as the quantity and cost of raw material used, the number of parts in various products, and the number of raw-material shipments received.

In identifying a cost driver, the managerial accountant should consider the extent to which a cost or pool of costs varies in accordance with the cost driver. The higher the correlation between the cost and the cost driver, the more -accurate will be the resulting understanding of cost behavior. Another important consideration is the cost of measuring the cost driver. Thus, there is a cost-benefit trade-off in the identification of cost drivers. As the number of cost drivers used in explaining an organization's cost behavior increases, the accuracy of the resulting information will increase. However, the cost of the information will increase also. The concept of a cost driver will be an important aspect of many of the topics discussed in subsequent chapters.

---

[8]Such cost driver teams have been established by many companies. For descriptions of such efforts at Deere and Company and Hewlett-Packard Corporation, see the management cases: John Deere Component Works and Hewlett-Packard-Queensferry Telecommunications Division (Harvard Business School).

Variable and Fixed Costs

After identifying costs and cost drivers for Comet Computer Corporation's operations, the cost driver team went on to examine the relationship of various costs to the activities performed. Such a relationship is referred to as *cost behavior* and will be the focus of Chapter 7. At this juncture, though, let's look at two types of cost behavior identified at Comet Computer Corporation: *variable* and *fixed costs.*

Learning Objective **8**

Describe the behavior of variable and fixed costs, in total and on a per-unit basis.

Variable Costs
A **variable cost** changes in total in direct proportion to a change in the level of activity (or cost driver). If activity increases by 20 percent, total variable cost increases by 20 percent also. For example, the cost of sheet metal used by Chrysler will increase by approximately 5 percent if automobile production increases by 5 percent. The cost of napkins and other paper products used at a KFC will increase by roughly 10 percent if the restaurant's patronage increases by 10 percent.

At Comet Computer Corporation, the cost management team identified direct material as a variable cost. One purchased component, a power bus assembly, costs $100 per computer manufactured. The cost behavior for this direct material cost is graphed and tabulated in Exhibit 2–8.

Panel A of Exhibit 2–8 displays a graph of this variable cost. As this graph shows, *total* variable cost increases proportionately with activity. When activity doubles, from 10 to 20 units, total variable cost doubles, from $1,000 to $2,000. However, the variable cost *per unit* remains the same as activity changes. The variable cost associated with each unit of activity is $100, whether it is the first unit, the fourth, or the eighteenth. The table in panel B of Exhibit 2–8 illustrates this point.

To summarize, as activity changes, total variable cost increases or decreases proportionately with the activity change, but unit variable cost remains the same.

Exhibit 2–8
Variable Cost

Cömet
Cömetcomp.com

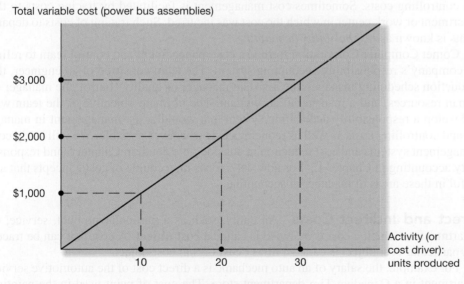

A. Graph of Total Variable Cost

Total variable cost (power bus assemblies)

$3,000		
$2,000		
$1,000		
	10 20 30	Activity (or cost driver): units produced

B. Tabulation of Variable Cost

Activity (or cost driver)	Variable Cost per Unit	Total Variable Cost
1	$100	$ 100
4	100	400
18	100	1,800
30	100	3,000

Fixed Costs A **fixed cost** remains unchanged in total as the level of activity (or cost driver) varies. If activity increases or decreases by 20 percent, total fixed cost remains the same. Examples of fixed costs include depreciation of plant and equipment at a Nike factory, the cost of property taxes at a Taj Hotel, and the salary of a subway train operator employed by the New York Transit Authority.

Comet Computer Corporation's cost driver team identified the salary of the manager of Web sales operations as a fixed cost. Her $150,000 annual salary does not vary with the number of units produced or sold.

This fixed cost is graphed in panel A of Exhibit 2–9.

From the graph in Exhibit 2–9, it is apparent that *total* fixed cost remains unchanged as activity changes. When activity triples, from 10 to 30 units, total fixed cost remains constant at $150,000. However, the fixed cost *per unit* does change as activity changes. If the activity level is only 1 unit, then the fixed cost per unit is $150,000 per unit ($150,000 ÷ 1). If the activity level is 10 units, then the fixed cost per unit declines to $15,000 per unit ($150,000 ÷ 10). The behavior of total fixed cost and unit fixed cost is illustrated by the table in panel B of Exhibit 2–9.

Another way of viewing the change in unit fixed cost as activity changes is in a graph, as shown in panel C of Exhibit 2–9. Unit fixed cost declines steadily as activity increases. Notice that the decrease in unit fixed cost when activity changes from 1 to 2 units is much larger than the decrease in unit fixed cost when activity changes from 10 to 11 units or from 20 to 21 units. Thus, the amount of the change in unit fixed cost declines as the activity level increases.

To summarize, as the activity level increases, total fixed cost remains constant but unit fixed cost declines. As you will see in subsequent chapters, it is vital in managerial accounting to thoroughly understand the behavior of both total fixed costs and unit fixed costs.

The Cost Management and Control Team

An important objective of managerial accounting is to assist managers in managing and controlling costs. Sometimes cost management is facilitated by tracing costs to the department or work center in which the cost was incurred. Such tracing of costs to departments is known as *responsibility accounting.*

Comet Computer Corporation formed a cost management and control team to refine the company's responsibility accounting system. The team consisted of an engineer, the production scheduling manager, the assistant manager of quality control, the manager of human resources, and a managerial accountant. The ultimate objective of the team was to develop a responsibility accounting system that would assist management in managing and controlling costs as well as reducing costs whenever possible. We will study cost management systems and cost reduction in considerable detail in Chapter 5 and responsibility accounting in Chapter 12. For now, let's focus on a couple of cost concepts that are useful in these areas of managerial accounting.

Learning Objective 9

Distinguish among direct, indirect, controllable, and uncontrollable costs.

Direct and Indirect Costs An entity, such as a particular product, service, or department, to which a cost is assigned is called a **cost object.** A cost that can be traced to a particular cost object is called a **direct cost** of that cost object.

For example, the salary of an auto mechanic is a direct cost of the automotive service department in a Canadian Tire department store. The cost of paint used in the painting department of a Toyota plant is a direct cost of the painting department.

A cost that is not directly traceable to a particular cost object is called an **indirect cost** of that cost object. For example, the costs of national advertising for Walt Disney World are indirect costs of each of the departments or subunits of the recreational complex, such as the Magic Kingdom and Epcot. The salary of a Saudi Basic Industries (SABIC) plant manager

A. Graph of Total Fixed Cost

Total fixed cost (Web sales manager's salary)

$150,000

Activity (or cost driver): units produced

10   20   30

B. Tabulation of Fixed Cost

Activity (or cost driver)	Fixed Cost per Unit	Total Fixed Cost
1	$150,000	$150,000
2	75,000	150,000
5	30,000	150,000
10	15,000	150,000
11	13,636*	150,000
20	7,500	150,000
21	7,143*	150,000
30	5,000	150,000

*Rounded

C. Graph of Unit Fixed Cost

Unit fixed cost

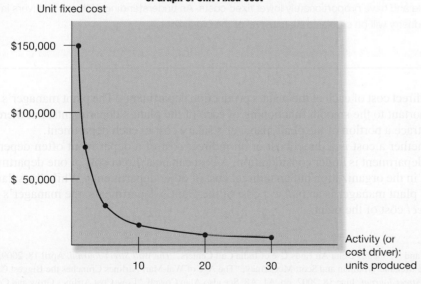

$150,000

$100,000

$ 50,000

Activity (or cost driver): units produced

10   20   30

Exhibit 2–9
Fixed Cost

Cómet
Cómetcomp**.**com

Management
Accounting
Practice

US Airways, Continental, American, United, Delta, JetBlue, Frontier, and Air-Tran

THE U.S. AIRLINE INDUSTRY: COST STRUCTURE, COST DRIVERS, AND A SHIFTING BUSINESS MODEL

"American business has changed its flying habits. The bottom line: business travel is being 'Walmarted' by low-cost operators. Just as Walmart did in retailing, the discounters of the air—Southwest Airlines and others such as JetBlue Airways—are proving that even some of the most finicky corporate fliers can't resist a bargain.

"Low-cost carriers now account for nearly 20 percent of U.S. domestic air capacity. A second force behind the fundamental shift in airline economics is the Internet, which has given travelers, travel agents, and corporate travel managers powerful tools to find and take advantage of deeply discounted fares.

"The shift is dire news for the big airlines, the full-service retailers of flight. The carriers, which are bleeding red ink, have massive fixed costs that aren't easy to scale back. Most of them have built expensive hub-and-spoke route systems and signed costly labor contracts that they had hoped to finance by charging high-margin business fares. But now, there is 'a low-fare network in this country that did not exist previously.' A senior vice president at Continental Airlines told a recent aviation conference, 'We've finally reached the point, perhaps, where [its] penetration may be fatal' to the major carriers' high-cost business models.

"Some carriers, including American Airlines and United Airlines, are now rethinking their entire operations, even considering whether they should cut back their high-cost route systems." At American, "a special task force is hunting for immediate money-saving ideas and another is studying longer-range restructuring."

It won't be easy, however, for major U.S. airlines to cut their costs. "Consider the current advantages low-fare carriers have over full-service rivals. They tend to have younger fleets, which require less maintenance, and younger labor forces that aren't tied to complicated, inefficient labor contracts. That's why labor costs are equivalent to just 25 percent of revenue at discounters Air-Tran Airways, Frontier Airlines, and JetBlue and 30 percent at Southwest. At United and Delta, labor costs exceed 40 percent of revenue. Moreover, low-fare carriers typically stick to one airplane model, thus minimizing maintenance, operating, and training costs." Many of the biggest carriers still fly six or seven types of aircraft.[9]

The bottom line is that the U.S. airline industry is undergoing a sea-change in its business model, and it is driven by the very different cost structures that characterize the largest carriers versus their smaller discount competitors. The discounters are more flexible and have proportionately lower fixed costs. An understanding of the cost drivers in the industry will be crucial to the survival of the big airlines.

---

is an indirect cost of each of the plant's production departments. The plant manager's duties are important to the smooth functioning of each of the plant's departments, but there is no way to trace a portion of the plant manager's salary cost to each department.

Whether a cost is a direct cost or an indirect cost of a department often depends on which department is under consideration. A cost can be a direct cost of one department or subunit in the organization but an indirect cost of other departments. While the salary of a SABIC plant manager is an *indirect* cost of the plant's departments, the manager's salary is a *direct* cost of the plant.

"The flight crew's salaries on a flight, say from Atlanta to St. Louis, would be considered a direct cost of that flight. The salaries of the flight scheduling folks, on the other hand, would be an indirect cost of any given flight." (2g)

Delta Air Lines

---

[9]P. Prada and N. Sheth, "Delta Air Ends Use of India Call Centers," *The Wall Street Journal,* April 18, 2009, p. B1; and Melanie Trottman and Scott McCartney, "The Age of Wal-Mart Airlines Crunches the Biggest Carriers," *The Wall Street Journal,* June 18, 2002, pp. A1, A8. See also Alan Cowell, "Low-Cost Airlines Grow and Compete in Europe," *The New York Times,* July 28, 2002, p. 3.

Comet Computer Corporation's cost management and control team determined that many of the company's costs were traceable to various departments or to specific activities of those departments. In the purchasing department, for example, costs were traced not just to the department, but to the specific activities of identifying vendors, qualifying vendors, securing design specifications from the engineering design department, negotiating prices, placing orders, expediting orders, receiving materials and components, inspecting materials, and releasing materials to the material-handling operation.

An important objective of a cost management system is to trace as many costs as possible directly to the activities that cause them to be incurred. Sometimes called *activity accounting,* this process is vital to management's objective of eliminating *non-value-added costs.* These are costs of activities that can be eliminated without deterioration of product quality, performance, or perceived value. (We will study the elimination of non-value-added costs in greater detail in Chapter 5.)

Controllable and Uncontrollable Costs   Another cost classification that can be helpful in cost control involves the controllability of a cost item by a particular manager. If a manager can control or heavily influence the level of a cost, then that cost is classified as a **controllable cost** of that manager. Costs that a manager cannot influence significantly are classified as *uncontrollable costs* of that manager. Many costs are not completely under the control of any individual. In classifying costs as controllable or uncontrollable, managerial accountants generally focus on a manager's ability to influence costs. The question is not, Who controls the cost? but, Who is in the best position to influence the level of a cost item? Exhibit 2–10 lists several cost items along with their typical classification as controllable or uncontrollable.

Comet Computer's cost management and control team was able to designate many of Comet's costs as controllable or uncontrollable by various managers. Take the cost of raw materials and components, for example. The team determined that the *quantity* of materials used was largely controllable by the production supervisor, but the *price* of the materials was influenced more by the purchasing manager.

The Outsourcing Action Team

Another of Comet Computer Corporation's interdisciplinary management teams was formed to take a close look at which of the raw materials and components used in Comet's products should be manufactured by Comet and which ones should be outsourced (purchased from outside vendors).[10] This team consisted of the assistant

---

[10]The outsourcing decision, as well as several other common management decisions, is covered in detail in Chapter 14.

Cost Item	Manager	Classification
Cost of raw material used to produce computer chips in an Intel factory	Supervisor of the production department for computer chips	Controllable (The production supervisor can exercise some control over the quantity of material used by ensuring that waste and defective units are minimized.)
Cost of food used in a Subway restaurant	Restaurant manager	Controllable (The restaurant manager exercises some control over the quantity of food used by scheduling production to ensure that excess food is not produced and wasted.)
Cost of national advertising for the EuropCar car rental company	Manager of the EuropCar rental agency at the Marseilles airport	Uncontrollable
Cost of national accounting and data processing operations for Target	Manager of a Target store in Seattle	Uncontrollable

Exhibit 2–10
Controllable and Uncontrollable Costs

Learning Objective **10**

Define and give examples of
an opportunity cost, an out-of-
pocket cost, a sunk cost, a
differential cost, a marginal
cost, and an average cost.

manager of purchasing, a product design engineer, a product group sales manager, and a managerial accountant. As the team pursued its assignment, its members soon found that they were once again dealing with several different cost concepts.

In addition to accounting cost classifications, such as product costs and period costs, the team's members also found themselves using economic concepts in classifying costs. Such concepts are often useful in helping managerial accountants decide what cost information is relevant to the decisions faced by the organization's managers. Several of the most important economic cost concepts are discussed next.

Opportunity Costs   An **opportunity cost** is defined as the benefit that is sacrificed when the choice of one action precludes taking an alternative course of action. If beef and fish are the available choices for dinner, the opportunity cost of eating beef is the forgone pleasure associated with eating fish.

Opportunity costs arise in many business decisions. For example, suppose a sporting goods manufacturer receives a special order for footballs from the city of Osaka. If the firm accepts the football order, it will not have enough productive capacity (labor and machine time) to produce its usual output of baseballs for sale to a large chain of sporting-goods stores. The opportunity cost of accepting the football order is the forgone benefit from the baseball production that cannot be achieved. This forgone benefit is measured by the potential revenue from the baseball sales minus the cost of manufacturing the baseballs.

Opportunity costs also arise in personal decisions. The opportunity cost of a student's college education includes the salary that is forgone as a result of not taking a full-time job during the student's years in college.

From an economic perspective, a dollar of opportunity cost associated with an action should be treated as equivalent to a dollar of out-of-pocket cost. **Out-of-pocket costs** are those that require the payment of cash or other assets as a result of their incurrence. The out-of-pocket costs associated with the football order consist of the manufacturing costs required to produce the footballs. In making the decision to accept or reject the football order, the firm's management should consider *both* the out-of-pocket cost and the opportunity cost of the order.

Studies by behavioral scientists and economists have shown that many people have a tendency to ignore or downplay the importance of opportunity costs. For example, in one study people were asked if they would pay $500 for two tickets to the American football Super Bowl. Most people responded that they would not. However, many of the same people said that they would not sell the Super Bowl tickets for $500 if they were given the tickets free of charge. These people refused to incur the $500 *out-of-pocket cost* of buying the Super Bowl tickets. However, they were willing to incur the $500 *opportunity cost* of going to the game rather than sell the tickets. In each case, a couple that attends the game ends up $500 poorer than a couple that does not attend the game. (Try surveying your friends with this scenario and the World Cup.)

Behavior such as that illustrated in the Super Bowl example is economically inconsistent. Ignoring or downplaying the importance of opportunity costs can result in inconsistent and faulty business decisions.

Comet Computer's outsourcing action team found that the opportunity cost of using constrained production resources (such as space, machine time, and employee time) to produce a computer component in-house was an important factor to consider in deciding whether to outsource the component.[11]

Sunk Costs   **Sunk costs** are costs that have been incurred in the past. Consequently, they do not affect future costs and cannot be changed by any current or future action.

---

[11]The details of the outsourcing decision, including its relevant costs and the role of opportunity costs, are covered in Chapter 14.

Examples of such costs include the acquisition cost of equipment previously purchased and the manufacturing cost of inventory on hand. Regardless of the current usefulness of the equipment or the inventory, the costs of acquiring them cannot be changed by any prospective action. Hence, these costs are irrelevant to all future decisions.

Suppose, for example, that a university's traffic department purchased a desktop computer to assist in the vehicle registration process. A year has passed, the computer's warranty has expired, and the computer is not working well. An investigation reveals that this brand of computer is very sensitive to humidity and temperature changes. The traffic department is located in an old building with poor heating and no air-conditioning. As a result, the computer works only intermittently, repair bills have been high, and the office staff is fed up. The office manager requests that the department director junk the computer and instruct the staff to return to the old manual registration system. The director responds by insisting, "We can't afford to junk the computer! We paid $3,400 for it."

This illustration is a typical example of the inappropriate attention paid to sunk costs. The $3,400 paid for the computer is sunk. No future decision about the computer or the office's procedures can affect that cost. Future decisions should be based on future costs, such as the computer repair bills or the costs of upgrading the building's heating and air-conditioning systems.

Although it is incorrect, from an economic perspective, to allow sunk costs to affect future decisions, people often do so. It is human nature to attempt to justify past decisions. When there is a perceived need to demonstrate competence, either to themselves or to others, managers may seek to justify their decisions. The response of the traffic department director that "We can't afford to junk the computer!" may represent the director's need to justify the past decision to purchase the computer. It is important for managerial accountants to be aware of such behavioral tendencies. Such an awareness enables the accountant to prepare the most relevant data for managers' decisions and, sometimes, to assist the managers in using the information.

Comet Computer's outsourcing action team encountered a sunk cost as it considered outsourcing production of a component called a monitor interface unit (MIU) from an electronics producer in Vietnam. The team discovered that the automatic insertion robot used to insert components into the MIU at Comet's production facility was difficult to maintain and expensive to operate. Nevertheless, the department supervisor was inclined to keep the robot and continue in-house production of the MIU, because, as he put it, "Comet paid an arm and a leg for this robot." The team was able to demonstrate that the robot's acquisition cost was a sunk cost and was irrelevant to the outsourcing decision. We will explore sunk costs in more detail in Chapter 14.

Differential Costs   A **differential cost** is the amount by which the cost differs under two alternative actions. Suppose, for example, that a regional government is considering two competing sites for a new landfill. If the northern site is chosen, the annual cost of transporting refuse to the site is projected at $85,000. If the southern site is selected, annual transportation charges are expected to be $70,000. The annual differential cost of transporting refuse is calculated as follows:

Annual cost of transporting refuse to northern site	$85,000
Annual cost of transporting refuse to southern site	70,000
Annual differential cost	$15,000

The increase in cost from one alternative to another is called an **incremental cost.** In the landfill example, the annual incremental cost of refuse transportation is $15,000 if the site is moved from the southern location to the northern location. Differential or incremental costs are found in a variety of economic decisions. The additional cost incurred by Gulliver's Travels, a travel agency, in locating a new office in the suburbs of Dublin is the incremental cost of the new business location. The difference in the total cost incurred by the travel agency with or without the suburban location is the differential cost of the decision whether to establish the new office. Decisions about establishing new airline routes, adding additional shifts in a manufacturing firm, or increasing the nursing staff in a hospital all involve differential costs.

At Comet Computer, the outsourcing action team estimated that the differential cost between outsourcing the production of the MIU (monitor interface unit) and producing it in-house would be $200,000 annually in favor of outsourcing, based on current projections of annual production.

Marginal Costs and Average Costs   A special case of the differential-cost concept is the **marginal cost,** which is the extra cost incurred when one additional unit is produced. The additional cost incurred by Comet Computer when one additional high-performance laptop computer is made is the marginal cost of manufacturing the computer. The table in Exhibit 2–11 shows how marginal cost can change across different ranges of production quantities.

Marginal costs typically differ across different ranges of production quantities because the efficiency of the production process changes. At Comet Computer, the marginal cost of producing a laptop computer declines as output increases. It is much more efficient for the company to manufacture 101 computers than to make only one.

It is important to distinguish between *marginal costs* and *average costs.* In the Comet Computer example, the marginal cost of the second computer is $1,900. However, the average cost per unit when two laptops are manufactured is $3,900 divided by 2, or $1,950. Similarly, the marginal cost of the eleventh laptop is $1,690, but the average cost per unit when 11 laptops are produced is $1,790 (calculated by dividing $19,690 by 11). What is the marginal cost of the 101st laptop computer? The average cost per unit when 101 laptops are manufactured?[12]

To summarize, the marginal cost of production is the extra cost incurred when one more unit is produced. The **average cost per unit** is the total cost, for whatever quantity is manufactured, divided by the number of units manufactured. Marginal costs and average costs arise in a variety of economic situations. A McGill University administrator might be interested in the marginal cost of educating one additional student, and a Toyota executive might want to know the marginal cost of producing one more Toyota van. A Greyhound bus route manager might be interested in the average cost per mile on the Pittsburgh to New York City route.

---

[12]Marginal cost of 101st laptop computer is $995 (from Exhibit 2–11). Average cost per unit when 101 laptops are produced is $1,495 ($150,995 ÷ 101).

Exhibit 2–11
Marginal Cost of Producing Laptop Computers at Comet Computer Corporation

Number of Laptop Computers Produced	Total Cost of Producing Laptops	Marginal Cost of Producing a Laptop
1	$ 2,000	Difference is $1,900 ⟶ Marginal cost of 2nd laptop is $1,900
2	3,900	
10	18,000	Difference is $1,690 ⟶ Marginal cost of 11th laptop is $1,690
11	19,690	
100	150,000	Difference is $995 ⟶ Marginal cost of 101st laptop is $995
101	150,995	

Costs and Benefits of Information

Many different cost concepts have been explored in this chapter. An important task of the managerial accountant is to determine which of these cost concepts is most appropriate in each situation. Then the accountant strives to *communicate* the cost information to the user in the most effective manner possible. The accountant attempts to structure the organization's accounting information system to record data that will be useful for a variety of purposes. The benefits of measuring and classifying costs in a particular way are realized through the improvements in planning, control, and decision making that the information facilitates.

Another important task of the managerial accountant is to weigh the benefits of providing information against the costs of generating, communicating, and using that information. Some accountants, eager to show that they have not overlooked anything, tend to provide too much information. But when managers receive more data than they can utilize effectively, *information overload* occurs. Struggling to process large amounts of information, managers may be unable to recognize the most important facts. In deciding how much and what type of information to provide, managerial accountants should consider these human limitations.

> "If you can't communicate information to the individual, then the information is . . . lost. So, your communication skills are very important."
> (2h)
> **Abbott Labs**

Costs in the Service Industry

The cost terms and concepts that we have studied in this chapter are just as relevant in the service industry as in a manufacturing firm like Comet Computer Corporation. Here we will explore those cost issues in the context of a well-known automotive service company.

Midas, Inc. is one of the world's largest providers of automotive service, including exhaust system, brake, steering, suspension, and routine maintenance services. There are more than 1,600 franchised and company-owned Midas locations in the United States and Canada and over 800 licensed and franchised locations in 14 other countries on five continents. In recent years, Midas has undergone some significant changes. First, the company intentionally transitioned from an under-car repair specialist to a full-service automotive repair and maintenance provider. Second, Midas has sold its exhaust system manufacturing business to concentrate fully on automotive service provision. To this end, Midas has established relationships with automobile parts vendors who distribute their products directly to Midas auto service shops.

A typical Midas automotive maintenance and repair shop has approximately 4,000 square feet (approximately 370 square meters) and six service bays. A company-owned shop usually is staffed with a manager, an assistant manager, and three to four automotive service technicians. Midas supports the franchise dealer network with 34 district managers and five regional managers. Each district manager covers approximately 52 franchised Midas shops and assists franchisees with operations, retail initiatives, training, and monitoring of the franchise agreement.[13]

Now let's think about a typical Midas-owned auto service shop to explore the various cost issues we have studied in a service-industry environment.

Product and Period Costs   Midas purchases auto parts and supplies, such as exhaust pipes, brake pads, oil filters, and engine oil, from vendors. These costs are stored in inventory as *product costs* (or *inventoriable costs*) until the time period when they are consumed in the repair process. At that time, these *product costs* become part of *cost of goods sold,* an *expense.* All of Midas' other costs are *period costs,* and they are expensed as *operating expenses* during the period they are incurred. Examples of

---

[13]Recent Midas, Inc. annual reports and the company's Web site.

these period costs include employee salaries and wages, utilities, and depreciation on equipment and facilities.

Variable and Fixed Costs

The costs incurred in the Midas service shop that vary directly with activity are *variable costs.* For example, the cost of lubricant, engine oil, and oil filters is a variable cost, because it varies in proportion to the number of lube-oil-filter (LOF) jobs the shop provides. Thus, a likely *cost driver* for this cost would be the number of LOF jobs performed. In contrast, any costs that do not tend to vary with service activity are *fixed costs.* Examples include the Midas shop's managerial salaries, depreciation on equipment and facilities, insurance, and property taxes.

Direct and Indirect Costs

Consider a typical service and repair job. The customer has requested a routine lube-oil-filter job and an exhaust system repair, which requires a new muffler. The *direct costs* of this service and repair job (the *cost object*) include the parts and supplies used (lubricant, engine oil, oil filter, and a new muffler) and the wages of the automotive service technician for the time spent on this job. The many *indirect costs* of this service job include the shop manager's salary, the depreciation on the building, and national media advertising purchased in that country by Midas, Inc.

Now consider a different cost object—this Midas shop. For this cost object, the shop manager's salary is a direct cost of the Midas shop. However, the Midas CEO's salary is an indirect cost of this particular shop.

Controllable and Uncontrollable Costs

Costs that are *controllable* by the manager of this Midas auto shop include local advertising, assuming the shop manager is responsible for such local ad buys. A cost that is partially controllable by the manager might include heating costs. Although the manager has little control over electricity or heating oil prices, the manager can ensure that the shop's heating system is properly maintained and the windows and doors have the proper weather stripping. Many of the shop's costs are largely *uncontrollable* by the shop manager. The depreciation, insurance, and property taxes on the building, for example, are the result of decisions made higher up in the Midas organization.

Opportunity, Out-of-Pocket, and Sunk Costs

These cost types all are represented in the Midas auto service business. Suppose the Midas shop manager decides to shut down one of the service bays on a particular day to inspect and maintain the auto lift and other equipment. Any customer business that is lost that day due to a shortage of service bays would be an *opportunity cost* of the shut-down decision. (Note that such an opportunity cost does not necessarily mean the shut-down decision was a poor one. The opportunity cost of any lost business could well be exceeded by the additional operating costs that could be incurred if the service bay was not properly maintained or the revenues lost if the auto lift were to break down.) The wages paid to service technicians and utility costs are examples of *out-of-pocket costs.* The money spent last year to replace an auto lift is an example of a *sunk cost.*

Differential, Marginal, and Average Costs

Suppose the Midas shop owns a small van to make short runs to pick up auto parts needed on short notice. The van needs to be replaced, and two vehicles are under consideration. The difference in the cost of these two alternative vehicles is a *differential cost* of the vehicle replacement decision. The cost of performing one additional lube-oil-filter (LOF) job in a given time period is the *marginal cost* of that type of service. The total cost of all LOF jobs in a time period, divided by the number of jobs, is the average cost of an LOF job.

Focus on Ethics

WAS WORLDCOM'S CONTROLLER JUST FOLLOWING ORDERS?

Through a series of mergers and acquisitions, WorldCom, Inc. grew to become the nation's second-largest long-distance telecommunications company. WorldCom's core communication services included network data transmission over public and private networks. Trouble arose for WorldCom because of the immense overcapacity in the telecommunications industry due to overly optimistic growth projections during the Internet boom. The combination of overcapacity, decreased demand, and high fixed costs still poses a serious problem for many of the major players in the industry.

In June 2002, the company disclosed that it had overstated earnings for 2001 and the first quarter of 2002 to the tune of $3.8 billion. The overstatement arose because the company incorrectly classified period expenses as capital expenditures. This maneuver had two major effects on the company's financial statements: the company's assets were artificially inflated and the capitalization allowed the company to spread the recognition of its expenses into the future, which increased net income in the current period. The expenses in question related to line costs—the fees that WorldCom pays outside providers for access to their communications networks. In addition, the company announced in July 2002 that it had also manipulated reserve accounts, which affected another $3.8 billion in earnings in 1999 and 2000.

The problems at WorldCom were discovered during an internal audit and brought to the attention of the company's new auditors, KPMG. Arthur Andersen served as WorldCom's auditors during the period covered by the alleged accounting scandal. Arthur Andersen maintained that the details of the accounting fraud were kept from them by senior WorldCom management. The firm's controller and chief financial officer (CFO), who was a former KPMG employee, were fired after the alleged accounting frauds were revealed. WorldCom's CEO maintained that he knew nothing of the accounting decisions made by the CFO, but many observers question how almost $8 billion in expenses could slip by senior management.[14]

According to an Associated Press article that ran on September 27, 2002, "the former controller of WorldCom, Inc. pleaded guilty to securities fraud charges, saying he was instructed by 'senior management,' to falsify records. His plea was the first admission of guilt to fall from the largest corporate accounting scandal in U.S. history."[15] Subsequently, Worldcom's CFO pleaded guilty to his part in the accounting scandal.[16] In March of 2005, the company's CEO was convicted by a jury of nine criminal counts in the accounting fraud, including conspiracy and securities fraud.[17]

The CFO and controller were the top two financial and managerial accountants in the WorldCom organization. They were ultimately responsible for all of the company's financial and managerial accounting reports. (Note that this case also involves the alleged intentional misclassification of period costs.) What ethical issues are involved here? What do you make of the controller's assertion that he was just following orders given by senior management? What steps should WorldCom's controller have taken? (Review the Institute of Management Accountants' Statement of Ethical Professional Practice on pages 63 and 64.)

To summarize, although manufacturers, like Zara, Motorola, or Nike, and service-industry firms, like Allianz, Europcar, or Midas, are in very different businesses, they all must understand their costs in order to be successful in a competitive environment.

---

[14]Jared Sandberg, Rebecca Blumenstein, and Shawn Young, "WorldCom Admits $3.8 Billion Error in Its Accounting—Firm Ousts Financial Chief and Struggles for Survival; SEC Probe Likely to Widen," *The Wall Street Journal,* June 26, 2002, p. A1; Jared Sandberg, Deborah Solomon, and Rebecca Blumenstein, "Disconnected: Inside WorldCom's Unearthing of a Vast Accounting Scandal," *The Wall Street Journal,* June 27, 2002, p. A1; and Jared Sandberg, "Leading the News: Was Ebbers Aware of Accounting Move at His WorldCom?" *The Wall Street Journal,* July 1, 2002, p. A3.

[15]Devlin Barrett, "Ex-WorldCom Exec Pleads Guilty," Associated Press, September 27, 2002 (as it appeared in the *Ithaca Journal*). See also Kurt Eichenwald and Simon Romero, "Plea Deals Are Seen for Three WorldCom Executives," *The New York Times,* August 29, 2002, pp. C1, C4.

[16]T. Richardson, "Worldcom CFO Lied, He Admits in Court," *The Register,* February 17, 2005, www.theregister.co.uk.

[17]A. Latour, S. Young, and L. Yuan, "Ebbers Is Convicted in Massive Fraud," *The Wall Street Journal,* March 16, 2005, p. A1.

Chapter Summary

LO1 Explain what is meant by the word *cost*. The word *cost* can have a variety of meanings in different situations. In general, a cost is the sacrifice made, usually measured by the resources given up, to achieve a particular purpose.

LO2 Distinguish among product costs, period costs, and expenses. A product cost is a cost assigned to manufactured or purchased goods. Period costs are those associated with the period of time in which they are incurred. An expense is the cost incurred when an asset is used up for the purpose of generating revenue.

LO3 Describe the role of costs in published financial statements. The cost of goods sold is an expense on the income statement. Inventory on the balance sheet is measured at its cost, as are all assets.

LO4 List five types of manufacturing operations and describe mass customization. The five basic types of manufacturing operations are job shop, batch, assembly line, mass customization, and continuous flow. In a mass-customization production environment, many standardized components are used to manufacture customized products to customer order.

LO5 Give examples of three types of manufacturing costs. Manufacturing costs are categorized as direct-material, direct-labor, and manufacturing-overhead.

LO6 Prepare a schedule of cost of goods manufactured, a schedule of cost of goods sold, and an income statement for a manufacturer. These accounting schedules, which are illustrated in the chapter, provide information to management about the costs incurred in a production operation.

LO7 Understand the importance of identifying an organization's cost drivers. A cost driver is any activity or event that causes costs to be incurred. Understanding the cost drivers in an organization is an essential component of managing those costs.

LO8 Describe the behavior of variable and fixed costs, in total and on a per-unit basis. As activity in an organization increases, a variable cost increases proportionately to activity in total, but remains constant on a per-unit basis. In contrast, as activity in an organization increases, a fixed cost remains constant in total but decreases on a per-unit basis.

LO9 Distinguish among direct, indirect, controllable, and uncontrollable costs. Direct and indirect costs refer to the ability of the accountant to trace costs to various departments in the organization. The terms *controllable* and *uncontrollable* are used to describe the extent to which a manager can influence a cost.

LO10 Define and give examples of an opportunity cost, an out-of-pocket cost, a sunk cost, a differential cost, a marginal cost, and an average cost. An opportunity cost is the benefit forgone because the choice of one action precludes another action. An out-of-pocket cost requires the payment of cash or other assets. Sunk costs are costs incurred in the past that cannot be altered by a current or future decision. A differential (or incremental) cost refers to the difference in the costs incurred under two alternative actions. A marginal cost is the cost of producing one additional unit. Finally, the average cost per unit is the total cost for whatever quantity is produced, divided by the number of units produced.

Review Problems on Cost Classifications

Problem 1

Several costs incurred by St. Andrews Golf Equipment, plc. are listed below. For each cost, indicate which of the following classifications best describe the cost. More than one classification may apply to the same cost item. For example, a cost may be both a variable cost *and* a product cost.

Cost Classifications

a. Variable

b. Fixed

c. Period

d. Product

e. Administrative

f. Selling

g. Manufacturing

h. Research and development

i. Direct material

j. Direct labor

k. Manufacturing overhead

Cost Items

1. Metal used in golf clubs.

2. Salary of the plant manager.

3. Cost of natural gas used to heat factory.

4. Commissions paid to sales personnel.

5. Wages paid to employees who assemble golf bags.

6. Salary of an engineer who is working on a prototype of a new solar-powered golf cart.

7. Depreciation on the word processing equipment used by the company president's secretary.

Problem 2

Listed below are several costs incurred in the loan department of Suwanee Bank and Trust Company. For each cost, indicate which of the following classifications best describe the cost. More than one classification may apply to the same cost item.

Cost Classifications

a. Controllable by the loan department manager

b. Uncontrollable by the loan department manager

c. Direct cost of the loan department

d. Indirect cost of the loan department

e. Differential cost

f. Marginal cost

g. Opportunity cost

h. Sunk cost

i. Out-of-pocket cost

Cost Items

1. Salary of the loan department manager.

2. Cost of office supplies used in the loan department.

3. Cost of the department's personal computers purchased by the loan department manager last year.

4. Cost of general advertising by the bank, which is allocated to the loan department.

5. Revenue that the loan department would have generated for the bank if a branch loan office had been located downtown instead of in the next county.

6. Difference in the cost incurred by the bank when one additional loan application is processed.

Solutions to Review Problems
Problem 1

1. a, d, g, i   2. b, d, g, k   3. a, d, g, k   4. a, c, f   5. a, d, g, j

6. b, c, h   7. b, c, e

Problem 2

1. b, c, i   2. a, c, i   3. a, c, h   4. b, d, i   5. g   6. e, f

Key Terms

For each term's definition refer to the indicated page, or turn to the glossary at the end of the text.

activity, 84

average cost per unit, 92

controllable cost, 89

conversion costs, 81

cost, 72

cost driver, 84

cost object, 86

cost of goods manufactured, 81

cost of goods sold, 73

differential cost, 91

direct cost, 86

direct-labor cost, 79

direct material, 79

expense, 73

finished goods, 77

fixed cost, 86

idle time, 80

incremental cost, 91

indirect cost, 86

indirect labor, 80

indirect material, 80

inventoriable cost, 74

manufacturing overhead, 80

marginal cost, 92

mass-customization, 78

operating expenses, 76

opportunity cost, 90

out-of-pocket costs, 90

overtime premium, 80

period costs, 74

prime costs, 81

product cost, 73

raw material, 77

schedule of cost of goods manufactured, 81

schedule of cost of goods sold, 81

service departments (or support departments), 80

sunk costs, 90

variable cost, 85

work in process, 77

Review Questions

2–1. Distinguish between product costs and period costs.

2–2. Why are product costs also called inventoriable costs?

2–3. What is the most important difference between a manufacturing firm and a service industry firm, with regard to the classification of costs as product costs or period costs?

2–4. List, describe, and give an example of each of the five different types of production processes.

2–5. "The words *mass* and *customization* in the term *mass customization* seem contradictory." Do you agree or disagree? Explain.

2–6. Why is the cost of idle time treated as manufacturing overhead?

2–7. Explain why an overtime premium is included in manufacturing overhead.

2–8. What is meant by the phrase "different costs for different purposes"?

2–9. Give examples to illustrate how the city of Tampa could use cost information in planning, controlling costs, and making decisions.

2–10. Distinguish between fixed costs and variable costs.

2–11. How does the fixed cost per unit change as the level of activity (or cost driver) increases? Why?

2–12. How does the variable cost per unit change as the level of activity (or cost driver) increases? Why?

2–13. Distinguish between volume-based and operations-based cost drivers in the airline industry.

2–14. Would each of the following characteristics be a volume-based or an operations-based cost driver in a college: (*a*) number of students, (*b*) number of disciplines offered for study, and (*c*) urban versus rural location?

2–15. List three direct costs of the food and beverage department in a hotel. List three indirect costs of the department.

2–16. List three costs that are likely to be controllable by a city's airport manager. List three costs that are likely to be uncontrollable by the manager.

2–17. Which of the following costs are likely to be controllable by the chief of nursing in a hospital?

   a. Cost of medication administered.

   b. Cost of overtime paid to nurses due to scheduling errors.

   c. Cost of depreciation of hospital beds.

2–18. Distinguish between out-of-pocket costs and opportunity costs.

2–19. Define the terms *sunk cost* and *differential cost.*

2–20. Distinguish between marginal and average costs.

2–21. Think about the process of registering for classes at your college or university. What additional information would you like to have before you register? How would it help you? What sort of information might create information overload for you?

2–22. Two years ago the manager of a large department store purchased new bar code scanners costing $39,000. A salesperson recently tried to sell the manager a new computer-integrated checkout system for the store. The new system would save the store a substantial amount of money each year. The recently purchased scanners could be sold in the secondhand market for $19,000. The store manager refused to listen to the salesperson, saying, "I just bought those scanners. I can't get rid of them until I get my money's worth out of them."

   What type of cost is the cost of purchasing the old bar code scanners? What common behavioral tendency is the manager exhibiting?

2–23. Indicate whether each of the following costs is a direct cost or an indirect cost of the restaurant in a hotel.

   a. Cost of food served.

   b. Chef's salary and fringe benefits.

   c. Part of the cost of maintaining the grounds around the hotel, which is allocated to the restaurant.

   d. Part of the cost of advertising the hotel, which is allocated to the restaurant.

Exercises

All applicable Exercises are available with McGraw-Hill's *Connect Accounting*™.

For each case below, find the missing amount.

	Case I	Case II	Case III
Beginning inventory of finished goods	?	$12,000	$ 7,000
Cost of goods manufactured during period	$419,000	$95,000	?
Ending inventory of finished goods	98,000	8,000	21,000
Cost of goods sold	405,000	?	304,000

■ **Exercise 2–24**
Cost of Goods Manufactured
and Sold; Missing Data
(LO 1, 3, 6)

A foundry employee worked a normal 40-hour shift, but five hours were idle due to a small fire in the plant. The employee earns $20 per hour.

■ **Exercise 2–25**
Idle Time
(LO 5)

Required:

1. Calculate the employee's total compensation for the week.
2. How much of this compensation is a direct-labor cost? How much is overhead?

A loom operator in a textiles factory earns $16 per hour. By contract, the employee earns $20 for over-time hours. The operator worked 45 hours during the first week of May, instead of the usual 40 hours.

■ **Exercise 2–26**
Overtime Cost
(LO 5)

Required:

1. Compute the loom operator's compensation for the week.
2. Calculate the employee's total overtime premium for the week.
3. How much of the employee's total compensation for the week is direct-labor cost? How much is overhead?

Find Dell Inc.'s Web site on the Internet, www.dell.com.

■ **Exercise 2–27**
Mass Customization; Use of
Internet
(LO 4)

Required: Read on the company's Web site about how Dell operates and serves its customers. Then briefly explain whether you believe mass customization to be the best type of manufacturing process for Dell.

Consider the following costs that were incurred during the current year:

■ **Exercise 2–28**
Cost Classifications
(LO 2, 8, 9)

1. Tire costs incurred by Ford Motor Company.
2. Sales commissions paid to the sales force of Dell Inc.
3. Wood glue consumed in the manufacture of Thomasville furniture.
4. Hourly wages of refinery security guards employed by ExxonMobil Corporation.
5. The salary of a financial vice president of Hewlett Packard.
6. Advertising costs of Coca-Cola.
7. Straight-line depreciation on factory machinery of Boeing Corporation.
8. Wages of assembly-line personnel of Whirlpool Corporation.
9. Delivery costs on customer shipments of Ben & Jerry's ice cream.
10. Newsprint consumed in printing *The New York Times*.
11. Plant insurance costs of Texas Instruments.
12. Glass costs incurred in light-bulb manufacturing of General Electric.

Required: Evaluate each of the preceding and determine whether the cost is (*a*) a product cost or a period cost, (*b*) variable or fixed in terms of behavior, and (*c*) for the product costs only, whether the cost is properly classified as direct material, direct labor, or manufacturing overhead. Item 1 is done as an example:

Tire costs: Product cost, variable, direct material

Alexandria Aluminum Company, a manufacturer of recyclable soda cans, had the following inventory balances at the beginning and end of 20x1.

Inventory Classification	January 1, 20x1	December 31, 20x1
Raw material	$ 50,000	$ 70,000
Work in process	120,000	115,000
Finished goods	100,000	165,000

During 20x1, the company purchased $250,000 of raw material and spent $400,000 on direct labor. Manufacturing overhead costs were as follows:

Indirect material	$ 10,000
Indirect labor	25,000
Depreciation on plant and equipment	100,000
Utilities	25,000
Other	30,000

Sales revenue was $1,105,000 for the year. Selling and administrative expenses for the year amounted to $110,000. The firm's tax rate is 40 percent.

Required:

1. Prepare a schedule of cost of goods manufactured.
2. Prepare a schedule of cost of goods sold.
3. Prepare an income statement.
4. *Build a spreadsheet:* Construct an Excel spreadsheet to solve all of the preceding requirements. Show how both cost schedules and the income statement will change if the following data change: direct labor is $390,000 and utilities cost $35,000.

Mighty Muffler, Inc. operates an automobile service facility that specializes in replacing mufflers on compact cars. The following table shows the costs incurred during a month when 600 mufflers were replaced.

	Muffler Replacements		
	500	600	700
Total costs:			
Fixed costs	a	$42,000	b
Variable costs	c	30,000	d
Total costs	e	$72,000	f
Cost per muffler replacement:			
Fixed cost	g	h	i
Variable cost	j	k	l
Total cost per muffler replacement	m	n	o

Required: Fill in the missing amounts, labeled (*a*) through (*o*), in the table.

A hotel pays the phone company $125 per month plus $.25 for each call made. During January 8,000 calls were made. In February 5,000 calls were made.

Required:

1. Calculate the hotel's phone bills for January and February.
2. Calculate the cost per phone call in January and in February.

3. Separate the January phone bill into its fixed and variable components.

4. What is the marginal cost of one additional phone call in January?

5. What was the average cost of a phone call in January?

Martin Shrood purchased a vacant lot outside of London for £13,500, because he heard that a shopping mall was going to be built on the other side of the road. He figured that he could make a bundle by putting in a fast-food outlet on the site. As it turned out, the rumor was false. A sanitary landfill was located on the other side of the road, and Martin's land was worthless. (£ denotes the British monetary unit, pounds sterling.)*

Required: What type of cost is the £13,500 that Martin paid for the vacant lot?

■ **Exercise 2–32**
Economic Characteristics of Costs
(LO 1, 10)

Orbital Communications, Inc. manufactures communications satellites used in TV signal transmission. The firm currently purchases one component for its satellites from a European firm. An Orbital Communications engineering team has found a way to use the company's own component, part number A200, instead of the European component. However, the Orbital Communications component must be modified at a cost of $750 per part. The European component costs $8,900 per part. Orbital Communications' part number A200 costs $4,900 before it is modified. Orbital Communications currently uses 20 of the European components per year.

Required: Calculate the annual differential cost between Orbital Communications' two production alternatives.

■ **Exercise 2–33**
Differential Cost
(LO 1, 10)

The state Department of Education owns a computer system, which its employees use for word processing and keeping track of education statistics. The governor's office recently began using this computer also. As a result of the increased usage, the demands on the computer soon exceeded its capacity. The director of the Department of Education was soon forced to lease several personal computers to meet the computing needs of her employees. The annual cost of leasing the equipment is $14,000.

Required:

1. What type of cost is this $14,000?

2. Should this cost be associated with the governor's office or the Department of Education? Why?

■ **Exercise 2–34**
Computing Costs;
Government Agency
(LO 1, 9, 10)

Suppose you paid $10 for a ticket to see your university's football team compete in a championship match. Someone offered to buy your ticket for $25, but you decided to go to the match.

Required:

1. What did it really cost you to see the game?

2. What type of cost is this?

■ **Exercise 2–35**
Economic Characteristics of Costs
(LO 1, 10)

List the costs that would likely be included in each of the following marginal-cost calculations.

1. The marginal cost of one additional passenger on an American Airlines flight.

2. The marginal cost of serving one additional customer in a Pizza Hut.

3. The marginal cost of United Airlines adding a flight from Honolulu to Seattle.

4. The marginal cost of keeping a Wachovia branch bank open one additional hour on Saturdays.

5. The marginal cost of manufacturing one additional pair of Nordica skis.

■ **Exercise 2–36**
Marginal Costs
(LO 1, 10)

---

*Although the euro is used in most European markets, Great Britain still uses the British pound sterling.

Problems

■ **Problem 2–37**
Content of Financial
Statements and Reports;
Mass Customization
(LO 3, 4)

Consider the following cost items:

1. Salaries of players on the Arsenal football squad.
2. Year-end completed goods of Levi Strauss jeans.
3. Executive compensation costs at Tata Motors.
4. Advertising costs for Sony.
5. Costs incurred during the period to insure a Philips plant against fire and flood losses.
6. Current year's depreciation on a Carnival Cruise Line ship.
7. The cost of Chocolate used during the period by Nestlé.
8. Assembly-line wage cost incurred at a Kona bicycle plant.
9. Year-end production in process at Acer Computer.
10. The cost of products sold to customers of a Target store.
11. The cost of products sold to distributors of Safavieh carpets.

Required:

1. Evaluate the costs just cited, and determine whether the associated dollar amounts would be found on the firm's balance sheet, income statement, or schedule of cost-of-goods-manufactured. (*Note:* In some cases, more than one answer will apply.)

2. What major asset will normally be insignificant for service enterprises and relatively substantial for retailers, wholesalers, and manufacturers? Briefly discuss.

3. Briefly explain the major differences between income statements of service enterprises versus those of retailers, wholesalers, and manufacturers.

4. Picture the operations of a firm such as Dell Inc, one that is involved in direct sales and mass customization of products. What would be the major difference in the balance sheet of this type of organization versus the balance sheet of a company that engages in more traditional manufacturing activities, that is, producing goods and waiting for customer orders to arrive?

■ **Problem 2–38**
Financial Statement
Elements: Manufacturer
(LO 5, 6)

2. Cost of goods manufactured: $913,200
4. Net income: $154,420

For most problems selected key figures from the solution appear in the margin.

The following selected information was extracted from the 20x1 accounting records of Lone Oak Products:

Raw material purchases	$ 175,000
Direct labor	254,000
Indirect labor	109,000
Selling and administrative salaries	133,000
Building depreciation*	80,000
Other selling and administrative expenses	195,000
Other factory costs	344,000
Sales revenue ($130 per unit)	1,495,000

*Seventy-five percent of the company's building was devoted to production activities; the remaining 25 percent was used for selling and administrative functions.

Inventory data:

	January 1	December 31
Raw material	$ 15,800	$18,200
Work in process	35,700	62,100
Finished goods*	111,100	97,900

*The January 1 and December 31 finished-goods inventory consisted of 1,350 units and 1,190 units, respectively.

Required:

1. Calculate Lone Oak's manufacturing overhead for the year.
2. Calculate Lone Oak's cost of goods manufactured.

3. Compute the company's cost of goods sold.
4. Determine net income for 20x1, assuming a 30% income tax rate.
5. Determine the number of completed units manufactured during the year.
6. *Build a spreadsheet:* Construct an Excel spreadsheet to solve all of the preceding requirements. Show how the solution will change if the following data change: indirect labor is $115,000 and other factory costs amount to $516,000.

■ **Problem 2–39**
Inventory Estimates; Partial Data
(LO 5, 6)

Direct material used: $40,000

On April 12, after the close of business, Singh & Sons had a devastating fire that destroyed the company's work-in-process and finished-goods inventories. Fortunately, all raw materials escaped damage because materials owned by the firm were stored in another warehouse. The following information is available:

Sales revenue through April 12	$330,000
Income before taxes through April 12	68,000
Direct labor through April 12	120,000
Cost of goods available for sale, April 12	275,000
Work-in-process inventory, January 1	21,000
Finished-goods inventory, January 1	37,000
Gross margin	30% of sales

The firm's accountants determined that the cost of direct materials used normally averages 25 percent of prime costs (i.e., direct material + direct labor). In addition, manufacturing overhead is 50 percent of the firm's total production costs.

Required: Singh & Sons is in the process of negotiating a settlement with its insurance company. Prepare an estimate of the cost of work-in-process and finished-goods inventories that were destroyed by the fire.

■ **Problem 2–40**
Financial-Statement Elements; Cost Behavior
(LO 5, 6, 8)

2. Net income: $168,000

Mason Corporation began operations at the beginning of the current year. One of the company's products, a refrigeration element, sells for $185 per unit. Information related to the current year's activities follows.

Variable costs per unit:	
Direct material	$ 20
Direct labor	37
Manufacturing overhead	48
Annual fixed costs:	
Manufacturing overhead	$600,000
Selling and administrative	860,000
Production and Sales activity:	
Production (units)	24,000
Sales (units)	20,000

Mason carries its finished-goods inventory at the average unit cost of production and is subject to a 30% income tax rate. There was no work in process at year-end.

Required:
1. Determine the cost of the December 31 finished-goods inventory.
2. Compute Mason's net income for the current year ended December 31.
3. If next year's production decreases to 23,000 units and general cost behavior patterns do not change, what is the likely effect on:
   a. The direct-labor cost of $37 per unit? Why?
   b. The fixed manufacturing overhead cost of $600,000? Why?
   c. The fixed selling and administrative cost of $860,000? Why?
   d. The average unit cost of production? Why?

■ **Problem 2–41**
Incomplete Data; Manufacturing Costs
(LO 2, 5)

Net income, case A: $110,000

Determine the missing amounts in each of the following independent cases.

	Case A	Case B	Case C
Beginning inventory, raw material	?	$ 10,000	$ 10,000
Ending inventory, raw material	$ 90,000	?	$ 45,000
Purchases of raw material	100,000	85,000	?
Direct material	70,000	95,000	?
Direct labor	?	100,000	125,000
Manufacturing overhead	250,000	?	160,000
Total manufacturing costs	520,000	345,000	340,000
Beginning inventory, work in process	35,000	20,000	?
Ending inventory, work in process	?	35,000	5,000
Cost of goods manufactured	525,000	?	350,000
Beginning inventory, finished goods	50,000	40,000	?
Cost of goods available for sale	?	?	370,000
Ending inventory, finished goods	?	?	25,000
Cost of goods sold	545,000	330,000	?
Sales	?	?	480,000
Gross margin	255,000	170,000	?
Selling and administrative expenses	?	70,000	?
Income before taxes	150,000	?	90,000
Income tax expense	40,000	45,000	?
Net income	?	?	50,000

■ **Problem 2–42**
Cost Terminology
(LO 2, 5, 10)

1(a). Total prime costs:
$2,680,000
1(d). Manufacturing overhead:
$534,000

The following cost data for the year just ended pertain to Sentiments, Inc., a greeting card manufacturer:

Direct material	$2,100,000
Advertising expense	99,000
Depreciation on factory building	115,000
Direct labor: wages	485,000
Cost of finished goods inventory at year-end	115,000
Indirect labor: wages	140,000
Production supervisor's salary	45,000
Service department costs*	100,000
Direct labor: fringe benefits	95,000
Indirect labor: fringe benefits	30,000
Fringe benefits for production supervisor	9,000
Total overtime premiums paid	55,000
Cost of idle time: production employees§	40,000
Administrative costs	150,000
Rental of office space for sales personnel†	15,000
Sales commissions	5,000
Product promotion costs	10,000

*All services are provided to manufacturing departments.

§Cost of idle time is an overhead item; it is not included in the direct-labor wages given above.

†The rental of sales space was made necessary when the sales offices were converted to storage space for raw material.

Required:

1. Compute each of the following costs for the year just ended: (*a*) total prime costs, (*b*) total manufacturing overhead costs, (*c*) total conversion costs, (*d*) total product costs, and (*e*) total period costs.

2. One of the costs listed above is an opportunity cost. Identify this cost, and explain why it is an opportunity cost.

The following data refer to San Fernando Fashions Company for the year 20x2:

Sales revenue	$980,000
Work-in-process inventory, December 31	20,000
Work-in-process inventory, January 1	40,000
Selling and administrative expenses	150,000
Income tax expense	90,000
Purchases of raw material	200,000
Raw-material inventory, December 31	25,000
Raw-material inventory, January 1	40,000
Direct labor	200,000
Utilities: plant	40,000
Depreciation: plant and equipment	80,000
Finished-goods inventory, December 31	50,000
Finished-goods inventory, January 1	20,000
Indirect material	10,000
Indirect labor	15,000
Other manufacturing overhead	80,000

Problem 2–43
Schedules of Cost of Goods Manufactured and Sold; Income Statement
(LO 1, 3, 5, 6)

2. Cost of goods sold: $630,000

Required:

1. Prepare San Fernando Fashions' schedule of cost of goods manufactured for the year.
2. Prepare San Fernando Fashions' schedule of cost of goods sold for the year.
3. Prepare San Fernando Fashions' income statement for the year.
4. *Build a spreadsheet:* Construct an Excel spreadsheet to solve all of the preceding requirements. Show how both cost schedules and the income statement will change if raw-material purchases amounted to $190,000 and indirect labor was $20,000.

Highlander Cutlery manufactures kitchen knives. One of the employees, whose job is to cut out wooden knife handles, worked 48 hours during a week in January. The employee earns $12 per hour for a 40-hour week. For additional hours, the employee is paid an overtime rate of $16 per hour. The employee's time was spent as follows:

Problem 2–44
Direct and Indirect Labor
(LO 1, 3, 5, 9)

2. Total cost of wages: $608

Regular duties involving cutting out knife handles	38 hours
General shop cleanup duties	9 hours
Idle time due to power outage	1 hour

Required:

1. Calculate the total cost of the employee's wages during the week described above.
2. Determine the portion of this cost to be classified in each of the following categories:
    a. Direct labor
    b. Manufacturing overhead (idle time)
    c. Manufacturing overhead (overtime premium)
    d. Manufacturing overhead (indirect labor)

Cod Verde Shirt Shop manufactures T-shirts and decorates them with custom designs for retail sale on the premises. Several costs incurred by the company are listed below. For each cost, indicate which of the following classifications best describe the cost. More than one classification may apply to the same cost item.

Problem 2–45
Cost Classifications
(LO 5, 8, 9)

Cost Classifications

a. Variable
b. Fixed
c. Period
d. Product
e. Administrative
f. Selling

   g.   Manufacturing

   h.   Research and development

   i.   Direct material

   j.   Direct labor

   k.   Manufacturing overhead

Cost Items

   1.   Cost of fabric used in T-shirts.

   2.   Wages of shirtmakers.

   3.   Cost of insurance for the production employees.

   4.   Cost of new sign in front of retail T-shirt shop.

   5.   Wages of the employee who repairs the firm's sewing machines.

   6.   Cost of electricity used in the sewing department.

   7.   Wages of T-shirt designers and painters.

   8.   Wages of sales personnel.

   9.   Depreciation on sewing machines.

   10.   Rent on the building. Part of the building's first floor is used to make and print T-shirts. Part of it is used for the retail sales shop. The second floor is used for administrative offices and storage of raw material and finished goods.

   11.   Cost of daily advertisements in local media.

   12.   Wages of designers who experiment with new inks, paints, and T-shirt designs.

   13.   Cost of hiring a pilot to fly along the beach pulling a banner advertising the shop.

   14.   Salary of the owner's secretary.

   15.   Cost of repairing the gas furnace.

■ **Problem 2–46**
Overtime Premiums and
Fringe Benefit Costs; Airline
(LO 1, 3, 5, 9,10)

Heartland Airways operates commuter flights in three Midwestern states. Due to a political convention held in Topeka, the airline added several extra flights during a two-week period. Additional cabin crews were hired on a temporary basis. However, rather than hiring additional flight attendants, the airline used its current attendants on overtime. Monica Gaines worked the following schedule on August 10. All of Gaines's flights on that day were extra flights that the airline would not normally fly.

Regular time:	2 round-trip flights between Topeka and St. Louis (8 hours)
Overtime:	1 one-way flight from Topeka to Kansas City (3 hours)

Gaines earns $12 per hour plus time and a half for overtime. Fringe benefits cost the airline $3 per hour for any hour worked, regardless of whether it is a regular or overtime hour.

Required:

   1.   Compute the direct cost of compensating Gaines for her services on the flight from Topeka to Kansas City.

   2.   Compute the cost of Gaines's services that is an indirect cost.

   3.   How should the cost computed in requirement (2) be treated for cost accounting purposes?

   4.   Gaines ended her workday on August 10 in Kansas City. However, her next scheduled flight departed Topeka at 11:00 a.m. on August 11. This required Gaines to "dead-head" back to Topeka on an early-morning flight. This means she traveled from Kansas City to Topeka as a passenger, rather than as a working flight attendant. Since the morning flight from Kansas City to Topeka was full, Gaines displaced a paying customer. The revenue lost by the airline was $82. What type of cost is the $82? To what flight, if any, is it chargeable? Why?

■ **Problem 2–47**
Variable Costs; Graphical and
Tabular Analyses
(LO 8, 9)

San Diego Sheet Metal, Inc. incurs a variable cost of $55 per pound for raw material to produce a special alloy used in manufacturing aircraft.

Required:

   1.   Draw a graph of the firm's raw material cost, showing the total cost at the following production levels: 10,000 pounds, 20,000 pounds, and 30,000 pounds.

   2.   Prepare a table that shows the unit cost and total cost of raw material at the following production levels: 1 pound, 10 pounds, and 1,000 pounds.

Hightide Upholstery Company manufactures a special fabric used to upholster the seats in power boats. The company's annual fixed production cost is $100,000.

Required:

1. Draw a graph of the company's fixed production cost showing the total cost at the following production levels of upholstery fabric: 10,000 yards, 20,000 yards, 30,000 yards, and 40,000 yards.

2. Prepare a table that shows the unit cost and the total cost for the firm's fixed production costs at the following production levels: 1 yard, 10 yards, 10,000 yards, and 40,000 yards.

3. Prepare a graph that shows the unit cost for the company's fixed production cost at the following production levels: 10,000 yards, 20,000 yards, 30,000 yards, and 40,000 yards.

■ **Problem 2–48**
Fixed Costs; Graphical and Tabular Analyses
(LO 8, 9)

For each of the following costs, indicate whether the amount is a direct or indirect cost of the equipment maintenance department. Also indicate whether each cost is at least partially controllable by the department supervisor.

1. Cost of plant manager's salary, which is allocated to the maintenance department.
2. Cost of property taxes allocated to the maintenance department.
3. Cost of electricity used in the maintenance department.
4. Depreciation on the building space occupied by the maintenance department.
5. Idle time of maintenance department employees.

■ **Problem 2–49**
Direct, Indirect, Controllable, and Uncontrollable Costs
(LO 1, 3, 9)

Indicate for each of the following costs whether it is a product cost or a period cost.

1. Wages of aircraft mechanics employed by an airline.
2. Wages of drill-press operators in a manufacturing plant.
3. Cost of food in a microwavable dinner.
4. Cost incurred by a department store chain to transport merchandise to its stores.
5. Cost of grapes purchased by a winery.
6. Depreciation on pizza ovens in a pizza restaurant.
7. Cost of plant manager in a computer production facility.
8. Wages of security personnel in a department store.
9. Cost of utilities in a manufacturing facility.

■ **Problem 2–50**
Product Costs and Period Costs
(LO 1, 2, 3)

Water Technology, Inc. incurred the following costs during 20x1. The company sold all of its products manufactured during the year.

Direct material	$3,000,000
Direct labor	2,200,000
Manufacturing overhead:	
Utilities (primarily electricity)	140,000
Depreciation on plant and equipment	250,000
Insurance	160,000
Supervisory salaries	300,000
Property taxes	210,000
Selling costs:	
Advertising	195,000
Sales commissions	100,000
Administrative costs:	
Salaries of top management and staff	372,000
Office supplies	40,000
Depreciation on building and equipment	80,000

During 20x1, the company operated at about half of its capacity, due to a slowdown in the economy. Prospects for 20x2 are slightly better. Jared Lowes, the marketing manager, forecasts a 30 percent growth in sales over the 20x1 level.

■ **Problem 2–51**
Fixed and Variable Costs; Forecasting
(LO 7, 8)

Direct material, 20x2 forecast: $3,900,000

Required: Categorize each of the costs listed above as to whether it is most likely variable or fixed. Forecast the 20x2 cost amount for each of the cost items listed above.

■ **Problem 2–52**
Economic Charactersitics
of Costs
(LO 4, 10)

The following terms are used to describe various economic characteristics of costs.

a. Opportunity cost

b. Out-of-pocket cost

c. Sunk cost

d. Differential cost

e. Marginal cost

f. Average cost

Required: Choose one of the terms listed above to characterize each of the amounts described below.

1. The cost of feeding 500 children in a public school cafeteria is $800 per day, or $1.60 per child per day. What economic term describes this $1.60 cost?

2. The cost of including one extra child in a day-care center.

3. The cost of merchandise inventory purchased two years ago, which is now obsolete.

4. The management of a high-rise office building uses 2,500 square feet of space in the building for its own management functions. This space could be rented for $250,000. What economic term describes this $250,000 in lost rental revenue?

5. The cost of building an automated assembly line in a factory is $800,000. The cost of building a manually operated assembly line is $375,000. What economic term is used to describe the difference between these two amounts?

6. Referring to the preceding question, what economic term is used to describe the $800,000 cost of building the automated assembly line?

7. The cost incurred by a mass customizer such as Dell Inc. to produce one more unit in its most popular line of laptop computers.

■ **Problem 2–53**
Cost Classifications; Hotel
(LO 1, 3, 9, 10)

Several costs incurred by Bayview Hotel and Restaurant are given in the following list. For each cost, indicate which of the following classifications best describe the cost. More than one classification may apply to the same cost item.

Cost Classifications

a. Direct cost of the food and beverage department

b. Indirect cost of the food and beverage department

c. Controllable by the kitchen manager

d. Uncontrollable by the kitchen manager

e. Controllable by the hotel general manager

f. Uncontrollable by the hotel general manager

g. Differential cost

h. Marginal cost

i. Opportunity cost

j. Sunk cost

k. Out-of-pocket cost

Cost Items

1. The cost of general advertising by the hotel, which is allocated to the food and beverage department.

2. The cost of food used in the kitchen.

3. The difference in the total cost incurred by the hotel when one additional guest is registered.

4. The cost of space (depreciation) occupied by the kitchen.

5. The cost of space (depreciation) occupied by a sauna next to the pool. The space could otherwise have been used for a magazine and bookshop.

6. The profit that would have been earned in a magazine and bookshop, if the hotel had one.

7. The discount on room rates given as a special offer for a "Labor Day Getaway Special."

8. The wages earned by table-service personnel.

9. The salary of the kitchen manager.

10. The cost of the refrigerator purchased 13 months ago. The unit was covered by a warranty for 12 months, during which time it worked perfectly. It conked out after 13 months, despite an original estimate that it would last five years.

11. The hotel has two options for obtaining fresh pies, cakes, and pastries. The goodies can be purchased from a local bakery for approximately $1,600 per month, or they can be made in the hotel's kitchen. To make the pastries on the premises, the hotel will have to hire a part-time pastry chef. This will cost $600 per month. The cost of ingredients will amount to roughly $700 per month. Thus, the savings from making the goods in the hotel's kitchen amount to $300 per month.

12. The cost of dishes broken by kitchen employees.

13. The cost of leasing a computer used for reservations, payroll, and general hotel accounting.

14. The cost of a pool service that cleans and maintains the hotel's swimming pool.

15. The wages of the hotel's maintenance employees, who spent 11 hours (at $14 per hour) repairing the dishwasher in the kitchen.

Refer to Exhibit 2–3, and answer the following questions.

Problem 2–54
Interpretation of Accounting Reports
(LO 1, 3)

Required:

1. List the major differences between the income statements shown for Caterpillar, Inc., Walmart Stores, Inc., and Southwest Airlines Company.

2. Explain how cost-accounting data were used to prepare these income statements.

3. On the income statement for Southwest Airlines Company, where would the ticket agents' salaries be shown? Where would the costs of the computer equipment used to keep track of reservations be included on the statement?

4. On the income statement for Walmart Stores, Inc., where would the cost of newspaper advertising be shown? How about the cost of merchandise?

5. Refer to the income statement for Caterpillar, Inc. Where would the salary of the brand manager who plans advertising for Caterpillar equipment be shown? How about the salary of a production employee? Where would the cost of the raw materials used in the company's products be included on the statement?

Juanita Garcia makes custom mooring covers for boats. Each mooring cover is hand sewn to fit a particular boat. If covers are made for two or more identical boats, each successive cover generally requires less time to make. Garcia has been approached by a local boat dealer to make mooring covers for all of the boats sold by the dealer. Garcia has developed the following cost schedule for mooring covers made to fit six-meter outboard power boats.

Problem 2–55
Marginal Costs and Average Costs
(LO 7, 10)

6. $420

Mooring Covers Made	Total Cost of Covers
1	$ 500
2	950
3	1,360
4	1,740
5	2,100

Required: Compute the following:

1. Marginal cost of second mooring cover.

2. Marginal cost of fourth mooring cover.

3. Marginal cost of fifth mooring cover.

4. Average cost if two mooring covers are made.

5. Average cost if four mooring covers are made.

6. Average cost if five mooring covers are made.

■ **Problem 2–56**
Cost Classifications;
Government Agency
(LO 3, 8, 9, 10)

The Department of Natural Resources is responsible for maintaining the state's parks and forest lands, stocking the lakes and rivers with fish, and generally overseeing the protection of the environment. Several costs incurred by the agency are listed below. For each cost, indicate which of the following classifications best describe the cost. More than one classification may apply to the same cost item.

Cost Classifications

a. Variable

b. Fixed

c. Controllable by the department director

d. Uncontrollable by the department director

e. Differential cost

f. Marginal cost

g. Opportunity cost

h. Sunk cost

i. Out-of-pocket cost

j. Direct cost of the agency

k. Indirect cost of the agency

l. Direct cost of providing a particular service

m. Indirect cost of providing a particular service

Cost Items

1. Cost of the automobiles used by the department's rangers. These cars were purchased by the state, and they would otherwise have been used by the state police.

2. Cost of live-trapping and moving beaver that were creating a nuisance in recreational lakes.

3. The department director's salary.

4. Cost of containing naturally caused forest fires, which are threatening private property.

5. Cost of the fish purchased from private hatcheries, which are used to stock the state's public waters.

6. The difference between (*a*) the cost of purchasing fish from private hatcheries and (*b*) the cost of running a state hatchery.

7. Cost of producing literature that describes the department's role in environmental protection. This literature is mailed free, upon request, to schools, county governments, libraries, and private citizens.

8. Cost of sending the department's hydroengineers to inspect one additional dam for stability and safety.

9. Cost of operating the state's computer services department, a portion of which is allocated to the Department of Natural Resources.

10. Cost of administrative supplies used in the agency's head office.

11. Cost of providing a toll-free number for the state's residents to report environmental problems.

12. The cost of replacing batteries in sophisticated monitoring equipment used to evaluate the effects of acid rain on the state's lakes.

13. Cost of a ranger's wages, when the ranger is giving a talk about environmental protection to elementary school children.

14. Cost of direct-mailing to 1 million state residents a brochure explaining the benefits of voluntarily recycling cans and bottles.

15. The cost of producing a TV show to be aired on public television. The purpose of the show is to educate people on how to spot and properly dispose of hazardous waste.

The controller for Vrede Vineyards has predicted the following costs at various levels of wine output.

■ **Problem 2–57**
Unit Costs; Profit-Maximizing
Output
(LO 7, 8, 10)

2. Output of 20,000 bottles,
profit: $26,000

	Wine Output (.75 Liter Bottles)		
	10,000 Bottles	**15,000 Bottles**	**20,000 Bottles**
Variable production costs	$ 37,000	$ 55,500	$ 74,000
Fixed production costs	120,000	120,000	120,000
Fixed selling and administrative costs	40,000	40,000	40,000
Total	$157,000	$175,500	$194,000

The company's marketing manager has predicted the following prices for the firm's fine wines at various levels of sales.

	Wine Sales		
	10,000 Bottles	**15,000 Bottles**	**20,000 Bottles**
Sales price per .75 liter bottle	$18.00	$15.00	$12.00

Required:

1. Calculate the unit costs of wine production and sales at each level of output. At what level of output is the unit cost minimized?

2. Calculate the company's profit at each level of production. Assume that the company will sell all of its output. At what production level is profit maximized?

3. Which of the three output levels is best for the company?

4. Why does the unit cost of wine decrease as the output level increases? Why might the sales price per bottle decline as sales volume increases?

■ **Problem 2–58**
Variable and Fixed Costs;
Make or Buy a Component
(LO 8, 10)

Hoboken Industries currently manufactures 30,000 units of part MR24 each month for use in production of several of its products. The facilities now used to produce part MR24 have a fixed monthly cost of $150,000 and a capacity to produce 84,000 units per month. If the company were to buy part MR24 from an outside supplier, the facilities would be idle, but its fixed costs would continue at 40 percent of their present amount. The variable production costs of part MR24 are $11 per unit.

Required:

1. If Hoboken Industries continues to use 30,000 units of part MR24 each month, it would realize a net benefit by purchasing part MR24 from an outside supplier only if the supplier's unit price is less than what amount?

2. If Hoboken Industries is able to obtain part MR24 from an outside supplier at a unit purchase price of $12.875, what is the monthly usage at which it will be indifferent between purchasing and making part MR24?

(CMA, adapted)

Cases

CompTech, Inc. manufactures printers for use with home computing systems. The firm currently manufactures both the electronic components for its printers and the plastic cases in which the devices are enclosed. Jim Cassanitti, the production manager, recently received a proposal from Universal Plastics Corporation to manufacture the cases for CompTech's printers. If the cases are purchased outside, CompTech will be able to close down its Printer Case Department. To help decide whether to accept the bid from Universal Plastics Corporation, Cassanitti asked CompTech's controller to prepare an analysis of the costs that would be saved if the Printer Case Department were closed. Included in the controller's list of annual cost savings were the following items:

■ **Case 2–59**
Economic Characteristics of
Costs; Closing a Department;
Ethics
(LO 1, 9, 10)

Building rental (The Printer Case Department occupies one-sixth of the factory building, which CompTech rents for $177,000 per year.)	$29,500
Salary of the Printer Case Department supervisor	$50,000

In a lunchtime conversation with the controller, Cassanitti learned that CompTech was currently renting space in a warehouse for $39,000. The space is used to store completed printers. If the Printer Case Department were discontinued, the entire storage operation could be moved into the factory building and occupy the space vacated by the closed department. Cassanitti also learned that the supervisor of the Printer Case Department would be retained by CompTech even if the department were closed. The supervisor would be assigned the job of managing the assembly department, whose supervisor recently gave notice of his retirement. All of CompTech's department supervisors earn the same salary.

Required:

1. You have been hired as a consultant by Cassanitti to advise him in his decision. Write a memo to Cassanitti commenting on the costs of space and supervisory salaries included in the controller's cost analysis. Explain in your memo about the "real" costs of the space occupied by the Printer Case Department and the supervisor's salary. What types of costs are these?

2. Independent of your response to requirement (1), suppose that CompTech's controller had been approached by his friend Jack Westford, the assistant supervisor of the Printer Case Department. Westford is worried that he will be laid off if the Printer Case Department is closed down.

    Westford has asked his friend to understate the cost savings from closing the department, in order to slant the production manager's decision toward keeping the department in operation. Comment on the controller's ethical responsibilities.

■ **Case 2–60**
Understanding Cost Concepts
(LO 7, 8, 10)

1(a). 60,000 copies

You just started a summer internship with the successful management consulting firm of Kirk, Spock, and McCoy. Your first day on the job was a busy one, as the following problems were presented to you.

Required: Supply the requested comments in each of the following independent situations.

1. FastQ Company, a specialist in printing, has established 500 convenience copying centers throughout the country. In order to upgrade its services, the company is considering three new models of laser copying machines for use in producing high-quality copies. These high-quality copies would be added to the growing list of products offered in the FastQ shops. The selling price to the customer for each laser copy would be the same, no matter which machine is installed in the shop. The three models of laser copying machines under consideration are 1024S, a small-volume model; 1024M, a medium-volume model; and 1024G, a large-volume model. The annual rental costs and the operating costs vary with the size of each machine. The machine capacities and costs are as follows:

	Copier Model		
	1024S	**1024M**	**1024G**
Annual capacity (copies)	100,000	350,000	800,000
Costs:			
Annual machine rental	$8,000	$11,000	$20,000
Direct material and direct labor	.02	.02	.02
Variable overhead costs	.12	.07	.03

   a. Calculate the volume level in copies where FastQ Company would be indifferent to acquiring either the small-volume model laser copier, 1024S, or the medium-volume model laser copier, 1024M.

   b. The management of FastQ Company is able to estimate the number of copies to be sold at each establishment. Present a decision rule that would enable FastQ Company to select the most profitable machine without having to make a separate cost calculation for each establishment. (*Hint:* To specify a decision rule, determine the volume at which FastQ would be indifferent between the small and medium copiers. Then determine the volume at which FastQ would be indifferent between the medium and large copiers.)

2. Alderon Enterprises is evaluating a special order it has received for a ceramic fixture to be used in aircraft engines. Alderon has recently been operating at less than full capacity, so the firm's management will accept the order if the price offered exceeds the costs that will be incurred in

producing it. You have been asked for advice on how to determine the cost of two raw materials that would be required to produce the order.

a. The special order will require 800 gallons of endor, a highly perishable material that is purchased as needed. Alderon currently has 1,200 gallons of endor on hand, since the material is used in virtually all of the company's products. The last time endor was purchased, Alderon paid $5.00 per gallon. However, the average price paid for the endor in stock was only $4.75. The market price for endor is quite volatile, with the current price at $5.50. If the special order is accepted, Alderon will have to place a new order next week to replace the 800 gallons of endor used. By then the price is expected to reach $5.75 per gallon.

Using the cost terminology introduced in Chapter 2, comment on each of the cost figures mentioned in the preceding discussion. What is the real cost of endor if the special order is produced?

b. The special order also would require 1,500 kilograms of tatooine, a material not normally required in any of Alderon's regular products. The company does happen to have 2,000 kilograms of tatooine on hand, since it formerly manufactured a ceramic product that used the material. Alderon recently received an offer of $14,000 from Solo Industries for its entire supply of tatooine. However, Solo Industries is not interested in buying any quantity less than Alderon's entire 2,000-kilogram stock. Alderon's management is unenthusiastic about Solo's offer, since Alderon paid $20,000 for the tatooine. Moreover, if the tatooine were purchased at today's market price, it would cost $11.00 per kilogram. Due to the volatility of the tatooine, Alderon will need to get rid of its entire supply one way or another. If the material is not used in production or sold, Alderon will have to pay $1,000 for each 500 kilograms that is transported away and disposed of in a hazardous waste disposal site.

Using the cost terminology introduced in Chapter 2, comment on each of the cost figures mentioned in the preceding discussion. What is the real cost of tatooine to be used in the special order?

3. A local PBS station has decided to produce a TV series on state-of-the-art manufacturing. The director of the TV series, Justin Tyme, is currently attempting to analyze some of the projected costs for the series. Tyme intends to take a TV production crew on location to shoot various manufacturing scenes as they occur. If the four-week series is shown in the 8:00–9:00 P.M. prime-time slot, the station will have to cancel a wildlife show that is currently scheduled. Management projects a 10 percent viewing audience for the wildlife show, and each 1 percent is expected to bring in donations of $10,000. In contrast, the manufacturing show is expected to be watched by 15 percent of the viewing audience. However, each 1 percent of the viewership will likely generate only $5,000 in donations. If the wildlife show is canceled, it can be sold to network television for $25,000.

Using the cost terminology introduced in Chapter 2, comment on each of the financial amounts mentioned in the scenario above. What are the relative merits of the two shows regarding the projected revenue to the station?

(CMA, adapted)

THIS CHAPTER'S FOCUS COMPANY is Barcos Belém, a small manufacturer of canoes and small boats in the city of Belém, a busy Brazilian port on the Pará River in the Amazon estuary. Barcos Belém uses job-order costing to accumulate the costs of each of its products. Job-order costing is well suited to companies like Barcos Belém that manufacture relatively small numbers of distinct products. In a job-order costing system, direct material, direct labor, and manufacturing overhead are first assigned to each production job, such as a set number of canoes of a particular type. Then the cost of the production job is averaged across the number of units in the job.

3 Product Costing and Cost Accumulation in a Batch Production Environment

In contrast to the manufacturing setting of Barcos Belém, we explore job-order costing in a service industry environment. Publicidades Paulista is a small advertising agency in São Paulo, Brazil. The firm has two managing partners, six artistic staff personnel, and an office support staff. Publicidades Paulista calculates predetermined overhead rates based on two cost drivers: partner direct professional labor and artistic staff direct professional labor. The ad agency's cost of completing the work for an advertising contract with ice cream company Sorvete Atlântico includes direct material, direct professional labor for both partner and artistic staff time, and applied overhead.

PAULISTA
PUBLICIDADES

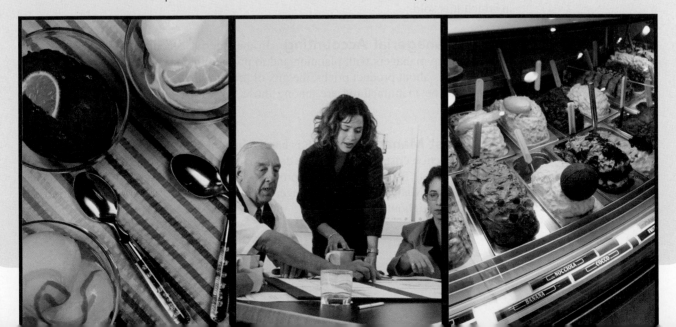

1 Discuss the role of product and service costing in manufacturing and non-manufacturing firms.

2 Diagram and explain the flow of costs through the manufacturing accounts used in product costing.

3 Distinguish between job-order costing and process costing.

4 Compute a predetermined overhead rate and explain its use in job-order costing for job-shop and batch-production environments.

5 Prepare journal entries to record the costs of direct material, direct labor, and manufacturing overhead in a job-order costing system.

6 Prepare a schedule of cost of goods manufactured, a schedule of cost of goods sold, and an income statement for a manufacturer.

7 Describe the two-stage allocation process used to assign manufacturing overhead costs to production jobs.

8 Describe the process of project costing used in service industry firms and nonprofit organizations.

Product and Service Costing

Learning Objective 1

Discuss the role of product and service costing in manufacturing and nonmanufacturing firms.

A **product-costing system** accumulates the costs incurred in a production process and assigns those costs to the organization's final products. Product costs are needed for a variety of purposes in financial accounting, managerial accounting, and cost management.

Use in Financial Accounting In financial accounting, product costs are needed to value inventory on the balance sheet and to compute cost-of-goods-sold expense on the income statement. Under generally accepted accounting principles, inventory is valued at its cost until it is sold. Then the cost of the inventory becomes an expense of the period in which it is sold.

Use in Managerial Accounting In managerial accounting, product costs are needed to help managers with planning and to provide them with data for decision making. Decisions about product prices, the mix of products to be produced, and the quantity of output to be manufactured are among those for which product cost information is needed.

Use in Cost Management It is hard to imagine how management can control or reduce production costs if management does not have a clear idea of how much it costs to make its product. Thus, product costs provide crucial data for a variety of cost management purposes. Many of the cost management uses of product-costing information will be covered throughout this book.

Use in Reporting to Interested Organizations In addition to financial statement preparation and internal decision making, there is an ever-growing need for product cost information in relationships between firms and various outside organizations. Public utilities, such as electric and gas companies, record product costs to justify rate increases that must be approved by state and national regulatory agencies. Hospitals keep track of the costs of medical procedures that are paid by insurance companies or by the national government. Manufacturing firms often sign cost-plus contracts with the government, where the contract price depends on the cost of manufacturing the product.

> "We recognized that our key competitors were overseas. We realized that in order to compete, we had to be extremely cost conscious." (3a)
> **Micrus**
> (joint venture of IBM and Cirrus Logic)

Product Costing in Nonmanufacturing Firms

The need for product costs is not limited to manufacturing firms. Merchandising companies include the costs of buying and transporting merchandise in their product costs. Producers of inventoriable goods, such as mining products, petroleum, and agricultural products, also record the costs of producing their goods. The role of product costs in these companies is identical to that in manufacturing firms. For example, the pineapples grown and sold by Dole are inventoried at their product cost until they are sold. Then the product cost becomes cost-of-goods-sold expense.

Service Firms and Nonprofit Organizations The production output of service firms and nonprofit organizations consists of services that are consumed as they are produced. Since services cannot be stored and sold later like manufactured goods, there are no inventoriable costs in service industry firms and nonprofit organizations. However, such organizations need information about the costs of producing services. Banks, insurance companies, restaurants, airlines, law firms, hospitals, and city governments all record the costs of producing various services for the purposes of planning, cost control, and decision making. For example, in making a decision about adding a flight from Dubai to Taipei, Emirates Airline's management needs to know the cost of flying the proposed route. Before building a new branch bank, HSBC's management would want to know the cost of maintaining the branch, as well as the additional revenue to be generated. A Los Angeles city manager can make a better decision as to whether the city government should begin a drug counseling program if the cost of providing similar, existing services is known.

> "The closer we get to the client physically, the more likely it is that we're going to have an opportunity to participate in what's going on in the business. The more remote you are from where the business decision makers are, the less likely they are to think about you." (3b)
> **Qwest**

Flow of Costs in Manufacturing Firms

Manufacturing costs consist of direct material, direct labor, and manufacturing overhead. The product-costing systems used by manufacturing firms employ several manufacturing accounts. As production takes place, all manufacturing costs are added to the *Work-in-Process Inventory* account. Work in process is partially completed inventory. A debit to the account increases the cost-based valuation of the asset represented by the unfinished products. As soon as products are completed, their product costs are transferred from Work-in-Process Inventory to *Finished-Goods Inventory*. This is accomplished with a credit to Work in Process and a debit to Finished Goods. During the time period when products are sold, the product cost of the inventory sold is removed from Finished Goods and added to *Cost of Goods Sold*, which is an expense of the period in which the sale occurred. A credit to Finished Goods and a debit to Cost of Goods Sold completes this step. Cost of Goods Sold is closed into the Income Summary account at the end of the accounting period, along with all other expenses and revenues of the period. Exhibit 3–1 depicts the flow of costs through the manufacturing accounts.

> **Learning Objective 2**
>
> Diagram and explain the flow of costs through the manufacturing accounts used in product costing.

Exhibit 3–1
Flow of Costs through
Manufacturing Accounts

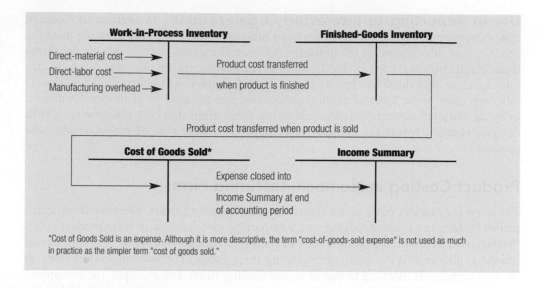

*Cost of Goods Sold is an expense. Although it is more descriptive, the term "cost-of-goods-sold expense" is not used as much in practice as the simpler term "cost of goods sold."

Example of Manufacturing Cost Flows

Suppose that the Ontario Paper Company incurred the following manufacturing costs during 20x1.

Direct material	$30,000
Direct labor	20,000
Manufacturing overhead	40,000

During 20x1, products costing $60,000 were finished and products costing $25,000 were sold for $32,000. Exhibit 3–2 shows the flow of costs through the Ontario Paper

Exhibit 3–2
Example of Manufacturing
Cost Flows for Ontario Paper
Company

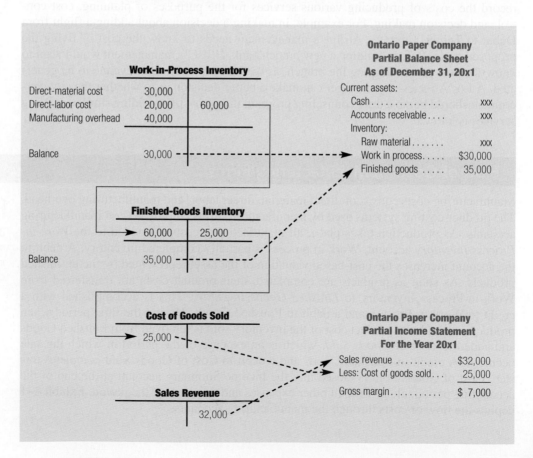

Company's manufacturing accounts and the effect of the firm's product costs on its balance sheet and income statement.

Types of Product-Costing Systems

The detailed accounting procedures used in product-costing systems depend on the type of industry involved. Two basic sets of procedures are used: job-order costing and process costing.

Job-Order Costing Systems

Job-order costing is used by companies with *job-shop* operations or *batch-production* operations. In a job-shop environment, products are manufactured in very low volumes or one at a time. Examples of a job-shop environment include feature film production, custom house building, ship building, aircraft manufacture, and custom machining operations. In a batch-production environment, multiple products are produced in batches of relatively small quantity. Examples include furniture manufacture, printing, agricultural equipment, and pleasure boat production.

> **Learning Objective 3**
>
> Distinguish between job-order costing and process costing.

In **job-order costing,** each distinct batch of production is called a *job* or *job order.* The cost-accounting procedures are designed to assign costs to each job. Then the costs assigned to each job are averaged over the units of production in the job to obtain an average cost per unit. For example, suppose that AccuPrint worked on two printing jobs during October, and the following costs were incurred.

	Job A27 (1,000 campaign posters)	Job B39 (100 wedding invitations)
Direct material	$100	$ 36
Direct labor	250	40
Manufacturing overhead	150	24
Total manufacturing cost	$500	$100

The cost per campaign poster is $.50 per poster ($500 divided by 1,000 posters), and the cost per wedding invitation is $1.00 ($100 divided by 100 invitations).

Procedures similar to those used in job-order costing also are used in many service industry firms, although these firms have no work-in-process or finished-goods inventories. In a public accounting firm, for example, costs are assigned to audit engagements in much the same way they are assigned to a batch of products by a furniture manufacturer. Similar procedures are used to assign costs to "cases" in health care facilities, to "programs" in government agencies, to research "projects" in universities, and to "contracts" in consulting and architectural firms.

> "We have to be the best in cost throughout the world." (3C)
>
> **Micrus**
> (joint venture of IBM and Cirrus Logic)

The cost-accounting system keeps track of production costs as they flow from raw material, through work in process and finished goods, and into cost of goods sold.

Process-Costing Systems

Process costing is used by companies that produce large numbers of identical units. Firms that produce chemicals, microchips, gasoline, beer, fertilizer, textiles, processed food, and electricity are among those using process costing. In these kinds of firms, there is no need to trace costs to specific batches of production, because the products in the different batches are identical. A **process-costing system** accumulates all the production costs for a large number of units of output, and then these costs are averaged over all of the units. For example, suppose Pearl River Ltd. produced 40,000 microchips during November. The following manufacturing costs were incurred in November.

Direct material	$1,000
Direct labor	2,000
Manufacturing overhead	3,000
Total manufacturing cost	$6,000

The cost per microchip is $.15 (total manufacturing cost of $6,000 ÷ 40,000 units produced).

Summary of Alternative Product-Costing Systems

The distinction between job-order and process costing hinges on the type of production process involved. Job-order costing systems assign costs to distinct production jobs that are significantly different. Then an average cost is computed for each unit of product in each job. Process-costing systems average costs over a large number of identical (or very similar) units of product.

The remainder of this chapter examines the details of job-order costing. The next chapter covers process costing.

Accumulating Costs in a Job-Order Costing System

BARCOS BELÉM

To illustrate job-order costing, we will focus on Barcos Belém. This small company, perched on the banks of the Pará River in the city of Belém, Brazil, manufactures canoes and small boats that are sold and used throughout the Amazon estuary.

In a job-order costing system, costs of direct material, direct labor, and manufacturing overhead are assigned to each production job. These costs comprise the *inputs* of the product-costing *system.* As costs are incurred, they are added to the Work-in-Process Inventory account in the ledger. To keep track of the manufacturing costs assigned to *each job,* a subsidiary ledger is maintained. The subsidiary ledger account assigned to each job is a document called a **job-cost record.**

Job-Cost Record

An example of a job-cost record is displayed in Exhibit 3–3. At this juncture, just focus on the major sections and headings, which are printed in blue. (For now just ignore the detailed entries, printed in black, which will be explained in due course.)

This job-cost record is for job F16 consisting of 80 deluxe aluminum fishing boats, which was produced during November 20x1. Three major sections on the job-cost record are used to accumulate the costs of direct material, direct labor, and manufacturing overhead assigned to the job. The other two sections are used to record the total cost and average unit cost for the job, and to keep track of units shipped to customers. A job-cost record may be a paper document upon which the entries for direct material, direct labor, and manufacturing overhead are written. Increasingly, it is a computer file where entries are made using a computer.

JOB-COST RECORD		
Job Number F16	**Description** 80 deluxe aluminum fishing boats	
Date Started Nov. 1, 20x1	**Date Completed** Nov. 22, 20x1	
	Number of Units Completed 80	

Direct Material

Date	Requisition Number	Quantity	Unit Price	Cost
11/1	803	720 m^2	$25	$18,000

Direct Labor

Date	Time Card Number	Hours	Rate	Cost
Various dates	Various time cards	600	$20	$12,000

Manufacturing Overhead

Date	Cost Driver (Activity Base)	Quantity	Application Rate	Cost
11/30	Machine hours	2,000	$9.00	$18,000

Cost Summary

Cost Item	Amount
Total direct material	$18,000
Total direct labor	12,000
Total manufacturing overhead	18,000
Total cost	$48,000
Unit cost	$600

Shipping Summary

Date	Units Shipped	Units Remaining in Inventory	Cost Balance
11/30	60	20	$12,000

Exhibit 3–3
Job-Cost Record:
Barcos Belém.

BARCOS BELÉM

The procedures used to accumulate the costs of direct material, direct labor, and manufacturing overhead for a job constitute the *set of activities* performed by the job-order costing *system*. These procedures are discussed next.

Direct-Material Costs

As raw materials are needed for the production process, they are transferred from the warehouse to the production department. To authorize the release of materials, the production department supervisor completes a **material requisition form** and presents it to the warehouse supervisor. A copy of the material requisition form goes to the cost accounting department. There it is used as the basis for transferring the cost of the requisitioned material from the Raw-Material Inventory account to the Work-in-Process

Exhibit 3–4
Material Requisition Form

Material-Requisition Number	352				Date	1/28/x1	
Job Number to Be Charged	J621				Department	Painting	
Department Supervisor	António Santos						

Item	Quantity	Unit Cost	Amount
White enamel paint	32 liters	$3.50	$112
Clear lacquer	8 liters	2.75	22

Inventory account, and for entering the direct-material cost on the job-cost record for the production job in process. A document such as the material requisition form, which is used as the basis for an accounting entry, is called a **source document.** Exhibit 3–4 shows an example of a material requisition form.

In many production facilities, material requisitions are entered directly into a computer by the production department supervisor. The requisition is automatically transmitted to computers in the warehouse and in the cost accounting department. Such automation reduces the flow of paperwork, minimizes clerical errors, and speeds up the product-costing process.

Supply Chain Management
An organization's **supply chain** refers to the flow of all goods, services, and information into and out of the organization. Thus, Barcos Belém's supply chain looks like this:

A supply chain often includes many companies and other organizations. *Supply chain management* means proactively working with some or all of the organizations in a company's supply chain to improve service and to manage or reduce costs. For example, Barcos Belém's managers might work with the vendor supplying aluminum sheet metal to improve delivery schedules or reduce material costs. Barcos Belém's managers also might consult with retailers about more effective displays for the company's products or more timely information about the retailers' restocking needs.

Material-Requirements Planning
For products and product components that are produced routinely, the required materials are known in advance. For these products and components, material requisitions are based on a **bill of materials** that lists all of the materials needed.

In complex manufacturing operations, in which production takes place in several stages, *material-requirements planning* (or *MRP*) may be used. MRP is an operations-management tool that assists managers in scheduling production in each stage of the manufacturing process. Such careful planning ensures that, at each stage in the production process, the required subassemblies, components, or partially processed materials will be ready for the next stage. MRP systems, which are generally computerized, include files that list all of the component parts and materials in inventory and all of the parts and materials needed in each stage of the production process.

Barcos Belém's operations are too limited to need an MRP system.

Direct-Labor Costs

The assignment of direct-labor costs to jobs is based on time records filled out by employees. A **time record** is a form that records the amount of time an employee spends on each production job. The time record is the source document used in the cost-accounting department as the basis for adding direct-labor costs to Work-in-Process Inventory and to the job-cost records for the various jobs in process. In some factories, a computerized time-clock system may be used. Employees enter the time they begin and stop work on each job into the time clock. The time clock is connected to a computer, which records the time spent on various jobs and transmits the information to the accounting department.

   Exhibit 3–5 displays an example of a time record. As the example shows, most of the employee's time was spent working on two different production jobs. In the accounting department, the time spent on each job will be multiplied by the employee's wage rate, and the cost will be recorded in Work-in-Process Inventory and on the appropriate job-cost records. The employee also spent one-half hour on shop cleanup duties. This time will be classified by the accounting department as indirect labor, and its cost will be included in manufacturing overhead.

Manufacturing-Overhead Costs

It is relatively simple to trace direct-material and direct-labor costs to production jobs, but manufacturing overhead is not easily traced to jobs. By definition, manufacturing overhead is a heterogeneous pool of indirect production costs, such as indirect material, indirect labor, utility costs, and depreciation. These costs often bear no obvious relationship to individual jobs or units of product, but they must be incurred for production to take place. Therefore, it is necessary to assign manufacturing-overhead costs to jobs in order to have a complete picture of product costs. This process of assigning manufacturing-overhead costs to production jobs is called **overhead application** (or sometimes **overhead absorption**).

Overhead Application   For product-costing information to be useful, it must be provided to managers on a timely basis. Suppose the cost-accounting department waited until the end of an accounting period so that the *actual* costs of manufacturing overhead could be determined before applying overhead costs to the firm's products. The result would be very accurate overhead application. However, the information might be useless because it was not available to managers for planning, control, and decision making during the period.

Predetermined Overhead Rate   The solution to this problem is to apply overhead to products on the basis of estimates made at the beginning of the accounting period. The accounting department chooses some measure of productive activity to use as the basis for overhead application. In traditional product-costing systems, this measure is usually some **volume-based cost driver** (or **activity base**), such as direct-labor hours, direct-labor cost, or machine hours. An estimate is made of (1) the amount of manufacturing

<table>
<tr><td colspan="3">Employee Name ___João Almeida_____   Date ___12/19/x1_____
Employee Number ___12_____   Department ___Painting_____</td></tr>
<tr><th>Time Started</th><th>Time Stopped</th><th>Job Number</th></tr>
<tr><td>8:00</td><td>11:30</td><td>A267</td></tr>
<tr><td>11:30</td><td>12:00</td><td>Shop cleanup</td></tr>
<tr><td>1:00</td><td>5:00</td><td>J122</td></tr>
</table>

> **Learning Objective 4**
>
> Compute a predetermined overhead rate and explain its use in job-order costing for job-shop and batch-production environments.

Exhibit 3–5
Time Record

BARCOS BELÉM

Management Accounting Practice

Caterpillar, Inc. and Kerry Logistics

SUPPLY CHAIN MANAGEMENT

Supply chain management has become a critically important issue in many companies and other organizations. Here are several examples of how organizations are managing their supply chains to get or provide better service at lower costs.

Caterpillar, Inc.—The Inventory "Bullwhip Effect"

Managing the supply chain is particularly critical for management during an economic slump and as the economy starts to emerge from a downturn. "Caterpillar, Inc. recently told its steel suppliers that it will more than double its purchases of the metal" within a year, even if there is no increase in sales of Caterpillar's own products. "In fact, the heavy equipment manufacturer has been boosting orders to suppliers for everything from big tires and hydraulic tubes to shatterproof glass." Why would Caterpillar be making such a large inventory resupply effort even in the face of nearly flat sales? "Chalk it up to the 'bullwhip effect,' which is reverberating" throughout the global economy.

"This phenomenon occurs when companies significantly cut or add inventories. Economists call it a bullwhip because even small increases in demand can cause a big snap in the need for parts and materials further down the supply chain. The bullwhip has broad implications" for the economy as "companies rush to fill orders while also restocking warehouse shelves. It touches everyone from retailers to the industrial companies that supply" the many resources needed to manufacture more products. "The manner in which companies, large and small, respond to market shifts determines which ones emerge first" from an economic downturn and start to grow again.[1]

Kerry Logistics and the Shenzhen Special Economic Zone

"Amid piles of cardboard cartons in the dimly lit upper storeys of Kerry Logistics' Yantian warehouse in southern China, workers fill boxes for export, pulling shirts in the right mix of sizes for each destination store from a row of shelves.

The boxes will later be put into a container, taken to the neighouring Yantian container terminal and put on a ship, probably to the U.S. – the main destination for goods from this eastern side of the Shenzhen Special Economic Zone bordering Hong Kong.

...The Yantian warehouse is among the most sophisticated logistics facilities in mainland China, carrying out packing, assembly and labelling work on products for clients, sometimes including final assembly in Yantian of parts made in different countries. It increasingly sends goods out packed in the right order to go straight from the destination port to customers' factories or stores, cutting out the need for expensive distribution centres in receiving countries.

Randy Rogers, a senior executive in China of Excel Supply Chain, part of the DHL Group, says his company is regularly asked to redesign customers' supply chains to cut the costs of their increasingly complex Chinese businesses. In over-complex supply chains, goods are often moved too frequently in and out of warehouses and between vehicles. 'It's not unusual to see customers touching a product four or five times before it hits the shelf,' Mr Rogers says. 'There's a lot of cost involved in doing that.'"[2]

overhead that will be incurred during a specified period of time and (2) the amount of the cost driver (or activity base) that will be used or incurred during the same time period. Then a **predetermined overhead rate** is computed as follows:

$$\text{Predetermined overhead rate} = \frac{\text{Budgeted manufacturing-overhead cost}}{\text{Budgeted amount of cost driver (or activity base)}}$$

[1]Timothy Aeppel, *The Wall Street Journal*, January 27, 2010, p. A1.

[2]Robert Wright, "Logistics: Customs' Lack of Practice," *Financial Times*, March 25, 2008.

For example, Barcos Belém has chosen machine hours as its cost driver (or activity base). For the year 20x1, the firm estimates that overhead cost will amount to $360,000 and that total machine hours used will be 40,000 hours. The 40,000 budgeted machine hours represent the company's *practical capacity* for production. This means that 40,000 machine hours are expected to be available for production under normal operating conditions. Recall from the discussion in Chapter 1 (pp. 52–54) that normal operating conditions allow for such issues as routine machine maintenance, employee fatigue, and so forth.

Barcos Belém's predetermined overhead rate is computed as follows:

$$\text{Predetermined overhead rate} = \frac{\$360,000}{40,000 \text{ hours}} = \$9.00 \text{ per machine hour}$$

In our discussion of the predetermined overhead rate, we have emphasized the term *cost driver,* because increasingly this term is replacing the more traditional term *activity base.* Furthermore, we have emphasized that *traditional* product-costing systems tend to rely on a *single, volume-based cost driver.* We will discuss more elaborate product-costing systems based on multiple cost drivers later in this chapter. This topic is examined in even greater detail in Chapter 5.

Applying Overhead Costs The predetermined overhead rate is used to apply manufacturing overhead costs to production jobs. The quantity of the cost driver (or activity base) required by a particular job is multiplied by the predetermined overhead rate to determine the amount of overhead cost applied to the job. For example, suppose Barcos Belém's job number D22 requires 30 machine hours. The overhead applied to the job is computed as follows:

Predetermined overhead rate	$ 9
Machine hours required by job D22	× 30
Overhead applied to job D22	$270

The $270 of applied overhead will be added to Work-in-Process Inventory and recorded on the job-cost record for job D22. The accounting entries made to add manufacturing overhead to Work-in-Process Inventory may be made daily, weekly, or monthly, depending on the time required to process production jobs. Before the end of an accounting period, entries should be made to record all manufacturing costs incurred to date in Work-in-Process Inventory. This is necessary to properly value Work-in-Process Inventory on the balance sheet.

Summary of Event Sequence in Job-Order Costing

The flowchart in Exhibit 3–6 summarizes the sequence of activities performed by the job-order costing system. The role of the various documents used in job-order costing also is emphasized in the flowchart.

Illustration of Job-Order Costing

Now let's examine the accounting entries made by Barcos Belém during November of 20x1. The company worked on two production jobs:

> Job number C12, 80 deluxe wooden canoes
> Job number F16, 80 deluxe aluminum fishing boats

The job numbers designate these as the 12th canoe production job and the 16th fishing boat production job undertaken during the year. The events of November are described below along with the associated accounting entries.

Learning Objective 5

Prepare journal entries to record the costs of direct material, direct labor, and manufacturing overhead in a job-order costing system.

BARCOS BELÉM

Exhibit 3-6

Summary of Event Sequence
in a Job-Order Costing
System

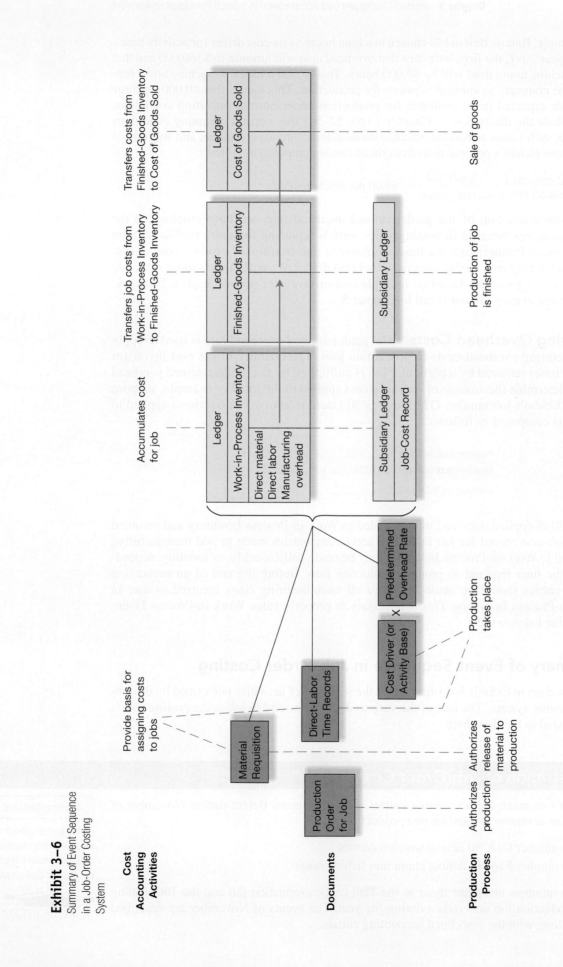

Purchase of Material

Four hundred square meters of rolled aluminum sheet metal were purchased on account for $10,000. The purchase is recorded with the following journal entry.

(1)	Raw-Material Inventory...	10,000	
	Accounts Payable		10,000

The postings of this and all subsequent journal entries to the ledger are shown in Exhibit 3–11, which appears on page 136.

Use of Direct Material

On November 1, the following material requisitions were submitted.

Requisition number 802:   16 cubic meters of lumber, at $1,000 per cubic
(for job number C12)   meter, for a total of $16,000

Requisition number 803:   720 square meters of aluminum sheet metal, at
(for job number F16) $25 per square meter, for a total of $18,000

The following journal entry records the release of these raw materials to production.

(2)	Work-in-Process Inventory	34,000	
	Raw-Material Inventory		34,000

The associated ledger posting is shown in Exhibit 3–11. These direct-material costs are also recorded on the job-cost record for each job. The job-cost record for job number F16 is displayed in Exhibit 3–3 on page 121. Since the job-cost record for job number C12 is similar, it is not shown.

Use of Indirect Material

On November 15, the following material requisition was submitted.

Requisition number 804:   20 liters of bonding glue, at $2.50 per liter, for a
                            total cost of $50

Small amounts of bonding glue are used in the production of all classes of boats manufactured by Barcos Belém. Since the cost incurred is small, no attempt is made to trace the cost of glue to specific jobs. Instead, glue is considered an indirect material, and its cost is included in manufacturing overhead. The company accumulates all manufacturing-overhead costs in the Manufacturing Overhead account. All actual overhead costs are recorded by debiting this account. The account is debited when indirect materials are requisitioned, when indirect-labor costs are incurred, when utility bills are paid, when depreciation is recorded on manufacturing equipment, and so forth. The journal entry made to record the usage of glue is as follows:

(3)	Manufacturing Overhead	50	
	Manufacturing Supplies Inventory		50

The posting of this journal entry to the ledger is shown in Exhibit 3–11. No entry is made on any job-cost record for the usage of glue, since its cost is not traced to individual production jobs.

This small production facility records the cost of manufacturing canoes and other boats, which are manufactured in small batches. Direct material, direct labor, and manufacturing-overhead costs are tracked.

Use of Direct Labor

At the end of November, the cost accounting department uses the labor time records filed during the month to determine the following direct-labor costs of each job.

Direct labor: job number C12	$ 9,000
Direct labor: job number F16	12,000
Total direct labor	$21,000

The journal entry made to record these costs is as follows:

(4)	Work-in-Process Inventory	21,000	
	Wages Payable		21,000

The associated ledger posting is shown in Exhibit 3–11. These direct-labor costs also are recorded on the job-cost record for each job. The job-cost record for job number F16 is displayed in Exhibit 3–3 on page 121. Only one direct-labor entry is shown on the job-cost record. In practice, there would be numerous entries made on different dates at a variety of wage rates for different employees.

Use of Indirect Labor

The analysis of labor time records undertaken on November 30 also revealed the following use of indirect labor:

Indirect labor: not charged to any particular job, $14,000

This cost comprises the production supervisor's salary and the wages of various employees who spent some of their time on maintenance and general cleanup duties during November. The following journal entry is made to add indirect-labor costs to manufacturing overhead:

(5)	Manufacturing Overhead	14,000	
	Wages Payable		14,000

No entry is made on any job-cost record, since indirect-labor costs are not traceable to any particular job. In practice, journal entries (4) and (5) are usually combined into one compound entry as follows:

Work-in-Process Inventory	21,000	
Manufacturing Overhead	14,000	
Wages Payable		35,000

Incurrence of Manufacturing-Overhead Costs

The following manufacturing-overhead costs were incurred during November:

Manufacturing overhead:	
Rent on factory building	$ 3,000
Depreciation on equipment	5,000
Utilities (electricity and natural gas)	4,000
Property taxes	2,000
Insurance	1,000
Total	$15,000

The following compound journal entry is made on November 30 to record these costs:

(6)	Manufacturing Overhead	15,000	
	Prepaid Rent		3,000
	Accumulated Depreciation—Equipment		5,000
	Accounts Payable (utilities and property taxes)		6,000
	Prepaid Insurance		1,000

The entry is posted in Exhibit 3–11. No entry is made on any job-cost record, since manufacturing-overhead costs are not traceable to any particular job.

Application of Manufacturing Overhead

Various manufacturing-overhead costs were incurred during November, and these costs were accumulated by debiting the Manufacturing Overhead account. However, no manufacturing-overhead costs have yet been added to Work-in-Process Inventory or recorded on the job-cost records. The application of overhead to the firm's products is based on a predetermined overhead rate. This rate was computed by the accounting department at the beginning of 20x1 as follows:

$$\text{Predetermined overhead rate} = \frac{\text{Budgeted total manufacturing overhead for 20x1}}{\text{Budgeted total machine hours for 20x1}}$$

$$= \frac{\$360,000}{40,000} = \$9.00 \text{ per machine hour}$$

As explained previously, the 40,000 budgeted machine hours represent the company's annual practical capacity for production.

Factory machine-usage records indicate the following actual usage of machine hours during November:

Machine hours used: job number C12	1,200 hours
Machine hours used: job number F16	2,000 hours
Total machine hours	3,200 hours

The total manufacturing overhead applied to Work-in-Process Inventory during November is calculated as follows:

	Machine Hours		Predetermined Overhead Rate		Manufacturing Overhead Applied
Job number C12	1,200	×	$9.00	=	$10,800
Job number F16	2,000	×	$9.00	=	18,000
Total manufacturing overhead applied					$28,800

The following journal entry is made to add **applied manufacturing overhead** to Work-in-Process Inventory.

(7)	Work-in-Process Inventory	28,800	
	Manufacturing Overhead		28,800

The entry is posted in Exhibit 3–11, and the manufacturing overhead applied to job number F16 is entered on the job-cost record in Exhibit 3–3 on page 121.

Summary of Overhead Accounting

As the following time line shows, three concepts are used in accounting for overhead. Overhead is *budgeted* at the *beginning* of the accounting period, it is *applied during* the period, and *actual* overhead is measured at the *end* of the period.

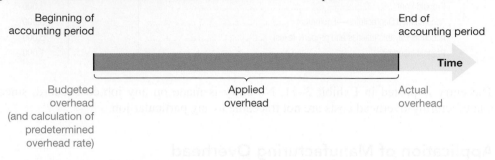

> "As production processes are becoming more automated, manufacturing overhead is becoming a greater and greater portion of total manufacturing costs. This is true of almost all manufacturing firms." (3d)
> **Chrysler**

Exhibit 3–7 summarizes the accounting procedures used for manufacturing overhead. The left side of the Manufacturing Overhead account is used to accumulate **actual manufacturing-overhead** costs as they are incurred throughout the accounting period. The actual costs incurred for indirect material, indirect labor, factory rental, equipment depreciation, utilities, property taxes, and insurance are recorded as debits to the account.

The right side of the Manufacturing Overhead account is used to record overhead *applied* to Work-in-Process Inventory.

While the left side of the Manufacturing Overhead account accumulates *actual* overhead costs, the right side applies overhead costs using the predetermined overhead rate, based on *estimated* overhead costs. The estimates used to calculate the predetermined overhead rate will generally prove to be incorrect to some degree. Consequently, there will usually be a nonzero balance left in the Manufacturing Overhead account at the end of the year. This balance is usually relatively small, and its disposition is covered later in this illustration.

Selling and Administrative Costs

During November, Barcos Belém incurred selling and administrative costs as follows:

Rental of sales and administrative offices	$ 1,500
Salaries of sales personnel	4,000
Salaries of management	8,000
Advertising	1,000
Office supplies used	300
Total	$14,800

Since these are not manufacturing costs, they are not added to Work-in-Process Inventory. Selling and administrative costs are period costs, not product costs.

Exhibit 3–7
Manufacturing Overhead Account

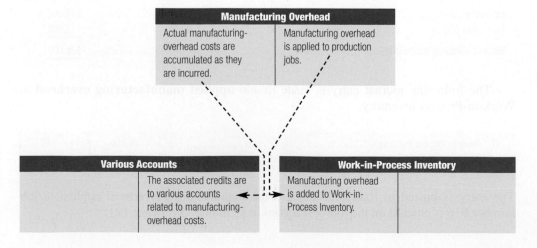

They are treated as expenses of the accounting period in which they are incurred. The following journal entry is made.

(8) Selling and Administrative Expenses	14,800	
Wages Payable		12,000
Accounts Payable		1,000
Prepaid Rent		1,500
Office Supplies Inventory		300

The entry is posted in Exhibit 3–11.

Completion of a Production Job

Job number F16 was completed during November, whereas job number C12 remained in process. As the job-cost record in Exhibit 3–3 (page 131) indicates, the total cost of job number F16 was $48,000. The following journal entry records the transfer of these job costs from Work-in-Process Inventory to Finished-Goods Inventory.

(9) Finished-Goods Inventory	48,000	
Work-in-Process Inventory		48,000

The entry is posted in Exhibit 3–11.

Sale of Goods

Sixty deluxe aluminum fishing boats manufactured in job number F16 were sold for $900 each during November. The cost of each unit sold was $600, as shown on the job-cost record in Exhibit 3–3 (page 121). The following journal entries are made.

(10) Accounts Receivable	54,000	
Sales Revenue		54,000

(11) Cost of Goods Sold	36,000	
Finished-Goods Inventory		36,000

These entries are posted in Exhibit 3–11.

The remainder of the manufacturing costs for job number F16 remain in Finished-Goods Inventory until some subsequent accounting period when the units are sold. Therefore, the cost balance for job number F16 remaining in inventory is $12,000 (20 units remaining times $600 per unit). This balance is shown on the job-cost record in Exhibit 3–3 (page 121).

Underapplied and Overapplied Overhead

During November, Barcos Belém incurred total *actual* manufacturing-overhead costs of $29,050, but only $28,800 of overhead was *applied* to Work-in-Process Inventory. The amount by which actual overhead exceeds applied overhead, called **underapplied overhead,** is calculated below.

Actual manufacturing overhead*	$ 29,050
Applied manufacturing overhead†	28,800
Underapplied overhead	$ 250

*Sum of debit entries in the Manufacturing-Overhead account: $50 + $14,000 + $15,000 = $29,050. See Exhibit 3–11.
†Applied overhead: $9.00 per machine hour × 3,200 machine hours.

If actual overhead had been less than applied overhead, the difference would have been called **overapplied overhead.** Underapplied or overapplied overhead is caused by errors in the estimates of overhead and activity used to compute the predetermined overhead rate. In this illustration, Barcos Belém's predetermined rate was underestimated by a small amount.

Disposition of Underapplied or Overapplied Overhead

At the end of an accounting period, the managerial accountant has two alternatives for the disposition of underapplied or overapplied overhead. Under the most common alternative, the underapplied or overapplied overhead is closed into Cost of Goods Sold. This is the method used by Barcos Belém, and the required journal entry is shown below.

| (12) | Cost of Goods Sold .... | 250 | |
| | Manufacturing Overhead .... | | 250 |

This entry, which is posted in Exhibit 3–11, brings the balance in the Manufacturing Overhead account to zero. The account is then clear to accumulate manufacturing-overhead costs incurred in the next accounting period. Journal entry (12) has the effect of increasing cost-of-goods-sold expense. This reflects the fact that the cost of the units sold had been underestimated due to the slightly underestimated predetermined overhead rate. Most companies use this approach because it is simple and the amount of underapplied or overapplied overhead is usually small. Moreover, most firms wait until the end of the year to close underapplied or overapplied overhead into Cost of Goods Sold, rather than making the entry monthly as in this illustration.

Proration of Underapplied or Overapplied Overhead

Some companies use a more accurate procedure to dispose of underapplied or overapplied overhead. This approach recognizes that underestimation or overestimation of the predetermined overhead rate affects not only Cost of Goods Sold, but also Work-in-Process Inventory and Finished-Goods Inventory. As the following diagram shows, applied overhead passes through all three of these accounts. Therefore, all three accounts are affected by any inaccuracy in the predetermined overhead rate.

When underapplied or overapplied overhead is allocated among the three accounts shown above, the process is called **proration.** The amount of the current period's applied overhead remaining in each account is the basis for the proration procedure. In the Barcos Belém illustration, the amounts of applied overhead remaining in the three accounts on November 30 are determined as follows:

Applied Overhead Remaining in Each Account on November 30				
Account	**Explanation**	**Amount**	**Percentage**	**Calculation of Percentages**
Work in Process	Job C12 only	$10,800	37.5%	10,800 ÷ 28,800
Finished Goods	¼ of units in job F16	4,500	15.6%*	4,500 ÷ 28,800
Cost of Goods Sold	¾ of units in job F16	13,500	46.9%*	13,500 ÷ 28,800
Total overhead applied in November		$28,800	100.0%	

*Rounded

Using the percentages calculated above, the proration of Barcos Belém's underapplied overhead is determined as follows:

Account	Underapplied Overhead	×	Percentage	=	Amount Added to Account
Work in Process	$250	×	37.5%	=	$ 93.75
Finished Goods	250	×	15.6%	=	39.00
Cost of Goods Sold	250	×	46.9%	=	117.25
Total underapplied overhead prorated					$250.00

If Barcos Belém had chosen to prorate underapplied overhead, the following journal entry would have been made.

Work-in-Process Inventory	93.75	
Finished-Goods Inventory	39.00	
Cost of Goods Sold	117.25	
Manufacturing Overhead		250.00

Since this is *not* the method used by Barcos Belém in our continuing illustration, this entry is *not* posted to the ledger in Exhibit 3–11.

Although proration is the most accurate way of correcting account balances for under- or overapplied overhead, as mentioned above most companies choose to apply the entire amount to Cost of Good Sold because any misstatement is usually immaterial. However, if misstatement is material, proration should be used. In addition, a small number of firms may be required to use proration under the rules specified by a governing regulatory agency. For example, in the United States the Cost Accounting Standards Board (CASB) regulates significant government contracts and under certain conditions requires that proration be used.

Schedule of Cost of Goods Manufactured

The Excel spreadsheet in Exhibit 3–8 displays the November **schedule of cost of goods manufactured** for Barcos Belém. The schedule details the costs of direct material, direct labor, and manufacturing overhead *applied* to work in process during November and shows the change in Work-in-Process Inventory. The **cost of goods manufactured,** shown in the last line of the schedule, is $48,000. This is the amount transferred from Work-in-Process Inventory to Finished-Goods Inventory during November, as recorded in journal entry number (9).

Schedule of Cost of Goods Sold

A **schedule of cost of goods sold** for Barcos Belém is displayed as an Excel spreadsheet in Exhibit 3–9. This schedule shows the November cost of goods sold and details the changes in Finished-Goods Inventory during the month. The Excel spreadsheet in Exhibit 3–10 displays the company's November income statement. As the income statement shows, income before taxes is $2,950, from which income tax expense of $1,420 is subtracted, yielding net income of $1,530.

> **Learning Objective 6**
>
> Prepare a schedule of cost of goods manufactured, a schedule of cost of goods sold, and an income statement for a manufacturer.

Exhibit 3–8

Schedule of Cost of Goods Manufactured

BARCOS BELÉM

	Microsoft Excel - Barcos Belém - Schedule of Cost of Goods Manufactured									
	File Edit View Insert Format Tools Data Window Help							Type a question for help		
	I33		f_x =I31-I32							
	A	B	C	D	E	F	G	H	I	J
1				BARCOS BELÉM						
2			Schedule of Cost of Goods Manufactured							
3			For the Month of November, 20x1							
4										
5	Direct material:									
6		Raw-material inventory, November 1						$ 30,000		
7		Add: November purchases of raw material						10,000		
8		Raw material available for use						$ 40,000		
9		Deduct: Raw-material inventory, November 30						6,000		
10		Raw material used							$ 34,000	
11										
12										
13	Direct labor								21,000	
14										
15	Manufacturing overhead:									
16		Indirect material						$ 50		
17		Indirect labor						14,000		
18		Rent on factory building						3,000		
19		Depreciation on equipment						5,000		
20		Utilities						4,000		
21		Property taxes						2,000		
22		Insurance						1,000		
23			Total actual manufacturing overhead					$ 29,050		
24			Deduct: Underapplied overhead*					250		
25		Overhead applied to work in process							28,800	
26										
27										
28	Total manufacturing costs								$ 83,800	
29	Add: Work-in-process inventory, November 1								4,000	
30										
31	Subtotal								$ 87,800	
32	Deduct: Work-in-process inventory, November 30								39,800	
33	Cost of goods manufactured								$ 48,000	
34										
35	*The schedule of cost of goods manufactured lists the manufacturing costs applied to work in									
36	process. Therefore, the underapplied overhead, $250, must be deducted from total actual overhead									
37	to arrive at the amount of overhead applied to work in process during November. If there had been									
38	overapplied overhead, the balance would have been added to total manufacturing overhead.									
	Sheet1 / Sheet2 / Sheet3 /									
	Ready									

Posting Journal Entries to the Ledger

All of the journal entries in the Barcos Belém illustration are posted to the ledger in Exhibit 3–11. An examination of these T-accounts provides a summary of the cost flows discussed throughout the illustration.

Further Aspects of Overhead Application

Actual and Normal Costing

Most firms use a predetermined overhead rate, based on overhead and activity estimates for a relatively long time period. When direct material and direct labor are added to Work-in-Process Inventory at their actual amounts, but overhead is applied to Work-in-Process Inventory using a *predetermined overhead rate,* the product-costing system is referred to as **normal costing.** This approach, which takes its name from the use of an overhead rate that is *normalized* over a fairly long period, is used in the Barcos Belém illustration.

Exhibit 3–9
Schedule of Cost of Goods Sold

Microsoft Excel - Barcos Belém - Schedule of Cost of Goods Sold

File Edit View Insert Format Tools Data Window Help

H11   =H9+H10

	A	B	C	D	E	F	G	H
1	BARCOS BELÉM							
2	Schedule of Cost of Goods Sold							
3	For the Month of November, 20x1							
4								
5	Finished-goods inventory, November 1							$ 12,000
6	Add: Cost of goods manufactured*							48,000
7	Cost of goods available for sale							$ 60,000
8	Deduct: Finished-goods inventory, November 30							24,000
9	Cost of goods sold							$ 36,000
10	Add: Underapplied overhead**							250
11	Cost of goods sold (adjusted for underapplied overhead)							$ 36,250
12								
13	*From the Schedule of Cost of Goods Manufactured in Exhibit 3-8.							
14								
15	**The company closes underapplied or overapplied overhead into cost of							
16	goods sold. Hence, the $250 balance in underapplied overhead is added to							
17	the cost of goods sold for the month.							

Sheet1 / Sheet2 / Sheet3 /

Ready

Exhibit 3–10
Income Statement

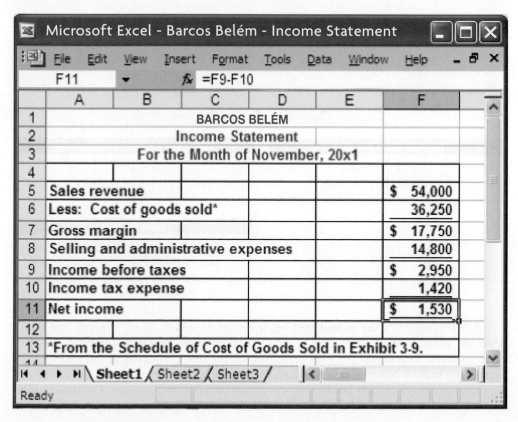

Microsoft Excel - Barcos Belém - Income Statement

File Edit View Insert Format Tools Data Window Help

F11   =F9-F10

	A	B	C	D	E	F
1	BARCOS BELÉM					
2	Income Statement					
3	For the Month of November, 20x1					
4						
5	Sales revenue					$ 54,000
6	Less: Cost of goods sold*					36,250
7	Gross margin					$ 17,750
8	Selling and administrative expenses					14,800
9	Income before taxes					$ 2,950
10	Income tax expense					1,420
11	Net income					$ 1,530
12						
13	*From the Schedule of Cost of Goods Sold in Exhibit 3-9.					

Sheet1 / Sheet2 / Sheet3 /

Ready

Exhibit 3–11
Ledger Accounts for
Barcos Belém Illustration*

Accounts Receivable		
Bal.	11,000	
(10)	54,000	

Accounts Payable		
	3,000	Bal.
	10,000	(1)
	6,000	(6)
	1,000	(8)

Prepaid Insurance		
Bal.	2,000	1,000	(6)

Wages Payable		
	10,000	Bal.
	21,000	(4)
	14,000	(5)
	12,000	(8)

Prepaid Rent		
Bal.	5,000		
		3,000	(6)
		1,500	(8)

Office Supplies Inventory		
Bal.	900	300	(8)

Manufacturing Supplies Inventory		
Bal.	750	50	(3)

Accumulated Depreciation: Equipment		
	105,000	Bal.
	5,000	(6)

Raw-Material Inventory		
Bal.	30,000	34,000	(2)
(1)	10,000		

Manufacturing Overhead			
(3)	50	28,800	(7)
(5)	14,000	250	(12)
(6)	15,000		

Work-in-Process Inventory		
Bal.	4,000	48,000	(9)
(2)	34,000		
(4)	21,000		
(7)	28,800		

Cost of Goods Sold		
(11)	36,000	
(12)	250	

Finished-Goods Inventory		
Bal.	12,000	36,000	(11)
(9)	48,000		

Selling and Administrative Expenses		
(8)	14,800	

Sales Revenue		
	54,000	(10)

*The numbers in parentheses relate T-account entries to the associated journal entries. The numbers in color are the November 1 account balances.

A few companies use **actual costing,** a system in which direct material and direct labor are added to work in process at their actual amounts, and actual overhead is allocated to work in process using an *actual overhead rate* computed at the *end* of each accounting period. Note that even though an actual overhead rate is used, the amount of overhead assigned to each production job is still an allocated amount. Overhead costs, which are by definition indirect costs, cannot be traced easily to individual production jobs. A significant drawback of actual costing is that product-cost information is not available until the end of the accounting period, when the actual overhead rate is computed. Actual and normal costing may be summarized as follows:

ACTUAL COSTING Work-in-Process Inventory		NORMAL COSTING Work-in-Process Inventory	
Actual direct- material costs		Actual direct- material costs	
Actual direct- labor costs		Actual direct- labor costs	
Overhead allocated:		Overhead applied:	
Actual overhead rate (computed at *end* of period)	Actual amount of cost driver used (e.g., direct-labor hours)	*Predetermined* overhead rate (computed at *beginning* of period)	Actual amount of cost driver used (e.g., direct-labor hours)

Choosing the Cost Driver for Overhead Application

Manufacturing overhead includes various indirect manufacturing costs that vary greatly in their relationship to the production process. If a single, volume-based cost driver (or activity base) is used in calculating the predetermined overhead rate, it should be some productive input that is common across all of the firm's products. If, for example, all of the firm's products require direct labor, but only some products require machine time, direct-labor hours would be a preferable activity base. If machine time were used as the base, products not requiring machine time would not be assigned any overhead cost.

In selecting a volume-based cost driver (or activity base), the goal is to choose an input that varies in a pattern that is most similar to the pattern with which overhead costs vary. Products that indirectly cause large amounts of overhead costs also should require large amounts of the cost driver, and vice versa. During periods when the cost driver is at a low level, the overhead costs incurred should be low. Thus, there should be a correlation between the incurrence of overhead costs and use of the cost driver.

Limitation of Direct Labor as a Cost Driver In traditional product-costing systems, the most common volume-based cost drivers are direct-labor hours and direct-labor cost. However, there is a trend away from using direct labor as the overhead application base. Many production processes are becoming increasingly automated, through the use of robotics and computer-integrated manufacturing systems. Increased automation brings two results. First, manufacturing-overhead costs represent a larger proportion of total production costs. Second, direct labor decreases in importance as a factor of production. As direct labor declines in importance as a productive input, it becomes less appropriate as a cost driver. For this reason, some firms have switched to machine hours, process time, or throughput time as cost drivers that better reflect the pattern of overhead cost incurrence. **Throughput time** (or **cycle time**) is the average amount of time required to convert raw materials into finished goods ready to be shipped to customers. Throughput time includes the time required for material handling, production processing, inspection, and packaging.

"As we continue to automate our production processes, direct labor is becoming less and less appropriate as a basis for the application of manufacturing overhead." (3f)
Chrysler

Departmental Overhead Rates

In the Barcos Belém illustration presented earlier in this chapter, all of the firm's manufacturing overhead was combined into a single cost pool. Then the overhead was applied to products using a single predetermined overhead rate based on machine hours.

Since only one overhead rate is used in Barcos Belém's entire factory, it is known as a **plantwide overhead rate.** In some production processes, the relationship between overhead costs and the firm's products differs substantially across production departments. In such cases, the firm may use **departmental overhead rates,** which differ across production departments. This usually results in a more accurate assignment of overhead costs to the firm's products. An even more accurate assignment of overhead costs can be achieved with *activity-based costing (ABC),* which is covered extensively in Chapter 5.

Two-Stage Cost Allocation

Learning Objective 7

Describe the two-stage allocation process used to assign manufacturing overhead costs to production jobs.

When a company uses departmental overhead rates, the assignment of manufacturing-overhead costs to production jobs is accomplished in two stages, comprising what is called **two-stage cost allocation.** In the first stage, all manufacturing-overhead costs are assigned to the production departments, such as machining and assembly. In the second stage, the overhead costs that have been assigned to each production department are applied to the production jobs that pass through the department. Let's examine this two-stage process in more detail.

Stage One In the first stage, all manufacturing-overhead costs are assigned to the firm's production departments. However, stage one often involves two different types of allocation processes. First, all manufacturing-overhead costs are assigned to **departmental overhead centers.** This step is called **cost distribution** (or sometimes **cost allocation**). For example, the costs of heating a factory with natural gas would be distributed among all of the departments in the factory, possibly in proportion to the cubic meters of space in each department. In the cost distribution step, manufacturing-overhead costs are assigned to *both* production departments and service departments. **Service departments,** such as equipment-maintenance and material-handling departments, are departments that do not work directly on the firm's products but are necessary for production to take place.

Second, all service department costs are reassigned to the production departments through a process called **service department cost allocation.** In this step, an attempt is made to allocate service department costs on the basis of the relative proportion of each service department's output that is used by the various production departments. For example, production departments with more equipment would be allocated a larger share of the maintenance department's costs.

At the conclusion of stage one, all manufacturing-overhead costs have been assigned to the production departments.

> "We're going to need much more general knowledge of how the business works." (3g)
>
> **Boeing**

Stage Two In the second stage, all of the manufacturing-overhead costs accumulated in each production department are assigned to the production jobs on which the department has worked. This process is called overhead application (or sometimes overhead absorption). In stage two, each production department has its own predetermined overhead rate. These rates often are based on different cost drivers.

The two-stage process of assigning overhead costs to production jobs is portrayed in Exhibit 3–12. Notice the roles of cost distribution, service department cost allocation, and overhead application in the exhibit. The techniques of overhead distribution and service department cost allocation will be covered later in the text. In this chapter, we are focusing primarily on the process of overhead application.[3]

---

[3]One might legitimately ask why this is called two-stage cost allocation when there are three types of allocation involved. The term *two-stage allocation* is entrenched in the literature and in practice. It stems from the fact that there are two *cost objects,* or entities, to which costs are assigned: production *departments* in stage one and production *jobs* in stage two.

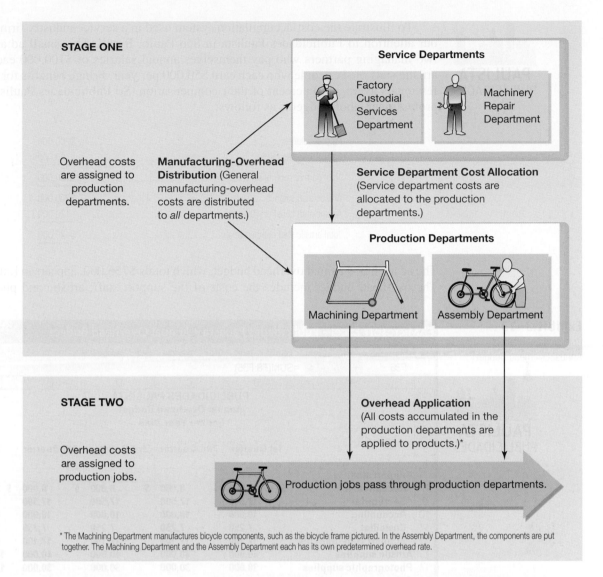

STAGE ONE

Service Departments

Factory Custodial Services Department

Machinery Repair Department

Overhead costs are assigned to production departments.

Manufacturing-Overhead Distribution (General manufacturing-overhead costs are distributed to *all* departments.)

Service Department Cost Allocation (Service department costs are allocated to the production departments.)

Production Departments

Machining Department

Assembly Department

STAGE TWO

Overhead costs are assigned to production jobs.

Overhead Application (All costs accumulated in the production departments are applied to products.)*

Production jobs pass through production departments.

* The Machining Department manufactures bicycle components, such as the bicycle frame pictured. In the Assembly Department, the components are put together. The Machining Department and the Assembly Department each has its own predetermined overhead rate.

Exhibit 3–12
Developing Departmental Overhead Rates Using Two-Stage Allocation

Project Costing: Job-Order Costing in Nonmanufacturing Organizations

Job-order costing also is used in service industry companies and other nonmanufacturing organizations. However, rather than referring to production "jobs," such organizations use terminology that reflects their operations. For example, hospitals such as the Philadelphia Children's Hospital assign costs to "cases," and consulting firms like McKinsey track "contract" costs. Law firms assign costs to cases, while government agencies typically refer to "programs" or "missions." The need for cost accumulation exists in these and similar organizations for the same reasons found in manufacturing firms. For example, a mission to launch a commercial satellite by NASA or Arianespace is assigned a cost for the purposes of planning, cost control, and pricing of the launch service.

Learning Objective 8

Describe the process of project costing used in service industry firms and nonprofit organizations.

PAULISTA
PUBLICIDADES

To illustrate the cost-accumulation system used in a service industry firm, let's turn our attention to Publicidades Paulista in São Paulo, Brazil. This small ad agency has two managing partners who pay themselves annual salaries of $100,000 each, and an artistic staff of six people who each earn $50,000 per year. Fringe benefits for these professionals average 40 percent of their compensation. So Publicidades Paulista's direct professional labor budget is as follows:

Partner salaries	$200,000
Partner benefits (40%)	80,000
Total partner compensation	$280,000
Artistic staff salaries	$300,000
Artistic staff benefits (40%)	120,000
Total artistic staff compensation	$420,000

The ad agency's annual overhead budget, which totals $756,000, appears in Exhibit 3–13. The overhead budget includes the costs of the support staff, artistic and photographic

Exhibit 3–13
Publicidades Paulista:
Annual Overhead Budget

PAULISTA
PUBLICIDADES

Microsoft Excel - Publicidades Paulista - Annual Overhead Budget

File   Edit   View   Insert   Format   Tools   Data   Window   Help   Adobe PDF

F36   =SUM(F8:F35)

	A	B	C	D	E	F
1		PUBLICIDADES PAULISTA				
2		Annual Overhead Budget				
3		For the Year 20x6				
4						
5		1st Quarter	2nd Quarter	3rd Quarter	4th Quarter	Year
6						
7	Support staff:					
8	Receptionist	$ 8,000	$ 8,000	$ 8,000	$ 8,000	$ 32,000
9	Secretarial	17,500	17,500	17,500	17,500	70,000
10	Accounting	10,000	10,000	10,000	10,000	40,000
11	Custodial	7,250	7,250	7,250	7,250	29,000
12	Support staff benefits	17,100	17,100	17,100	17,100	68,400
13	Artistic supplies	40,000	40,000	40,000	40,000	160,000
14	Photographic supplies	30,000	30,000	30,000	30,000	120,000
15	Office:					
16	Computer	5,000	5,000	5,000	5,000	20,000
17	Photocopying	3,750	3,750	3,750	3,750	15,000
18	Office supplies	4,500	4,500	4,500	4,500	18,000
19	Postage	525	525	525	525	2,100
20	Utilities:					
21	Electricity	3,250	3,250	3,250	3,250	13,000
22	Heat/air conditioning	4,000	4,000	4,000	4,000	16,000
23	Internet access	375	375	375	375	1,500
24	Cable TV	500	500	500	500	2,000
25	Telephone	775	775	775	775	3,100
26	Trash collection	600	600	600	600	2,400
27	Other	625	625	625	625	2,500
28	Building rent	12,500	12,500	12,500	12,500	50,000
29	Insurance	3,750	3,750	3,750	3,750	15,000
30	Advertising	5,000	5,000	5,000	5,000	20,000
31	Vehicle maintenance	1,000	1,000	1,000	1,000	4,000
32	Depreciation					
33	Equipment	3,000	3,000	3,000	3,000	12,000
34	Vehicles	5,000	5,000	5,000	5,000	20,000
35	Other	5,000	5,000	5,000	5,000	20,000
36	Total overhead	$ 189,000	$ 189,000	$ 189,000	$ 189,000	$756,000

Sheet1 / Sheet2 / Sheet3 /

Ready

supplies, office operation, utilities, rent, insurance, advertising, vehicle maintenance, and depreciation. Publicidades Paulista's accountant has estimated that one-third of the budgeted overhead cost is incurred to support the ad agency's two partners, and two-thirds of it goes to support the artistic staff. Thus, the following two overhead rates are calculated.

$$\frac{\text{Budgeted annual partner support overhead}}{\text{Budgeted annual partner compensation}} = \frac{\$756,000 \times \frac{1}{3}}{\$280,000} = 90\%$$

$$\frac{\text{Budgeted annual artistic staff support overhead}}{\text{Budgeted annual artistic staff compensation}} = \frac{\$756,000 \times \frac{2}{3}}{\$420,000} = 120\%$$

> "Every research contract negotiated between Cornell and the federal government includes an overhead component to cover the university's indirect costs." (3h)
> **Cornell University**

Overhead is assigned to each ad contract at the rate of 90 percent of partner direct professional labor plus 120 percent of artistic staff direct professional labor. During May, Publicidades Paulista completed an advertising project for ice cream company Sorvete Atlântico. The contract required \$1,800 in direct material, \$1,200 of partner direct professional labor, and \$2,000 of artistic staff direct professional labor. The total cost of the contract is computed as follows:

Contract MJH0207: Advertising Program for Sorvete Atlântico

Direct material	\$1,800
Direct professional labor (partner)	1,200
Direct professional labor (artistic staff)	2,000
Applied overhead:	
Partner support (\$1,200 × 90%)	1,080
Artistic staff support (\$2,000 × 120%)	2,400
Total cost	\$8,480

The total contract cost of \$8,480 includes actual direct material and direct professional labor costs, and applied overhead based on the predetermined overhead rates for partner support costs and artistic staff support costs. The contract cost can be used by the firm in controlling costs, for planning cash flows and operations, and as one informational input in its contract-pricing decisions. In addition to the contract cost, the firm also should consider the demand for its advertising services and the prices charged by its competitors.

The discussion above provides only a brief overview of cost-accumulation procedures in service industry and nonprofit organizations. The main point is that job-order costing systems are used in a wide variety of organizations, and these systems provide important information to managers for planning, decision making, and control.

Changing Technology in Manufacturing Operations

The technology of manufacturing is changing rapidly. These technological changes often affect the managerial accounting procedures used to collect data and transmit information to the intended users. Three such technological changes are electronic data interchange (or EDI), Extensible Markup Language (or XML), and the use of bar codes.

EDI and XML

Electronic data interchange (or *EDI*) is the direct exchange of data between organizations via a computer-to-computer interface. EDI is used to transmit such documents as purchase orders, shipping notices, receiving notices, invoices, and a host of other production-related data. This eliminates the need for paperwork, speeding up the flow of information and substantially reducing errors. EDI is now in widespread use. For example, Walmart places most of its merchandise orders to its suppliers using this information technology.

A recently developed alternative to EDI is *Extensible Markup Language* (or *XML*), which is Web-based and less expensive to implement than EDI. Its purpose is to allow users to share structured data (e.g., product order lists or price data) via the Internet. XML allows its users to define "tags," which the computer then interprets as a particular type of information. For example, a tag might indicate a product's in-stock date or price. See www.XML.com for a primer on this rapidly growing Web-based data-sharing tool.

Use of Bar Codes

> "Each production job, from beginning to end, can take several weeks. Bar code technology is used extensively. The container that carries the work in process is bar-coded, and we use that to track each job." (3i)
>
> **Micrus**
> (joint venture of IBM and Cirrus Logic)

We all have seen bar codes used to record inventory and sales information in retail stores. This efficient means of recording data also is becoming widely used in recording important events in manufacturing processes. Production employees can record the time they begin working on a particular job order by scanning the bar code on their employee ID badge and a bar code assigned to the production job order. When raw materials arrive at the production facility, their bar code is scanned and the event is recorded. Inventory records are updated automatically. Raw materials and partially completed components are assigned bar codes, and their movement throughout the production process is efficiently recorded. For example, raw materials may be requisitioned by a production employee simply by scanning the bar code assigned to the needed raw materials. When the materials are sent from the warehouse to the requisitioning production department, the bar code is scanned again. Inventory records are updated instantly. Bar codes represent one more instance where technology is changing both the production environment and the procedures used in accounting for production operations.

Management
Accounting
Practice

Walmart,
GlaxoSmithKline, and
Adani Grain
Logistics

RADIO FREQUENCY IDENTIFICATION SYSTEMS (RFID)

Bar codes are in some places being replaced by radio frequency identification systems (RFID). Unlike bar codes, which can be read by a scanner only when visible, the RFID system allows the information to be read from longer distances and without visibility. For example, a raw-material shipment that embeds the RFID system could be identified while still unpacked or in a delivery truck. Among the benefits attributed to RFID systems are reduced labor costs, fewer supply delays, and a reduction of waste in the supply chain. Major retailers such as Walmart "have mandated that their suppliers comply with their RFID guidelines." GlaxoSmithKline is putting RFID tags on bottles of some of its medications.[4] And "Adani Grain Logistics, which operates several grain storage facilities in India, has implemented an automated, RFID-based system for receiving, testing and tracking food grain harvested in the states of Haryana and Punjab."[5]

[4]C.T. Stambaugh and F.W. Carpenter, "RFID: Wireless Innovations in Inventory Monitoring and Accounting," *Strategic Finance,* December 2009, pp. 35–40; and Ariel Markelevich and Ronald Bell, "RFID: The Changes It Will Bring," *Strategic Finance* 88, no. 2 (August 2006), pp. 46–49.

[5]Mary Catherine O'Connor, "RFID Facilitates Grain Storage in India," *RFID Journal* (April 19, 2010).

Focus on Ethics

DID BOEING EXPLOIT ACCOUNTING RULES TO CONCEAL COST OVERRUNS AND PRODUCTION SNAFUS?

Aircraft manufacturers use job-order costing to determine the cost of an airplane. As this chapter discusses, supply chain management and production controls are also important tools used by manufacturers to manage production costs. As *BusinessWeek* reports, however, things don't always go according to plan.

For three years, Boeing's top management had been seeking a merger with McDonnell-Douglas Corporation, whose board of directors was reluctant to approve the deal. Finally, the deal went through, and the world's largest aerospace company was born—"the first manufacturer ever with the ability to build everything that flies, from helicopters and fighter jets to space stations."

Unfortunately, "a disaster was quietly unfolding Inside Boeing's sprawling factories—one that would ultimately wind up costing billions of dollars, cause several executives to lose their jobs, and lead to claims of accounting fraud. Facing an unprecedented surge in orders because of a booming economy, workers were toiling around the clock, pushing the assembly line to the breaking point. At the same time, the company was struggling to overhaul outdated production methods. These pressures were building up to what was, in essence, a manufacturing nervous breakdown. In the weeks after the merger announcement, parts shortages and overtime approached all-time highs. As costs went through the roof, the profitability of airliners such as the 777 swooned. A special team formed to study the crisis issued a report with a blunt conclusion: 'Our production system is broken.'"

Had investors "understood the scope of the problems, the stock would probably have tumbled and the McDonnell deal—a stock swap that hinged on Boeing's ability to maintain a lofty share price—would have been jeopardized."

In May of 2002, *BusinessWeek* reported the results of its three-month investigation, which "reconstructed this hidden chapter in the company's history—and analyzed its current implications." The *BusinessWeek* article alleges that "new details supplied by several inside witnesses indicate that Boeing did more than simply fail to tell investors about its production disaster. It also engaged in a wide variety of aggressive accounting techniques that papered over the mess. Critics say the company should have taken charges for the assembly-line disaster in the first half of 1997, even if it meant jeopardizing the McDonnell merger. They also claim that Boeing took advantage of the unusual flexibility provided by *program accounting*—a system that allows the huge upfront expense of building a plane to be spread out over several years—to cover up cost overruns and to book savings from efficiency initiatives that never panned out. 'Boeing managed its earnings to the point where it got caught,' says Debra A. Smith, a partner at Constraints Management, a Seattle-area manufacturing consultancy, and a former senior auditor at Deloitte & Touche who worked on the company's account during the early 1980s. 'Boeing basically decided in the short run that [managing earnings] was a lesser evil than losing the merger,' adds Smith. At a time when investors are asking themselves how far Corporate America can be trusted, the Boeing saga provides rich new evidence that companies have much greater leeway to manipulate their numbers than most people suspect."[6]

Boeing allegedly used a system they called *program accounting* to spread their huge cost overruns across several years, thereby propping up earnings and the company's share price. After the merger with McDonnell-Douglas, however, the truth came out in the form of much lower earnings.

What is your view of how Boeing handled its cost overruns, its production problems, and the merger with McDonnell-Douglas? Did the company's top executives act ethically? How about their accountants?

[6]Stanley Holmes and Mike France, "Boeing's Secret: Did the Aircraft Giant Exploit Accounting Rules to Conceal a Huge Factory Snafu?" *BusinessWeek,* May 20, 2002, pp. 110–120. Also see Andy Pasztor and Anne Soueo, "Boeing Could Pay Large Penalty to Settle Probes, Avoid Prosecution," *The Wall Street Journal,* September 17, 2005, pp. A1, A8. For recent information on Boeing, see P. Sanders and A. Keeton, "Boeing Reports Signs of Recovery as It Shakes off a Troubling Year," *The Wall Street Journal,* January 28, 2010, p. B1.

Chapter Summary

LO1 Discuss the role of product and service costing in manufacturing and nonmanufacturing firms. Product costing is the process of accumulating the costs of a production process and assigning them to the firm's products. Product costs are needed for three major purposes: (1) to value inventory and cost of goods sold in financial accounting; (2) to provide managerial accounting information to managers for planning, cost control, and decision making; and (3) to provide cost data to various organizations outside the firm.

LO2 Diagram and explain the flow of costs through the manufacturing accounts used in product costing. The costs of direct material, direct labor, and manufacturing overhead are first entered into the Work-in-Process Inventory account. When goods are completed, the accumulated manufacturing costs are transferred from Work-in-Process Inventory to Finished-Goods Inventory. Finally, these product costs are transferred from Finished-Goods Inventory to Cost of Goods Sold when sales occur.

LO3 Distinguish between job-order costing and process costing. Job-order costing is used by firms that engage in either job-shop or batch-production operations. Such firms produce relatively small numbers of dissimilar products. Process costing is used by companies that produce relatively large numbers of nearly identical products.

LO4 Compute a predetermined overhead rate and explain its use in job-order costing for job-shop and batch-production environments. Overhead is applied to production jobs using a predetermined overhead rate, which is based on estimates of manufacturing overhead (in the numerator) and the level of some cost driver or activity base (in the denominator).

LO5 Prepare journal entries to record the costs of direct material, direct labor, and manufacturing overhead in a job-order costing system. Journal entries, as illustrated in the chapter, are used to track the flow of manufacturing costs through the various accounts, such as Raw-Material Inventory, Work-in-Process Inventory, Finished-Goods Inventory, and Cost of Goods Sold.

LO6 Prepare a schedule of cost of goods manufactured, a schedule of cost of goods sold, and an income statement for a manufacturer. These accounting schedules, which are illustrated in the chapter, provide information to management about the costs incurred in a production operation.

LO7 Describe the two-stage allocation process used to assign manufacturing overhead costs to production jobs. In stage one, cost distribution and service-department cost allocation are used to assign all manufacturing overhead costs to production departments. In stage two, cost application is used to assign overhead costs from production departments to production jobs using a predetermined overhead rate.

LO8 Describe the process of project costing used in service industry firms and nonprofit organizations. Job-order costing methods are used in a variety of service industry firms and nonprofit organizations. Accumulating costs of projects, contracts, cases, programs, or missions provides important information to managers in such organizations as hospitals, law firms, and government agencies.

Review Problem on Job-Order Costing

Piedmont Paint Company uses a job-order costing system, and the company had two jobs in process at the beginning of the current year. Job JY65 currently has a cost of $134,400 assigned to it, and job DC66 currently has a cost of $85,600 assigned to it. The following additional information is available.

- The company applies manufacturing overhead on the basis of machine hours. Budgeted overhead and machine activity (based on practical capacity) for the year were $1,344,000 and 16,000 hours, respectively.
- The company worked on four jobs during the first quarter. Direct materials used, direct labor incurred, and machine hours consumed were as follows:

Job No.	Direct Material	Direct Labor	Machine Hours
JY65	$33,600	$ 56,000	1,200
DC66	—	35,200	700
SG78	70,400	104,000	2,000
RG82	24,000	14,080	500

- Manufacturing overhead during the first quarter included charges for depreciation ($54,400), indirect labor ($96,000), indirect materials used ($8,000), and other factory costs ($223,200).
- Piedmont Paint Company completed job JY65 and job DC66. Job DC66 was sold on account, producing a profit of $55,520 for the firm.

Required:

1. Determine Piedmont Paint Company's predetermined overhead application rate.

2. Prepare journal entries as of March 31 to record the following. (*Note:* Use summary entries where appropriate by combining individual job data.)

   a. The issuance of direct material to production and the direct labor incurred.

   b. The manufacturing overhead incurred during the quarter.

   c. The application of manufacturing overhead to production.

   d. The completion of jobs JY65 and DC66.

   e. The sale of job DC66.

3. Determine the cost of the jobs still in production as of March 31.

4. Did the finished-goods inventory increase or decrease during the first quarter? By how much?

5. Was manufacturing overhead under- or overapplied for the first quarter of the year? By how much?

Solution to Review Problem

1. Predetermined overhead rate = budjeted overhead ÷ budgeted machine hours
   = $1,344,000 ÷ 16,000 = $84 per machine hour

2. *(a)* Work-in-Process Inventory 128,000*
   Raw-Material Inventory 128,000

   Work-in-Process Inventory .... 209,280†
   Wages Payable 209,280

   *$33,600 + $70,400 + $24,000 = $128,000

   †$56,000 + $35,200 + $104,000 + $14,080 = $209,280

   (b) Manufacturing Overhead... 381,600
   Accumulated Depreciation... 54,400
   Wages Payable 96,000
   Manufacturing Supplies Inventory.................................... 8,000
   Miscellaneous Accounts.. 223,200

   (c) Work-in-Process Inventory 369,600*
   Manufacturing Overhead.. 369,600

   *(1,200 + 700 + 2,000 + 500) × $84 = $369,600

   (d) Finished-Goods Inventory... 504,400*
   Work-in-Process Inventory 504,400

   *Job JY65: $134,400 + $33,600 + $56,000 + (1,200 × $84) = $324,800

   Job DC66: $85,600 + $35,200 + (700 × $84) = $179,600

   $504,400 = $324,800 + $179,600

   (e) Accounts Receivable... 235,120*
   Sales Revenue... 235,120

   *$179,600 + $55,520 = $235,120

   Cost of Goods Sold... 179,600
   Finished-Goods Inventory... 179,600

3. Job SG78 and RG82 are in production as of March 31:
   Job SG78: $70,400 + $104,000 + (2,000 × $84)........................ $342,400
   Job RG82: $24,000 + $14,080 + (500 × $84)............................ 80,080
   Total... $422,480

4. Finished-goods inventory increased by $324,800 ($504,400 − $179,600).

5. The company's actual overhead amounted to $381,600, whereas applied overhead totaled $369,600. Thus, overhead was underapplied by $12,000.

Key Terms

For each term's definition refer to the indicated page, or turn to the glossary at the end of the text.

activity base, 123

actual costing, 136

actual manufacturing overhead, 130

applied manufacturing overhead, 129

bill of materials, 122

cost distribution (sometimes called cost allocation), 138

cost of goods manufactured, 133

cycle time, 137

departmental overhead centers, 138

departmental overhead rate, 138

job-cost record, 120

job-order costing, 119

material requisition form, 121

normal costing, 134

overapplied overhead, 131

overhead application (or absorption), 123

plantwide overhead rate, 138

predetermined overhead rate, 124

process-costing system, 120

product-costing system, 116

proration, 132

schedule of cost of goods manufactured, 133

schedule of cost of goods sold, 133

service department cost allocation, 138

service departments, 138

source document, 122

supply chain, 122

throughput time, 137

time record, 123

two-stage cost allocation, 138

underapplied overhead, 131

volume-based cost driver, 123

Review Questions

3–1. List and explain four purposes of product costing.

3–2. Explain the difference between job-order and process costing.

3–3. How is the concept of product costing applied in service industry firms?

3–4. What are the purposes of the following documents: (*a*) material requisition form, (*b*) labor time record, and (*c*) job-cost record.

3–5. Why is manufacturing overhead applied to products when product costs are used in making pricing decisions?

3–6. Explain the benefits of using a predetermined overhead rate instead of an actual overhead rate.

3–7. Describe one advantage and one disadvantage of prorating overapplied or underapplied overhead.

3–8. Describe an important cost-benefit issue involving accuracy versus timeliness in accounting for overhead.

3–9. Explain the difference between actual and normal costing.

3–10. When a single, volume-based cost driver (or activity base) is used to apply manufacturing overhead, what is the managerial accountant's primary objective in selecting the cost driver?

3–11. Describe some costs and benefits of using multiple overhead rates instead of a plantwide overhead rate.

3–12. Describe the process of two-stage cost allocation in the development of departmental overhead rates.

3–13. Define each of the following terms, and explain the relationship among them: (*a*) overhead cost distribution, (*b*) service department cost allocation, and (*c*) overhead application.

3–14. Describe how job-order costing concepts are used in professional service firms, such as law practices and consulting firms.

3–15. What is meant by the term *cost driver?* What is a *volume-based cost driver?*

3–16. Describe the flow of costs through a product-costing system. What special accounts are involved, and how are they used?

3–17. Give an example of how a hospital, such as the Ahmedabad Civil Hospital, might use job-order costing concepts.

3–18. Why are some manufacturing firms switching from direct-labor hours to machine hours or throughput time as the basis for overhead application?

3–19. What is the cause of overapplied or underapplied overhead?

3–20. Briefly describe two ways of closing out overapplied or underapplied overhead at the end of an accounting period.

3–21. Describe how a large retailer such as Walmart could use EDI.

3–22. Explain how a Sony engineer might use bar code technology to record the time she spends on various activities.

Exercises

All applicable Exercises are available with McGraw-Hill's *Connect Accounting*™.

■ **Exercise 3–23**
Job-Order versus Process
Costing
(LO 1, 3)

For each of the following companies, indicate whether job-order or process costing is more appropriate.

1. Manufacturer of swimming pool chemicals.

2. Manufacturer of custom hot tubs and spas.

3. Architectural firm.

4. Manufacturer of ceramic tile.

5. Producer of yogurt.
6. Manufacturer of custom tool sheds.
7. Manufacturer of papers clips.
8. Engineering consulting firm.
9. Manufacturer of balloons.
10. Manufacturer of custom emergency rescue vehicles.

Exercise 3–24
Fixed and Variable Costs; Overhead Rate; Agribusiness
(LO 1, 4)

The controller for Tender Bird Poultry, Inc. estimates that the company's fixed overhead is $100,000 per year. She also has determined that the variable overhead is approximately $.10 per chicken raised and sold. Since the firm has a single product, overhead is applied on the basis of output units, chickens raised and sold.

Required:

1. Calculate the predetermined overhead rate under each of the following output predictions: 200,000 chickens, 300,000 chickens, and 400,000 chickens.
2. Does the predetermined overhead rate change in proportion to the change in predicted production? Why?

Exercise 3–25
Basic Journal Entries in Job-Order Costing
(LO 5)

Queensland Educational Products started and finished job number B67 during June. The job required $4,600 of direct material and 40 hours of direct labor at $18 per hour. The predetermined overhead rate is $4.50 per direct-labor hour.

Required: Prepare journal entries to record the incurrence of production costs and the completion of job number B67.

Exercise 3–26
Job-Order Costing; Feature Film Production; Use of Internet
(LO 1, 3)

Visit the Web site of a film producer, such as Disney, MGM, or Warner Brothers.

Walt Disney Studios	www.disney.com
MGM	www.mgm.com
Warner Brothers	www.warnerbros.com

Required: Read about one of the company's recent (or upcoming) film releases. Then discuss why or why not job-order costing would be an appropriate costing method for feature film production. Would your answer be any different depending on the type of film being produced (e.g., animation in a studio versus filming on location in Timbuktu)?

Exercise 3–27
Job-Order Costing Basics
(LO 2, 4, 5, 6)

Bodin Company manufactures finger splints for kids who get tendonitis from playing video games. The firm had the following inventories at the beginning and end of the month of January.

	January 1	January 31
Finished goods	$125,000	$117,000
Work in process	235,000	251,000
Raw material	134,000	124,000

The following additional data pertain to January operations.

Raw material purchased	$191,000
Direct labor	300,000
Actual manufacturing overhead	175,000
Actual selling and administrative expenses	115,000

The company applies manufacturing overhead at the rate of 60 percent of direct-labor cost. Any over-applied or underapplied manufacturing overhead is accumulated until the end of the year.

Required: Compute the following amounts.

1. The company's prime cost for January.
2. The total manufacturing cost for January.

3. The cost of goods manufactured for January.

4. The cost of goods sold for January.

5. The balance in the Manufacturing Overhead account on January 31. Debit or credit?

(CMA, adapted)

■ **Exercise 3–28**
Cost Relationships;Normal
Costing System
(LO 2, 4, 6)

McAllister, Inc. employs a normal costing system. The following information pertains to the year just ended.

- Total manufacturing costs were $2,500,000.
- Cost of goods manufactured was $2,425,000.
- Applied manufacturing overhead was 30 percent of total manufacturing costs.
- Manufacturing overhead was applied to production at a rate of 80 percent of direct-labor cost.
- Work-in-process inventory on January 1 was 75 percent of work-in-process inventory on December 31.

Required:

1. Compute the total direct-labor cost for the year.

2. Calculate the total cost of direct material used during the year.

3. Compute the value of the company's work-in-process inventory on December 31.

(CMA, adapted)

■ **Exercise 3–29**
Job-Cost Record
(LO 2, 3, 4)

Schwarzwald Toy Company incurred the following costs in April to produce job number TB78, which consisted of 1,000 stuffed bears that can walk, talk, and play cards.

Direct Material:

4/1/x0 Requisition number 101: 40 square meters of fabric at $8 per square meter

4/5/x0 Requisition number 108: 12.5 cubic meters of stuffing at $12 per cubic meter

Direct Labor:

From employee time cards for 4/1/x0 through 4/8/x0: 500 hours at $15 per hour

Manufacturing Overhead:

Applied on the basis of direct-labor hours at $2.00 per hour.

On April 30, 700 of the bears were shipped to a local toy store.

Required: Prepare a job-cost record using the information given above. (Use Exhibit 3–3 as a guide.)

■ **Exercise 3–30**
Schedule of Cost of Goods
Manufactured
(LO 2, 4, 6)

Crunchem Cereal Company incurred the following actual costs during 20x1.

Direct material used	$275,000
Direct labor	120,000
Manufacturing overhead	252,000

The firm's predetermined overhead rate is 210 percent of direct-labor cost. The January 1 inventory balances were as follows:

Raw material	$30,000
Work in process	39,000
Finished goods	42,000

Each of these inventory balances was 10 percent higher at the end of the year.

Required:

1. Prepare a schedule of cost of goods manufactured for 20x1.

2. What was the cost of goods sold for the year?

3. *Build a spreadsheet:* Construct an Excel spreadsheet to solve all of the preceding requirements. Show how the solution will change if the following data change: direct material used amounted to $281,000 and raw-material inventory on December 31 was $28,000.

Reimel Furniture Company, Inc. incurred the following costs during 20x2.

■ **Exercise 3–31**
Manufacturing Cost Flows
(LO 2, 5, 6)

Direct material used	$174,000
Direct labor	324,000
Manufacturing overhead applied	180,000

During 20x2, products costing $120,000 were finished, and products costing $132,000 were sold on account for $195,000. There were no purchases of raw material during the year. The beginning balances in the firm's inventory accounts are as follows:

Raw material	$227,000
Work in process	18,000
Finished goods	30,000

Required:

1. Prepare T-accounts to show the flow of costs through the company's manufacturing accounts during 20x2.
2. Prepare a partial balance sheet and a partial income statement to reflect the information given above. (*Hint:* See Exhibit 3–2.)

Selected data concerning the past year's operations of the Ozarks Manufacturing Company are as follows:

■ **Exercise 3–32**
Basic Manufacturing Cost
Flows
(LO 2, 6)

	Inventories	
	Beginning	**Ending**
Raw material	$71,000	$ 81,000
Work in process	80,000	30,000
Finished goods	90,000	110,000

Other data:	
Direct material used	$326,000
Total manufacturing costs charged to production during the year (includes direct material, direct labor, and manufacturing overhead applied at a rate of 60% of direct-labor cost)	686,000
Cost of goods available for sale	826,000
Selling and administrative expenses	31,500

Required:

1. What was the cost of raw materials purchased during the year?
2. What was the direct-labor cost charged to production during the year?
3. What was the cost of goods manufactured during the year?
4. What was the cost of goods sold during the year?

(CMA, adapted)

Kansai Confectionary incurred $173,000 of manufacturing overhead costs during the year just ended. However, only $141,000 of overhead was applied to production. At the conclusion of the year, the following amounts of the year's applied overhead remained in the various manufacturing accounts.

■ **Exercise 3–33**
Proration of Underapplied
Overhead
(LO 5)

	Applied Overhead Remaining in Account on December 31
Work-in-Process Inventory	$35,250
Finished-Goods Inventory	49,350
Cost of Goods Sold	56,400

Required: Prepare a journal entry to close out the balance in the Manufacturing Overhead account and prorate the balance to the three manufacturing accounts.

■ **Exercise 3–34**
Overapplied or Underapplied
Overhead
(LO 4, 5)

The following information pertains to Trenton Glass Works for the year just ended.

Budgeted direct-labor cost:	75,000 hours (practical capacity) at $16 per hour
Actual direct-labor cost:	80,000 hours at $17.50 per hour
Budgeted manufacturing overhead:	$997,500
Actual selling and administrative expenses:	435,000

Actual manufacturing overhead:

Depreciation	$231,000
Property taxes	21,000
Indirect labor	82,000
Supervisory salaries	200,000
Utilities	59,000
Insurance	30,000
Rental of space	300,000
Indirect material (see data below)	79,000

Indirect material:

Beginning inventory, January 1	48,000
Purchases during the year	94,000
Ending inventory, December 31	63,000

Required:

1. Compute the firm's predetermined overhead rate, which is based on direct-labor hours.
2. Calculate the overapplied or underapplied overhead for the year.
3. Prepare a journal entry to close out the Manufacturing Overhead account into Cost of Goods Sold.
4. *Build a spreadsheet:* Construct an Excel spreadsheet to solve requirements (1) and (2) above. Show how the solution will change if the following data change: budgeted manufacturing overhead was $990,000, property taxes were $25,000, and purchases of indirect material amounted to $97,000.

■ **Exercise 3–35**
Predetermined Overhead
Rate; Various Cost Drivers
(LO 4)

The following data pertain to the Oneida Restaurant Supply Company for the year just ended.

Budgeted sales revenue	$205,000
Actual manufacturing overhead	340,000
Budgeted machine hours (based on practical capacity)	10,000
Budgeted direct-labor hours (based on practical capacity)	20,000
Budgeted direct-labor rate	$ 14
Budgeted manufacturing overhead	$378,000
Actual machine hours	11,000
Actual direct-labor hours	18,000
Actual direct-labor rate	$ 15

Required:

1. Compute the firm's predetermined overhead rate for the year using each of the following common cost drivers: (*a*) machine hours, (*b*) direct-labor hours, and (*c*) direct-labor dollars.
2. Calculate the overapplied or underapplied overhead for the year using each of the cost drivers listed above.

■ **Exercise 3–36**
Actual versus Normal Costing
(LO 4, 5)

Refer to the data for the preceding exercise for Oneida Restaurant Supply Company. Prepare a journal entry to add to work-in-process inventory the total manufacturing overhead cost for the year, assuming:

1. The firm uses actual costing.
2. The firm uses normal costing, with a predetermined overhead rate based on machine hours.

Design Arts Associates is an interior decorating firm in Berlin. The following costs were incurred in the firm's contract to redecorate the mayor's offices.

Direct material used	3,500 euros
Direct professional labor	6,000 euros

The firm's budget for the year included the following estimates:

Budgeted overhead	400,000 euros
Budgeted direct professional labor	250,000 euros

Overhead is applied to contracts using a predetermined overhead rate calculated annually. The rate is based on direct professional labor cost.

Required: Calculate the total cost of the firm's contract to redecorate the mayor's offices. (Remember to express your answer in terms of euros.)

Exercise 3–37
Project Costing; Interior Decorating
(LO 1, 8)

Suppose you are the controller for a company that produces handmade glassware.

1. Choose a volume-based cost driver upon which to base the application of overhead. Write a memo to the company president explaining your choice.
2. Now you have changed jobs. You are the controller of a microchip manufacturer that uses a highly automated production process. Repeat the same requirements stated above.

Exercise 3–38
Choice of a Cost Driver for Overhead Application
(LO 1, 4)

Kolkata Leather Manufacturing has three departments. The Assembly Department manufactures various leather products, such as belts, purses, and saddlebags, using an automated production process. The Saddle Department produces handmade saddles and uses very little machinery. The Tanning Department produces leather. The tanning process requires little in the way of labor or machinery, but it does require space and process time. Due to the different production processes in the three departments, the company uses three different cost drivers for the application of manufacturing overhead. The cost drivers and overhead rates are as follows:

Exercise 3–39
Cost Drivers; Different Production Methods
(LO 4, 5)

	Cost Driver	Predetermined Overhead Rate
Tanning Department	Square meters of leather	$30 per square meter
Assembly Department	Machine time	$9 per machine hour
Saddle Department	Direct-labor time	$4 per direct-labor hour

The company's deluxe saddle and accessory set consists of a handmade saddle, two saddlebags, a belt, and a vest, all coordinated to match. The entire set uses 10 square meters of leather from the Tanning Department, 2 machine hours in the Assembly Department, and 30 direct-labor hours in the Saddle Department.

Required: Job number DS-20 consisted of 20 deluxe saddle and accessory sets. Prepare journal entries to record applied manufacturing overhead in the Work-in-Process Inventory account for each department.

Refer to Exhibit 3–12, which portrays the three types of allocation procedures used in two-stage allocation. Give an example of each of these allocation procedures in a hospital setting. The ultimate cost object is a patient-day of hospital care. This is one day of care for one patient. (*Hint:* First think about the various departments in a hospital. Which departments deal directly with patients; which ones are service departments and do not deal directly with patients? What kinds of costs does a hospital incur that should be distributed among all of the hospital's departments? Correct hospital terminology is not important here. Focus on the *concepts* of cost allocation portrayed in Exhibit 3–12.)

Exercise 3–40
Two-Stage Allocation
(LO 1, 7)

Refer to the illustration of overhead application in the Publicidades Paulista on pp. 140–141. Suppose the firm used a single cost driver, total staff compensation, to apply overhead costs to each ad contract.

Exercise 3–41
Overhead Application in a Service Industry Firm
(LO 8)

Required:

1. Compute the total budgeted staff compensation: both partner and artistic staff compensation.

2. Compute Publicidades Paulista's overhead rate on the basis of this single cost driver.

3. Recalculate the applied overhead for the Sorvete Atlântico ice cream company contract.

4. Compare the applied overhead using the single cost driver with the applied overhead computed using the two cost drivers used in the text illustration.

Problems

All applicable Problems are available with McGraw-Hill's *Connect Accounting™*.

■ **Problem 3–42**
Schedule of Cost of Goods
Manufactured and Sold;
Income Statement
(LO 6)

1. Total manufacturing costs: $175,100
3. Net income: $7,100

The following data refer to Twisto Pretzel Company for the year 20x1.

Work-in-process inventory, 12/31/x0	$ 8,100
Selling and administrative salaries	13,800
Insurance on factory and equipment	3,600
Work-in-process inventory, 12/31/x1	8,300
Finished-goods inventory, 12/31/x0	14,000
Cash balance, 12/31/x1	6,000
Indirect material used	4,900
Depreciation on factory equipment	2,100
Raw-material inventory, 12/31/x0	10,100
Property taxes on factory	2,400
Finished-goods inventory, 12/31/x1	15,400
Purchases of raw material in 20x1	39,000
Utilities for factory	6,000
Utilities for sales and administrative offices	2,500
Other selling and administrative expenses	4,000
Indirect-labor cost incurred	29,000
Depreciation on factory building	3,800
Depreciation on cars used by sales personnel	1,200
Direct-labor cost incurred	79,000
Raw-material inventory, 12/31/x1	11,000
Accounts receivable, 12/31/x1	4,100
Rental for warehouse space to store raw material	3,100
Rental of space for company president's office	1,700
Applied manufacturing overhead	58,000
Sales revenue	205,800
Income tax expense	5,100

Required:

1. Prepare Twisto Pretzel Company's schedule of cost of goods manufactured for 20x1.

2. Prepare the company's schedule of cost of goods sold for 20x1. The company closes overapplied or underapplied overhead into Cost of Goods Sold.

3. Prepare the company's income statement for 20x1.

■ **Problem 3–43**
Basic Job-Order Costing;
Journal Entries
(LO 4, 5)

1. Predetermined overhead rate: $12.50 per hour

Zurich Clock Works manufactures fine, handcrafted clocks. The firm uses a job-order costing system, and manufacturing overhead is applied on the basis of direct-labor hours. Estimated manufacturing overhead for the year is $250,000. The firm employs 10 master clockmakers, who constitute the direct-labor force. Each of these employees is expected to work 2,000 hours during the year, which represents each employee's practical capacity. The following events occurred during October.

a. The firm purchased six cubic meters of mahogany veneer at $6,000 per cubic meter.

b. Twenty brass counterweights were requisitioned for production. Each weight cost $23.

c. Twenty liters of glue were requisitioned for production. The glue cost $5 per liter. Glue is treated as an indirect material.

d. Depreciation on the clockworks building for October was $8,000.

e. A $400 utility bill was paid in cash.

f. Time cards showed the following usage of labor:

   Job number G60: 12 grandfather's clocks, 1,000 hours of direct labor

   Job number C81: 20 cuckoo clocks, 700 hours of direct labor

   The master clockmakers (direct-labor personnel) earn $20 per hour.

g. The October property tax bill for $910 was received but has not yet been paid in cash.

h. The firm employs laborers who perform various tasks such as material handling and shop cleanup. Their wages for October amounted to $2,500.

i. Job number G60, which was started in July, was finished in October. The total cost of the job was $14,400.

j. Nine of the grandfather's clocks from job number G60 were sold in October for $1,500 each.

Required:

1. Calculate the firm's predetermined overhead rate for the year.

2. Prepare journal entries to record the events described above.

Perfecto Pizza Company produces microwavable pizzas. The following accounts appeared in Perfecto's ledger as of December 31.

■ **Problem 3–44**
Manufacturing Cost Flows;
Analysis of T-Accounts
(LO 2, 5)

Raw-Materials Inventory		
Bal. 1/1	21,000	
	?	?
Bal. 12/31	36,000	

Accounts Payable		
		2,500 Bal. 1/1
136,500		?
1,000		Bal. 12/31

Work-in-Process Inventory		
Bal. 1/1	17,000	
Direct material	?	?
Direct labor	?	
Manufacturing overhead	?	
Bal. 12/31	19,000	

Finished-Goods Inventory		
Bal. 1/1	12,000	
	?	?
Bal. 12/31	20,000	

Manufacturing Overhead		
?		?

Cost of Goods Sold		
710,000		

Wages Payable		
2,000		Bal. 1/1
147,000		?
5,000		Bal. 12/31

Sales Revenue		
		?

Accounts Receivable		
Bal. 1/1	11,000	
	?	806,000
Bal. 12/31	15,000	

Additional information:

a. Accounts payable is used only for direct-material purchases.

b. Underapplied overhead of $2,500 for the year has not yet been closed into cost of goods sold.

Required: Complete the T-accounts by computing the amounts indicated by a question mark.

■ **Problem 3–45**
Job-Order Costing; Journal
Entries
(LO 2, 4, 5)

4. Finished-goods inventory
increased by $204,200

Stellar Sound, Inc. which uses a job-order costing system, had two jobs in process at the start of 20x1: job no. 64 ($84,000) and job no. 65 ($53,500). The following information is available:

a.   The company applies manufacturing overhead on the basis of machine hours (based on practical capacity). Budgeted overhead and machine activity for the year were anticipated to be $856,000, and 16,000 hours, respectively.

b.   The company worked on four jobs during the first quarter. Direct materials used, direct labor incurred, and machine hours consumed were as follows:

Job No.	Direct Material	Direct Labor	Machine Hours
64	$21,000	$35,000	1,200
65	—	22,000	700
66	44,000	65,000	2,000
67	15,000	8,800	500

c.   Manufacturing overhead during the first quarter included charges for depreciation ($34,000), indirect labor ($60,000), indirect materials used ($5,000), and other factory costs ($139,500).

d.   Stellar Sound completed job no. 64 and job no. 65. Job no. 65 was sold on account, producing a profit of $34,700 for the firm.

Required:

1.   Determine the company's predetermined overhead application rate.

2.   Prepare journal entries as of March 31 to record the following. (*Note:* Use summary entries where appropriate by combining individual job data.)

   a.   The issuance of direct material to production and the direct labor incurred.

   b.   The manufacturing overhead incurred during the quarter.

   c.   The application of manufacturing overhead to production.

   d.   The completion of jobs no. 64 and no. 65.

   e.   The sale of job no. 65.

3.   Determine the cost of the jobs still in production as of March 31.

4.   Did the finished-goods inventory increase or decrease during the first quarter? By how much?

5.   Was manufacturing overhead under- or overapplied for the first quarter of the year? By how much?

■ **Problem 3–46**
Job-Order Costing; Focus on
Manufacturing Overhead
(LO 2, 4, 5)

1. Predetermined overhead
rate: 130% of direct labor
cost
6. Cost of goods sold:
$15,309,300

Finlon Upholstery, Inc. uses a job-order costing system to accumulate manufacturing costs. The company's work-in-process on December 31, 20x1, consisted of one job (no. 2077), which was carried on the year-end balance sheet at $156,800. There was no finished-goods inventory on this date.

Finlon applies manufacturing overhead to production on the basis of direct-labor cost. (The budgeted direct-labor cost is the company's practical capacity, in terms of direct-labor hours, multiplied by the budgeted direct-labor rate.) Budgeted totals for 20x2 for direct labor and manufacturing overhead are $4,200,000 and $5,460,000, respectively. Actual results for the year follow.

Direct material used	$ 5,600,000
Direct labor	4,350,000
Indirect material used	65,000
Indirect labor	2,860,000
Factory depreciation	1,740,000
Factory insurance	59,000
Factory utilities	830,000
Selling and administrative expenses	2,160,000
Total	$17,664,000

Job no. 2077 was completed in January 20x2; there was no work in process at year-end. All jobs produced during 20x2 were sold with the exception of job no. 2143, which contained direct-material costs of $156,000 and direct-labor charges of $85,000. The company charges any under- or overapplied overhead to Cost of Goods Sold.

Required:

1. Determine the company's predetermined overhead application rate.

2. Determine the additions to the Work-in-Process Inventory account for direct material used, direct labor, and manufacturing overhead.

3. Compute the amount that the company would disclose as finished-goods inventory on the December 31, 20x2, balance sheet.

4. Prepare the journal entry needed to record the year's completed production.

5. Compute the amount of under- or overapplied overhead at year-end, and prepare the necessary journal entry to record its disposition.

6. Determine the company's 20x2 cost of goods sold.

7. Would it be appropriate to include selling and administrative expenses in either manufacturing overhead or cost of goods sold? Briefly explain.

JLR Enterprises provides consulting services throughout Australia and uses a job-order costing system to accumulate the cost of client projects. Traceable costs are charged directly to individual clients; in contrast, other costs incurred by JLR, but not identifiable with specific clients, are charged to jobs by using a predetermined overhead application rate. Clients are billed for directly chargeable costs, overhead, and a markup.

JLR's director of cost management, Brent Dean, anticipates the following costs for the upcoming year:

■ **Problem 3–47**
Job-Order Costing in a
Consulting Firm
(LO 1, 2, 4, 8)

1. Traceable costs:
$2,900,000

	Cost		Percentage of Cost Directly Traceable to Clients
Professional staff salaries	$3,000,000		80%
Administrative support staff	300,000		60%
Travel	250,000		90%
Photocopying	50,000		90%
Other operating costs	100,000		50%
Total	$3,700,000		

The firm's partners desire to make a $640,000 profit for the firm and plan to add a percentage markup on total cost to achieve that figure.

On March 10, JLR completed work on a project for Martin Manufacturing. The following costs were incurred: professional staff salaries, $41,000; administrative support staff, $2,600; travel, $4,500; photocopying, $500; and other operating costs, $1,400.

Required:

1. Determine JLR's total traceable costs for the upcoming year and the firm's total anticipated overhead.

2. Calculate the predetermined overhead rate. The rate is based on total costs traceable to client jobs.

3. What percentage of cost will JLR add to each job to achieve its profit target?

4. Determine the total cost of the Martin Manufacturing project. How much would Martin be billed for services performed?

5. Notice that only 50 percent of JLR's other operating cost is directly traceable to specific client projects. Cite several costs that would be included in this category and difficult to trace to clients.

6. Notice that 80 percent of the professional staff cost is directly traceable to specific client projects. Cite several reasons that would explain why this figure isn't 100 percent.

■ **Problem 3–48**

Job-Order Costing; Focus on
Overhead and Cost Drivers
(LO 2, 4, 5, 7)

2. Ending work-in-process
inventory cost: $153,530

Garcia, Inc. uses a job-order costing system for its products, which pass from the Machining Department, to the Assembly Department, to finished-goods inventory. The Machining Department is heavily automated; in contrast, the Assembly Department performs a number of manual-assembly activities. The company applies manufacturing overhead using machine hours in the Machining Department and direct-labor cost in the Assembly Department. The following information relates to the year just ended:

	Machining Department	Assembly Department
Budgeted manufacturing overhead	$4,000,000	$3,080,000
Actual manufacturing overhead	4,260,000	3,050,000
Budgeted direct-labor cost (based on practical capacity)	1,500,000	5,600,000
Actual direct-labor cost	1,450,000	5,780,000
Budgeted machine hours (based on practical capacity)	400,000	100,000
Actual machine hours	425,000	110,000

The data that follow pertain to job no. 775, the only job in production at year-end.

	Machining Department	Assembly Department
Direct material	$24,500	$ 6,700
Direct labor	27,900	58,600
Machine hours	360	150

Selling and administrative expense amounted to $2,500,000.

Required:

1. Assuming the use of normal costing, determine the predetermined overhead rates used in the Machining Department and the Assembly Department.

2. Compute the cost of the company's year-end work-in-process inventory.

3. Determine whether overhead was under- or overapplied during the year in the Machining Department.

4. Repeat requirement (3) for the Assembly Department.

5. If the company disposes of under- or overapplied overhead as an adjustment to Cost of Goods Sold, would the company's Cost of Goods Sold account increase or decrease? Explain.

6. How much overhead would have been charged to the company's Work-in-Process account during the year?

7. Comment on the appropriateness of the company's cost drivers (i.e., the use of machine hours in Machining and direct-labor cost in Assembly).

■ **Problem 3–49**

Journal Entries in Job-Order
Costing
(LO 4, 5)

1. Predetermined overhead
rate: $22 per machine hour

MarineCo, Inc. manufactures outboard motors and an assortment of other marine equipment. The company uses a job-order costing system. Normal costing is used, and manufacturing overhead is applied on the basis of machine hours. Estimated manufacturing overhead for the year is $1,610,400, and management estimates the firm's practical capacity at 73,200 machine hours.

Required:

1. Calculate MarineCo's predetermined overhead rate for the year.

2. Prepare journal entries to record the following events, which occurred during April.

   a. The firm purchased marine propellers from Peninsula Marine Corporation for $7,850 on account.

   b. A requisition was filed by the Gauge Department supervisor for 150 kilograms of clear plastic. The material cost $1.20 per kilogram when it was purchased.

   c. The Motor Testing Department supervisor requisitioned 100 meters of electrical wire, which is considered an indirect material. The wire cost $.30 per meter when it was purchased.

   d. An electric utility bill of $800 was paid in cash.

e. Direct-labor costs incurred in April were $75,000.

f. April's insurance cost was $1,800 for insurance on the cars driven by sales personnel. The policy had been prepaid in March.

g. Metal tubing costing $3,000 was purchased on account.

h. A cash payment of $1,700 was made on outstanding accounts payable.

i. Indirect-labor costs of $21,000 were incurred during April.

j. Depreciation on equipment for April amounted to $7,000.

k. Job number G22, consisting of 50 tachometers, was finished during April. The total cost of the job was $1,100.

l. During April, 7,000 machine hours were used.

m. Sales on account for April amounted to $176,000. The cost of goods sold in April was $139,000.

The following data refers to Huron Corporation for the year 20x2.

Sales revenue	$2,105,000
Raw-material inventory, 12/31/x1	89,000
Purchases of raw material in 20x2	731,000
Raw-material inventory, 12/31/x2	59,000
Direct-labor cost incurred	474,000
Selling and administrative expenses	269,000
Indirect labor cost incurred	150,000
Property taxes on factory	90,000
Depreciation on factory building	125,000
Income tax expense	25,000
Indirect material used	45,000
Depreciation on factory equipment	60,000
Insurance on factory and equipment	40,000
Utilities for factory	70,000
Work-in-process inventory, 12/31/x1	-0-
Work-in-process inventory, 12/31/x2	40,000
Finished-goods inventory, 12/31/x1	35,000
Finished-goods inventory, 12/31/x2	40,000
Applied manufacturing overhead	577,500

Problem 3–50
Schedule of Cost of Goods
Manufactured and Sold;
Income Statement
(LO 5, 6)

2. Cost of goods sold
(adjusted for underapplied
overhead): $1,770,000

Required:

1. Prepare Huron's schedule of cost of goods manufactured for 20x2.

2. Prepare the company's schedule of cost of goods sold for 20x2. The company closes overapplied or underapplied overhead into Cost of Goods Sold.

3. Prepare the company's income statement for 20x2.

4. *Build a spreadsheet:* Construct an Excel spreadsheet to solve all of the preceding requirements. Show how the solution will change if the following data change: sales revenue was $2,115,000, applied manufacturing overhead was $580,000, and utilities amounted to $78,000.

Refer to the schedule of cost of goods manufactured prepared for Huron Corporation in the preceding problem.

Problem 3–51
Interpreting the Schedule of
Cost of Goods Manufactured
(LO 2, 6)

Required:

1. How much of the manufacturing costs incurred during 20x2 remained associated with work-in-process inventory on December 31, 20x2?

2. Suppose the company had increased its production in 20x2 by 20 percent. Would the direct-material cost shown on the schedule have been larger or the same? Why?

3. Answer the same question as in requirement (2) for depreciation on the factory building.

4. Suppose only half of the $60,000 in depreciation on equipment had been related to factory machinery, and the other half was related to selling and administrative equipment. How would this have changed the schedule of cost of goods manufactured?

■ **Problem 3–52**

Cost of Goods Manufactured;
Prime and Conversion Costs
(LO 2, 6)

1. Cost of goods manufactured:
$348,000

Marco Polo Map Company's cost of goods sold for March was $345,000. March 31 work-in-process inventory was 90 percent of March 1 work-in-process inventory. Manufacturing overhead applied was 50 percent of direct-labor cost. Other information pertaining to the company's inventories and production for the month of March is as follows:

Beginning inventories, March 1:	
Raw material	$ 17,000
Work in process	40,000
Finished goods	102,000
Purchases of raw material during March	113,000
Ending inventories, March 31:	
Raw material	26,000
Work in process	?
Finished goods	105,000

Required:

1. Prepare a schedule of cost of goods manufactured for the month of March.
2. Prepare a schedule to compute the prime costs (direct material and direct labor) incurred during March.
3. Prepare a schedule to compute the conversion costs (direct labor and manufacturing overhead) charged to work in process during March.

(CMA, adapted)

■ **Problem 3–53**

Proration of Overapplied or
Underapplied Overhead
(LO 2, 4, 5, 6)

3. Underapplied overhead:
$7,000

Midnight Sun Apparel Company uses normal costing, and manufacturing overhead is applied to work-in-process on the basis of machine hours. On January 1 of the current year, there were no balances in work-in-process or finished-goods inventories. The following estimates were included in the current year's budget.

Total budgeted manufacturing overhead	$235,000
Total budgeted machine hours	47,000

During January, the firm began the following production jobs:

A79:	1,000 machine hours
N08:	2,500 machine hours
P82:	500 machine hours

During January, job numbers A79 and N08 were completed, and job number A79 was sold. The actual manufacturing overhead incurred during January was $27,000.

Required:

1. Compute the company's predetermined overhead rate for the current year.
2. How much manufacturing overhead was applied to production during January?
3. Calculate the overapplied or underapplied overhead for January.
4. Prepare a journal entry to close the balance calculated in requirement (3) into Cost of Goods Sold.
5. Prepare a journal entry to prorate the balance calculated in requirement (3) among the Work-in-Process Inventory, Finished-Goods Inventory, and Cost of Goods Sold accounts.

■ **Problem 3–54**

Ethical Issues; Underap-
plication of Manufacturing
Overhead
(LO 1, 2, 4, 6)

Marc Jackson has recently been hired as a cost accountant by Offset Press Company, a privately held company that produces a line of offset printing presses and lithograph machines. During his first few months on the job, Jackson discovered that Offset has been underapplying factory overhead to the Work-in-Process Inventory account, while overstating expenses through the General and Administrative Expense account. This practice has been going on since the start of the company, which is in its sixth year of operation. The effect in each year has been favorable, having a material impact on the company's tax position. No internal audit function exists at Offset, and the external auditors have not yet discovered the underapplied factory overhead.

Prior to the sixth-year audit, Jackson had pointed out the practice and its effect to Mary Brown, the corporate controller, and had asked her to let him make the necessary adjustments. Brown directed him not to make the adjustments, but to wait until the external auditors had completed their work and see what they uncovered.

The sixth-year audit has now been completed, and the external auditors have once again failed to discover the underapplication of factory overhead. Jackson again asked Brown if he could make the required adjustments and was again told not to make them. Jackson, however, believes that the adjustments should be made and that the external auditors should be informed of the situation.

Since there are no established policies at Offset Press Company for resolving ethical conflicts, Jackson is considering one of the following three alternative courses of action:

- Follow Brown's directive and do nothing further.

- Attempt to convince Brown to make the proper adjustments and to advise the external auditors of her actions.

- Tell the Audit Committee of the Board of Directors about the problem and give them the appropriate accounting data.

Required:

1. For each of the three alternative courses of action that Jackson is considering, explain whether or not the action is appropriate.

2. Independent of your answer to requirement (1), assume that Jackson again approaches Brown to make the necessary adjustments and is unsuccessful. Describe the steps that Jackson should take in proceeding to resolve this situation.

(CMA, adapted)

■ **Problem 3–55**
Predetermined Overhead Rate; Different Time Periods; Pricing
(LO 4)

4. Predetermined rate: $4.64 per hour

Kuwait Electronics Ltd. calculates its predetermined overhead rate on a quarterly basis. The following estimates were made for the current year.

	Estimated Manufacturing Overhead	Estimated Direct-Labor Hours	Quarterly Predetermined Overhead Rate (per direct-labor hour)
First quarter	$90,000	20,000	?
Second quarter	80,000	16,000	?
Third quarter	50,000	12,500	?
Fourth quarter	70,000	14,000	?
Total	$290,000	62,500	

The firm's main product, part number A200, requires $100 of direct material and 20 hours of direct labor per unit. The labor rate is $15 per hour.

Required:

1. Calculate the firm's *quarterly* predetermined overhead rate for each quarter.

2. Determine the cost of one unit of part number A200 if it is manufactured in January versus April.

3. Suppose the company's pricing policy calls for a 10 percent markup over cost. Calculate the price to be charged for a unit of part number A200 if it is produced in January versus April.

4. Calculate the company's predetermined overhead rate for the year if the rate is calculated *annually*.

5. Based on your answer to requirement (4), what is the cost of a unit of part number A200 if it is manufactured in January? In April?

6. What is the price of a unit of part A200 if the predetermined overhead rate is calculated annually?

■ **Problem 3–56**
Overhead Application Using a Predetermined Overhead Rate
(LO 2, 4, 5, 6)

2. Cost of job 77: $200,675
6. Underapplied overhead for November: $4,575

Tiana Shar, the controller for Bondi Furniture Company, is in the process of analyzing the overhead costs for the month of November. She has gathered the following data for the month.

Labor

Direct-labor hours:

Job 77	3,500
Job 78	3,000
Job 79	2,000

Labor costs:

Direct-labor wages	$204,000
Indirect-labor wages	15,000
Supervisory salaries	6,000

Material

Inventories, November 1:

Raw material and supplies	$ 10,500
Work in process (job 77)	54,000
Finished goods	112,500

Purchases of raw material and supplies:

Raw material	$135,000
Supplies (indirect material)	15,000

Direct material and supplies requisitioned for production:

Job 77	$ 45,000
Job 78	37,500
Job 79	25,500
Supplies (indirect material)	12,000
Total	$120,000

Other

Building occupancy costs (heat, light, depreciation, etc.)

Factory facilities	$ 6,400
Sales offices	1,600
Administrative offices	1,000
Total	$ 9,000

Production equipment costs:

Power	$ 4,100
Repairs and maintenance	1,500
Depreciation	1,500
Other	1,000
Total	$ 8,100

The firm's job-order costing system uses direct-labor hours (measured at practical capacity) as the cost driver for overhead application. In December of the preceding year, Shar had prepared the following budget for direct-labor and manufacturing-overhead costs for the current year. The plant is theoretically capable of operating at 150,000 direct-labor hours per year. However, Shar estimates that the practical capacity is 120,000 hours in a typical year.

	Manufacturing Overhead	
Direct-Labor Hours	**Variable**	**Fixed**
100,000	$325,000	$216,000
120,000	390,000	216,000
140,000	455,000	216,000

During November the following jobs were completed:

Job 77	Side chairs
Job 78	End tables

Required: Assist Shar by making the following calculations.

1. Calculate the predetermined overhead rate for the current year.
2. Calculate the total cost of job 77.
3. Compute the amount of manufacturing overhead applied to job 79 during November.

4. What was the total amount of manufacturing overhead applied during November?
5. Compute the actual manufacturing overhead incurred during November.
6. Calculate the overapplied or underapplied overhead for November.

(CMA, adapted)

Scholastic Brass Corporation manufactures brass musical instruments for use by high school students. The company uses a normal costing system, in which manufacturing overhead is applied on the basis of direct-labor hours. The company's budget for the current year included the following predictions.

Budgeted total manufacturing overhead	$426,300
Budgeted total direct-labor hours (based on practical capacity)	20,300

During March, the firm worked on the following two production jobs:

Job number T81, consisting of 76 trombones
Job number C40, consisting of 110 cornets

The events of March are described as follows:

a. One thousand square feet of rolled brass sheet metal were purchased on account for $5,000.
b. Four hundred pounds of brass tubing were purchased on account for $4,000.
c. The following requisitions were submitted on March 5:

Requisition number 112: 250 square feet of brass sheet metal at $5 per square foot (for job number T81)
Requisition number 113: 1,000 pounds of brass tubing, at $10 per pound (for job number C40)
Requisition number 114: 10 gallons of valve lubricant, at $10 per gallon

All brass used in production is treated as direct material. Valve lubricant is an indirect material.

d. An analysis of labor time cards revealed the following labor usage for March.

Direct labor: Job number T81, 800 hours at $20 per hour
Direct labor: Job number C40, 900 hours at $20 per hour
Indirect labor: General factory cleanup, $4,000
Indirect labor: Factory supervisory salaries, $9,000

e. Depreciation of the factory building and equipment during March amounted to $12,000.
f. Rent paid in cash for warehouse space used during March was $1,200.
g. Utility costs incurred during March amounted to $2,100. The invoices for these costs were received, but the bills were not paid in March.
h. March property taxes on the factory were paid in cash, $2,400.
i. The insurance cost covering factory operations for the month of March was $3,100. The insurance policy had been prepaid.
j. The costs of salaries and fringe benefits for sales and administrative personnel paid in cash during March amounted to $8,000.
k. Depreciation on administrative office equipment and space amounted to $4,000.
l. Other selling and administrative expenses paid in cash during March amounted to $1,000.
m. Job number T81 was completed on March 20.
n. Half of the trombones in job number T81 were sold on account during March for $700 each.

The March 1 balances in selected accounts are as follows:

Cash	$ 10,000
Accounts Receivable	21,000
Prepaid Insurance	5,000
Raw-Material Inventory	149,000
Manufacturing Supplies Inventory	500
Work-in-Process Inventory	91,000
Finished-Goods Inventory	220,000
Accumulated Depreciation: Buildings and Equipment	102,000
Accounts Payable	13,000
Wages Payable	8,000

■ **Problem 3–57**
Comprehensive Job-Order Costing Problem
(LO 2, 4, 5, 6)

1. Predetermined overhead rate: $21 per direct-labor hour
4. Total actual overhead: $33,900
7. Income (loss): $(1,625)

Required:

1. Calculate the company's predetermined overhead rate for the year.
2. Prepare journal entries to record the events of March.
3. Set up T-accounts, and post the journal entries made in requirement (2).
4. Calculate the overapplied or underapplied overhead for March. Prepare a journal entry to close this balance into Cost of Goods Sold.
5. Prepare a schedule of cost of goods manufactured for March.
6. Prepare a schedule of cost of goods sold for March.
7. Prepare an income statement for March.

■ **Problem 3–58**
Job-Cost Record; Continuation of Preceding Problem
(LO 2, 4, 6)

Total cost of job T81:
$34,050

Refer to the preceding problem regarding Scholastic Brass Corporation. Complete the following job-cost record for job number T81.

SCHOLASTIC BRASS CORPORATION:
JOB-COST RECORD

Job Number _____ T81 _____   Description _____
Date Started _____   Date Completed _____
                                     Number of Units Completed _____

Direct Material

Date	Requisition Number	Quantity	Unit Price	Cost

Direct Labor

Date	Time Card Number	Hours	Rate	Cost
3/8 to 3/12	3–08 through 3–12			

Manufacturing Overhead

Date	Cost Driver (Activity Base)	Quantity	Application Rate	Cost
3/8 to 3/12				

Cost Summary

Cost Item	Amount
Total direct material Total direct labor Total manufacturing overhead	
Total cost	
Unit cost	

Shipping Summary

Date	Units Shipped	Units Remaining in Inventory	Cost Balance

■ **Problem 3–59**
Flow of Manufacturing Costs;
Incomplete Data
(LO 2, 4, 5)

5. $80,000

Lisboa Ltda. manufactures furniture. Due to a fire in the administrative offices, the accounting records for November of the current year were partially destroyed. You have been able to piece together the following information from the ledger.

Raw-Materials Inventory	
	40,000
Bal. 11/30 45,000	

Accounts Payable	
	12,000 Bal. 10/31

Work-in-Process Inventory	
Bal. 10/31 8,000	

Finished-Goods Inventory	
Bal. 10/31 35,000	

Manufacturing Overhead	
60,000	

Cost of Goods Sold	

Wages Payable	
	1,500 Bal. 11/30

Sales Revenue	

Accounts Receivable	
Bal. 10/31 8,000	

Upon examining various source documents and interviewing several employees, you were able to gather the following additional information.

a.   Collections of accounts receivable during November amounted to $205,000.

b.   Sales revenue in November was 125 percent of cost of goods sold. All sales are on account.

c.   Overhead is applied using an annual predetermined overhead rate using direct-labor hours (based on practical capacity).

d.   The budgeted overhead for the current year is $768,000.

e.   Budgeted direct-labor cost for the current year is $960,000. The direct-labor rate is $20 per hour.

f.   The accounts payable balance on November 30 was $1,000. Only purchases of raw material are credited to accounts payable. A payment of $81,000 was made on November 15.

g.   November's cost of goods sold amounted to $180,000.

h.   The November 30 balance in finished-goods inventory was $5,000.

i.   Payments of $79,500 were made to direct-labor employees during November. The October 31 balance in the Wages Payable account was $1,000.

j.   The *actual* manufacturing overhead for November was $60,000.

k.   An analysis of the furniture still in process on November 30 revealed that so far these items have required 500 hours of direct labor and $24,000 of direct material.

Required: Calculate the following amounts. Then complete the T-accounts given in the problem.

1.   Sales revenue for November.
2.   November 30 balance in accounts receivable.
3.   Cost of raw material purchased during November.
4.   November 30 balance in work-in-process inventory.
5.   Direct labor added to work in process during November.
6.   Applied overhead for November.
7.   Cost of goods manufactured (completed) during November.
8.   Raw material used during November.
9.   October 31 balance in raw-material inventory.
10.   Overapplied or underapplied overhead for November.

■ **Problem 3–60**
Plantwide versus Departmental Overhead Rates; Product Pricing
(LO 1, 4, 7)

1. Total budgeted overhead (departments A and B): $800,000
3. Departmental overhead rate, Department A: $26 per direct-labor hour

TeleTech Corporation manufactures two different fax machines for the business market. Cost estimates for the two models for the current year are as follows:

	Basic System	Advanced System
Direct material	$ 400	$ 800
Direct labor (20 hours at $15 per hour)	300	300
Manufacturing overhead*	400	400
Total	$1,100	$1,500

*The predetermined overhead rate is $20 per direct-labor hour.

Each model of fax machine requires 20 hours of direct labor. The basic system requires 5 hours in department A and 15 hours in department B. The advanced system requires 15 hours in department A and 5 hours in department B. The overhead costs budgeted in these two production departments are as follows:

	Department A	Department B
Variable cost	$16 per direct-labor hour	$4 per direct-labor hour
Fixed cost	$200,000	$200,000

The firm's management expects to operate at a level of 20,000 direct-labor hours in each production department during the current year. (This estimate is based on the practical capacity of each department.)

Required:

1. Show how the company's predetermined overhead rate was determined.
2. If the firm prices each model of fax machines at 10 percent over its cost, what will be the price of each model?
3. Suppose the company were to use departmental predetermined overhead rates. Calculate the rate for each of the two production departments.
4. Compute the product cost of each model using the departmental overhead rates calculated in requirement (3).
5. Compute the price to be charged for each model, assuming the company continues to price each product at 10 percent above cost. Use the revised product costs calculated in requirement (4).
6. Write a memo to the president of TeleTech Corporation making a recommendation as to whether the firm should use a plantwide overhead rate or departmental rates. Consider the potential implications of the overhead rates and the firm's pricing policy. How might these considerations affect the firm's ability to compete in the marketplace?

Cases

■ **Case 3–61**
Interpreting Information from a Job-Order Costing System
(LO 2, 3, 4, 6)

3. Finished-goods inventory, 12/31: 13,400 units
4. Actual manufacturing overhead: $4,392,000

CompuFurn, Inc. manufactures furniture for computer work stations. CompuFurn uses a job-order costing system and employs absorption costing. ComuFurn's work-in-process inventory on November 30 consisted of the following jobs.

Job No.	Description	Units	Accumulated Cost
CC723	Computer caddy	20,000	$ 900,000
CH291	Chair	15,000	431,000
PS812	Printer stand	25,000	250,000
Total			$1,581,000

On November 30, the company's finished-goods inventory, which is evaluated using the first-in, first-out (FIFO) method, consisted of four items.

Item	Quantity and Unit Cost	Accumulated Cost
Computer caddy	7,500 units @ $64 each	$ 480,000
Chair	19,400 units @ $35 each	679,000
Printer stand	21,000 units @ $55 each	1,155,000
Desk	11,200 units @ $102 each	1,142,400
Total		$3,456,400

At the end of November, the balance in CompuFurn's Materials Inventory account, which includes both raw materials and purchased parts, was $668,000. Additions to and requisitions from the materials inventory during the month of December included the following.

Additions	Raw Materials	Purchased Parts
Additions	$242,000	$396,000
Requisitions:		
Job CC723	51,000	104,000
Job CH291	3,000	10,800
Job PS812	124,000	87,000
Job DS444 (5,000 desks)	65,000	187,000

CompuFurn applies manufacturing overhead on the basis of machine hours. The company's manufacturing overhead budget for the year totaled $4,500,000. The company planned to use 900,000 machine hours during this period, which is the firm's estimated practical capacity. Through the first 11 months of the year, a total of 830,000 machine hours were used, and actual manufacturing overhead amounted to $4,140,000.

During the month of December, machine hours and labor hours consisted of the following:

Account	Machine Hours	Labor Hours	Labor Cost
CC723	12,000	11,600	$122,400
CH291	4,400	3,600	43,200
PS812	19,500	14,300	200,500
DS444	14,000	12,500	138,000
Indirect labor	—	3,000	29,400
Supervision	—	—	57,600
Total	49,900	45,000	$591,100

The jobs completed in December and the unit sales for that month are as follows:

Job No.	Production Items	Quantity Completed	Item	Quantity Shipped
CC723	Computer caddy	20,000	Computer caddy	17,500
CH291	Chair	15,000	Chair	21,000
DS444	Desks	5,000	Printer stand	18,000
			Desk	6,000

Required:

1. Describe when it is appropriate for a company to use a job-order costing system.
2. Calculate the balance in CompuFurn, Inc.'s Work-in-Process Inventory account as of December 31.
3. Calculate the cost of the chairs in CompuFurn, Inc.'s finished-goods Inventory as of December 31.
4. Actual manufacturing overhead incurred in December amounted to $252,000. Calculate CompuFurn's overapplied or underapplied overhead for the year.
5. Explain two alternative accounting treatments for overapplied or underapplied overhead balances when using a job-order costing system.

(CMA, adapted)

FiberCom, Inc., a manufacturer of fiber optic communications equipment, uses a job-order costing system. Since the production process is heavily automated, manufacturing overhead is applied on the basis of machine hours using a predetermined overhead rate. The current annual rate of $15 per machine hour is based on budgeted manufacturing overhead costs of $1,200,000 and a budgeted activity level of 80,000 machine hours (the company's estimated practical capacity). Operations for the year have been completed, and all of the accounting entries have been made for the year except the application of manufacturing overhead to the jobs worked on during December, the transfer of costs from Work in Process to Finished Goods for the jobs completed in December, and the transfer of costs from Finished Goods to Cost of Goods Sold for the jobs that have been sold during December. Summarized data as of November 30 and for the month of December are presented in the

■ **Case 3–62**
Cost Flows in a Job-Order Costing System; Schedule of Cost of Goods Manufactured; Automation
(LO 2, 3, 4, 5, 6)

3. Manufacturing overhead applied in December: $90,000
6. Cost of goods manufactured: $2,968,800

following table. Jobs T11-007, N11-013, and N11-015 were completed during December. All completed jobs except Job N11-013 had been turned over to customers by the close of business on December 31.

	Work-in-Process		December Activity	
Job No.	Balance November 30	Direct Material	Direct Labor	Machine Hours
T11-007	$ 87,000	$ 1,500	$ 4,500	300
N11-013	55,000	4,000	12,000	1,000
N11-015	-0-	25,600	26,700	1,400
D12-002	-0-	37,900	20,000	2,500
D12-003	-0-	26,000	16,800	800
Total	$142,000	$95,000	$80,000	6,000

Operating Activity	Activity through November 30	December Activity
Actual manufacturing overhead incurred:		
Indirect material	$ 125,000	$ 9,000
Indirect labor	345,000	30,000
Utilities	245,000	22,000
Depreciation	385,000	35,000
Total overhead	$1,100,000	$96,000
Other data:		
Raw-material purchases*	$ 965,000	$98,000
Direct-labor costs	$ 845,000	$80,000
Machine hours	73,000	6,000

Account Balances at Beginning of Year	January 1
Raw-material inventory*	$105,000
Work-in-process inventory	60,000
Finished-goods inventory	125,000

*Raw-material purchases and raw-material inventory consist of both direct and indirect materials. The balance of the Raw-Material Inventory account as of December 31 of the year just completed is $85,000.

Required:

1. Explain why manufacturers use a predetermined overhead rate to apply manufacturing overhead to their jobs.

2. How much manufacturing overhead would FiberCom have applied to jobs through November 30 of the year just completed?

3. How much manufacturing overhead would have been applied to jobs during December of the year just completed?

4. Determine the amount by which manufacturing overhead is overapplied or underapplied as of December 31 of the year just completed.

5. Determine the balance in the Finished-Goods Inventory account on December 31 of the year just completed.

6. Prepare a Schedule of Cost of Goods Manufactured for FiberCom, Inc. for the year just completed. (*Hint:* In computing the cost of direct material used, remember that FiberCom includes both direct and indirect material in its Raw-Material Inventory account.)

(CMA, adapted)

THIS CHAPTER'S FOCUS COMPANY is the Fuji Sports Equipment Company. The Japanese company manufactures baseball gloves in its Osaka plant. Fuji's Osaka plant uses a product-costing method called process costing. Under process costing, direct material and conversion costs (direct labor and manufacturing overhead) are first assigned to each of the processes (or departments) used in the manufacturing operation. Then, the costs of each process (or department) are assigned to the units worked on in the department. Process costing is used only by manufacturing companies that produce relatively large numbers of similar products.

4 Process Costing and Hybrid Product-Costing Systems

In contrast to the process-costing system used in Fuji's Osaka plant, we explore a different product-costing system in the company's Nagoya plant. This Fuji plant manufactures two types of footballs (soccer balls). The match balls are covered with a premium synthetic leather, whereas the practice balls are covered with PVC plastic. Except for the different exterior material, though, each football requires the same production steps. Fuji's Nagoya plant uses a product-costing system called operation costing, which is well suited to its production environment. Operation costing is used only by manufacturing companies.

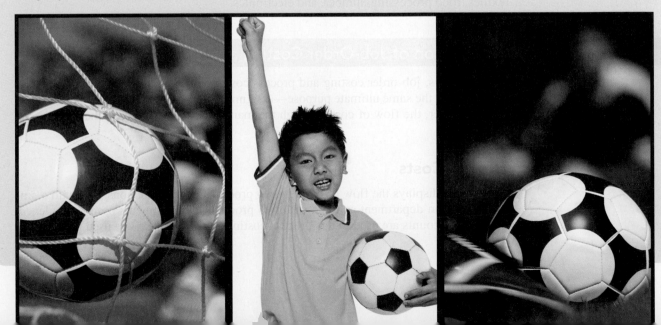

1 List and explain the similarities and important differences between job-order and process costing.

2 Prepare journal entries to record the flow of costs in a process-costing system with sequential production departments.

3 Prepare a table of equivalent units under weighted-average process costing.

4 Compute the cost per equivalent unit under the weighted-average method of process costing.

5 Analyze the total production costs for a department under the weighted-average method of process costing.

6 Prepare a departmental production report under weighted-average process costing.

7 Describe how an operation costing system accumulates and assigns the costs of direct-material and conversion activity in a batch manufacturing process.

We have seen that a product-costing system performs two primary functions:

1. Accumulating production costs.
2. Assigning those production costs to the firm's products.

Product costs are needed for the purposes of planning, cost management, decision making, and reporting to various outside organizations, such as governmental regulatory agencies.

Job-order costing was described in Chapter 3. This type of product-costing system is used when relatively small numbers of products are produced in distinct batches or job orders and these products differ significantly from each other. This chapter covers **process-costing systems.** Process costing is used in **repetitive production** environments, where large numbers of identical or very similar products are manufactured in a continuous flow. Industries using process costing include paper, petroleum, chemicals, textiles, food processing, lumber, and electronics.

Comparison of Job-Order Costing and Process Costing

Learning Objective 1

List and explain the similarities and important differences between job-order and process costing.

In many ways, job-order costing and process costing are similar. Both product-costing systems have the same ultimate purpose—assignment of production costs to units of output. Moreover, the flow of costs through the manufacturing accounts is the same in the two systems.

Flow of Costs

Exhibit 4–1 displays the flow of costs in two process-costing situations: one with a single production department and one with two production departments used in sequence. The same accounts are used in this process-costing illustration as were used in job-order

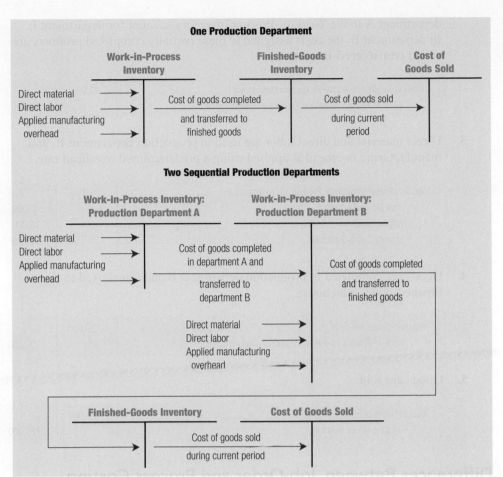

Exhibit 4–1
Flow of Costs in Process-Costing Systems

costing in the preceding chapter. As the illustration shows, direct-material, direct-labor, and manufacturing-overhead costs are added to a Work-in-Process Inventory account. As goods are finished, costs are transferred to Finished-Goods Inventory. During the period when goods are sold, the product costs are transferred to Cost of Goods Sold. In the two-department case, when goods are finished in the first production department, costs accumulated in the Work-in-Process Inventory account for production department A are transferred to the Work-in-Process Inventory account for production department B.

The journal entries for the case of two sequential production departments, as illustrated in Exhibit 4–1, are as follows. (The numbers used in the journal entries are assumed for the purpose of showing the form of the entries.)

1. As direct material and direct labor are used in production department A, these costs are added to the Work-in-Process Inventory account for department A. Overhead is applied using a predetermined overhead rate. The predetermined overhead rate is computed in the same way in job-order and process costing.

Work-in-Process Inventory: Production Department A..	100,000	
Raw-Material Inventory		50,000
Wages Payable...		20,000
Manufacturing Overhead...		30,000

2. When production department A completes its work on some units of product, these units are transferred to production department B. The costs assigned to these goods are transferred from the Work-in-Process Inventory account for

Learning Objective 2

Prepare journal entries to record the flow of costs in a process-costing system with sequential production departments.

department A to the Work-in-Process Inventory account for department B. In department B, the costs assigned to these partially completed products are called **transferred-in costs.**

Work-in-Process Inventory: Production Department B	80,000	
Work-in-Process Inventory: Production Department A		80,000

3. Direct material and direct labor are used in production department B, and manufacturing overhead is applied using a predetermined overhead rate.

Work-in-Process Inventory: Production Department B	75,000	
Raw-Material Inventory		40,000
Wages Payable		15,000
Manufacturing Overhead		20,000

4. Goods are completed in production department B and transferred to the finished-goods warehouse.

Finished-Goods Inventory	130,000	
Work-in-Process Inventory: Production Department B		130,000

5. Goods are sold.

Cost of Goods Sold	125,000	
Finished-Goods Inventory		125,000

Differences Between Job-Order and Process Costing

In job-order costing, *costs are accumulated by job order* and recorded on job-cost records. The cost of each unit in a particular job order is found by dividing the total cost of the job order by the number of units in the job.

In process costing, *costs are accumulated by department,* rather than by job order or batch. The cost per unit is found by averaging the total costs incurred over the units produced. Exhibit 4–2 summarizes this key difference between job-order and process costing.

Equivalent Units: A Key Concept

Material, labor, and overhead costs often are incurred at different rates in a production process. Direct material is usually placed into production at one or more discrete points in the process. In contrast, direct labor and manufacturing overhead, called *conversion costs,* usually are incurred continuously throughout the process. When an accounting period ends, the partially completed goods that remain in process generally are at different stages of completion with respect to material and conversion activity. For example, the in-process units may be 75 percent complete with respect to conversion, but they may already include all of their direct materials. This situation is portrayed in Exhibit 4–3.

Equivalent Units

The graphical illustration in Exhibit 4–3 supposes there are 1,000 physical units in process at the end of an accounting period. Each of the physical units is 75 percent complete with respect to conversion (direct labor and manufacturing overhead). How much conversion activity has been applied to these partially completed units? Conversion activity occurs uniformly throughout the production process. Therefore, the amount of conversion activity

A. Job-Order Costing: Accumulates Costs by Job Order

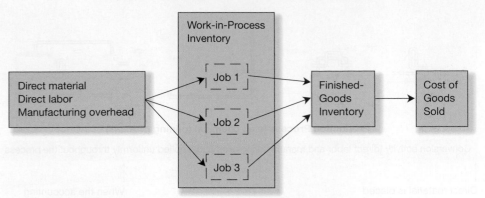

B. Process Costing: Accumulates Costs by Production Department

Exhibit 4–2
Comparison of Job-Order and Process Costing

required to do 75 percent of the conversion on 1,000 units is *equivalent* to the amount of conversion activity required to do all of the conversion on 750 units. This number is computed as follows:

$$\underset{\text{physical units in process}}{1{,}000 \text{ partially completed}} \times \underset{\text{respect to conversion}}{75\% \text{ complete with}} = 750 \text{ equivalent units}$$

The term **equivalent units** is used in process costing to refer to the amount of manufacturing activity that has been applied to a batch of physical units. The *1,000 physical units* in process represent *750 equivalent units* of conversion activity.

The term *equivalent units* also is used to measure the amount of direct materials represented by the partially completed goods. Since direct materials are incorporated at the beginning of the production process, the *1,000 physical units* represent *1,000 equivalent units of direct material* (1,000 physical units × 100% complete with respect to direct materials).

The most important feature of process costing is that the costs of direct material and conversion are assigned to equivalent units rather than to physical units. Refer again to Exhibit 4–3. For simplicity, suppose that the only production activity of the current accounting period was to start work on the 1,000 physical units and complete 75 percent of the required conversion activity. Assume that the costs incurred were $1,500 for conversion (direct labor and manufacturing overhead) and $5,000 for direct material. These costs would then be assigned as follows:

$$\frac{\$1{,}500 \text{ conversion cost}}{750 \text{ equivalent units of conversion}} = \underset{\text{for conversion}}{\$2.00 \text{ per equivalent unit}}$$

$$\frac{\$5{,}000 \text{ direct-material cost}}{1{,}000 \text{ equivalent units of direct material}} = \underset{\text{for direct material}}{\$5.00 \text{ per equivalent unit}}$$

"Operations [managers] have a keen interest in cost management. To truly manage costs, you must look at the processes involved." (4b)
John Deere Health Care, Inc.

Exhibit 4–3
Direct Material and
Conversion Activity in a
Typical Production Process

Production Process (e.g., chemical refining process)

Conversion activity (direct labor and manufacturing overhead) applied uniformly throughout the process

Direct material is placed into production at the beginning of the production process.

When the accounting period ends, the partially completed goods are 75% complete with respect to conversion. The goods are 100% complete with respect to direct material.

This is a highly simplified example because there is no work-in-process inventory at the beginning of the accounting period and no goods were completed during the period. Nevertheless, it illustrates the important concept that under process costing, costs are assigned to equivalent units rather than physical units.

Illustration of Process Costing

The key document in a typical process-costing system is the **departmental production report,** prepared for each production department at the end of every accounting period. This report replaces the job-cost record, which is used to accumulate costs by job in a job-order costing system. The departmental production report summarizes the flow of production quantities through the department, and it shows the amount of production cost transferred out of the department's Work-in-Process Inventory account during the period. The following four steps are used in preparing a departmental production report.

1. Analysis of physical flow of units.
2. Calculation of equivalent units (for direct material and conversion activity).

Process costing is used in the wine industry. First, raw material (in this case, grapes) is harvested and entered into production. Then conversion costs are incurred in the production process. At the end of the accounting period, partially completed units of wine remain in process as the wine ages.

3. Computation of unit costs (i.e., the cost per equivalent unit for direct material and conversion).

4. Analysis of total costs (determine the cost to be removed from work in process and transferred either to the next production department or to finished goods).

The method of process costing that we will focus on in this chapter is called the **weighted-average method.** *This method is almost always used in practice* by companies using process costing. There is another process-costing method called the *first-in, first-out,* or *FIFO, method.* This method is covered in some cost accounting courses, but it is rarely used in practice.[1]

Basic Data for Illustration

The Osaka plant of Fuji Sports Equipment Company manufactures baseball gloves. In the Cutting Department, direct material consisting of imitation leather is placed into production at the beginning of the process. Direct-labor and manufacturing overhead costs are incurred uniformly throughout the process. The material is rolled to make it softer and then cut into the pieces needed to produce baseball gloves. The predetermined overhead rate used in the Cutting Department is 125 percent of direct-labor *cost.*

The Excel spreadsheet in Exhibit 4–4 presents a summary of the activity and costs in the Cutting Department during March. The direct-material and conversion

---

[1]The FIFO method of process costing is also covered in a supplement to this text titled *Process Costing: The First-In, First-Out Method.* This supplement is available to students on the text Web site at http://www.mhhe.com/hilton9e.

Microsoft Excel - Basic Data for Illustration - Cutting Department		
File Edit View Insert Format Tools Data Window Help — Type a question for help		
B22 ▼ *fx* =SUM(B20:B21)		
A	B	C
1 Information for Illustration	Amount	
2		
3 Work in process, March 1 - 20,000 units		
4 Direct material: 100% complete, cost of*	$ 50,000	
5 Conversion: 10% complete, cost of*	7,200	
6 Balance in work in process, March 1*	$ 57,200	
7		
8 Units started during March	30,000	units
9		
10 Units completed during March and transferred out of the Cutting Department	40,000	units
11		
12 Work in process, March 31	10,000	units
13 Direct material: 100% complete		
14 Conversion: 50% complete		
15		
16 Costs Incurred during March:		
17 Direct material	$ 90,000	
18		
19 Conversion costs:		
20 Direct labor	$ 86,000	
21 Applied manufacturing overhead**	107,500	
22 Total conversion costs	$ 193,500	
23		
24 *These costs were incurred during the prior month, February		
25		
26 **(Predetermined overhead rate) x (Direct labor cost) = 125% x $86,000 = $107,500		
◄ ► ►I \Sheet1 / Sheet2 / Sheet3 /		
Ready		

Exhibit 4–4
Basic Data for Illustration—
Cutting Department

THE GLOBAL WINE INDUSTRY

The wine industry circles the globe, with significant wine production found in western and central Europe, the United States, South America (especially Chile and Argentina), South Africa, Australia, and New Zealand. The coming decade promises to be a dynamic one for the industry, with two major factors playing leading roles: industry consolidation and the emergence of the Asian wine consumer. As the *Financial Times* noted recently, ". . . western auctioneers are heavily reliant on Asian buyers, who last year [2009] represented 37 percent of Sotheby's London sales (and 99 percent of its Hong Kong sales) . . . Furthermore, a significant proportion of lots sold to trade buyers will end up on the Asian continent . . . Wine consumption in Greater China grew faster than in any other region in 2008, according to a report by the *International Wines & Spirits Record*, which predicts that across Asia consumption will rise more than 25 percent between 2009 and 2013."

Wine production provides an excellent example of a production setting where process costing would be used. The processes in a typical vineyard include most or all of the following:[2]

- *Trimming:* At the end of a growing season, the vines are trimmed, which helps prepare them for the next harvest.
- *Tying:* The vines are tied onto wires to help protect them from the weather. (This also occurs at the end of the season.)
- *Hilling:* Dirt is piled up around the roots to further protect them.
- *Conditioning:* In the spring, dirt is leveled back from the roots.
- *Untying:* The vines are untied from the wires to allow them freedom to grow during the spring and summer months.
- *Chemical spraying:* The vines are sprayed in the spring to protect them from disease and insects.
- *Harvesting:* The highest-quality grapes are picked by hand to minimize damage.
- *Stemming and crushing:* Batches of grapes are loaded into a machine, which gently removes the stems and mildly crushes them.
- *Pressing:* After removal from the stemmer/crusher, the juice runs freely from the grapes.
- *Filtering:* The grapes are crushed mechanically to render more juice from them.
- *Fermentation:* This process varies, depending on the type of wine. For example, riesling grape juice is placed in stainless-steel tanks for fermentation. Chardonnay grape juice undergoes a two-stage fermentation process in oak barrels.
- *Aging:* Again, this process varies. Riesling wines are aged in the stainless-steel tanks for approximately a year. Chardonnays are aged in the oak barrels for about two years.
- *Bottling:* A machine bottles the wine and corks the bottles.
- *Labeling:* Each bottle is labeled with the name of the vintner, vintage, and variety.
- *Packing:* The bottles are packed in 12-bottle cases.
- *Case labeling:* The cases are stamped with the same information as is on the bottles.
- *Shipping:* The wine is shipped to wine distributors and retailers.

costs listed in Exhibit 4–4 for the March 1 work in process consist of costs that were incurred during February. These costs were assigned to the units remaining in process at the end of February.

---

[2]Based on the authors' research, and Ella Lister, "Auctions: China Uncorks the Market," *Financial Times*, June 18, 2010.

Based on the data in Exhibit 4–4, the Cutting Department's Work-in-Process Inventory account has the following balance on March 1:

Work-in-Process Inventory: Cutting Department		
March 1 balance	57,200	

The following journal entry is made during March to add the costs of direct material, direct labor, and manufacturing overhead to Work-in-Process Inventory.

Work-in-Process Inventory: Cutting Department	283,500	
Raw-Material Inventory		90,000
Wages Payable		86,000
Manufacturing Overhead		107,500

Weighted-Average Method of Process Costing

We now present the four steps used to prepare a departmental production report using weighted-average process costing.

Step 1: Analysis of Physical Flow of Units
The first step is to prepare a table summarizing the physical flow of production units during March. The table is shown in Exhibit 4–5 and reflects the following inventory formula.

$$\begin{pmatrix} \text{Physical units} \\ \text{in beginning} \\ \text{work in process} \end{pmatrix} + \begin{pmatrix} \text{Physical} \\ \text{units} \\ \text{started} \end{pmatrix} - \begin{pmatrix} \text{Physical units} \\ \text{completed and} \\ \text{transferred out} \end{pmatrix} = \begin{pmatrix} \text{Physical units} \\ \text{in ending work} \\ \text{in process} \end{pmatrix}$$

Step 2: Calculation of Equivalent Units
The second step in the process-costing procedure is to calculate the equivalent units of direct material and conversion activity. A table of equivalent units, displayed in Exhibit 4–6, is based on the table of physical flows prepared in step 1 (Exhibit 4–5). The 40,000 physical units that were completed and transferred out of the Cutting Department were 100 percent complete. Thus, they represent 40,000 equivalent units for both direct material and conversion. The 10,000 units in the ending work-in-process inventory are complete with respect to direct material, and they represent 10,000 equivalent units of direct material. However, they are only 50 percent complete with respect to conversion. Therefore, the ending work-in-process inventory represents 5,000 equivalent units of conversion activity (10,000 physical units × 50% complete).

As Exhibit 4–6 indicates, the total number of equivalent units is calculated:

Learning Objective 3

Prepare a table of equivalent units under weighted-average process costing.

$$\begin{pmatrix} \text{Equivalent units of} \\ \text{activity in units completed} \\ \text{and transferred out} \end{pmatrix} + \begin{pmatrix} \text{Equivalent units of} \\ \text{activity in ending} \\ \text{work in process} \end{pmatrix} = \begin{pmatrix} \text{Total} \\ \text{equivalent units} \\ \text{of activity} \end{pmatrix}$$

	Physical Units
Work in process, March 1	20,000
Units started during March	30,000
Total units to account for	50,000
Units completed and transferred out during March	40,000
Work in process, March 31	10,000
Total units accounted for	50,000

Exhibit 4–5
Step 1: Analysis of Physical Flow of Units—Cutting Department

Exhibit 4–6

Step 2: Calculation of Equivalent Units—Cutting Department (weighted-average method)

	Physical Units	Percentage of Completion with Respect to Conversion	Equivalent Units	
			Direct Material	Conversion
Work in process, March 1	20,000	10%		
Units started during March	30,000			
Total units to account for	50,000			
Units completed and transferred out during March	40,000	100%	40,000	40,000
Work in process, March 31	10,000	50%	10,000	5,000
Total units accounted for	50,000			
Total equivalent units			50,000	45,000

Note that the total equivalent units of activity, for both direct material and conversion, exceeds the activity accomplished in the current period alone. Since only 30,000 physical product units were started during March and direct material is added at the beginning of the process, only 30,000 equivalent units of direct material were actually placed into production during March. However, the total number of equivalent units of direct material used for weighted-average process costing is 50,000 (see Exhibit 4–6). The other 20,000 equivalent units of direct material were actually entered into production during the preceding month. *This is the key feature of the weighted-average method. The number of equivalent units of activity is calculated without making a distinction as to whether the activity occurred in the current accounting period or the preceding period.*

Step 3: Computation of Unit Costs   The third step in the process-costing procedure, calculating the cost per equivalent unit for both direct material and conversion activity, is presented in Exhibit 4–7. The cost per equivalent unit for direct material is computed by dividing the total direct-material cost, including the cost of the beginning work in process *and* the cost incurred during March, by the total equivalent units (from step 2, Exhibit 4–6). An analogous procedure is used for conversion costs.

Step 4: Analysis of Total Costs   Now we can complete the process-costing procedure by determining the total cost to be transferred out of the Cutting Department's Work-in-Process Inventory account and into the Stitching Department's Work-in-Process Inventory account. Exhibit 4–8 provides the required calculations. For convenience, the computations in step 3 are repeated in Exhibit 4–8. At the bottom of Exhibit 4–8, a check is made to be sure that the total costs of $340,700 have been fully accounted for in the cost of goods completed and transferred out and the balance remaining in work-in-process inventory.

Exhibit 4–7

Step 3: Computation of Unit Costs—Cutting Department (weighted-average method)

	Direct Material	Conversion	Total
Work in process, March 1 (from Exhibit 4–4)	$ 50,000	$ 7,200	$ 57,200
Costs incurred during March (from Exhibit 4–4)	90,000	193,500	283,500
Total costs to account for	$140,000	$200,700	$340,700
Equivalent units (from step 2, Exhibit 4–6)	50,000	45,000	
Costs per equivalent unit	$ 2.80 ↑	$ 4.46 ↑	$ 7.26 ↑
	$140,000 / 50,000	$200,700 / 45,000	$2.80 + $4.46

	Direct Material	Conversion	Total
Work in process, March 1 (from Exhibit 4–4)	$ 50,000	$ 7,200	$ 57,200
Costs incurred during March (from Exhibit 4–4)	90,000	193,500	283,500
Total costs to account for	$140,000	$200,700	$340,700
Equivalent units (from step 2, Exhibit 4–6)	50,000	45,000	
Costs per equivalent unit	$ 2.80	$ 4.46	$ 7.26

$$\frac{\$140,000}{50,000} \qquad \frac{\$200,700}{45,000} \qquad \$2.80 + \$4.46$$

Cost of goods completed and transferred out of the Cutting Department during March:

$\left(\begin{array}{c}\text{Number of units}\\\text{transferred out}\end{array}\right) \times \left(\begin{array}{c}\text{Total cost per}\\\text{equivalent unit}\end{array}\right)$ .... 40,000 × $7.26 .... $290,400

Cost remaining in March 31 work-in-process inventory in the Cutting Department:

Direct material:

$\left(\begin{array}{c}\text{Number of equivalent}\\\text{units of direct material}\end{array}\right) \times \left(\begin{array}{c}\text{Cost per equivalent}\\\text{unit of direct material}\end{array}\right)$ .... 10,000 × $2.80 .... $ 28,000

Conversion:

$\left(\begin{array}{c}\text{Number of equivalent}\\\text{units of conversion}\end{array}\right) \times \left(\begin{array}{c}\text{Cost per equivalent}\\\text{unit of conversion}\end{array}\right)$ .... 5,000 × $4.46 22,300

Total cost of March 31 work in process .... $ 50,300

Check: Cost of goods completed and transferred out $290,400
         Cost of March 31 work-in-process inventory 50,300
         Total costs accounted for $340,700

The calculations in Exhibit 4–8 are used as the basis for the following journal entry to transfer the cost of goods completed and transferred out of the Cutting Department.

Work-in-Process Inventory: Stitching Department	290,400	
Work-in-Process Inventory: Cutting Department		290,400

On March 31, the Cutting Department's Work-in-Process Inventory account appears as follows. The March 31 balance in the account agrees with that calculated in Exhibit 4–8.

Work-in-Process Inventory: Cutting Department			
March 1 balance	57,200		
March cost of direct material, direct labor, and applied manufacturing overhead	283,500	290,400	Cost of goods completed and transferred out of Cutting Department
March 31 balance	50,300		

Departmental Production Report We have now completed all four steps necessary to prepare the March production report for the Cutting Department. The report, which is displayed in Exhibit 4–9, simply combines the tables presented in Exhibits 4–6 and 4–8. The report provides a convenient summary of all of the process-costing calculations made under the weighted-average method.

Why is this process-costing method called the *weighted-average* method? Because the cost per equivalent unit for March, for both direct material and conversion activity, is computed as a weighted average of the costs incurred during two different accounting periods, February and March. To demonstrate this fact, we will focus on direct material. Since direct material is placed into production at the beginning of the

Learning Objective 6

Prepare a departmental production report under weighted-average process costing.

Exhibit 4–9
March Production Report:
Cutting Department
(weighted-average method)

FUJI SPORTS EQUIPMENT COMPANY
March Production Report: Cutting Department

	Physical Units	Percentage of Completion with Respect to Conversion	Equivalent Units Direct Material	Conversion
Work in process, March 1	20,000	10%		
Units started during March	30,000			
Total units to account for	50,000			
Units completed and transferred out during March	40,000	100%	40,000	40,000
Work in process, March 31	10,000	50%	10,000	5,000
Total units accounted for	50,000			
Total equivalent units			50,000	45,000

	Direct Material	Conversion	Total
Work in process, March 1 (from Exhibit 4–4)	$ 50,000	$ 7,200	$ 57,200
Costs incurred during March (from Exhibit 4–4)	90,000	193,500	283,500
Total costs to account for	$140,000	$200,700	$340,700
Equivalent units (from step 2, Exhibit 4–6)	50,000	45,000	
Costs per equivalent unit	$ 2.80	$ 4.46	$ 7.26

$$\frac{\$140,000}{50,000} \qquad \frac{\$200,700}{45,000} \qquad \$2.80 + \$4.46$$

Cost of goods completed and transferred out of the Cutting Department during March:

$\left(\begin{array}{c}\text{Number of units}\\\text{transferred out}\end{array}\right) \times \left(\begin{array}{c}\text{Total cost per}\\\text{equivalent unit}\end{array}\right)$ .... 40,000 × $7.26 .... **$290,400**

Cost remaining in March 31 work-in-process inventory in the Cutting Department:

Direct material:

$\left(\begin{array}{c}\text{Number of equivalent}\\\text{units of direct material}\end{array}\right) \times \left(\begin{array}{c}\text{Cost per equivalent}\\\text{unit of direct material}\end{array}\right)$ .... 10,000 × $2.80 .... $ 28,000

Conversion:

$\left(\begin{array}{c}\text{Number of equivalent}\\\text{units of conversion}\end{array}\right) \times \left(\begin{array}{c}\text{Cost per equivalent}\\\text{unit of conversion}\end{array}\right)$ .... 5,000 × $4.46 22,300

Total cost of March 31 work in process .... $ 50,300

Check:	Cost of goods completed and transferred out	$290,400
	Cost of March 31 work-in-process inventory	50,300
	Total costs accounted for	$340,700

process, the 20,000 physical units in the March 1 work in process already have their direct material. The direct-material cost per equivalent unit in the March 1 work in process is $2.50 ($50,000 ÷ 20,000, from Exhibit 4–4). This cost was actually incurred in *February*.

In March, 30,000 physical units were entered into work in process and received their direct material. The direct-material cost incurred in March was $90,000. Thus, the direct-material cost per equivalent unit experienced in *March* was $3.00 ($90,000 ÷ 30,000).

Under the weighted-average method of process costing, the cost per equivalent unit for direct material was calculated in Exhibit 4–7 to be $2.80. *This $2.80 unit-cost figure is a weighted average,* as the following calculation shows.

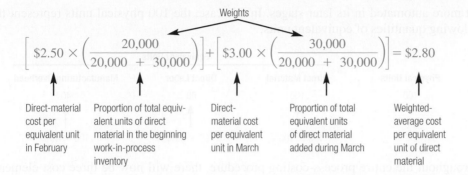

The point of this demonstration is that under weighted-average process costing, unit-cost figures are weighted averages of costs incurred over two or more accounting periods.

Other Issues in Process Costing

Several other issues related to process costing are worth discussion.

Actual versus Normal Costing

Our illustration of process costing assumed that *normal costing* was used. As explained in Chapter 3, in a normal-costing system, direct material and direct labor are applied to Work-in-Process Inventory at their *actual* amounts, but manufacturing overhead is applied to Work-in-Process Inventory using a predetermined overhead rate. In contrast, under an *actual-costing* system, the actual costs of direct material, direct labor, *and manufacturing overhead* are entered into Work-in-Process Inventory.

Either actual or normal costing may be used in conjunction with a process-costing system. Our illustration used normal costing since a predetermined overhead rate was used to compute applied manufacturing overhead in Exhibit 4–4. This resulted in applied overhead for March of $107,500 (125% × $86,000). If actual costing had been used, the manufacturing overhead cost for March would have been the actual overhead cost incurred instead of the applied overhead amount given in Exhibit 4–4. In all other ways, the process-costing procedures used under actual and normal costing are identical.

When normal costing is used, there may be overapplied or underapplied overhead at the end of the period. This amount is either closed into Cost of Goods Sold or prorated, as explained in Chapter 3.

Other Cost Drivers for Overhead Application

Our illustration used a predetermined overhead rate based on direct-labor cost. Since the application of manufacturing overhead was based on direct-labor cost, direct labor and manufacturing overhead were combined into the single cost element *conversion costs*. This procedure is quite common in practice. If some cost driver (or activity base) other than direct labor had been used to apply manufacturing overhead, then overhead costs would be accounted for separately from direct-labor costs in the process-costing calculations.

Suppose, for example, that manufacturing overhead is applied on the basis of machine hours. A group of 100 physical units is 100 percent complete as to direct material, 60 percent complete as to direct labor, and 40 percent complete as to machine time. This situation could arise in a production process that is labor-intensive in its early stages but more automated in its later stages. In this case, the 100 physical units represent the following quantities of equivalent units:

	Equivalent Units		
Physical Units	Direct Material	Direct Labor	Manufacturing Overhead
100	100	60	40
	↑	↑	↑
	100 × 100%	100 × 60%	100 × 40%

Throughout the entire process-costing procedure, there will now be three cost elements (direct material, direct labor, and manufacturing overhead) instead of only two (direct material and conversion). In all other respects, the process-costing calculations will be identical to those illustrated earlier in the chapter.

Subsequent Production Departments

In our illustration, production requires two sequential production operations: cutting and stitching. Although the process-costing procedures for the second department are similar to those illustrated for the first, there is one additional consideration. The cost of goods completed and transferred out of the Cutting Department must remain assigned to the partially completed product units as they undergo further processing in the Stitching Department. Process-costing procedures for subsequent production departments are covered in cost accounting texts.[3]

Hybrid Product-Costing Systems

Job-order and process costing represent the polar extremes of product-costing systems. However, some production processes exhibit characteristics of both job-order and process-costing environments. Examples of such production processes include some clothing and food-processing operations. In these production processes, the conversion activities may be very similar or identical across all of the firm's product lines, even though the direct materials may differ significantly. Different clothing lines require significantly different direct materials, such as cotton, silk, or wool. However, the conversion of these materials, involving direct labor and manufacturing overhead, may not differ much across product types. In the food industry, production of economy-grade or premium applesauce differs with regard to the quality and cost of the direct-material input, apples. However, the cooking, straining, and canning operations for these two product lines are nearly identical.

Operation Costing for Batch Manufacturing Processes

The production processes described above often are referred to as **batch manufacturing** processes. Such processes are characterized by high-volume production of several product lines that differ in some important ways but are nearly identical in others. Since batch manufacturing operations have characteristics of both job-order costing and process-costing environments, a **hybrid product-costing system** is required. One common approach is called **operation costing.** This product-costing system is used when conversion activities are very similar across product lines, but the direct materials

---

[3]Sequential production operations are also covered in a supplement to this textbook titled *Process Costing in Sequential Production Departments*. This supplement is available to students on the text Web site at http://www.mhhe.com/hilton9e.

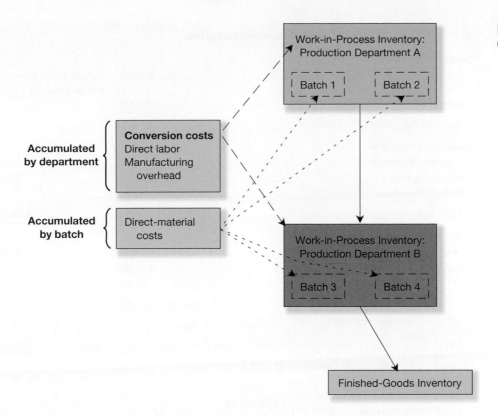

Exhibit 4–10
Operation Costing

differ significantly. *Conversion costs* are accumulated by *department,* and process-costing methods are used to assign these costs to products. In contrast, *direct-material costs* are accumulated by *job order or batch,* and job-order costing is used to assign material costs to products.

The main features of operation costing are illustrated in Exhibit 4–10. Notice in the exhibit that products pass sequentially through production departments A and B. Direct-material costs are traced directly to each batch of goods, but conversion costs are applied on a departmental basis. Direct labor and manufacturing overhead are combined in a single cost category called conversion costs, rather than separately identifying direct labor. Moreover, under operation costing, conversion costs are applied to products using a *predetermined application rate.* This predetermined rate is based on *budgeted conversion costs,* as follows:[4]

$$\frac{\text{Predetermined application}}{\text{rate for conversion costs}} = \frac{\text{Budgeted conversion costs}}{\text{(direct labor and manufacturing overhead)}}{\text{Budgeted cost driver (or activity base)}}$$

As an illustration of operation costing, we will focus on the Nagoya plant of Fuji Sports Equipment Company. This division manufactures two different grades of footballs (soccer balls): match balls, which have premium synthetic leather exteriors, and practice balls, which use PVC plastic covers. The cutting and stitching operations for the two different products are identical. Practice balls are sold without special packaging, but match balls are packaged in an attractive cardboard box.

During October two batches were entered into production and finished. There was no beginning or ending inventory of work in process for October. Cost and production data are given in Exhibit 4–11. Notice in Exhibit 4–11 that the direct-material costs are

---

[4]The budgeted amount for the cost driver is based on the company's practical capacity for production.

Exhibit 4–11
Basic Data for Illustration of
Operation Costing

Operation Costing Data		
Direct-material costs:		
Batch P19 (1,000 match balls)	$20,000	(includes $1,000 for packaging material)
Batch S28 (3,000 practice balls)	30,000	
Total direct-material costs	$50,000	
Conversion costs (budgeted):		
Preparation Department		$ 30,000
Finishing Department		24,000
Packaging Department		500
Total		$ 54,500
Total costs:		
Direct material		50,000
Conversion: Preparation	$ 30,000	
Finishing	24,000	
Packaging	500	
Total conversion costs		54,500
Total		$104,500

Predetermined application rates for conversion costs:*

Preparation Department:
$$\frac{\text{Budgeted conversion costs}}{\text{Budgeted production}} = \frac{\$30,000}{4,000 \text{ units}} = \$7.50 \text{ per unit}$$

Finishing Department:
$$\frac{\text{Budgeted conversion costs}}{\text{Budgeted production}} = \frac{\$24,000}{4,000 \text{ units}} = \$6.00 \text{ per unit}$$

Packaging Department:
$$\frac{\text{Budgeted conversion costs}}{\text{Budgeted units packaged}} = \frac{\$500}{1,000 \text{ units}} = \$.50 \text{ per unit}$$

*The cost driver (or activity base) is the number of units processed.

identified by *batch*. The conversion costs, however, are associated with the two production departments and the Packaging Department.

The product cost for each of the footballs is computed as follows:

	Match	Practice
Direct material:		
Batch P19 ($20,000 ÷ 1,000)	$20.00	
Batch S28 ($30,000 ÷ 3,000)		$10.00
Conversion: Preparation Department		
(conversion costs of $30,000 ÷ 4,000 units produced)*	7.50	7.50
Conversion: Finishing Department		
(conversion costs of $24,000 ÷ 4,000 units produced)*	6.00	6.00
Conversion: Packaging Department		
(conversion costs of $500 ÷ 1,000 units packaged)*	.50	–0–
Total product cost	$34.00	$23.50

*The two production departments each worked on a total of 4,000 balls, but the Packaging Department handled only the 1,000 match balls.

Notice in the preceding display that each ball receives the same conversion costs in the Preparation Department and the Finishing Department, since these operations are identical for the two products. Direct-material costs and packaging costs, though, differ for the products. The total costs of $104,500 (Exhibit 4–11) are accounted for in the product costs, as shown below.

Match balls: 1,000 × $34.00	$ 34,000
Practice balls: 3,000 × $23.50	70,500
Total	$104,500

The following journal entries are made to record the Nagoya plant's flow of costs. The first entry is made to record the requisition of raw material by the Preparation Department, when batch P19 is entered into production. (This amount excludes the $1,000 in packaging costs to be incurred subsequently for batch P19.)

Work-in-Process Inventory: Preparation Department	19,000	
Raw-Material Inventory		19,000

The following entry is made to record the requisition of raw material by the Preparation Department, when batch S28 is entered into production.

Work-in-Process Inventory: Preparation Department	30,000	
Raw-Material Inventory		30,000

Conversion costs are applied in the Preparation Department with the following journal entry.

Work-in-Process Inventory: Preparation Department	30,000	
Applied Conversion Costs		30,000

The following entry records the transfer of the partially completed match and practice balls to the Finishing Department.

Work-in-Process Inventory: Finishing Department	79,000	
Work-in-Process Inventory: Preparation Department		79,000

The conversion costs applied in the Finishing Department are recorded as follows:

Work-in-Process Inventory: Finishing Department	24,000	
Applied Conversion Costs		24,000

Next, the match balls are transferred to the Packaging Department, and the practice balls are transferred to finished goods.

Work-in-Process Inventory: Packaging Department	32,500	
Finished-Goods Inventory	70,500	
Work-in-Process Inventory: Finishing Department		103,000

Raw-material (packaging) costs and conversion costs are recorded in the Packaging Department as follows:

Work-in-Process Inventory: Packaging Department	1,500	
Raw-Material Inventory		1,000
Applied Conversion Costs		500

Finally, the match balls are transferred to finished goods.

Finished-Goods Inventory	34,000	
Work-in-Process Inventory: Packaging Department		34,000

Suppose that at the end of an accounting period, applied conversion costs differ from the actual conversion costs incurred. Then the difference, called overapplied or underapplied conversion costs, would be closed into Cost of Goods Sold. This accounting treatment is similar to that described in Chapter 3 for overapplied or underapplied overhead.

Chapter Summary

LO1 List and explain the similarities and important differences between job-order and process costing. Process costing is used in production processes where relatively large numbers of nearly identical products are manufactured. The purpose of a process-costing system is the same as that of a job-order costing system—to accumulate costs and assign these costs to units of product. Job-order costing is used by firms that produce relatively small numbers of dissimilar products.

LO2 Prepare journal entries to record the flow of costs in a process-costing system with sequential production departments. Costs of direct material, direct labor, and manufacturing overhead are added to a Work-in-Process Inventory account. Direct labor and manufacturing overhead often are combined into a single cost category termed *conversion costs*. When products are completed, the costs assigned to them are transferred either to Finished-Goods Inventory or to the next production department's Work-in-Process Inventory account. Finally, when goods are sold, their costs are transferred to the expense account called Cost of Goods Sold.

LO3 Prepare a table of equivalent units under weighted-average process costing. The table of equivalent units, illustrated in the chapter, computes the equivalent units of activity for the period for both direct material and conversion costs.

LO4 Compute the cost per equivalent unit under the weighted-average method of process costing. The cost per equivalent unit, for both direct material and conversion, is calculated as shown in the chapter. For each factor input, direct material and conversion, the cost of that input is divided by the number of equivalent units for that input.

LO5 Analyze the total production costs for a department under the weighted-average method of process costing. The total production costs incurred during the period, for both direct material and conversion, are assigned to either ending work-in-process inventory or to the cost of goods completed and transferred out.

LO6 Prepare a departmental production report under weighted-average process costing. As illustrated in the chapter, there are four steps in preparing a departmental production report: (1) analyze the physical flow of units, (2) calculate the equivalent units, (3) compute the cost per equivalent unit, and (4) analyze the total costs of the department. In the weighted-average method of process costing, the cost per equivalent unit, for each cost category, is a weighted average of (1) the costs assigned to the beginning work-in-process inventory and (2) the costs incurred during the current period.

LO7 Describe how an operation costing system accumulates and assigns the costs of direct material and conversion activity in a batch manufacturing process. Operation costing is a hybrid of job-order and process costing. It is designed for production processes in which the direct material differs significantly among product lines, but the conversion activities are essentially the same. Direct-material costs are accumulated by batches of products using job-order costing methods. Conversion costs are accumulated by production departments and are assigned to product units using process-costing methods.

Review Problem on Process Costing

The following data have been compiled for Fuji's Cutting Department for the month of June. Conversion activity occurs uniformly throughout the production process.

Work in process, June 1—25,000 units:	
Direct material: 100% complete, cost of	$ 73,750
Conversion: 40% complete, cost of	46,000
Balance in work in process, June 1	$119,750

Units started during June...	40,000
Units completed during June and transferred out	60,000

Work in process, June 30:
    Direct material: 100% complete
    Conversion: 60% complete

Costs incurred during June:

Direct material..	$121,250
Conversion costs: direct labor and applied manufacturing overhead........................	237,500

Required: Prepare the Cutting Department's June production report using weighted-average process costing. (*Hint:* Follow the format of Exhibit 4–9.)

Solution to Review Problem

The Cutting Department's June production report is displayed in Exhibit 4–12.

FUJI SPORTS EQUIPMENT COMPANY
June Production Report: Cutting Department

Exhibit 4–12
June Production Report:
Cutting Department
(weighted-average method)

	Physical Units	Percentage of Completion with Respect to Conversion	Direct Material	Conversion
			Equivalent Units	
Work in process, June 1	25,000	40%		
Units started during June	40,000			
Total units to account for	65,000			
Units completed and transferred out during June	60,000	100%	60,000	60,000
Work in process, June 30	5,000	60%	5,000	3,000
Total units accounted for	65,000			
Total equivalent units			65,000	63,000

	Direct Material	Conversion	Total
Work in process, June 1	$ 73,750	$ 46,000	$119,750
Costs incurred during June	121,250	237,500	358,750
Total costs to account for	$195,000	$283,500	$478,500
Equivalent units	65,000	63,000	
Costs per equivalent unit	$ 3.00	$ 4.50	$ 7.50
	↑	↑	↑
	$195,000 / 65,000	$283,500 / 63,000	$3.00 + $4.50

Cost of goods completed and transferred out of the Cutting Department during June:

$$\left(\begin{array}{c}\text{Number of units}\\\text{transferred out}\end{array}\right) \times \left(\begin{array}{c}\text{Total cost per}\\\text{equivalent unit}\end{array}\right) \quad 60,000 \times \$7.50 \qquad \$450,000$$

Cost remaining in June 30 work-in-process inventory in the Cutting Department:

Direct material:

$$\left(\begin{array}{c}\text{Number of equivalent}\\\text{units of direct material}\end{array}\right) \times \left(\begin{array}{c}\text{Cost per equivalent}\\\text{unit of direct material}\end{array}\right) \quad 5,000 \times \$3.00 \qquad \$ 15,000$$

Conversion:

$$\left(\begin{array}{c}\text{Number of equivalent}\\\text{units of conversion}\end{array}\right) \times \left(\begin{array}{c}\text{Cost per equivalent}\\\text{unit of conversion}\end{array}\right) \quad 3,000 \times \$4.50 \qquad 13,500$$

Total cost of June 30 work in process	$ 28,500
Check: Cost of goods completed and transferred out	$450,000
Cost of June 30 work-in-process inventory	28,500
Total costs accounted for	$478,500

Key Terms

For each term's definition refer to the indicated page, or turn to the glossary at the end of the text.

batch manufacturing, 182
departmental production
   report, 174

equivalent units, 173
hybrid product-costing
   system, 182

operation costing, 182
process-costing system, 170
repetitive production, 170

transferred-in costs, 172
weighted-average method,
   175

Review Questions

4–1. Explain the primary differences between job-order and process costing.

4–2. List five types of manufacturing in which process costing would be an appropriate product-costing system. What is the key characteristic of these products that makes process costing a good choice?

4–3. List three nonmanufacturing businesses in which process costing could be used. For example, a public accounting firm could use process costing to accumulate the costs of processing clients' tax returns.

4–4. What are the purposes of a product-costing system?

4–5. Define the term *equivalent unit* and explain how the concept is used in process costing.

4–6. List and briefly describe the purpose of each of the four process-costing steps.

4–7. Show how to prepare a journal entry to enter direct-material costs into the Work-in-Process Inventory account for the first department in a sequential production process. Show how to prepare the journal entry recording the transfer of goods from the first to the second department in the sequence.

4–8. What are *transferred-in costs?*

4–9. A food processing company has two sequential production departments: mixing and cooking. The cost of the January 1 work in process in the cooking department is detailed as follows:

Direct material	$ 79,000
Conversion	30,000
Transferred-in costs	182,000

During what time period and in what department were the $182,000 of costs listed above incurred? Explain your answer.

4–10. Explain the reasoning underlying the name of the weighted-average method.

4–11. How does process costing differ under normal or actual costing?

4–12. How would the process-costing computations differ from those illustrated in the chapter if overhead were applied on some activity base other than direct labor?

4–13. Explain the concept of *operation costing.* How does it differ from process or job-order costing? Why is operation costing well suited for batch manufacturing processes?

4–14. What is the purpose of a departmental production report prepared using process costing?

Exercises

All applicable Exercises are available with McGraw-Hill's *Connect Accounting*™.

■ **Exercise 4–15**
Physical Flow of Units
(LO 1, 3)

In each case below, fill in the missing amount.

1.	Work in Process, September 1	10,000 tonnes
	Units started during September	?
	Units completed during September	19,000 tonnes
	Work in process, September 30	2,000 tonnes
2.	Work in process, February 1	13,000 kilograms
	Units started during February	1,500 kilograms
	Units completed during February	9,800 kilograms
	Work in process, February 28	?
3.	Work in process, January 1	100,000 liters
	Units started during the year	950,000 liters
	Units completed during the year	?
	Work in process, December 31	200,000 liters

■ **Exercise 4–16**
Process Costing; Use of Internet
(LO 1)

Use the Internet to access the Web site for Weyerhaeuser (www.weyerhaeuser.com), International Paper (www.internationalpaper.com), or Boise Cascade (www.boisecascade.com).

Required: Skim over the information presented on the Web site about the company's products and operations. Then discuss why process costing is an appropriate product-costing method for this company.

Rainbow Glass Company manufactures decorative glass products. The firm employs a process-costing system for its manufacturing operations. All direct materials are added at the beginning of the process, and conversion costs are incurred uniformly throughout the process. The company's production schedule for October follows.

■ **Exercise 4–17**
Equivalent Units;
Weighted-Average
(LO 1, 3)

	Units
Work in process on October 1 (70% complete as to conversion)	1,000
Units started during October	5,000
Total units to account for	6,000
Units from beginning work in process, which were completed and transferred out during October	1,000
Units started and completed during October	3,000
Work in process on October 31 (10% complete as to conversion)	2,000
Total units accounted for	6,000

Required: Calculate each of the following amounts using weighted-average process costing.

1. Equivalent units of direct material during October.
2. Equivalent units of conversion activity during October.

(CMA, adapted)

Terra Energy Company refines a variety of petrochemical products. The following data are from the firm's Lodi plant.

■ **Exercise 4–18**
Equivalent Units;
Weighted-Average
(LO 1, 3)

Work in process, November 1	2,000,000 gallons
Direct material	100% complete
Conversion	25% complete
Units started in process during November	950,000 gallons
Work in process, November 30	240,000 gallons
Direct material	100% complete
Conversion	80% complete

Required: Compute the equivalent units of direct material and conversion for the month of November. Use the weighted-average method of process costing.

The Seoul plant of Lucky Foods Corporation produces kimchi. The following data pertain to the year just ended.

■ **Exercise 4–19**
Physical Flow and Equivalent Units; Weighted-Average
(LO 1, 3)

		Percentage of Completion	
	Units	Direct Material	Conversion
Work in process, January 1	10,000 kg.	80%	60%
Work in process, December 31	7,500 kg.	70%	30%

During the year, the company started 70,000 kilograms of material in production.

Required: Prepare a schedule analyzing the physical flow of units and computing the equivalent units of both direct material and conversion for the year. Use weighted-average process costing.

Idaho Lumber Company grows, harvests, and processes timber for use in construction. The following data pertain to the firm's sawmill during November.

■ **Exercise 4–20**
Cost per Equivalent Unit;
Weighted-Average
(LO 1, 3, 4)

Work in process, November 1:	
Direct material	$ 65,000
Conversion	180,000
Costs incurred during November:	
Direct material	$425,000
Conversion	690,000

The equivalent units of activity for November were as follows: 7,000 equivalent units of direct material and 1,740 equivalent units of conversion activity.

Required: Calculate the cost per equivalent unit, for both direct material and conversion, during November. Use weighted-average process costing.

■ **Exercise 4–21**
Cost per Equivalent Unit;
Weighted-Average
(LO 1, 3, 4)

Otsego Glass Company manufactures window glass for automobiles. The following data pertain to the Plate Glass Department.

Work in process, June 1:	
Direct material	$ 37,000
Conversion	36,750
Costs incurred during June:	
Direct material	$150,000
Conversion	230,000

The equivalent units of activity for June were as follows: 17,000 equivalent units of direct material and 48,500 equivalent units of conversion activity.

Required: Calculate the cost per equivalent unit, for both direct material and conversion, during June. Use weighted-average process costing.

■ **Exercise 4–22**
Analysis of Total Costs;
Weighted-Average
(LO 5)

Savannah Textiles Company manufactures a variety of natural fabrics for the clothing industry. The following data pertain to the Weaving Department for the month of September.

Equivalent units of direct material (weighted-average method)	60,000
Equivalent units of conversion (weighted-average method)	52,000
Units completed and transferred out during September	50,000

The cost data for September are as follows:

Work in process, September 1	
Direct material	$ 94,000
Conversion	44,400
Costs incurred during September	
Direct material	$164,000
Conversion	272,800

There were 20,000 units in process in the Weaving Department on September 1 (100% complete as to direct material and 40% complete as to conversion).

Required: Compute each of the following amounts using weighted-average process costing.

1. Cost of goods completed and transferred out of the Weaving Department.
2. Cost of the September 30 work-in-process inventory in the Weaving Department.
3. *Build a spreadsheet:* Construct an Excel spreadsheet to solve all of the preceding requirements. Show how the solution will change if the following data change: the costs incurred in September were $328,000 for direct material and $818,400 for conversion.

■ **Exercise 4–23**
Analysis of Total Costs;
Weighted-Average
(LO 5)

The following data pertain to Taipei Paperboard Company, a manufacturer of cardboard boxes.

Work in process, February 1	10,000 units*
Direct material	$ 5,500
Conversion	25,800
Costs incurred during February	
Direct material	$115,500
Conversion	171,600

*Complete as to direct material; 40% complete as to conversion.

The equivalent units of activity for February were as follows:

Direct material (weighted-average method)	110,000
Conversion (weighted-average method)	94,000
Completed and transferred out	90,000

Required: Compute the following amounts using weighted-average process costing.

1. Cost of goods completed and transferred out during February.
2. Cost of the February 28 work-in-process inventory.

■ **Exercise 4–24**
Operation Costing
(LO 7)

November production of Fuji's Nagoya plant consisted of batch P25 (2,000 match footballs) and batch S33 (4,000 practice footballs). Each batch was started and finished during November, and there was no beginning or ending work in process. Costs incurred were as follows:

Direct Material:

Batch P25, $42,000, including $2,500 for packaging material; batch S33, $45,000.

Conversion Costs:

Preparation Department, predetermined rate of $7.50 per unit; Finishing Department, predetermined rate of $6.00 per unit; Packaging Department, predetermined rate of $.50 per unit. (Only the match balls are packaged.)

Required:

1. Draw a diagram depicting the division's batch manufacturing process. Refer to Exhibit 4–10 for guidance.
2. Compute the November product cost for each type of football.
3. Prepare journal entries to record the cost flows during November.

Problems

All applicable Problems are available with McGraw-Hill's *Connect Accounting*™.

Timing Technology, Inc. manufactures timing devices. During 20x1, 1,000,000 units were completed and transferred to finished-goods inventory. On December 31, 20x1, there were 300,000 units in work in process. These units were 50 percent complete as to conversion and 100 percent complete as to direct material. Finished-goods inventory consisted of 150,000 units. Materials are added to production at the beginning of the manufacturing process, and overhead is applied to each product at the rate of 60 percent of direct-labor costs. There was no finished-goods inventory on January 1, 20x1. A review of the inventory cost records disclosed the following information:

■ **Problem 4–25**
Step-by-Step Weighted-Average Process Costing
(LO 3, 4, 5)

3. Cost per equivalent unit, total: $4.82

		Costs	
	Units	**Materials**	**Labor**
Work in process, January 1, 20x1			
(80% complete as to conversion)	200,000	$ 200,000	$ 315,000
Units started in production	1,100,000		
Direct-material costs		$1,438,000	
Direct-labor costs			$2,243,750

Required: Prepare schedules as of December 31, 20x1, to compute the following:

1. Physical flow of units.
2. Equivalent units of production using the weighted-average method.
3. Costs per equivalent unit for material and conversion.
4. Cost of the December 31, 20x1, finished-goods inventory and work-in-process inventory.

(CMA, adapted)

■ **Problem 4–26**
Straightforward Weighted-Average Process Costing, Step-by-Step Approach
(LO 3, 4, 5)

2. Total equivalent units, conversion: 226,000

Piscataway Plastics Company manufactures a highly specialized plastic that is used extensively in the automobile industry. The following data have been compiled for the month of June. Conversion activity occurs uniformly throughout the production process.

Work in process, June 1—50,000 units:

Direct material: 100% complete cost of	$120,000
Conversion: 40% complete, cost of	34,400
Balance in work in process, June 1	$154,400
Units started during June	200,000
Units completed during June and transferred out to finished-goods inventory	190,000

Work in process, June 30:

Direct material: 100% complete

Conversion: 60% complete

Costs incurred during June:

Direct material	$492,500
Conversion costs:	
Direct labor	$ 87,450
Applied manufacturing overhead	262,350
Total conversion costs	$349,800

Required: Prepare schedules to accomplish each of the following process-costing steps for the month of June. Use the weighted-average method of process costing.

1.   Analysis of physical flow of units.
2.   Calculation of equivalent units.
3.   Computation of unit costs.
4.   Analysis of total costs.

■ **Problem 4–27**
Missing Data; Production Report; Weighted-Average
(LO 4, 5, 6)

Cost remaining in ending work-in-process inventory, direct material: $123,750
Total cost of July 31 work in process: $202,950

The following data pertain to the Vesuvius Tile Company for July.

Work in process, July 1 (in units)	20,000
Units started during July	?
Total units to account for	65,000
Units completed and transferred out during July	?
Work in process, July 31 (in units)	15,000
Total equivalent units: direct material	65,000
Total equivalent units: conversion	?
Work in process, July 1: direct material	$164,400
Work in process, July 1: conversion	?
Costs incurred during July: direct material	?
Costs incurred during July: conversion	659,400
Work in process, July 1: total cost	244,200
Total costs incurred during July	1,031,250
Total costs to account for	1,275,450
Cost per equivalent unit: direct material	8.25
Cost per equivalent unit: conversion	?
Total cost per equivalent unit	21.45
Cost of goods completed and transferred out during July..	?
Cost remaining in ending work-in-process inventory: direct material	?
Cost remaining in ending work-in-process inventory: conversion	79,200
Total cost of July 31 work in process	202,950

Additional Information:

a.   Direct material is added at the beginning of the production process, and conversion activity occurs uniformly throughout the process.

b.   The company uses weighted-average process costing.

c. The July 1 work in process was 30 percent complete as to conversion.

d. The July 31 work in process was 40 percent complete as to conversion.

Required: Compute the missing amounts, and prepare the firm's July production report.

Triangle Fastener Corporation accumulates costs for its single product using process costing. Direct material is added at the beginning of the production process, and conversion activity occurs uniformly throughout the process. A partially completed production report for the month of May follows.

■ **Problem 4–28**
Partial Production Report;
Journal Entries; Weighted-
Average Method
(LO 2, 3, 4, 5)

1(b). Cost per equivalent unit, direct material: $5.60

Production Report
For the Month of May

	Physical Units	Percentage of Completion with Respect to Conversion	Equivalent Units	
			Direct Material	Conversion
Work in process, May 1	25,000	40%		
Units started during May	30,000			
Total units to account for	55,000			
Units completed and transferred out during May	35,000		35,000	35,000
Work in process, May 31	20,000	80%	20,000	16,000
Total units accounted for	55,000			

	Direct Material	Conversion	Total
Work in process, May 1	$143,000	$ 474,700	$ 617,700
Costs incurred during May	165,000	2,009,000	2,174,000
Total costs to account for	$308,000	$2,483,700	$2,791,700

Required:

1. Complete each of the following process-costing steps using the weighted-average method:
   a. Calculation of equivalent units.
   b. Computation of unit costs.
   c. Analysis of total costs.
2. Prepare a journal entry to record the transfer of the cost of goods completed and transferred out during May.

Moravia Company processes and packages cheese. The following data have been compiled for the month of April. Conversion activity occurs uniformly throughout the production process.

■ **Problem 4–29**
Straightforward Weighted-
Average Process Costing;
Step-by-Step Approach
(LO 3, 4, 5)

2. Equivalent units, direct material: 110,000

Work in process, April 1—10,000 units:	
Direct material: 100% complete, cost of	$ 22,000
Conversion: 20% complete, cost of	4,500
Balance in work in process, April 1	$ 26,500
Units started during April	100,000
Units completed during April and transferred out to finished-goods inventory	80,000
Work in process, April 30:	
Direct material: 100% complete	
Conversion: 33⅓% complete	
Costs incurred during April:	
Direct material	$198,000
Conversion costs:	
Direct labor	$ 55,800
Applied manufacturing overhead	111,600
Total conversion costs	$167,400

Required: Prepare schedules to accomplish each of the following process-costing steps for the month of April. Use the weighted-average method of process costing.

1.   Analysis of physical flow of units.
2.   Calculation of equivalent units.
3.   Computation of unit costs.
4.   Analysis of total costs.
5.   *Build a spreadsheet:* Construct an Excel spreadsheet to solve all of the preceding requirements. Show how the solution will change if the following data change: the April 1 work-in-process costs were $66,000 for direct material and $18,000 for conversion.

■ **Problem 4–30**
Partial Production Report; Journal Entries; Weighted-Average Method
(LO 2, 3, 4, 5)

2. Cost per equivalent unit, total: $11.43
5. Work-in-Process Inventory (credit): $1,143,000

Albany Company accumulates costs for its product using process costing. Direct material is added at the beginning of the production process, and conversion activity occurs uniformly throughout the process.

Production Report
For August 20x1

	Physical Units	Percentage of Completion with Respect to Conversion	Equivalent Units Direct Material	Conversion
Work in process, August 1	40,000	80%		
Units started during August	80,000			
Total units to account for	120,000			
Units completed and transferred out during August	100,000		100,000	100,000
Work in process, August 31	20,000	30%	20,000	6,000
Total units accounted for	120,000			

	Direct Material	Conversion	Total
Work in process, August 1	$ 42,000	$ 305,280	$ 347,280
Costs incurred during August	96,000	784,400	880,400
Total costs to account for	$138,000	$1,089,680	$1,227,680

Required: Use weighted-average process costing in completing the following requirements.

1.   Prepare a schedule of equivalent units.
2.   Compute the costs per equivalent unit.
3.   Compute the cost of goods completed and transferred out during August.
4.   Compute the cost remaining in the work-in-process inventory on August 31.
5.   Prepare a journal entry to record the transfer of the cost of goods completed and transferred out during August.

■ **Problem 4–31**
Determination of Production Costs; Analysis of Equivalent Units
(LO 3, 4, 5)

1. Overhead applied: $379,500
3. Cost of ending work-in-process inventory: $324,000

Goodson Corporation assembles various components used in the telecommunications industry. The company's major product, a relay switch, is the result of assembling three parts: XY634, AA788, and GU321. The following information relates to activities of April:

• Beginning work-in-process inventory: 4,000 units, 75 percent complete as to conversion; cost, $286,000 (direct materials, $220,000; conversion cost, $66,000).

• Production started: 25,000 units.

• Production completed: 24,000 units.

• Ending work-in-process inventory: 5,000 units, 40 percent complete as to conversion.

• Direct materials used: XY634, $267,000; AA788, $689,000; GU321, $448,000.

• Hourly wage of direct laborers, $20; total direct-labor payroll, $126,500.

• Overhead application rate: $60 per direct-labor hour.

All parts are introduced at the beginning of Goodson's manufacturing process; conversion cost is incurred uniformly throughout production.

Required:

1. Calculate the total cost of direct material and conversion during April.
2. Determine the cost of goods completed during the month.
3. Determine the cost of the work-in-process inventory on April 30.
4. With regard to the ending work-in-process inventory:
   a. How much direct-material cost would be added to these units in May?
   b. What percentage of conversion would be performed on these units in May?
5. Assume that the relay switch required the addition of another part (HH887) at the 70 percent stage of completion. How many equivalent units with respect to part HH887 would be represented in April's ending work-in-process inventory?

A-1 Products manufactures wooden furniture using an assembly-line process. All direct materials are introduced at the start of the process, and conversion cost is incurred evenly throughout manufacturing. An examination of the company's Work-in-Process Inventory account for June revealed the following selected information:

Debit side:

    June 1 balance: 300 units, 30% complete as to conversion, cost $21,300*

    Production started: 900 units

    Direct material used during June: $45,000

    June conversion cost: $25,700

Credit side:

    Production completed: 700 units

*Supplementary records revealed direct-material cost of $15,000 and conversion cost of $6,300.

Conversations with manufacturing personnel revealed that the ending work in process was 60 percent complete as to conversion.

Required:

1. Determine the number of units in the June 30 work-in-process inventory.
2. Calculate the cost of goods completed during June and prepare the appropriate journal entry to record completed production.
3. Determine the cost of the June 30 work-in-process inventory.
4. Briefly explain the meaning of equivalent units. Why are equivalent units needed to properly allocate costs between completed production and production in process?

The following data pertain to the Hercules Tire and Rubber Company for the month of May.

■ **Problem 4–32**
Analysis of Work-in-Process
Inventory Account
(LO 3, 4, 5)

3. Cost of June 30 work-in-process inventory: $34,600

■ **Problem 4–33**
Missing Data; Production
Report; Weighted-Average
(LO 4, 5, 6)

Total equivalent units, conversion: 71,000
Total cost of May 31 work-in-process: $170,000

Work in process, May 1 (in units)	?
Units started during May	60,000
Total units to account for	75,000
Units completed and transferred out during May	?
Work in process, May 31 (in units)	10,000
Total equivalent units: direct material	75,000
Total equivalent units: conversion	?
Work in process, May 1: direct material	$135,000
Work in process, May 1: conversion	?
Costs incurred during May: direct material	?
Costs incurred during May: conversion	850,000
Work in process, May 1: total cost	172,500
Total costs incurred during May	1,427,500
Total costs to account for	1,600,000
Cost per equivalent unit: direct material	9.50
Cost per equivalent unit: conversion	?
Total cost per equivalent unit	22.00
Cost of goods completed and transferred out during May	?
Cost remaining in ending work-in-process inventory: direct material	?
Cost remaining in ending work-in-process inventory: conversion	75,000
Total cost of May 31 work in process	170,000

Additional Information:

a.   Direct material is added at the beginning of the production process, and conversion activity occurs uniformly throughout the process.

b.   Hercules uses weighted-average process costing.

c.   The May 1 work in process was 20 percent complete as to conversion.

d.   The May 31 work in process was 60 percent complete as to conversion.

Required: Compute the missing amounts, and prepare the firm's May production report.

■ **Problem 4–34**
Process Costing in a Public Accounting Firm
(LO 3, 4, 5)

2. Total cost of returns in process, February 28: £14,250

Scrooge and Zilch, a public accounting firm in London, is engaged in the preparation of income tax returns for individuals. The firm uses the weighted-average method of process costing for internal reporting. The following information pertains to February. (£ denotes the British monetary unit, pounds sterling.)[*]

Returns in process, February 1:	
(25% complete)	200
Returns started in February	825
Returns in process, February 28:	
(80% complete)	125
Returns in process, February 1:	
Labor	£ 6,000
Overhead	2,500
Labor, February (4,000 hours)	89,000
Overhead, February	45,000

*Although the euro is used in most European markets, day-to-day business in the United Kingdom continues to be conducted in pounds sterling.

Required:

1.   Compute the following amounts for labor and for overhead:

   a.   Equivalent units of activity.

   b.   Cost per equivalent unit. (Remember to express your answer in terms of the British pound sterling, denoted by £.)

2.   Compute the cost of returns in process as of February 28.

(CMA, adapted)

■ **Problem 4–35**
Process Costing; Production Report; Journal Entries; Weighted-Average Method
(LO 2, 3, 4, 5, 6)

Cost of goods completed and transferred out, November: $306,750

Hyderabad Fertilizer Company manufactures a high-quality fertilizer, which is used primarily by commercial vegetable growers. Two departments are involved in the production process. In the Mixing Department, various chemicals are entered into production. After processing, the Mixing Department transfers a chemical called Chemgro to the Finishing Department. There the product is completed, packaged, and shipped under the brand name Vegegro.

In the Mixing Department, the raw material is added at the beginning of the process. Labor and overhead are applied continuously throughout the process. All direct departmental overhead is traced to the departments, and plant overhead is allocated to the departments on the basis of direct-labor. The plant overhead rate for 20x2 is $.40 per direct-labor dollar.

The following information relates to production during November 20x2 in the Mixing Department.

a.   Work in process, November 1 (4,000 kilograms, 75 percent complete as to conversion):

Raw material	$22,800
Direct labor at $5.00 per hour	24,200
Departmental overhead	8,000
Allocated plant overhead	9,680

b. Raw material:

Inventory, November 1, 2,000 kilograms	$10,000
Purchases, November 3, 10,000 kilograms	51,000
Purchases, November 18, 10,000 kilograms	51,500
Released to production during November, 16,000 kilograms	

c. Direct-labor cost, $107,000

d. Direct departmental overhead costs, $52,000

e. Transferred to Finishing Department, 15,000 kilograms

f. Work in process, November 30, 5,000 kilograms, 20 percent complete

The company uses weighted-average process costing to accumulate product costs. However, for raw-material inventories, the firm uses the FIFO inventory method.

Required:

1. Prepare a production report for the Mixing Department for November 20x2. The report should show:
   a. Equivalent units of production by cost factor (i.e., direct material and conversion).
   b. Cost per equivalent unit for each cost factor.
   c. Cost of Chemgro transferred to the Finishing Department.
   d. Cost of the work-in-process inventory on November 30 20x2, in the Mixing Department.

2. Prepare journal entries to record the following events:
   a. Release of direct material to production during November.
   b. Incurrence of direct-labor costs in November.
   c. Application of overhead costs for the Mixing Department (direct departmental and allocated plant overhead costs.)
   d. Transfer of Chemgro out of the Mixing Department.

(CMA, adapted)

■ Problem 4–36
Operation Costing; Unit Costs; Journal Entries
(LO 7)

1. Total product cost, deluxe model: $207,900

Plasto Corporation manufactures a variety of plastic products including a series of molded chairs. The three models of molded chairs, which are all variations of the same design, are Standard (can be stacked), Deluxe (with arms), and Executive (with arms and padding). The company uses batch manufacturing and has an operation-costing system. The production process includes an extrusion operation and subsequent operations to form, trim, and finish the chairs. Plastic sheets are produced by the extrusion operation, some of which are sold directly to other manufacturers. During the forming operation, the remaining plastic sheets are molded into chair seats and the legs are added; the Standard model is sold after this operation. During the trim operation, the arms are added to the Deluxe and Executive models and the chair edges are smoothed. Only the Executive model enters the finish operation where the padding is added. All of the units produced receive the same steps within each operation. The March production run had a total manufacturing cost of $898,000. The units of production and direct-material costs incurred were as follows:

	Units Produced	Extrusion Materials	Form Materials	Trim Materials	Finish Materials
Plastic sheets	5,000	$ 60,000			
Standard model	6,000	72,000	$24,000		
Deluxe model	3,000	36,000	12,000	$ 9,000	
Executive model	2,000	24,000	8,000	6,000	$12,000
Total	16,000	$192,000	$44,000	$15,000	$12,000

Manufacturing costs applied during the month of May were as follows:

	Extrusion Operation	Form Operation	Trim Operation	Finish Operation
Direct labor	$152,000	$60,000	$30,000	$18,000
Manufacturing overhead	240,000	72,000	39,000	24,000

Required:

1. For each product produced by Plasto Corporation during the month of May, determine the (*a*) unit cost and (*b*) total cost. Be sure to account for all costs incurred during the month.

2. Prepare journal entries to record the flow of production costs during May.

(CMA, adapted)

■ **Problem 4–37**
Operation Costing; Unit Costs
(LO 7)

2. Conversion cost per unit,
department II: $10.00
5. Cost of etched, colored
glass sheet: $76.25 per sheet

(Contributed by Roland Minch.) Glass Glow Company manufactures a variety of glass windows in its Glasgow plant. In department I, clear glass sheets are produced, and some of these sheets are sold as finished goods. Other sheets made in department I have metallic oxides added in department II to form colored glass sheets. Some of these colored sheets are sold; others are moved to department III for etching and then are sold. The company uses operation costing.

Glass Glow Company's production costs applied to products in May are given in the following table. There was no beginning or ending inventory of work in process for May.

Cost Category	Dept. I	Dept. II	Dept. III
Direct material	$450,000	$72,000	–0–
Direct labor	38,000	22,000	$38,000
Manufacturing overhead	230,000	68,000	73,750

Products	Units	Dept. I Dir. Mat.	Dept. II Dir. Mat.
Clear glass, sold after dept. I	11,000	$247,500	–0–
Unetched colored glass, sold after dept. II	4,000	90,000	$32,000
Etched colored glass, sold after dept. III	5,000	112,500	40,000

Each sheet of glass requires the same steps within each operation.

Required: Compute each of the following amounts.

1. The conversion cost per unit in department I.
2. The conversion cost per unit in department II.
3. The cost of a clear glass sheet.
4. The cost of an unetched colored glass sheet.
5. The cost of an etched colored glass sheet.

■ **Problem 4–38**
Operation Costing; Unit Cost;
Cost Flow; Journal Entries
(LO 7)

2. Unit cost, reflective
ceralam housing: $200.00

Orbital Industries of Canada, Inc. manufactures a variety of materials and equipment for the aerospace industry. A team of R & D engineers in the firm's Winnipeg plant has developed a new material that will be useful for a variety of purposes in orbiting satellites and spacecraft. Trademarked Ceralam, the material combines some of the best properties of both ceramics and laminated plastics. Ceralam is already being used for a variety of housings in satellites produced in three different countries. Ceralam sheets are produced in an operation called rolling, in which the various materials are rolled together to form a multilayer laminate. Orbital Industries sells many of these Ceralam sheets just after the rolling operation to aerospace firms worldwide. However, Orbital also processes many of the Ceralam sheets further in the Winnipeg plant. After rolling, the sheets are sent to the molding operation, where they are formed into various shapes used to house a variety of instruments. After molding, the sheets are sent to the punching operation, where holes are punched in the molded sheets to accommodate protruding instruments, electrical conduits, and so forth. Some of the molded and punched sheets are then sold. The remaining units are sent to the dipping operation, in which the molded sheets are dipped in a special chemical mixture to give them a reflective surface.

During the month of March, the following products were manufactured at the Winnipeg plant. The direct-material costs also are shown.

	Units	Direct Materials Used in Ceralam Sheets	Direct Materials Used in Dipping
Ceralam sheets (sold after the rolling operation)	12,000	$480,000	
Nonreflective housings (sold after the punching operation)	5,000	200,000	
Reflective housings (sold after the dipping operation)	3,000	120,000	$30,000
Total	20,000	$800,000	$30,000

The costs incurred in producing the various Ceralam products in the Winnipeg plant during March are shown in the following table. Manufacturing overhead is applied on the basis of direct-labor dollars at the rate of 150 percent.

	Rolling	Molding	Punching	Dipping
Direct material	$ 800,000	–0–	–0–	$ 30,000
Direct labor	300,000	$112,000	$128,000	45,000
Manufacturing overhead	450,000	168,000	192,000	67,500
Total	$1,550,000	$280,000	$320,000	$142,500

Orbital Industries of Canada uses operation costing for its Ceralam operations in the Winnipeg plant.

Required:

1. Prepare a table that includes the following information *for each of the four operations.*
   - Total conversion costs.
   - Units manufactured.
   - Conversion cost per unit.

2. Prepare a second table that includes the following information *for each product* (i.e., rolled Ceralam sheets, nonreflective Ceralam housings, and reflective Ceralam housings).
   - Total manufacturing costs.
   - Units manufactured.
   - Total cost per unit.

3. Prepare journal entries to record the flow of all manufacturing costs through the Winnipeg plant's Ceralam operations during March. (Ignore the journal entries to record sales revenue.)

4. *Build a spreadsheet:* Construct an Excel spreadsheet to solve requirements 1 and 2 above. Show how the solution will change if the following data change: the cost of direct material used in dipping was $45,000 and the overhead application rate is 200% of direct-labor cost.

Case

Laredo Leather Company manufactures high-quality leather goods. The company's profits have declined during the past nine months. In an attempt to isolate the causes of poor profit performance, management is investigating the manufacturing operations of each of its products.

One of the company's main products is leather belts. The belts are produced in a single, continuous process in the Dallas Plant. During the process, leather strips are sewn, punched, and dyed. The belts then enter a final finishing stage to conclude the process. Labor and overhead are applied continuously during the manufacturing process. All materials, leather strips, and buckles are introduced at the beginning of the process. The firm uses the weighted-average method to calculate its unit costs.

The leather belts produced at the Dallas Plant are sold wholesale for $9.95 each. Management wants to compare the current manufacturing costs per unit with the market prices for leather belts. Top management has asked the Dallas plant controller to submit data on the cost of manufacturing the leather belts for the month of October. These cost data will be used to determine whether modifications

■ **Case 4–39**
Weighted-Average Process Costing; Ethics
(LO 3,4, 5, 6)

4. Weighted-average unit cost of completed leather belts: $6.10
Total cost of October 31 work in process: $4,700

in the production process should be initiated or whether an increase in the selling price of the belts is justified. The cost per belt used for planning and control is $5.35.

The work-in-process inventory consisted of 400 partially completed units on October 1. The belts were 25 percent complete as to conversion. The costs included in the inventory on October 1 were as follows:

Leather strips	$ 990
Buckles	260
Conversion costs	300
Total	$1,550

During October 7,600 leather strips were placed into production. A total of 7,000 leather belts were completed. The work-in-process inventory on October 31 consisted of 1,000 belts, which were 50 percent complete as to conversion.

The costs charged to production during October were as follows:

Leather strips	$19,900
Buckles	5,250
Conversion costs	20,700
Total	$45,850

Required: In order to provide cost data regarding the manufacture of leather belts in the Dallas Plant to the top management of Laredo Leather Company, compute the following amounts for the month of October.

1. The equivalent units for material and conversion.

2. The cost per equivalent unit of material and conversion.

3. The assignment of production costs to the October 31 work-in-process inventory and to goods transferred out.

4. The weighted-average unit cost of leather belts completed and transferred to finished goods. Comment on the company's cost per belt used for planning and control.

5. Laredo Leather Company's production manager, Jack Murray, has been under pressure from the company president to reduce the cost of conversion. In spite of several attempts to reduce conversion costs, they have remained more or less constant. Now Murray is faced with an upcoming meeting with the company president, at which he will have to explain why he has failed to reduce conversion costs. Murray has approached his friend, Jeff Daley, who is the corporate controller, with the following request: "Jeff, I'm under pressure to reduce costs in the production process. There is no way to reduce material cost, so I've got to get the conversion costs down. If I can show just a little progress in next week's meeting with the president, then I can buy a little time to try some other cost-cutting measures I've been considering. I want you to do me a favor. If we raise the estimate of the percentage of completion of October's inventory to 60 percent, that will increase the number of equivalent units. Then the unit conversion cost will be a little lower." By how much would Murray's suggested manipulation lower the unit conversion cost? What should Daley do? Discuss this situation, citing specific ethical standards for managerial accountants.

(CMA, adapted)

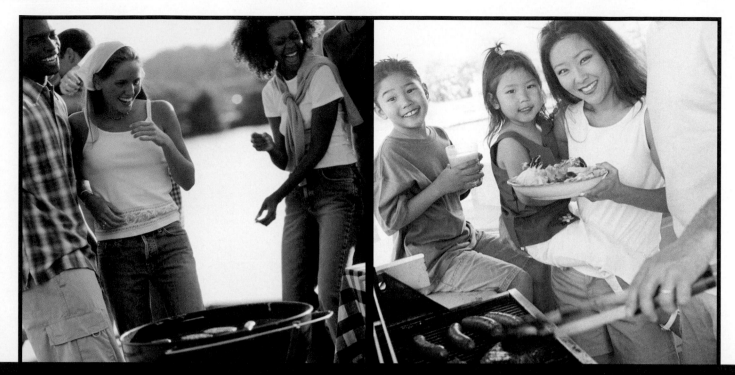

THIS CHAPTER'S FOCUS COMPANY is the Patio Grill Company, which manufactures high-end gas barbeque grills in its Denver plant. The company has recently experienced intense competition in its two high-volume product lines, forcing management to drop these products' prices below their target levels. A careful study of this situation revealed that

Patio Grill Company's traditional product-costing system distorted the product costs by assigning too much cost to the high-volume gas-grill lines and not enough cost to the low-volume, complex line of grills. Management then implemented a new costing system, called activity-based costing, or ABC, which assigns product costs more accurately than traditional product-costing systems. Armed with the cost insights from the ABC system, management was able to change its pricing structure to compete more effectively in the gas-grill market.

5 Activity-Based Costing and Management

In contrast to the manufacturing setting of the Patio Grill Company, we explore the use of activity-based costing by the Delaware Medical Center's Primary Care Unit. ABC is used in this health care services setting to assign treatment costs to categories of patient visits, such as routine, extended, and complex visits, as well as new and continuing patients.

1 Compute product costs under a traditional, volume-based product-costing system.

2 Explain how an activity-based costing system operates, including the use of a two-stage procedure for cost assignment, the identification of activity cost pools, and the selection of cost drivers.

3 Explain the concept of cost levels, including unit-level, batch-level, product-sustaining-level, and facility-level costs.

4 Compute product costs under an activity-based costing system.

5 Explain why traditional, volume-based costing systems tend to distort product costs.

6 Explain three criteria for selecting cost drivers.

7 Discuss several key issues in activity-based costing, including data collection and storyboarding.

8 Explain the concepts of activity-based management and two-dimensional ABC.

9 Explain and execute a customer-profitability analysis.

10 Understand and discuss how activity-based costing is used in service-industry organizations.

11 List and explain eight important features of just-in-time inventory and production management systems (Appendix).

A revolution is transforming the world of business. Not since the mid-19th century have we seen changes as sweeping and dramatic. The growth of global competition, the break-neck pace of technological innovation, and startling advances in computerized systems have created a new playing field for manufacturers around the world. Some manufacturers have emerged as world-class producers, while others have fallen by the wayside. World-class companies such as Hyundai, Coca-Cola, Johnson & Johnson, and GlaxoSmithKline are among the many manufacturers that have changed key business processes to compete effectively in the 21st century.

The service industry also is undergoing dramatic transformation. The growth of the Internet, the trend toward a service economy, and the willingness of businesses to outsource many critical service functions have caused many service organizations to reinvent the way they do business. Among the many service-industry firms that have adapted most successfully to the changing business environment are American Express, HSBC, FedEx, Google, and Singapore Airlines.

What is the role of managerial accounting in this rapidly changing environment? To explore this issue, we will review recent events in the life of Patio Grill Company, a manufacturer of barbeque grills and accessories. The company's Denver plant manufactures three product lines, all high-end gas barbeque grills. The plant's three gas grill lines are the Patio Standard (STD), the Deluxe (DEL), and the Ultimate (ULT).

Traditional, Volume-Based Product-Costing System

Until recently, Patio Grill Company's Denver plant used a job-order product-costing system similar to the one described in Chapter 3 for Barcos Belém. The cost of each product was the sum of its actual direct-material cost, actual direct-labor cost, and applied manufacturing overhead. Overhead was applied using a predetermined overhead rate based on direct-labor hours. Exhibit 5–1 provides the basic data upon which the traditional costing system was based.

> **Learning Objective 1**
>
> Compute product costs under a traditional, volume-based product-costing system.

The Excel spreadsheet in Exhibit 5–2 shows the calculation of the product cost for each of three gas-grill lines (STD, DEL, and ULT). Overhead is applied to the products at the rate of $24 per direct-labor hour. Notice that all of the Denver plant's budgeted manufacturing overhead costs are lumped together in a single cost pool. This total budgeted overhead amount ($4,896,000) then is divided by the plant's total budgeted direct-labor hours (204,000 hours). The 204,000 direct-labor hours is also equal to the plant's practical capacity for production, as expressed in terms of direct-labor hours.

Patio Grill Company's labor-hour-based product-costing system is typical of many manufacturing companies. Labor hours are related closely to the volume of activity in the factory, which sometimes is referred to as *throughput*. Consequently, these traditional product-costing systems often are said to be **volume-based** (or **throughput-based**) **costing systems.**

Trouble in Denver

The profitability of Patio Grill Company's Denver operation has been faltering in recent years. The company's pricing policy has been to set a target price for each grill equal to 120 percent of the full product cost. Thus, the prices were determined as shown in Exhibit 5 3. Also shown are the actual prices that Patio Grill Company has been obtaining for its products.

Due to price competition from other grill manufacturers, Patio Standard (STD) grills were selling at $585, approximately $10 below their target price of $595.20. Moreover, Patio Grill Company's competition had forced management to reduce the price of the Deluxe grill (DEL) to $705, almost $20 below its target price of $724.80. Even at this lower price, the sales team was having difficulty getting orders for its planned volume of Deluxe grill production. Fortunately, the disappointing profitability of the Patio Standard and Deluxe model grills was partially offset by greater-than-expected profits on the Ultimate (ULT) line of grills. Patio Grill Company's sales personnel had discovered that the company was swamped with orders when the Ultimate grill's target price of $902.40 was charged. Consequently, management had raised the price on the Ultimate grills several times, and eventually the product was selling for $940. Even at this price, Patio Grill Company's customers did not seem to hesitate to place orders. Moreover, the company's

	Patio Standard Grill STD	Deluxe Grill DEL	Ultimate Grill ULT
Planned annual production:			
Volume in units	10,000	8,000	2,000
Production runs	80 runs of 125 units each	80 runs of 100 units each	40 runs of 50 units each
Direct material	$100	$120	$180
Direct labor (not including setup time)	$180 (9 hours @ $20 per hour)	$220 (11 hours @ $20 per hour)	$260 (13 hours @ $20 per hour)
Machine hours (MH) per product unit	10 MH	12 MH	17 MH
Total machine hours consumed by product line	100,000 (10 MH × 10,000 units)	96,000 (12 MH × 8,000 units)	34,000 (17 MH × 2,000 units)

Exhibit 5–1
Basic Production and Cost Data: Patio Grill Company

Exhibit 5-2

Product Costs from
Traditional, Volume-Based
Product-Costing System:
Patio Grill Company

Microsoft Excel - Product Costs from Traditional, Volume-Based Product-Costing System

File Edit View Insert Format Tools Data Window Help   Type a question for help

G7   fx =SUM(G3:G6)

	A	B	C	D	E	F	G	H
1			STD		DEL		ULT	
2								
3	Direct material		$100.00		$120.00		$180.00	
4	Direct labor							
5	(not including set-up time)		180.00	(9 hr. @ $20)	220.00	(11 hr. @ $20)	260.00	(13 hr. @ $20)
6	Manufacturing overhead*		216.00	(9 hr. @ $24)	264.00	(11 hr. @ $24)	312.00	(13 hr. @ $24)
7	Total		$496.00		$604.00		$752.00	
8								
9								
10	*Calculation of predetermined-overhead rate:							
11								
12	Budgeted manufacturing overhead			$4,896,000				
13								
14	Direct labor, budgeted hours:							
15	STD: 10,000 units x 9 hours			90,000				
16	DEL: 8,000 units x 11 hours			88,000				
17	ULT: 2,000 units x 13 hours			26,000				
18	Total direct-labor hours			204,000	hours			
19								
20	Predetermined overhead rate:							
21	(Budgeted manufacturing overhead / Budgeted direct-labor hours) = $4,896,000 / 204,000 = $24 per hour							

Sheet1 / Sheet2 / Sheet3 /

Ready

competitors did not mount a challenge in the market for the Ultimate line of grills. Patio's management was pleased to have a niche for the Ultimate grill market, which appeared to be a highly profitable, low-volume specialty product. Nevertheless, concern continued to mount in Denver about the difficulty in the Patio Standard and Deluxe grill markets. After all, these were the Denver plant's core products, with projected annual sales of 10,000 Patio Standard grills and 8,000 Deluxe grills.

Activity-Based Costing System

Learning Objective 2

Explain how an activity-based
costing system operates,
including the use of a two-
stage procedure for cost
assignment, the identification
of activity cost pools, and the
selection of cost drivers.

Patio Grill Company's director of cost management, Hamilton Burger, had been thinking for some time about a refinement in the Denver plant's product-costing system. He wondered if the traditional, volume-based system was providing management with accurate data about product costs. Burger had read about **activity-based costing (ABC) systems,** which follow a two-stage procedure to assign overhead costs to products. The first stage identifies significant activities in the production of the three products and assigns overhead costs to each activity in accordance with the cost of the organization's resources used by the activity. The overhead costs assigned to each activity comprise an **activity cost pool.**

After assigning overhead costs to activity cost pools in stage one, cost drivers appropriate for each cost pool are identified in stage two. Then the overhead costs are allocated from each activity cost pool to each product line in proportion to the amount of the cost driver consumed by the product line.

Exhibit 5-3

Target and Actual Selling
Prices: Patio Grill Company

	Patio Standard Grill STD	Deluxe Grill DEL	Ultimate Grill ULT
Production cost under traditional, volume-based system (Exhibit 5–2)	$496.00	$604.00	$752.00
Target selling price (cost × 120%)	595.20	724.80	902.40
Actual current selling price	585.00	705.00	940.00

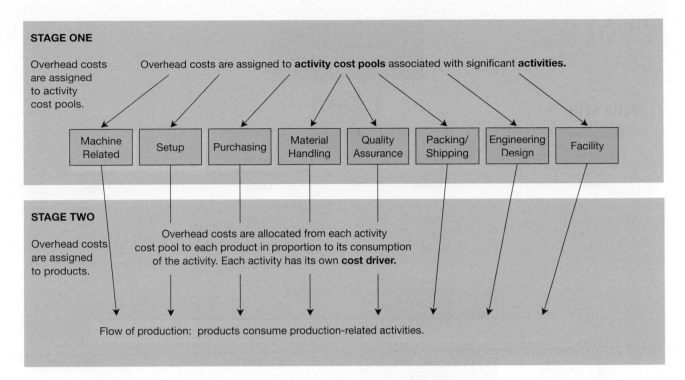

Exhibit 5–4
Activity-Based Costing System

The two-stage cost-assignment process of activity-based costing is depicted in Exhibit 5–4.

Burger discussed activity-based costing with Patty Cook, the assistant director of cost management. Together they met with all of Patio Grill Company's department supervisors to discuss development of an ABC system. After initial discussion, an ABC proposal was made to the company's top management. Approval was obtained, and an ABC project team was formed, which included Burger, Cook, and representatives of various functional departments. Through several months of painstaking data collection and analysis, the project team was able to gather the data necessary to implement an ABC system.

ABC Stage One

Patio Grill Company's ABC project team identified eight activity cost pools, which fall into four broad categories.

1. *Unit level.* This type of activity must be done for each unit of production. The machine-related activity cost pool represents a **unit-level activity** since every product unit requires machine time.

2. *Batch level.* These activities must be performed for each batch of products, rather than each unit. Patio Grill Company's **batch-level activities** include the setup, purchasing, material handling, quality assurance, and packing/shipping activity cost pools.

3. *Product-sustaining level.* This category includes activities that are needed to support an entire product line but are not performed every time a new unit or batch of products is produced. Patio Grill Company's project team identified engineering design costs as a **product-sustaining-level activity** cost pool.

4. *Facility (or general operations) level.* **Facility-level activities** are required in order for the entire production process to occur. Examples of such activity costs include plant management salaries, plant depreciation, property taxes, plant maintenance, and insurance.

This classification of activities into unit-level, batch-level, product-sustaining-level, and facility-level activities is called a **cost hierarchy.**

Learning Objective 3

Explain the concept of cost levels, including unit-level, batch-level, product-sustaining-level, and facility-level costs.

Exhibit 5–5
Stage One of Activity-Based
Costing: Identification of
Activity Cost Pools

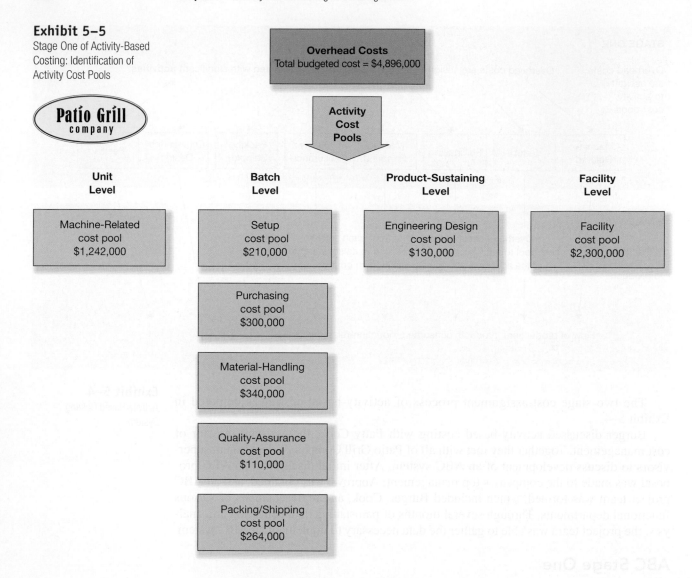

Patio Grill Company's eight activity cost pools are depicted in Exhibit 5–5. Notice that the total overhead cost for all eight activity cost pools, $4,896,000, is shown at the top of Exhibit 5–5. This amount is the same as the total overhead cost shown in Exhibit 5–2, which shows the details of the product costs calculated under Patio Grill Company's traditional product-costing system.

ABC Stage Two

In stage two of the activity-based costing project, Burger and Cook identified cost drivers for each activity cost pool. Then they used a three-step process to compute unit activity costs for each of Patio Grill Company's three product lines, and for each of the eight activity cost pools. In the following sections, we will discuss in detail how stage two of the ABC project was carried out for the various activity cost pools identified in stage one. Then we will complete the ABC project by developing new product costs for each of the company's gas-grill product lines.

Machine-Related Cost Pool Let's begin by focusing on only one of the eight activity cost pools. The machine-related cost pool, a unit-level activity, totals $1,242,000 and includes the costs of machine maintenance, depreciation, computer

Learning Objective 4

Compute product costs under an activity-based costing system.

support, lubrication, electricity, and calibration. Burger and Cook selected machine hours for the cost driver, since a product that uses more machine hours should bear a larger share of machine-related costs. Exhibit 5–6 shows how machinery costs are assigned to products in stage two of the ABC analysis. Notice that Exhibit 5–6 includes just a portion of a larger spreadsheet that we will examine in due course. The spreadsheet rows shown in Exhibit 5–6 focus just on the machine-related activity cost pool. Most of the columns in Exhibit 5–6 contain ABC data that were collected by the ABC project team. We will learn more later in this chapter about how that information is collected. For now, though, let's just take this ABC information as a given. As noted in Exhibit 5–6, the following columns contain *data collected by the ABC project team.*

Data Collected by ABC Project Team (Exhibit 5–6)

Column A   Activity: machine related

Column B   Activity cost pool: $1,242,000 (from Exhibit 5–5)

Column C   Cost driver: machine hours

Column D   Cost driver quantity: 230,000 machine hours (total of machine hours for the three product lines in column G)[1]

Column F   Product lines: STD, DEL, ULT

Column G   Cost driver quantity for each product line: STD, 100,000 machine hours (from Exhibit 5–1)
            DEL, 96,000 machine hours (from Exhibit 5–1)
            ULT, 34,000 machine hours (from Exhibit 5–1)

Column I   Product line production volume: STD, 10,000 units (from Exhibit 5–1)
            DEL, 8,000 units (from Exhibit 5–1)
            ULT, 2,000 units (from Exhibit 5–1)

Notice that only three columns in Exhibit 5–6 remain: columns E, H, and J. These columns contain the *amounts that are computed* during the ABC calculations, and they appear in red in Exhibit 5–6.

Amounts Computed During ABC Calculations (Exhibit 5–6)

Column E   Pool rate

Column H   Activity cost for each product line

Column J   Activity cost per unit of product for each product line

Exhibit 5–6, below the spreadsheet excerpt, shows in detail how each of these amounts (shown in red) is computed. Take time now to examine Exhibit 5–6 carefully, in order to understand how these amounts are computed in the ABC calculations.

A key number computed in Exhibit 5–6 (column E) is the **pool rate,** which is defined as the cost per unit of the *cost driver* for a particular activity cost pool. The pool rate for the machine-related cost pool is $5.40, which means that Patio Grill Company's machine-related cost is $5.40 per machine hour. Each activity cost pool will have its own pool rate.

Now we have seen the type of data that the ABC project team must supply for the machine-related cost pool. In addition, we have studied how the ABC calculations are carried out in order to determine the machine-related activity cost per unit of each type of product (STD, DEL, and ULT). The final conclusion of the ABC analysis *for the machine-related cost pool only* is given in column J of Exhibit 5–6. Thus, under activity-based costing, the following machine-related costs per product unit should be assigned to each of the three product lines.

STD: $54.00 of machine-related cost per grill

DEL: $64.80 of machine-related cost per grill

ULT: $91.80 of machine-related cost per grill

---

[1]The 230,000 machine hours used to compute the pool rate for the machine-related cost pool is also equal to management's estimate of the company's practical capacity of production, as expressed in terms of machine hours.

Exhibit 5–6
ABC Data and Calculations
for the Machine-Related Cost
Pool: Patio Grill Company

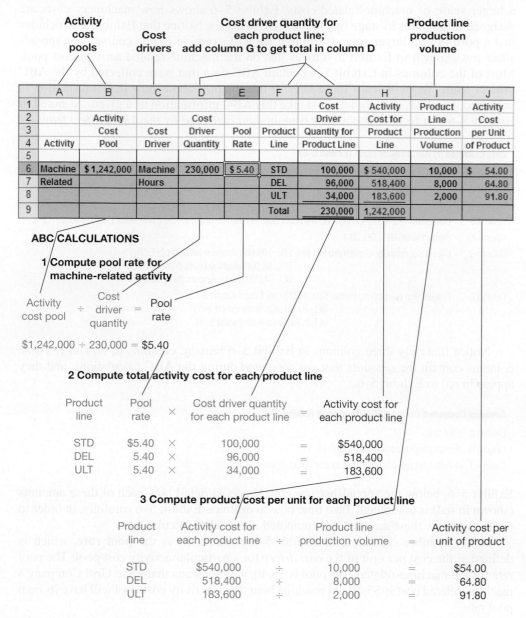

Completing the ABC Calculations Now that we have studied the ABC data requirements and calculations for the machine-related cost pool (Exhibit 5–6), we can complete the ABC calculations by including all eight of the activity cost pools. These eight cost pools were given in Exhibit 5–5. The entire Excel spreadsheet for Patio Grill Company's activity-based costing project is displayed in Exhibit 5–7. As the cliché goes, there is good news and bad news. The bad news is that the spreadsheet in Exhibit 5–7 contains eight times as many rows as the one we just examined in detail for the machine-related cost pool. The good news, though, is that the ABC data requirements and calculations are conceptually *identical* for each of the eight activity cost pools. In other words, the same type of ABC data is supplied for each activity cost pool, and the three steps of ABC computations are performed for each activity cost pool in exactly the same manner as they were for the machine-related cost pool. So if we understand the computations in Exhibit 5–6 (for the machine-related costs), then we will understand

Learning Objective 4

Compute product costs under an activity-based costing system.

Microsoft Excel - Activity-Based Costing Data and Calculations

File Edit View Insert Format Tools Data Window Help   Type a question for help

E6   fx =B6/D6

	A	B	C	D	E	F	G	H	I	J
1							Cost	Activity	Product	Activity
2		Activity		Cost			Driver	Cost for	Line	Cost
3		Cost	Cost	Driver	Pool	Product	Quantity for	Product	Production	per Unit
4	Activity	Pool	Driver	Quantity	Rate	Line	Product Line	Line	Volume	of Product
5										
6	Machine	$ 1,242,000	Machine	230,000	$ 5.40	STD	100,000	$ 540,000	10,000	$ 54.00
7	Related		Hours			DEL	96,000	518,400	8,000	64.80
8						ULT	34,000	183,600	2,000	91.80
9						Total	230,000	1,242,000		
10	Setup	210,000	Production	200	1,050.00	STD	80	84,000	10,000	8.40
11			Runs			DEL	80	84,000	8,000	10.50
12						ULT	40	42,000	2,000	21.00
13						Total	200	210,000		
14	Purchasing	300,000	Purchase	600	500.00	STD	200	100,000	10,000	10.00
15			Orders			DEL	192	96,000	8,000	12.00
16						ULT	208	104,000	2,000	52.00
17						Total	600	300,000		
18	Material	340,000	Production	200	1,700.00	STD	80	136,000	10,000	13.60
19	Handling		Runs			DEL	80	136,000	8,000	17.00
20						ULT	40	68,000	2,000	34.00
21						Total	200	340,000		
22	Quality	110,000	Inspection	2,200	50.00	STD	800	40,000	10,000	4.00
23	Assurance		Hours			DEL	800	40,000	8,000	5.00
24						ULT	600	30,000	2,000	15.00
25						Total	2,200	110,000		
26	Packing/	264,000	Shipments	2,200	120.00	STD	1,000	120,000	10,000	12.00
27	Shipping					DEL	800	96,000	8,000	12.00
28						ULT	400	48,000	2,000	24.00
29						Total	2,200	264,000		
30	Engineering	130,000	Engineering	1,300	100.00	STD	500	50,000	10,000	5.00
31	Design		Hours			DEL	400	40,000	8,000	5.00
32						ULT	400	40,000	2,000	20.00
33						Total	1,300	130,000		
34	Facility	2,300,000	Machine	230,000	10.00	STD	100,000	1,000,000	10,000	100.00
35			Hours			DEL	96,000	960,000	8,000	120.00
36						ULT	34,000	340,000	2,000	170.00
37						Total	230,000	2,300,000		
38										
39	Grand Total	$ 4,896,000				Grand Total		$ 4,896,000		

Sheet1 / Sheet2 / Sheet3 /

Ready

the computations in Exhibit 5–7 for all eight activity cost pools. (The amounts that are *computed* in Exhibit 5–7 are shown in red.)

Pause here and take a few moments to examine Exhibit 5–7. Select an activity other than the machine-related activity we studied earlier. Try to verify the computations of the pool rate in column E, the activity cost for each product line in column H, and the ABC overhead cost per unit of product in column J.

Now that we have the activity cost per unit of product for each activity cost pool and each product line, it is straightforward to compute the total unit product cost for each type of grill. To do so, we need only add the direct-material and direct-labor costs for each grill type (given in Exhibit 5–1) to the ABC activity costs calculated in Exhibit 5–7. We do this in the Excel spreadsheet displayed as Exhibit 5–8.

Exhibit 5–7
Activity-Based Costing Data and Calculations: Patio Grill Company

Patio Grill company

Exhibit 5–8
Product Costs from Activity-Based Costing System: Patio Grill Company

Microsoft Excel - Product Costs from Activity-Based Costing System

File Edit View Insert Format Tools Data Window Help   Type a question for help

G17   fx =SUM(G9:G16)

	A	B	C	D	E	F	G	H
1			STD		DEL		ULT	
2								
3	Direct material		$100.00		$120.00		$180.00	
4	Direct labor							
5	(not including set-up time)		180.00	(9 hr. @ $20)	220.00	(11 hr. @ $20)	260.00	(13 hr. @ $20)
6	Total direct costs per unit		$280.00		$340.00		$440.00	
7								
8	Manufacturing overhead (based on ABC):*							
9	Machine-related		$ 54.00		$ 64.80		$ 91.80	
10	Setup		8.40		10.50		21.00	
11	Purchasing		10.00		12.00		52.00	
12	Material handling		13.60		17.00		34.00	
13	Quality assurance		4.00		5.00		15.00	
14	Packing/shipping		12.00		12.00		24.00	
15	Engineering design		5.00		5.00		20.00	
16	Facility		100.00		120.00		170.00	
17	Total ABC overhead cost per unit		$207.00		$246.30		$427.80	
18	Total product cost per unit		$487.00		$586.30		$867.80	
19								
20	*ABC overhead costs from Exhibit 5-7							

Sheet1 Sheet2 Sheet3

Ready

Interpreting the ABC Product Costs

Hamilton Burger was amazed to see the product costs reported under the activity-based costing system. Both the STD and DEL grills exhibited lower product costs under the ABC system than under the traditional system. This could explain the price competition Patio Grill Company faced on its STD and DEL grills. Patio Grill Company's competitors could sell their comparable standard and deluxe grills at a lower price because they realized it cost less to produce these grills than Patio Grill Company's traditional costing system had indicated. However, as Burger scanned the new product costs shown in Exhibit 5–8, he was alarmed by the substantial increase in the reported cost of an ULT grill. The cost of an ULT grill had risen by more than $100 above the company's original estimate. The complexity of the ULT grills, and its impact on costs, was hidden by the traditional, volume-based costing system. To compare the results of the two alternative costing systems, Burger prepared Exhibit 5–9.

As shown in Exhibit 5–9, the STD grills emerged as a profitable product, selling for approximately 120 percent of their reported cost under the activity-based costing system ($585 ÷ $487). The DEL grills also were selling at approximately 120 percent of their new reported product cost ($705 ÷ $586.30). "No wonder we couldn't sell the deluxe

This forklift operator is engaged in material handling, which is usually a batch-level activity in an ABC system. The engineer using this computer-aided design (CAD) system is engaged in the product-sustaining-level activity of product design.

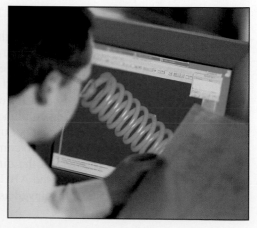

	STD	DEL	ULT
Reported unit *overhead* cost:			
Traditional, volume-based costing system (Exhibit 5–2)	$216.00	$264.00	$ 312.00
Activity-based costing system (Exhibit 5–8)	207.00	246.30	427.80
Reported unit *product* cost (direct material, direct labor, and overhead):			
Traditional, volume-based costing system (Exhibit 5–2)	496.00	604.00	752.00
Activity-based costing system (Exhibit 5–8)	487.00	586.30	867.80
Sales price data:			
Original target price (120% of product cost based on traditional, volume-based costing system (Exhibit 5–3)	595.20	724.80	902.40
New target price (120% of product cost based on activity-based costing system	584.40	703.56	1,041.36
Actual current selling price (Exhibit 5–3)	585.00	705.00	940.00

Exhibit 5–9

Comparison of Product Costs and Target Prices from Alternative Product-Costing Systems: Patio Grill Company

grills at the old target price of $724.80," said Burger to Cook, as they looked over the data. "Our competitors probably knew their deluxe grills cost around $586, and they priced them accordingly." When he got to the ULT column in Exhibit 5–9, Burger was appalled. "We thought those ultimate grills were a winner," lamented Burger, "but we've been selling them at a price that is just about 8 percent over their cost!" (Burger had made this calculation: actual current selling price of $940 ÷ ABC product cost of $867.80.) "And worse yet," Burger continued, "we've been selling the ultimate grills for $940, which is more than a hundred dollars below the new target price of $1,041.36." After looking over the data, Burger made a beeline for the president's office. "We've got to get this operation straightened out," he thought.

Burger also realized that the comparison of the two product-costing systems was even more striking when he focused on just the reported *overhead* costs. He commented to Cook, "The direct-material and direct-labor costs for each product line don't change under ABC. They're the same under both costing systems. Since these are direct costs, it's straightforward to trace these costs to each product with considerable accuracy. It's the overhead costs that cause the problem." To see what Burger was getting at, look again at Exhibit 5–9 and focus on the top two rows. The overhead cost of a STD grill dropped from the old reported cost of $216 to $207 under ABC. Similarly, the overhead cost of a DEL grill dropped from the old reported cost of $264 to $246.30 under ABC. Now look at the ULT column, though. Here the overhead cost rose from the old reported cost of $312 to $427.80 under ABC! This represents an increase of more than a third. ($427.80 ÷ $312.00 is a little over 137 percent, which yields an *increase* of over 37 percent.)

The Punch Line

What has happened at Patio Grill Company's Denver plant? The essence of the problem is that the traditional, volume-based costing system was overcosting the high-volume product lines (STD and DEL) and undercosting the complex, relatively low-volume product line (ULT). The high-volume products basically subsidized the low-volume line. The activity-based costing system revealed this problem by more accurately assigning overhead costs to the three product lines.

Exhibit 5–10 summarizes the effects of the cost distortion under the traditional product-costing system. Patio Grill Company's traditional system *overcosted* each STD grill by $9.00, for a total of $90,000 for the STD product line on a volume of 10,000 units. Each DEL grill was *overcosted* by $17.70, for a total of $141,600 on a volume of 8,000 units for the DEL product line. These excess costs had to come from somewhere, and that place was the ULT product line. Each ULT grill was *undercosted* by $115.80, for a total of $231,600 for the ULT product line on a volume of 2,000 units. Notice that the *total* amount by which the STD and DEL grill lines were overcosted equals the *total* amount by which the ULT grill line was undercosted.

Learning Objective 5

Explain why traditional, volume-based costing systems tend to distort product costs.

	STD	DEL	ULT
Traditional, volume based-costing system: reported product cost	$496.00	$604.00	$ 752.00
Activity based-costing system: reported product cost	487.00	586.30	867.80
Amount of cost distortion per unit	$ 9.00	$ 17.70	$(115.80)

Traditional system *overcosts* STD grills by $9.00 per unit.

Traditional system *overcosts* DEL grills by $17.70 per unit.

Traditional system *undercosts* ULT grills by $(115.80) per unit.

	STD	DEL	ULT
× Production volume	× 10,000	× 8,000	× 2,000
Total amount of cost distortion for entire product line	$90,000	$141,600	$(231,600)

Sum of these three amounts is zero.

STD   DEL   ULT

Traditional system shifts costs from ULT product line to STD and DEL product lines.

Exhibit 5–10
Cost Distortion under Patio Grill Company's Traditional Product-Costing System

Why Traditional, Volume-Based Systems Distort Product Costs

Why did Patio Grill Company's traditional product-costing system distort its product costs? The answer lies in the use of a single, volume-based cost driver. The company's old costing system assigned overhead to products on the basis of their relative usage of direct labor. Since the STD and DEL grill lines use substantially more direct labor than the ULT grill line, *in total,* the traditional system assigned them more overhead costs.

The problem with this result is that for every one of Patio Grill Company's overhead activities, the proportion of the activity actually consumed by the ULT grill line is far greater than its low volume would suggest. The ULT grill line has a budgeted production volume of just 2,000 units, which is only 10 percent of Patio Grill Company's total budgeted production volume of 20,000 units. (20,000 units = 10,000 STD units + 8,000 DEL units + 2,000 ULT units.) Now examine the ABC calculations in Exhibit 5–7. Focus on column G, which details the consumption of the cost driver by each product line for each activity cost pool. Notice that for every one of the overhead activities, the ULT grill line consumes much more than a 10 percent share of the activity, even though the ULT line accounts for only 10 percent of budgeted production volume. The relatively heavy consumption of overhead activities by the ULT product line is due to its greater complexity and small production runs. We must conclude, therefore, that direct labor is not a suitable cost driver for Patio Grill Company's overhead costs. Usage of direct labor does not drive most overhead costs in this company.

There are actually two factors working against Patio Grill Company's old product-costing system. First, many of the activities that result in the company's overhead costs are *not unit-level activities.* Second, the company manufactures a *diverse set of products.*

Non-Unit-Level Overhead Costs

Non-Unit-Level Overhead Costs When Patio Grill Company's ABC project team designed the activity-based costing system, only the machine-related overhead cost pool was classified as a unit-level activity. All of the other activities were classified as batch-level, product-sustaining-level, or facility-level activities. This means that many of the company's overhead costs are not incurred every time a unit is produced. Instead, many of these overhead costs are related to starting new production batches, supporting an entire product line, or running the entire operation. Since direct labor is a unit-level cost driver, it fails to capture the forces that drive these other types of costs. In Patio Grill Company's new ABC system, cost drivers were chosen that were appropriate for each activity cost pool. For example, since setting up machinery for a new production run is a batch-level activity, the number of production runs is an appropriate batch-level cost driver.

Product Diversity Patio Grill Company manufactures three different products. Although all three are gas barbeque grills, the three grills are quite different. The STD and DEL grills are high-volume, relatively simple products. The ULT grills constitute a considerably more complex, and relatively low-volume, product line. As a result of this *product line diversity,* Patio Grill Company's three product lines consume overhead activities in different proportions. For example, compare the *consumption ratios* for the purchasing and material-handling activity cost pools shown below. The **consumption ratio** is the proportion of an activity consumed by a particular product.

Activity Cost Pool	Consumption Ratios*		
	STD	DEL	ULT
Purchasing activity (cost driver is purchase orders, or POs)	200 POs (33%)	192 POs (32%)	208 POs (35%)
Material-handling activity (cost driver is production runs)	80 runs (40%)	80 runs (40%)	40 runs (20%)

*The purchase order and production run data come from Exhibit 5–7.

These widely varying consumption ratios result from Patio Grill Company's product line diversity. A single cost driver will not capture the widely differing usage of these activities by the three products. The activity-based costing system uses two different cost drivers to assign these costs to the company's diverse products.

Two Key Points To summarize, each of the following characteristics will undermine the ability of a volume-based product-costing system to assign overhead costs accurately.

*   *A large proportion of non-unit-level activities.* A unit-level cost driver, such as direct labor, machine hours, or throughput, will not be able to assign the costs of non-unit-level activities accurately.
*   *Product diversity.* When the consumption ratios differ widely between activities, no single cost driver will accurately assign the resulting overhead costs.

When either of these characteristics is present, a volume-based product-costing system is likely to distort product costs.

Does the sort of product-cost distortion experienced by Patio Grill Company occur in other companies? The answer is yes, as illustrated by the following examples from Rockwell International and DHL express transport service. (See tops of next two pages.)

Management Accounting Practice

Rockwell International

COST DISTORTION AT ROCKWELL INTERNATIONAL

When managers at Rockwell International noticed erratic sales in one of the company's lines of truck axles, they investigated. One of the company's best axle products was losing market share. A special cost study revealed that the firm's costing system, which applied costs to products in proportion to direct-labor costs, had resulted in major distortions. The reported product costs for high-volume axles were approximately 20 percent too high, and the low-volume axles were being undercosted by roughly 40 percent. The firm's practice of basing prices on reported product costs resulted in the overpricing of the high-volume axles. As a consequence, Rockwell's competitors entered the market for the high-volume axle business.[2]

Activity-Based Costing: Some Key Issues

> "Before the industry really became wide open in long-distance competition [as the result of deregulation], you could get by with knowing less. You could get by with having price structures that were not based on the underlying activities and the costs associated with those activities, but were instead based on broad averages. It was okay. It worked. It's not good enough anymore. We have to get more precise in our costs. We have to deliver the kinds of prices to our customers that they're willing to pay." (5a)
> **TELUS**

Patio Grill Company's movement toward activity-based costing is typical of changes currently underway in many companies. Added domestic and foreign competition is forcing manufacturers to strive for a better understanding of their cost structures. Moreover, the cost structures of many manufacturers have changed significantly over the past decade. Years ago, a typical manufacturer produced a relatively small number of products that did not differ much in the amount and types of manufacturing support they required. Labor was the dominant element in such a firm's cost structure. Now, products are more numerous, are more complicated, and vary more in their production requirements. Perhaps most important, labor is becoming an ever-smaller component of total production costs. All these factors mean manufacturers must take a close look at their traditional, volume-based costing systems and consider a move toward activity-based costing. Among the many well-known manufacturers that have benefited from ABC are Boise Cascade, Caterpillar, Coca-Cola, Chrysler, Hewlett-Packard, John Deere, Johnson & Johnson, Pennzoil, and Pfizer to name only a few.

The service sector also has undergone dynamic change in recent years. Increasing competition, outsourcing of key business processes, and the growth of the Internet have changed many service companies' business models. As their business environment changes, many service-industry firms have made use of activity-based costing. Service companies benefiting from ABC include American Airlines, AT&T, Blue Cross/Blue Shield, DHL, FedEx, Gemico (GE Capital Mortgage Insurance Company), and Summit Bank, among many others. Governmental units also have implemented activity-based costing. Among the governmental units that have benefited from ABC are such diverse organizations as the British Navy, the California Department of Taxation, the City of Indianapolis, and several agencies of the U.S. government.

An important factor in the move toward ABC systems is related to the information requirements of such systems. The data required for activity-based costing are more readily available than in the past. Increasing automation, coupled with sophisticated real-time information systems, provides the kind of data necessary to implement highly accurate product-costing systems. Some key issues related to activity-based costing systems are discussed in the following sections.

---

[2]Ford S. Worthy, "Accounting Bores You? Wake Up," *Fortune* 116, no. 8, pp. 43–53. For another example of cost distortion, see S. L. Mintz, "Compaq's Secret Weapon," *CFO* 10, no. 10, pp. 93–97.

COST DISTORTION AT DHL

DHL, the express transport company, ships packages to 220 countries and territories throughout the world. Management at DHL found that its cost accounting system had distorted costs between the various types of express transport services the firm provided. Before implementation of a full activity-based costing system at DHL, express transport services provided to banks appeared to be unprofitable, whereas transport services provided to heavy manufacturers appeared to be highly profitable. "This was bad news because we (DHL) had a lot more banking customers than heavy manufacturing customers." After fully implementing ABC, however, management found that the previous costing system had used cost drivers that failed to account for package weights, thereby distorting costs between services to banks and services to heavy manufacturers. The ABC analysis revealed that express transport services to banks were actually quite profitable after all.[3]

Cost Drivers

A **cost driver** is a characteristic of an event or activity that results in the incurrence of costs. In activity-based costing systems, the most significant cost drivers are identified. Then a database is created, which shows how these cost drivers are distributed across products. Three factors are important in selecting appropriate cost drivers.

> **Learning Objective 6**
>
> Explain three criteria for selecting cost drivers.

1. *Degree of correlation.* The central concept of an activity-based costing system is to assign the costs of each activity to product lines on the basis of how each product line consumes the cost driver identified for that activity. The idea is to *infer* how each product line consumes the activity by *observing* how each product line consumes the cost driver. Therefore, the accuracy of the resulting cost assignments depends on the *degree of correlation* between consumption of the activity and consumption of the cost driver.

   Say that inspection cost is selected as an activity cost pool. The objective of the ABC system is to assign inspection costs to product lines on the basis of their consumption of the inspection activity. Two potential cost drivers come to mind: number of inspections and hours of inspection time. If every inspection requires the same amount of time for all products, then the number of inspections on a product line will be highly correlated with the consumption of inspection activity by that product line. On the other hand, if inspections vary significantly in the time required, then simply recording the number of inspections will not adequately portray the consumption of inspection activity. In this case, hours of inspection time would be more highly correlated with the actual consumption of the inspection activity.

> "ABC is not a magic bullet, but it is a tool to help you understand your business better." (5b)
>
> **Braas Company**

2. *Cost of measurement.* Designing any information system entails cost-benefit trade-offs. The more activity cost pools there are in an activity-based costing system, the greater will be the accuracy of the cost assignments. However, more activity cost pools also entail more cost drivers, which results in greater costs of implementing and maintaining the system.

   Similarly, the higher the correlation between a cost driver and the actual consumption of the associated activity, the greater the accuracy of

---

[3]See DHL Web site; S. Kranz, "Sitting Pretty in Prague: DHL's Tech Triumph," *BusinessWeek*, December 12, 2005, p. 56; and S. Player and C. Cobble, *Cornerstones of Decision Making: Profiles of Enterprise ABM* (Greensboro, NC: Oakhill Press, 1999), pp. 131–44.

the cost assignments. However, it also may be more costly to measure the more highly correlated cost driver. Returning to our example of the inspection activity, it may be that inspection hours make a more accurate cost driver than the number of inspections. It is likely, however, that inspection hours also will be more costly to measure and track over time.

3. *Behavioral effects.* Information systems have the potential not only to facilitate decisions but also to influence the behavior of decision makers. This can be good or bad, depending on the behavioral effects. In identifying cost drivers, an ABC analyst should consider the possible behavioral consequences. For example, in a just-in-time (JIT) production environment, a key goal is to reduce inventories and material-handling activities to the absolute minimum level possible. The number of material moves may be the most accurate measure of the consumption of the material-handling activity for cost assignment purposes. It also may have a desirable behavioral effect of inducing managers to reduce the number of times materials are moved, thereby reducing material-handling costs.

Dysfunctional behavioral effects are also possible. For example, the number of vendor contacts may be a cost driver for the purchasing activity of vendor selection. This could induce purchasing managers to contact fewer vendors, which could result in the failure to identify the lowest-cost or highest-quality vendor.

Collecting ABC Data

The output of an organization's various departments consists of the activities performed by personnel or machines in those departments. Activities usually result in paperwork or the generation of computer documents. For example, engineering departments typically deal with documents such as specification sheets and engineering change orders. Purchasing departments handle requisitions and orders, which may be either hard-copy or computer documents. In an ABC system, analysis of documents such as these can be used to assign the costs of activities to product lines on the basis of the amount of activity generated by each product.

Interviews and Paper Trails The information used in Patio Grill Company's ABC system came initially from extensive interviews with key employees in each of the organization's support departments and a careful review of each department's records. In the engineering area, for example, ABC project team members interviewed each engineer to determine the breakdown of time spent on each of the three products. They also examined every engineering change order completed in the past two years. The team concluded that engineering costs were driven largely by engineering hours and that the breakdown was 500 hours for the STD grill line, 400 hours for the DEL grill line, and 400 hours for the ULT grill line.

Storyboarding As Patio Grill Company's project team delved further into the ABC analysis, they made considerable use of another technique for collecting activity data. **Storyboarding** is a procedure used to develop a detailed process flowchart, which visually represents activities and the relationships among the activities. A storyboarding session involves all or most of the employees who participate in the activities oriented toward achieving a specific objective. A facilitator helps the employees identify the key activities involved in their jobs. These activities are written on small cards and placed on a large board in the order they are accomplished. Relationships among the activities are shown by the order and proximity of the cards. Other information about the activities is recorded on the cards, such as the amount of time and other resources that are expended on each activity and the events that trigger the activity. After several storyboarding sessions, a completed storyboard emerges, recording key activity information vital to the ABC project. Historically, storyboards have been used by Sony Pictures and other film producers in the development of plots for animated films. More recently, storyboarding has been used by advertising agencies in developing event sequences for TV commercials.

Interviews with department personnel and storyboarding sessions are often used by activity-based costing project teams to accumulate the data needed for an ABC study. In the interview sessions, an ABC project team member asks departmental employees to detail their activities, as well as the time and other resources consumed by the activities. Storyboards, like the one depicted here, visually show the relationships between the activities performed in an organization.

Storyboarding provides a powerful tool for collecting and organizing the data needed in an ABC project. Patio Grill Company's ABC project team used storyboarding very effectively to study each of the firm's activity cost pools. The team concluded that purchasing costs were driven by the number of purchase orders. Material-handling costs were driven by the number of production runs. Quality-assurance costs were driven by the number of inspection hours devoted to each product line. Packaging and shipping costs were driven by the number of shipments made.

In summary, the ABC project team conducted a painstaking and lengthy analysis involving many employee interviews, the examination of hundreds of documents, and storyboarding sessions. The final result was the data used in the ABC calculations displayed in Exhibits 5–7 and 5–8.

Multidisciplinary ABC Project Teams   In order to gather information from all facets of an organization's operations, it is essential to involve personnel from a variety of functional areas. A typical ABC project team includes accounting and finance people as well as engineers, marketing personnel, production and operations managers, and so forth. A multidisciplinary project team not only designs a better ABC system but also helps in gaining credibility for the new system throughout the organization.

Activity Dictionary and Bill of Activities

Many organizations' ABC teams compile an **activity dictionary,** which is a complete listing of the activities identified and used in the ABC analysis. An activity dictionary helps in the implementation of activity-based costing across several divisions of an organization, because it provides for consistency in the ABC system terminology and the complexity of the ABC analyses in the various divisions.

A **bill of activities** is another commonly used element in an ABC analysis. A bill of activities for a product or service is a complete listing of the activities required for the product or service to be produced. As a familiar analogy, think about a recipe for chocolate chip cookies. The *bill of materials* for the cookies is the list of ingredients provided

> "Having a plant-level activity dictionary allows the plant to manage its activities locally and serves as a standard reference that employees can use to see which activities roll up into which processes." (5e)
>
> **Navistar International Corporation**

in the recipe. The *bill of activities* is the list of steps given in the recipe for making the cookies (e.g., combine ingredients in a bowl, stir in chocolate chips, place spoon-size globs of dough on greased cookie sheet, bake for 10 minutes or until done).

Activity-Based Management

Learning Objective 8

Explain the concepts of activity-based management and two-dimensional ABC.

Using activity-based costing (ABC) information to support organizational strategy, improve operations, and manage costs is called **activity-based management** or **ABM.** We have already caught a glimpse of activity-based management earlier in this chapter, where the management of Patio Grill Company used ABC information to better understand its product-pricing decisions. The company's management discovered through the ABC analysis that some products were overcosted and some products were undercosted by their traditional product-costing system. This important insight presented management with the opportunity to revise its product pricing in order to reflect the more accurate product costs provided by the ABC analysis. When management followed up on this product-pricing opportunity, it was engaging in activity-based management. However, ABM is a much broader concept than this. Activity-based management involves any use of ABC information to support the organization's strategy, improve operations, or manage activities and their resulting costs.

Two-Dimensional ABC

One way of picturing the relationship between ABC and ABM is in terms of the **two-dimensional ABC model** depicted in Exhibit 5–11.[4] The vertical dimension of the model depicts the cost assignment view of an ABC system. From the *cost assignment viewpoint,* the ABC system uses two-stage cost allocation to *assign* the costs of resources to the firm's cost objects. These cost objects could be products manufactured, services produced, or customers served.

Now focus on the horizontal dimension of the model. Depicted here is the *process view* of an ABC system. The emphasis now is on the activities themselves, the various processes by which work is accomplished in the organization. The left-hand side of Exhibit 5–11 depicts **activity analysis,** which is the detailed identification and description of the activities conducted in the enterprise. Activity analysis entails identification not only of the activities but also of their *root causes,* the events that *trigger* activities, and the *linkages* among activities. The right-hand side of Exhibit 5–11 depicts the evaluation of activities through performance measures. It is these processes of *activity analysis and evaluation* that comprise activity-based management. Notice that the *activities,* which appear in the center of both dimensions in Exhibit 5–11, are the focal point of ABC and ABM.

Using ABM to Identify Non-Value-Added Activities and Costs

An important goal of activity-based management is to identify and eliminate non-value-added activities and costs. **Non-value-added activities** are operations that are either (1) unnecessary and dispensable or (2) necessary, but inefficient and improvable.[5] **Non-value-added costs,** which result from such activities, are the costs of activities that can be eliminated without deterioration of product quality, performance, or perceived value.

---

[4]This section draws on Lewis J. Soloway, "Using Activity-Based Management in Aerospace and Defense Companies," *Journal of Cost Management* 6, no. 4 (Winter 1993), pp. 56–66; and Peter B. B. Turney, "What an Activity-Based Cost Model Looks Like," *Journal of Cost Management* 5, no. 4 (Winter 1992), pp. 54–60.

[5]This definition, as well as other material in this section, is drawn from James A. Brimson, "Improvement and Elimination of Non-Value-Added Costs," *Journal of Cost Management* 2, no. 2 (Summer 1988), pp. 62–65.

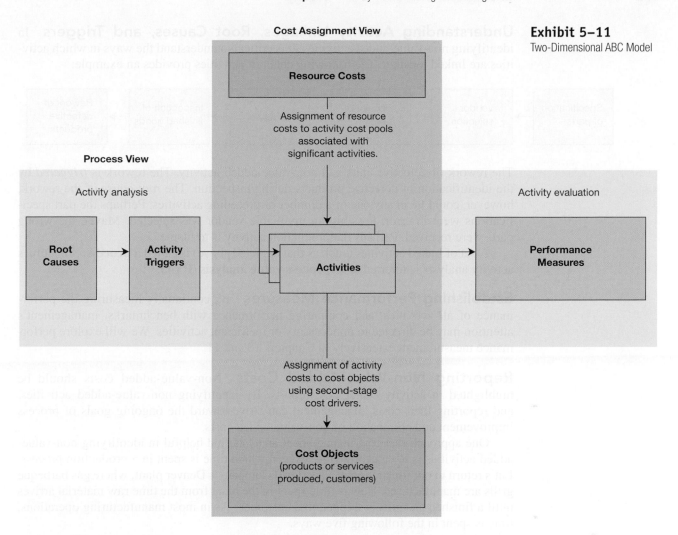

Exhibit 5–11
Two-Dimensional ABC Model

Cost Assignment View

Resource Costs

Assignment of resource costs to activity cost pools associated with significant activities.

Process View

Activity analysis

Activity evaluation

Root Causes → **Activity Triggers** → **Activities** → **Performance Measures**

Assignment of activity costs to cost objects using second-stage cost drivers.

Cost Objects
(products or services produced, customers)

The following five steps provide a strategy for eliminating non-value-added costs in both manufacturing and service industry firms.

Identifying Activities   The first step is activity analysis, which identifies all of the organization's significant activities. The resulting activity list should be broken down to the most fundamental level practical. For example, rather than listing purchasing as an activity, the list should break down the purchasing operation into its component activities, such as obtaining part specifications, compiling vendor lists, selecting vendors, negotiating prices, ordering, and expediting.

Identifying Non-Value-Added Activities   Three criteria for determining whether an activity adds value are as follows:

- *Is the activity necessary?* If it's a duplicate or nonessential operation, it is non-value-added.
- *Is the activity efficiently performed?* In answering this question, it is helpful to compare the actual performance of the activity to a value-added baseline established using budgets, targets, or external benchmarks.
- *Is an activity sometimes value-added and sometimes non-value-added?* For example, it may be necessary to move work-in-process units between production operations, but unnecessary to move raw materials around while in storage.

> "Putting a spotlight on non-value-added activities, such as [correcting] errors in procurement, provided the focus for ultimately implementing process improvements." (5f)
> **GTE Supply**
> (currently a part of Verizon)

Understanding Activity Linkages, Root Causes, and Triggers

In identifying non-value-added activities, it is critical to understand the ways in which activities are linked together. The following chain of activities provides an example:

The rework of defective units is a non-value-added activity. The rework is *triggered* by the identification of defective products during inspection. The *root cause* of the rework, however, could lie in any one of a number of preceding activities. Perhaps the part specifications were in error. Possibly an unreliable vendor was selected. Maybe the wrong parts were received. Perhaps the production activity is to blame.

A set of linked activities (such as that depicted above) is called a **process.** Sometimes activity analysis is referred to as **process value analysis (PVA).**

Establishing Performance Measures

By continually measuring the performance of all activities, and comparing performance with benchmarks, management's attention may be directed to unnecessary or inefficient activities. We will explore performance measurement extensively in Chapters 10 and 11.

Reporting Non-Value-Added Costs

Non-value-added costs should be highlighted in activity center cost reports. By identifying non-value-added activities, and reporting their costs, management can strive toward the ongoing goals of process improvement and elimination of non-value-added costs.

One approach that cost-management analysts find helpful in identifying non-value-added activities is to categorize the ways in which time is spent in a production process. Let's return to our illustration of Patio Grill Company's Denver plant, where gas barbeque grills are manufactured. How is time spent in the plant from the time raw material arrives until a finished gas grill is shipped to a customer? As in most manufacturing operations, time is spent in the following five ways.

1. *Process time.* The time during which a product is undergoing conversion activity.
2. *Inspection time.* The amount of time spent ensuring that the product is of high quality.
3. *Move time.* The time spent moving raw materials, work in process, or finished goods between operations.
4. *Waiting time.* The amount of time that raw materials or work in process spend waiting for the next operation.
5. *Storage time.* The time during which materials, partially completed products, or finished goods are held in stock before further processing or shipment to customers.

Thinking about the production operation in these terms allows management to ask the questions, "Does the time spent in all of these activities add value to the product? Will the customer pay for it? Can the time spent on inspection be reduced without diminishing product quality? Can production efficiency be improved by reducing the number of times materials, work-in-process, or finished goods are moved from one place to another? Can production be scheduled so that partially completed products spend less time just waiting for the next operation? Can storage time be reduced by ordering raw material and producing products only as they are needed?" Many companies have implemented just-in-time (JIT) inventory and production management systems to reduce move, waiting, and storage time. JIT systems are covered in the appendix to this chapter.

If reductions can be made in any of these time-consuming activities, without diminishing product quality or functionality, management has a real opportunity to reduce non-value-added costs.

Some companies have begun making a distinction between *customer-value-added activities* and *business-value-added activities.* For example, the addition of a 24/7 customer-service hotline to assist customers in maximizing their benefits from the products or services they have purchased would likely be an activity that customers would value. In contrast, most customers would not value a company's expenditures on information technology (IT) or accounting, whereas these activities are likely to be critical to the success of the company's business model.

Customer-Profitability Analysis

It is quite possible for a company to have profitable products and, at the same time, incur customer-related costs that make certain customer relationships unprofitable. **Customer-profitability analysis** uses activity-based costing to determine the activities, costs, and profit associated with serving particular customers. Suppose, for example, that customer X frequently changes its orders after they are placed, but customer Y typically does not. Then the costs incurred in updating sales orders for changes should be recorded in a manner that reflects the fact that customer X is more responsible for those activities and costs than is customer Y. An effective cost management system should allow managers to derive such cost details.

> **Learning Objective 9**
>
> Explain and execute a customer-profitability analysis.

Many factors can result in some customers being more profitable than others. Customers that order in small quantities, order frequently, often change their orders, require special packaging or handling, demand faster delivery, or need special parts or engineering design generally are less profitable than customers who demand less in terms of customized services. If managers have a good understanding of which customers are generating the greatest profit, they can make more-informed decisions about customer service. Moreover, this allows customers to be educated as to the costs they are causing when demanding special services. In many cases, customers' behavior can be changed in a way that reduces costs to the supplier. Then these cost savings can be shared by the supplier and the customer.

The task of assigning costs to customers is a challenge. A system must be in place that enables the company to identify which customers are using customer support services and how frequently they do so. How much time must the company spend on a customer to make the sale and to provide ongoing support services? These costs are in addition to the cost of manufacturing the product or initially providing a service for the customer.

Illustration of Customer-Profitability Analysis

To illustrate customer-profitability analysis, let's focus again on Patio Grill Company. Two more years have passed, and the company has successfully implemented its activity-based costing system in its Denver plant. At a recent strategy meeting with her senior management team, Patio Grill Company's president and CEO expressed interest in assessing the profitability of the entire company's various customer relationships. She found support for the idea from the director of cost management, who had been reading about customer-profitability analysis in some of his professional journals. The company's marketing manager also expressed interest in customer-profitability analysis, since he was concerned about the profitability of a couple of Patio Grill Company's customers in particular. "We have a few customers who seem to want the moon and the stars when it comes to customer service," he complained. "I know the customer is always right and all, but you really have to wonder if we're making any money from a couple of these customers, what with all the extra design and packaging they demand. And some of our other customers seem to require an awful lot of extra attention in sales calls, order processing, and billing. If we had a better idea of each customer's profitability, it would help our marketing and sales staffs to focus their efforts."

The controller soon had his cost management staff attacking the customer-profitability analysis that the president had requested. The first step required an activity-based costing analysis of certain *customer-related costs* that could seriously

Exhibit 5–12
ABC Analysis for Customer-Related Costs: Patio Grill Company

Customer-Related Activities	Cost Driver Base	Cost Driver Rate
Order processing	Purchase orders	$ 150
Sales contacts (phone calls, faxes, etc.)	Contacts	100
Sales visits	Visits	1,000
Shipment processing	Shipments	200
Billing and collection	Invoices	160
Design/engineering change orders	Engineering/design changes	4,000
Special packaging	Units packaged	40
Special handling	Units handled	60

"When we saw what some of our customers were costing us, we were quite surprised. We shared this information with them, and they were also surprised to see how much work went into servicing them. At this point, we negotiated with them to eliminate certain discounts they were receiving." (5g)

Pfizer

affect a customer's profitability. Recall that ABC analysis relies on a cost hierarchy with cost levels, such as unit-level, batch-level, product-line-level, customer-level, and facility- or general-operations-level costs. In this use of activity-based costing, the cost management team is focusing on the customer-related costs. After an extensive analysis and several interviews with personnel throughout Patio Grill Company, the cost management team came up with the ABC analysis in Exhibit 5–12.[6]

Based on the activity-based costing information, the cost management team assessed the profitability of each of Patio Grill Company's customer relationships. Detailed information from that analysis for five of these customers appears in the Excel spreadsheet in Exhibit 5–13. These five customers were singled out because three of them are key customers (i.e., customers 106, 112, and 113), and two of them (107 and 119) were suspected by the marketing manager to be at best marginally profitable. As it turned out, suspicions about customers 107 and 119 were well founded. Both customers were found to be unprofitable; in fact, customer 119 had caused a loss of almost $120,000 during the year.

---

[6]An important point that could be overlooked here is that activity-based costing analysis can be used in a very specific, targeted manner to address a particular management problem. In this case, the ABC focus is customer-profitability analysis. This is the essence of activity-based management, using the results of an ABC analysis to manage an enterprise more effectively.

Exhibit 5–13
Customer-Profitability Analysis for Five Designated Customers: Patio Grill Company

Microsoft Excel - Customer-Profitability Analysis for Five Designated Customers

File Edit View Insert Format Tools Data Window Help

F20   =F6-F19

	A	B	C	D	E	F
1		Designated Customers (By 3-Digit Customer Code)				
2		Customer 106	Customer 107	Customer 112	Customer 113	Customer 119
3						
4	Sales revenue	$ 4,320,000	$ 3,480,000	$ 6,500,000	$ 4,490,000	$ 1,960,000
5	Cost of goods sold	3,220,000	2,810,000	4,890,000	3,380,000	1,480,000
6	Gross margin	$ 1,100,000	$ 670,000	$ 1,610,000	$ 1,110,000	$ 480,000
7	Selling and administrative costs:					
8	General selling costs	$ 362,000	$ 220,000	$ 530,000	$ 366,000	$ 160,000
9	General administrative costs	181,000	110,000	265,000	183,000	80,000
10	Customer-related costs					
11	Order processing	11,100	80,250	16,050	22,200	38,400
12	Sales contacts	22,000	13,400	32,000	24,100	28,800
13	Sales visits	44,000	20,000	47,000	38,000	32,000
14	Shipment processing	33,000	27,800	64,200	44,600	19,200
15	Billing and collection	33,600	14,000	80,480	22,400	9,600
16	Design/engineering changes	93,000	96,000	84,000	112,000	68,000
17	Special packaging	88,000	27,200	64,440	44,480	76,800
18	Special handling	33,000	80,400	48,300	33,300	86,400
19	Total selling and administrative cost	$ 900,700	$ 689,050	$ 1,231,470	$ 890,080	$ 599,200
20	Operating income	$ 199,300	$ (19,050)	$ 378,530	$ 219,920	$ (119,200)

Sheet1 / Sheet2 / Sheet3 /

Ready

CUSTOMER PROFITABILITY ANALYSIS AT BANK ONE CORP.

The Wall Street Journal described how Bank One Corp. (now part of JPMorgan Chase Bank) has used customer-profitability analysis to guide decisions about customer service.

At Bank One Corp., at the time one of the largest banks, "the line in the sand between preferred and nonpreferred customers has become strikingly obvious." The bank is redesigning its 218 branches in Louisiana so its "Premier One" customers can be whisked away to a special teller window with no wait or to the desk of an appropriate bank officer. "Customers qualify by keeping at least $2,500 in a checking account or a total of $25,000 in a combination of certain bank accounts," or by paying a $17 monthly fee. "Management estimates that the extra attention will go only to the top 20 percent of its customers."[7]

Management Accounting Practice

Bank One Corp.

A complete customer-profitability analysis for all of Patio Grill Company's customers appears in the spreadsheet in Exhibit 5–14. This exhibit reveals several interesting aspects of the customer-profitability scenario. Seventeen of 20 customers are profitable. The three unprofitable customers (107, 134, and 119) resulted in losses of over $240,000 in operating income for Patio Grill Company in a single year! Notice that over 25 percent of the company's profit is generated by its top three customers. Almost half the company's profit comes from its top six customers, and fully three-quarters of its

"Almost any person in any organization that implements ABM has some real surprises when they start seeing the data about customer profitability and product profitability." (5h)
Shiloh Industries, Inc.

[7]"Alienating Customers Isn't Always a Bad Idea Many Firms Discover," *The Wall Street Journal*, January 7, 1999.

Exhibit 5–14
Customer-Profitability Analysis with Customers Ranked by Operating Income: Patio Grill Company

Microsoft Excel - Customer-Profitability Analysis - Customers Ranked by Operating Income						
File Edit View Insert Format Tools Data Window Help					Type a question for help	
E25		fx =SUM(D6:D25)				
	A	B	C	D	E	F	G
1						Cumulative Operating	
2	3-Digit	Customer	Customer	Customer	Cumulative	Income as a	
3	Customer	Sales	Gross	Operating	Operating	Percentage of Total	
4	Code	Revenue	Margin	Income	Income	Operating Income	
5							
6	112	$ 6,500,000	$ 1,610,000	$ 378,530	$ 378,530	8.8%	
7	108	6,964,000	1,570,000	370,000	748,530	17.3%	
8	114	6,694,000	1,484,300	351,000	1,099,530	25.5%	
9	116	5,846,000	1,461,600	340,000	1,439,530	33.4%	
10	110	5,602,000	1,430,000	336,070	1,775,600	41.1%	
11	121	5,400,000	1,413,000	331,000	2,106,600	48.8%	
12	124	5,601,000	1,405,520	330,000	2,436,600	56.5%	
13	127	5,090,000	1,280,020	300,000	2,736,600	63.4%	
14	128	4,760,000	1,160,200	281,400	3,018,000	69.9%	
15	125	5,000,200	1,181,000	276,000	3,294,000	76.3%	
16	135	4,431,000	1,150,000	270,000	3,564,000	82.6%	
17	133	4,008,000	1,059,800	251,400	3,815,400	88.4%	
18	113	4,490,000	1,110,000	219,920	4,035,320	93.5%	
19	111	4,200,000	875,220	205,000	4,240,320	98.2%	
20	106	4,320,000	1,100,000	199,300	4,439,620	102.9%	
21	136	1,920,000	351,200	82,000	4,521,620	104.8%	
22	137	1,641,000	139,400	35,600	4,557,220	105.6%	
23	107	3,480,000	670,000	(19,050)	4,538,170	105.1%	
24	134	2,820,000	582,000	(102,600)	4,435,570	102.8%	
25	119	1,960,000	480,000	(119,200)	4,316,370	100.0%	

Chart1 \ Sheet1 \ Sheet2 \ Sheet3

Ready

Exhibit 5–15

Customer-Profitability Profile in Terms of Cumulative Operating Income as a Percentage of Total Operating Income: Patio Grill Company

Cumulative Operating Income as a Percentage of Total Operating Income

*Customers ranked by operating income.

profit is generated by half its customers. This sort of customer-profitability scenario is quite typical for manufacturers. The lion's share of most companies' profits comes from a handful of their customers. Such an insight is important for management as it determines where to devote the company's resources in serving customers.[8]

A graphical portrayal of Patio Grill Company's complete customer-profitability analysis is given in Exhibit 5–15. This graph is called a **customer-profitability profile,** and it is a common and useful way of presenting a customer-profitability analysis to management.

Activity-Based Costing in the Service Industry

"As bankers become more familiar with the [ABC] numbers and start to embrace them, their decision making improves, their profitability increases, and the growth of the business improves." (5i)
Summit Bancorp

We conclude this chapter with the important point that activity-based costing has found widespread usage in the service industry as well as in manufacturing. There have been many ABC success stories in such diverse organizations as airlines, insurance companies, banks, hospitals, financial services firms, hotels, railroads, and government agencies. Among the service organizations that used activity-based costing are Air France, American Airlines, American Express, Bank of America, Cambridge Hospital Community Health Care Network, City of Indianapolis, FedEx, Owens & Minor, Telus, Union Pacific, U.S. Naval Supply Center, and the U.S. Postal Service.

The overall objectives of ABC in service firms are no different than they are in manufacturing companies. Managers want more accurate information about the cost of producing the services they are selling. Moreover, they want to use this information to improve operations and to better meet the needs of their customers in a more cost-effective manner. The general approach of identifying activities, activity cost pools, and cost drivers is used in the service industry as well as in manufacturing. The classification of activities into unit-level, batch-level, product-sustaining-level, and facility-level activities

---

[8]In a conversation with a vice president from a large consumer-products manufacturer, the author was struck by the executive's statement that, "You can bet we pay a lot of attention to the needs and desires of the 'Mart Brothers,' K and Wal."

Management
Accounting
Practice

Best Buy

CUSTOMER PROFITABILITY ANALYSIS AT BEST BUY

After Circuit City's recent liquidation, Best Buy, with over $45 billion in annual revenue, became the last major consumer electronics retailer in the U.S.[9] Best Buy's CEO "is embracing a heretical notion for a retailer. He wants to separate the best customers among the 1.5 million people who visit Best Buy's stores every day from the worst customers." Best Buy's preferred customers "boost profits at the consumer-electronics giant by snapping up high-definition televisions, portable electronics, and newly released DVDs without waiting for markdowns or rebates."[10] The retailer's worst customers, on the other hand, "buy products, apply for rebates, return the purchases, and then buy them back at returned-merchandise discounts. They load up on loss-leaders, severely discounted merchandise designed to boost store traffic, then "flip" the goods at a profit on eBay. They slap down rock-bottom price quotes from Web sites and demand that Best Buy make good on its lowest-price pledge." According to Best Buy's CEO, these customers "can wreak enormous economic havoc." The company estimates "that as many as 100 million of its 500 million customer visits each year are undesirable." And Best Buy's CEO "wants to be rid of these customers." The company's new approach "upends what has long been standard practice for mass merchants. Most chains use their advertising budgets chiefly to maximize customer traffic." Best Buy's new plan is to "rate its customers according to profitability, and then dump the up to 20 percent that are unprofitable." Best Buy rolled

out its new strategy in about 100 of its 670 stores. Best Buy "is examining its sales records and demographic data and sleuthing through computer databases to identify good and bad customers. To lure the high spenders, it is stocking more merchandise and providing more appealing service. To deter the undesirables, it is cutting back on promotions and sales tactics that tend to draw them, and culling them from the marketing lists."[11]

also applies in service industry settings. For example, insurance company Pennsylvania Blue Shield used these activity classifications in its ABC system.[12] Examples from the Blue Shield system are as follows:

- *Unit level:* Entering initial claim data into the computer (for each claim received).
- *Batch level:* Moving a batch of claims from one processing step to the next.
- *Product-sustaining level:* Maintenance of the medical-services provider network (i.e., maintaining relationships with physicians and hospitals providing medical care to claimants).
- *Facility (general operations) level:* General administration of the claims business unit.

[9]"Why Tech Bows to Best Buy," *BusinessWeek*, December 21, 2009, and recent Best Buy annual reports.

[10]G. McWilliams, "Analyzing Customers, Best Buy Decides Not All Are Welcome," *The Wall Street Journal*, November 8, 2004.

[11]Ibid.

[12]Angela Norkiewicz, "Nine Steps to Implementing ABC," *Management Accounting* 75, no. 10 (April 1994), pp. 28–33.

Activity-Based Costing at Delaware Medical Center

To see how management can use activity-based costing in a service-industry setting, let's explore how ABC is used at Delaware Medical Center's Primary Care Unit.[13] The Primary Care Unit is the medical center's outpatient clinic and provides nearly 25,000 patient appointments in a typical year. The Primary Care Unit's administration implemented activity-based costing in order to determine how much it costs to serve patients in various categories. The Primary Care Unit classifies patient appointments as routine, extended, or complex, depending on the appointment length and complexity. In addition, each appointment is classified as either a new-patient appointment or a continuing-patient appointment. Thus, every patient appointment is one of the following six types.

	Routine	Extended	Complex
New patient	New patient; routine appointment	New patient; extended appointment	New patient; complex appointment
Continuing patient	Continuing patient; routine appointment	Continuing patient; extended appointment	Continuing patient; complex appointment

Every patient appointment involves a registered nurse (or RN), who takes vital signs and prepares the patient for the primary health care professional. Then, every patient is seen by one primary health care professional, which can be a physician, a nurse practitioner, an intern, or a resident. No appointment involves more than one of these types of primary health care professionals.

The Primary Care Unit's ABC project team designated the following activities and cost drivers.

Activity	Cost Driver
Physician time	Physician minutes with patient
Nurse practitioner time	Nurse practitioner minutes with patient
Intern or resident time	Intern or resident minutes with patient
Registered nurse time	Registered nurse minutes with patient
Clerical time: new patients	New patient visits
Clerical time: continuing patients	Continuing patient visits
Billing	Billing lines (i.e., number of line items on bill)
Facility	Patient visits (both new and continuing)

The activity-based costing analysis is displayed in the Excel spreadsheet in Exhibit 5–16. Notice that this ABC spreadsheet for Delaware Medical Center's Primary Care Unit has a format that is identical to the ABC spreadsheet prepared for Patio Grill Company (Exhibit 5–7 on page 211). The column headings are different, because the Primary Care Unit provides medical services to patients, whereas Patio Grill Company manufactures barbeque grills. Conceptually and computationally, however, the two Excel spreadsheets are identical.

The *information supplied by the primary care unit's ABC project team* is located in the following columns.

Column A: Activity
Column B: Activity cost pool
Column C: Cost driver
Column D: Cost driver quantity

---

[13]For a more elaborate example of activity-based costing in a hospital's primary care unit, see V. G. Narayanan, R. Moore, and L. Brem, "Cambridge Hospital Community Health Care Network—The Primary Care Unit" (Boston: The President and Fellows of Harvard College, 2000). In this case, minutes of time with a health care professional is a key cost driver.

Column F: Patient visit type (routine, extended, or complex)

Column G: Cost driver quantity for each type of patient visit

Column I: Patient volume for each type of visit

The *ABC computations* are in columns E, H, and J and are shown in red.

Column E: Pool rate

Pool rate   =   Activity cost pool   ÷   Cost driver quantity
(column E)   (column B)   (column D)

For example, the pool rate for physician time (cell E6) is calculated as follows:

$4.00 per physician minute = $960,000 ÷ 240,000 minutes of physician time

Column H: Activity cost for patient type

Activity cost for patient type   =   Pool rate   ×   Cost driver quantity for patient type
            (column H)   (column E)   (column G)

For example, the physician activity cost for a routine visit (cell H6) is calculated as follows:

$320,000 = $4.00 per physician minute × 80,000 physician minutes on routine visits

Column J: Activity cost per patient of each type

Activity cost per patient of each type = Activity cost for patient type ÷ Patient type volume
                (column J)   (column H)   (column I)

For example, the physician activity cost per routine patient visit (cell J6) is calculated as follows:

$40 per routine visit
attended by a physician = $320,000 ÷ 8,000 routine visits attended by a physician

Interpreting the Primary Care Unit's ABC Information

The Primary Care Unit's administration can use the ABC information in Exhibit 5–16 to determine the cost of each of the six types of patient appointments discussed earlier. Notice, though, that there is an important conceptual difference in the interpretation of the Primary Care Unit's ABC data (Exhibit 5–16) versus the interpretation of Patio Grill Company's ABC data (Exhibit 5–7 on page 211). In the Patio Grill Company manufacturing illustration, *all eight of the activities* identified in the ABC analysis were required by each line of barbeque grills manufactured. However, that is not true in the Primary Care Unit example. In this health care services setting, each patient sees *either* a physician, *or* a nurse practitioner, *or* an intern, *or* a resident—not all four. Moreover, each patient is *either* a new patient *or* a continuing patient—not both. Therefore, to compute the cost of a particular type of appointment, we must *select only one of the primary health care professionals,* which are highlighted by the red bar on the right-hand side of Exhibit 5–16. Moreover, we select *just one of the two categories for clerical time,* new patient or continuing patient, which are highlighted by the green bar on the right-hand side of Exhibit 5–16. Finally, since every patient appointment involves a registered nurse, *and* billing, *and* use of the primary care unit facility, *all* of these activities must be included in the cost calculation. (These activities are highlighted by the yellow bars on the right-hand side of Exhibit 5–16.)

Let's compute the cost of an extended appointment in which a new patient sees a nurse practitioner.

Exhibit 5–16
Activity-Based Costing
Analysis: Delaware Medical
Center

Delaware
Medical
Center

Microsoft Excel - Activity-Based Costing Analysis - Delaware Medical Center

File   Edit   View   Insert   Format   Tools   Data   Window   Help   Type a question for help

E6   *fx* =B6/D6

	A	B	C	D	E	F	G	H	I	J
1							Cost Driver	Activity	Patient	Activity
2		Activity		Cost		Patient	Quantity for	Cost for	Type	Cost per
3		Cost	Cost	Driver	Pool	Visit	Patient	Patient	Visit	Patient of
4	Activity	Pool	Driver	Quantity	Rate	Type	Visit Type	Type	Volume	Each Type
5										
6	Physician	$ 960,000	Physician	240,000	$4.00	Routine	80,000	$ 320,000	8,000	$ 40.00
7	Time		Minutes			Extended	100,000	400,000	5,000	80.00
8			With Patient			Complex	60,000	240,000	2,000	120.00
9						Total	240,000	960,000		
10	Nurse	90,000	NP	30,000	3.00	Routine	12,000	36,000	1,200	30.00
11	Practitioner		Minutes			Extended	10,000	30,000	500	60.00
12	(NP) Time		With Patient			Complex	8,000	24,000	320	75.00
13						Total	30,000	90,000		
14	Intern or	412,500	I/R	125,000	3.30	Routine	40,000	132,000	4,000	33.00
15	Resident		Minutes			Extended	50,000	165,000	2,500	66.00
16	(I/R) Time		With Patient			Complex	35,000	115,500	1,000	115.50
17						Total	125,000	412,500		
18	Registered	281,980	RN	245,200	1.15	Routine	132,000	151,800	13,200	11.50
19	Nurse		Minutes			Extended	80,000	92,000	8,000	11.50
20	(RN) Time		With Patient			Complex	33,200	38,180	3,320	11.50
21						Total	245,200	281,980		
22	Clerical Time	135,300	New	12,300	11.00	Routine	7,200	79,200	7,200	11.00
23	New		Patient			Extended	3,000	33,000	3,000	11.00
24	Patients		Visits			Complex	2,100	23,100	2,100	11.00
25						Total	12,300	135,300		
26	Clerical Time	61,100	Continuing	12,220	5.00	Routine	6,000	30,000	6,000	5.00
27	Continuing		Patient			Extended	5,000	25,000	5,000	5.00
28	Patients		Visits			Complex	1,220	6,100	1,220	5.00
29						Total	12,220	61,100		
30	Billing	38,480	Billing	76,960	0.50	Routine	26,400	13,200	13,200	1.00
31			Lines			Extended	24,000	12,000	8,000	1.50
32						Complex	26,560	13,280	3,320	4.00
33						Total	76,960	38,480		
34	Facility	245,200	Patient	24,520	10.00	Routine	13,200	132,000	13,200	10.00
35			Visits			Extended	8,000	80,000	8,000	10.00
36			(Both New &			Complex	3,320	33,200	3,320	10.00
37			Continuing)			Total	24,520	245,200		
38										
39	Grand Total	$2,224,560				Grand Total		$2,224,560		

Sheet1 / Sheet2 / Sheet3 /

Ready

Activity	Cost (spreadsheet cell)
Nurse practitioner time	$60.00 (cell J11 in Exhibit 5–16)
Registered nurse time	11.50 (cell J19 in Exhibit 5–16)
Clerical time: new patients	11.00 (cell J23 in Exhibit 5–16)
Billing	1.50 (cell J31 in Exhibit 5–16)
Facility	10.00 (cell J35 in Exhibit 5–16)
Total	$94.00

Now let's compute the cost of a routine appointment in which a continuing patient sees a physician.

Activity	Cost (spreadsheet cell)
Physician time	$40.00 (cell J6 in Exhibit 5–16)
Registered nurse time	11.50 (cell J18 in Exhibit 5–16)
Clerical time: continuing patients	5.00 (cell J26 in Exhibit 5–16)
Billing	1.00 (cell J30 in Exhibit 5–16)
Facility	10.00 (cell J34 in Exhibit 5–16)
Total	$67.50

With a good understanding of how much it costs the Primary Care Unit to provide various types of patient appointments, the clinic's administration is in a much better position to make decisions. Determining appropriate charges for appointments, justifying third-party reimbursements from insurance companies and government agencies, and adding or discontinuing services are among the types of decisions that will be enhanced by the ABC information.

Focus on Ethics

ETHICAL ISSUES SURROUNDING ACTIVITY-BASED COSTING

Aztec Auto Parts, Ltda. manufactures a wide range of auto parts in Mexico, which it sells to auto manufacturers in Mexico, the United States and Canada.* The company's Engine Parts Division operated three plants in Mexico and specialized in engine parts. The division's Monterrey plant manufactured some 6,500 different parts.

Trouble Brewing

Both the Engine Parts Division, as well as the Monterrey plant in particular, had shown satisfactory profitability for the past 20 years. In 2009, however, the Monterrey plant's profitability took a sharp downward turn, in spite of rising sales. The trend continued through the next several years. Management at both the division and plant levels took note of the plant's declining profits and held several strategy meetings as a result.

Division Strategy

The Engine Parts Division had always positioned itself as the industry's full-line producer. If a customer wanted a product, the division would make it. Although occasionally very-low-volume products were discontinued due to lack of consistent orders, the division's product line remained a full line of engine parts. As part of its strategy review, division management did two things. First, an activity-based costing study was initiated in the Monterrey plant in order to give management a better picture of each product line's profitability. Second, a high-level review was undertaken to determine whether the full-line-producer strategy continued to make sense.

Activity-based Costing

An ABC project team was formed, and a successful pilot study was conducted on two of the Monterrey plant's

product lines. Then the ABC project was extended to the entire Monterrey operation. Management was astonished to find that fully a quarter of the plant's products were selling at a loss. Moreover, the ABC project highlighted the extent of the product-line proliferation at the Monterrey plant. It turned out that in many instances, unprofitable products had been dropped only to creep back into the product line-up after a customer requested it and a salesperson acquiesced. It became a joke around the plant that the only way to be sure a dropped product was really gone was to burn the engineering drawings and destroy the special tools required to make it.

ABC Team Recommendations

The ABC project team made sweeping recommendations to division management, beginning with a suggestion that the Monterrey plant's product lines be pruned and that roughly 20 percent of its products be dropped. New emphasis would then be devoted to increasing the profitability of the remaining 80 percent of the Monterrey plant's products. Attention would be given to identifying inefficient processes, and process improvements would be evaluated.

Top Management Response

Top management balked at the recommendations of the ABC project team. Some top managers did not believe the ABC results. It just seemed impossible to them that so many of the Monterrey plant's products were losers. Other members of the management team largely accepted the validity of the ABC study, but they, too, hesitated to drop so many products. To do so would most likely have meant massive layoffs and even the possibility of closing the Monterrey plant altogether, while shifting its remaining production to the division's other two plants. Some members of the ABC project team quietly speculated that some of the division's managers were more concerned about their own pay and perks than they were about the well-being of the division. In the final analysis, only a handful of products were dropped, and then only if they were suspected to be unprofitable before the ABC study was undertaken.

*The scenario described here, while fictitious, is based on several real-world events described in the ABC literature. Anecdotes in various ABC cases and other sources, as well as the author's research, form the basis for the events described. A key source is the well-known "Schrader-Bellows" case, by R. Cooper (Boston: President and Fellows of Harvard College), which remains a classic case describing issues surrounding activity-based costing.

Aftermath

The Monterrey plant's profits continued to deteriorate, as did the Engine Parts Division's profitability. Eventually, Aztec's corporate management cut its losses by selling off the Engine Parts Division to a competitor at bargain-basement prices. The division's new owners closed the Monterrey plant and changed the division's focus to be a boutique producer of high-quality engine parts, which was more in line with its own corporate strategy.

Ethical Issues

What ethical issues do you see in this scenario? How would you resolve them?

Chapter Summary

LO1 Compute product costs under a traditional, volume-based product-costing system. Traditional product-costing systems are structured on single, volume-based cost drivers, such as direct labor or machine hours. Overhead is applied to production jobs using a predetermined overhead rate, which is based on estimates of manufacturing overhead (in the numerator) and the level of some cost driver (in the denominator).

LO2 Explain how an activity-based costing system operates, including the use of a two-stage procedure for cost assignment, the identification of activity cost pools, and the selection of cost drivers. In the first stage of ABC, resource costs are identified and divided into activity cost pools. In the second stage, a cost driver is selected for each activity cost pool, and the costs in each pool are assigned to cost objects, such as products, services, product lines, customers, and so forth.

LO3 Explain the concept of cost levels, including unit-level, batch-level, product-sustaining-level, and facility-level costs. Unit-level costs are incurred for each unit produced. Batch-level costs are incurred once for each batch of products (i.e., one production run). Product-sustaining-level costs are incurred once for each product line. Facility-level costs are incurred to keep the overall facility in operation.

LO4 Compute product costs under an activity-based costing system. A product's cost is the sum of its direct-material cost, its direct-labor cost, and its overhead cost, which is the accumulation of all the resource costs driven to the product by the various cost drivers selected for the ABC system.

LO5 Explain why traditional, volume-based costing systems tend to distort product costs. Traditional, volume-based costing systems tend to distort product costs because of two factors: (1) product-line diversity and (2) non-unit-level overhead costs. No single cost driver can capture the complex relationships between products and the myriad activities necessary to produce and sell them.

LO6 Explain three criteria for selecting cost drivers. Three criteria for selecting cost drivers are: (1) the degree of correlation between the cost driver and the incurrence of costs in the activity cost pool associated with the cost driver; (2) the cost of measurement of the cost driver; and (3) the behavioral effects that might result from the selection of a cost driver.

LO7 Discuss several key issues in activity-based costing, including data collection and storyboarding. Collecting ABC data is difficult and costly. Techniques for data collection include interviews, examination of work product and other documentation, and sometimes storyboarding, which is a detailed map of the processes used in the organization.

LO8 Explain the concepts of activity-based management and two-dimensional ABC. Activity-based management (ABM) is the use of activity-based costing information to improve operations and eliminate non-value-added costs. One way of depicting ABM is the two-dimensional ABC model. This model combines the cost assignment role of ABC with the process and activity evaluation view of an ABC system.

LO9 Explain and execute a customer-profitability analysis. Customer profitability analysis is an application of ABM in which management determines the cost drivers for customer-related costs. The resulting ABC information is then used to assess the profitability of key customer relationships.

LO10 Understand and discuss how activity-based costing is used in service-industry organizations. Activity-based costing has found widespread successful implementation in the service industry. The application of ABC in the service industry is similar to that in manufacturing, wherein a two-stage costing model is used that first assigns resource costs to activity cost pools and then uses cost drivers to assign the costs in these pools to the various services provided and customers served. Many service-industry firms are implementing ABC and ABM systems to better meet the needs of management.

LO11 List and explain eight important features of just-in-time inventory and production management systems (Appendix). The key features of JIT systems are: (1) a smooth, uniform production rate; (2) a pull method of coordinating steps in the production process; (3) purchase and manufacturing in small lot sizes; (4) quick and inexpensive machine setups; (5) high quality levels for raw materials and finished products; (6) effective preventive maintenance of equipment; (7) an atmosphere of teamwork to improve the production process; and (8) multiskilled workers and flexible facilities.

Review Problem on Cost Drivers and Product-Cost Distortion

Euro Box Corporation manufactures a variety of special packaging boxes used in the pharmaceutical industry. The company's Zurich plant is semiautomated, but the special nature of the boxes requires some manual labor. The controller has chosen the following activity cost pools, cost drivers, and pool rates for the Zurich plant's product-costing system.

Activity Cost Pool	Overhead Cost	Cost Driver	Budgeted Level for Cost Driver	Pool Rate
Purchasing, storage, and material handling	$ 200,000	Raw-material costs	$ 1,000,000	20% of material cost
Engineering and product design	100,000	Hours in design department	5,000 hrs.	$20 per hour
Machine setup costs	70,000	Production runs	1,000 runs	$70 per run
Machine depreciation and maintenance	300,000	Machine hours	100,000 hrs.	$3 per hour
Factory depreciation, taxes, insurance, and utilities	200,000	Machine hours	100,000 hrs.	$2 per hour
Other manufacturing-overhead costs	150,000	Machine hours	100,000 hrs.	$1.50 per hour
Total	$1,020,000			

Two recent production orders had the following requirements.

	20,000 Units of Box C52	10,000 Units of Box W29
Direct-labor hours	42 hr.	21 hr.
Raw-material cost	$40,000	$35,000
Hours in design department	10	25
Production runs	2	4
Machine hours	24	20

Required:

1. Compute the total overhead that should be assigned to each of the two production orders, C52 and W29.

2. Compute the overhead cost per box in each order.

3. Suppose the Zurich plant were to use a single predetermined overhead rate based on direct-labor hours. The direct-labor budget calls for 4,000 hours.

   a. Compute the predetermined overhead rate per direct-labor hour.

   b. Compute the total overhead cost that would be assigned to the order for box C52 and the order for box W29.

   c. Compute the overhead cost per box in each order.

4. Why do the two product-costing systems yield such widely differing overhead costs per box?

Solution to Review Problem

1.

	Box C52	Box W29
Purchasing, storage, and material handling	$8,000 (20% × $40,000)	$7,000 (20% × $35,000)
Engineering and product design	200 (10 × $20/hr.)	500 (25 × $20/hr.)
Machine setup costs	140 (2 × $70/run)	280 (4 × $70/run)
Machine depreciation and maintenance	72 (24 × $3/hr.)	60 (20 × $3/hr.)
Factory depreciation, taxes, insurance, and utilities	48 (24 × $2/hr.)	40 (20 × $2/hr.)
Other manufacturing overhead costs	36 (24 × $1.50/hr.)	30 (20 × $1.50/hr.)
Total overhead assigned to production order	$8,496	$7,910

2. Overhead cost per box: $.4248 per box $\left(\dfrac{\$8,496}{20,000}\right)$ $.791 per box $\left(\dfrac{\$7,910}{10,000}\right)$

3. Computations based on a single predetermined overhead rate based on direct-labor hours:

   a. $\dfrac{\text{Total budgeted overhead}}{\text{Total budgeted direct-labor hours}} = \dfrac{\$1,020,000}{4,000} = \$255/\text{hr.}$

   b. Total overhead assigned to each order:

   Box C52 order: 42 direct-labor hours × $255/hr. = $10,710

   Box W29 order: 21 direct-labor hours × $255/hr. = $5,355

   c. Overhead cost per box:

   Box C52: $10,710 ÷ 20,000 = $.5355 per box

   Box W29: $5,355 ÷ 10,000 = $.5355 per box

4. The widely differing overhead costs are assigned as a result of the inherent inaccuracy of the single, volume-based overhead rate. The relative usage of direct labor by the two production orders does not reflect their relative usage of other manufacturing support services.

Key Terms

For each term's definition refer to the indicated page, or turn to the glossary at the end of the text.

activity analysis, 220

activity-based costing (ABC) system, 206

activity-based management (ABM), 220

activity cost pool, 206

activity dictionary, 219

batch-level activity, 207

bill of activities, 219

consumption ratio, 215

cost driver, 217

cost hierarchy, 207

customer-profitability analysis, 223

customer-profitability profile, 226

facility- (or general-operations) level activity, 207

just-in-time (JIT) inventory and production management system,* 235

just-in-time (JIT) purchasing,* 236

non-value-added activities, 220

non-value-added costs, 220

pool rate, 209

process, 222

process value analysis (PVA), 222

production Kanban,* 235

product-sustaining-level activity, 207

pull method,* 235

storyboarding, 218

total quality control (TQC),* 236

two-dimensional ABC model, 220

unit-level activity, 207

volume-based (or throughput-based) costing system, 205

withdrawal Kanban,* 235

*Term appears in appendix.

Just-in-Time Inventory and Production Management

A cost management tool that is widely used in manufacturing is the *just-in-time* (or *JIT*) system. A **just-in-time (JIT) inventory and production management system** is a comprehensive inventory and manufacturing control system in which no materials are purchased and no products are manufactured until they are needed. Raw materials and parts are purchased only as they are needed in some phase of the production process. Component parts and subassemblies are not manufactured in any stage of production until they are required in the next stage. Finished goods are manufactured only as they are needed to fill customer orders. A primary goal of a JIT production system is to *reduce or eliminate inventories* at every stage of production, from raw materials to finished goods. The JIT philosophy, made famous by Toyota, has been credited with the success of many of the world's leading manufacturers. Tremendous cost savings have been realized by many companies that have adopted the JIT approach.

How does a JIT system achieve its vast reductions in inventory and associated cost savings? A production-systems expert lists the following key features of the JIT approach.[14]

> **Learning Objective 11**
>
> List and explain eight important features of just-in-time inventory and production management systems.

1. *A smooth, uniform production rate.* An important goal of a JIT system is to establish a smooth production flow, beginning with the arrival of materials from suppliers and ending with the delivery of goods to customers.

2. *A pull method of coordinating steps in the production process.* Most manufacturing processes occur in multiple stages. Under the **pull method,** goods are produced in each manufacturing stage only as they are needed at the next stage. This approach reduces or eliminates work-in-process inventory between production steps. The result is a reduction in waiting time and its associated non-value-added cost.

   The pull method of production begins at the last stage of the manufacturing process.[15] When additional materials and parts are needed for final assembly, a message is sent to the immediately preceding work center to send the amount of materials and parts that will be needed over the next few hours. Often this message is in the form of a **withdrawal Kanban,** a card indicating the number and type of parts requested from the preceding work center. The receipt of the withdrawal Kanban in the preceding work center triggers the release of a **production Kanban,** which is another card specifying the number of parts to be manufactured in that work center. Thus, the parts are "pulled" from a particular work center by a need for parts in the subsequent work center. This *pull approach* to production is repeated all the way back through the manufacturing sequence toward the beginning. Nothing is manufactured at any stage until its need is signaled from the subsequent process via a Kanban.[16]

3. *Purchase of materials and manufacture of subassemblies and products in small lot sizes.* This is an outgrowth of the pull method of production planning. Materials are purchased and goods are produced only as required, rather than for the sake of building up stocks.

4. *Quick and inexpensive setups of production machinery.* In order to produce in small lot sizes, a manufacturer must be able to set up production runs quickly. Advanced manufacturing technology aids in this process, as more and more machines are computer-controlled.

5. *High quality levels for raw material and finished products.* If raw materials and parts are to arrive "just in time" for production, they must be "just right" for their intended purpose. Otherwise, the production line will be shut down and significant non-value-added costs of waiting will result. Moreover, if very small stocks of finished goods are to be maintained, then finished

---

[14]James B. Dilworth, *Production and Operations Management,* 3rd ed. (New York: Random House, 1996), pp. 354–61.

[15]You may find it helpful to review Exhibit 1–5 on page 58, which depicts the pull method of the JIT system.

[16]Toyota's ground-breaking JIT system originally was referred to as *Kanban,* a Japanese word meaning "signboard." See Takeo Tanaka, "Kaizen Budgeting: Toyota's Cost Control System under TQC," *Journal of Cost Management* 8, no. 3 (Fall 1994), p. 57.

products must be of uniform high quality. For this reason, a **total quality control (TQC)** program often accompanies a just-in-time production environment.

6. *Effective preventive maintenance of equipment.* If goods are to be manufactured just in time to meet customer orders, a manufacturer cannot afford significant production delays. By strictly adhering to routine maintenance schedules, the firm can avoid costly down time from machine breakdowns.

7. *An atmosphere of teamwork to improve the production system.* A company can maintain a competitive edge in today's worldwide market only if it is constantly seeking ways to improve its product or service, achieve more efficient operations, and eliminate non-value-added costs. My favorite football coach often says that a team must improve from one week to the next. Otherwise the team will get worse, because it rarely will stay at the same level. So it goes in business as well. If a company's employees are not constantly seeking ways to improve the firm's performance, before long its competitors will pass it by.

8. *Multiskilled workers and flexible facilities.* To facilitate just-in-time production, manufacturing equipment must be flexible enough to produce a variety of components and products. Otherwise, if a particular production line can produce only one item, bottlenecks may result. A bottleneck can hold up production in subsequent manufacturing stages and result in the non-value-added costs associated with waiting time.

JIT Purchasing   Along with a JIT production approach, many companies implement *JIT purchasing.* Under this approach, materials and parts are purchased from outside vendors only as they are needed. This avoids the costly and wasteful buildup of raw-material inventories. The following are five key features of **JIT purchasing.**

1. *Only a few suppliers.* This results in less time spent on vendor relations. Only highly reliable vendors, who can invariably deliver high-quality goods on time, are used.

2. *Long-term contracts negotiated with suppliers.* This eliminates costly paperwork and negotiations with each individual transaction. The need for delivery can be communicated via a telephone call or computer message. The long-term contracts state the price, quality, and delivery terms of the goods.

3. *Materials and parts delivered in small lot sizes immediately before they are needed.* This is the essence of the just-in-time approach. Costly inventories are avoided by having supplies arrive "just-in-time" to be placed into production.

4. *Only minimal inspection of delivered materials and parts.* The long-term contracts clearly state the quality of material required. Vendors are selected on the basis of their reliability in meeting these stringent standards and in delivering the correct amount of materials on time.

5. *Grouped payments to each vendor.* Instead of paying for each delivery, payments are made for batches of deliveries according to the terms of the contract. This reduces costly paperwork for both the vendor and the purchaser.

JIT purchasing is widely used in a variety of organizations. In manufacturing firms, it goes hand in hand with JIT production. In retail and service industry firms, JIT purchasing reduces costly warehouse inventories and streamlines the purchasing function.

Review Questions

5–1.   Briefly explain how a traditional, volume-based product-costing system operates.

5–2.   Why was Patio Grill Company's management being misled by the traditional product-costing system? What mistakes were being made?

5–3.   Explain how an activity-based costing system operates.

5–4.   What are cost drivers? What is their role in an activity-based costing system?

5–5.   List and briefly describe the four broad categories of activities identified in stage one of an activity-based costing system.

5–6.   How can an activity-based costing system alleviate the problems Patio Grill Company's management was having under its traditional, volume-based product-costing system?

5–7.   Why do product-costing systems based on a single, volume-based cost driver tend to overcost high-volume products? What undesirable strategic effects can such distortion of product costs have?

5–8.   How is the distinction between direct and indirect costs handled differently under volume-based versus activity-based costing systems?

5–9. Explain the concept of a *pool rate* in activity-based costing. (Refer to Exhibit 5–6.)

5–10. Briefly explain two factors that tend to result in product cost distortion under traditional, volume-based product-costing systems.

5–11. List three factors that are important in selecting cost drivers for an ABC system.

5–12. What is the role of *activity dictionary* in an ABC project?

5–13. Explain why a new product-costing system may be needed when line managers suggest that an apparently profitable product be dropped.

5–14. Explain why a manufacturer with diverse product lines may benefit from an ABC system.

5–15. Are activity-based costing systems appropriate for the service industry? Explain.

5–16. Explain why the maintenance of the medical-services provider network is treated as a product-sustaining-level activity by Pennsylvania Blue Shield.

5–17. How could the administration at Delaware Medical Center's Primary Care Unit use the activity-based costing information developed by the ABC project team?

5–18. Explain a key difference in the interpretation of the ABC data in Exhibit 5–7 (Patio Grill Company) and Exhibit 5–16 (Delaware Medical Center).

5–19. Explain the concept of *two-dimensional ABC.* Support your explanation with a diagram.

5–20. What is meant by the term *activity analysis?* Give three criteria for determining whether an activity adds value.

5–21. Distinguish between an activity's *trigger* and its *root cause.* Give an example of each.

5–22. What is meant by *customer-profitability analysis?* Give an example of an activity that might be performed more commonly for one customer than for another.

5–23. Explain the relationship between customer profitability analysis and activity-based costing.

5–24. What is a customer profitability profile?

5–25. (Appendix) Explain in words and then draw a diagram depicting the pull method of coordinating steps in a JIT system. (Refer to the JIT discussion in this chapter and to the JIT exhibit in Chapter 1.)

Exercises

All applicable Exercises are available with McGraw-Hill's *Connect Accounting*™.

Tioga Company manufactures sophisticated lenses and mirrors used in large optical telescopes. The company is now preparing its annual profit plan. As part of its analysis of the profitability of individual products, the controller estimates the amount of overhead that should be allocated to the individual product lines from the following information.

■ **Exercise 5–26**
Volume-Based Cost Driver versus ABC
(LO 1, 2, 4)

	Lenses	Mirrors
Units produced	25	25
Material moves per product line	5	15
Direct-labor hours per unit	200	200

The total budgeted material-handling cost is $50,000.

Required:

1. Under a costing system that allocates overhead on the basis of direct-labor hours, the material-handling costs allocated to one lens would be what amount?

2. Answer the same question as in requirement (1), but for mirrors.

3. Under activity-based costing (ABC), the material-handling costs allocated to one lens would be what amount? The cost driver for the material-handling activity is the number of material moves.

4. Answer the same question as in requirement (3), but for mirrors.

(CMA, adapted)

Urban Africa Cosmetics has used a traditional cost accounting system to apply quality-control costs uniformly to all products at a rate of 14 percent of direct-labor cost. Monthly direct-labor cost for Nile Blush makeup is $27,500. In an attempt to more equitably distribute quality-control costs, management is considering activity-based costing. The monthly data shown in the following chart have been gathered for Nile Blush makeup.

■ **Exercise 5–27**
Activity-Based Costing; Quality Control Costs
(LO 1, 2, 4)

Activity Cost Pool	Cost Driver	Pool Rates	Quantity of Driver for Nile Blush
Incoming material inspection	Type of material	$11.50 per type	10 types
In-process inspection	Number of units	.14 per unit	18,000 units
Product certification	Per order	77.00 per order	20 orders

Required:

1. Calculate the monthly quality-control cost to be assigned to the Nile Blush product line under each of the following product-costing systems.

    a. Traditional system, which assigns overhead on the basis of direct-labor cost.

    b. Activity-based costing.

2. Does the traditional product-costing system overcost or undercost the Nile Blush product line with respect to quality-control costs? By what amount?

(CMA, adapted)

■ **Exercise 5–28**
Cost Drivers; Activity Cost Pools
(LO 2, 3, 6)

Kentaro Corporation manufactures VCRs in its Tokyo plant. The following costs are budgeted for January.

Raw materials and components	2,950,000 *yen*
Insurance, plant	600,000
Electricity, machinery	120,000
Electricity, light	60,000
Engineering design	610,000
Depreciation, plant	700,000
Depreciation, machinery	1,400,000
Custodial wages, plant	40,000
Equipment maintenance, wages	150,000
Equipment maintenance, parts	30,000
Setup wages	40,000
Inspection of finished goods	30,000
Property taxes	120,000
Natural gas, heating	30,000

Required: Divide these costs into activity cost pools, and identify a cost driver for assigning each pool of costs to products. Calculate the total cost in each activity cost pool.

■ **Exercise 5–29**
Categorizing Activity Cost Pools
(LO 2, 3)

Refer to the information given in the preceding exercise. For each of the activity cost pools identified, indicate whether it represents a unit-level, batch-level, product-sustaining-level, or facility-level activity.

■ **Exercise 5–30**
Activity-Based Costing in a Government Agency; Use of Internet
(LO 2, 7, 10)

Visit the Web site of a city, of your choosing (e.g., for Paris, www.paris.fr; note that site is available in English and Spanish by clicking the appropriate buttons).

Required: Read about the services offered to the public by this governmental unit. Then discuss how activity-based costing could be used effectively by the governmental unit to determine the cost of providing these services.

■ **Exercise 5–31**
Distortion of Product Costs
(LO 2, 5)

Czech manufacturer Big Wheels Ltd (BWL) makes automobile and truck wheels. The company produces four basic, high-volume wheels used by large automobile and pickup truck manufacturers. BWL also has two specialty wheel lines. These are fancy, complicated wheels used in expensive sports cars.

Lately, BWL's profits have been declining. Asian competitors have been undercutting BWL's prices in three of its bread-and-butter product lines, and BWL's sales volume and market share have declined. In contrast, BWL's specialty wheels have been selling steadily, although in relatively small numbers, in spite of three recent price increases. At a recent staff meeting. BWL's president made the following remarks: "Our profits are falling dramatically. It costs us 29 dollars to manufacture our A22 wheel. That's our best seller, with a volume last year of 17,000 units. But our chief competitor is selling basically the same wheel for 27 dollars. I don't see how they can do it. I think it's just one more example of unfair foreign competition. I'm going to write the Prime Minister about it! Thank goodness for our specialty wheels. I think we've got to get our salespeople to sell more of them. Take the D52 model, for example.

It's a complicated thing to make, and we don't sell many. But look at the profit margin. Those wheels cost us 49 dollars to make, and we're selling them for 105 dollars each."

Required: What do you think is behind the problems faced by BWL? Comment on the president's remarks. Do you think his strategy is a good one? What do you recommend, and why?

Refer to the description given for Big Wheels Ltd. in the preceding exercise. Suppose the firm's president has decided to implement an activity-based costing system.

Required:

1. List and briefly describe the key features that BWL's new product-costing system should have.
2. What impact will the new system be likely to have on the company's situation?
3. What strategic options would you expect to be suggested by the product-costing results from the new system?

■ **Exercise 5–32**
Key Features of Activity-Based Costing
(LO 2, 5, 7)

Queenstown Vintners is a small, family-run vineyard and wine-making operation in southern New Zealand. The winery produces two varieties of wine: sauvignon blanc and chardonnay. Among the activities engaged in by the winery are the following:

■ **Exercise 5–33**
Winery; Classification of Activities
(LO 2, 3, 7)

1. Trimming: At the end of a growing season, the vines are trimmed, which helps prepare them for the next harvest.

2. Tying: The vines are tied onto wires to help protect them from the cold. (This also occurs at the end of the season.)

3. Hilling: Dirt is piled up around the roots to help protect them from frost.

4. Conditioning: After the snow melts in the spring, dirt is leveled back from the roots.

5. Untying: The vines are untied from the wires to allow them freedom to grow during the spring and summer months.

6. Chemical spraying: The vines are sprayed in the spring to protect them from disease and insects.

7. Harvesting: All of the grapes of both varieties are picked by hand to minimize damage.

8. Stemming and crushing: Batches of grapes are hand-loaded into a machine, which gently removes the stems and mildly crushes them.

9. Pressing: After removal from the stemmer/crusher, the juice runs freely from the grapes.

10. Filtering: The grapes are crushed mechanically to render more juice from them.

11. Fermentation: The sauvignon blanc grape juice is placed in stainless steel tanks for fermentation. The chardonnay grape juice undergoes a two-stage fermentation process in oak barrels.

12. Aging: The sauvignon blanc wines are aged in the stainless steel tanks for approximately a year. The chardonnays are aged in the oak barrels for about two years.

13. Bottling: A machine bottles the wine and corks the bottles.

14. Labeling: Each bottle is manually labeled with the name of the vintner, vintage, and variety.

15. Packing: The bottles are manually packed in 12-bottle cases.

16. Case labeling: The cases are hand-stamped with the same information that the bottles received.

17. Shipping: The wine is shipped to wine distributors and retailers, mainly in Asia. Generally, about 100 cases are shipped at a time.

18. Maintenance on buildings: This is done during the slow winter months.

19. Maintenance on equipment: This is done when needed, and on a routine basis for preventive maintenance.

Required: Classify each of the activities listed as a unit-, batch-, product-sustaining-, or facility-level activity.

United Technologies Corporation is using activity-based costing in two of its subsidiaries: Otis Elevator Company and Carrier Corporation. The following table shows 27 activities and eight accounts identified at Carrier, along with the classification determined by the ABC project team.[17]

Name of Activity or Account	Classification by Activity level
Acquiring material	Batch
Inspecting incoming materials	Batch
Moving materials	Batch
Planning production	Batch
Processing special orders	Batch
Processing supplier invoices	Batch
Receiving material	Batch
Scheduling production	Batch
Inspecting production processes	Batch
Processing purchase orders	Batch
Building occupancy	Facility
Depreciation	Facility
General management	Facility
Maintaining facilities	Facility
Managing the environment	Facility
Assuring quality	Sustaining
Expediting	Sustaining
Maintaining tools and dies	Sustaining
Maintaining/improving production processes	Sustaining
Managing human resources	Sustaining
Managing waste disposal	Sustaining
Processing payroll	Sustaining
Processing production information	Sustaining
Providing product cost	Sustaining
Setting manufacturing methods	Sustaining
Supervising production	Sustaining
Sustaining accounting	Sustaining
Maintaining production equipment	Sustaining
Direct-labor allowances	Unit
Direct-labor fringes	Unit
Utilities (equipment)	Unit
Overtime (hourly)	Unit
Rework	Unit
Shift differential	Unit
Spoilage	Unit

Required: Choose two activities or accounts from each of the four classifications and explain why you agree or disagree with the ABC project team's classification.

Hebrides Crafts Company sells craft kits and supplies to retail outlets and through its catalog. Some of the items are manufactured by Hebrides, while others are purchased for resale. For the products it manufactures, the company currently bases its selling prices on a product-costing system that accounts for direct material, direct labor, and the associated overhead costs. In addition to these product costs, Hebrides incurs substantial selling costs, and Angus McAdams, controller, has suggested that these selling costs should be included in the product pricing structure.

---

[17]Robert Adams and Ray Carter, "United Technologies' Activity-Based Accounting Is a Catalyst for Success," *As Easy as ABC* 18, p 4. United Technologies uses the term "*structural*-level activity." instead of "*facility*-level activity" as we have done in the chapter and in the table presented here.

After studying the costs incurred over the past two years for one of its products, skeins of knitting yarn, McAdams has selected four categories of selling costs and chosen cost drivers for each of these costs. The selling costs actually incurred during the past year and the cost drivers are as follows:

Cost Category	Amount	Cost Driver
Sales commissions	$ 787,500	Boxes of yarn sold to retail stores
Catalogs	295,400	Catalogs distributed
Cost of catalog sales	105,000	Skeins sold through catalog
Credit and collection	60,000	Number of retail orders
Total selling costs	$1,247,900	

The knitting yarn is sold to retail outlets in boxes, each containing 12 skeins of yarn. The sale of partial boxes is not permitted. Commissions are paid on sales to retail outlets but not on catalog sales. The cost of catalog sales includes telephone costs and the wages of personnel who take the catalog orders. McAdams believes that the selling costs vary significantly with the size of the order. Order sizes are divided into three categories as follows:

Order Size	Catalog Sales	Retail Sales
Small	1–10 skeins	1–10 boxes
Medium	11–20 skeins	11–20 boxes
Large	Over 20 skeins	Over 20 boxes

An analysis of the previous year's records produced the following statistics.

	Order Size			
	Small	Medium	Large	Total
Retail sales in boxes (12 skeins per box)	2,000	45,000	178,000	225,000
Catalog sales in skeins	79,000	52,000	44,000	175,000
Number of retail orders	485	2,415	3,100	6,000
Catalogs distributed	254,300	211,300	125,200	590,800

Required:

1. Prepare a schedule showing Hebrides Crafts Company's total selling cost for each order size and the per-skein selling cost within each order size.

2. Explain how the analysis of the selling costs for skeins of knitting yarn is likely to impact future pricing and product decisions at Hebrides.

(CMA, adapted)

As a group, discuss the activities of your college or university (e.g., admission, registration, etc.). List as many activities as you can.

Required: Make a presentation to your class that includes the following:
1. Your list of activities.
2. The classification of each activity (e.g., unit level).
3. An appropriate cost driver for each activity.

■ **Exercise 5–36**
Classification of Activities in a University; Cost Drivers
(LO 2, 3, 6, 7, 10)

Non-value-added costs occur in nonmanufacturing organizations, just as they do in manufacturing firms.

Required: Identify four potential non-value-added costs in (1) an airline, (2) a bank, and (3) a hotel.

■ **Exercise 5–37**
Non-Value-Added Costs
(LO 8)

Since you have always wanted to be an industrial baron, invent your own product and describe at least five steps used in its production.

Required: Explain how you would go about identifying non-value-added costs in the production process.

■ **Exercise 5–38**
Design Your Own Production Process; Non-Value-Added Costs
(LO 8)

■ **Exercise 5–39**
College Registration; Activity Analysis
(LO 8, 10)

As a group, think carefully about the various activities and steps involved in the course selection and registration process at your college or university.

Required:

1. List the steps in the registration process in the sequence in which they occur.
2. Prepare an activity analysis of the registration process. Discuss the activity linkages, triggers, and root causes.
3. Redesign your institution's course registration process with these goals in mind:
   a. Improve the convenience and effectiveness of the process for a student registering.
   b. Improve the effectiveness and cost efficiency of the process from the standpoint of the institution.

■ **Exercise 5–40**
Activity Analysis; Non-Value-Added Activities
(LO 8, 10)

Visit a restaurant for a meal or think carefully about a recent visit to a restaurant. List as many activities as you can think of that would be performed by the restaurant's employees for its customers.

Required: For each activity on your list, indicate the following:

1. Value-added or non-value-added.
2. The trigger of the activity.
3. The possible root causes of the activity.

■ **Exercise 5–41**
Performance Measures in Two-Dimensional ABC; ABM
(LO 8, 10)

List five activities performed by the employees of an airline *on the ground.*.

Required: For each of these activities, suggest a performance measure that could be used in activity-based management.

■ **Exercise 5–42**
Customer Profitability Analysis; Customers Ranked by Sales Revenue
(LO 9)

The customer-profitability analysis for Patio Grill Company, which is displayed in Exhibit 5–14, ranks customers by operating income. An alternative, often-used approach is to rank customers by sales revenue.

Required:

1. List the customer numbers in the left-hand column of Exhibit 5–14 by sales revenue, from highest to lowest. Is the ranking different from that in Exhibit 5–14?
2. Patio Grill Company's smallest customers, in terms of sales revenue, are last in the listing prepared for requirement (1). Are these customers the company's least profitable?
3. Would the customer-profitability profile in Exhibit 5–15 be different if the customers were ranked by sales revenue instead of operating income? Explain.
4. What factors could cause a larger customer (in terms of sales revenue) to be less profitable than a smaller customer?

■ **Exercise 5–43**
Customer-Profitability Graph
(LO 9)

Mariposa Design Company specializes in designing commercial office space in Mexico City. The firm's president recently reviewed the following income statement and noticed that operating profits were below her expectations. She had a hunch that certain customers were not profitable for the company and asked the controller to perform a customer-profitability analysis showing profitability by customer for the month of March.

MARIPOSA DESIGN COMPANY
Income Statement
For the Month Ended March 31

Sales revenue	$320,000
Cost of services billed	255,000
Gross margin	$ 65,000
Marketing and administrative costs	50,000
Operating profit	$ 15,000

The controller provided the following customer-profitability graph:

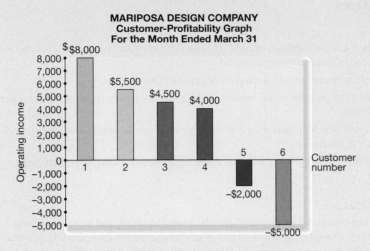

MARIPOSA DESIGN COMPANY
Customer-Profitability Graph
For the Month Ended March 31

Required: Put yourself in the position of Mariposa's controller and write a memo to the president to accompany the customer-profitability graph. Comment on the implications of the customer-profitability analysis and raise four or more questions that should be addressed by the firm's management team.

Service-industry firms can make effective use of ABC systems as well as manufacturers. For each of the following businesses, list five key activities that are important in the provision of the firm's service. For each activity cost pool, suggest an appropriate cost driver to use in assigning costs from the activity cost pool to the services provided to customers.

1. Air Canada
2. Pizza Hut
3. Island Health & Fitness Club
4. Bank Hapoalim branch bank
5. Ibis Hotels
6. Fatmawati Hospital

■ **Exercise 5–44**
Activity-Based Costing
(LO 2, 3, 10)

Problems

All applicable Problems are available with McGraw-Hill's *Connect Accounting*™.

Lotus Manufacturing has just completed a major change in its quality control (QC) process. Previously, products had been reviewed by QC inspectors at the end of each major process, and the company's five QC inspectors were charged as direct labor to the operation or job. In an effort to improve efficiency and quality, a computerized video QC system was purchased for $200,000. The system consists of a minicomputer, 10 video cameras, other peripheral hardware, and software. The new system uses cameras stationed by QC engineers at key points in the production process. Each time an operation changes or there is a new operation, the cameras are moved, and a new master picture is loaded into the computer by a QC engineer. The camera takes pictures of the units in process, and the computer compares them to the picture of a "good" unit. Any differences are sent to a QC engineer, who removes the bad units and discusses the flaws with the production supervisors. The new system has replaced the five QC inspectors with two QC engineers.

The operating costs of the new QC system, including the salaries of the QC engineers, have been included as factory overhead in calculating the company's plantwide manufacturing-overhead rate, which is based on direct-labor dollars. The company's president is confused. His vice president of production has told him how efficient the new system is. Yet there is a large increase in the overhead rate. The computation of the rate before and after automation is as follows:

■ **Problem 5–45**
Overhead Application;
Activity-Based Costing
(LO 1, 2, 7)

	Before	After
Budgeted manufacturing overhead	$1,900,000	$2,062,500
Budgeted direct-labor cost	1,000,000	750,000
Budgeted overhead rate	190%	275%

"Two-hundred seventy-five percent," lamented the president. "How can we compete with such a high overhead rate?"

Required:

1.   *a.*   Define "manufacturing overhead," and cite three examples of typical costs that would be included in manufacturing overhead.

     b.   Explain why companies develop predetermined overhead rates.

2.   Explain why the increase in the overhead rate should not have a negative financial impact on Lotus Manufacturing.

3.   Explain how Lotus Manufacturing could change its overhead application system to eliminate confusion over product costs.

4.   Discuss how an activity-based costing system might benefit Lotus Manufacturing.

(CMA, adapted)

■ **Problem 5–46**
Activity-Based Costing; Cost Analysis
(LO 1, 2, 4, 5, 7)

1. Total cost, standard: $157
2. Manufactured cost, standard unit: $181

Ontario, Inc. manufactures two products, Standard and Enhanced, and applies overhead on the basis of direct-labor hours. Anticipated overhead and direct-labor time for the upcoming accounting period are $800,000 and 25,000 hours, respectively. Information about the company's products follows.

Standard:

   Estimated production volume, 3,000 units

   Direct-material cost, $25 per unit

   Direct labor per unit, 3 hours at $12 per hour

Enhanced:

   Estimated production volume, 4,000 units

   Direct-material cost, $40 per unit

   Direct labor per unit, 4 hours at $12 per hour

Ontario's overhead of $800,000 can be identified with three major activities: order processing ($150,000), machine processing ($560,000), and product inspection ($90,000). These activities are driven by number of orders processed, machine hours worked, and inspection hours, respectively. Data relevant to these activities follow.

	Orders Processed	Machine Hours Worked	Inspection Hours
Standard	300	18,000	2,000
Enhanced	200	22,000	8,000
Total	500	40,000	10,000

Top management is very concerned about declining profitability despite a healthy increase in sales volume. The decrease in income is especially puzzling because the company recently undertook a massive plant renovation during which new, highly automated machinery was installed—machinery that was expected to produce significant operating efficiencies.

Required:

1.   Assuming use of direct-labor hours to apply overhead to production, compute the unit manufacturing costs of the Standard and Enhanced products if the expected manufacturing volume is attained.

2.   Assuming use of activity-based costing, compute the unit manufacturing costs of the Standard and Enhanced products if the expected manufacturing volume is attained.

3.   Ontario's selling prices are based heavily on cost.

     a.   By using direct-labor hours as an application base, which product is overcosted and which product is undercosted? Calculate the amount of the cost distortion for each product.

     b.   Is it possible that overcosting and undercosting (i.e., cost distortion) and the subsequent determination of selling prices are contributing to the company's profit woes? Explain.

4.   *Build a spreadsheet:* Construct an Excel spreadsheet to solve requirements 1, 2, and 3(*a*) above. Show how the solution will change if the following data change: the overhead associated with order processing is $300,000 and the overhead associated with product inspection is $270,000.

World Cuisine's Ho Chi Minh City plant manufactures three product lines, all premium induction cook tops. The plant's three product models are the Regular (REG), the Advanced (ADV), and the Gourmet (GMT). Until recently, the plant used a job-order product-costing system, with manufacturing overhead applied on the basis of direct-labor hours. The following table displays the basic data upon which the traditional costing system was based.

	REG	ADV	GMT
Planned annual production:			
Volume in units	5,000	4,000	1,000
Production runs	40 runs of 125 units	40 runs of 100 units	20 runs of 50 units
Direct material	$134	$156	$208
Direct labor:			
(not including setup)	$171 (9 hrs. @ $19 per hr.)	$209 (11 hrs. @ $19 per hr.)	$247 (13 hrs. @ $19 per hr.)
Machine hours (MH)			
per product unit	10 MH	12 MH	17 MH
Total machine hours consumed			
by product line in a year	50,000 (10 MH × 5,000)	48,000 (12 MH × 4,000)	17,000 (17 MH × 1,000)

The annual budgeted overhead is $1,224,000, and the company's predetermined overhead rate is $12 per direct-labor hour. The product costs for the three product models, as reported under the plant's traditional costing system, are shown in the following table.

	REG	ADV	GMT
Direct material	$134.00	$156.00	$208.00
Direct labor (not including set-up time)	171.00 (9 hr. @ $19)	209.00 (11 hr. @ $19)	247.00 (13 hr. @ $19)
Manufacturing overhead	108.00 (9 hr. @ $12)	132.00 (11 hr. @ $12)	156.00 (13 hr. @ $12)
Total	$413.00	$497.00	$611.00

World Cuisine's pricing policy is to set a target price for each product equal to 130 percent of the full product cost. Due to price competition from other appliance manufacturers, REG units were selling at $525, and ADV units were selling for $628. These prices were somewhat below the firm's target prices. However, these results were partially offset by greater-than-expected profits on the GMT product line. Management had raised the price on the GMT model to $800, which was higher than the original target price. Even at this price, World Cuisine's customers did not seem to hesitate to place orders, Moreover, the company's competitiors did not mount a challenge in the market for the GMT product line. Neverthless, concern continued to mount in Ho Chi Minh City about the difficulty in the REG and ADV markets. After all, these were the plant's bread-and-butter products, with projected annual sales of 5,000 REG units and 4,000 ADV units.

World Cuisine's director of cost management, Le Hung Thành, had been thinking for some time about a refinement in the Ho Chi Minh City plant's product-costing system. Thành wondered if the traditional, volume-based system was providing management with accurate data about product costs. He had read about activity-based costing, and wondered if ABC would be an improvement to the plant's product-costing system. After some discussion, an ABC proposal was made to the company's top management, and approval was obtained. The data collected for the new ABC system is displayed in the following table.

Activity	Activity Cost Pool	Cost Driver	Product Line	Cost Driver Quantity for Product Line
Machine related	$310,500	Machine Hours	REG	50,000
			ADV	48,000
			GMT	17,000
			Total	115,000
Material handling	52,500	Production Runs	REG	40
			ADV	40
			GMT	20
			Total	100

(continues)

■ **Problem 5–47**
Straightforward ABC calculations
(LO 1, 2, 4, 5)

2. Machine-related cost, REG line: $135,000
3. Total cost per unit, under ABC, GMT line: $668.90
4. Cost distortion per unit, ADV line: overcosted by $8.85

Activity	Activity Cost Pool	Cost Driver	Product Line	Cost Driver Quantity for Product Line
Purchasing	$ 75,000	Purchase Orders	REG	100
			ADV	96
			GMT	104
			Total	300
Setup	85,000	Production Runs	REG	40
			ADV	40
			GMT	20
			Total	100
Inspection	27,500	Inspection Hours	REG	400
			ADV	400
			GMT	300
			Total	1,100
Shipping	66,000	Shipments	REG	500
			ADV	400
			GMT	200
			Total	1,100
Engineering	32,500	Engineering Hours	REG	250
			ADV	200
			GMT	200
			Total	650
Facility	575,000	Machine Hours	REG	50,000
			ADV	48,000
			GMT	17,000
			Total	115,000

Required:

1. Show how the company's overhead rate of $12 per direct-labor hour was calculated.

2. Complete an activity-based costing analysis for World Cuisine's three product lines. Display the results of your ABC analysis in a table similar to Exhibit 5–7 in the text.

3. Prepare a table similar to Exhibit 5–8, which computes the new product cost for each product line under ABC.

4. Prepare a table similar to Exhibit 5–9, which compares the overhead cost, total product cost, and target price for each product line under the two alternative costing systems.

5. Was each of World Cuisine's three product lines overcosted or undercosted? By how much per unit?

6. *Build a spreadsheet:* Construct an Excel spreadsheet to solve requirement (2) above. Show how the solution would change if the machine-related cost pool was $621,000, and the facility cost pool was $1,150,000.

■ **Problem 5–48**
Continuation of Preceding Problem; Explaining ABC
(LO 2, 4)

Refer to your solution to requirement (2) of the preceding problem.

Required: Prepare an exhibit similar to Exhibit 5–6 in the text to explain the ABC calculations for the material-handling activity. Use your exhibit to explain ABC to a friend who is not a business major.

■ **Problem 5–49**
Activity-Based Costing;
Product Promotion
(LO 1, 2, 4, 5)

Chonju Furniture manufactures two types of home storage units—the Inch'on and the Pusan—and applies manufacturing overhead to all units at the rate of $80 per machine hour. Production information follows.

1. Inch'on manufacturing overhead cost: $160 per unit
2. Manufactured cost of Inch'on unit: $248.50

	Inch'on	Pusan
Anticipated volume (units)	8,000	15,000
Direct-material cost per unit	$ 35	$ 60
Direct-labor cost per unit	25	25

The controller, who is studying the use of activity-based costing, has determined that the firm's overhead can be identified with three activities: manufacturing setups, machine processing, and product shipping. Data on the number of setups, machine hours, and outgoing shipments, which are the activities' three respective cost drivers, follow.

	Inch'on	Pusan	Total
Setups	50	30	80
Machine hours	16,000	22,500	38,500
Outgoing shipments	100	75	175

The firm's total overhead of $3,080,000 is subdivided as follows: manufacturing setups, $672,000; machine processing, $1,848,000; and product shipping, $560,000.

Required:

1. Compute the unit manufacturing cost of the Inch'on and Pusan storage units by using the company's current overhead costing procedures.

2. Compute the unit manufacturing cost of the Inch'on and Pusan storage units by using activity-based costing.

3. Is the cost of the Inch'on storage unit overstated or understated (i.e., distorted) by the use of machine hours to allocate total manufacturing overhead to production? By how much?

4. Assume that the current selling price of an Inch'on storage unit is $270 and the marketing manager is contemplating a $35 discount to stimulate volume. Is this discount advisable? Briefly discuss.

Grady and Associates performs a variety of activities related to information systems and e-commerce consulting in Toronto, Canada. The firm, which bills $125 per hour for services performed, is in a very tight local labor market and is having difficulty finding quality help for its overworked professional staff. The cost per hour for professional staff time is $45. Selected information follows.

- Billable hours to clients for the year totaled 5,000, consisting of information systems services, 3,100; e-commerce consulting, 1,900.

- Administrative cost of $342,000 was (and continues to be) allocated to both services based on billable hours. These costs consist of staff support, $180,000; in-house computing, $136,400; and miscellaneous office charges, $25,600.

   A recent analysis of staff support costs found a correlation with the number of clients served. In-house computing and miscellaneous office charges varied directly with the number of computer hours logged and number of client transactions, respectively. A tabulation revealed the following data:

	Information Systems Services	E-Commerce Consulting	Total
Number of clients	200	50	250
Number of computer hours	2,600	1,800	4,400
Number of client transactions	400	600	1,000

Required:

1. Activity-based costing (ABC) is said to result in improved costing accuracy when compared with traditional costing procedures. Briefly explain how this improved accuracy is attained.

2. Assume that the firm uses traditional costing procedures, allocating total costs on the basis of billable hours. Determine the profitability of the firm's information systems and e-commerce activities, expressing your answer both in dollars and as a percentage of activity revenue.

3. Repeat requirement (2), using activity-based costing.

■ **Problem 5–50**
Activity-Based Costing;
Analysis of Operations
(LO 1, 2, 4, 7, 10)

2. E-commerce consulting,
income: $22,040
3. Activity-based application
rate, staff support: $720 per
client
Billings, information systems
services: $387,500

4. Jeffrey Grady, one of the firm's partners, doesn't care where his professionals spend their time because, as he notes, "many clients have come to expect both services and we need both to stay in business. Also, information systems and e-commerce professionals are paid the same hourly rate." Should Grady's attitude change? Explain.

5. Is an aggressive expansion of either service currently desirable? Briefly discuss.

■ **Problem 5–51**
Automation; Robotics;
Overhead Application;
Activity-Based Costing
(LO 1, 2, 5, 8)

John Patrick has recently been hired as controller of Valdosta Vinyl Company (VVC), a manufacturer of vinyl siding used in residential construction. VVC has been in the vinyl siding business for many years and is currently investigating ways to modernize its manufacturing process. At the first staff meeting Patrick attended, Jack Kielshesky, chief engineer, presented a proposal for automating the Molding Department. Kielshesky recommended that the company purchase two robots that would have the capability of replacing the eight direct-labor employees in the department. The cost savings outlined in the proposal include the elimination of direct-labor cost in the Molding Department plus a reduction of manufacturing overhead cost in the department to zero, because VVC charges manufacturing overhead on the basis of direct-labor dollars using a plantwide rate. The president of VVC was puzzled by Kielshesky's explanation: "This just doesn't make any sense. How can a department's overhead rate drop to zero by adding expensive, high-tech manufacturing equipment? If anything, it seems like the rate ought to go up."

Kielshesky responded by saying "I'm an engineer, not an accountant. But if we're charging overhead on the basis of direct labor, and we eliminate the labor, then we eliminate the overhead."

Patrick agreed with the president. He explained that as firms become more automated, they should rethink their product-costing systems. The president then asked Patrick to look into the matter and prepare a report for the next staff meeting. Patrick gathered the following data on the manufacturing-overhead rates experienced by VVC over the years. Patrick also wanted to have some departmental data to present at the meeting and, by using VVC's accounting records, he was able to estimate the following annual averages for each manufacturing department over the five decades since VVC's formation.

Historical Plantwide Data

Decade	Average Annual Manufacturing-Overhead Cost	Average Annual Direct-Labor Cost	Average Manufacturing-Overhead Application Rate
1st	$ 2,200,000	$2,000,000	110%
2nd	6,240,000	2,400,000	260
3rd	13,600,000	4,000,000	340
4th	24,600,000	6,000,000	410
5th	38,710,000	7,900,000	490

Annual Averages during Recent Years

	Cutting Department	Finishing Department	Molding Department
Manufacturing overhead	$22,000,000	$14,000,000	$4,000,000
Direct labor	4,000,000	3,500,000	500,000

Required:

1. Disregarding the proposed use of robots in the Molding Department, describe the shortcomings of the system for applying overhead that is currently used by Valdosta Vinyl Company.

2. Explain the misconceptions underlying Kielshesky's statement that the manufacturing-overhead cost in the Molding Department will be reduced to zero if the automation proposal is implemented.

3. Recommend ways to improve VVC's method for applying overhead by describing how it should revise its product-costing system for each of the following departments:

   a. In the Cutting and Finishing Departments.

   b. To accommodate automation in the Molding Department.

(CMA, adapted)

The controller for Mumbai Fertilizers Limited has established the following activity cost pools and cost drivers.

Activity Cost Pool	Budgeted Overhead Cost	Cost Driver	Budgeted Level for Cost Driver	Pool Rate
Machine setups	$250,000	Number of setups	125	$2,000 per setup
Material handling	75,000	Weight of raw material	18,750 kg.	$4 per kg.
Hazardous waste control	25,000	Weight of hazardous chemicals used	2,500 kg.	$10 per kg.
Quality control	75,000	Number of inspections	1,000	$75 per inspection
Other overhead costs	200,000	Machine hours	20,000	$10 per machine hour
Total	$625,000			

An order for 1,000 bags of Nitrogen Plus fertilizer has the following production requirements.

Machine setups	5 setups
Raw material	5,000 kg.
Hazardous materials	1,000 kg.
Inspections	10 inspections
Machine hours	500 machine hours

Required:

1. Compute the total overhead that should be assigned to the Nitrogen Plus fertilizer.
2. What is the overhead cost per bag of fertilizer?
3. Suppose Mumbai Fertilizers Limited were to use a single predetermined overhead rate based on machine hours. Compute the rate per hour.
4. Under the approach in requirement (3), how much overhead would be assigned to the Nitrogen Plus fertilizer order?

    a. In total.

    b. Per bag of fertilizer.

5. Explain why these two product-costing systems result in such widely differing costs. Which system do you recommend? Why?
6. *Build a spreadsheet:* Construct an Excel spreadsheet to solve requirements (1), (2), (3), and (4) above. Show how the solution will change if the following data change. The overhead associated with machine setups is $375,000, and there are 500 inspections budgeted.

Refer to the original data given in the preceding problem for Mumbai Fertilizers Limited.

Required:

1. Calculate the per-bag cost of a production order for 100 bags of Clear Field weed killer. In addition to direct material costing $140 per bag and direct labor costing $40 per bag, the order requires the following:

Machine setups	3
Raw material	450 kg.
Hazardous materials	150 kg.
Inspections	3
Machine hours	50

2. *Build a spreadsheet:* Construct an Excel spreadsheet to solve the preceding requirement. (This will be an extension of the spreadsheet constructed for the preceding problem.) Show how the solution will change if the data *given in the preceding problem* change as follows: the overhead associated with machine setups is $375,000, and there are 500 inspections budgeted.

■ **Problem 5–52**
Activity Cost Pools; Cost Drivers; Pool Rates
(LO 1, 2, 3, 4, 5, 7)

3. Predetermined overhead rate: $31.25 per machine hr.

■ **Problem 5–53**
Overhead Cost Drivers
(LO 2, 3, 4)

1. Unit cost per bag: $280.25

■ **Problem 5–54**
Activity-Based Costing;
Activity-Based Management
(LO 2, 3, 4, 5, 7)

2. Total cost, royal:
$4,431,900

Montreal Electronics Company manufactures two large-screen television models: the Nova, which has been produced for five years and sells for $900, and the Royal, a new model introduced in early 20x0, which sells for $1,140. Based on the following income statement for 20x1, a decision has been made to concentrate Montreal's marketing resources on the Royal model and to begin to phase out the Nova model.

MONTREAL ELECTRONICS COMPANY
Income Statement
For the Year Ended December 31, 20x1

	Royal	Nova	Total
Sales	$4,560,000	$19,800,000	$24,360,000
Cost of goods sold	3,192,000	12,540,000	15,732,000
Gross margin	$1,368,000	$ 7,260,000	$ 8,628,000
Selling and administrative expense	978,000	5,830,000	6,808,000
Net income	$ 390,000	$ 1,430,000	$ 1,820,000
Units produced and sold	4,000	22,000	
Net income per unit sold	$ 97.50	$ 65.00	

The standard unit costs for the Royal and Nova models are as follows:

	Royal	Nova
Direct material	$584	$208
Direct labor:		
Royal (3.5 hr. × $12)	42	
Nova (1.5 hr. × $12)		18
Machine usage:		
Royal (4 hr. × $18)	72	
Nova (8 hr. × $18)		144
Manufacturing overhead*	100	200
Standard cost	$798	$570

*Manufacturing overhead was applied on the basis of machine hours at a predetermined rate of $25 per hour.

Montreal Electronics Company's controller is advocating the use of activity-based costing and activity-based management and has gathered the following information about the company's manufacturing-overhead costs for 20x1.

Activity Center (cost driver)	Traceable Costs	Number of Events		
		Royal	Nova	Total
Soldering (number of solder joints)	$ 942,000	385,000	1,185,000	1,570,000
Shipments (number of shipments)	860,000	3,800	16,200	20,000
Quality control (number of inspections)	1,240,000	21,300	56,200	77,500
Purchase orders (number of orders)	950,400	109,980	80,100	190,080
Machine power (machine hours)	57,600	16,000	176,000	192,000
Machine setups (number of setups)	750,000	14,000	16,000	30,000
Total traceable costs	$4,800,000			

Required:

1. Briefly explain how an activity-based costing system operates.

2. Using activity-based costing, determine if Montreal Electronics should continue to emphasize the Royal model and phase out the Nova model.

(CMA, adapted)

Birmingham Circuits plc manufactures several different types of printed circuit boards; however, two of the boards account for the majority of the company's sales. The first of these boards, a standard-definition video (SD) board, has been a standard in the industry for several years. The market for this type of board is competitive and price-sensitive. Birmingham plans to sell 65,000 of the SD boards in 20x1 at a price of $170 per unit. The second high-volume product, a high-definition circuit board (HD) used in flat-panel televisions, is a recent addition to Birmingham's product line. Because the HD board incorporates the latest technology, it can be sold at a premium price. The 20x1 plans include the sale of 40,000 HD boards at $330 per unit.

Birmingham's management group is meeting to discuss how to spend the sales and promotion dollars for 20x1. The sales manager believes that the market share for the SD board could be expanded by concentrating Birmingham's promotional efforts in this area. In response to this suggestion, the production manager said, "Why don't you go after a bigger market for the HD board? The cost sheets that I get show that the contribution from the HD board is more than double the contribution from the SD board. I know we get a premium price for the HD board. Selling it should help overall profitability."

The cost-accounting system shows that the following costs apply to the HD and SD boards.

	HD Board	SD Board
Direct material	$160	$100
Direct labor	4 hr.	1.5 hr.
Machine time	1.5 hr.	.5 hr.

Variable manufacturing overhead is applied on the basis of direct-labor hours. For 20x1, variable overhead is budgeted at $1,120,000, and direct-labor hours are estimated at 280,000. The hourly rates for machine time and direct labor are $10 and $14, respectively. The company applies a material handling charge at 10 percent of material cost. This material-handling charge is not included in variable manufacturing overhead. Total 20x1 expenditures for direct material are budgeted at $10,800,000.

Andrew Fulton, Birmingham's controller, believes that before the management group proceeds with the discussion about allocating sales and promotional dollars to individual products, it might be worthwhile to look at these products on the basis of the activities involved in their production. Fulton has prepared the following schedule to help the management group understand this concept.

"Using this information," Fulton explained, "we can calculate an activity-based cost for each SD board and each HD board and then compare it to the standard cost we have been using. The only cost that remains the same for both cost methods is the cost of direct material. The cost drivers will replace the direct labor, machine time, and overhead costs in the old standard cost figures."

Budgeted Cost		Cost Driver	Budgeted Annual Activity for Cost Driver
Procurement	$ 400,000	Number of parts	4,000,000 parts
Production scheduling	220,000	Number of boards	110,000 boards
Packaging and shipping	440,000	Number of boards	110,000 boards
Total	$ 1,060,000		
Machine setup	$ 446,000	Number of setups	278,750 setups
Hazardous waste disposal	48,000	Kilograms of waste	8,000 kilograms
Quality control	560,000	Number of inspections	160,000 inspections
General supplies	66,000	Number of boards	110,000 boards
Total	$ 1,120,000		
Machine insertion	$ 1,200,000	Number of parts	3,000,000 parts
Manual insertion	4,000,000	Number of parts	1,000,000 parts
Wave-soldering	132,000	Number of boards	110,000 boards
Total	$ 5,332,000		

Required per Unit	HD Board	SD Board
Parts:	55	25
Machine insertions	35	24
Manual insertions	20	1
Machine setups	3	2
Hazardous waste disposal	.175 kg.	.01 kg.
Inspections	2	1

■ **Problem 5–55**
Activity-Based Costing
(LO 1, 2, 4, 5)

2. Total contribution margin from HD board: $2,760,000
3. Using ABC, total contribution margin from SD board: $2,557,100

Required:

1. Identify at least four general advantages associated with activity-based costing.

2. On the basis of Birmingham's unit cost data given in the problem, calculate the total amount that each of the two product lines will contribute toward covering fixed costs and profit in 20x1. (In other words, for each product line, calculate the total sales revenue minus the total *variable* costs. This amount is often referred to as a product's total *contribution margin.*)

3. Repeat requirement (2) but now use the cost data from the activity-based costing system.

4. Explain how a comparison of the results of the two costing methods may impact the decisions made by Birmingham's management group.

(CMA, adapted)

■ **Problem 5–56**
Activity-Based Costing
(LO 1, 2, 4, 5, 7)

2. New product cost, under ABC: $7.46 per pound of Kona

World Gourmet Coffee Company (WGCC) is a distributor and processor of different blends of coffee. The company buys coffee beans from around the world and roasts, blends, and packages them for resale in the United States. WGCC currently has 15 different coffees that it offers to gourmet shops in one-pound bags. The major cost is raw materials; however, there is a substantial amount of manufacturing overhead in the predominantly automated roasting and packing process. The company uses relatively little direct labor.

Some of the coffees are very popular and sell in large volumes, while a few of the newer blends have very low volumes. WGCC prices its coffee at full product cost, including allocated overhead, plus a markup of 30 percent. If prices for certain coffees are significantly higher than market, adjustments are made. The company competes primarily on the quality of its products, but customers are price-conscious as well.

Data for the 20x1 budget include manufacturing overhead of $3,000,000, which has been allocated on the basis of each product's direct-labor cost. The budgeted direct-labor cost for 20x1 totals $600,000. Based on the sales budget and raw-material budget, purchases and use of raw materials (mostly coffee beans) will total $6,000,000.

The expected prime costs for one-pound bags of two of the company's products are as follows:

	Kona	Malaysian
Direct material	$3.20	$4.20
Direct labor	.30	.30

WGCC's controller believes the traditional product-costing system may be providing misleading cost information. She has developed an analysis of the 20x1 budgeted manufacturing-overhead costs shown in the following chart.

Activity	Cost Driver	Budgeted Activity	Budgeted Cost
Purchasing	Purchase orders	1,158	$ 579,000
Material handling	Setups	1,800	720,000
Quality control	Batches	720	144,000
Roasting	Roasting hours	96,100	961,000
Blending	Blending hours	33,600	336,000
Packaging	Packaging hours	26,000	260,000
Total manufacturing-overhead cost			$3,000,000

Data regarding the 20x1 production of Kona and Malaysian coffee are shown in the following table. There will be no raw-material inventory for either of these coffees at the beginning of the year.

	Kona	Malaysian
Budgeted sales	2,000 lb.	100,000 lb.
Batch size	500 lb.	10,000 lb.
Setups	3 per batch	3 per batch
Purchase order size	500 lb.	25,000 lb.
Roasting time	1 hr. per 100 lb.	1 hr. per 100 lb.
Blending time	.5 hr. per 100 lb.	.5 hr. per 100 lb.
Packaging time	.1 hr. per 100 lb.	.1 hr. per 100 lb.

Required:

1. Using WGCC's current product-costing system:

   a. Determine the company's predetermined overhead rate using direct-labor cost as the single cost driver.

   b. Determine the full product costs and selling prices of one pound of Kona coffee and one pound of Malaysian coffee.

2. Develop a new product cost, using an activity-based costing approach, for one pound of Kona coffee and one pound of Malaysian coffee.

3. What are the implications of the activity-based costing system with respect to

   a. The use of direct labor as a basis for applying overhead to products?

   b. The use of the existing product-costing system as the basis for pricing?

(CMA, adapted)

Dragon Metal Works dedicates its Guangzhou plant to the manufacture of two industrial valves, Valve CX and Valve KV. The firm uses a single, plantwide overhead rate based on direct-labor hours. Production and product-costing data are as follows:

■ **Problem 5–57**
Activity-Based Costing; Activity Cost Pools; Pool Rates; Calculation of Product Costs; Cost Distortion
(LO 1, 2, 3, 4, 5)

2. Pool rate, plant-related costs: $500 per m^2

5. New target price, Valve CX: $615.36

	Valve CX	Valve KV
Production quantity	1,000 units	5,000 units
Direct material	$ 40	$ 60
Direct labor (not including setup time)	30 (2 hr. at $15)	45 (3 hr. at $15)
Manufacturing overhead*	98 (2 hr. at $49)	147 (3 hr. at $49)
Total cost per unit	$ 168	$ 252

*Calculation of predetermined overhead rate:

Manufacturing overhead budget:

Machine-related costs	$450,000
Setup and inspection	$197,000
Engineering	90,000
Plant-related costs	96,000
Total	$833,000

Predetermined overhead rate:

$$\frac{\text{Budgeted manufacturing overhead}}{\text{Budgeted direct-labor hours}} = \frac{\$833,000}{(1,000)(2) + (5,000)(3)} = \$49 \text{ per direct-labor hour}$$

Dragon Metal Works prices its products at 120 percent of cost, which yields target prices of $201.60 for Valve CX and $302.40 for Valve KV. Recently, however, Dragon has been challenged in the market for Valve KV by an Indian competitor, Ganges Metal Products. A new entrant in this market, Ganges has been selling a product virtually identical to Valve KV for $220 each. Dragon's president is puzzled by Ganges' ability to sell its Valve KV clone at such a low cost. She has asked you (the controller) to look into the matter. You have determined that cost of labor and materials are similar for the two companies, so you suspect that Dragon's traditional, volume-based product-costing system may be causing cost distortion between the firm's two products. Valve KV is a high-volume, relatively simple product. Valve CX, on the other hand, is quite complex and is produced in much lower volume. As a result, you have begun work on an activity-based costing system.

Required:

1. Let each of the overhead categories in the budget represent an activity cost pool. Categorize each in terms of the type of activity (e.g., unit-level activity).

2. The following cost drivers have been identified for the four activity cost pools.

Activity Cost Pool	Cost Driver	Budgeted Level of Cost Driver
Machine-related costs	Machine hours	9,000 hr.
Setup and inspection	Number of production runs	40 runs
Engineering	Engineering change orders	100 change orders
Plant-related costs	Plant area used	192 m^2

You have gathered the following additional information:

- Each Valve CX requires 4 machine hours, whereas each Valve KV requires 1 machine hour.

- Valve CX are manufactured in production runs of 50 units each. Valve KV are manufactured in 250-unit batches.

- Three-quarters of the engineering activity, as measured in terms of change orders, is related to Valve CX.

- The plant has 192 m² of space, 80 percent of which is used in the production of Valve CX.

  For each activity cost pool, compute a pool rate. (*Hint:* Regarding the pool rate refer to Exhibit 5–6.)

3. Determine the unit cost, for each activity cost pool, for Valve CX and Valve KV.
4. Compute the new product cost per unit for Valve CX and Valve KV, using the ABC system.
5. Using the same pricing policy as in the past, compute prices for Valve CX and Valve KV. Use the product costs determined by the ABC system.
6. Show that the ABC system fully assigns the total budgeted manufacturing overhead costs of $833,000.
7. Show how Dragon Metal Works traditional, volume-based costing system distorted its product costs. (Refer to Exhibit 5–10 for guidance.)

■ **Problem 5–58**
Activity-Based Costing;
Forecasting; Ethics
(LO 1, 2, 4, 5)

1. Total Material-Handling Department costs: $288,000
3. Reduction in material-handling costs allocated to government contracts: $74,600
4. Cumulative impact of recommended change in allocating Material-Handling Department costs: $234,346

Industrie Aéronautique Grenoble (IAG) was founded 25 years ago by Francois Chastres as a small machine shop producing machined parts for the aircraft industry, which is prominent in southeastern France. By the end of its first decade, IAG's annual sales had reached $15 million, almost exclusively under government contracts. The next 15 years brought slow but steady growth as cost-reimbursement government contracts continued to be the main source of revenue. Realizing that IAG could not depend on government contracts for long-term growth and stability, Michel Chastres, son of the founder and now president of the company, began planning for diversified commercial growth. As a result of these efforts, three years ago IAG had succeeded in reducing the ratio of government contract sales to 50 percent of total sales.

Traditionally, the costs of the Material-Handling Department have been allocated to direct material as a percentage of direct-material dollar value. This was adequate when the majority of the manufacturing was homogeneous and related to government contracts. Recently, however, government auditors have rejected some proposals, stating that "the amount of Material-Handling Department costs allocated to these proposals is disproportionate to the total effort involved."

Ann-Marie Barré, the newly hired cost-accounting manager, was asked by the manager of the Government Contracts Unit, Björn Andersson, to find a more equitable method of allocating Material-Handling Department costs to the user departments. Her review has revealed the following information.

- The majority of the direct-material purchases for government contracts are high-dollar, low-volume purchases, while commercial materials represent low-dollar, high-volume purchases.

- Administrative departments such as marketing, finance and administration, human resources, and maintenance also use the services of the Material-Handling Department on a limited basis but have never been charged in the past for material-handling costs.

- One purchasing agent with a direct phone line is assigned exclusively to purchasing high-dollar, low-volume material for government contracts at an annual salary of $36,000. Supplemental employee benefits (beyond those included in base salary/payroll) are estimated to be 20 percent of the annual salary. The annual dedicated phone line costs are $2,800.

The components of the Material-Handling Department's budget for 20x1, as proposed by Barré's predecessor, are as follows:

Payroll	$ 180,000
Supplemental employee benefits	36,000
Telephone	38,000
Other utilities	22,000
Materials and supplies	6,000
Depreciation	6,000
Direct-material budget:	
Government contracts	2,006,000
Commercial products	874,000

Barré has estimated the number of purchase orders to be processed in 20x1 to be as follows:

Government contracts*	80,000
Commercial products	156,000
Marketing	1,800
Finance and administration	2,700
Human resources	500
Maintenance	1,000
Total	242,000

*Exclusive of high dollar, low-volume materials.

Barré recommended to Andersson that material-handling costs be allocated on a per-purchase-order basis. Andersson realizes and accepts that the company has been allocating to government contracts more material-handling costs than can be justified. However, the implication of Barré's analysis could be a decrease in his unit's earnings and, consequently, a cut in his annual bonus. Andersson told Barré to "adjust" her numbers and modify her recommendation so that the results will be more favorable to the Government Contracts Unit.

Being new in her position, Barré is not sure how to proceed. She feels ambivalent about Andersson's instructions and suspects his motivation. To complicate matters for Barré, Chastres has asked her to prepare a three-year forecast of the Government Contracts Unit's results, and she believes that the newly recommended allocation method would provide the most accurate data. However, this would put her in direct opposition to Andersson's directives.

Barré has assembled the following data to project the material-handling costs.

- Total direct-material costs increase 2.5 percent per year.
- Material-handling costs remain the same percentage of direct-material costs.
- Direct government costs (payroll, employee benefits, and direct phone line) remain constant.
- The number of purchase orders increases 5 percent per year.
- The ratio of government purchase orders to total purchase orders remains at 33 percent.
- In addition, she has assumed that government material in the future will be 70 percent of total material.

Required:

1. Calculate the material-handling rate that would have been used by Ann-Marie Barré's predecessor at IAG.
2. *a.* Calculate the revised material-handling costs to be allocated on a per-purchase-order basis.
   b. Discuss why purchase orders might be a more reliable cost driver than the dollar amount of direct material.
3. Calculate the difference due to the change to the new method of allocating material-handling costs to government contracts.
4. Prepare a forecast of the cumulative dollar impact over a three-year period from 20x1 through 20x3 of Ann-Marie Barré's recommended change for allocating Material-Handling Department costs to the Government Contracts Unit. Round all calculations to the nearest whole number.
5. Referring to the standards of ethical conduct for management accountants:
   a. Discuss why Ann-Marie Barré's has an ethical conflict.
   b. Identify several steps that Barré could take to resolve the ethical conflict.

(CMA, adapted)

Marconi Manufacturing produces two items in its Trumbull Plant: Tuff Stuff and Ruff Stuff. Since inception, Marconi has used only one manufacturing-overhead cost pool to accumulate costs. Overhead has been allocated to products based on direct-labor hours. Until recently, Marconi was the sole producer of Ruff Stuff and was able to dictate the selling price. However, last year Marvella Products began marketing a comparable product at a price below the cost assigned by Marconi. Market share has declined rapidly, and Marconi must now decide whether to meet the competitive price or to discontinue the product line. Recognizing that discontinuing the product line would place an additional burden on its remaining product, Tuff Stuff, management is using activity-based costing to determine if it would show a different cost structure for the two products.

■ **Problem 5–59**
Activity-Based Costing; Production and Pricing Decisions
(LO 1, 2, 3, 4, 5)

1(b). Tuff Stuff unit cost: $28.00
3. Fabricating cost per unit, Tuff Stuff: $4.93 per unit (rounded)

The two major indirect costs for manufacturing the products are power usage and setup costs. Most of the power is used in fabricating, while most of the setup costs are required in assembly. The setup costs are predominantly related to the Tuff Stuff product line.

A decision was made to separate the Manufacturing Department costs into two activity cost pools as follows:

Fabricating: machine hours will be the cost driver.

Assembly: number of setups will be the cost driver.

The controller has gathered the following information.

MANUFACTURING DEPARTMENT
Annual Budget before Separation of Overhead

		Product Line	
	Total	Tuff Stuff	Ruff Stuff
Number of units..		20,000	20,000
Direct-labor hours*..		2 hours per unit	3 hours per unit
Total direct-labor cost...	$800,000		
Direct material..		$5.00 per unit	$3.00 per unit
Budgeted overhead:			
Indirect labor	24,000		
Fringe benefits...	5,000		
Indirect material..	31,000		
Power	180,000		
Setup	75,000		
Quality assurance	10,000		
Other utilities...	10,000		
Depreciation...	15,000		

*Direct-labor hourly rate is the same in both departments.

MANUFACTURING DEPARTMENT
Cost Structure after Separation of Overhead into Activity Cost Pools

	Fabrication	Assembly
Direct-labor cost	75%	25%
Direct material (no change)	100%	0%
Indirect labor	75%	25%
Fringe benefits	80%	20%
Indirect material	$ 20,000	$11,000
Power	$160,000	$20,000
Setup	$ 5,000	$70,000
Quality assurance	80%	20%
Other utilities	50%	50%
Depreciation	80%	20%

Cost driver:

	Product Line	
	Tuff Stuff	Ruff Stuff
Machine-hours per unit	4.4	6.0
Setups	1,000	272

Required:

1. Assigning overhead based on direct-labor hours, calculate the following:
   a. Total budgeted cost of the Manufacturing Department.
   b. Unit cost of Tuff Stuff and Ruff Stuff.
2. After separation of overhead into activity cost pools, compute the total budgeted cost of each department: fabricating and assembly.

3. Using activity-based costing, calculate the unit costs for each product. (In computing the pool rates for the fabricating and assembly activity cost pools, round to the nearest cent. Then, in computing unit product costs, round to the nearest cent.)

4. Discuss how a decision regarding the production and pricing of Ruff Stuff will be affected by the results of your calculations in the preceding requirements.

(CMA, adapted)

Gigabyte, Inc. manufactures three products for the computer industry:

Grandes (product G): annual sales, 8,000 units

Trucos (product T): annual sales, 15,000 units

Walkirias (product W): annual sales, 4,000 units

The company uses a traditional, volume-based product-costing system with manufacturing overhead applied on the basis of direct-labor dollars. The product costs have been computed as follows:

■ Problem 5–60
Traditional versus Activity-Based Costing Systems
(LO 1, 2, 3, 4, 5)

5. Reported product costs with ABC, product G: $141.67
6. Reported product costs with ABC, product T: $163.74

	Product G	Product T	Product W
Raw material	$ 35.00	$ 52.50	$17.50
Direct labor	16.00 (.8 hr. at $20)	12.00 (.6 hr. at $20)	8.00 (.4 hr. at $20)
Manufacturing overhead*	140.00	105.00	70.00
Total product cost	$191.00	$169.50	$95.50

*Calculation of predetermined overhead rate:

Manufacturing overhead budget:

Machine setup	$ 5,250
Machinery	1,225,000
Inspection	525,000
Material handling	875,000
Engineering	344,750
Total	$2,975,000

Direct-labor budget (based on budgeted annual sales):

Product G:	8,000 × $16.00	=	$128,000
Product I:	15,000 × $12.00	=	180,000
Product W:	4,000 × $8.00	=	32,000
Total			$340,000

Predetermined overhead rate $= \dfrac{\text{Budgeted overhead}}{\text{Budgeted direct labor}} = 875\%$

Gigabyte's pricing method has been to set a target price equal to 150 percent of full product cost. However, only the Trucos have been selling at their target price. The target and actual current prices for all three products are the following:

	Product G	Product T	Product W
Product cost	$191.00	$169.50	$ 95.50
Target price	286.50	254.25	143.25
Actual current selling price	213.00	254.25	200.00

Gigabyte has been forced to lower the price of Grandes in order to get orders. In contrast, Gigabyte has raised the price of Walkirias several times, but there has been no apparent loss of sales. Gigabyte, Inc. has been under increasing pressure to reduce the price even further on Grandes. In contrast, Gigabyte's competitors do not seem to be interested in the market for Walkirias. Gigabyte apparently has this market to itself.

Required:

1. Is product G the company's least profitable product?
2. Is product W a profitable product for Gigabyte, Inc.?
3. Comment on the reactions of Gigabyte's competitors to the firm's pricing strategy. What dangers does Gigabyte, Inc. face?
4. Gigabyte's controller, Paula Campos, recently attended a conference at which activity-based costing systems were discussed. She became convinced that such a system would help Gigabyte's management to understand its product costs better. She got top management's approval to design an activity-based costing system, and an ABC project team was formed. In stage one of the ABC project, each of the overhead items listed in the overhead budget was placed into its own activity cost pool. Then a cost driver was identified for each activity cost pool. Finally, the ABC project team compiled data showing the percentage of each cost driver that was consumed by each of Gigabyte's product lines. These data are summarized as follows:

Activity Cost Pool	Cost Driver	Product G	Product T	Product W
Machine setup	Number of setups	20%	30%	50%
Machinery	Machine hours	25%	50%	25%
Inspection	Number of inspections	15%	45%	40%
Material handling	Raw-material costs	25%	69%	6%
Engineering	Number of change orders	35%	10%	55%

   Show how the controller determined the percentages given above for raw-material costs. (Round to the nearest whole percent.)

5. Develop product costs for the three products on the basis of an activity-based costing system. (Round to the nearest cent.)
6. Calculate a target price for each product, using Gigabyte's pricing formula. Compare the new target prices with the current actual selling prices and previously reported product costs.
7. *Build a spreadsheet:* Construct an Excel spreadsheet to solve requirements (5) and (6) above. Show how the solution will change if the inspection activity was divided among the three products in the following manner: product G, 20%; product T, 40%, and product W, 40%.

■ **Problem 5–61**

Strategic Cost Analysis;
Continuation of Preceding
Problem

(LO 2, 5, 7)

Refer to the new target prices for Gigabyte's three products, based on the new activity-based costing system calculated in the preceding problem.

Required: Write a memo from Paula Campos to the company president commenting on the situation Gigabyte, Inc. has been facing regarding the market for its products and the actions of its competitors. Discuss the strategic options available to management. What should she recommend, and why?

■ **Problem 5–62**

Cost Distortion; Continuation
of Problem 5–60

(LO 2, 5)

Traditional system undercosts
product W by $120.25 per unit

Refer to the product costs developed in requirement (5) of Problem 5–60. Prepare a table showing how Gigabyte's traditional, volume-based product-costing system distorts the product costs of Grandes, Trucos, and Walkirias. (You may wish to refer to Exhibit 5–10 for guidance. Because of rounding in the calculation of the product costs, there will be a small rounding error in this cost distortion analysis as well.)

■ **Problem 5–63**

Basic Elements of a
Production Process;
Non-Value-Added Costs

(LO 7, 8, 10)

Better Bagels, Inc. manufactures a variety of bagels, which are frozen and sold in grocery stores. The production process consists of the following steps.

1. Ingredients, such as flour and raisins, are received and inspected. Then they are stored until needed.
2. Ingredients are carried on hand carts to the mixing room.
3. Dough is mixed in 20-kilogram batches in four heavy-duty mixers.
4. Dough is stored on large boards in the mixing room until a bagel machine is free.
5. A board of dough is carried into the bagel room. The board is tipped, and the dough slides into the hopper of a bagel machine. This machine pulls off a small piece of dough, rolls it into a cylindrical shape, and then squeezes it into a doughnut shape. The bagel machines can be adjusted in a setup

procedure to accommodate different sizes and styles of bagels. Workers remove the uncooked bagels and place them on a tray, where they are kept until a boiling vat is free.

6. Next the trays of uncooked bagels are carried into an adjoining room, which houses three 250-liter vats of boiling water. The bagels are boiled for approximately one minute.

7. Bagels are removed from the vats with a long-handled strainer and placed on a wooden board. The boards full of bagels are carried to the oven room, where they are kept until an oven rack is free. The two ovens contain eight racks which rotate but remain upright, much like the seats on a Ferris wheel. A rack full of bagels is finished baking after one complete revolution in the oven. When a rack full of bagels is removed from the oven, a fresh rack replaces it. The oven door is opened and closed as each rack completes a revolution in the oven.

8. After the bagels are removed from the oven, they are placed in baskets for cooling.

9. While the bagels are cooling, they are inspected. Misshapen bagels are removed and set aside. (Most are eaten by the staff.)

10. After the bagels are cool, the wire baskets are carried to the packaging department. Here the bagels are dumped into the hopper on a bagging machine. This machine packages a half-dozen bagels in each bag and seals the bag with a twist tie.

11. Then the packaged bagels are placed in cardboard boxes, each holding 24 bags. The boxes are placed on a forklift and are driven to the freezer, where the bagels are frozen and stored for shipment.

Required:

1. Identify the steps in the bagel-production process that fall into each of the following categories: process time, inspection time, move time, waiting time, storage time.

2. List the steps in the production process that could be candidates for non-value-added activities.

Refer to the information given in the preceding problem for Better Bagels, Inc.

Required: Redesign the bagel production process so that it adheres to the JIT philosophy. Explain how the eight key features of JIT systems would be present in the new production process. What new equipment would the company need to purchase in order to implement the JIT approach fully?

■ **Problem 5–64**
Key Features of JIT Production Systems (Appendix)
(LO 11)

Middle Eastern Trading Company (METC) manufactures a variety of housewares for export to the European consumer market. The company's three major product lines are cooking utensils, tableware, and flatware. METC implemented activity-based costing four years ago and now has a well-developed ABC system in place for determining product costs. Only recently, however, has the ABC system been systematically used for the purposes of activity-based management. As a pilot project, METC's controller asked the ABC project team to do a detailed activity analysis of the purchasing activity. The following specific activities were identified.

■ **Problem 5–65**
Two-Dimensional Activity-Based Costing; Activity Analysis; ABM
(LO 8)

1. Receipt of parts specifications from the Design Engineering Department.
2. Follow-up with design engineers to answer any questions.
3. Vendor (supplier) identification.
4. Vendor consultations (by phone or in person).
5. Price negotiation.
6. Vendor selection.
7. Ordering (by phone or mail).
8. Order follow-up.
9. Expediting (attempting to speed up delivery).
10. Order receiving.
11. Inspection of parts.
12. Return of parts not meeting specifications.
13. Consultation with design engineers and production personnel if parts do not satisfy intended purpose.
14. Further consultation and/or negotiation with vendor if necessary.
15. Ship parts back to vendor if necessary.
16. If satisfactory, move parts to storage.

Required:

1. Draw a diagram to depict METC's two-dimensional activity-based costing efforts. The diagram should include the following:

   a. The cost assignment role of ABC, with the cost pools, activities, and product lines represented.

   b. The process view of ABC, with the purchasing activities displayed. Also indicated here will be the linkages among the activities. (To save space, indicate the activities by their numbers.)

   c. The activity evaluation phase of two-dimensional ABC.

2. Identify the triggers for each of the following activities in METC's purchasing activity analysis:

   Follow-up with design engineers (activity 2)

   Expediting (activity 9)

   Inspection of parts (activity 11)

   Return of parts (activity 12)

   Consultation with design engineers and production personnel (activity 13)

3. For each of the activities listed in requirement (2), identify the possible root causes.

4. Choose four activities in METC's purchasing function, and suggest a performance measure for each of these activities.

■ **Problem 5–66**
Customer-Profitability
Analysis; Activity-Based
Costing
(LO 9)

1. Operating income, Trace
Telecom: $7,000

Deutsche Fiber Optics GmbH (DFO) manufactures fiber optic cables for the computer and telecommunications industries. At the request of the company vice president of marketing, the cost management staff has recently completed a customer-profitability study. The following activity-based costing information was the basis for the analysis.

Customer-Related Activities	Cost Driver Base	Cost Driver Rate
Sales activity	Sales visits	$500
Order taking	Purchase orders	100
Special handling	Units handled	50
Special shipping	Shipments	1,000

Cost-driver data for two of DFO's customers, Krondor Computing and Feist Cables, for the most recent year are

Customer-Related Activities	Krondor Computing	Feist Cables
Sales activity	16 visits	12 visits
Order taking	30 orders	40 orders
Special handling	800 units handled	600 units handled
Special shipping	9 shipments	10 shipments

The following additional information has been compiled for DFO, also with respect to those two customers, for the most recent year:

	Krondor Computing	Feist Cables
Sales revenue	$200,000	$123,800
Cost of goods sold	90,000	62,000
General selling costs	24,000	19,000
General administrative costs	19,000	15,000

Required:

1. Prepare a customer profitability analysis for Krondor Computing and Feist Cables. (*Hint:* Refer to Exhibit 5–13 for guidance.)

2. ***Build a spreadsheet:*** Construct an Excel spreadsheet to solve requirement (1) above. Show how the solution will change if the following information changes: Krondor Computing's sales revenue was $185,000 and Feist Cables' cost of goods sold was $59,000.

Refer to the information given in the preceding problem for Deutsche Fiber Optics GmbH (DFO) and two of its customers, Krondor Computing and Feist Cables. Additional information for six of DFO's other customers for the most recent year follows:

Customer	Operating Income
Hillpert Service Associates	$71,000
Tele-Install, GmbH	(18,000)
Hossfeld Computer Company	60,000
Lindenstrasse Computing Company	42,000
Nettwerk Telekom	93,000
The Bavaria Group	6,000

Problem 5–67
Customer-Profitability Profile; Continuation of Preceding Problem
(LO 9)

Required:

1. Prepare DFO's customer profitability profile for the most recent year.
2. As DFO's director of cost management, write a memo to the company's vice president of marketing that will accompany the customer profitability profile. Include a brief explanation of the methodology used and comment on the results.

Cases

Whitestone Company produces two subassemblies, JR-14 and RM-13, used in manufacturing trucks. The company is currently using an absorption costing system that applies overhead based on direct-labor hours. The budget for the current year ending December 31, 20x1, is as follows:

Case 5–68
Activity-Based Costing; Budgeted Operating Margin
(LO 1, 2, 4, 5, 7)

3. Total cost, JR-14, estimated 20x2 product cost: $1,540,000
4. Gross margin, RM-13: $(113,000)

WHITESTONE COMPANY
Budgeted Statement of Gross Margin for 20x1

	JR-14	RM-13	Total
Sales in units	5,000	5,000	10,000
Sales revenue	$1,700,000	$2,200,000	$3,900,000
Cost of goods manufactured and sold:			
Beginning finished-goods inventory	$ 240,000	$ 300,000	$ 540,000
Add: Direct material	1,000,000	1,750,000	2,750,000
Direct labor	185,185	92,593	277,778
Applied manufacturing overhead*	544,025	272,013	816,038
Cost of goods available for sale	$1,969,210	$2,414,606	$4,383,816
Less: Ending finished-goods inventory	240,000	300,000	540,000
Cost of goods sold	$1,729,210	$2,114,606	$3,843,816
Gross margin	$ (29,210)	$ 85,394	$ 56,184

*Applied on the basis of direct-labor hours:

Machining	$ 424,528
Assembly	216,981
Material handling	56,604
Inspection	117,925
Total	$ 816,038

Mark Ward, Whitestone's president, has been reading about a product-costing method called activity-based costing. Ward is convinced that activity-based costing will cast a new light on future profits. As a result, Brian Walters, Whitestone's director of cost management, has accumulated cost pool information for this year shown on the following chart. This information is based on a product mix of 5,000 units of JR-14 and 5,000 units of RM-13.

Cost Pool Information for 20x1

Cost Pool	Activity	JR-14	RM-13
Direct labor	Direct-labor hours	10,000	5,000
Machining	Machine hours	15,000	30,000
Assembly	Assembly hours	6,000	5,500
Material handling	Number of parts	5	10
Inspection	Inspection hours	5,000	7,500

In addition, the following information is projected for the next calendar year, 20x2.

	JR-14	RM-13
Beginning inventory, finished goods (in units)	800	600
Ending inventory, finished goods (in units)	700	700
Sales (in units)	5,100	4,900

On January 1, 20x2, Whitestone is planning to increase the prices of JR-14 to $355 and RM-13 to $455. Material costs are not expected to increase in 20x2, but direct labor will increase by 8 percent, and all manufacturing overhead costs will increase by 6 percent. Due to the nature of the manufacturing process, the company does not have any beginning or ending work-in-process inventories.

Whitestone uses a just-in-time inventory system and has materials delivered to the production facility directly from the vendors. The raw-material inventory at both the beginning and the end of the month is immaterial and can be ignored for the purposes of a budgeted income statement. The company uses the first-in, first-out (FIFO) inventory method.

Required:

1. Explain how activity-based costing differs from traditional product-costing methods.

2. Using activity-based costing, calculate the total cost for the following activity cost pools: machining, assembly, material handling, and inspection. (Round to the nearest dollar.) Then, calculate the pool rate per unit of the appropriate cost driver for each of the four activities. (*Hint:* Refer to Exhibit 5–6, regarding calculation of the pool rate.)

3. Prepare a table showing for each product line the estimated 20x2 cost for each of the following cost elements: direct material, direct labor, machining, assembly, material handling, and inspection. (Round to the nearest dollar.)

4. Prepare a budgeted statement showing the gross margin for Whitestone Company for 20x2, using activity-based costing. The statement should show each product and a total for the company. Be sure to include detailed calculations for the cost of goods manufactured and sold. (Round each amount in the statement to the nearest dollar.)

(CMA, adapted)

■ **Case 5–69**
Traditional versus Activity-Based Costing Systems
(LO 1, 2, 3, 4, 5)

2. Product costs with ABC, Standard Model: $437.75
3. New target price, Heavy-Duty Model: $248.73

Morelli Electric Motor Corporation manufactures electric motors for commercial use. The company produces three models, designated as standard, deluxe, and heavy-duty. The company uses a job-order cost-accounting system with manufacturing overhead applied on the basis of direct-labor hours. The system has been in place with little change for 25 years. Product costs and annual sales data are as follows:

	Standard Model	Deluxe Model	Heavy-Duty Model
Annual sales (units)	20,000	1,000	10,000
Product costs:			
Raw material	$ 10	$ 25	$ 42
Direct labor	10 (.5 hr. at $20)	20 (1 hr. at $20)	20 (1 hr. at $20)
Manufacturing overhead*	85	170	170
Total product cost	$105	$215	$232

*Calculation of predetermined overhead rate:

Manufacturing-overhead budget:

Depreciation, machinery	$1,480,000
Maintenance, machinery	120,000
Depreciation, taxes, and insurance for factory	300,000
Engineering	350,000
Purchasing, receiving and shipping	250,000
Inspection and repair of defects	375,000
Material handling	400,000
Miscellaneous manufacturing overhead costs	295,000
Total	$3,570,000

Direct-labor budget:

Standard model:	10,000 hours
Deluxe model:	1,000 hours
Heavy-duty model:	10,000 hours
Total	21,000 hours

Predetermined overhead rate: $\dfrac{\text{Budgeted overhead}}{\text{Budgeted direct-labor hours}} = \dfrac{\$3,570,000}{21,000 \text{ hours}} = \$170 \text{ per hour}$

For the past 10 years, the company's pricing formula has been to set each product's target price at 110 percent of its full product cost. Recently, however, the standard-model motor has come under increasing price pressure from offshore competitors. The result was that the price on the standard model has been lowered to $110.

The company president recently asked the controller, "Why can't we compete with these other companies? They're selling motors just like our standard model for 106 dollars. That's only a buck more than our production cost. Are we really that inefficient? What gives?"

The controller responded by saying, "I think this is due to an outmoded product-costing system. As you may remember, I raised a red flag about our system when I came on board last year. But the decision was to keep our current system in place. In my judgment, our product-costing system is distorting our product costs. Let me run a few numbers to demonstrate what I mean."

Getting the president's go-ahead, the controller compiled the basic data needed to implement an activity-based costing system. These data are displayed in the following table. The percentages are the proportion of each cost driver consumed by each product line.

		Product Lines		
Activity Cost Pool	**Cost Driver**	**Standard Model**	**Deluxe Model**	**Heavy-Duty Model**
I: Depreciation, machinery Maintenance, machinery	Machine time	40%	13%	47%
II: Engineering Inspection and repair of defects	Engineering hours	47%	6%	47%
III: Purchasing, receiving, and shipping Material handling	Number of material orders	47%	8%	45%
IV: Depreciation, taxes, and insurance for factory Miscellaneous manufacturing overhead	Factory space usage	42%	15%	43%

Required:

1. Compute the target prices for the three models, based on the traditional, volume-based product-costing system.

2. Compute new product costs for the three products, based on the new data collected by the controller. Round to the nearest cent.

3. Calculate a new target price for the three products, based on the activity-based costing system. Compare the new target price with the current actual selling price for the standard-model electric motor.

4. Write a memo to the company president explaining what has been happening as a result of the firm's traditional, volume-based product-costing system.

5. What strategic options does Morelli Electric Motor Corporation have? What do you recommend, and why?

■ **Case 5–70**
Cost Distortion; Continuation
of Preceding Case
(LO 2, 5)

Traditional system undercosts
Deluxe Model by $222.75
per unit

Refer to the product costs developed in requirement (2) of the preceding case. Prepare a table showing how Morelli Electric Motor Corporation's traditional, volume-based product-costing system distorts the product costs of the standard, deluxe, and heavy-duty models. (You may wish to refer to Exhibit 5–10 for guidance. Because of rounding in the calculation of the product costs, there will be a small rounding error in this cost distortion analysis as well.)

■ **Case 5–71**
Ethical Issues Related to
Product-Cost Distortion;
Activity-Based Costing;
Continuation of Case
5–69
(LO 2, 5, 7)

Morelli Electric Motor Corporation's controller, Erin Jackson, developed new product costs for the standard, deluxe, and heavy-duty models using activity-based costing. It was apparent that the firm's traditional product-costing system had been undercosting the deluxe-model electric motor by a significant amount. This was due largely to the low volume of the deluxe-model motor. Before she could report back to the president, Jackson received a phone call from her friend, Alan Tyler. He was the production manager for the deluxe-model electric motor. Tyler was upset, and he let Jackson know it. "Erin, I've gotten wind of your new product-cost analysis. There's no way the deluxe model costs anywhere near what your numbers say. For years and years, this line has been highly profitable, and its reported product cost was low. Now you're telling us it costs more than twice what we thought. I just don't buy it."

Jackson briefly explained to her friend about the principles of activity-based costing and why it resulted in more accurate product costs. "Alan, the deluxe model is really losing money. It simply has too low a volume to be manufactured efficiently."

Tyler was even more upset now. "Erin, if you report these new product costs to the president, he's going to discontinue the deluxe model. My job's on the line, Erin! How about massaging those numbers a little bit. Who's going to know?"

"I'll know, Alan. And you'll know," responded Jackson. "Look, I'll go over my analysis again, just to make sure I haven't made an error."

Required: Discuss the ethical issues involved in this scenario.

1. Is the controller, Erin Jackson, acting ethically?
2. Is the production manager, Alan Tyler, acting ethically?
3. What are Jackson's ethical obligations? To the president? To her friend?

THIS CHAPTER'S FOCUS COMPANY is Tasty Donuts, Inc., a Canadian chain of 10 donut shops in Toronto, Ontario. Using the Tasty Donuts illustration, we explore cost behavior, cost estimation, and cost prediction. Cost behavior refers to the relationship between cost and activity. Variable and fixed costs, which we studied in Chapter 2, are two examples of the many types of cost behavior. Cost estimation is the process of determining how a particular cost behaves, often relying on historical cost data. Cost prediction means using our knowledge of cost behavior to forecast the cost to be incurred at a particular level of activity. Cost analysis helps Tasty Donuts' management plan for the costs to be incurred at various levels of donut sales activity.

6 Activity Analysis, Cost Behavior, and Cost Estimation

1 Explain the relationship between activity and cost.

2 Explain cost behavior and cost predictors, including variable, fixed, step, mixed, and curvilinear cost behavior.

3 Define and give examples of cost prediction.

4 Define and give examples of engineered costs, committed costs, and discretionary costs.

5 Describe and use the following cost estimation methods: account classification, visual fit, high-low, and least-squares regression.

6 Describe the multiple regression, engineered, and learning-curve approaches to cost estimation.

IN CONTRAST   >>>

COSMOS COMMUNICATIONS TECHNOLOGY

In contrast to the service-industry setting of Tasty Donuts, we turn to a manufacturing environment to explore the effect of the learning curve on cost behavior. In many production processes, production efficiency increases with experience. As cumulative production output increases, the average labor time required per unit declines. As the labor time declines, labor cost declines as well. This phenomenon is called the learning curve. To illustrate the learning-curve concept, we explore its use by Cosmos Communications Technology (CCT), a Canadian manufacturer of sophisticated communications satellites in Vancouver, British Columbia. CCT's management has found that the learning curve applies to the labor-intensive assembly operation for each new satellite design.

1 Explain the relationships between cost estimation, cost behavior, and cost prediction.

2 Define and describe the behavior of the following types of costs: variable, step-variable, fixed, step-fixed, semivariable (or mixed), and curvilinear.

3 Explain the importance of the relevant range in using a cost behavior pattern for cost prediction.

4 Define and give examples of engineered costs, committed costs, and discretionary costs.

5 Describe and use the following cost estimation methods: account classification, visual fit, high-low, and least-squares regression.

6 Describe the multiple regression, engineering, and learning-curve approaches to cost estimation.

7 Describe some problems often encountered in collecting data for cost estimation.

8 Perform and interpret a least-squares regression analysis with a single independent variable (appendix).

Managers in almost any organization want to know how costs will be affected by changes in the organization's activity. The relationship between cost and activity, called **cost behavior,** is relevant to the management functions of planning, control, and decision making. In order to *plan* operations and prepare a budget, managers at Kraft Foods need to predict the costs that will be incurred at different levels of production and sales. To *control* the costs of providing commercial-loan services at Arab Bank, executives need to have a feel for the costs that the bank should incur at various levels of commercial-loan activity. In *deciding* whether to add a new intensive care unit, Apollo Hospitals administrators need to predict the cost of operating the new unit at various levels of patient demand. In each of these situations, knowledge of *cost behavior* will help the manager to make the desired cost prediction. A **cost prediction** is a forecast of cost at a particular level of activity. In the first half of this chapter, we will study cost behavior patterns and their use in making cost predictions.

How does a managerial accountant determine the cost behavior pattern for a particular cost item? The determination of cost behavior, which is often called **cost estimation,** can be accomplished in a number of ways. One way is to analyze historical data concerning costs and activity levels. Cost estimation is covered in the second half of this chapter.

The following diagram summarizes the key points in the preceding discussion.

Learning Objective 1

Explain the relationships between cost estimation, cost behavior, and cost prediction.

Cost estimation	Cost behavior	Cost prediction
The process of determining cost behavior. Often focuses on historical data.	The relationship between cost and activity.	Using knowledge of cost behavior to forecast the level of cost at a particular level of activity. Focus is on the future.

Cost Behavior Patterns

Our discussion of cost behavior patterns, also called *cost functions,* will be set in the context of a donut shop business. Tasty Donuts, Inc. operates a chain of 10 donut shops in the city of Toronto, Ontario. Each shop sells a variety of donuts, muffins, and sweet rolls as well as various beverages. Beverages, such as coffee and fruit juices, are prepared in each donut shop, but all of the company's donuts and baked products are made in a centrally located bakery. The company leases several small delivery trucks to transport the bakery items to its donut shops. Use of a central bakery is more cost-efficient. Moreover, this approach allows the firm to smooth out fluctuations in demand for each type of product. For example, the demand for glazed donuts may change from day to day in each donut shop, but these fluctuations tend to cancel each other out when the total demand is aggregated across all 10 shops.

The corporate controller for Tasty Donuts has recently completed a study of the company's cost behavior to use in preparing the firm's budget for the coming year. The controller studied the following costs.

Direct material: ingredients for donuts, muffins, and sweet rolls; beverages; paper products, such as napkins and disposable cups.

Direct labor: wages and fringe benefits of bakers, donut shop sales personnel, and delivery-truck drivers.

Overhead:

Facilities costs: property taxes; depreciation on bakery building, donut shops, and equipment; salaries and fringe benefits of maintenance personnel.

Indirect labor: salaries and fringe benefits of managers and assistant managers for bakery and donut shops.

Delivery trucks: rental payments under lease contract; costs of gasoline, oil, tires, and maintenance.

Utilities: electricity, telephone, and trash collection.

In studying the behavior of each of these costs, the controller measured company *activity* in terms of *dozens of bakery items sold.* Thus, dozens of bakery items sold is the *cost driver* for each of the costs studied. A bakery item is one donut, muffin, or sweet roll. The costs to make each of these products are nearly identical. The number of bakery items sold each day is roughly the same as the number produced, since bakery goods are produced to keep pace with demand as reported by the company's donut shop managers.

"Failure to understand costs would have left Portugal Telecom vulnerable to competition. Understanding the company's costs became essential to cost reduction efforts and to the company's long-term viability." (6a)
Accenture, regarding its client Portugal Telecom

Variable Costs

Variable costs were discussed briefly in Chapter 2. We will summarize that discussion here in the context of the Tasty Donuts illustration. A **variable cost** changes *in total* in direct proportion to a change in the activity level (or cost driver). Tasty Donuts' direct-material cost is a variable cost. As the company sells more donuts, muffins, and sweet rolls, the total cost of the ingredients for these goods increases in direct proportion to the number of items sold. Moreover, the quantities of beverages sold and paper products used by customers also increase in direct proportion to the number of bakery items sold. As a result, the costs of beverages and paper products are also variable costs.

Panel A of Exhibit 6–1 displays a graph of Tasty Donuts' direct-material cost. As the graph shows, *total* variable cost increases in proportion to the activity level (or cost driver). When activity triples, for example, from 50,000 dozen items to 150,000 dozen items, total direct-material costs triple, from $55,000 to $165,000. However, the variable cost *per unit* remains the same as activity changes. The total direct-material cost incurred *per dozen* items sold is constant at $1.10 per dozen. The table in panel B of Exhibit 6–1 illustrates this

Learning Objective 2

Define and describe the behavior of the following types of costs: variable, step-variable, fixed, step-fixed, semivariable (or mixed), and curvilinear.

Exhibit 6–1

Variable Cost: Direct-Material
Cost, Tasty Donuts, Inc.

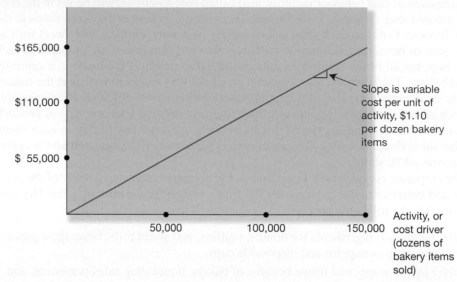

A. Graph of Total Direct-Material Cost

Total direct-material cost
(food ingredients, beverages, paper products)

Slope is variable cost per unit of activity, $1.10 per dozen bakery items

Activity, or cost driver (dozens of bakery items sold)

B. Tabulation of Direct-Material Cost

Activity (or cost driver)	Direct-Material Cost per Dozen Bakery Items Sold	Total Direct-Material Cost
50,000	$1.10	$ 55,000
100,000	1.10	110,000
150,000	1.10	165,000

point. The variable cost per unit also is represented in the graph in panel A of Exhibit 6–1 as the slope of the cost line.

To summarize, as activity changes, total variable cost increases in direct proportion to the change in activity level, but the variable cost per unit remains constant.

Step-Variable Costs

Some costs are nearly variable, but they increase in small steps instead of continuously. Such costs, called **step-variable costs,** usually include inputs that are purchased and used in relatively small increments. At Tasty Donuts, Inc., the direct-labor cost of bakers, counter-service personnel, and delivery-truck drivers is a step-variable cost. Many of these employees are part-time workers, called upon for relatively small increments of time, such as a few hours. On a typical day, for example, Tasty Donuts may have 35 employees at work in the bakery and the donut shops. If activity increases slightly, these employees can handle the extra work. However, if activity increases substantially, the bakery manager or various restaurant managers may call on additional help. Exhibit 6–2, a graph of Tasty Donuts' monthly direct-labor cost, shows that this cost remains constant within an activity range of about 5,000 dozen bakery items per month. When monthly activity increases beyond this narrow range, direct-labor costs increase.

Approximating a Step-Variable Cost   If the steps in a step-variable cost behavior pattern are small, the step-variable cost function may be approximated by a variable cost function without much loss in accuracy. Exhibit 6–3 shows such an approximation for Tasty Donuts' direct-labor cost.

Total direct-labor cost (wages and fringe benefits of bakers, sales personnel, and delivery-truck drivers)

Size of activity range in one step is 5,000 dozen bakery items per month

Size of cost increment in one step is $1,500 of direct-labor cost per month

Activity, or cost driver
(dozens of bakery items sold)

Exhibit 6–2
Step-Variable Cost: Direct-Labor Cost, Tasty Donuts

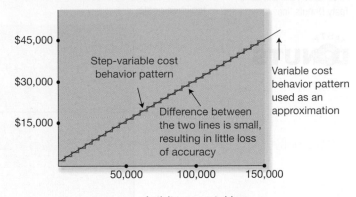

Total direct-labor cost (wages and fringe benefits of bakers, sales personnel, and delivery-truck drivers)

Step-variable cost behavior pattern

Variable cost behavior pattern used as an approximation

Difference between the two lines is small, resulting in little loss of accuracy

Activity, or cost driver
(dozens of bakery items sold)

Exhibit 6–3
Approximating a Step-Variable Cost, Tasty Donuts

Fixed Costs

Fixed costs were covered briefly in Chapter 2. We will summarize that discussion here, using the Tasty Donuts illustration. A **fixed cost** remains unchanged *in total* as the activity level (or cost driver) varies. Facilities costs, which include property taxes, depreciation on buildings and equipment, and the salaries of maintenance personnel, are fixed costs for Tasty Donuts, Inc. These fixed costs are graphed in panel A of Exhibit 6–4. This graph shows that the *total* monthly cost of property taxes, depreciation, and maintenance personnel is $200,000 regardless of how many dozen bakery items are produced and sold during the month.

The fixed cost *per unit* does change as activity varies. Exhibit 6–4 (panel B) shows that the company's facilities cost per dozen bakery items is $4.00 when 50,000 dozen items are produced and sold. However, this unit cost declines to $2.00 when 100,000 dozen items are produced and sold. If activity increases to 150,000 dozen items, unit fixed cost will decline further, to about $1.33.

A graph provides another way of viewing the change in unit fixed cost as activity changes. Panel C of Exhibit 6–4 displays a graph of Tasty Donuts' cost of property taxes, depreciation, and maintenance personnel *per dozen bakery items.* As the graph shows, the fixed cost per dozen bakery items declines steadily as activity increases.

To summarize, as the activity level increases, total fixed cost does not change, but unit fixed cost declines. For this reason, it is preferable in any cost analysis to work with total fixed cost rather than fixed cost per unit.

Step-Fixed Costs

Some costs remain fixed over a wide range of activity but jump to a different amount for activity levels outside that range. Such costs are called **step-fixed costs.** Tasty Donuts' cost of indirect labor is a step-fixed cost. Indirect-labor cost consists of the salaries and fringe benefits for the managers and assistant managers of the company's bakery and donut shops. Tasty Donuts' monthly indirect-labor cost is graphed in Exhibit 6–5.

> "By understanding the costs and workload associated with the real business activities we undertake . . . we are better positioned to understand where value is created. . . . From this information, we can then make better decisions as to the management and direction of the business." (6b)
>
> **Transco**

Exhibit 6–4

Fixed Cost: Facilities Costs, Tasty Donuts, Inc.

A. Graph of Total Monthly Fixed Costs: Facilities Costs

Total monthly fixed costs: facilities costs

$200,000

50,000   100,000   150,000

Activity, or cost driver (dozens of bakery items sold per month)

B. Tabulation of Monthly Fixed Costs: Facilities Costs

Activity (or cost driver)	Cost of Facilities per Dozen Bakery Items Sold	Total Monthly Cost of Facilities
50,000	$4.00	$200,000
100,000	2.00	200,000
150,000	1.33*	200,000

*Rounded.

C. Graph of Unit Fixed Costs: Cost of Facilities per Dozen Bakery Items Sold

Unit fixed cost: facilities costs

$4.00

$2.00

$1.33

50,000   100,000   150,000

Activity, or cost driver (dozens of bakery items sold per month)

As Exhibit 6–5 shows, for activity in the range of 50,000 to 100,000 dozen bakery items per month, Tasty Donuts' monthly indirect-labor cost is $35,000. For this range of activity, the company employs a full-time manager and a full-time assistant manager in the bakery and in each donut shop. When monthly activity exceeds this range during the summer tourist season, the company employs additional part-time assistant managers in the bakery and in its busiest donut shops. The company hires college students who are majoring in restaurant management for these summer positions. Their salaries boost the monthly indirect-labor cost to $45,000. Tasty Donuts has not experienced demand of less than 50,000 dozen bakery items per month. However, the controller anticipates that if

Exhibit 6–5

Step-Fixed Cost: Indirect-Labor Cost, Tasty Donuts, Inc.

such a decrease in demand were to occur, the company would reduce the daily operating hours for its donut shops. This would allow the firm to operate each donut shop with only a full-time manager and no assistant manager. As the graph in Exhibit 6–5 indicates, such a decrease in managerial personnel would reduce monthly indirect-labor cost to $25,000.

Semivariable Cost

A **semivariable** (or **mixed**) **cost** has both a fixed and a variable component. The cost of operating delivery trucks is a semivariable cost for Tasty Donuts, Inc. These costs are graphed in Exhibit 6–6. As the graph shows, the company's delivery-truck costs have two components. The fixed-cost component is $3,000 per month, which is the monthly rental payment paid under the lease contract for the delivery trucks. The monthly rental payment is constant, regardless of the level of activity (or cost driver). The variable-cost

Exhibit 6–6

Semivariable Cost: Cost of Operating Delivery Trucks, Tasty Donuts, Inc.

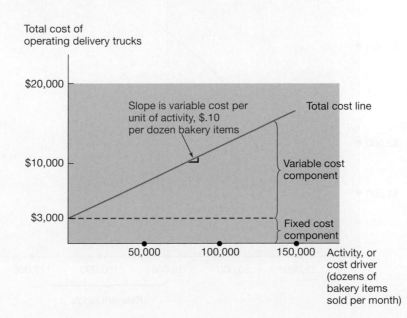

component consists of the costs of gasoline, oil, routine maintenance, and tires. These costs vary with activity, since greater activity levels result in more deliveries. The distance between the fixed-cost line (dashed line) and the total-cost line in Exhibit 6–6 is the amount of variable cost. For example, at an activity level of 100,000 dozen bakery items, the total variable-cost component is $10,000.

The slope of the total-cost line is the variable cost per unit of activity. For Tasty Donuts, the variable cost of operating its delivery trucks is $.10 per dozen bakery items sold.

Curvilinear Cost

The graphs of all of the cost behavior patterns examined so far consist of either straight lines or several straight-line sections. A **curvilinear cost** behavior pattern has a curved graph. Tasty Donuts' utilities cost, depicted as the *solid curve* in Exhibit 6–7, is a curvilinear cost. For low levels of activity, this cost exhibits *decreasing marginal costs*. As the discussion in Chapter 2 indicated, a marginal cost is the cost of producing the next unit, in this case the next dozen bakery items. As the graph in Exhibit 6–7 shows, the marginal utilities cost of producing the next dozen bakery items declines as activity increases in the range zero to 100,000 dozen items per month. For activity greater than 100,000 dozen bakery items per month, the graph in Exhibit 6–7 exhibits *increasing marginal costs*.

Tasty Donuts' utilities cost includes electricity, telephone, and trash-collection costs. The utilities cost is curvilinear as a result of the company's pattern of electricity usage in the bakery. If the demand in a particular month is less than 100,000 dozen bakery items, the goods can be produced entirely in the modernized section of the bakery. This section uses

Exhibit 6–7
Curvilinear Cost: Utilities Cost, Tasty Donuts, Inc.

recently purchased deep-fat fryers and ovens that are very energy-efficient. As long as the bakery operates only the modernized section, the utilities cost per dozen items declines as production increases.

During the summer tourist months, when Tasty Donuts' sales exceed 100,000 dozen items per month, the older section of the bakery also must be used. This section uses much older cooking equipment that is less energy-efficient. As a result, the marginal utilities cost per dozen bakery items rises as monthly activity increases in the range above 100,000 dozen items per month.

Relevant Range The cost behavior graphed in Exhibit 6–7 is very different at low activity levels (below 50,000) than it is at high activity levels (above 125,000). However, management need not concern itself with these extreme levels of activity if it is unlikely that Tasty Donuts, Inc. will operate at those activity levels. Management is interested in cost behavior within the company's **relevant range,** the range of activity within which management expects the company to operate. Tasty Donuts' management believes the firm's relevant range to be 75,000 to 120,000 dozen bakery items per month. Based on past experience and sales projections, management does not expect the firm to operate outside that range of monthly activity. Tasty Donuts' relevant range is shown in Exhibit 6–7 as the section of the graph between the dashed lines.

Approximating a Curvilinear Cost within the Relevant Range The
straight, dashed line in Exhibit 6–7 may be used to approximate Tasty Donuts' utilities cost. Notice that the approximation is quite accurate for activity levels within the relevant range. However, as the activity level gets further away from the boundary of the relevant range, the approximation declines in accuracy. For monthly activity levels of 25,000 or 150,000, for example, the approximation is very poor.

The straight, dashed line used to approximate Tasty Donuts' utilities cost *within the relevant range* represents a semivariable cost behavior pattern. This straight-line graph has a slope of $.05, which represents a unit variable-cost component of $.05 per dozen bakery items. The line intersects the vertical axis of the graph at $1,500, which represents a fixed-cost component of $1,500 per month. Managerial accountants often use a semivariable-cost behavior pattern to approximate a curvilinear cost. However, it is important to limit this approximation to the range of activity in which its accuracy is acceptable.

Using Cost Behavior Patterns to Predict Costs

How can Tasty Donuts' corporate controller use the cost behavior patterns identified in the cost study to help in the budgeting process? First, a sales forecast is made for each month during the budget year. Suppose management expects Tasty Donuts' activity level to be 110,000 dozen bakery items during the month of June. Second, a *cost prediction* is made for each of the firm's cost items. The following cost predictions are based on the cost behavior patterns discussed earlier. (Try to verify these cost predictions by referring to the graphs in Exhibits 6–1 through 6–7.)

Cost Item	Cost Prediction for June (110,000 dozen bakery items per month)
Direct material	$121,000
Direct labor	33,000
Overhead:	
Facilities costs	200,000
Indirect labor	45,000
Delivery trucks	14,000
Utilities	7,000

M anagement
A ccounting
P ractice

The World Bank,
Microsoft, and Hilton
Hotels

IS DIRECT LABOR A VARIABLE OR A FIXED COST?

Are labor costs variable or fixed? It depends on the ability and willingness of a company's management to continually fine-tune the size of its workforce. If labor contracts or government regulations make it difficult to lay off workers during an economic downturn, or if top management adopts a policy of maintaining a stable workforce, labor costs will tend to be largely fixed (or step-fixed). However, if management can *and is willing to* reduce the labor force when activity declines, then labor cost will be a variable (or step-variable) cost.

The World Bank

In its research project on "Doing Business . . . ," The World Bank Group reports on the regulations that affect business operations in many countries around the world, including difficulty and cost of redundancy and flexibility of work hours. "Governments all over the world face the challenge of finding the right balance between worker protection and labor market flexibility. [The EU and others] have embraced the concept of 'flexicurity,' combining flexible regulation, safety nets (such as unemployment insurance) and active social policies."[1]

They also note that worker protection regulations "increase the likelihood that employed workers will stay in their job," resulting in labor costs that are more fixed than variable. Based on this, we would expect to find labor costs more variable in the countries listed on the left in the table below and more fixed in the countries on the right.

Rigidity of employment index (0–100)			
Least		**Most**	
Australia	0	Panama	66
Hong Kong, China	0	Niger	68
United States	0	Venezuela, R.B.	69
Singapore	0	Bolivia	77

Source: The World Bank Group, "Doing Business 2010," Palgrave MacMillan, p. 22.

Nevertheless, in countries such as Australia and the United States, we find companies taking actions that suggest that even there labor costs are quite inflexible.

Microsoft

"Temp employment in the United States fluctuates wildly, by design. The whole purpose of bringing on workers who are employed by temporary staffing firms such as Manpower, Adecco, and Kelly Services is that they're easy to shuck off when unneeded . . . For years Microsoft has been an avid user of temporary-staffing firms such as Volt Information Sciences for a variety of short-term projects, including writing chunks of software, says Microsoft spokesman Lou Gellos. 'Our contingent workforce fluctuates wildly depending on the different projects that are going on,' Gellos says."[2]

Hilton Hotels

"Many employers, wary of losing valued workers altogether, are reducing the workweek rather than the workforce. Officials of Hilton Hotels Corp. . . . boast that they have laid off relatively few workers [but] workweek reductions are widespread among its 77,000 workers."[3]

By relying more on part-time workers and shortening the workweek, Microsoft and Hilton Hotels are treating their regular workers as a fixed cost while using these other techniques to induce as much variability into labor costs as possible. As a result, their direct-labor cost does, in fact, behave like a variable cost *within the relevant range of operations*, moving up and down as production volumes move up and down.

---

[1]The World Bank, *Doing Business 2010,* Palgrave MacMillan.
[2]P. Coy, M. Conlin, and M. Herbst, "The Disposable Worker," *BusinessWeek,* January 18, 2010, pp. 33–45.
[3]Jonathan Eig, "Do Part-Time Workers Hold Key to When the Recession Breaks?" *The Wall Street Journal,* January 3, 2002, p. A1.

The preparation of a complete budget involves much more analysis and detailed planning than is shown here.[4] The point is that cost prediction is an important part of the planning process. The cost behavior patterns discussed in this chapter make those cost predictions possible.

Engineered, Committed, and Discretionary Costs

In the process of budgeting costs, it is often useful for management to make a distinction between engineered, committed, and discretionary costs. An **engineered cost** bears a definitive physical relationship to the activity measure. Tasty Donuts' direct-material cost is an engineered cost. It is impossible to produce more donuts without incurring greater material cost for food ingredients.

A **committed cost** results from an organization's ownership or use of facilities and its basic organization structure. Property taxes, depreciation on buildings and equipment, costs of renting facilities or equipment, and the salaries of management personnel are examples of committed fixed costs. Tasty Donuts' facilities cost is a committed fixed cost.

A **discretionary cost** arises as a result of a *management decision* to spend a particular amount of money for some purpose. Examples of discretionary costs include amounts spent on research and development, advertising and promotion, management development programs, and contributions to charitable organizations. For example, suppose Tasty Donuts' management decided to spend $12,400 each month on promotion and advertising.

The distinction between committed and discretionary costs is an important one. Management can change committed costs only through relatively major decisions that have long-term implications. Decisions to build a new production facility, lease a fleet of vehicles, or add more management personnel to oversee a new division are examples of such decisions. These decisions will generally influence costs incurred over a long period of time. In contrast, discretionary costs can be changed in the short run much

---

[4]The budgeting process is covered in Chapter 9.

Learning Objective 4

Define and give examples of engineered costs, committed costs, and discretionary costs.

"... there are many other costs in producing sustainable products ... We invest in these and many other choices because they add comfort, performance, and beauty to our products, while helping to mitigate the environmental impacts of producing, using and recycling our clothing." (6d)

Nau, Inc.

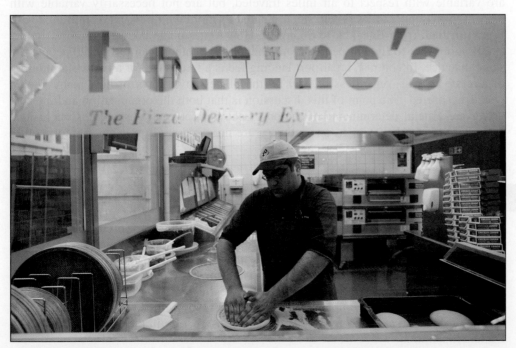

The raw material (ingredients) in these Domino's Pizzas represents an engineered cost. The depreciation on the equipment is a committed cost. Expenditures on advertising and promotion are discretionary costs.

more easily. Management can be flexible about expenditures for advertising, promotion, employee training, or research and development. This does not imply that such programs are unimportant, but simply that management can alter them over time. For example, the management of a manufacturing firm may decide to spend $100,000 on research and development in the current year, but cut back to $60,000 in the next year because of an anticipated economic downturn.

Cost Behavior in Other Industries

> "Operational test costs commonly consist of a combination of personnel costs, maintenance costs, and facility costs. More specifically, personnel costs typically roll up from the operators and technicians, while maintenance costs reflect the cost of maintaining spares to prevent downtime in the event of a failure or need to remove an instrument for routine calibration." (6e)
>
> **National Instruments**

We have illustrated a variety of cost behavior patterns for Tasty Donuts' restaurant business. The same cost behavior patterns are used in other industries. The cost behavior pattern appropriate for a particular cost item depends on the organization and the activity base (or cost driver). In manufacturing firms, production quantity, direct-labor hours, and machine hours are common cost drivers. Direct-material and direct-labor costs are usually considered variable costs. Other variable costs include some manufacturing-overhead costs, such as indirect material and indirect labor. Fixed manufacturing costs are generally the costs of creating production capacity. Examples include depreciation on plant and equipment, property taxes, and the plant manager's salary. Such overhead costs as utilities and equipment maintenance are usually semivariable or curvilinear costs. A semivariable-cost behavior pattern is generally used to approximate a curvilinear cost within the relevant range. Supervisory salaries are usually step-fixed costs, since one person can supervise production over a range of activity. When activity increases beyond that range, such as when a new shift is added, an additional supervisor is added.

In merchandising firms, such as Tesco, the activity base (or cost driver) usually is sales revenue. The cost of merchandise sold is a variable cost. Most labor costs are fixed or step-fixed costs, since a particular number of sales and stock personnel can generally handle sales activity over a fairly wide range of sales. Store facility costs, such as rent, depreciation on buildings and furnishings, and property taxes, are fixed costs.

In some industries, the choice of the cost driver is not obvious, and the cost behavior pattern can depend on the cost driver selected. At Thai Airways International, for instance, the cost driver could be air miles flown, passengers flown, or passenger miles flown. A passenger mile is the transportation of one passenger for one mile. Fuel costs are variable with respect to air miles traveled, but are not necessarily variable with respect to passenger miles flown. An airplane uses more fuel in flying from Bangkok to Frankfurt than from Bangkok to Shanghai. However, a plane does not require significantly more fuel to fly 200 people from one city to another than to fly 190 people the same distance. In contrast, an airport landing fee is a fixed cost for a particular number of aircraft arrivals, regardless of how far the planes have flown or how many people were transported. The point of this discussion is that both the organization and the cost driver are crucial determinants of the cost behavior for each cost item. Conclusions drawn about cost behavior in one industry are not necessarily transferable to another industry.

Cost Estimation

Learning Objective 5

Describe and use the following cost estimation methods: account classification, visual fit, high-low, and least-squares regression.

As the preceding discussion indicates, different costs exhibit a variety of cost behavior patterns. Cost estimation is the process of determining how a particular cost behaves. Several methods are commonly used to estimate the relationship between cost and activity. Some of these methods are simple, while some are quite sophisticated. In some firms, managers use more than one method of cost estimation. The results of the different methods are then combined by the cost analyst on the basis of experience and judgment. We will examine five methods of cost estimation in the context of the Tasty Donuts illustration.

Account-Classification Method

The **account-classification method** of cost estimation, also called **account analysis,** involves a careful examination of the organization's ledger accounts. The cost analyst classifies each cost item in the ledger as a variable, fixed, or semivariable cost. The classification is based on the analyst's knowledge of the organization's activities and experience with the organization's costs. For example, it may be obvious to the analyst going through the ledger that direct-material cost is variable, building depreciation is fixed, and utility costs are semivariable.

Once the costs have been classified, the cost analyst estimates cost amounts by examining job-cost records, paid bills, labor time cards, or other source documents. A property-tax bill, for example, will provide the cost analyst with the information needed to estimate this fixed cost. This examination of historical source documents is combined with other knowledge that may affect costs in the future. For example, the municipal government may have recently enacted a 10 percent property-tax increase, which takes effect the following year.

For some costs, particularly those classified as semivariable, the cost analyst may use one of several more systematic methods of incorporating historical data in the cost estimate. These methods are discussed next.

Visual-Fit Method

When a cost has been classified as semivariable, or when the analyst has no clear idea about the behavior of a cost item, it is helpful to use the **visual-fit method** to plot recent observations of the cost at various activity levels. The resulting **scatter diagram** helps the analyst visualize the relationship between cost and the level of activity (or cost driver). To illustrate, suppose Tasty Donuts' controller has compiled the following historical data for the company's utility costs.

Month	Utility Cost for Month	Activity or Cost Driver (dozens of bakery items sold per month)
January	$5,100	75,000
February	5,300	78,000
March	5,650	80,000
April	6,300	92,000
May	6,400	98,000
June	6,700	108,000
July	7,035	118,000
August	7,000	112,000
September	6,200	95,000
October	6,100	90,000
November	5,600	85,000
December	5,900	90,000

The scatter diagram of these data is shown in Exhibit 6–8. The cost analyst can *visually fit a line* to these data by laying a ruler on the plotted points. The line is positioned so that roughly equal numbers of plotted points lie above and below the line. Using this method, Tasty Donuts' controller visually fit the line shown in Exhibit 6–8.

Just a glance at the visually fit cost line reveals that Tasty Donuts' utilities cost is a semivariable cost *within the relevant range*. The scatter diagram provides little or no information about the cost relationship outside the relevant range. Recall from the discussion of Tasty Donuts' utilities cost (see Exhibit 6–7) that the controller believes the cost behavior pattern to be curvilinear over the *entire range* of activity. This judgment is based on the controller's knowledge of the firm's facilities and an understanding of electricity

Exhibit 6–8

Scatter Diagram of Cost Data with Visually Fit Cost Line, Tasty Donuts, Inc.

Utilities cost (for one month)

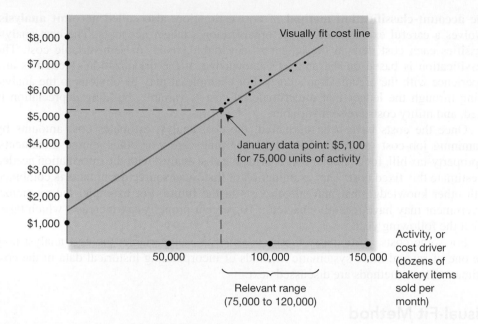

usage by the modern bakery equipment and the older bakery equipment. As Exhibit 6–7 shows, however, the curvilinear utilities cost can be approximated closely by a semivariable cost *within the relevant range*. The data plotted in the scatter diagram lie within the relevant range. Consequently, the data provide a sound basis for the semivariable approximation that the controller has chosen to use.

The visually fit cost line in Exhibit 6–8 intercepts the vertical axis at $1,500. Thus, $1,500 is the estimate of the fixed-cost component in the semivariable-cost approximation. To determine the variable cost per unit, subtract the fixed cost from the total cost at any activity level. The remainder is the total variable cost for that activity level. For example, the total variable cost for an activity level of 50,000 dozen items is $2,500 (total cost of $4,000 minus fixed cost of $1,500). This yields a variable cost of $.05 per dozen bakery items ($.05 = $2,500 ÷ 50,000).

These variable and fixed cost estimates were used for the semivariable-cost approximation discussed earlier in the chapter (Exhibit 6–7). These estimates are valid only *within the relevant range*.

Evaluation of Visual-Fit Method   The scatter diagram and visually fit cost line provide a valuable first step in the analysis of any cost item suspected to be semivariable or curvilinear. The method is easy to use and to explain to others, and it provides a useful view of the overall cost behavior pattern.

The visual-fit method also enables an experienced cost analyst to spot *outliers* in the data. An **outlier** is a data point that falls far away from the other points in the scatter diagram and is not representative of the data. Suppose, for example, that the data point for January had been $6,000 for 75,000 units of activity. Exhibit 6–8 reveals that such a data point would be way out of line with the rest of the data. The cost analyst would follow up on such a cost observation to discover the reasons behind it. It could be that the data point is in error. Perhaps a utility bill was misread when the data were compiled, or possibly the billing itself was in error. Another possibility is that the cost observation is correct but due to unusual circumstances. Perhaps Toronto experienced a record cold wave during January that required the company's donut shops to use unusually high amounts of electric heat. Perhaps an oven in the bakery had a broken thermostat during January that caused the oven to overheat consistently until discovered and repaired. An outlier can result from many causes. If the outlier is due to an error or very unusual circumstances, the data point should be ignored in the cost analysis.

A significant drawback of the visual-fit method is its lack of objectivity. Two cost analysts may draw two different visually fit cost lines. This is not usually a serious problem, however, particularly if the visual-fit method is combined with other, more objective methods.

High-Low Method

In the **high-low method,** the semivariable-cost approximation is computed using exactly two data points. The high and low *activity levels* are chosen from the available data set. These activity levels, together with their associated cost levels, are used to compute the variable and fixed cost components as follows:

$$\begin{aligned}\text{Variable cost per}\atop\text{dozen bakery items}\end{aligned} = \frac{\begin{aligned}\text{Difference between the } costs \text{ corresponding}\\\text{to the highest and lowest activity levels}\end{aligned}}{\begin{aligned}\text{Difference between the highest}\\\text{and lowest } activity \text{ levels}\end{aligned}}$$

$$= \frac{\$7{,}035 - \$5{,}100}{118{,}000 - 75{,}000} = \frac{\$1{,}935}{43{,}000}$$

$$= \$.045 \text{ per dozen items}$$

Now we can compute the total variable cost at either the high or low activity level. At the low activity of 75,000 dozen items, the total variable cost is $3,375 ($.045 × 75,000). Subtracting the total variable cost from the total cost at the 75,000 dozen activity level, we obtain the fixed-cost estimate of $1,725 ($5,100 − $3,375). Notice that the high and low *activity* levels are used to choose the two data points. In general, these two points need not necessarily coincide with the high and low cost levels in the data set.

Exhibit 6–9 presents a graph of Tasty Donuts' utilities cost, which is based on the high-low method of cost estimation. As in any cost estimation method, this estimate of the cost behavior pattern should be *restricted to the relevant range.*

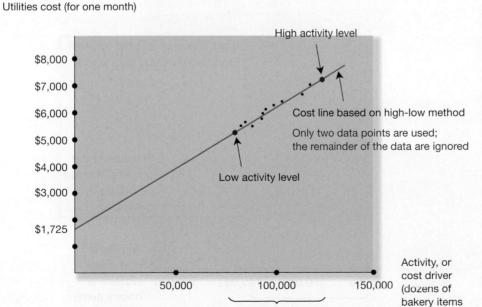

Utilities cost (for one month)

Exhibit 6–9
Graph of Utilities Cost Using High-Low Method, Tasty Donuts, Inc.

Evaluation of High-Low Method   The high-low method is more objective than the visual-fit method, since it leaves no room for the cost analyst's judgment. However, the high-low method suffers from a major weakness. Only two data points are used to estimate the cost behavior pattern; the remainder of the data points are ignored. In this regard, the visual-fit method is superior to the high-low method, since the former approach uses all of the available data.

Least-Squares Regression Method

Statistical techniques may be used to estimate objectively a cost behavior pattern using all of the available data. The most common of these methods is called *least-squares regression*. To understand this method, examine Exhibit 6–10, which repeats the scatter diagram of Tasty Donuts' utilities cost data. The Exhibit also includes a cost line that has been drawn through the plotted data points. Since the data points do not lie along a perfectly straight line, any cost line drawn through this scatter diagram will miss some or most of the data points. The objective is to draw the cost line so as to make the deviations between the cost line and the data points as small as possible.

In the **least-squares regression method,** the cost line is positioned so as to *minimize* the sum of the *squared deviations* between the cost line and the data points. The inset to Exhibit 6–10 depicts this technique graphically. Note that the deviations between the cost line and the data points are measured vertically on the graph rather than perpendicular to the line. The cost line fit to the data using least-squares regression is called a *least-squares regression line* (or simply a **regression line**).

Exhibit 6–10

Graph of Utilities Cost Using Least-Squares Regression Method, Tasty Donuts, Inc.

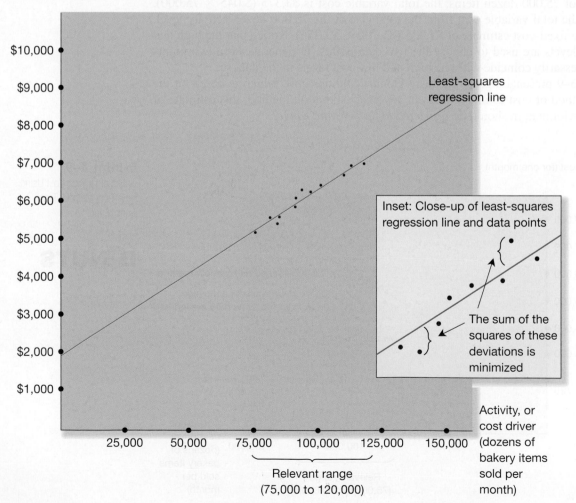

Why is the regression method based on minimizing the *squares* of the deviations between the cost line and the data points? A complete answer to this question lies in the theory of statistics. In short, statistical theorists have proved that a least-squares regression line possesses some very desirable properties for making cost predictions and drawing inferences about the estimated relationship between cost and activity. As always, the least-squares regression estimate of the cost behavior pattern should be restricted to the relevant range.

Equation Form of Least-Squares Regression Line The least-squares regression line shown in Exhibit 6–10 may be represented by the equation of a straight line. In the following equation, X denotes Tasty Donuts' activity level for a month, and Y denotes the estimated utilities cost for that level of activity. The intercept of the line on the vertical axis is denoted by $a,$ and the slope of the line is denoted by $b.$ *Within the relevant range, a* is interpreted as an estimate of the fixed-cost component, and *b* is interpreted as an estimate of the variable cost per unit of activity.

$$Y = a + bX \tag{1}$$

In regression analysis, X is referred to as the **independent variable,** since it is the variable upon which the estimate is based. Y is called the **dependent variable,** since its estimate depends on the independent variable.

The least-squares regression line for Tasty Donuts' utilities cost is shown below in equation form.

$$Y = 1{,}920 + .0448X$$

Estimated utilities cost for one month Activity level for one month

Within the relevant range of activity, the regression estimate of the fixed-cost component is \$1,920 per month, and the regression estimate of the variable-cost component is \$.0448 per dozen bakery items.

There are several statistical software packages available that do regression analysis. However, a common method of computing the least-squares regression estimates is to use a spreadsheet application such as Microsoft® Excel. This approach is covered in this chapter's appendix, which you may want to read now.

Evaluation of Least-Squares Regression Method We have seen that least-squares regression is an objective method of cost estimation that makes use of all available data. Moreover, the regression line has desirable statistical properties for making cost predictions and drawing inferences about the relationship between cost and activity. The method does require considerably more computation than either the visual-fit or high-low method. However, computer programs are readily available to perform least-squares regression.

Evaluating a Particular Least-Squares Regression Line We have seen the benefits of least-squares regression *in general.* How does a cost analyst evaluate a *particular* regression line based on a specific set of data? A number of criteria may be used, including *economic plausibility* and *goodness of fit.*

The cost analyst should always evaluate a regression line from the perspective of *economic plausibility.* Does the regression line make economic sense? Is it intuitively plausible to the cost analyst? If not, the analyst should reconsider using the regression line to make cost predictions. It may be that the chosen independent variable is not a good predictor of the cost behavior being analyzed. Perhaps another independent variable should be considered. Alternatively, there may be errors in the data upon which the regression is based. Rechecking the data will resolve this issue. It could be that fundamental assumptions that underlie the regression method have been violated. In this case, the analyst may have to resort to some other method of cost estimation.

Another criterion commonly used to evaluate a particular regression line is to assess its **goodness of fit.** Statistical methods can be used to determine objectively how well a regression line fits the data upon which it is based. If a regression line fits the data well, a large proportion of the variation in the dependent variable will be explained by the variation in the independent variable. One frequently used measure of goodness of fit is described in the appendix at the end of this chapter.[5]

Multiple Regression

Learning Objective 6

Describe the multiple regression, engineering, and learning-curve approaches to cost estimation.

In each of the cost estimation methods discussed so far, we have based the estimate on a single independent variable. Moreover, all of Tasty Donuts' cost behavior patterns were specified with respect to a single activity (or cost driver), dozens of bakery items produced and sold. However, there may be two or more independent variables that are important predictors of cost behavior.

To illustrate, we will continue our analysis of Tasty Donuts' utilities costs. The company uses electricity for two primary purposes: operating cooking equipment, such as deep-fat fryers and ovens, and heating the bakery and donut shops. The cost of electricity for food production is a function of the firm's activity, as measured in dozens of bakery items produced and sold. However, the cost of electricity for donut shop heating is related more closely to the number of customers than to the number of bakery items sold. A donut shop's heating costs go up each time the shop's door is opened, resulting in loss of heat. Two customers purchasing half a dozen donuts each result in greater heating cost than one customer buying a dozen donuts.

Suppose Tasty Donuts' controller wants to estimate a cost behavior pattern for utilities cost that is based on both units of sales and number of customers. The method of *multiple regression* may be used for this purpose. **Multiple regression** is a statistical method that estimates a linear (straight-line) relationship between one dependent variable and two or more independent variables. In Tasty Donuts' case, the following regression equation would be estimated.

$$Y = a + b_1 X_1 + b_2 X_2 \qquad (2)$$

where Y denotes the dependent variable, utilities cost

X_1 denotes the first independent variable, dozens of bakery items sold

X_2 denotes the second independent variable, number of customers served

In regression equation (2), a denotes the regression estimate of the fixed-cost component, b_1 denotes the regression estimate of the variable utilities cost per dozen bakery items, and b_2 denotes the regression estimate of the variable utilities cost per customer served. The multiple-regression equation will likely enable Tasty Donuts' controller to make more accurate cost predictions than could be made with the *simple regression* discussed previously. A **simple regression** is based on a single independent variable. Multiple regression is covered more extensively in cost accounting and statistics texts.

Data Collection Problems

Learning Objective 7

Describe some problems often encountered in collecting data for cost estimation.

Regardless of the method used, the resulting cost estimation will be only as good as the data upon which it is based. The collection of data appropriate for cost estimation requires a skilled and experienced cost analyst. Six problems frequently complicate the process of data collection:

1. *Missing data.* Misplaced source documents or failure to record a transaction can result in missing data.

---

[5]We have only scratched the surface of regression analysis as a tool for cost estimation. For an expanded discussion of the least-squares regression method, see any statistics text.

2. *Outliers.* We have discussed these extreme observations of cost-activity relationships. If outliers are determined to represent errors or highly unusual circumstances, they should be eliminated from the data set.

3. *Mismatched time periods.* The units of time for which the dependent and independent variables are measured may not match. For example, production activity may be recorded daily, but costs may be recorded monthly. A common solution is to aggregate the production data to get monthly totals.

4. *Trade-offs in choosing the time period.* In choosing the length of the time period for which data are collected, there are conflicting objectives. One objective is to obtain as many data points as possible, which implies a short time period. Another objective is to choose a long enough time period to ensure that the accounting system has accurately associated costs with time periods. If, for example, a cost that resulted from production activity in one period is recorded in a later period, the cost and activity data will not be matched properly. Longer time periods result in fewer recording lags in the data.

5. *Allocated and discretionary costs.* Fixed costs are often *allocated* on a per-unit-of-activity basis. For example, fixed manufacturing-overhead costs such as depreciation are allocated to units of production. As a result, such costs may appear to be variable in the cost records. *Discretionary costs* often are budgeted in a manner that makes them appear variable. A cost such as advertising, for example, may be fixed once management decides on the level of advertising. If management's policy is to budget advertising on the basis of sales dollars, however, the cost will appear to be variable to the cost analyst. An experienced analyst will be wary of such costs and take steps to learn how their amounts are determined.

6. *Inflation.* During periods of inflation, historical cost data may not reflect future cost behavior. One solution is to choose historical data from a period of low inflation and then factor in the current inflation rate. Other, more sophisticated approaches are also available, and they are covered in cost accounting texts.

Engineering Method of Cost Estimation

All of the methods of cost estimation examined so far are based on historical data. Each method estimates the relationship between cost and activity by studying the relationship observed in the past. A completely different method of cost estimation is to study the process that results in cost incurrence. This approach is called the **engineering method** of cost estimation. In a manufacturing firm, for example, a detailed study is made of the production technology, materials, and labor used in the manufacturing process. Rather than asking what the cost of material was last period, the engineering approach is to ask how much material should be needed and how much it should cost. Industrial engineers sometimes perform *time and motion studies,* which determine the steps required for people to perform the manual tasks that are part of the production process. Cost behavior patterns for various types of costs are then estimated on the basis of the engineering analysis. Engineering cost studies are time-consuming and expensive, but they often provide highly accurate estimates of cost behavior. Moreover, in rapidly evolving, high-technology industries, there may not be any historical data on which to base cost estimates. Such industries as genetic engineering, superconductivity, and electronics are evolving so rapidly that historical data are often irrelevant in estimating costs.

> **Learning Objective 6**
>
> Describe the multiple regression, engineering, and learning-curve approaches to cost estimation.

Effect of Learning on Cost Behavior

In many production processes, production efficiency increases with experience. As cumulative production output increases, the average labor time required per unit declines. As the labor time declines, labor cost declines as well. This phenomenon is called the **learning curve.** First documented by aeronautical engineer P. T. Wright in the 1930s, the learning curve concept was popularized by the Boston Consulting Group (BCG) in the 1970s. BCG broadened the learning curve idea to include costs other than direct labor and named this phenomenon the **experience curve.** The learning-curve and experience-curve concepts have been applied primarily to complex, labor-intensive manufacturing operations, such as aircraft assembly and shipbuilding. Boeing and Airbus, for example, make extensive use of the learning and experience curve concepts when budgeting the cost for a new aircraft design. However, the learning curve also has seen limited application in the health care services industry, mainly focusing on complex surgical procedures.

    To illustrate the learning curve concept, let's explore its use by Cosmos Communications Technology (CCT), a Canadian manufacturer of sophisticated communications satellites in Vancouver, British Columbia. The company's satellites transmit voice and data communications around the world. CCT's management has found that the learning curve applies to the labor-intensive assembly operation for each new satellite design. A graphical portrayal of CCT's learning curve is shown in panel A of Exhibit 6–11. On this learning curve, when cumulative output doubles, the average labor time per unit declines by 20 percent. Panel B of Exhibit 6–11 displays the total labor time and average labor time per unit for various levels of cumulative output. As cumulative output doubles from 5 to 10 units, for example, the average labor time per unit declines by 20 percent, from 100 hours per unit to 80 hours per unit. As CCT gains experience with a new satellite design, estimates of the cost of direct labor should be adjusted downward to take this learning effect into account.

    When the learning-curve concept is applied to a broader set of costs than just labor costs, it is referred to as an *experience curve.* Suppose, for example, that all labor and variable overhead costs are observed to decline by 20 percent every time cumulative output doubles. Then we would change the vertical axis of Exhibit 6–11 to *labor and variable overhead costs.* The graph would then be called an *experience curve.*

Exhibit 6–11
Learning Curve

A. Graphical Presentation of Learning Curve

Average labor time per unit (hours)

B. Tabular Presentation of Learning Curve

Cumulative Output (In units)	Average Labor Time per Unit (hours)	Total Labor Time (hours)
5	100.0	500.0
10	80.0	800.0
20	64.0	1,280.0
40	51.2	2,048.0

Focus on Ethics

CISCO SYSTEMS, WALMART, TACO BELL, STARBUCKS, U-HAUL, GENERAL DYNAMICS, AND FARMER'S INSURANCE: IS DIRECT LABOR A VARIABLE COST?

The question as to whether direct labor is a variable cost is interesting from a cost estimation perspective, but it also presents an interesting ethical issue.

Direct material is always a variable cost. At the other extreme, depreciation on fixed facilities and infrastructure typically is not. What about direct labor? Here it depends on the ability and willingness of management to adjust the labor force to current needs. If management is able *and willing* to hire workers as needed and lay them off when activity declines, direct labor would be a variable cost. The contemporary trend at many U.S. companies seems to be in this direction. "Companies are looking first to bring in contract workers that they can quickly *tap and zap* without paying any benefits or severance."* In fact, the temps have recently been the fastest-growing sector of employment. "And they aren't accounted for as regular employees. This helps companies that use a lot of them, like Cisco Systems Inc., to drive up revenue per employee."

"The growing use of the *just-in-time workforce* is not the only means by which companies are priming the productivity pump. Workers complain that many employers are taking advantage of outdated labor laws by misclassifying them as salaried-exempt so they can skirt overtime pay. Walmart, Taco Bell, Starbucks, and U-Haul, among others, have been slapped with class actions. In the case of General Dynamics Corp., this resulted in a $100 million award that is now on appeal. At Farmer's Insurance, employees got $90 million. Some employers are so worried about the issue that they are now doing wage-and-hour audits."

Is it ethical to "tap and zap" employees? What do you think? (For a more global perspective on this issue, see the Management Accounting Practice inset on page 276.)

*The information and quotations in this box are from Michelle Conlin, "The Big Squeeze on Workers," *BusinessWeek,* May 13, 2002, pp. 96, 97. See also P. Coy, M. Conlin, and M. Herbst, "The Disposable Worker," *BusinessWeek,* January 18, 2010, pp. 33–39.

Learning curves have been used extensively in such industries as aircraft production, shipbuilding, and electronics to assist cost analysts in predicting labor costs. These cost predictions are then used in scheduling production, budgeting, setting product prices, and other managerial decisions.

Chapter Summary

LO1 Explain the relationships between cost estimation, cost behavior, and cost prediction. Cost behavior is the relationship between cost and activity. Cost estimation refers to the determination of a cost's behavior. A cost prediction is a forecast of a cost at a particular level of activity.

LO2 Define and describe the behavior of the following types of costs: variable, step-variable, fixed, step-fixed, semivariable (or mixed), and curvilinear. A variable cost changes in total in direct proportion to a change in the activity level (or cost driver). A step-variable cost is nearly variable, but increases in small steps instead of continuously. A fixed cost remains unchanged in total as the activity level (or cost driver) varies. A step-fixed cost remains constant over a wide range of activity but jumps to a different amount for activity levels outside that range. A semivariable (or mixed) cost has both a variable and a semivariable component. A curvilinear cost behavior pattern has a curved graph.

LO3 Explain the importance of the relevant range in using a cost behavior pattern for cost prediction. Cost predictions should be confined to the relevant range, which is the range of activity expected for the organization. If the organization operates at an activity level outside the relevant range, any cost predictions based on data from the relevant range may not be very accurate.

LO4 Define and give examples of engineered costs, committed costs, and discretionary costs. An engineered cost bears a definitive physical relationship to the activity measure. Direct material cost is an example. A committed cost results from an organization's ownership or use of facilities and its basic organization structure. Examples include property taxes and depreciation on buildings and equipment. A discretionary cost arises as a result of a management decision to spend a particular amount of money for some purpose. Examples include research and development, advertising, and promotion.

LO5 Describe and use the following cost-estimation methods: account classification, visual fit, high-low, and least-squares regression. The account-classification, visual-fit, high-low, and least-squares regression methods of cost estimation are all based on an analysis of historical cost data observed at a variety of activity levels. The account-classification method involves a careful examination of an organization's ledger accounts. In the visual-fit method, a cost analyst plots recent observations of cost at various activity levels. In the high-low method, a semivariable cost is estimated using only two data points: the high and the low activity levels. In the least-squares regression method, the cost line is estimated so as to minimize the sum of the squared deviations between the cost line and the data points.

LO6 Describe the multiple regression, engineering, and learning-curve approaches to cost estimation. Multiple regression is a statistical method that estimates a linear (straight-line) relationship between one dependent variable and two or more independent variables. The engineering method of cost estimation is based on a detailed analysis of the process that results in cost incurrence. Under the learning-curve approach, the labor cost is estimated by studying the relationship between the cumulative production quantity and the average labor time required per unit. When this approach is applied to costs other than labor, it is referred to as the experience-curve approach.

LO7 Describe some problems often encountered in collecting data for cost estimation. Some common data collection problems include missing data, outliers (highly unusual observations), mismatched time periods, and cost inflation. Allocated and discretionary costs create other challenges in data collection and cost estimation.

LO8 Perform and interpret a least-squares regression analysis with a single independent variable (Appendix). In the least-squares regression method, the cost line is estimated so as to minimize the sum of the squared deviations between the cost line and the data points. The resulting regression line has an intercept on the vertical (cost) axis and a slope, which measures how steeply the cost line rises as activity increases.

Review Problems on Cost Behavior and Estimation

Problem 1

Irie Hardware operates a chain of four retail stores in Jamaica. Data on the company's maintenance costs for its store buildings and furnishings are as follows:

Month	Maintenance Cost	Sales
January	$53,000	$600,000
February	55,000	700,000
March	47,000	550,000
April	51,000	650,000
May	45,000	500,000
June	49,000	610,000

Using the high-low method, estimate and graph the cost behavior for the firm's maintenance costs.

Problem 2

The Rasta Rag is a weekly newspaper sold throughout Jamaica. The following costs were incurred by its publisher during a week when circulation was 100,000 newspapers: total variable costs, $40,000; total fixed costs, $66,000. Fill in your predictions for the following cost amounts.

	Circulation	
	110,000 Newspapers	**120,000 Newspapers**
Total variable cost	_____	_____
Variable cost per unit	_____	_____
Total fixed cost	_____	_____
Fixed cost per unit	_____	_____

Solutions to Review Problems
Problem 1

	Sales	Cost
At high activity level, February	$700,000	$55,000
At low activity level, May	500,000	45,000
Difference	$200,000	$10,000

$$\text{Variable cost per sales dollar} = \frac{\$10,000}{200,000} = \$.05 \text{ per sales dollar}$$

Total cost at $700,000 of sales	$55,000
Total variable cost at $700,000 of sales (700,000 × $.05)	35,000
Difference is total fixed cost	$20,000

The company's maintenance cost may be expressed by the following equation.

Total maintenance cost = $20,000 + $.05 (sales dollars)

Alternatively, the maintenance cost can be expressed in the following graph.

Problem 2

	Circulation			
	110,000 Newspapers		120,000 Newspapers	
Total variable cost	$40,000 × $\left(\frac{110,000}{100,000}\right)$ = $44,000		$40,000 × $\left(\frac{120,000}{100,000}\right)$ = $48,000	
Variable cost per unit	$44,000 ÷ 110,000 = $.40		$48,000 ÷ 120,000 = $.40	
Total fixed cost	$66,000		$66,000	
Fixed cost per unit	$66,000 ÷ 110,000 = $.60		$66,000 ÷ 120,000 = $.55	

Key Terms

For each term's definition refer to the indicated page, or turn to the glossary at the end of the text.

account-classification method (also called account analysis), 279
coefficient of determination,* 291
committed cost, 277
cost behavior, 268
cost estimation, 268
cost prediction, 268

curvilinear cost, 274
dependent variable, 283
discretionary cost, 277
engineered cost, 277
engineering method, 285
experience curve, 286
fixed cost, 271
goodness of fit, 284
high-low method, 281

independent variable, 283
learning curve, 286
least-squares regression method, 282
multiple regression, 284
outlier, 280
regression line, 282
relevant range, 275
scatter diagram, 279

semivariable (or mixed) cost, 273
simple regression, 284
step-fixed costs, 271
step-variable costs, 270
variable cost, 269
visual-fit method, 279

---

*Term appears in the appendix.

APPENDIX TO CHAPTER 6

Least-Squares Regression Using Microsoft® Excel

The least-squares regression line, which is shown below in equation form, includes two estimates. These estimates, which are called *parameters,* are the *intercept* (denoted by *a*) and the *slope coefficient* (denoted by *b*).

$$Y = a + bX \tag{3}$$

where X denotes the independent variable (activity level for one month)

        Y denotes the dependent variable (cost for one month)

Learning Objective 8

Perform and interpret a least-squares regression analysis with a single independent variable (Appendix).

Statistical theorists have shown that these parameters are defined by the following two equations.[6]

$$a = \frac{(\Sigma Y)(\Sigma X^2) - (\Sigma X)(\Sigma XY)}{n(\Sigma X^2) - (\Sigma X)(\Sigma X)} \tag{4}$$

$$b = \frac{n(\Sigma XY) - (\Sigma X)(\Sigma Y)}{n(\Sigma X^2) - (\Sigma X)(\Sigma X)} \tag{5}$$

where n denotes the number of data points

        Σ denotes summation; for example, ΣY denotes the sum of the Y (cost) values in the data

Calculating the intercept (a) and the slope coefficient (b) would be very laborious to do manually. Fortunately, there are many statistical software programs available to do the regression calculations. Alternatively, Microsoft® Excel can calculate the regression estimates, as the next section demonstrates.

Using Microsoft® Excel to Calculate the Regression Parameters

A cost analyst can use commands in Microsoft® Excel to easily calculate the regression estimate for the intercept (a) and the slope (b). All the analyst needs to do is input the data in a spreadsheet. The spreadsheet in Exhibit 6–12 displays the data used to compute Tasty Donuts' utilities cost. The dependent variable (utilities cost) is in column B, and the independent variable (activity) is in column C. Then the Excel functions INTERCEPT and SLOPE are used to compute the parameters. To use each command, the analyst specifies the range of cells in the spreadsheet in which the values of the dependent variable reside and the range of cells in which the values of the independent variable reside. This is illustrated in the Excel worksheet in Exhibit 6–12 as follows:

       Cell B24 contains the following formula: =INTERCEPT(B7:B18,C7:C18)

       Cell B25 contains the following formula: =SLOPE(B7:B18,C7:C18)

In these formulas, B7:B18 specifies the range of cells where the values of the dependent variable reside, and C7:C18 specifies the range of cells where the values of the independent variable reside.

       As the Excel calculations show in Exhibit 6–12, the regression estimates are as follows:

Intercept: $a = 1,920$

Slope: $b = .0448$

So the regression equation is the following:

$$Y = 1,920 + .0448X$$

     ↑   ↑

Estimated utilities   Activity level
cost for one month   for one month

---

[6]The derivation of these equations, which requires calculus, is covered in any introductory statistics text.

Goodness of Fit

The goodness of fit for Tasty Donuts' regression line may be measured by the **coefficient of determination,** commonly denoted by R^2. This measure is defined as the percentage of the variability of the dependent variable about its mean that is explained by the variability of the independent variable about its mean. The higher the R^2, the better the regression line fits the data. The interpretation for a high R^2 is that the independent variable is a good predictor of the behavior of the dependent variable. In cost estimation, a high R^2 means that the cost analyst can be relatively confident in the cost predictions based on the estimated cost behavior pattern.

Statistical theorists have shown that R^2 can be computed using the following formula:

$$R^2 = 1 - \frac{\Sigma(Y - Y')^2}{\Sigma(Y - \overline{Y})^2} \qquad (6)$$

where Y denotes the observed value of the dependent variable (cost) at a particular activity level

Y' denotes the predicted value of the dependent variable (cost), based on the regression line, at a particular activity level

$\overline{Y}$ denotes the mean (average) observation of the dependent variable (cost)

Excel can be used once again to calculate the R^2. The analyst simply uses the RSQ command in Excel. As shown in cell B26 of the Excel worksheet in Exhibit 6–12, the R^2 is .949.

Cell B26 contains the following formula: =RSQ(B7:B18,C7:C18)

This is a high value for R^2, and Tasty Donuts' controller may be quite confident in the resulting cost predictions. As always, these predictions should be confined to the relevant range.

Exhibit 6–12
Using Microsoft® Excel to Compute the Least-Squares Regression Estimates

Microsoft Excel - Computation of Regression Estimates

File Edit View Insert Format Tools Data Window Help

B24   fx =INTERCEPT(B7:B18,C7:C18)

	A	B	C	D
1		Utility		
2	Month	Cost	Activity	
3	of	for	during	
4	Preceding	Month	Month	
5	Year	Y	X	
6				
7	January	5,100	75,000	
8	February	5,300	78,000	
9	March	5,650	80,000	
10	April	6,300	92,000	
11	May	6,400	98,000	
12	June	6,700	108,000	
13	July	7,035	118,000	
14	August	7,000	112,000	
15	September	6,200	95,000	
16	October	6,100	90,000	
17	November	5,600	85,000	
18	December	5,900	90,000	
19	Total	73,285	1,121,000	
20				
21	Computation of Regression Parameters			
22	Using Spreadsheet Functions			
23				
24	Intercept	1,920		
25	Slope	0.0448		
26	R^2	0.949		

Sheet1 / Sheet2 / Sheet3

Ready

Review Questions

6–1. Describe the importance of cost behavior patterns in planning, control, and decision making.

6–2. Define the following terms, and explain the relationship between them: (*a*) cost estimation, (*b*) cost behavior, and (*c*) cost prediction.

6–3. Suggest an appropriate activity base (or cost driver) for each of the following organizations: (*a*) hotel, (*b*) hospital, (*c*) computer manufacturer, (*d*) computer sales store, (*e*) computer repair service, and (*f*) public accounting firm.

6–4. Draw a simple graph of each of the following types of cost behavior patterns: (*a*) variable, (*b*) step-variable, (*c*) fixed, (*d*) step-fixed, (*e*) semivariable, and (*f*) curvilinear.

6–5. Explain the impact of an increase in the level of activity (or cost driver) on (*a*) total fixed cost and (*b*) fixed cost per unit of activity.

6–6. Explain why a manufacturer's cost of supervising production might be a step-fixed cost.

6–7. Explain the impact of an increase in the level of activity (or cost driver) on (*a*) total variable cost and (*b*) variable cost per unit.

6–8. Using graphs, show how a semivariable (or mixed) cost behavior pattern can be used to approximate (*a*) a step-variable cost and (*b*) a curvilinear cost.

6–9. Indicate which of the following descriptions is most likely to describe each cost listed below.

Description	Costs
Engineered cost	Annual cost of maintaining a major highway
Committed cost	Cost of ingredients in a breakfast cereal
Discretionary cost	Cost of advertising for a credit card company
	Depreciation on an insurance company's computer
	Cost of charitable donations that are budgeted as 1 percent of sales revenue
	Research and development costs, which have been budgeted at $45,000 per year

6–10. A cost analyst showed the company president a graph that portrayed the firm's utility cost as semivariable. The president criticized the graph by saying, "This fixed-cost component doesn't look right to me. If we shut down the plant for six months, we wouldn't incur half of these costs." How should the cost analyst respond?

6–11. What is meant by a *learning curve?* Explain its role in cost estimation.

6–12. Suggest an appropriate independent variable to use in predicting the costs of the following tasks.
  a. Handling materials at a loading dock.
  b. Registering vehicles at a motor vehicle registry office.
  c. Picking oranges.
  d. Inspecting computer components in an electronics firm.

6–13. What is an *outlier?* List some possible causes of outliers. How should outliers be handled in cost estimation?

6–14. Explain the cost estimation problem caused by allocated and discretionary costs.

6–15. Describe the visual-fit method of cost estimation. What are the main strengths and weaknesses of this method?

6–16. What is the chief drawback of the high-low method of cost estimation? What problem could an outlier cause if the high-low method were used?

6–17. Explain the meaning of the term *least squares* in the least-squares regression method of cost estimation.

6–18. Use an equation to express a least-squares regression line. Interpret each term in the equation.

6–19. Distinguish between *simple regression* and *multiple regression.*

6–20. List several possible cost drivers that could be used by a cruise line such as Carnival.

6–21. Briefly describe two methods that can be used to evaluate a particular least-squares regression line.

Exercises

All applicable Exercises are available with McGraw-Hill's *Connect Accounting*™.

■ **Exercise 6–22**
Graphing Cost Behavior
Patterns; Hospital
(LO 1, 2)

Draw a graph of the cost behavior for each of the following costs incurred by the Mountain Summit Hospital. The hospital measures monthly activity in patient days. Label both axes and the cost line in each graph.

1. The cost of food varies in proportion to the number of patient days of activity. In January, the hospital provided 3,000 patient days of care, and food costs amounted to $24,000.

2. The cost of salaries and fringe benefits for the administrative staff totals $12,000 per month.

3. The hospital's laboratory costs include two components: (*a*) $40,000 per month for compensation of personnel and depreciation on equipment and (*b*) $10 per patient day for chemicals and other materials used in performing the tests.

4. The cost of utilities depends on how many wards the hospital needs to use during a particular month. During months with activity under 2,000 patient days of care, two wards are used, resulting in utility costs of $10,000. During months with greater than 2,000 patient days of care, three wards are used, and utility costs total $15,000.

5. Many of the hospital's nurses are part-time employees. As a result, the hours of nursing care provided can be easily adjusted to the amount required at any particular time. The cost of wages and fringe benefits for nurses is approximately $2,500 for each block of 200 patient days of care provided during a month. For example, nursing costs total $2,500 for 1 to 200 patient days, $5,000 for 201 to 400 patient days, $7,500 for 401 to 600 patient days, and so forth.

The behavior of the annual maintenance and repair cost of Sinaloa Bus Lines is shown by the solid line in the following graph. The dashed line depicts a semivariable-cost approximation of the department's repair and maintenance cost.

■ **Exercise 6–23**
Approximating a Curvilinear Cost;
(LO 1, 2, 3)

Required:

1. What is the actual (curvilinear) and estimated (semivariable) cost shown by the graph for each of the following activity levels?

	Actual	Estimated

a. 20,000 kilometers
b. 40,000 kilometers
c. 60,000 kilometers
d. 90,000 kilometers

2. How good an approximation does the semivariable cost pattern provide if the department's relevant range is 40,000 to 60,000 kilometers per month? What if the relevant range is 20,000 to 90,000 kilometers per month?

U-TV television channel is run by a major university in the northen hemisphere. The station's broadcast hours vary during the year depending on whether the university is in session. The station's production-crew and supervisory costs are as follows for July and October.

■ **Exercise 6–24**
Behavior of Fixed and Variable Costs; Television Station
(LO 1, 2)

Cost Item	Cost Behavior	Cost Amount	Broadcast Hours during Month
Production crew	Variable		
July..		$4,875	390
October		8,000	640
Supervisory employees	Fixed		
July..		5,500	390
October		5,500	640

Required:

1. Compute the cost per broadcast hour during July and October for each of these cost items.
2. What will be the total amount incurred for each of these costs during December, when the station's activity will be 450 broadcast hours?
3. What will be the cost per broadcast hour in December for each of the cost items?

■ **Exercise 6–25**
Estimating Cost Behavior;
High-Low Method
(LO 1, 2, 5)

Luis Ibañez owns a very successful apple orchard in Chile. He has formed his own company to produce and package applesauce. Apples can be stored for several months in cold storage, so applesauce production is relatively uniform throughout the year. The recently hired controller for the firm is about to apply the high-low method in estimating the company's energy cost behavior. The following costs were incurred during the past 12 months:

Month	Liters of Applesauce Produced	Energy Cost
January	35,000	$23,400
February	21,000	22,100
March	22,000	22,000
April	24,000	22,450
May	30,000	22,900
June	32,000	23,350
July	40,000	28,000
August	30,000	22,800
September	30,000	23,000
October	28,000	22,700
November	41,000	24,100
December	39,000	24,950

Required:

1. Use the high-low method to estimate the company's energy cost behavior and express it in equation form.
2. Predict the energy cost for a month in which 28,000 liters of applesauce are produced.

■ **Exercise 6–26**
Estimating Cost Behavior;
Visual-Fit Method
(LO 1, 2, 5)

Refer to the data in the preceding exercise.

Required:

1. Draw a scatter diagram and graph the company's energy cost behavior using the visual-fit method.
2. Predict the energy cost for a month in which 28,000 liters of applesauce are produced.
3. What peculiarity is apparent from the scatter diagram? What should the cost analyst do?

■ **Exercise 6–27**
Cost Behavior; Use of Internet
(LO 2)

Visit the Web site of one of the following companies, or a different company of your choosing.

Boeing	www.boeing.com	América Móvil	www.americamovil.com
Renault	www.renault.com	Hertz	www.hertz.com
ABB	www.abb.com	Gazprom	www.gazprom.com
Inditex Group	www.inditex.com	McDonald's	www.mcdonalds.com
Acer	www.acer.com	Teva Pharmaceuticals	www.tevapharm.com
General Electric	www.ge.com	Investec	www.investec.com

Required: Read about the company's products and operations. Then list five costs that the company would incur and explain what type of cost behavior you believe would be appropriate for each of these cost items.

■ **Exercise 6–28**
Visual-Fit Method; Veterinary
Laboratory
(LO 1, 2, 5)

The Stockholm Veterinary Laboratory performs a variety of diagnostic tests on commercial and domestic animals. The lab has incurred the following costs over the past year.

Month	Diagnostic Tests Completed	Cost
January	3,050	$121,000
February	4,500	149,000
March	7,100	149,000
April	6,200	191,200
May	4,700	149,600
June	5,900	178,000
July	6,000	182,000
August	6,100	180,000
September	5,300	174,000
October	4,900	152,400
November	4,800	156,200
December	5,050	161,400

Required:

1. Plot the data above in a scatter diagram. Assign cost to the vertical axis and the number of diagnostic tests to the horizontal axis. Visually fit a line to the plotted data.
2. Using the visually fit line, estimate the monthly fixed cost and the variable cost per diagnostic test.

■ **Exercise 6–29**
Account-Classification
Method; Food Processing
(LO 1, 2, 5)

Bavarian Wurst Company produces premium sausage products in southern Germany. The company's controller used the account-classification method to compile the following information.

a. Depreciation schedules revealed that monthly depreciation on buildings and equipment is $19,000.
b. Inspection of several invoices from meat packers indicated that meat costs the company $2.20 per kilogram of sausage produced.
c. Wage records showed that compensation for production employees costs $1.40 per kilogram of sausage produced.
d. Payroll records showed that supervisory salaries total $12,000 per month.
e. Bills revealed that the company incurs utility costs of $4,000 per month plus $.60 per kilogram of sausage produced.

Required:

1. Classify each cost item as variable, fixed, or semivariable.
2. Write a cost formula to express the cost behavior of the firm's production costs. (Use the formula $Y = a + bX$, where Y denotes production cost and X denotes quantity of sausage produced.)

■ **Exercise 6–30**
High-Low Method; Tour
Company
(LO 1, 2, 5)

Rio Bus Tours has incurred the following bus maintenance costs during the recent tourist season.

Month	Kilometers Traveled by Tour Buses	Cost
November	8,500	$11,400
December	10,600	11,600
January	12,700	11,700
February	15,000	12,000
March	20,000	12,500
April	8,000	11,000

Required:

1. Use the high-low method to estimate the variable cost per tour kilometer traveled and the fixed cost per month.
2. Develop a formula to express the cost behavior exhibited by the company's maintenance cost.

3. Predict the level of maintenance cost that would be incurred during a month when 22,000 tour kilometers are driven.

4. *Build a spreadsheet:* Construct an Excel spreadsheet to solve all of the preceding requirements. Show how the solution will change if the following information changes: in March there were 21,000 kilometers traveled and the cost was $12,430.

■ **Exercise 6–31**
Work Measurement;
Government Agency
(LO 2, 6)

The Department of Taxation processes and audits income-tax returns. The tax commissioner has recently begun a program of work measurement to help in estimating the costs of running the department. The independent variable used in the program is the number of returns processed. The analysis revealed that the following variable costs are incurred in auditing a typical tax return.

> Time spent by clerical employees, 10 hours at $12 per hour
>
> Time spent by tax professional, 20 hours at $25 per hour
>
> Computer time, $50 per audit
>
> Telephone charges, $10 per audit
>
> Postage, $2 per audit

In addition, the department incurs $10,000 of fixed costs each month that are associated with the process of auditing returns.

Required: Draw a graph depicting the monthly costs of auditing tax returns. Label the horizontal axis "Tax returns audited."

■ **Exercise 6–32**
Learning Curve; High
Technology
(LO 1, 6)

Weathereye, Inc. manufactures weather satellites. The final assembly and testing of the satellites is a largely manual operation involving dozens of highly trained electronics technicians. The following learning curve has been estimated for the firm's newest satellite model, which is about to enter production.

Assembly and Testing

Required:

1. What will be the average labor time required to assemble and test each satellite when the company has produced four satellites? Eight satellites?

2. What will be the total labor time required to assemble and test all satellites produced if the firm manufactures only four satellites? Eight satellites?

3. How can the learning curve be used in the company's budgeting process? In setting cost standards?

■ **Exercise 6–33**
Airline; Least-Squares
Regression (Appendix)
(LO 1, 2, 5, 8)

Recent monthly costs of providing on-board flight service incurred by Lotus Airlines are shown in the following table.

Month	Number of Passengers	Cost of On-Board Flight Service
January	16,000	$18,000
February	17,000	18,000
March	16,000	19,000
April	18,000	20,000
May	15,000	18,000
June	17,000	19,000

Required:

1. *Build a spreadsheet:* Construct an Excel spreadsheet and use the Excel commands to perform a least-squares regression. Estimate the cost behavior of the airline's on-board flight service. Express the cost behavior in equation form.

2. Use Excel to calculate and interpret the R^2 value for the regression.

Hill Island Markets, a chain of convenience grocery stores on Phuket, has store hours that fluctuate from month to month with the tourist trade. The utility costs for one of the company's stores are listed below for the past six months.

■ **Exercise 6–34**
Estimating Cost Behavior by Multiple Methods (Appendix)
(LO 1, 2, 5, 8)

Month	Total Hours of Operation	Total Utility Cost
January	550	$1,620
February	600	1,700
March	700	1,960
April	500	1,600
May	450	1,350
June	400	1,300

Required:

1. Use the high-low method to estimate the cost behavior for the store's utility costs. Express the cost behavior in formula form ($Y = a + bX$). What is the variable utility cost per hour of operation?

2. Draw a scatter diagram of the store's utility costs. Visually fit a cost line to the plotted data. Estimate the variable utility cost per hour of operation.

3. *Build a spreadsheet:* Construct an Excel spreadsheet and use the Excel commands to perform a least-squares regression. Estimate the cost behavior for the store's utility cost. Express the cost behavior in formula form. What is the variable utility cost per hour of operation?

4. During July, the store will be open 300 hours. Predict the store's total utility cost for July using each of the cost-estimation methods employed in requirements (1), (2), and (3).

5. Use your Excel sheet from requirement (3) to calculate and interpret the R^2 value for the regression.

Problems

All applicable Problems are available with McGraw-Hill's *Connect Accounting™*.

For each of the cost items described below, choose the graph (on the next page) that best represents it.

■ **Problem 6–35**
Cost Behavior Patterns in a Variety of Settings;
(LO 1, 2)

1. The salaries of the security personnel at a factory. The security guards are on duty around the clock.

2. The wages of table-service personnel in a restaurant. The employees are part-time workers, who can be called upon for as little as two hours at a time.

3. The cost of electricity during peak-demand periods is based on the following schedule.

Up to 9,500 kilowatt-hours (kwh)	$.10 per kwh
Above 9,500 kilowatt-hours	$.13 per kwh

The price schedule is designed to discourage overuse of electricity during periods of peak demand.

4. The cost of sheet metal used to manufacture automobiles.

5. The cost of utilities at a university. For low student enrollments, utility costs increase with enrollment, but at a decreasing rate. For large student enrollments, utility costs increase at an increasing rate.

6. The cost of telephone service, which is based on the number of message units per month. The charge is $.08 per message unit, for up to 700 message units. Additional message units (above 700) are free.

7. The cost of the nursing staff in a hospital. The staff always has a minimum of nine nurses on duty. Additional nurses are used depending on the number of patients in the hospital. The hospital administrator estimates that this additional nursing staff costs approximately $195 per patient per day.

8. The cost of chartering a private airplane. The cost is $390 per hour for the first three hours of a flight. Then the charge drops to $280 per hour.

9. Under a licensing agreement with an import/export company, your firm has begun shipping machine tools to several countries. The terms of the agreement call for an annual licensing fee of $100,000 to be paid to the import/export company if total exports are under $5,000,000. For sales in excess of $5,000,000, an additional licensing fee of 10 percent of sales is due.

10. Your winery exports wine to several Asian countries. In one nation, you must pay a tariff for every case of wine brought into the country. The tariff schedule is the following:

0 to 5,500 cases per year	$12 per case
5,501 to 11,000 cases per year	$15 per case
Above 11,000 cases per year	$20 per case

11. The salary costs of the shift supervisors at a truck depot. Each shift is eight hours. The depot operates with one, two, or three shifts at various times of the year.

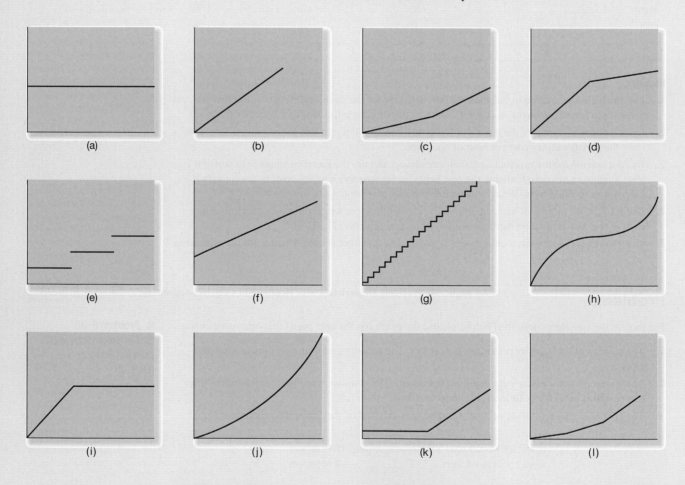

■ **Problem 6–36**

Cost Behavior and Analysis; High-Low Method
(LO 2, 5)

2. Variable maintenance cost: $9 per hour

The following selected data were taken from the accounting records of Metcalf Manufacturing. The company uses direct-labor hours as its cost driver for overhead costs.

Month	Direct-Labor Hours	Manufacturing Overhead
January...	23,000...	$454,000
February..	30,000...	517,000
March	34,000...	586,000
April	26,000...	499,500
May	25,000...	480,000
June	28,000...	515,000

March's costs consisted of machine supplies ($102,000), depreciation ($15,000), and plant maintenance ($469,000). These costs exhibit the following respective behavior: variable, fixed, and semivariable.

The manufacturing overhead figures presented in the preceding table do not include Metcalf's supervisory labor cost, which is step-fixed in nature. For volume levels of less than 15,000 hours, supervisory labor amounts to $45,000. The cost is $90,000 from 15,000–29,999 hours and $135,000 when activity reaches 30,000 hours or more.

Required:

1. Determine the machine supplies cost and depreciation for January.

2. Using the high-low method, analyze Metcalf's plant maintenance cost and calculate the monthly fixed portion and the variable cost per direct-labor hour.

3. Assume that present cost behavior patterns continue into the latter half of the year. Estimate the *total* amount of manufacturing overhead the company can expect in November if 29,500 direct-labor hours are worked.

4. Briefly explain the difference between a fixed cost and a step-fixed cost.

5. Assume that a company has a step-fixed cost. Generally speaking, where on a step should the firm attempt to operate if it desires to achieve a maximum return on its investment?

───────────────

Kalimantan Extraction, which mines ore in Indonesia, uses a calendar year for both financial-reporting and tax purposes. The following selected costs were incurred in December, the low point of activity, when 1,500 tons of ore were extracted:

Straight-line depreciation	$ 25,000	Royalties	$135,000
Charitable contributions*	11,000	Trucking and hauling	275,000
Mining labor/fringe benefits	360,000		

*Incurred only in December.

Peak activity of 2,600 tons occurred in June, resulting in mining labor/fringe benefit costs of $624,000, royalties of $201,000, and trucking and hauling outlays of $325,000. The trucking and hauling outlays exhibit the following behavior:

Less than 1,500 tons	$250,000
From 1,500–1,899 tons	275,000
From 1,900–2,299 tons	300,000
From 2,300–2,699 tons	325,000

Kalimantan uses the high-low method to analyze costs.

Required:

1. Classify the five costs listed in terms of their behavior: variable, step-variable, committed fixed, discretionary fixed, step-fixed, or semivariable. Show calculations to support your answers for mining labor/fringe benefits and royalties.

2. Calculate the total cost for next February when 1,650 tons are expected to be extracted.

3. Comment on the cost-effectiveness of hauling 1,500 tons with respect to Kalimantan's trucking/hauling cost behavior. Can the company's effectiveness be improved? How?

4. Distinguish between committed and discretionary fixed costs. If Kalimantan were to experience severe economic difficulties, which of the two types of fixed costs should management try to cut? Why?

5. Speculate as to why the company's charitable contribution cost arises only in December.

───────────────

Capital Fitness operates a chain of fitness centers in Canberra. The firm's controller is accumulating data to be used in preparing its annual profit plan for the coming year. The cost behavior pattern of the firm's equipment maintenance costs must be determined. The accounting staff has suggested the use of an equation, in the form of $Y = a + bX$, for maintenance costs. Data regarding the maintenance hours and costs for last year are as follows:

■ **Problem 6–37**
Cost Behavior and Analysis; High-Low Method
(LO 2, 4, 5)

2. Total cost for 1,650 tons: $840,000

■ **Problem 6–38**
High-Low Method; Fitness Centers
(LO 1, 2, 5)

3. Cost prediction at 590 hours of activity, maintenance cost: $4,995

Month	Hours of Maintenance Service	Maintenance Costs
January	520	$ 4,470
February	490	4,260
March	300	2,820
April	500	4,350
May	310	2,960
June	480	4,200
July	320	3,000
August	400	3,600
September	470	4,050
October	350	3,300
November	340	3,160
December	320	3,030
Total	4,800	$43,200
Average	400	$ 3,600

Required:

1. Using the high-low method of cost estimation, estimate the behavior of the maintenance costs incurred by Capital Fitness. Express the cost behavior pattern in equation form.

2. Using your answer to requirement (1), what is the variable component of the maintenance cost?

3. Compute the predicted maintenance cost at 590 hours of activity.

4. Compute the variable cost per hour and the fixed cost per hour at 600 hours of activity. Explain why the fixed cost per hour could be misleading.

(CMA, adapted)

■ **Problem 6–39**
Account-Classification Method; Private School
(LO 1, 2, 5)

The Versailles School of Music has hired you as a consultant to help in analyzing the behavior of the school's costs. Use the account-classification method of cost estimation to classify each of the following costs as variable, fixed, or semivariable. Before classifying the costs, choose an appropriate measure for the school's activity.

1. Salaries and fringe benefits of the school's full-time teachers.

2. Salaries and fringe benefits of the school's full-time administrative staff.

3. Cost of buying books, sheet music, and other academic materials that are supplied to the students by the school.

4. Repairs on musical instruments. The school employs a full-time repair technician. Repair jobs that are beyond the technician's capability are taken to a local musical-instrument dealer for repairs.

5. Fee charged by a local accounting firm to audit the school's accounting records.

6. Wages of the school's part-time assistant recital instructors. These employees are hired on a temporary basis. For each student enrolled in the school's music programs, four hours of assistant instructor time are needed per week.

7. Depreciation on the school's musical instruments.

8. Rent for the building in which the school operates.

9. Electricity for the school. The school pays a fixed monthly charge plus $.11 per kilowatt-hour of electricity.

■ **Problem 6–40**
Approximating a StepVariable Cost; Visual-Fit Method; Golf Course
(LO 1, 2, 5)

3. Fixed-cost component: $12,520

Kansai Golf Association is a nonprofit, private organization that operates three 18-hole golf courses near Osaka. The organization's financial director has just analyzed the course maintenance costs incurred by the golf association during recent summers. The courses are maintained by a full-time crew of four people, who are assisted by part-time employees. These employees are typically college students on their summer vacations. The course maintenance costs vary with the number of people using the course. Since a large part of the maintenance work is done by part-time employees, the maintenance crew size can easily be adjusted to reflect current needs. The financial director's analysis revealed that the course maintenance cost includes two components:

1. A fixed component of $12,500 per month (when the courses are open).

2. A step-variable cost component. For each additional 1 to 10 people teeing off in one day, $20 in costs are incurred. Thus, if 101 to 110 people tee off, $220 of additional cost will be incurred. If 111 to 120 people tee off, $240 of additional cost will be incurred.

Required:

1. Draw a graph of Kansai Golf Association's course maintenance costs. Show on the graph the fixed-cost component and the step-variable cost component. Label each clearly.

2. Use a semivariable-cost behavior pattern to approximate the golf association's course maintenance cost behavior. Visually fit the semivariable cost line to your graph.

3. Using your graph, estimate the variable- and fixed-cost components included in your semivariable approximation. Express this approximate cost behavior pattern in equation form.

4. Fill in the following table of cost predictions.

	Predicted Course Maintenance Costs	
	Using Fixed Cost Coupled with Step-Variable Cost Behavior Pattern	Using Semivariable Cost Approximation
150 people tee off	?	?
158 people tee off	?	?

Cape Verde Marine Supply is a wholesaler for a large variety of boating and fishing equipment. The company's controller, Carlos Pereira, has recently completed a cost study of the firm's material-handling department in which he used work measurement to quantify the department's activity. The control factor unit used in the work-measurement study was hundreds of kilograms of equipment unloaded or loaded at the company's loading dock. Pereira compiled the following data.

■ **Problem 6–41**
Work Measurement; Cost Estimation with Different Methods; Wholesaler
(LO 1, 2, 5, 6)

3. Variable cost per unit of activity: $2.00

Month	Units of Activity (hundreds of kilograms of equipment loaded or unloaded)	Material-Handling Department Costs
January	700	$11,350
February	600	11,350
March	550	11,050
April	1,300	12,120
May	900	11,400
June	1,000	12,000
July	1,200	12,550
August	1,100	11,100
September	500	10,200
October	650	11,250
November	800	11,300
December	900	11,700

Required:

1. Draw a scatter diagram of the cost data for the material-handling department.

2. Visually fit a cost line to the scatter diagram.

3. Estimate the variable and fixed components of the department's cost behavior pattern using the visually fit cost line.

4. Using your estimate from requirement (3), specify an equation to express the department's cost behavior.

5. Estimate the material-handling department's cost behavior using the high-low method. Use an equation to express the results of this estimation method.

6. Help Carlos Pereira write a brief memo to the company's president explaining why the cost estimates developed in requirements (4) and (5) differ.

7. Predict the company's material-handling costs for a month when 1,150 units of activity are recorded. Use each of your cost equations to make the prediction. Which prediction would you prefer to use? Why?

■ **Problem 6–42**
Continuation of Preceding Problem; Computing Least-Squares Regression Estimates; Comparing Multiple Methods (Appendix)
(LO 1, 2, 5, 6, 8)

2. Total monthly cost: $9,943 + $1.77 per unit of activity

Refer to the orginal data in the preceding problem for Cape Verde Marine Supply.

Required:

1. *Build a spreadsheet:* Construct an Excel spreadsheet and use the Excel commands to perform a least-squares regression. Estimate of the variable- and fixed-cost components in the company's material-handling department costs.

2. Write the least-squares regression equation for the department's costs.

3. Predict the firm's material-handling department's costs for a month when 1,150 units of activity are recorded.

4. Why do the three cost predictions computed in this and the preceding problem differ? Which method do you recommend? Why?

5. *Build a spreadsheet:* Use your Excel spreadsheet from requirement (1) to compute the R^2 value for the regression. Interpret the R^2 value.

■ **Problem 6–43**
Cost Estimation Methods; Cost Analysis; E-Commerce
(LO 2, 5)

4. C: $1,567,000

Shortly after being hired as an analyst with Global Airlines, Kim Williams was asked to prepare a report that focused on passenger ticketing cost. The airline writes most of its own tickets (largely through reservations personnel), makes little use of travel agents, and has seen an ever-increasing passenger interest in e-ticketing. (i.e., electronic reservations and tickets handled over the Internet).

   After some discussion, Williams thought it would be beneficial to begin her report with an overview of three different cost estimation tools: scatter diagrams, least-squares regression, and the high-low method. She would then present the results of her analysis of the past year's monthly ticketing cost, which was driven largely by the number of tickets written. These results would be presented in the form of algebraic equations that were derived by the three tools just cited. The equations follow. (C denotes ticketing cost, and PT denotes number of passenger tickets written.)

   Scatter diagram: C = $320,000 + $2.15PT

   Least-squares regression: C = $312,000 + $2.30PT

   High-low method: C = $295,000 + $2.55PT

Williams had analyzed data over the past 12 months and built equations on these data, purposely including the slowest month of the year (February) and the busiest month (November) so that things would ". . . tend to average out." She observed that November was especially busy because of passengers purchasing tickets for holiday travel, and the effects of a strike by Western Airlines, Global's chief competitor. The lengthy strike resulted in many of Western's passengers being rerouted on Global flights.

Required:

1. Prepare a bullet-point list suitable for use in Williams's report that describes the features of scatter diagrams, least-squares regression, and the high-low method. Determine which of the three tools will typically produce the most accurate results.

2. Will the three cost estimation tools normally result in different equations? Why?

3. Assuming the use of least-squares regression, explain what the $312,000 and $2.30 figures represent.

4. Assuming the use of a scatter diagram, predict the cost of an upcoming month when Global expects to write 580,000 tickets.

5. Did Williams err in constructing the equations on data of the past 12 months? Briefly explain.

6. Assume that over the next few years, more of Global's passengers will take advantage of e-ticketing over the Internet. What will likely happen to the airline's cost structure in terms of variable and fixed cost incurred?

The controller of Chittenango Chain Company believes that the identification of the variable and fixed components of the firm's costs will enable the firm to make better planning and control decisions. Among the costs the controller is concerned about is the behavior of indirect-materials cost. She believes there is a correlation between machine hours and the amount of indirect materials used.

A member of the controller's staff has suggested that least-squares regression be used to determine the cost behavior of indirect materials. The regression equation shown below was developed from 40 pairs of observations.

$$S = \$200 + \$4H$$

> where S = Total monthly cost of indirect materials
>
> H = Machine hours per month

■ **Problem 6–44**
Comparing Regression
and High-Low Estimates;
Manufacturer
(LO 1, 2, 5, 7)

5. Fixed cost: $150

Required:

1. Explain the meaning of "200" and "4" in the regression equation $S = \$200 + \$4H$.
2. Calculate the estimated cost of indirect materials if 900 machine hours are to be used during a month.
3. To determine the validity of the cost estimate computed in requirement (2), what question would you ask the controller about the data used for the regression?
4. The high and low activity levels during the past four years, as measured by machine hours, occurred during April and August, respectively. Data concerning machine hours and indirect-material usage follow.

	April	August
Machine hours	1,100	800
Indirect supplies:		
Beginning inventory	$1,200	$ 950
Ending inventory	1,550	2,900
Purchases	6,000	6,100

Determine the cost of indirect materials used during April and August.

5. Use the high-low method to estimate the behavior of the company's indirect-material cost. Express the cost behavior pattern in equation form.
6. Which cost estimate would you recommend to the controller, the regression estimate or the high-low estimate? Why?

(CMA, adapted)

■ **Problem 6–45**
Interpreting Regression
Analysis in Cost Estimation
(LO 1, 2, 5)

3. Minimum bid for 200-person
cocktail party: $4,400

Dana Rand owns a catering company that prepares banquets and parties for both individual and business functions throughout the year. Rand's business is seasonal, with a heavy schedule during the summer months and the year-end holidays and a light schedule at other times. During peak periods, there are extra costs; however, even during nonpeak periods Rand must work more to cover her expenses.

One of the major events Rand's customers request is a cocktail party. She offers a standard cocktail party and has developed the following cost structure on a per-person basis.

Food and beverages	$15
Labor (.5 hr. @ $10 per hour)	5
Overhead (.5 hr. @ $14 per hour)	7
Total cost per person	$27

When bidding on cocktail parties, Rand adds a 15 percent markup to this cost structure as a profit margin. Rand is quite certain about her estimates of the prime costs but is not as comfortable with the overhead estimate. This estimate was based on the actual data for the past 12 months presented in the following table. These data indicate that overhead expenses vary with the direct-labor hours expended. The $14 estimate was determined by dividing total overhead expended for the 12 months ($805,000) by total labor hours (57,600) and rounding to the nearest dollar.

Month	Labor Hours	Overhead Expenses
January	2,500	$ 55,000
February	2,800	59,000
March	3,000	60,000
April	4,200	64,000
May	4,500	67,000
June	5,500	71,000
July	6,500	74,000
August	7,500	77,000
September	7,000	75,000
October	4,500	68,000
November	3,100	62,000
December	6,500	73,000
Total	57,600	$805,000

Rand recently attended a meeting of the local chamber of commerce and heard a business consultant discuss regression analysis and its business applications. After the meeting, Rand decided to do a regression analysis of the overhead data she had collected. The following results were obtained.

Intercept *(a)*	48,000
Coefficient *(b)*	4

Required:

1. Explain the difference between the overhead rate originally estimated by Dana Rand and the overhead rate developed from the regression method.

2. Using data from the regression analysis, develop the following cost estimates per person for a cocktail party.

   a. Variable cost per person

   b. Absorption cost per person

   Assume that the level of activity remains within the relevant range.

3. Dana Rand has been asked to prepare a bid for a 200-person cocktail party to be given next month. Determine the minimum bid price that Rand should be willing to submit.

4. What other factors should Dana Rand consider in developing the bid price for the cocktail party?

(CMA, adapted)

■ **Problem 6–46**
Computing Least-Squares Regression Estimates; Airport Costs (Appendix)
(LO 1, 2, 5, 8)

2. Variable: $7.65 per flight
2. Fixed: $10,894 per month
4. Cost prediction, 1,600 flights: $23,134

Metropolitan Airport handles several daily commuter flights and many private flights. The municipal budget officer has compiled the following data regarding airport costs and activity over the past year.

Month	Flights Originating at Metropolitan Airport	Airport Costs
January	1,100	$20,000
February	800	16,000
March	1,400	19,000
April	900	18,000
May	1,000	19,000
June	1,200	20,000
July	1,100	18,000
August	1,400	24,000
September	1,000	19,000
October	1,200	23,000
November	900	17,000
December	1,500	21,000

Required:

1. Draw a scatter diagram of the airport costs shown above.
2. *Build a spreadsheet:* Construct an Excel spreadsheet and use the Excel commands to perform a least-squares regression. Estimate the variable- and fixed-cost components in the airport's cost behavior pattern.
3. Write the least-squares regression equation for the airport's costs.
4. Predict the airport's costs during a month when 1,600 flights originate at the airport.
5. Using the Excel spreadsheet prepared for requirement (2), compute the coefficient of determination (R^2) for the regression equation. Briefly interpret R^2.

Cases

Earth and Artistry, Inc. provides commercial landscaping services. Sasha Cairns, the firm's owner, wants to develop cost estimates that she can use to prepare bids on jobs. After analyzing the firm's costs, Cairns has developed the following preliminary cost estimates for each 1,000 square feet of landscaping.

■ **Case 6–47**
Interpreting Least-Squares Regression; Landscaping Service; Activity-Based Costing
(LO 1, 2, 5)

Direct material	$400
Direct labor (5 direct-labor hours at $10 per hour)	50
Overhead (at $18 per direct-labor hour)	90
Total cost per 1,000 square feet	$540

2. Total variable cost per 1,000 square feet: $496.25

5(b). Total incremental variable overhead: $3,285

Cairns is quite certain about the estimates for direct material and direct labor. However, she is not as comfortable with the overhead estimate. The estimate for overhead is based on the overhead costs that were incurred during the past 12 months as presented in the following schedule. The estimate of $18 per direct-labor hour was determined by dividing the total overhead costs for the 12-month period ($648,000) by the total direct-labor hours (36,000).

	Total Overhead	Regular Direct-Labor Hours	Overtime Direct-Labor Hours*	Total Direct-Labor Hours
January	$ 54,000	2,910	190	3,100
February	47,000	2,380	20	2,400
March	48,000	2,210	40	2,250
April	56,000	2,590	210	2,800
May	57,000	3,030	470	3,500
June	65,000	3,240	760	4,000
July	64,000	3,380	620	4,000
August	56,000	3,050	350	3,400
September	53,000	2,760	40	2,800
October	47,000	2,770	30	2,800
November	47,000	2,120	30	2,150
December	54,000	2,560	240	2,800
Total	$648,000	33,000	3,000	36,000

*The overtime premium is 50 percent of the direct-labor wage rate.

Cairns believes that overhead is affected by total monthly direct-labor hours. Cairns decided to perform a least-squares regression of overhead (OH) on total direct-labor hours (DLH). The following regression formula was obtained.

$$OH = 26{,}200 + 9.25DLH$$

Required:

1. The overhead rate developed from the least-squares regression is different from Cairns' preliminary estimate of $18 per direct-labor hour. Explain the difference in the two overhead rates.
2. Using the overhead formula that was derived from the least-squares regression, determine a total variable-cost estimate for each 1,000 square feet of landscaping.
3. Cairns has been asked to submit a bid on a landscaping project for the city government consisting of 60,000 square feet. Cairns estimates that 40 percent of the direct-labor hours required for the project

will be on overtime. Calculate the incremental costs that should be included in any bid that Cairns would submit on this project. Use the overhead formula derived from the least-squares regression.

4. Should management rely on the overhead formula derived from the least-squares regression as the basis for the variable overhead component of its cost estimate? Explain your answer.

5. After attending a seminar on activity-based costing, Cairns decided to further analyze the company's activities and costs. She discovered that a more accurate portrayal of the firm's cost behavior could be achieved by dividing overhead into three separate pools, each with its own cost driver. Separate regression equations were estimated for each of the cost pools, with the following results.

$OH_1 = 10,000 + 4.10DLH$,

where *DLH* denotes direct-labor hours

$OH_2 = 9,100 + 13.50SFS$,

where *SFS* denotes the number of square feet of turf seeded (in thousands)

$OH_3 = 8,000 + 6.60PL$,

where *PL* denotes the number of individual plantings (e.g., trees and shrubs)

Assume that 5 direct-labor hours will be needed to landscape each 1,000 square feet, regardless of the specific planting material used.

a. Suppose the landscaping project for the city will involve seeding all 60,000 square feet of turf and planting 80 trees and shrubs. Calculate the incremental *variable overhead* cost that Cairns should include in the bid.

b. Recompute the incremental variable overhead cost for the city's landscaping project assuming half of the 60,000-square-foot landscaping area will be seeded and there will be 250 individual plantings. The plantings will cover the entire 60,000-square-foot area.

c. Briefly explain, using concepts from activity-based costing, why the incremental costs differ in requirements (a) and (b).

(CMA, adapted)

Case 6–48
Approximating a Curvilinear
Cost; Visual-Fit Method;
Pediatrics Clinic
(LO 1, 2, 5)

6. Administrative cost
= $7,000 + $3.00X, where X
denotes number of patients

(*Note:* Instructors who wish to cover all three cost-estimation methods with the same data set may assign this case in conjunction with the following case.)

"I don't understand this cost report at all," exclaimed Jeff Mahoney, the newly appointed administrator of Mountainview General Hospital. "Our administrative costs in the new pediatrics clinic are all over the map. One month the report shows $8,300, and the next month it's $16,100. What's going on?"

Mahoney's question was posed to Megan McDonough, the hospital's director of Cost Management. "The main problem is that the clinic has experienced some widely varying patient loads in its first year of operation. There seems to be some confusion in the public's mind about what services we offer in the clinic. When do they come to the clinic? When do they go to the emergency room? That sort of thing. As the patient load has varied, we've frequently changed our clinic administrative staffing."

Mahoney continued to puzzle over the report. "Could you pull some data together, Megan, so we can see how this cost behaves over a range of patient loads?"

"You'll have it this afternoon," McDonough responded. Later that morning, she gathered the following data:

Month	Patient Load	Administrative Cost
January	1,400	$13,900
February	500	7,000
March	400	6,000
April	1,000	10,000
May	1,300	11,900
June	900	9,200
July	1,100	10,200
August	300	4,100
September	700	9,400
October	1,200	11,100
November	600	8,300
December	1,500	16,100

McDonough does not believe the first year's widely fluctuating patient load will be experienced again in the future. She has estimated that the clinic's relevant range of monthly activity in the future will be 600 to 1,200 patients.

Required:

1. Draw a scatter diagram of the clinic's administrative costs during its first year of operation.

2. Visually fit a curvilinear cost line to the plotted data.

3. Mark the clinic's relevant range of activity on the scatter diagram.

4. Visually fit a semivariable-cost line to approximate the curvilinear cost behavior pattern within the clinic's relevant range.

5. Estimate the fixed- and variable-cost components of the visually fit semivariable-cost line.

6. Use an equation to express the semivariable-cost approximation of the clinic's administrative costs.

7. What is your prediction of the clinic's administrative cost during a month when 800 patients visit the clinic? When 300 patients visit? Which one of your visually fit cost lines did you use to make each of these predictions? Why?

Refer to the data and accompanying information in the preceding case.

Required:

1. Use the high-low method to estimate the cost behavior for the clinic's administrative costs. Express the cost behavior in formula form ($Y = a + bX$). What is the variable cost per patient?

2. *Build a spreadsheet:* Construct an Excel spreadsheet and use the Excel commands to perform a least-squares regression and estimate the administrative cost behavior. Express the cost behavior in formula form. What is the variable cost per patient? Compute and interpret the R^2 value for the regression.

3. Help McDonough write a memo to the hospital administrator comparing the cost estimates using (*a*) least-squares regression, (*b*) the high-low method, and (*c*) the scatter diagram and visually fit semivariable-cost line from the preceding case (requirement (4)). Make a recommendation as to which estimate should be used, and support your recommendation. Make any other suggestions you feel are appropriate.

4. After receiving the memo comparing the three cost estimates, Mahoney called McDonough to discuss the matter. The following exchange occurred.

> **Mahoney:** "As you know, Megan, I was never in favor of this clinic. It's going to be a drag on our administrative staff, and we'd have been far better off keeping the pediatrics operation here in the hospital."
>
> **McDonough:** "I was aware that you felt the clinic was a mistake. Of course, the board of trustees had other issues to consider. I believe the board felt the clinic should be built to make pediatric care more accessible to the economically depressed area on the other side of the city."
>
> **Mahoney:** "That's true, but the board doesn't realize how difficult it's going to make life for us here in the hospital. In any case, I called to tell you that when you and I report to the board next week, I'm going to recommend that the clinic be shut down. I want you to support my recommendation with one of your cost estimates showing that administrative costs will soar at high activity levels."
>
> **McDonough:** "But that estimate was based on the high-low method. It's not an appropriate method for this situation."
>
> **Mahoney:** "It *is* an estimate, Megan, and it's based on a well-known estimation method. This is just the ammunition I need to make the board see things my way."
>
> **McDonough:** "I don't know, Jeff. I just don't think I can go along with that."
>
> **Mahoney:** "Be a team player, Megan. I've got a meeting now. Got to run."

That night McDonough called to discuss the matter with her best friend, you. What would you advise her?

■ **Case 6–49**
Comparing Multiple Cost Estimation Methods; Ethics (Appendix)
(LO 1, 2, 3, 5, 8)

1. High-low method, variable administrative cost per patient: $10
2. Total monthly administrative cost = $2,671 + $7.81X, where X denotes number of patients per month

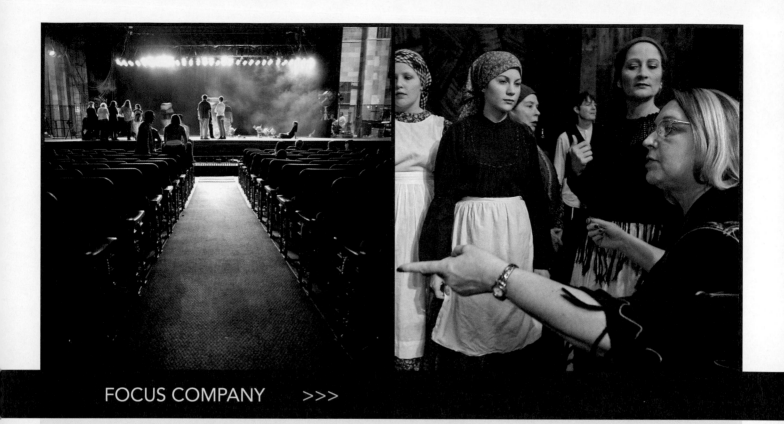

THIS CHAPTER'S FOCUS is on the St. Petersburg Repertory Theater Company in St. Petersburg, Russia.

ST. PETERSBURG REP

Known as St. Petersburg Rep, this not-for-profit enterprise was formed to bring classic Russian drama to the St. Petersburg region. The theater operates in a historic theater building owned by the city, for which St. Petersburg Rep pays the city a fixed monthly rental charge and a portion of the price of each ticket sold. The theater must cover its operating expenses with ticket revenue in order to break even. Using St. Petersburg Rep as an illustration, we will explore a technique called cost-volume-profit (or CVP) analysis, which the theater's managing director and business manager use to better understand the relationships between the theater's costs, ticket sales volume, and revenue.

7 Cost-Volume-Profit Analysis

In contrast to the nonprofit, entertainment-service setting of St. Petersburg Rep, we explore the use of cost-volume-profit analysis by AccuTime Company. The management of this manufacturer of digital clocks located outside of Moscow uses CVP analysis to better understand the relationships between the company's costs, sales volume, and profit. The company's management also analyzes the firm's cost structure, which refers to the relative proportion of fixed and variable costs.

1 Compute a break-even point using the contribution-margin approach and the equation approach.

2 Compute the contribution-margin ratio and use it to find the break-even point in sales dollars.

3 Prepare a cost-volume-profit (CVP) graph and explain how it is used.

4 Apply CVP analysis to determine the effect on profit of changes in fixed expenses, variable expenses, sales prices, and sales volume.

5 Compute the break-even point and prepare a profit-volume graph for a multiproduct enterprise.

6 List and discuss the key assumptions of CVP analysis.

7 Prepare and interpret a contribution income statement.

8 Explain the role of cost structure and operating leverage in CVP relationships.

9 Understand the implications of activity-based costing for CVP analysis.

10 Be aware of the effects of advanced manufacturing technology on CVP relationships.

11 Understand the effect of income taxes on CVP analysis (appendix).

What effect on profit can Aeroflot expect if it adds a flight on the Moscow to New York route? How will NBC's profit change if the ratings increase for its evening news program? How many patient days of care must Tokyo Metropolitan Hiroo Hospital provide to break even for the year? What happens to this break-even patient load if the hospital leases a new computerized system for patient records?

Each of these questions concerns the effects on costs and revenues when the organization's activity changes. The analytical technique used by managerial accountants to address these questions is called **cost-volume-profit analysis.** Often called **CVP analysis** for short, this technique summarizes the effects of changes in an organization's *volume* of activity on its *costs,* revenue, and *profit.* Cost-volume-profit analysis can be extended to cover the effects on profit of changes in selling prices, service fees, costs, income-tax rates, and the organization's mix of products or services. What will happen to profit, for example, if Manchester United raises ticket prices for stadium seats? In short, CVP analysis provides management with a comprehensive overview of the effects on revenue and costs of all kinds of short-run financial changes.

Although the word *profit* appears in the term, cost-volume-profit analysis is not confined to profit-seeking enterprises. Managers in nonprofit organizations also routinely use CVP analysis to examine the effects of activity and other short-run changes on revenue and costs. For example, as the State of Florida gains approximately 1,000 people a day in population, the state's political leaders must analyze the effects of this change on sales-tax revenues and the cost of providing services, such as education, transportation, and police protection. Managers at such diverse nonprofit institutions as Massachusetts General Hospital, Tsinghua University, and Doctors Without Borders all could use CVP analysis as a routine operational tool.

Illustration of Cost-Volume-Profit Analysis

To illustrate the various analytical techniques used in cost-volume-profit analysis, we will focus on a performing arts organization. St. Petersburg Rep was recently formed as a not-for-profit enterprise to bring classic Russian drama to St. Petersburg. The organization has a part-time, unpaid board of trustees comprising local professional people who are avid theater fans. The board has hired the following full-time employees.

ST. PETERSBURG REP

> *Managing director:* Responsibilities include overall management of the organization; direction of six plays per year.
>
> *Artistic director:* Responsibilities include hiring of actors and production crews for each play; direction of six plays per year.
>
> *Business manager and producer:* Responsibilities include managing the organization's business functions and ticket sales; direction of the production crews, who handle staging, lighting, costuming, and makeup.

The board of trustees has negotiated an agreement with the city of St. Petersburg to hold performances in a historic theater owned by the city. The theater has not been used for 30 years, but the city has agreed to refurbish it and to provide lighting and sound equipment. In return, the city will receive a rental fee of $10,000 per month plus $8 for each theater ticket sold.

> "Accounting is changing. You're no longer sitting behind a desk just working on a computer, just crunching the numbers. You're actually getting to be a part of the day-to-day functions of the business." (7a)
>
> **Abbott Laboratories**

Projected Expenses and Revenue

The theater's business manager and producer, Dmitri Katkalo, has made the following projections for the first few years of operation.

Fixed expenses per month:	
Theater rental	$10,000
Employees' salaries and fringe benefits	8,000
Actors' wages	15,000
(to be supplemented with local volunteer talent)	
Production crew's wages	5,600
(to be supplemented with local volunteers)	
Playwrights' royalties for use of plays	5,000
Insurance	1,000
Utilities—fixed portion	1,400
Advertising and promotion	800
Administrative expenses	1,200
Total fixed expenses per month	$48,000
Variable expenses per ticket sold:	
City's charge per ticket for use of theater	$ 8
Other miscellaneous expenses (for example, printing of playbills and tickets, variable portion of utilities)	2
Total variable cost per ticket sold	$10
Revenue:	
Price per ticket	$16

Importance of Cost Behavior   Notice that the theater's expenses have been categorized according to their cost behavior: fixed or variable. Analyzing an organization's cost behavior, the topic of Chapter 6, is a necessary first step in any cost-volume-profit analysis. As we proceed through this chapter, the data pertaining to St. Petersburg Rep will be an important part of our cost-volume-profit analysis.

The Break-Even Point

As the first step in the CVP analysis for St. Petersburg Rep, we will find the **break-even point.** The break-even point is the volume of activity where the organization's revenues and expenses are equal. At this amount of sales, the organization has no profit or loss; it *breaks even.*

> **Learning Objective 1**
>
> Compute a break-even point using the contribution-margin approach and the equation approach.

Suppose St. Petersburg Rep sells 8,000 tickets during a play's one-month run. The following income statement shows that the profit for the month will be zero; thus, the theater will break even.

Sales revenue (8,000 × $16)	$128,000
Less variable expenses (8,000 × $10)	80,000
Total contribution margin	$ 48,000
Less fixed expenses	48,000
Profit	$ 0

> "[Companies are asking] how do we reduce our break-even point so as to ensure that we are prepared in the event we see a recurrence of the 2007–2009 downturn? One of the most effective ways of doing that is by sharing technologies." (7b)
>
> **Spyker Cars N.V.**

Notice that this income statement highlights the distinction between variable and fixed expenses. The statement also shows the **total contribution margin,** which is defined as total sales revenue minus total variable expenses. This is the amount of revenue that is available to *contribute* to covering fixed expenses after all variable expenses have been covered. The contribution income statement will be covered in more depth later in the chapter. At this juncture, it provides a useful way to think about the meaning of breaking even.

How could we compute St. Petersburg Rep's break-even point if we did not already know it is 8,000 tickets per month? This is the question to which we turn our attention next.

Contribution-Margin Approach

St. Petersburg Rep will break even when the organization's revenue from ticket sales is equal to its expenses. How many tickets must be sold during one month (one play's run) for the organization to break even?

Each ticket sells for $16, but $10 of this is used to cover the variable expense per ticket. This leaves $6 per ticket to *contribute* to covering the fixed expenses of $48,000. When enough tickets have been sold in one month so that these $6 contributions per ticket add up to $48,000, the organization will break even for the month. Thus, we may compute the break-even volume of tickets as follows:

$$\frac{\text{Fixed expenses}}{\substack{\text{Contribution of each ticket toward} \\ \text{covering fixed expenses}}} = \frac{\$48,000}{\$6} = 8,000$$

St. Petersburg Rep must sell 8,000 tickets during a play's one-month run to break even for the month.

Whether running a small business or a worldwide enterprise, understanding cost-volume-profit relationships is crucial in managing any organization.

The $6 amount that remains of each ticket's price, after the variable expenses are covered, is called the **unit contribution margin.** The general formula for computing the break-even sales volume in units is given below.

$$\frac{\text{Fixed expenses}}{\text{Unit contribution margin}} = \text{Break-even point (in units)} \qquad (1)$$

Contribution-Margin Ratio Sometimes management prefers that the break-even point be expressed in sales *dollars* rather than *units*. St. Petersburg Rep's break-even point in sales dollars is computed as follows.

Break-even point in units (tickets)	8,000
Sales price per unit	× $16
Break-even point in sales dollars	$128,000

The following computation provides an alternative way to determine the break-even point in sales dollars.

$$\frac{\text{Fixed expenses}}{\dfrac{\text{Unit contribution margin}}{\text{Unit sales price}}} = \frac{\$48,000}{\dfrac{\$6}{\$16}} = \frac{\$48,000}{.375} = \$128,000$$

The unit contribution margin divided by the unit sales price is called the **contribution-margin ratio.** This ratio also can be expressed as a percentage, in which case it is called the *contribution-margin percentage*. St. Petersburg Rep's contribution-margin ratio is .375 (in percentage form, 37.5%). Thus, the organization's break-even point in sales dollars may be found by dividing its fixed expenses by its contribution-margin ratio. The logic behind this approach is that 37.5 percent of each sales dollar is available to make a contribution toward covering fixed expenses. The general formula is given below.

$$\frac{\text{Fixed expenses}}{\text{Contribution-margin ratio}} = \text{Break-even point in sales dollars} \qquad (2)$$

Equation Approach

An alternative approach to finding the break-even point is based on the profit equation. Income (or profit) is equal to sales revenue minus expenses. If expenses are separated into variable and fixed expenses, the essence of the income (profit) statement is captured by the following equation.

Sales revenue − Variable expenses − Fixed expenses = Profit

This equation can be restated as follows:

$$\left[\binom{\text{Unit}}{\text{sales}}_{\text{price}} \times \binom{\text{Sales}}{\text{volume}}_{\text{in units}}\right] - \left[\binom{\text{Unit}}{\text{variable}}_{\text{expense}} \times \binom{\text{Sales}}{\text{volume}}_{\text{in units}}\right] - \binom{\text{Fixed}}{\text{expenses}} = \text{Profit} \qquad (3)$$

To find St. Petersburg Rep's break-even volume of ticket sales per month, we define profit in equation (3) to be zero.

$$(\$16 \times X) - (\$10 \times X) - \$48,000 = 0$$

$$\left[\binom{\text{Unit}}{\text{sales}}_{\text{price}} \times \binom{\text{Sales}}{\text{volume}}_{\text{in units}}\right] - \left[\binom{\text{Unit}}{\text{variable}}_{\text{expense}} \times \binom{\text{Sales}}{\text{volume}}_{\text{in units}}\right] - \binom{\text{Fixed}}{\text{expenses}} = \frac{\text{Break-even}}{\text{profit (zero)}} \qquad (4)$$

where

X denotes the number of sales units (tickets) required to break even.

Equation (4) can be solved for X as shown below.

$$\$16X - \$10X - \$48{,}000 = 0$$
$$\$6X = \$48{,}000$$
$$X = \frac{\$48{,}000}{\$6} = 8{,}000$$

Using the equation approach, we have arrived at the same general formula for computing the break-even sales volume (formula (1)).

The contribution-margin and equation approaches are two equivalent techniques for finding the break-even point. Both methods reach the same conclusion, and so personal preference dictates which approach should be used.

Graphing Cost-Volume-Profit Relationships

While the break-even point conveys useful information to management, it does not show how profit changes as activity changes. To capture the relationship between profit and volume of activity, a **cost-volume-profit (CVP) graph** is commonly used. The following steps are used to prepare a CVP graph for St. Petersburg Rep. The graph is displayed in Exhibit 7–1. Notice that the graph shows the *relevant range,* which is the range of activity within which management expects the theater to operate.

Step 1: Draw the axes of the graph. Label the vertical axis in dollars and the horizontal axis in units of sales (tickets).

Step 2: Draw the fixed-expense line. It is parallel to the horizontal axis, since fixed expenses do not change with activity.

Step 3: Compute *total* expense at any convenient volume. For example, select a volume of 6,000 tickets.

Variable expenses (6,000 × $10 per ticket)	$ 60,000
Fixed expenses	48,000
Total expenses (at 6,000 tickets)	$108,000

Plot this point ($108,000 at 6,000 tickets) on the graph. See point *A* on the graph in Exhibit 7–1.

Step 4: Draw the total-expense line. This line passes through the point plotted in step 3 (point *A*) and the intercept of the fixed-expense line on the vertical axis ($48,000).

Step 5: Compute total sales revenue at any convenient volume. We will choose 6,000 tickets again. Total revenue is $96,000 (6,000 × $16 per ticket). Plot this point ($96,000 at 6,000 tickets) on the graph. See point *B* on the graph in Exhibit 7–1.

Step 6: Draw the total revenue line. This line passes through the point plotted in step 5 (point *B*) and the origin.

Step 7: Label the graph as shown in Exhibit 7–1.

Interpreting the CVP Graph

Several conclusions can be drawn from the CVP graph in Exhibit 7–1.

Break-Even Point   The break-even point is determined by the intersection of the total-revenue line and the total-expense line. St. Petersburg Rep breaks even for the

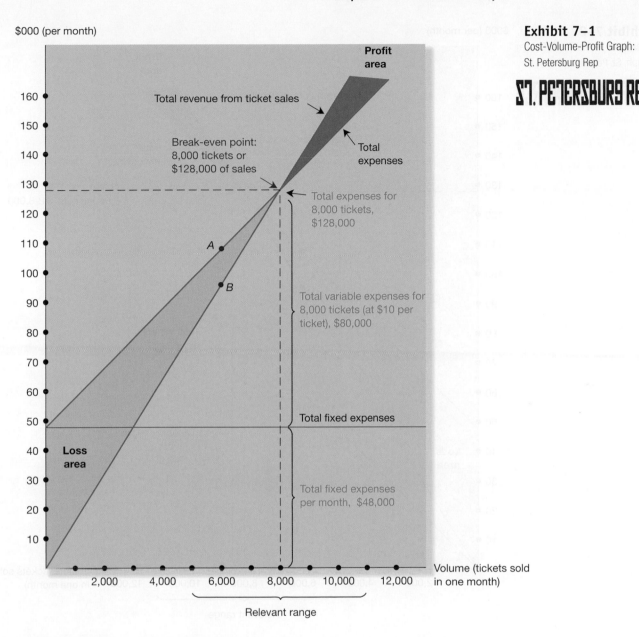

$000 (per month)

Exhibit 7–1
Cost-Volume-Profit Graph:
St. Petersburg Rep

ST. PETERSBURG REP

Profit area

Total revenue from ticket sales

Total expenses

Break-even point:
8,000 tickets or
$128,000 of sales

Total expenses for
8,000 tickets,
$128,000

A

B

Total variable expenses for
8,000 tickets (at $10 per
ticket), $80,000

Total fixed expenses

Loss area

Total fixed expenses
per month, $48,000

Volume (tickets sold
in one month)

2,000   4,000   6,000   8,000   10,000   12,000

Relevant range

month at 8,000 tickets, or $128,000 of ticket sales. This agrees with our calculations in the preceding section.

Profit and Loss Areas   The CVP graph discloses more information than the break-even calculation. From the graph, a manager can see the effects on profit of changes in volume. The vertical distance between the lines on the graph represents the profit or loss at a particular sales volume. If St. Petersburg Rep sells fewer than 8,000 tickets in a month, the organization will suffer a loss. The magnitude of the loss increases as ticket sales decline. The theater organization will have a profit if sales exceed 8,000 tickets in a month.

Implications of the Break-Even Point   The position of the break-even point within an organization's relevant range of activity provides important information to management. The St. Petersburg Rep building seats 450 people. The agreement with the city of St. Petersburg calls for 20 performances during each play's one-month run. Thus, the maximum number of tickets that can be sold each month is 9,000 (450 seats × 20 performances). The organization's break-even point is quite close to the maximum possible

Exhibit 7–2
Alternative Format for CVP
Graph: St. Petersburg Rep

ST. PETERSBURG REP

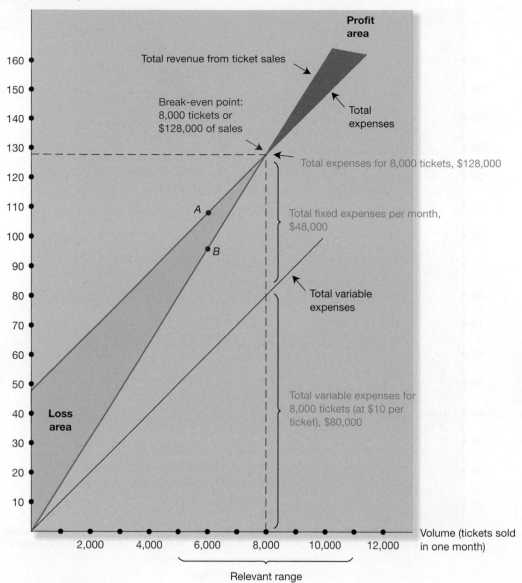

$000 (per month)

Profit area

Total revenue from ticket sales

Break-even point:
8,000 tickets or
$128,000 of sales

Total expenses

Total expenses for 8,000 tickets, $128,000

A

B

Total fixed expenses per month, $48,000

Total variable expenses

Loss area

Total variable expenses for 8,000 tickets (at $10 per ticket), $80,000

Volume (tickets sold in one month)

2,000   4,000   6,000   8,000   10,000   12,000

Relevant range

sales volume. This could be cause for concern in a nonprofit organization operating on limited resources.

What could management do to improve this situation? One possibility is to renegotiate with the city to schedule additional performances. However, this might not be feasible, because the actors need some rest each week. Also, additional performances would likely entail additional costs, such as increased theater-rental expenses and increased compensation for the actors and production crew. Other possible solutions are to raise ticket prices or reduce costs. These kinds of issues will be explored later in the chapter.

The CVP graph will not resolve this potential problem for the management of St. Petersburg Rep. However, the graph will *direct management's attention* to the situation.

Alternative Format for the CVP Graph

An alternative format for the CVP graph, preferred by some managers, is displayed in Exhibit 7–2. The key difference is that fixed expenses are graphed above variable expenses, instead of the reverse as they were in Exhibit 7–1.

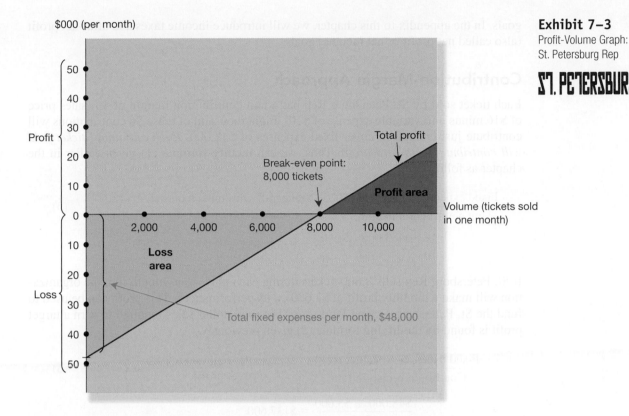

Exhibit 7–3
Profit-Volume Graph:
St. Petersburg Rep

Profit-Volume Graph

Yet another approach to graphing cost-volume-profit relationships is displayed in Exhibit 7–3. This format is called a **profit-volume graph,** since it highlights the amount of profit or loss. Notice that the graph intercepts the vertical axis at the amount equal to fixed expenses at the zero activity level. The graph crosses the horizontal axis at the break-even point. The vertical distance between the horizontal axis and the profit line, at a particular level of sales volume, is the profit or loss at that volume.

Target Profit

The board of trustees for St. Petersburg Rep would like to run free workshops and classes for young actors and aspiring playwrights. This program would cost $3,600 per month in fixed expenses, including teachers' salaries and rental of space at a local university. No variable expenses would be incurred. If St. Petersburg Rep could make a profit of $3,600 per month on its performances, the St. Petersburg Drama Workshop could be opened. The board has asked Dmitri Katkalo, the organization's business manager and producer, to determine how many theater tickets must be sold during each play's one-month run to make a profit of $3,600.

The desired profit level of $3,600 is called a **target profit** (or **income).** The problem of computing the volume of sales required to earn a particular target profit is very similar to the problem of finding the break-even point. After all, the break-even point is the number of units of sales required to earn a target profit of zero.

Because St. Petersburg Rep is a not-for-profit organization, it make no distinction between profits before taxes and profits after taxes. However, the profits of for-profit companies are subject to income taxes. In this chapter, we will address pre-tax profit

Learning Objective 4

Apply CVP analysis to determine the effect on profit of changes in fixed expenses, variable expenses, sales prices, and sales volume.

goals. In the appendix to this chapter, we will introduce income taxes and after-tax profit (also called net profit or net income) goals.

Contribution-Margin Approach

Each ticket sold by St. Petersburg Rep has a unit contribution margin of $6 (sales price of $16 minus unit variable expense of $10). Eight thousand of these $6 contributions will contribute just enough to cover fixed expenses of $48,000. *Each additional ticket sold will contribute $6 toward profit.* Thus, we can modify formula (1) given earlier in the chapter as follows:

$$\frac{\text{Fixed expenses} + \text{Target Profit}}{\text{Unit contribution margin}} = \frac{\text{Number of sales units required}}{\text{to earn target profit}} \tag{5}$$

$$\frac{\$48,000 + \$3,600}{\$6} = 8,600 \text{ tickets}$$

If St. Petersburg Rep sells 8,600 tickets during each play's one-month run, the organization will make a monthly profit of $3,600 on its performances. This profit can be used to fund the St. Petersburg Drama Workshop. The total dollar sales required to earn a target profit is found by modifying formula (2) given previously.

$$\frac{\text{Fixed expenses} + \text{Target profit}}{\text{Contribution-margin ratio}} = \frac{\text{Dollar sales required to earn}}{\text{target profit}} \tag{6}$$

$$\frac{\$48,000 + \$3,600}{.375} = \$137,600$$

$$\text{where the contribution margin ratio} = \frac{\$6}{\$16} = .375$$

This dollar sales figure also can be found by multiplying the required sales of 8,600 tickets by the ticket price of $16 (8,600 × $16 = $137,600).

Equation Approach

The equation approach also can be used to find the units of sales required to earn a target profit. (Again, note that in a for-profit company this would be target pre-tax profit.) We can modify the profit equation given previously as follows:

$$\left[\left(\begin{array}{c}\text{Unit} \\ \text{sales} \\ \text{price}\end{array}\right) \times \left(\begin{array}{c}\text{Sales volume} \\ \text{required to} \\ \text{earn target} \\ \text{profit}\end{array}\right)\right] - \left[\left(\begin{array}{c}\text{Unit} \\ \text{variable} \\ \text{expense}\end{array}\right) \times \left(\begin{array}{c}\text{Sales volume} \\ \text{required to} \\ \text{earn target} \\ \text{profit}\end{array}\right)\right]$$

$$- \left(\begin{array}{c}\text{Fixed} \\ \text{expenses}\end{array}\right) = \text{Target profit}$$

Filling in the values for St. Petersburg Rep, we have the following equation.

$$(\$16 \times X) - (\$10 \times X) - \$48,000 = \$3,600 \tag{7}$$

where X denotes the sales volume required to earn the target profit.

Equation (7) can be solved for X as follows:

$$\$16X - \$10X - \$48,000 = \$3,600$$

$$\$6X = \$51,600$$

$$X = \frac{\$51,600}{\$6} = 8,600$$

Graphical Approach

The profit-volume graph in Exhibit 7–3 also can be used to find the sales volume required to earn a target profit. First, locate St. Petersburg Rep's target profit of $3,600 on the vertical axis. Then move horizontally until the profit line is reached. Finally, move down from the profit line to the horizontal axis to determine the required sales volume.

Applying CVP Analysis

The cost-volume-profit relationships that underlie break-even calculations and CVP graphs have wide-ranging applications in management. We will look at several common applications illustrated by St. Petersburg Rep.

Safety Margin

The **safety margin** of an enterprise is the difference between the budgeted sales revenue and the break-even sales revenue. Suppose St. Petersburg Rep's business manager expects every performance of each play to be sold out. Then budgeted monthly sales revenue is $144,000 (450 seats × 20 performances of each play × $16 per ticket). Since break-even sales revenue is $128,000, the organization's safety margin is $16,000 ($144,000 − $128,000). The safety margin gives management a feel for how close projected operations are to the organization's break-even point. We will further discuss the safety margin concept later in the chapter.

Changes in Fixed Expenses

What would happen to St. Petersburg Rep's break-even point if fixed expenses change? Suppose the business manager is concerned that the estimate for fixed utilities expenses, $1,400 per month, is too low. What would happen to the break-even point if fixed utilities expenses prove to be $2,600 instead? The break-even calculations for both the original and the new estimate of fixed utilities expenses are as follows:

	Original Estimate	New Estimate
Fixed utilities expenses	$ 1,400	$ 2,600
Total fixed expenses	$48,000	$49,200
Break-even calculation	$48,000	$49,200
(Fixed expenses ÷ Unit contribution margin)	$6	$6
Break-even point (units)	8,000 tickets	8,200 tickets
Break-even point (dollars)	$128,000	$131,200

The estimate of fixed expenses has increased by 2.5 percent, since $1,200 is 2.5 percent of $48,000. Notice that the break-even point also increased by 2.5 percent (200 tickets is 2.5 percent of 8,000 tickets). This relationship will always exist.

$$\frac{\text{Fixed expenses}}{\text{Unit contribution margin}} = \text{Break-even point (in units)}$$

$$\frac{\text{Fixed expenses} \times 1.025}{\text{Unit contribution margin}} = (\text{Break-even point in units}) \times 1.025$$

Learning Objective 4

Apply CVP analysis to determine the effect on profit of changes in fixed expenses, variable expenses, sales prices, and sales volume.

"Basically the role of the [accountant] on the team [is] analyzing the financial impact of the business decision and providing advice. Does this make sense financially or not?" (7d)

Abbott Laboratories

Donations to Offset Fixed Expenses   Nonprofit organizations often receive cash donations from people or organizations desiring to support a worthy cause. A donation is equivalent to a reduction in fixed expenses, and it reduces the organization's break-even point. In our original set of data, St. Petersburg Rep's monthly fixed expenses total $48,000. Suppose that various people pledge donations amounting to $6,000 per month. The new break-even point is computed as follows:

$$\frac{\text{Fixed expenses} - \text{Donations}}{\text{Unit contribution margin}} = \text{Break-even point (in units)}$$

$$\frac{\$48,000 - \$6,000}{\$6} = 7,000 \text{ tickets}$$

Changes in the Unit Contribution Margin

What would happen to St. Petersburg Rep's break-even point if miscellaneous variable expenses were $3 per ticket instead of $2? Alternatively, what would be the effect of raising the ticket price to $18?

Change in Unit Variable Expenses   If the theater organization's miscellaneous variable expenses increase from $2 to $3 per ticket, the unit contribution margin will fall from $6 to $5. The original and new break-even points are computed as follows:

	Original Estimate	New Estimate
Miscellaneous variable expenses	$2 per ticket	$3 per ticket
Unit contribution margin	$6	$5
Break-even calculation	$48,000	$48,000
(Fixed expenses ÷ Unit contribution margin)	$6	$5
Break-even point (units)	8,000 tickets	9,600 tickets
Break-even point (dollars)	$128,000	$153,600

If this change in unit variable expenses actually occurs, it will no longer be possible for the organization to break even. Only 9,000 tickets are available for each play's one-month run (450 seats × 20 performances), but 9,600 tickets would have to be sold to break even. Once again, CVP analysis will not solve this problem for management, but it will direct management's attention to potentially serious difficulties.

Change in Sales Price   Changing the unit sales price will also alter the unit contribution margin. Suppose the ticket price is raised from $16 to $18. This change will raise the unit contribution margin from $6 to $8. The new break-even point will be 6,000 tickets ($48,000 ÷ $8).

A $2 increase in the ticket price will lower the break-even point from 8,000 tickets to 6,000 tickets. Is this change desirable? A lower break-even point decreases the risk of operating with a loss if sales are sluggish. However, the organization may be more likely to at least break even with a $16 ticket price than with an $18 ticket price. The reason is that the lower ticket price encourages more people to attend the theater's performances. It could be that break-even sales of 8,000 tickets at $16 are more likely than break-even sales of 6,000 tickets at $18. Ultimately, the desirability of the ticket-price increase depends on management's assessment of the likely reaction by theater patrons.

Management's decision about the ticket price increase also will reflect the fundamental goals of St. Petersburg Rep. This nonprofit drama organization was formed to bring classic Russian drama to the people of St. Petersburg. The lower the ticket price, the more accessible the theater's productions will be to people of all income levels.

The point of this discussion is that CVP analysis provides valuable information, but it is only one of several elements that influence management's decisions.

Predicting Profit Given Expected Volume

So far, we have focused on finding the required sales volume to break even or achieve a particular target profit. Thus, we have asked the following question.

Given: $\begin{cases} \text{Fixed expenses} \\ \text{Unit contribution margin} \\ \text{Target profit} \end{cases}$, Find: {required sales volume}

We also can use CVP analysis to turn this question around and make the following query.

Given: $\begin{cases} \text{Fixed expenses} \\ \text{Unit contribution margin} \\ \text{Expected sales volume} \end{cases}$, Find: {expected profit}

Suppose the management of St. Petersburg Rep expects fixed monthly expenses of $48,000 and unit variable expenses of $10 per ticket. The organization's board of trustees is considering two different ticket prices, and the business manager has forecast monthly demand at each price.

Ticket Price	Forecast Monthly Demand
$16	9,000
$20	6,000

Expected profit may be calculated at each price as shown in the following table. In these profit calculations, the **total contribution margin** is the difference between *total* sales revenue and *total* variable expenses. This use of the term *contribution margin* is a "total" concept rather than the "per unit" concept used earlier in the chapter. The *total contribution margin* is the *total* amount left to contribute to covering fixed expenses after *total* variable expenses have been covered.

	Ticket Price $16	Ticket Price $20
Sales revenue:		
9,000 × $16	$144,000	
6,000 × $20		$120,000
Less variable expenses:		
9,000 × $10	90,000	
6,000 × $10		60,000
Total contribution margin	$ 54,000	$ 60,000
Less fixed expenses	48,000	48,000
Profit	$ 6,000	$ 12,000

The difference in expected profit at the two ticket prices is due to two factors:

1. A different *unit* contribution margin, defined previously as *unit* sales price minus *unit* variable expenses
2. A different sales volume

Incremental Approach Rather than presenting the entire income statement under each ticket price alternative, we can use a simpler incremental approach. This analysis focuses only on the difference in the total contribution margin under the two prices. Thus, the combined effect of the change in unit contribution margin and the change in sales volume is as follows:

Expected *total* contribution margin at $20 ticket price:	
6,000 × ($20 − $10)	$60,000
Expected *total* contribution margin at $16 ticket price:	
9,000 × ($16 − $10)	54,000
Difference in *total* contribution margin	$ 6,000

The $6,000 difference in expected profit, at the two ticket prices, is due to a $6,000 difference in the total contribution margin. The board of trustees will consider these projected profits as it decides which ticket price is best. Even though St. Petersburg Rep is a nonprofit organization, it may still have legitimate reasons for attempting to make a profit on its theater performances. For example, the board might use these profits to fund a free drama workshop, provide scholarships for local young people to study drama at university, or produce a free outdoor play for St. Petersburg's residents.

Interdependent Changes in Key Variables

Sometimes a change in one key variable will cause a change in another key variable. Suppose the board of trustees is choosing between ticket prices of $16 and $20, and the business manager has projected demand as shown in the preceding section. A famous retired actress who lives in St. Petersburg has offered to donate $10,000 per month to St. Petersburg Rep if the board will set the ticket price at $16. The actress is interested in making the theater's performances affordable for as many people as possible. The facts are now as follows:

Ticket Price	Unit Contribution Margin	Forecast Monthly Demand	Net Fixed Expenses (after subtracting donation)
$16	$ 6	9,000	$38,000 ($48,000 − $10,000)
20	10	6,000	48,000

The organization's expected profit at each price is computed as follows:

	Ticket Price	
	$16	**$20**
Sales revenue:		
9,000 × $16	$144,000	
6,000 × $20		$120,000
Less variable expenses:		
9,000 × $10	90,000	
6,000 × $10		60,000
Total contribution margin	$ 54,000	$ 60,000
Less net fixed expenses (net of donation)	38,000	48,000
Profit	$ 16,000	$ 12,000

Now the difference in expected profit at the two ticket prices is due to three factors:

1. A different *unit* contribution margin.
2. A different sales volume.
3. A difference in the *net* fixed expenses, after deducting the donation.

Incremental Approach The combined effect of these factors is shown in the following analysis, which focuses on the effects of the price alternatives on the total contribution margin and the net fixed expenses.

Expected *total* contribution margin at $20 ticket price:	
6,000 × ($20 − $10)	$60,000
Expected *total* contribution margin at $16 ticket price:	
9,000 × ($16 − $10)	54,000
Difference in *total* contribution margin	$ 6,000
(higher with $20 ticket price)	
Net fixed expenses at $20 ticket price	$48,000
Net fixed expenses at $16 ticket price	38,000
Difference in net fixed expenses (higher with $20 ticket price)	$10,000

The expected total contribution margin is $6,000 higher with the $20 ticket price, but net fixed expenses are $10,000 higher. Thus, St. Petersburg Rep will make $4,000 more in profit at the $16 price ($10,000 − $6,000).

CVP Information in Published Annual Reports

Cost-volume-profit relationships are so important to understanding an organization's operations that some companies disclose CVP information in their published annual reports. The following illustration is from the airline industry.

Management **A**ccounting **P**ractice

Air France-KLM, Emirates Airways, and SpiceJet

AIRLINES KEEP A CLOSE EYE ON BREAK-EVEN LOAD FACTORS

Some airlines disclose their systemwide break-even load factors in their annual reports. The Emirates Group, for example, listed its break-even load factor as 64.4 percent in a recent annual report. Utilization of that load capacity is critical to the financial success of an airline. When Indian budget carrier SpiceJet Ltd. announced that they would break even in 2009, they said "It (the break-even) will be backed by our business plan, which primarily includes higher utilization of our capacity."[1]

Load factors can be improved either by attracting more business or by reducing the capacity available and its related costs. Air France-KLM responded to the economic recession with a " . . . sharp reduction in cargo capacity and a rationalization of existing cargo assets [that] should bring the cargo division back to break-even during the 2011–2012 financial year . . . and the airline will reduce its passenger capacity by a further 2% for the coming winter season." Simultaneously, the airline attacked the problem through cost reduction: "The airline said it will pursue its cost-cutting efforts in an effort to return to break even at the operating level . . . 'Lack of visibility over the timing and strength of the economic recovery means we must pursue our efforts in terms of cost reduction.'" These efforts included "stabilizing its activity levels, and plans to reduce headcount through the voluntary departure of 1,700 employees..."[2]

---

[1]Anirban Chowdhury, "Spicejet, Kingfisher Expect to Break Even This Financial Year," *The Wall Street Journal India,* July 1, 2009. Also see "British Air's Net Soars Amid Strong Demand," *The Wall Street Journal,* February 4, 2008, p. A6.

[2]David Pearson, "Air France-KLM Swings to Loss on Charge, Lower Traffic," *The Wall Street Journal,* November 18, 2009.

CVP Analysis with Multiple Products

Major airlines keep a close watch on the break-even passenger load factor.

Our CVP illustration for St. Petersburg Rep has assumed that the organization has only one product, a theater seat at a dramatic performance. Most firms have a *sales mix* consisting of more than one product, and this adds some complexity to their CVP analyses.

As we have seen, St. Petersburg Rep's monthly fixed expenses total $48,000, and the unit variable expense per ticket is $10. Now suppose that the city of St. Petersburg has agreed to refurbish 10 theater boxes in the historic theater building. Each box has five seats, which are more comfortable and afford a better view of the stage than the theater's general seating. The board of trustees has decided to charge $16 per ticket for general seating and $20 per ticket for box seats. These facts are summarized as follows:

Seat Type	Ticket Price	Unit Variable Expense	Unit Contribution Margin	Seats in Theater	Seats Available per Month (20 performances)
Regular	$16	$10	$ 6	450	9,000
Box	20	10	10	50	1,000

Notice that 90 percent of the available seats are regular seats, and 10 percent are box seats. The business manager estimates that tickets for each type of seat will be sold in the same proportion as the number of seats available. If, for example, 5,000 tickets are sold during a month, sales will be as follows:

Regular seats:	90% × 5,000	4,500
Box seats:	10% × 5,000	500
Total		5,000

For any organization selling multiple products, the relative proportion of each type of product *sold* is called the **sales mix.** The business manager's estimate of St. Petersburg Rep's *sales mix* is 90 percent regular seats and 10 percent box seats.

The sales mix is an important assumption in multiproduct CVP analysis. The sales mix is used to compute a **weighted-average unit contribution margin.** This is the *average* of the several products' *unit contribution margins, weighted* by the relative sales proportion of each product. St. Petersburg Rep's weighted-average unit contribution margin is computed below.

$$\text{Weighted-average unit contribution margin} = (\$6 \times 90\%) + (\$10 \times 10\%) = \$6.40$$

The organization's break-even point in units is computed using the following formula.

$$\text{Break-even point} = \frac{\text{Fixed expenses}}{\text{Weighted-average unit contribution margin}} \qquad (8)$$

$$= \frac{\$48,000}{\$6.40} = 7,500 \text{ tickets}$$

The break-even point of 7,500 tickets must be interpreted in light of the sales mix. St. Petersburg Rep will break even for the month if it sells 7,500 tickets as follows:

Break-even			
sales in	Regular seats: 7,500 × 90%	6,750 tickets
units	Box seats: 7,500 × 10%	750 tickets
	Total	7,500 tickets

The following income calculation verifies the break-even point.

Sales revenue:		
Regular seats: 6,750 × $16	$108,000
Box seats: 750 × $20	15,000
Total revenue: 7,500 seats in total	$123,000
Less variable expenses: 7,500 × $10	75,000
Total contribution margin	$ 48,000
Less fixed expenses	48,000
Profit	$ 0

The break-even point of 7,500 tickets per month is *valid only for the sales mix assumed* in computing the weighted-average unit contribution margin. If 7,500 tickets are sold in any other mix of regular and box seats, the organization might not break even.

Notice that break-even formula (8) is a modification of formula (1) given earlier in the chapter. The only difference is that formula (8) uses the *weighted-average* unit contribution margin.

St. Petersburg Rep's business manager has constructed the profit-volume graph in Exhibit 7–4. The PV graph shows the organization's profit at any level of total monthly sales, assuming the sales mix of 90 percent regular seats and 10 percent box seats. For example, if 9,000 tickets are sold in total, at the assumed sales mix, the PV graph indicates that profit will be $9,600.

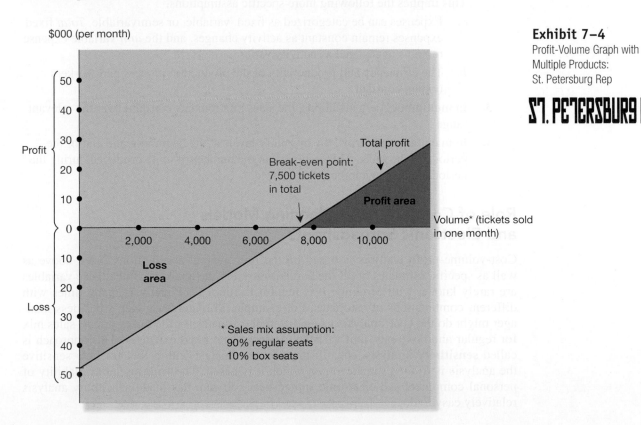

Exhibit 7–4
Profit-Volume Graph with
Multiple Products:
St. Petersburg Rep

ST. PETERSBURG REP

With multiproduct CVP analysis, a managerial accountant can investigate the impact on profit of changes in sales volume, prices, variable costs, fixed costs, or the sales mix itself. For example, what would be the effect on St. Petersburg Rep's break-even point if the sales mix were 95 percent regular seats and 5 percent box seats? With this sales mix, the weighted-average unit contribution margin is computed as follows:

$$\text{Weighted-average unit contribution margin} = (\$6 \times 95\%) + (\$10 \times 5\%) = \$6.20$$

The break-even point increases from 7,500 tickets to approximately 7,742 tickets as a result of the lower proportion of expensive seats in the sales mix.

$$\text{Break-even point} = \frac{\text{Fixed expenses}}{\text{Weighted-average unit contribution margin}}$$

$$= \frac{\$48,000}{\$6.20} = 7,742 \text{ tickets*}$$

*Rounded

Assumptions Underlying CVP Analysis

For any cost-volume-profit analysis to be valid, the following important assumptions must be reasonably satisfied *within the relevant range.*

1. The behavior of total revenue is linear (straight-line). This implies that the price of the product or service will not change as sales volume varies within the relevant range.
2. The behavior of total expenses is linear (straight-line) over the relevant range. This implies the following more specific assumptions.
    a. Expenses can be categorized as fixed, variable, or semivariable. *Total* fixed expenses remain constant as activity changes, and the *unit* variable expense remains unchanged as activity varies.
    b. The efficiency and productivity of the production process and workers remain constant.
3. In multiproduct organizations, the sales mix remains constant over the relevant range.
4. In manufacturing firms, the inventory levels at the beginning and end of the period are the same. This implies that the number of units produced during the period equals the number of units sold.

Role of Computerized Planning Models and Electronic Spreadsheets

Cost-volume-profit analysis is based on the four general assumptions listed above as well as specific estimates of all the variables used in the analysis. Since these variables are rarely known with certainty, it is helpful to run a CVP analysis many times with different combinations of estimates. For example, St. Petersburg Rep's business manager might do the CVP analysis using different estimates for the ticket prices, sales mix for regular and box seats, unit variable expenses, and fixed expenses. This approach is called **sensitivity analysis,** since it provides the analyst with a feel for how sensitive the analysis is to the estimates upon which it is based. The widespread availability of personal computers and electronic spreadsheet software has made sensitivity analysis relatively easy to do.

A. Traditional Format

ACCUTIME COMPANY
Income Statement
For the Year Ended December 31, 20x1

Sales		$500,000
Less: Cost of goods sold		380,000
Gross margin		$120,000
Less: Operating expenses:		
Selling expenses	$ 35,000	
Administrative expenses	35,000	70,000
Operating income		$ 50,000

B. Contribution Format

ACCUTIME COMPANY
Income Statement
For the Year Ended December 31, 20x1

Sales		$500,000
Less: Variable expenses:		
Variable manufacturing	$280,000	
Variable selling	15,000	
Variable administrative	5,000	300,000
Contribution margin		$200,000
Less: Fixed expenses:		
Fixed manufacturing	$100,000	
Fixed selling	20,000	
Fixed administrative	30,000	150,000
Operating income		$ 50,000

Exhibit 7–5

Income Statement: Traditional and Contribution Formats

CVP Relationships and the Income Statement

The management functions of planning, control, and decision making all are facilitated by an understanding of cost-volume-profit relationships. These relationships are important enough to operating managers that some businesses prepare income statements in a way that highlights CVP issues. Before we examine this new income-statement format, we will review the more traditional income statement used in the preceding chapters.

Traditional Income Statement

An income statement for AccuTime Company, a manufacturer of digital clocks located outside of Moscow, is shown in Exhibit 7–5 (panel A). During 20x1 the firm manufactured and sold 20,000 clocks at a price of $25 each. This income statement is prepared in the traditional manner. *Cost of goods sold* includes both variable and fixed manufacturing costs, as measured by the firm's product-costing system. The *gross margin* is computed by subtracting cost of goods sold from sales. Selling and administrative expenses are then subtracted; each expense includes both variable and fixed costs. *The traditional income statement does not disclose the breakdown of each expense into its variable and fixed components.*

In discussing operational decisions, companies often focus on profits from operations, excluding nonoperating profits such as interest income as well as interest expense and taxes. This level of profit is referred to as **operating income.** When taxes and interest are excluded, the income statement ends with *operating income* rather than *net income.* (Income taxes are introduced in the appendix at the end of this chapter.)

Contribution Income Statement

Many operating managers find the traditional income-statement format difficult to use, because it does not separate variable and fixed expenses. Instead they prefer the **contribution income statement.** A contribution income statement for AccuTime is shown in Exhibit 7–5 (panel B). *The contribution format highlights the distinction between variable and fixed expenses.* The variable manufacturing cost of each clock is $14, and the total fixed manufacturing cost is $100,000. On the contribution income statement, all variable expenses are subtracted from sales to obtain the *contribution margin.* For AccuTime, $200,000 remains from total sales revenue, after all variable costs have been covered, to contribute to covering fixed costs and making a profit. All fixed costs are then subtracted from the contribution margin to obtain operating income.

Comparison of Traditional and Contribution Income Statements

Operating managers frequently prefer the contribution income statement, because its separation of fixed and variable expenses highlights cost-volume-profit relationships. It is readily apparent from the contribution format statement how income will be affected when sales volume changes by a given percentage. Suppose management projects that sales volume in 20x2 will be 20 percent greater than in 20x1. No changes are anticipated in the sales price, variable cost per unit, or fixed costs. Examination of the contribution income statement shows that if sales volume increases by 20 percent, the following changes will occur.

Income Statement Item	20x1 Amount	Change	20x2 Amount
Sales	$500,000	$100,000	$600,000
		(20% × $500,000)	
Total variable expenses	$300,000	$60,000	$360,000
		(20% × $300,000)	
Contribution margin	$200,000	$40,000	$240,000
		(20% × $200,000)	
Total fixed expenses	$150,000	–0–	$150,000
		(no change in fixed expenses when volume changes)	
Operating income	$ 50,000	$40,000	$ 90,000
		(income changes by the amount of the contribution-margin change)	

Notice that operating income increases by the same amount as the increase in the contribution margin. Moreover, the contribution margin changes in direct proportion to the change in sales volume. These two facts enable us to calculate the increase in operating income using the following shortcut. Recall that the *contribution-margin ratio* is the percentage of contribution margin to sales.

$$\left(\begin{array}{c} \text{Increase in} \\ \text{sales revenue} \end{array} \right) \times \left(\begin{array}{c} \text{Contribution-margin} \\ \text{ratio} \end{array} \right) = \left(\begin{array}{c} \text{Increase in} \\ \text{operating income} \end{array} \right)$$

$$\$100{,}000 \quad \times \quad .40 \quad = \quad \$40\ 000$$

$$\text{where} \quad \left(\begin{array}{c} \text{Contribution-margin} \\ \text{ratio} \end{array} \right) = \frac{\text{Contribution margin}}{\text{Sales revenue}}$$

$$.40 = \frac{\$200{,}000}{\$500{,}000}$$

Exhibit 7–6
Comparison of Cost
Structures

```
Microsoft Excel - Comparison of Cost Structures                                          _ □ X
 File  Edit  View  Insert  Format  Tools  Data  Window  Help     Type a question for help  ▾ _ ᵆ ×
   B10        ▾        fx  =B8-B9
```

	A	B	C	D	E	F	G
1		Company A		Company B		Company C	
2		(AccuTime Company)		(Manual System)		(Automated System)	
3							
4		Amount	%	Amount	%	Amount	%
5							
6	Sales	$ 500,000	100	$ 500,000	100	$ 500,000	100
7	Variable expenses	300,000	60	400,000	80	50,000	10
8	Contribution margin	$ 200,000	40	$ 100,000	20	$ 450,000	90
9	Fixed expenses	150,000	30	50,000	10	400,000	80
10	Operating income	$ 50,000	10	$ 50,000	10	$ 50,000	10

```
I◄ ◄ ▶ ▶I \ Sheet1 ⟨ Sheet2 ⟨ Sheet3 /           ◄                    ▶
Ready
```

The preceding analysis makes use of cost-volume-profit relationships that are disclosed in the contribution income statement. Such an analysis cannot be made with the information presented in the traditional income statement.

Cost Structure and Operating Leverage

The **cost structure** of an organization is the relative proportion of its fixed and variable costs. Cost structures differ widely among industries and among firms within an industry. A company using a computer-integrated manufacturing system has a large investment in plant and equipment, which results in a cost structure dominated by fixed costs. In contrast, a home building contractor's cost structure has a much higher proportion of variable costs. The highly automated manufacturing firm is capital-intensive, whereas the home building contractor is labor-intensive.

> **Learning Objective 8**
>
> Explain the role of cost structure and operating leverage in CVP relationships.

An organization's cost structure has a significant effect on the sensitivity of its profit to changes in volume. A convenient way to portray a firm's cost structure is shown in the Excel spreadsheet in Exhibit 7–6.[3] The data for AccuTime Company (company A) comes from the firm's 20x1 contribution income statement in Exhibit 7–5. For comparison purposes, two other firms' cost structures also are shown. Although these three firms have the same sales revenue ($500,000) and operating income ($50,000), they have very different cost structures. Company B's production process is largely manual, and its cost structure is dominated by variable costs. It has a low contribution-margin ratio of only 20 percent. In contrast, company C employs a highly automated production process, and its cost structure is dominated by fixed costs. The firm's contribution-margin ratio is 90 percent. Company A falls between these two extremes with a contribution-margin ratio of 40 percent.

Suppose sales revenue increases by 10 percent, or $50,000, in each company. The resulting increase in each company's profit is calculated in Exhibit 7–7.

Notice that company B, with its high variable expenses and low contribution-margin ratio, shows a relatively low *percentage* increase in profit. In contrast, the high fixed expenses and large contribution-margin ratio of company C result in a relatively high *percentage* increase in profit. Company A falls in between these two extremes.

To summarize, the greater the proportion of fixed costs in a firm's cost structure, the greater the impact on profit will be from a given percentage change in sales revenue.

---

[3]This form of income statement, in which each item on the statement is expressed as a percentage of sales revenue, is often called a *common-size income statement.*

Exhibit 7–7

Effect on Profit of Increase in Sales Revenue

	$\left(\begin{array}{c}\text{Increase}\\\text{In Sales}\\\text{Revenue}\end{array}\right)$	×	$\left(\begin{array}{c}\text{Contribution}\\\text{Margin}\\\text{Ratio}\end{array}\right)$	=	$\left(\begin{array}{c}\text{Increase}\\\text{In Operating}\\\text{Income}\end{array}\right)$	Percentage Increase in Operating Income
Company A						
(AccuTime)	$50,000	×	40%	=	$20,000	40% ($20,000 ÷ $50,000)
Company B						
(high variable expenses)	$50,000	×	20%	=	$10,000	20% ($10,000 ÷ $50,000)
Company C						
(high fixed expenses)	$50,000	×	90%	=	$45,000	90% ($45,000 ÷ $50,000)

Operating Leverage

The extent to which an organization uses fixed costs in its cost structure is called **operating leverage.** The operating leverage is greatest in firms with a large proportion of fixed costs, low proportion of variable costs, and the resulting high contribution-margin ratio. Exhibit 7–6 shows that company B has low operating leverage, company C has high operating leverage, and company A falls in between. To a physical scientist, *leverage* refers to the ability of a small force to move a heavy weight. To the managerial accountant, *operating leverage* refers to the ability of the firm to generate an increase in operating income when sales revenue increases.

Measuring Operating Leverage   The managerial accountant can measure a firm's operating leverage, *at a particular sales volume,* using the **operating leverage factor:**

$$\text{Operating leverage factor} = \frac{\text{Contribution margin}}{\text{Operating income}}$$

Using the data in Exhibit 7–6, the operating leverage factors of companies A, B, and C are computed as follows:

	$\left(\begin{array}{c}\text{Contribution}\\\text{Margin}\end{array}\right)$	÷	$\left(\begin{array}{c}\text{Operating}\\\text{Income}\end{array}\right)$	=	$\left(\begin{array}{c}\text{Operating}\\\text{Leverage}\\\text{Factor}\end{array}\right)$
Company A (AccuTime)	$200,000	÷	$50,000	=	4
Company B (high variable expenses)	$100,000	÷	$50,000	=	2
Company C (high fixed expenses)	$450,000	÷	$50,000	=	9

The operating leverage factor is a measure, at a particular level of sales, of the *percentage* impact on operating income of a given *percentage* change in sales revenue. Multiplying the *percentage* change in sales revenue by the operating leverage factor yields the *percentage* change in operating income.

	$\left(\begin{array}{c}\text{Percentage}\\\text{Increase in}\\\text{Sales Revenue}\end{array}\right)$	×	$\left(\begin{array}{c}\text{Operating}\\\text{Leverage}\\\text{Factor}\end{array}\right)$	=	$\left(\begin{array}{c}\text{Percentage}\\\text{Change in}\\\text{Operating}\\\text{Income}\end{array}\right)$
Company A (AccuTime)	10%	×	4	=	40%
Company B (high variable expenses)	10%	×	2	=	20%
Company C (high fixed expenses)	10%	×	9	=	90%

The percentage change in operating income shown above for each company may be verified by re-examining Exhibit 7–7.

Break-Even Point and Safety Margin

A firm's operating leverage also affects its break-even point. Since a firm with relatively high operating leverage has proportionally high fixed expenses, the firm's break-even point will be relatively high. This fact is illustrated using the data from Exhibit 7–6.

	$\left(\begin{array}{c}\textbf{Fixed}\\\textbf{Expenses}\end{array}\right)$	÷	$\left(\begin{array}{c}\textbf{Contribution}\\\textbf{Margin Ratio}\end{array}\right)$	=	$\left(\begin{array}{c}\textbf{Break-Even}\\\textbf{Sales Revenue}\end{array}\right)$
Company A (AccuTime)	$150,000	÷	40%	=	$375,000
Company B (high variable expenses)	$ 50,000	÷	20%	=	$250,000
Company C (high fixed expenses)	$400,000	÷	90%	=	$444,444*

*Rounded

The safety margin also is affected by a firm's operating leverage. Suppose the budgeted sales revenue for each of the three companies is $500,000. Then the safety margin, defined as budgeted sales revenue minus break-even sales revenue, is calculated as shown on the next page:

Management **A**ccounting **P**ractice

Expedia, Amazon.com, Tencent.com, Netflix, Google, and Priceline.com

OPERATING LEVERAGE: FRIEND *AND* FOE

The *BusinessWeek* InfoTech 100 is a ranking of the top-performing information technology companies. A few years ago, when the first Web companies were breaking into the ranking, *BusinessWeek* observed that, "The leaders of the Web pack are showing that once they turn profitable, they can quickly become big moneymakers. The reason is operating leverage. That's accounting-speak for a simple concept: Once you invest enough to build a Web site and your basic operations, you don't need to spend much money as sales rise. After you cover your fixed costs, the expense of processing each sale is so little that profits grow faster than revenues."

BusinessWeek also noted that, "Online travel agency Expedia Inc. is a textbook example of leverage in action." In one quarter alone, "Expedia doubled its sales, to $116 million. Yet its overhead, including administrative and marketing costs, rose only 8 percent, to $63 million. One big reason is that the company already had paid for the computing gear it needed to handle the higher volume of ticket sales. . . . What's holding Amazon.com Inc. and other e-tailers back is simple: Every time someone buys a book on Amazon, the company has to buy a new copy from the publisher. The upshot is that Amazon's gross margins are around 26 percent, compared with 70 percent at Expedia."[4]

But operating leverage can work both ways. In recent years, Amazon.com has been the #1 company on the InfoTech 100 list after moving beyond selling books to take advantage of its operating leverage by using partnerships to run additional business through its fixed investment in a Web presence. And Expedia, the leader in years past, has fallen off of the list completely as the global recession has reduced travel: when sales volume drops, the high fixed costs associated with high operating leverage become a heavy burden indeed!

Other leading Web companies on the InfoTech 100 have included Chinese Internet giant Tencent.com, as well as U.S. Web sites Netflix, Google, and Priceline.com.[5] As their business models evolve, these Web high-fliers need to keep an eye out for the downside of operating leverage.

---

[4]Timothy J. Mullancy and Robert D. Hof, "Finally, the Pot of Gold," *BusinessWeek,* June 24, 2002, p. 106.

[5]Bloomberg BusinessWeek, "The InfoTech 100," http://www.businessweek.com/interactive_reports/it100_2009. html (2009).

Exhibit 7–8
Labor-Intensive Production
Processes versus Advanced
Manufacturing Systems

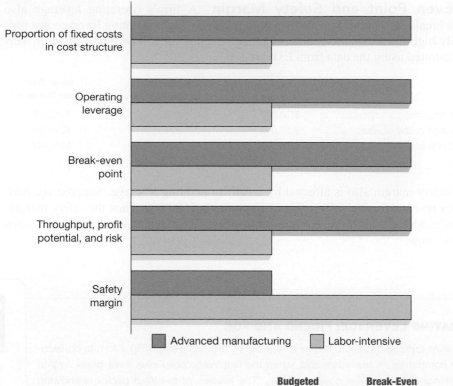

	Budgeted Sales Revenue	Break-Even Sales Revenue	Safety Margin
Company A (AccuTime)	$500,000	$375,000	$125,000
Company B (high variable expenses)	500,000	250,000	250,000
Company C (high fixed expenses)	500,000	444,444	55,556

To summarize, company C's high fixed expenses result in a high break-even point and low safety margin. Company B displays the opposite characteristics, and company A falls in between the two extremes.

Labor-Intensive Production Processes versus Advanced Manufacturing Systems

The effects of labor-intensive (manual) production processes and highly automated, advanced manufacturing systems illustrated by companies A, B, and C are typical. As Exhibit 7–8 shows, a movement toward an advanced manufacturing environment often results in a higher break-even point, lower safety margin, and higher operating leverage. However, high-technology manufacturing systems generally have greater throughput, thus allowing greater potential for profitability. Along with the increased potential for profitability comes increased risk. In an economic recession, for example, a highly automated company with high fixed costs will be less able to adapt to lower consumer demand than will a firm with a more labor-intensive production process.

Cost Structure and Operating Leverage: A Cost-Benefit Issue

A firm's cost structure plays an important role in determining its cost-volume-profit relationships. A company with proportionately high fixed costs has relatively high operating leverage. The result of high operating leverage is that the firm can generate a large percentage increase in operating income from a relatively small percentage increase in sales revenue. On the other hand, a firm with high operating leverage has a relatively high break-even point. This entails some risk to the firm.

The optimal cost structure for an organization involves a trade-off. Management must weigh the benefits of high operating leverage against the risks of large committed fixed costs and the associated high break-even point.

CVP Analysis, Activity-Based Costing, and Advanced Manufacturing Systems

Traditional cost-volume-profit analysis focuses on the number of units sold as the only cost and revenue driver. Sales revenue is assumed to be linear in units sold. Moreover, costs are categorized as fixed or variable, with respect to the number of units sold, within the relevant range. This approach is consistent with traditional product-costing systems, in which cost assignment is based on a single, volume-related cost driver. In CVP analysis, as in product costing, the traditional approach can be misleading or provide less than adequate information for various management purposes. An activity-based costing system can provide a much more complete picture of cost-volume-profit relationships and thus provide better information to managers.

To illustrate the potential impact of activity-based costing on CVP analysis, we will continue our discussion of AccuTime Company. The basic data underlying the contribution income statement shown in Exhibit 7–5 are as follows:

AccuTime

Sales volume	20,000 units
Sales price	$25
Unit variable costs:	
Variable manufacturing	$14
Variable selling and administrative	1
Total unit variable cost	$15
Unit contribution margin	$10
Fixed costs:	
Fixed manufacturing	$100,000
Fixed selling and administrative	50,000
Total fixed costs	$150,000

These data are adequate for a traditional CVP analysis of various questions management may ask. For example, the break-even point is easily calculated as 15,000 units, as the following analysis shows:

$$\text{Break-even point} = \frac{\text{Fixed costs}}{\text{Unit contribution margin}} = \frac{\$150,000}{\$10} = 15,000 \text{ units}$$

Alternatively, management may determine how many clocks must be sold to earn a target profit (operating income) of $200,000, as the following calculation demonstrates:

$$\begin{aligned}\text{Sales volume required to earn} \\ \text{target profit of } \$200,000\end{aligned} = \frac{\text{Fixed costs} + \text{Target profit}}{\text{Unit contribution margin}}$$

$$= \frac{\$150,000 + \$200,000}{\$10} = 35,000 \text{ units}$$

What do these questions have in common? They both focus on *sales volume* as the sole revenue and cost driver. The CVP analysis depends on a distinction between costs that are fixed and costs that are variable *with respect to sales volume.*

A Move Toward JIT and Flexible Manufacturing

Now let's examine another question AccuTime's management could face. Suppose management is considering the installation of a *flexible manufacturing system* and a move toward just-in-time (JIT) production. A flexible manufacturing system uses highly automated material-handling and production equipment to manufacture a variety of similar products. In the new production process, setups would be quicker and more frequent and production runs would be smaller. Fewer inspections would be required, due to the total quality control (TQC) philosophy that often accompanies JIT. Variable manufacturing costs would be lower, due to savings in direct labor. Finally, general factory overhead costs would increase, due to the greater depreciation charges on the new production equipment.

Suppose management wants to answer the same two questions addressed previously, under the assumption that the production process changes are adopted. To properly address this issue, we need a much more detailed understanding of the impact of other, *non-volume-based cost drivers* on AccuTime's costs. This type of detail is the hallmark of an activity-based costing system. Suppose AccuTime's controller completes an ABC analysis of the company's 20x1 activity before the new equipment is installed. The results are shown in Exhibit 7–9.

There is a subtle but important point to realize about the cost behavior depicted in Exhibit 7–9. Setup, inspection, and material handling are listed as fixed costs. *They are largely fixed with respect to sales volume.* However, they are *not* fixed with respect to *other cost drivers,* such as the number of setups, inspections, and hours of material handling. This is the fundamental distinction between a traditional CVP analysis and an activity-based costing CVP analysis. The traditional CVP analysis recognizes a single, volume-based cost driver, namely, sales volume. The activity-based costing CVP analysis recognizes multiple cost drivers. As a result, some costs viewed as fixed under the traditional analysis are considered variable (with respect to the appropriate cost drivers) under the ABC approach.

Now let's return to management's decision regarding the installation of a flexible manufacturing system and the adoption of the JIT and TQC philosophies. The activity-based costing analysis of the proposed production technology is displayed in Exhibit 7–10. Due to the decreased use of direct labor, the unit variable manufacturing cost has declined from $14 to $9, thus bringing the total unit variable cost down to $10. This results in an increase in the unit contribution margin to $15. The installation of sophisticated new manufacturing equipment has more than tripled general factory overhead, from $60,000

Pictured here is a production cell in a flexible manufacturing system engaged in the production of disks for computer hard disk drives. In such a high-tech manufacturing environment, setups are quicker and more frequent, and production runs are smaller. An activity-based costing CVP analysis will give management a better understanding of cost-volume-profit relationships.

Sales price	$25
Unit variable costs:	
Variable manufacturing	$14
Variable selling and administrative	1
Total unit variable costs	$15
Unit contribution margin	$10
Fixed costs (fixed with respect to sales volume):	
General factory overhead (including depreciation on plant and equipment)	$ 60,000
Setup (52 setups at $100 per setup)*	5,200
Inspection [(52)(21) inspections at $20 per inspection]†	21,840
Material handling (1,080 hours at $12 per hour)	12,960
Total fixed manufacturing costs	$100,000
Fixed selling and administrative costs	50,000
Total fixed costs	$150,000

*One setup per week.
†Three inspections per day, seven days a week (52 weeks per year).

Exhibit 7–9
Activity-Based Costing Data under Current Production Process (20x1)

 AccuTime

to $184,000. Under the proposed JIT approach, setups will be daily instead of weekly; each setup will be quicker and less expensive. As a result of the emphasis on total quality control, only one inspection per day will be necessary, instead of three as before. Moreover, each inspection will be less expensive. Finally, the amount of material-handling activity will decline dramatically, although there will be a slight increase in the cost per hour. This is due to the higher skill grade of labor required to operate the new automated material-handling system.

Using the ABC data in Exhibit 7–10, we can answer the two CVP questions posed by management. If the new production technology is adopted, the following CVP computations will be appropriate.

$$\text{Break-even point} = \frac{\text{Fixed costs}}{\text{Unit contribution margin}} = \frac{\$250,000}{\$15} = \begin{array}{c} 16,667 \text{ units} \\ (\text{rounded}) \end{array}$$

$$\begin{array}{l} \text{Sales volume required to earn} \\ \text{target profit of } \$200,000 \end{array} = \text{Fixed costs} + \frac{\text{Target profit}}{\text{Unit contribution margin}}$$

$$= \frac{\$250,000 + \$200,000}{\$15} = 30,000 \text{ units}$$

Notice that AccuTime's break-even point increased with the introduction of the advanced manufacturing system (from 15,000 to 16,667 units). However, the number of sales units required to earn a target profit of $200,000 declined (from 35,000 to 30,000 units). These kinds of CVP changes are typical when firms install an advanced manufacturing system. Typically, the cost structure of an advanced manufacturing environment is characterized by a lower proportion of variable costs and a larger proportion of costs that are fixed (with respect to sales volume).

ABC Provides a Richer Understanding of Cost Behavior and CVP Relationships
The point of this section is that activity-based costing provides a richer description of a company's cost behavior. AccuTime's traditional costing system treated setup, inspection, and material handling as fixed costs. However, the ABC analysis showed that while these costs are largely fixed with respect to sales volume, they are

Exhibit 7–10
Activity-Based Costing Data
under Proposed Production
Technology

Sales price	$25
Unit variable costs:	
Variable manufacturing	$ 9
Variable selling and administrative	1
Total unit variable costs	$10
Unit contribution margin	$15
Fixed costs (fixed with respect to sales volume):	
General factory overhead (including depreciation on plant and equipment)	$184,000
Setup (365 setups at $30 per setup)	10,950
Inspection (365 inspections at $10 per inspection)	3,650
Material handling (100 hours at $14 per hour)	1,400
Total fixed manufacturing costs	$200,000
Fixed selling and administrative costs	50,000
Total fixed costs	$250,000

not fixed with respect to other appropriate cost drivers. In analyzing the cost-volume-profit implications of the proposed changes in manufacturing technology, it was crucial to have an understanding of how these costs would change with respect to such cost drivers as the number of setups, number of quality-assurance inspections, and amount of material-handling activity.

Just as ABC can improve an organization's product-costing system, it also can facilitate a deeper understanding of cost behavior and CVP relationships.

Chapter Summary

LO1 Compute a break-even point using the contribution-margin approach and the equation approach. These two approaches result in the same general formula for computing the break-even point (in units). Under the equation approach, the profit equation is specified as follows: Sales revenue − Variable expenses − Fixed expenses = Profit. When this equation is manipulated, the contribution-margin approach to the break-even point results, as follows: Break-even point (in units) = Fixed expenses ÷ Unit contribution margin.

LO2 Compute the contribution-margin ratio and use it to find the break-even point in sales dollars. The contribution-margin ratio is defined as follows: Unit contribution margin ÷ Unit sales price. The break-even point (in sales dollars) can be computed as follows: Fixed expenses ÷ Contribution-margin ratio.

LO3 Prepare a cost-volume-profit (CVP) graph and explain how it is used. A cost-volume-profit graph shows the break-even point (in sales dollars) as the intersection of the total revenue line and the total expense line. The graph can be used to help management understand how changes in the volume of activity affect cost and profit.

LO4 Apply CVP analysis to determine the effect on profit of changes in fixed expenses, variable expenses, sales prices, and sales volume. Management can use the break-even equation to predict the effects on the break-even point of changes in any component of the equation, e.g., sales price, unit variable cost, fixed cost, and so forth. Such prediction can help management in making a variety of operational decisions.

LO5 Compute the break-even point and prepare a profit-volume graph for a multiproduct enterprise. Break-even analysis in a multiproduct firm is accomplished by computing a weighted-average contribution margin, which is based on the expected sales mix. The same break-even formulas are used as in a single-product analysis, except that the unit contribution margin is replaced by the weighted-average contribution margin. This analysis is limited by the assumption of a constant sales mix across the range of total sales volume.

LO6 List and discuss the key assumptions of CVP analysis. CVP analysis involves several key assumptions, which follow: (1) Total revenue is linear (i.e., a straight line) with respect to changes in the volume of activity. (2) Total expense is linear (i.e., a straight line) with respect to changes in the volume of activity. An implication of this assumption is that the efficiency and productivity of the production process remains constant. (3) The sales mix remains constant over the relevant range. (4) The beginning and ending inventory levels are the same in a manufacturing firm.

LO7 Prepare and interpret a contribution income statement. Cost-volume-profit relationships are important enough to operating managers that some firms prepare a contribution income statement. This income-statement format separates fixed and variable expenses and computes the aggregate contribution margin. This statement format helps managers discern the effects on profit from changes in volume. The contribution income statement also discloses an organization's cost structure, which is the relative proportion of its fixed and variable costs.

LO8 Explain the role of cost structure and operating leverage in CVP relationships. An organization's cost structure is the relative proportions of its fixed and variable costs. The extent to which an organization uses fixed costs in its cost structure is called operating leverage. Firms with high operating leverage tend to have higher break-even points, other things being equal.

LO9 Understand the implications of activity-based costing for CVP analysis. Activity-based costing (ABC) provides a richer description of an organization's cost behavior and CVP relationships than is provided by a traditional costing system. An ABC cost-volume-profit analysis recognizes that some costs that are fixed with respect to sales volume may not be fixed with respect to other important cost drivers. In many cases, management can benefit substantially from such an improved understanding of cost behavior and CVP relationships.

LO10 Be aware of the effects of advanced manufacturing technology on CVP relationships. Companies with advanced manufacturing technology tend to have higher fixed costs, lower variable costs, and higher break-even points.

LO11 Understand the effect of income taxes on CVP analysis (Appendix). When a firm is required to pay taxes on income, it is important to distinguish between net income and operating or pre-tax income. Net income is equal to pre-tax income minus income tax expense. Therefore, pre-tax income is equal to net income ÷ (1 − tax rate). The number of units of sales required to earn a specified net income is equal to (pre-tax income + fixed expenses) ÷ unit contribution margin.

Review Problem on Cost-Volume-Profit Analysis

Overlook Inn is a small bed-and-breakfast inn located in the Scottish Highlands. The charge is $50 per person for one night's lodging and a full breakfast in the morning. The retired couple who own and manage the inn estimate that the variable expense per person is $20. This includes such expenses as food, maid service, and utilities. The inn's fixed expenses total $42,000 per year. The inn can accommodate 10 guests each night.

Required: Compute the following:
1. Contribution margin per unit of service. (A unit of service is one night's lodging for one guest.)
2. Contribution-margin ratio.
3. Annual break-even point in units of service and in dollars of service revenue.
4. The number of units of service required to earn a target operating income of $60,000 for the year.

Solution to Review Problem

1. Contribution margin per unit of service = Nightly room charge − Variable expense per person

   $30 = $50 − $20

2.   Contribution-margin ratio $= \dfrac{\text{Contribution margin per unit}}{\text{Nightly room charge}}$

$$.60 \quad = \dfrac{\$30}{\$50}$$

3. $\dfrac{\text{Break-even point}}{\text{in units of service}} = \dfrac{\text{Fixed expenses}}{\text{Contribution margin per unit}}$

$$1,400 = \dfrac{\$42,000}{\$30}$$

$\dfrac{\text{Break-even point in}}{\text{dollars of revenue}} = \dfrac{\text{Fixed expenses}}{\text{Contribution-margin ratio}}$

$$\$70,000 = \dfrac{\$42,000}{.60}$$

4. $\dfrac{\text{Number of units of service}}{\text{required to earn target profit}} = \dfrac{\text{Fixed expenses} + \text{Target profit}}{\text{Contribution margin per unit of service}}$

$$3,400 \quad = \dfrac{\$42,000 + \$60,000}{\$30}$$

Key Terms

For each term's definition refer to the indicated page, or turn to the glossary at the end of the text.

after-tax net income,* 338

break-even point, 311

contribution income statement, 328

contribution-margin ratio, 313

cost structure, 329

cost-volume-profit (CVP) analysis, 310

cost-volume-profit (CVP) graph, 314

operating income, 327

operating leverage, 330

operating leverage factor, 330

pre-tax income,* 338

profit-volume graph, 317

safety margin, 319

sales mix, 324

sensitivity analysis, 326

target profit (or income), 317

total contribution margin, 312

unit contribution margin, 313

weighted-average unit contribution margin, 324

---

*Term appears in the appendix.

APPENDIX TO CHAPTER 7

Effect of Income Taxes

Learning Objective 11

Understand the effect of income taxes on CVP analysis (Appendix).

Profit-seeking enterprises must pay income taxes on their profits. A firm's **after-tax net income,** the amount of income remaining after subtracting the firm's income-tax expense, is less than its **pre-tax income.** This fact is expressed in the following formula.

(After-tax net income) = (Pre-tax income) $-\ t$(Pre-tax income)

where t denotes the income-tax rate.

Rearranging this equation yields the following formula.

(After-tax net income) = (Pre-tax income)$(1 - t)$ (9)

To illustrate this formula, suppose AccuTime Company must pay income taxes of 40 percent of its pre-tax income. The company's contribution income statement for 20x1 appears below.

Sales, 20,000 units at $25 each	$500,000
Variable expenses, 20,000 units at $15 each*	300,000
Contribution margin	$200,000
Fixed expenses	150,000
Income before taxes	$ 50,000
Income-tax expense, .40 × $50,000	20,000
Net income, $50,000 × (1 − .40)	$ 30,000

*Variable cost per unit is $15: variable manufacturing cost of $14 plus variable selling and administrative costs of $1.

The requirement that companies pay income taxes affects their cost-volume-profit relationships. To earn a particular after-tax net income will require greater pre-tax income than if there were no tax. For example, if AccuTime's target after-tax net income were $30,000, the company would have to earn pre-tax income of $50,000. AccuTime's income statement shows this relationship.

How much pre-tax income must be earned in order to achieve a particular target after-tax net income? Rearranging equation (9) above yields the following formula.

$$\begin{pmatrix} \text{Target} \\ \text{after-tax} \\ \text{net income} \end{pmatrix} = \begin{pmatrix} \text{Target} \\ \text{pre-tax} \\ \text{income} \end{pmatrix}(1 - t)$$

Divide both sides by $(1 - t)$

$$\frac{\begin{pmatrix} \text{Target} \\ \text{after-tax} \\ \text{net income} \end{pmatrix}}{1 - t} = \begin{pmatrix} \text{Target} \\ \text{pre-tax} \\ \text{income} \end{pmatrix}\frac{1 - t}{1 - t}$$

$$\frac{\begin{pmatrix} \text{Target} \\ \text{after-tax} \\ \text{net income} \end{pmatrix}}{1 - t} = \begin{matrix} \text{Target} \\ \text{pre-tax} \\ \text{income} \end{matrix}$$

If AccuTime Company's target after-tax net income is $30,000, its target pre-tax income is calculated as follows:

$$\frac{\begin{matrix}\text{Target after-tax}\\ \text{net income}\end{matrix}}{1 - t} = \frac{\$30,000}{1 - .40} = \$50,000 = \text{Target pre-tax income}$$

Now we are in a position to compute the number of digital clocks that AccuTime must sell in order to achieve a particular after-tax net income. We begin with the following pre-tax income equation.

$$\text{Sales} - \text{Variable expenses} - \text{Fixed expenses} = \text{Pre-tax income}$$

Now we use our formula for pre-tax pre-income.

$$\text{Sales} - \text{Variable expenses} - \text{Fixed expenses} = \frac{\text{After-tax net income}}{1 - t}$$

$$\left[\begin{pmatrix}\text{Unit}\\\text{sales}\\\text{price}\end{pmatrix} \times \begin{pmatrix}\text{Sales}\\\text{volume}\\\text{in units}\end{pmatrix}\right] - \left[\begin{pmatrix}\text{Unit}\\\text{variable}\\\text{expense}\end{pmatrix} \times \begin{pmatrix}\text{Sales}\\\text{volume}\\\text{in units}\end{pmatrix}\right] - \begin{pmatrix}\text{Fixed}\\\text{expenses}\end{pmatrix} = \frac{\begin{matrix}\text{After-tax}\\\text{net income}\end{matrix}}{1 - t}$$

Using the data for AccuTime Company, and assuming target after-tax net income of $30,000:

$$(\$25 \times X) - (\$15 \times X) - \$150,000 = \frac{\$30,000}{1 - .40}$$

where X denotes the number of units that must be sold to achieve the target after-tax net income.

Now we solve for X as follows:

$$(\$25 - \$15) \times X = \$150,000 + \frac{\$30,000}{1 - .40}$$

$$\$10 \quad \times X = \$150,000 + \frac{\$30,000}{1 - .40}$$

$$X = \frac{\$150,000 + \dfrac{\$30,000}{1 - .40}}{\$10}$$

$$= 20,000 \text{ units}$$

In terms of sales revenue, AccuTime must achieve a sales volume of $500,000 (20,000 units × $25 sales price). We can verify these calculations by examining AccuTime's income statement given previously.

Notice in the calculations above that $10 is the unit contribution margin ($25 sales price minus $15 variable expense). Thus, the general formula illustrated above is the following:

$$\begin{array}{l}\text{Number of units of sales} \\ \text{required to earn target} \\ \text{after-tax net income}\end{array} = \frac{\text{Fixed expenses} + \dfrac{\text{Target after-tax net income}}{1 - t}}{\text{Unit contribution margin}}$$

where t denotes the income tax rate.

A cost-volume-profit graph for AccuTime Company is displayed in Exhibit 7–11. As the graph shows, 20,000 units must be sold to achieve $30,000 in after-tax net income. The company's break-even

Exhibit 7–11
Cost-Volume-Profit Graph
(with income taxes)

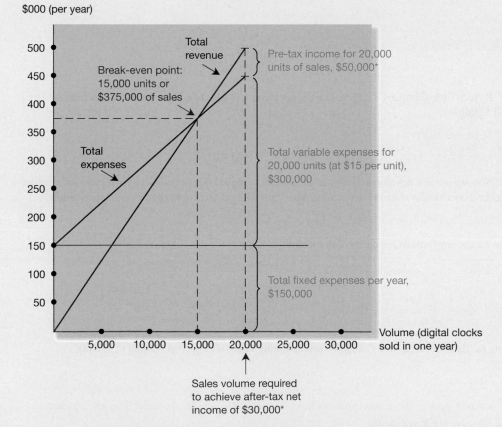

AccuTime Company

$000 (per year)

Total revenue

Break-even point:
15,000 units or
$375,000 of sales

Pre-tax income for 20,000 units of sales, $50,000*

Total expenses

Total variable expenses for 20,000 units (at $15 per unit), $300,000

Total fixed expenses per year, $150,000

Volume (digital clocks sold in one year)

Sales volume required to achieve after-tax net income of $30,000*

*(Pre-tax income) × (1 − Tax rate) = After-tax income
$50,000 × (1 − .40) = $30,000

point is 15,000 units. The break-even point is not affected by income taxes, because at the break-even point, there is no income.

Notice that AccuTime Company must sell 5,000 units *beyond the break-even point* in order to achieve after-tax net income of $30,000. Each unit sold beyond the break-even point contributes $10 toward *pre-tax* income. However, of that $10 contribution margin, $4 will have to be paid in income taxes. This leaves an *after-tax contribution* of $6 toward after-tax net income. Thus, selling 5,000 units beyond the break-even point results in after-tax net income of $30,000 (5,000 units $\times$ $6 after-tax contribution per unit).

The tax rate, *t,* in the discussion above is a flat rate that applies to all profits. However, many tax jurisdictions apply a progressive tax structure (where tax rates increase with increasing levels of profit). Full modeling of a progressive tax structure results in cost functions that are beyond the scope of this text. However, because the highest tax rate often applies beginning at a relatively low level of profitability, performing cost-volume-profit analysis with the tax rate set at the highest tax rate will generally result in solutions that are reasonable for most levels of profitability.

Review Questions

7–1. Briefly explain each of the following methods of computing a break-even point in units: (*a*) contribution-margin approach, (*b*) equation approach, and (*c*) graphical approach.

7–2. What is the meaning of the term *unit contribution margin?* Contribution to what?

7–3. What information is conveyed by a cost-volume-profit graph in addition to a company's break-even point?

7–4. What does the term *safety margin* mean?

7–5. Suppose the fixed expenses of a travel agency increase. What will happen to its break-even point, measured in number of clients served? Why?

7–6. Delmarva Oyster Company has been able to decrease its variable expenses per pound of oysters harvested. How will this affect the firm's break-even sales volume?

7–7. In a strategy meeting, a manufacturing company's president said, "If we raise the price of our product, the company's break-even point will be lower." The financial vice president responded by saying, "Then we should raise our price. The company will be less likely to incur a loss." Do you agree with the president? Why? Do you agree with the financial vice president? Why?

7–8. What will happen to a company's break-even point if the sales price and unit variable cost of its only product increase by the same dollar amount?

7–9. An art museum covers its operating expenses by charging a small admission fee. The objective of the nonprofit organization is to break even. A local arts enthusiast has just pledged an annual donation of $10,000 to the museum. How will the donation affect the museum's break-even attendance level?

7–10. How can a profit-volume graph be used to predict a company's profit for a particular sales volume?

7–11. List the most important assumptions of cost-volume-profit analysis.

7–12. Why do many operating managers prefer a contribution income statement instead of a traditional income statement?

7–13. What is the difference between a manufacturing company's *gross margin* and its total *contribution margin?*

7–14. East Company manufactures DVD players using a completely automated production process. West Company also manufactures DVD players, but its products are assembled manually. How will these two firms' cost structures differ? Which company will have a higher operating leverage factor?

7–15. When sales volume increases, which company will experience a larger percentage increase in profit: company X, which has mostly fixed expenses, or company Y, which has mostly variable expenses?

7–16. What does the term *sales mix* mean? How is a *weighted-average unit contribution margin* computed?

7–17. A car rental agency rents subcompact, compact, and full-size automobiles. What assumptions would be made about the agency's sales mix for the purpose of a cost-volume-profit analysis?

7–18. How can a hotel's management use cost-volume-profit analysis to help in deciding on room rates?

7–19. How could cost-volume-profit analysis be used in budgeting? In making a decision about advertising?

7–20. Two companies have identical fixed expenses, unit variable expenses, taxes, and profits. Yet one company has set a much lower price for its product. Explain how this can happen.

7–21. A company with an advanced manufacturing environment typically will have a higher break-even point, greater operating leverage, and larger safety margin than a labor-intensive firm. True or false? Explain.

7–22. Explain briefly how activity-based costing (ABC) affects cost-volume-profit analysis.

Exercises

■ **Exercise 7–23**
Fill in Blanks; Basic CVP
Relationships
(LO 1, 2)

Fill in the missing data for each of the following independent cases.

	Sales Revenue	Variable Expenses	Total Contribution Margin	Fixed Expenses	Operating Income	Break-Even Sales Revenue
1.	?	$40,000	?	$30,000	?	$40,000
2.	$ 80,000	?	$15,000	?	?	80,000
3.	?	40,000	80,000	?	$50,000	?
4.	110,000	22,000	?	?	38,000	?

■ **Exercise 7–24**
Pizza Delivery Business;
Basic CVP Analysis
(LO 1, 2, 4)

Smart Pizza delivers pizzas to the dormitories and apartments near a major university. The company's annual fixed expenses are $40,000. The sales price of a pizza is $10, and it costs the company $6 to make and deliver each pizza.

Required:

1. Using the contribution-margin approach, compute the company's break-even point in units (pizzas).
2. What is the contribution-margin ratio?
3. Compute the break-even sales revenue. Use the contribution-margin ratio in your calculation.
4. How many pizzas must the company sell to earn a target operating income of $80,000? Use the equation method.

■ **Exercise 7–25**
Manufacturing; Using CVP
Analysis
(LO 1, 4)

Rosario Company, which is located in Buenos Aires, Argentina, manufactures a component used in farm machinery. The firm's fixed costs are $4,000,000 per year. The variable cost of each component is $2,000 and the components are sold for $3,000 each. The company sold 5,000 components during the prior year.

Required: Answer requirements (1) through (4) independently.

1. Compute the break-even point in units.
2. What will the new break-even point be if fixed costs increase by 10 percent?
3. What was the company's operating income for the prior year?
4. The sales manager believes that a reduction in the sales price to $2,500 will result in orders for 1,200 more components each year. What will the break-even point be if the price is changed?
5. Should the price change discussed in requirement (4) be made?

■ **Exercise 7–26**
Sports Franchise; CVP Graph
(LO 3, 4)

The Houston Armadillos, a minor-league baseball team, play their weekly games in a small stadium just outside Houston. The stadium holds 10,000 people and tickets sell for $10 each. The franchise owner estimates that the team's annual fixed expenses are $180,000, and the variable expense per ticket sold is $1. (In the following requirements, ignore income taxes.)

Required:

1. Draw a cost-volume-profit graph for the sports franchise. Label the axes, break-even point, profit and loss areas, fixed expenses, variable expenses, total-expense line, and total-revenue line.
2. If the stadium is half full for each game, how many games must the team play to break even?

■ **Exercise 7–27**
Continuation of Preceding
Exercise; Profit-Volume
Graph; Safety Margin
(LO 3, 4)

Refer to the data given in the preceding exercise. (Ignore income taxes.)

Required:

1. Prepare a fully labeled profit-volume graph for the Houston Armadillos.
2. What is the safety margin for the baseball franchise if the team plays a 12-game season and the team owner expects the stadium to be 30 percent full for each game?
3. If the stadium is half full for each game, what ticket price would the team have to charge in order to break even?

■ **Exercise 7–28**
Publishing; Contribution
Income Statement
(LO 7, 8)

Europa Publications, Inc. specializes in reference books that keep abreast of the rapidly changing political and economic issues in Europe. The results of the company's operations during the prior year are given in the following table. All units produced during the year were sold.

Sales revenue	$2,200,000
Manufacturing costs:	
Fixed	500,000
Variable	1,000,000
Selling costs:	
Fixed	50,000
Variable	100,000
Administrative costs:	
Fixed	120,000
Variable	30,000

Required:

1. Prepare a traditional income statement and a contribution income statement for the company's operating income.

2. What is the firm's operating leverage for the sales volume generated during the prior year?

3. Suppose sales revenue increases by 10 percent. What will be the percentage increase in operating income?

4. Which income statement would an operating manager use to answer requirement (3)? Why?

■ **Exercise 7–29**
Retail; CVP Analysis with
Multiple Products
(LO 1, 2, 5)

Tim's Bicycle Shop sells 21-speed bicycles. For purposes of a cost-volume-profit analysis, the shop owner has divided sales into two categories, as follows:

Product Type	Sales Price	Invoice Cost	Sales Commission
High-quality	$500	$275	$25
Medium-quality	300	135	15

Three-quarters of the shop's sales are medium-quality bikes. The shop's annual fixed expenses are $65,000.

Required:

1. Compute the unit contribution margin for each product type.

2. What is the shop's sales mix?

3. Compute the weighted-average unit contribution margin, assuming a constant sales mix.

4. What is the shop's break-even sales volume in dollars? Assume a constant sales mix.

5. How many bicycles of each type must be sold to earn a target operating income of $48,750? Assume a constant sales mix.

■ **Exercise 7–30**
Cost-Volume-Profit Analysis
in an Airline; Use of Internet
(LO 4)

Use the Internet to access the Web site of one of these airlines, or a different airline of your choosing.

Air Canada	www.aircanada.com
British Airways	www.britishairways.com
Air New Zealand	www.airnewzealand.com
Cathay Pacific Airways	www.cathaypacific.com
Emirates Airlines	www.emirates.com

Required: Find the company's most recent annual report (hint: look for an "About . . ." or "Investor Relations" link). What does the report disclose about the airline's load factor? Does it disclose the break-even load factor for the most recent year? If so, what is it?

■ **Exercise 7–31**
Hotel and Restaurant; Cost
Structure and Operating
Leverage
(LO 4, 8)

A contribution income statement for the Penzance Inn is shown below.

Revenue	$550,000
Less: Variable expenses	300,000
Contribution margin	$250,000
Less: Fixed expenses	200,000
Operating income	$ 50,000

Required:

1. Show the inn's cost structure by indicating the percentage of revenue represented by each item on the income statement.
2. Suppose revenue declines by 10 percent. Use the contribution-margin percentage to calculate the resulting decrease in operating income.
3. What is the operating leverage factor when revenue is $550,000?
4. Use the operating leverage factor to calculate the increase in operating income resulting from a 20 percent increase in sales revenue.

■ **Exercise 7–32**
Continuation of Preceding
Exercise
(LO 4, 7)

Refer to the income statement given in the preceding exercise. Prepare a new contribution income statement for the Penzance Inn in each of the following independent situations. (Ignore income taxes.)

1. The inn's volume of activity increases by 20 percent, and fixed expenses increase by 40 percent.
2. The ratio of variable expenses to revenue doubles. There is no change in the inn's volume of activity. Fixed expenses decline by $25,000.

■ **Exercise 7–33**
Consulting Firm; CVP Analysis
with Income Taxes (Appendix)
(LO 1, 4, 11)

Hydro Systems GmbH provides consulting services to city water authorities. The consulting firm's contribution-margin ratio is 20 percent, and its annual fixed expenses are $120,000. The firm's income-tax rate is 40 percent.

Required:

1. Calculate the firm's break-even volume of service revenue.
2. How much pre-tax income must the firm earn to make an after-tax net income of $48,000?
3. What level of revenue for consulting services must the firm generate to earn an after-tax net income of $48,000?
4. Suppose the firm's income-tax rate rises to 45 percent. What will happen to the break-even level of consulting service revenue?

Problems

All applicable Problems are available with McGraw-Hill's *Connect Accounting*™.

■ **Problem 7–34**
Basic CVP Relationships;
Retailer
(LO 1, 2, 4)

2. Operating income:
$280,000

Disk City, Inc. is a retailer for digital video disks. The projected operating income for the current year is $200,000 based on a sales volume of 200,000 video disks. Disk City has been selling the disks for $16 each. The variable costs consist of the $10 unit purchase price of the disks and a handling cost of $2 per disk. Disk City's annual fixed costs are $600,000.

  Management is planning for the coming year, when it expects that the unit purchase price of the video disks will increase 30 percent.

Required:

1. Calculate Disk city's break-even point for the current year in number of video disks.
2. What will be the company's operating income for the current year if there is a 10 percent increase in projected unit sales volume?
3. What volume of sales (in dollars) must Disk City achieve in the coming year to maintain the same operating income as projected for the current year if the unit selling price remains at $16?
4. In order to cover a 30 percent increase in the disk's purchase price for the coming year and still maintain the current contribution-margin ratio, what selling price per disk must Disk City establish for the coming year?
5. *Build a spreadsheet:* Construct an Excel spreadsheet to solve requirements (1), (2), and (3) above. Show how the solution will change if the following information changes: the selling price is $17 and the annual fixed costs are $640,000.

(CMA, adapted)

CollegePak Company produced and sold 50,000 backpacks during the year just ended at an average price of $20 per unit. Variable manufacturing costs were $8 per unit, and variable marketing costs were $2 per unit sold. Fixed costs amounted to $180,000 for manufacturing and $72,000 for marketing. There was no year-end work-in-process inventory.

Required:

1. Compute CollegePak's break-even point in sales dollars for the year.
2. Compute the number of sales units required to earn operating income of $180,000 during the year.
3. CollegePak's variable manufacturing costs are expected to increase by 10 percent in the coming year. Compute the firm's break-even point in sales dollars for the coming year.
4. If CollegePak's variable manufacturing costs do increase by 10 percent, compute the selling price that would yield the same contribution-margin ratio in the coming year.

(CMA, adapted)

■ **Problem 7–35**
Basic CVP Computations
(LO 1, 2, 4)

2. Sales units required for $180,000 income: 43,200 units

Corrigan Enterprises is studying the acquisition of two electrical component insertion systems for producing its sole product, the universal gismo. Data relevant to the systems follow.

Model no. 6754:
    Variable costs, $16.00 per unit
    Annual fixed costs, $985,600

Model no. 4399:
    Variable costs, $12.80 per unit
    Annual fixed costs, $1,113,600

Corrigan's selling price is $64 per unit for the universal gismo, which is subject to a 5 percent sales commission.

Required:

1. How many units must the company sell to break even if Model 6754 is selected?
2. Which of the two systems would be more profitable if sales and production are expected to average 46,000 units per year?
3. Assume Model 4399 requires the purchase of additional equipment that is not reflected in the preceding figures. The equipment will cost $450,000 and will be depreciated over a five-year life by the straight-line method. How many units must Corrigan sell to earn $956,400 of operating income if Model 4399 is selected? As in requirement (2), sales and production are expected to average 46,000 units per year.
4. Ignoring the information presented in requirement (3), at what volume level will management be indifferent between the acquisition of Model no. 6754 and Model no. 4399? In other words, at what volume level will the annual total cost of each system be equal? (*Hint:* At any given sales volume, sales commissions will be the same amount regardless of which model is selected.)

■ **Problem 7–36**
CVP Relationships; Indifference Point
(LO 1, 4)

2. Operating income, model no. 4399: $1,094,400

Madrid-based Advanced Electronics manufactures audio speakers for desktop computers. The following data relate to the period just ended when the company produced and sold 42,000 speaker sets:

Sales	$3,360,000
Variable costs	924,000
Fixed costs	2,280,000

Management is considering relocating its manufacturing facilities to Slovakia to reduce costs. Variable costs are expected to average $16 per set; annual fixed costs are anticipated to be $1,984,000.

■ **Problem 7–37**
CVP Analysis; Impact of Operating Changes
(LO 1, 4)

2. Break-even point: 31,000 units

Required:

1. Calculate the company's current operating income and determine the level of sales needed to double that figure, assuming that manufacturing operations remain in Spain.

2. Determine the break-even point in speaker sets if operations are shifted to Slovakia.

3. Assume that management desires to achieve the Slovak break-even point; however, operations will remain in Spain.

   a. If variable costs remain constant, what must management do to fixed costs? By how much must fixed costs change?

   b. If fixed costs remain constant, what must management do to the variable cost per unit? By how much must unit variable cost change?

4. Determine the impact (increase, decrease, or no effect) of the following operating changes.

   a. Effect of an increase in direct material costs on the break-even point.

   b. Effect of an increase in fixed administrative costs on the unit contribution margin.

   c. Effect of an increase in the unit contribution margin on operating income.

   d. Effect of a decrease in the number of units sold on the break-even point.

■ **Problem 7–38**
Sales Mix and Employee Compensation; Operating Changes
(LO 4, 5)

2(c). Commissions, total: $535,600

Lawrence Corporation sells two ceiling fans, Deluxe and Basic. Current sales total 60,000 units, consisting of 39,000 Deluxe units and 21,000 Basic units. Selling price and variable cost information follow.

	Deluxe	Basic
Selling price	$86	$74
Variable cost	65	41

Salespeople currently receive flat salaries that total $400,000. Management is contemplating a change to a compensation plan that is based on commissions in an effort to boost the company's presence in the marketplace. Two plans are under consideration:

Plan A: 10% commission computed on gross dollar sales. Deluxe sales are expected to total 45,500 units; Basic sales are anticipated to be 19,500 units.

Plan B: 30% commission computed on the basis of production contribution margins. Deluxe sales are anticipated to be 26,000 units; Basic sales are expected to total 39,000 units.

Required:

1. Define the term *sales mix*.

2. Comparing Plan A to the current compensation arrangement:

   a. Will Plan A achieve management's objective of an increased presence in the marketplace? Briefly explain.

   b. From a sales-mix perspective, will the salespeople be promoting the product that one would logically expect? Briefly discuss.

   c. Will the sales force likely be satisfied with the results of Plan A? Why?

   d. Will Lawrence likely be satisfied with the resulting impact of Plan A on company profitability? Why?

3. Assume that Plan B is under consideration.

   a. Compare Plan A and Plan B with respect to total units sold and the sales mix. Comment on the results.

   b. In comparison with flat salaries, is Plan B more attractive to the sales force? To the company? Show calculations to support your answers.

■ **Problem 7–39**
Leverage; Analysis of Operating Change
(LO 1, 4, 8)

1. Plan B break-even point: 1,800 units
3. Operating leverage factor, plan A: 1.22

Consolidated Industries is studying the addition of a new valve to its product line. The valve would be used by manufacturers of irrigation equipment. The company anticipates starting with a relatively low sales volume and then boosting demand over the next several years. A new salesperson must be hired because Consolidated's current sales force is working at capacity. Two compensation plans are under consideration:

Plan A: An annual salary of $34,100 plus a 10% commission based on gross dollar sales.
Plan B: An annual salary of $72,000 and no commission.

Consolidated Industries will purchase the valve for $50 and sell it for $90. Anticipated demand during the first year is 6,000 units.

Required:

1. Compute the break-even point for Plan A and Plan B.

2. What is meant by the term *operating leverage*?

3. Analyze the cost structures of both plans at the anticipated demand of 6,000 units. Which of the two plans has a higher operating leverage factor?

4. Assume that a general economic downturn occurred during year 2, with product demand falling from 6,000 to 5,000 units. Determine the percentage decrease in company net income if Consolidated had adopted Plan A.

5. Repeat requirement (4) for Plan B. Compare Plan A and Plan B, and explain a major factor that underlies any resulting differences.

6. Briefly discuss the likely profitability impact of an economic recession for highly automated manufacturers. What can you say about the risk associated with these firms?

■ Problem 7–40
Basic CVP Relationships
(LO 1, 2, 4)

3. Sales units required for target operating income: 140,000 units
6. Old contribution-margin ratio: .208

Serendipity Sound, Inc. manufactures and sells compact discs. Price and cost data are as follows:

Selling price per unit (package of two CDs)	$25.00
Variable costs per unit:	
Direct material	$6.00
Direct labor	5.00
Artist's royalties	4.50
Manufacturing overhead	3.00
Selling expenses	1.30
Total variable costs per unit	$19.80
Annual fixed costs:	
Manufacturing overhead	$ 192,000
Selling and administrative	276,000
Total fixed costs	$ 468,000
Forecasted annual sales volume (120,000 units)	$ 3,000,000

Required:

1. What is Serendipity Sound's break-even point in units?

2. What is the company's break-even point in sales dollars?

3. How many units would Serendipity Sound have to sell in order to earn operating income of $260,000?

4. What is the firm's margin of safety?

5. Management estimates that direct-labor costs will increase by 8 percent next year. How many units will the company have to sell next year to reach its break-even point?

6. If the company's direct-labor costs do increase by 8 percent, what selling price per unit of product must it charge to maintain the same contribution-margin ratio?

(CMA, adapted)

■ Problem 7–41
CVP Graph; Cost Structure; Operating Leverage
(LO 2, 3, 4, 8)

3. Margin of safety: $8,000,000

Athletico, Ltda. manufactures athletic shoes. The company's projected operating income for the coming year, based on sales of 160,000 units, is as follows:

Sales		$16,000,000
Operating expenses:		
Variable expenses	$4,000,000	
Fixed expenses	6,000,000	
Total expenses		10,000,000
Operating income		$6,000,000

Required:

1. Prepare a CVP graph for Athletico, Ltda. for the coming year.

2. Calculate the firm's break-even point for the year in sales dollars.

3. What is the company's margin of safety for the year?

4. Compute Athletico's operating leverage factor, based on the budgeted sales volume for the year.

5. Compute Athletico's required sales in dollars in order to earn operating income of $9,000,000 in the coming year.

6. Describe the firm's cost structure. Calculate the percentage relationships between variable and fixed expenses and sales revenue.

(CMA, adapted)

■ Problem 7–42
Break-Even Point; After-Tax
Net Income; Profit-Volume
Graph; International Issues
(Appendix)
(LO 1, 2, 3, 4, 11)

3. Break-even point (units):
80,500 units

The European Division of Worldwide Reference Corporation produces a pocket dictionary containing popular phrases in six European languages. Annual budget data for the coming year follow. Projected sales are 100,000 books.

	Fixed	Variable	
Sales			$1,000,000
Costs:			
Direct material	$ –0–	$300,000	
Direct labor	–0–	200,000	
Manufacturing overhead	100,000	150,000	
Selling and administrative	110,000	50,000	
Total costs	$210,000	$700,000	910,000
Budgeted operating income			$ 90,000

Required:

1. Calculate the break-even point in units and in sales dollars.

2. If the European Division is subject to an income-tax rate of 40 percent, compute the number of units the company would have to sell to earn an after-tax net income of $90,000.

3. If fixed costs increased $31,500 with no other cost or revenue factor changing, compute the firm's break-even sales in units.

4. Prepare a profit-volume graph for the European Division.

5. Due to an unstable political situation in the country in which the European Division is located, management believes the country may split into two independent nations. If this happens, the tax rate could rise to 50 percent. Assuming all other data as in the original problem, how many pocket dictionaries must be sold to earn $90,000 after taxes?

6. **Build a spreadsheet:** Construct an Excel spreadsheet to solve requirements (1), (2), (3), and (5) above. Show how the solution will change if the following information changes: sales amounted to $1,100,000 and fixed manufacturing overhead was $110,000.

(CMA, adapted)

■ Problem 7–43
Break-Even Point; Safety
Margin; Law Firm
(LO 1, 4)

1. Total fixed expenses:
$1,466,980
2. Safety margin: $1,192,800

Martin Wong and two of his colleagues are considering opening a law office in Rio de Janeiro that would make inexpensive legal services available to those who could not otherwise afford services. The intent is to provide easy access for their clients by having the office open 360 days per year, 16 hours each day from 7:00 a.m. to 11:00 p.m. The office would be staffed by a lawyer, paralegal, legal secretary, and clerk-receptionist for each of the two eight-hour shifts.

In order to determine the feasibility of the project, Wong hired a marketing consultant to assist with market projections. The results of this study show that if the firm spends $350,000 on advertising the first year, the number of new clients expected each day will be 50. Wong and his associates believe this number is reasonable and are prepared to spend the $350,000 on advertising. Other pertinent information about the operation of the office follows:

- The only charge to each new client would be $30 for the initial consultation. All cases that warrant further legal work will be accepted on a contingency basis with the firm earning 30 percent of any favorable settlements or judgments. Wong estimates that 20 percent of new client consultations will result in favorable settlements or judgments averaging $2,000 each. It is not expected that there will be repeat clients during the first year of operations.
- The hourly wages of the staff are projected to be $25 for the lawyer, $20 for the paralegal, $15 for the legal secretary, and $10 for the clerk-receptionist. Fringe benefit expense will be 40 percent of the wages paid. A total of 400 hours of overtime is expected for the year; this will be divided equally between the legal secretary and the clerk-receptionist positions. Overtime will be paid at one and one-half times the regular wage, and the fringe benefit expense will apply to the full wage.
- Wong has located 600 square meters of suitable office space that rents for $480 per square meter annually. Asssociated expenses will be $27,000 for property insurance and $37,000 for utilities.
- It will be necessary for the group to purchase malpractice insurance, which is expected to cost $160,000 annually.
- The initial investment in the office equipment will be $120,000. This equipment has an estimated useful life of four years.
- The cost of office supplies has been estimated to be $4 per expected new client consultation.

Required:

1. Determine how many new clients must visit the law office being considered by Martin Wong and his colleagues in order for the venture to break even during its first year of operations.
2. Compute the law firm's safety margin.

(CMA, adapted)

Celestial Products, Inc. has decided to introduce a new product, which can be manufactured by either a computer-assisted manufacturing system or a labor-intensive production system. The manufacturing method will not affect the quality of the product. The estimated manufacturing costs by the two methods are as follows:

	Computer-Assisted Manufacturing System	Labor-Intensive Production System
Direct material	$5.00	$5.60
Direct labor (DLH denotes direct-labor hours)	.5DLH @ $12 6.00	.8DLH @ $9 7.20
Variable overhead	.5DLH @ $6 3.00	.8DLH @ $6 4.80
Fixed overhead*	$2,440,000	$1,320,000

*These costs are directly traceable to the new product line. They would not be incurred if the new product were not produced.

The company's marketing research department has recommended an introductory unit sales price of $30. Selling expenses are estimated to be $500,000 annually plus $2 for each unit sold. (Ignore income taxes.)

Required:

1. Calculate the estimated break-even point in annual unit sales of the new product if the company uses the (*a*) computer-assisted manufacturing system; (*b*) labor-intensive production system.
2. Determine the annual unit sales volume at which the firm would be indifferent between the two manufacturing methods.
3. Management must decide which manufacturing method to employ. One factor it should consider is operating leverage. Explain the concept of operating leverage. How is this concept related to Celestial Products' decision?
4. Describe the circumstances under which the firm should employ each of the two manufacturing methods.
5. Identify some business factors other than operating leverage that management should consider before selecting the manufacturing method.

(CMA, adapted)

■ **Problem 7–44**
Break-Even Analysis; Operating Leverage; New Manufacturing Environment **(LO 1, 8, 10)**

1(a). Computer-assisted manufacturing system, break-even point: 210,000 units

■ **Problem 7–45**

Break-Even Analysis;
Profit-Volume Graph; Movie
Theaters
(LO 1, 3, 4)

1. Break-even sales volume,
regular model: 27,500 liters
3. Volume at which both
machines produce same
profit: 37,500 liters

Silver Screen Group owns and operates a chain of movie theaters. The 500 properties in the Silver Screen chain vary from low-volume, small-town, single-screen theaters to high-volume, urban, multi-screen theaters. The firm's management is considering installing popcorn machines, which would allow the theaters to sell freshly popped corn rather than prepopped corn. This new feature would be advertised to increase patronage at the company's theaters. The fresh popcorn will be sold for $1.75 per liter. The annual rental costs and the operating costs vary with the size of the popcorn machines. The machine capacities and costs are shown below.

	Popper Model		
	Economy	**Regular**	**Super**
Annual capacity	45,000 liters	90,000 liters	140,000 liters
Costs:			
Annual machine rental	$8,000	$11,000	$20,000
Popcorn cost per liter	.13	.13	.13
Other costs per liter	1.22	1.14	1.05
Cost of each liter	.08	.08	.08

Required:

1. Calculate each theater's break-even sales volume (measured in liters of popcorn) for each model of popcorn popper.
2. Prepare a profit-volume graph for one theater, assuming that the Super Popper is purchased.
3. Calculate the volume (in liters) at which the Economy Popper and the Regular Popper earn the same profit or loss in each movie theater.

(CMA, adapted)

■ **Problem 7–46**

CVP Analysis of Changes in
Sales Prices and Costs
(LO 1, 4)

3. New break-even point:
19,250 units
5. New contribution-margin
ratio: .40 (rounded)

Halong Game Company manufactures pocket electronic games. Last year Halong sold 25,000 games at $25 each. Total costs amounted to $525,000, of which $150,000 were considered fixed.

In an attempt to improve its product, the company is considering replacing a component part that has a cost of $2.50 with a new and better part costing $4.50 per unit in the coming year. A new machine also would be needed to increase plant capacity. The machine would cost $24,000 with a useful life of six years and no salvage value. The company uses straight-line depreciation on all plant assets.

Required:

1. What was Halong's break-even point in number of units last year?
2. How many units of product would the company have had to sell in the last year to earn operating income of $140,000?
3. If management holds the sales price constant and makes the suggested changes, how many units of product must be sold in the coming year to break even?
4. If the firm holds the sales price constant and makes the suggested changes, how many units of product will the company have to sell to make the same operating income as last year?
5. If Halong wishes to maintain the same contribution-margin ratio, what selling price per unit of product must it charge next year to cover the increased direct-material cost?

(CMA, adapted)

■ **Problem 7–47**

Continuation of Preceding
Problem; Activity-Based
Costing; Advanced
Manufacturing Systems;
Ethical Issues
(LO 4, 9, 10)

2. Break-even point: 17,500 units

Refer to the original data given for Halong Game Company in the preceding problem. An activity-based costing study has revealed that Halong's $150,000 of fixed costs include the following components:

Setup (40 setups at $400 per setup)	$ 16,000
Engineering (500 hours at $25 per hour)	12,500
Inspection (1,000 inspections at $30 per inspection)	30,000
General factory overhead	61,500
Total	$120,000
Fixed selling and administrative costs	30,000
Total fixed costs	$150,000

Management is considering the installation of new, highly automated manufacturing equipment that would significantly alter the production process. In addition, management plans a move toward just-in-time inventory and production management. If the new equipment is installed, setups will be quicker and less expensive. Under the proposed JIT approach, there would be 300 setups per year at $40 per setup. Since a total quality control program would accompany the move toward JIT, only 100 inspections would be anticipated annually, at a cost of $45 each. After the installation of the new production system, 800 hours of engineering would be required at a cost of $28 per hour. General factory overhead would increase to $176,100. However, the automated equipment would allow Halong to cut its unit variable cost by 20 percent. Moreover, the more consistent product quality anticipated would allow management to raise the price of electronic games to $26 per unit.

Required:

1. Upon seeing the ABC analysis given in the problem, Halong's vice president for manufacturing exclaimed to the controller, "I thought you told me this $150,000 cost was fixed. These don't look like fixed costs at all. What you're telling me now is that setup costs us $400 every time we set up a production run. Please explain."

   As Halong's controller, write a short memo explaining to the vice president what is going on.

2. Compute Halong's new break-even point if the proposed automated equipment is installed.

3. Determine how many units Halong will have to sell to show operating income of $140,000, assuming the new technology is adopted.

4. If Halong adopts the new manufacturing technology, will its break-even point be higher or lower? Will the number of sales units required to earn operating income of $140,000 be higher or lower? (Refer to your answers for the first two requirements of the preceding problem.) Are the results in this case consistent with what you would typically expect to find? Explain.

5. The decision as to whether to purchase the automated manufacturing equipment will be made by Halong's board of directors. In order to support the proposed acquisition, the vice president for manufacturing asked the controller to prepare a report on the financial implications of the decision. As part of the report, the vice president asked the controller to compute the new break-even point, assuming the installation of the equipment. The controller complied, as in requirement (2) of this problem.

   When the vice president for manufacturing saw that the break-even point would increase, he asked the controller to delete the break-even analysis from the report. What should the controller do? Which ethical standards for managerial accountants are involved here?

■ **Problem 7–48**
CVP Relationships; Retail
(LO 1, 4)

2. Decrease in operating income: $(1,400)

Condensed monthly income data for Thurber Book Stores are presented in the following table for November 20x1. (Ignore income taxes.)

	Mall Store	Downtown Store	Total
Sales	$80,000	$120,000	$200,000
Less: Variable expenses	32,000	84,000	116,000
Contribution margin	$48,000	$ 36,000	$ 84,000
Less: Fixed expenses	20,000	40,000	60,000
Operating income	$28,000	$ (4,000)	$ 24,000

Additional Information:

- Management estimates that closing the downtown store would result in a 10 percent decrease in mall store sales, while closing the mall store would not affect downtown store sales.

- One-fourth of each store's fixed expenses would continue through December 31, 20x2, if either store were closed.

- The operating results for November 20x1 are representative of all months.

Required:

1. Calculate the increase or decrease in Thurber's monthly operating income during 20x2 if the downtown store is closed.

2. The management of Thurber Book Stores is considering a promotional campaign at the downtown store that would not affect the mall store. Annual promotional expenses at the downtown store would be increased by $60,000 in order to increase downtown store sales by 10 percent. What

would be the effect of this promotional campaign on the company's monthly operating income during 20x2?

3. One-half of the downtown store's dollar sales are from items sold at their variable cost to attract customers to the store. Thurber's management is considering the deletion of these items, a move that would reduce the downtown store's direct fixed expenses by 15 percent and result in the loss of 20 percent of the remaining downtown store's sales volume. This change would not affect the mall store. What would be the effect on Thurber's monthly operating income if the items sold at their variable cost are eliminated?

4. *Build a spreadsheet:* Construct an Excel spreadsheet to solve all of the preceding requirements. Show how the solution will change if the following information changes: the downtown store's sales amounted to $126,000 and its variable expenses were $86,000.

(CMA, adapted)

■ **Problem 7–49**
CVP; Multiple Products;
Changes in Costs and Sales
Mix
(LO 4, 5)

2. Total sales to break even:
172,500 units
3. Weighted-average unit
contribution margin: $13.00

Chennai Tool Company (CTC) manufactures a line of electric garden tools that are sold in general hardware stores. The company's controller, T.R. Subramanian, has just received the sales forecast for the coming year for CTC's three products: hedge clippers, weeders, and leaf blowers. CTC has experienced considerable variations in sales volumes and variable costs over the past two years, and Subramanian believes the forecast should be carefully evaluated from a cost-volume-profit viewpoint. The preliminary budget information for 20x2 follows:

	Weeders	Hedge Clippers	Leaf Blowers
Unit sales	50,000	50,000	100,000
Unit selling price	$28	$36	$48
Variable manufacturing cost per unit	13	12	25
Variable selling cost per unit	5	4	6

For 20x2, CTC's fixed manufacturing overhead is budgeted at $2,160,000 and the company's fixed selling and administrative expenses are forecasted to be $600,000. CTC has a tax rate of 40 percent.

Required:

1. Determine CTC's budgeted after-tax net income for 20x2.

2. Assuming the sales mix remains as budgeted, determine how many units of each product CTC must sell in order to break even in 20x2.

3. After preparing the original estimates, management determined that its variable manufacturing cost of leaf blowers would increase by 20 percent, and the variable selling cost of hedge clippers could be expected to increase by $1.00 per unit. However, management has decided not to change the selling price of either product. In addition, management has learned that its leaf blower has been perceived as the best value on the market, and it can expect to sell three times as many leaf blowers as each of its other products. Under these circumstances, determine how many units of each product CTC would have to sell in order to break even in 20x2.

(CMA, adapted)

■ **Problem 7–50**
CVP Relationships;
International Business;
Automation
(LO 1, 4, 10)

3. Variable cost per ton: $275
per ton
6. Dollar sales required for
target operating income:
$1,140,000

Ohio Limestone Company produces thin limestone sheets used for cosmetic facing on buildings. The following income statement represents the operating results for the year just ended. The company had sales of 1,800 tons during the year. The manufacturing capacity of the firm's facilities is 3,000 tons per year.

OHIO LIMESTONE COMPANY
Income Statement
For the Year Ended December 31, 20x1

Sales	$900,000
Variable costs:	
Manufacturing	$315,000
Selling costs	180,000
Total variable costs	$495,000
Contribution margin	$405,000
Fixed costs:	
Manufacturing	$100,000
Selling	107,500
Administrative	40,000
Total fixed costs	$247,500
Operating income	$157,500

Required:

1. Calculate the company's break-even volume in tons for 20x1.

2. If the sales volume is estimated to be 2,100 tons in the next year, and if the prices and costs stay at the same levels and amounts, what is the operating income that management can expect for 20x2?

3. Ohio Limestone has been trying for years to get a foothold in the European market. The company has a potential German customer that has offered to buy 1,500 tons at $450 per ton. Assume that all of the firm's costs would be at the same levels and rates as in 20x1. What operating income would the firm earn if it took this order and rejected some business from regular customers so as not to exceed capacity?

4. Ohio Limestone plans to market its product in a new territory. Management estimates that an advertising and promotion program costing $61,500 annually would be needed for the next two or three years. In addition, a $25 per ton sales commission to the sales force in the new territory, over and above the current commission, would be required. How many tons would have to be sold in the new territory to maintain the firm's current operating income? Assume that sales and costs will continue as in 20x1 in the firm's established territories.

5. Management is considering replacing its labor-intensive process with an automated production system. This would result in an increase of $58,500 annually in fixed manufacturing costs. The variable manufacturing costs would decrease by $25 per ton. Compute the new break-even volume in tons and in sales dollars.

6. Ignore the facts presented in requirement (5). Assume that management estimates that the selling price per ton would decline by 10 percent next year. Variable costs would increase by $40 per ton, and fixed costs would not change. What sales volume in dollars would be required to earn operating income of $94,500 next year?

(CMA, adapted)

Alpine Ski Company recently expanded its manufacturing capacity. The firm will now be able to produce up to 15,000 pairs of cross-country skis of either the mountaineering model or the touring model. The sales department assures management that it can sell between 9,000 and 13,000 units of either product this year. Because the models are very similar, the company will produce only one of the two models.

The following information was compiled by the accounting department.

	Model	
	Mountaineering	**Touring**
Selling price per unit	$180.00	$162.50
Variable costs per unit	117.00	117.00

Fixed costs will total $693,000 if the mountaineering model is produced but will be only $540,650 if the touring model is produced. Alpine Ski Company is subject to a 40 percent income tax rate. (Round each answer to the nearest whole number.)

■ **Problem 7–51**
Cost-Volume-Profit Analysis with Income Taxes and Multiple Products (Appendix)
(LO 1, 2, 4, 5, 11)

3. Break-even point, mountaineering model: 11,000 units

Required:

1. Compute the contribution-margin ratio for the touring model.

2. If Alpine Ski Company desires an after-tax net income of $44,160, how many pairs of touring skis will the company have to sell?

3. How much would the variable cost per unit of the touring model have to change before it had the same break-even point in units as the mountaineering model?

4. Suppose the variable cost per unit of touring skis decreases by 10 percent, and the total fixed cost of touring skis increases by 10 percent. Compute the new break-even point.

5. Suppose management decided to produce both products. If the two models are sold in equal proportions, and total fixed costs amount to $616,825, what is the firm's break-even point in units?

(CMA, adapted)

■ **Problem 7–52**
CVP Analysis; Marketing
Decisions; Income Taxes
(Appendix)
(LO 1, 4, 11)

2. Required sales dollars to
break even: $19,692,308

Syracuse Telecom, Inc. manufactures telecommunications equipment. The company has always been production oriented and sells its products through agents. Agents are paid a commission of 15 percent of the selling price. Syracuse Telecom's budgeted income statement for 20x2 follows:

SYRACUSE TELECOM, INC.
Budgeted Income Statement
For the Year Ended December 31, 20x2
(in thousands)

Sales		$16,000
Manufacturing costs:		
Variable	$7,200	
Fixed overhead	2,340	9,540
Gross margin		$ 6,460
Selling and administrative expenses:		
Commissions	$2,400	
Fixed marketing expenses	140	
Fixed administrative expenses	1,780	4,320
Operating income		$ 2,140
Less fixed interest expense		540
Income before income taxes		$ 1,600
Less income taxes (30%)		480
Net income		$ 1,120

After the profit plan was completed for the coming year, Syracuse Telecom's sales agents demanded that the commissions be increased to 22½ percent of the selling price. This demand was the latest in a series of actions that Constantine Solomos, the company's president, believed had gone too far. He asked Ada Prokopiou, the most sales-oriented officer in his production-oriented company, to estimate the cost to Syracuse Telecom of employing its own sales force. Prokopiou's estimate of the additional annual cost of employing its own sales force, exclusive of commissions, follows. Sales personnel would receive a commission of 10 percent of the selling price in addition to their salary.

Estimated Annual Cost of
Employing a Company Sales Force
(in thousands)

Salaries:	
Sales manager	$ 100
Sales personnel	1,000
Travel and entertainment	400
Fixed marketing costs	900
Total	$2,400

Required:

1. Calculate Syracuse Telecom's estimated break-even point in sales dollars for 20x2.

    a. If the events that are represented in the budgeted income statement take place.

    b. If the company employs its own sales force.

2. If Syracuse Telecom continues to sell through agents and pays the increased commission of 22½ percent of the selling price, determine the estimated volume in sales dollars for 20x2 that would be required to generate the same net income as projected in the budgeted income statement.

3. Determine the estimated volume in sales dollars that would result in equal net income for 20x2 regardless of whether the company continues to sell through agents and pays a commission of 22½ percent of the selling price or employs its own sales force.

(CMA, adapted)

Cases

Dubai Medical Center operates a general hospital. The medical center also rents space and beds to separately owned entities rendering specialized services, such as Pediatrics and Psychiatric Care. Dubai Medical Center charges each separate entity for common services, such as patients' meals and laundry, and for administrative services, such as billings and collections. Space and bed rentals are fixed charges for the year, based on bed capacity rented to each entity. Dubai Medical Center charged the following costs to Pediatrics for the year ended June 30, 20x1:

■ **Case 7–53**
Break-Even Analysis; Hospital CVP Relationships
(LO 1, 4)

1. Contribution margin per patient day: $200
2. Increase in revenue: $540,000

	Patient Days (variable)	Bed Capacity (fixed)
Dietary	$ 600,000	—
Janitorial	—	$ 70,000
Laundry	300,000	—
Laboratory	450,000	—
Pharmacy	350,000	—
Repairs and maintenance	—	30,000
General and administrative	—	1,300,000
Rent	—	1,500,000
Billings and collections	300,000	—
Total	$2,000,000	$2,900,000

During the year ended June 30, 20x1, Pediatrics charged each patient an average of $300 per day, had a capacity of 60 beds, and had revenue of $6 million for 365 days. In addition, Pediatrics directly employed personnel with the following annual salary costs per employee: supervising nurses, $25,000; nurses, $20,000; and aides, $9,000.

Dubai Medical Center has the following minimum departmental personnel requirements, based on total annual patient days:

Annual Patient Days	Aides	Nurses	Supervising Nurses
Up to 22,000	20	10	4
22,001 to 26,000	25	14	5
26,001 to 29,200	31	16	5

Pediatrics always employs only the minimum number of required personnel. Salaries of supervising nurses, nurses, and aides are therefore fixed within ranges of annual patient days.

Pediatrics operated at 100 percent capacity on 90 days during the year ended June 30, 20x1. Administrators estimate that on these 90 days, Pediatrics could have filled another 20 beds above capacity. Dubai Medical Center has an additional 20 beds available for rent for the year ending June 30, 20x2. Such additional rental would increase Pediatrics' fixed charges based on bed capacity. (In the following requirements, ignore income taxes.)

Required:

1. Calculate the minimum number of patient days required for Pediatrics to break even for the year ending June 30, 20x2, if the additional 20 beds are not rented. Patient demand is unknown, but assume that revenue per patient day, cost per patient day, cost per bed, and salary rates will remain the same as for the year ended June 30, 20x1.

2. Assume that patient demand, revenue per patient day, cost per patient day, cost per bed, and salary rates for the year ending June 30, 20x2, remain the same as for the year ended June 30, 20x1. Prepare a schedule of Pediatrics' increase in revenue and increase in costs for the year ending June 30, 20x2. Determine the net increase or decrease in Pediatrics' earnings from the additional 20 beds if Pediatrics rents this extra capacity from Dubai Medical Center.

(CPA, adapted)

■ **Case 7–54**

CVP Analysis with Production and Marketing Decisions; Taxes (Appendix)
(LO 1, 4, 11)

1(b). To achieve after-tax profit objective, Oakley must sell 2,500 units
2. Alternative (3), after-tax profit: $204,000

Oakley Company manufactures and sells adjustable canopies that attach to motor homes and trailers. The market covers both new units as well as replacement canopies. Oakley developed its 20x2 business plan based on the assumption that canopies would sell at a price of $400 each. The variable cost of each canopy is projected at $200, and the annual fixed costs are budgeted at $100,000. Oakley's after-tax profit objective is $240,000; the company's tax rate is 40 percent.

While Oakley's sales usually rise during the second quarter, the May financial statements reported that sales were not meeting expectations. For the first five months of the year, only 350 units had been sold at the established price, with variable costs as planned. It was clear the 20x2 after-tax profit projection would not be reached unless some actions were taken. Oakley's president, Melanie Grand, assigned a management committee to analyze the situation and develop several alternative courses of action. The following mutually exclusive alternatives were presented to the president.

*   Reduce the sales price by $40. The sales organization forecasts that with the significantly reduced sales price, 2,700 units can be sold during the remainder of the year. Total fixed and variable unit costs will stay as budgeted.

*   Lower variable costs per unit by $25 through the use of less expensive raw materials and slightly modified manufacturing techniques. The sales price also would be reduced by $30, and sales of 2,200 units for the remainder of the year are forecast.

*   Cut fixed costs by $10,000 and lower the sales price by 5 percent. Variable costs per unit will be unchanged. Sales of 2,000 units are expected for the remainder of the year.

Required:

1. If no changes are made to the selling price or cost structure, determine the number of units that Oakley Company must sell

    a. In order to break even.

    b. To achieve its after-tax profit objective.

2. Determine which one of the alternatives Oakley Company should select to achieve its annual after-tax profit objective.

(CMA, adapted)

■ **Case 7–55**

Sales Commissions in a Wholesale Firm; Income Taxes (Appendix)
(LO 1, 2, 4, 11)

1. Break-even point: $500,000
3. New contribution-margin ratio: .15

Maple Leaf Sporting Goods Company, a wholesale supply company, engages independent sales agents to market the company's products throughout the United States and Canada. These agents currently receive a commission of 20 percent of sales, but they are demanding an increase to 25 percent of sales made during the year ending December 31, 20x2. The controller already prepared the 20x2 budget before learning of the agents' demand for an increase in commissions. The budgeted 20x2 income statement is shown below. Assume that cost of goods sold is 100 percent variable cost.

MAPLE LEAF SPORTING GOODS COMPANY
Budgeted Income Statement
For the Year Ended December 31, 20x2

Sales		$10,000,000
Cost of goods sold		6,000,000
Gross margin		$ 4,000,000
Selling and administrative expenses:		
Commissions	$2,000,000	
All other expenses (fixed)	100,000	2,100,000
Operating income		$ 1,900,000
Income tax (30%)		570,000
Net income		$ 1,330,000

The company's management is considering the possibility of employing full-time sales personnel. Three individuals would be required, at an estimated annual salary of $30,000 each, plus commissions of 5 percent of sales. In addition, a sales manager would be employed at a fixed annual salary of $160,000. All other fixed costs, as well as the variable cost percentages, would remain the same as the estimates in the 20x2 budgeted income statement.

Required:

1. Compute Maple Leaf Sporting Goods' estimated break-even point in sales dollars for the year ending December 31, 20x2, based on the budgeted income statement prepared by the controller.

2. Compute the estimated break-even point in sales dollars for the year ending December 31, 20x2, if the company employs its own sales personnel.

3. Compute the estimated volume in sales dollars that would be required for the year ending December 31, 20x2, to yield the same net income as projected in the budgeted income statement, if management continues to use the independent sales agents and agrees to their demand for a 25 percent sales commission.

4. Compute the estimated volume in sales dollars that would generate an identical net income for the year ending December 31, 20x2, regardless of whether Maple Leaf Sporting Goods Company employs its own sales personnel or continues to use the independent sales agents and pays them a 25 percent commission.

(CPA, adapted)

THIS CHAPTER'S FOCUS COMPANY is Quikmath.com, an Indian manu- Quikmath.com facturer of handheld calculators and other electronic gadgetry. Quikmath specializes in the school-age and college markets, producing products that are perceived as "educational," and virtually all of its sales are Web-based. In this chapter, we explore two product-costing systems called absorption and variable costing. Under absorption costing, all manufacturing costs, including fixed manufacturing overhead, are assigned as product costs and stored in inventory until the products are sold. Under variable costing, fixed manufacturing overhead is not included in inventory as a product cost. Instead, fixed manufacturing overhead is treated as a period cost, and it is expensed during the period in which it is incurred. The choice between absorption and variable costing arises only in manufacturing firms.

8 Absorption and Variable Costing

IN CONTRAST   >>>

In contrast to the absorption and variable costing systems discussed **Quikmath.com** in the first part of the chapter, we explore yet another product-costing method called throughput costing. We continue our illustration with Quikmath.com to explain how this product-costing method works. Throughput costing assigns only the unit-level spending for direct costs as the cost of a product. A unit-level cost is one that is incurred every time a unit is manufactured.

1 Explain the accounting treatment of fixed manufacturing overhead under absorption and variable costing.

2 Prepare an income statement under absorption costing.

3 Prepare an income statement under variable costing.

4 Reconcile reported income under absorption and variable costing.

5 Explain the implications of absorption and variable costing for cost-volume-profit analysis.

6 Evaluate absorption and variable costing.

7 Explain the rationale behind throughput costing.

8 Prepare an income statement under throughput costing.

Income is one of many important measures used to evaluate the performance of companies and segments of companies. There are two commonly used methods for determining product costs and reporting income in a manufacturing firm, depending on the accounting treatment of fixed manufacturing overhead. In this chapter, we will examine these two income-reporting alternatives, called *absorption costing* and *variable costing*. In addition, we will study a third alternative for product costing and income reporting, which is called *throughput costing*.

Product Costs

In the product-costing systems we have studied so far, manufacturing overhead is applied to Work-in-Process Inventory as a product cost along with direct material and direct labor. When the manufactured goods are finished, these product costs flow from Work-in-Process Inventory into Finished-Goods Inventory. Finally, during the accounting period when the goods are sold, the product costs flow from Finished-Goods Inventory into Cost of Goods Sold, an expense account. The following diagram summarizes this flow of costs.

Since the costs of production are stored in inventory accounts until the goods are sold, these costs are said to be *inventoried costs*.

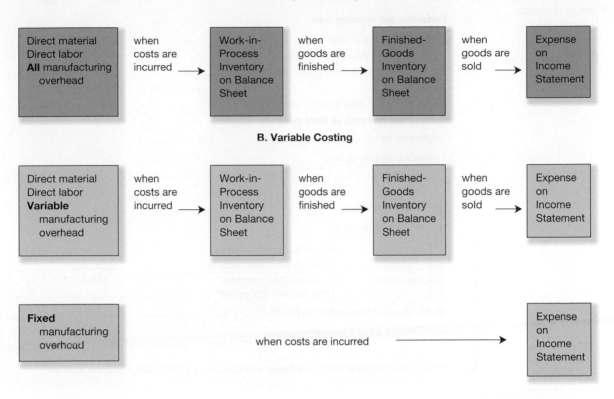

Exhibit 8–1
Absorption versus Variable Costing

Explain the accounting treatment of fixed manufacturing overhead under absorption and variable costing.

Fixed Manufacturing Overhead: The Key In our study of product-costing systems, we have included both variable and fixed manufacturing overhead in the product costs that flow through the manufacturing accounts. This approach to product costing is called **absorption costing** (or **full costing**), because *all* manufacturing-overhead costs are applied to (or absorbed by) manufactured goods. An alternative approach to product costing is called **variable costing** (or **direct costing**), in which *only variable* manufacturing overhead is applied to Work-in-Process Inventory as a product cost.

The distinction between absorption and variable costing is summarized in Exhibit 8–1. Notice that the distinction involves the *timing* with which fixed manufacturing overhead becomes an expense. Eventually, fixed overhead is expensed under both product-costing systems. Under variable costing, however, fixed overhead is expensed *immediately*, as it is incurred. Under absorption costing, fixed overhead is *inventoried* until the accounting period during which the manufactured goods are sold.

Illustration of Absorption and Variable Costing

Quikmath.com began operations in Hyderabad on January 1, 20x0, to manufacture hand-held electronic calculators. The company uses a standard-costing system. Cost, production, and sales data for the first three years of Quikmath's operations are given in Exhibit 8–2. Comparative income statements for 20x0, 20x1, and 20x2 are presented in Exhibit 8–3, using both absorption and variable costing.

Exhibit 8–2

Data for Illustration:
Quikmath.com

Quikmath.com

	20x0	20x1	20x2
Production and inventory data:			
Planned production (in units)	50,000	50,000	50,000
Finished-goods inventory (in units), January 1	–0–	–0–	15,000
Actual production (in units)	50,000	50,000	50,000
Sales (in units)	50,000	35,000	65,000
Finished-goods inventory (in units), December 31	–0–	15,000	–0–
Revenue and cost data, all three years:			
Sales price per unit			$12
Manufacturing costs per unit:			
Direct material			$ 3
Direct labor			2
Variable manufacturing overhead			1
Total variable cost per unit			$ 6

Used only under absorption costing

Fixed manufacturing overhead:

$$\text{Total absorption cost per unit} = \frac{\text{Budgeted annual fixed overhead} \quad \$150{,}000}{\text{Planned annual production*} \quad 50{,}000} = 3$$

Total absorption cost per unit			$ 9
Variable selling and administrative cost per unit			$ 1
Fixed selling and administrative cost per year			$25,000

*Planned annual production of 50,000 units is management's estimate of the company's practical capacity for production.

Learning Objective 2

Prepare an income statement under absorption costing.

The fixed costs of operating this manufacturing plant include such costs as the depreciation on plant and equipment, property taxes, insurance, and the salary of the plant manager. Fixed manufacturing costs are incurred in order to generate production capacity. Under absorption costing, these costs are treated as product costs and included in the cost of inventory. Under variable costing, they are expensed during the period incurred. Pictured here is a Kawasaki machine that presses steel at a heavy-duty truck factory in Maahshan, China.

Absorption-Costing Income Statements

Examine the absorption-costing income statements in the upper half of Exhibit 8–3. Two features of these income statements are highlighted in the left-hand margin. First, notice that the Cost of Goods Sold expense for each year is determined by multiplying the year's sales by the absorption manufacturing cost per unit, $9. Included in the $9 cost per unit is the predetermined fixed manufacturing-overhead cost of $3 per unit. Second, notice that on Quikmath's absorption-costing income statements, the only period expenses are the selling and administrative expenses. There is no deduction of fixed-overhead costs as a lump-sum period expense at the bottom of each income statement. As mentioned above, fixed manufacturing-overhead costs are included in Cost of Goods Sold on these absorption-costing income statements.

Variable-Costing Income Statements

Now examine the income statements based on variable costing in the lower half of Exhibit 8–3. Notice that the format of the statements is different from the format used in the absorption-costing statements. In the variable-costing statements, the contribution format is used to highlight the separation of variable and fixed costs. Let's focus

QUIKMATH.COM
Absorption-Costing Income Statement

		20x0	20x1	20x2
1	Sales revenue (at $12 per unit)	$600,000	$420,000	$780,000
	Less: Cost of goods sold (at absorption cost of $9 per unit)	450,000	315,000	585,000
	Gross margin	$150,000	$105,000	$195,000
	Less: Selling and administrative expenses:			
2 No fixed overhead	Variable (at $1 per unit)	50,000	35,000	65,000
	Fixed	25,000	25,000	25,000
	Operating income	$ 75,000	$ 45,000	$105,000

QUIKMATH.COM
Variable-Costing Income Statement

		20x0	20x1	20x2
	Sales revenue (at $12 per unit)	$600,000	$420,000	$780,000
1	Less: Variable expenses:			
	Variable manufacturing costs (at variable cost of $6 per unit)	300,000	210,000	390,000
	Variable selling and administrative costs (at $1 per unit)	50,000	35,000	65,000
	Contribution margin	$250,000	$175,000	$325,000
	Less: Fixed expenses:			
2	Fixed manufacturing overhead	150,000	150,000	150,000
	Fixed selling and administrative expenses	25,000	25,000	25,000
	Operating income	$ 75,000	$ 0	$150,000

Exhibit 8–3
Income Statements under Absorption and Variable Costing

Quikmath.com

Learning Objective 3
Prepare an income statement under variable costing.

on the same two aspects of the variable-costing statements that we discussed for the absorption-costing statements. First, the manufacturing expenses subtracted from sales revenue each year include only the variable costs, which amount to $6 per unit. Second, fixed manufacturing overhead is subtracted as a lump-sum period expense at the bottom of each year's income statement.

Reconciling Income under Absorption and Variable Costing

Examination of Exhibit 8–3 reveals that the income reported under absorption and variable costing is sometimes different. Although income is the same for the two product-costing methods in 20x0, it is different in 20x1 and 20x2. Let's figure out why these results occur.

No Change in Inventory In 20x0 there is no change in inventory over the course of the year. Beginning and ending inventory are the same, because actual production and sales are the same. Think about the implications of the stable inventory level for the treatment of fixed manufacturing overhead. On the variable-costing statement, the $150,000 of fixed manufacturing overhead incurred during 20x0 is an expense in 20x0. Under absorption costing, however, fixed manufacturing overhead was applied to production at the predetermined rate of $3 per unit. Since all of the units produced in 20x0 also were sold in 20x0, all of the fixed manufacturing-overhead cost flowed through into Cost of Goods Sold. Thus, $150,000 of fixed manufacturing overhead was expensed in 20x0 under absorption costing also.

Learning Objective 4
Reconcile reported income under absorption and variable costing.

Exhibit 8–4

Reconciliation of Income under Absorption and Variable Costing: Quikmath.com

Quik**math**.com

		20x0	20x1	20x2
1	Cost of goods sold under absorption costing	$450,000	$ 315,000	$585,000
	Variable manufacturing costs under variable costing	300,000	210,000	390,000
	Subtotal	$150,000	$ 105,000	$195,000
2	Fixed manufacturing overhead as period expense under variable costing	150,000	150,000	150,000
	Total	$ 0	$ (45,000)	$ 45,000
	Operating income under variable costing	$ 75,000	$ 0	$150,000
	Operating income under absorption costing	75,000	45,000	105,000
	Difference in operating income	$ 0	$ (45,000)	$ 45,000

The 20x0 column of Exhibit 8–4 reconciles the 20x0 operating income reported under absorption and variable costing. The reconciliation focuses on the two places in the income statements where differences occur between absorption and variable costing. The numbers in the left-hand margin of Exhibit 8–4 correspond to the numbers in the left-hand margin of the income statements in Exhibit 8–3.

Increase in Inventory   In 20x1 inventory increased from zero on January 1 to 15,000 units on December 31. The increase in inventory was the result of production exceeding sales. Under variable costing, the $150,000 of fixed overhead cost incurred in 20x1 is expensed, just as it was in 20x0. Under absorption costing, however, only a portion of the 20x1 fixed manufacturing overhead is expensed in 20x1. Since the fixed overhead is inventoried under absorption costing, some of this cost *remains in inventory* at the end of 20x1.

The 20x1 column of Exhibit 8–4 reconciles the 20x1 operating income reported under absorption and variable costing. As before, the reconciliation focuses on the two places in the income statements where differences occur between absorption and variable costing.

Decrease in Inventory   In 20x2 inventory decreased from 15,000 units to zero. Sales during the year exceeded production. As in 20x0 and 20x1, under variable costing, the $150,000 of fixed manufacturing overhead incurred in 20x2 is expensed in 20x2. Under absorption costing, however, *more than* $150,000 of fixed overhead is expensed in 20x2. Why? Because some of the fixed overhead incurred during the prior year, which was inventoried then, is now expensed in 20x2 as the goods are sold.

The 20x2 column of Exhibit 8–4 reconciles the 20x2 income under absorption and variable costing. Once again, the numbers on the left-hand side of Exhibit 8–4 correspond to those on the left-hand side of the income statements in Exhibit 8–3.

A Shortcut to Reconciling Income   When inventory increases or decreases during the year, reported income differs under absorption and variable costing. This results from the fixed overhead that is inventoried under absorption costing but expensed immediately under variable costing. The following formula may be used to compute the difference in the amount of fixed overhead expensed in a given time period under the two product-costing methods.[1]

$$\begin{pmatrix} \text{Difference in fixed overhead} \\ \text{expensed under absorption} \\ \text{and variable costing} \end{pmatrix} = \begin{pmatrix} \text{Change in} \\ \text{inventory,} \\ \text{in units} \end{pmatrix} \times \begin{pmatrix} \text{Predetermined} \\ \text{fixed-overhead} \\ \text{rate per unit} \end{pmatrix}$$

[1]This approach assumes that the predetermined fixed-overhead rate per unit does not change across time periods.

As the following table shows, this difference in the amount of fixed overhead expensed explains the difference in reported income under absorption and variable costing.

Year	Change in Inventory (in units)		Predetermined Fixed-Overhead Rate		Difference in Fixed Overhead Expensed		Absorption-Costing Income Minus Variable-Costing Income
20x0	–0–	×	$3	=	–0–	=	–0–
20x1	15,000 increase	×	$3	=	$ 45,000	=	$ 45,000
20x2	15,000 decrease	×	$3	=	$(45,000)	=	$(45,000)

Length of Time Period

The discrepancies between absorption-costing and variable-costing income in Exhibit 8–3 occur because of the changes in inventory levels during 20x1 and 20x2. It is common for production and sales to differ over the course of a week, month, or year. Therefore, the income measured for those time periods often will differ between absorption and variable costing. This discrepancy is likely to be smaller over longer time periods. Over the course of a decade, for example, Quikmath.com cannot sell much more or less than it produces. Thus, the income amounts under the two product-costing methods, when added together over a lengthy time period, will be approximately equal under absorption and variable costing.

Notice in Exhibit 8–3 that Quikmath.com's total income over the three-year period is $225,000 under *both* absorption and variable costing. This results from the fact that the company produced and sold the same total amount over the three-year period.

Cost-Volume-Profit Analysis

One of the tools used by managers to plan and control business operations is cost-volume-profit analysis, which we studied in Chapter 7. Quikmath.com's break-even point in units can be computed as follows:

$$\text{Break-even point} = \frac{\text{Fixed costs}}{\text{Unit contribution margin}} = \frac{\$150,000 + \$25,000}{\$12 - \$6 - \$1}$$

$$= \frac{\$175,000}{\$5} = 35,000 \text{ units}$$

If Quikmath.com sells 35,000 calculators, operating income should be zero, as Exhibit 8–5 confirms.

Learning Objective 5

Explain the implications of absorption and variable costing for cost-volume-profit analysis.

Exhibit 8–5
Break-Even Graph:
Quikmath.com

Quikmath.com

Now return to Exhibit 8–3 and examine the 20x1 income statements under absorption and variable costing. In 20x1 Quikmath.com sold 35,000 units, the break-even volume. This fact is confirmed on the variable-costing income statement, since operating income is zero. On the absorption-costing income statement, however, the 20x1 operating income is $45,000. What has happened here?

The answer to this inconsistency lies in the different treatment of fixed manufacturing overhead under absorption and variable costing. Variable costing highlights the separation between fixed and variable costs, as do cost-volume-profit analysis and break-even calculations. Both of these techniques account for fixed manufacturing overhead as a lump sum. In contrast, *absorption costing is inconsistent with CVP analysis,* because fixed overhead is applied to goods as a product cost on a per-unit basis.

Evaluation of Absorption and Variable Costing

Learning Objective 6

Evaluate absorption and variable costing.

Some managers find the inconsistency between absorption costing and CVP analysis troubling enough to warrant using variable costing for internal income reporting. Variable costing dovetails much more closely than absorption costing with any operational analyses that require a separation between fixed and variable costs.

Pricing Decisions   Many managers prefer to use absorption-costing data in cost-based pricing decisions. They argue that fixed manufacturing overhead is a necessary cost incurred in the production process. To exclude this fixed cost from the inventoried cost of a product, as is done under variable costing, is to understate the cost of the product. For this reason, most companies that use cost-based pricing base their prices on absorption-costing data.

Proponents of variable costing argue that a product's variable cost provides a better basis for the pricing decision. They point out that any price above a product's variable cost makes a positive contribution to covering fixed cost and profit.

Definition of an Asset   Another controversy about absorption and variable costing hinges on the definition of an asset. An *asset* is a thing of value owned by the organization with future service potential. By accounting convention, assets are valued at their cost. Since fixed costs comprise part of the cost of production, advocates of absorption costing argue that inventory (an asset) should be valued at its full (absorption) cost of production. Moreover, they argue that these costs have future service potential since the inventory can be sold in the future to generate sales revenue.

Proponents of variable costing argue that the fixed-cost component of a product's absorption-costing value has no future service potential. Their reasoning is that the fixed manufacturing-overhead costs during the current period will not prevent these costs from having to be incurred again next period. Fixed-overhead costs will be incurred every period, regardless of production levels. In contrast, the incurrence of variable costs in manufacturing a product does allow the firm to avoid incurring these costs again.

To illustrate, Quikmath.com produced 15,000 more calculators in 20x1 than it sold. These units will be carried in inventory until they are sold in some future year. Quikmath.com will never again have to incur the costs of direct material, direct labor, and variable overhead incurred in 20x1 to produce those calculators. Yet Quikmath.com will have to incur approximately $150,000 of fixed-overhead costs every year, even though the firm has the 15,000 units from 20x1 in inventory.

External Reporting   For external reporting purposes, generally accepted accounting principles require that income reporting be based on absorption costing. Federal tax laws also require the use of absorption costing in reporting income for tax purposes.

IRS: UNIQUE PRODUCT PACKAGING IS AN INVENTORIABLE COST

Most national tax authorities require the use of absorption costing for tax purposes. Thus, absorption costing must be used in valuing inventory and in determining cost-of-goods-sold expense, which in turn affects taxable income. In the United States, the Internal Revenue Service (IRS) defines inventoriable costs (i.e., product costs) that must be included in valuing inventory and cost-of-goods-sold expense to include the following: (1) direct material consumed in the production of the product and (2) direct labor, and (3) all indirect costs deemed to be necessary for the production of the company's product. These necessary indirect costs include fixed-overhead costs.

One interesting nuance in the IRS interpretation of what constitutes inventoriable costs concerns a company's expenditures on the design of the packaging for the company's products. Packaging design costs can run into hundreds of thousands of dollars for large consumer products companies. The IRS has specified that packaging design costs must be inventoried as product costs if the resulting design is successful—that is, it remains in use for several years. If, however, a package design fails in the marketplace, the company can deduct the package design costs early as an expense. Examples of unique packaging designs that would be affected by this ruling include Pringles potato chips cans, Yoplait yogurt containers, and Perrier sparkling water bottles.

Why Not Both? Using computerized accounting systems, it is straightforward for a company to prepare income statements under both absorption and variable costing. Since absorption-costing statements are required for external reporting, managers will want to keep an eye on the effects of their decisions on financial reports to outsiders. Yet the superiority of variable-costing income reporting as a method for dovetailing with operational analyses cannot be denied. Preparation of both absorption-costing and variable-costing data is perhaps the best solution to the controversy.

JIT Manufacturing Environment In a just-in-time inventory and production management system, all inventories are kept very low. Since finished-goods inventories are minimal, there is little change in inventory from period to period. Thus, in a JIT environment, the income differences under absorption and variable costing generally will be insignificant.

Throughput Costing

Some managers advocate *throughput costing* as an alternative to either absorption or variable costing for product costing and income reporting. **Throughput costing** assigns *only* the unit-level *spending* for direct costs as the cost of products or services. A unit-level cost is one that is incurred every time a unit of product is manufactured and will *not* be incurred if another unit is not manufactured.[2] Advocates of throughput costing argue that classifying any other past or committed cost as a product cost creates an

Learning Objective 7

Explain the rationale behind throughput costing.

---

[2]See Chapter 5 for a thorough discussion of the concept of unit-level costs and cost hierarchies in the context of an activity-based costing system.

incentive to drive down the average cost per unit simply by manufacturing more units on nonbottleneck processes.

Throughput-Costing Income Statements

Suppose Quikmath.com's management team decided that only direct material qualified as a throughput cost. This implies that Quikmath.com's management has *committed,* at least for the time being, to provide *all* other resources (i.e., direct labor and all manufacturing support costs included in manufacturing overhead) regardless of how many calculators and other devices Quikmath.com produces. Under throughput costing, then, Quikmath.com's income statements for the three years in our illustration would appear as in the Excel spreadsheet shown in Exhibit 8–6. Notice that all costs other than the throughput cost (only direct material in this hypothetical illustration) are considered to be operating cost of the period.

A comparison of the reported income under throughput costing (Exhibit 8–6) with the reported income under either variable or absorption costing (Exhibit 8–3) reveals substantial differences in the "bottom line" under the three methods for each year. Proponents of throughput costing argue that this method alone eliminates the incentive to produce excess inventory simply to reduce unit costs by spreading *committed* resource costs (i.e., direct labor and variable and fixed manufacturing overhead) across more units. The incentive for such overproduction disappears under throughput costing, because all nonthroughput costs (direct labor and manufacturing overhead in our illustration) will be expensed as period costs regardless of how many units are produced.

Exhibit 8–6
Income Statements under Throughput Costing

Quikmath.com

Microsoft Excel - Income Statements Under Throughput Costing

File Edit View Insert Format Tools Data Window Help   Type a question for help

E17   *fx* =E9-E16

	A	B	C	D	E
1	QUIKMATH.COM				
2	Throughput-Costing Income Statement				
3					
4			20x0	20x1	20x2
5					
6	Sales revenue (at $12 per unit)		$ 600,000	$ 420,000	$ 780,000
7	Less: Cost of goods sold (at throughput cost:				
8	standard direct-material cost)ᵃ		150,000	105,000	195,000
9	Gross margin		$ 450,000	$ 315,000	$ 585,000
10	Less: Operating costs:				
11	Direct laborᵇ		$ 100,000	$ 100,000	$ 100,000
12	Variable manufacturing overheadᶜ		50,000	50,000	50,000
13	Fixed manufacturing overheadᶜ		150,000	150,000	150,000
14	Variable selling and administrative costsᵈ		50,000	35,000	65,000
15	Fixed selling and administrative costsᵈ		25,000	25,000	25,000
16	Total operating costs		$ 375,000	$ 360,000	$ 390,000
17	Operating Income		$ 75,000	$ (45,000)	$ 195,000
18					
19	ᵃStandard direct-material cost per unit of $3 multiplied by sales volume in units.				
20					
21	ᵇAssumes management has committed to direct labor sufficient to produce the planned annual production				
22	volume of 50,000; direct-labor cost is used at a rate of $2 per unit produced.				
23					
24	ᶜAssumes management has committed to support resources sufficient to produce the planned annual				
25	production volume of 50,000 units; variable-overhead cost is used at a rate of $1 per unit produced. Fixed				
26	overhead is $150,000 per year.				
27					
28	ᵈVariable selling and administrative costs used amount to $1 per unit sold. Fixed selling and				
29	administrative costs are $25,000 per year.				

Sheet1 / Sheet2 / Sheet3 /

Ready

Focus on Ethics

INCENTIVE TO OVERPRODUCE INVENTORY

This classic case is based on an actual company's experience.* Brandolino Company uses an actual-cost system to apply all production costs to units produced. The plant has a maximum production capacity of 40 million units but produced and sold only 10 million units during year 1. There were no beginning or ending inventories. The company's absorption-costing income statement for year 1 follows:

BRANDOLINO COMPANY
Income Statement
For Year 1

Sales (10,000,000 units at $6)		$ 60,000,000
Cost of goods sold:		
Direct costs (material and labor)		
(10,000,000 at $2)	$20,000,000	
Manufacturing overhead	48,000,000	68,000,000
Gross margin		$ (8,000,000)
Less: Selling and administrative expenses		10,000,000
Operating profit (loss)		$(18,000,000)

The board of directors is upset about the $18 million loss. A consultant approached the board with the following offer: "I agree to become president for no fixed salary. But I insist on a year-end bonus of 10 percent of operating profit (before considering the bonus)." The board of directors agreed to these terms and hired the consultant as Brandolino's new president. The new president promptly stepped up production to an annual rate of 30 million units. Sales for year 2 remained at 10 million units. The resulting absorption-costing income statement for year 2 is displayed in the right-hand column.

The day after the year 2 statement was verified, the president took his check for $1,400,000 and resigned to take a job with another corporation. He remarked, "I enjoy challenges. Now that Brandolino Company is in the black, I'd prefer tackling another challenging situation." (His contract with his new employer is similar to the one he had with Brandolino Company.)

BRANDOLINO COMPANY
Income Statement
For Year 2

Sales (10,000,000 units at $6)		$60,000,000
Cost of goods sold:		
Costs of goods manufactured:		
Direct costs (material and labor)		
(30,000,000 at $2)	$ 60,000,000	
Manufacturing overhead	48,000,000	
Total cost of goods manufactured	$108,000,000	
Less: Ending inventory:		
Direct costs (material and labor)		
(20,000,000 at $2)	$ 40,000,000	
Manufacturing overhead		
(20/30 × $48,000,000)	32,000,000	
Total ending inventory costs	$ 72,000,000	
Cost of goods sold		36,000,000
Gross margin		$24,000,000
Less: Selling and administrative expenses		10,000,000
Operating profit before bonus		$14,000,000
Bonus		1,400,000
Operating profit after bonus		$12,600,000

What do you think is going on here? How would you evaluate the company's year 2 performance? Using variable costing, what would operating profit be for year 1? For year 2? (Assume that all selling and administrative costs are committed and unchanged.) Compare those results with the absorption-costing statements. Comment on the ethical issues in this scenario.

---

*This scenario is based on the case "I Enjoy Challenges," originally written by Michael W. Maher. It is used here with permission.

Chapter Summary

LO1 Explain the accounting treatment of fixed manufacturing overhead under absorption and variable costing. Under absorption (or full) costing, fixed overhead is applied to manufactured goods as a product cost. The fixed-overhead cost remains in inventory until the goods are sold. Under variable (or direct) costing, fixed overhead is a period cost expensed during the period when it is incurred.

LO2 Prepare an income statement under absorption costing. On an absorption-costing income statement, the cost of goods sold is measured at absorption cost (i.e., includes direct material, direct labor, and both variable and fixed manufacturing overhead) and, therefore, fixed overhead is not a period cost.

LO3 Prepare an income statement under variable costing. On a variable-costing income statement, the cost of goods sold is measured at variable cost (i.e., includes direct material, direct labor, and only variable manufacturing overhead), and fixed overhead is treated as a period cost.

LO4 Reconcile reported income under absorption and variable costing. Income reported under absorption and variable costing can be reconciled by focusing on the effects of the two places where the two statements differ: (1) calculation of cost of goods sold and (2) period costs.

LO5 Explain the implications of absorption and variable costing for cost-volume-profit analysis. Variable costing highlights the separation between fixed and variable costs, as do cost-volume-profit analysis and break-even calculations. Both of these techniques account for fixed manufacturing overhead as a lump-sum period cost. In contrast, absorption costing is inconsistent with CVP analysis, because fixed overhead is applied to goods as a product cost on a per-unit basis.

LO6 Evaluate absorption and variable costing. There are pros and cons to both costing methods. Variable costing dovetails much more closely than absorption costing with any operational analysis that requires a separation between fixed and variable costs (e.g., CVP analysis). On the other hand, variable costing understates a product's cost, because it excludes fixed manufacturing overhead from the unit cost calculation. In contrast, absorption costing alleviates that objection by including fixed overhead on a per-unit basis in a product's cost. However, this distorts the cost behavior of fixed costs, which do not in fact vary with production activity.

LO7 Explain the rationale behind throughput costing. Some accountants and managers advocate throughput costing, in which only throughput costs are inventoried as product costs. They argue that throughput costing reduces the incentive for management to produce excess inventory simply for the purpose of spreading committed (non-throughput) costs across a larger number of units produced.

LO8 Prepare an income statement under throughput costing. A throughput-costing income statement assigns only unit-level spending for direct costs as the cost of products or services. A unit-level cost is incurred every time a unit is manufactured and will not be incurred if another unit is not manufactured. All other costs are treated as period costs.

Review Problem on Absorption and Variable Costing

ScholasticPak Company manufactures backpacks used by students. A typical backpack has the following price and variable costs.

Sales price	$45
Direct material	15
Direct labor	6
Variable overhead	9

Budgeted fixed overhead in the company's first year of operations, was $900,000. Actual and planned production was 150,000 units, of which 125,000 were sold. ScholasticPak incurred the following selling and administrative expenses.

Fixed	$150,000 for the year
Variable	$3 per unit sold

Required:

1. Compute the product cost per backpack under (*a*) variable costing and (*b*) absorption costing.
2. Prepare income statements for the year using (*a*) variable costing and (*b*) absorption costing.
3. Reconcile the income reported under the two methods by analyzing the two key places where the income statements differ.

Solution to Review Problem

1. Predetermined fixed overhead rate $= \dfrac{\text{Budgeted fixed overhead}}{\text{Budgeted production}}$

$$= \frac{\$900,000}{150,000} = \$6 \text{ per unit}$$

Product Cost per Unit

Direct material	$15
Direct labor	6
Variable overhead	9
a. Cost per unit under variable costing	$30
Fixed overhead per unit under absorption costing	6
b. Cost per unit under absorption costing	$36

2. *a.*
Variable-Costing Income Statement

Sales revenue (125,000 units sold at $45 per unit)		$5,625,000
Less: Variable expenses:		
Variable manufacturing costs (at variable cost of $30 per unit)	3,750,000	
Variable selling and administrative costs (at $3 per unit × 125,000 units sold)	375,000	
Contribution margin		$1,500,000
Less: Fixed expenses:		
Fixed manufacturing overhead	900,000	
Fixed selling and administrative expenses	150,000	
Operating income		$ 450,000

b.
Absorption-Costing Income Statement

Sales revenue (125,000 units sold at $45 per unit)		$5,625,000
Less: Cost of goods sold (at absorption cost of $36 per unit)		4,500,000
Gross margin		$1,125,000
Less: Selling and administrative expenses:		
Variable (at $3 per unit × 125,000 units sold)	375,000	
Fixed	150,000	
Operating income		$ 600,000

3.

Cost of goods sold under absorption costing		$4,500,000
Less: Variable manufacturing costs under variable costing		3,750,000
Subtotal		$ 750,000
Less: Fixed manufacturing overhead as period expense under variable costing		900,000
Total		$ (150,000)
Operating income under variable costing		$ 450,000
Less: Operating income under absorption costing		600,000
Difference in operating income		$ (150,000)

Key Terms

For each term's definition refer to the indicated page, or turn to the glossary at the end of the text.

absorption (or **full**) costing, 361

throughput costing, 367

variable (or **direct**) costing, 361

Review Questions

8–1. Briefly explain the difference between absorption costing and variable costing.

8–2. Timing is the key in distinguishing between absorption and variable costing. Explain this statement.

8–3. The term *direct costing* is a misnomer. *Variable costing* is a better term for the product-costing method. Do you agree or disagree? Why?

8–4. When inventory increases, will absorption-costing or variable-costing income be greater? Why?

8–5. Why do many managers prefer variable costing over absorption costing?

8–6. Explain how throughput costing differs from absorption and variable costing.

8–7. Explain why some management accountants believe that absorption costing may provide an incentive for managers to overproduce inventory. How does throughput costing avoid this problem?

8–8. Will variable and absorption costing result in significantly different income measures in a JIT setting? Why?

8–9. Why do proponents of absorption costing argue that absorption costing is preferable as the basis for pricing decisions?

8–10. Why do proponents of variable costing prefer variable costing when making pricing decisions?

8–11. Which is more consistent with cost-volume-profit analysis, variable costing or absorption costing? Why?

8–12. Explain how the accounting definition of an asset is related to the choice between absorption and variable costing.

Exercises

All applicable Exercises are available with McGraw-Hill's *Connect Accounting*™.

■ **Exercise 8–13**
Difference in Income under Absorption and Variable Costing
(LO 1, 4)

Great Northern Ltd. produces fishing rods with a variable cost of $25. The fishing rods sell for $34. Budgeted fixed manufacturing overhead for the most recent year was $814,000. Actual production was equal to planned production.

Required: Under each of the following conditions, state (*a*) whether income is higher under variable or absorption costing and (*b*) the amount of the difference in reported income under the two methods. Treat each condition as an independent case.

1.	Production	110,000 units
	Sales	108,000 units
2.	Production	90,000 units
	Sales	95,000 units
3.	Production	79,200 units
	Sales	79,200 units

■ **Exercise 8–14**
Absorption, Variable, and Throughput Costing
(LO 1, 7)

Information taken from Yangtze Minerals Group's records for the most recent year is as follows:

Direct material used	$290,000
Direct labor	100,000
Variable manufacturing overhead	50,000
Fixed manufacturing overhead	80,000
Variable selling and administrative costs	40,000
Fixed selling and administrative costs	20,000

Required:

1. Assuming Yangtze Minerals Group uses variable costing, compute the inventoriable costs for the year.

2. Compute the year's inventoriable costs using absorption costing.

3. Now assume that Yangtze Minerals Group uses throughput costing, and the company has *committed* to spending for direct labor, variable overhead, and fixed overhead in the amounts given in the problem. Under this scenario, compute the company's inventoriable costs for the year.

(CMA, adapted)

Easton Pump Company's planned production for the year just ended was 20,000 units. This production level was achieved, and 21,000 units were sold. Other data follow:

Direct material used	$600,000
Direct labor incurred	300,000
Fixed manufacturing overhead	420,000
Variable manufacturing overhead	200,000
Fixed selling and administrative expenses	350,000
Variable selling and administrative expenses	105,000
Finished-goods inventory, January 1	2,000 units

There were no work-in-process inventories at the beginning or end of the year.

Required:

1. What would be Easton Pump Company's finished-goods inventory cost on December 31 under the variable-costing method?
2. Which costing method, absorption or variable costing, would show a higher operating income for the year? By what amount?

(CMA, adapted)

■ **Exercise 8–15**
Absorption and Variable Costing
(LO 1, 4)

Hungarian Down Pillow Company's planned production for the year just ended was 12,000 units. This production level was achieved, but only 9,000 units were sold. Other data follow:

Direct material used	$240,000
Direct labor incurred	60,000
Fixed manufacturing overhead	42,000
Variable manufacturing overhead	18,000
Fixed selling and administrative expenses	30,000
Variable selling and administrative expenses	6,000
Finished-goods inventory, January 1	None

There were no work-in-process inventories at the beginning or end of the year.

Required:

1. What would be Hungarian Down Pillow Company's finished-goods inventory cost on December 31 under the variable-costing method?
2. Which costing method, absorption or variable costing, would show a higher operating income for the year? By what amount?
3. Suppose Hungarian Down Pillow Company uses throughput costing, and direct material is its only unit-level cost. What would be Hungarian Down's finished-goods inventory on December 31?

■ **Exercise 8–16**
Absorption, Variable, and Throughput Costing
(LO 1, 4, 7)

Bianca Bicycle Company manufactures mountain bikes with a variable cost of $200. The bicycles sell for $350 each. Budgeted fixed manufacturing overhead for the most recent year was $2,200,000. Planned and actual production for the year were the same.

Required: Under each of the following conditions, state (*a*) whether income is higher under variable or absorption costing and (*b*) the amount of the difference in reported income under the two methods. Treat each condition as an independent case.

■ **Exercise 8–17**
Difference in Income under Absorption and Variable Costing
(LO 1, 4)

1.	Production	20,000 units
	Sales	23,000 units
2.	Production	10,000 units
	Sales	10,000 units
3.	Production	11,000 units
	Sales	9,000 units

■ **Exercise 8–18**
Variable Costing and
Cost-Volume-Profit Analysis
(LO 5)

Refer to the data given in the preceding exercise for Bianca Bicycle Company.

Required:

1. Prepare a cost-volume-profit graph for the company. (Scale the vertical axis in millions of dollars, and draw the CVP graph up through 15,000 units on the horizontal axis.)

2. Calculate Bianca Bicycle Company's break-even point in units, and show the break-even point on the CVP graph.

3. Explain why variable costing is more compatible with your CVP graph than absorption costing would be.

■ **Exercise 8–19**
Absorption versus Variable
Costing
(LO 1)

Information taken from Anatolian Pipe Company's records for the most recent year is as follows:

Direct material used	$420,000
Direct labor	90,000
Variable manufacturing overhead	75,000
Fixed manufacturing overhead	240,000
Variable selling and administrative costs	40,000
Fixed selling and administrative costs	37,000

Required:

1. Assuming Anatolian Pipe Company uses absorption costing, compute the inventoriable costs for the year.

2. Compute the year's inventoriable costs using variable costing.

(CMA, adapted)

■ **Exercise 8–20**
Absorption, Variable, and
Throughput Costing; Use of
Internet
(LO 1, 6)

Visit the Web site for one of the following companies, or a different company of your choosing.

Coca-Cola	www.cocacola.com
Yokohama Rubber Company	www.yrc.co.jp/english/
Motorola	www.motorola.com
Haier	www.haier.com
Toyota	www.toyota.com
Xerox Corporation	www.xerox.com

Required: Read about the company's products and operations. Discuss the pros and cons of absorption, variable, and throughput costing as the basis for product costing if the firm uses cost-based pricing.

Problems

All applicable Problems are available with McGraw-Hill's *Connect Accounting*™.

■ **Problem 8–21**
Straightforward Problem on
Absorption versus Variable
Costing
(LO 2, 3, 4)

2(a). Operating income:
$370,000
3. Cost of goods sold
under absorption costing:
$1,950,000

Delizioso S.p.A. produces gelato for distribution to restaurants. The product is sold in 10-liter containers, which have the following price and variable costs.

Sales price	$20
Direct material	6
Direct labor	4
Variable overhead	3

Budgeted fixed overhead in 20x1, the company's first year of operations, was $300,000. Planned and actual production was 150,000 10-liter containers, of which 130,000 were sold. Delizioso incurred the following selling and administrative expenses.

Fixed	$150,000 for the year
Variable	$1 per container sold

Required:

1. Compute the product cost per container of gelato under (*a*) variable costing and (*b*) absorption costing.

2. Prepare income statements for 20x1 using (*a*) absorption costing and (*b*) variable costing.

3. Reconcile the income reported under the two methods by listing the two key places where the income statements differ.

4. Reconcile the income reported under the two methods using the shortcut method.

5. *Build a spreadsheet:* Construct an Excel spreadsheet to solve all of the preceding requirements. Show how the solution will change if the following information changes: the selling price and direct-material cost per unit are $16.00 and $4.50, respectively.

Refer to the information given in the preceding problem for Delizioso S.p.A. Assume that the company has *committed* spending for direct labor and manufacturing overhead; direct material is the only unit-level production cost.

Required:

1. Compute the cost of Delizioso's year-end finished-goods inventory using throughput costing.

2. Prepare an income statement for 20x1 using throughput costing.

3. Briefly explain the difference between gross margin computed under absorption costing and gross margin computed under throughput costing.

4. *Build a spreadsheet:* Construct an Excel spreadsheet to solve requirement (2) above. Show how the solution will change if the following information changes: the selling price and direct-material cost per unit are $16.00 and $4.50, respectively.

■ **Problem 8–22**
Straightforward Problem on Throughput Costing
(LO 7, 8)

2. Operating income: $190,000

Everest Company began operations on January 1 to produce a single product. It used an absorption costing system with a planned production volume of 100,000 units. During its first year of operations, the planned production volume was achieved, and there were no fixed selling or administrative expenses. Inventory on December 31 was 20,000 units, and operating income for the year was $240,000.

Required:

1. If Everest Company had used variable costing, its operating income would have been $220,000. Compute the break-even point in units under variable costing.

2. Draw a profit-volume graph for Everest Company. (Use variable costing.)

■ **Problem 8–23**
Absorption and Variable Costing; CVP Analysis
(LO 2, 3, 4, 5)

1. Total contribution margin: $320,000
2. Break-even point: 25,000 units

Outback Corporation manufactures rechargeable flashlights in Brisbane, Australia. The firm uses an absorption costing system for internal reporting purposes; however, the company is considering using variable costing. Data regarding Outback's planned and actual operations for 20x1 follow:

■ **Problem 8–24**
Variable versus Absorption Costing; JIT
(LO 1, 4)

2. Budgeted variable manufacturing costs: $3,500,000
3. Increase in inventory (in units): 5,000 units

	Budgeted Costs		
	Per Unit	Total	Actual Costs
Direct material	$12.00	$1,680,000	$1,560,000
Direct labor	9.00	1,260,000	1,170,000
Variable manufacturing overhead	4.00	560,000	520,000
Fixed manufacturing overhead	5.00	700,000	715,000
Variable selling expenses	8.00	1,120,000	1,000,000
Fixed selling expenses	7.00	980,000	980,000
Variable administrative expenses	2.00	280,000	250,000
Fixed administrative expenses	3.00	420,000	425,000
Total	$50.00	$7,000,000	$6,620,000

	Planned Activity	Actual Activity
Beginning finished-goods inventory in units	35,000	35,000
Sales in units	140,000	125,000
Production in units	140,000	130,000

The budgeted per-unit cost figures were based on Outback producing and selling 140,000 units in 20x1. Outback uses a predetermined overhead rate for applying manufacturing overhead to its product. A total manufacturing overhead rate of $9.00 per unit was employed for absorption costing purposes in 20x1. Any overapplied or underapplied manufacturing overhead is closed to the Cost of Goods Sold account at the end of the year. The 20x1 beginning finished-goods inventory for absorption costing purposes was valued at the 20x0 budgeted unit manufacturing cost, which was the same as the 20x1 budgeted unit manufacturing cost. There are no work-in-process inventories at either the beginning or the end of the year. The planned and actual unit selling price for 20x1 was $70 per unit.

Required: Was Outback's 20x1 income higher under absorption costing or variable costing? Why? Compute the following amounts.

1. The value of Outback Corporation's 20x1 ending finished-goods inventory under absorption costing.

2. The value of Outback Corporation's 20x1 ending finished-goods inventory under variable costing.

3. The difference between Outback Corporation's 20x1 reported income calculated under absorption costing and calculated under variable costing.

4. Suppose Outback Corporation had introduced a JIT production and inventory management system at the beginning of 20x1.

    a. What would likely be different about the scenario as described in the problem?

    b. Would reported income under variable and absorption costing differ by the magnitude you found in requirement (3)? Explain.

(CMA, adapted)

■ **Problem 8–25**
Variable-Costing and Absorption-Costing Income Statements; FMS; JIT
(LO 2, 3, 4, 6)

1. Total variable cost: $61 per unit
2(b). Operating income: $451,000

Stars Above Ltd. manufactures telescopes, which sell for $95 each. The variable costs of production are as follows:

Direct material	$35
Direct labor	16
Variable manufacturing overhead	10

Budgeted fixed overhead in 20x1 was $210,000 and budgeted production was 30,000 telescopes. The year's actual production was 30,000 units, of which 27,000 were sold. Variable selling and administrative costs were $1 per unit sold; fixed selling and administrative costs were $230,000. The firm does not prorate variances.

Required:

1. Calculate the product cost per telescope under (a) absorption costing and (b) variable costing.

2. Prepare income statements for the year using (a) absorption costing and (b) variable costing.

3. Reconcile reported income under the two methods using the shortcut method.

4. Suppose that Stars Above Ltd. implemented a JIT inventory and production management system at the beginning of 20x1. In addition, the firm installed a flexible manufacturing system. Would you expect reported income under variable and absorption costing to be different by as great a magnitude as you found in requirement (3)? Explain.

■ **Problem 8–26**
Throughput Costing
(LO 7, 8)

2. Operating income: $370,000

Refer to the information given in the preceding problem for Stars Above Ltd. Assume that direct material is the *only unit-level* manufacturing cost. The company has *committed* its spending for direct labor and overhead (variable and fixed).

Required:

1. Calculate the product cost per telescope under throughput costing.

2. Prepare a 20x1 income statement using throughput costing.

3. Give an argument for and against throughput costing.

Xiamen Lighting Company had operating income for the first 10 months of the current year of $200,000. One hundred thousand units were manufactured during this period (the same as the planned production), and 100,000 units were sold. Fixed manufacturing overhead was $2,000,000 over the 10-month period (i.e., $200,000 per month). There are no selling and administrative expenses for Xiamen Lighting Company. Both variable and fixed costs are expected to continue at the same rates for the balance of the year (i.e., fixed costs at $200,000 per month and variable costs at the same variable cost per unit). Twenty thousand units are to be produced and 19,000 units are to be sold in total over the last two months of the current year. Assume the unit variable cost is the same in the current year as in the previous year. (*Hint:* You cannot calculate revenue or cost of goods sold; you must work directly with contribution margin or gross margin.)

Required:

1. If operations proceed as described, will operating income be higher under variable or absorption costing for the current year in total? Why?

2. If operations proceed as described, what will operating income for the year *in total* be under (*a*) variable costing and (*b*) absorption costing?

3. Discuss the advantages and disadvantages of absorption and variable costing.

■ **Problem 8–27**
Variable and Absorption Costing
(LO 1, 4)

2(a). Contribution margin per unit: $22
2(b). Projected operating income for the year under absorption costing: $178,000

Emerson Corporation, which uses throughput costing, just completed its first year of operations. Planned and actual production equaled 10,000 units, and sales totaled 9,600 units at $72 per unit. Cost data for the year are as follows:

Direct material (per unit)	$12
Conversion cost:	
Direct labor	45,000
Variable manufacturing overhead	65,000
Fixed manufacturing overhead	220,000
Selling and administrative costs:	
Variable (per unit)	8
Fixed	118,000

The company classifies only direct material as a throughput cost.

Required:

1. Compute the company's total cost for the year assuming that variable manufacturing costs are driven by the number of units produced, and variable selling and administrative costs are driven by the number of units sold.

2. How much of this cost would be held in year-end inventory under (*a*) absorption costing, (*b*) variable costing, and (*c*) throughput costing?

3. How much of the company's total cost for the year would be included as an expense on the period's income statement under (*a*) absorption costing, (*b*) variable costing, and (*c*) throughput costing?

4. Prepare Emerson's throughput-costing income statement.

5. *Build a spreadsheet:* Construct an Excel spreadsheet to solve requirements (1) and (2) above. Show how the solution will change if the following information changes: the direct-material cost is $11 per unit, and the total direct-labor cost is $46,000.

■ **Problem 8–28**
Throughput Costing, Absorption Costing, and Variable Costing
(LO 1, 2, 3, 7, 8)

1. Total cost: $644,800
2. Year-end inventory, throughput costing: $4,800
4. Operating income: $51,200

Warsaw Can Company manufactures metal cans used in the food-processing industry. A case of cans sells for $50. The variable costs of production for one case of cans are as follows:

Direct material	$15
Direct labor	5
Variable manufacturing overhead	12
Total variable manufacturing cost per case	$32

■ **Problem 8–29**
Variable-Costing and Absorption Costing Income Statements; Reconciling Reported Income
(LO 2, 3, 4)

1(a). Absorption cost per case is $42
1(b). Variable costing, operating income, year 2: $145,000

Variable selling and administrative costs amount to $1 per case. Budgeted fixed manufacturing overhead is $800,000 per year, and fixed selling and administrative cost is $75,000 per year. The following data pertain to the company's first three years of operation.

	Year 1	Year 2	Year 3
Planned production (in units)	80,000	80,000	80,000
Finished-goods inventory (in units), January 1	0	0	20,000
Actual production (in units)	80,000	80,000	80,000
Sales (in units)	80,000	60,000	90,000
Finished-goods inventory (in units), December 31	0	20,000	10,000

Actual costs were the same as the budgeted costs.

Required:

1. Prepare operating income statements for Warsaw Can Company for its first three years of operations using:

    a. Absorption costing.

    b. Variable costing.

2. Reconcile Warsaw Can Company's operating income reported under absorption and variable costing for each of its first three years of operation. Use the shortcut method.

3. Suppose that during Warsaw Can's fourth year of operation actual production equals planned production, actual costs are equal to budgeted or standard costs, and the company ends the year with no inventory on hand.

    a. What will be the difference between absorption-costing income and variable-costing income in year 4?

    b. What will be the relationship between total operating income for the four-year period as reported under absorption and variable costing? Explain.

■ **Problem 8–30**
Throughput Costing
(LO 7, 8)

Operating income, year 1:
$485,000

Refer to the information in the preceding problem for Warsaw Can Company. Assume that direct material is the *only unit-level* manufacturing cost.

Required: Prepare income statements for all three years using throughput costing.

Cases

■ **Case 8–31**
Comparison of Absorption
and Variable Costing; Actual
Costing
(LO 2, 3, 4)

1. Operating income, year 1:
$27,500
2. Operating income, year 2:
$20,500

Lucknow Lighting Ltd. manufactures blackboard chalk for educational uses. The company's product is sold by the box at $50 per unit. Lucknow Lighting uses an actual costing system, which means that the actual costs of direct material, direct labor, and manufacturing overhead are entered into work-in-process inventory. The actual application rate for manufacturing overhead is computed each year; actual manufacturing overhead is divided by actual production (in units) to compute the application rate. Information for Lucknow Lighting's first two years of operation is as follows:

	Year 1	Year 2
Sales (in units)	2,500	2,500
Production (in units)	3,000	2,000
Production costs:		
Variable manufacturing costs	$21,000	$14,000
Fixed manufacturing overhead	42,000	42,000
Selling and administrative costs:		
Variable	25,000	25,000
Fixed	20,000	20,000

Required: Lucknow Lighting Ltd. had no beginning or ending work-in-process inventories for either year.

1. Prepare operating income statements for both years based on absorption costing.
2. Prepare operating income statements for both years based on variable costing.
3. Prepare a numerical reconciliation of the difference in income reported under the two costing methods used in requirements (1) and (2).

Refer to the information given in the preceding case for Lucknow Lighting Ltd.

Required:

1. Reconcile Lucknow Lighting's income reported under absorption and variable costing, during each year, by comparing the following two amounts on each income statement:
   - Cost of goods sold
   - Fixed cost (expensed as a period expense)
2. What was Lucknow Lighting's total income across both years under absorption costing and under variable costing?
3. What was the total sales revenue across both years under absorption costing and under variable costing?
4. What was the total of all costs expensed on the income statements across both years under absorption costing and under variable costing?
5. Subtract the total costs expensed across both years [requirement (4)] from the total sales revenue across both years [requirement (3)]: (*a*) under absorption costing and (*b*) under variable costing.
6. Comment on the results obtained in requirements (1), (2), (3), and (4) in light of the following assertion: *Timing is the key in distinguishing between absorption and variable costing.*

Refer to the information given in Case 8–31 for Lucknow Lighting Ltd. Selected information from Lucknow Lighting's year-end balance sheets for its first two years of operation is as follows:

LUCKNOW LIGHTING LTD.
Selected Balance Sheet Information

Based on absorption costing	End of Year 1	End of Year 2
Finished-goods inventory	$10,500	$ 0
Retained earnings	16,500	24,600
Based on variable costing	**End of Year 1**	**End of Year 2**
Finished-goods inventory	$3,500	$ 0
Retained earnings	9,500	24,600

Required:

1. Why is the year 1 ending balance in finished-goods inventory higher if absorption costing is used than if variable costing is used?
2. Why is the year 2 ending balance in finished-goods inventory the same under absorption and variable costing?
3. Notice that the ending balance of finished-goods inventory under absorption costing is greater than or equal to the ending finished-goods inventory balance under variable costing *for both years 1 and 2*. Will this relationship always hold true at any balance sheet date? Explain.
4. Compute the amount by which the year-end balance in finished-goods inventory declined during year 2 (i.e., between December 31 of year 1 and December 31 of year 2):
   - Using the data from the balance sheet prepared under absorption costing.
   - Using the data from the balance sheet prepared under variable costing.
5. Refer to your calculations from requirement (4). Compute the difference in the amount by which the year-end balances in finished-goods inventory declined under absorption versus variable costing. Then compare the amount of this difference with the difference in the company's reported income for year 2 under absorption versus variable costing. (Refer to the income statements prepared in Case 8–31.)
6. Notice that the retained earnings balance at the end of both years 1 and 2 on the balance sheet prepared under absorption costing is greater than or equal to the corresponding retained earnings balance on the statement prepared under variable costing. Will this relationship hold true at any balance sheet date? Explain.

■ Case 8–32
Analysis of Differences in Absorption-Costing and Variable-Costing Income Statements; Continuation of Preceding Case
(LO 1, 6)

1. Cost of goods sold, year 1, absorption costing income statement: $52,500
Cost of goods sold, year 2, variable costing income statement: $17,500
5(a). Total sales revenue minus total costs expensed across both years, absorption costing: $41,000

■ Case 8–33
Absorption and Variable Costing; Effect on the Balance Sheet; Continuation of Preceding Case
(LO 1, 4)

4. Absorption costing, finished-goods inventory, end of year 1: $10,500
5. Variable costing, reported income for year 2, $20,500

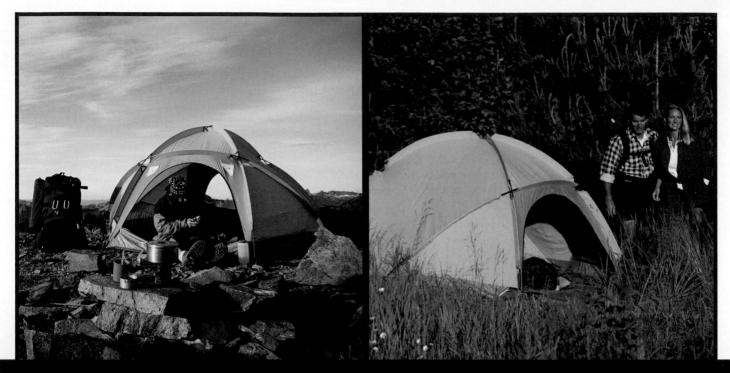

THIS CHAPTER'S FOCUS COMPANY is Cozycamp Company, a manufacturer of backpacking tents based in Berlin, Germany. Cozycamp uses a highly automated manufacturing process to produce its tents, and 75 percent of its sales are made through its Cozycamp.com Web site. In this chapter, we will explore how Cozycamp.com goes about developing its annual budget. A **budget**

cozycamp.com

is a detailed plan, expressed in quantitative terms, that specifies how resources will be acquired and used during a specific period of time. Cozycamp .com's management uses the budget for many purposes, including planning, communication, resource allocation, control of operations, evaluation of performance, and provision of incentives.

9 Profit Planning and Activity-Based Budgeting

In contrast to the manufacturing setting of Cozycamp.com, we explore budgeting at SportStudio. This service organization, located in Munich, Germany, operates as a cooperative. The members of the fitness club elect a board of directors who hire a manager and assistant manager to run the fitness club. SportStudio does not seek to make a profit. Each year, the membership fees are adjusted with the intention of bringing in just enough revenue to cover projected expenses. The fitness club's budget is an important part of that process.

SportStudio

1 List and explain five purposes of budgeting systems.

2 Describe the similarities and differences in the operational budgets prepared by manufacturers, service-industry firms, merchandisers, and nonprofit organizations.

3 Explain the concept of activity-based budgeting and the benefits it brings to the budgeting process.

4 Prepare each of the budget schedules that make up the master budget.

5 Discuss the role of assumptions and predictions in budgeting.

6 Describe a typical organization's process of budget administration.

7 Understand the importance of budgeting product life-cycle costs.

8 Discuss the behavioral implications of budgetary slack and participative budgeting.

Developing a budget is a critical step in planning any economic activity. This is true for businesses, for governmental agencies, and for individuals. We all must budget our money to meet day-to-day expenses and to plan for major expenditures, such as buying a car or paying for college tuition. Similarly, businesses of all types and governmental units at every level must make financial plans to carry out routine operations, to plan for major expenditures, and to help in making financial decisions.

Purposes of Budgeting Systems

Learning Objective 1

List and explain five purposes of budgeting systems.

A **budget** is a detailed plan, expressed in quantitative terms, that specifies how resources will be acquired and used during a specified period of time. The procedures used to develop a budget constitute a **budgeting system.** Budgeting systems have five primary purposes: planning; facilitating communication and coordination; allocating resources; controlling profit and operations; and evaluating performance and providing incentives.

Planning The most obvious purpose of a budget is to quantify a plan of action. The budgeting process forces the individuals who make up an organization to plan ahead. The development of a quarterly budget for a Le Meridien Hotel, for example, forces the hotel manager, the reservation manager, and the food and beverage manager to plan for the staffing and supplies needed to meet anticipated demand for the hotel's services.

Facilitating Communication and Coordination For any organization to be effective, each manager throughout the organization must be aware of the plans made by other managers. In order to plan reservations and ticket sales effectively, the reservations manager for Lufthansa Air Lines must know the flight schedules developed by the airline's route manager. The budgeting process pulls together the plans of each manager in an organization.

Allocating Resources Generally, an organization's resources are limited, and budgets provide one means of allocating resources among competing uses. The city of Amsterdam, for example, must allocate its revenue among basic life services (such as police and fire protection), maintenance of property and equipment (such as city streets, parks, and vehicles), and other community services (such as child-care services and programs to prevent alcohol and drug abuse).

Controlling Profit and Operations A budget is a plan, and plans are subject to change. Nevertheless, a budget serves as a useful benchmark with which actual results can be compared. For example, Allianz Insurance can compare its actual sales of insurance policies for a year against its budgeted sales. Such a comparison can help managers evaluate the firm's effectiveness in selling insurance. The next two chapters examine the control purpose of budgets in more depth.

> "Budgeting is used extensively for cost control. Each plant manager develops a plant budget, and then each department supervisor is responsible for his or her own cost center. . . . There are budgets for every department in the company." (9a)
>
> **Best Foods**
> (a subsidiary of Unilever)

Evaluating Performance and Providing Incentives Comparing actual results with budgeted results also helps managers evaluate the performance of individuals, departments, divisions, or entire companies. Since budgets are used to evaluate performance, they also can be used to provide incentives for people to perform well. For example, Renault Group, like many other companies, provides incentives for managers to improve profits by awarding bonuses to managers who meet or exceed their budgeted profit goals.

Types of Budgets

Different types of budgets serve different purposes. A **master budget,** or **profit plan,** is a comprehensive set of budgets covering all phases of an organization's operations for a specified period of time. We will examine a master budget in detail later in this chapter.

Budgeted financial statements, often called **pro forma financial statements,** show how the organization's financial statements will appear at a specified time if operations proceed according to plan. Budgeted financial statements include a *budgeted income statement, a budgeted balance sheet,* and *a budgeted statement of cash flows.*

A **capital budget** is a plan for the acquisition of capital assets, such as buildings and equipment. Capital budgeting is covered in depth later in the text. A **financial budget** is a plan that shows how the organization will acquire its financial resources, such as through the issuance of stock or incurrence of debt.

Budgets are developed for specific time periods. *Short-range budgets* cover a year, a quarter, or a month, whereas *long-range budgets* cover periods longer than a year. **Rolling budgets** are continually updated by periodically adding a new incremental time period, such as a quarter, and dropping the period just completed. Rolling budgets are also called **revolving budgets** or **continuous budgets.**

Diverse organizations use budgets for a variety of reasons. A cruise line, such as Carnival, uses budgets to plan for meeting the payroll and operating expenses and to coordinate operations by matching staffing with projected cruise demand. Carnival also uses its budgeting process to allocate capital improvement funds among competing projects, such as expanding its fleet or improving landside facilities.

Sales
Budget

Operational
Budgets

Budgeted
Financial
Statements

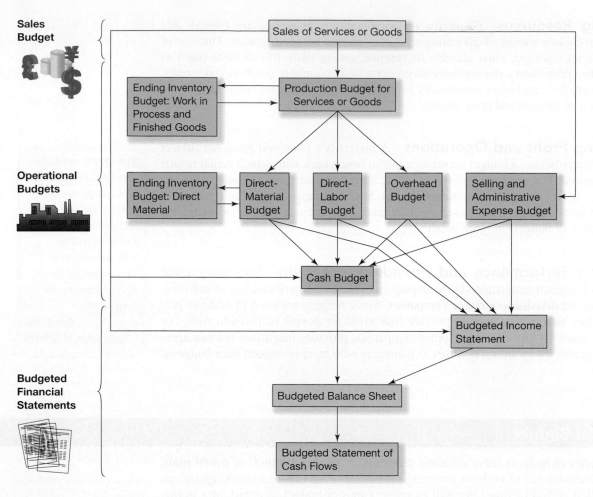

Exhibit 9–1
Components of a Master Budget

The Master Budget: A Planning Tool

The master budget, the principal output of a budgeting system, is a comprehensive profit plan that ties together all phases of an organization's operations. The master budget comprises many separate budgets, or schedules, that are interdependent. Exhibit 9–1 portrays these interrelationships in a flowchart.

Sales of Services or Goods

The starting point for any master budget is a sales revenue budget based on a sales forecast for services or goods. Airlines forecast the number of passengers on each of their routes. Banks forecast the number and dollar amount of consumer loans and home mortgages to be provided. Hotels forecast the number of rooms that will be occupied during various seasons. Manufacturing and merchandising companies forecast sales of their goods. Some companies sell both goods and services. For example, Sears is a large merchandising company, but its Sears Auto Service Centers provide the firm with substantial service revenue.

Sales Forecasting

All companies have two things in common when it comes to forecasting sales of services or goods. **Sales forecasting** is a critical step in the budgeting process, and it is very difficult to do accurately.

Various procedures are used in sales forecasting, and the final forecast usually combines information from many different sources. Many firms have a top-management-level market research staff whose job is to coordinate the company's sales forecasting efforts. Typically, everyone from key executives to the firm's sales personnel will be asked to contribute sales projections.

Major factors considered when forecasting sales include the following:

1. Past sales levels and trends:
   a. For the firm developing the forecast (for example, Royal Dutch Shell).
   b. For the entire industry (for example, the petroleum industry).
2. General economic trends. (Is the economy growing? How fast? Is a recession or economic slowdown expected?)
3. Economic trends in the company's industry. (In the petroleum industry, for example, is personal travel likely to increase, thereby implying increased demand for gasoline?)
4. Other factors expected to affect sales in the industry. (Is an unusually cold winter expected, which would result in increased demand for home heating oil in northern climates?)
5. Political and legal events. (For example, is any legislation pending in Congress that would affect the demand for petroleum, such as tax incentives to use alternative energy sources?)
6. The intended pricing policy of the company.
7. Planned advertising and product promotion.
8. Expected actions of competitors.
9. New products contemplated by the company or other firms. (For example, automobile manufacturers are continuing to develop hybrids, which run on a combination of gasoline and battery power, thereby reducing the demand for gasoline.)
10. Market research studies.

The starting point in the sales forecasting process is generally the sales level of the prior year. Then the market research staff considers the information discussed above along with input from key executives and sales personnel. In many firms, elaborate *econometric models* are built to incorporate all the available information systematically. (*Econometric* means economic measurement.) Statistical methods, such as regression analysis and probability distributions for sales, are often used. All in all, a great deal of effort generally goes into the sales forecast, since it is such a critical step in the budgeting process. Making a sales forecast is like shooting an arrow. If the archer's aim is off by only a fraction of an inch, the arrow will go further and further astray and miss the bull's eye by a wide margin. Similarly, a slightly inaccurate sales forecast, coming at the very beginning of the budgeting process, will throw off all of the other schedules comprising the master budget.

> "Historically, the personality types that drive sales and those that drive finance and operations are very different. They tend not to spend time with each other. And that's a mistake...The whole point of a forecast is that it's supposed to give you guideposts for what your actions are, how you allocate your resources, what you spend your time focusing on. At the very base of that, you need to involve the person who is out there actually driving the sale." (9b)
> **ePartners Inc.**

> "I see more and more forecasting and less time spent on what has happened." (9c)
> **Caterpillar**

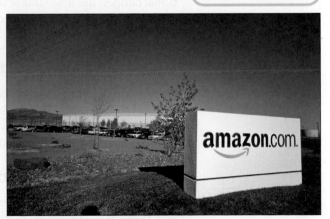

One advantage that "etailers," such as *Amazon.com*, have in the sales-forecasting process is the large amount of information collected online about their customers' buying patterns. This data, in theory at least, helps these firms in forecasting future sales.

Operational Budgets

Based on the sales budget, a company develops a set of **operational budgets** that specify how its operations will be carried out to meet the demand for its goods or services. The budgets constituting this operational portion of the master budget are depicted in the middle portion of Exhibit 9–1.

Manufacturing Firms   A manufacturing company develops a production budget, which shows the number of product units to be manufactured. Coupled with the production budget are ending-inventory budgets for raw material, work in process, and finished goods. Manufacturers plan to have some inventory on hand at all times to meet peak demand while keeping production at a stable level. From the production budget, a manufacturer develops budgets for the direct materials, direct labor, and overhead that will be required in the production process. A budget for selling and administrative expenses also is prepared.

Merchandising Firms   The operational portion of the master budget is similar in a merchandising firm, but instead of a production budget for goods, a merchandiser develops a budget for merchandise purchases. A merchandising firm will not have a budget for direct material, because it does not engage in production. However, the merchandiser will develop budgets for labor (or personnel), overhead, and selling and administrative expenses.

Service-Industry Firms   Based on the sales budget for its services, a service-industry firm develops a set of budgets that show how the demand for those services will be met. An airline, for example, prepares the following operational budgets: a budget of planned air miles to be flown; material budgets for spare aircraft parts, aircraft fuel, and in-flight food; labor budgets for flight crews and maintenance personnel; and an overhead budget.

Cash Budget   Every business prepares a cash budget. This budget shows expected cash receipts, as a result of selling goods or services, and planned cash disbursements, to pay the bills incurred by the firm.

Summary of Operational Budgets   Operational budgets differ since they are adapted to the operations of individual companies in various industries. However, operational budgets are also similar in important ways. In each firm, they encompass a detailed plan for using the basic factors of production—material, labor, and overhead—to produce a product or provide a service.

Budgeted Financial Statements

The final portion of the master budget, depicted in Exhibit 9–1, includes a budgeted income statement, a budgeted balance sheet, and a budgeted statement of cash flows. These budgeted financial statements show the overall financial results of the organization's planned operations for the budget period.

Nonprofit Organizations

The master budget for a nonprofit organization includes many of the components shown in Exhibit 9–1. However, there are some important differences. Many nonprofit organizations provide services free of charge. Hence, there is no sales budget as shown in Exhibit 9–1. However, such organizations do begin their budgeting process with a budget that shows the level of services to be provided. For example, the budget for the city of Houston would show the planned levels of various public services, such as the hours of operation for libraries and parks.

Nonprofit organizations also prepare budgets showing their anticipated funding. The city of Houston budgets for such revenue sources as city taxes, state and federal revenue sharing, and sale of municipal bonds.

In summary, all organizations begin the budgeting process with plans for (1) the goods or services to be provided and (2) the revenue to be available, whether from sales or from other funding sources.

ACTIVITY-BASED BUDGETING (ABB) AT AMERICAN EXPRESS AND AT&T PARADYNE

American Express has successfully used ABB for its travel-related services in its New York operations. This approach has been used to identify and implement cost reduction and process improvement initiatives. Then, an activity-by-activity analysis of each department has allowed process improvement savings to be factored into the forecasted costs for each department in the next budget cycle.[1]

AT&T Paradyne designs and produces medium- and high-speed data communications equipment, which provides an interface between telephone networks and computers. The company's activity-based costing project ultimately led to activity-based budgeting. As ABM and ABB matured at AT&T Paradyne, the company began to experience a culture change. A key lesson learned in this case was that linking activity-based costing to the budgeting process and performance evaluation led to the integration of ABC into the management of the company.[2]

Activity-Based Budgeting

The process of constructing a master budget can be significantly enhanced if the concepts of activity-based costing are applied.[3] Activity-based costing uses a two-stage cost-assignment process. In stage I, overhead costs are assigned to cost pools that represent the most significant *activities* constituting the production process. The activities identified vary across manufacturers, but such activities as engineering design, material handling, machine setup, production scheduling, inspection, quality control, and purchasing provide examples.

After assigning costs to the activity cost pools in stage I, cost drivers are identified that are appropriate for each cost pool. Then, in stage II, the overhead costs are allocated from each activity cost pool to cost objects (e.g., products, services, and customers) in proportion to the amount of activity consumed.

Exhibit 9–2 portrays the two-stage allocation process used in activity-based costing systems.

Applying ABC concepts to the budgeting process yields **activity-based budgeting (ABB).**[4] Under ABB, the first step is to specify the products or services to be produced and the customers to be served. Then the activities that are necessary to produce these products and services are determined. Finally, the resources necessary to perform the specified activities are quantified. Conceptually, ABB takes the ABC model and reverses the flow of the analysis, as depicted in Exhibit 9–3. As portrayed in the diagram, ABC assigns resource costs to activities, and then it assigns activity costs to

> **Learning Objective 3**
>
> Explain the concept of activity-based budgeting and the benefits it brings to the budgeting process.

> Commenting on how the company's ABC and ABM initiatives led to activity-based budgeting: "We are using ABM as a means to execute our strategic management process." (9d)
>
> **AT&T Paradyne Corporation**

---

[1]David M. Aldea and David E. Bullinger, "Using ABC for Shared Services, Charge-Outs, Activity-Based Budgeting, and Benchmarking," in *Activity-Based Management: Arthur Andersen's Lessons from the ABM Battlefield,* ed. Steve Player and David E. Keys (New York: John Wiley & Sons, 1999), pp. 138–45.

[2]Jay Collins, "Advanced Use of ABM: Using ABC for Target Costing, Activity-Based Budgeting, and Benchmarking," in *Activity-Based Management: Arthur Andersen's Lessons from the ABM Battlefield,* ed. Steve Player and David E. Keys (New York: John Wiley & Sons, 1999), pp. 152–58.

[3]Activity-based costing (ABC) was introduced conceptually in Chapter 3, and it is covered in depth in Chapter 5.

[4]This section is based on the following references: James A. Brimson and John Antos, *Driving Value Using Activity-Based Budgeting* (New York: John Wiley & Sons, 1999); Sofia Börjesson, "A Case Study on Activity-Based Budgeting," *Journal of Cost Management* 10, no. 4 (Winter 1997), pp. 7–18; and Robert S. Kaplan and Robin Cooper, *Cost and Effect* (Boston: Harvard Business School Press, 1998), pp. 301–15.

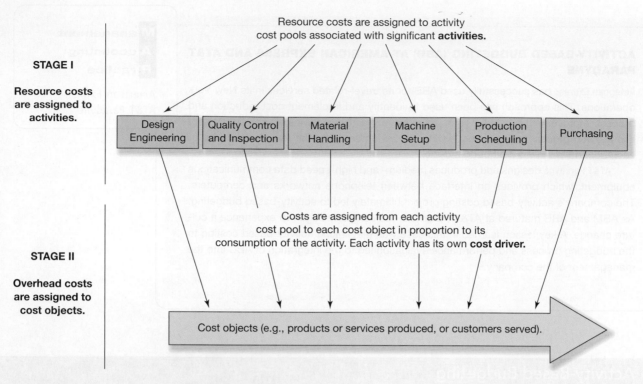

Exhibit 9–2
Activity-Based Costing
System

products and services produced and customers served. ABB, on the other hand, begins by forecasting the demand for products and services as well as the customers to be served. These forecasts then are used to plan the activities for the budget period and budget the resources necessary to carry out the activities.

In the next section of the chapter, we will illustrate the process of constructing a master budget. Notice how the conceptual activity-based budgeting model is employed in the budgeting process. In the context of the master-budget illustration, we will explore the benefits and implications of the ABB approach.

Exhibit 9–3
Activity-Based Costing versus
Activity-Based Budgeting

Source: Robert S. Kaplan and Robin Cooper, *Cost and Effect* (Boston: Harvard Business School Press, 1998), p. 303.

Using Activity-Based Budgeting to Prepare the Master Budget

To illustrate the steps in developing a master budget, or profit plan, we will focus on Cozycamp.com, a manufacturer of backpacking tents based in Berlin, Germany. The company is wholly owned by Annika Reusch, who started the company 15 years ago. After a difficult two to three years, success came quickly for the company, and Reusch eventually built a production facility outside Berlin. The manufacturing process is highly automated, using several machines to cut out pieces of tent fabric and sew them together to form a lightweight but durable backpacking tent. Production of the aluminum tent poles is outsourced to a company in Bratislava, Slovakia, and the poles are purchased on a just-in-time basis so they can be packaged with the finished tents just before they are shipped. Initially, Reusch called her firm Cozycamp Company, and its sales were made to regional retailers throughout Germany using a traditional sales approach. Three years ago, however, Reusch changed the company's name to Cozycamp.com and made a major foray into the world of Internet sales. Now almost 75 percent of Cozycamp.com's sales are made through the company's Web site and its customers are found throughout Europe. Although Cozycamp.com retained several of its sales personnel to handle the traditional sales to area retailers, new personnel had to be hired to handle the company's Internet sales environment. Tents are shipped to Internet customers via DHL, FedEx, and other express delivery services.

The 20x2 master budget for Cozycamp.com has just been completed. It contains the following schedules, which are displayed and explained in the following pages.

Learning Objective 4

Prepare each of the budget schedules that make up the master budget.

cozycamp.com

Schedule	Title of Schedule
1	Sales Budget
2	Production Budget
3	Direct-Material Budget
4	Direct-Labor Budget
5	Manufacturing-Overhead Budget
6	Selling, General, and Administrative Expense Budget
7	Cash Receipts Budget
8	Cash Disbursements Budget
9	Cash Budget
10	Budgeted Schedule of Cost of Goods Manufactured and Sold
11	Budgeted Income Statement
12	Budgeted Statement of Cash Flows
13	Budgeted Balance Sheet

Sales Budget

The first step in developing Cozycamp.com's 20x2 master budget is to prepare the **sales budget,** which is displayed as schedule 1. This budget displays the projected sales in units for each quarter and then multiplies the unit sales by the sales price to determine sales revenue. Notice that there is a significant seasonal pattern in the sales forecast, with the bulk of the sales coming in the spring and summer.

Schedule 1

cozycamp.com

COZYCAMP.COM
Sales Budget
For the Year Ending December 31, 20x2

	Quarter				
	1st	2nd	3rd	4th	Year
Sales in units	5,000	15,000	20,000	10,000	50,000
Unit sales price	× $225	× $225	× $225	× $225	× $225
Total sales revenue	$1,125,000	$3,375,000	$4,500,000	$2,250,000	$11,250,000

Production Budget

The **production budget** shows the number of units of services or goods that are to be produced during a budget period. Cozycamp.com's production budget, displayed as schedule 2, determines the number of tents to be produced each quarter based on the quarterly sales projections in the sales budget. Schedule 2 is based on the following formula.

$$\text{Sales in units} + \text{Desired ending inventory of finished goods} = \text{Total units required}$$

$$\text{Total units required} - \text{Expected beginning inventory of finished goods} = \text{Units to be produced}$$

Focus on the second-quarter column in schedule 2, which is shaded. Expected sales are 15,000 tents, and Reusch desires to have 2,000 finished units on hand at the end of the quarter. This is 10 percent of the expected sales for the third quarter. However, 1,500 tents are expected to be in inventory at the beginning of the second quarter. Thus, only 15,500 tents need to be produced.

Schedule 2

cozycamp.com

COZYCAMP.COM
Production Budget
For the Year Ending December 31, 20x2

	1st	2nd	3rd	4th	Year
	Quarter				
Sales in units (from schedule 1)	5,000	15,000	20,000	10,000	50,000
Add desired ending inventory of finished goods*	1,500	2,000	1,000	500†	500
Total units required	6,500	17,000	21,000	10,500	50,500
Less expected beginning inventory of finished goods	500	1,500	2,000	1,000	500
Units to be produced	6,000	15,500	19,000	9,500	50,000

*Ten percent of the next quarter's expected sales.

†Ten percent of the expected sales for the 1st quarter of the next year, 20x3, which is predicted to be 5,000 units.

Direct-Material Budget

The **direct-material budget** shows the number of units and the cost of material to be purchased and used during a budget period. Cozycamp.com's direct-material budget, which is displayed as schedule 3, has two sections: one for tent fabric and one for tent poles. As is true for almost all manufacturers, Cozycamp.com's direct-material cost is a unit-level cost.[5] Each tent requires 12 meters of fabric and one tent pole kit. The tent poles required for each tent are prepackaged in a kit by the vendor in Bratislava and delivered to Cozycamp.com on a just-in-time basis.[6] The top section of Cozycamp.com's direct-material budget shows the total amount of tent fabric needed to make tents during each quarter. The shaded portion of schedule 3 computes the amount of tent fabric to be purchased each quarter. This part of the schedule is based on the following formula.

---

[5]A unit-level cost is one that must be incurred each time a unit is produced.

[6]Just-in-time production and inventory control systems are covered in Chapter 5.

| Raw material required for production | + | Desired ending inventory of raw material | = | Total raw material required |
| | | | | |

| Total raw material required | − | Expected beginning inventory of raw material | = | Raw material to be purchased |

The darker-shaded portion of schedule 3 also computes the cost of each quarter's tent fabric purchases. (This information also will be needed later in the budgeting process, in schedule 10.)

The lower, lighter-shaded section of schedule 3 calculates the quantity and cost of tent pole kits to be purchased each quarter.

Finally, the last row of schedule 3 (shown in blue) totals the cost of tent fabric and tent pole kits to yield the total cost of raw material to be purchased each quarter.

Schedule 3

cozycamp.com

COZYCAMP.COM					
Direct-Material Budget					
For the Year Ending December 31, 20x2					
	Quarter				
	1st	**2nd**	**3rd**	**4th**	**Year**
Tent fabric:					
Tents to be produced (from schedule 2)	6,000	15,500	19,000	9,500	50,000
Raw material required per unit (meters of fabric)	× 12	× 12	× 12	× 12	× 12
Raw material required for production (meters)	72,000	186,000	228,000	114,000	600,000
Add desired ending inventory of raw material (meters)*	18,600	22,800	11,400	7,200[†]	7,200
Total raw material required	90,600	208,800	239,400	121,200	607,200
Less expected beginning inventory of raw material (meters)	7,200	18,600	22,800	11,400	7,200
Raw material to be purchased (meters)	83,400	190,200	216,600	109,800	600,000
Cost per meter	× $9	× $9	× $9	× $9	× $9
Total cost of tent fabric purchases	$750,600	$1,711,800	$1,949,400	$ 988,200	$5,400,000
Tent poles:					
Tents to be produced (from schedule 2)	6,000	15,500	19,000	9,500	50,000
Tent pole kits required per tent	× 1	× 1	× 1	× 1	× 1
Tent pole kits to be purchased[‡]	6,000	15,500	19,000	9,500	50,000
Cost per tent pole kit	× $20	× $20	× $20	× $20	× $20
Total cost of tent pole kit purchases	$120,000	$ 310,000	$ 380,000	$ 190,000	$1,000,000
Total cost of raw material purchases (fabric and poles)	$870,600	$2,021,800	$2,329,400	$1,178,200	$6,400,000

*Ten percent of the next quarter's expected raw material requirements.

[†]Ten percent of the expected raw material requirements for the 1st quarter of the next year, 20x3, which is assumed to be 72,000 meters. (Sales, and therefore production, is predicted to be the same in each quarter of 20x3 as in the corresponding quarter of 20x2.)

[‡]Since the tent pole kits are prepackaged by the vendor and delivered on a just-in-time basis, there is no need for buffer inventory stocks. Thus, the number of tent pole kits purchased each quarter is the same as the number needed each quarter.

Production and Purchasing: An Important Link   Notice the important link between planned production and purchases of raw material. This link is apparent in schedule 3, and it is also emphasized in the formula preceding the schedule. Let's focus on the second quarter. Since 15,500 tents are to be produced, 186,000 meters of tent material will be needed (15,500 tents times 12 meters per unit). In addition, Reusch desires to have 22,800 meters of material in inventory at the end of the quarter.[7] Thus, total needs are 208,800 meters. Does Cozycamp.com need to purchase this much raw material? No it does not, because 18,600 meters will be in inventory at the beginning of the quarter. Therefore, the firm needs to purchase only 190,200 meters of material during the quarter (208,800 meters less 18,600 meters in the beginning inventory).

Inventory Management   The linkage between planned production and raw material purchases is a particularly critical linkage in manufacturing firms. Thus, considerable effort is devoted to careful inventory planning and management. How did Reusch decide how much raw material to have in inventory at the end of each quarter? Examination of schedule 3 reveals that each quarter's desired ending inventory of raw material is 10 percent of the *material needed for production* in the next quarter. For example, 22,800 meters of raw material will be in inventory at the end of the second quarter, because 228,000 meters will be needed for production in the third quarter (22,800 = 10% × 228,000). The effect of this approach is to have a larger ending inventory when the next quarter's planned production is greater. Inventories are drawn down when the subsequent quarter's planned production is lower.

    Further discussion of inventory management can be found in Appendix III on page 814.

Direct-Labor Budget

The **direct-labor budget** shows the number of hours and the cost of the direct labor to be used during the budget period. Cozycamp.com's direct-labor budget is displayed as schedule 4. Based on each quarter's planned production, this schedule computes the amount of direct labor needed each quarter and the cost of the required labor. Cozycamp.com is a relatively small company, and owner Annika Reusch hires all of her direct-labor production employees on a part-time basis only. This allows Cozycamp.com to meet the labor demands of a given time period, which vary significantly with the seasonal pattern of demand and production. Thus, Cozycamp.com's direct labor may be adjusted up or down to meet short-term needs. As a result, direct labor for this company is a unit-level cost. As schedule 4 shows, each tent manufactured requires half an hour of direct labor.

A Note on Direct Labor and the Cost Hierarchy   Where direct labor belongs in the cost hierarchy depends on management's ability to adjust the organization's labor force to match short-term requirements, as well as management's attitude about making such adjustments.[8] Either for strategic business reasons or due to ethical concerns, many companies strive to maintain a relatively stable labor force. If production employees are retained when production declines, then direct labor will not be a unit-level cost. In the extreme case, where employees are virtually never laid off, direct labor becomes a facility-level, or general-operations-level, cost. Cozycamp.com's ability to easily adjust the total hours of its part-time workforce results in a unit-level designation for direct-labor cost in this situation.

---

[7]It often is desirable to have a buffer inventory just before a bottleneck manufacturing operation.

[8]A typical cost hierarchy includes costs incurred at the unit level, batch level, product-sustaining level, customer level, and facility or general-operations level. Cost hierarchies are discussed in detail in Chapter 5.

Schedule 4

	Quarter				
COZYCAMP.COM **Direct-Labor Budget** **For the Year Ending December 31, 20x2**					
	1st	2nd	3rd	4th	Year
Units to be produced (from schedule 2)	6,000	15,500	19,000	9,500	50,000
Direct-labor required per unit (hours)	× .5	× .5	× .5	× .5	× .5
Total direct-labor hours required	3,000	7,750	9,500	4,750	25,000
Direct-labor cost per hour	× $15	× $15	× $15	× $15	× $15
Total direct-labor cost	$45,000	$116,250	$142,500	$71,250	$375,000

cozycamp.com

Manufacturing-Overhead Budget

The **manufacturing-overhead budget** shows the cost of overhead expected to be incurred in the production process during the budget period. Cozycamp.com's manufacturing overhead budget, displayed as schedule 5, lists the expected cost of each overhead item by quarter. At the bottom of the schedule, the total budgeted overhead for each quarter is shown. Then each quarter's depreciation is subtracted to determine the total cash disbursements to be expected for overhead during each quarter. This cash disbursement information will be needed later in the budgeting process when the cash disbursements budget is constructed (schedule 8).

Activity-Based Budgeting and the Cost Hierarchy Cozycamp.com uses an activity-based budgeting (ABB) approach in the construction of the manufacturing-overhead budget. This budget explicitly uses activity-based costing information in that the budgeted costs for various overhead items are based on the expected quantity of the appropriate cost driver. For example, the cost driver used to budget setup costs is the number of production runs.

In Cozycamp.com's cost hierarchy, unit-level costs include indirect material and electricity used to run the production machinery.[9] Batch-level costs include machine setup, purchasing and material handling, and quality control and inspection. The cost driver for these costs is the number of production runs. A run typically produces 500 tents. Cozycamp.com's only product-level cost is design engineering. The company typically develops one new tent design each quarter. Each new design costs $1,200. The remaining overhead costs in schedule 5 are costs incurred at the facility, or general-operations, level.

Benefits of ABB Proponents of ABB believe that real, sustainable payoffs from activity-based costing and activity-based management will not be forthcoming until an organization's budgeting process embraces the ABM approach. Utilizing ABC information in the budgeting process provides solid reasoning for budgeting costs at particular levels, since the underlying ABC information is based explicitly on the relationships among cost drivers, activities, and resources consumed. Moreover, the resulting budget is more useful to management, because it reveals how cost levels will change if the predicted quantities of the cost drivers change. For example, what will happen to Cozycamp.com's setup costs in the 1st quarter if the quantity produced is 6,000 units as reflected in the budget (see schedule 5), but 15 production runs are used to produce these 6,000 units instead of 12 runs as specified in the budget? According to schedule 5, setup cost is $400 per production run ($4,800/12 runs). Therefore, 15 runs would result in $6,000 of setup

Learning Objective 3

Explain the concept of activity-based budgeting and the benefits it brings to the budgeting process.

---

[9]A typical cost hierarchy includes costs incurred at the unit level, batch level, product-sustaining level, customer level, and facility or general-operations level. Cost hierarchies are discussed in detail in Chapter 5.

cozycamp.com

cost in the first quarter, instead of $4,800 as forecast in the budget. This will be true even if 6,000 units are produced as forecast in the budget.[10]

Traditional budgeting processes, which do not embrace the ABB approach, often classify such costs as setup, purchasing and material handling, quality control and inspection, or design engineering as *fixed* costs, since they do not vary with the number of units produced. The ABB approach, however, recognizes that these costs are really *variable* if the budget analyst is careful to identify the appropriate cost driver with which each of these costs varies.

Schedule 5

COZYCAMP.COM
Manufacturing-Overhead Budget
For the Year Ending December 31, 20x2

	Quarter				
	1st	2nd	3rd	4th	Year
Unit-level costs:					
Units	*6,000*	*15,500*	*19,000*	*9,500*	*50,000*
Indirect material	$ 18,000	$ 46,500	$ 57,000	$ 28,500	$ 150,000
Electricity (for machinery)	6,000	15,500	19,000	9,500	50,000
Total unit-level costs	$ 24,000	$ 62,000	$ 76,000	$ 38,000	$ 200,000
Batch-level costs:					
Production runs	*12*	*31*	*38*	*19*	*100*
Setup	$ 4,800	$ 12,400	$ 15,200	$ 7,600	$ 40,000
Purchasing and material handling	7,200	18,600	22,800	11,400	60,000
Quality control and inspection	6,000	15,500	19,000	9,500	50,000
Total batch-level costs	$ 18,000	$ 46,500	$ 57,000	$ 28,500	$ 150,000
Product-level costs:					
New tent designs	*1*	*1*	*1*	*1*	*4*
Design engineering	$ 1,200	$ 1,200	$ 1,200	$ 1,200	$ 4,800
Total product-level costs	$ 1,200	$ 1,200	$ 1,200	$ 1,200	$ 4,800
Facility- and general-operations-level costs:					
Supervisory salaries	$ 52,500	$ 52,500	$ 52,500	$ 52,500	$ 210,000
Insurance and property taxes	11,300	11,300	11,300	11,300	45,200
Maintenance	47,500	47,500	47,500	47,500	190,000
Utilities	40,000	40,000	40,000	40,000	160,000
Depreciation	110,000	110,000	110,000	110,000	440,000
Total facility- and general-operations-level costs	$261,300	$261,300	$261,300	$261,300	$1,045,200
Total overhead	$304,500	$371,000	$395,500	$329,000	$1,400,000
Less depreciation	110,000	110,000	110,000	110,000	440,000
Total cash disbursements for overhead	$194,500	$261,000	$285,500	$219,000	$ 960,000

Selling, General, and Administrative (SG&A) Expense Budget

The **selling, general, and administrative (SG&A) expense budget** shows the planned amounts of expenditures for selling, general, and administrative expenses during the budget period. Cozycamp.com's selling, general, and administrative expense budget is displayed as schedule 6. This budget lists the expenses of administering the firm and selling its product.

---

[10]These management consulting firms specialize in ABC, ABM, ABB, and cost management systems.

Activity-Based Budgeting and the Cost Hierarchy Similar to the manufacturing-overhead budget, Cozycamp.com's SG&A expense budget reflects the activity-based budgeting (ABB) approach. Activity-based costing information was used to develop this budget. For example, the cost driver used to budget sales commissions (for sales in the firm's traditional market) is the number of units sold.

In Cozycamp.com's cost hierarchy, the only unit-level marketing expenses consist of sales commissions.[11] For Cozycamp's traditional sales through German retail outlets, sales personnel are paid commissions based on the number of units sold. The SG&A budget reflects a $5 commission paid on each tent sold through traditional outlets, which account for 25 percent of Cozycamp.com's sales. In the second quarter, for example, sales commissions are predicted to be $18,750 (15,000 tents × 25% traditional sales × $5).

The customer-level expenses incurred by Cozycamp.com are the sales personnel salaries, which differ depending on whether the customers are traditional retailers or Web shoppers. In order to sell its tents in the traditional marketplace, Cozycamp.com employs sales personnel who travel to the retailers throughout Germany and personally take orders. These sales personnel receive both a salary and sales commissions. (The sales commissions are unit-level expenses, as noted above.) To serve its Internet customers, Cozycamp .com employs computer operators to update the company's Web site and a couple of telephone operators to provide customer service over the phone. For example, some Internet customers are hesitant to give their credit card numbers to Cozycamp.com online, so they place their orders online and then phone in to an authorized telephone number to submit their credit card information.

The remainder of Cozycamp.com's selling, general, and administrative expenses are incurred at the facility or general-operations level.

Schedule 6

cozycamp.com

COZYCAMP.COM
Selling, General, and Administrative Expense Budget
For the Year Ending December 31, 20x2

	Quarter				
	1st	2nd	3rd	4th	Year
Unit-level expenses:					
Units	5,000	15,000	20,000	10,000	50,000
Sales commissions (traditional market)	$ 6,250	$ 18,750	$ 25,000	$ 12,500	$ 62,500
Total unit-level expenses	$ 6,250	$ 18,750	$ 25,000	$ 12,500	$ 62,500
Customer-level expenses:					
Sales personnel salaries (traditional market)	$ 16,000	$ 16,000	$ 16,000	$ 16,000	$ 64,000
Computer operator salaries	18,000	18,000	18,000	18,000	72,000
Telephone operator salaries	6,000	6,000	6,000	6,000	24,000
Total customer-level expenses	$ 40,000	$ 40,000	$ 40,000	$ 40,000	$ 160,000
Facility- and general-operations-level expenses:					
Sales manager's salary	$ 15,000	$ 15,000	$ 15,000	$ 15,000	$ 60,000
Media advertising	61,000	61,000	61,000	61,000	244,000
Administrative salaries	220,000	220,000	220,000	220,000	880,000
Total facility- and general-operations-level expenses	$296,000	$296,000	$296,000	$296,000	$1,184,000
Total expenses	$342,250	$354,750	$361,000	$348,500	$1,406,500

---

[11]A typical cost hierarchy includes costs incurred at the unit level, batch level, product-sustaining level, customer level, and facility, or general-operations, level. Cost hierarchies are discussed in detail in Chapter 5.

Cash Receipts Budget

The **cash receipts budget** details the expected cash collections during a budget period. Cozycamp.com's cash receipts budget is displayed as schedule 7. The firm collects 80 percent of its billings during the same quarter in which the sale is made, and another 18 percent in the following quarter. Two percent of each quarter's sales are expected to be uncollectible accounts.

Schedule 7

cozycamp.com

COZYCAMP.COM
Cash Receipts Budget
For the Year Ending December 31, 20x2

	Quarter				
	1st	2nd	3rd	4th	Year
Sales revenue (from schedule 1)	$1,125,000	$3,375,000	$4,500,000	$2,250,000	$11,250,000
Collections in quarter of sale (80% of revenue)	$ 900,000	$2,700,000	$3,600,000	$1,800,000	$ 9,000,000
Collections in quarter following sale (18% of prior quarter's revenue)*	405,000†	202,500	607,500	810,000	2,025,000
Total cash receipts	$1,305,000	$2,902,500	$4,207,500	$2,610,000	$11,025,000

*Two percent of each quarter's sales are expected to be uncollectible, as follows:

	Quarter				
	1st	2nd	3rd	4th	Year
Uncollectible accounts	$22,500	$67,500	$90,000	$45,000	$225,000

†The revenue in the prior quarter (i.e., the 4th quarter of 20x1) is assumed to be $2,250,000. Therefore, the $405,000 is 18% of $2,250,000.

How to Budget Cash Receipts   To understand how the cash receipts budget is prepared, let's focus again on the second quarter column, which is shaded. The $3,375,000 of total revenue comes directly from schedule 1, the sales budget (second column, last row). Since most of Cozycamp.com's sales are on account, not all of the second quarter's revenue will be collected during the second quarter. The cash that the firm will collect during the second quarter comprises two components, as depicted in the following diagram.

	1st Quarter	2nd Quarter
Total revenue	$1,125,000	$3,375,000
		× 80%
Collections in quarter of sale (80% of sales)		$2,700,000
	× 18%	
Collections in quarter following sale (18% of sales)		$202,500
Total cash receipts ($2,700,000 + $202,500)		$2,902,500

The second quarter's total cash receipts are the sum of $2,700,000 (80 percent of second quarter sales) and $202,500 (18 percent of first quarter sales).

One final point to notice is that 2 percent of each quarter's sales are not expected to be collected. Thus, the $67,500 of second quarter uncollectible accounts amounts to

2 percent of the second quarter's revenue ($67,500 = 2% × $3,375,000). Almost all of Cozycamp.com's uncollectible accounts relate to the company's traditional sales.

Cash Disbursements Budget

The **cash disbursements budget** details the expected cash payments during a budget period. Schedule 8 displays Cozycamp.com's cash disbursements budget. The darker-shaded, top portion shows the schedule of cash payments for raw material purchases, which are made on account. The company pays for 60 percent of its purchases on account during the quarter in which the purchase is made. The remaining 40 percent of each quarter's purchases are paid for during the quarter following the purchase.

The lighter-shaded, lower portion of schedule 8 shows all of Cozycamp.com's direct-labor, manufacturing overhead, and selling, general, and administrative expenditures.

Schedule 8

COZYCAMP.COM
Cash Disbursements Budget
For the Year Ending December 31, 20x2

	1st	2nd	3rd	4th	Year
		Quarter			
Cost of raw material purchases (from schedule 3)	$ 870,600	$2,021,800	$2,329,400	$1,178,200	$6,400,000
Cash payments for purchases made during the quarter (60% of current quater's purchases)	$ 522,360	$1,213,080	$1,397,640	$ 706,920	$3,840,000
Cash payments for prior quarter's purchases (40% of prior quarter's purchases)	471,280*	348,240	808,720	931,760	2,560,000
Total cash payments for raw material purchases	$ 993,640	$1,561,320	$2,206,360	$1,638,680	$6,400,000
Other cash disbursements					
Direct labor (schedule 4)	$ 45,000	$ 116,250	$ 142,500	$ 71,250	$ 375,000
Indirect material (schedule 5)	18,000	46,500	57,000	28,500	150,000
Electricity (schedule 5)	6,000	15,500	19,000	9,500	50,000
Setup (schedule 5)	4,800	12,400	15,200	7,600	40,000
Purchasing and material handling (schedule 5)	7,200	18,600	22,800	11,400	60,000
Quality control and inspection (schedule 5)	6,000	15,500	19,000	9,500	50,000
Design engineering (schedule 5)	1,200	1,200	1,200	1,200	4,800
Supervisory salaries (schedule 5)	52,500	52,500	52,500	52,500	210,000
Insurance and property taxes (schedule 5)	11,300	11,300	11,300	11,300	45,200
Maintenance (schedule 5)	47,500	47,500	47,500	47,500	190,000
Utilities (schedule 5)	40,000	40,000	40,000	40,000	160,000
Sales commissions (schedule 6)	6,250	18,750	25,000	12,500	62,500
Sales personnel (schedule 6)	16,000	16,000	16,000	16,000	64,000
Computer operators (schedule 6)	18,000	18,000	18,000	18,000	72,000
Telephone operators (schedule 6)	6,000	6,000	6,000	6,000	24,000
Sales manager (schedule 6)	15,000	15,000	15,000	15,000	60,000
Media advertising (schedule 6)	61,000	61,000	61,000	61,000	244,000
Administration (schedule 6)	220,000	220,000	220,000	220,000	880,000
Total of other cash disbursements	$ 581,750	$ 732,000	$ 789,000	$ 638,750	$2,741,500
Total cash disbursements	$1,575,390	$2,293,320	$2,995,360	$2,277,430	$9,141,500

*Forty percent of the purchases in the 4th quarter of the prior year, 20x1, which is assumed to be $1,178,200.

cozycamp.com

How to Budget Cash Disbursements

Cozycamp.com purchases raw material, direct labor, and various services. The raw material purchases are made on account, which means payment is not made in cash at the time of the purchase. The shaded top portion of schedule 8 shows the purchases on account. Let's focus on the second quarter column. The second quarter's raw material purchases on account amount to $2,021,800. Does the company pay for all of the $2,021,800 purchases on account during the same quarter? No, it does not. As the following diagram shows, the second quarter's actual cash payment for purchases made on account comprises two components.

The second quarter's total cash payments *for purchases made on account* are the sum of $1,213,080 (which relates to second quarter purchases on account) and $348,240 (which relates to first quarter purchases on account).

We are not finished with the second quarter's cash disbursements yet, because Cozycamp.com *also pays for some of its purchases in cash at the time of purchase.* These cash expenditures are detailed in the unshaded lower portion of schedule 8. The amounts are drawn from schedules 4, 5, and 6, which detail expenditures for direct-labor, manufacturing-overhead, and selling, general, and administrative expenses, respectively. For example, schedule 4 lists $116,250 for direct labor in the second quarter; schedule 5 lists $261,000 for cash expenditures on manufacturing-overhead costs; and schedule 6 lists $354,750 for selling, general, and administrative expenditures.

Finally, the last row in the cash disbursements budget (schedule 8) shows the total cash disbursements during each quarter. Thus, the $2,293,320 total payment in the second quarter is the sum of $1,561,320 (for raw material purchases on account) and $732,000 for other purchases made in cash.

Cash Budget: Combining Receipts and Disbursements

The **cash budget** details the expected cash receipts and disbursements during a budget period. Cozycamp.com's completed cash budget is displayed as schedule 9. The darker-shaded, top portion pulls together the cash receipts and cash disbursements detailed in schedules 7 and 8. The lower portion of schedule 9 discloses the company's plans to take out a short-term bank loan on January 2, 20x2, for the purpose of building an addition to its production facility. The pattern of construction payments reflects high outlays early in the year as the major construction takes place. The high payment in the fourth quarter is due to the costs of reconfiguring the production line after the addition is finished. The company will repay the loan (with interest) in four equal installments on the last day of each quarter in 20x2. The funds for this repayment will come from excess cash generated from operations during 20x2.

Also shown in schedule 9 are the interest payments on the short-term bank loan.

Schedule 9

cozycamp.com

COZYCAMP.COM					
Cash Budget					
For the Year Ending December 31, 20x2					
			Quarter		
	1st	2nd	3rd	4th	Year
Cash receipts (from schedule 7)	$1,305,000	$2,902,500	$4,207,500	$2,610,000	$11,025,000
Less cash disbursements (from schedule 8)	(1,575,390)	(2,293,320)	(2,995,360)	(2,277,430)	(9,141,500)
Change in cash balance during quarter due to operations	$ (270,390)	$ 609,180	$1,212,140	$ 332,570	$ 1,883,500
Proceeds from bank loan (1/2/x2)	1,000,000				1,000,000
Payments for construction of plant addition	(500,000)	(120,000)	(80,000)	(300,000)	(1,000,000)
Repayment of principal on bank loan (at the end of each quarter)	(250,000)	(250,000)	(250,000)	(250,000)	(1,000,000)
Interest on bank loan (at 10% per year)*	(25,000)	(18,750)	(12,500)	(6,250)	(62,500)
Change in cash balance during the year					$ 821,000
Cash balance 1/1/x2					10,000
Cash balance 12/31/x2					$ 831,000

*Interest computations:

Quarter	Unpaid Principal during the Quarter	Annual Interest Rate	Portion of Year	Interest Payment†
1st	$1,000,000	10%	1/4	$25,000‡
2nd	750,000	10%	1/4	18,750
3rd	500,000	10%	1/4	12,500
4th	250,000	10%	1/4	6,250

†Unpaid principal × Annual interest rate × 1/4.
‡$1,000,000 × .10 × 1/4 = $25,000.

Budgeted Schedule of Cost of Goods Manufactured and Sold

The **budgeted schedule of cost of goods manufactured and sold** details the direct material, direct-labor, and manufacturing-overhead costs to be incurred, and shows the cost of the goods to be sold during the budget period. Schedule 10 shows Cozycamp.com's budgeted schedule of cost of goods manufactured and sold. The following Excel spreadsheet shows how the cost of the beginning and ending inventories of finished goods in schedule 10 are determined. From schedule 2, we see that the expected beginning and ending inventories of finished goods for 20x2 consist of 500 units. The absorption manufacturing cost for one unit of product is $163.50. The direct-material cost per unit is $128.00 ($108.00 + $20.00) (schedule 3), and the unit direct-labor cost is $7.50 (schedule 4). Recall that the *absorption* cost includes the direct-material and direct-labor costs and an allocation of all manufacturing overhead costs (i.e., overhead at the unit, batch, product, and facility, or general-operations, levels). The overhead cost data come from schedule 5.

Schedule 10

cozycamp.com

COZYCAMP.COM Budgeted Schedule of Cost of Goods Manufactured and Sold For the Year Ending December 31, 20x2		
Direct material (see schedule 3 for details):		
Raw-material inventory, January 1	$ 64,800[a]	
Add: Purchases of raw material	6,400,000[b]	
Raw material available for use	$6,464,800	
Deduct: Raw-material inventory, December 31	64,800[a]	
Direct material used		$6,400,000[b]
Direct labor (see schedule 4 for details)		375,000
Manufacturing overhead (see schedule 5 for details)		1,400,000
Total manufacturing costs		$8,175,000
Add: Work-in-process inventory, January 1		0[c]
Subtotal		$8,175,000
Deduct: Work-in-process inventory, December 31		0[c]
Cost of goods manufactured		$8,175,000
Add: Finished-goods inventory, January 1		81,750[d]
Cost of goods available for sale		$8,256,750
Deduct: Finished-goods inventory, December 31		81,750[d]
Cost of goods sold		$8,175,000

[a]From schedule 3: 7,200 meters of tent fabric × $9 per meter, and zero inventory of tent pole kits.
[b]From schedule 3: $5,400,000 for tent fabric + $1,000,000 for tent pole kits.
[c]The company's production cycle is short enough that there is no work-in-process inventory at any time.
[d]From schedule 2: 500 units × $163.50 per unit, which is the absorption manufacturing cost per unit.

Budgeted Income Statement

The **budgeted income statement** shows the expected revenue and expenses for the budget period, assuming that planned operations are carried out. Cozycamp.com's budgeted income statement is displayed as schedule 11.

Schedule 11

cozycamp.com

COZYCAMP.COM Budgeted Income Statement For the Year Ending December 31, 20x2		
Sales revenue (from schedule 1)		$11,250,000
Less: Cost of goods sold (from schedule 10)		8,175,000
Gross margin		$ 3,075,000
Other expenses:		
Selling, general, and administrative expenses (from schedule 6)	$1,406,500	
Uncollectible accounts expense (from schedule 7: 2% × $11,250,000)*	225,000	
Interest expense (from schedule 9)*	62,500	
Total other expenses		1,694,000
Net income		$ 1,381,000

*Usually these two expenses would be included in selling, general, and administrative expenses. They are listed separately in our illustration because they were determined after the selling, general, and administrative expense budget had already been explained.

Budgeted Statement of Cash Flows

The **budgeted statement of cash flows** provides information about the expected sources and uses of cash for operating activities, investing activities, and financing activities during a particular period of time. Cozycamp.com's budgeted statement of cash flows for 20x2 is displayed as schedule 12. Notice that the format used in the budgeted statement of cash flows follows that specified under the *direct method* of preparing the statement, which is favored by both the International Accounting Standards Board (AISB) and the Financial Accounting Standards Board (FASB).[12] The format used in the statement of cash flows, which is a statement prepared by companies for *external* reporting purposes, generally differs from the format used in the cash receipts and cash disbursements budgets, which are prepared for *internal* use by management. Notice the differences in the format of schedule 11 when compared with schedules 7, 8, and 9. Notice also the greater detail in schedules 7, 8, and 9, which are designed for internal managerial use.

Schedule 12

cozycamp.com

COZYCAMP.COM
Budgeted Statement of Cash Flows
For the Year Ending December 31, 20x2

Cash flows from operating activities:		
Cash receipts from customers[a]		$11,025,000
Cash payments:		
To suppliers of raw material[b]	$6,400,000	
For direct labor[c]	375,000	
For manufacturing-overhead expenditures[d]	960,000	
For selling, general, and administrative expenses[e]	1,406,500	
For interest[f]	62,500	
Total cash payments		9,204,000
Net cash flow from operating activities		$ 1,821,000
Cash flows from investing activities:		
Construction of building addition[g]	(1,000,000)	
Net cash used by investing activities		(1,000,000)
Cash flows from financing activities:		
Principle of bank loan[f]	$1,000,000	
Repayment of bank loan[f]	(1,000,000)	
Net cash provided by financing activities		0
Net increase in cash and cash equivalents		$ 821,000
Balance in cash and cash equivalents, beginning of year		10,000
Balance in cash and cash equivalents, end of year		$ 831,000

[a]From Schedule 7. [e]From Schedule 6.
[b]From Schedule 8. [f]From Schedule 9.
[c]From Schedule 4. [g]From Schedule 9.
[d]From Schedule 5.

---

[12]The direct and indirect methods of preparing the statement of cash flows are covered in financial accounting texts. They also are covered in the supplement to this text entitled *The Statement of Cash Flows and Financial Statement Analysis,* which is available from the publisher. This supplement is *not* needed in order to understand the preparation of the budget, as explained in this chapter.

Exhibit 9–4
Balance Sheet for December
31, 20x1

cozycamp.com

COZYCAMP.COM Balance Sheet December 31, 20x1		
Assets		
Current assets:		
Cash		$ 10,000
Accounts receivable (net of allowance for uncollectible accounts)		405,000
Inventory:		
Raw material	$ 64,800	
Finished goods	81,750	
Supplies	42,000	
Total inventory		188,550
Total current assets		$ 603,550
Long-lived assets:		
Building	$8,200,000	
Equipment	2,280,000	
Less accumulated depreciation on building and equipment	(1,883,550)	
Building and equipment, net of accumulated depreciation		8,596,450
Total assets		$9,200,000
Liabilities and Owner's Equity		
Current liabilities:		
Accounts payable		$ 471,280
Total current liabilities		$ 471,280
Long-term liabilities:		
Note payable (non-interest bearing; due on December 31, 20x4)		4,100,000
Total liabilities		$4,571,280
Owner's equity		4,628,720
Total liabilities and owner's equity		$9,200,000

Budgeted Balance Sheet

The **budgeted balance sheet** shows the expected end-of-period balances for the company's assets, liabilities, and owner's equity, assuming that planned operations are carried out. Cozycamp.com's budgeted balance sheet for December 31, 20x2, is displayed as schedule 13. To construct this budgeted balance sheet, we start with the firm's balance sheet projected for the *beginning* of the budget year (Exhibit 9–4) and adjust each account balance for the changes expected during 20x2. These expected changes are reflected in the various 20x2 budget schedules.

Balance sheet December 31, 20x1 (Exhibit 9–4)	→	Expected changes in account balances during 20x2	→	Balance sheet December 31, 20x2 (schedule 13)

Explanations for the account balances on the budgeted balance sheet for December 31, 20x2, are given in the second half of schedule 13. Examine these explanations carefully. Notice how the budgeted balance sheet pulls together information from most of the schedules constituting the master budget.

Schedule 13

cozycamp.com

COZYCAMP.COM
Budgeted Balance Sheet
December 31, 20x2

Assets

Current assets:

Cash (from schedule 9)		$ 831,000
Accounts receivable (net of allowance for uncollectible accounts)		405,000[a]
Inventory:		
Raw material (from schedule 10)	$ 64,800	
Finished goods (from schedule 10)	81,750	
Supplies	42,000	
Total inventory		188,550
Total current assets		$ 1,424,550
Long-lived assets:		
Building	$9,200,000[b]	
Equipment	2,280,000	
Less accumulated depreciation on building and equipment	(2,323,550)[c]	
Building and equipment, net of accumulated depreciation		9,156,450
Total assets		$10,581,000

Liabilities and Owner's Equity

Current liabilities:

Accounts payable		$ 471,280[d]
Total current liabilities		$ 471,280
Long-term liabilities:		
Note payable (non-interest-bearing; due on December 31, 20x4)		4,100,000
Total liabilities		4,571,280
Owner's equity		6,009,720[e]
Total liabilities and owner's equity		$10,581,000

[a]From schedule 7: 4th quarter sales of $2,250,000 times 18% amounts to $405,000.

[b]Balance in the Building account on the December 31, 20x1, balance sheet, plus the $1,000,000 cost of the building construction project in 20x2 (schedule 9).

[c]Balance in the Accumulated Depreciation account on the December 31, 20x1, balance sheet, plus the $440,000 in depreciation during 20x2 (schedule 5).

[d]From schedule 8: 4th quarter raw-material purchases of $1,178,200 times 40% amounts to $471,280.

[e]Balance in Owner's Equity on the December 31, 20x1, balance sheet, plus the 20x2 budgeted net income of $1,381,000 (schedule 11).

Assumptions and Predictions Underlying the Master Budget

A master budget is based on many assumptions and estimates of unknown parameters. Some estimates tend to be quite accurate, while other predictions are much more difficult to make accurately.

To explore the role of assumptions and predictions in the budgeting process, let's turn our attention away from the manufacturing environment of Cozycamp.com and consider the budget prepared for SportStudio. This service organization, located in Munich, Germany, operates as a cooperative. The members of the club elect a board of directors who hire a manager and assistant manager to run the fitness club. Sport-Studio does not seek to make a profit. Each year the membership fees are adjusted

Learning Objective 5

Discuss the role of assumptions and predictions in budgeting

SportStudio

Exhibit 9–5
Annual Budget: SportStudio

Microsoft Excel - SportStudio - Annual Budget						
B20	=SUM(B11:B19)					

	A	B	C	D	E	F
1				SPORTSTUDIO		
2				ANNUAL BUDGET		
3				For the Year 20x6		
4						
5						
6		1st Quarter	2nd Quarter	3rd Quarter	4th Quarter	Year
7						
8	Revenue:					
9	Membership revenue:					
10	Individual adult memberships					
11	Monthly	$ 52,200	$ 36,000	$ 14,400	$ 52,200	$ 154,800
12	Annual	30,000	30,000	30,000	30,000	120,000
13	Family memberships					
14	Monthly	22,500	18,000	3,000	22,500	66,000
15	Annual	48,750	48,750	48,750	48,750	195,000
16	Youth/student memberships	9,000	8,100	900	9,000	27,000
17	Fees for professional space:					
18	Massage therapists	5,460	5,460	1,820	5,460	18,200
19	Nutritionists	3,640	3,640	1,300	3,640	12,220
20	Total revenue	$ 171,550	$ 149,950	$ 100,170	$ 171,550	$ 593,220
21						
22	Operating expenses:					
23	Salaries and wages:					
24	Administration	$ 20,000	$ 20,000	$ 20,000	$ 20,000	$ 80,000
25	Yoga/pilates instruction	14,700	13,200	4,200	14,700	46,800
26	Aerobics instruction	14,700	13,200	4,200	14,700	46,800
27	Weight training/fitness instruction	9,600	6,400	2,200	9,600	27,800
28	Personal trainers	6,400	4,200	1,200	6,400	18,200
29	Other instruction (e.g., racquetball)	5,400	3,400	800	5,400	15,000
30	Reception/cashier	13,650	13,650	7,800	13,650	48,750
31	Maintenance/custodial	13,000	13,000	13,000	13,000	52,000
32	Employee fringe benefits	29,235	26,115	16,020	29,235	100,605
33	Utilities:					
34	Electricity	3,000	3,000	1,800	3,000	10,800
35	Heat/air conditioning	2,500	2,500	2,500	2,500	10,000
36	Telephone	600	600	600	600	2,400
37	Satellite TV	450	450	450	450	1,800
38	Trash collection	200	200	200	200	800
39	Other	1,000	1,000	1,000	1,000	4,000
40	Insurance	3,200	3,200	3,200	3,200	12,800
41	Supplies	900	700	450	900	2,950
42	Administrative	800	800	800	800	3,200
43	Maintenance/repair	2,500	2,500	4,000	2,500	11,500
44	Property taxes	9,000	9,000	9,000	9,000	36,000
45	Advertising	1,100	1,100	500	1,100	3,800
46	Depreciation:					
47	Building	10,000	10,000	10,000	10,000	40,000
48	Equipment	2,500	2,500	2,500	2,500	10,000
49	Other	1,300	1,300	1,300	1,300	5,200
50	Total operating expenses	$ 165,735	$ 152,015	$ 107,720	$ 165,735	$ 591,205
51						
52	Revenue less operating expenses	$ 5,815	$ (2,065)	$ (7,550)	$ 5,815	$ 2,015

Sheet1 / Sheet2 / Sheet3 /

Ready

with the intention of bringing in just enough revenue to cover projected expenses. The fitness club's budget is an important part of that process.

SportStudio's annual budget is displayed in Exhibit 9–5. The fitness cooperative sells individual adult, family, and youth/student memberships. The individual adult and family memberships can be monthly or annual, with a significant price break offered on the annual memberships. The fitness cooperative also allows licensed massage therapists and nutritional counselors to meet clients in the club's facilities and charges a fee to the professional offering the service. The staff of the cooperative includes the following personnel: a manager and assistant manager to administer the operation; various part-time instructors who teach classes such as yoga, pilates, aerobic exercise, weight training, and proper use of the club's fitness equipment; reception and cashier personnel; and custodians. Other operating expenses include such items as utilities, insurance, supplies, maintenance, property taxes, advertising, and depreciation.

Notice the differences and similarities between the budgets for Cozycamp.com and SportStudio. Cozycamp.com's budgeted income statement (schedule 11 on page 400) subtracts cost of goods sold expense from sales revenue to calculate the gross margin. In contrast, SportStudio does not show cost of goods sold because the fitness cooperative does not sell a physical product. Nor does it show a gross margin. The SportStudio budget shows revenue from membership dues and rental of space to licensed massage therapists and nutritional counselors, and operating expenses. While Cozycamp.com's budget shows net income, the SportStudio budget refers to revenue less operating expenses. This emphasizes the fitness cooperative's status as a nonprofit enterprise.

There are also similarities between these two budgets. For example, both businesses experience significant seasonality in activity. Cozycamp.com sells more tents in the second and third quarters than in the first and fourth quarters. SportStudio sells more monthly memberships in the cold months (first and fourth quarters) than in the warmer months (second and third quarters). During quarters with increased sales activity, both businesses show correspondingly higher expenses.

Now let's briefly discuss some of the assumptions and predictions that are reflected in SportStudio's budget. First, the fitness club's managers have assumed that people will continue to use the club more in the colder months of the year than in the warmer months as they have in the past. Second, the managers have assumed that the split between monthly and annual memberships for both individuals and families will be about the same as in the past. Based on these assumptions, the managers have predicted membership sales for each quarter. For example, the budget reflects the following predictions for memberships and prices in the first and second quarters. Notice that the monthly memberships decline in the second quarter, whereas the annual memberships are constant across the entire year.

Membership Type	1st Quarter	2nd Quarter
Individual adult, monthly	290 @ $60 per month	200 @ $60 per month
Individual adult, annual	200 @ $600 per year	200 @ $600 per year
Family, monthly	50 @ $150 per month	40 @ $50 per month
Family, annual	130 @ $1,500 per year	130 @ $1,500 per year
Youth/student	100 @ $30 per month	90 @ $30 per month

The SportStudio budget reflects many other predictions, such as salaries, wage rates, electric and other utility rates, insurance and property tax rates, and so forth. Some of these predictions—property tax rates, for example—would likely be quite accurate. Other predictions would be more difficult, as, for example, the cost of natural gas for heating purposes due to its dependence on the weather.

Financial Planning Models

Managers must make assumptions and predictions in preparing budgets because organizations operate in a world of uncertainty. One way of coping with that uncertainty is to supplement the budgeting process with a *financial planning model*. A **financial planning model** is a set of mathematical relationships that express the interactions among the various operational, financial, and environmental events that determine the overall results of an organization's activities. A financial planning model is a mathematical expression of all the relationships expressed in the flowchart of Exhibit 9–1.

To illustrate this concept, focus on the following equation, which is used to budget SportStudio's employee fringe benefits.

(Employee fringe benefits) $= .30 \times$ (Total salaries and wages)

However, suppose the cooperative's managers are uncertain about this 30 percent estimate. A financial planning model might include the following equation instead.

(Employee fringe benefits) $= p \times$ (Total salaries and wages)

where $0 \leq p \leq 1.0$.

The budget staff can run the financial planning model as many times as desired on a computer, using a different value for p each time. Perhaps the following values would be tried: .29, .295, .30, .305, and .31. Now management can answer the question, What if employee fringe benefits cost 29 percent of salaries and wages? In a fully developed financial planning model, all of the key estimates and assumptions are expressed as general mathematical relationships. Then the model is run on a computer many times to determine the impact of different combinations of these unknown variables. "What if" questions can be answered about such unknown variables as inflation, interest rates, the value of the dollar, demand, competitors' actions, union demands in forthcoming wage negotiations, and a host of other factors. The widespread availability of personal computers and electronic-spreadsheet software has made financial planning models a more and more common management tool.

Budget Administration

Learning Objective 6

Describe a typical organization's process of budget administration.

In small organizations, the procedures used to gather information and construct a master budget are usually informal. In contrast, larger organizations use a formal process to collect data and prepare the master budget. Such organizations usually designate a **budget director** or **chief budget officer.** This is often the organization's controller. The budget director specifies the process by which budget data will be gathered, collects the information, and prepares the master budget. To communicate budget procedures and deadlines to employees throughout the organization, the budget director often develops and disseminates a **budget manual.** The budget manual states who is responsible for providing various types of information, when the information is required, and what form the information is to take. For example, the budget manual for a manufacturing firm might specify that each regional sales director is to send an estimate of the following year's sales, by product line, to the budget director by September 1. The budget manual also states who should receive each schedule when the master budget is complete.

A **budget committee,** consisting of key senior executives, often is appointed to advise the budget director during the preparation of the budget. The authority to give final approval to the master budget usually belongs to the board of directors, or a board of trustees in many nonprofit organizations. Usually the board has a subcommittee whose task is to examine the proposed budget carefully and recommend approval or any changes deemed necessary. By exercising its authority to make changes in the budget and grant final approval, the board of directors, or trustees, can wield considerable influence on the overall direction the organization takes.

As more and more companies operate globally, the Internet is playing an ever-greater role in the budgeting process. E-budgeting is an increasingly popular, Internet-based budgeting tool that can help streamline and speed up an organization's budgeting process. The *e* in **e-budgeting** stands for both *electronic* and *enterprisewide;* employees throughout an organization, at all levels and around the globe, can submit and retrieve budget information electronically via the Internet. Budgeting software is utilized and made available on the Web, so that budget information electronically submitted from any location is in a consistent companywide format. Managers in organizations using e-budgeting have found that it greatly streamlines the entire budgeting process. In the past, these organizations have compiled their master budgets on hundreds of spreadsheets, which had to

"Implementing a Web-based, enterprise-wide budgeting solution will help us develop business plans and allow our analysts to be proactive in monitoring quarterly results." (9f)
Toronto Dominion Bank

BUDGET ADMINISTRATION AT CORNELL UNIVERSITY

Cornell University's annual budget covers the period from July 1 through the following June 30. The budgeting process begins in October, when the deans and senior vice presidents have meetings to discuss the programs the university will conduct during the following budget year. The university's priorities in educational, research, and public service programs are established during these meetings. In early January, the university's budget director, together with other members of the Operating Plans Committee, settles on a set of assumptions to be used during the remainder of the budgeting process. These assumptions include such key forecasts as the next year's inflation rate, interest rates, and tuition levels. Based on these assumptions, the dean of each of Cornell's colleges or professional schools must develop a detailed budget for salaries and general expenses. These detailed budgets are prepared during January and February by the financial staff in each college or professional school. In March, the university president and provost review these budgets with the deans. After any needed revisions have been made, the budgets for the various colleges and professional schools are consolidated by the university controller's staff into a master budget. This budget is presented to the university's board of trustees in May for final approval.

be collected and integrated by the corporate controller's office. One result of this cumbersome approach was that a disproportionate amount of time was spent compiling and verifying data from multiple sources. Under e-budgeting, both the submission of budget information and its compilation are accomplished electronically by the Web-based budgeting software. Thus, e-budgeting is just one more area where the Internet has transformed how the workplace operates in the era of e-business.[13]

International Aspects of Budgeting

As the economies and cultures of countries throughout the world become intertwined, more and more companies are becoming multinational in their operations. Firms with international operations face a variety of additional challenges in preparing their budgets. First, a multinational firm's budget must reflect the translation of foreign currencies into the company's official corporate currency, which is usually determined by the location of the corporate headquaters or the stock exchange on which the company has its primary listing. Since almost all the world's currencies fluctuate in their relative values, this makes budgeting for those translations difficult. Although multinationals have sophisticated financial ways of hedging against such currency fluctuations, the budgeting task is still more challenging. Second, it is difficult to prepare budgets when inflation is high or unpredictable. Most countries occasionally experience periods of high inflation, and some coun-

As this photo from Thailand shows, McDonald's operates throughout the world. Multinational companies face special challenges in preparing their budgets.

tries have experienced hyperinflation, sometimes with annual inflation rates well over 100 percent. Predicting such high inflation rates is difficult and further complicates a

---

[13]Steve Hornyak, "Budgeting Made Easy," *Management Accounting* 80, no. 4 (October 1998), pp. 18–23.

multinational's budgeting process. Finally, the economies of all countries fluctuate in terms of consumer demand, availability of skilled labor, laws affecting commerce, and so forth. Companies with offshore operations face the task of anticipating such changing conditions in their budgeting processes.

Budgeting Product Life-Cycle Costs

Learning Objective **7**

Understand the importance of budgeting product life-cycle costs.

A relatively recent focus of the budgeting process is to plan for all of the costs that will be incurred throughout a product's life cycle, before a commitment is made to the product.[14] Product life-cycle costs encompass the following five phases in a product's life cycle

- Product planning and concept design.
- Preliminary design.
- Detailed design and testing.
- Production.
- Distribution and customer service.

In order to justify a product's introduction, the sales revenues it will generate over its life must be sufficient to cover all of these costs. Thus, planning these life-cycle costs is a crucial step in making a decision about the introduction of a new product. This is particularly true for firms with very short product life cycles, such as some products in the computer and electronics industries. When product life cycles are as short as a year or two, the firm does not have time to adjust its pricing strategy or production methods to ensure that the product turns a profit. Management must be fairly certain before a commitment is made to the product that its life-cycle costs will be covered. As Exhibit 9–6 shows, most of a product's life-cycle costs are committed rather early in the product's life. By the time the planning, design, and testing phases are complete, roughly 85 percent of this product's life-cycle costs have been committed, while only about 5 percent actually have been incurred.

---

[14]This section draws on Norm Raffish, "How Much Does That Product Really Cost?" in *Readings in Management Accounting,* 3d ed., ed. S. Mark Young (Upper Saddle River, NJ: Prentice Hall, 2001), pp. 61, 62; and Callie Berliner and James A. Brimson, eds., *Cost Management for Today's Advanced Manufacturing* (Boston: Harvard Business School Press, 1988).

Exhibit 9–6
Product Life-Cycle Costs and Cost Commitment for a Typical Product

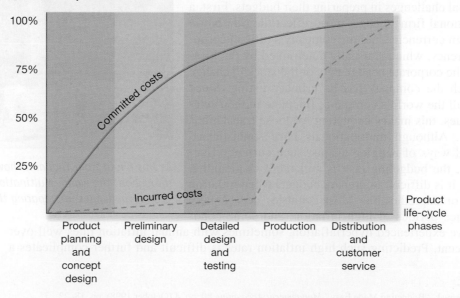

Life-Cycle Phase	Year				
	20x5	20x6	20x7	20x8	20x9
Product planning and concept design	$300,000				
Preliminary design	100,000				
Detail design and testing		$600,000			
Production		300,000	$2,000,000	$2,700,000	$1,200,000
Distribution and customer service		50,000	750,000	1,000,000	1,000,000

Exhibit 9–7
Product Life-Cycle Cost
Budget

Given the early commitment that must be made to significant downstream costs in a product's life cycle, it is crucial to budget these costs as early as possible.

Exhibit 9–7 displays a product life-cycle cost budget for an ancillary computer device with an anticipated five-year life cycle.

Behavioral Impact of Budgets

One of the underlying themes stressed in this text is the behavioral impact of managerial accounting practices. There is no other area where the behavioral implications are more important than in the budgeting area. A budget affects virtually everyone in an organization: those who prepare the budget, those who use the budget to facilitate decision making, and those who are evaluated using the budget. The human reactions to the budgeting process can have considerable influence on an organization's overall effectiveness.

A great deal of study has been devoted to the behavioral effects of budgets. Here we will barely scratch the surface by briefly considering two issues: budgetary slack and participative budgeting.

Learning Objective 8

Discuss the behavioral
implications of budgetary slack
and participative budgeting.

Budgetary Slack: Padding the Budget

The information upon which a budget is based comes largely from people throughout an organization. For example, the sales forecast relies on market research and analysis by market research staff but also incorporates the projections of sales personnel. If a territorial sales manager's performance is evaluated on the basis of whether the sales budget for the territory is exceeded, what is the incentive for the sales manager in projecting sales? The incentive is to give a conservative, or cautiously low, sales estimate. The sales manager's performance will look much better in the eyes of top management when a conservative estimate is exceeded than when an ambitious estimate is not met. At least that is the *perception* of many sales managers, and, in the behavioral area, perceptions are what count most.

When a supervisor provides a departmental cost projection for budgetary purposes, there is an incentive to overestimate costs. When the actual cost incurred in the department proves to be less than the inflated cost projection, the supervisor appears to have managed in a cost-effective way.

These illustrations are examples of **padding the budget.** Budget padding means underestimating revenue or overestimating costs. The difference between the revenue or cost projection that a person provides and a realistic estimate of the revenue or cost is called **budgetary slack.** For example, if a manager believes the annual utilities cost will be $18,000, but gives a budgetary projection of $20,000, the manager has built $2,000 of slack into the budget.

Why do people pad budgets with budgetary slack? There are three primary reasons. First, people often *perceive* that their performance will look better in their superiors' eyes if they can "beat the budget." Second, budgetary slack often is used to cope with uncertainty. A departmental supervisor may feel confident in the cost projections for 10 cost items. However, the supervisor also may feel that some unforeseen event during the budgetary period could result in unanticipated costs. For example, an unexpected machine breakdown could occur. One way of dealing with that unforeseen event is to pad the budget. If nothing goes wrong, the supervisor can beat the cost budget. If some negative event does occur, the supervisor can use the budgetary slack to absorb the impact of the event and still meet the cost budget.

The third reason why cost budgets are padded is that budgetary cost projections are often cut in the resource-allocation process. Thus, we have a vicious circle. Budgetary projections are padded because they will likely be cut, and they are cut because they are likely to have been padded.

How does an organization solve the problem of budgetary slack? First, it can avoid relying on the budget as a negative evaluation tool. If a departmental supervisor is harassed by the budget director or some other top manager every time a budgetary cost projection is exceeded, the likely behavioral response will be to pad the budget. In contrast, if the supervisor is allowed some managerial discretion to exceed the budget when necessary, there will be less tendency toward budgetary padding. Second, managers can be given incentives not only to achieve budgetary projections but also to *provide accurate projections*. This can be accomplished by asking managers to justify all or some of their projections and by rewarding managers who consistently provide accurate estimates.

Participative Budgeting

Most people will perform better and make greater attempts to achieve a goal if they have been consulted in setting the goal. The idea of **participative budgeting** is to involve employees throughout an organization in the budgetary process. Such participation can give employees the feeling that "this is our budget," rather than the all-too-common feeling that "this is the budget you imposed on us."

While participative budgeting can be very effective, it also can have shortcomings. Too much participation and discussion can lead to vacillation and delay. Also, when those involved in the budgeting process disagree in significant and irreconcilable ways, the process of participation can accentuate those differences. Finally, the problem of budget padding can be severe unless incentives for accurate projections are provided.

Focus on Ethics

IS PADDING THE BUDGET UNETHICAL?

A departmental or divisional budget often is used as the basis for evaluating a manager's performance. Actual results are compared with budgeted performance levels, and those who outperform the budget often are rewarded with promotions or salary increases. In many cases, bonuses are tied explicitly to performance relative to a budget. For example, the top-management personnel of a division may receive a bonus if divisional profit exceeds budgeted profit by a certain percentage.

Serious ethical issues can arise in situations where a budget is the basis for rewarding managers. For example, suppose a division's top-management personnel will split a bonus equal to 10 percent of the amount by which actual divisional profit exceeds the budget. This may create an incentive for the divisional budget officer, or other managers supplying data, to pad the divisional profit budget. Such padding would make the budget easier to achieve, thus increasing the chance of a bonus. Alternatively, there may be an incentive to manipulate the actual divisional

results in order to maximize management's bonus. For example, year-end sales could be shifted between years to increase reported revenue in a particular year. Budget personnel could have such incentives for either of two reasons: (1) they might share in the bonus or (2) they might feel pressure from the managers who would share in the bonus.

Put yourself in the position of the division controller. Your bonus, and that of your boss, the division vice president, will be determined in part by the division's income in comparison to the budget. When your division has submitted budgets in the past, the corporate management has usually cut your budgeted expenses, thereby increasing the division's budgeted profit. This, of course, makes it more difficult for your division to achieve the budgeted profit. Moreover, it makes it less likely that you and your divisional colleagues will earn a bonus.

Now your boss is pressuring you to pad the expense budget, because "the budgeted expenses will just be cut anyway at the corporate level." Is padding the budget ethical under these circumstances? What do you think?

Chapter Summary

LO1 List and explain five purposes of budgeting systems. The budget is a key tool for planning, control, and decision making in virtually every organization. The five purposes of budgeting systems are: to force planning, to facilitate communication and coordination, to allocate resources, to control profit and operations, and to evaluate performance and provide incentives.

LO2 Describe the similarities and differences in the operational budgets prepared by manufacturers, service industry firms, merchandisers, and nonprofit organizations. The key difference in the operational budgets of manufacturers and merchandisers versus service-industry and nonprofit organizations is that the operational budgets of manufacturers and merchandisers must account for the production or purchase and holding of inventory. In contrast, the budgets of service-industry and nonprofit organizations generally do not have inventories of manufactured or purchased inventories.

LO3 Explain the concept of activity-based budgeting and the benefits it brings to the budgeting process. Activity-based budgeting (ABB) applies the concepts of activity-based costing (ABC) to the budgeting process. Utilizing ABC information in the budgeting process through ABB provides sound information for budgeting costs, because the underlying ABC information is based explicitly on the relationships among cost drivers, activities, and resources consumed.

LO4 Prepare each of the budget schedules that make up the master budget. As shown in the chapter, the master budget includes the following key budget schedules: sales; production; direct-material; direct-labor; manufacturing overhead; selling, general, and administrative expense; cash receipts; cash disbursements; cash; and the cost of goods manufactured and sold. Also included are the following budgeted financial statements: income statement; statement of cash flows; and balance sheet.

LO5 Discuss the role of assumptions and predictions in budgeting. A master budget is based on many assumptions and predictions of unknown parameters. Some estimates tend to be quite accurate, while other predictions are much more difficult.

LO6 Describe a typical organization's process of budget administration. Most organizations have a well-defined process by which budget data is collected and the budget is prepared. This administrative process often includes a budget director or chief budget officer, a budget manual, and a budgeting committee.

LO7 Understand the importance of budgeting product life-cycle costs. A relatively recent focus of the budgeting process is to plan for product life-cycle costs. A large portion of these costs often are committed early in a product's life cycle. It is important for management to be fairly certain that the revenue to be generated by a product will cover all of its life-cycle costs.

LO8 Discuss the behavioral implications of budgetary slack and participative budgeting. A common problem in budgeting is the tendency of people to pad budgets. The resulting budgetary slack makes the budget less useful because the padded budget does not present an accurate picture of expected revenue and expenses. Participative budgeting is the process of allowing employees throughout the organization to have a significant role in developing the budget. Participative budgeting can result in greater commitment to meet the budget by those who participated in the process.

Review Problem on Preparing Master Budget Schedules

SolarTech, Inc. manufactures a special ceramic tile used as a component in residential solar energy systems. Sales are seasonal due to the seasonality in the home-building industry.

- The expected pattern of sales for the next year (20x8) is as follows:

	Quarter				
	1st	2nd	3rd	4th	Year
Sales in units	2,000	6,000	8,000	4,000	20,000

- Each tile sells for $25. All sales are on account, and SolarTech's experience with cash collections is that 60 percent of each quarter's sales are collected during the same quarter as the sale. The remaining 40 percent of sales is collected in the quarter after the sale. SolarTech experiences negligible bad debts, and so this is ignored in the budgeting process. Sales in the fourth quarter of 20x7 are expected to be $100,000 (4,000 units).

- SolarTech desires to have 10 percent of the following quarter's sales needs in finished-goods inventory at the end of each quarter. (On December 31, 20x7, SolarTech expects to have 200 units in inventory.)

- Each tile requires two kilograms of raw material. SolarTech desires to have 10 percent of the next quarter's raw material in inventory at the end of each quarter. (On December 31, 20x7, SolarTech expects to have 480 kilograms of raw material in inventory.)

- The raw material price is $5 per kilogram. The company buys its raw material on account and pays 70 percent of the resulting accounts payable during the quarter of the purchase. The remaining 30 percent is paid during the following quarter. (The raw-material purchases in the fourth quarter of 20x7 are expected to be $36,600.)

Required: Prepare the following budget schedules for 20x8. Include a column for each quarter and for the year.

1. Sales budget (in units and dollars).
2. Cash receipts budget.
3. Production budget.
4. Direct material budget. (*Hint:* The desired ending inventory in the fourth quarter is 480 kilograms.)
5. Cash disbursements budget for raw material purchases.

Solution to Review Problem

1. Sales budget for 20x8:

| | Quarter | | | | |
	1st	2nd	3rd	4th	Year
Sales in units	2,000	6,000	8,000	4,000	20,000
Unit sales price	$ 25	$ 25	$ 25	$ 25	$ 25
Total sales revenue	$50,000	$150,000	$200,000	$100,000	$500,000

2. Cash receipts budget for 20x8:

| | Quarter | | | | |
	1st	2nd	3rd	4th	Year
Sales revenue (from sales budget)	$50,000	$150,000	$200,000	$100,000	$500,000
Collections in quarter of sale (60% of revenue)	$30,000	$ 90,000	$120,000	$ 60,000	$300,000
Collections in quarter after sale (40% of prior quarter's revenue)*	40,000*	20,000	60,000	80,000	200,000
Total cash receipts	$70,000	$110,000	$180,000	$140,000	$500,000

*Forty percent of sales revenue from the 4th quarter of 20x7, which was given at $100,000.

3. Production budget for 20x8:

| | Quarter | | | | |
	1st	2nd	3rd	4th	Year
Sales in units (from sales budget)	2,000	6,000	8,000	4,000	20,000
Add desired ending inventory of finished goods*	600	800	400	200†	200
Total units required	2,600	6,800	8,400	4,200	20,200
Less expected beginning inventory of finished goods	200	600	800	400	200
Units to be produced	2,400	6,200	7,600	3,800	20,000

*Ten percent of the next quarter's expected sales.

†Ten percent of the expected sales for the first quarter of the next year 20x9, which is predicted to be 2,000 units.

4. Direct-material budget for 20x8:

	\multicolumn{5}{c}{Quarter}
	1st	2nd	3rd	4th	Year
Units to be produced (from production budget)	2,400	6,200	7,600	3,800	20,000
Raw material required per unit (kilograms)	x 2	x 2	x 2	x 2	x 2
Raw material required for production (kilograms)	4,800	12,400	15,200	7,600	40,000
Add desired ending inventory of raw material (kilograms)*	1,240	1,520	760	480†	480
Total raw material required	6,040	13,920	15,960	8,080	40,480
Less expected beginning inventory of raw material (kilograms)	480‡	1,240	1,520	760	480
Raw material to be purchased (kilograms)	5,560	12,680	14,440	7,320	40,000
Cost per kilogram	x $5	x $5	x $5	x $5	x $5
Total cost of raw material purchases	$27,800	$63,400	$72,200	$36,600	$200,000

*Ten percent of the next quarter's raw material requirements.

†The desired ending raw material inventory for the fourth quarter of 20x8 is given at 480 kilograms. However, it can also be computed independently by noting that the expected sales pattern for 20x9 is the same as that for 20x8. Therefore, the first quarter budgets for 20x9 will be the same as those for the first quarter of 20x8. So the desired ending raw-material inventory for the fourth quarter of 20x8 is 480 kilograms (10% × 4,800 kilograms required for production in the first quarter of 20x9.)

‡Given in problem.

5. Cash disbursements budget for raw material purchases for 20x8:

	\multicolumn{5}{c}{Quarter}
	1st	2nd	3rd	4th	Year
Cost of raw material purchases (from direct-material budget)	$27,800	$63,400	$72,200	$36,600	$200,000
Cash payments for purchases made during the quarter (70% of current quarter's purchases)	$19,460	$44,380	$50,540	$25,620	$140,000
Cash payments for prior quarter's purchases (30% of prior quarter's purchases)	10,980*	8,340	19,020	21,660	60,000
Total cash payments for raw material purchases	$30,440	$52,720	$69,560	$47,280	$200,000

*Purchases in the fourth quarter of 20x7 were given at $36,600.

Key Terms

For each term's definition refer to the indicated page, or turn to the glossary at the end of the text.

Review Questions

9–1. Explain how a budget facilitates communication and coordination.

9–2. Use an example to explain how a budget could be used to allocate resources in a university.

9–3. Explain what a *master budget* is, and list five of its parts.

9–4. Draw a flowchart similar to the one in Exhibit 9–1 for a gasoline service station. The service station provides automotive maintenance services in addition to selling gasoline and related products.

9–5. Give an example of how general economic trends would affect sales forecasting in the airline industry.

9–6. What is meant by the term *operational budgets?* List three operational budgets that would be prepared by Central Military Hospital in Prague.

9–7. How does activity-based budgeting differ from more traditional budgeting methods?

9–8. How does e-budgeting make use of the Internet?

9–9. Give three examples of how the city of London could use a budget for planning purposes.

9–10. Describe the role of a *budget director.*

9–11. What is the purpose of a *budget manual?*

9–12. How can a company's board of directors use the budget to influence the future direction of the firm?

9–13. Discuss the importance of predictions and assumptions in the budgeting process.

9–14. Define the term *budgetary slack,* and briefly describe a problem it can cause.

9–15. How can an organization help to reduce the problems caused by budgetary slack?

9–16. Why is participative budgeting often an effective management tool?

9–17. Discuss this comment by a small-town bank president: "Budgeting is a waste of time. I've been running this business for 40 years. I don't need to plan."

9–18. List the steps you would go through in developing a budget to meet your college expenses.

9–19. Briefly describe three issues that create special challenges for multinational firms in preparing their budgets.

9–20. List five phases in a product's *life cycle,* and explain why it is important to budget the costs in each of these phases.

9–21. Find an article in a current newspaper or news magazine that discusses budgeting problems in your country. Summarize the article.

Exercises

All applicable Exercises are available with McGraw-Hill's *Connect Accounting*™.   connect
ACCOUNTING

■ **Exercise 9–22**
Missing Amounts; Various
Types of Budgets
(LO 2, 4)

Fill in the missing amounts in the following schedules.

	April	May	June
1. Sales*	$80,000	$60,000	$?
Cash receipts:			
From cash sales	$?	$?	$50,000
From sales on account†	?	34,000	?
Total cash receipts	$?	$?	$?
2. Accounts payable, 12/31/x0		$ 300,000	
Purchase of goods and services on account during 20x1		1,200,000	
Payments of accounts payable during 20x1		?	
Accounts payable, 12/31/x1		400,000	
3. Accounts receivable, 12/31/x0		$ 340,000	
Sales on account during 20x1		900,000	
Collections of accounts receivable during 20x1		780,000	
Accounts receivable, 12/31/x1		?	
4. Accumulated depreciation, 12/31/x0		$ 810,000	
Depreciation expense during 20x1		150,000	
Accumulated depreciation, 12/31/x1		?	
5. Retained earnings, 12/31/x0		$2,050,000	
Net income for 20x1		400,000	
Dividends paid in 20x1		-0-	
Retained earnings, 12/31/x1		?	

*Half of each month's sales are on account. March sales amounted to $40,000.

†60% of credit sales is collected in the month of sale; 40% is collected in the following month.

Choose a municipality or regional government (state, department, province, etc.) and use the Internet to explore the annual budget of the governmental unit you selected. For example, you could check out the budget for Austin, Texas (U.S.) at www.ci.austin.tx.us/budget/, or for the State of Texas at www.texastransparency.org/budget/.

Required: List three items in the budget that you found surprising or particularly interesting, and explain why.

■ **Exercise 9–23**
City or State Budget; Use of Internet
(LO 1, 2)

Bodin Company budgets on an annual basis. The following beginning and ending inventory levels (in units) arc plannned for the year 20x1. Two units of raw material are required to produce each unit of finished product.

	January 1	December 31
Raw material	35,000	45,000
Work in process	12,000	12,000
Finished goods	80,000	50,000

■ **Exercise 9–24**
Budgeting Production and Direct-Material Purchases
(LO 2, 4)

Required:

1. If Bodin Company plans to sell 480,000 units during the year, compute the number of units the firm would have to manufacture during the year.
2. If 500,000 finished units were to be manufactured by Bodin Company during the year, determine the amount of raw material to be purchased.

(CMA, adapted)

Coyote Loco, Inc., a manufacturer of salsa, has the following historical collection pattern for its credit sales.

70 percent collected in the month of sale.
15 percent collected in the first month after sale.
10 percent collected in the second month after sale.
4 percent collected in the third month after sale.
1 percent uncollectible.

■ **Exercise 9–25**
Cash Collections
(LO 2, 4)

   The sales on account have been budgeted for the last seven months as follows:

June	$ 49,000
July	60,000
August	70,000
September	80,000
October	90,000
November	100,000
December	85,000

Required:

1. Compute the estimated total cash collections during October from credit sales.
2. Compute the estimated total cash collections during the fourth quarter from sales made on account during the fourth quarter.
3. *Build a spreadsheet:* Construct an Excel spreadsheet to solve both of the preceding requirements. Show how the solution will change if the following information changes: sales in June and July were $50,000 and $65,000, respectively.

(CMA, adapted)

Flower Bright Fertilizer Company plans to sell 200,000 units of finished product in July and anticipates a growth rate in sales of 5 percent per month. The desired monthly ending inventory in units of finished product is 80 percent of the next month's estimated sales. There are 320,000 finished units in inventory on June 30. Each unit of finished product requires two kilograms of raw material at a cost of $2.30 per kilogram. There are 300,000 kilograms of raw material in inventory on June 30.

■ **Exercise 9–26**
Budgeting Production and Raw-Material Purchases
(LO 2, 4)

Required:

1. Compute the company's total required production in units of finished product for the entire three-month period ending September 30.

2. Independent of your answer to requirement (1), assume the company plans to produce 600,000 units of finished product in the three-month period ending September 30, and to have raw-material inventory on hand at the end of the three-month period equal to 25 percent of the amount used during that period. Compute the total estimated cost of raw-material purchases for the entire three-month period ending September 30.

(CMA, adapted)

■ **Exercise 9–27**
Cash Budgeting
(LO 2, 4)

The following information is from Birmingham Film Corporation's financial records.

Month	Sales	Purchases
April	$72,000	$42,000
May	66,000	48,000
June	60,000	36,000
July	78,000	54,000

Collections from customers are normally 70 percent in the month of sale, 20 percent in the month following the sale, and 9 percent in the second month following the sale. The balance is expected to be uncollectible. All purchases are on account. Management takes full advantage of the 2 percent discount allowed on purchases paid for by the tenth of the following month. Purchases for August are budgeted at $60,000, and sales for August are forecasted at $66,000. Cash disbursements for expenses are expected to be $14,400 for the month of August. The company's cash balance on August 1 was $22,000.

Required: Prepare the following schedules.

1. Expected cash collections during August.

2. Expected cash disbursements during August.

3. Expected cash balance on August 31.

■ **Exercise 9–28**
Budgetary Slack; Bank
(LO 8)

Chung Wing Wah is the new accounts manager at Asian Banking Corp.'s Macau branch. She has just been asked to project how many new bank accounts she will generate during 20x2. Macau's local economy has been strong and the bank has experienced a 10 percent increase in its number of bank accounts over each of the past five years. In 20x1, the bank had 12,000 accounts.

The new accounts manager is paid a salary plus a bonus of $15 for every new account she generates above the budgeted amount. Thus, if the annual budget calls for 500 new accounts, and 540 new accounts are obtained, Williams's bonus will be $600 (40 × $15).

Williams believes the economy of the county will continue to grow at the same rate in 20x2 as it has in recent years. She has decided to submit a budgetary projection of 900 new accounts for 20x2.

Required: Your consulting firm has been hired by the branch vice-president to make recommendations for improving its operations. Write a memorandum to the vice-president defining and explaining the negative consequences of budgetary slack. Also discuss the bank's bonus system for the new accounts manager and how the bonus program tends to encourage budgetary slack.

■ **Exercise 9–29**
Using Budgets for Financial Planning
(LO 1, 4, 5)

Sound Investments, Inc. is a large retailer of stereo equipment. The controller is about to prepare the budget for the first quarter of 20x2. Past experience has indicated that 75 percent of the store's sales are cash sales. The collection experience for the sales on account is as follows:

80 percent during month of sale
15 percent during month following sale
5 percent uncollectible

The total sales for December 20x1 are expected to be $190,000. The controller feels that sales in January 20x2 could range from $100,000 to $160,000.

Required:

1. Demonstrate how financial planning can be used to project cash receipts in January of 20x2 for three different levels of January sales. Use the following columnar format.

	Total Sales in January 20x2		
	$100,000	$130,000	$160,000
Cash receipts in January 20x2:			
From December sales on account	$	$	$
From January cash sales			
From January sales on account			
Total cash receipts	$	$	$

2. How could the controller of Sound Investments, Inc. use this financial planning approach to help in planning operations for January?

■ **Exercise 9–30**
Budgeted Financial
Statements; Retailer
(LO 2, 4)

Handy Hardware is a retail hardware store. Information about the store's operations follows.

- November 20x1 sales amounted to $200,000.
- Sales are budgeted at $220,000 for December 20x1 and $200,000 for January 20x2.
- Collections are expected to be 60 percent in the month of sale and 38 percent in the month following the sale. Two percent of sales are expected to be uncollectible. Bad debts expense is recognized monthly.
- The store's gross margin is 25 percent of its sales revenue.
- A total of 80 percent of the merchandise for resale is purchased in the month prior to the month of sale, and 20 percent is purchased in the month of sale. Payment for merchandise is made in the month following the purchase.
- Other monthly expenses paid in cash amount to $22,600.
- Annual depreciation is $216,000.

The company's balance sheet as of November 30, 20x1, is as follows:

HANDY HARDWARE, INC.
Balance Sheet
November 30, 20x1

Assets

Cash	$ 22,000
Accounts receivable (net of $3,500 allowance for uncollectible accounts)	76,000
Inventory	140,000
Property, plant, and equipment (net of $590,000 accumulated depreciation)	862,000
Total assets	$1,100,000

Liabilities and Stockholders' Equity

Accounts payable	$ 162,000
Common stock	795,000
Retained earnings	143,000
Total liabilities and stockholders' equity	$1,100,000

Required: Compute the following amounts.

1. The budgeted cash collections for December 20x1.
2. The budgeted income (loss) before income taxes for December 20x1.
3. The projected balance in accounts payable on December 31, 20x1.

(CMA, adapted)

■ **Exercise 9–31**
Professional Services Budget;
Medical Practice; Activity-
Based Budgeting
(LO 2, 3, 4)

BA Pediatrics Group is a large children's health care practice in Buenos Aires. The firm's controller is preparing the budget for the next year. The controller projects a total of 48,000 office visits, to be evenly distributed throughout the year. Seventy-five percent of the visits will be half-hour appointments, and the remainder will be one-hour visits. The average rates for pediatric medical services are $40 for half-hour appointments and $70 for one-hour office visits. Ninety percent of each month's professional service revenue is collected during the month when services are rendered, and the remainder is collected the month following service. Uncollectible billings are negligible. The practice's physicians earn $60 per hour.

BA Pediatrics Group uses activity-based budgeting to budget office overhead and administrative expenses. Two cost drivers are used: office visits and direct professional labor. The cost-driver rates are as follows:

Patient registration and records	$2.00 per office visit (of any length)
All other overhead and administrative expenses	$6.00 per direct professional labor hour

Required: Prepare the following budget schedules.

1. Direct-professional-labor budget for the month of June.
2. Cash collections during June for professional services rendered during May and June.
3. Overhead and administrative expense budget for the month of June.
4. *Build a spreadsheet:* Construct an Excel spreadsheet to solve all of the preceding requirements. Show how the solution will change if the following information changes: a total of 54,000 office visits are expected for the year and 70 percent of the office visits are half-hour appointments.

Problems

All applicable Problems are available with McGraw-Hill's *Connect Accounting*™.

■ **Problem 9–32**
Production and Direct-Labor
Budgets; Activity-Based
Overhead Budget
(LO 2, 3, 4)

1. Total direct-labor cost for
the quarter: $470,155

Spiffy Shades Corporation manufactures artistic frames for sunglasses. Talia Demarest, controller, is responsible for preparing the company's master budget. In compiling the budget data for 20x1, Demarest has learned that new automated production equipment will be installed on March 1. This will reduce the direct labor per frame from 1 hour to .75 hour.

Labor-related costs include pension contributions of $.50 per hour, workers' compensation insurance of $.20 per hour, employee medical insurance of $.80 per hour, and employer contributions to Social Security equal to 7 percent of direct-labor wages. The cost of employee benefits paid by the company on its employees is treated as a direct-labor cost. Spiffy Shades Corporation has a labor contract that calls for a wage increase to $18.00 per hour on April 1, 20x1. Management expects to have 16,000 frames on hand at December 31, 20x0, and has a policy of carrying an end-of-month inventory of 100 percent of the following month's sales plus 50 percent of the second following month's sales.

These and other data compiled by Demarest are summarized in the following table.

	January	February	March	April	May
Direct-labor hours per unit	1.0	1.0	.75	.75	.75
Wage per direct-labor hour	$16.00	$16.00	$16.00	$18.00	$18.00
Estimated unit sales	10,000	12,000	8,000	9,000	9,000
Sales price per unit	$50.00	$47.50	$47.50	$47.50	$47.50
Manufacturing overhead:					
Shipping and handling (per unit sold)	$2.00	$2.00	$2.00	$2.00	$2.00
Purchasing, material handling,					
and inspection (per unit produced)	$3.00	$3.00	$3.00	$3.00	$3.00
Other manufacturing overhead					
(per direct-labor hour)	$7.00	$7.00	$7.00	$7.00	$7.00

Required:

1. Prepare a production budget and a direct-labor budget for Spiffy Shades Corporation by month and for the first quarter of 20x1. Both budgets may be combined in one schedule. The direct-labor budget should include direct-labor hours and show the detail for each direct-labor cost category.
2. For each item used in the firm's production budget and direct-labor budget, identify the other components of the master budget that also would use these data.
3. Prepare a manufacturing overhead budget for each month and for the first quarter.

(CMA, adapted)

National Science University (NSU) is preparing its master budget for the upcoming academic year. Currently, 10,000 students are enrolled; however, the admissions office is forecasting a 5 percent growth in the student enrollment despite a tuition fee of $80 per class. The following additional information has been gathered from an examination of university records and conversations with university officials:

- NSU is planning to award 120 tuition-free scholarships.

- The university has a target average class size of 25 students, and the typical student takes five classes each semester.

- NSU's faculty members are evaluated on the basis of teaching, research, and university service. Each faculty member teaches five classes during the academic year.

Required:

1. Prepare a tuition revenue budget for the upcoming academic year.
2. Determine the number of faculty members needed to achieve the class-size target.
3. Assume there is a shortage of full-time faculty members. List at least five actions that NSU might take to accommodate the growing student enrollment.
4. You have been requested by the university's administrative vice president (AVP) to construct budgets for other areas of operation (e.g., the library, grounds, dormitories, and maintenance). The AVP noted: "The most important resource of the university is its faculty. Now that you know the number of faculty needed, you can prepare the other budgets. Faculty members are indeed the key driver—without them we don't operate." Does the administrative vice president really understand the linkages within the budgeting process? Explain.

■ **Problem 9–33**
Revenue and Labor Budgeting for a University; Budget Linkages
(LO 4, 6)

2. Faculty needed: 840

Worldwide Beauty Products, Ltd., a global distributor of cosmetics, is in the process of assembling a cash budget for the first quarter of 20x1. The following information has been extracted from the company's accounting records:

- All sales are on account. Sixty percent of customer accounts are collected in the month of sale; 35 percent are collected in the following month. Uncollectibles amounting to 5 percent of sales are anticipated, and management believes that only 20 percent of the accounts outstanding on December 31, 20x0, will be recovered and that the recovery will be in January 20x1.

- Seventy percent of the merchandise purchases are paid for in the month of purchase; the remaining 30 percent are paid for in the month after acquisition.

- The December 31, 20x0, balance sheet disclosed the following selected figures: cash, $20,000,000; accounts receivable, $55,000,000; and accounts payable, $22,000,000.

- Worldwide Beauty Products, Ltd. maintains a $20,000,000 minimum cash balance at all times. Financing is available (and retired) in $1,000,000 multiples at an 8 percent interest rate, with borrowings taking place at the beginning of the month and repayments occurring at the end of the month. Interest is paid at the time of repaying principal and computed on the portion of principal repaid at that time.

- Additional data (in thousands):

■ **Problem 9–34**
Cash budgeting
(LO 2, 4)

2. Total cash disbursements, February: $121,000,000

	January	February	March
Sales revenue	$150,000	$180,000	$185,000
Merchandise purchases	90,000	100,000	140,000
Cash operating costs	31,000	24,000	45,000
Proceeds from sale of equipment	—	—	5,000

Required:

1. Prepare a schedule that discloses the firm's total cash collections for January through March.
2. Prepare a schedule that discloses the firm's total cash disbursements for January through March.
3. Prepare a schedule that discloses the firm's cash needs, if any, for January through March. The schedule should present the following information in the order cited: Beginning cash balance, total receipts (from requirement (1)), total payments (from requirement (2)), the cash excess (deficiency) before financing, borrowing needed to maintain minimum balance, loan principal repaid, loan interest paid, and ending cash balance.

■ **Problem 9–35**
Relationships of the Master-
Budget Components
(LO 2, 4)

5. December 31 inventory:
1,900 units

Highlands, Inc. manufactures a household fan that sells for $40 per unit. All sales are on account, with 40 percent of sales collected in the month of sale and 60 percent collected in the following month. The data that follow were extracted from the company's accounting records.

- Highlands maintains a minimum cash balance of $30,000. Total payments in January 20x1 are budgeted at $390,000.

- A schedule of cash collections for January and February of 20x1 revealed the following receipts for the period:

	Cash Receipts	
	January	**February**
From December 31 accounts receivable	$216,000	
From January sales	152,000	$228,000
From February sales		156,800

- March 20x1 sales are expected to total 10,000 units.
- Finished-goods inventories are maintained at 20 percent of the following month's sales.
- The December 31, 20x0, balance sheet revealed the following selected figures: cash, $45,000; accounts receivable, $216,000; and finished goods, $44,700.

Required:

1. Determine the number of units that Highlands sold in December 20x0.
2. Compute the sales revenue for March 20x1.
3. Compute the total sales revenue to be reported on Highlands' budgeted income statement for the first quarter of 20x1.
4. Determine the accounts receivable balance to be reported on the March 31, 20x1, budgeted balance sheet.
5. Calculate the number of units in the December 31, 20x0, finished-goods inventory.
6. Calculate the number of units of finished goods to be manufactured in January 20x1.
7. Calculate the financing required in January, if any, to maintain the firm's minimum cash balance.

■ **Problem 9–36**
Cash Budget; Wholesaler
(LO 1, 2, 4)

1. Total cash disbursements,
April: $9,785,000
Ending cash balance, June:
$2,605,000

Alpha-Tech, a rapidly growing distributor of electronic components, is formulating its plans for 20x5. Carolina Reyes, the firm's marketing director, has completed the following sales forecast.

ALPHA-TECH			
20x5 Forecasted Sales			
(in thousands)			
Month	**Sales**	**Month**	**Sales**
January	$ 9,000	July	$15,000
February	10,000	August	15,000
March	9,000	September	16,000
April	11,500	October	16,000
May	12,500	November	15,000
June	14,000	December	17,000

Gustav Larsson, an accountant in the Planning and Budgeting Department, is responsible for preparing the cash flow projection. The following information will be used in preparing the cash flow projection.

- Alpha-Tech's excellent record in accounts receivable collection is expected to continue. Sixty percent of billings are collected the month after the sale, and the remaining 40 percent two months after.

- The purchase of electronic components is Alpha-Tech's largest expenditure, and each month's cost of goods sold is estimated to be 40 percent of sales. Seventy percent of the parts are received by Alpha-Tech one month prior to sale, and 30 percent are received during the month of sale.

- Historically, 75 percent of accounts payable has been paid one month after receipt of the purchased components, and the remaining 25 percent has been paid two months after receipt.

- Hourly wages and fringe benefits, estimated to be 30 percent of the current month's sales, are paid in the month incurred.

- General and administrative expenses are projected to be $15,620,000 for the year. The breakdown of these expenses is presented in the following schedule. All cash expenditures are paid uniformly throughout the year, except the property taxes, which are paid in four equal installments at the end of each quarter.

20x5 Forecasted General and Administrative Costs
(in thousands)

Salaries and fringe benefits	$ 3,200
Promotion	3,800
Property taxes	1,360
Insurance	2,000
Utilities	1,800
Depreciation	3,460
Total	$15,620

- Income-tax payments are made at the beginning of each calendar quarter based on the income of the prior quarter. Alpha-Tech is subject to an income-tax rate of 40 percent. Alpha-Tech's operating income for the first quarter of 20x5 is projected to be $3,200,000. The company pays 100 percent of the estimated tax payment.

- Alpha-Tech maintains a minimum cash balance of $500,000. If the cash balance is less than $500,000 at the end of each month, the company borrows amounts necessary to maintain this balance. All amounts borrowed are repaid out of the subsequent positive cash flow. The projected April 1, 20x5, opening balance is $500,000.

- Alpha-Tech has no short-term debt as of April 1, 20x5.

- Alpha-Tech uses a calendar year for both financial reporting and tax purposes.

Required:

1. Prepare a cash budget for Alpha-Tech by month for the second quarter of 20x5. For simplicity, ignore any interest expense associated with borrowing.

2. Discuss why cash budgeting is important for Alpha-Tech.

(CMA, adapted)

■ Problem 9–37
Ethics; Budgetary Pressure; Management Bonuses; Budgetary Constraints
(LO 4, 5, 7)

Total Chemical Company (TCC) produces and distributes industrial chemicals, TCC's earnings increased sharply in 20x1, and bonuses were paid to the management staff for the first time in several years. Bonuses are based in part on the amount by which reported income exceeds budgeted income.

Martin Kern, vice president of finance, was pleased with TCC's 20x1 earnings and thought that the pressure to show financial results would ease. However, Hildegard Ritter, TCC's president, told Kern that she saw no reason why the 20x2 bonuses should not be double those of 20x1. As a result, Kern felt pressure to increase reported income in order to exceed budgeted income by an even greater amount. This would assure increased bonuses.

Kern met with Wilhelm Keller of Pristeel, Inc., a primary vendor of TCC's manufacturing supplies and equipment. Kern and Keller have been close business contacts for many years. Kern asked Keller to identify all of TCC's purchases of perishable supplies as equipment on Pristeel's sales invoices. The reason Kern gave for his request was that TCC's president had imposed stringent budget constraints on operating expenses but not on capital expenditures. Kern planned to capitalize the purchase of perishable supplies, and include them with the Equipment account on the balance sheet. In this way Kern could defer the expense recognition for these items to a later year. This procedure would increase reported earnings, leading to increased bonuses. Keller agreed to do as Kern had asked.

While analyzing the second quarter financial statements, Mats Günther, TCC's controller, noticed a large decrease in supplies expense from one year ago. Günther reviewed the Supplies Expense account and noticed that only equipment and no supplies had been purchased from Pristeel, a major source for supplies. Günther, who reports to Kern, immediately brought this to Kern's attention.

Kern told Günther of Ritter's high expectations and of the arrangement made with Keller of Pristeel. Günther told Kern that his action was an improper accounting treatment for the supplies purchased from Pristeel. Günther requested that he be allowed to correct the accounts and urged that the arrangement with Pristeel be discontinued. Kern refused the request and told Günther not to become involved in the arrangement with Pristeel.

After clarifying the situation in a confidential discussion with an objective and qualified peer within TCC, Günther arranged to meet with Ritter, TCC's president. At the meeting, Günther disclosed the arrangement Kern had made with Pristeel.

Required:

1. Explain why the use of alternative accounting methods to manipulate reported earnings is unethical.

2. Is Mats Günther, TCC's controller, correct in saying that the supplies purchased from Pristeel, Inc. were accounted for improperly? Explain your answer.

3. Assuming that Martin Kern's arrangement with Pristeel, Inc. was in violation of the standards of ethical conduct for managerial accountants, discuss whether the actions of Günther were appropriate or inappropriate. (The standards are given in Chapter 1.)

(CMA, adapted)

■ **Problem 9–38**
Completion of Budget Schedules
(LO 2, 4)

2. Planned production, June: 15,000 sets
4. Planned direct-labor cost, May: $415,800

Reliable Furniture Company manufactures a variety of desks, chairs, tables, and shelf units that are marketed to small businesses. The controller of the company's Desk Division is currently preparing a budget for the second quarter of the year. The following sales forecast has been made by the division's sales manager.

April	10,000 desk-and-chair sets
May	12,000 desk-and-chair sets
June	15,000 desk-and-chair sets

Each desk-and-chair set requires .02 cubic meters of pine planks and 1.5 hours of direct labor. Each set sells for $54. Pine planks cost $250 per cubic meter, and the division ends each month with enough wood to cover 10 percent of the next month's production requirements. The division incurs a cost of $22 per hour for direct-labor wages and fringe benefits. The division ends each month with enough finished-goods inventory to cover 20 percent of the next month's sales.

Required: Complete the following budget schedules.

1. Sales budget:

	April	May	June
Sales (in sets)	10,000		
Sales price per set	× $54		
Sales revenue	$540,000		

2. Production budget (in sets):

	April	May	June
Sales	10,000		
Add: Desired ending inventory	2,400		3,000
Total requirements	12,400		
Less: Projected beginning inventory	2,000		
Planned production	10,400		

3. Raw-material purchases:

	April	May	June
Planned production (sets)	10,400		
Raw material required per set (cubic meters)	×.02		
Raw material required for production (cubic meters)	208.0		
Add: Desired ending inventory of raw material, in cubic meters (10% of next month's requirement)	25.2		32.0
Total requirements	233.2		
Less: Projected beginning inventory of raw material, in cubic meters (10% of current month's requirement)	20.8		
Planned purchases of raw material (cubic meters)	212.4		
Cost per cubic meter	× $250		
Planned purchases of raw material (dollars)	$53,100		

4. Direct-labor budget:

	April	May	June
Planned production (sets)	10,400		
Direct-labor hours per set	× 1.5		
Direct-labor hours required	15,600		
Cost per hour	× $22		
Planned direct-labor cost	$343,200		

5. *Build a spreadsheet:* Construct an Excel spreadsheet to solve all of the preceding requirements. Show how the solution will change if the following information changes: each set sells for $55 and the direct-labor cost per hour is $21.

■ **Problem 9–39**
Production and Materials Budgets
(LO 2, 4)

2. Conversion cost budget: $245,040
4. Increase in cost of raw material: $100,820

Empire Chemical Company produces three products using three different continuous processes. The products are Yarex, Darol, and Norex. Projected sales in gallons for the three products for the years 20x2 and 20x3 are as follows:

	20x2	20x3
Yarex	60,000	65,000
Darol	40,000	35,000
Norex	25,000	30,000

- Inventories are planned for each product so that the projected finished-goods inventory at the beginning of each year is equal to 8 percent of that year's projected sales.
- Because of the continuous nature of Empire's processes, work-in-process inventory for each of the products remains constant throughout the year.
- The raw-material requirements of the three products are shown in the following chart.

Raw Material	Units	Unit Price	Yarex	Darol	Norex
Gamma	pounds	$ 8.00	.2	.4	—
Murad	pounds	6.00	.4	—	.5
Islin	gallons	5.00	1.0	.7	.5
Tarden	gallons	10.00	—	.3	.5

- Raw-material inventories are planned so that each raw material's projected inventory at the beginning of a year is equal to 10 percent of the previous year's usage of that raw material.

The conversion requirements in hours per gallon for the three products are Yarex, .07 hour; Darol, .10 hour; and Norex, .16 hour. The conversion cost of $20 per hour is considered 100 percent variable.

Required:

1. Determine Empire Chemical Company's production budget (in gallons) for the three products for 20x2.

2. Determine Empire Chemical Company's conversion cost budget for 20x2.

3. Assuming the 20x1 usage of Islin is 100,000 gallons, determine the company's raw-material purchases budget (in dollars) for Islin for 20x2.

4. Assume that for 20x2 production, Empire Chemical Company could replace the raw material Islin with the raw material Philin. The usage of Philin would be the same as the usage of Islin. However, Philin would cost 20 percent more than Islin and would cut production times on all three products by 10 percent. Determine whether management should use Philin or Islin for the 20x2 production, supporting your decision with appropriate calculations. For this requirement, ignore any impact of beginning and ending inventory balances.

(CMA, adapted)

■ **Problem 9–40**
Sales, Production, and
Purchases Budgets; Activity-
Based Overhead Budget
(LO 2, 3, 4)

2. Production required (units),
heavy coils: 41,000
6. Manufacturing overhead
budget for 20x0, total
manufacturing overhead:
$1,482,375

Vista Electronics, Inc. manufactures two different types of coils used in electric motors. In the fall of the current year, Chung-Hua Lee, the controller, compiled the following data.

• Sales forecast for 20x0 (all units to be shipped in 20x0):

Product	Units	Price
Light coil	60,000	$120
Heavy coil	40,000	170

• Raw-material prices and inventory levels:

Raw Material	Expected Inventories, January 1, 20x0	Desired Inventories, December 31, 20x0	Anticipated Purchase Price
Sheet metal	16,000 kg.	18,000 kg.	$16
Copper wire	14,500 kg.	16,000 kg.	10
Platforms	6,000 units	7,000 units	3

• Use of raw material:

| Raw Material | Amount Used per Unit | |
	Light Coil	Heavy Coil
Sheet metal	2 kg.	2.5 kg.
Copper wire	1 kg.	1.5 kg.
Platforms		1 unit

• Direct-labor requirements and rates:

Product	Hours per Unit	Rate per Hour
Light coil	2	$15
Heavy coil	3	20

• Finished-goods inventories (in units):

Product	Expected January 1, 20x0	Desired December 31, 20x0
Light coil	20,000	25,000
Heavy coil	8,000	9,000

- Manufacturing overhead:

Overhead Cost Item	Activity-Based Budget Rate
Purchasing and material handling	$.55 per kilogram of sheet metal and copper wire purchased
Depreciation, utilities, and inspection	$4.00 per coil produced (either type)
Shipping	$1.00 per coil shipped (either type)
General manufacturing overhead	$3.00 per direct-labor hour

Required: Prepare the following budgets for 20x0.

1. Sales budget (in dollars).
2. Production budget (in units).
3. Raw-material purchases budget (in quantities).
4. Raw-material purchases budget (in dollars).
5. Direct-labor budget (in dollars).
6. Manufacturing-overhead budget (in dollars).

(CPA, adapted)

United Security Systems, Inc. (USSI) manufactures and sells security systems. The company started by installing photoelectric security systems in offices and has expanded into the private-home market. USSI has a basic security system that has been developed into three standard products, each of which can be adapted to meet the specific needs of customers. The manufacturing operation is moderate in size, as the bulk of the component manufacturing is completed by independent contractors. The security systems are approximately 85 percent complete when received from contractors and require only final assembly in the USSI plant. Each product passes through at least one of three assembly operations.

USSI operates in a rapidly growing community. There is evidence that a great deal of new commercial construction will take place in the near future, and management has decided to pursue this new market. In order to be competitive, the firm will have to expand its operations.

In view of the expected increase in business, Sandra Feldman, the controller, believes that USSI should implement a complete budgeting system. Feldman has decided to make a formal presentation to the company's president explaining the benefits of a budgeting system and outlining the budget schedules and reports that would be necessary.

Required:

1. Explain the benefits that USSI would gain from implementing a budgeting system.
2. If Sandra Feldman develops a master budget:
   a. Identify, in order, the schedules that will have to be prepared.
   b. Identify the subsequent schedules that would be based on the schedules identified above. Use the following format for your answer.

   Schedule   **Subsequent Schedule**

(CMA, adapted)

■ **Problem 9–41**
Interrelationships Between Components of Master Budget
(LO 1, 2, 4, 6)

Toronto Business Associates, a division of Maple Leaf Services Corporation, offers management and computer consulting services to clients throughout Canada and the northwestern United States. The division specializes in Web site development and other Internet applications. The corporate management at Maple Leaf Services is pleased with the performance of Toronto Business Associates for the first nine months of the current year and has recommended that the division manager, Richard Howell, submit a revised forecast for the remaining quarter, as the division has exceeded the annual plan year-to-date by 20 percent of operating income. An unexpected increase in billed hour volume over the original plan is the main reason for this increase in income. The original operating budget for the first three quarters for Toronto Business Associates follows.

■ **Problem 9–42**
Revised Operating Budget; Consulting Firm
(LO 1, 4, 5)

1. Operating income: $179,600
Total compensation, management consulting: $245,000

TORONTO BUSINESS ASSOCIATES
20x1 Operating Budget

	1st Quarter	2nd Quarter	3rd Quarter	Total for First Three Quarters
Revenue:				
Consulting fees:				
Computer system consulting	$421,875	$421,875	$421,875	$1,265,625
Management consulting	315,000	315,000	315,000	945,000
Total consulting fees	$736,875	$736,875	$736,875	$2,210,625
Other revenue	10,000	10,000	10,000	30,000
Total revenue	$746,875	$746,875	$746,875	$2,240,625
Expenses:				
Consultant salary expenses	$386,750	$386,750	$386,750	$1,160,250
Travel and related expenses	45,625	45,625	45,625	136,875
General and administrative expenses	100,000	100,000	100,000	300,000
Depreciation expense	40,000	40,000	40,000	120,000
Corporate expense allocation	50,000	50,000	50,000	150,000
Total expenses	$622,375	$622,375	$622,375	$1,867,125
Operating income	$124,500	$124,500	$124,500	$ 373,500

Howell will reflect the following information in his revised forecast for the fourth quarter.

- Toronto Business Associates currently has 25 consultants on staff, 10 for management consulting and 15 for computer systems consulting. Three additional management consultants have been hired to start work at the beginning of the fourth quarter in order to meet the increased client demand.

- The hourly billing rate for consulting revenue will remain at $90 per hour for each management consultant and $75 per hour for each computer consultant. However, due to the favorable increase in billing hour volume when compared to the plan, the hours for each consultant will be increased by 50 hours per quarter.

- The budgeted annual salaries and actual annual salaries, paid monthly, are the same: $50,000 for a management consultant and $46,000 for a computer consultant. Corporate management has approved a merit increase of 10 percent at the beginning of the fourth quarter for all 25 existing consultants, while the new consultants will be compensated at the planned rate.

- The planned salary expense includes a provision for employee fringe benefits amounting to 30 percent of the annual salaries. However, the improvement of some corporatewide employee programs will increase the fringe benefits to 40 percent.

- The original plan assumes a fixed hourly rate for travel and other related expenses for each billing hour of consulting. These are expenses that are not reimbursed by the client, and the previously determined hourly rate has proven to be adequate to cover these costs.

- Other revenue is derived from temporary rentals and interest income and remains unchanged for the fourth quarter.

- General and administrative expenses have been favorable at 7 percent below the plan; this 7 percent savings on fourth quarter expenses will be reflected in the revised plan.

- Depreciation of office equipment and personal computers will stay constant at the projected straight-line rate.

- Due to the favorable experience for the first three quarters and the division's increased ability to absorb costs, the corporate management at Maple Leaf Services has increased the corporate expense allocation by 50 percent.

Required:

1. Prepare a revised operating budget for the fourth quarter for Toronto Business Associates that Richard Howell will present to corporate management.

2. Discuss the reasons why an organization would prepare a revised operating budget.

(CMA, adapted)

FreshPak Corporation manufactures two types of cardboard boxes used in shipping canned food, fruit, and vegetables. The canned food box (type C) and the perishable food box (type P) have the following material and labor requirements.

	Type of Box	
	C	**P**
Direct material required per 100 boxes:		
Paperboard ($.40 per kilogram)	15 kilograms	35 kilograms
Corrugating medium ($.20 per kilogram)	10 kilograms	15 kilograms
Direct labor required per 100 boxes ($12.00 per hour)	.25 hour	.50 hour

Problem 9–43
Preparation of Master Budget
(LO 2, 3, 4)

1. Total sales revenue: $1,100,000
3. Cost of purchases (paperboard): $97,000
5. Total overhead: $148,500
7. Predetermined overhead rate: $40 per hour

The following manufacturing-overhead costs are anticipated for the next year. The predetermined overhead rate is based on a production volume of 495,000 units for each type of box. Manufacturing overhead is applied on the basis of direct-labor hours.

Indirect material	$ 10,500
Indirect labor	50,000
Utilities	25,000
Property taxes	18,000
Insurance	16,000
Depreciation	29,000
Total	$148,500

The following selling and administrative expenses are anticipated for the next year.

Salaries and fringe benefits of sales personnel	$ 85,000
Advertising	15,000
Management salaries and fringe benefits	90,000
Clerical wages and fringe benefits	26,000
Miscellaneous administrative expenses	4,000
Total	$220,000

The sales forecast for the next year is as follows:

	Sales Volume	Sales Price
Box type C	500,000 boxes	$ 90.00 per hundred boxes
Box type P	500,000 boxes	130.00 per hundred boxes

The following inventory information is available for the next year. The unit production costs for each product are expected to be the same this year and next year.

	Expected Inventory January 1	Desired Ending Inventory December 31
Finished goods:		
Box type C	10,000 boxes	5,000 boxes
Box type P	20,000 boxes	15,000 boxes
Raw material:		
Paperboard	7,500 kilograms	2,500 kilograms
Corrugating medium	2,500 kilograms	5,000 kilograms

Required: Prepare a master budget for FreshPak Corporation for the next year. Assume an income tax rate of 40 percent. Include the following schedules.

1. Sales budget.
2. Production budget.
3. Direct-material budget.
4. Direct-labor budget.
5. Manufacturing-overhead budget.
6. Selling and administrative expense budget.
7. Budgeted income statement. (*Hint:* To determine cost of goods sold, first compute the manufacturing cost per unit for each type of box. Include applied manufacturing overhead in the cost.)

■ **Problem 9–44**
Budgeting; Financial
Objectives; Ethics
(LO 1, 2, 4)

2. Increase in sales: 11.5%

Healthful Foods Inc., a manufacturer of breakfast cereals and snack bars, has experienced several years of steady growth in sales, profits, and dividends while maintaining a relatively low level of debt. The board of directors has adopted a long-run strategy to maximize the value of the shareholders' investment. In order to achieve this goal, the board of directors established the following five-year financial objectives.

- Increase sales by 12 percent per year.
- Increase income before taxes by 15 percent per year.
- Maintain long-term debt at a maximum of 16 percent of assets.

These financial objectives have been attained for the past three years. At the beginning of last year, the president of Healthful Foods, Andrea Donis, added a fourth financial objective of maintaining cost of goods sold at a maximum of 70 percent of sales. This goal also was attained last year.

The budgeting process at Healthful Foods is to be directed toward attaining these goals for the forthcoming year, a difficult task with the economy in a prolonged recession. In addition, the increased emphasis on eating healthful foods has driven up the price of ingredients used by the company significantly faster than the expected rate of inflation. John Winslow, cost accountant at Healthful Foods, has responsibility for preparation of the profit plan for next year. Winslow assured Donis that he could present a budget that achieved all of the financial objectives. Winslow believed that he could overestimate the ending inventory and reclassify fruit and grain inspection costs as administrative rather than manufacturing costs to attain the desired objective. The actual statements for 20x1 and the budgeted statements for 20x2 that Winslow prepared are as follows:

HEALTHFUL FOODS INC.
Income Statement

	20x1 Actual	20x2 Budgeted
Sales	$850,000	$947,750
Less: Variable costs:		
Cost of goods sold	510,000	574,725
Selling and administrative	90,000	87,500
Contribution margin	$250,000	$285,525
Less: Fixed costs:		
Manufacturing	85,000	94,775
Selling and administrative	60,000	70,000
Income before taxes	$105,000	$120,750

HEALTHFUL FOODS INC.
Balance Sheet

	20x1 Actual	20x2 Budgeted
Assets:		
Cash	$ 10,000	$ 17,000
Accounts receivable	60,000	68,000
Inventory	300,000	365,000
Plant and equipment (net of accumulated depreciation)	1,630,000	1,600,000
Total	$2,000,000	$2,050,000
Liabilities:		
Accounts payable	$ 110,000	$ 122,000
Long-term debt	320,000	308,000
Stockholders' equity:		
Common stock	400,000	400,000
Retained earnings	1,170,000	1,220,000
Total	$2,000,000	$2,050,000

The company paid dividends of $27,720 in 20x1, and the expected tax rate for 20x2 is 34 percent.

Required:

1. Describe the role of budgeting in a firm's strategic planning.
2. For each of the financial objectives established by the board of directors and the president of Healthful Foods Inc., determine whether John Winslow's budget attains these objectives. Support your conclusion in each case by presenting appropriate calculations, and use the following format for your answer.

Objective	Attained/Not Attained	Calculations

3. Explain why the adjustments contemplated by John Winslow are unethical, citing specific standards of ethical conduct for management accountants.

(CMA, adapted)

"We really need to get this new material-handling equipment in operation just after the new year begins. I hope we can finance it largely with cash and marketable securities, but if necessary we can get a short-term loan down at MetroBank." This statement by Beth Davies-Lowry, president of Intercoastal Electronics Company, concluded a meeting she had called with the firm's top management. Intercoastal is a small, rapidly growing wholesaler of consumer electronic products. The firm's main product lines are small kitchen appliances and power tools. Marcia Wilcox, Intercoastal's General Manager of Marketing, has recently completed a sales forecast. She believes the company's sales during the first quarter of 20x1 will increase by 10 percent each month over the previous month's sales. Then Wilcox expects sales to remain constant for several months. Intercoastal's projected balance sheet as of December 31, 20x0, is as follows:

Cash	$ 35,000
Accounts receivable	270,000
Marketable securities	15,000
Inventory	154,000
Buildings and equipment (net of accumulated depreciation)	626,000
Total assets	$1,100,000
Accounts payable	$ 176,400
Bond interest payable	12,500
Property taxes payable	3,600
Bonds payable (10%; due in 20x6)	300,000
Common stock	500,000
Retained earnings	107,500
Total liabilities and stockholders' equity	$1,100,000

Jack Hanson, the assistant controller, is now preparing a monthly budget for the first quarter of 20x1. In the process, the following information has been accumulated:

1. Projected sales for December of 20x0 are $400,000. Credit sales typically are 75 percent of total sales. Intercoastal's credit experience indicates that 10 percent of the credit sales are collected during the month of sale, and the remainder are collected during the following month.
2. Intercoastal's cost of goods sold generally runs at 70 percent of sales. Inventory is purchased on account, and 40 percent of each month's purchases are paid during the month of purchase. The remainder is paid during the following month. In order to have adequate stocks of inventory on hand, the firm attempts to have inventory at the end of each month equal to half of the next month's projected cost of goods sold.
3. Hanson has estimated that Intercoastal's other monthly expenses will be as follows:

Sales salaries	$21,000
Advertising and promotion	16,000
Administrative salaries	21,000
Depreciation	25,000
Interest on bonds	2,500
Property taxes	900

In addition, sales commissions run at the rate of 1 percent of sales.

■ **Problem 9–45**
Comprehensive Master Budget; Borrowing; Acquisition of Automated Material-Handling System **(LO 1, 2, 4)**

2. Total cash receipts, first quarter: $1,367,030
4. Total cash disbursements, first quarter: $1,213,576
6. Required short-term borrowing: $(100,000)
7. Net income: $160,656

4. Intercoastal's president, Davies-Lowry, has indicated that the firm should invest $125,000 in an automated inventory-handling system to control the movement of inventory in the firm's warehouse just after the new year begins. These equipment purchases will be financed primarily from the firm's cash and marketable securities. However, Davies-Lowry believes that Intercoastal needs to keep a minimum cash balance of $25,000. If necessary, the remainder of the equipment purchases will be financed using short-term credit from a local bank. The minimum period for such a loan is three months. Hanson believes short-term interest rates will be 10 percent per year at the time of the equipment purchases. If a loan is necessary, Davies-Lowry has decided it should be paid off by the end of the first quarter if possible.

5. Intercoastal's board of directors has indicated an intention to declare and pay dividends of $50,000 on the last day of each quarter.

6. The interest on any short-term borrowing will be paid when the loan is repaid. Interest on Intercoastal's bonds is paid semiannually on January 31 and July 31 for the preceding six-month period.

7. Property taxes are paid semiannually on February 28 and August 31 for the preceding six-month period.

Required: Prepare Intercoastal Electronics Company's master budget for the first quarter of 20x1 by completing the following schedules and statements.

1. Sales budget:

	20x0	20x1			
	December	January	February	March	1st Quarter
Total sales					
Cash sales					
Sales on account					

2. Cash receipts budget:

	20x1			
	January	February	March	1st Quarter
Cash sales				
Cash collections from credit sales made during current month				
Cash collections from credit sales made during preceding month				
Total cash receipts				

3. Purchases budget:

	20x0	20x1			
	December	January	February	March	1st Quarter
Budgeted cost of goods sold					
Add: Desired ending inventory					
Total goods needed					
Less: Expected beginning inventory					
Purchases					

4. Cash disbursements budget:

	20x1			
	January	**February**	**March**	**1st Quarter**
Inventory purchases:				
Cash payments for purchases during the current month*				
Cash payments for purchases during the preceding month†				
Total cash payments for inventory purchases				
Other expenses:				
Sales salaries				
Advertising and promotion				
Administrative salaries				
Interest on bonds‡				
Property taxes‡				
Sales commissions				
Total cash payments for other expenses				
Total cash disbursements				

*40% of the current month's purchases (schedule 3).

†60% of the prior month's purchases (schedule 3).

‡Bond interest is paid every six months, on January 31 and July 31. Property taxes also are paid every six months, on February 28 and August 31.

5. Complete the first three lines of the summary cash budget. Then do the analysis of short-term financing needs in requirement (6). Then finish requirement (5).

Summary cash budget:

	20x1			
	January	**February**	**March**	**1st Quarter**
Cash receipts (from schedule 2)				
Less: Cash disbursements (from schedule 4)				
Change in cash balance during period due to operations				
Sale of marketable securities (1/2/x1)				
Proceeds from bank loan (1/2/x1)				
Purchase of equipment				
Repayment of bank loan (3/31/x1)				
Interest on bank loan				
Payment of dividends				
Change in cash balance during first quarter				
Cash balance, 1/1/x1				
Cash balance, 3/31/x1				

6. Analysis of short-term financing needs:

Projected cash balance as of December 31, 20x0	$
Less: Minimum cash balance	
Cash available for equipment purchases	$
Projected proceeds from sale of marketable securities	
Cash available	$
Less: Cost of investment in equipment	
Required short-term borrowing	$

7. Prepare Intercoastal Electronics' budgeted income statement for the first quarter of 20x1. (Ignore income taxes.)

8. Prepare Intercoastal Electronics' budgeted statement of retained earnings for the first quarter of 20x1.

9. Prepare Intercoastal Electronics' budgeted balance sheet as of March 31, 20x1. (*Hint:* On March 31, 20x1, Bond Interest Payable is $5,000 and Property Taxes Payable is $900.)

Cases

■ **Case 9–46**
Using Budgets to Evaluate
Business Decisions
(LO 1, 2, 5)

City Racquetball Club (CRC) offers racquetball and other physical fitness facilities to its members. There are four of these clubs in the metropolitan area. Each club has between 1,800 and 2,500 members. Revenue is derived from annual membership fees and hourly court fees. The annual membership fees are as follows:

Individual	$ 40
Student	25
Family	95

The hourly court fees vary from $6 to $10 depending upon the season and the time of day (prime versus nonprime time).

The peak racquetball season is considered to run from September through April. During this period, court usage averages 90 to 100 percent of capacity during prime time (5:00–9:00 p.m.) and 50 to 60 percent of capacity during the remaining hours. Daily court usage during the off-season (i.e., summer) averages only 20 to 40 percent of capacity.

Most of CRC's memberships have September expirations. A substantial amount of the cash receipts are collected during the early part of the racquetball season due to the renewal of the annual membership fees and heavy court usage. However, cash receipts are not as large in the spring and drop significantly in the summer months.

CRC is considering changing its membership and fee structure in an attempt to change its cash receipts. Under the new membership plan, only an annual membership fee would be charged, rather than a membership fee plus hourly court fees. There would be two classes of membership as follows:

Individual	$250
Family	400

The annual fee would be collected in advance at the time the membership application is completed. Members would be allowed to use the racquetball courts as often as they wish during the year under the new plan.

All future memberships would be sold under these new terms. Current memberships would be honored on the old basis until they expire. However, a special promotional campaign would be instituted to attract new members and to encourage current members to convert to the new membership plan immediately.

The annual fees for individual and family memberships would be reduced to $200 and $300, respectively, during the two-month promotional campaign. In addition, all memberships sold or renewed during this period would be for 15 months rather than the normal one-year period. Current members also would be given a credit toward the annual fee for the unexpired portion of their membership fee, and for all prepaid hourly court fees for league play that have not yet been used.

CRC's management estimates that 60 to 70 percent of the present membership would continue with the club. The most active members (45 percent of the present membership) would convert immediately to the new plan, while the remaining members who continue would wait until their current memberships expire. Those members who would not continue are not considered active (i.e., they play five or less times during the year). Management estimates that the loss of members would be offset fully by new members within six months of instituting the new plan. Furthermore, many of the new members would be individuals who would play during nonprime time. Management estimates that adequate court time will be available for all members under the new plan.

If the new membership plan is adopted, it would be instituted on February 1, well before the summer season. The special promotional campaign would be conducted during March and April. Once the plan is implemented, annual renewal of memberships and payment of fees would take place as each individual or family membership expires.

Required: Your consulting firm has been hired to help CRC evaluate its new fee structure. Write a letter to the club's president answering the following questions.

1. Will City Racquetball Club's new membership plan and fee structure improve its ability to plan its cash receipts? Explain your answer.

2. City Racquetball Club should evaluate the new membership plan and fee structure completely before it decides to adopt or reject it.

   a. Identify the key factors that CRC should consider in its evaluation.

   b. Explain what type of financial analyses CRC should prepare in order to make a complete evaluation.

3. Explain how City Racquetball Club's cash management would differ from the present if the new membership plan and fee structure were adopted.

(CMA, adapted)

■ Case 9–47
Participative Budgeting
(LO 1, 2, 8)

Patrica Eklund, controller in the division of social services for the state, recognizes the importance of the budgetary process for planning, control, and motivational purposes. She believes that a properly implemented participative budgetary process for planning purposes and an evaluation procedure will motivate the managers to improve productivity within their particular departments. Based upon this philosophy, Eklund has implemented the following budgetary procedures.

- An appropriation target figure is given to each department manager. This amount is the maximum funding that each department can expect to receive in the next year.

- Department managers develop their individual budgets within the following spending constraints as directed by the controller's staff.

  - Expenditure requests cannot exceed the appropriation target.

  - All fixed expenditures should be included in the budget. Fixed expenditures would include such items as contracts and salaries at current levels.

  - All government projects directed by higher authority should be included in the budget in their entirety.

- The controller's staff consolidates the budget requests from the various departments into a master budget submission for the entire division.

- Upon final budget approval by the legislature, the controller's staff allocates the appropriation to the various departments on instructions from the division manager. However, a specified percentage of each department's appropriation is held back in anticipation of potential budget cuts and special funding needs. The amount and use of this contingency fund is left to the discretion of the division manager.

- Each department is allowed to adjust its budget when necessary to operate within the reduced appropriation level. However, as stated in the original directive, specific projects authorized by higher authority must remain intact.

- The final budget is used as the basis of control. Excessive expenditures by account for each department are highlighted on a monthly basis. Department managers are expected to account for all expenditures over budget. Fiscal responsibility is an important factor in the overall performance evaluation of department managers.

Eklund believes her policy of allowing the department managers to participate in the budgetary process and then holding them accountable for their performance is essential, especially during times of limited resources. She further believes that the department managers will be positively motivated to increase the efficiency and effectiveness of their departments because they have provided input into the initial budgetary process and are required to justify any unfavorable performances.

Required:

1. Describe several operational and behavioral benefits that are generally attributed to a participative budgetary process.

2. Identify at least four deficiencies in Patricia Eklund's participative policy for planning and performance evaluation purposes. For each deficiency identified, recommend how it can be corrected.

(CMA, adapted)

■ **Case 9–48**
Comprehensive Master
Budget; Short-Term
Financing; Acquisition of
Robotic Equipment
(LO 1, 2, 4)

1. Total sales revenue, entire
year: $5,650,000
3. Production budget, S
frames, units to be produced,
entire year: 254,000
4. Cost of metal strips to
be purchased, entire year:
$1,150,000
5. Total cash payments for
direct labor, entire year:
$936,000
7. Cost of goods sold:
$3,850,000
8. Net income: $1,337,500
10. Total assets: $9,634,700

Jeffrey Vaughn, president of Frame-It Company, was just concluding a budget meeting with his senior staff. It was November of 20x0, and the group was discussing preparation of the firm's master budget for 20x1. "I've decided to go ahead and purchase the industrial robot we've been talking about. We'll make the acquisition on January 2 of next year, and I expect it will take most of the year to train the personnel and reorganize the production process to take full advantage of the new equipment."

In response to a question about financing the acquisition, Vaughn replied as follows: "The robot will cost $1,000,000. We'll finance it with a one-year $1,000,000 loan from Shark Bank and Trust Company. I've negotiated a repayment schedule of four equal installments on the last day of each quarter. The interest rate will be 10 percent, and interest payments will be quarterly as well." With that the meeting broke up, and the budget process was on.

Frame-It Company is a manufacturer of metal picture frames. The firm's two product lines are designated as S (small frames; 5 × 7 inches) and L (large frames; 8 × 10 inches). The primary raw materials are flexible metal strips and 9-inch by 24-inch glass sheets. Each S frame requires a 2-foot metal strip; an L frame requires a 3-foot strip. Allowing for normal breakage and scrap glass, Frame-It can get either four S frames or two L frames out of a glass sheet. Other raw materials, such as cardboard backing, are insignificant in cost and are treated as indirect materials. Emily Jackson, Frame-It's controller, is in charge of preparing the master budget for 20x1. She has gathered the following information:

1. Sales in the fourth quarter of 20x0 are expected to be 50,000 S frames and 40,000 L frames. The sales manager predicts that over the next two years, sales in each product line will grow by 5,000 units each quarter over the previous quarter. For example, S frame sales in the first quarter of 20x1 are expected to be 55,000 units.

2. Frame-It's sales history indicates that 60 percent of all sales are on credit, with the remainder of the sales in cash. The company's collection experience shows that 80 percent of the credit sales are collected during the quarter in which the sale is made, while the remaining 20 percent is collected in the following quarter. (For simplicity, assume the company is able to collect 100 percent of its accounts receivable.)

3. The S frame sells for $10, and the L frame sells for $15. These prices are expected to hold constant throughout 20x1.

4. Frame-It's production manager attempts to end each quarter with enough finished-goods inventory in each product line to cover 20 percent of the following quarter's sales. Moreover, an attempt is made to end each quarter with 20 percent of the glass sheets needed for the following quarter's production. Since metal strips are purchased locally, Frame-It buys them on a just-in-time basis; inventory is negligible.

5. All of Frame-It's direct-material purchases are made on account, and 80 percent of each quarter's purchases are paid in cash during the same quarter as the purchase. The other 20 percent is paid in the next quarter.

6. Indirect materials are purchased as needed and paid for in cash. Work-in-process inventory is negligible.

7. Projected manufacturing costs in 20x1 are as follows:

	S Frame	L Frame
Direct material:		
Metal strips:		
S: 2 ft. @ $1 per foot	$2	
L: 3 ft. @ $1 per foot		$ 3
Glass sheets:		
S: ¼ sheet @ $8 per sheet	2	
L: ½ sheet @ $8 per sheet		4
Direct labor:		
.1 hour @ $20 per hour	2	2
Manufacturing overhead:		
.1 direct-labor hour × $10 per hour..	1	1
Total manufacturing cost per unit	$7	$10

8. The predetermined overhead rate is $10 per direct-labor hour. The following manufacturing overhead costs are budgeted for 20x1.

	1st Quarter	2nd Quarter	3rd Quarter	4th Quarter	Entire Year
Indirect material	$ 10,200	$ 11,200	$ 12,200	$ 13,200	$ 46,800
Indirect labor	40,800	44,800	48,800	52,800	187,200
Other overhead	31,000	36,000	41,000	46,000	154,000
Depreciation	20,000	20,000	20,000	20,000	80,000
Total overhead	$102,000	$112,000	$122,000	$132,000	$468,000

All of these costs will be paid in cash during the quarter incurred except for the depreciation charges.

9. Frame-It's quarterly selling and administrative expenses are $100,000, paid in cash.

10. Jackson anticipates that dividends of $50,000 will be declared and paid in cash each quarter.

11. Frame-It's projected balance sheet as of December 31, 20x0, follows:

Cash	$ 95,000
Accounts receivable	132,000
Inventory:	
Raw material	59,200
Finished goods	167,000
Plant and equipment (net of accumulated depreciation)	8,000,000
Total assets	$8,453,200
Accounts payable	$ 99,400
Common stock	5,000,000
Retained earnings	3,353,800
Total liabilities and stockholders' equity	$8,453,200

Required: Prepare Frame-It Company's master budget for 20x1 by completing the following schedules and statements.

1. Sales budget:

	20x0	20x1				
	4th Quarter	1st Quarter	2nd Quarter	3rd Quarter	4th Quarter	Entire Year
S frame unit sales						
× S sales price						
S frame sales revenue						
L frame unit sales						
× L sales price						
L frame sales revenue						
Total sales revenue						
Cash sales*						
Sales on account†						

*40% of total sales.
†60% of total sales.

2. Cash receipts budget:

	20x1				
	1st Quarter	2nd Quarter	3rd Quarter	4th Quarter	Entire Year
Cash sales					
Cash collections from credit sales made during current quarter*					
Cash collections from credit sales made during previous quarter†					
Total cash receipts					

*80% of current quarter's credit sales.
†20% of previous quarter's credit sales.

3.   Production budget:

	20x0	20x1				
	4th Quarter	1st Quarter	2nd Quarter	3rd Quarter	4th Quarter	Entire Year
S frames:						
Sales (in units)						
Add: Desired ending inventory						
Total units needed						
Less: Expected beginning inventory						
Units to be produced						
L frames:						
Sales (in units)						
Add: Desired ending inventory						
Total units needed						
Less: Expected beginning inventory						
Units to be produced						

4.   Direct-material budget:

	20x0	20x1				
	4th Quarter	1st Quarter	2nd Quarter	3rd Quarter	4th Quarter	Entire Year
Metal strips:						
S frames to be produced						
× Metal quantity per unit (ft.)						
Needed for S frame production						
L frames to be produced						
× Metal quantity per unit (ft.)						
Needed for L frame production						
Total metal needed for production; to be purchased (ft.)						
× Price per foot						
Cost of metal strips to be purchased						
Glass sheets:						
S frames to be produced						
× Glass quantity per unit (sheets)						
Needed for S frame production						
L frames to be produced						
× Glass quantity per unit (sheets)						
Needed for L frame production						
Total glass needed for production (sheets)						
Add: Desired ending inventory					10,400	10,400
Total glass needs						
Less: Expected beginning inventory						
Glass to be purchased						
× Price per glass sheet						
Cost of glass to be purchased						
Total raw-material purchases (metal and glass)						

5. Cash disbursements budget:

	20x1				
	1st Quarter	2nd Quarter	3rd Quarter	4th Quarter	Entire Year
Raw-material purchases:					
Cash payments for purchases during the current quarter					
Cash payments for purchases during the preceding quarter					
Total cash payments for raw-material purchases					
Direct labor:					
Frames produced (S and L)					
× Direct-labor hours per frame					
Direct-labor hours to be used					
× Rate per direct-labor hour					
Total cash payments for direct labor					
Manufacturing overhead:					
Indirect material					
Indirect labor					
Other					
Total cash payments for manufacturing overhead					
Cash payments for selling and administrative expenses					
Total cash disbursements					

6. Summary cash budget:

	20x1				
	1st Quarter	2nd Quarter	3rd Quarter	4th Quarter	Entire Year
Cash receipts (from schedule 2)					
Less: Cash disbursements (from schedule 5)					
Change in cash balance due to operations					
Payment of dividends					
Proceeds from bank loan (1/2/x1)					
Purchase of equipment					
Quarterly installment on loan principal					
Quarterly interest payment					
Change in cash balance during the period					
Cash balance, beginning of period					
Cash balance, end of period					

7. Prepare a budgeted schedule of cost of goods manufactured and sold for the year 20x1. (*Hint:* In the budget, actual and applied overhead will be equal.)

8. Prepare Frame-It's budgeted income statement for 20x1. (Ignore income taxes.)

9. Prepare Frame-It's budgeted statement of retained earnings for 20x1.

10. Prepare Frame-It's budgeted balance sheet as of December 31, 20x1.

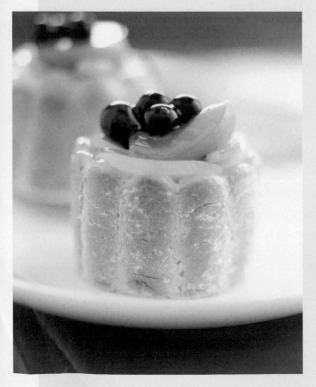

THIS CHAPTER'S FOCUS COMPANY is Pâtisserie Cézanne, which **Pâtisserie Cézanne** supplies fancy desserts to a variety of restaurants, caterers, and upscale food stores in Lyon, France. The company's order-taking system is entirely Web-based. Each day, Pâtisserie Cézanne posts its pastry and desserts menu on its Web site, and orders are accepted via the Internet. In this chapter, we explore Pâtisserie Cézanne's use of standard costing. A standard-costing system sets predetermined (or standard) costs for each of a product's inputs, such as direct material and direct labor. Then the actual costs to produce the product are compared with the standard costs that should have been incurred. Pâtisserie Cézanne's management uses the standard-costing system to help control the company's production costs.

10 Standard Costing, Operational Performance Measures, and the Balanced Scorecard

In contrast to the food-processing setting of Pâtisserie Cézanne, we will turn our attention to the financial-services industry. Here we will explore Banque Tournesol's use of the balanced scorecard. Banque Tournesol, headquartered in Marseilles, France, uses a balanced scorecard to help management and employees focus on the customer, internal operations, and learning and growth areas of the business, so that ultimately the bank's long-term financial goals will be attained.

Banque Tournesol

1 Explain how standard costing is used to help manage costs.

2 Describe two ways to set standards and distinguish between perfection and practical standards.

3 Compute and interpret the direct-material price and quantity variances and the direct-labor rate and efficiency variances.

4 Explain several methods for determining the significance of cost variances.

5 Describe some behavioral effects of standard costing.

6 Explain how standard costs are used in product costing.

7 Summarize some advantages of standard costing.

8 Explain several common criticisms of standard costing.

9 Describe the operational performance measures appropriate for today's manufacturing environment.

10 Describe the balanced scorecard concept and explain the reasoning behind it.

11 Prepare journal entries to record and close out cost variances (appendix).

A budget provides a plan for managers to follow in making decisions and directing an organization's activities. At the end of a budget period, the budget serves another useful purpose. At that time, managers use the budget as a benchmark against which to compare the results of actual operations. Did the company make as much profit as anticipated in the budget? Were costs greater or less than expected? These questions involve issues of cost management and control. In this chapter, we will study one of the tools used by managerial accountants to assist managers in controlling an organization's operations and costs.

Managing Costs

Learning Objective 1

Explain how standard costing is used to help manage costs.

How can managers use a control system as a cost management tool? Any control system has three basic parts: a predetermined or *standard* performance level, a measure of *actual* performance, and a *comparison* between standard and actual performance. A thermostat is a control system with which we are all familiar. First, a thermostat has a predetermined or standard temperature, which can be set at any desired level. If you want the temperature in a room to be 21 degrees Celsius, you set the thermostat at the *standard* of 21 degrees. Second, the thermostat has a thermometer, which measures the *actual* temperature in the room. Third, the thermostat *compares* the preset or standard temperature with the actual room temperature. If the actual temperature falls below the preset or standard temperature, the thermostat activates a heating device. The three features of a control system are depicted in Exhibit 10–1.

A managerial accountant's budgetary-control system works like a thermostat. First, a predetermined or **standard cost** is set. In essence, a standard cost is a budget for the production of one unit of product or service. It is the cost chosen by the managerial

1. **Predetermined or standard performance** (The thermostat is set to a standard temperature.)

2. **Measure of actual performance** (The thermometer measures the actual room temperature.)

3. **Comparison of actual and standard performance** (The thermostat compares the preset or standard temperature with the actual temperature.)

Exhibit 10–1

Control System: A Thermostat

accountant to serve as the benchmark in the budgetary-control system. When the firm produces many units, the managerial accountant uses the standard unit cost to determine the total standard or budgeted cost of production. For example, suppose the standard direct-material cost for one unit of product is $5 and 100 units are manufactured. The total standard or budgeted direct-material cost, given an actual output of 100 units, is $500 ($5 × 100).

Second, the managerial accountant measures the actual cost incurred in the production process.

Third, the managerial accountant compares the actual cost with the budgeted or standard cost. Any difference between the two is called a **cost variance.** Cost variances then are used in controlling costs.

Management by Exception

Managers are busy people. They do not have time to look into the causes of every variance between actual and standard costs. However, they do take the time to investigate the causes of significant cost variances. This process of following up on only significant cost variances is called **management by exception.** When operations are going along as planned, actual costs and profit will typically be close to the budgeted amounts. However, if there are significant departures from planned operations, such effects will show up as significant cost variances. Managers investigate these variances to determine their causes, if possible, and take corrective action when indicated.

What constitutes a significant variance? No precise answer can be given to this question, since it depends on the size and type of the organization and its production process. We will consider this issue later in the chapter when we discuss common methods for determining the significance of cost variances. First, however, we will turn our attention to the process of setting standards.

Setting Standards

Methods for Setting Standards

Managerial accountants typically use two methods for setting cost standards: analysis of historical data and task analysis.

Analysis of Historical Data   One indicator of future costs is historical cost data. In a mature production process, where the firm has a lot of production experience, historical costs can provide a good basis for predicting future costs. The methods for analyzing cost behavior that we studied in Chapter 6 are used in making cost predictions. The managerial accountant often will need to adjust these predictions to reflect movements in price levels or technological changes in the production process. For example, the amount

Learning Objective 2

Describe two ways to set standards and distinguish between perfection and practical standards.

of rubber required to manufacture a particular type of tire will likely be the same this year as last year, unless there has been a significant change in the process used to manufacture tires. However, the price of rubber is likely to be different this year than last, and this fact must be reflected in the new standard cost of a tire.

Despite the relevance of historical cost data in setting cost standards, managerial accountants must guard against relying on them excessively. Even a seemingly minor change in the way a product is manufactured may make historical data almost totally irrelevant. Moreover, new products also require new cost standards. For new products, such as genetically engineered medicines, there are no historical cost data upon which to base standards. In such cases, the managerial accountant must turn to another approach.

Task Analysis   Another way to set cost standards is to analyze the process of manufacturing a product to determine what it *should* cost. The emphasis shifts from what the product *did* cost in the past to what it *should* cost in the future. In using **task analysis,** the managerial accountant typically works with engineers who are intimately familiar with the production process. Together they conduct studies to determine exactly how much direct material should be required and how machinery should be used in the production process. Time and motion studies are conducted to determine how long each step performed by direct laborers should take.

A Combined Approach   Managerial accountants often apply both historical cost analysis and task analysis in setting cost standards. It may be, for example, that the technology has changed for only one step in the production process. In such a case, the managerial accountant would work with engineers to set cost standards for the technologically changed part of the production process. However, the accountant would likely rely on the less expensive method of analyzing historical cost data to update the cost standards for the remainder of the production process.

Participation in Setting Standards

Standards should not be determined by the managerial accountant alone. People generally will be more committed to meeting standards if they are allowed to participate in setting them. For example, production supervisors should have a role in setting production cost standards, and sales managers should be involved in setting targets for sales prices and volume. In addition, knowledgeable staff personnel should participate in the standard-setting process. For example, task analysis should be carried out by a team consisting of production engineers, production supervisors, and managerial accountants.

Perfection versus Practical Standards: A Behavioral Issue

How difficult should it be to attain standard costs? Should standards be set so that actual costs rarely exceed standard costs? Or should it be so hard to attain standards that actual costs frequently exceed them? The answers to these questions depend on the purpose for which standards will be used and how standards affect behavior.

Perfection Standards   A **perfection** (or **ideal**) **standard** is one that can be attained only under nearly perfect operating conditions. Such standards assume peak efficiency, the lowest possible input prices, the best-quality materials obtainable, and no disruptions in production due to such causes as machine breakdowns or power failures. Some managers believe that perfection standards motivate employees to achieve the lowest cost possible. They claim that since the standard is theoretically attainable, employees will have an incentive to come as close as possible to achieving it.

Other managers and many behavioral scientists disagree. They feel that perfection standards discourage employees, since they are so unlikely to be attained. Moreover, setting unrealistically difficult standards may encourage employees to sacrifice product quality to achieve lower costs. By skimping on raw-material quality or the attention given manual production tasks, employees may be able to lower the production cost. However, this lower cost may come at the expense of a higher rate of defective units. Thus, the firm ultimately may incur higher costs than necessary as defective products are returned by customers or scrapped upon inspection.

Practical Standards Standards that are as tight as practical, but still are expected to be attained, are called **practical (or attainable) standards.** Such standards assume a production process that is as efficient as practical under normal operating conditions. Practical standards allow for such occurrences as occasional machine breakdowns and normal amounts of raw-material waste. Attaining a practical standard keeps employees on their toes, without demanding miracles. Most behavioral theorists believe that practical standards encourage more positive and productive employee attitudes than do perfection standards.

> "At Best Foods, standard costs are set at attainable levels." (10a)
>
> **Best Foods**
> (a subsidiary of Unilever)

Use of Standards by Service Organizations

Many service industry firms, nonprofit organizations, and governmental units make use of standards. For example, FedEx allows its crews 18 minutes to unload the 9 to 12 containers of packages from a Boeing 727. A delay of over a minute must be explained at a daily 5 a.m. meeting. Burger King sets a standard for the amount of meat in a hamburger. Airlines such as Japan Airlines or Chilean airline LAN set standards for fuel and maintenance costs. Insurance companies such as Dai-Ichi Life or ING Groep set standards for the amount of time to process an insurance application. Even government offices may have standards such as the number of days required to process and return an application for vehicle registration. These and similar organizations use standards in budgeting and cost control in much the same way that manufacturers use standards.

Governmental organizations like the National Health Service in Great Britain may use standards to plan staffing levels and measure customer service.

Cost Variance Analysis

To illustrate the use of standards in managing costs, we will focus on a producer of fancy desserts located in Lyon, France. Pâtisserie Cézanne supplies fresh and frozen desserts to a variety of restaurants, caterers, and upscale food stores. The company's order-taking system is entirely Web-based. Pâtisserie Cézanne posts its menu of fresh desserts and pastries for each day on its Web site four days in advance of the delivery date. Orders are accepted via the Internet three days in advance of delivery. For example, the menu of desserts to be available for delivery on Friday afternoon is posted to Pâtisserie Cézanne's Web site on Monday, and orders are accepted up to midnight on Tuesday. The company places orders for ingredients on Wednesday and accepts delivery on Thursday. Pâtisserie Cézanne's ordering is also done largely via the Internet. Production then takes place throughout the day on Friday, and the desserts are delivered Friday afternoon. Pâtisserie Cézanne uses independent delivery services to deliver its products.

Pâtisserie Cézanne also produces frozen dessert products for upscale grocery stores. Unlike the fresh desserts, which vary daily, the frozen desserts are stock items that are varied less frequently. Like the fresh desserts, however, the frozen dessert menu is posted to Pâtisserie Cézanne's Web site, and orders are accepted entirely via the Internet.

Pâtisserie Cézanne

Learning Objective 3

Compute and interpret the direct-material price and quantity variances and the direct-labor rate and efficiency variances.

Pâtisserie Cézanne produces its fresh desserts and frozen desserts in two different bakeries, both located on the outskirts of Lyon.

The production process for the fresh desserts involves a combination of semiauto-mated equipment and manual labor. Even in this era of widespread automation, making desserts and pastries still involves considerable direct labor. The basic steps in the production process are much as you might expect. These steps include selecting ingredients, mixing, baking, cooling, and finishing. The finishing work, of course, involves the most skilled direct labor. In making a six-layer chocolate raspberry torte, for example, each individual cake layer must be sliced into two pieces, and then fillings and icings are spread on each layer. The cake's top is finished artistically, and any additional toppings are carefully applied.

Pâtisserie Cézanne's director of cost management has set standards for direct material and direct labor as follows for a category of dessert products generically referred to as multilayer fancy cakes.

Direct-Material Standards

The standard quantity and price of ingredients for one multilayer fancy cake, such as a Linzer torte, are shown in the following table:

Standard quantity:	
Ingredients in finished product	2.4 kilograms
Allowance for normal waste	.1 kilograms
Total standard quantity required per multilayer fancy cake	2.5 kilograms
Standard price:	
Purchase price per kilogram of ingredients (net of purchase discounts)	$2.60
Transportation cost per kilogram	.20
Total standard price per kilogram of ingredients	$2.80

The standard quantity of ingredients needed to produce one cake is 2.5 kilograms, even though only 2.4 kilograms actually remain in the finished product. One-hundred grams of ingredients are wasted as a normal result of the production process. Therefore, the entire amount of ingredients needed to produce a fancy cake is included in the standard quantity of material.

The standard price of ingredients reflects all of the costs incurred to acquire the material and transport it to the plant. Notice that the cost of transportation is added to the purchase price. Any purchase discounts would be subtracted out from the purchase price to obtain a net price.

To summarize, the **standard direct-material quantity** is the total amount of direct material normally required to produce a finished product, including allowances for normal waste or inefficiency. The **standard direct-material price** is the total delivered cost, after subtracting any purchase discounts.

Direct-Labor Standards

The standard quantity and rate for direct labor for the production of one multilayer fancy cake are as follows:

Standard quantity:	
Direct labor required per multilayer fancy cake	.5 hour
Standard rate:	
Hourly wage rate	$16
Fringe benefits (25% of wages)	4
Total standard rate per hour	$20

The **standard direct-labor quantity** is the number of direct-labor hours normally needed to manufacture one unit of product. The **standard direct-labor rate** is the total hourly cost of compensation, including fringe benefits.

Standard Costs Given Actual Output

During September, Pâtisserie Cézanne produced 2,000 multilayer fancy cakes. The total standard or budgeted costs for direct material and direct labor are computed as follows:

Direct material:

Standard direct-material cost per cake (2.5 kilograms x $2.80 per kilogram)	$ 7
Actual output	× 2,000
Total standard direct-material cost	$14,000

Direct labor:

Direct-labor cost per cake (.5 hour × $20.00 per hour)	$ 10
Actual output	× 2,000
Total standard direct-labor cost	$20,000

Notice that the total standard cost for the direct-material and direct-labor inputs is based on Pâtisserie Cézanne's actual *output*. The company should incur costs of $34,000 for direct material and direct labor, *given that it produced 2,000 multilayer fancy cakes*. The total standard costs for direct material and direct labor serve as the managerial accountant's benchmarks against which to compare actual costs. This comparison then serves as the basis for controlling direct-material and direct-labor costs.

Analysis of Cost Variances

During September, Pâtisserie Cézanne incurred the following actual costs for direct material and direct labor in the production of multilayer fancy cakes.

Direct material purchased: actual cost 6,250 kilograms at $2.84 per kilogram	$17,750
Direct material used: actual cost 5,125 kilograms at $2.84 per kilogram	$14,555
Direct labor: actual cost 980 hours at $21 per hour	$20,580

Compare these actual expenditures with the total standard costs for the production of 2,000 multilayer fancy cakes. Pâtisserie Cézanne spent more than the budgeted amount for both direct material and direct labor. But why were these excess costs incurred? Is there any further analysis the managerial accountant can provide to help answer this question?

Direct-Material Variances

What caused Pâtisserie Cézanne to spend more than the anticipated amount on direct material? First, the company purchased ingredients at a higher price ($2.84 per kilogram) than the standard price ($2.80 per kilogram). Second, the company used more ingredients than the standard amount. The amount actually used was 5,125 kilograms instead of the standard amount of 5,000 kilograms, which is based on actual output of 2,000 multilayer fancy cakes. The managerial accountant can show both of these deviations from standards by computing a **direct-material price variance** (or **purchase price variance**) and a **direct-material quantity variance**. The computation of these variances is depicted in Exhibit 10–2.

Exhibit 10–2
Direct-Material Price and
Quantity Variances

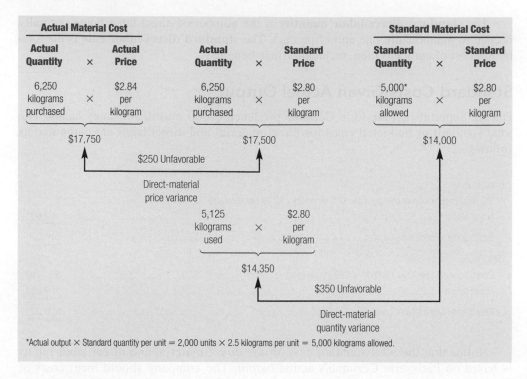

*Actual output × Standard quantity per unit = 2,000 units × 2.5 kilograms per unit = 5,000 kilograms allowed.

The formula for the direct-material price variance is as follows:

Direct-material price variance = (PQ × AP) − (PQ × SP) = PQ(AP − SP)

where

PQ = Quantity purchased
AP = Actual price
SP = Standard price

Pâtisserie Cézanne's direct-material price variance for September's production of multilayer fancy cakes is computed as follows:

$$\text{Direct-material price variance} = PQ(AP - SP)$$
$$= 6,250\ (\$2.84 - \$2.80)$$
$$= \$250\ \text{Unfavorable}$$

This variance is unfavorable, because the actual purchase price exceeded the standard price. Notice that the price variance is based on the quantity of material *purchased* (PQ), not the quantity actually used in production.

As Exhibit 10–2 shows, the following formula defines the direct-material quantity variance.

Direct-material quantity variance = (AQ × SP) − (SQ × SP) = SP(AQ − SQ)

where

AQ = Actual quantity used
SQ = Standard quantity allowed

Pâtisserie Cézanne's direct-material quantity variance for September's production of multilayer fancy cakes is computed as follows:

$$\text{Direct-material quantity variance} = SP(AQ - SQ)$$
$$= \$2.80\ (5,125 - 5,000)$$
$$= \$350\ \text{Unfavorable}$$

This variance is unfavorable, because the actual quantity of direct material used in September exceeded the standard quantity allowed, *given actual September output* of 2,000 multilayer fancy cakes. The quantity variance is based on the quantity of material actually *used* in production (AQ).

Quantity Purchased versus Quantity Used   As stated above, the direct-material price variance is based on the quantity purchased (PQ). This makes sense, because deviations between the actual and standard price, which are highlighted by the price variance, relate to the *purchasing* function in the firm. Timely action to follow up a significant price variance will be facilitated by calculating this variance as soon as possible after the material is *purchased*.

In contrast, the direct-material quantity variance is based on the amount of material *used* in production (AQ). The quantity variance highlights deviations between the quantity of material actually used (AQ) and the standard quantity allowed (SQ). Thus, it makes sense to compute this variance at the time the material is *used* in production.

"In most cases, purchases account for one of the largest if not the largest part of the total cost . . . Deciding what to purchase from which supplier is a key purchasing decision, and one of the key factors in this decision is the net cost of goods." (10b)
Vereeniging Refractories

Basing the Quantity Variance on Actual Output   Notice that the standard quantity of material must be based on the actual production output in order for the quantity variance to be meaningful. It would not make any sense to compare standard or budgeted material usage at one level of output (say, 1,000 multilayer fancy cakes) with the actual material usage at a *different* level of output (say, 2,000 multilayer fancy cakes). Everyone would expect more direct material to be used in the production of 2,000 cakes than in the production of 1,000 cakes. For the direct-material

Standard quantity allowed, given *actual output*		Actual quantity used in the production of *actual output*
	Comparison of these quantities is the basis of the **direct-material quantity variance**	

quantity variance to provide helpful information for management, the standard or budgeted quantity must be based on *actual output*. Then the quantity variance compares the following two quantities.

Direct-Labor Variances

Why did Pâtisserie Cézanne spend more than the anticipated amount on direct labor during September? First, the division incurred a cost of $21 per hour for direct labor instead of the standard amount of $20 per hour. Second, the division used only 980 hours of direct labor, which is less than the standard quantity of 1,000 hours, given actual output of 2,000 multilayer fancy cakes. The managerial accountant analyzes direct-labor costs by computing a **direct-labor rate variance** and a **direct-labor efficiency variance.** Exhibit 10–3 depicts the computation of these variances.

The formula for the direct-labor rate variance is shown below.

Direct-labor rate variance $= (\text{AH} \times \text{AR}) - (\text{AH} \times \text{SR}) = \text{AH}(\text{AR} - \text{SR})$

where

AH = Actual hours used

AR = Actual rate per hour

SR = Standard rate per hour

Exhibit 10–3
Direct-Labor Rate and
Efficiency Variances

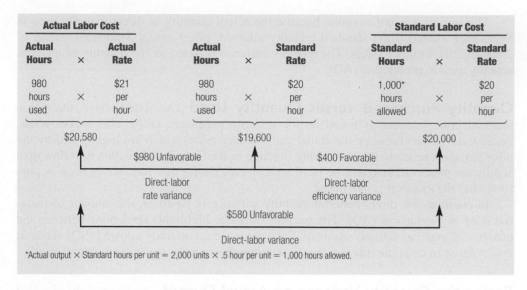

	Actual Labor Cost					Standard Labor Cost	
Actual Hours	×	**Actual Rate**	**Actual Hours**	×	**Standard Rate**	**Standard Hours**	× **Standard Rate**
980 hours used	×	$21 per hour	980 hours used	×	$20 per hour	1,000* hours allowed	× $20 per hour
	$20,580			$19,600		$20,000	

$980 Unfavorable $400 Favorable

Direct-labor rate variance   Direct-labor efficiency variance

$580 Unfavorable

Direct-labor variance

*Actual output × Standard hours per unit = 2,000 units × .5 hour per unit = 1,000 hours allowed.

Pâtisserie Cézanne's direct-labor rate variance for September's production of multilayer fancy cakes is computed as follows:

$$\text{Direct-labor rate variance} = AH(AR - SR)$$
$$= 980(\$21 - \$20) = \$980 \text{ Unfavorable}$$

This variance is unfavorable because the actual rate exceeded the standard rate during September.

As Exhibit 10–3 shows, the formula for the direct-labor efficiency variance is as follows:

$$\text{Direct-labor efficiency variance} = (AH \times SR) - (SH \times SR) = SR(AH - SH)$$

where

$$SH = \text{Standard hours allowed}$$

Pâtisserie Cézanne's direct-labor efficiency variance for September is computed as follows:

$$\text{Direct-labor efficiency variance} = SR(AH - SH)$$
$$= \$20(980 - 1,000)$$
$$= \$400 \text{ Favorable}$$

This variance is favorable, because the actual direct-labor hours used in September were less than the standard hours allowed, *given actual September output of 2,000* multilayer fancy cakes.

Notice that the direct-labor rate and efficiency variances add up to the total direct-labor variance. However, the rate and efficiency variances have opposite signs, since one variance is unfavorable and the other is favorable.

Direct-labor rate variance	$980 Unfavorable	Different signs of variances cancel just as plus
Direct-labor efficiency variance	400 Favorable	and minus signs cancel in arithmetic.
Direct-labor variance	$580 Unfavorable	

Basing the Efficiency Variance on Actual Output

The number of standard hours of direct labor allowed is based on the *actual* production output. It would not be meaningful to compare standard or budgeted labor usage at one level of output with the actual hours used at a different level of output.

PARKER HANNIFIN CORPORATION'S BRASS PRODUCTS DIVISION

Parker Hannifin's Brass Products Division, a world-class manufacturer of brass fittings, valves, and tubing, is a standard-costing success story.[1] "Parker Brass uses its standard-costing system and variance analyses as important business tools to target problem areas so it can develop solutions for continuous improvement. Variances are reported for each product line, and if any production variance exceeds 5 percent of product-line sales, the product-line manager is required to provide an explanation. Also required is a plan to correct the problems underlying any unfavorable variances. Variance reports, which are generated within one day of the completion of a job order, are distributed to managers and production schedulers. A variance database is kept, which can be accessed by product-line managers, to provide variance data by part number, by job-order number, or by dollar amount."

From the perspective of Parker Brass's management, the division has modified its standard-costing system to provide disaggregated and timely cost information to enable timely corrective action in a rapidly changing business environment.

Multiple Types of Direct Material or Direct Labor

Manufacturing processes usually involve several types of direct material. In such cases, direct-material price and quantity variances are computed for each type of material. Then these variances are added to obtain a total price variance and a total quantity variance, as follows:

	Price Variance	Quantity Variance
Direct material A	$1,000 F	$1,600 U
Direct material B	2,500 U	200 U
Direct material C	800 U	500 F
Total variance	$2,300 U	$1,300 U

Similarly, if a production process involves several types of direct labor, rate and efficiency variances are computed for each labor type. Then they are added to obtain a total rate variance and a total efficiency variance.

Allowing for Spoilage or Defects

In some manufacturing processes, a certain amount of spoilage or defective production is normal. This must be taken into account when the standard quantity of material is computed. To illustrate, suppose that 400 liters of chemicals are normally required in a chemical process in order to obtain 320 liters of good output. If total good output in January is 2,000 liters, what is the standard allowed quantity of input?

$$\text{Good output quantity} = 80\% \times \text{Input quantity}$$

Dividing both sides of the equation by 80%

$$\frac{\text{Good output quantity}}{80\%} = \text{Input quantity allowed}$$

Using the numbers in the illustration

$$\frac{2,000 \text{ liters of good output}}{80\%} = 2,500 \text{ liters of input allowed}$$

The total standard allowed input is 2,500 liters to achieve 2,000 liters of good output.

---

[1]David Johnsen and Parvez Sopariwala, "Standard Costing Is Alive and Well at Parker Brass," *Management Accounting Quarterly* 1, no. 2 (Winter 2000), pp. 12–20.

Significance of Cost Variances

Managers do not have time to investigate the causes of every cost variance. Management by exception enables managers to look into the causes of only significant variances. But what constitutes an exception? How does the manager know when to follow up on a cost variance and when to ignore it?

These questions are difficult to answer, because to some extent the answers are part of the art of management. A manager applies judgment and experience in making guesses, pursuing hunches, and relying on intuition to determine when a variance should be investigated. Nevertheless, there are guidelines and rules of thumb that managers often apply.

Size of Variances   The absolute size of a variance is one consideration. Managers are more likely to follow up on large variances than on small ones. The relative size of the variance is probably even more important. A manager is more likely to investigate a $20,000 material quantity variance that is 20 percent of the standard direct-material cost of $100,000 than a $50,000 labor efficiency variance that is only 2 percent of the standard direct-labor cost of $2,500,000. The *relative* magnitude of the $20,000 material quantity variance (20 percent) is greater than the *relative* magnitude of the $50,000 labor efficiency variance (2 percent). For this reason, managerial accountants often show the relative magnitude of variances in their cost variance reports. For example, the September cost variance report for Pâtisserie Cézanne's production of multilayer fancy cakes is shown in Exhibit 10–4.

Managers often apply a rule of thumb that takes into account both the absolute and the relative magnitudes of a variance. An example of such a rule is the following: Investigate variances that are either greater than $10,000 or greater than 10 percent of standard cost.

Recurring Variances   Another consideration in deciding when to investigate a variance is whether the variance occurs repeatedly or only infrequently. Suppose a manager uses the rule of thumb stated above and direct-material quantity variances occur as shown in the following Excel spreadsheet.

	A	B	C	D	E
1		Standard	Direct-Material		Percentage
2		Direct-Material	Quantity		of Standard
3	Month	Cost	Variance		Cost
4					
5	January	$ 50,000	$ 3,000 F*		6.0%
6	February	50,000	3,200 F		6.4%
7	March	50,000	1,800 F		3.6%
8	April	50,000	3,100 F		6.2%
9					
10	*F denotes a favorable variance.				

Microsoft Excel - Direct-Material Quantity Variances
E8 = C8/B8

A strict adherence to the rule of thumb indicates no investigation, since none of the monthly variances is greater than $10,000 or 10 percent of standard cost. Nevertheless, the manager might investigate this variance in April, since it has *recurred* at a reasonably high level for several consecutive months. In this case, the consistency of the variance triggers an investigation, not its absolute or relative magnitude.

	Amount		Percentage of Standard Cost
Direct material			
Standard cost, given actual output	$14,000		
Direct-material price variance	$250	Unfavorable	1.79%
Direct-material quantity variance	$350	Unfavorable	2.50%
Direct labor			
Standard cost, given actual output	$20,000		
Direct-labor rate variance	$980	Unfavorable	4.9%
Direct-labor efficiency variance	$400	Favorable	(2.0%)

Exhibit 10–4

Cost Variance Report for September: Pâtisserie Cézanne

Pâtisserie
Cézanne

Trends   A trend in a variance also may call for investigation. Suppose a manager observes the direct-labor efficiency variances shown in the following Excel spreadsheet.

None of these variances is large enough to trigger an investigation if the manager uses the "$10,000 or 10 percent" rule of thumb. However, the four-month *trend* is worrisome. An alert manager will likely follow up on this unfavorable trend to determine its causes before costs get out of hand.

```
Microsoft Excel - Direct-Labor Efficiency Variances
File  Edit  View  Insert  Format  Tools  Data  Window  Help
E8          fx  =C8/B8
         A              B            C         D          E
1                    Standard    Direct-Labor          Percentage
2                   Direct-Labor   Efficiency           of Standard
3      Month          Cost        Variance                Cost
4
5  January        $   100,000  $       100  U*           0.10%
6  February           100,000          550  U            0.55%
7  March              100,000        3,000  U            3.00%
8  April              100,000        9,100  U            9.10%
9
10 *U denotes an unfavorable variance.
   Sheet1 / Sheet2 / Sheet3 /
Ready
```

Controllability   Another important consideration in deciding when to look into the causes of a variance is the manager's view of the **controllability** of the cost item. A manager is more likely to investigate the variance for a cost that is controllable by someone in the organization than one that is not. For example, there may be little point to investigating a material price variance if the organization has no control over the price. This could happen, for example, if the firm has a long-term contract with a supplier of the material at a price determined on the international market. In contrast, the manager is likely to follow up on a variance that should be controllable, such as a direct-labor efficiency variance or a direct-material quantity variance.

Favorable Variances   It is just as important to investigate significant favorable variances as significant unfavorable variances. For example, a favorable direct-labor efficiency variance may indicate that employees have developed a more efficient way of performing a production task. By investigating the variance, management can learn about the improved method. It may be possible to use a similar approach elsewhere in the organization.

Costs and Benefits of Investigation   The decision whether to investigate a cost variance is a cost-benefit decision. The costs of investigation include the time spent by the investigating manager and the employees in the department where the investigation occurs. Other potential costs include disruption of the production process as the investigation is conducted, and corrective actions taken to eliminate the cause of a variance. The benefits of a variance investigation include reduced future production costs if the cause of an unfavorable variance is eliminated. Another potential benefit is the cost saving associated with the lowering of cost standards when the cause of a favorable variance is discovered.

Weighing these considerations takes the judgment of skillful and experienced managers. Key to this judgment is an intimate understanding of the organization's production process and day-to-day contact with its operations.

A Statistical Approach

There are many reasons for cost variances. For example, a direct-labor efficiency variance could be caused by inexperienced employees, employee inefficiency, poor-quality raw materials, poorly maintained machinery, an intentional work slowdown due to employee grievances, or many other factors. In addition to these substantive reasons, there are purely random causes of variances. People are not robots, and they are not perfectly consistent in their work habits. Random fluctuations in direct-labor efficiency variances can be caused by such factors as employee illnesses, workers experimenting with different production methods, or simply random fatigue. Ideally, managers would be able to sort out the randomly caused variances from those with substantive and controllable underlying causes. It is impossible to accomplish this with 100 percent accuracy, but a **statistical control chart** can help.

A statistical control chart plots cost variances across time and compares them with a statistically determined *critical value* that triggers an investigation. This critical value is usually determined by assuming that cost variances have a normal probability distribution with a mean of zero. The critical value is set at some multiple of the distribution's standard deviation. Variances greater than the critical value are investigated.

Exhibit 10–5 shows a statistical control chart with a critical value of 1 standard deviation. The manager would investigate the variance observed in May, since it falls further than 1 standard deviation from the mean (zero). The variances for the remaining five months would not be investigated. The presumption is that these minor variances are due to random causes and are not worth investigating.

Exhibit 10–5
Statistical Control Chart

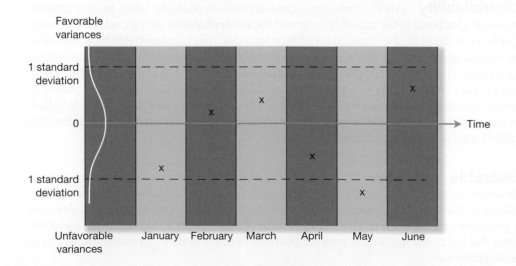

Behavioral Impact of Standard Costing

Standard costs and variance analysis are useful in diagnosing organizational performance. These tools help managers discern "the story behind the story"—the details of operations that underlie reported cost and profit numbers. Standard costs, budgets, and variances also are used to evaluate the performance of individuals and departments. The performance of individuals, relative to standards or budgets, often is used to help determine salary increases, bonuses, and promotions. When standards and variances affect employee reward structures, they can profoundly influence behavior.

For example, suppose a hotel's food and beverage department manager earns a bonus when food and beverage costs are below the budgeted amount. This reward structure will provide a concrete incentive for the manager to keep food and beverage costs under control. But such an incentive can have either positive or negative effects. The bonus may induce the manager to seek the most economical food suppliers and to watch more carefully for employee theft and waste. However, the bonus also could persuade the manager to buy cheaper but less tender cuts of meat for the restaurant. This could ultimately result in lost patronage for the restaurant and the hotel. One aspect of skillful management is knowing how to use standards, budgets, and variances to get the most out of an organization's employees. Unfortunately, there are no simple answers or formulas for success in this area. Despite such difficulties, standards, budgets, and variances are used in the executive compensation schemes of many well-known companies.

> **Learning Objective 5**
>
> Describe some behavioral effects of standard costing.

Controllability of Variances

Cost control is accomplished through the efforts of individual managers in an organization. By determining which managers are in the best position to influence each cost variance, the managerial accountant can assist managers in deriving the greatest benefit from cost variance analysis.

Who is responsible for the direct-material price and quantity variances? The direct-labor rate and efficiency variances? Answering these questions is often difficult, because it is rare that any one person completely controls any event. Nevertheless, it is often possible to identify the manager who is *most able to influence* a particular variance, even if he or she does not exercise complete control over the outcome.

Direct-Material Price Variance The purchasing manager is generally in the best position to influence material price variances. Through skillful purchasing practices, an expert purchasing manager can get the best prices available for purchased goods and services. To achieve this goal, the purchasing manager uses such practices as buying in quantity, negotiating purchase contracts, comparing prices among vendors, and global sourcing.

Despite these purchasing skills, the purchasing manager is not in complete control of prices. The need to purchase component parts with precise engineering specifications, the all-too-frequent rush requests from the production department, and worldwide shortages of critical materials all contribute to the challenges faced by the purchasing manager.

Direct-Material Quantity Variance The production supervisor is usually in the best position to influence material quantity variances. Skillful supervision and motivation of production employees, coupled with the careful use and handling of materials, contribute to minimal waste. Production engineers are also partially responsible for material quantity variances, since they determine the grade and technical specifications of

> "We designate variances as controllable or uncontrollable. Plant managers are held accountable for the controllable variances." (10c)
> **Best Foods**
> (a subsidiary of Unilever)

materials and component parts. In some cases, using a low-grade material may result in greater waste than using a high-grade material.

Direct-Labor Rate Variance   Direct-labor rate variances generally result from using a different mix of employees than that anticipated when the standards were set. Wage rates differ among employees due to their skill levels and their seniority with the organization. Using a higher proportion of more senior or more highly skilled employees than a task requires can result in unfavorable direct-labor rate variances. The production supervisor is generally in the best position to influence the work schedules of employees.

Direct-Labor Efficiency Variance   Once again, the production supervisor is usually most responsible for the efficient use of employee time. Through motivation toward production goals and effective work schedules, the efficiency of employees can be maximized.

Interaction among Variances

Interactions among variances often occur, making it even more difficult to determine the responsibility for a particular variance. To illustrate, consider the following anecdote from a manufacturer of brass musical instruments. The purchasing manager obtained a special price on brass alloy from a new supplier. When the material was placed into production, it turned out to be a lower grade of material than the production employees were used to. The alloy was of a slightly different composition, which made the material bend less easily during the formation of brass instruments. The company could have returned the material to the supplier, but that would have interrupted production and kept the division from filling its orders on time. Since using the off-standard material would not affect the quality of the company's finished products, the division manager decided to keep the material and make the best of the situation.

The ultimate result was that the company incurred four interrelated variances during May. The material was less expensive than normal, so the direct-material price variance was favorable. However, the employees had difficulty using the material, which resulted in more waste than expected. Hence, the division incurred an unfavorable direct-material quantity variance.

What were the labor implications of the off-standard material? Due to the difficulty in working with the metal alloy, the employees required more than the standard amount of time to form the instruments. This resulted in an unfavorable direct-labor efficiency variance. Finally, the production supervisor had to use his most senior employees to work with the off-standard material. Since these people earned relatively high wages, the direct-labor rate variance was also unfavorable.

To summarize, the purchase of off-standard material resulted in the following interrelated variances.

$$\text{Purchase of off-standard material} => \begin{cases} \text{Favorable direct-material price variance} \\ \text{Unfavorable direct-material quantity variance} \\ \text{Unfavorable direct-labor rate variance} \\ \text{Unfavorable direct-labor efficiency variance} \end{cases}$$

Such interactions of variances make it more difficult to assign responsibility for any particular variance.

Trade-Offs among Variances   Does the incident described above mean that the decision to buy and use the off-standard material was a poor one? Not necessarily. Perhaps these variances were anticipated, and a conscious decision was made to buy the material anyway. How could this be a wise decision? Suppose the amounts of the variances were as follows:

$(8,500)	Favorable direct-material price variance
1,000	Unfavorable direct-material quantity variance
2,000	Unfavorable direct-labor rate variance
1,500	Unfavorable direct-labor efficiency variance
$(4,000)	Favorable net overall variance

The company saved money overall on the decision to use a different grade of brass alloy. Given that the quality of the final product was not affected, the company's management acted wisely.

Standard Costs and Product Costing

Our discussion of standard costing has focused on its use in controlling costs. But firms that use standard costs for control also use them for product costing. Recall from Chapter 3 that *product costing* is the process of accumulating the costs of a production process and assigning them to the completed products. Product costs are used for various purposes in both financial and managerial accounting.

As production takes place, product costs are added to the Work-in-Process Inventory account. The flow of product costs through a firm's manufacturing accounts is depicted in Exhibit 10–6.

Different types of product-costing systems are distinguished by the type of costs that are entered into Work-in-Process Inventory. In Chapter 3, we studied *actual-* and *normal-costing* systems. In these product-costing systems, the *actual* costs of direct material and direct labor are charged to Work-in-Process Inventory. In a **standard-costing system,** the *standard* costs of direct material and direct labor are entered into Work-in-Process Inventory.

Further explanation of the use of standard costs for product-costing purposes is provided in the appendix at the end of this chapter, which can be studied now if desired.

> **Learning Objective 6**
>
> Explain how standard costs are used in product costing.

> "... [his] innovation and knowledge of the technology led to ... a significant reduction in standard costs, enabling new business opportunities in the government transport market." (10d)
>
> **Rockwell Collins**
> *Engineer of the Year* Award

Exhibit 10–6
Flow of Product Costs through Manufacturing Accounts

*Cost of Goods Sold is an expense. Although it is more descriptive, the term *cost-of-goods-sold expense* is not used as much in practice as the simpler term *cost of goods sold*.

Evaluation of Standard Costing Systems

Learning Objective 7

Summarize some advantages of standard costing.

Standard costing has been the predominant accounting system in manufacturing companies, for both cost control and product-costing purposes, for several decades. This remains true today, and the use of standard costing is spreading to nonmanufacturing firms as well. The widespread use of standard costing over such a long time period suggests that it has traditionally been perceived as offering several advantages. However, today's manufacturing environment is changing dramatically. Some managers are calling into question the usefulness of the traditional standard-costing approach. They argue that the role of standard-costing systems must change.

Advantages of Standard Costing

In this section, we will list some of the advantages traditionally attributed to standard-costing systems. In the next section, we will discuss some of the contemporary criticisms of the standard-costing approach, and suggest several ways in which the role of standard costing is beginning to change.

"Many people have condemned standard costing, saying it is irrelevant to the current just-in-time, fast-paced business environment. Yet surveys consistently show that most industrial companies in the U.S. and abroad still use it. Apparently, these companies have successfully adapted their standard-costing system to their particular business environments." (10e)

Brass Products Division, Parker Hannifin Corporation

Some advantages traditionally attributed to standard costing include the following:

1. Standard costs provide a basis for *sensible cost comparisons.* As we discussed earlier, it would make no sense to compare budgeted costs at one (planned) activity level with actual costs incurred at a different (actual) activity level. Standard costs enable the managerial accountant to compute the standard allowed cost, given actual output, which then serves as a sensible benchmark to compare with the actual cost.

2. Computation of standard costs and cost variances enables managers to employ *management by exception.* This approach conserves valuable management time.

3. Variances provide a means of *performance evaluation* and rewards for employees.

4. Since the variances are used in performance evaluation, they provide *motivation* for employees to adhere to standards.

5. Use of standard costs in product costing results in *more stable product costs* than if actual production costs are used. Actual costs often fluctuate erratically, whereas standard costs are changed only periodically.

Like any tool, a standard-costing system can be misused. When employees are criticized for every cost variance, the positive motivational effects will quickly vanish. Moreover, if standards are not revised often enough, they will become outdated. Then the benefits of cost benchmarks and product costing will disappear.

Criticisms of Standard Costing in Today's Manufacturing Environment

Learning Objective 8

Explain several common criticisms of standard costing.

Listed below are several drawbacks attributed to standard costing in an advanced manufacturing setting.[2]

---

[2]The sources for this material are Robert S. Kaplan, "Limitations of Cost Accounting in Advanced Manufacturing Environments," in *Measures for Manufacturing Excellence,* ed. Robert S. Kaplan (Boston: Harvard Business School Press, 1990), pp. 1–14; H. Thomas Johnson, "Performance Measurement for Competitive Excellence," in *Measures for Manufacturing Excellence,* ed. Robert S. Kaplan (Boston: Harvard Business School Press, 1990), pp. 63–90; Robert A. Bonsack, "Does Activity-Based Costing Replace Standard Costing?" *Journal of Cost Management* 4, no. 4 (Winter 1991), pp. 46, 47; and Michiharu Sukurai, "The Influence of Factory Automation on Management Accounting Practices: A Study of Japanese Companies," in *Measures for Manufacturing Excellence,* ed. Robert S. Kaplan (Boston: Harvard Business School Press, 1990), pp. 39–62.

1.   The variances calculated under standard costing are at too aggregate a level and come too late to be useful. A production process comprises many activities that result in costs. By focusing on the activities that cause costs to be incurred, by eliminating non-value-added activities, and by continually improving performance in value-added activities, costs will be minimized and profit maximized.[3] What is needed are performance measures that focus directly on performance in the activities that management wants to improve. For example, such activities could include product quality, processing time, and delivery performance. (We will explore such measures later in this chapter.)

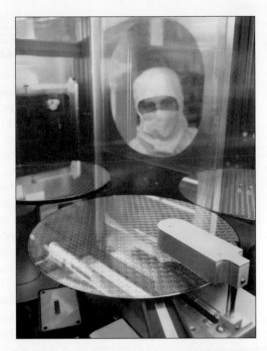

This Texas Instruments manufacturing facility relies on its suppliers for high-quality raw materials delivered on a timely basis. Texas Instruments, like many other companies, employs a sophisticated supplier rating system to measure the performance of its vendors.

2.   Traditional cost variances are also too aggregate in the sense that they are not tied to specific product lines or production batches. The aggregate nature of the variances makes it difficult for managers to determine their cause.

3.   Traditional standard-costing systems focus too much on the cost and efficiency of direct labor, which is rapidly becoming a relatively unimportant factor of production.

4.   One of the most important conditions for the successful use of standard costing is a stable production process. Yet the introduction of flexible manufacturing systems has reduced this stability, with frequent switching among a variety of products on the same production line.

5.   Shorter product life cycles mean that standards are relevant for only a short time. When new products are introduced, new standards must be developed.

6.   Traditional standard costs are not defined broadly enough to capture various important aspects of performance. For example, the standard direct-material price does not capture all of the *costs of ownership*. In addition to the purchase price and transportation costs, the *cost of ownership* includes the costs of ordering, paying bills, scheduling delivery, receiving, inspecting, handling and storing, and any production-line disruptions resulting from untimely or incorrect delivery.

7.   Traditional standard-costing systems tend to focus too much on cost minimization, rather than increasing product quality or customer service. For example, buying the least expensive materials of a given quality, in order to avoid a material price variance, may result in using a vendor whose delivery capabilities are not consistent with JIT requirements.

---

[3]Cost management systems and activity-based management are covered in Chapter 5. Elimination of non-value-added costs also is covered in Chapter 5.

Management
Accounting
Practice

ABB, Bosch
Chassis Systems,
and Hewlett-Packard

WORKING WITH SUPPLIERS TO MANAGE COSTS

Many companies have developed supplier rating systems that contribute to cost competitiveness by helping identify the various costs of ownership. Standard costs often serve as a reference point in such systems. By targeting aspects of performance that affect the standard cost of production, these rating systems help companies to achieve cost control and even reductions in standards costs. ABB has developed a supplier rating system that is designed to minimize the costs of direct materials by focusing on costly defects and shipping errors. "The process consists of a data-driven approach to regularly measure and provide feedback to suppliers. This feedback enables ongoing communication, continuous process improvement, and supplier development." [4]

Bosch Chassis Systems tracks various elements of supplier performance through its Monthly Supplier Performance Rating System. Bosch's model provides for an annual "Supplier of the Year Award," which includes criteria relating to cost reduction, achieving cost targets, and the supplier's role in "value management activities which bring about incremental improvement." [5]

Cost of quality is a significant component of standard cost but one that is difficult to measure. Hewlett-Packard uses a supplier measurement system to engage suppliers in the effort to identify and reduce these costs. "By forming a concrete set of standards regarding product technology, quality, responsiveness, delivery, cost, and environmental impact, HP has been able to weed out noncompliant suppliers and drive performance higher in others . . . Several quality metrics are measured weekly for cost of quality impact, including annualized failure rate (AFR), annualized return rate (ARR), defects parts per million (PPM), and component failure rate." [6]

Operational Performance Measures in Today's Manufacturing Environment

Learning Objective 9

Describe the operational performance measures appropriate for today's manufacturing environment.

In today's advanced manufacturing environment, operational performance measures are taking on ever-greater importance.[7] Under the philosophy of *activity-based management,* the goal is to focus on continually improving each activity. As a result, the emerging operational control measures focus on the key *activities* in which the organization engages. Exhibit 10–7 lists some commonly used operational performance measures. The measures listed in Exhibit 10–7 are representative, but not exhaustive, of those used in practice. In using these measures to control operations, management emphasizes trends over time. The goal is to continually improve all aspects of the plant's operations.

Raw Material and Scrap
Raw material continues to be a significant cost element in any manufacturing process, whether labor-intensive or highly automated. Worldwide material sourcing and international competition have resulted in the purchasing function taking on greater importance in many firms. As a result, purchasing performance has

[4]ABB Web site, "Supplier Performance Assessment" (March 15, 2006) at www.abb.com/cawp/seitp161/e4d128636caefa9ec12569ac0032f1c2.aspx.

[5]Bosch Chassis Systems Work Instruction WIG 11-005, "Monthly Supplier Performance Rating System" (May 8, 2008) at www.pbr.com.au/supplier/documents/WIG11-005.pdf.

[6]Maria Varmazis, "How HP Measures Supplier Performance and Compliance," *Purchasing* 135, Issue 13 (September 21, 2006), pp. 47–49.

[7]This section draws on Howard M. Armitage and Anthony A. Atkinson, "The Choice of Productivity Measures in Organizations," in *Measures for Manufacturing Excellence,* ed. Robert S. Kaplan (Boston: Harvard Business School Press, 1990), pp. 91–128; and Robert S. Kaplan and David P. Norton, *The Strategy-Focused Organization: How Balanced-Scorecard Companies Thrive in the New Business Environment* (Boston: Harvard Business School Press, 2001).

Raw Material and Scrap

Number of vendors

Number of unique parts

Number of common parts

Raw material as a percentage of total cost

Lead time for material delivery

Percentage of orders received on time

Total raw-material cost

Deviations between actual and budgeted raw-material prices

Scrap as a percentage of raw-material cost

Cost of scrap

Quality of raw material

Inventory

Average value of inventory

Average amount of time various inventory items are held

Ratio of inventory value to sales revenue

Number of inventoried parts

Machinery

Hours of machine downtime

Percentage of machine downtime

Percentage of machine availability

Bottleneck machine downtime

Percentage of bottleneck machine downtime

Percentage of bottleneck machine availability

Detailed maintenance records

Percentage of on-time routine maintenance procedures

Setup time

Machine flexibility:

    Product switchover times in an FMS cell

    Number of different products manufactured in an FMS cell

Product Quality

Customer acceptance measures:

    Number of customer complaints

    Number of warranty claims

    Number of products returned

    Cost of repairing returned products

In-process quality measures:

    Number of defects found

    Cost of rework

Quality costs

Production and Delivery

Manufacturing cycle time

Velocity

Manufacturing cycle efficiency

Percentage of on-time deliveries

Percentage of orders filled

Delivery cycle time

Productivity

Financial measures:

    Aggregate or total productivity (output in dollars ÷ total input in dollars)

    Partial or component productivity (output in dollars ÷ a particular input in dollars)

Operational (physical) measures:

    Partial or component productivity measures. These measures express relationships between inputs and outputs, in physical terms. For example:

        Finished products produced per day per employee

        Square feet of floor space required per finished product per day

        Electricity required per finished product

Innovation and Learning

New products:

    Percentage of sales from new products

    New products introduced by this firm versus introductions by competitors

Process improvements:

    Number of process improvements made

    Cost savings from process improvements

Exhibit 10–7

Operational Performance Measures for an Advanced Manufacturing Environment

become an important area of measurement; criteria include total raw-material cost, deviations between actual and budgeted material prices, the quality of raw materials, and the delivery performance of vendors.

Inventory The essence of the just-in-time production environment is low inventories at every stage of production. Thus, inventory control is of paramount importance in achieving the benefits of the JIT philosophy. Inventory control measures include the average value of inventory, the average amount of time various inventory items are held, and other inventory turnover measures, such as the ratio of inventory value to sales revenue.

Machinery If inventories are to be kept low, as the JIT philosophy demands, then the production process must be capable of producing goods quickly. This goal requires that production machinery must work when it is needed, which means that routine maintenance schedules must be adhered to scrupulously. Performance controls in this area include measures of machine downtime and machine availability, and detailed maintenance records. Some manufacturers make a distinction between *bottleneck machinery* and nonbottleneck machinery. A bottleneck operation is one that limits the production capacity of the entire facility. It is vital that the machinery in bottleneck operations be available 100 percent of the time, excluding time for routine required maintenance. This emphasis on bottleneck operations is consistent with the management philosophy known as the **theory of constraints (TOC),** which seeks to maximize long-run profit through proper management of organizational bottlenecks or constrained resources. The key idea in TOC is to identify the constraints in a system that are preventing the organization from achieving a higher level of success and then to seek to relieve or relax those constraints. Moreover, TOC recommends subordinating all other management goals to the objective of solving the constraint problems.[8]

Product Quality   A JIT inventory management system demands adherence to strict quality standards for raw materials, manufactured components, and finished products. Various nonfinancial data are vital for assessing a manufacturer's effectiveness in maintaining product quality. **Customer-acceptance measures** focus on the extent to which a firm's customers perceive its product to be of high quality. Typical performance measures include the number of customer complaints, the number of warranty claims, the number of products returned, and the cost of repairing returned products. **In-process quality controls** refer to procedures designed to assess product quality before production is completed. For example, in a *quality audit program,* partially completed products are randomly inspected at various stages of production. Defect rates are measured, and corrective actions are suggested.

Production and Delivery   A company will achieve little success if it manufactures a great product but delivers it to the customer a week late. World-class manufacturers are striving toward a goal of filling 100 percent of their orders on time. Common measures of product delivery performance include the percentage of on-time deliveries and the percentage of orders filled. Another measure is **delivery cycle time,** the average time between the receipt of a customer order and delivery of the goods.

Delivering goods on time requires that they be produced on time. Various operational performance measures have been developed to assess the timeliness of the production process. **Manufacturing cycle time** is the total amount of production time (or throughput time) required per unit. It can be computed by dividing the total time required to produce a batch by the number of units in the batch. **Velocity** is defined as the number of units produced in a given time period. Perhaps an even more important operational measure is the **manufacturing cycle efficiency (MCE),** defined as follows:

$$\text{Manufacturing cycle efficiency} = \frac{\text{Processing time}}{\text{Processing time} + \text{Inspection time} + \text{Waiting time} + \text{Move time}}$$

The value of the MCE measure lies in its comparison between value-added time (processing) and non-value-added time (inspection, waiting, and moving). In many manufacturing companies, MCE is less than 10 percent. Firms with advanced manufacturing systems strive for as high an MCE measure as possible.

Productivity   Global competitiveness has forced virtually all manufacturers to strive for greater productivity. One *financial* productivity measure is **aggregate** (or **total**) **productivity,** defined as total output divided by total input. A firm's total output is measured as the sum, across all of the goods and services produced, of those products and services times their sales prices. Total input is the sum of the direct-material, direct-labor,

> "We have to be the best in cost throughout the world. And cycle time is also very important." (10f)
>
> **MiCRUS**
> (joint venture of IBM and Cirrus Logic, now part of NXP Semiconductor)

[8]Eliyahu M. Goldratt, *Theory of Constraints* (Croton-on-Hudson, New York: North River Press, 1990).

and overhead costs incurred in production. Another financial measure is a **partial** (or **component**) **productivity** measure, in which total output (in dollars) is divided by the cost of a particular input.

A preferable approach to productivity measurement is to record multiple physical measures that capture the most important determinants of a company's productivity. These *operational* (or *physical*) measures are also partial productivity measures, since each one focuses on a particular input. For example, a large automobile manufacturer routinely records the following data for one of its plants: the number of engines produced per day per employee and the number of square meters of floor space required per engine produced in a day. Data such as these convey more information to management than a summary financial measure such as aggregate productivity.

Innovation and Learning Global competition requires that companies continually improve and innovate. New products must be developed and introduced to replace those that have become obsolete. New processes must continually be developed to make production more efficient. In a world-class manufacturer or service firm, the one thing that is most constant is change.

To summarize, nonfinancial measures are being used increasingly to augment standard-costing systems. These operational performance measures assist management in its goal of continuous process improvement. To be most effective, operational controls should be tied to the strategic objectives of the organization. Specific improvement targets can be set for various measures to provide motivation for improvement in the areas deemed most important by management.

One widely used method to improve operational efficiency is **benchmarking**. This is the continual search for the most effective method of accomplishing a task by comparing existing methods and performance levels with those of other organizations, or with other subunits within the same organization. For example, hospitals routinely benchmark their costs of patient care by diagnostic-related groups (such as circulatory disorders) by comparing them with the costs of other hospitals.

Gain-Sharing Plans

One widely used method of providing incentives to employees to improve their performance on various operational control measures is gain sharing. A **gain-sharing plan** is an incentive system that specifies a formula by which cost or productivity gains achieved by a company are shared with the workers who helped accomplish the improvements. For example, suppose an electronics manufacturer reduced its defect rate in the Manual Insertion Department by 2 percent for a savings of $100,000. A gain-sharing formula might call for 25 percent of the savings to be shared with the employees in that department.

The Balanced Scorecard

Managers of the most successful organizations do not rely on either financial or nonfinancial performance measures alone. They recognize that financial performance measures summarize the results of past actions. These measures are important to a firm's owners, creditors, employees, and so forth. Thus, they must be watched carefully by management as well. Nonfinancial performance measures concentrate on *current* activities, which will be the drivers of *future* financial performance. Thus, effective management requires a balanced perspective on performance measurement, a viewpoint that some call the *balanced scorecard* perspective.

To illustrate the balanced scorecard, we will explore its use by Banque Tournesol, located in Marseilles, France. The bank's balanced scorecard, which is depicted in

Learning Objective 10

Describe the balanced scorecard concept and explain the reasoning behind it.

 Banque Tournesol

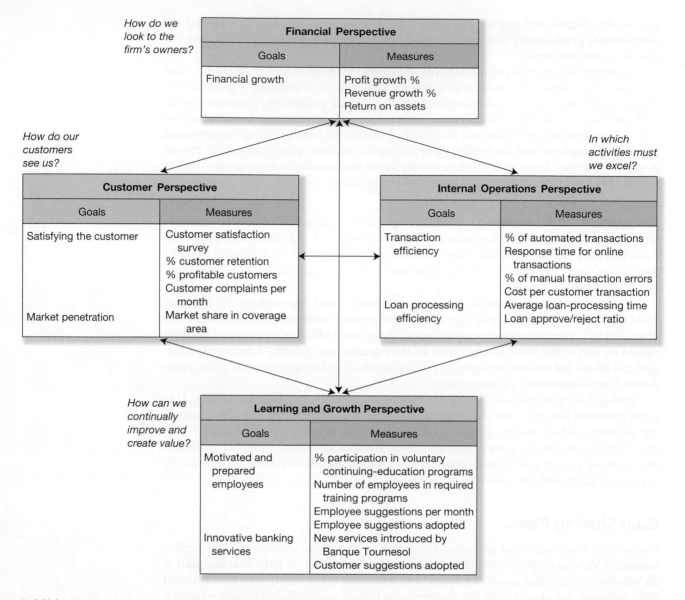

How do we look to the firm's owners?

How do our customers see us?

In which activities must we excel?

How can we continually improve and create value?

Exhibit 10–8

Balanced Scorecard: Banque Tournesol

Exhibit 10–8, integrates performance measures in four key areas: financial, internal operations, customer, and learning and growth.[9] What is the rationale behind Banque Tournesol's balanced scorecard? The bank's overarching, *long-term* goal is financial growth. This goal will be assessed by the following financial measures: profit growth percentage, revenue growth percentage, and return on assets.

This begs the question, though, as to what Banque Tournesol must be doing right now to ensure that its long-term financial goals will be met. The bank's management has decided on several key goals that must be achieved in the near term in order for the company's long-term financial goals to be met.

---

[9]Many banking institutions have developed a balanced scorecard. This balanced scorecard is an amalgamation of bank scorecards from a number of sources, including the author's research as well as the following resources: Robert S. Kaplan and David P. Norton, *The Strategy-Focused Organization: How Balanced Scorecard Companies Thrive in the New Business Environment* (Boston: Harvard Business School Press, 2001); Robert S. Kaplan, "Wells Fargo Online Financial Services," an HBS management case (Boston: President and Fellows of Harvard College, 1998); and Norman Klein and Robert S. Kaplan, "Chemical Bank: Implementing the Balanced Scorecard," an HBS management case (Boston: President and Fellows of Harvard College, 1995).

Let's first look at the customer perspective in the balanced scorecard. The question for Banque Tournesol's management is "How do the bank's customers see us?" Management has expressed its customer-perspective goal as "satisfying the customer." How, then, can management measure progress on this short-term, day-to-day objective? Management has chosen five measures: (1) A customer satisfaction survey is conducted annually among all the bank's customers. Moreover, a more detailed customer satisfaction survey is aimed at the bank's key customers, which account for about 20 percent of the customer base. (2) Banque Tournesol's management keeps track of the percentage of its customers that it retains from one year to the next. The assumption is that a customer who stays with Banque Tournesol is largely satisfied with the service. (3) Not all of Banque Tournesol's customers are profitable. (This is true of almost all banks.) For example, customers that keep low account balances, pay off their credit cards each month, and avoid service charges tend to be unprofitable. Therefore, the percentage of profitable customers is a very important measure. A trend in the wrong direction here would almost certainly spell trouble for the company's financial goals in the future. (4) Banque Tournesol's management has found that a particularly sensitive customer-satisfaction measure is the number of complaints received in a month. If something is going awry in Banque Tournesol's customer interface, customers are not shy about letting the bank know about it—and quickly. (5) Finally, Banque Tournesol's market share in its coverage area is a key measure of market penetration. Increasing this key measure would most likely translate into revenue and profit growth in the future.

What about Banque Tournesol's internal operations? In what business processes must Banque Tournesol excel in order to achieve its long-term financial goals? Management has decided to focus on two important goals: completing routine bank transactions efficiently and processing loan applications efficiently. For routine bank transactions (e.g., making deposits, withdrawals, or loan payments), Banque Tournesol's management focuses on three key measures: (1) Customers can complete automated transactions in three ways. They can bank online, use an ATM, or use a touch-tone telephone to make phone-automated inquiries. Banque Tournesol's management believes that the greater the percentage of automated transactions, as opposed to transactions involving a bank teller, the more efficient will be the bank's transaction operations. (2) Another measure of transaction efficiency is the average time that it takes a customer to complete an online transaction. The smaller this time interval is, Banque Tournesol's management believes, the more likely customers will be to use online banking. (3) As far as manual, teller-assisted transactions go, Banque Tournesol's management keeps track of the percentage of these transactions that exhibit errors.

On the loan side of Banque Tournesol's internal operations, management tracks two measures of loan processing efficiency: (1) The average time to process a loan application is a key indicator of how smoothly this aspect of the bank's operations is running. (2) Banque Tournesol's management also believes that the higher the ratio of approved to rejected loans, the more successful the bank has been in communicating its loan criteria to the bank's customer base.

Finally, let's look at the learning and growth perspective in Banque Tournesol's balanced scorecard. Management has highlighted two goals: motivated and prepared employees and innovative banking services. To assess the goal of motivated and prepared employees, Banque Tournesol's management has established three measures: (1) The bank's human resource management team believes that the percentage of employees participating in voluntary continuing-education programs is an indicator of both employee motivation and preparation. (2) On the other hand, the number of employees in required training programs speaks to both the company's training program offerings as well as employee preparation. (3) The number of employee suggestions per month, as well as the number of those suggestions adopted, also speaks to both employee motivation and preparation. A motivated employee is more likely to submit a suggestion, and a well-prepared employee is more likely to make an adoptable suggestion.

"When you buy into [the balanced scorecard] you've got to be willing to put the time and energy and commitment into it. At the end of the day, the rewards and benefits you can reap from this are tremendous." (10g)
FMC Corporation

The second goal under innovation and learning on Banque Tournesol's scorecard involves innovative banking services. (1) The number of new banking services first offered by Banque Tournesol in its coverage area, as opposed to those first offered by competing banks, is a measure of just how innovative Banque Tournesol's management is. (2) When the bank is able to act positively on a customer suggestion, this too speaks to Banque Tournesol's ability to learn from its customer base.

All in all, Banque Tournesol's management team believes that if the bank meets its current goals for its customer, internal operations, and learning and growth perspectives, the bank will ultimately be successful in achieving its long-term goal of financial growth.

Lead and Lag Measures: The Key to the Balanced Scorecard

Key to understanding the balanced scorecard is the distinction between lead and lag indicators of performance. *Lead indicators* of performance are measures of nonfinancial and financial outcomes that guide management in making current decisions that will result in desirable results in the future. In other words, lead indicators guide management to take actions *now* that will have positive effects on enterprise performance *later.* For example, Banque Tournesol's scorecard includes the bank's market share in its coverage area as an indicator of future market growth, which will ultimately translate into growth of the bank's profitability. By including this key lead indicator in its scorecard, management is directed to take actions now that will increase the bank's market share.

Lag indicators are measures of the final outcomes of earlier management decisions. Examples of lag indicators are a company's profit and cash flow. These key financial measures, while important, only improve in later time periods, well after management has taken important actions to affect key operational results.

The whole idea of the balanced scorecard is to *use lead indicators to communicate with, motivate, and evaluate individuals* with the expectation that their current actions will result in improvements in the company's important lag measures (e.g., profitability) in the future. Exhibit 10–9 gives examples of several key lead and lag measures used in a variety of organizations' balanced scorecards. In addition, note that most of the

Rockwater, which is now owned by Halliburton, is a global undersea oil services company headquartered in Aberdeen, Scotland. Doing the undersea engineering and construction for drilling rigs such as the one pictured here requires diverse technical operations, both on- and offshore. Rockwater's management found the balanced scorecard to be an invaluable tool in clarifying the company's goals and communicating them to the employees. Among the measures in Rockwater's balanced scorecard are the following: cash flow and project profitability (financial); safety index and hours spent with customers on new work (internal); project pricing and customer satisfaction (customer); percentage of revenue from new services and number of employee suggestions (innovation and learning).[10]

---

[10]Robert S. Kaplan and David P. Norton, *The Strategy-Focused Organization: How Balanced Scorecard Companies Thrive in the New Business Environment* (Boston: Harvard Business School Press, 2001).

Exhibit 10–9
Selected Performance Measures Used in Balanced Scorecards

Financial Perspective

Earnings	Cash flow
Earnings per share	Cash flow from operations

Customer Perspective

Customer contacts	Customer satisfaction (surveyed)
Repeat customers	Customer complaints
New customers	Market share

Learning and Growth Perspective

Employee training hours	New processes
Employee promotion rate	Employee suggestions
New products or services	Employee retention

Internal Operations Perspective

Product quality/defect rates	Finished products per day per employee
Number of vendors	Floor space per finished product
Cycle time	Cost of inventories held
Throughput	Number of common parts
Machine downtime	Number of part numbers

operational performance measures listed in Exhibit 10–7 (page 459) could be (and are) used in balanced scorecards.

Many companies, in all types of industries, have developed a balanced scorecard to help management and employees understand the important lead indicators of performance that will ultimately bring success on the company's key long-term goals. Among the many service-industry firms that have developed a balanced scorecard are AT&T of Canada, Bank of America, CIGNA Property and Casualty Division, Citicorp, Duke Children's Hospital, Fannie Mae, J. P. Morgan Chase, Northwestern Mutual, and United Parcel Service. Retailers too have made use of the balanced scorecard. Among them are Best Buy and IKEA.

Among the well-known manufacturers making use of the balanced score card concept are Anheuser-Busch, Apple Computer, Caterpillar, Chrysler, Exxon Mobil, General Motors, Microsoft, Motorola, Phillips Electronics, and Pfizer. Finally, governmental units also have benefited from a balanced scorecard, among them the Republic of South Africa, which designed its Black Economic Empowerment Act around a balanced scorecard model, and the United States Department of Defense.

> "Because of the balanced scorecard, the nature of the monthly financial meetings changed from a focus on the things Pitney Bowes is doing well to the three things we need to improve, with the emphasis on an appropriate action plan." (10h)
> **Pitney Bowes**

Linking the Balanced Scorecard to Organizational Strategy

A key to making successful use of the balanced scorecard is linking the scorecard's lead and lag measures to the organization's strategy. As depicted in the diagram in Exhibit 10–10, the organization's vision and strategy drive the specification of both goals and metrics in the scorecard's financial, customer, internal operations, and learning and growth perspectives.[11]

---

[11]Robert S. Kaplan and David P. Norton, *The Strategy-Focused Organization: How Balanced Scorecard Companies Thrive in the New Business Environment* (Boston: Harvard Business School Press, 2001). See also Raef Lawson, William Stratton, and Toby Hatch, "Scorecarding Goes Global," *Strategic Finance* 87, no. 9 (March 2006), pp. 35–41.

Exhibit 10–10
Linkage between the
Balanced Scorecard and
Organizational Strategy

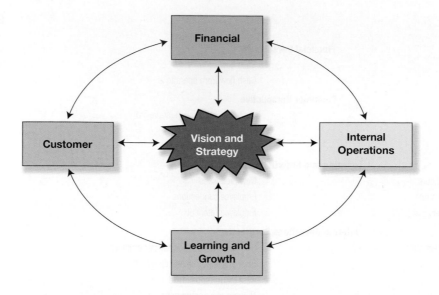

The precise form of the linkage between strategy and the goals and measures in the balanced scorecard will, of course, depend on the nature of the organization and its strategy. The following case in point explores this linkage for Dell Inc. (See also the Management Accounting Practice inset on page 78 in Chapter 2.)

M anagement
A ccounting
P ractice

Dell Inc.

LINKING THE BALANCED SCORECARD TO ORGANIZATIONAL STRATEGY

Key to successfully using the balanced scorecard is linking the scorecard's lead and lag measures to the organization's strategy. According to Dell Inc.'s Web site, the company's strategy is "to be the most successful computer company in the world at delivering the best customer experience in markets we serve."[12]

As the following diagram shows, Dell's strategy of using its direct-sales model to provide unparalleled customer service drives through each of the perspectives that comprise a balanced scorecard.

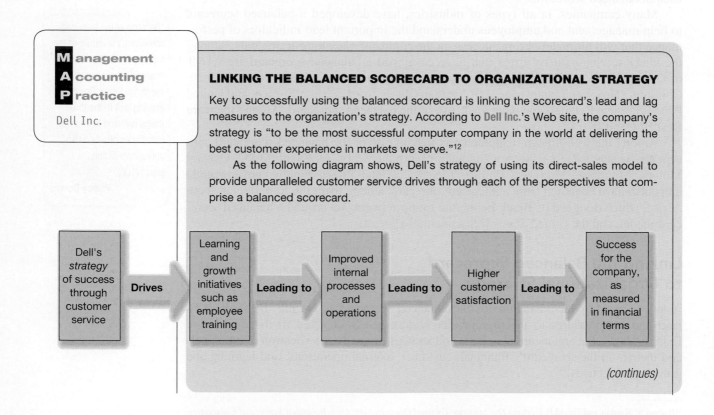

(continues)

[12]This material is based on "Putting Strategy into the Balanced Scorecard," *Strategic Finance* 83, no. 7 (January 2002), pp. 44–52; and Robert S. Kaplan and David P. Norton, *The Strategy-Focused Organization: How Balanced Scorecard Companies Thrive in the New Business Environment* (Boston: Harvard Business School Press, 2001).

The following selected balanced scorecard measures are among those relevant for Dell Inc. to successfully implement its strategy. Notice the frequency of the words *customer* and *sales* in these measures. Dell's strategy and its relevant balanced scorecard measures are dominated by its customer-focused direct-sales business model.

Financial
Profit (in relation to assets invested)
Cash flow
Revenue growth by customer segment
Gross margin by customer segment

↑

Customer
Customer perception of value (i.e., product quality relative to cost)
Customer retention
Customer perception of ease of interacting with Dell
Customer perception of customer response by Dell

↑

Internal processes and operations
Defect rate within Dell's manufacturing operations
Defect rate by Dell's suppliers
Order-to-delivery cycle time
Time spent in contact with customers
Number of customer-focused process innovations

↑

Learning and growth
Training expenditures per full-time employees
Number of customer-initiated product innovations
Number of patents that improve Dell's direct-sales business model
Number of emerging technologies evaluated

↑

Dell's vision and strategy

Focus on Ethics

SACRIFICING QUALITY TO CUT STANDARD COSTS

Pressures to control costs, coupled with bonus systems based on adherence to standards, can present the opportunity to engage in ethical lapses. The following hypothetical scenario describes such a situation.

Amazonia Products manufactures small wooden household items such as cutting boards and knife racks. Amazonia's controller, João Costa, recently completed the installation of a new standard-costing system, which has been in place now for six months. Pedro Ribeiro, the purchasing manager, is about to place an order for wood to be used in Amazonia's cutting boards. Ribeiro has found a supplier that will furnish the necessary wood at $800 per cubic meter, rather than the standard cost of $1,200. This is very appealing to Ribeiro, since his annual bonus is influenced by any favorable price variances he is able to obtain. Ribeiro is due to be transferred at the end of the year to Amazonia's Northwestern Division, which manufactures metal kitchen utensils. The transfer is a promotion for Ribeiro.

After further discussions with the potential supplier, Ribeiro realized that the wood being offered would not be well-suited for use in cutting boards. Although the wood would seem fine in the manufacturing process, and it would result in an attractive product, it would not hold up well over time. This particular type of wood, after repeated cycles of getting wet and then drying out, would tend to crack. Ribeiro figured that it would take about a year for the cutting boards to deteriorate, and then Amazonia Products would be beset with customer complaints.

Ribeiro mulled over the situation for a while and then decided to accept the new supplier's offer. The $800 price would help him get a nice annual bonus, which he could use to help with the down payment on a new home. By the time the cutting boards cracked and customers started to complain, he would be long gone. Someone else could worry about the problem then, he reasoned. After all, he thought, people shouldn't expect a cutting board to last forever.

Several weeks later, when the invoice for the first shipment of wood came through, Costa noticed the large, favorable price variance. When he ran into Ribeiro on the golf course, Costa congratulated Ribeiro on the purchase. The following conversation resulted.

Costa (C): "That was quite a price break on that wood, Pedro. How'd you manage it?"

Ribeiro (PM): "Tough negotiating, João. It's as simple as that."

Costa (C): "Is it good wood? And how about the supplier, Pedro? Will they deliver on time?"

Ribeiro (PM): "This supplier is very timely in their deliveries. I made sure of that."

Costa (C): "How about the quality, Pedro? Did you check into that?"

Ribeiro (PM): "Sure I did, João. Hey, what is this? An interrogation? I thought we were here to play golf."

Costa was left feeling puzzled and disconcerted by Ribeiro's evasiveness. The next day, Costa talked to the production manager, Roberto Creuza, about his concerns. Later that day, Creuza raised the issue with Ribeiro. After a lengthy and sometimes heated exchange, the story came out.

Discuss the ethical issues involved in this scenario. Did the purchasing manager, Pedro Ribeiro, act ethically? Did the controller, João Costa, act ethically when he asked Ribeiro about the quality of the wood? Did Costa act ethically when he went to the production manager with his concerns? What should the controller do now?

Chapter Summary

LO1 Explain how standard costing is used to help manage costs. The managerial accountant works with others in the organization to set standard costs for direct material, direct labor, and manufacturing overhead through either historical cost analysis or task analysis. The accountant then uses the standard cost as a benchmark against which to compare actual costs incurred. Managers use management by exception to determine the causes of significant cost variances.

LO2 Describe two ways to set standards and distinguish between perfection and practical standards. One way to set standards is to analyze historical data, which will show how much it has cost in the past to produce a product. Another way to set standards is to perform task analysis, in which the manufacturing process is analyzed to determine what it should cost to produce the product. A perfection (or ideal) standard is one that can be attained only under nearly perfect operating conditions. A practical (or attainable) standard can be achieved with a production process that is as efficient as practical under normal operating conditions.

LO3 Compute and interpret the direct-material price and quantity variances and the direct-labor rate and efficiency variances. The direct-material price variance calculates the effect on production cost of deviations between actual and standard direct-material prices. The direct-material quantity variance calculates the effect on production cost of deviations between actual and standard direct-material quantities allowed, given actual production output. The direct-labor rate variance calculates the effect on production cost of deviations between actual and standard direct-labor rates. The direct-labor efficiency variance calculates the effect on production cost of deviations between actual and standard direct-labor hours allowed, given actual production output.

LO4 Explain several methods for determining the significance of cost variances. Managers determine the significance of cost variances through judgment and rules of thumb. The absolute and relative sizes of variances, recurrence of variances, variance trends, and controllability of variances are all considered in deciding whether variances warrant investigation. In some cases a statistical control chart can help determine the significance of cost variances.

LO5 Describe some behavioral effects of standard costing. When variances can affect employees' reward structures, such as pay increases or promotions, they can significantly affect employee behavior. For example, an unfavorable direct-material price variance may cause a purchasing manager to purchase a lower quality of material than what is specified or needed.

LO6 Explain how standard costs are used in product costing. The managerial accountant achieves the product-costing purpose of the standard-costing system by entering the standard cost of production into Work-in-Process Inventory as a product cost. This standard cost then flows through the Finished-Goods Inventory account and into the Cost of Goods Sold account.

LO7 Summarize some advantages of standard costing. Standard-costing systems offer an organization many advantages. Among these are: sensible cost comparisons; management by exception; performance evaluation; employee motivation; and more stable product costs.

LO8 Explain several common criticisms of standard costing. Some common criticisms of standard costing include: too high a level of aggregation exhibited by variances; untimely reporting of variances; excessive focus on direct labor; inconsistency with flexible manufacturing systems; quick outdating of standards; narrow focus of standard costs, such as ignoring the total cost of ownership; and an excessive focus on cost minimization.

LO9 Describe the operational performance measures appropriate for today's manufacturing environment. Nonfinancial measures of operational performance are widely used to augment the control information provided by standard costing. These measures typically focus on raw material and scrap, inventory, machinery, product quality, production and delivery, productivity, and innovation and learning.

LO10 Describe the balanced scorecard concept and explain the reasoning behind it. The balanced scorecard is an important tool designed to focus management's attention on key current goals, which, if achieved, will facilitate the attainment of the organization's long-term goals. By achieving current goals in the customer, internal operations, and learning and growth perspectives, the company will ultimately achieve its long-term financial goals.

LO11 Prepare journal entries to record and close out cost variances (appendix). The managerial accountant prepares journal entries: to enter the standard cost of production into Work-in-Process Inventory as a product cost; to transfer the standard production cost to Finished-Goods Inventory; and to close the standard production cost into Cost of Goods Sold.

Review Problems on Standard Costing and Operational Performance Measures

Problem 1

In November Pâtisserie Cézanne produced 3,000 multilayer fancy cakes and incurred the following actual costs for direct material and direct labor.

Purchased 8,250 kilograms of ingredients at $2.88 per kilogram.

Used 7,750 kilograms of ingredients at $2.88 per kilogram.

Used 1,520 hours of direct labor at $22 per hour.

The standard costs for production of multilayer fancy cakes were the same in November as those given earlier in the chapter for September.

Compute Pâtisserie Cézanne's direct-material and direct-labor variances for November using the format shown in Exhibits 10–2 and 10–3.

Problem 2

Toscano Door Company manufactures high-quality wooden doors used in home construction. The following information pertains to operations during April.

Processing time (average per batch)	6 hours
Inspection time (average per batch)	1 hour
Waiting time (average per batch)	4 hours
Move time (average per batch)	5 hours
Units per batch	40 units

Compute the following operational measures: (1) average value-added time per batch; (2) average non-value-added time per batch; (3) manufacturing cycle efficiency; (4) manufacturing cycle time; (5) velocity.

Solutions to Review Problems

Problem 1

Direct-Material Price and Quantity Variances

Actual Material Cost					Standard Material Cost	
Actual Quantity × **Actual Price**		**Actual Quantity** × **Standard Price**			**Standard Quantity** × **Standard Price**	
8,250 kilograms purchased × $2.88 per kilogram		8,250 kilograms purchased × $2.80 per kilogram			7,500 kilograms allowed × $2.80 per kilogram	

$23,760 $23,100 $21,000

$660 Unfavorable

Direct-material price variance

7,750 kilograms used × $2.80 per kilograms

$21,700

$700 Unfavorable

Direct-material quantity variance

*Actual output × Standard quantity per unit = 3,000 units × 2.5 kilograms per unit = 7,500 kilograms allowed.

Using Formulas

$$\text{Direct-material price variance} = PQ(AP - SP)$$
$$= 8{,}250(\$2.88 - \$2.80)$$
$$= \$660 \text{ Unfavorable}$$
$$\text{Direct-material quantity variance} = SP(AQ - SQ)$$
$$= \$2.80(7{,}750 - 7{,}500)$$
$$= \$700 \text{ Unfavorable}$$

Direct-Labor Rate and Efficiency Variances

Actual Labor Cost					Standard Labor Cost	
Actual Hours	× Actual Rate	Actual Hours	× Standard Rate	Standard Hours	× Standard Rate	
1,520 hours used	× $22 per hour	1,520 hours used	× $20 per hour	1,500* hours allowed	× $20 per hour	
$33,440		$30,400		$30,000		

$3,040 Unfavorable ← → $400 Unfavorable

Direct-labor rate variance   Direct-labor efficiency variance

*Actual output × Standard hours per unit = 3,000 units × .5 hour per unit = 1,500 hours allowed.

Using Formulas

$$\text{Direct-labor rate variance} = AH(AR - SR)$$
$$= 1,520(\$22 - \$20)$$
$$= \$3,040 \text{ Unfavorable}$$
$$\text{Direct-labor efficiency variance} = SR(AH - SH)$$
$$= \$20(1,520 - 1,500)$$
$$= \$400 \text{ Unfavorable}$$

Problem 2

1. Average value-added time per batch = Processing time = 6 hours

2. Average non-value-added time per batch = Inspection time + Waiting time + Move time
   = 10 hours

3. Manufacturing cycle efficiency $= \dfrac{\text{Processing time}}{\text{Processing time} + \text{Inspection time} + \text{Waiting time} + \text{Move time}}$

   $= \dfrac{6 \text{ hours}}{6 \text{ hours} + 1 \text{ hour} + 4 \text{ hours} + 5 \text{ hours}} = 37.5\%$

4. Manufacturing cycle time $= \dfrac{\text{Total production time per batch}}{\text{Units per batch}}$

   $= \dfrac{16 \text{ hours}}{40 \text{ units per batch}} = .4$ hour (or 24 minutes) per unit

5. Velocity $= \dfrac{\text{Units per batch}}{\text{Total production time per batch}}$

   $= \dfrac{40 \text{ units}}{16 \text{ hours}} = 2.5$ units per hour

Key Terms

For each term's definition refer to the indicated page, or turn to the glossary at the end of the text.

aggregate (or total) productivity, 460
benchmarking, 461
controllability, 451
cost variance, 441
customer-acceptance measures, 460
delivery cycle time, 460
direct-labor efficiency variance, 447
direct-labor rate variance, 447

direct-material price variance (or purchase price variance), 445
direct-material quantity variance, 445
gain-sharing plan, 461
in-process quality controls, 460
management by exception, 441
manufacturing cycle efficiency (MCE), 460

manufacturing cycle time, 460
partial (or component) productivity, 461
perfection (or ideal) standard, 442
practical (or attainable) standard, 443
standard cost, 440
standard-costing system, 455
standard direct-labor quantity, 445

standard direct-labor rate, 445
standard direct-material price, 444
standard direct-material quantity, 444
statistical control chart, 452
task analysis, 442
theory of constraints (TOC), 460
velocity, 460

APPENDIX TO CHAPTER 10

Use of Standard Costs for Product Costing

Learning Objective **11**

Prepare journal entries to record and close out cost variances (Appendix).

Pâtisserie Cézanne

In addition to providing a tool for *cost management,* standard-costing systems also provide the necessary information to be used in *product costing.* As shown in Exhibit 10–6, under standard costing, it is the *standard costs* that are entered into Work-in-Process Inventory as a product cost.

Journal Entries under Standard Costing   To illustrate the use of standard costs in product costing, we will continue our illustration of Pâtisserie Cézanne. For September's production of multilayer fancy cakes, the company purchased 6,250 kilograms of direct material for $17,750. The actual quantity of material used in production was 5,125 kilograms. However, the standard cost of direct material, given September's actual output of 2,000 multilayer fancy cakes, was only $14,000. The following journal entries record these facts and isolate the direct-material price and quantity variances.

Raw-Material Inventory	17,500	
Direct-Material Price Variance	250	
Accounts Payable		17,750
To record the purchase of raw material and the incurrence of an unfavorable price variance.		

Work-in-Process Inventory	14,000	
Direct-Material Quantity Variance	350	
Raw-Material Inventory		14,350
To record the use of direct material in production and the incurrence of an unfavorable quantity variance.		

Notice that the material purchase is recorded in the Raw-Material Inventory account at its standard price ($17,500 = 6,250 kilograms purchased × $2.80 per kilogram). The $14,000 debit entry to Work-in-Process Inventory adds only the standard cost of the material to Work-in-Process Inventory as a product cost ($14,000 = 5,000 kilograms allowed × $2.80 per kilogram). The two variances are isolated in their own variance accounts. Since they are both unfavorable, they are represented by debit entries.

The following journal entry records the actual September cost of direct labor, as an addition to Wages Payable. The entry also adds the standard cost of direct labor to Work-in-Process Inventory and isolates the direct-labor variances.

Work-in-Process Inventory	20,000	
Direct-Labor Rate Variance	980	
Direct-Labor Efficiency Variance		400
Wages Payable		20,580
To record the usage of direct labor and the direct-labor variances for September.		

Since the direct-labor efficiency variance is favorable, it is recorded as a credit entry.

Disposition of Variances   Variances are temporary accounts, like revenue and expense accounts, and they are closed out at the end of each accounting period. Most companies close their variance accounts directly into Cost of Goods Sold. The journal entry required to close out the September variances incurred in the production of multilayer fancy cakes is as follows:

Cost of Goods Sold	1,180	
Direct-Labor Efficiency Variance	400	
Direct-Labor Rate Variance		980
Direct-Material Price Variance		250
Direct-Material Quantity Variance		350

The increase of $1,180 in Cost of Goods Sold is explained as follows:

	Unfavorable Variances Increase Cost of Goods Sold	Favorable Variance Decreases Cost of Goods Sold	Net Increase in Cost of Goods Sold
Direct-labor efficiency variance		$400	
Direct-labor rate variance	$ 980		
Direct-material price variance	250		
Direct-material quantity variance	350		
Total	$1,580 −	$400 =	$1,180

The unfavorable variances represent costs of operating inefficiently, relative to the standards, and thus cause Cost of Goods Sold to be higher. The opposite is true for favorable variances.

An alternative method of variance disposition is to apportion all variances among Work-in-Process Inventory, Finished-Goods Inventory, and Cost of Goods Sold. This accounting treatment reflects the effects of unusual inefficiency or efficiency in all of the accounts through which the manufacturing costs flow. This method, called *variance proration,* is covered more fully in cost accounting texts.

Cost Flow Under Standard Costing

In a standard-costing system, since standard costs are entered into Work-in-Process Inventory, standard costs flow through all of the manufacturing accounts. Thus, as depicted in Exhibit 10–6, all of the product costs flowing through the accounts are standard costs. To illustrate, suppose Pâtisserie Cézanne produced 2,000 multilayer fancy cakes in September and sold all 2,000 of them. The journal entries to record the flow of standard direct-material and direct-labor costs are shown below.

Finished-Goods Inventory	34,000*	
Work-in-Process Inventory		34,000

*Total standard cost of direct material and direct labor: $34,000 = $14,000 + $20,000.

Cost of Goods Sold	34,000*	
Finished-Goods Inventory		34,000

*All 2,000 multilayer fancy cakes were sold.

Our illustration is not really complete yet, because we have not discussed manufacturing-overhead costs. This topic is covered in the next chapter. The important point at this juncture is that in a standard-costing system, *standard costs rather than actual costs flow through the manufacturing accounts.*

A Note on Perishable Products and JIT Production Management Systems

Traditional manufacturing systems typically exhibit the cost flows explained in this section. Direct-material, direct-labor, and manufacturing-overhead costs are entered in Work-in-Process Inventory, from which they flow into Finished-Goods Inventory when the goods are finished, and then on into Cost of Goods Sold. Since Pâtisserie Cézanne produces perishable goods, which are produced and sold on the same day, a simpler procedure could be used. In Pâtisserie Cézanne's case, the *standard* costs of direct material, direct labor, and manufacturing overhead could be entered directly into Cost of Goods Sold as they are incurred. This simplified procedure could be used, because the production process is very short and the goods are sold immediately. Thus, there is never any work-in-process inventory or finished-goods inventory on hand. Such situations are common with producers of perishable goods.

An analogous situation occurs in manufacturers that employ a just-in-time (JIT) production and inventory control system. In a JIT environment, raw materials are delivered just in time to be entered into production, and parts or components are manufactured in each stage of the production process just in time for the next production stage. Thus, like the case of perishable goods, there is little or no work-in-process or finished-goods inventory at any given time in a JIT environment. For this reason, many manufacturers that employ the JIT approach make use of highly simplified cost accounting procedures similar to those explained in the preceding paragraph for Pâtisserie Cézanne.

Review Questions

10–1. List the three parts of a control system, and explain how such a system works.

10–2. What is meant by the phrase *management by exception?*

10–3. Describe two methods of setting standards.

10–4. Distinguish between *perfection* and *practical* standards. Which type of standard is likely to produce the best motivational effects?

10–5. Describe how a bank might use standards.

10–6. Explain how standard material prices and quantities are set.

10–7. What is the interpretation of the *direct-material price variance?*

10–8. What manager is usually in the best position to influence the direct-material price variance?

10–9. What is the interpretation of the *direct-material quantity variance?*

10–10. What manager is usually in the best position to influence the direct-material quantity variance?

10–11. Explain why the quantity purchased (PQ) is used in computing the direct-material price variance, but the actual quantity consumed (AQ) is used in computing the direct-material quantity variance.

10–12. What is the interpretation of the *direct-labor rate variance?* What are some possible causes?

10–13. What manager is generally in the best position to influence the direct-labor rate variance?

10–14. What is the interpretation of the *direct-labor efficiency variance?*

10–15. What manager is generally in the best position to influence the direct-labor efficiency variance?

10–16. Refer to Review Question 10–11. Why does an analogous question *not* arise in the context of the direct-labor variances?

10–17. Describe five factors that managers often consider when determining the significance of a variance.

10–18. Discuss several ways in which standard-costing systems should be adapted in today's manufacturing environment.

10–19. Describe how standard costs are used for product costing.

10–20. List six advantages of a standard-costing system.

10–21. List seven areas in which nonfinancial, operational performance measures are receiving increased emphasis in today's manufacturing environment.

10–22. Define the term *manufacturing cycle efficiency.*

10–23. List four examples of customer acceptance measures.

10–24. What is meant by *aggregate productivity,* and what are its limitations?

10–25. List seven criticisms of standard costing in an advanced manufacturing environment.

10–26. Suggest two performance measures in each of the four balanced scorecard categories for a service industry firm of your choosing. Using these measures as examples, explain the difference between lead and lag measures.

10–27. Give an example of a gain-sharing plan that could be implemented by an airline.

Exercises

All applicable Exercises are available with McGraw-Hill's *Connect Accounting*™.

■ **Exercise 10–28**
Straightforward Computation of Variances
(LO 1, 3)

Saskatewan Can Company manufactures recyclable soft-drink cans. A unit of production is a case of 12 dozen cans. The following standards have been set by the production-engineering staff and the controller.

Direct labor:	Direct material:
Quantity, .25 hour	Quantity, 4 kilograms
Rate, $16 per hour	Price, $.80 per kilogram

Actual material purchases amounted to 240,000 kilograms at $.81 per kilogram. Actual costs incurred in the production of 50,000 units were as follows:

Direct labor:	$211,900 for 13,000 hours
Direct material:	$170,100 for 210,000 kilograms

Required:

1. Use the variance formulas to compute the direct-material price and quantity variances and the directlabor rate and efficiency variances. Indicate whether each variance is favorable or unfavorable.

2. *Build a spreadsheet:* Construct an Excel spreadsheet to solve the preceding requirement. Show how the solution will change if the following information changes: the standard direct-labor rate is $15 per hour, and the standard direct-material price is $.79 per kilogram.

Refer to the data in the preceding exercise. Use diagrams similar to those in Exhibits 10–2 and 10–3 to determine the direct-material and direct-labor variances. Indicate whether each variance is favorable or unfavorable.

■ **Exercise 10–29**
Determination of Variances Using Diagrams
(LO 3)

Choose one of the following manufacturers (or any manufacturer of your choosing), and use the Internet to gather information about any new products the company has recently introduced or plans to introduce.

Airbus	www.airbus.com	Fuji	www.fujifilm.com
Komatsu	www.komatsu.com	Pfizer	www.pfizer.com
Ford	www.ford.com/us	Xerox	www.xerox.com

Required: Discuss the steps you think the company would go through in establishing standard costs for its new product.

■ **Exercise 10–30**
Developing Standards for New Products; Use of Internet
(LO 2)

China Hardwoods mass produces jewelry boxes. A production lot of standard-size boxes requires 8 cubic meters of hardwood in the finished product. In addition, 2 cubic meters of scrap lumber are normally left from the production of one production lot. Hardwood costs $1600 per cubic meter, plus $600 in transportation charges per cubic meter..

Required: Compute the standard direct-material cost of a jewelry box.

■ **Exercise 10–31**
Computing Standard Direct-Material Cost
(LO 2)

During June, Danby Company's material purchases amounted to 6,000 kilograms at a price of $7.20 per kilogram. Actual costs incurred in the production of 2,000 units were as follows:

Direct labor:	$117,390 ($18.20 per hour)
Direct material:	$30,240 ($7.20 per kilogram)

The standards for one unit of Danby Company's product are as follows:

Direct labor:	Direct material:
Quantity, 3 hours per unit	Quantity, 2 kilograms per unit
Rate, $18 per hour	Price, $7 per kilogram

Required: Compute the direct-material price and quantity variances and the direct-labor rate and efficiency variances. Indicate whether each variance is favorable or unfavorable.

■ **Exercise 10–32**
Straightforward Calculation of Variances
(LO 1, 3)

Refer to the data in the preceding exercise. Draw diagrams depicting the direct-material and direct-labor variances similar to the diagrams in Exhibits 10–2 and 10–3.

■ **Exercise 10–33**
Diagramming Direct-Material and Direct-Labor Variances
(LO 3)

The director of cost management for Odessa Company uses a statistical control chart to help management determine when to investigate variances. The critical value is 1 standard deviation. The company incurred the following direct-labor efficiency variances during the first six months of the current year.

■ **Exercise 10–34**
Cost Variance Investigation
(LO 4)

January	$250 F	April	$ 900 U
February	800 U	May	1,050 U
March	700 U	June	1,200 U

The standard direct-labor cost during each of these months was $19,000. The controller has estimated that the firm's monthly direct-labor variances have a standard deviation of $950.

Required:

1. Draw a statistical control chart and plot the variance data given above. Which variances will be investigated?

2. Suppose the controller's rule of thumb is to investigate all variances equal to or greater than 6 percent of standard cost. Then which variances will be investigated?

3. Would you investigate any of the variances listed above other than those indicated by the rules discussed in requirements (1) and (2)? Why?

■ **Exercise 10–35**
Standard Allowed Input
(LO 2)

Due to evaporation during production, Plano Plastics Company requires 8 kilograms of material input for every 7 kilograms of good plastic sheets manufactured. During May, the company produced 3,500 kilograms of good sheets.

Required: Compute the total standard allowed input quantity, given the good output produced.

■ **Exercise 10–36**
Reconstructing Standard-Cost Information from Partial Data
(LO 1, 3)

Part of your company's accounting database was destroyed by a malicious computer virus. You have been able to gather the following data from your files. Reconstruct the remaining information using the available data. All of the raw material purchased during the period was used in production. (*Hint:* It is helpful to solve for the unknowns in the order indicated by the letters in the following table.)

	Direct Labor	Direct Material
Standard price or rate per unit of input	e	$8 per kilogram
Standard quantity per unit of output	f	c
Actual quantity used per unit of output	3.5 hours	a
Actual price or rate per unit of input	$21 per hour	$7 per kilogram
Actual output	10,000 units	10,000 units
Direct-material price variance	—	$30,000 F
Direct-material quantity variance	—	b
Total of direct-material variances	—	$10,000 F
Direct-labor rate variance	d	—
Direct-labor efficiency variance	$100,000 F	—
Total of direct-labor variances	$ 65,000 F	—

■ **Exercise 10–37**
Operational Performance Measures; JIT/FMS Setting
(LO 9)

Zagreb Valve Company manufactures flow control valves. The following information pertains to operations during May.

Processing time (average per batch)	8.5 hours
Inspection time (average per batch)	.5 hour
Waiting time (average per batch)	.5 hour
Move time (average per batch)	.5 hour
Units per batch	30 units

Required: Compute the following operational measures: (1) manufacturing cycle efficiency; (2) manufacturing cycle time; (3) velocity.

■ **Exercise 10–38**
Performance Measures for Production and Delivery
(LO 9)

Data Screen Corporation is a highly automated manufacturing firm. The vice president of finance has decided that traditional standards are inappropriate for performance measures in an automated environment. Labor is insignificant in terms of the total cost of production and tends to be fixed, material quality is considered more important than minimizing material cost, and customer satisfaction is the number one priority. As a result, production and delivery performance measures have been chosen to evaluate performance. The following information is considered typical of the time involved to complete and ship orders.

Waiting time:

From order being placed to start of production	8.0 days
From start of production to completion	7.0 days
Inspection time	1.5 days
Processing time	3.0 days
Move time	2.5 days

Required:

1. Calculate the manufacturing cycle efficiency.
2. Calculate the delivery cycle time.

(CMA, adapted)

Managerial accounting procedures developed for the manufacturing industry often are applied in nonmanufacturing settings also. Belfast Banking Group PLC's total output of financial services during the year just ended was valued at $10 million. The total cost of the firm's inputs, primarily direct labor and overhead, was $8 million.

Required:

1. Compute the bank's aggregate (or total) productivity for the year.
2. Do you believe this is a useful measure? Why? Suggest an alternative approach that Belfast Banking Group might use to measure productivity.

■ **Exercise 10–39**
Productivity Measurement
(LO 9)

Refer to the data in Exercise 10–28, regarding Saskatewan Can Company. Prepare journal entries to:

1. Record the purchase of direct material on account.
2. Add direct-material and direct-labor cost to Work-in-Process Inventory.
3. Record the direct-material and direct-labor variances.
4. Close these variances into Cost of Goods Sold.

■ **Exercise 10–40**
Journal Entries under
Standard Costing (Appendix)
(LO 6, 11)

Refer to your answer for Exercise 10–40. Set up T-accounts, and post the journal entries to the general ledger.

■ **Exercise 10–41**
Posting Journal Entries for
Variances (Appendix)
(LO 6, 11)

Problems

All applicable Problems are available with McGraw-Hill's *Connect Accounting*™.

Patni Auto Parts Mfg. Ltd. manufactured 7,800 units during January of a control valve used in the production of fuel injectors in its nearby Mumbai plant. Records indicated the following:

Direct labor	40,100 hr. at $14.60 per hr.
Direct material purchased	12,500 kg. at $5.20 per kg.
Direct material used	11,550 kg.

The control valve has the following standard prime costs:

Direct material:	1.5 kg. at $5.00 per kg.	$ 7.50
Direct labor:	5 hr. at $15.00 per hr.	75.00
Standard prime cost per unit		$82.50

■ **Problem 10–42**
Direct-Material and
Direct-Labor Variances
(LO 1, 3)

2. Direct-material quantity
variance: $750 F

Required:

1. Prepare a schedule of standard production costs for January, based on actual production of 7,800 units.
2. For the month of January, compute the following variances, indicating whether each is favorable or unfavorable.

    a. Direct-material price variance.

    b. Direct-material quantity variance.

    c. Direct-labor rate variance.

    d. Direct-labor efficiency variance.

3. ***Build a spreadsheet:*** Construct an Excel spreadsheet to solve all of the preceding requirements. Show how the solution will change if the following information changes: the standard direct-labor rate is $16 per hour, and the standard direct-material price is $5.20 per kilogram.

■ **Problem 10–43**
Determining Standard
Material Cost
(LO 2)

South Atlantic Chemical Company manufactures industrial chemicals in Rio de Janeiro, Brazil. The company plans to introduce a new chemical solution and needs to develop a standard product cost. The new chemical solution is made by combining a chemical compound (nyclyn) and a solution (salex), heating the mixture, adding a second compound (protet), and bottling the resulting solution in 10-liter containers. The initial mix, which is 11 liters in volume, consists of 12 kilograms of nyclyn and 9.6 liters of salex. A 1-liter reduction in volume occurs during the boiling process. The solution is cooled slightly before 5 kilograms of protet are added. The addition of protet does not affect the total liquid volume.

    The purchase price of the direct materials used in the manufacture of this new chemical solution are given below.

Nyclyn	$1.45 per kilogram
Salex	$1.80 per liter
Protet	$2.40 per kilogram

Required: Determine the standard material cost of a 10-liter container of the new product.

(CMA, adapted)

■ **Problem 10–44**
Direct-Material and Direct-
Labor Variances
(LO 1, 3)

1. Direct-material price variance: $540 U

During May, Milan Fabrics manufactured 500 units of a special multilayer fabric with the trade name Stylex. The following information from the Stylex production department also pertains to May.

Direct material purchased: 18,000 meters at $1.38 per meter	$24,840
Direct material used: 9,500 meters at $1.38 per meter	13,110
Direct labor: 2,100 hours at $9.15 per hour	19,215

The standard prime costs for one unit of Stylex are as follows:

Direct material: 20 meters at $1.35 per meter	$27
Direct labor: 4 hours at $8.90 per hour	36
Total standard prime cost per unit of output	$63

Required: Compute the following variances for the month of May, indicating whether each variance is favorable or unfavorable.

1. Direct-material price variance.

2. Direct-material quantity variance.

3. Direct-labor rate variance.

4. Direct-labor efficiency variance.

(CPA, adapted)

■ **Problem 10–45**
Variance Calculation;
Analysis; Service Business
(LO 1, 3)

2. Direct-labor efficiency
variance: $495.00 F
4. Total material and labor
variances: $852.50 F

Salvatore Amato operates a residential landscaping business in an affluent district of Florence. In an effort to provide quality service, he has concentrated solely on the design and installation of upscale landscaping plans (e.g., trees, shrubs, fountains, and lighting). With his clients continually requesting additional services, Amato recently expanded into lawn maintenance, including fertilization.

    The following data relate to his first year's experience with 55 fertilization clients:

• Each client required six applications throughout the year and was billed $40 per application.

• Two applications involved Type I fertilizer, which contains a special ingredient for weed control. The remaining four applications involved Type II fertilizer.

- Amato purchased 2,500 kilograms of Type I fertilizer at $1.08 per kilogram and 5,000 kilograms of Type II fertilizer at $.80 per kilogram. Actual usage amounted to 1,850 kilograms of Type I and 3,900 kilograms of Type II.

- A new, part-time employee was hired to spread the fertilizer. Amato had to pay premium wages of $11.50 per hour because of a very tight labor market; the employee logged a total of 165 hours at client residences.

- Based on previous knowledge of the operation, articles in trade journals, and conversations with other landscapers, Amato established the following standards:

> Fertilizer purchase price per kilogram: Type I, $1.00; Type II, $.84
>
> Fertilizer usage: 20 kilograms per application
>
> Typical hourly wage rate of landscape personnel: $9
>
> Labor time per application: 40 minutes

- The operation did not go as smoothly as planned, with customer complaints actually much higher than expected.

Required:

1. Compute Amato's direct-material variances of each type of fertilizer.
2. Compute the direct-labor variances.
3. Compute the actual cost of the client applications. (*Note:* Exclude any fertilizer in inventory, as remaining fertilizer can be used next year.) Was the new service a financial success? Explain.
4. Analyze the variances that you computed in requirements (1) and (2).
   a. Was the new service a success from an overall cost-control perspective? Briefly discuss.
   b. What seems to have happened that would give rise to customer complaints?
5. In view of the complaints, should the fertilizer service be continued next year? Why?

■ **Problem 10–46**
Variance Computation;
Analysis of Performance and
Responsibility
(LO 1, 3)

Direct-labor rate variance:
$41,800 U

Santa Rosa Industries uses a standard-costing system to assist in the evaluation of operations. The company has had considerable trouble in recent months with suppliers and employees, so much so that management hired a new production supervisor (Frank Schmidt). The new supervisor has been on the job for five months and has seemingly brought order to an otherwise chaotic situation.

The vice president of manufacturing recently commented that ". . . Schmidt has really done the trick. The change to a new direct-material supplier and Schmidt's team-building/morale-boosting training exercises have truly brought things under control." The VP's comments were based on both a plant tour, where he observed a contented workforce, and a review of the following data, which was excerpted from a performance report:

Direct-material variances, favorable	$4,620
Direct-labor variances, favorable	$11,400

These variances are especially outstanding, given that the amounts are favorable and small. (Santa Rosa's budgeted material and labor costs generally each average about $350,000 for similar periods.) Additional data follow.

- The company purchased and consumed 22,500 kilograms of direct materials at $15.40 per kilogram, and paid $16.00 per hour for 20,900 direct-labor hours of activity. Total completed production amounted to 9,500 units.

- A review of the firm's standard cost records found that each completed unit requires 2.1 kilograms of direct material at $17.60 per kilogram and 2.6 direct-labor hours at $14 per hour.

Required:

1. On the basis of the information contained in the performance report, should Santa Rosa be concerned about its variances? Why?
2. Calculate the company's direct-material variances and direct-labor variances.
3. On the basis of your answers to requirement (2), should Santa Rosa be concerned about its variances? Why?
4. Are things going as smoothly as the vice president believes? Evaluate the company's variances and determine whether the change to a new supplier and Schmidt's team-building/morale-boosting training exercises appear to be working. Explain.
5. Is it possible that some of the company's current problems lie outside Schmidt's area of responsibility? Explain.

■ **Problem 10–47**
Direct-Labor Variances at
Colgate Palmolive Company;
Cost Variance Investigation
(LO 4)

2(a). Standard direct-labor
cost, January: $9,983
(rounded)

The following data pertain to Colgate Palmolive's liquid filling line during the first 10 months of a particular year. The standard ratio of direct-labor hours to machine hours is 4:1. The standard direct-labor rate is $15.08.

Colgate Palmolive: Direct-Labor Efficiency Variance Data*

	Units Produced		Machine Hours		Standard Direct-Labor Hours		Actual Direct-Labor Hours		Direct-Labor Efficiency Variance
January	50,478	.....	165.5	.....	662.00	.....	374.00	.....	$ 4,343
February	31,943	.....	100.3	.....	401.20	.....	214.00	.....	2,823
March	185,179	.....	552.0	.....	2,208.00	.....	1,068.00	.....	17,191
April	212,274	.....	713.8	.....	2,855.20	.....	1,495.75	.....	20,501
May	48,390	.....	160.0	.....	640.00	.....	364.00	.....	4,162
June	82,436	.....	232.0	.....	928.00	.....	536.50	.....	5,904
July	36,208	.....	104.0	.....	416.00	.....	283.00	.....	2,006
August	33,483	.....	96.0	.....	384.00	.....	317.50	.....	1,003
September	31,560	.....	96.0	.....	384.00	.....	328.50	.....	837
October	28,191	.....	72.0	.....	288.00	.....	158.00	.....	1,960

*Source of data: Alan S. Levitan and Sidney J. Baxendale, "Analyzing the Labor Efficiency Variance to Signal Process Engineering Problems," *Journal of Cost Management* 6, no. 2, p. 70.

Required:

1. Show how the following amounts were calculated for the month of January:
   a. Standard direct-labor hours.
   b. Direct-labor efficiency variance.
2. Calculate the following amounts.
   a. The standard direct-labor cost for each of the 10 months.
   b. For each month, 20 percent of the standard direct-labor cost.
3. Suppose management investigates all variances in excess of 20 percent of standard cost. Which variances will be investigated?
4. Suppose the standard deviation for the direct-labor efficiency variance is $5,000. Draw a statistical control chart, and plot the variance data.
5. Using the chart developed in requirement (4), which variances will be investigated?
6. The variances for March, April, and June are much larger than the others. Suggest at least one reason for this.

■ **Problem 10–48**
Direct-Material and Direct-
Labor Variances
(LO 1, 3)

2. Direct-material quantity
variance: $16,625 F

Orion Corporation has established the following standards for the prime costs of one unit of its chief product, dartboards.

	Standard Quantity	Standard Price or Rate	Standard Cost
Direct material	8 pounds	$1.75 per pound	$14.00
Direct labor	.25 hour	$8.00 per hour	2.00
Total			$16.00

During June, Orion purchased 160,000 pounds of direct material at a total cost of $304,000. The total wages for June were $42,000, 90 percent of which were for direct labor. Orion manufactured 19,000 dartboards during June, using 142,500 pounds of direct material and 5,000 direct-labor hours.

Required: Compute the following variances for June, and indicate whether each is favorable or unfavorable.

1. The direct-material price variance.
2. The direct-material quantity variance.
3. The direct-labor rate variance.
4. The direct-labor efficiency variance.

(CMA, adapted)

Associated Media Graphics (AMG) is a rapidly expanding company involved in the mass reproduction of instructional materials. Ralph Boston, owner and manager of AMG, has made a concentrated effort to provide a quality product at a fair price, with delivery on the promised date. Boston is finding it increasingly difficult to personally supervise the operations of AMG, and he is beginning to institute an organizational structure that would facilitate management control.

One change recently made was the transfer of control over departmental operations from Boston to each departmental manager. However, the Quality Control Department still reports directly to Boston, as do the Finance and Accounting Departments. A materials manager was hired to purchase all raw materials and to oversee the material-handling (receiving, storage, etc.) and recordkeeping functions. The materials manager also is responsible for maintaining an adequate inventory based on planned production levels.

The loss of personal control over the operations of AMG caused Boston to look for a method of efficiently evaluating performance. Dave Cress, a new managerial accountant, proposed the use of a standard-costing system. Variances for material and labor could then be calculated and reported directly to Boston.

Required:

1. Assume that Associated Media Graphics is going to implement a standard-costing system and establish standards for materials and labor. Identify and discuss for each of these cost components:
   a. Who should be involved in setting the standards?
   b. What factors should be considered in establishing the standards?
2. Describe the basis for assignment of responsibility for variances under a standard-costing system.

(CMA, adapted)

■ **Problem 10–49**
Setting Standards;
Responsibility for Variances
(LO 2)

The director of cost management for Portland Instrument Corporation compares each month's actual results with a monthly plan. The standard direct-labor rates for the year just ended and the standard hours allowed, given the actual output in April, are shown in the following schedule.

	Standard Direct-Labor Rate per Hour	Standard Direct-Labor Hours Allowed, Given April Output
Labor class III	$16.00	500
Labor class II	14.00	500
Labor class I	10.00	500

A new union contract negotiated in March resulted in actual wage rates that differed from the standard rates. The actual direct-labor hours worked and the actual direct-labor rates per hour experienced for the month of April were as follows:

	Actual Direct-Labor Rate per Hour	Actual Direct-Labor Hours
Labor class III	$17.20	550
Labor class II	15.00	650
Labor class I	10.80	375

Required:

1. Compute the following variances for April. Indicate whether each is favorable or unfavorable.
   a. Direct-labor rate variance for *each* labor class.
   b. Direct-labor efficiency variance for *each* labor class.
2. Discuss the advantages and disadvantages of a standard-costing system in which the standard direct-labor rates are not changed during the year to reflect such events as a new labor contract.
3. *Build a spreadsheet:* Construct an Excel spreadsheet to solve requirements (1) above. Show how the solution will change if the following information changes: the actual labor rates were $16.95, $15.10, and $10.60 for labor classes III, II, and I, respectively.

(CMA, adapted)

■ **Problem 10–50**
Direct-Labor Variances
(LO 1, 3)

1(b). Direct-labor efficiency variance, labor class III: $800 U

■ **Problem 10–51**
Development of Standard Costs
(LO 1, 2, 5)

1. Total standard unit cost: $7.42

QuickSteel Manufacturing produces metal products for sale to food manufacturers. Keita Ozawa, controller of the Nagoya Division, plans to implement a standard-costing system. Ozawa has collected information from several co-workers that will assist him in developing standards. One of the Nagoya Division's products is a pastry cooling rack. Each cooling rack requires 1.25 meters of stainless steel wire and 12 minutes of direct-labor time to prepare and weld the wire. The cooling racks are inspected after they are welded. Because the cooling rack welds must be flawless, one cooling rack is normally rejected for each five that are accepted. Four rubber footpads are attached to each good cooling rack. A total of six minutes of direct-labor time is required to attach all four footpads and polish and package each cooling rack. The stainless steel wire for the cooling racks costs $3.00 per meter, and each footpad costs $.05. Direct labor is paid at the rate of $8.00 per hour.

Required:

1. Develop the standard cost for direct material and direct labor of a cooling rack.

2. Explain the role of each of the following people in developing standards.

    a. Purchasing manager.

    b. Industrial engineer.

    c. Managerial accountant.

3. The production manager complained that the standards are unrealistic, stifle motivation by concentrating only on unfavorable variances, and are out of date too quickly. He noted that his recent switch to high-grade stainless wire for the cooling racks has resulted in higher material costs but decreased labor hours. The net result was no increase in the total cost to produce the product. The monthly reports continue to show an unfavorable material variance and a favorable labor variance despite indications that the workers are slowing down.

    a. Explain why a standard-costing system can strengthen cost management.

    b. Give at least two reasons to explain why a standard-costing system could negatively impact the motivation of production employees.

■ **Problem 10–52**
Determining Standard Costs; Ethics
(LO 1, 2)

1. Total standard cost per 10-gallon batch: $30.20

Quincy Farms produces items made from local farm products that are distributed to supermarkets. For many years, Quincy's products have had strong regional sales on the basis of brand recognition: however, other companies have begun marketing similar products in the area, and price competition has become increasingly important. Doug Gilbert, the company's controller, is planning to implement a standard cost system for Quincy and has gathered considerable information from his co-workers on production and material requirements for Quincy's products. Gilbert believes that the use of standard costing will allow Quincy to improve cost control and make better pricing decisions.

Quincy's most popular product is strawberry jam. The jam is produced in 10-gallon batches, and each batch requires six quarts of good strawberries. The fresh strawberries are sorted by hand before entering the production process. Because of imperfections in the strawberries and normal spoilage, one quart of berries is discarded for every four quarts of acceptable berries. Three minutes is the standard direct-labor time for sorting required to obtain one quart of acceptable strawberries. The acceptable strawberries are then blended with the other ingredients. Blending requires 12 minutes of direct-labor time per batch. After blending, the jam is packaged in quart containers. Gilbert has gathered the following information from Joe Adams, Quincy's cost accountant.

•   Quincy purchases strawberries at a cost of $.80 per quart. All other ingredients cost a total of $.45 per gallon.

•   Direct labor is paid at the rate of $9.00 per hour.

•   The total cost of material and labor required to package the jam is $.38 per quart.

Adams has a friend who owns a strawberry farm that has been losing money in recent years. Because of good crops, there has been an oversupply of strawberries, and prices have dropped to $.50 per quart. Adams has arranged for Quincy to purchase strawberries from his friend and hopes that $.80 per quart will help his friend's farm become profitable again.

Required:

1. Develop the standard cost for the direct-cost components of a 10-gallon batch of strawberry jam. The standard cost should identify the following amounts for each direct-cost component of a batch of strawberry jam: (*a*) standard quantity. (*b*) standard price or rate, and (*c*) standard cost per batch.

2. Citing the specific ethical standards of competence, confidentiality, integrity, and credibility for management accountants, explain why Joe Adams' behavior regarding the cost information provided to Doug Gilbert is unethical.

3. As part of the implementation of a standard-costing system at Quincy Farms, Doug Gilbert plans to train those responsible for maintaining the standards in the use of variance analysis. Gilbert is particularly concerned with the causes of unfavorable variances. Discuss the possible causes of the following unfavorable variances and identify the individual(s) who should be held responsible: (*a*) direct-material price variance and (*b*) direct-labor efficiency variance.

(CMA, adapted)

■ **Problem 10–53**
Investigating Cost Variances
(LO 4)

Schiffer Corporation manufactures agricultural machinery. At a recent staff meeting, the following direct-labor variance report for the year just ended was presented by the controller.

SCHIFFER CORPORATION
Direct-Labor Variance Report

	Direct-Labor Rate Variance			Direct-Labor Efficiency Variance	
	Amount	Standard Cost, %		Amount	Standard Cost, %
January	$ 800 F	.16%	.....	$ 5,000 U	1.00%
February	4,900 F	.98%	.....	7,500 U	1.50%
March	100 U	.02%	.....	9,700 U	1.94%
April	2,000 U	.40%	.....	12,800 U	2.56%
May	3,800 F	.76%	.....	20,100 U	4.02%
June	3,900 F	.78%	.....	17,000 U	3.40%
July	4,200 F	.84%	.....	28,500 U	5.70%
August	5,100 F	1.02%	.....	38,000 U	7.60%
September	4,800 F	.96%	.....	37,000 U	7.40%
October	5,700 F	1.14%	.....	42,000 U	8.40%
November	4,200 F	.84%	.....	60,000 U	12.00%
December	4,300 F	.86%	.....	52,000 U	10.40%

Schiffer's controller uses the following rule of thumb: Investigate all variances equal to or greater than $30,000, which is 6 percent of standard cost.

Required:

1. Which variances would have been investigated during the year? (Indicate month and type of variance.)

2. What characteristics of the variance pattern shown in the report should draw the controller's attention, regardless of the usual investigation rule? Explain. Given these considerations, which variances would you have investigated? Why?

3. Is it important to follow up on favorable variances, such as those shown in the report? Why?

4. The controller believes that the firm's direct-labor rate variance has a normal probability distribution with a mean of zero and a standard deviation of $5,000. Prepare a statistical control chart, and plot the company's direct-labor rate variances for each month. The critical value is one standard deviation. Which variances would have been investigated under this approach?

■ **Problem 10–54**
Production Efficiency Report;
Operational Performance
Measures
(LO 9)

Yonsei Plastics Ltd. manufactures a range of molded plastic products, such as kitchen utensils and desk accessories. The production process in the Seoul plant is a JIT system, which operates in four FMS cells. An AMHS is used to transport products between production operations. Each month, the controller prepares a production efficiency report, which is sent to corporate headquarters. The data compiled in these reports, for the first six months of the year, are as follows:

PRODUCTION EFFICIENCY REPORT
Yonsei Plastics Ltd.
Seoul Plant
January through June

	Jan.	Feb.	Mar.	Apr.	May	June	Average
Overtime hours	60	70	75	80	85	105	79.2
Total setup time	70	70	65	64	62	62	65.5
Cycle time (average in hours)	20	20	19	18	19	17	18.8
Manufacturing-cycle efficiency	95%	94%	96%	90%	89%	90%	92.3%
Percentage of orders filled	100%	100%	100%	100%	100%	100%	100%
Percentage of on-time deliveries	99%	98%	99%	100%	96%	94%	97.7%
Inventory value/sales revenue	5%	5%	5%	4%	5%	5%	4.8%
Number of defective units, finished goods	80	82	75	40	25	22	54
Number of defective units, in process	10	30	35	40	60	60	39.2
Number of raw-material shipments with defective materials	3	3	2	0	0	0	1.3
Number of products returned	0	0	0	0	0	0	0
Aggregate productivity	1.3	1.3	1.2	1.25	1.2	1.15	1.23
Power consumption (thousands of kilowatt-hours)	800	795	802	801	800	800	800
Machine downtime (hours)	30	25	25	20	20	10	21.7
Bottleneck machine downtime	0	0	2	0	15	2	3.2
Number of unscheduled machine maintenance calls	0	0	1	0	2	3	1

Required:

1. Write a memo to the company president evaluating the Seoul plant's performance. Structure your report by dividing it into the following parts: (*a*) production processing and productivity; (*b*) product quality and customer acceptance; (*c*) delivery performance; (*d*) raw material, scrap, and inventory; and (*e*) machine maintenance.

2. If you identify any areas of concern in your memo, indicate an appropriate action for management.

■ **Problem 10–55**
Manufacturing Performance Measurement
(LO 9)

MedTech, Inc. manufactures diagnostic testing equipment used in hospitals. The company practices JIT production management and has a state-of-the-art manufacturing system, including an FMS and an AMHS. The following nonfinancial data were collected biweekly in the Singapore plant during the first quarter of the current year.

	Biweekly Measurement Period					
	1	2	3	4	5	6
Cycle time (days)	1.5	1.3	1.3	1.2	1.2	1.1
Number of defective finished products	4	4	3	4	3	3
Manufacturing-cycle efficiency	94%	94%	96%	96%	97%	96%
Customer complaints	6	7	6	5	7	8
Unresolved complaints	2	1	0	0	0	0
Products returned	3	3	2	2	1	1
Warranty claims	2	2	2	0	1	0
In-process products rejected	5	5	7	9	10	10
Aggregate productivity	1.5	1.5	1.5	1.5	1.4	1.5
Number of units produced per day per employee	410	405	412	415	415	420
Percentage of on-time deliveries	94%	95%	95%	97%	100%	100%
Percentage of orders filled	100%	100%	100%	98%	100%	100%
Inventory value/sales revenue	2%	2%	2%	1.5%	2%	1.5%
Machine downtime (minutes)	80	80	120	80	70	75
Bottleneck machine downtime (minutes)	25	20	15	0	60	10
Overtime (minutes) per employee	20	0	0	10	20	10
Average setup time (minutes)	120	120	115	112	108	101

Required:

1. For each nonfinancial performance measure, indicate which of the following areas of manufacturing performance is involved: (*a*) production processing, (*b*) product quality, (*c*) customer acceptance, (*d*) in-process quality control, (*e*) productivity, (*f*) delivery performance, (*g*) raw material and scrap, (*h*) inventory, (*i*) machine maintenance. Some measures may relate to more than one area.

2. Write a memo to management commenting on the performance data collected for the Singapore plant. Be sure to note any trends or other important results you see in the data. Evaluate the Singapore plant in each of the areas listed in requirement (1).

■ **Problem 10–56**
Gain-Sharing; Operational Performance Measures; Cost Reduction
(LO 9)

1. Charter Division, total bonus awarded for the year: $6,600

MedLine Equipment Corporation specializes in the manufacture of medical equipment, a field that has become increasingly competitive. Approximately two years ago, Ben Harrington, president of MedLine, became concerned that the company's bonus plan, which focused on division profitability, was not helping MedLine remain competitive. Harrington decided to implement a gain-sharing plan that would encourage employees to focus on operational areas that were important to customers and that added value without increasing cost. In addition to a profitability incentive, the revised plan also includes incentives for reduced rework costs, reduced sales returns, and on-time deliveries. Bonuses are calculated and awarded semiannually on the following basis. The bonuses are distributed among the relevant employees according to a formula developed by the division manager.

- Profitability: Two percent of operating income.
- Rework: Costs in excess of 2 percent of operating income are deducted from the bonus amount.
- On-time delivery: $5,000 if over 98 percent of deliveries are on time, $2,000 if 96 to 98 percent of deliveries are on time, and no increment if on-time deliveries are below 96 percent.
- Sales returns: $3,000 if returns are less than 1.5 percent of sales. Fifty percent of any amount in excess of 1.5 percent of sales is deducted from the bonus amount.
- *Note:* If the calculation of the bonus results in a negative amount for a particular period, there is no bonus, and the negative amount is not carried forward to the next period.

The revised bonus plan was implemented on January 1, 20x1. Presented in the following table are the results for two of Medline's divisions, Charter and Mesa Divisions, for the first year under the new bonus plan. Both of these divisions had similar sales and operating income results for the prior year, when the old bonus plan was in effect. Based on the 20x0 results, the employees of the Charter Division earned a bonus of $27,060 while the employees of the Mesa Division earned $22,440.

	Charter Division		Mesa Division	
	January 20x1– June 20x1	July 20x1– December 20x1	January 20x1– June 20x1	July 20x1– December 20x1
Sales	$4,200,000	$4,400,000	$2,850,000	$2,900,000
Operating income	$ 462,000	$ 440,000	$ 342,000	$ 406,000
On-time delivery	95.4%	97.3%	98.2%	94.6%
Rework costs	$ 11,500	$ 11,000	$ 6,000	$ 8,000
Sales returns	$ 84,000	$ 70,000	$ 44,750	$ 42,500

Required:

1. For the Charter Division:
   a. Compute the semiannual installments and total bonus awarded for 20x1.
   b. Discuss the likely behavior of the Charter Division employees under the revised bonus plan.

2. For the Mesa Division:
   a. Compute the semiannual installments and total bonus awarded for 20x1.
   b. Discuss the likely behavior of the Mesa Division employees under the revised bonus plan.

3. Citing specific examples, evaluate whether or not Harrington's revisions to the bonus plan at MedLine Equipment Corporation have achieved the desired results, and recommend any changes that might improve the plan.

(CMA, adapted)

■ **Problem 10–57**
Variances; Journal Entries;
Missing Data (Appendix)
(LO 3, 6, 11)

1(b). Total standard hours
allowed: 37,200 hours
2. Direct-material price
variance: $750 F

Aquafloat Corporation manufactures rafts for use in swimming pools. The standard cost for material and labor is $89.20 per raft. This includes 8 kilograms of direct material at a standard cost of $5.00 per kilogram, and 6 hours of direct labor at $8.20 per hour. The following data pertain to November:

- Work-in-process inventory on November 1: none.
- Work-in-process inventory on November 30: 800 units (75 percent complete as to labor; material is issued at the beginning of processing).
- Units completed: 5,600 units.
- Purchases of materials: 50,000 kilograms for $249,250.
- Total actual labor costs: $300,760.
- Actual hours of labor: 36,500 hours.
- Direct-material quantity variance: $ 1,500 unfavorable.

Required:

1. Compute the following amounts. Indicate whether each variance is favorable or unfavorable.
   a. Direct-labor rate variance for November.
   b. Direct-labor efficiency variance for November.
   c. Actual kilograms of material used in the production process during November.
   d. Actual price paid per kilogram of direct material in November.
   e. Total amounts of direct-material and direct-labor cost transferred to Finished-Goods Inventory during November.
   f. The total amount of direct-material and direct-labor cost in the ending balance of Work-in-Process Inventory at the end of November.

2. Prepare journal entries to record the following:

   - Purchase of raw material.
   - Adding direct material to Work-in-Process Inventory.
   - Adding direct labor to Work-in-Process Inventory.
   - Recording of variances.

(CMA, adapted)

■ **Problem 10–58**
Direct-Material Variances;
Journal Entries (Appendix)
(LO 1, 3, 11)

1. Direct-material quantity
variance: $300 U

Aoraki Camping Equipment has established the following direct-material standards for its two products.

	Standard Quantity	Standard Price
Standard camping tent	6 meters	$12 per meter
Deluxe backpacking tent	3 meters	$16 per meter

During March, the company purchased 1,050 meters of tent fabric for its standard model at a cost of $13,440. The actual March production of the standard tent was 100 tents, and 625 meters of fabric were used. Also during March, the company purchased 400 meters of tent fabric for its deluxe backpacking tent at a cost of $6,320. The firm used 360 meters of the fabric during March in the production of 120 deluxe tents.

Required:

1. Compute the direct-material price variance and quantity variance for March.
2. Prepare journal entries to record the purchase of material, use of material, and incurrence of variances in March.

Segovia Guitar Company manufactures classical guitars. The company uses a standard, job-order cost-accounting system in two production departments. In the Construction Department, the wooden guitars are built by highly skilled craftsmen and coated with several layers of lacquer. Then the units are transferred to the Finishing Department, where the bridge of the guitar is attached and the strings are installed. The guitars also are tuned and inspected in the Finishing Department. The diagram below depicts the production process.

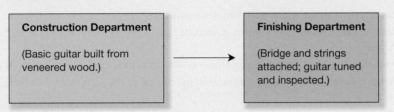

Each finished guitar contains 3.5 kilograms of veneered wood. In addition, one-half kilogram of wood is typically wasted in the production process. The veneered wood used in the guitars has a standard price of $24 per kilogram. The other parts needed to complete each guitar, such as the bridge and nylon strings, cost $20 per guitar. The labor standards for Segovia's two production departments are as follows:

Construction Department: 6 hours of direct labor at $20 per hour

Finishing Department: 3 hours of direct labor at $15 per hour

The following pertains to the month of July.

1. There were no beginning or ending work-in-process inventories in either production department.
2. There was no beginning finished-goods inventory.
3. Actual production was 500 guitars, and 300 guitars were sold on account for $400 each.
4. The company purchased 3,000 kilograms of veneered wood at a price of $25 per kilogram.
5. Actual usage of veneered wood was 2,250 kilograms.
6. Enough parts (bridges and strings) to finish 600 guitars were purchased at a cost of $9,000.
7. The Construction Department used 2,850 direct-labor hours. The total direct-labor cost in the Construction Department was $54,150.
8. The Finishing Department used 1,570 direct-labor hours. The total direct-labor cost in that department was $25,120.
9. There were no direct-material variances in the Finishing Department.

Required:

1. Prepare a schedule that computes the standard costs of direct material and direct labor in each production department.
2. Prepare three exhibits that compute the July direct-material and direct-labor variances in the Construction Department and the July direct-labor variances in the Finishing Department. (Refer to Exhibits 10–2 and 10–3 for guidance.)
3. Prepare a cost variance report for July similar to that shown in Exhibit 10–4.

Refer to your solution for the preceding problem regarding Segovia Guitar Company.

Required:

1. Prepare journal entries to record all of the events listed for Segovia Guitar Company during July. Specifically, these journal entries should reflect the following events.
   a. Purchase of direct material.
   b. Use of direct material.
   c. Incurrence of direct-labor costs.
   d. Addition of production costs to the Work-in-Process Inventory account for each department.
   e. Incurrence of all variances.
   f. Completion of 500 guitars.
   g. Sale of 300 guitars.
   h. Closing of all variance accounts into Cost of Goods Sold.

■ **Problem 10–59**
Comprehensive Problem on Variance Analysis
(LO 1, 3, 6)

1. Total standard cost of direct material in July, Finishing Dept: $10,000
2. Construction Dept, standard material cost: $48,000
3. Direct-material quantity variance, Construction Dept: $6,000 U

■ **Problem 10–60**
Journal Entries under Standard Costing; Continuation of Preceding Problem (Appendix)
(LO 7, 11)

To close variances into Cost of Goods Sold (CGS): $5,770 (debit to CGS)

2. Draw T-accounts, and post the journal entries prepared in requirement (1). Assume the beginning balance in all accounts is zero.

■ **Problem 10–61**
Balanced scorecard; Banking;
Use of Internet
(LO 10)

Visit the Web site of a major bank, e.g., Deutsche Bank Group at www.db.com. Explore the Web site to learn about the bank's services and operations.

Required:

1. What do you think the bank's overall, long-term goals are?

2. Develop a balanced scorecard for the bank. Include two to five measures in each of the scorecard's perspectives.

3. How would the balanced scorecard affect the way managers develop the bank's strategy?

4. Explain the concept of lead and lag measures in the context of the scorecard you have developed.

Cases

■ **Case 10–62**
Direct-Material and Direct-
Labor Variances; Job-Order
Costing; Journal Entries
(Appendix)
(LO 1, 3, 6, 11)

2. Direct-material price
variance: $1,900 U
3. Direct-material price
variance (debit): $1,900

European Styles, Inc. manufactures women's blouses of one quality, which are produced in lots to fill each special order. Its customers are department stores in various cities. European Styles sews the particular stores' labels on the blouses. During November, the company worked on three orders, for which the month's job-cost records disclose the following data.

Lot Number	Boxes in Lot	Material Used (yards)	Hours Worked
22	1,000	24,100	2,980
23	1,700	40,440	5,130
24	1,200	28,825	2,890

The following additional information is available:

1. The firm purchased 95,000 yards of material during November at a cost of $106,400.

2. Direct labor during November amounted to $165,000. According to payroll records, production employees were paid $15.00 per hour.

3. There was no work in process on November 1. During November, lots 22 and 23 were completed. All material was issued for lot 24, which was 80 percent completed as to direct labor.

4. The standard costs for a box of six blouses are as follows:

Direct material	24 yards at $1.10 per yard	$ 26.40
Direct labor	3 hours at $14.70 per hr.	44.10
Manufacturing overhead	3 hours at $12.00 per hr.	36.00
Standard cost per box		$106.50

Required:

1. Prepare a schedule computing the standard cost of lots 22, 23, and 24 for November.

2. Prepare a schedule showing, for each lot produced during November:

    a. Direct-material price variance.

    b. Direct-material quantity variance.

    c. Direct-labor efficiency variance.

    d. Direct-labor rate variance.

    Indicate whether each variance is favorable or unfavorable.

3. Prepare journal entries to record each of the following events.

    • Purchase of material.

    • Incurrence of direct-labor cost.

    • Addition of direct-material and direct-labor cost to Work-in-Process Inventory.

    • Recording of direct-material and direct-labor variances.

(CPA, adapted)

MacGyver Corporation manufactures a product called Miracle Goo, which comes in handy for just about anything. The thick tarry substance is sold in six-gallon drums. Two raw materials are used; these are referred to by people in the business as A and B. Two types of labor are required also. These are mixers (labor class I) and packers (labor class II). You were recently hired by the company president, Pete Thorn, to be the controller. You soon learned that MacGyver uses a standard-costing system. Variances are computed and closed into Cost of Goods Sold monthly. After your first month on the job, you gathered the necessary data to compute the month's variances for direct material and direct labor. You finished everything up by 5:00 p.m. on the 31st, including the credit to Cost of Goods Sold for the sum of the variances. You decided to take all your notes home to review them prior to your formal presentation to Thorn first thing in the morning. As an afterthought, you grabbed a drum of Miracle Goo as well, thinking it could prove useful in some unanticipated way.

You spent the evening boning up on the data for your report and were ready to call it a night. As luck would have it though, you knocked over the Miracle Goo as you rose from the kitchen table. The stuff splattered everywhere, and, most unfortunately, obliterated most of your notes. All that remained legible is the following information.

■ **Case 10–63**
Missing Data; Variances, Ledger Accounts (Appendix)
(LO 1, 3, 11)

1. Actual output (in drums): 1,000 drums
2. Direct material, quantity variance, A: $2,500 U
3. Direct labor, actual hours, (mixers): 2,000 hr
4. Total of all variances for the month: $1,510 F

Direct Material A: Quantity Variance	
2,500	

Direct Material B: Price Variance	
1,200	

Direct Labor I: Rate Variance	
600	

Direct Labor II: Efficiency Variance	
1,200	

Cost of Goods Sold	
143,000	
	1,510

Accounts Payable	
	1,500 Beg. bal.
70,000	73,200
	4,700 End. bal.

Other assorted data gleaned from your notes:

- The standards for each drum of Miracle Goo include 10 pounds of material A at a standard price of $5 per pound.

- The standard cost of material B is $15 for each drum of Miracle Goo.

- Purchases of material A were 12,000 pounds at $4.50 per pound.

- Given the actual output for the month, the standard allowed quantity of material A was 10,000 pounds. The standard allowed quantity of material B was 5,000 gallons.

- Although 6,000 gallons of B were purchased, only 4,800 gallons were used.

- The standard wage rate for mixers is $15 per hour. The standard labor cost per drum of product for mixers is $30 per drum.

- The standards allow 4 hours of direct labor II (packers) per drum of Miracle Goo. The standard labor cost per drum of product for packers is $48 per drum.

- Packers were paid $11.90 per hour during the month.

You happened to remember two additional facts. There were no beginning or ending inventories of either work in process or finished goods for the month. The increase in accounts payable relates to direct-material purchases only.

Required: Now you've got a major problem. Somehow you've got to reconstruct all the missing data in order to be ready for your meeting with the president. You start by making the following list of the facts you want to use in your presentation. Before getting down to business, you need a brief walk to clear your head. Out to the trash you go, and toss the remaining Miracle Goo.

1. Actual output (in drums): _____

2. Direct material: **A**   **B**

   a. Standard quantity per drum: _____   _____

   b. Standard price: _____   _____

   c. Standard cost per drum: _____   _____

   d. Standard quantity allowed, given actual output: _____   _____

   e. Actual quantity purchased: _____   _____

   f. Actual price: _____   _____

   g. Actual quantity used: _____   _____

   h. Price variance: _____   _____

   i. Quantity variance: _____   _____

3. Direct labor: **I (mixers)**   **II (packers)**

   a. Standard hours per drum: _____   _____

   b. Standard rate per hour: _____   _____

   c. Standard cost per drum: _____   _____

   d. Standard quantity allowed, given actual output: _____   _____

   e. Actual rate per hour: _____   _____

   f. Actual hours: _____   _____

   g. Rate variance: _____   _____

   h. Efficiency variance: _____   _____

4. Total of all variances for the month: _____

   Fill in the missing amounts in the list, using the available facts.

THIS CHAPTER'S FOCUS COMPANY is Pâtisserie Cézanne, and continues our discussion from the previous chapter. Pâtisserie Cézanne supplies fancy desserts to a variety of restaurants, caterers, and upscale food stores in Lyon, France. In this chapter, we explore Pâtisserie Cézanne's use of flexible budgeting to plan for and control overhead costs. A flexible budget allows for a variety of levels of activity. As activity increases, the costs in the flexible budget rise as well. This tool enables management to compare the actual overhead costs incurred with the costs that should have been incurred, given the actual level of production activity.

Pâtisserie
Cézanne

11

Flexible Budgeting and the Management of Overhead and Support Activity Costs

In contrast to the food-processing setting of Pâtisserie Cézanne, we turn our attention to flexible budgeting in the service industry. Riviera Rentals is a small automobile rental company based in Nice, France. The company has four rental locations in towns on the French Riviera and specializes in short-term car rentals, primarily for local use by tourists. Riviera Rentals' flexible budget uses two cost drivers: the distance driven by its rental cars and the number of customer contracts.

1 Distinguish between static and flexible budgets and explain the advantages of a flexible overhead budget.

2 Prepare a flexible overhead budget, using both a formula and a columnar format.

3 Explain how overhead is applied to Work-in-Process Inventory under standard costing.

4 Explain some important issues in choosing an activity measure for overhead budgeting and application.

5 Compute and interpret the variable-overhead spending and efficiency variances and the fixed-overhead budget and volume variances.

6 Prepare an overhead cost performance report.

7 Explain how an activity-based flexible budget differs from a conventional flexible budget.

8 Prepare journal entries to record manufacturing overhead under standard costing (Appendix A).

9 Compute and interpret the sales-price and sales-volume variances (Appendix B).

How do service industry companies, such as Aetna insurance, Hertz car rental, BNP Paribas bank, Four Seasons Hotels, and Royal Jordanian Airlines control the overhead costs they incur in producing their services? Similarly, how do manufacturing firms such as Toyota, Hewlett-Packard, and Haier control the many overhead costs incurred in their production processes? Unlike direct material and direct labor, overhead costs are not traceable to individual products. Moreover, overhead is a pool of many different kinds of costs. Indirect material, indirect labor, and other indirect production costs often exhibit different relationships to productive activity. Some overhead costs are variable, and some are fixed. Moreover, different individuals in an organization are responsible for different types of overhead costs.

Considering all of these issues together, controlling overhead presents a challenge for managerial accountants. In this chapter, we will study an accounting system that is widely used to control overhead costs.

Overhead Budgets

<table>
<tr><td>

Learning Objective 1

Distinguish between static and flexible budgets and explain the advantages of a flexible overhead budget.

</td><td>

Since direct material and direct labor are traceable to products, it is straightforward to determine standard costs for these inputs. If the top of a conference table requires 30 square meters of mahogany lumber at $40 per square meter, the standard direct-material cost for the tabletop is $1,200. But how much electricity does it take to produce a conference table? How much supervisory time, equipment depreciation, or machinery repair services does the table require? Since all of these overhead costs are indirect costs of production, we cannot set overhead cost standards for the oak table. If standard costs do not provide the answer to controlling overhead, what does?

</td></tr>
</table>

Flexible Budgets

The tool used by most companies to control overhead costs is called a **flexible budget.** A flexible budget resembles the budgets we studied in Chapter 9, with one important difference: *A flexible budget is not based on only one level of activity.* Instead, a flexible budget covers a range of activity within which the firm may operate. A *flexible overhead budget* is defined as a detailed plan for controlling overhead costs that is valid in the firm's relevant range of activity. In contrast, a **static budget** is based on a particular planned level of activity.

At Pâtisserie Cézanne, the measure of activity used for flexible budgeting purposes is process time. The process time for a dessert is the total amount of time the product is in process, including selecting ingredients, mixing, baking, cooling, assembly and finishing, and packaging. Pâtisserie Cézanne's director of cost management estimates that the average process time required for fancy desserts is three hours.

To illustrate the flexible budgeting concept, suppose Pâtisserie Cézanne's director of cost management has determined that electricity is a variable cost, incurred at the rate of $.50 per hour of process time. Two different budgets for electricity cost are shown in Exhibit 11–1. The static budget is based on management's predicted level of activity for September—7,500 hours of process time. This estimate is based on planned production of 2,500 multilayer fancy cakes, where each cake requires three hours of total process time. The flexible budget includes three different production activity levels within the relevant range: 6,000, 7,500, and 9,000 hours of process time.

Advantages of Flexible Budgets

Why is the distinction between static and flexible budgets so important? Suppose Pâtisserie Cézanne produced 2,000 multilayer fancy cakes during September, used 6,000 hours of process time, and incurred electricity costs of $3,200. Does this constitute good control or poor control of electricity costs? Which budget in Exhibit 11–1 is more useful in answering this question?

A manager using the static budget makes the following comparison.

Actual Electricity Cost	Budgeted Electricity Cost (static budget)	Cost Variance
$3,200	$3,750	$550 Favorable

This comparison suggests that operating personnel maintained excellent control over electricity costs during September, generating a favorable variance of $550. Is this a valid analysis and conclusion?

The fault with this analysis is that the manager is comparing the electricity cost incurred at the *actual* activity level, 2,000 multilayer fancy cakes, with the budgeted electricity cost at the *planned* activity level, 2,500 multilayer fancy cakes. Since these activity levels are different, we should expect the electricity cost to be different.

Static Budget		Flexible Budget			
Activity (process hours)*	7,500	Activity (process hours)	6,000	7,500	9,000
Budgeted electricity cost	$3,750	Budgeted electricity cost	$3,000	$3,750	$4,500

Static budget: based on only one anticipated activity level.

Flexible budget: includes several possible activity levels.

*Based on planned September production of 2,500 multilayer fancy cakes, at three hours of process time per cake.

Exhibit 11–1
Static Budget versus Flexible Budget

A more sensible approach is to compare the actual electricity cost incurred with the cost that should be incurred when 2,000 multilayer fancy cakes are produced. At this production level, 6,000 process hours should be used (3 per cake). The flexible budget in Exhibit 11–1 shows that the manager should expect $3,000 of electricity cost at the 6,000 process-hour level of activity. Therefore, an analysis based on the flexible budget gives the following comparison.

Actual Electricity Cost	Budgeted Electricity Cost (flexible budget)	Cost Variance
$3,200	$3,000	$200 Unfavorable

Now the manager's conclusion is different; the revised analysis indicates an unfavorable variance. Electricity cost was greater than it should have been, given the actual level of output. The flexible budget provides the correct basis for comparison between actual and expected costs, given actual activity.

The Activity Measure

Notice that the flexible budget for electricity cost in Exhibit 11–1 is based on hours of process time, which is an input in the production process. The process-hour activity levels shown in the flexible budget are the standard allowed process hours given various levels of output. If 2,000 multilayer fancy cakes are produced, and the standard allowance per cake is 3 process hours, then the standard allowed number of process hours is 6,000.

Why are the activity levels in the flexible budget based on process hours, an *input* measure, instead of the number of multilayer fancy cakes produced, an *output* measure? When only a single product is manufactured, it makes no difference whether the flexible budget is based on input or output. In our illustration, either of the flexible budgets shown in Exhibit 11–2 could be used.

Now suppose that during August, Pâtisserie Cézanne produced three different products: 1,000 multilayer fancy cakes, 1,500 single-layer sheet cakes, and 600 specialty cakes (such as wedding cakes). The following standards have been assigned to these products.

Product	Standard Process Hours per Unit
Multilayer fancy cakes	3
Single-layer sheet cakes	2
Specialty cakes	6

During August, the company's production output was 3,100 cakes. Is 3,100 cakes a meaningful output measure? Adding numbers of multilayer fancy cakes, sheet cakes, and specialty cakes, which require different amounts of productive inputs, is like adding apples and oranges. It would not make sense to base a flexible budget for electricity cost on units of output when the output consists of different products with different electricity requirements. In this case, the flexible budget must be based on an *input* measure. The standard allowed number of process hours for the August production is computed as follows:

Product	Units Produced	Standard Process Hours per Unit	Total Standard Allowed Process Hours
Multilayer fancy cakes	1,000	3	3,000
Single-layer sheet cakes	1,500	2	3,000
Specialty cakes	600	6	3,600
Total			9,600

Exhibit 11-2
Flexible Budgets: Input versus
Output

Flexible Budget (based on input)			
Activity: standard allowed process hours	6,000	7,500	9,000
Budgeted electricity cost	$3,000	$3,750	$4,500
Flexible Budget (based on output)			
Activity: multilayer fancy cakes produced	2,000	2,500	3,000
Budgeted electricity cost	$3,000	$3,750	$4,500

3 standard allowed process hours per multilayer fancy cake

Recall that the controller estimates electricity cost at $.50 per process hour. Thus, the flexible-budget cost of electricity during August is computed as follows:

Standard allowed process hours given August output	9,600
Electricity cost per process hour	× $.50
Flexible budget for electricity cost	$4,800

The important point is that *units of output* usually is not a meaningful measure in a multiproduct firm, because it would require us to add numbers of unlike products. To avoid this problem, output is measured in terms of the *standard allowed input, given actual output*. The flexible overhead budget is then based on this standard input measure.

Flexible Overhead Budget Illustrated

Pâtisserie Cézanne's monthly flexible overhead budget is shown in the Excel spreadsheet in Exhibit 11–3. The overhead costs on the flexible budget are divided into variable and fixed costs. The total budgeted variable cost increases proportionately with increases in the activity. Thus, when the number of process hours increases by 50 percent, from 6,000 hours to 9,000 hours, the total budgeted variable overhead cost also increases by 50 percent, from $30,000 to $45,000. In contrast, the total budgeted fixed overhead does not change with increases in activity; it remains constant at $15,000 per month.

Learning Objective 2

Prepare a flexible overhead budget, using both a formula and a columnar format.

Formula Flexible Budget

When overhead costs can be divided into variable and fixed categories, we can express the flexible overhead budget differently. The format used in Exhibit 11–3 is called a *columnar flexible budget*. The budgeted overhead cost for each overhead item is listed in a column under a particular activity level. Notice that the columnar format allows for only a limited number of activity levels. Pâtisserie Cézanne's flexible budget shows only three.

A more general format for expressing a flexible budget is called a *formula flexible budget*. In this format, the managerial accountant expresses the relationship between activity and total budgeted overhead cost by the following formula:

$$\text{Total budgeted monthly overhead cost} = \left(\text{Budgeted variable-overhead cost per activity unit} \times \text{Total activity units} \right) + \text{Budgeted fixed-overhead cost per month}$$

To use this formula for Pâtisserie Cézanne, we first need to compute the budgeted variable-overhead cost per process hour. Dividing total budgeted variable-overhead cost by the associated activity level yields a budgeted variable-overhead rate of $5 per process hour. Notice that we can use any activity level in Exhibit 11–3 to compute this rate.

Exhibit 11–3
Flexible Overhead Budget

Pâtisserie Cézanne

Microsoft Excel - Flexible Overhead Budget - Pâtisserie Cézanne

File Edit View Insert Format Tools Data Window Help

G32   =G19+G31

	A	B	C	D	E	F	G
1			Pâtisserie Cézanne				
2			Monthly Flexible Overhead Budget				
3							
4						Process Hours	
5							
6					6,000	7,500	9,000
7	Budgeted costs:						
8							
9	Variable costs:						
10	Indirect material:						
11	Nonstick cooking spray				$ 12,000	$ 15,000	$ 18,000
12	Waxed paper				2,000	2,500	3,000
13	Other paper products				2,000	2,500	3,000
14	Miscellaneous supplies				6,000	7,500	9,000
15	Indirect labor: maintenance				4,000	5,000	6,000
16	Utilities						
17	Electricity				3,000	3,750	4,500
18	Natural gas				1,000	1,250	1,500
19	Total variable cost				$ 30,000	$ 37,500	$ 45,000
20							
21							
22	Fixed costs:						
23	Indirect labor:						
24	Inspection				$ 2,200	$ 2,200	$ 2,200
25	Production supervisors				6,000	6,000	6,000
26	Setup				3,000	3,000	3,000
27	Material handling				2,000	2,000	2,000
28	Depreciation: plant and equipment				500	500	500
29	Insurance and property taxes				100	100	100
30	Test kitchen				1,200	1,200	1,200
31	Total fixed cost				$ 15,000	$ 15,000	$ 15,000
32	Total overhead cost				$ 45,000	$ 52,500	$ 60,000

Sheet1 / Sheet2 / Sheet3 /

Ready

$$\frac{\$30,000}{6,000} = \frac{\$37,500}{7,500} = \frac{\$45,000}{9,000} = \$5 \text{ per process hour}$$

Pâtisserie Cézanne's formula flexible overhead budget is shown below.

$$\text{Total budgeted monthly overhead cost} = (\$5 \times \text{Total process hours}) + \$15,000$$

To check the accuracy of the formula, compute the total budgeted overhead cost at each of the activity levels shown in Exhibit 11–3.

Activity (process hours)	Formula Flexible Overhead Budget		Budgeted Monthly Overhead Cost
6,000	($5 × 6,000) + $15,000	=	$45,000
7,500	($5 × 7,500) + $15,000	=	$52,500
9,000	($5 × 9,000) + $15,000	=	$60,000

The budgeted monthly overhead cost computed above is the same as that shown in Exhibit 11–3 for each activity level.

The formula flexible budget is more general than the columnar flexible budget, because the formula allows the managerial accountant to compute budgeted overhead costs at any activity level. Then the flexible-budgeted overhead cost can be used at the end of the period as a benchmark against which to compare the actual overhead costs incurred.

> "It's critical to understand variable and fixed overhead costs. When activity levels change, what costs will change and how?" (11b)
>
> **A.T.Kearney**

Overhead Application in a Standard-Costing System

Recall that *overhead application* refers to the addition of overhead cost to the Work-in-Process Inventory account as a product cost. In the normal-costing system, described in Chapter 3, overhead is applied as shown in the top panel of Exhibit 11–4. Overhead application is based on *actual* hours. In a standard-costing system, overhead application is based on standard hours allowed, given actual output. This system is depicted in the bottom panel of Exhibit 11–4. Notice that the difference between normal costing and standard costing, insofar as overhead is concerned, lies in the quantity of hours used.

Both normal- and standard-costing systems use a predetermined overhead rate. In a standard-costing system, the predetermined overhead rate also is referred to as the standard overhead rate. Pâtisserie Cézanne calculates its predetermined or standard overhead rate annually. The rate for the current year, computed in Exhibit 11–5, is based on *planned* activity of 7,500 process hours per month. Notice that Pâtisserie Cézanne breaks its predetermined overhead rate into a variable rate and a fixed rate. We will discuss further the use of standard costs for product costing in Appendix A at the end of this chapter.

Learning Objective 3

Explain how overhead is applied to Work-in-Process Inventory under standard costing.

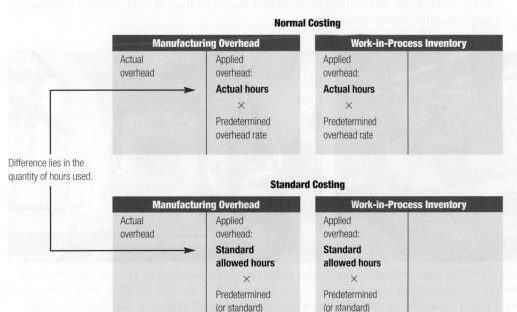

Exhibit 11–4
Overhead Application

Exhibit 11–5
Predetermined Overhead
Rate: Pâtisserie Cézanne

Pâtisserie Cézanne

	Budgeted Overhead		Planned Monthly Activity		Predetermined Overhead Rate
Variable	$37,500*		7,500 process hours		$5.00 per process hour
Fixed	15,000*		7,500 process hours		2.00 per process hour
Total	$52,500		7,500 process hours		$7.00 per process hour

*From the flexible budget (Exhibit 11–3) for planned monthly activity of 7,500 process hours.

Choice of Activity Measure

Learning Objective 4

Explain some important issues in choosing an activity measure for overhead budgeting and application.

Pâtisserie Cézanne's flexible overhead budget is based on process hours. A variety of activity measures are used in practice. Machine hours, direct-labor hours, direct-labor cost, total process time, and direct-material cost are among the most common measures. Choosing the appropriate activity measure for the flexible overhead budget is important, because the flexible budget is the chief tool for managing overhead costs.

Criteria for Choosing the Activity Measure

How should the managerial accountant select the activity measure for the flexible budget? The activity measure should be one that varies in a similar pattern to the way that variable overhead varies. As productive activity increases, both variable-overhead cost and the activity measure should increase in roughly the same proportion. As productive activity declines, both variable-overhead cost and the activity measure should decline in roughly the same proportion. In short, variable-overhead cost and the activity measure should *move together* as overall productive activity changes.

Changing Manufacturing Technology: Computer-Integrated Manufacturing
Direct-labor time has traditionally been a popular activity measure in manufacturing firms. However, as automation increases, more and more firms are switching to such measures as machine hours or process time for their flexible overhead budgets. Machine hours and process time are linked more closely than direct-labor hours to the robotic technology and computer-integrated manufacturing (CIM) systems common in today's manufacturing environment.

As manufacturing has become increasingly automated, direct labor is becoming less appropriate as an activity measure in flexible budgeting. Moreover, computer-integrated manufacturing entails a shift in the cost structure away from direct-labor costs and toward greater overhead costs. Left, employees inspect and pack clothes at the Zipsa industrial park near Managua, Nicaragua (a labor-intensive activity). Right, a robot assembles washing machines at the BSH Bosch und Siemens consumer appliances factory in Nauen, Germany (a high-tech process).

Cost Drivers

As we discussed in Chapter 5, some companies have refined their cost management systems even further. *Cost drivers* are identified as the most significant factors affecting overhead costs. Then multiple overhead rates based on these cost drivers are used to compute product costs and control overhead expenditures. A relentless search for *non-value-added* costs is an integral part of such a cost management system. We will discuss the role of *activity-based costing* in flexible budgeting later in the chapter.

Beware of Dollar Measures

Dollar measures, such as direct-labor or raw-material costs, often are used as the basis for flexible overhead budgeting. However, such measures have significant drawbacks, and they should be avoided. Dollar measures are subject to price-level changes and fluctuate more than physical measures. For example, the direct-labor *hours* required to produce a fancy dessert will be relatively stable over time. However, the direct-labor *cost* will vary as wage levels and fringe-benefit costs change with inflation and conditions in the labor market.

The choice of an activity measure upon which to base the flexible budget for variable overhead is really a cost-estimation problem, which is the topic addressed in Chapter 7.

Cost Management Using Overhead Cost Variances

The flexible overhead budget is one of the managerial accountant's primary tools for the control of manufacturing-overhead costs. At the end of each accounting period, the managerial accountant uses the flexible overhead budget to determine the level of overhead cost that should have been incurred, given the actual level of activity. Then the accountant compares the overhead cost in the flexible budget with the actual overhead cost incurred. The managerial accountant then computes four separate overhead variances, each of which conveys information useful in controlling overhead costs.

To illustrate overhead variance analysis, we will continue our illustration for Pâtisserie Cézanne.

Learning Objective 5

Compute and interpret the variable-overhead spending and efficiency variances and the fixed-overhead budget and volume variances.

Flexible Budget

Pâtisserie Cézanne's monthly flexible overhead budget, displayed in Exhibit 11–3, shows budgeted variable and fixed manufacturing-overhead costs at three levels of production activity. During September, Pâtisserie Cézanne produced 2,000 multilayered fancy cakes. Since production standards allow three process hours per cake, the total standard allowed number of process hours is 6,000 hours.

Actual production output	2,000 multilayered fancy cakes
Standard allowed process hours per multilayered fancy cake	× 3
Total standard allowed process hours	6,000 process hours

From the 6,000 process-hour column in Exhibit 11–3, the budgeted overhead cost for September is as follows:

	Budgeted Overhead Cost for September
Variable overhead	$30,000
Fixed overhead	15,000

From the cost accounting records, Pâtisserie Cézanne's director of cost management determined that the following overhead costs were actually incurred during September.

	Actual Cost for September
Variable overhead	$34,650
Fixed overhead	16,100
Total overhead	$50,750

The production supervisor's records indicate that the actual total process time in September was as follows:

Actual process hours for September 6,300

Notice that the actual number of process hours used (6,300) exceeds the standard allowed number of process hours, given actual production output (6,000).

We now have assembled all of the information necessary to compute Pâtisserie Cézanne's overhead variances for September.

Variable Overhead

Pâtisserie Cézanne's total variable-overhead variance for September is computed below.

Actual variable overhead $34,650
Budgeted variable overhead 30,000
Total variable-overhead variance .... $ 4,650 Unfavorable

What caused the company to spend $4,650 more than the budgeted amount on variable overhead? To discover the reasons behind this performance, the managerial accountant computes a **variable-overhead spending variance** and a **variable-overhead efficiency variance.** The computation of these variances is depicted in Exhibit 11–6.

Two equivalent formulas for the variable-overhead spending variance are shown below.

1. $\dfrac{\text{Variable-overhead}}{\text{spending variance}} = \text{Actual variable overhead} - (AH \times SVR)$, or

2. $\dfrac{\text{Variable-overhead}}{\text{spending variance}} = (AH \times AVR) - (AH \times SVR)$

where   AH denotes actual process hours

             AVR denotes actual variable-overhead rate

             (actual variable overhead ÷ AH)

             SVR denotes standard variable-overhead rate

Exhibit 11–6
Variable-Overhead Spending and Efficiency Variances

Pâtisserie Cézanne

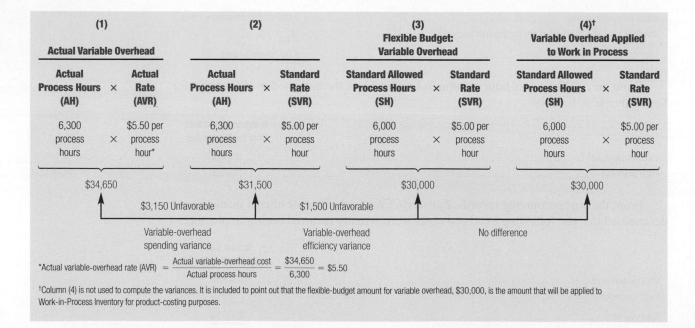

(1)		(2)		(3) Flexible Budget: Variable Overhead		(4)† Variable Overhead Applied to Work in Process	
Actual Variable Overhead							
Actual Process Hours (AH) ×	**Actual Rate (AVR)**	**Actual Process Hours (AH)** ×	**Standard Rate (SVR)**	**Standard Allowed Process Hours (SH)** ×	**Standard Rate (SVR)**	**Standard Allowed Process Hours (SH)** ×	**Standard Rate (SVR)**
6,300 process hours ×	$5.50 per process hour*	6,300 process hours ×	$5.00 per process hour	6,000 process hours ×	$5.00 per process hour	6,000 process hours ×	$5.00 per process hour
$34,650		$31,500		$30,000		$30,000	

$3,150 Unfavorable $1,500 Unfavorable   No difference

Variable-overhead spending variance   Variable-overhead efficiency variance

*Actual variable-overhead rate (AVR) $= \dfrac{\text{Actual variable-overhead cost}}{\text{Actual process hours}} = \dfrac{\$34,650}{6,300} = \$5.50$

†Column (4) is not used to compute the variances. It is included to point out that the flexible-budget amount for variable overhead, $30,000, is the amount that will be applied to Work-in-Process Inventory for product-costing purposes.

These two formulas are equivalent because actual variable overhead is equal to actual hours times the actual variable overhead rate (AH × AVR). Formula 2 above can be simplified as follows:

3. Variable-overhead spending variance = AH(AVR − SVR)

Pâtisserie Cézanne's variable-overhead spending variance for September is computed as follows (using formula 1):

$$
\begin{aligned}
\text{Variable-overhead spending variance} &= \text{Actual variable overhead} - (\text{AH} \times \text{SVR}), \\
&= \$34{,}650 - (6{,}300 \times \$5.00) \\
&= \$3{,}150 \text{ Unfavorable}
\end{aligned}
$$

This variance is unfavorable because the actual variable-overhead cost exceeded the expected amount, after adjusting that expectation for the actual number of process hours used.

As Exhibit 11–6 shows, the following formula defines the variable-overhead efficiency variance.

Variable-overhead efficiency variance = (AH × SVR) − (SH × SVR)

where   SH denotes standard process hours

Writing this formula more simply, we have the following expression.

Variable-overhead efficiency variance = SVR(AH − SH)

Pâtisserie Cézanne's variable-overhead efficiency variance for September is computed as follows:

$$
\begin{aligned}
\text{Variable-overhead efficiency variance} &= \text{SVR}(\text{AH} - \text{SH}) \\
&= \$5.00(6{,}300 - 6{,}000) \\
&= \$1{,}500 \text{ Unfavorable}
\end{aligned}
$$

This variance is unfavorable because actual process hours exceeded standard allowed process hours, given actual output.

Product Costing versus Cost Management Columns (1), (2), and (3) in Exhibit 11–6 are used to compute the variances for *cost management purposes.* Column (4) in the exhibit shows the variable overhead applied to work in process for the *product-costing purpose.* Notice that the variable-overhead cost on the flexible budget, $30,000, is the same as the amount applied to work in process.

Graphing Variable-Overhead Variances Exhibit 11–7 provides a graphical analysis of Pâtisserie Cézanne's variable-overhead variances for September. The graph shows the variable-overhead rate per process hour on the vertical axis. The standard rate is $5.00 per process hour, while the actual rate is $5.50 per process hour (actual variable-overhead cost of $34,650 divided by actual process hours of 6,300). Process hours are shown on the horizontal axis.

The green area on the graph represents the flexible-budget amount for variable overhead, given actual September output of 2,000 multilayered fancy cakes. The large area on the graph enclosed by colored lines on the top and right sides represents actual variable-overhead cost. The colored area in between, representing the total variable-overhead variance, is divided into the spending and efficiency variances.

Managerial Interpretation of Variable-Overhead Variances What do the variable-overhead variances mean? What information do they convey to management? The formulas for computing the variable-overhead variances resemble

Exhibit 11–7

Graphical Analysis of Variable-Overhead Variances

Key:
Total variable-overhead variance: blue areas
Variable-overhead spending variance: dark blue area
Variable-overhead efficiency variance: light blue area

those used to compute the direct-labor variances. To see this, compare Exhibit 11–6 (variable overhead) with Exhibit 10–3 (direct labor).

Despite the similar formulas, the interpretation of the variable-overhead variances is quite different from that applicable to the direct-labor variances.

Efficiency Variance   Recall that an unfavorable direct-labor efficiency variance results when more direct labor is used than the standard allowed quantity. Thus, direct labor has been used inefficiently, relative to the standard. However, that is not the proper interpretation of an unfavorable variable-overhead efficiency variance. Pâtisserie Cézanne's variable-overhead efficiency variance did *not* result from using more of the variable-overhead items, such as electricity and indirect material, than the standard allowed amount. Instead, this variance resulted when the division used *more process hours* than the standard quantity, given actual output. Recall that the company's director of cost management has found that variable-overhead cost varies in a pattern similar to that with which process hours vary. Since 300 more process hours were used than the standard quantity, the division's management should expect that variable-overhead costs will be greater. Thus, the variable-overhead efficiency variance has nothing to do with efficient or inefficient usage of electricity, indirect material, and other variable-overhead items. This variance simply reflects an adjustment in the managerial accountant's expectation about variable-overhead cost, because the division used more than the standard quantity of process hours.

What is the important difference between direct labor and variable overhead that causes this different interpretation of the efficiency variance? Direct labor is a traceable cost and is budgeted on the basis of direct-labor hours. Variable overhead, on the other hand, is a pool of *indirect* costs that are budgeted on the basis of *process hours*. The indirect nature of variable-overhead costs causes the different interpretation.

Spending Variance   An unfavorable direct-labor rate variance is straightforward to interpret; the actual labor rate *per hour* exceeds the standard rate. Although the formula for computing the variable-overhead spending variance is similar to that for the direct-labor rate variance, its interpretation is quite different.

An unfavorable spending variance simply means that the total actual cost of variable overhead is greater than expected, after adjusting for the actual quantity of process hours used. An unfavorable spending variance could result from paying a higher-than-expected price per unit for variable-overhead items. Or the variance could result from using more of the variable-overhead items than expected.

Suppose, for example, that electricity were the only variable-overhead cost item. An unfavorable variable-overhead spending variance could result from paying a higher-than-expected price per kilowatt-hour for electricity, from using more than the expected amount of electricity, or from both.

Management of Variable Overhead Costs Since the variable-overhead efficiency variance says nothing about efficient or inefficient usage of variable overhead, the spending variance is the real control variance for variable overhead. Managers can use the spending variance to alert them if variable-overhead costs are out of line with expectations.

Fixed Overhead

To analyze performance with regard to fixed overhead, the managerial accountant calculates two fixed-overhead variances.

Fixed-Overhead Budget Variance The variance used by managers to control fixed overhead is called the **fixed-overhead budget variance.** It is defined as follows:

$$\text{Fixed-overhead budget variance} = \text{Actual fixed overhead} - \text{Budgeted fixed overhead}$$

Pâtisserie Cézanne's fixed-overhead budget variance for September is as follows:

$$\begin{aligned}\text{Fixed-overhead budget variance} &= \text{Actual fixed overhead} - \text{Budgeted fixed overhead} \\ &= \quad\quad \$16,100 \quad\quad - \quad\quad \$15,000^* \\ &= \$1,100 \text{ Unfavorable}\end{aligned}$$

*From the flexible budget (Exhibit 11–3).

The fixed-overhead budget variance is unfavorable, because the company spent more than the budgeted amount on fixed overhead. Notice that we need not specify an activity level to determine budgeted fixed overhead. All three columns in the flexible budget (Exhibit 11–3) specify $15,000 as budgeted fixed overhead.

Fixed-Overhead Volume Variance The **fixed-overhead volume variance** is defined as follows:

$$\text{Fixed-overhead volume variance} = \text{Budgeted fixed overhead} - \text{Applied fixed overhead}$$

Pâtisserie Cézanne's applied fixed overhead for September is $12,000:

$$\begin{aligned}\text{Applied fixed overhead} &= \text{Predetermined fixed overhead rate} \times \text{Standard allowed hours} \\ &= \$2.00 \text{ per process hour} \times 6,000 \text{ process hours} \\ &= \$12,000\end{aligned}$$

The $2.00 predetermined fixed-overhead rate was calculated in Exhibit 11–5. The 6,000 standard allowed process hours is based on actual September production of 2,000 multi-layered fancy cakes, each with a standard allowance of three process hours.

Pâtisserie Cézanne's fixed-overhead volume variance is calculated below.

$$\begin{aligned}\text{Fixed-overhead volume variance} &= \text{Budgeted fixed overhead} - \text{Applied fixed overhead} \\ &= \quad\quad \$15,000 \quad\quad - \quad\quad \$12,000 \\ &= \$3,000 \text{ Unfavorable}\end{aligned}$$

Exhibit 11–8
Fixed-Overhead Budget and
Volume Variances

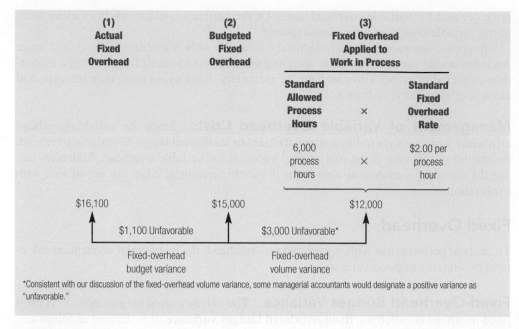

(1) **Actual Fixed Overhead**	(2) **Budgeted Fixed Overhead**	(3) **Fixed Overhead Applied to Work in Process**	
		Standard Allowed Process Hours ×	**Standard Fixed Overhead Rate**
		6,000 process hours ×	$2.00 per process hour
$16,100	$15,000	$12,000	

$1,100 Unfavorable $3,000 Unfavorable*

Fixed-overhead   Fixed-overhead
budget variance   volume variance

*Consistent with our discussion of the fixed-overhead volume variance, some managerial accountants would designate a positive variance as "unfavorable."

Managerial Interpretation of Fixed-Overhead Variances

Exhibit 11–8 shows Pâtisserie Cézanne's two fixed-overhead variances for September. The budget variance is the real control variance for fixed overhead, because it compares actual expenditures with budgeted fixed-overhead costs.

The volume variance provides a way of reconciling two different purposes of the cost management system. For the *control purpose,* the system recognizes that fixed overhead does not change as production activity varies. Hence, budgeted fixed overhead is the same at all activity levels in the flexible budget. (Review Exhibit 11–3 to verify this.) Budgeted fixed overhead is the basis for controlling fixed overhead, because it provides the benchmark against which actual expenditures are compared.

For the *product-costing purpose* of the system, budgeted fixed overhead is divided by planned activity to obtain a predetermined (or standard) fixed-overhead rate. For Pâtisserie Cézanne, this rate is $2.00 per process hour (budgeted fixed overhead of $15,000 divided by planned activity of 7,500 process hours). This predetermined rate is then used to apply fixed overhead to Work-in-Process Inventory. During any period in which the standard allowed number of process hours, given actual output, differs from the planned level of process hours, the budgeted fixed overhead differs from applied fixed overhead.

Exhibit 11–9 illustrates this point graphically. Budgeted fixed overhead is constant at $15,000 for all levels of activity. However, applied fixed overhead increases with activity, since fixed overhead is applied to Work-in-Process Inventory at the rate of $2.00 per standard allowed process hour. Notice that budgeted and applied fixed overhead are equal *only* if the number of standard allowed hours equals the planned activity level of 7,500 process hours. When this happens, there is no fixed-overhead volume variance. Pâtisserie Cézanne has a $3,000 volume variance in September because the standard allowed hours and planned hours are different.

Capacity Utilization

A common, but faulty, interpretation of a positive volume variance is that it measures the cost of underutilizing productive capacity. Some firms even designate a positive volume variance as unfavorable. The reasoning behind this view is that the planned activity level used to compute the predetermined fixed-overhead rate is a measure of normal capacity utilization. Moreover, fixed-overhead costs, such as depreciation and property taxes, are costs incurred to create productive capacity.

Exhibit 11–9
Budgeted versus Applied
Fixed Overhead

Pâtisserie
Cézanne

Therefore, the predetermined fixed-overhead rate measures the cost of providing an hour of productive capacity. If 7,500 process hours are planned, but output is such that only 6,000 standard process hours are allowed, then capacity has been underutilized by 1,500 hours. Since each hour costs $2.00 (Pâtisserie Cézanne's predetermined fixed-overhead rate), the cost of underutilization is $3,000 (1,500 × $2.00), which is Pâtisserie Cézanne's volume variance.

The fault with this interpretation of the volume variance is that it ignores the real cost of underutilizing productive capacity. The real cost is due to the lost contribution margins of the products that are not produced when capacity is underutilized. Moreover, this interpretation fails to recognize that underutilizing capacity and reducing inventory may be a wise managerial response to slackening demand.

For this reason, many managerial accountants interpret the volume variance merely as a way of reconciling the two purposes of the cost management system. Moreover, these managerial accountants would choose not to designate the volume variance as either favorable or unfavorable. However, some accountants designate a positive volume variance as *unfavorable*. Their reasoning is that when the volume variance is closed into Cost of Goods Sold expense at the end of the accounting period (as explained in Appendix A), the effect is to increase Cost of Goods Sold, which in turn has an *unfavorable* effect on income. In contrast, other accountants argue that no sign (favorable or unfavorable) should be assigned to the fixed-overhead volume variance.

Overhead Cost Performance Report

The variable-overhead spending and efficiency variances and the fixed-overhead budget variance can be computed for each overhead cost item in the flexible budget. When these itemized variances are presented along with actual and budgeted costs for each overhead item, the result is an **overhead cost performance report.** Pâtisserie Cézanne's performance report is displayed in Exhibit 11–10. This report would be used by management to exercise control over each of the division's overhead costs.

Notice that the performance report includes only spending and efficiency variances for the variable items, and only a budget variance for the fixed items. Upon receiving this report, a manager might investigate the relatively large variances for indirect maintenance labor, electricity, and production supervisory labor.

Learning Objective 6

Prepare an overhead cost performance report.

COST MANAGEMENT SYSTEMS IN GERMANY

Throughout the world, flexible budgeting is found in cost management systems as a means of controlling overhead costs. However, differences in terminology and design may be present in managerial accounting practices due to geographic variations in the evolution of industrial practice or accounting philosophy. In Germany, for example, *grenzplankostenrechnung* (or "flexible standard costing") exhibits many of the features illustrated in this chapter. Under the German approach, "each cost center distinguishes between variable costs (e.g., energy) and fixed costs (e.g., a manager's salary)." The number of machine hours is a common activity measure. "For purposes of cost planning and control, companies budget each cost center's expenses and then distribute the expenses to each month of the budget year. The budgeted costs are standards for efficient resource consumption. . . ." The cost and performance information "allows for effective discussions about productivity improvement" among department managers, management accountants, and plant managers.

Among the companies using the flexible standard costing system is Stihl, a well-known German manufacturer of chain saws and other landscaping equipment.[1]

Learning Objective 7

Explain how an activity-based flexible budget differs from a conventional flexible budget.

Activity-Based Flexible Budget

The flexible budget shown in Exhibit 11–3, which underlies our variance analysis for Pâtisserie Cézanne, is based on a single cost driver. Overhead costs that vary with respect to *process hours* are categorized as variable; all other overhead costs are treated as fixed. This approach is consistent with traditional, volume-based product-costing systems.

Under the more accurate product-costing method called activity-based costing, several cost drivers are identified.[2] Costs that may appear fixed with respect to a single volume-based cost driver, such as process hours, may be variable with respect to some other cost driver. The activity-based costing approach also can be used as the basis for a flexible budget for planning and cost management purposes. Exhibit 11–11 displays an **activity-based flexible budget** for Pâtisserie Cézanne, using the same data as Exhibit 11–3.

Compare the conventional flexible budget (Exhibit 11–3) and the activity-based flexible budget (Exhibit 11–11). The key difference lies in the costs that were categorized as fixed on the conventional flexible budget. These costs are fixed with respect to process hours but are not fixed with respect to other more appropriate cost drivers. For example, cost pool II includes inspection and setup costs, which vary with respect to the number of production runs.

Effect on Performance Reporting

The activity-based flexible budget provides a more accurate prediction (and benchmark) of overhead costs. For example, suppose that activity in December is as follows:

	Process hours	6,000
December	Production runs	12
Activity	New products tested	40
	Direct material handled (pounds)	30,000

---

[1]Kip R. Krumwiede, "Rewards and Realities of German Cost Accounting," *Strategic Finance* 86, no. 10 (April 2005), pp. 27–34; Carl S. Smith, "Going for GPK," *Strategic Finance* 86, no. 10 (April 2005), pp. 36–39; and Bernd Gaiser, "German Cost Management Systems," *Journal of Cost Management* 11, no. 5 (September/October 1997), pp. 35–41.

[2]Activity-based costing, introduced conceptually in Chapter 3, is explored in detail in Chapter 5.

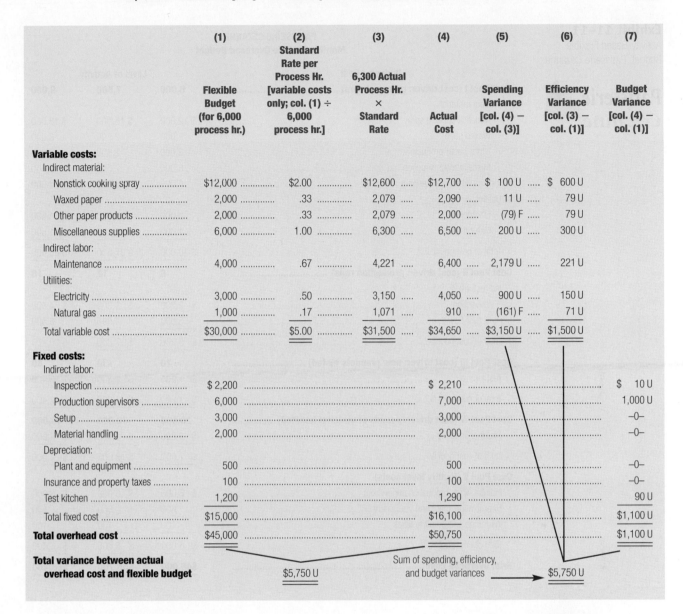

	(1) Flexible Budget (for 6,000 process hr.)	(2) Standard Rate per Process Hr. [variable costs only; col. (1) ÷ 6,000 process hr.]	(3) 6,300 Actual Process Hr. × Standard Rate	(4) Actual Cost	(5) Spending Variance [col. (4) − col. (3)]	(6) Efficiency Variance [col. (3) − col. (1)]	(7) Budget Variance [col. (4) − col. (1)]
Variable costs:							
Indirect material:							
Nonstick cooking spray	$12,000	$2.00	$12,600	$12,700	$ 100 U	$ 600 U	
Waxed paper	2,000	.33	2,079	2,090	11 U	79 U	
Other paper products	2,000	.33	2,079	2,000	(79) F	79 U	
Miscellaneous supplies	6,000	1.00	6,300	6,500	200 U	300 U	
Indirect labor:							
Maintenance	4,000	.67	4,221	6,400	2,179 U	221 U	
Utilities:							
Electricity	3,000	.50	3,150	4,050	900 U	150 U	
Natural gas	1,000	.17	1,071	910	(161) F	71 U	
Total variable cost	$30,000	$5.00	$31,500	$34,650	$3,150 U	$1,500 U	
Fixed costs:							
Indirect labor:							
Inspection	$ 2,200			$ 2,210			$ 10 U
Production supervisors	6,000			7,000			1,000 U
Setup	3,000			3,000			–0–
Material handling	2,000			2,000			–0–
Depreciation:							
Plant and equipment	500			500			–0–
Insurance and property taxes	100			100			–0–
Test kitchen	1,200			1,290			90 U
Total fixed cost	$15,000			$16,100			$1,100 U
Total overhead cost	$45,000			$50,750			$1,100 U
Total variance between actual overhead cost and flexible budget		$5,750 U		Sum of spending, efficiency, and budget variances		$5,750 U	

The following table compares the budgeted cost levels for several overhead items on the conventional and activity-based flexible budgets.

Overhead Cost Item	Conventional Flexible Budget	Activity-Based Flexible Budget
Electricity	$3,000	$3,000
Inspection	2,200	3,300
Setup	3,000	4,500
Test kitchen	1,200	2,400
Material handling	2,000	3,000
Insurance and property taxes	100	100

The budgeted electricity cost is the same on both budgets, because both use the same cost driver (process hours). Insurance and property taxes are also the same, because both budgets recognize these as facility-level fixed costs. However, the other overhead costs are budgeted at different levels, because the conventional and activity-based flexible budgets use *different cost drivers* for these items. While the conventional budget treats inspection, setup, test kitchen, and material-handling costs as fixed, the activity-based flexible budget shows that they are all variable with respect to the appropriate cost driver.

Exhibit 11–10
Overhead Cost Performance
Report: Pâtisserie Cézanne

Pâtisserie
Cézanne

"In the past decade, Whirlpool has faced increasing competition, higher overhead, and greater product diversity. Managers initiated and supported ABC to obtain accurate information for dealing with these challenges." (11d)

Whirlpool

Exhibit 11–11
Activity-Based Flexible
Budget: Pâtisserie Cézanne

*Pâtisserie
Cézanne*

PÂTISSERIE CÉZANNE
Monthly Flexible Overhead Budget

Budgeted Cost	Level of Activity		
Cost Pool I (cost driver: process hours)	**6,000**	**7,500**	**9,000**
Indirect material:			
Nonstick cooking spray	$ 12,000	$ 15,000	$ 18,000
Waxed paper	2,000	2,500	3,000
Other paper products	2,000	2,500	3,000
Miscellaneous supplies	6,000	7,500	9,000
Indirect labor: maintenance	4,000	5,000	6,000
Utilities:			
Electricity	3,000	3,750	4,500
Natural gas	1,000	1,250	1,500
Total of cost pool I	$ 30,000	$ 37,500	$ 45,000
Cost Pool II (cost driver: production runs)	**8**	**12**	**16**
Indirect labor:			
Inspection	$ 2,200	$ 3,300	$ 4,400
Setup	3,000	4,500	6,000
Total of cost pool II	$ 5,200	$ 7,800	$ 10,400
Cost Pool III (cost driver: new products tested)	**20**	**30**	**40**
Test kitchen	$ 1,200	$ 1,800	$ 2,400
Total of cost pool III	$ 1,200	$ 1,800	$ 2,400
Cost Pool IV (cost driver: pounds of material handled)	**20,000**	**30,000**	**40,000**
Material handling	$ 2,000	$ 3,000	$ 4,000
Total of cost pool IV	$ 2,000	$ 3,000	$ 4,000
Cost Pool V (facility level costs)			
Indirect labor: production supervisors	$ 6,000	$ 6,000	$ 6,000
Depreciation: plant and equipment	500	500	500
Insurance and property taxes	100	100	100
Total of cost pool V	$ 6,600	$ 6,600	$ 6,600
Total overhead cost	**$45,000**	**$56,700**	**$68,400**

These differences are important for performance reporting. The activity-based flexible budget provides a more accurate benchmark against which to compare actual costs. Suppose the actual inspection cost in December is $3,000. Using the conventional flexible budget would result in an unfavorable variance of $800 ($3,000 − $2,200). However, the activity-based flexible budget yields a favorable variance of $300 ($3,000 − $3,300).

To summarize, activity-based flexible budgeting provides a richer view of cost behavior and the underlying cost drivers, and it provides a valuable tool for cost management.

Flexible Budgeting in the Service Industry

All kinds of organizations benefit from the concept of a flexible budget. Like manufacturing firms, service-industry organizations incur overhead costs that vary with appropriately chosen cost drivers. At University of Cambridge in England, for example, the cost of operating the admissions department depends in part on the number of applicants. At National Takaful Insurance Company in Kuwait, the cost of administering the claims department depends in part on the number of claims. At the Siloam Hospitals in Indonesia, the cost of operating the patient records department depends in part on the number of patients.

Exhibit 11–12
Flexible Budget: Riviera Rentals

RIVIERA
RENTALS

```
Microsoft Excel - Flexible Budget - Riviera Rentals
File  Edit  View  Insert  Format  Tools  Data  Window  Help
B30            fx  =B12+B20+B28
```

	A	B	C	D
1	RIVIERA RENTALS			
2	Annual Flexible Budget: Operating Expenses			
3				
4	Budgeted Operating Expenses		Level of Activity	
5				
6	Cost Pool I (cost driver: kilometers driven)	750,000	1,000,000	1,250,000
7	Automobile maintenance	$ 240,000	$ 320,000	$ 400,000
8	Tire replacement	6,000	8,000	10,000
9	Automobile insurance	27,000	36,000	45,000
10	New York State registration and inspection	900	1,200	1,500
11	Leasing costs	36,000	48,000	60,000
12	Total of cost pool I	$ 309,900	$ 413,200	$ 516,500
13				
14	Cost Pool II (cost driver: customer contracts	3,000	6,000	9,000
15	Reservations	$ 16,000	$ 32,000	$ 48,000
16	Registration of contract information	18,000	36,000	54,000
17	Inspection of vehicle by employee/customer	8,000	16,000	24,000
18	Employee commissions	20,000	40,000	60,000
19	Cleaning/washing automobile	17,000	34,000	51,000
20	Total of cost pool II	$ 79,000	$ 158,000	$ 237,000
21				
22	Cost Pool III (overall organization: fixed costs)			
23	Office managers' salaries	240,000	240,000	240,000
24	Rent: buildings	36,000	36,000	36,000
25	Utilities: buildings	13,000	13,000	13,000
26	Liability insurance: rental offices	12,000	12,000	12,000
27	Depreciation: equipment	11,000	11,000	11,000
28	Total of cost pool III	$ 312,000	$ 312,000	$ 312,000
29				
30	Total operating expenses	$ 700,900	$ 883,200	$1,065,500

```
Sheet1 / Sheet2 / Sheet3 /
Ready
```

We briefly turn our attention to Riviera Rentals, a small automobile rental company in Nice, France. The company has four rental locations in towns on the French Riviera and specializes in short-term car rentals, primarily for local use by tourists. Riviera Rental's flexible budget is displayed in Exhibit 11–12. Notice that unlike Pâtisserie Cézanne's flexible overhead budget, Riviera Rentals' flexible budget lists its operating expenses. All of this service industry firm's costs are operating expenses. Riviera Rentals' management has chosen two cost drivers for its activity-based flexible budget: the number of kilometers driven and the number of customer contracts.

An activity-based flexible budget is based on many cost drivers. Think about the costs that are incurred at your college. The cost of staffing the college's faculty, for example, depends on factors such as the number of students enrolled, the number of courses offered, and the average class size. The cost of operating the admissions department would depend in part on the number of applicants.[3]

---

[3]Key cost drivers used in activity-based flexible budgeting at Cornell University include the number of students enrolled and the number of student credit hours. For further reading on activity-based budgeting, see Jay Collins, "Advanced Use of ABM: Using ABC for Target Costing, Activity-Based Budgeting, and Benchmarking," in *Activity-Based Management: Arthur Andersen's Lessons from the ABM Battlefield,* ed. Steve Player and David E. Keys (New York: John Wiley & Sons, 1999), pp. 152–58.

Some operating expenses (cost pool I in the flexible budget) vary with the number of kilometers driven by the rental cars. Automobile maintenance and tire replacement expenses increase as the cars drive more kilometers. Similarly, such operating expenses as insurance and leasing costs increase with the number of kilometers driven, because the company needs more cars on hand. Other operating expenses (cost pool II) vary with the number of customer contracts, regardless of how many kilometers each customer drives a rental car. Such expenses as rental reservations, filling out contracts, and cleaning up a rental car upon return depend on the number of times the cars are rented. Finally, some fixed operating expenses (cost pool III), such as the office managers' salaries and rental charges on the office locations, do not vary with any cost driver.

Riviera Rentals' management can use this flexible budget to predict operating expenses at varying levels of activity, as measured by the two cost drivers.

Focus on Ethics

MISSTATED STANDARDS AFFECT ACCURACY OF REPORTS

The scenario described here, while placed in the context of a fictitious enterprise, is based on an actual situation that occurred at NuTone Housing Group, which at the time was a subsidiary of Scoville, Inc.*

To set the stage, consider these facts about the standard-costing system in place at Shrood Division, a subsidiary of Gigantic Enterprises, Inc. Shrood Division manufactures a wide range of electric household products, such as lighting, fans, water pumps, and security systems. The division manufactures approximately 10,000 products, made from over 70,000 components. Tom Cleverly has run the division in what he calls a hands-on manner for over a quarter century. When Shrood Division was acquired by Gigantic Enterprises a decade ago, Cleverly was at first unhappy with the merger, but it soon became apparent that Gigantic's top management would let him run the business the way he was used to running it. Three aspects of Cleverly's management style are noteworthy. First, he insists on being involved in all major pricing decisions; he's not a delegator. Second, he has developed a second-level management that is loyal and supportive of his approach. Third, he has refused to lower the direct-labor time standards for years, even though many productivity improvements have been made. At present, the actual direct-labor times are on average only about a third of the standard times. Moreover, since manufacturing overhead is applied on the basis of direct labor, both the standard direct-labor and the standard overhead costs are inflated relative to actual costs.

The implications of this practice are that huge favorable variances are experienced all year long in both direct labor and overhead. Cleverly has used these favorable variances to "manage the quarterly earnings" reported by Shrood Division to corporate. Cleverly has instructed his manager of accounting, Evan Twixt, to release just enough of the favorable variances into Cost of Goods Sold (CGS) on a quarterly basis to ensure that Shrood Division just meets its earnings target in the budget. Then, at the end of the year, the remainder of this large favorable variance is released into CGS, with the result that Shrood Division ends each year with fourth-quarter earnings far in excess of the target. Like a knight in shining white armor, Shrood Division saves the day for Gigantic Enterprises year after year. Shrood has come to be known in corporate circles as "the jewel in the crown of Gigantic Enterprises."

Now for the conflict. Gigantic has hired a new corporate controller, Jeffrey Fixit, whose charge is to introduce more consistency in the reporting methods of Gigantic's various divisions. When Fixit visited Shrood Division and discovered what was going on, he tried to get Tom Cleverly to instruct Evan Twixt to correct the direct-labor standards to reflect attainable results (i.e., reality). Cleverly has refused, though, and Fixit doesn't have the power to force him to do so. Meanwhile, poor Twixt is caught in the middle.

Here is what each of them had to say about the situation.

Cleverly (division manager): "I've been running this business for 25 years. And you know what? We've been profitable for 25 years! The high labor standards help me make sure that neither I nor my salespeople shave prices too much. It's like setting the clock 10 minutes ahead to make sure you're not late. We always make budget. We always report the highest profits in

*K. Merchant and L. Ferreira, "Scoville: NuTone Housing Group," a management accounting case (Boston: President and Fellows of Harvard College).

the company. And we are, in fact, the 'jewel in the crown.'"

Fixit (corporate controller): "This is a really bad situation. Shrood is reporting fictitious numbers to corporate on a quarterly basis, which then get rolled up into Gigantic's quarterly results. Then these numbers get published to the shareholders. We're misleading them. I don't have the authority to get Tom Cleverly to fix the problem. I can, however, go to the board of directors and explain to them that they need to get Cleverly to do what needs to be done."

Twixt (Shrood's accounting manager): "I'm caught in the middle. We basically have two sets of books: the ones based on Mr. Cleverly's labor standards, and the ones based on the more accurate results that Mr. Fixit wants. I can report either set of results. I feel like I'm serving two gods—and so far I'm getting away with it."

What do you make of this situation? Can a company that keeps two sets of books be well managed? What ethical issues do you see here? What actions should Cleverly, Twixt, and Fixit take?

Chapter Summary

LO1 Distinguish between static and flexible budgets and explain the advantages of a flexible overhead budget. A static budget is based on a single, predicted volume of production activity. A flexible budget allows for many possible activity levels. The flexible overhead budget is based on some activity measure that varies in a pattern similar to that of variable overhead. The managerial accountant uses the amount of overhead cost specified by the flexible budget, given actual output, as a benchmark against which to compare actual overhead costs.

LO2 Prepare a flexible overhead budget, using both a formula and a columnar format. A columnar flexible budget is based on several distinct activity levels, while a formula flexible budget is valid for a continuous range of activity. The flexible overhead budget is based on some activity measure that varies in a pattern similar to that of variable overhead.

LO3 Explain how overhead is applied to Work-in-Process Inventory under standard costing. The amount of overhead cost entered into Work-in-Process Inventory is equal to the standard overhead rate multiplied by the standard allowed amount of the activity base, given actual output.

LO4 Explain some important issues in choosing an activity measure for overhead budgeting and application. The flexible overhead budget is based on some activity measure that varies in a pattern similar to that of variable overhead. Machine hours, process time, and direct-labor hours are common activity bases.

LO5 Compute and interpret the variable-overhead spending and efficiency variances and the fixed overhead budget and volume variances. The variable-overhead spending variance calculates the effect on production cost of deviations between the actual and standard variable overhead rates. The variable-overhead efficiency variance calculates the effect on production cost of deviations between actual and standard amounts of the cost driver, multiplied by the standard variable overhead rate. The fixed overhead budget variance calculates the effect on production cost of deviations between actual and budgeted fixed overhead. The fixed overhead volume variance calculates the effect of deviations between budgeted and applied fixed overhead.

LO6 Prepare an overhead cost performance report. The overhead cost performance report shows the actual and budgeted costs for each overhead item, along with the four overhead variances: the variable-overhead spending and efficiency variances, and the fixed-overhead budget and volume variances. These variances help management to control overhead costs.

LO7 Explain how an activity-based flexible budget differs from a conventional flexible budget. In an activity-based flexible budget, each overhead item may have a different cost driver identified upon which the flexible overhead budget for that cost item is based. Such a flexible budget is more accurate than conventional flexible budgets, because multiple cost drivers are identified to explain the behavior of overhead costs.

LO8 Prepare journal entries to record manufacturing overhead under standard costing (Appendix A). The left (debit) side of the manufacturing overhead account accumulates actual overhead costs incurred. The right (credit) side of the overhead account records manufacturing overhead applied to Work-in-Process Inventory. The cumulative difference between the amounts on the left and right sides of the overhead account is equal to the sum of the four overhead variances.

LO9 Compute and interpret the sales-price and sales-volume variances (Appendix B). The sales-price variance is the difference between the actual and budgeted sales prices multiplied by the actual sales volume. This variance measures the effect on sales revenue of sales price deviations. The sales-volume variance is the difference between the actual and budgeted sales volumes multiplied by the budgeted sales price. This variance measures the effect on sales revenue of deviations in sales volume.

Review Problem on Overhead Variances

In November, Pâtisserie Cézanne produced 3,000 multilayered fancy cakes, used 9,100 hours of process time, and incurred the following manufacturing-overhead costs.

Variable overhead	$45,955
Fixed overhead	$15,800

Pâtisserie Cézanne's monthly flexible overhead budget for November is the same as that given in Exhibit 11–3.

Compute Pâtisserie Cézanne's variable-overhead variances using the format shown in Exhibit 11–6. Compute the company's fixed-overhead variances using the format shown in Exhibit 11–8.

Solution to Review Problem
The solution to the review problem is given in Exhibits 11–13 and 11–14.

(1)		(2)		(3)		(4)†	
Actual Variable Overhead		**Actual Variable Overhead**		**Flexible Budget: Variable Overhead**		**Variable Overhead Applied to Work in Process**	
Actual Process Hours (AH) ×	**Actual Rate (AVR)**	**Actual Process Hours (AH)** ×	**Standard Rate (SVR)**	**Standard Allowed Process Hours (SH)** ×	**Standard Rate (SVR)**	**Standard Allowed Process Hours (SH)** ×	**Standard Rate (SVR)**
9,100 process hours ×	$5.05 per process hour*	9,100 process hours ×	$5.00 per process hour	9,000 process hours ×	$5.00 per process hour	9,000 process hours ×	$5.00 per process hour
$45,955		$45,500		$45,000		$45,000	

$455 Unfavorable ← Variable-overhead spending variance

$500 Unfavorable ← Variable-overhead efficiency variance

No difference

*Actual variable-overhead rate (AVR) = $\dfrac{\text{Actual variable-overhead cost}}{\text{Actual process hours}}$ = $\dfrac{\$45,955}{9,100}$ = $5.05

†Column (4) is not used to compute the variances. It is included to point out that the flexible-budget amount for variable overhead, $45,000, is the amount that will be applied to Work-in-Process Inventory for product-costing purposes.

Exhibit 11–13
Variable-Overhead
Spending and Efficiency
Variances: Review Problem

Pâtisserie
Cézanne

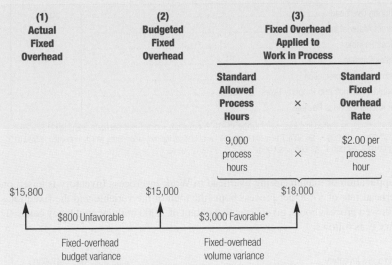

Exhibit 11–14
Fixed-Overhead Budget and
Volume Variances: Review
Problem

Pâtisserie Cézanne

*Some managerial accountants would designate a negative fixed-overhead volume variance as "favorable."

Key Terms

For each term's definition refer to the indicated page, or turn to the glossary at the end of the text.

activity-based flexible
   budget, 508
fixed-overhead budget
   variance, 505
fixed-overhead volume
   variance, 505

flexible budget, 495
overhead cost performance
   report, 507
sales-price variance,* 518
sales-volume variance,* 518

static budget, 495
total contribution margin,*
   517
unit contribution margin,*
   517

variable-overhead efficiency
   variance, 502
variable-overhead spending
   variance, 502

---

*Term appears in Appendix B.

APPENDIX A TO CHAPTER 11

Standard Costs and Product Costing

In a standard-costing system, the standard costs are used for product costing as well as for cost control. The costs of direct material, direct labor, and manufacturing overhead are all entered into Work-in-Process Inventory at their standard costs. (Review Exhibit 11–4.)

Learning Objective 8

Prepare journal entries to record manufacturing overhead under standard costing.

Journal Entries under Standard Costing   During September, Pâtisserie Cézanne incurred actual manufacturing-overhead costs of $50,750, which includes $34,650 of variable overhead and $16,100 of fixed overhead. A summary journal entry to record these actual expenditures follows.

Manufacturing Overhead	50,750	
Indirect-Material Inventory		23,290*
Wages Payable		20,610*
Utilities Payable		4,960
Accumulated Depreciation		500
Prepaid Insurance and Property Taxes		100
Test Kitchen Salaries Payable		1,290

*The credit amounts can be verified in column (4) of Exhibit 11–10. For example, indirect-material costs amounted to $23,290 ($12,700 + $2,090 + $2,000 + $6,500). The credit to Wages Payable is for indirect-labor costs, which amounted to $20,610 ($6,400 + $2,210 + $7,000 + $3,000 + $2,000).

The application of manufacturing overhead to Work-in-Process Inventory is based on a predetermined overhead rate of $7.00 per process hour (the total of the variable and the fixed rates) and 6,000 standard allowed process hours, given an actual output of 2,000 multilayered fancy cakes. The summary journal entry is as follows:

Work-in-Process Inventory	42,000	
Manufacturing Overhead		42,000*

*Applied overhead = $7.00 × 6,000 = $42,000

Now the Manufacturing Overhead account appears as follows:

Manufacturing Overhead			
Actual	$50,750	$42,000	Applied

The *underapplied overhead* for September is $8,750 ($50,750 − $42,000). This means that the overhead applied to Work-in-Process Inventory in September was $8,750 less than the actual overhead cost incurred. Notice that the underapplied overhead is equal to the sum of the four overhead variances for September. The total of the four overhead variances will always be equal to the overapplied or underapplied overhead for the accounting period.[4]

Disposition of Variances   As explained in the preceding chapter, variances are temporary accounts, and most companies close them directly into Cost of Goods Sold at the end of each accounting period. The journal entry required to close out Pâtisserie Cézanne's underapplied overhead for September is as follows:

Cost of Goods Sold	8,750	
Manufacturing Overhead		8,750

The journal entry to close out underapplied or overapplied overhead typically is made annually, rather than monthly.

An alternative accounting treatment is to prorate underapplied or overapplied overhead among Work-in-Process Inventory, Finished-Goods Inventory, and Cost of Goods Sold, as explained in Chapter 3.

A Note on Perishable Products and JIT Production Management Systems   As noted in the preceding chapter, traditional manufacturing systems typically exhibit the cost flows explained in this section. Direct-material, direct-labor, and manufacturing-overhead costs are entered in Work-in-Process Inventory, from which they flow into Finished-Goods Inventory when the goods are finished, and then on into Cost of Goods Sold. Since Pâtisserie Cézanne produces perishable goods, which are produced and sold on the same day, a simpler procedure could be used. In Pâtisserie Cézanne's case, the *standard* costs of direct material, direct labor, and manufacturing overhead could be entered directly into Cost of Goods Sold as they are incurred. This simplified procedure could be used, because the production process is very short and the goods are sold immediately. Thus, there is never any work-in-process inventory or finished-goods inventory on hand. Such situations are common with producers of perishable goods.

---

[4]Overapplied and underapplied manufacturing overhead are discussed in Chapter 3.

An analogous situation occurs in manufacturers that employ a just-in-time (JIT) production and inventory control system. In a JIT environment, raw materials are delivered just in time to be entered into production, and parts or components are manufactured in each stage of the production process just in time for the next production stage. Thus, like the case of perishable goods, there is little or no work-in-process or finished-goods inventory at any given time in a JIT environment. For this reason, many manufacturers that employ the JIT approach make use of highly simplified cost accounting procedures similar to those explained in the preceding paragraph for Pâtisserie Cézanne.

APPENDIX B TO CHAPTER 11

Sales Variances

The variances discussed in Chapters 10 and 11 focus on production costs. Managerial accountants also compute variances to help management analyze the firm's sales performance. To illustrate two commonly used sales variances, we will continue our discussion of Pâtisserie Cézanne. The expected sales price and standard variable cost for a multilayered fancy cake are as follows:

> **Learning Objective 9**
>
> Compute and interpret the sales-price and sales-volume variances.

Budgeted sales price	$38
Standard variable costs:	
Direct material	$ 7
Direct labor	10
Variable overhead (3 process hours at $5 per hour)	15
Total unit variable cost	$32

The difference between the sales price and the unit variable cost is called the **unit contribution margin.** Pâtisserie Cézanne's unit contribution margin is $6 per multilayered fancy cake ($38 − $32). This is the amount that the sale of one multilayered fancy cake contributes toward covering the company's fixed costs and making a profit.

During October, Pâtisserie Cézanne's management expects to sell 1,500 multilayered fancy cakes. Based on this sales forecast, the controller computed the following budgeted **total contribution margin.**

Budgeted sales revenue (1,500 multilayered fancy cakes × $38)	$57,000
Budgeted variable costs (1,500 multilayered fancy cakes × $32)	48,000
Budgeted total contribution margin (1,500 multilayered fancy cakes × $6)	$ 9,000

The *actual* results for October were as follows:

Actual sales volume	1,600 cakes
Actual sales price	$37
Actual unit variable cost	$32

Using these actual results, the actual total contribution margin for October is as follows:

Actual sales revenue (1,600 multilayered fancy cakes × $37)	$59,200
Actual variable costs (1,600 multilayered fancy cakes × $32)	51,200
Actual total contribution margin (1,600 multilayered fancy cakes × $5)	$ 8,000

Pâtisserie Cézanne's actual and budgeted results for October are summarized in the following table. Notice that actual sales revenue exceeded budgeted sales revenue by $2,200. However, this favorable variance was more than offset by the additional $3,200 in variable costs resulting from actual sales volume exceeding budgeted sales volume. So the actual total contribution margin was $1,000 less than the budgeted total contribution margin, as the table shows.

	Budget	Actual	Variance
Revenue	$57,000	$59,200	$2,200 F
Variable costs	48,000	51,200	3,200 U
Contribution margin	$ 9,000	$ 8,000	$1,000 U

The managerial accountant computes two sales variances to explain the $2,200 favorable variance in sales revenue. These variances are defined and computed as follows:

$$\text{Sales-price variance} = \left(\begin{array}{c}\text{Actual} \\ \text{sales} \\ \text{price}\end{array} - \begin{array}{c}\text{Budgeted} \\ \text{sales} \\ \text{price}\end{array}\right) \times \text{Actual sales volume}$$

$$= (\$37 - \$38) \times 1,600$$

$$= \$1,600 \text{ Unfavorable}$$

$$\text{Sales-volume variance} = \left(\begin{array}{c}\text{Actual} \\ \text{sales} \\ \text{volume}\end{array} - \begin{array}{c}\text{Budgeted} \\ \text{sales} \\ \text{volume}\end{array}\right) \times \text{Budgeted sales price}$$

$$= (1,600 - 1,500) \times \$38$$

$$= \$3,800 \text{ Favorable}$$

Together, the **sales-price** and **sales-volume variances** explain the $2,200 favorable variance between actual and budgeted sales revenue.

Sales-price variance	$1,600 Unfavorable
Sales-volume variance	3,800 Favorable
Variance between actual and budgeted sales revenue	$2,200 Favorable

We have only just introduced sales variance analysis here. This topic is covered more extensively in cost management textbooks.[5]

---

[5]For example, see Ronald W. Hilton, Michael W. Maher, and Frank H. Selto, *Cost Management: Strategies for Business Decisions,* 4th ed. (New York: McGraw-Hill/Irwin, 2008), pp. 728–735.

Review Questions

11–1. Distinguish between static and flexible budgets.

11–2. Explain the advantage of using a flexible budget.

11–3. Why are flexible overhead budgets based on an activity measure, such as hours of process time, machine time, or direct-labor hours?

11–4. Distinguish between a columnar and a formula flexible budget.

11–5. Show, using T-accounts, how manufacturing overhead is added to Work-in-Process Inventory when standard costing is used.

11–6. How has computer-integrated-manufacturing (CIM) technology affected overhead application?

11–7. What is the interpretation of the variable-overhead spending variance?

11–8. Jeddah Company's only variable-overhead cost is electricity. Does an unfavorable variable-overhead spending variance imply that the company paid more than the anticipated rate per kilowatt-hour?

11–9. What is the interpretation of the variable-overhead efficiency variance?

11–10. Distinguish between the interpretations of the direct-labor and variable-overhead efficiency variances.

11–11. What is the fixed-overhead budget variance?

11–12. What is the correct interpretation of the fixed-overhead volume variance?

11–13. Describe a common but misleading interpretation of the fixed-overhead volume variance. Why is this interpretation misleading?

11–14. Draw a graph showing budgeted and applied fixed overhead, and show an unfavorable (or positive) volume variance on the graph.

11–15. What types of organizations use flexible budgets?

11–16. What is the conceptual problem of applying fixed manufacturing overhead as a product cost?

11–17. Distinguish between the control purpose and the product-costing purpose of standard costing and flexible budgeting.

11–18. Why are fixed-overhead costs sometimes called capacity-producing costs?

11–19. Draw a graph showing both budgeted and applied variable overhead. Explain why the graph appears as it does.

11–20. Give one example of a plausible activity base to use in flexible budgeting for each of the following organizations: an insurance company, an express delivery service, a restaurant, and a governmental tax-collection agency.

11–21. Explain how an activity-based flexible budget differs from a conventional flexible budget.

Exercises

Murano Glassware Company has the following standards and flexible-budget data.

Standard variable-overhead rate	$6.10 per direct-labor hour
Standard quantity of direct labor	2 hours per unit of output
Budgeted fixed overhead	$100,000
Budgeted output	25,000 units

Actual results for April are as follows:

Actual output	20,000 units
Actual variable overhead	$320,000
Actual fixed overhead	$99,000
Actual direct labor	50,000 hours

Required: Use the variance formulas to compute the following variances. Indicate whether each variance is favorable or unfavorable, where appropriate.

1. Variable-overhead spending variance.
2. Variable-overhead efficiency variance.
3. Fixed-overhead budget variance.
4. Fixed-overhead volume variance.

■ **Exercise 11–22**
Straightforward Computation
of Overhead Variances
(LO 5)

Refer to the data in the preceding exercise. Use diagrams similar to those in Exhibits 11–6 and 11–8 to compute the variable-overhead spending and efficiency variances, and the fixed-overhead budget and volume variances.

■ **Exercise 11–23**
Diagram of Overhead
Variances
(LO 5)

Refer to the data in the Exercise 11–22 for Murano Glassware Company. Draw graphs similar to those in Exhibit 11–7 (variable overhead) and Exhibit 11–9 (fixed overhead) to depict the overhead variances.

■ **Exercise 11–24**
Graphing Overhead Variances
(LO 5)

Choose a city and use the Internet to explore the annual budget for the governmental unit you selected. For example, you could check out the annual budget for Cape Town at www.capetown.gov.za/en/budget/.

Required:

1. Select three items in the budget and explain how these items would be treated if the budget were converted to an activity-based flexible budget.
2. What would be appropriate cost drivers for the budgetary items you selected?

■ **Exercise 11–25**
City or State Budget; Activity-
Based Flexible Budget; Cost
Drivers; Use of Internet
(LO 4, 7)

The following data are the actual results for Montreal Marshmallow Company for October.

Actual output	9,000 cases
Actual variable overhead	$405,000
Actual fixed overhead	$126,000
Actual machine time	40,500 machine hours

■ **Exercise 11–26**
Straightforward Computation
of Overhead Variances
(LO 5)

Standard cost and budget information for Montreal Marshmallow Company follows:

Standard variable-overhead rate	$9.00 per machine hour
Standard quantity of machine hours	4 hours per case of marshmallows
Budgeted fixed overhead	$120,000 per month
Budgeted output	10,000 cases per month

Required:

1. Use any of the methods explained in the chapter to compute the following variances. Indicate whether each variance is favorable or unfavorable, where appropriate.
   a. Variable-overhead spending variance.
   b. Variable-overhead efficiency variance.

      c. Fixed-overhead budget variance.

      d. Fixed-overhead volume variance.

  2. ***Build a spreadsheet:*** Construct an Excel spreadsheet to solve the preceding requirement. Show how the solution will change if the following information changes: actual output was 9,100 cases, and actual variable overhead was $395,000.

■ **Exercise 11–27**
Standard Hours Allowed;
Flexible Budgeting; Multiple
Products
(LO 1, 2)

Evening Star, Inc. produces binoculars of two quality levels: field and professional. The field model requires three direct-labor hours, while the professional binoculars require five hours. The firm uses direct-labor hours for flexible budgeting.

Required:

1. How many standard hours are allowed in May, when 200 field models and 300 professional binoculars are manufactured?

2. Suppose the company based its flexible overhead budget for May on the number of binoculars manufactured, which is 500. What difficulties would this approach cause?

■ **Exercise 11–28**
Construct a Flexible Overhead
Budget; Hospital
(LO 1, 2)

The controller for Rainbow Children's Hospital, located in Munich, Germany, estimates that the hospital uses 30 kilowatt-hours of electricity per patient-day, and that the electric rate will be $.10 per kilowatt-hour. The hospital also pays a fixed monthly charge of $1,000 to the electric utility to rent emergency backup electric generators.

Required: Construct a flexible budget for the hospital's electricity costs using each of the following techniques.

1. Formula flexible budget.

2. Columnar flexible budget for 30,000, 40,000 and 50,000 patient-days of activity. List variable and fixed electricity costs separately.

■ **Exercise 11–29**
Interpretation of Variable-
Overhead Efficiency Variance
(LO 5)

You recently received the following note from the production supervisor of the company where you serve as controller. "I don't understand these crazy variable-overhead efficiency variances. My employees are very careful in their use of electricity and manufacturing supplies, and we use very little indirect labor. What are we supposed to do?" Write a brief memo responding to the production supervisor's concern.

■ **Exercise 11–30**
Reconstruct Missing
Information from Partial Data
(LO 2, 5)

You brought your work home one evening, and your nephew spilled his chocolate milk shake on the variance report you were preparing. Fortunately, you were able to reconstruct the obliterated information from the remaining data. Fill in the missing numbers below. (*Hint:* It is helpful to solve for the unknowns in the order indicated by the letters in the following table.)

Standard machine hours per unit of output	4 hours
Standard variable-overhead rate per machine hour	$8.00
Actual variable-overhead rate per machine hour	b
Actual machine hours per unit of output	d
Budgeted fixed overhead	$50,000
Actual fixed overhead	a
Budgeted production in units	25,000
Actual production in units	c
Variable-overhead spending variance	$ 72,000 U
Variable-overhead efficiency variance	$192,000 F
Fixed-overhead budget variance	$ 15,000 U
Fixed-overhead volume variance	g
Total actual overhead	$713,000
Total budgeted overhead (flexible budget)	e
Total budgeted overhead (static budget)	f
Total applied overhead	$816,000

Refer to Pâtisserie Cézanne's activity-based flexible budget in Exhibit 11–11. Suppose that the company's activity in June is described as follows:

Process hours	7,500
Production runs	16
New products tested	30
Direct material handled (pounds)	40,000

Exercise 11–31
Activity-Based Flexible Budget
(LO 2, 7)

Required:

1. Determine the flexible budgeted cost for each of the following:
   a. Indirect material   d. Test kitchen
   b. Utilities   e. Material handling
   c. Inspection   f. Total overhead cost
2. Compute the variance for setup cost during the month, assuming that the actual setup cost was $3,000:
   a. Using the activity-based flexible budget.
   b. Using Pâtisserie Cézanne's conventional flexible budget (Exhibit 11–3).

Madrid Controls Ltda., which manufactures electrical switches, uses a standard-costing system. The standard manufacturing overhead costs per switch are based on direct-labor hours and are as follows:

Exercise 11–32
Overhead Variances
(LO 5)

Variable overhead (5 hours @ $8.00 per hour)	$ 40
Fixed overhead (5 hours @ $11.00 per hour)*	55
Total overhead	$ 95

*Based on capacity of 300,000 direct-labor hours per month.

The following information is available for the month of October.

- Variable overhead costs were $2,340,000.
- Fixed overhead costs were $3,750,000.
- 56,000 switches were produced, although 60,000 switches were scheduled to be produced.
- 275,000 direct-labor hours were worked at a total cost of $2,550,000.

Required: Compute the variable-overhead spending and efficiency variances and the fixed-overhead budget and volume variances for October. Indicate whether a variance is favorable or unfavorable where appropriate.

(CMA, adapted)

Refer to the data in Exercise 11–22 for Murano Glassware Company. Prepare journal entries to

Exercise 11–33
Journal Entries for Overhead
(Appendix A)
(LO 8)

- Record the incurrence of actual variable overhead and actual fixed overhead.
- Add variable and fixed overhead to Work-in-Process Inventory.
- Close underapplied or overapplied overhead into Cost of Goods Sold.

The following data pertain to Aurora Electronics for the month of February.

Exercise 11–34
Sales Variances (Appendix B)
(LO 9)

	Static Budget	Actual
Units sold	10,000	9,000
Sales revenue	$120,000	$103,500
Variable manufacturing cost	40,000	36,000
Fixed manufacturing cost	20,000	20,000
Variable selling and administrative cost	10,000	9,000
Fixed selling and administrative cost	10,000	10,000

Required: Compute the sales-price and sales-volume variances for February.

Problems

■ **Problem 11–35**
Straightforward Overhead
Variances
(LO 5)

Actual variable-overhead rate:
$3.10

Calgary Paper Company produces paper for photocopiers. The company has developed standard overhead rates based on a monthly capacity of 180,000 direct-labor hours as follows:

Standard costs per unit (one box of paper):	
Variable overhead (2 hours @ $3 per hour)	$ 6
Fixed overhead (2 hours @ $5 per hour)	10
Total	$16

During April, 90,000 units were scheduled for production: however, only 80,000 units were actually produced. The following data relate to April.

1. Actual direct-labor cost incurred was $1,567,500 for 165,000 actual hours of work.
2. Actual overhead incurred totaled $1,371,500, of which $511,500 was variable and $860,000 was fixed.

Required: Prepare two exhibits similar to Exhibits 11–6 and 11–8 in the chapter, which show the following variances. State whether each variance is favorable or unfavorable, where appropriate.

1. Variable-overhead spending variance.
2. Variable-overhead efficiency variance.
3. Fixed-overhead budget variance.
4. Fixed-overhead volume variance.

(CMA, adapted)

■ **Problem 11–36**
Standard Hours Allowed;
Flexible Budget; Multiple
Products; Insurance Company
(LO 1, 2, 4)

4. Budgeted overhead cost for
July: $11,800

Gibraltar Insurance Company uses a flexible overhead budget for its application-processing department. The firm offers five types of policies, with the following standard hours allowed for clerical processing.

Automobile	1 hour
Renter's	1 hour
Homeowner's	2 hours
Health	2 hours
Life	5 hours

The following numbers of insurance applications were processed during July.

Automobile	250
Renter's	200
Homeowner's	100
Health	400
Life	200

The controller estimates that the variable-overhead rate in the application-processing department is $4.00 per hour, and that fixed-overhead costs will amount to $2,000 per month.

Required:

1. How many standard clerical hours are allowed in July, given actual application activity?
2. Why would it not be sensible to base the company's flexible budget on the number of applications processed instead of the number of clerical hours allowed?
3. Construct a formula flexible overhead budget for the company.
4. What is the flexible budget for total overhead cost in July?

■ **Problem 11–37**
Graphing Budgeted and
Applied Overhead;
Recording Studio
(LO 1, 2, 3)

Mbalax Studios is a music recording studio in Dakar Senegal. The studio budgets and applies overhead costs on the basis of production time. Mbalax's financial manager anticipates 8,000 hours of production time to be available during the year. The following overhead amounts have been budgeted for the year.

Variable overhead	$32,000
Fixed overhead	$72,000

Required:

1. Draw two graphs, one for variable overhead and one for fixed overhead. The variable on the horizontal axis of each graph should be production time, in hours, ranging from 4,000 to 12,000

hours. The variable on the vertical axis of each graph should be overhead cost (variable or fixed). Each graph should include two lines, one for the flexible-budget amount of overhead and one for applied overhead.

2. Write a brief memo to Mbalax Studio's general manager, explaining the graph so that she will understand the concepts of budgeted and applied overhead.

■ **Problem 11–38**
Overhead Variances
(LO 5)

1(d). Variable-overhead
efficiency variance: $8,850 F

Neustadt Plastics Corporation developed its overhead application rate from the annual budget. The budget is based on an expected total output of 720,000 units requiring 3,600,000 machine hours. The company is able to schedule production uniformly throughout the year.

A total of 66,000 units requiring 315,000 machine hours were produced during May. Actual overhead costs for May amounted to $375,000. The actual costs, as compared to the annual budget and to one-twelfth of the annual budget, are as follows:

NEUSTADT PLASTICS CORPORATION
Annual Budget

	Total Amount	Per Unit	Per Machine Hour	Monthly Budget	Actual Costs for May
Variable overhead:					
Indirect material	$1,224,000	$1.70	$ .34	$102,000	$111,000
Indirect labor	900,000	1.25	.25	75,000	75,000
Fixed overhead:					
Supervision	648,000	.90	.18	54,000	51,000
Utilities	540,000	.75	.15	45,000	54,000
Depreciation	1,008,000	1.40	.28	84,000	84,000
Total	$4,320,000	$6.00	$1.20	$360,000	$375,000

Required:

1. Prepare a schedule showing the following amounts for Neustadt Plastics for May.

   a. Applied overhead costs.

   b. Variable-overhead spending variance.

   c. Fixed-overhead budget variance.

   d. Variable-overhead efficiency variance.

   e. Fixed-overhead volume variance.

   Where appropriate, be sure to indicate whether each variance is favorable or unfavorable.

2. Draw a graph similar to Exhibit 11–7 to depict the variable-overhead variances.

3. Why does your graph differ from Exhibit 11–7, other than the fact that the numbers differ?

(CMA, adapted)

■ **Problem 11–39**
Budgets and Performance
Evaluation
(LO 1, 6)

3. Direct material used:
$20.00 per unit
Variable manufacturing
overhead: $6.25 per unit
Supervisory salaries: $36,000
per month

Johnson Electrical produces industrial ventilation fans. The company plans to manufacture 72,000 fans evenly over the next quarter at the following costs: direct material, $1,440,000; direct labor, $360,000; variable manufacturing overhead, $450,000; and fixed manufacturing overhead, $900,000. The $900,000 amount includes $72,000 of straight-line depreciation and $108,000 of supervisory salaries.

Shortly after the conclusion of the quarter's first month, Johnson reported the following costs:

Direct material	$432,500
Direct labor	110,600
Variable manufacturing overhead	152,000
Depreciation	24,000
Supervisory salaries	37,800
Other fixed manufacturing overhead	239,000
Total	$995,900

Dave Kellerman and his crews turned out 20,000 fans during the month—a remarkable feat given that the firm's manufacturing plant was closed for several days because of storm damage and flooding.

Kellerman was especially pleased with the fact that overall financial performance for the period was favorable when compared with the budget. His pleasure, however, was very short-lived, as Johnson's general manager issued a stern warning that performance must improve, and improve quickly, if Kellerman had any hopes of keeping his job.

Required:

1. Explain the difference between a static budget and a flexible budget.
2. Which of the two budgets would be more useful when planning the company's cash needs over a range of activity?
3. Prepare a performance report that compares budgeted and actual costs for the period just ended (i.e., the report that Kellerman likely used when assessing his performance).
4. Prepare a performance report that compares budgeted and actual costs for the period just ended (i.e., the report that the general manager likely used when assessing Kellerman's performance).
5. Which of the two reports is preferred? Should Kellerman be praised for outstanding performance or is the general manager's warning appropriate? Explain, citing any apparent problems for the firm.

■ **Problem 11–40**

Linkages Between the Flexible Budget and Variances
(LO 1, 2, 5)

1. Medical assistants, budget: $11,060
Medical assistants, actual: $13,020
3. Variable-overhead spending variance: $20,856 F

Golden City Hospital has an outpatient clinic. Su-Huei Huang, the hospital's chief administrator, is very concerned about cost control and has asked that performance reports be prepared that compare budgeted and actual amounts for medical assistants, clinic supplies, and lab tests. Past financial studies have shown that the cost of clinic supplies used is driven by the number of medical assistant labor hours worked, whereas lab tests are highly correlated with the number of patients served.

The following information is available for June:

- *Medical assistants* Golden City's Hospital standard wage rate is $14 per hour, and each assistant is expected to spend 30 minutes with a patient. Assistants totaled 840 hours in helping the 1,580 patients seen, at an average pay rate of $15.50 per hour.
- *Clinic supplies* The cost of clinic supplies used is budgeted at $12 per labor hour, and the actual cost of supplies used was $9,180.
- *Lab tests* Each patient is anticipated to have three lab tests, at an average budgeted cost of $65 per test. Actual lab tests for June cost $318,054 and averaged 3.3 per patient.

Required:

1. Prepare a report that shows budgeted and actual costs for the 1,580 patients served during June. Compute the differences (variances) between these amounts and label them as favorable or unfavorable.
2. On the basis of your answer to requirement (1), determine whether Golden City Hospital has any significant problems with respect to clinic supplies and lab tests. Briefly discuss your findings.
3. By performing a detailed analysis, determine the spending and efficiency variances for lab tests. Does it appear that Golden City Hospital has any significant problems with the cost of its lab tests? Briefly explain. (*Hint:* In applying the overhead variance formulas, think of the number of tests as analogous to the number of hours, and think of the cost per test as analogous to the variable overhead rate.)
4. Compare the lab test variance computed in requirement (1), a flexible-budget variance, with the sum of the variances in requirement (3). Discuss your findings and explain the relationship of flexible-budget variances and standard cost variances for variable overhead.

■ **Problem 11–41**

Overhead Calculations; Variance Interpretation
(LO 5)

2. Variable-overhead spending variance: $2,310 F
5. Variable-overhead is underapplied by $42,065

Maxwell Company uses a standard cost accounting system and applies manufacturing overhead to products on the basis of machine hours. The following information is available for the year just ended:

Standard variable overhead rate per hour: $2.50

Standard fixed overhead rate per hour: $4.00

Planned activity during the period: 20,000 machine hours

Actual production: 10,700 finished units

Machine-hour standard: Two completed units per machine hour

Actual variable overhead: $55,440

Actual total overhead: $155,900

Actual machine hours worked: 23,100

Required:

1. Calculate the budgeted fixed overhead for the year.
2. Compute the variable-overhead spending variance.

3. Calculate the company's fixed-overhead volume variance.
4. Did Maxwell spend more or less than anticipated for fixed overhead? How much?
5. Was variable overhead underapplied or overapplied during the year? By how much?
6. On the basis of the data presented, does it appear that Maxwell suffered a lengthy strike during the year by its production workers? Briefly explain.

Faiz Ibrahim, president of SoftGro, Inc., was looking forward to seeing the performance reports for November because he knew the company's sales for the month had exceeded budget by a considerable margin. SoftGro, a distributor of educational software packages, had been growing steadily for approximately two years. Ibrahim's biggest challenge at this point was to ensure that the company did not lose control of expenses during this growth period. When Ibrahim received the November reports, he was dismayed to see the large unfavorable variance in the company's Monthly Selling Expense Report that follows.

■ **Problem 11–42**
Flexible Budget;
Performance Report
(LO 1, 6)

2. Advertising, flexible budget:
$1,650,000

SOFTGRO, INC.
Monthly Selling Expense Report
For the Month of November

	Annual Budget	November Budget	November Actual	November Variance
Unit sales	2,000,000	280,000	310,000	30,000
Dollar sales	$80,000,000	$11,200,000	$12,400,000	$1,200,000
Orders processed	54,000	6,500	5,800	(700)
Sales personnel per month	90	90	96	(6)
Advertising	$19,800,000	$ 1,650,000	$ 1,660,000	$ 10,000 U
Staff salaries	1,500,000	125,000	125,000	—
Sales salaries	1,296,000	108,000	115,400	7,400 U
Commissions	3,200,000	448,000	496,000	48,000 U
Per diem expense	1,782,000	148,500	162,600	14,100 U
Office expenses	4,080,000	340,000	358,400	18,400 U
Shipping expenses	6,750,000	902,500	976,500	74,000 U
Total expenses	$38,408,000	$ 3,722,000	$ 3,893,900	$ 171,900 U

Ibrahim called in the company's new controller, Fatima Oudoud, to discuss the implications of the variances reported for November and to plan a strategy for improving performance. Oudoud suggested that the company's reporting format might not be giving Ibrahim a true picture of the company's operations. She proposed that SoftGro implement flexible budgeting. Oudoud offered to redo the Monthly Selling Expense Report for November using flexible budgeting so that Ibrahim could compare the two reports and see the advantages of flexible budgeting.

Oudoud discovered the following information about the behavior of SoftGro's selling expenses.

• The total compensation paid to the sales force consists of a monthly base salary and a commission; the commission varies with sales dollars.

• Sales office expense is a semivariable cost with the variable portion related to the number of orders processed. The fixed portion of office expense is $3,000,000 annually and is incurred uniformly throughout the year.

• Subsequent to the adoption of the annual budget for the current year, SoftGro decided to open a new sales territory. As a consequence, approval was given to hire six additional salespeople effective November 1. Oudoud decided that these additional six people should be recognized in her revised report.

• Per diem reimbursement to the sales force, while a fixed amount per day, is variable with the number of sales personnel and the number of days spent traveling. SoftGro's original budget was based on an average sales force of 90 people throughout the year with each salesperson traveling 15 days per month.

• The company's shipping expense is a semivariable cost with the variable portion, $3.00 per unit, dependent on the number of units sold. The fixed portion is incurred uniformly throughout the year.

Required:

1. Citing the benefits of flexible budgeting, explain why Fatima Oudoud would propose that SoftGro use flexible budgeting in this situation.

2. Prepare a revised Monthly Selling Expense Report for November that would permit Faiz Ibrahim to more clearly evaluate SoftGro's control over selling expenses. The report should have a line for each selling expense item showing the appropriate budgeted amount, the actual selling expense, and the monthly dollar variance.

(CMA, adapted)

■ **Problem 11–43**

Flexible Budgeting; Variances; Impact on Behavior

(LO 1, 2, 5)

1. Operating income: $102,400

2. Operating income, flexible budget variance: $45,400 U

LawnMate Company manufactures power mowers that are sold throughout the United States and Canada. The company uses a comprehensive budgeting process and compares actual results to budgeted amounts on a monthly basis. Each month, LawnMate's accounting department prepares a variance analysis and distributes the report to all responsible parties. Cheng Li, production manager, is upset about the results for May. Cheng, who is responsible for the cost of goods manufactured, has implemented several cost-cutting measures in the manufacturing area and is discouraged by the unfavorable variance in variable costs.

LAWNMATE COMPANY
Operating Results
For the Month of May

	Master Budget	Actual	Variance
Units sold	5,000	4,800	200 U
Revenue	$1,200,000	$1,152,000	$48,000 U
Variable cost	760,000	780,000	20,000 U
Contribution margin	$ 440,000	$ 372,000	$68,000 U
Fixed overhead	180,000	180,000	—
Fixed general and administrative cost	140,000	135,000	5,000 F
Operating income	$ 120,000	$ 57,000	$63,000 U

When the master budget was prepared, LawnMate's cost accountant, Xu Lifen, supplied the following unit costs: direct material, $60; direct labor, $44; variable overhead, $36; and variable selling, $12.

The total variable costs of $780,000 for May include $320,000 for direct material, $192,000 for direct labor, $176,000 for variable overhead, and $92,000 for variable selling expenses. Xu believes that LawnMate's monthly reports would be more meaningful to everyone if the company adopted flexible budgeting and prepared more detailed analyses.

Required:

1. Prepare a flexible budget for LawnMate Company for the month of May that includes separate variable-cost budgets for each type of cost (direct material, etc.).

2. Determine the variance between the flexible budget and actual cost for each cost item.

3. Discuss how the revised budget and variance data are likely to impact the behavior of Cheng Li, the production manager.

4. *Build a spreadsheet:* Construct an Excel spreadsheet to solve requirements (1) and (2) above. Show how the solution will change if the following information changes: actual sales amounted to 4,700 units, and actual fixed overhead was $179,000.

(CMA, adapted)

■ **Problem 11–44**

Finding Missing Data; Overhead Accounting

(LO 1, 5)

2. Case A: $7.00 per hour
5. Case B: $18,000
14. Case B: 1,000 units

For each of the following independent cases, fill in the missing information. The company budgets and applies manufacturing-overhead costs on the basis of direct-labor hours. (U denotes *unfavorable variance;* F denotes *favorable variance.*)

		Case A	Case B
1.	Standard variable-overhead rate	$2.50 per hour	? per hour
2.	Standard fixed-overhead rate	? per hour	? per hour
3.	Total standard overhead rate	? per hour	$13.00 per hour
4.	Flexible budget for variable overhead	$90,000	?

	Case A	Case B
5. Flexible budget for fixed overhead	$210,000	?
6. Actual variable overhead	?	?
7. Actual fixed overhead	$207,000	?
8. Variable-overhead spending variance	$5,550 U	$2,000 U
9. Variable-overhead efficiency variance	?	$400 F
10. Fixed-overhead budget variance	?	$1,080 U
11. Fixed-overhead volume variance	?	$3,600 U
12. Under- (or over-) applied variable overhead	?	?
13. Under- (or over-) applied fixed overhead	?	?
14. Budgeted production (in units)	5,000 units	?
15. Standard direct-labor hours per unit	6 hours per unit	2 hours per unit
16. Actual production (in units)	?	?
17. Standard direct-labor hours allowed, given actual production	36,000 hours	1,600 hours
18. Actual direct-labor hours	37,000 hours	1,500 hours
19. Applied variable overhead	?	?
20. Applied fixed overhead	?	?

Goa Sky Tours is a small sightseeing tour company in southwestern India. The firm specializes in aerial tours of the state of Goa and the Goan coastline. Until recently, the company had not had an accounting department. Routine bookkeeping tasks, such as billing, had been handled by an individual who had little formal training in accounting. As the business began to grow, however, the owner recognized the need for more formal accounting procedures. Lakshmi Srikumar has recently been hired as the new controller.

During her first week on the job, Srikumar was given the following performance report. The report was prepared by Joe Gomes, the company's manager of aircraft operations, who was planning to present it to the owner the next morning. "Look at these favorable variances for fuel and so forth," Gomes pointed out, as he showed the report to Srikumar. "My operations people are doing a very good job." Later that day, Srikumar looked at the performance report more carefully. She immediately realized that it was improperly prepared and would be misleading to the company's owner.

■ **Problem 11–45**
Preparing and Using a Columnar Flexible Budget; Tour Company; Ethical Issues
(LO 1, 2, 6)

Total variable expenses, activity level (air miles), 38,000: $93,100
4. Total variable expenses, flexible budget: $78,400

GOA SKY TOURS
Performance Report
For the Month of September

	Formula Flexible Budget (per air mile)	Actual (32,000 air miles)	Static Budget (35,000 air miles)	Variance
Passenger revenue	$3.50	$112,000	$122,500	$10,500 U
Less: Variable expenses:				
Fuel	.50	17,000	17,500	500 F
Aircraft maintenance	.75	23,500	26,250	2,750 F
Flight crew salaries	.40	13,100	14,000	900 F
Selling and administrative	.80	24,900	28,000	3,100 F
Total variable expenses	$2.45	$ 78,500	$ 85,750	$ 7,250 F
Contribution margin	$1.05	$ 33,500	$ 36,750	$ 3,250 U
Less: Fixed expenses:	Per Month			
Depreciation on aircraft	$ 2,900	$ 2,900	$ 2,900	$ 0
Landing fees	900	1,000	900	100 U
Supervisory salaries	9,000	8,600	9,000	400 F
Selling and administrative	11,000	12,500	11,000	1,500 U
Total fixed expenses	$23,800	$ 25,000	$ 23,800	$ 1,200 U
Operating income		$ 8,500	$ 12,950	$ 4,450 U

Required:

1. Prepare a columnar flexible budget for Goa Sky Tours' expenses, based on the following activity levels: 32,000 air miles, 35,000 air miles, and 38,000 air miles.

2. In spite of several favorable expense variances shown on the report above, the company's September operating income was only about two-thirds of the expected level. Why?

3. Write a brief memo from the controller to the manager of aircraft operations explaining why the original variance report is misleading.

4. Prepare a revised expense variance report for September, which is based on the flexible budget prepared in requirement (1).

5. Lakshmi Srikumar presented the revised expense report to Gomes along with the memo explaining why the original performance report was misleading. Gomes did not react well. He complained of Srikumar's "interference" and pointed out that the company had been doing just fine without her. "I'm taking my report to the owner tomorrow," Gomes insisted. "Yours just makes us look bad." What are Srikumar's ethical obligations in this matter? What should she do?

■ Problem 11–46
Interactions Between
Variances; Flexible
Manufacturing System
(LO 5)

Eastern Auto Parts Company manufactures replacement parts for automobile repair. The company recently installed a flexible manufacturing system, which has significantly changed the production process. The installation of the new FMS was not anticipated when the current year's budget and cost structure were developed. The installation of the new equipment was hastened by several major breakdowns in the company's old production machinery.

The new equipment was very expensive, but management expects it to cut the labor time required by a substantial amount. Management also expects the new equipment to allow a reduction in direct-material waste. On the negative side, the FMS requires a more highly skilled labor force to operate it than the company's old equipment.

The following cost variance report was prepared for the month of July, the first full month after the equipment was installed.

EASTERN AUTO PARTS COMPANY
Cost Variance Report
For the Month of July

Direct material:

Standard cost	$602,450
Actual cost	598,700
Direct-material price variance	150 U*
Direct-material quantity variance	3,900 F

Direct labor:

Standard cost	393,000
Actual cost	383,800
Direct-labor rate variance	4,800 U
Direct-labor efficiency variance	14,000 F

Manufacturing overhead:

Applied to work in process	400,000
Actual cost	408,000
Variable-overhead spending variance	8,000 U
Variable-overhead efficiency variance	10,000 F
Fixed-overhead budget variance	30,000 U
Fixed-overhead volume variance	(20,000)†

*F denotes favorable variance; U denotes unfavorable variance.

†The sign of the volume variance is negative; applied fixed overhead exceeded budgeted fixed overhead.

Required: Comment on the possible interactions between the variances listed in the report. Which ones are likely to have been caused by the purchase of the new production equipment? The company budgets and applies manufacturing overhead on the basis of direct-labor hours. (You may find it helpful to review the discussion of variance interactions in Chapter 10.)

WoodCrafts, Inc. is a manufacturer of furniture for specialty shops and has an annual sales volume of $12 million. The company has four major product lines: bookcases, magazine racks, end tables, and bar stools. Each line is managed by a production manager. Since production is spread fairly evenly over the 12 months of operation, Dusan Markovic, WoodCrafts' controller, has prepared an annual budget divided into 12 periods for monthly reporting purposes.

WoodCrafts uses a standard-costing system and applies variable overhead on the basis of process hours. Fixed production cost is allocated on the basis of square footage occupied using a predetermined plantwide rate; the size of the space occupied varies considerably among the product lines. All other costs are assigned on the basis of revenue dollars earned. At the monthly meeting to review November performance, Milica Djuric, manager of the bookcase line, received the following report.

■ **Problem 11–47**
Flexible Budget; Improved
Performance Report;
Behavioral Issues
(LO 1, 6)

Contribution margin, actual:
$59,400

WOODCRAFTS, INC.
Bookcase Production Performance Report
For the Month of November

	Actual	Budget	Variance
Units	3,000	2,500	500 F
Revenue	$161,000	$137,500	$23,500 F
Variable production costs:			
Direct material	$ 23,100	$ 20,000	$ 3,100 U
Direct labor	18,300	15,000	3,300 U
Machine time	19,200	16,250	2,950 U
Manufacturing overhead	41,000	35,000	6,000 U
Fixed production costs:			
Indirect labor	9,400	6,000	3,400 U
Depreciation	5,500	5,500	—
Property taxes	2,400	2,300	100 U
Insurance	4,500	4,500	—
Administrative expenses	12,000	9,000	3,000 U
Marketing expenses	8,300	7,000	1,300 U
Research and development	6,000	4,500	1,500 U
Total expenses	$149,700	$125,050	$24,650 U
Operating income	$ 11,300	$ 12,450	$ 1,150 U

While distributing the monthly reports at the meeting, Markovic remarked to Djuric, "We need to talk about getting your division back on track. Be sure to see me after the meeting."

Djuric had been so convinced that her division did well in November that Markovic's remark was a real surprise. She spent the balance of the meeting avoiding the looks of her fellow managers and trying to figure out what could have gone wrong. The monthly performance report was no help.

Required:

1. *a.* Identify three weaknesses in WoodCrafts, Inc.'s monthly Bookcase Production Performance Report.

   b. Discuss the behavioral implications of Dusan Markovic's remarks to Milica Djuric during the meeting.

2. WoodCrafts, Inc. could do a better job of reporting monthly performance to the production managers.

   a. Recommend how the report could be improved to eliminate weaknesses, and revise it accordingly.

   b. Discuss how the recommended changes in reporting are likely to affect Milica Djuric's behavior.

(CMA, adapted)

■ **Problem 11–48**
Using a Flexible Budget
(LO 1, 2, 5)

3. $11 per machine hour
5. Standard variable-overhead
rate per machine hour:
$10.10 per machine hour
8. Variable-overhead efficiency variance: $10,100 U
11. Fixed overhead cost:
$324,000

Rutherford Wheel and Axle, Inc. has an automated production process, and production activity is quantified in terms of process hours. A standard-costing system is used. The annual static budget for 20x1
called for 6,000 units to be produced, requiring 30,000 machine hours. The standard overhead rate for
the year was computed using this planned level of production. The 20x1 manufacturing cost report
follows.

RUTHERFORD WHEEL AND AXLE, INC.
Manufacturing Cost Report
For 20x1
(in thousands of dollars)

Cost Item	Static Budget 30,000 Machine Hours	Flexible Budget 31,000 Machine Hours	Flexible Budget 32,000 Machine Hours	Actual Cost
Direct material:				
G27 aluminum	$ 252.0	$ 260.4	$ 268.8	$ 270.0
M14 steel alloy	78.0	80.6	83.2	83.0
Direct labor:				
Assembler	273.0	282.1	291.2	287.0
Grinder	234.0	241.8	249.6	250.0
Manufacturing overhead:				
Maintenance	24.0	24.8	25.6	25.0
Supplies	129.0	133.3	137.6	130.0
Supervision	80.0	82.0	84.0	81.0
Inspection	144.0	147.0	150.0	147.0
Insurance	50.0	50.0	50.0	50.0
Depreciation	200.0	200.0	200.0	200.0
Total cost	$1,464.0	$1,502.0	$1,540.0	$1,523.0

Rutherford develops flexible budgets for different levels of activity for use in evaluating performance. A total of 6,200 units was produced during 20x1, requiring 32,000 machine hours. The preceding manufacturing cost report compares the company's actual cost for the year with the static budget and
the flexible budget for two different activity levels.

Required: Compute the following amounts. For variances, indicate whether favorable or unfavorable
where appropriate. Answers should be rounded to two decimal places when necessary.

1. The standard number of machine hours allowed to produce one unit of product.
2. The actual cost of direct material used in one unit of product.
3. The cost of material that should be processed per machine hour.
4. The standard direct-labor cost for each unit produced.
5. The variable-overhead rate per machine hour in a flexible-budget formula (*Hint:* Use the high-
    low method to estimate cost behavior.)
6. The standard fixed-overhead rate per machine hour used for product costing.
7. The variable-overhead spending variance. (Assume management has determined that the actual
    fixed overhead cost in 20x1 amounted to $324,000.)
8. The variable-overhead efficiency variance.
9. The fixed-overhead budget variance.
10. The fixed-overhead volume variance. [Make the same assumption as in requirement (7).]
11. The total budgeted manufacturing cost (in thousands of dollars) for an output of 6,050 units.
    (*Hint:* Use the flexible-budget formula.)

(CMA, adapted)

Chillco Corporation produces containers of frozen food. During April, Chillco produced 1,450 cases of food and incurred the following actual costs.

Variable overhead	$ 11,000
Fixed overhead	26,000
Actual labor cost (8,000 direct-labor hours)	151,200
Actual material cost (30,000 pounds purchased and used)	66,000

Standard cost and annual budget information are as follows:

Standard Costs per Case

Direct labor (5 hours at $18 per hour)	$ 90.00
Direct material (20 pounds at $2 per pound)	40.00
Variable overhead (5 hours at $1.50 per hour)	7.50
Fixed overhead (5 hours at $3 per hour)	15.00
Total	$152.50

Annual Budget Information

Variable overhead	$150,000
Fixed overhead	$300,000
Planned activity for year	100,000 direct-labor hours

Required:

1. Prepare as complete an analysis of cost variances as is possible from the available data.
2. *Build a spreadsheet:* Construct an Excel spreadsheet to solve the preceding requirement. Show how the solution will change if the following information changes: the standard rates were $17.50 per hour for direct labor, and $1.60 per direct-labor hour for variable overhead.

■ **Problem 11–49**
Complete Analysis of Cost Variances; Review of Chapters 10 and 11
(LO 5)

Direct-labor efficiency variance: $13,500 U
Fixed-overhead budget variance: $1,000 U

Montreal Scholastic Supply Company uses a standard-costing system. The firm estimates that it will operate its manufacturing facilities at 800,000 machine hours for the year. The estimate for total budgeted overhead is $2,000,000. The standard variable-overhead rate is estimated to be $2 per machine hour or $6 per unit. The actual data for the year are presented below.

Actual finished units	250,000
Actual machine hours	764,000
Actual variable overhead	$1,701,000
Actual fixed overhead	$ 392,000

Required:

1. Compute the following variances. Indicate whether each is favorable or unfavorable, where appropriate.
   a. Variable-overhead spending variance.
   b. Variable-overhead efficiency variance.
   c. Fixed-overhead budget variance.
   d. Fixed-overhead volume variance.
2. Prepare journal entries to
   • Record the incurrence of actual variable overhead and actual fixed overhead.
   • Add variable and fixed overhead to Work-in-Process Inventory.
   • Close underapplied or overapplied overhead into Cost of Goods Sold.

(CMA, adapted)

■ **Problem 11–50**
Overhead Variances; Journal Entries (Appendix A)
(LO 5, 8)

1(a). Variable-overhead spending variance: $173,000 U
2. Cost of goods sold (debit): $218,000

■ **Problem 11–51**
Comprehensive Problem on
Overhead Accounting under
Standard Costing; Journal
Entries (Appendix A)
(LO 2, 3, 5, 8)

Flexible budget, variable
overhead: $18,000
5. Fixed overhead applied to
work in process: $25,600
8. Cost of goods sold (debit):
$13,530

Treasured Memories, Inc. (TMI) publishes consumer photobooks using an on-line business model. Customers use software provided free of charge by TMI to create photobooks on their home computers and then TMI prints and ships the book designed by the customer. A monthly flexible overhead budget for the firm's photobook printing division follows.

TREASURED MEMORIES, INC.
Photobook Printing Division
Monthly Flexible Overhead Budget

	Direct-Labor Hours		
Budgeted Cost	**1,500**	**1,750**	**2,000**
Variable costs:			
Indirect material:			
Glue	$ 750	$ 875	$ 1,000
Tape	300	350	400
Miscellaneous supplies	3,000	3,500	4,000
Indirect labor	7,500	8,750	10,000
Utilities:			
Electricity	1,500	1,750	2,000
Natural gas	450	525	600
Total variable cost	$13,500	$15,750	$18,000
Fixed costs:			
Supervisory labor	12,500	12,500	12,500
Depreciation	3,400	3,400	3,400
Property taxes and insurance	4,580	4,580	4,580
Total fixed cost	$20,480	$20,480	$20,480
Total overhead cost	$33,980	$35,230	$38,480

The planned monthly production is 6,400 photobooks. The standard direct-labor allowance is .25 hour per book. During February, TMI produced 8,000 photobooks and actually used 2,100 direct-labor hours. The actual overhead costs for the month were as follows:

Actual variable overhead	$19,530
Actual fixed overhead	37,600

Required:

1. Determine the formula-style flexible overhead budget for TMI.

2. Prepare a display similar to Exhibit 11–6, which shows TMI's variable-overhead variances for February. Indicate whether each variance is favorable or unfavorable.

3. Draw a graph similar to Exhibit 11–7, which shows TMI's variable-overhead variances for February.

4. Explain how to interpret each of the variances computed in requirement (2).

5. Prepare a display similar to Exhibit 11–8, which shows TMI's fixed-overhead variances for February.

6. Draw a graph similar to Exhibit 11–9, which depicts the company's applied and budgeted fixed overhead for February. Show the firm's February volume variance on the graph.

7. Explain the interpretation of the variances computed in requirement (5).

8. Prepare journal entries to record each of the following:
   - Incurrence of February's actual overhead cost.
   - Application of February's overhead cost to Work-in-Process Inventory.
   - Close underapplied or overapplied overhead into Cost of Goods Sold.

9. Draw T-accounts for all of the accounts used in the journal entries of requirement (8). Then post the journal entries to the T-accounts.

White Mountain Sled Company manufactures children's snow sleds. The company's performance report for November is as follows.

■ **Problem 11–52**
Sales Variances (Appendix B)
(LO 9)

2. Sales volume variance: $50,000 U

	Actual	Budget
Sleds sold	5,000	6,000
Sales	$240,000	$300,000
Variable costs	150,000	180,000
Contribution margin	$ 90,000	$120,000
Fixed costs	84,000	80,000
Operating income	$ 6,000	$ 40,000

The company uses sales variance analysis to explain the difference between budgeted and actual sales revenue.

Required: Compute the following variances and indicate whether each is favorable or unfavorable.

1. November sales price variance.
2. November sales volume variance.

(CMA, adapted)

Canberra Computer Accessory Company (CCAC) distributes keyboard trays to computer stores. The keyboard trays can be attached to the underside of a desk, effectively turning it into a computer table. The keyboard trays are purchased from a manufacturer that attaches CCAC's private label to the trays. The wholesale selling prices to the computer stores are $120 for the business-grade keyboard tray and $60 for the residential-grade product. The 20x2 budget and actual results are as follows. The budget was adopted in late 20x1 and was based on CCAC's estimated share of the market for the two types of keyboard trays.

■ **Problem 11–53**
Analyzing Sales Variances
(Appendix B)
(LO 9)

1. Sales price variance: $456,000 U

CANBERRA COMPUTER ACCESSORY COMPANY
Income Statement
For the Year Ending December 31, 20x2
(in thousands)

	Business Grade		Residential Grade		Total		
	Budget	Actual	Budget	Actual	Budget	Actual	Variance
Sales in units	80	74	120	86	200	160	40
Revenue	$9,600	$8,510	$7,200	$5,074	$16,800	$13,584	$(3,216)
Cost of goods sold	6,400	6,068	6,000	4,300	12,400	10,368	2,032
Gross margin	$3,200	$2,442	$1,200	$ 774	$ 4,400	$ 3,216	$(1,184)
Unallocated costs:							
Selling					$ 1,000	$ 1,000	$ —
Advertising					1,000	1,060	(60)
Administrative					400	406	(6)
Income taxes (45%)					900	338	562
Total unallocated costs					$ 3,300	$ 2,804	$ 496
Net income					$ 1,100	$ 412	$ (688)

During the first quarter of 20x2, management estimated that the total market for these products actually would be 10 percent below the original estimates. In an attempt to prevent unit sales from declining as much as industry projections, management implemented a marketing program. Included in the program were dealer discounts and increased direct advertising. The business-grade line was emphasized in this program.

Required:

1. Compute the sales-price and sales-volume variances for each product line. Indicate whether each variance is favorable or unfavorable.

2. Discuss the apparent effect of CCAC's special marketing program (i.e., dealer discounts and additional advertising) on the 20x2 operating results.

(CMA, adapted)

Cases

■ **Case 11–54**

Integrative Case on Chapters 10 and 11; Drawing Conclusion from Missing Data **(LO 1, 3, 5)**

3. Actual fixed overhead: $43,250

7. Actual variable-overhead rate: $6.30 per hr

10. Applied fixed overhead: $36,000

Your cousin recently began a new job as assistant controller for Conundrum Corporation. As her first assignment, she prepared a performance report for January. She is nervous about this first big assignment, so she asks you to review it with her. Unfortunately, as you are reviewing it together on her laptop, the hard drive crashes. Your spouse, an engineer, is able to help you retrieve some, but not all, of the spreadsheet file, and only certain data are legible on the report. This information follows:

CONUNDRUM CORPORATION
Performance Report For the Month of January

	Direct Material	Direct Labor	Variable Overhead	Fixed Overhead
Standard allowed cost given actual output	?	?		
	(? kilograms at $12 per kilogram)	(2 hours at $14 per hour)		
Flexible overhead budget			?	$40,000
Actual cost	$189,000	?	?	?
	(14,000 kilograms at $13.50 per kilogram)	(8,800 hours at ? per hour)		
Direct-material price variance	?			
Direct-material quantity variance	$6,000 U			
Direct-labor rate variance		$8,800 U		
Direct-labor efficiency variance		2,800 F		
Variable-overhead spending variance			$2,640 U	
Variable-overhead efficiency variance			1,200 F	
Fixed-overhead budget variance				$3,250 U
Fixed-overhead volume variance				?

In addition to the fragmentary data still legible on the performance report, your neighbor happened to remember the following facts.

*   Planned production of Conundrum's sole product was 500 units more than the actual production.
*   All of the direct material purchased in January was used in production.
*   There were no beginning or ending inventories.
*   Variable and fixed overhead are applied on the basis of direct-labor hours. The fixed overhead rate is $4.00 per hour.

Required: Using the data still available to her on the spreadsheet, help your cousin reconstruct the following numbers, which will be necessary for her presentation.

1. Planned production (in units).
2. Actual production (in units).
3. Actual fixed overhead.
4. Total standard allowed direct-labor hours.
5. Actual direct-labor rate.
6. Standard variable-overhead rate.
7. Actual variable-overhead rate.
8. Standard direct-material quantity per unit.
9. Direct-material price variance.
10. Applied fixed overhead.
11. Fixed-overhead volume variance.

■ **Case 11–55**
Comprehensive Variance
Analysis Used to Explain
Operational Results; Review
of Chapters 10 and 11;
Activity-Based Costing
(Appendix B)
(LO 4, 5, 7)

4(a). Direct-material price
variance, total: $133,000 U
4(e). Variable-overhead
spending variance: $75,000 U
4(h). Sales-price variance:
$45,000 U

Aunt Molly's Old Fashioned Cookies bakes cookies for retail stores. The company's best-selling cookie is chocolate nut supreme, which is marketed as a gourmet cookie and regularly sells for $8.00 per pound. The standard cost per pound of chocolate nut supreme, based on Aunt Molly's normal monthly production of 400,000 pounds, is as follows:

Cost Item	Quantity	Standard Unit Cost	Total Cost
Direct materials:			
Cookie mix	10 oz.	$ .02 per oz.	$ .20
Milk chocolate	5 oz.	.15 per oz.	.75
Almonds	1 oz.	.50 per oz.	.50
			$1.45
Direct labor:*			
Mixing	1 min.	14.40 per hr.	$ .24
Baking	2 min.	18.00 per hr.	.60
			$ .84
Variable overhead[†]	3 min.	32.40 per hr.	$1.62
Total standard cost per pound			$3.91

*Direct-labor rates include employee benefits.
[†]Applied on the basis of direct-labor hours.

Aunt Molly's management accountant, Karen Blair, prepares monthly budget reports based on these standard costs. April's contribution report, which compares budgeted and actual performance, is shown in the following schedule.

	Static Budget	Actual	Variance
Contribution Report for April			
Units (in pounds)	400,000	450,000	50,000 F
Revenue	$3,200,000	$3,555,000	$355,000 F
Direct material	$ 580,000	$ 865,000	$285,000 U
Direct labor	336,000	348,000	12,000 U
Variable overhead	648,000	750,000	102,000 U
Total variable costs	$1,564,000	$1,963,000	$399,000 U
Contribution margin	$1,636,000	$1,592,000	$ 44,000 U

Justine Madison, president of the company, is disappointed with the results. Despite a sizable increase in the number of cookies sold, the product's expected contribution to the overall profitability of the firm decreased. Madison has asked Blair to identify the reason why the contribution margin decreased. Blair has gathered the following information to help in her analysis of the decrease.

Usage Report for February

Cost Item	Quantity	Actual Cost
Direct materials:		
Cookie mix	4,650,000 oz.	$ 93,000
Milk chocolate	2,660,000 oz.	532,000
Almonds	480,000 oz.	240,000
Direct labor:		
Mixing	450,000 min.	108,000
Baking	800,000 min.	240,000
Variable overhead		750,000
Total variable costs		$1,963,000

Required:

1. Prepare a new contribution report for April, in which:
   - The static budget column in the contribution report is replaced with a flexible budget column.
   - The variances in the contribution report are recomputed as the difference between the flexible budget and actual columns.

2. What is the total contribution margin in the flexible budget column of the new report prepared for requirement (1)?

3. Explain (i.e., interpret) the meaning of the total contribution margin in the flexible budget column of the new report prepared for requirement (1).

4. What is the total variance between the flexible budget contribution margin and the actual contribution margin in the new report prepared for requirement (1)? Explain this total contribution margin variance by computing the following variances. (Assume that all materials are used in the month of purchase.)
   - *a.* Direct-material price variance.
   - *b.* Direct-material quantity variance.
   - *c.* Direct-labor rate variance.
   - *d.* Direct-labor efficiency variance.
   - *e.* Variable-overhead spending variance.
   - *f.* Variable-overhead efficiency variance.
   - *g.* Sales-price variance.

5. *a.* Explain the problems that might arise in using direct-labor hours as the basis for applying overhead.
   b. How might activity-based costing (ABC) solve the problems described in requirement (5a)?

(CMA, adapted)

THIS CHAPTER'S FOCUS COMPANY is Oasis Hotels and Resorts, a chain of luxury hotels and resorts based in Abu Dhabi. In this chapter, we will explore this hospitality company's responsibility-accounting system. Responsibility accounting refers to the various concepts and tools used to measure the performance of both people and departments in an organization. The management of Oasis Hotels and Resorts uses detailed performance reports about the company's divisions, hotels, and departments to help ensure that everyone in the organization is working toward the same overall corporate goals.

12 Responsibility Accounting, Quality Control, and Environmental Cost Management

In contrast to the hospitality-services setting of Oasis Hotels and Resorts, we will turn to a manufacturing company to explore the management of **Labban** ◎ **Enterprises** product quality and environmental costs. Labban Enterprises manufactures cellular telephones. Using the Labban Enterprises illustration, we will explore various types of quality-related costs incurred in manufacturing companies. We also will discuss how companies try to identify and manage a variety of environmental costs.

1 Explain the role of responsibility accounting in fostering goal congruence.

2 Define and give an example of a cost center, a revenue center, a profit center, and an investment center.

3 Prepare a performance report and explain the relationships between the performance reports for various responsibility centers.

4 Use a cost allocation base to allocate costs.

5 Prepare a segmented income statement.

6 Prepare a quality-cost report.

7 Discuss the traditional and contemporary views of the optimal level of product quality.

8 Understand the different types of environmental costs and discuss environmental cost management.

Learning Objective 1

Explain the role of responsibility accounting in fostering goal congruence.

Most organizations are divided into smaller units, each of which is assigned particular responsibilities. These units are called by various names, including divisions, segments, business units, and departments. Each department is composed of individuals who are responsible for particular tasks or managerial functions. The managers of an organization should ensure that the people in each department are striving toward the same overall goals. **Goal congruence** results when the managers of subunits throughout an organization strive to achieve the goals set by top management.

How can an organization's managerial accounting system promote goal congruence? **Responsibility accounting** refers to the various concepts and tools used by managerial accountants to measure the performance of people and departments in order to foster goal congruence.

Responsibility Centers

Learning Objective 2

Define and give an example of a cost center, a revenue center, a profit center, and an investment center.

The basis of a responsibility-accounting system is the designation of each subunit in the organization as a particular type of *responsibility center*. A **responsibility center** is a subunit in an organization whose manager is held accountable for specified financial results of the subunit's activities. There are four common types of responsibility centers.

Cost Center A **cost center** is an organizational subunit, such as a department or division, whose manager is held accountable for the costs incurred in the subunit. The Painting Department in an automobile plant is an example of a cost center.

Revenue Center The manager of a **revenue center** is held accountable for the revenue attributed to the subunit. For example, the Reservations Department of an airline and the Sales Department of a manufacturer are revenue centers.

Profit Center A **profit center** is an organizational subunit whose manager is held accountable for profit. Since profit is equal to revenue minus expenses, profit-center managers are held accountable for both the revenue and expenses attributed to their subunits. An example of a profit center is a company-owned restaurant in a fast-food chain.

Investment Center   The manager of an **investment center** is held accountable for the subunit's profit *and the invested capital* used by the subunit to generate its profit. A division of a large corporation is typically designated as an investment center.[1]

Illustration of Responsibility Accounting

To illustrate the concepts used in responsibility accounting, we will focus on a hotel chain. Oasis Hotels and Resorts operates 10 luxury hotels along the Persian (Arabian) Gulf. The company is divided into the South Division, which operates seven hotels along the southern Gulf in the United Arab Emirates, Qatar, and Oman, and the North Division, with three properties in Kuwait and Saudi Arabia. Exhibit 12–1 shows the company's organization chart, and Exhibit 12–2 depicts the responsibility-accounting system.

Clockwise from upper left: This aircraft maintenance department is a cost center. However, a sales office like the one shown next is usually treated as a revenue center. This McDonalds in Riyadh, Saudi Arabia is a profit center. And this power plant in the Loire Valley, France, is an investment center. What sort of responsibility center designation would be appropriate for your local auto repair shop, hair salon, and dry cleaner?

---

[1]Although there is an important conceptual difference between profit centers and investment centers, the latter term is not always used in practice. Some managers use the term *profit center* to refer to both types of responsibility centers. Hence, when businesspeople use the term *profit center,* they may be referring to a true profit center (as defined in this chapter) or to an investment center.

Exhibit 12–1
Organization Chart: Oasis
Hotels and Resorts

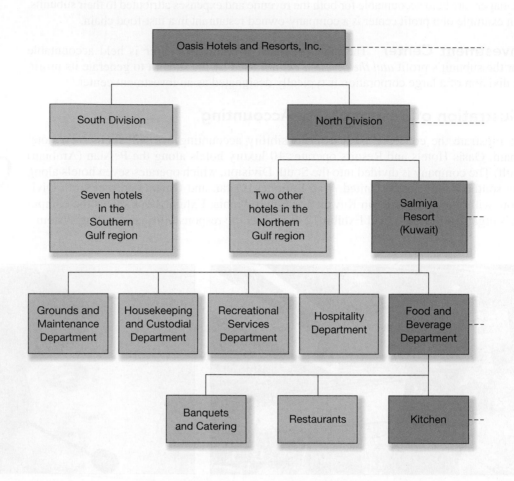

Corporate Level   The chief executive officer of Oasis Hotels and Resorts, Inc. is the company's president. The president, who is responsible to the company's owners, is accountable for corporate profit in relation to the capital (assets) invested in the company. Therefore, the entire company is an *investment center*. The president has the autonomy to make significant decisions that affect the company's profit and invested capital. For example, the final decision to add a new luxury tower to any of the company's resort properties would be made by the president.

> "Responsibility accounting is an integral part of our reporting process in this company. Always has been. Always will." (12a)
>
> **Chryster**

Division Level   The vice president of the North Division is accountable for the profit earned by the three resort hotels in Kuwait and Saudi Arabia in relation to the capital invested in those properties. Hence, the North Division is also an *investment center*. The vice president has the authority to make major investment decisions regarding the properties in the northern Gulf region, up to a limit of $300,000. For example, the vice president could decide to landscape a swimming pool at one of the North Division resort hotels, but could not decide to add a new wing.

Hotel Level   The Salmiya Resort, in Kuwait, is one of the properties in the North Division. The general manager of the Salmiya Resort is accountable for the profit earned by the hotel. The general manager does not have the authority to make major investment decisions, but is responsible for operational decisions. For example, the general manager hires all of the hotel's departmental managers, sets wage rates, determines procedures and standards for operations, approves decorating decisions, and generally oversees the hotel's operation. Since the hotel's general manager has no authority to

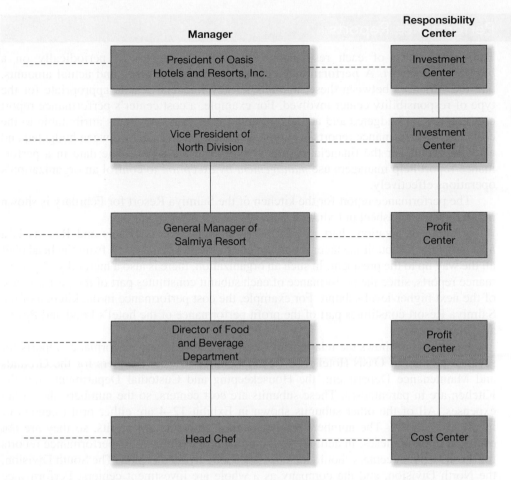

Exhibit 12–2
Responsibility Accounting
System: Oasis Hotels and
Resorts

make major investment decisions, he is held accountable only for the hotel's profit, not the capital invested in the property. Thus, the Salmiya Resort is a *profit center.*

Departmental Level   The Salmiya Resort has five departments, as shown in Exhibit 12–1. The Grounds and Maintenance Department includes landscaping, building and equipment maintenance, and hotel security. The Housekeeping and Custodial Services Department covers laundry and janitorial services. These two departments are called service departments, since they provide services to the hotel's other departments but do not deal directly with hotel guests. The Recreational Services Department operates the hotel's swimming pools, saunas, fitness center, and tennis courts. The Hospitality Department includes the hotel's reservations desk, rooms, bell staff, and shopping facilities. Finally, the Food and Beverage Department operates the resort's restaurants, coffee shop, lounges, poolside snack bar, banquet operations, and catering service.

The director of the Food and Beverage Department is accountable for the profit earned on all food and beverage operations. Therefore, this department is a *profit center.* The director has the authority to approve the menu, set food and beverage prices, hire the wait staff, schedule entertainers, and generally oversee all food and beverage operations.

Kitchen Level   The Food and Beverage Department is divided further into subunits responsible for Banquets and Catering, Restaurants, and the Kitchen.

The head chef manages the kitchen and is accountable for the costs incurred there. Thus, the Kitchen is a *cost center.* The head chef hires the kitchen staff, orders food supplies, and oversees all food preparation. The head chef is responsible for providing high-quality food at the lowest possible cost.

"But you have to wear the hat of the management team you are on to help them achieve the goals. You also have to wear the corporate finance hat to recognize that you have a duty, to the corporate finance function, to do things right and do them correctly, to stand up for what has to be done, and to say no when no is the appropriate thing to say." (12b)

Abbott Laboratories

Performance Reports

Learning Objective 3

Prepare a performance report and explain the relationships between the performance reports for various responsibility centers.

The performance of each responsibility center is summarized periodically on a *performance report*. A **performance report** shows the budgeted and actual amounts, and the variances between these amounts, of key financial results appropriate for the type of responsibility center involved. For example, a cost center's performance report concentrates on budgeted and actual amounts for various cost items attributable to the cost center. Performance reports also typically show the variance between budgeted and actual amounts for the financial results conveyed in the report. The data in a performance report help managers use *management by exception* to control an organization's operations effectively.

The performance report for the kitchen of the Salmiya Resort for February is shown in the Excel spreadsheet in Exhibit 12–3.

As the organization chart in Exhibit 12–1 shows, Oasis Hotels and Resorts is a *hierarchy*. Each subunit manager reports to one higher-level manager, from the head chef all the way up to the president. In such an organization, there is also a hierarchy of performance reports, since the performance of each subunit constitutes part of the performance of the next higher-level subunit. For example, the cost performance in the kitchen of the Salmiya Resort constitutes part of the profit performance of the hotel's Food and Beverage Department.

Exhibit 12–4 shows the relationships between the February performance reports for several subunits of Oasis Hotels and Resorts. Notice that the numbers for the Grounds and Maintenance Department, the Housekeeping and Custodial Department, and the Kitchen are in parentheses. These subunits are cost centers, so the numbers shown are expenses. All of the other subunits shown in Exhibit 12–4 are either profit centers or investment centers. The numbers shown for these subunits are profits, so they are not enclosed in parentheses. In addition to the profit figures shown, the performance reports for the investment centers should include data about invested capital. The South Division, the North Division, and the company as a whole are investment centers. Performance evaluation in investment centers is covered in the next chapter.

Notice the relationships between the performance reports in Exhibit 12–4. The kitchen is the lowest-level subunit shown, and its performance report is the same as that displayed in Exhibit 12–3. The *total expense* line from the kitchen performance report is included as one line in the performance report for the Food and Beverage Department.

Oasis
HOTELS & RESORTS

Exhibit 12–3
Performance Report for
February: Kitchen, Salmiya
Resort

Microsoft Excel - Performance Report for February - Kitchen, Salmiya Resort

File Edit View Insert Format Tools Data Window Help   Type a question for help

F9   fx =B9-D9

	A	B	C	D	E	F	G	H	I
1		Flexible Budget		Actual Results		Variance*			
2		February	Year to Date	February	Year to Date	February		Year to Date	
3									
4	Kitchen staff wages	$ 80,000	$ 168,000	$ 78,000	$ 169,000	$ 2,000	F	$ 1,000	U
5	Food	675,000	1,420,000	678,000	1,421,000	3,000	U	1,000	U
6	Paper products	120,000	250,000	115,000	248,000	5,000	F	2,000	F
7	Variable overhead	70,000	150,000	71,000	154,000	1,000	U	4,000	U
8	Fixed overhead	85,000	180,000	83,000	181,000	2,000	F	1,000	U
9	Total expense	$ 1,030,000	$ 2,168,000	$ 1,025,000	$ 2,173,000	$ 5,000	F	$ 5,000	U
10									
11	*F denotes favorable variance, U denotes unfavorable variance.								

Sheet1 / Sheet2 / Sheet3 /

Ready

	Flexible Budget*		Actual Results*		Variance†	
	February	Year to Date	February	Year to Date	February	Year to Date
Company	$ 30,660	$ 64,567	$ 30,716	$64,570	$56 F	$ 3 F
South Division	$ 18,400	$ 38,620	$ 18,470	$38,630	$70 F	$10 F
North Division	12,260	25,947	12,246	25,940	14 U	7 U
Total profit	$ 30,660	$ 64,567	$ 30,716	$64,570	$56 F	$ 3 F
North Division						
Al Khobar Hotel	$ 6,050	$ 12,700	$ 6,060	$12,740	$10 F	$40 F
Dasman Tower	2,100	4,500	2,050	4,430	50 U	70 U
Salmiya Resort	4,110	8,747	4,136	8,770	26 F	23 F
Total profit	$ 12,260	$ 25,947	$ 12,246	$25,940	$14 U	$ 7 U
Salmiya Resort						
Grounds and Maintenance	$ (45)	$ (90)	$ (44)	$ (90)	$ 1 F	—
Housekeeping and Custodial	(40)	(90)	(41)	(90)	1 U	—
Recreational Services	40	85	41	88	1 F	$ 3 F
Hospitality	2,800	6,000	2,840	6,030	40 F	30 F
Food and Beverage	1,355	2,842	1,340	2,832	15 U	10 U
Total profit	$ 4,110	$ 8,747	$ 4,136	$ 8,770	$26 F	$23 F
Food and Beverage Department						
Banquets and Catering	$ 600	$ 1,260	$ 605	$ 1,265	$ 5 F	$ 5 F
Restaurants	1,785	3,750	1,760	3,740	25 U	10 U
Kitchen	(1,030)	(2,168)	(1,025)	(2,173)	5 F	5 U
Total profit	$ 1,355	$ 2,842	$ 1,340	$ 2,832	$15 U	$10 U
Kitchen						
Kitchen staff wages	$ (80)	$ (168)	$ (78)	$ (169)	$ 2 F	$ 1 U
Food	(675)	(1,420)	(678)	(1,421)	3 U	1 U
Paper products	(120)	(250)	(115)	(248)	5 F	2 F
Variable overhead	(70)	(150)	(71)	(154)	1 U	4 U
Fixed overhead	(85)	(180)	(83)	(181)	2 F	1 U
Total expense	$ (1,030)	$ (2,168)	$ (1,025)	$ (2,173)	$ 5 F	$ 5 U

*Numbers without parentheses denote profit; numbers with parentheses denote expenses; numbers in thousands.

†F denotes favorable variance; U denotes unfavorable variance.

Exhibit 12–4

Performance Reports for February: Selected Subunits of Oasis Hotels and Resorts (numbers in thousands)

Also included are the total profit figures for the department's other two subunits: Banquets and Catering, and Restaurants. How is the *total profit* line for the Food and Beverage Department used in the performance report for the Salmiya Resort? Follow the relationships emphasized with arrows in Exhibit 12–4.

The hierarchy of performance reports starts at the bottom and builds toward the top, just as the organization structure depicted in Exhibit 12–1 builds from the bottom upward. Each manager in the organization receives the performance report for his or her own subunit in addition to the performance reports for the major subunits in the next lower level. For example, the general manager of the Salmiya Resort receives the reports for the hotel, and each of its departments: Grounds and Maintenance, Housekeeping and Custodial, Recreational Services, Hospitality, and Food and Beverage. With these reports, the hotel's general manager can evaluate his subordinates as well as his own performance. This will help the general manager in improving the hotel's performance, motivating employees, and planning future operations.

Budgets, Variance Analysis, and Responsibility Accounting

Notice that the performance reports in Exhibit 12–4 make heavy use of budgets and variance analysis. Thus, the topics of budgeting, variance analysis, and responsibility accounting are closely interrelated. The flexible budget provides the benchmark against which actual revenues, expenses, and profits are compared. As you saw in Chapter 11, it is important to use a flexible budget so that appropriate comparisons can be made. It would make no sense, for example, to compare the actual costs incurred in the kitchen at Salmiya Resort with budgeted costs established for a different level of hotel occupancy.

The performance reports in Exhibit 12–4 also show variances between budgeted and actual performance. These variances often are broken down into smaller components to help management pinpoint responsibility and diagnose performance. Variance analysis, which was discussed in detail in Chapters 10 and 11, is an important tool in a responsibility-accounting system.

Learning Objective 4

Use a cost allocation base to allocate costs.

Cost Allocation

Many costs incurred by an organization are the joint result of several subunits' activities. For example, the property taxes and utility costs incurred by Oasis Hotels and Resorts for the Salmiya Resort are the joint result of all of the hotel's activities. One function of a responsibility-accounting system is to assign all of an organization's costs to the subunits that cause them to be incurred.

A collection of costs to be assigned is called a **cost pool.** At the Salmiya Resort, for example, all utility costs are combined into a *utility cost pool,* which includes the costs of electricity, water, sewer, trash collection, television cable, and telephone. The responsibility centers, products, or services to which costs are to be assigned are called **cost objects.** The Salmiya Resort's cost objects are its major departments. (See the organization chart in Exhibit 12–1.) The process of assigning the costs in the *cost pool* to the *cost objects* is called **cost allocation** or **cost distribution.**

Cost Allocation Bases

To distribute (or allocate) costs to responsibility centers, the managerial accountant chooses an *allocation base* for each cost pool. An **allocation base** is a measure of activity, physical characteristic, or economic characteristic that is associated with the responsibility centers, which are the cost objects in the allocation process. The allocation base chosen for a cost pool should reflect some characteristic of the various responsibility centers that is related to the incurrence of costs. An allocation base also may be referred to as a *cost driver.*

Exhibit 12–5 shows the Salmiya Resort's February cost distribution for selected cost pools. Each cost pool is distributed to each responsibility center in proportion to that center's relative amount of the allocation base. For example, the Food and Beverage Department receives 30 percent of the total administrative costs, $25,000, because that department's 36 employees constitute 30 percent of the hotel's employees. Notice that no marketing costs are allocated to either the Grounds and Maintenance Department or the Housekeeping and Custodial Department. Neither of these responsibility centers generates any sales revenue.

Allocation Bases Based on Budgets

At the Salmiya Resort, administrative and marketing costs are distributed on the basis of *budgeted* amounts of the relevant allocation bases, rather than *actual* amounts.

Cost Pool	Responsibility Center	Allocation Base	Percentage of Total	Costs Distributed
Administration	Grounds and Maintenance	12 employees	10.0%	$ 2,500
	Housekeeping and Custodial	24 employees	20.0	5,000
	Recreational Services	12 employees	10.0	2,500
	Hospitality	36 employees	30.0	7,500
	Food and Beverage	36 employees	30.0	7,500
	Total	120 employees	100.0%	$25,000
Facilities	Grounds and Maintenance	2,000 sq. ft.	1.0%	$ 300
	Housekeeping and Custodial	2,000 sq. ft.	1.0	300
	Recreational Services	5,000 sq. ft.	2.5	750
	Hospitality	175,000 sq. ft.	87.5	26,250
	Food and Beverage	16,000 sq. ft.	8.0	2,400
	Total	200,000 sq. ft.	100.0%	$30,000
Marketing	Grounds and Maintenance	—	—	—
	Housekeeping and Custodial	—	—	—
	Recreational Services	$ 20,000 of sales	4.0%	$ 2,000
	Hospitality	400,000 of sales	80.0	40,000
	Food and Beverage	80,000 of sales	16.0	8,000
	Total	$500,000 of sales	100.0%	$50,000

Exhibit 12–5
Cost Distribution to
Responsibility Centers:
Salmiya Resort

The managerial accountant should design an allocation procedure so that the behavior of one responsibility center does not affect the costs allocated to other responsibility centers.

Suppose, for example, that the budgeted and actual February sales revenues for the hotel were as shown in Exhibit 12–6. Notice that the Hospitality Department's actual sales revenue is close to the budget. However, the actual sales of the Recreational Services Department and the Food and Beverage Department are substantially below the budget. If the distribution of marketing costs is based on actual sales, instead of budgeted sales, then the cost distributed to the Hospitality Department jumps from $40,000 to $45,000, an increase of 12.5 percent. Why does this happen? As a result of a sales performance substantially below the budget for the *other two departments,* the Hospitality Department is penalized with a hefty increase in its cost distribution. This is misleading and unfair to the Hospitality Department manager. A preferable cost distribution procedure is to use budgeted sales revenue as the allocation base, rather than actual sales revenue. Then the marketing costs distributed to each department do not depend on the performance in the other two departments.

			Marketing Cost Distribution	
Responsibility Center	**Budgeted Sales Revenue**	**Actual Sales Revenue**	**Based on Budget**	**Based on Actual**
Recreational Services	$ 20,000 (4%)*	$ 4,500 (1%)*	$ 2,000	$ 500
Hospitality	400,000 (80%)	405,000 (90%)	40,000	45,000
Food and Beverage	80,000 (16%)	40,500 (9%)	8,000	4,500
Total	$ 500,000	$450,000	$50,000	$50,000

*Percentage of column total.

Exhibit 12–6
Cost Distribution: Budgeted
versus Actual Allocation
Bases

Activity-Based Responsibility Accounting

Traditional responsibility-accounting systems tend to focus on the financial performance measures of cost, revenue, and profit for the *subunits* of an organization. Contemporary cost management systems, however, are beginning to focus more and more on *activities*. Costs are incurred in organizations and their subunits because of activities. *Activity-based costing (ABC)* systems associate costs with the activities that drive those costs. The database created by an ABC system, coupled with nonfinancial measures of operational performance for each activity, enables management to employ **activity-based responsibility accounting.** Under this approach, management's attention is directed not only to the cost incurred in an activity but also to the activity itself. Is the activity necessary? Does it add value to the organization's product or service? Can the activity be improved? By seeking answers to these questions, managers can eliminate non-value-added activities and increase the cost-effectiveness of the activities that do add value.[2]

Behavioral Effects of Responsibility Accounting

Responsibility-accounting systems can influence behavior significantly. Whether the behavioral effects are positive or negative, however, depends on how responsibility accounting is implemented.

Information versus Blame

The proper focus of a responsibility-accounting system is *information*. The system should identify the individual in the organization who is in the best position to explain each particular event or financial result. The emphasis should be on providing that individual and higher-level managers with information to help them understand the reasons behind the organization's performance. When properly used, a responsibility-accounting system *does not emphasize blame.* If managers feel they are beaten over the head with criticism and rebukes when unfavorable variances occur, they are unlikely to respond in a positive way. Instead, they will tend to undermine the system and view it with skepticism. But when the responsibility-accounting system emphasizes its informational role, managers tend to react constructively, and strive for improved performance.

Controllability

" . . . Profitability improved sufficiently to absorb uncontrollable cost . . . [This] was accomplished through continuous improvement activities . . . that enhance efficiency and productivity" (12d)

Univar N.V.

Some organizations use performance reports that distinguish between controllable and uncontrollable costs or revenues. For example, the head chef at the Salmiya Resort can influence the hours and efficiency of the kitchen staff, but he probably cannot change the wage rates. A performance report that distinguishes between the financial results influenced by the head chef and those he does not influence has the advantage of providing complete information to the head chef. Yet the report recognizes that certain results are beyond his control.

Identifying costs as controllable or uncontrollable is not always easy. Many cost items are influenced by more than one person. The time frame also may be important in determining controllability. Some costs are controllable over a long time frame, but not within a short time period. To illustrate, suppose the Salmiya Resort's head chef has signed a one-year contract with a local seafood supplier. The cost of seafood can be influenced by the head chef if the time period is a year or more, but the cost cannot be controlled on a weekly basis.

---

[2]Activity-based costing is covered in Chapter 5. Activity analysis and the elimination of non-value-added activities are also covered in Chapters 5.

Motivating Desired Behavior

Managerial accountants often use the responsibility-accounting system to motivate actions considered desirable by upper-level management. Sometimes the responsibility-accounting system can solve behavioral problems as well. As a case in point, consider the problem of rush orders. To accept or reject a rush order is a cost-benefit decision:

Costs of Accepting Rush Order	Benefits of Accepting Rush Order
Disrupted production	Satisfied customers
More setups	Greater future sales
Higher costs	

The following real-world example involving rush orders provides a case in point.

The production scheduler in a manufacturing firm was frequently asked to interrupt production of one product with a rush order for another product. Rush orders typically resulted in greater costs because more product setups were required. Since the production scheduler was evaluated on the basis of costs, he was reluctant to accept rush orders. The sales manager, on the other hand, was evaluated on the basis of sales revenue. By agreeing to customers' demands for rush orders, the sales manager satisfied his customers. This resulted in more future sales and favorable performance ratings for the sales manager.

As the rush orders became more and more frequent, the production manager began to object. The sales manager responded by asking if the production scheduler wanted to take the responsibility for losing a customer by refusing a rush order. The production scheduler did not want to be blamed for lost sales, so he grudgingly accepted the rush orders. However, considerable ill will developed between the sales manager and production scheduler.

The company's managerial accountant came to the rescue by redesigning the responsibility-accounting system. The system was modified to accumulate the extra costs associated with rush orders and charge them to the sales manager's responsibility center, rather than the production scheduler's center. The ultimate result was that the sales manager chose more carefully which rush-order requests to make, and the production manager accepted them gracefully.

The problem described in the preceding illustration developed because two different managers were considering the costs and benefits of the rush-order decision. The production manager was looking only at the costs, while the sales manager was looking only at the benefits. The modified responsibility-accounting system made the sales manager look at *both the costs and the benefits* associated with each rush order. Then the sales manager could make the necessary trade-off between costs and benefits in considering each rush order. Some rush orders were rejected, because the sales manager decided the costs exceeded the benefits. Other rush orders were accepted, when the importance of the customer and potential future sales justified it.

This example illustrates how a well-designed responsibility-accounting system can make an organization run more smoothly and achieve higher performance.

Segmented Reporting

Subunits of an organization are often called *segments. Segmented reporting* refers to the preparation of accounting reports by segment and for the organization as a whole. Many organizations prepare **segmented income statements,** which show the income for major segments and for the entire enterprise.

In preparing segmented income statements, the managerial accountant must decide how to treat costs that are incurred to benefit more than one segment. Such costs are called **common costs.** The salary of the president of Oasis Hotels and Resorts is a common cost. The president manages the entire company. Some of his time is spent on matters related

> Learning Objective 5
>
> Prepare a segmented income statement.

specifically to the South Division or the North Division, but much of it is spent on tasks that are not traced easily to either division. The president works with the company's board of directors, develops strategic plans for the company, and helps set policy and goals for the entire enterprise. Thus, the president's compensation is a common cost, which is not related easily to any segment's activities.

Many managerial accountants believe that it is misleading to allocate common costs to an organization's segments. Since these costs are not traceable to the activities of segments, they can be allocated to segments only on the basis of some highly arbitrary allocation base. Consider the salary of Oasis Hotels and Resorts' president. What allocation base would you choose to reflect the contribution of the president's managerial efforts to the company's two divisions? The possible allocation bases include budgeted divisional sales revenue, the number of hotels or employees in each division, or some measure of divisional size, such as total assets. However, all of these allocation bases would yield arbitrary cost allocations and possibly misleading segment profit information. For this reason, many organizations choose not to allocate common costs on segmented income statements.

Exhibit 12–7 shows February's segmented income statement (on a budgeted basis) for Oasis Hotels and Resorts. Each segment's income statement is presented in the *contribution format* discussed in Chapter 8. Notice that Exhibit 12–7 shows income statements for the following segments.

$$\text{Oasis Hotels and Resorts} \begin{cases} \text{South Division} \\ \text{North Division} \end{cases} \begin{cases} \text{Al Khobar Hotel} \\ \text{Dasman Tower} \\ \text{Salmiya Resort} \end{cases}$$

Three numbers in Exhibit 12–7 require special emphasis. First, the $10,000,000 of common fixed expenses in the left-hand column is not allocated to the company's two divisions. Included in this figure are such costs as the company president's salary. These costs cannot be allocated to the divisions, except in some arbitrary manner.

Second, $1,000,000 of controllable fixed expense in the right-hand column constitutes part of the North Division's $9,000,000 of controllable fixed expense. All $9,000,000 of expense is controllable by the vice president of the North Division. However, $1,000,000 of these expenses cannot be traced to the division's three hotels, except on an arbitrary basis. For example, this $1,000,000 of expense includes the salary of the North Division's vice president. Therefore, the $1,000,000 of expense is *not allocated* among the division's three hotels. This procedure illustrates an important point. Costs that are traceable to segments at one level in an organization may become common costs at a lower level in the organization. The vice president's salary is traceable to the North Division, but it cannot be allocated among the division's three hotels except arbitrarily. Thus, the vice president's salary is a traceable cost at the divisional level, but it becomes a common cost at the hotel level.

Third, the $200,000,000 of fixed expenses controllable by others in the right-hand column constitutes part of the North Division's $250,000,000 of fixed expenses controllable by others. However, the $200,000,000 portion cannot be allocated among the division's three hotels, except arbitrarily.

Segments versus Segment Managers

One advantage of segmented reports like the one in Exhibit 12–7 is that they make a distinction between segments and segment managers. Some costs that are traceable to a segment may be completely beyond the influence of the segment manager. Property taxes on the Salmiya Resort, for example, are traceable to the hotel, but the hotel's general manager cannot influence them. To properly evaluate the Salmiya Resort *as an investment* of the company's resources, the property taxes should be included in the hotel's costs. However, in evaluating the general manager's performance, the property-tax cost should be *excluded,* since the manager has no control over it.

	Oasis Hotels and Resorts	Segment of Company		Segment of North Division			
		South Division	North Division	Al Khobar Hotel	Dasman Tower	Salmiya Resort	Not Allocated
Sales revenue	$2,500,000	$1,600,000	$900,000	$450,000	$150,000	$300,000	—
Variable operating expenses:							
Personnel	$ 820,900	$ 510,400	$310,500	$155,500	$ 50,000	$105,000	—
Food, beverages, and supplies	738,000	458,600	279,400	139,700	46,400	93,300	—
Other	83,000	58,000	25,000	12,500	4,000	8,500	—
Total	$1,641,900	$1,027,000	$614,900	$307,700	$100,400	$206,800	—
Segment contribution margin	$ 858,100	$ 573,000	$285,100	$142,300	$ 49,600	$ 93,200	
Less: Fixed expenses controllable by segment manager	30,000	21,000	9,000	4,000	1,000	3,000	$ 1,000
Profit margin controllable by segment manager	$ 828,100	$ 552,000	$276,100	$138,300	$ 48,600	$ 90,200	$ (1,000)
Less: Fixed expenses, traceable to segment, but controllable by others	750,000	500,000	250,000	26,000	8,000	16,000	200,000
Segment profit margin	$ 78,100	$ 52,000	$ 26,100	$112,300	$ 40,600	$ 74,200	$(201,000)
Less: Common fixed expenses	10,000						
Income before taxes	$ 68,100						
Less: Income tax expense	37,440						
Net income	$ 30,660						

Key Features of Segmented Reporting

Exhibit 12–7
Segmented Income Statements: Oasis Hotels and Resorts (in thousands)

To summarize, Exhibit 12–7 illustrates three important characteristics of segmented reporting:

1. *Contribution format.* These income statements use the contribution format. The statements subtract variable expenses from sales revenue to obtain the *contribution margin.*

2. *Controllable versus uncontrollable expenses.* The income statements in Exhibit 12–7 highlight the costs that can be controlled, or heavily influenced, by each segment manager. This approach is consistent with *responsibility accounting.*

3. *Segmented income statement. Segmented reporting* shows income statements for the company as a whole and for its major segments.

Customer-Profitability Analysis and Activity-Based Costing

Analyzing profitability by segments of the company can help managers gain insight into the factors that are driving the company's performance. In addition to focusing on the major organizational subunits in the company, profitability analysis can focus on major market segments, geographical regions, distribution channels, or customers.

Customer-profitability analysis uses the concept of activity-based costing to determine how serving particular customers causes activities to be performed and costs to be incurred. Suppose, for example, that customer A frequently changes its orders after they are placed, but customer B typically does not. Then the costs incurred in updating sales orders for changes should be recorded in a manner that reflects the fact that customer A is more responsible for those activities and costs than is customer B.

Many factors can result in some customers being more profitable than others. Customers that order in small quantities, order frequently, often change their orders, require special packaging or handling, demand faster delivery, or need special parts or engineering design generally are less profitable than customers who demand less in terms of customized services. If managers have a good understanding of which customers are generating the greatest profit, they can make more-informed decisions about customer service. Moreover, customers can be educated as to the costs they are causing by demanding special services. In many cases, customers' behavior can be changed in a way that reduces costs to the supplier. Then these cost savings can be shared by the supplier and the customer. (Customer-profitability analysis is covered more extensively in Chapter 6.)

Total Quality Management

Traditional responsibility-accounting systems focus primarily on the financial performance of an organization's subunits. However, it is crucial for organizations to monitor performance in many nonfinancial areas as well. For many companies, quality is at the forefront of the areas in which nonfinancial performance is critically important. The quality of the product or service that an organization provides can spell the difference between future profitability and disaster. Quality is equally important in the service and manufacturing industries. For Oasis Hotels and Resorts, the quality of service includes the comfort of the guest rooms, the amenities provided to guests, the friendliness of the staff, the quality of food served in the restaurant, and so forth. Hotel guests are ever more discriminating as they assess the overall quality of service and then select their accommodations accordingly. Similar comments apply to the airlines, long-distance telecommunications companies, banks, car rental firms, and financial investment firms.

In the manufacturing industry, product quality has become a key factor in determining a firm's success or failure in the global marketplace. Advanced, highly reliable manufacturing methods have made it possible to achieve very high standards of product quality. As a result, relatively few firms now include product quality as a keystone of their competitive strategy because it is a condition of entry in the market. Producing high-quality products has become, instead, part of their fundamental mission

Measuring and Reporting Quality Costs

Learning Objective 6

Prepare a quality-cost report.

Recognizing the importance of maintaining high product quality, companies often measure and report the costs of doing so. Before we examine the costs that companies incur to maintain high product quality, let's consider what product quality means.

Product Quality What is meant by a high-quality product? There are two concepts of quality that determine a product's degree of excellence or the product's ultimate fitness for its intended use. A product's **grade** refers to the extent of its capability in performing its intended purpose, in relation to other products with the same functional use. For example, a laser printer that prints in color is of a higher grade than a laser printer that only prints in black and white. A product's **quality of design** refers to how well it is conceived or designed for its intended use. For example, a coffee mug designed with a handle that is too small for the user's fingers is a poorly designed mug. The **quality of conformance** refers to the extent to which a product meets the specifications of its design. A coffee mug with an appropriately sized handle could be well designed, but if the handle breaks off due to shoddy manufacturing, it will be useless. This mug fails to conform to its design specifications. Both quality of design and quality of conformance are required in order to achieve a high-quality finished product.

Costs of Quality Due to the increasing importance of maintaining high product quality, many companies routinely measure and report the costs of ensuring high quality. Four types of costs are monitored.

First are **prevention costs,** the costs of preventing defects. Second are **appraisal costs,** the costs of determining whether defects exist. The third type of costs are **internal failure costs,** those costs of repairing defects found prior to product delivery. The last type of costs are **external failure costs,** those costs incurred after defective products have been delivered.

Exhibit 12–8 shows a quality-cost report prepared by Labban Enterprises, a manufacturer of cellular telephones.[3] As is always true in cost monitoring, quality-cost reporting is most useful when cost trends are examined over a period of time. Through trend analysis, management can see where improvement is occurring and where difficulties exist. Goals can be set to achieve a particular cost target in an area of concern. For example, Labban Enterprises' management might strive to reduce warranty costs to zero by a certain date.

Observable versus Hidden Quality Costs

The quality costs discussed in the preceding section are *observable*. They can be measured and reported, often on the basis of information in the accounting records. In addition to these observable quality costs, however, companies incur *hidden* quality costs. When products of inferior quality make it to market, customers are dissatisfied. Their dissatisfaction can result in decreased

Exhibit 12–8
Quality-Cost Report: Labban Enterprises

Labban ◎
Enterprises

	Current Month's Cost	Percent of Total
Prevention costs		
Quality training	$ 2,000	1.3
Reliability engineering	10,000	6.5
Pilot studies	5,000	3.3
Systems development	8,000	5.2
Total prevention costs	$ 25,000	16.3
Appraisal costs		
Materials inspection	$ 6,000	3.9
Supplies inspection	3,000	2.0
Reliability testing	5,000	3.3
Metallurgical laboratory	25,000	16.3
Total appraisal costs	$ 39,000	25.5
Internal failure costs		
Scrap	$ 15,000	9.8
Repair	18,000	11.8
Rework	12,000	7.8
Downtime	6,000	3.9
Total internal failure costs	$ 51,000	33.3
External failure costs		
Warranty costs	$ 14,000	9.2
Out-of-warranty repairs and replacement	6,000	3.9
Customer complaints	3,000	2.0
Product liability	10,000	6.5
Transportation losses	5,000	3.3
Total external failure costs	$ 38,000	24.9
Total quality costs	$ 153,000	100.00

Labban ◎
Enterprises

---

[3]For further information on cost of quality, see Zafar U. Khan, "Cost of Quality," in Barry J. Brinker, ed., *Guide to Cost Management* (New York: John Wiley & Sons, 2000), pp. 319–44. For examples of quality cost reporting, see Lawrence Carr, "Cost of Quality: Making It Work," *Journal of Cost Management* 9, no. 1 (Spring 1995), pp. 61–65; and S. Brinkman and M. Applebaum, "The Quality Cost Report: It's Alive and Well," *Management Accounting* 76, no. 3 (September 1994), pp. 61–65.

sales and a tarnished reputation for the company. Not only does the company experience lost sales for the inferior products but it will also likely experience lost sales in its other product lines. The opportunity cost of these lost sales and decreased market share can represent a significant hidden cost. Such hidden costs are difficult to estimate or report.

Changing Views of Optimal Product Quality

Learning Objective 7

Discuss the traditional and contemporary views of the optimal level of product quality.

One way to express product quality is in the percentage of products that fail to conform to their specifications, that is, the percentage of defects. Given this perspective, what is the optimal level of product quality?[4]

Traditional Perspective The traditional viewpoint holds that finding the optimal level of product quality is a balancing act between incurring costs of prevention and appraisal on one hand and incurring costs of failure on the other. Panel A of Exhibit 12–9 depicts this trade-off. As the percentage of defective products decreases, the costs of prevention and appraisal increase. However, the costs of internal and external failure decrease. Adding the costs of prevention, appraisal, and internal and external failure yields total quality costs. The optimal product quality level is the point that minimizes total quality costs.

Contemporary Perspective Due largely to the influence of Japanese product quality expert Genichi Taguchi, the contemporary viewpoint of optimal product quality differs from the traditional perspective. The contemporary view is that if both observable and hidden costs of quality are considered, *any* deviation from a product's target specifications results in the incurrence of increasing quality costs. Under the contemporary viewpoint, as depicted in Panel B of Exhibit 12–9, the optimal level of product quality occurs at the *zero defect level*. As Panel B shows, the observable and hidden costs of internal and external failure increase as the percentage of defective products increases. The observable and hidden costs of prevention and appraisal increase slightly and then decrease as the percentage of defects increases. The most important point, though, is that the total costs of quality are minimized at the zero defect level.

Whether the traditional or contemporary view of optimal product quality is most accurate is still being debated by quality control experts. Moreover, the exact shape of the cost functions in Exhibit 12–9 is largely an empirical question, and the cost functions probably differ among industries and product types. One thing is certain, though. To compete successfully in today's global market, any company must pay very close attention to achieving a very high level of product quality.

Exhibit 12–9
Quality Costs and the Optimal
Level of Product Quality

---

[4]This discussion is based on the following sources: Wayne J. Morse, Harold P. Roth, and Kay M. Poston, *Measuring, Planning and Controlling Quality Costs* (Montvale, NJ: National Association of Accountants, 1987); Jack Campanella, ed., *Principles of Quality Costs* (Milwaukee, WI: ASQC Quality Press, 1990); and Alahassane Diallo, Zafar V. Kahn, and Curtis F. Vail, "Cost of Quality in the New Manufacturing Environment," *Management Accounting* 77, no. 2 (August 1993), pp. 20–25.

Total Quality Management Monitoring product quality coupled with measuring and reporting quality costs helps companies maintain programs of **total quality management,** or **TQM.** This refers to the broad set of management and control processes designed to focus the entire organization and all of its employees on providing products or services that do the best possible job of satisfying the customer. Among the tools used in total quality management is the **Six Sigma** program, an analytical method that aims at achieving near-perfect results in a production process. (See the Management Accounting Practice illustration on the next page for details.)

Identifying Quality Control Problems An effective TQM program includes methods for identifying quality control problems. One method of identifying quality problems is the cause-and-effect diagram (also called an Ishikawa diagram or a fishbone diagram). Exhibit 12–10 displays a cause-and-effect diagram used by Xerox Corporation to identify the causes of errors in its customer billing process. As the diagram shows, the quality improvement team has identified a wide range of possible causes for billing errors. After identifying possible causes for billing errors, the Xerox team, nicknamed the Billing Bloopers Team, could take systematic steps to eliminate the root causes of the errors.

Another helpful tool in quality improvement programs is the Pareto diagram. Depicted in Exhibit 12–11, the Pareto diagram shows graphically the frequency with which various quality control problems are observed for a particular model of cordless

> "Today's competitive environment leaves no room for error . . . This is why Six Sigma Quality has become a part of our culture." (12f)
> **General Electric Company**

Exhibit 12–10
Cause-and-Effect Diagram: Billing Quality at Xerox Corporation

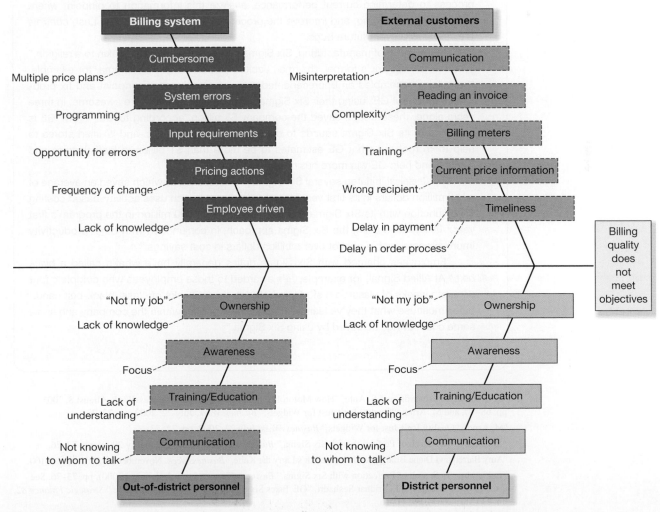

Source: David M. Buehlman and Donald Stover, "How Xerox Solves Quality Problems," *Management Accounting* 75, no. 3 (September 1993), pp. 33–36.

telephone. The Pareto diagram helps the TQM team visualize and communicate to others what the most serious types of defects are. Steps can be taken then to attack the most serious and most frequent problems first.

Management
Accounting
Practice

Motorola, General
Electric, Dell Inc.,
Walmart, Dow Chemical,
Allied Signal, and
Honeywell

SIX SIGMA FOR QUALITY MANAGEMENT AND COST REDUCTION

"Originally conceived by Motorola Inc. as a quality-improvement device" two decades ago, "Six Sigma soon morphed into a cost-cutting utensil for manufacturers of all stripes. Now, it's fast becoming the Swiss army knife of the business world. Goods producers still make up the bulk of users, who typically rely on statistics to uncover and then reduce product variance in order to boost quality and efficiency. But increasingly, manufacturers are applying Six Sigma to functions as varied as accounts receivable, sales, and research and development. And their success in these nonfactory domains has inspired Six Sigma projects at financial institutions, retailers, health-care concerns, and in other areas of the service sector."

Six Sigma is "an analytical method aimed at achieving *near-perfect results* in a production process. In statistics, the Greek letter *sigma* denotes variation in a standard bell curve. One sigma equals 690,000 defects per 1 million. Most companies do no better than three sigma, or 66,000 errors per million. Six Sigma reduces that count to *3.4 defects per million.* That saves money by preventing waste."

Six Sigma "achieves results by reducing subjective errors in the assessment of problems. First, auditors *define* a process where results are subpar. Then they *measure* the process to determine current performance, *analyze* this information to pinpoint where things are going wrong, and *improve* the process and eliminate the error. Last, *controls* are set up to prevent future bugs."

"In the world of manufacturing, Six Sigma has become something akin to a religion." When General Electric's former chairman Jack Welch embraced Six Sigma, for example, "he quickly assembled an unprecedented army of employees to pinpoint and fix problems throughout GE" using their Six Sigma training. "The results were awesome: In three years alone, these troops saved the company $8 billion, according to GE." Now "GE is sending out its Six Sigma squads to customers such as Dell Inc. and Walmart stores to help them root out what GE estimates to be more than $1 billion in inefficiencies and waste—and help GE win more business."[5]

Dow Chemical initiated several Six Sigma projects, each of which saved an average of a half million dollars in its first year alone.[6] Allied Signal, which uses activity-based costing in conjunction with its Six Sigma program, saved over $500 million in the program's first year.[7] Honeywell is using the Six Sigma approach, in conjunction with other productivity improvements, with a goal of over a billion dollars in cost savings.[8]

"Employees charged with Six Sigma duties generally have what's called a *black belt.*" At Allied Signal, for example, "it's awarded to those employees who complete four separate weeks of classroom study. In between those weeks of class, black-belt candidates must use what they've learned to focus on a project within the company and show some cost savings achieved by using Six Sigma."[9]

---

[5]R. Crockett, C. Edwards, and S. Ante, "How Motorola Got Its Groove Back," *BusinessWeek,* August 8, 2005, pp. 68–70; and M. Arndt, "Quality Isn't Just for Widgets," *BusinessWeek,* July 22, 2002, pp. 72, 73.

[6]M. Arndt, "Quality Isn't Just for Widgets," *BusinessWeek,* July 22, 2002, pp. 72, 73.

[7]Tad Leahy, "In Search of Perfection with Six Sigma," *Business Finance* 5, no. 1 (January 2000), pp. 73–76.

[8]Amy Barrett and Diane Brady, "At Honeywell, It's Larry the Knife," *BusinessWeek,* November 26, 2001, pp. 98–100.

[9]Tad Leahy, "In Search of Perfection with Six Sigma," *Business Finance* 5, no. 1 (January 2000), pp. 73–76. See also, Gregory T. Lucier and Sridhar Seshadri, "GE Takes Six Sigma beyond the Bottom Line," *Strategic Finance* 82, no. 11 (May 2001), pp. 41–46.

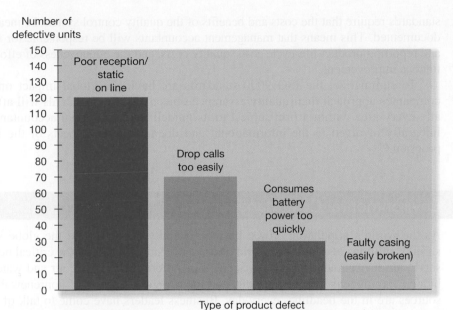

Exhibit 12–11
Pareto Diagram: Frequency of
Defect Types for Cellular Tele-
phone (Labban Enterprises)

Labban ◎
Enterprises

ISO 9000 Standards

A key factor in determining the quality of a company's products is its quality control system. The organizational structure, personnel, procedures, and policies that are in place to monitor product quality will greatly affect a firm's ability to achieve high-quality standards. In 1987, the International Standards Organization (ISO), based in Geneva, Switzerland, issued a set of quality control standards for companies selling products in Europe. The ISO 9000 standards, as they have come to be known, focus on a manufacturer's quality control system. The ISO 9000 standards basically require that a manufacturer have a well-defined quality control system in place, and that the target level of product quality be maintained consistently. Moreover, the ISO 9000 standards require a manufacturer to prepare extensive documentation of all aspects of the quality control system. The first standard, ISO 9000, lists three objectives:

- The company should sustain the quality of its product or service at a level that continually meets the purchaser's stated or implied needs.
- The quality control system should be sufficient to give the supplier's own management confidence that the intended quality is being maintained.
- The supplying company should give the purchaser confidence that the intended quality is consistently achieved in the delivered product or service.

The ISO 9000 standards consist of five major parts. ISO 9000 states the objectives of the standards, defines a quality-related vocabulary, and provides a guide to the other standards in the series. ISO 9001 provides a model for quality assurance in design, development, production, installation, and servicing. ISO 9002 focuses narrowly on quality assurance in production and installation. ISO 9003 addresses quality assurance in final inspection and testing. Finally, ISO 9004 provides guidelines for the design of a quality assurance system.

Implications for Managerial Accounting
The ISO 9000 standards have several implications for managerial accountants. First, the standards require extensive documentation of the quality control system. This task often falls to the controller's office. In fact, several of the largest public accounting firms are offering assurance services in helping companies meet the ISO documentation requirements for certification. Second, the ISO

standards require that the costs and benefits of the quality control system be measured and documented. This means that management accountants will be responsible for measuring and reporting product life-cycle costs, quality costs, and the effectiveness of efforts at continuous improvement.

To summarize, the ISO 9000 standards are having a global impact on the way companies approach their quality assurance objectives. The standards will affect virtually every area within a firm subject to its guidelines. Managerial accountants will be integrally involved in the informational and documentation aspects of the ISO 9000 program.[10]

Environmental Cost Management

As the world's population grows, business activity expands, and the globe seemingly shrinks, millions of people the world over are ever-more aware of the critical need to preserve our environment for ourselves and our posterity. Issues like air and water quality, hidden carcinogens, global warming, and the overconsumption of nonrenewable energy sources are in the headlines every day. Business leaders have come to talk of the desirability of **sustainable development,** which means business activity that produces the goods and services needed in the present without limiting the ability of future generations to meet their needs. Many companies are striving for greater *ecoefficiency,* which means increasing their production of goods and services while at the same time decreasing the deleterious effects on the environment of that production.

Besides being a very important issue to all of us due to the clear health and quality-of-life implications, what does any of this have to do with managerial accounting? The answer is that the *costs* of dealing with environmental issues in one way or another are enormous. These **environmental costs** take many forms, such as installing scrubbers on a smokestack to comply with government regulations, improving a production process to reduce or eliminate certain pollutants, or cleaning up a contaminated river. In the next section, we will systematically explore these costs with the goal of having a better understanding of how to manage them.

Classifying Environmental Costs

There are many types of environmental costs.

Private versus Social Environmental Costs One important distinction is between private costs and social (or public) costs. *Private environmental costs* are those borne by a company or individual. Examples would be costs incurred by a company to comply with a government's environmental regulations or to clean up a polluted lake. *Social environmental costs* are those borne by the public at large. Examples of these include costs borne by the taxpayers to staff the government's environmental overseer; costs borne by the taxpayers to clean up a polluted lake or river; costs borne by individuals as well as private and public health insurance systems due to health problems caused by pollutants; and the unquantifiable quality-of-life costs we all bear from a degraded environment.

The recent tragic oil spill in the Gulf of Mexico stemming from an explosion at the Deepwater Horizon oil rig provides an unfortunate example of both social and private environmental costs. The social environmental costs associated with this disaster, which will be borne for years to come, include such costs as cleaning up fouled beaches and fragile wetlands, severe harm to the region's recreational and fishing industries, and

---

[10]The ISO standards are available on the Internet at http://www.iso.org or from the American National Standards Institute, 105–111 South State Street, Hackensack, NJ 07601.

possible human health hazards from the hydrocarbons contaminating the Gulf's waters, marshes, and beaches. Huge private environmental costs will be borne by the companies involved in the Deepwater Horizon's drilling operations, such as BP and its partners. While these social environmental costs are of great importance to all of us, we will focus our attention here on **environmental cost management,** which is the systematic attempt to measure and control or reduce the private environmental costs borne by a company or other organization.[11]

Visible versus Hidden Environmental Costs

Both social and private environmental costs can be *visible* or *hidden*. *Visible social environmental costs* are those that are known and clearly identified as tied to environmental issues, such as the taxpayers' costs of staffing the government's environmental overseer; or cleaning up a polluted lake. *Hidden social environmental costs* include those that are caused by environmental issues but have not been so identified, such as the costs borne by individuals as well as private and public health insurance systems due to cancers caused by pollutants but not clearly identified as such. For example, is melanoma (a serious type of skin cancer) caused by a genetic predisposition, failure to use sun block, or a thinning of the ozone layer resulting from industrial emissions of chlorofluorocarbons? No one knows for sure.

Managing Private Environmental Costs

Let's focus our attention now on environmental cost management, or the measuring and control or reduction of private environmental costs.

Visible versus Hidden Private Environmental Costs

Once again, we need to distinguish between visible and hidden costs. *Visible private environmental costs* are those that are measurable and have been clearly identified as tied to environmental issues. *Hidden private environmental costs* are those that are caused by environmental issues but have not been so identified by the accounting system.[12] Exhibit 12–12 provides examples of both visible and hidden private environmental costs.[13] Notice that the visible and the hidden costs listed in Exhibit 12–12 are further classified as follows:

- *Monitoring costs.* Costs of monitoring the production process to determine if pollution is being generated (e.g., costs of testing wastewater for contaminants).
- *Abatement costs.* Costs incurred to reduce or eliminate pollution (e.g., changing a product's design to use more expensive materials that do not result in environmental contamination).
- *Remediation costs* (i.e., clean-up costs).
- *On-site remediation.* Costs of reducing or preventing the discharge into the environment of pollutants that have been generated in the production process (e.g., cost of installing scrubbers on a smokestack to remove certain air pollutants in the smoke).
- *Off-site remediation.* Costs of reducing or eliminating pollutants from the environment after they have been discharged (e.g., cost of cleaning up a river polluted by a company's operations).

---

[11]Based on the discussion in German Böer, Margaret Curtin, and Louis Hoyt, "Environmental Cost Management," *Management Accounting* 80, no. 3 (September 1998), pp. 28–38. See also Ramona Dzinkowski, "Saving the Environment," *Strategic Finance* 89, no. 1 (July 2007), pp. 51–53.

[12]Based on Satish Joshi, Ranjani Krishnan, and Lester Lave, "Estimating the Hidden Costs of Environmental Regulation," *The Accounting Review* 76, no. 2 (April 2001), pp. 171–98. See also Kathryn Kranhold, "GE's Environmental Push Hits Business Realities," *The Wall Street Journal,* September 14, 2007, p. A1.

[13]Ibid.

Exhibit 12–12
Private Environmental Costs

	Visible Costs	Hidden Costs*
Monitoring	Inspecting products for contamination	Inspection of products
	Measuring contamination of processes or machinery	Incremental costs of procurement staff to ensure vendor compliance with environmental standards
	Verifying vendor compliance with environmental standards	
Abatement	Qualifying vendors for environmental compliance	Incremental material costs incurred to use less-polluting materials
	Recycling materials, containers, or water	Incremental direct-labor costs incurred to perform duties related to reducing pollution
	Designing products and processes to reduce or eliminate negative environmental impacts	Incremental costs of more expensive processes installed all or in part to reduce pollution
	Doing environmental impact analyses	Incremental costs of purchasing hybrid (electric and gasoline powered) vehicles to reduce air pollution
Remediation		
On-site	Installing pollution reduction or elimination devices	Incremental direct-labor costs incurred to maintain remediation equipment
	Disposing of toxic waste in an environmentally sound manner	Incremental energy or other overhead costs incurred to operate remediation equipment
	Treating toxic waste	
Off-site	Cleaning up polluted sites (e.g., water, soil, or buildings)	Incremental direct-labor costs for workers used to perform environmental clean-up tasks
	Defending or settling environmental lawsuits	
	Paying government fines	Forgone contribution margins on lost sales due to an unfavorable environmental record or reputation

*Each of the costs listed in the *hidden costs* column is included under the assumption that although these costs are caused by environmental concerns, the accounting system has not identified them as such. A study by Joshi et al. provides evidence for the plausibility of this assumption. See Satish Joshi, Ranjani Krishnan, and Lester Lave, "Estimating the Hidden Costs of Environmental Regulation," *The Accounting Review* 76, no. 2 (April 2001), pp. 171–98.

The distinction between the visible and hidden costs listed in Exhibit 12–12 is an important but subtle one. Consider, for example, the incremental cost of using a more expensive material because it causes less (or no) negative environmental impact. Is this a visible or a hidden cost? The answer is *it depends* on whether the accounting system has measured this cost and identified it as an environmental cost. Studies show that many environmental costs are hidden, because the accounting system does not measure and identify them as environmental costs. "Most accounting systems accumulate visible costs into environmental cost pools, separate from other overhead cost pools . . . For example, many steel mills compile separate cost pools for wastewater treatment, remediation, hazardous waste disposal, pollution-abatement capital expenditures, and depreciation on pollution abatement equipment."[14] However, a steel mill's incremental material costs caused by changing from sinters to less-polluting pellets in response to more stringent environmental regulations is typically not separately reported by the accounting system as an environmental cost.[15] Hence, it remains a *hidden* environmental cost.

Why is this point about visible versus hidden costs so important? Because many observers believe that the visible costs reported by most accounting systems may be only a small proportion of the hidden costs. A steel-industry study, for example, concluded that the hidden costs were nearly 10 times the visible costs!

---

[14]Ibid.

[15]Ibid

Environmental Cost Strategies

We have only scratched the surface in our discussion of environmental costs, and it is an area certain to receive much greater attention in the future—both in practice and in academia. Let's conclude our discussion with a brief mention of three strategies for managing environmental costs.[16]

1. *End-of-pipe strategy.* Under this approach, companies produce the waste or pollutant, and then clean it up before it is discharged into the environment. Smokestack scrubbers, wastewater treatment, and carbon air filters are examples of end-of-pipe strategies.
2. *Process improvement strategy.* Under this approach, companies modify products and production processes to produce little or no pollutants, or find ways to recycle wastes internally.
3. *Prevention strategy.* "The ultimate strategy for maximizing the value of pollution-related activities involves . . . not producing any pollutants in the first place. With this strategy, companies avoid all problems with regulatory authorities and, in many cases, generate significant profit improvements."[17]

Tie-In to the Responsibility-Accounting System

As a concluding thought, consider why our discussion of environmental costs—and in the preceding section, quality costs—is located in the chapter covering responsibility accounting. For any type of cost, an important key to managing or controlling the cost is to make it someone's responsibility. "Line managers make the decisions that cause waste and environmental costs, and these managers should see the financial consequences of their decisions. Without a tight link between decision makers and environmental costs, any cost-control efforts will be difficult and prone to failure."[18]

Focus on Ethics

SHORT-SIGHTED VIEW OF COST CUTTING

The hypothetical scenario described here is based on a compilation of anecdotes taken from the literature on responsibility accounting, quality management, and environmental cost accounting. Houda Kabbaj, the controller for Labban Enterprises, has just compiled a cost report for the second quarter. The report is prepared each quarter for corporate headquarters. She has taken particular notice of several major cost categories that show significant reductions in expenditures when compared to the first quarter. She made the following list of the major cost cuts:

Cost Item	Cost Reduction ($)	Cost Reduction (%)
General employee training	$12,000	25%
Routine machine maintenance	13,500	20
Process improvement	12,000	12
Quality training*	18,000	8
Raw-material inspection*	6,500	9
Product redesign for compliance with environmental policies†	7,100	13
Random testing of materials for environmental contaminants†	11,200	10

*Categorized as quality costs.
†Categorized as environmental costs.

(continues)

---

[16]German Boër, Margaret Curtin, and Louis Hoyt, "Environmental Cost Management," *Management Accounting* 80, no. 3 (September 1998), pp. 28–38.

[17]Ibid.

[18]Ibid.

Concerned that there may have been errors in compiling the data, Kabbaj scheduled an appointment with the divisional vice president, Ahmed Edelbi. At the meeting, the conversation went like this.

Kabbaj (C): "Ahmad, I'm concerned about these cost cuts. Are these mistakes, or are we really making such substantial cuts in these areas?"

Edelbi (VP): "Your numbers look right, Houda. I ordered these cutbacks myself. I think there's a lot of fat in this operation that can be cut, and I'm just getting started."

Kabbaj (C): "But these are all important areas to invest in, Ahmad. I see the invoices for these costs every month, and I don't think it's wasted money at all."

Edelbi (VP): "Corporate wants a lean company, Houda. I'm just trying to give them one."

Kabbaj (C): "Have you thought through the implications, Ahmad? Cutting general employee training will eventually take a toll on our productivity gains. Same thing for the cuts in process improvements. And cutting routine machine maintenance could mean breakdowns later on. Maybe not for a year or so, but eventually it'll take its toll."

Edelbi (VP): Becoming annoyed, "Those are my concerns, Ms. Kabbaj, not yours."

Kabbaj (C): "Look, Ahmad, we're all on the same team. I'm just concerned, that's all. I'm especially worried about these cuts in quality and environmental costs. These quality costs are in the areas of prevention and appraisal. If we make these cuts now, we'll likely have higher costs for internal, or even external, failure down the road. And the same goes for these environmental cost cuts.

If we scrimp on monitoring and abatement costs, we're just going to be shelling out more for remediation costs in the future."

Edelbi (VP): "Those are all hypotheticals. You don't know any of that for sure."

Kabbaj (C): "I feel as though I need to highlight these cost cuts in my report to corporate. They should at least be made aware of these issues. I'll need your authorization for that."

Edelbi (VP): "No, Houda. You are instructed to make your usual quarterly report using the standard format."

After the meeting, Kabbaj was commiserating with Faisan Ali, the chief of engineering.

Kabbaj (C): "Faisan, I just had a very unsatisfactory meeting with Ahmad Edelbi. I shouldn't go into the details, but I'm concerned about some things."

Ali (E): "Well, I have good news for you then. The grapevine has it that Ahmad is on the very short list for taking over as president of our French subsidiary. That would be a huge promotion for him. Word is that all he's got to do is turn in a good performance for the year here. If he does that, the job's his."

Kabbaj (C): "That explains a lot, Faisan. Thanks for the information. I've got some thinking to do."

What do you think is going on here? What is the VP, Ahmad Edelbi, trying to do? Is he acting ethically? What steps should the controller, Houda Kabbaj, take? Also, how could a balanced scorecard help mitigate the problems apparent in this scenario?*

---

*The balanced scorecard was introduced in Chapter 1 and covered extensively in Chapter 10.

Chapter Summary

LO1 Explain the role of responsibility accounting in fostering goal congruence. Responsibility-accounting systems are designed to foster goal congruence among the managers in decentralized organizations by specifying the performance measures upon which managers of various organizational subunits will be evaluated.

LO2 Define and give an example of a cost center, a revenue center, a profit center, and an investment center. A cost center is an organizational subunit, the manager of which is held accountable for the subunit's costs. Examples include the assembly department of an auto manufacturer and the maintenance department of a hotel. A revenue center is an organizational subunit, the manager of which is held accountable for the subunit's revenue. Examples include the sales departments of a cruise line or an insurance company. A profit center is an organizational subunit, the manager of which is held accountable for the subunit's profit. Examples include an individual branch bank or an individual fast food restaurant. An investment center is an organizational subunit, the manager of which is held accountable for the relationship between the subunit's profit and its invested capital. A division of a large corporation (manufacturing, service, or retail) is usually designated as an investment center.

LO3 Prepare a performance report and explain the relationships between the performance reports for various responsibility centers. The performance of each of an organization's responsibility accounting centers is summarized periodically on a performance report. This report shows the budgeted and actual performance results for a specified time period for each responsibility accounting center.

LO4 Use a cost allocation base to allocate costs. A cost allocation base is a measure of activity, physical characteristic, or economic characteristic associated with a group of organizational subunits or activities, which is the basis for allocating costs among those subunits or activities.

LO5 Prepare a segmented income statement. Segmented income statements often are included in a responsibility-accounting system to show the performance of the organization and its various segments. To be most effective, such reports should distinguish between the performance of segments and segment managers.

LO6 Prepare a quality cost report. As product quality becomes ever more important, many firms are beginning to carefully monitor the costs of maintaining product quality. Quality costs often are categorized as follows: prevention costs, appraisal costs, internal failure costs, and external failure costs. These quality costs are periodically listed on a quality cost report, which is used by management as it seeks to ensure quality products and services and manage the costs of providing them.

LO7 Discuss the traditional and contemporary views of the optimal level of product quality. In addition to observable quality costs, companies experience hidden quality costs, such as the opportunity cost associated with lost market share. The contemporary perspective on product quality holds that if both observable and hidden costs of product quality are considered, the optimal level of product quality occurs at the zero defect level. In contrast, the traditional viewpoint holds that the optimal level of product quality occurs at the minimum point on the total quality cost curve, which typically is above the zero-defect level.

LO8 Understand the different types of environmental costs and discuss environmental cost management. Companies incur a variety of environmental costs. These costs include private versus social environmental costs, and the private environmental costs include some visible and some hidden costs. These visible and hidden environmental costs include the costs of monitoring, abatement, and both on-site and off-site remediation.

Review Problem on Responsibility Accounting

Crescent Bank has two divisions, Commercial and Consumer. Each divisional vice president is held accountable for both profit and invested capital. Each division consists of two branch banks, East and West. Each branch manager is responsible for that bank's profit. The Commercial Division's East Branch has a Deposit Department, an Investment Department, and an Administrative Services Department. The department supervisors of the Investment and Deposit Departments are accountable for departmental revenues; the Administrative Services Department supervisor is accountable for costs.

All of Crescent Bank's advertising and promotion is done centrally. The advertising and promotion cost pool for the year just ended, which amounted to $40,000, is allocated across the four branch banks on the basis of budgeted branch revenue. Budgeted revenue for the year is shown below.

Commercial Division:	West Branch	$400,000
	East Branch	200,000
Consumer Division:	West Branch	250,000
	East Branch	150,000

Required:
1. Draw an organization chart for Crescent Bank that shows each subunit described above, its manager's title, and its designation as a responsibility center.
2. Distribute (allocate) the bank's advertising cost pool to the four branch banks.

Solution to Review Problem

1.   Organization chart (subunits, managers, responsibility center designation) is shown below.

2.   Cost distribution (or allocation):

Cost Pool	Responsibility Center	Allocation Base: Revenue	Percentage of Total*	Costs Distributed
Advertising	Commercial, West Branch	$ 400,000	40%	$16,000
and	Commercial, East Branch	200,000	20	8,000
promotion	Consumer, West Branch	250,000	25	10,000
costs	Consumer, East Branch	150,000	15	6,000
	Total	$1,000,000	100%	$40,000

*Branch revenue as a percentage of total revenue, $1,000,000.

Key Terms

For each term's definition refer to the indicated page, or turn to the glossary at the end of the text.

Review Questions

12–1. Why is goal congruence important to an organization's success? How does a responsibility-accounting system foster goal congruence?

12–2. Define and give examples of the following terms: *cost center, revenue center, profit center,* and *investment center.*

12–3. Under what circumstances would it be appropriate to change the Salmiya Resort from a profit center to an investment center?

12–4. Explain the relationship between performance reports and flexible budgeting.

12–5. What is the key feature of activity-based responsibility accounting? Briefly explain.

12–6. Explain how to get positive behavioral effects from a responsibility-accounting system.

12–7. "Performance reports based on controllability are impossible. Nobody really *controls* anything in an organization!" Do you agree or disagree? Explain your answer.

12–8. Define and give examples of the following terms: *cost pool, cost object,* and *cost allocation* (or *distribution*).

12–9. Give an example of a common resource in an organization. List some of the opportunity costs associated with using the resource. Why might allocation of the cost of the common resource to its users be useful?

12–10. Explain how and why cost allocation might be used to assign the costs of a mainframe computer system used for research purposes in a university.

12–11. Define the term *cost allocation base.* What would be a sensible allocation base for assigning advertising costs to the various components of a large amusement park?

12–12. Referring to Exhibit 12–5, why are marketing costs distributed to the Salmiya Resort's departments on the basis of *budgeted* sales dollars?

12–13. Explain what is meant by a *segmented income statement.*

12–14. Why do some managerial accountants choose not to allocate common costs in segmented reports?

12–15. Why is it important in responsibility accounting to distinguish between segments and segment managers?

12–16. List and explain three key features of the segmented income statement shown in Exhibit 12–7.

12–17. Can a common cost for one segment be a traceable cost for another segment? Explain your answer.

12–18. What is meant by *customer profitability analysis?* Give an example of an activity that might be performed more commonly for one customer than for another.

12–19. List and define four types of product quality costs.

12–20. Explain the difference between observable and hidden quality costs.

12–21. Distinguish between a product's quality of design and its quality of conformance.

12–22. What is meant by a product's *grade,* as a characteristic of quality? Give an example in the service industry.

12–23. "An ounce of prevention is worth a pound of cure." Interpret this old adage in light of Exhibit 12–8.

12–24. Briefly explain the purpose of a cause-and-effect (or fishbone) diagram.

12–25. Define the following types of environmental costs: private, social, visible, hidden, monitoring, abatement, and both on-site and off-site remediation.

12–26. Explain three strategies of environmental cost management.

Exercises

All applicable Exercises are available with McGraw-Hill's *Connect Accounting*™.

For each of the following organizational subunits, indicate the type of responsibility center that is most appropriate.

1. A movie theater in a company that operates a chain of theaters.
2. A radio station owned by a large broadcasting network.
3. The claims department in an insurance company.
4. The ticket sales division of a major airline.
5. A bottling plant of a soft drink company.
6. An orange juice factory operated by a large orange grower.
7. The College of Engineering at a large university.
8. The Middle Eastern Division of a multinational manufacturing company.
9. The outpatient clinic in a profit-oriented hospital.
10. The Mayor's Office in a large city.

■ **Exercise 12–27**
Designating Responsibility Centers
(LO 2)

How should a responsibility-accounting system handle each of the following scenarios?

1. Department A manufactures a component, which is then used by Department B. Department A recently experienced a machine breakdown that held up production of the component. As a result, Department B was forced to curtail its own production, thereby incurring large costs

■ **Exercise 12–28**
Responsibility Accounting;
Equipment Breakdown
(LO 1, 2)

of idle time. An investigation revealed that Department A's machinery had not been properly maintained.

2. Refer to the scenario above, but suppose the investigation revealed the machinery in Department A had been properly maintained.

■ **Exercise 12–29**
Assigning Responsibility for Skilled Employees' Wages
(LO 1)

KL Electronics Company manufactures complex circuit boards for the aerospace industry. Demand for the company's products has fallen in recent months, and the firm has cut its production significantly. Many unskilled workers have been temporarily laid off. Top management has made a decision, however, not to lay off any highly skilled employees, such as inspectors and machinery operators. Management was concerned that these highly skilled employees would easily find new jobs elsewhere and not return when production returned to normal levels.

To occupy the skilled employees during the production cutback, they have been reassigned temporarily to the Maintenance Department. Here they are performing general maintenance tasks, such as repainting the interior of the factory, repairing the loading dock, and building wooden storage racks for the warehouse. The skilled employees continued to receive their normal wages, which average $22 per hour. However, the normal wages for Maintenance Department employees average $12 per hour.

The supervisor of the Maintenance Department recently received the March performance report, which indicated that his department's labor cost exceeded the budget by $19,360. The department's actual labor cost was approximately 90 percent over the budget. The department supervisor complained to the controller.

Required: As the controller, how would you respond? Would you make any modification in KL Electronics' responsibility-accounting system? If so, list the changes you would make. Explain your reasoning.

■ **Exercise 12–30**
Responsibility-Accounting Centers; Xerox Corporation
(LO 1, 2)

Xerox Corporation has been an innovator in its responsibility-accounting system. In one initiative, management changed the responsibility-center orientation of its Logistics and Distribution Department from a cost center to a profit center. The department manages the inventories and provides other logistical services to the company's Business Systems Group. Formerly, the manager of the Logistics and Distribution Department was held accountable for adherence to an operating expense budget. Now the department "sells" its services to the company's other segments, and the department's manager is evaluated partially on the basis of the department's profit. Xerox Corporation's management feels that the change has been beneficial. The change has resulted in more innovative thinking in the department and has moved decision making down to lower levels in the company.

Required: Comment on the new responsibility-center designation for the Logistics and Distribution Department.

■ **Exercise 12–31**
Performance Report; Hotel
(LO 3)

The following data pertain to the Salmiya Resort for the month of March.

	Flexible Budget March (in thousands)*	Actual Results March (in thousands)*
Banquets and Catering	$ 650	$ 658
Restaurants	1,800	1,794
Kitchen staff wages	(85)	(86)
Food	(690)	(690)
Paper products	(125)	(122)
Variable overhead	(75)	(78)
Fixed overhead	(95)	(99)

*Numbers without parentheses denote profit; numbers with parentheses denote expenses.

Required: Prepare a March performance report similar to the lower portion of Exhibit 12–4. The report should have six numerical columns with headings analogous to those in Exhibit 12–4. Your performance report should cover only the Food and Beverage Department and the Kitchen. Draw arrows to show the relationships between the numbers in the report. Refer to Exhibit 12–4 for guidance. For the year-to-date columns in your report, use the data given in Exhibit 12–4. You will need to update those figures using the March data given above.

■ **Exercise 12–32**
Cost Allocation in a College
(LO 4)

Iberian College has three divisions: Liberal Arts, Sciences, and Business Administration. The college's comptroller is trying to decide how to allocate the costs of the Admissions Department, the Registrar's Department, and the Computer Services Department. The comptroller has compiled the following data for the year just ended.

Department	Annual Cost
Admissions	$ 90,000
Registrar	150,000
Computer Services	320,000

Division	Budgeted Enrollment	Budgeted Credit Hours	Planned Courses Requiring Computer Work
Liberal Arts	1,000	30,000	12
Sciences	900	28,000	24
Business Administration	600	22,000	24

Required:

1. For each department, choose an allocation base and distribute the departmental costs to the college's three divisions. Justify your choice of an allocation base.

2. Would you have preferred a different allocation base than those available using the data compiled by the comptroller? Why?

3. *Build a spreadsheet:* Construct an Excel spreadsheet to solve requirement (1) above. Show how the solution will change if the following information changes: the costs incurred by the departments were $120,000, $160,000, and $360,000, for Admissions, Registrar, and Computer Services, respectively.

■ **Exercise 12–33**
Segmented Income
Statement; TV Cable
Company
(LO 5)

Countywide Cable Services, Inc. is organized with three segments: Metro, Suburban, and Outlying. Data for these segments for the year just ended follow.

	Metro	Suburban	Outlying
Service revenue	$1,000,000	$800,000	$400,000
Variable expenses	200,000	150,000	100,000
Controllable fixed expenses	400,000	320,000	150,000
Fixed expenses controllable by others	230,000	200,000	90,000

In addition to the expenses listed above, the company has $95,000 of common fixed expenses. Income-tax expense for the year is $145,000.

Required:

1. Prepare a segmented income statement for Countywide Cable Services, Inc. Use the contribution format.

2. *Build a spreadsheet:* Construct an Excel spreadsheet to solve the preceding requirement. Show how the solution will change if the following information changes: the sales revenues were $950,000 and $815,000 for Metro and Suburban, respectively.

■ **Exercise 12–34**
Quality Costs
(LO 6)

The following costs were incurred by Osaka Metals Company to maintain the quality of its products.

1. Operating an X-ray machine to detect faulty welds, $110,000
2. Repairs of products sold last year, $116,000
3. Cost of rewelding faulty joints, $17,000
4. Cost of sending machine operators to a three-week training program so they could learn to use new production equipment with a lower defect rate, $18,100

Required: Classify each of these costs as a prevention, appraisal, internal failure, or external failure cost.

■ **Exercise 12–35**
Quality-Cost Report
(LO 6)

San Mateo Circuitry manufactures electrical instruments for a variety of purposes. The following costs related to maintaining product quality were incurred in May.

Training of quality-control inspectors	$21,000
Tests of instruments before sale	30,000
Inspection of electrical components purchased from outside suppliers	12,000
Costs of rework on faulty instruments	9,000
Replacement of instruments already sold, which were still covered by warranty	16,500
Costs of defective parts that cannot be salvaged	6,100

Required: Prepare a quality-cost report similar to the report shown in Exhibit 12–8.

■ **Exercise 12–36**
Costs of Quality; Airline
(LO 6)

List three observable and three hidden quality costs that could occur in the airline industry related to the quality of service provided.

■ **Exercise 12–37**
Responsibility Accounting;
Use of Internet
(LO 1, 2)

Visit the Web site for one of the following companies, or a different company of your choosing.

Le Méridien Hotels	www.starwoodhotels.com/lemeridien
McDonald's Corporation	www.mcdonald.com
HSBC Bank	www.hsbc.com
Brioche Dorée	www.groupeleduff.com/en
Couples Resorts	www.couples.com
Xerox Corporation	www.xerox.com

Required: Read about the company's activities and operations. Then do as good a job as you can in preparing an organization chart for the firm. For each subunit in the organization chart, indicate what type of responsibility accounting center designation you believe would be most appropriate. (Refer to Exhibits 12–1 and 12–2 for guidance.)

■ **Exercise 12–38**
Environmental Cost Management; Internet
(LO 8)

Visit the Web site of Interface, Inc. at http://www.ifsia.com. Then go to the part of the company's Web site about its efforts toward sustainable development at http://www.interfacesustainability.com.

Required: What is Interface's product? Describe the company's efforts toward sustainable development.

Problems

All applicable Problems are available with McGraw-Hill's *Connect Accounting*™.

■ **Problem 12–39**
Create an Organization
(LO 1, 2)

Here is your chance to be a tycoon. Create your own company. You will be the president and chief executive officer. It could be a manufacturer, retailer, or service industry firm, but *not* a hotel or bank. Draw an organization chart for your company, similar to the one in Exhibit 12–1. Identify divisions and departments at all levels in the organization. Then prepare a companion chart similar to the one in Exhibit 12–2. This chart should designate the title of the manager of a subunit at each level in the organization. It also should designate the type of responsibility center appropriate for each of these subunits. Finally, write a letter to your company's stockholders summarizing the major responsibilities of each of the managers you identified in your chart. For guidance, refer to the discussion of Exhibits 12–1 and 12–2 in the chapter. (Have some fun, and be creative.)

■ **Problem 12–40**
Design Performance Reports;
Continuation of Preceding
Problem
(LO 3)

After designing your company, design a set of performance reports for the subunits you identified in your chart. Make up numbers for the performance reports, and show the relationship between the reports. Refer to Exhibit 12–4 for guidance.

■ **Problem 12–41**
Designating Responsibility
Centers; Hotel
(LO 2)

The following partial organization chart is an extension of Exhibit 12–1 for Oasis Hotels and Resorts.

Each of the hotel's five main departments is managed by a director (e.g., director of hospitality). The Front Desk subunit, which is supervised by the front desk manager, handles the hotel's reservations, room assignments, guest payments, and key control. The Bell Staff, managed by the bell captain, is responsible for greeting guests, front door service, assisting guests with their luggage, and delivering room-service orders. The Guest Services subunit, supervised by the manager of Guest Services, is responsible for assisting guests with local transportation arrangements, advising guests on tourist attractions, and such conveniences as valet and floral services.

Required: As an outside consultant, write a memo to the hotel's general manager suggesting a responsibility-center designation for each of the subunits shown in the organization chart above. Justify your choices.

New South Wales Hospital provides broad-based medical and hospital services in southeastern Australia. The hospital is a nonprofit organization that is supported by patient billings, state funds, and private donations. The hospital's organization is shown in the following chart.

■ **Problem 12–42**
Preparation of Performance Reports; Hospital
(LO 3)

1. New South Wales Hospital, total cost, flexible budget, August: $583,700

The following cost information has been compiled for August.

	Budget		Actual	
	August	Year to Date	August	Year to Date
Cafeteria:				
Food servers' wages	$ 9,000	$ 64,000	$ 11,000	$ 72,000
Paper products	4,500	36,000	4,400	36,200
Utilities	1,000	8,000	1,050	8,100
Maintenance	400	3,200	100	1,100
Custodial	1,100	8,800	1,100	8,600
Supplies	1,200	9,600	900	9,600
Patient Food Service	17,000	136,000	18,500	137,000
Registered Dietitians' Section	7,500	60,000	7,500	60,000
Kitchen	31,000	248,000	29,400	246,000
Nursing Department	70,000	560,000	75,000	580,000
Radiology and Laboratory Department	18,000	144,000	18,100	144,000
Housekeeping Department	10,000	80,000	11,600	86,000
Maintenance Department	13,000	104,000	6,000	77,000
General Medicine Division	210,000	1,680,000	204,000	1,670,900
Surgical Division	140,000	1,120,000	141,000	1,115,800
Administrative Division	50,000	400,000	53,500	406,000

Required:

1. Prepare a set of cost performance reports similar to Exhibit 12–4. The report should have six columns, as in Exhibit 12–4. The first four columns will have the same headings as those used above. The last two columns will have the following headings: Variance—August, Variance—Year to Date.

      Since all of the information in the performance reports for New South Wales Hospital is cost information, you do not need to show these data in parentheses. Use F or U to denote whether each variance in the reports is favorable or unfavorable.

2. Using arrows, show the relationships between the numbers in your performance reports for New South Wales Hospital. Refer to Exhibit 12–4 for guidance.

3. Put yourself in the place of the hospital's administrator. Which August variances in the performance reports would you want to investigate further? Why?

■ **Problem 12–43**
Cost Distribution Using
Allocation Bases; Hospital
(LO 4)

Facilities, General Medicine:
$76,000

Refer to the organization chart for New South Wales Hospital given in the preceding problem. Ignore the rest of the data in that problem. The following table shows the cost allocation bases used to distribute various costs among the hospital's divisions.

Cost Pool	Cost Allocation Base	Annual Cost
Facilities:		
Building depreciation	Square feet of space	$190,000
Equipment depreciation		
Insurance		
Utilities:		
Electricity	Cubic feet of space	24,000
Waste disposal		
Water and sewer		
Cable TV and phone		
Heat		
General administration:		
Administrator	Budgeted number of employees	220,000
Administrative staff		
Office supplies		
Community outreach:		
Public education	Budgeted dollars of patient billings	40,000
School physical exams		

Shown below are the amounts of each cost allocation base associated with each division.

	Square Feet	Cubic Feet	Number of Employees	Patient Billings
General Medicine Division	20,000	135,000	30	$2,000,000
Surgical Division	8,000	100,000	20	1,250,000
Medical Support Division	14,000	90,000	20	750,000
Administrative Division	8,000	75,000	30	0
Total	50,000	400,000	100	$4,000,000

Required:

1. Prepare a table similar to Exhibit 12–5 that distributes each of the costs listed in the preceding table to the hospital's divisions.

2. Comment on the appropriateness of patient billings as the basis for distributing community outreach costs to the hospital's divisions. Can you suggest a better allocation base?

3. Is there any use in allocating utilities costs to the divisions? What purposes could such an allocation process serve?

4. *Build a spreadsheet:* Construct an Excel spreadsheet to solve requirement (1) above. Show how the solution will change if the following information changes: the costs incurred were $200,000, $25,000, $200,000, and $50,000, for facilities, utilities, general administration, and community outreach, respectively.

■ **Problem 12–44**
Segmented Income Statement; Responsibility Accounting
(LO 3, 5)

1. Segment profit margin, Paris: $151, 560

Showplace Homes, Inc. sells home decor merchandise through three retail outlets—in Paris, Milan, and Abu Dhabi—and operates a general corporate headquarters in Mumbai. A review of the company's income statement indicates a record year in terms of sales and profits. The owner, though, desires additional insights about the individual stores and has asked the controller to prepare a segmented income statement. The following information has been extracted from Showplace Homes' accounting records:

- The sales volume, sales price, and purchase price data follow:

	Paris	Milan	Abu Dhabi
Sales volume	37,000 units	41,000 units	46,000 units
Unit selling price	$12.00	$11.00	$9.50
Unit purchase price	5.50	5.50	6.00

- The following expenses were incurred for sales commissions, local advertising, property taxes, management salaries, and other noncontrollable (but traceable) costs:

	Paris	Milan	Abu Dhabi
Sales commissions	6%	6%	6%
Local advertising	$11,000	$22,000	$48,000
Local property taxes	4,500	2,000	6,000
Sales manager salary	—	—	32,000
Store manager salaries	41,000	49,000	48,000
Other noncontrollable costs	5,800	4,600	17,800

Local advertising decisions are made at the store manager level. The sales manager's salary in Abu Dhabi is determined by the Abu Dhabi store manager; in contrast, store manager salaries are set by Showplace Homes' vice president.

- Nontraceable fixed corporate expenses total $192,300.
- The company uses a responsibility accounting system.

Required:

1. Assume the role of the controller and prepare a segmented income statement for Show-Off.

2. Determine the weakest-performing store and present an analysis of the probable causes of poor performance.

3. Assume that an opening for a VP of Sales has arisen at the Mumbai corporate headquarters and the company's chief executive officer (CEO) desires to promote one of the three existing store managers. In evaluating the store managers' performance, should the CEO use a store's segment contribution margin, the profit margin controllable by the store manager, or a store's segment profit margin? Justify your answer.

■ **Problem 12–45**
Quality Costs: Identification and Analysis
(LO 6)

2. Total quality costs, no. 165: $439,900

Advanced Technologies (AT) produces two compression machines that are popular with manufacturers of plastics: no. 165 and no. 172. Machine no. 165 has an average selling price of $60,000, whereas no. 172 typically sells for approximately $55,000. The company is very concerned about quality and has provided the following information:

	No. 165	No. 172
Number of machines produced and sold	80	100
Warranty costs:		
Average repair cost per unit	$1,200	$400
Percentage of units needing repair	70%	10%
Reliability engineering at $150 per hour	1,600 hours	2,000 hours
Rework at AT's manufacturing plant:		
Average rework cost per unit	$1,900	$1,600
Percentage of units needing rework	35%	25%
Manufacturing inspection at $50 per hour	300 hours	500 hours
Transportation costs to customer sites to fix problems	$29,500	$15,000
Quality training for employees	$35,000	$50,000

Required:

1. Classify the preceding costs as prevention, appraisal, internal failure, or external failure.

2. Using the classifications in requirement (1), compute AT's quality costs for machine no. 165 in dollars and as a percentage of sales revenues. Also calculate prevention, appraisal, internal failure, and external failure costs as a percentage of total quality costs.

3. Repeat requirement (2) for machine no. 172.

4. Comment on your findings, noting whether the company is "investing" its quality expenditures differently for the two machines.

5. Quality costs can be classified as observable or hidden. What are hidden quality costs, and how do these costs differ from observable costs?

■ **Problem 12–46**
Prepare Segmented Income Statement; Contribution-Margin Format; Retail
(LO 5)

Profit margin traceable to segment, Sugar Land store: $795,000

Lone Star Department Stores, Inc. operates a chain of department stores in Texas. The company's organization chart appears below. Operating data for 20x1 follow.

LONE STAR DEPARTMENT STORES, INC.
Operating Data for 20x1
(in thousands)

	Houston Division			
	Sugar Land Store	Clear Lake Store	Galleria Store	Dallas (total for all stores)
Sales revenue	$5,000	$2,400	$11,000	$21,000
Variable expenses:				
Cost of merchandise sold	3,000	2,000	6,000	12,000
Sales personnel—salaries	400	300	750	1,600
Sales commissions	50	40	90	200
Utilities	80	60	150	300
Other	60	35	120	250
Fixed expenses:				
Depreciation—buildings	120	90	250	470
Depreciation—furnishings	80	50	140	290
Computing and billing	40	30	75	160
Warehouse	70	60	200	450
Insurance	40	25	90	200
Property taxes	35	20	80	170
Supervisory salaries	200	150	300	900
Security	30	30	80	210

The following fixed expenses are controllable at the divisional level: depreciation—furnishings, computing and billing, warehouse, insurance, and security. In addition to these expenses, each division annually incurs $50,000 of computing costs, which are not allocated to individual stores.

The following fixed expenses are controllable only at the company level: depreciation—building, property taxes, and supervisory salaries. In addition to these expenses, each division incurs costs for supervisory salaries of $100,000, which are not allocated to individual stores.

Lone Star Department Stores incurs common fixed expenses of $80,000, which are not allocated to the two divisions. Income-tax expense for 20x1 is $1,950,000.

Required:

1. Prepare a segmented income statement similar to Exhibit 12–7 for Lone Star Department Stores, Inc. The statement should have the following columns:

	Segments of Company		Segments of Houston Division			
Lone Star Department Stores, Inc.	Dallas Division	Houston Division	Sugar Land Store	Clear Lake Store	Galleria Store	Not Allocated

   Prepare the statement in the contribution format, and indicate the controllability of expenses. Subtract all variable expenses, including cost of merchandise sold, from sales revenue to obtain the contribution margin.

2. How would the segmented income statement help the president of Lone Star Department Stores manage the company?

■ **Problem 12–47**
Responsibility Accounting; Participation; Behavioral Issues
(LO 1, 2, 3)

Building Services Co. (BSC) was started a number of years ago by Michel and Jeanne Forgé to provide cleaning services to both large and small businesses in their home city. Over the years, as local businesses reduced underutilized building maintenance staffs, more and more cleaning services were subcontracted to BSC. BSC also expanded into other building services such as painting and local moving.

BSC maintains a pool of skilled workers who are contracted to perform the noncleaning services because these services do not recur on a day-to-day basis for the individual buildings. Many of BSC's full-time employees have been with the firm for a number of years. Five zone managers are each responsible for furnishing recurring nightly cleaning services to several businesses. In addition, the zone manager sells and schedules noncleaning service jobs for the company's central pool of skilled employees. Informal meetings are held periodically to discuss BSC's performance, personnel allocations, and scheduling problems. BSC's budgeting and planning have been done by the Forgés, who also manage variations from budgets.

The Forgés recently decided to retire and sold the business to Commercial Maintenance Inc. (CMI), which provides similar services in a number of metropolitan locations that surround BSC's business area. After news of the sale, several of BSC's long-term employees appeared resentful of the change in ownership and did not know what to expect.

CMI's senior management met with BSC's managers and announced that Rolf Bieger would become president of BSC and that BSC would continue to operate as a separate subsidiary of CMI. Furthermore, in accordance with CMI's management philosophy, a responsibility-accounting system is to be implemented at BSC. Also, in line with other CMI subsidiaries, a participatory budgeting process is being considered. However, no decision will be made until an evaluation of BSC's existing policies, operational culture, and management is completed. In view of the significant change in management philosophy, CMI has taken considerable time in explaining how each system operates and assuring BSC's managers that they are expected and encouraged to participate in both the planning and implementation of any of the systems that are to be adopted.

Required: Two new systems are being considered at Building Services Co.:

- Responsibility-accounting system
- Participatory budgeting system

For each of these systems:

1. Identify at least two behavioral advantages that could arise.
2. Identify at least two potential problems that could arise.
3. Discuss the likelihood that the system will contribute to the alignment of organizational and personal goals.

(CMA, adapted)

■ **Problem 12–48**
Designing a Responsibility-
Accounting System
(LO 1, 2)

Warriner Equipment Company, which is located in Ontario, Canada, manufactures heavy construction equipment. The company's primary product, an especially powerful bulldozer, is among the best produced in North America. The company operates in a very price-competitive industry, so it has little control over the price of its products. It must meet the market price. To do so, the firm has to keep production costs in check by operating as efficiently as possible. Mathew Basler, the company's president, has stated that, to be successful, the company must provide a very high-quality product and meet its delivery commitments to customers on time. Warriner Equipment Company is organized as shown below.

There is currently a disagreement between the company's two vice presidents regarding the responsibility-accounting system. The vice president for manufacturing claims that the 10 plants should be cost centers. He recently expressed the following sentiment: "The plants should be cost centers because the plant managers do not control the sales of our products. Designating the plants as profit centers would result in holding the plant managers responsible for something they can't control." A contrary view is held by the vice president for marketing. He recently made the following remarks: "The plants should be profit centers. The plant managers are in the best position to affect the company's overall profit."

Required: As the company's new controller, you have been asked to make a recommendation to Mathew Basler, the company president, regarding the responsibility center issue. Write a memo to the president making a recommendation and explaining the reasoning behind it. In your memo, address the following points.

1. Assuming that Warriner Equipment Company's overall goal is profitability, what are the company's critical success factors? A *critical success factor* is a variable that meets these two criteria: It is largely under the company's control and the company must succeed in this area in order to reach its overall goal of profitability.

2. Which responsibility-accounting arrangement is most consistent with achieving success on the company's critical success factors?

3. What responsibility-center designation is most appropriate for the company's sales districts?

4. As a specific example, consider the rush-order problem illustrated in the chapter. Suppose that Warriner Equipment Company often experiences rush orders from its customers. Which of the two proposed responsibility-accounting arrangements is best suited to making good decisions about accepting or rejecting rush orders? Specifically, should the plants be cost centers or profit centers?

■ **Problem 12–49**
Quality-Improvement Programs and Quality Costs
(LO 6)

Laser News Technology, Inc. manufactures computerized laser printing equipment used by newspaper publishers throughout North America. In recent years, the company's market share has been eroded by stiff competition from Asian and European competitors. Price and product quality are the two key areas in which companies compete in this market.

Ben McDonough, Laser News Technology's president, decided to devote more resources to the improvement of product quality after learning that his company's products had been ranked fourth in product quality in a recent survey of newspaper publishers. He believed that the company could no longer afford to ignore the importance of product quality. McDonough set up a task force that he headed to implement a formal quality-improvement program. Included on the task force were representatives from engineering, sales, customer service, production, and accounting, as McDonough believed this was a companywide program and all employees should share the responsibility for its success.

After the first meeting of the task force, Sheila Hayes, manager of sales, asked Tony Reese, the production manager, what he thought of the proposed program. Reese replied, "I have reservations. Quality is too abstract to be attaching costs to it and then to be holding you and me responsible for cost improvements. I like to work with goals that I can see and count! I don't like my annual income to be based on a decrease in quality costs; there are too many variables that we have no control over!"

Laser News Technology's quality-improvement program has now been in operation for 18 months, and the following quality cost report has recently been issued. As they were reviewing the report, Hayes asked Reese what he thought of the quality program now. "The work is really moving through the Production Department," replied Reese. "We used to spend time helping the Customer Service Department solve their problems, but they are leaving us alone these days. I have no complaints so far. I'll be anxious to see how much the program increases our bonuses."

LASER NEWS TECHNOLOGY, INC.
Cost of Quality Report
(in thousands)

	Quarter Ended					
	6/30/x0	9/30/x0	12/31/x0	3/31/x1	6/30/x1	9/30/x1
Prevention costs:						
Design review	$ 20	$ 102	$ 111	$ 100	$ 104	$ 95
Machine maintenance	215	215	202	190	170	160
Training suppliers	5	45	25	20	20	15
Total	$ 240	$ 362	$ 338	$ 310	$ 294	$ 270
Appraisal costs:						
Incoming inspection	$ 45	$ 53	$ 57	$ 36	$ 34	$ 22
Final testing	160	160	154	140	115	94
Total	$ 205	$ 213	$ 211	$ 176	$ 149	$ 116
Internal failure costs:						
Rework	$ 120	$ 106	$ 114	$ 88	$ 78	$ 62
Scrap	68	64	53	42	40	40
Total	$ 188	$ 170	$ 167	$ 130	$ 118	$ 102
External failure costs:						
Warranty repairs	$ 69	$ 31	$ 24	$ 25	$ 23	$ 23
Customer returns	262	251	122	116	87	80
Total	$ 331	$ 282	$ 146	$ 141	$ 110	$ 103
Total quality cost	$ 964	$1,027	$ 862	$ 757	$ 671	$ 591
Total production cost	$4,120	$4,540	$4,380	$4,650	$4,580	$4,510

Required:

1. Identify at least three factors that should be present for an organization to successfully implement a quality improvement program.

2. By analyzing the cost of quality report presented, determine if Laser News Technology's quality improvement program has been successful. List specific evidence to support your answer.

3. Discuss why Tony Reese's current reaction to the quality improvement program is more favorable than his initial reaction.

4. Laser News Technology's president believed that the quality improvement program was essential and that the firm could no longer afford to ignore the importance of product quality. Discuss how the company could measure the opportunity cost of not implementing the quality-improvement program.

(CMA, adapted)

■ **Problem 12–50**
Environmental Cost
Management
(LO 8)

As a group, take a walking tour of your campus and the surrounding community. Make a list of all of the environmental costs of which you see evidence.

Required: Make a presentation to the class about your findings. List and categorize the environmental costs you noted either for your college or for businesses in the community. (You might consider writing a letter to your campus newspaper regarding these environmental issues and their costs.)

Cases

■ **Case 12–51**
Segmented Income State-
ment; Responsibility Account-
ing; Bonuses; Motivation;
Ethics
(LO 1, 2, 5)

1. Net income, Windsor store:
$91,275
2. Sovereign store's net
income for May: $12,375

High Street Clothes is a retailer that sells to professional women. The firm leases space for stores in upscale shopping districts, and the organizational structure consists of regions, districts, and stores. Each region consists of two or more districts; each district consists of three or more stores. Each store, district, and region has been established as a profit center. At all levels, the company uses a responsibility-accounting system focusing on information and knowledge rather than blame and control. Each year, managers, in consultation with their supervisors, establish financial and nonfinancial goals, and these goals are integrated into the budget. Actual performance is measured each month.

The South Region consists of the Coastal District and the Inland District. The Coastal District includes the Excelsior, Windsor, and Sovereign stores. The Coastal District's performance has not been up to expectations in the past. For the month of May, the district manager has set performance goals with the managers of the Excelsior and Windsor stores, who will receive bonuses if certain performance measures are exceeded. The manager of the Sovereign store decided not to participate in the bonus scheme. Since the district manager is unsure what type of bonus will encourage better performance, the Excelsior manager will receive a bonus based on sales in excess of budgeted sales of $570,000, while the Windsor manager will receive a bonus based on net income in excess of budgeted net income. The company's net income goal for each store is 12 percent of sales. The budgeted sales revenue for the Windsor store is $530,000.

Other pertinent data for May are as follows:

- Coastal District sales revenue was $1,500,000, and its cost of goods sold amounted to $633,750.

- The Coastal District spent $75,000 on advertising.

- General and administrative expenses for the Coastal District amounted to $180,000.

- At the Excelsior store, sales were 40 percent of Coastal District sales, while sales at the Windsor store were 35 percent of district sales. The cost of goods sold in both Excelsior and Windsor was 42 percent of sales.

- Variable selling expenses (sales commissions) were 6 percent of sales for all stores, districts, and regions.

- Variable administrative expenses were 2.5 percent of sales for all stores, districts, and regions.

- Maintenance cost includes janitorial and repair services and is a direct cost for each store. The store manager has complete control over this outlay. Maintenance costs were incurred as follows: Excelsior, $7,500; Windsor, $600; and Sovereign, $4,500.

- Advertising is considered a direct cost for each store and is completely under the control of the store manager. The Excelsior store spent two-thirds of the Coastal District total outlay for advertising, which was 10 times the amount spent in Windsor on advertising.

- Coastal District rental expense amounted to $150,000.
- The rental expenses at the Excelsior store were 40 percent of the Coastal District's total, while the Windsor store incurred 30 percent of the district total.
- District expenses were allocated to the stores based on sales.
- South Region general and administrative expenses of $165,000 were allocated to the Coastal District. These expenses were, in turn, allocated equally to the district's three stores.

Required:

1. Prepare the May segmented income statement for the Coastal District and for the Excelsior and Windsor stores.
2. Compute the Sovereign store's net income for May.
3. Discuss the impact of the responsibility-accounting system and bonus structure on the managers' behavior and the effect of their behavior on the financial results for the Excelsior store and the Windsor store.
4. The assistant controller for the South Region, Jack Williams, has been a close friend of the Excelsior store manager for over 20 years. When Williams saw the segmented income statement [as prepared in requirement (1)], he realized that the Excelsior store manager had really gone overboard on advertising expenditures. To make his friend look better to the regional management, he reclassified $25,000 of the advertising expenditures as miscellaneous expenses, and buried them in rent and other costs. Comment on the ethical issues in the assistant controller's actions. (Refer to specific ethical standards for managerial accountants which were given in Chapter 1.)

(CMA, adapted)

Pacific Rim Industries is a diversified company whose products are marketed both domestically and internationally. The company's major product lines are furniture, sports equipment, and household appliances. At a recent meeting of Pacific Rim's board of directors, there was a lengthy discussion on ways to improve overall corporate profitability. The members of the board decided that they required additional financial information about individual corporate operations in order to target areas for improvement.

Danielle Murphy, the controller, has been asked to provide additional data that would assist the board in its investigation. Murphy believes that income statements, prepared along both product lines and geographic areas, would provide the directors with the required insight into corporate operations. Murphy had several discussions with the division managers for each product line and compiled the following information from these meetings.

■ **Case 12–52**
Segmented Income Statement; International Operations
(LO 1, 5)

1. Operating income (loss), Canada: $421,000

| | **Product Lines** | | | |
	Furniture	Sports	Appliances	Total
Production and sales in units	160,000	180,000	160,000	500,000
Average selling price per unit	$8.00	$20.00	$15.00	
Average variable manufacturing cost per unit	4.00	9.50	8.25	
Average variable selling expense per unit	2.00	2.50	2.25	
Fixed manufacturing overhead, excluding depreciation				$ 500,000
Depreciation of plant and equipment				400,000
Administrative and selling expense				1,160,000

1. The division managers concluded that Murphy should allocate fixed manufacturing overhead to both product lines and geographic areas on the basis of the ratio of the variable costs expended to total variable costs.
2. Each of the division managers agreed that a reasonable basis for the allocation of depreciation on plant and equipment would be the ratio of units produced per product line (or per geographical area) to the total number of units produced.
3. There was little agreement on the allocation of administrative and selling expenses, so Murphy decided to allocate only those expenses that were traceable directly to a segment. For example, manufacturing staff salaries would be allocated to product lines, and sales staff salaries would be allocated to geographic areas. Murphy used the following data for this allocation.

Manufacturing Staff		**Sales Staff**	
Furniture	$120,000	United States	$ 60,000
Sports	140,000	Canada	100,000
Appliances	80,000	Asia	250,000

4. The division managers were able to provide reliable sales percentages for their product lines by geographical area.

	Percentage of Unit Sales		
	United States	**Canada**	**Asia**
Furniture	40%	10%	50%
Sports	40%	40%	20%
Appliances	20%	20%	60%

Murphy prepared the following product-line income statement based on the data presented above.

PACIFIC RIM INDUSTRIES
Segmented Income Statement by Product Lines
For the Fiscal Year Ended April 30, 20x0

	Product Lines				
	Furniture	**Sports**	**Appliances**	**Unallocated**	**Total**
Sales in units	160,000	180,000	160,000		
Sales	$1,280,000	$3,600,000	$2,400,000	—	$7,280,000
Variable manufacturing and selling costs	960,000	2,160,000	1,680,000	—	4,800,000
Contribution margin	$ 320,000	$1,440,000	$ 720,000	—	$2,480,000
Fixed costs:					
Fixed manufacturing overhead	$ 100,000	$ 225,000	$ 175,000	$ —	$ 500,000
Depreciation	128,000	144,000	128,000	—	400,000
Administrative and selling expenses	120,000	140,000	80,000	820,000	1,160,000
Total fixed costs	$ 348,000	$ 509,000	$ 383,000	$ 820,000	$2,060,000
Operating income (loss)	$ (28,000)	$ 931,000	$ 337,000	$(820,000)	$ 420,000

Required:

1. Prepare a segmented income statement for Pacific Rim Industries based on the company's geographical areas. The statement should show the operating income for each segment.

2. As a result of the information disclosed by both segmented income statements (by product line and by geographic area), recommend areas where Pacific Rim Industries should focus its attention in order to improve corporate profitability.

(CMA, adapted)

THIS CHAPTER'S FOCUS COMPANY is GreenMarket Food Stores, a chain of

GreenMarket
FOOD STORES

retail grocery stores in South Korea. The company has three divisions. The

Capital and Regional divisions operate individual grocery stores in cities and towns located

throughout South Korea. The Capital division serves the population within 100 kilometers

of Seoul, and the Regional division serves the rest of the country. The Food Processing Divi-

sion operates dairy plants, bakeries, and fresh seafood processing facilities in Daegu, Seoul,

and Busan in order to supply the GreenMarket

grocery stores with fresh food products. In this

chapter, we will explore how companies evaluate

the performance of investment centers, such as

GreenMarket's three divisions. Investment centers

are organizational subunits whose managers have

the authority to make significant investment deci-

sions, such as building a new store or expanding

an existing one.

13 Investment Centers and Transfer Pricing

In contrast to the evaluation of investment center performance explored in the first part of the chapter, we will turn our attention to transfer pricing. The amount charged when one division of a company sells products or services to another division is called a transfer price. We can continue to use GreenMarket Food Stores for our illustration, because the GreenMarket food processing facilities sell their dairy, bakery, and fresh seafood products to the GreenMarket grocery stores at a transfer price. We will explore different ways to set such transfer prices.

GreenMarket
FOOD STORES

1 Explain the role of managerial accounting in achieving goal congruence.

2 Compute an investment center's return on investment (ROI), residual income (RI), and economic value added (EVA).

3 Explain how a manager can improve ROI by increasing either the sales margin or capital turnover.

4 Describe some advantages and disadvantages of both ROI and residual income as divisional performance measures.

5 Explain how to measure a division's income and invested capital.

6 Use the general economic rule to set an optimal transfer price.

7 Explain how to base a transfer price on market prices, costs, or negotiations.

8 Understand the behavioral issues of incentives, goal congruence, and internal controls.

How do the top managers of large companies such as BNP Paribas and Bharti Airtel evaluate their divisions and other major subunits? The largest subunits within these and similar organizations usually are designated as **investment centers.** The manager of this type of *responsibility center* is held accountable not only for the investment center's *profit* but also for the *capital invested* to earn that profit. Invested capital refers to assets, such as buildings and equipment, used in a subunit's operations. In this chapter, we will study the methods that managerial accountants use to evaluate investment centers and the performance of their managers.[1]

In many organizations, one subunit manufactures a product or produces a service that is then transferred to another subunit in the same organization. For example, automobile parts manufactured in one division of Hyundai Motors are then transferred to another Hyundai division that assembles vehicles.

The price at which products or services are transferred between two subunits in an organization is called a **transfer price.** Since a transfer price affects the profit of both the buying and selling divisions, the transfer price affects the performance evaluation of these responsibility centers. Later in this chapter, we will study the methods that managerial accountants use to determine transfer prices.

Delegation of Decision Making

Learning Objective 1

Explain the role of managerial accounting in achieving goal congruence.

Most large organizations are decentralized. Managers throughout these organizations are given autonomy to make decisions for their subunits. Decentralization takes advantage of the specialized knowledge and skills of managers, permits an organization to respond

---

[1]Recall from Chapter 12 that in practice the term *profit center* sometimes is used interchangeably with the term *investment center*. To be precise, however, the term *profit center* should be reserved for a subunit whose manager is held accountable for profit but not for invested capital.

quickly to events, and relieves top management of the need to direct the organization's day-to-day activities. The biggest challenge in making a decentralized organization function effectively is to obtain *goal congruence* among the organization's autonomous managers.

Obtaining Goal Congruence: A Behavioral Challenge

Goal congruence is obtained when the managers of subunits throughout an organization strive to achieve the goals set by top management. This desirable state of affairs is difficult to achieve for a variety of reasons. Managers often are unaware of the effects of their decisions on the organization's other subunits. Also, it is only human for people to be more concerned with the performance of their own subunit than with the effectiveness of the entire organization. The behavioral challenge in designing any management control system is to come as close as possible to obtaining goal congruence.

To obtain goal congruence, the behavior of managers throughout an organization must be directed toward top management's goals. Successful managers not only have their sights set on these organizational goals, but also have been given positive incentives to achieve them. *The managerial accountant's objective* in designing a responsibility-accounting system is to provide these incentives to the organization's subunit managers. *The key factor in deciding how well the responsibility-accounting system works is the extent to which it directs managers' efforts toward organizational goals.* Thus, the accounting measures used to evaluate investment-center managers should provide them with incentives to act in the interests of the overall organization.

Management by Objectives (MBO)   An emphasis on obtaining goal congruence is consistent with a broad managerial approach called **management by objectives,** or **MBO.** Under the MBO philosophy, managers participate in setting goals that they then strive to achieve. The goals usually are expressed in financial or other quantitative terms, and the responsibility-accounting system is used to evaluate performance in achieving them.

Adaptation of Management Control Systems

When an organization begins its operations, it is usually small and decision making generally is centralized. The chief executive can control operations without a formal responsibility-accounting system. It is relatively easy in a small organization for managers to keep in touch with routine operations through face-to-face contact with employees.

As an organization grows, however, its managers need more formal information systems, including managerial accounting information, in order to maintain control. Accounting systems are established to record events and provide the framework for internal and external financial reports. Budgets become necessary to plan the organization's activity. As the organization gains experience in producing its goods or services, cost standards and flexible budgets often are established to help control operations. As the organization continues to grow, some delegation of decision making becomes necessary. Decentralization is often the result of this tendency toward delegation. Ultimately, a fully developed responsibility-accounting system emerges. Managerial accountants designate cost centers, revenue centers, profit centers, and investment centers, and develop appropriate performance measures for each subunit.

Thus, an organization's accounting and managerial control systems usually adapt and become more complex as the organization grows and changes.

Measuring Performance in Investment Centers

In our study of investment-center performance evaluation, we will focus on GreenMarket Food Centers. This South Korean chain of retail grocery stores has three divisions, as depicted by the organization chart in Exhibit 13–1.

The Capital and Regional divisions consist of grocery stores located in cities and towns throughout South Korea. The Capital division serves the population within 100 kilometers of Seoul, and the Regional division serves the rest of the country. The company's Food Processing Division operates dairy plants, bakeries, and fresh seafood processing plants in Daegu, Seoul, and Busan. These facilities provide all GreenMarket Food Stores with milk, ice cream, yogurt, cheese, breads, desserts, and fresh seafood. These GreenMarket-brand food products are transferred to the company's Capital and Regional divisions at transfer prices established by the corporate controller's office.

GreenMarket Food Stores' three divisions are investment centers. This responsibility-center designation is appropriate, because each division manager has the authority to make decisions that affect both profit and invested capital. For example, the Capital Division manager approves the overall pricing policies in the Capital Division's stores, and also has the autonomy to sign contracts to buy food and other products for resale. These actions influence the division's profit. In addition, the Capital Division manager has the authority to build new GreenMarket Food Stores, rent space in shopping districts in and around Seoul, or close existing stores. These decisions affect the amount of capital invested in the division.

The primary goals of any profit-making enterprise include maximizing its profitability and using its invested capital as effectively as possible. Managerial accountants use three different measures to evaluate the performance of investment centers: return on investment (ROI), residual income (RI), and economic value added (EVA®). (EVA® is a registered trademark of Stern Stewart & Co.) We will illustrate each of these measures for GreenMarket Food Stores.

> "Accounting is changing. You're no longer sitting behind a desk just working on a computer, just crunching the numbers. You're actually getting to be a part of the day to day functions of the business." (13a)
>
> **Abbott Laboratories**

Return on Investment

> **Learning Objective 2**
>
> Compute an investment center's return on investment (ROI), residual income (RI), and economic value added (EVA).

The most common investment-center performance measure is **return on investment,** or **ROI,** which is defined as follows:

$$\text{Return on investment (ROI)} = \frac{\text{Income}}{\text{Invested capital}}$$

Exhibit 13–1
Organization Chart: Green-Market Food Stores

The most recent year's ROI calculations for GreenMarket Food Stores' three divisions are:

	$\dfrac{\text{Income}}{\text{Invested capital}}$	=	Return on investment (ROI)
Regional Division	$\dfrac{\$3,000,000}{\$20,000,000}$	=	15%
Food Processing Division	$\dfrac{\$3,600,000}{\$18,000,000}$	=	20%
Capital Division	$\dfrac{\$6,750,000}{\$45,000,000}$	=	15%

Notice how the ROI calculation for each division takes into account *both divisional income and the capital invested* in the division. Why is this important? Suppose each division were evaluated only on the basis of its divisional profit. The Capital Division reported a higher divisional profit than the Regional Division. Does this mean the Capital Division performed better than the Regional Division? The answer is no. Although the Capital Division's profit exceeded the Regional Division's profit, the Capital Division used a much larger amount of invested capital to earn its profit. The Capital Division's assets are more than two times the assets of the Regional Division.

Considering the relative size of the two divisions, we should expect the Capital Division to earn a larger profit than the Regional Division. The important question is not how much profit each division earned, but rather how effectively each division used its invested capital to earn a profit.

Factors Underlying ROI   We can rewrite the ROI formula as follows:

$$\text{Return on investment} = \frac{\text{Income}}{\text{Invested capital}} = \frac{\text{Income}}{\text{Sales revenue}} \times \frac{\text{Sales revenue}}{\text{Invested capital}}$$

Notice that the *sales revenue* term cancels out in the denominator and numerator when the two right-hand fractions are multiplied.

Writing the ROI formula in this way highlights the factors that determine a division's return on investment. Income divided by sales revenue is called the **sales margin.** This term measures the percentage of each sales dollar that remains as profit after all expenses are covered. Sales revenue divided by invested capital is called the **capital turnover.** This term focuses on the number of sales dollars generated by every dollar of invested capital. The sales margin and capital turnover for GreenMarket Food Stores' three divisions are calculated below for the most recent year.

> "The ROI of pollution prevention rises radically when 'hidden' environmental management costs are revealed." (13b)
> **Kestrel Management Services**
> (an environmental consulting firm)

	Sales margin	×	Capital turnover	=	ROI
	$\dfrac{\text{Income}}{\text{Sales revenue}}$	×	$\dfrac{\text{Sales revenue}}{\text{Invested capital}}$	=	ROI
Regional Division	$\dfrac{\$3,000,000}{\$60,000,000}$	×	$\dfrac{\$60,000,000}{\$20,000,000}$	=	15%
Food Processing Division	$\dfrac{\$3,600,000}{\$9,000,000}$	×	$\dfrac{\$9,000,000}{\$18,000,000}$	=	20%
Capital Division	$\dfrac{\$6,750,000}{\$135,000,000}$	×	$\dfrac{\$135,000,000}{\$45,000,000}$	=	15%

The Regional Division's sales margin is 5 percent ($3,000,000 of profit ÷ $60,000,000 of sales revenue). Thus, each dollar of divisional sales resulted in a five-cent profit. The division's capital turnover was 3 ($60,000,000 of sales revenue ÷ $20,000,000 of invested capital). Thus, three dollars of sales revenue were generated by each dollar of capital invested in the division's assets, such as store buildings, display shelves, checkout equipment, and inventory.

Learning Objective 3

Explain how a manager can improve ROI by increasing either the sales margin or capital turnover.

Improving ROI How could the Regional Division manager improve the division's return on investment? Since ROI is the product of the sales margin and the capital turnover, ROI can be improved by increasing either or both of its components. For example, if the Regional Division manager increased the division's sales margin to 6 percent while holding the capital turnover constant at 3, the division's ROI would climb from 15 percent to 18 percent, as follows:

$$\begin{array}{c} \text{Regional Division's} \\ \text{improved ROI} \end{array} = \begin{array}{c} \text{Improved} \\ \text{sales margin} \end{array} \times \begin{array}{c} \text{Same} \\ \text{capital turnover} \end{array}$$

$$= \quad 6\% \quad \times \quad 3 \quad = 18\%$$

To bring about the improved sales margin, the Regional Division manager would need to increase divisional profit to $3,600,000 on sales of $60,000,000 ($3,600,000 ÷ $60,000,000 = 6%). How could profit be increased without changing total sales revenue? There are two possibilities: increase sales prices while selling less quantity, or decrease expenses. Neither of these is necessarily easy to do. In increasing sales prices, the division manager must be careful not to lose sales to the extent that total sales revenue declines. Similarly, reducing the expenses must not diminish product quality, customer service, or overall store atmosphere. Any of these changes could also result in lost sales revenue.

An alternative way of increasing the Regional Division's ROI would be to increase its capital turnover. Suppose the Regional Division manager increased the division's capital turnover to 4 while holding the sales margin constant at 5 percent. The division's ROI would climb from 15 percent to 20 percent:

$$\begin{array}{c} \text{Regional Division's} \\ \text{improved ROI} \end{array} = \begin{array}{c} \text{Same} \\ \text{Sales margin} \end{array} \times \begin{array}{c} \text{Improved} \\ \text{capital turnover} \end{array}$$

$$= \quad 5\% \quad \times \quad 4 \quad = 20\%$$

To obtain the improved capital turnover, the Regional Division manager would need to either increase sales revenue or reduce the division's invested capital. For example, the improved ROI could be achieved by reducing invested capital to $15,000,000 while maintaining sales revenue of $60,000,000. This would be a very tall order. The division manager can lower invested capital somewhat by reducing inventories and can increase sales revenue by using store space more effectively. But reducing inventories may lead to stockouts and lost sales, and crowded aisles may drive customers away.

Improving ROI is a balancing act that requires all the skills of an effective manager. The ROI analysis above merely shows the arena in which the balancing act is performed.

Residual Income

Learning Objective 2

Compute an investment center's return on investment (ROI), residual income (RI), and economic value added (EVA).

Although ROI is the most popular investment-center performance measure, it has one major drawback. To illustrate, suppose GreenMarket's Food Processing Division manager can buy a new food processing machine for $500,000, which will save $80,000 in operating expenses and thereby raise divisional profit by $80,000. The return on this investment in new equipment is 16 percent:

$$\begin{array}{c} \text{Return on investment} \\ \text{in new equipment} \end{array} = \frac{\text{Increase in divisional profit}}{\text{Increase in invested capital}} = \frac{\$80,000}{\$500,000} = 16\%$$

Now suppose it costs GreenMarket Food Stores 12 cents for each dollar of capital to invest in operational assets. What is the optimal decision for the Food Processing Division manager to make, *viewed from the perspective of the company as a whole?* Since it costs GreenMarket Food Stores 12 percent for every dollar of capital, and the return on investment in new equipment is 16 percent, the equipment should be purchased. For goal congruence, the autonomous division manager should decide to buy the new equipment.

Now consider what is likely to happen. The Food Processing Division manager's performance is evaluated on the basis of his division's ROI. Without the new equipment, the divisional ROI is 20 percent ($3,600,000 of divisional profit ÷ $18,000,000 of invested capital). If he purchases the new equipment, his divisional ROI will decline:

Food Processing Division's Return on Investment	
Without Investment in New Equipment	**With Investment in New Equipment**
$\dfrac{\$3{,}600{,}000}{\$18{,}000{,}000} = 20\%$	$\dfrac{\$3{,}600{,}000 + \$80{,}000}{\$18{,}000{,}000 + \$500{,}000} < 20\%$

Why did this happen? Even though the investment in new equipment earns a return of 16 percent, which is greater than the company's cost of raising capital (12 percent), the return is less than the division's ROI without the equipment (20 percent). Averaging the new investment with those already in place in the Food Processing Division merely reduces the division's ROI. Since the division manager is evaluated using ROI, he will be reluctant to decide in favor of acquiring the new equipment.

The problem is that the ROI measure leaves out an important piece of information: it ignores the firm's cost of raising investment capital. For this reason, many managers prefer to use a different investment-center performance measure instead of ROI.

Computing Residual Income An investment center's **residual income** is defined as follows:

$$\frac{\text{Residual}}{\text{income}} = \frac{\text{Investment center's}}{\text{profit}} - \left(\frac{\text{Investment center's}}{\text{invested capital}} \times \frac{\text{Imputed}}{\text{interest rate}}\right)$$

where the imputed interest rate is the firm's cost of acquiring investment capital.

Residual income is a dollar amount, not a ratio like ROI. It is the amount of an investment center's profit that remains (as a residual) after subtracting an imputed interest charge. The term *imputed* means that the interest charge is estimated by the managerial accountant. This charge reflects the firm's minimum required rate of return on invested capital. In some firms, the imputed interest rate depends on the riskiness of the investment for which the funds will be used. Thus, divisions that have different levels of risk sometimes are assigned different imputed interest rates.

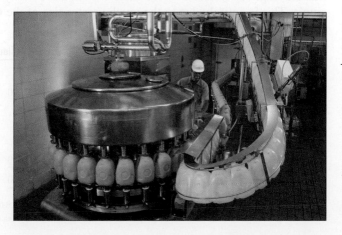

ROI and residual income are common performance measures for investment centers. Both measures relate the profit earned from selling the final product to the capital required to carry out production operations. Here the product is orange juice, and this bottling equipment represents the capital investment.

The residual income of GreenMarket's Food Processing Division is computed below, both with and without the investment in the new equipment. The imputed interest rate is 12 percent.

	Food Processing Division's Residual Income			
	Without Investment in New Equipment		**With Investment in New Equipment**	
Divisional profit		$3,600,000		$3,680,000
Less imputed interest charge:				
Invested capital	$18,000,000		$18,500,000	
× Imputed interest rate	× .12		× .12	
Imputed interest charge		2,160,000		2,220,000
Residual income		$1,440,000		$1,460,000

Investment in new equipment raises residual income by $20,000.

Notice that the Food Processing Division's residual income will *increase* if the new equipment is purchased. What will be the division manager's incentive if he is evaluated on the basis of residual income instead of ROI? He will want to make the investment because that decision will increase his division's residual income. Thus, goal congruence is achieved when the managerial accountant uses residual income to measure divisional performance.

Why does residual income facilitate goal congruence while ROI does not? Because the residual-income formula incorporates an important piece of data that is excluded from the ROI formula: the firm's minimum required rate of return on invested capital. To summarize, ROI and residual income are compared as follows:

$$\text{ROI} = \frac{\text{Investment center's profit}}{\text{Investment center's invested capital}}$$

Two pieces of data

$$\frac{\text{Residual}}{\text{income}} = \frac{\text{Investment center's}}{\text{profit}} - \left(\frac{\text{Investment center's}}{\text{invested capital}} \times \frac{\text{Imputed}}{\text{interest rate}}\right)$$

Three pieces of data

Unfortunately, residual income also has a serious drawback: It should not be used to compare the performance of different-sized investment centers because it incorporates a bias in favor of the larger investment center. To illustrate, the following table compares the residual income of GreenMarket Food Store's Regional and Capital divisions. Notice that the Capital Division's residual income is considerably higher than the Regional Division's. This is entirely due to the much greater size of the Capital Division, as evidenced by its far greater invested capital.

	Comparison of Residual Income: Two Divisions			
	Regional Division		**Capital Division**	
Divisional profit		$3,000,000		$6,750,000
Less imputed interest charge:				
Invested capital	$20,000,000		$45,000,000	
× Imputed interest rate	× .12		× .12	
Imputed interest charge		2,400,000		5,400,000
Residual income		$ 600,000		$1,350,000

The Capital Division's residual income is much higher simply because it is larger than the Regional Division.

Learning Objective 4

Describe some advantages and disadvantages of both ROI and residual income as divisional performance measures.

In short, neither ROI nor residual income provides a perfect measure of investment-center performance. ROI can undermine goal congruence. Residual income distorts comparisons between investment centers of different sizes. As a result, some companies routinely use both measures for divisional performance evaluation.

Shareholder Value Analysis

Some companies apply the residual income concept to individual product lines. **Shareholder value analysis** calculates the residual income for a major product line, with the objective of determining how the product line affects the firm's value to the shareholders. Suppose, for example, that GreenMarket Food Stores offers in-store, one-hour film development in selected stores. Let's say that the company's investment in this service is $200,000 and the annual profit is $40,000. Then the residual income on one-hour film development is $16,000 [$40,000 − ($200,000 × 12%)].

Economic Value Added

The most contemporary measure of investment center performance is **economic value added (EVA),** which is defined as follows:

Learning Objective 2

Compute an investment center's return on investment (ROI), residual income (RI), and economic value added (EVA).

$$\begin{pmatrix} \text{Economic} \\ \text{value} \\ \text{added} \end{pmatrix} = \begin{pmatrix} \text{Investment} \\ \text{center's after-tax} \\ \text{operating income} \end{pmatrix} - \left[\begin{pmatrix} \text{Investment} \\ \text{center's} \\ \text{total assets} \end{pmatrix} - \begin{pmatrix} \text{Investment} \\ \text{center's current} \\ \text{liabilities} \end{pmatrix} \times \begin{pmatrix} \text{Weighted-} \\ \text{average cost} \\ \text{of capital} \end{pmatrix} \right]$$

Like residual income, the economic value added is a dollar amount. However, it differs from residual income in two important ways. First, an investment center's current liabilities are subtracted from its total assets. Second, the weighted-average cost of capital is used in the calculation.

Weighted-Average Cost of Capital

GreenMarket Food Stores has two sources of long-term capital: debt and equity. The cost to GreenMarket of issuing debt is the after-tax cost of the interest payments on the debt, taking account of the fact that the interest payments are tax deductible. The cost of GreenMarket's equity capital is the investment opportunity rate of GreenMarket Food Stores' investors, that is, the rate they could earn on investments of similar risk to that of investing in GreenMarket Food Stores. The **weighted-average cost of capital (WACC)** is defined as follows:

$$\begin{pmatrix} \text{Weighted-average} \\ \text{cost of capital} \end{pmatrix} = \frac{\begin{pmatrix} \text{After-tax cost} \\ \text{of debt} \\ \text{capital} \end{pmatrix}\begin{pmatrix} \text{Market} \\ \text{value} \\ \text{of debt} \end{pmatrix} + \begin{pmatrix} \text{Cost of} \\ \text{equity} \\ \text{capital} \end{pmatrix}\begin{pmatrix} \text{Market} \\ \text{value} \\ \text{of equity} \end{pmatrix}}{\begin{matrix} \text{Market} \\ \text{value} + \\ \text{of debt} \end{matrix}\quad\begin{matrix} \text{Market} \\ \text{value} \\ \text{of equity} \end{matrix}}$$

The interest rate on GreenMarket Food Stores' $40 million of debt is 9 percent, and the company's tax rate is 30 percent. Therefore, GreenMarket's after-tax cost of debt is 6.3 percent [9% × (1 − 30%)]. Let's assume that the cost of GreenMarket's equity capital is 12 percent. Moreover, the market value of the company's equity is $60 million.[2] The following calculation shows that GreenMarket Food Stores' WACC is 9.72 percent.

---

[2]The *book value* of GreenMarket Food Stores' equity is $41 million, but that amount does not reflect the current value of the company's assets or the value of intangible assets such as the GreenMarket Food Stores name.

$$\text{Weighted-average} \atop \text{cost of capital} = \frac{(.063)(\$40{,}000{,}000) + (.12)(\$60{,}000{,}000)}{\$40{,}000{,}000 + \$60{,}000{,}000} = .0972$$

Finally, GreenMarket Food Stores had an average balance of $2 million in current liabilities, distributed as follows:

Division	Current Liabilities
Regional Division	$ 400,000
Food Processing Division	1,000,000
Capital Division	600,000

Now we can compute the economic value added (or EVA) for each of GreenMarket's three divisions.

Division	After-tax operating income (in millions)	−	Total assets (in millions)	−	Current liabilities (in millions)	× WACC	=	Economic value added
Regional	$3.00 × (1 − .30) −		[($20	−	$ .4)	× .0972]	=	$194,880
Food Processing	$3.60 × (1 − .30) −		[($18	−	$1.0)	× .0972]	=	867,600
Capital	$6.75 × (1 − .30) −		[($45	−	$ .6)	× .0972]	=	409,320

The EVA analysis reveals that all three of GreenMarket Food Stores' divisions are contributing substantially to the company's economic value.

What does an EVA analysis tell us? EVA indicates how much shareholder wealth is being created, as Roberto Goizueta, Coca-Cola's former CEO, explained: "We raise capital to make concentrate and sell it at an operating profit. Then we pay the cost of that capital. Shareholders pocket the difference (EVA amount)."

Management
Accounting
Practice

Siemens and Royal Bank
of Canada

PAY FOR PERFORMANCE BASED ON EVA

In the wake of the excesses in top management compensation over the past few years, at many companies pay for performance is back in vogue. Top executives earn hefty bonuses when times are good, but are expected to share in the pain during a decline in business.

Siemens, a global electronics firm, links the compensation of its top 500 managers to their business units' economic value added (EVA) measure. Similarly, the Royal Bank of Canada, upon observing that its lower-level managers were not acting in accordance with the bank's overall strategy, began linking their compensation to the bank's EVA and revenue growth.[3]

---

[3]Kara Seannell and Joann Lublin, "SEC Unhappy with Answers on Executive Pay," *The Wall Street Journal,* January 29, 2008, p. 31; Louis Lavelle, "The Gravy Train Just Got Derailed—'Pay for Performance' Is Back in Vogue," *BusinessWeek,* November 19, 2001; and Tad Leahy, "All the Right Moves," *Business Finance* 6, no. 1 (April 2000), p. 32.

Measuring Income and Invested Capital

The ROI, residual-income, and economic value added (EVA) measures of investment-center performance all use profit and invested capital in their formulas. This raises the question of how to measure divisional profit and invested capital. This section will illustrate various approaches to resolving these measurement issues.

Invested Capital

We will focus on GreenMarket Food Stores' Food Processing Division to illustrate several alternative approaches to measuring an investment center's capital. Exhibit 13–2 lists the assets and liabilities associated with the Food Processing Division. Notice that Exhibit 13–2 does not constitute a complete balance sheet. First, there are no long-term liabilities, such as bonds payable, associated with the Food Processing Division. Although GreenMarket Food Stores may have such long-term debt, it would not be meaningful to assign portions of that debt to the company's individual divisions. Second, there is no stockholders' equity associated with the Food Processing Division. The owners of the company own stock in GreenMarket Food Stores, not in its individual divisions.

> **Learning Objective 5**
>
> Explain how to measure a division's income and invested capital.

Average Balances   ROI, residual income, and EVA are computed for a period of time, such as a year or a month. Asset balances, on the other hand, are measured at a point in time, such as December 31. Since divisional asset balances generally will change over time, we use average balances in calculating ROI, residual income, and EVA. For example, if the Food Processing Division's balance in invested capital was $19,000,000 on January 1 and $17,000,000 on December 31, we would use the year's average invested capital of $18,000,000 in the ROI, residual income, and EVA calculations.

Should Total Assets Be Used?   Exhibit 13–2 shows that the Food Processing Division had average balances during the year of $2,000,000 in current assets, $15,000,000 in long-lived assets, and $1,000,000 tied up in a plant under construction. (GreenMarket Food Stores is building a new high-tech dairy plant in Daegu to produce its innovative zero-calorie ice cream.) In addition, Exhibit 13–2 discloses that the Food Processing Division's average balance of current liabilities was $1,000,000.

Assets*		
Current assets (cash, accounts receivable, inventories, etc.)		$ 2,000,000
Long-lived assets (land, buildings, equipment, vehicles, etc.):		
Gross book value (acquisition cost)	$19,000,000	
Less: Accumulated depreciation	4,000,000	
Net book value		15,000,000
Plant under construction		1,000,000
Total assets		$18,000,000
Liabilities		
Current liabilities (accounts payable, salaries payable, etc.)		$ 1,000,000

*This is not a balance sheet, but rather a listing of certain assets and liabilities associated with the Food Processing Division.

Exhibit 13–2
Assets and Liabilities Associated with Food Processing Division

GreenMarket
FOOD STORES

What is the division's invested capital? Several possibilities exist.

1. *Total assets.* The management of GreenMarket Food Stores has decided to use *average total assets* for the year in measuring each division's invested capital. Thus, $18,000,000 is the amount used in the ROI, residual-income, and EVA calculations discussed earlier in this chapter. This measure of invested capital is appropriate if the division manager has considerable authority in making decisions about *all* of the division's assets, *including nonproductive assets.* In this case, the Food Processing Division's partially completed dairy plant is a nonproductive asset. Since the division manager had considerable influence in deciding to build the new plant and he is responsible for overseeing the project, average total assets provides an appropriate measure.

2. *Total productive assets.* In other companies, division managers are directed by top management to keep nonproductive assets, such as vacant land or construction in progress. In such cases, it is appropriate to exclude nonproductive assets from the measure of invested capital. Then *average total productive assets* is used to measure invested capital. If GreenMarket Food Stores had chosen this alternative, $17,000,000 would have been used in the ROI, residual-income, and EVA calculations (total assets of $18,000,000 less $1,000,000 for the plant under construction).

3. *Total assets less current liabilities.* Some companies allow division managers to secure short-term bank loans and other short-term credit. In such cases, invested capital often is measured by *average total assets less average current liabilities.* This approach encourages investment-center managers to minimize resources tied up in assets and maximize the use of short-term credit to finance operations. If this approach had been used by GreenMarket Food Stores, the Food Processing Division's invested capital would have been $17,000,000, total assets of $18,000,000 less current liabilities of $1,000,000. (Note that current liabilities are always subtracted from total assets for the measure of invested capital used in the EVA measure.)

Gross or Net Book Value   Another decision to make in choosing a measure of invested capital is whether to use the *gross book value (acquisition cost)* or the *net book value* of long-lived assets. (Net book value is the acquisition cost less accumulated depreciation.) GreenMarket Food Stores' management has decided to use the average net book value of $15,000,000 to value the Food Processing Division's long-lived assets. If gross book value had been used instead, the division's measure of invested capital would have been $22,000,000, as the following calculation shows.

Current assets	$ 2,000,000
Long-lived assets (at gross book value)	19,000,000
Plant under construction	1,000,000
Total assets (at gross book value)	$22,000,000

There are advantages and disadvantages associated with both gross and net book value as a measure of invested capital. The advantages of net book value are:

1. Using net book value maintains consistency with the balance sheet prepared for external reporting purposes. This allows for more meaningful comparisons of return-on-investment measures across different companies.

2. Using net book value to measure invested capital is also more consistent with the definition of income, which is the numerator in ROI calculations. In computing income, the current period's depreciation on long-lived assets is deducted as an expense.

Exhibit 13–3
Increase in ROI over Time
(when net book value is used)

GreenMarket
FOOD STORES

				Acquisition cost of equipment	$500,000

Acquisition cost of equipment $500,000

Useful life .... 5 years

Salvage value at end of useful life 0

Annual straight-line depreciation $100,000

Annual income generated by asset (before deducting depreciation) $150,000

Year	Income before Depreciation	Annual Depreciation	Income Net of Depreciation	Average Net Book Value*	ROI Based on Net Book Value†	Average Gross Book Value	ROI Based on Gross Book Value
1	$150,000	$100,000	$50,000	$450,000	11.1%	$500,000	10%
2	150,000	100,000	50,000	350,000	14.3	500,000	10
3	150,000	100,000	50,000	250,000	20.0	500,000	10
4	150,000	100,000	50,000	150,000	33.3	500,000	10
5	150,000	100,000	50,000	50,000	100.0	500,000	10

*Average net book value is the average of the beginning and ending balances for the year in net book value. In year 1, for example, the average net book value is

$$\frac{\$500,000 + \$400,000}{2}$$

†ROI rounded to nearest tenth of 1 percent.

The following two advantages are often associated with using gross book value:

1. The usual methods of computing depreciation, such as the straight-line and the declining-balance methods, are arbitrary. Hence, they should not be allowed to affect ROI, residual-income, or EVA calculations.

2. When long-lived assets are depreciated, their net book value declines over time. This results in a misleading increase in ROI, residual income, and EVA across time. Exhibit 13–3 provides an illustration of this phenomenon for the ROI calculated on an equipment purchase under consideration by the Food Processing Division manager. Notice that the ROI rises steadily across the five-year horizon if invested capital is measured by net book value. However, using gross book value eliminates this problem. If an accelerated depreciation method were used instead of the straight-line method, the increasing trend in ROI would be even more pronounced.

A Behavioral Problem   The tendency for net book value to produce a misleading increase in ROI over time can have a serious effect on the incentives of investment-center managers. Investment centers with old assets will show much higher ROIs than investment centers with relatively new assets. This can discourage investment-center managers from investing in new equipment. If this behavioral tendency persists, a division's assets can become obsolete, making the division uncompetitive.

Allocating Assets to Investment Centers   Some companies control certain assets centrally, although these assets are needed to carry on operations in the divisions. Common examples are cash and accounts receivable. Divisions need cash in order to operate, but many companies control cash balances centrally in order to minimize their total cash holdings. Some large retail firms manage accounts receivable centrally. A credit customer of some national department store chains can make a payment either at the local store or by mailing the payment to corporate headquarters.

When certain assets are controlled centrally, some allocation basis generally is chosen to allocate these asset balances to investment centers, for the purpose of measuring invested capital. For example, cash may be allocated based on the budgeted cash needs in each division or on the basis of divisional sales. Accounts receivable usually are allocated on the basis of divisional sales. Divisions with less stringent credit terms are allocated proportionately larger balances of accounts receivable.

Measuring Investment-Center Income

In addition to choosing a measure of investment-center capital, an accountant must also decide how to measure a center's income. The key issue is controllability; the choice involves the extent to which uncontrollable items are allowed to influence the income measure. The Excel spreadsheet in Exhibit 13–4 illustrates several different possibilities for measuring the income of GreenMarket Food Stores' Food Processing Division.

GreenMarket Food Stores' top management uses the *profit margin controllable by division manager,* $3,600,000, to evaluate the Food Processing Division manager. This profit measure is used in calculating ROI, residual income, or EVA. Some fixed costs traceable to the division have not been deducted from this $3,600,000 amount, but the division manager cannot control or significantly influence these costs. Hence they are excluded from the ROI calculation in evaluating the division manager. In calculating EVA, the $3,600,000 profit-margin amount is converted to an after-tax basis by multiplying it by 1 minus the tax rate of 30 percent.

Pay for Performance Some companies reward investment-center managers with **cash bonuses** if they meet a predetermined target on a specified performance criterion, such as residual income, ROI, or EVA. Such payments often are referred to as **pay for performance, merit pay,** or **incentive compensation.** These cash bonuses generally are single payments, independent of a manager's base salary.

As the result of public outrage over the recent nearly catastrophic financial meltdown, as well as other perceived corporate excesses, many companies are beginning to rein in top management compensation packages. World governments have also reacted, but with mixed results. While France and the Netherlands decided to restrict banker bonuses, a similar proposal by the G20 group of government ministers was defeated due to opposition by the United States and the United Kingdom. The United States did, however, appoint a representative to oversee top management compensation for the various companies that received funds from government coffers during the recent financial crisis.[4]

Exhibit 13–4
Divisional Income Statement: Food Processing Division

GreenMarket
FOOD STORES

			FOOD PROCESSING DIVISION					
			Divisional Income Statement					
4		Sales revenue						$9,000,000
5		Variable expenses						3,800,000
6 (1)		Divisional contribution margin						$5,200,000
7		Fixed expenses controllable by division manager						1,600,000
8 (2)		Profit margin controllable by division manager						$3,600,000
9		Fixed expenses, traceable to division, but controlled by others						1,200,000
10 (3)		Profit margin traceable to division						$2,400,000
11		Common fixed expenses, allocated from corporate headquarters						400,000
12 (4)		Divisional income before interest and taxes						$2,000,000
13		Interest expense allocated from corporate headquarters						250,000
14 (5)		Divisional income before taxes						$1,750,000
15		Income taxes allocated from corporate headquarters						700,000
16 (6)		Divisional net income						$1,050,000

Microsoft Excel - Divisional Income Statement - Food Processing Division

File Edit View Insert Format Tools Data Window Help

H16   *fx* =H14-H15

---

[4]See, for example, G. Chazan, "Shell Plans to Reduce Executive Salaries," *The Wall Street Journal,* February 17, 2010, p. B1; K. Chibber, "Bonus Reform: Country by Country," *BBC News,* September 17, 2009; and D. Brady, "The Pay Czar on the End of His Empire," *Bloomberg Businessweek,* January 4, 2010, p. 15.

Managers versus Investment Centers It is important to make a distinction between an investment center and its manager. In evaluating the *manager's* performance, only revenues and costs that the manager can control or significantly influence should be included in the profit measure. Remember that the overall objective of the performance measure is to provide incentives for goal-congruent behavior. No performance measure can motivate a manager to make decisions about costs he or she cannot control. This explains why GreenMarket Food Stores' top management relies on the profit margin controllable by division manager to compute the manager's ROI performance measure.

Evaluating the Food Processing Division as a viable economic investment is a different matter altogether. In this evaluation, traceability of costs, rather than controllability, is the issue. For this purpose, GreenMarket Food Stores' top management uses the profit margin traceable to division to compute the divisional ROI, residual income, or EVA. As Exhibit 13–4 shows, this amount is $2,400,000.

Other Profit Measures The other measures of divisional profit shown in Exhibit 13–4 (lines 4, 5, and 6) also are used by some companies. The rationale behind these divisional income measures is that all corporate costs have to be covered by the operations of the divisions. Allocating corporate costs, interest, and income taxes to the divisions makes division managers aware of these costs.

Inflation: Historical-Cost versus Current-Value Accounting

Whether measuring investment-center income or invested capital, the impact of price-level changes should not be forgotten. During periods of inflation, historical-cost asset values soon cease to reflect the cost of replacing those assets. Therefore, some accountants argue that investment-center performance measures based on historical-cost accounting are misleading. Yet surveys of corporate managers indicate that an accounting system based on current values would not alter their decisions. Most managers believe that measures based on historical-cost accounting are adequate when used in conjunction with budgets and performance targets. As managers prepare those budgets, they build their expectations about inflation into the budgets and performance targets.

Another reason for using historical-cost accounting for internal purposes is that it is required for external reporting. Thus, historical-cost data already are available, while installing current-value accounting would add substantial incremental costs to the organization's information system.

Other Issues in Segment Performance Evaluation

Alternatives to ROI, Residual Income, and Economic Value Added (EVA)

ROI, residual income, and EVA are short-run performance measures. They focus on only one period of time. Yet an investment center is really a collection of assets (investments), each of which has a multiperiod life. Exhibit 13–5 portrays this perspective of an investment center.

To evaluate any one of these individual investments correctly requires a multiperiod viewpoint, which takes into account the timing of the cash flows from the investment. For example, investment E in Exhibit 13–5 may start out slowly in years 4 and 5, but it may be economically justified by its expected high performance in years 8, 9, and 10. Any evaluation of the investment center in year 5 that ignores the long-term performance of its various investments can result in a misleading conclusion. Thus, single-period

Exhibit 13–5
Investment Center Viewed as
a Collection of Investments

Assets or investments
comprising investment center

performance measures suffer from myopia. They focus on only a short time segment that slices across the division's investments as portrayed in Exhibit 13–5.

To avoid this short-term focus, some organizations downplay ROI, residual income, and EVA in favor of an alternative approach. Instead of relating profit to invested capital in a single measure, these characteristics of investment-center performance are evaluated separately. Actual divisional profit for a time period is compared to a flexible budget, and variances are used to analyze performance. The division's major investments are evaluated through a *postaudit* of the investment decisions. For example, investment E may have been undertaken because of expected high performance in years 8, 9, and 10. When that time comes, a review will determine whether the project lived up to expectations.

Evaluating periodic profit through flexible budgeting and variance analysis, coupled with postaudits of major investment decisions, is a more complicated approach to evaluating investment centers. However, it does help management avoid the myopia of single-period measures such as ROI, residual income, and EVA.

Importance of Nonfinancial Information

Although financial measures such as segment profit, ROI, residual income, and EVA are widely used in performance evaluation, nonfinancial measures are important also. Manufacturers collect data on rates of defective products, airlines record information on lost bags and aircraft delays, and hotels keep track of occupancy rates. The proper evaluation of an organization and its segments requires that multiple performance measures be defined and used. The *balanced scorecard,* with its *lead* and *lag measures* of performance, is one tool that is more and more widely used as a means of introducing nonfinancial measures into performance evaluation. See Chapter 10 for a discussion of the balanced scorecard.

Measuring Performance in Nonprofit Organizations

Management control in a nonprofit organization presents a special challenge. Such organizations often are managed by professionals, such as physicians in a hospital. Moreover, many people participate in a nonprofit organization at some personal sacrifice, motivated by humanitarian or public service ideals. Often, such people are less receptive to formal control procedures than their counterparts in business.

The goals of nonprofit organizations often are less clear-cut than those of businesses. Public service objectives may be difficult to specify with precision and even more difficult to measure in terms of achievement. For example, one community health center was established in an economically depressed area with three stated goals:

1. To reduce costs in a nearby hospital by providing a clinic for people to use instead of the hospital emergency room.
2. To provide preventive as well as therapeutic care, and establish outreach programs in the community.
3. To become financially self-sufficient.

There is some conflict between these objectives, since goal 2 does not provide revenue to the center, while goals 1 and 3 focus on financial efficiency. Moreover, the health center was staffed with physicians who could have achieved much greater incomes in private practice. The management control tools described in this and the preceding three chapters can be used in nonprofit organizations. However, the challenges in doing so effectively often are greater.

Transfer Pricing

Measuring performance in profit centers or investment centers is made more complicated by transfers of goods or services between responsibility centers. The amount charged when one division sells goods or services to another division is called a *transfer price.* This price affects the profit measurement for both the selling division and the buying division. A high transfer price results in high profit for the selling division and low profit for the buying division. A low transfer price has the opposite effect. Consequently, the transfer-pricing policy *can* affect the *incentives* of autonomous division managers as they decide whether to make the transfer. Exhibit 13–6 depicts this scenario.

Goal Congruence

What should be management's goal in setting transfer prices for internally transferred goods or services? In a decentralized organization, the managers of profit centers and investment centers often have considerable autonomy in deciding whether to accept or reject orders and whether to buy inputs from inside the organization or from outside. For example, a large manufacturer of farm equipment allows its Assembly Division managers to buy parts either from another division of the company or from independent manufacturers. The goal in setting transfer prices is to establish incentives for autonomous division managers to make decisions that support the overall goals of the organization.

Suppose it is in the best interests of GreenMarket Food Stores for the baked goods produced by the Food Processing Division's Seoul Bakery to be transferred to the Regional Division's stores elsewhere in the country. Thus, if the firm were centralized, bakery products would be transferred from the Food Processing Division to the Regional Division. However, GreenMarket Food Stores is a decentralized company, and the Regional Division manager is free to buy baked goods either from the Food Processing Division or from an outside bakery company. Similarly, the Food Processing Division manager is free to accept or reject an order for baked goods, at any given price, from the Regional Division. The goal of the company's controller in setting the transfer price is to provide incentives for each of these division managers to act in the company's best interests.

The transfer price should be chosen so that each division manager, when striving to maximize his or her own division's profit, makes the decision that maximizes the company's profit.

Transfer pricing is widely used in all kinds of businesses. When the wings for this Emirates Airlines airplane were transferred from the Airbus factory in Broughton, Wales, to the A380 assembly plant in Toulouse, France, a transfer price was specified.

Exhibit 13–6
The Transfer-Pricing Scenario

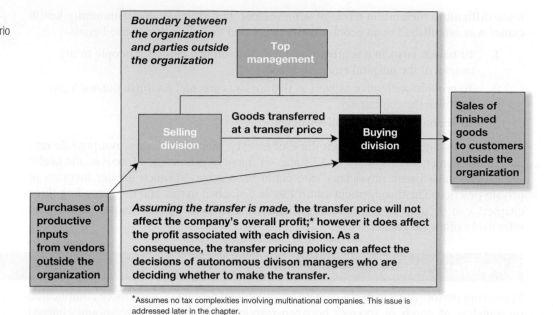

Boundary between the organization and parties outside the organization

Top management

Selling division

Goods transferred at a transfer price

Buying division

Sales of finished goods to customers outside the organization

Purchases of productive inputs from vendors outside the organization

Assuming the transfer is made, the transfer price will not affect the company's overall profit;* however it does affect the profit associated with each division. As a consequence, the transfer pricing policy can affect the decisions of autonomous divison managers who are deciding whether to make the transfer.

*Assumes no tax complexities involving multinational companies. This issue is addressed later in the chapter.

General Transfer-Pricing Rule

Management's objective in setting a transfer price is to encourage goal congruence among the division managers involved in the transfer. A general rule that will ensure goal congruence is given below.

$$\text{Transfer price} = \begin{array}{c}\text{Additional } \textit{outlay cost} \\ \text{per unit incurred because} \\ \text{good are transferred}\end{array} + \begin{array}{c}\textit{Opportunity cost} \text{ per unit} \\ \text{to the organization} \\ \text{because of the transfer}\end{array}$$

The general rule specifies the transfer price as the sum of two cost components. The first component is the outlay cost incurred by the division that produces the goods or services to be transferred. Outlay costs will include the direct variable costs of the product or service and any other outlay costs that are incurred only as a result of the transfer. The second component in the general transfer-pricing rule is the opportunity cost incurred by the organization as a whole because of the transfer. Recall from Chapter 2 that an *opportunity cost* is a benefit that is forgone as a result of taking a particular action.

"Transfer pricing is a business issue as well as a tax issue that should be considered in the board room." (13c)

Ernst & Young

We will illustrate the general transfer-pricing rule for GreenMarket Food Stores. The company's Food Processing Division produces bread in its Seoul bakery. The division transfers some of its products to the company's Capital and Regional divisions, and sells some of its products to other companies in the *external market* under different labels.

Bread is transported to stores in racks containing one dozen loaves of packaged bread. In the Seoul bakery, the following variable costs are incurred to produce bread and transport it to a buyer.

Production:
    Standard variable cost per rack (including packaging)....... $7.00
Transportation:
    Standard variable cost per rack to transport bread........... .25

In applying the general transfer-pricing rule, we will distinguish between two different scenarios.

Scenario I: No Excess Capacity

Suppose the Food Processing Division can sell all the bread it can produce to outside buyers at a market price of $11 per rack. Since the division can sell all of its production, it has *no excess capacity. Excess capacity* exists only when more goods can be produced than the producer is able to sell, due to low demand for the product.

What transfer price does the general rule yield under this scenario of no excess capacity? The transfer price is determined as follows:

Outlay cost:

Standard variable cost of production	$ 7.00 per rack
Standard variable cost of transportation	.25 per rack
Total outlay cost	$ 7.25 per rack

Opportunity cost:

Selling price per unit in external market	$11.00 per rack
Less: Variable cost of production and transportation	7.25 per rack
Opportunity cost (forgone contribution margin)	$ 3.75 per rack

General transfer-pricing rule:

Transfer price	=	Outlay cost	+	Opportunity cost
$11.00	=	$7.25	+	$3.75

The *outlay cost* incurred by the Food Processing Division in order to transfer a rack of bread includes the standard variable production cost of $7.00 and the standard variable transportation cost of $.25. The *opportunity cost* incurred by GreenMarket Food Stores when its Food Processing Division transfers a rack of bread to the Regional Division *instead* of selling it in the external market is the forgone contribution margin from the lost sale, equal to $3.75. Why does the company lose a sale in the external market for every rack of bread transferred to the Regional Division? The sale is lost because there is *no excess capacity* in the Food Processing Division. Every rack of bread transferred to another company division results in one less rack of bread sold in the external market.

Goal Congruence

How does the general transfer-pricing rule promote goal congruence? Suppose the Regional Division's grocery stores can sell a loaf of bread for $1.50, or $18 for a rack of 12 loaves ($18 = 12 × $1.50). What is the best way for GreenMarket Food Stores to use the limited production capacity in the Food Processing Division's Seoul bakery? The answer is determined as follows:

Contribution to GreenMarket Food Stores from Sale in External Market		**Contribution to GreenMarket Food Stores from Transfer to Regional Division**	
Wholesale selling price per rack	$11.00	Retail selling price per rack	$18.00
Less: Variable costs	7.25	Less: Variable costs	7.25
Contribution margin	$ 3.75	Contribution margin	$10.75

The best use of the bakery's limited production capacity is to produce bread for transfer to the Regional Division. If the transfer price is set at $11.00, as the general rule specifies, goal congruence is maintained. The Food Processing Division manager is willing to transfer bread to the Regional Division, because the transfer price of $11.00 is equal to the external market price. The Regional Division manager is willing to buy the bread, because her division will have a contribution margin of $7.00 on each rack of bread transferred ($18.00 sales price minus the $11.00 transfer price).

Now consider a different situation. Suppose a local organization makes a special offer to the Regional Division manager to buy several hundred loaves of bread to sell in a promotional campaign. The organization offers to pay $.80 per loaf, which is $9.60 per rack of a dozen loaves. What will the Regional Division manager do? She must pay a transfer price of $11.00 per rack, so the Regional Division would lose $1.40 per rack if the special offer were accepted ($1.40 = $11.00 − $9.60). The Regional Division manager will decline the special offer. Is this decision in the best interests of GreenMarket Food Stores as a whole? If the offer were accepted, the company as a whole would make a positive contribution of $2.35 per rack, as shown below.

Contribution to GreenMarket Food Stores If Special Offer Is Accepted

Special price per rack	$9.60 per rack
Less: Variable cost to company	7.25 per rack
Contribution to company, per rack	$2.35 per rack

However, the company can make even more if its Food Processing Division sells bread directly in its external market. Then the contribution to the company is $3.75, as we have just seen. (The external market price of $11.00 per rack minus a variable cost of $7.25 per rack equals $3.75 per rack.) Thus, GreenMarket Food Stores is better off, as a whole, if the Regional Division's special offer is rejected. Once again, the general transfer-pricing rule results in goal-congruent decision making.

Scenario II: Excess Capacity

Now let's change our basic assumption, and suppose the Food Processing Division's Seoul bakery has excess production capacity. This means that the total demand for its bread from all sources, including the Regional and Capital divisions and the external market, is less than the bakery's production capacity. Under this scenario of excess capacity, what does the general rule specify for a transfer price?

$$\text{Transfer price} = \text{Outlay cost} + \text{Opportunity cost}$$
$$\$7.25 = \$7.25 + 0$$

The *outlay cost* in the Food Processing Division's Seoul bakery is still $7.25, since it does not depend on whether there is idle capacity or not. The *opportunity cost,* however, is now zero. There is no opportunity cost to the company when a rack of bread is transferred to the Regional Division, because the Food Processing Division can still satisfy all of its external demand for bread. Thus, the general rule specifies a transfer price of $7.25, the total standard variable cost of production and transportation.

Goal Congruence

Let's reconsider what will happen when the Regional Division manager receives the local organization's special offer to buy bread at $9.60 per rack. The Regional Division will now show a positive contribution of $2.35 per rack on the special order.

Special price per rack	$9.60 per rack
Less: Transfer price paid by Regional Division	7.25 per rack
Contribution to Regional Division	$2.35 per rack

The Regional Division manager will accept the special offer. This decision is also in the best interests of GreenMarket Food Stores. The company, as a whole, also will make a contribution of $2.35 per rack on every rack transferred to the Regional Division to satisfy the special order. Once again, the general transfer-pricing rule maintains goal-congruent decision-making behavior.

Notice that the general rule yields a transfer price that leaves the Food Processing Division manager indifferent as to whether the transfer will be made. At a transfer price of $7.25, the contribution to the Food Processing Division will be zero (transfer price of $7.25 less variable cost of $7.25). To avoid this problem, we can view the general rule as providing a lower bound on the transfer price. Some companies allow the producing division to add a markup to this lower bound in order to provide a positive contribution margin. This in turn provides a positive incentive to make the transfer.

> "It is difficult for people 'doing the business' to stop and consult about the transfer pricing implications of their moves, but they have to." (13d)
>
> **Respondent, Ernst & Young Survey**

Difficulty in Implementing the General Rule The general transfer-pricing rule will always promote goal-congruent decision making *if the rule can be implemented.* However, the rule is often difficult or impossible to implement due to the difficulty of measuring opportunity costs. Such a cost-measurement problem can arise for a number of reasons. One reason is that the external market may not be perfectly competitive. Under **perfect competition,** the market price does not depend on the quantity sold by any one producer. Under **imperfect competition,** a single producer or group of producers can affect the market price by varying the amount of product available in the market. In such cases, the external market price depends on the production decisions of the producer. This in turn means that the opportunity cost incurred by the company as a result of internal transfers depends on the quantity sold externally. These interactions may make it impossible to measure accurately the opportunity cost caused by a product transfer.

Other reasons for difficulty in measuring the opportunity cost associated with a product transfer include uniqueness of the transferred goods or services, a need for the producing division to invest in special equipment in order to produce the transferred goods, and interdependencies among several transferred products or services. For example, the producing division may provide design services as well as production of the goods for a buying division. What is the opportunity cost associated with each of these related outputs of the producing division? In many such cases, it is difficult to sort out the opportunity costs.

The general transfer-pricing rule provides a good conceptual model for the managerial accountant to use in setting transfer prices. Moreover, in many cases, it can be implemented. When the general rule cannot be implemented, organizations turn to other transfer-pricing methods, as we shall see next.

Transfers Based on the External Market Price

A common approach is to set the transfer price equal to the price in the external market. In the GreenMarket Food Stores illustration, the Food Processing Division would set the transfer price for bread at $11.00 per rack, since that is the price the division can obtain in its external market. When the producing division has no excess capacity and perfect competition prevails, where no single producer can affect the market price, the general transfer-pricing rule and the external market price yield the same transfer price. This fact is illustrated for GreenMarket Food Stores as follows:

Learning Objective 7

Explain how to base a transfer price on market prices, costs, or negotiations.

$$\text{Transfer price} = \text{Outlay cost} + \text{Opportunity cost}$$

$$= \begin{array}{c}\text{Variable cost of} \\ \text{production and} \\ \text{transportation}\end{array} + \begin{array}{c}\text{Forgone contribution} \\ \text{margin of an external} \\ \text{sale}\end{array}$$

$$= \$7.25 + (\$11.00 - \$7.25) = \$11.00$$

Transfer price = External market price = $11.00

If the producing division has excess capacity or the external market is imperfectly competitive, the general rule and the external market price will not yield the same transfer price.

If the transfer price is set at the market price, the producing division should have the option of either producing goods for internal transfer or selling in the external market. The buying division should be required to purchase goods from inside its organization if the producing division's goods meet the product specifications. Otherwise, the buying division should have the autonomy to buy from a supplier outside its own organization. To handle pricing disputes that may arise, an arbitration process should be established.

Transfer prices based on market prices are consistent with the responsibility-accounting concepts of profit centers and investment centers. In addition to encouraging division managers to focus on divisional profitability, market-based transfer prices help to show the contribution of each division to overall company profit. Suppose the Food Processing Division of GreenMarket Food Stores transfers bread to the Regional Division at a market-based transfer price of $11.00 per rack. The following contribution margins will be earned by the two divisions and the company as a whole.

Food Processing Division		Regional Division	
Transfer price	$11.00 per rack	Retail sales price	$18.00 per rack
Less: Variable costs	7.25 per rack	Less: Transfer price	11.00 per rack
Contribution margin	$ 3.75 per rack	Contribution margin	$ 7.00 per rack

GreenMarket Food Stores	
Retail sales price	$18.00 per rack
Less: Variable costs	7.25 per rack
Contribution margin	$10.75 per rack

When aggregate divisional profits are determined for the year, and ROI and residual income are computed, the use of a market-based transfer price helps to assess the contributions of each division to overall corporate profits.

Distress Market Prices   Occasionally an industry will experience a period of significant excess capacity and extremely low prices. For example, when gasoline prices soared due to a foreign oil embargo, the market prices for recreational vehicles and power boats fell temporarily to very low levels.

Under such extreme conditions, basing transfer prices on market prices can lead to decisions that are not in the best interests of the overall company. Basing transfer prices on artificially *low distress market prices* could lead the producing division to sell or close the productive resources devoted to producing the product for transfer. Under distress market prices, the producing division manager might prefer to move the division into a more profitable product line. While such a decision might improve the division's profit in the short run, it could be contrary to the best interests of the company overall. It might be better for the company as a whole to avoid divesting itself of any productive resources and to ride out the period of market distress. To encourage an autonomous division manager to act in this fashion, some companies set the transfer price equal to the long-run average external market price, rather than the current (possibly depressed) market price.

Negotiated Transfer Prices

Many companies use negotiated transfer prices. Division managers or their representatives actually negotiate the price at which transfers will be made. Sometimes they start with the external market price and then make adjustments for various reasons. For example, the producing division may enjoy some cost savings on internal transfers that are not obtained on external sales. Commissions may not have to be paid to sales personnel on internally transferred products. In such cases, a negotiated transfer price may split the cost savings between the producing and buying divisions.

In other instances, a negotiated transfer price may be used because no external market exists for the transferred product.

Two drawbacks sometimes characterize negotiated transfer prices. First, negotiations can lead to divisiveness and competition between participating division managers. This can undermine the spirit of cooperation and unity that is desirable throughout an organization. Second, although negotiating skill is a valuable managerial talent, it should not be the sole or dominant factor in evaluating a division manager. If, for example, the producing division's manager is a better negotiator than the buying division's manager, then the producing division's profit may look better than it should, simply because of its manager's superior negotiating ability.

Cost-Based Transfer Prices

Organizations that do not base prices on market prices or negotiations often turn to a cost-based transfer-pricing approach.

Variable Cost One approach is to set the transfer price equal to the standard variable cost. The problem with this approach is that even when the producing division has excess capacity, it is not allowed to show any contribution margin on the transferred products or services. To illustrate, suppose the Food Processing Division has excess capacity and the transfer price is set at the standard variable cost of $7.25 per rack of bread. There is no positive incentive for the division to produce and transfer bread to the Regional Division. The Food Processing Division's contribution margin from a transfer will be zero (transfer price of $7.25 minus variable costs of $7.25 equals zero). Some companies avoid this problem by setting the transfer price at standard variable cost plus a markup to allow the producing division a positive contribution margin.

Full Cost An alternative is to set the transfer price equal to the *full cost* of the transferred product or service. **Full** (or **absorption**) **cost** is equal to the product's variable cost plus an allocated portion of fixed overhead.

Suppose the Food Processing Division's Seoul bakery has budgeted annual fixed overhead of $500,000 and budgeted annual production of 200,000 racks of bread. The full cost of the bakery's product is computed as follows:

$$\text{Full cost} = \text{Variable cost} + \text{Allocated fixed overhead}$$

$$= \$7.25 \text{ per rack} + \frac{\$500,000 \text{ budgeted fixed overhead}}{200,000 \text{ budgeted racks of bread}}$$

$$= \$7.25 + \$2.50$$

$$= \$9.75 \text{ per rack}$$

Under this approach, the transfer price is set at $9.75 per rack of bread.

Dysfunctional Decision-Making Behavior Basing transfer prices on full cost entails a serious risk of causing dysfunctional decision-making behavior. Full-cost-based transfer prices lead the buying division to view costs that are fixed for the company as a whole as variable costs to the buying division. This can cause faulty decision making.

To illustrate, suppose the Food Processing Division has excess capacity, and the transfer price of bread is equal to the full cost of $9.75 per rack. What will happen if the Regional Division receives the special offer discussed previously, where it can sell bread to a local organization at a special price of $9.60 per rack? The Regional Division manager will reject the special order, since otherwise her division would incur a loss of $.15 per rack.

Special price per rack	$9.60 per rack
Less: Transfer price based on full cost	9.75 per rack
Loss	$ .15 per rack

What is in the best interests of the company as a whole? GreenMarket Food Stores would make a positive contribution of $2.35 per rack on the bread sold in the special order.

Special price per rack	$9.60 per rack
Less: Variable cost in Food Processing Division	7.25 per rack
Contribution to company as a whole	$2.35 per rack

What has happened here? Setting the transfer price equal to the full cost of $9.75 has turned a cost that is fixed in the Food Processing Division, and hence is fixed for the company as a whole, into a variable cost from the viewpoint of the Regional Division manager. The manager would tend to reject the special offer, even though accepting it would benefit the company as a whole.

Although the practice is common, transfer prices should not be based on full cost. The risk is too great that the cost behavior in the producing division will be obscured. This can all too easily result in poor decisions in the buying division.

Standard versus Actual Costs

Throughout our discussion of transfer prices, we have used standard costs rather than actual costs. This was true in our discussion of the general transfer-pricing rule as well as for cost-based transfer prices. Transfer prices should not be based on actual costs, because such a practice would allow an inefficient producing division to pass its excess production costs on to the buying division in the transfer price. When standard costs are used in transfer-pricing formulas, the buying division is not forced to pick up the tab for the producer's inefficiency. Moreover, the producing division is given an incentive to control its costs, since any costs of inefficiency cannot be passed on.

Undermining Divisional Autonomy

Suppose the manager of GreenMarket Food Stores' Food Processing Division has excess capacity but insists on a transfer price of $9.75, based on full cost. The Regional Division manager is faced with the special offer for bread at $9.60 per rack. She regrets that she will have to decline the offer because it would cause her division's profit to decline, even though the company's interests would be best served by accepting the special order. The Regional Division manager calls the company president and explains the situation. She asks the president to intervene and force the Food Processing Division manager to lower his transfer price.

As the company president, what would you do? If you stay out of the controversy, your company will lose the contribution on the special order. If you intervene, you will run the risk of undermining the autonomy of your division managers. You established a decentralized organization structure for GreenMarket Food Stores and hired competent managers because you believed in the benefits of decentralized decision making.

There is no obvious answer to this dilemma. In practice, central managers are reluctant to intervene in such disputes unless the negative financial consequences to the organization are quite large. Most managers believe the benefits of decentralized decision making are important to protect, even if it means an occasional dysfunctional decision.

An International Perspective

The discussion above focuses on the use of transfer prices for aligning incentives and measuring performance. However, when goods or services are transferred between divisions of a company that are located in different countries, the company may have an incentive to set transfer prices to minimize the overall tax exposure of the company. And this incentive may be so strong that it overrides the approaches to setting transfer prices discussed earlier.

Income-Tax Rates   For example, suppose a company based in Europe has divisions in Europe and Asia. A European division produces a subassembly, which is transferred to an Asian division for assembly and sale of the final product. Suppose also that the income-tax rate for the European division is higher than the rate in the Asian division's country. How would these different tax rates affect the transfer price for the subassembly?

The company's management has an incentive to set a low transfer price for the subassembly. The low price for the European division's subassembly will result in relatively low profits for the company's European division, which is desirable due to the relatively high tax rate applied to profits in the European country. In turn, the low subassembly price from Europe results in a reduced materials cost to the Asian division. This yields a relatively high income for the Asian division. Since the tax rate is lower in the Asian country, the overall company will save on income tax. By setting a low transfer price, the

"[Transfer pricing] affects nearly every aspect of multinational operations—R&D, manufacturing, marketing and distribution, after-sale services." (13e)
Ernst & Young

"Transfer pricing has become the most difficult area of international taxation." (13f)
Ernst & Young

TRANSFER PRICING AND TAX ISSUES

The most difficult transfer-pricing issues arise in multinational corporations because of the complexity of the tax issues involved. According to a survey by Ernst & Young LLP, "transfer pricing is the top tax issue facing multinational corporations. Of the international tax directors at 582 multinational organizations polled in the survey, 75 percent expect their company to face a transfer-pricing audit within the next two years. Respondents cited related-party transactions (including the intercompany transfer of goods, services, properties, loans, and leases) involving administrative and management services as the most likely to be audited. Moreover, there has been an increase in transfer pricing audit activity in recent years.[5]

The Organization for Economic Cooperation and Development (OECD) notes that "Transfer pricing can deprive governments of their fair share of taxes from global corporations and expose multinationals to possible double taxation. No country—poor, emerging, or wealthy—wants its tax base to suffer because of transfer pricing . . . In a bid to avoid such problems, current OECD international guidelines are based on the armís length principle—that a transfer price should be the same as if the two companies involved were indeed two independents, not part of the same corporate structure."[6]

In the United States, the taxing authority takes a similar perspective.

"The Internal Revenue Service (IRS) is concerned that companies could use transfer prices to shift profits between related entities through cost of goods sold. Thus, transfer pricing manipulation could be used by taxpayers to shift income from high tax jurisdictions like the United States to low tax jurisdictions. The right price from the IRS's perspective is the market value price. Because it's difficult to prove that the transfer price was equal to the market price, companies often find themselves in disputes with the IRS. But now there's help. The IRS's Advanced Pricing Agreement Program provides companies an opportunity to avoid costly audits and litigation by allowing them to negotiate a prospective agreement with the IRS regarding the facts, the transfer pricing methodology, and an acceptable range of results. The program is aimed at multinational corporations interested in avoiding penalties, managing risk, and determining their tax liability with certainty."[7]

company will shift a portion of its income to a country with a lower tax rate. Tax laws vary among countries with regard to flexibility in setting transfer prices. Because of the potential for loss of tax revenue, most countries with relatively high tax rates have laws prohibiting the behavior described in our example.

Import Duties   Another international issue that can affect a firm's transfer pricing policy is the imposition of import duties, or tariffs. These are fees charged to an importer, generally on the basis of the reported value of the goods being imported. Consider again the example of a firm with divisions in Europe and Asia. If the Asian country imposes an import duty on goods transferred in from the European division, the company has an incentive to set a relatively low transfer price on the transferred goods. This will minimize

---

[5]Mahendra Gujarathi, "GlaxoSmithkline Plc.: International Transfer Pricing and Taxation," *Issues in Accounting Education* 22, no. 4 (November 2007), pp. 749–759; and Eric Krell, "Scrutiny of Transfer Pricing Grows," *Business Finance* 6, no. 4 (August 2000), p. 12.

[6]John Neighbor, "Transfer Pricing: Keeping it at Arm's Length," *OECD Observer* 230 (January 2002, updated July 2008).

[7]Steven C. Wrappe, Ken Milani, and Julie Joy, "The Transfer Price Is Right," *Strategic Finance* 81, no. 1 (July 1999), p. 40.

the duty to be paid and maximize the overall profit for the company as a whole. As in the case of taxation, countries sometimes pass laws to limit a multinational firm's flexibility in setting transfer prices for the purpose of minimizing import duties.

Transfer prices are used in the service industry as well as in manufacturing. Cornell University, for example, charges an accessory instruction fee to a campus unit when one of its students enrolls in a course offered in a different unit.

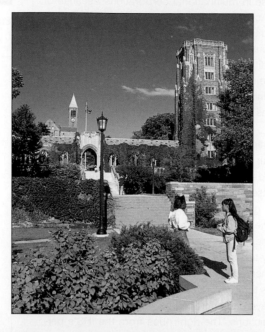

Transfer Pricing in the Service Industry

Service industry firms and nonprofit organizations also use transfer pricing when services are transferred between responsibility centers. In banks, for example, the interest rate at which depositors' funds are transferred to the loan department is a form of transfer price. At Cornell University, if a student in the law school takes a course in the business school, a transfer price is charged to the law school for the credit hours of instruction provided to the law student. Since the transfer price is based on tuition charges, it is a market-price-based transfer price.

Behavioral Issues: Risk Aversion and Incentives

Understand the behavioral issues of incentives, goal congruence, and internal controls.

The designer of a performance-evaluation system for responsibility-center managers must consider many factors. Trade-offs often must be made between competing objectives. The overall objective is to achieve goal congruence by providing *incentives* for managers to act in the best interests of the organization as a whole. Financial performance measures such as divisional income, ROI, and residual income go a long way toward achieving this objective. However, these measures do have the disadvantage of imposing *risk* on a manager, because the measures also are affected by factors beyond the manager's control. For example, the income of an orange-growing division of an agricultural company will be affected not only by the manager's diligence and ability, but also by the weather and insect infestations.

Since most people exhibit *risk aversion,* managers must be compensated for the risk they must bear. This compensation comes in the form of higher salaries or bonuses. Thus, the design of a managerial performance evaluation and reward system involves a trade-off between the following two factors:

Evaluation of a manager on the basis of financial performance measures, which provide incentives for the manager to act in the organization's interests.

Imposition of risk on a manager who exhibits risk aversion, because financial performance measures are controllable only partially by the manager.

Trade-offs in designing
managerial performance
evaluation and reward system.

Achieving the optimal trade-off between risk and incentives is a delicate balancing act that requires the skill and experience of top management.

Goal Congruence and Internal Control Systems

Although most business professionals have high ethical standards, there are unfortunately those who will cut corners. An **internal control system** is designed to provide reasonable assurance of the achievement of objectives in: (1) the effectiveness and efficiency of operations; (2) reliability of financial reporting; and (3) compliance with laws and regulations. Internal control procedures are designed to prevent the major lapses in responsible behavior described below.

Fraud   Theft or misuse of an organization's resources constitutes *fraud*. To prevent and detect fraud, organizations establish well-defined procedures that prescribe how valuable resources will be handled. For example, many organizations require all checks above a particular amount to be authorized by two people.

Financial Misrepresentation   Internal control systems also are designed to prevent managers from intentionally (or accidentally) misstating an organization's financial records. Most companies have an *internal audit* staff, which reviews financial records throughout the organization to ensure their accuracy. (Appendix I explores the Sarbanes-Oxley Act and other governmental regulations affecting internal controls over financial reporting.)

Corruption   Activities such as bribery, deceit, illegal political campaign contributions, and kickbacks constitute *corruption*. Most organizations have internal control procedures and codes of conduct to prevent and detect corrupt practices. For example, many organizations forbid their purchasing personnel from accepting gifts or gratuities from the sales personnel with whom they conduct business. In the United States, the Foreign Corrupt Practices Act (FCPA) prohibits U.S. companies (and other companies whose stock is listed on U.S. stock exchanges) from paying bribes to influence foreign officials and imposes accounting and record-keeping requirements on the companies. Violators are subject to civil and criminal penalties at the corporate and personal levels.

In addition, the Organization for Economic Cooperation and Development (OECD) has adopted a "Convention on Combating Bribery," and most recently, the United Nations has approved its "Convention Against Corruption." These documents, both modeled on the FCPA, together form the basis and model for anticorruption legislation being adopted by member countries.[8]

Unauthorized Action   Sometimes a well-meaning employee is tempted to take an action that is not illegal or even unethical, but it is contrary to the organization's policies. Internal control procedures also are designed to detect and prevent unauthorized actions by an organization's employees, when those actions could reflect unfavorably on the organization. For example, a company may prohibit its employees from using company facilities for a rally in support of a controversial social cause.

An internal control system constitutes an integral part of an organization's efforts to achieve its goals. To be effective, internal control procedures require top management's full support and intolerance of intentional violations.

---

[8]David C. Weiss, "The Foreign Corrupt Practices Act, SEC Disgorgement of Profits, and the Evolving International Bribery Regime: Weighing Proportionality, Retribution, and Deterrence," *Michigan Journal of International Law* 30 (2009), p. 471.

Chapter Summary

LO1 Explain the role of managerial accounting in achieving goal congruence. An important objective of any organization's managerial accounting system is to promote goal congruence among its employees. Thus, the primary criterion for judging the effectiveness of performance measures for responsibility-center managers is the extent to which the measures promote goal congruence.

LO2 Compute an investment center's return on investment (ROI), residual income (RI), and economic value added (EVA). An investment center's ROI is equal to its income divided by its invested capital. The investment center's RI is equal to its profit minus the product of its invested capital and an imputed interest rate. The investment center's EVA is computed as follows: After-tax operating income − [(Total assets − Current liabilities) × Weighted-average cost of capital].

LO3 Explain how a manager can improve ROI by increasing either the sales margin or capital turnover. An investment center's ROI equals sales margin multiplied by capital turnover. Therefore, an investment center's ROI may be improved by increasing either the sales margin or capital turnover.

LO4 Describe some advantages and disadvantages of both ROI and residual income as divisional performance measures. Each of these performance measures relates an investment center's income to the capital invested to earn it. However, residual income and EVA have the additional advantage of incorporating the organization's cost of acquiring capital in the performance measure.

LO5 Explain how to measure a division's income and invested capital. There are several ways that investment centers' invested capital is measured in practice. Among the commonly observed measures are: total assets, total productive assets, and total assets less current liabilities. Similarly, several measures of investment center income are observed in practice. As explained in the chapter, these income measures differ on the degree to which certain expenses are controllable at the investment center level.

LO6 Use the general economic rule to set an optimal transfer price. The general rule states that the transfer price should be equal to the outlay cost incurred to make the transfer plus the organization's opportunity cost associated with the transfer.

LO7 Explain how to base a transfer price on market prices, costs, or negotiations. Due to difficulties in implementing the general transfer pricing rule, most companies base transfer prices on external market prices, costs, or negotiations. Market prices may be the best practical measure, as long as an external market for the transferred product exists. Alternatively, transfer prices may be based on full, absorption product costs or variable product costs. Negotiation, although widely used in setting transfer prices, can be time-consuming and divisive.

LO8 Understand the behavioral issues of incentives, goal congruence, and internal controls. In general, companies use investment center performance measures and transfer pricing methods to provide incentives to managers to make goal-congruent decisions. In some cases, both investment center performance measures and transfer prices may result in dysfunctional decisions by mid-level managers. Top management then must weigh the benefits of intervening to prevent suboptimal decisions and the costs of undermining divisional autonomy. Internal controls also are used in organizations to promote the effectiveness and efficiency of operations, the reliability of financial reporting, and compliance with laws and regulations.

Review Problems on Investment Centers and Transfer Pricing

Problem 1

Stellar Systems Company manufactures guidance systems for rockets used to launch commercial satellites. The company's Software Division reported the following results for 20x7.

Income	$ 300,000
Sales revenue	2,000,000
Invested capital (total assets)	3,000,000
Average balance in current liabilities	20,000

Stellar Systems' weighted-average cost of capital (WACC) is 9 percent, and the company's tax rate is 40 percent. Moreover, the company's required rate of return on invested capital is 9 percent.

Required:

1. Compute the Software Division's sales margin, capital turnover, return on investment (ROI), residual income, and economic value added (EVA) for 20x7.

2. If income and sales remain the same in 20x8, but the division's capital turnover improves to 80 percent, compute the following for 20x8: (*a*) invested capital and (*b*) ROI.

Problem 2

Stellar Systems Company's Microprocessor Division sells a computer module to the company's Guidance Assembly Division, which assembles completed guidance systems. The Microprocessor Division has no excess capacity. The computer module costs $10,000 to manufacture, and it can be sold in the external market to companies in the computer industry for $13,500.

Required: Compute the transfer price for the computer module using the general transfer-pricing rule.

Solutions to Review Problems

Problem 1

1. Sales margin $= \dfrac{\text{Income}}{\text{Sales revenue}} = \dfrac{\$300,000}{\$2,000,000} = 15\%$

Capital turnover $= \dfrac{\text{Sales revenue}}{\text{Invested capital}} = \dfrac{\$2,000,000}{\$3,000,000} = 67\%$

Return on investment $= \dfrac{\text{Income}}{\text{Invested capital}} = \dfrac{\$300,000}{\$3,000,000} = 10\%$

Residual income:

Divisional income	$300,000
Less: Imputed interest charge:	
Invested capital	$3,000,000
× Imputed interest rate	× .09
Imputed interest charge	270,000
Residual income	$ 30,000

Economic value added (EVA):

$$EVA = \begin{pmatrix}\text{Investment center's} \\ \text{after-tax} \\ \text{operating income}\end{pmatrix} - \left[\left(\begin{matrix}\text{Investment center's} \\ \text{total assets}\end{matrix} - \begin{matrix}\text{Investment center's} \\ \text{current liabilities}\end{matrix}\right) \times \begin{matrix}\text{Weighted-average} \\ \text{cost of capital}\end{matrix}\right]$$

$= \$300,000\,(1 - .40) - [(\quad\$3,000,000\quad - \quad\$20,000\quad) \times \quad .09\quad]$

$= \$(88,200)$

2. *a.* Capital turnover $= \dfrac{\text{Sales revenue}}{\text{Invested capital}} = \dfrac{\$2,000,000}{?} = 80\%$

Therefore: Invested capital $= \dfrac{\$2,000,000}{.80} = \$2,500,000$

b. New ROI $= 15\% \times 80\% = 12\%$

Problem 2

Transfer price = Outlay cost + Opportunity cost

$= \$10,000 + (\$13,500 - \$10,000)$

$= \$13,500$

The $3,500 opportunity cost of a transfer is the contribution margin that will be forgone if a computer module is transferred instead of sold in the external market.

Key Terms

For each term's definition refer to the indicated page, or turn to the glossary at the end of the text.

capital turnover, 585

cash bonus, 594

economic value added
  (EVA), 589

full (or absorption) cost, 603

goal congruence, 583

imperfect competition, 601

incentive compensation, 594

internal control system, 607

investment center, 582

management by objectives
  (MBO), 583

merit pay, 594

pay for performance, 594

perfect competition, 601

residual income, 587

return on investment
  (ROI), 584

sales margin, 585

shareholder value
  analysis, 589

transfer price, 582

weighted-average cost of
  capital (WACC), 589

Review Questions

13–1. What is the managerial accountant's primary objective in designing a responsibility-accounting system?

13–2. Define *goal congruence,* and explain why it is important to an organization's success.

13–3. Describe the managerial approach known as *management by objectives* or *MBO.*

13–4. Define and give three examples of an *investment center.*

13–5. Write the formula for ROI, showing sales margin and capital turnover as its components.

13–6. Explain how the manager of the Automobile Division of an insurance company could improve her division's ROI.

13–7. Make up an example showing how residual income is calculated. What information is used in computing residual income that is not used in computing ROI?

13–8. What is the chief disadvantage of ROI as an investment-center performance measure? How does the residual-income measure eliminate this disadvantage?

13–9. Why is there typically a rise in ROI or residual income across time in a division? What undesirable behavioral implications could this phenomenon have?

13–10. Define the term *economic value added.* How does it differ from residual income?

13–11. Distinguish between the following measures of invested capital, and briefly explain when each should be used: (*a*) total assets, (*b*) total productive assets, and (*c*) total assets less current liabilities.

13–12. Why do some companies use gross book value instead of net book value to measure a division's invested capital?

13–13. Explain why it is important in performance evaluation to distinguish between investment centers and their managers.

13–14. How do organizations use pay for performance to motivate managers?

13–15. Describe an alternative to using ROI or residual income to measure investment-center performance.

13–16. How does inflation affect investment-center performance measures?

13–17. List three nonfinancial measures that could be used to evaluate a division of an insurance company.

13–18. Discuss the importance of nonfinancial information in measuring investment-center performance.

13–19. Identify and explain the managerial accountant's primary objective in choosing a transfer-pricing policy.

13–20. Describe four methods by which transfer prices may be set.

13–21. Explain the significance of excess capacity in the transferring division when transfer prices are set using the general transfer-pricing rule.

13–22. How do tax laws affect the transfer-pricing policies of multinational companies?

13–23. Explain the role of import duties, or tariffs, in affecting the transfer-pricing policies of multinational companies.

Exercises

All applicable Exercises are available with McGraw-Hill's *Connect Accounting*™.

■ **Exercise 13–24**
Components of ROI
(LO 2)

The following data pertain to Dubai Division's most recent year of operations.

Income	$ 5,000,000
Sales revenue	40,000,000
Average invested capital	20,000,000

Required: Compute Dubai Division's sales margin, capital turnover, and return on investment for the year.

■ **Exercise 13–25**
Improving ROI
(LO 3)

Refer to the preceding exercise.

Required: Demonstrate two ways Dubai Division's manager could improve the division's ROI to 30 percent.

Refer to the data for Exercise 13–24. Assume that the company's minimum desired rate of return on invested capital is 12 percent.

Required: Compute Dubai Division's residual income for the year.

■ **Exercise 13–26**
Residual Income
(LO 2)

Golden Gate Construction Associates, a real estate developer and building contractor, has two sources of long-term capital: debt and equity. The cost to Golden Gate of issuing debt is the after-tax cost of the interest payments on the debt, taking into account the fact that the interest payments are tax deductible. The cost of Golden Gate's equity capital is the investment opportunity rate of Golden Gate's investors, that is, the rate they could earn on investments of similar risk to that of investing in Golden Gate Construction Associates. The interest rate on Golden Gate's $60 million of long-term debt is 10 percent, and the company's tax rate is 40 percent. The cost of Golden Gate's equity capital is 15 percent. Moreover, the market value (and book value) of Golden Gate's equity is $90 million.

Required: Calculate Golden Gate Construction Associates' weighted-average cost of capital.

■ **Exercise 13–27**
Calculate Weighted-Average
Cost of Capital for EVA
(LO 2)

Refer to the data in the preceding exercise for Golden Gate Construction Associates. The company has two divisions: the real estate division and the construction division. The divisions' total assets, current liabilities, and before-tax operating income for the most recent year are as follows:

■ **Exercise 13–28**
Economic Value Added (EVA);
Continuation of Preceding
Exercise
(LO 2)

Division	Total Assets	Current Liabilities	Before-Tax Operating Income
Real estate	$100,000,000	$6,000,000	$20,000,000
Construction	60,000,000	4,000,000	18,000,000

Required: Calculate the economic value added (EVA) for each of Golden Gate Construction Associates' divisions. (You will need to use the weighted-average cost of capital, which was computed in the preceding exercise.)

Wyalusing Industries has manufactured prefabricated houses for over 20 years. The houses are constructed in sections to be assembled on customers' lots. Wyalusing expanded into the precut housing market when it acquired Fairmont Company, one of its suppliers. In this market, various types of lumber are precut into the appropriate lengths, banded into packages, and shipped to customers' lots for assembly. Wyalusing designated the Fairmont Division as an investment center. Wyalusing uses return on investment (ROI) as a performance measure with investment defined as average productive assets. Management bonuses are based in part on ROI. All investments are expected to earn a minimum return of 15 percent before income taxes. Fairmont's ROI has ranged from 19.3 to 22.1 percent since it was acquired. Fairmont had an investment opportunity in 20x1 that had an estimated ROI of 18 percent. Fairmont's management decided against the investment because it believed the investment would decrease the division's overall ROI. The 20x1 income statement for Fairmont Division follows. The division's productive assets were $12,600,000 at the end of 20x1, a 5 percent increase over the balance at the beginning of the year.

■ **Exercise 13–29**
ROI; Residual Income
(LO 1, 2)

FAIRMONT DIVISION
Income Statement
For the Year Ended December 31, 20x1
(in thousands)

Sales revenue		$24,000
Cost of goods sold		15,800
Gross margin		$ 8,200
Operating expenses:		
Administrative	$2,140	
Selling	3,600	5,740
Income from operations before income taxes		$ 2,460

Required:

1. Calculate the following performance measures for 20x1 for the Fairmont Division.
   a. Return on investment (ROI).
   b. Residual income.

2. Would the management of Fairmont Division have been more likely to accept the investment opportunity it had in 20x1 if residual income were used as a performance measure instead of ROI? Explain your answer.

3. *Build a spreadsheet:* Construct an Excel spreadsheet to solve requirement (1) above. Show how the solution will change if income from operations was $2,700,000.

(CMA, adapted)

■ **Exercise 13–30**
ROI and Residual Income; Annual Reports; Use of Internet
(LO 2)

Select one of the following companies (or any company of your choosing) and use the Internet to explore the company's most recent annual report.

Quantas Airlines	www.quantas.com.au
Hyundai	worldwide.hyundai.com
Michelin	www.michelin.com
IBM	www.ibm.com
Pizza Hut	www.pizzahut.com
Wyndham Hotels	www.wyndham.com
Walmart	www.walmart.com

Required:

1. Calculate the company's overall return on investment (ROI). Also, calculate the company's overall residual income. (Assume an imputed interest rate of 10 percent.) List and explain any assumptions you make.

2. Does the company include a calculation of ROI in its online annual report? If it does, do your calculations agree with those of the company? If not, what would be some possible explanations?

■ **Exercise 13–31**
Increasing ROI over Time
(LO 2, 4, 5)

Refer to Exhibit 13–3. Assume that you are a consultant who has been hired by GreenMarket Food Stores.

Required: Write a memorandum to the company president explaining why the ROI based on net book value (in Exhibit 13–3) behaves as it does over the five-year time horizon.

■ **Exercise 13–32**
Internal Control
(LO 8)

Dryden Company is an auto parts supplier. At the end of each month, the employee who maintains all of the inventory records takes a physical inventory of the firm's stock. When discrepancies occur between the recorded inventory and the physical count, the employee changes the physical count to agree with the records.

Required:

1. What problems could arise as a result of Dryden Company's inventory procedures?
2. How could the internal control system be strengthened to eliminate the potential problems?

■ **Exercise 13–33**
Improving ROI
(LO 2, 3)

The following data pertain to British Isles Aggregates Company, a producer of sand, gravel, and cement, for the year just ended.

Sales revenue	$2,000,000
Cost of goods sold	1,100,000
Operating expenses	800,000
Average invested capital	1,000,000

Required:

1. Compute the company's sales margin, capital turnover, and ROI.

2. If the sales and average invested capital remain the same during the next year, to what level would total expenses have to be reduced in order to improve the firm's ROI to 15 percent?

3. Assume expenses are reduced, as calculated in requirement (2). Compute the firm's new sales margin. Show how the new sales margin and the old capital turnover together result in a new ROI of 15 percent.

■ **Exercise 13–34**
General Transfer-Pricing Rule
(LO 6)

Tasman Metallurgy Corporation has two divisions. The Fabrication Division transfers partially completed components to the Assembly Division at a predetermined transfer price. The Fabrication Division's standard variable production cost per unit is $320. The division has no excess capacity, and it could sell all of its components to outside buyers at $420 per unit in a perfectly competitive market.

Required:

1. Determine a transfer price using the general rule.

2. How would the transfer price change if the Fabrication Division had excess capacity?

■ **Exercise 13–35**
Cost-Based Transfer Pricing
(LO 7)

Refer to the preceding exercise. The Fabrication Division's full (absorption) cost of a component is $370, which includes $50 of applied fixed-overhead costs. The transfer price has been set at $407, which is the Fabrication Division's full cost plus a 10 percent markup.

The Assembly Division has a special offer for its product of $475. The Assembly Division incurs variable costs of $110 in addition to the transfer price for the Fabrication Division's components. Both divisions currently have excess production capacity.

Required:

1. What is the Assembly Division's manager likely to do regarding acceptance or rejection of the special offer? Why?

2. Is this decision in the best interests of the company as a whole? Why?

3. How could the situation be remedied using the transfer price?

Problems

All applicable Problems are available with McGraw-Hill's *Connect Accounting*™.

■ **Problem 13–36**
Comparing the Performance of Two Divisions
(LO 2, 4)

Haryana Pharmaceutical Company has two divisions, which reported the following results for the most recent year.

	Division I	Division II
Income	$ 900,000	$ 200,000
Average invested capital	$6,000,000	$1,000,000
ROI	15%	20%

Required: Which was the more successful division during the year? Think carefully about this, and explain your answer.

■ **Problem 13–37**
ROI and Residual Income;
Missing Data
(LO 2)

Residual income, Division A:
$240,000

The following data pertain to three divisions of Czech EcoProducts, Ltd. The company's required rate of return on invested capital is 8 percent.

	Division A	Division B	Division C
Sales revenue	?	$16,000,000	?
Income	$400,000	$2,000,000	?
Average investment	?	$2,500,000	?
Sales margin	20%	?	25%
Capital turnover	1	?	?
ROI	?	?	20%
Residual income	?	?	$120,000

Required: Fill in the blanks above.

■ **Problem 13–38**
Improving ROI
(LO 3)

2. ROI: 25%

Refer to the preceding problem about Czech EcoProducts, Ltd.

Required:

1. Explain three ways the Division B manager could improve her division's ROI. Use numbers to illustrate these possibilities.

2. Suppose Division A's sales margin increased to 25 percent, while its capital turnover remained constant. Compute the division's new ROI.

■ **Problem 13–39**
Residual Income
(LO 2, 4)

Refer to the data for problem 13–36 regarding Haryana Pharmaceutical Company.

Required: Compute each division's residual income for the year under each of the following assumptions about the firm's cost of acquiring capital.

1. 12 percent.
2. 15 percent.
3. 18 percent.

Which division was more successful? Explain your answer.

■ **Problem 13–40**
Increasing ROI over Time;
Accelerated Depreciation
(LO 2, 4, 5)

Year 2, ROI based on net
book value: 12.5%

Refer to Exhibit 13–3. Prepare a similar table of the changing ROI assuming the following accelerated depreciation schedule. Assume the same income before depreciation as shown in Exhibit 13–3. (If there is a loss, leave the ROI column blank.)

Year	Depreciation
1	$200,000
2	120,000
3	72,000
4	54,000
5	54,000
Total	$500,000

Required:

1. How does your table differ from the one in Exhibit 13–3? Why?
2. What are the implications of the ROI pattern in your table?

■ **Problem 13–41**
Increasing Residual Income
over Time
(LO 2, 4, 5)

Year 1, residual income (based
on net book value): $5,000

Prepare a table similar to Exhibit 13–3, which focuses on residual income. Use a 10 percent rate to compute the imputed interest charge. The table should show the residual income on the investment during each year in its five-year life. Assume the same income before depreciation and the same depreciation schedule as shown in Exhibit 13–3.

■ **Problem 13–42**
ROI and Residual Income;
Investment Evaluation
(LO 2, 3, 4, 8)

1. Current ROI: 21%
5. Current residual income of
the Middle Eastern Division:
$166,500

Megatronics Corporation, a massive retailer of electronic products, is organized in four separate divisions. The four divisional managers are evaluated at year-end, and bonuses are awarded based on ROI. Last year, the company as a whole produced a 13 percent return on its investment.

During the past week, management of the company's Middle Eastern Division was approached about the possibility of buying a competitor that had decided to redirect its retail activities. (If the competitor is acquired, it will be acquired at its book value.) The data that follow relate to recent performance of the Middle Eastern Division and the competitor:

	Middle Eastern Division	Competitor
Sales	$8,400,000	$5,200,000
Variable costs	70% of sales	65% of sales
Fixed costs	$2,131,500	$1,670,000
Invested capital	$1,850,000	$625,000

Management has determined that in order to upgrade the competitor to Megatronics' standards, an additional $375,000 of invested capital would be needed.

Required: As a group, complete the following requirements.

1. Compute the current ROI of the Middle Eastern Division and the division's ROI if the competitor is acquired.

2. What is the likely reaction of divisional management toward the acquisition? Why?

3. What is the likely reaction of Megatronics' corporate management toward the acquisition? Why?

4. Would the division be better off if it acquired the competitor but didn't upgrade it to Megatronics' standards? Show computations to support your answer.

5. Assume that Megatronics uses residual income to evaluate performance and desires a 12 percent minimum return on invested capital. Compute the current residual income of the Middle Eastern Division and the division's residual income if the competitor is acquired. Will divisional management be likely to change its attitude toward the acquisition? Why?

■ **Problem 13–43**
ROI and Performance
Evaluations
(LO 2, 4, 8)

1. Capital turnover: 80%

Li Ling-Fung, head of the Sporting Goods Division of Reliable Products, has just completed a miserable nine months. "If it could have gone wrong, it did. Sales are down, income is down, inventories are too high, and quite frankly, I'm beginning to worry that I will lose my job," he explained. Li is evaluated on the basis of ROI. Selected figures for the past nine months follow.

Sales	$4,800,000
Operating income	348,000
Invested capital	6,000,000

In an effort to salvage the current year's performance, Li was contemplating implementation of some or all of the following four strategies:

a. Write off and discard $60,000 of obsolete inventory. The company will take a loss on the disposal.

b. Accelerate the collection of $80,000 of overdue customer accounts receivable.

c. Stop advertising through year-end and drastically reduce outlays for repairs and maintenance. These actions are expected to save the division $150,000 of expenses and will conserve cash resources.

d. Acquire two competitors that are expected to have the following financial characteristics:

	Projected Sales	Projected Operating Expenses	Projected Invested Capital
Kowloon Manufacturing	$3,000,000	$2,400,000	$5,000,000
Pearl River Enterprises	4,500,000	4,120,000	4,750,000

Required:

1. Briefly define sales margin, capital turnover, and return on investment and then compute these amounts for Reliable's Sporting Goods Division over the past nine months.

2. Evaluate each of the first two strategies listed, with respect to its effect on the Reliable's last nine months' performance, and make a recommendation to Li regarding which, if any, to adopt.

3. Are there possible long-term problems associated with strategy (c)? Briefly explain.

4. Determine the ROI of the investment in Kowloon Manufacturing and do the same for the investment in Pearl River Enterprises. Should Li reject both acquisitions, acquire one company, or acquire both companies? Assume that sufficient capital is available to fund investments in both organizations.

■ **Problem 13–44**
Weighted-Average Cost of
Capital; Economic Value
Added (EVA)
(LO 2)

1. Weighted-average cost of
capital: .1056

Costa Brava Seafood, Ltd. (CBSL) is a seafood restaurant chain operating throughout Europe. The company has two sources of long-term capital: debt and equity. The cost to CBSL of issuing debt is the after-tax cost of the interest payments on the debt, taking into account the fact that the interest payments are tax deductible. The cost of CBSL's equity capital is the investment opportunity rate of CBSL's investors, that is, the rate they could earn on investments of similar risk to that of investing in Costa Brava Seafood, Ltd. The interest rate on CBSL's $80 million of long-term debt is 9 percent, and the company's tax rate is 40 percent. The cost of CBSL's equity capital is 14 percent. Moreover, the market value (and book value) of CBSL's equity is $120 million.

Costa Brava Seafood, Ltd. consists of two divisions, the properties division and the food service division. The divisions' total assets, current liabilities, and before-tax operating income for the most recent year are as follows:

Division	Total Assets	Current Liabilities	Before-Tax Operating Income
Properties	$145,000,000	$3,000,000	$29,000,000
Food Service	64,000,000	6,000,000	15,000,000

Required:

1. Calculate the weighted-average cost of capital for Costa Brava Seafood, Ltd..
2. Calculate the economic value added (EVA) for each of CBSL's divisions.
3. *Build a spreadsheet:* Construct an Excel spreadsheet to solve both of the preceding requirements. Show how the solution will change if the following information changes: before-tax operating income was $30,000,000 and $14,000,000 for Properties and Food Service, respectively.

Problem 13–45
Weighted-Average Cost of Capital; Economic Value Added (EVA)
(LO 2)

1. The weighted-average cost of capital: .0972
2. Atlantic Division, economic value added: $(12,181,200)

All-Canadian, Ltd. is a multiproduct company with three divisions: Pacific Division, Plains Division, and Atlantic Division. The company has two sources of long-term capital: debt and equity. The interest rate on All-Canadian's $400 million debt is 9 percent, and the company's tax rate is 30 percent. The cost of All-Canadian's equity capital is 12 percent. Moreover, the market value of the company's equity is $600 million. (The book value of All-Canadian's equity is $430 million, but that amount does not reflect the current value of the company's assets or the value of intangible assets.)

The following data (in millions) pertain to All-Canadian's three divisions.

Division	Operating Income	Current Liabilities	Total Assets
Pacific	$14	$6	$ 70
Plains	45	5	300
Atlantic	48	9	480

Required:

1. Compute All-Canadian's weighted-average cost of capital (WACC).
2. Compute the economic value added (or EVA) for each of the company's three divisions.
3. What conclusions can you draw from the EVA analysis?

Problem 13–46
Comprehensive Transfer-Pricing Problem; Ethics
(LO 6, 7, 8)

2(a). Transfer price: $55

Clearview Window Company manufactures windows for the home-building industry. The window frames are produced in the Frame Division. The frames are then transferred to the Glass Division, where the glass and hardware are installed. The company's best-selling product is a 1000 mm × 1250 mm, doublepaned operable window.

The Frame Division also can sell frames directly to custom home builders, who install the glass and hardware. The sales price for a frame is $80. The Glass Division sells its finished windows for $190. The markets for both frames and finished windows exhibit perfect competition.

The standard variable cost of the window is detailed as follows:

	Frame Division	Glass Division
Direct material	$15	$30*
Direct labor	10	15
Variable overhead	30	30
Total	$55	$75

*Not including the transfer price for the frame.

Required:

1. Assume that there is no excess capacity in the Frame Division.
   a. Use the general rule to compute the transfer price for window frames.
   b. Calculate the transfer price if it is based on standard variable cost with a 10 percent markup.
2. Assume that there is excess capacity in the Frame Division.
   a. Use the general rule to compute the transfer price for window frames.
   b. Explain why your answers to requirements (1a) and (2a) differ.

    c. Suppose the predetermined fixed-overhead rate in the Frame Division is 125 percent of direct-labor cost. Calculate the transfer price if it is based on standard full cost plus a 10 percent markup.

    d. Assume the transfer price established in requirement (2c) is used. The Glass Division has been approached by the U.S. Army with a special order for 1,000 windows at $145. From the perspective of Clearview Window Company as a whole, should the special order be accepted or rejected? Why?

    e. Assume the same facts as in requirement (2d). Will an autonomous Glass Division manager accept or reject the special order? Why?

    f. Comment on any ethical issues you see in the questions raised in requirements (2d) and (2e).

3. Comment on the use of full cost as the basis for setting transfer prices.

■ **Problem 13–47**
Transfer Pricing; Negotiation
(LO 7, 8)

4. Produce diode and sell externally, contribution margin: $275

Cortez Enterprises has two divisions: Birmingham and Manchester. Birmingham currently sells a diode reducer to manufacturers of aircraft navigation systems for $775 per unit. Variable costs amount to $500, and demand for this product currently exceeds the division's ability to supply the marketplace.

    Despite this situation, Cortez is considering another use for the diode reducer, namely, integration into a satellite positioning system that would be made by Manchester. The positioning system has an anticipated selling price of $1,400 and requires an additional $670 of variable manufacturing costs. A transfer price of $750 has been established for the diode reducer.

    Top management is anxious to introduce the positioning system; however, unless the transfer is made, an introduction will not be possible because of the difficulty of obtaining needed diode reducers. Birmingham and Manchester are in the process of recovering from previous financial problems, and neither division can afford any future losses. The company uses responsibility accounting and ROI in measuring divisional performance, and awards bonuses to divisional management.

Required:

1. How would Birmingham's divisional manager likely react to the decision to transfer diode reducers to Manchester? Show computations to support your answer.

2. How would Manchester's divisional management likely react to the $750 transfer price? Show computations to support your answer.

3. Assume that a lower transfer price is desired. Should top management lower the price or should the price be lowered by another means? Explain.

4. From a contribution margin perspective, does Cortez benefit more if it sells the diode reducers externally or transfers the reducers to Manchester? By how much?

■ **Problem 13–48**
Setting a Transfer Price; International Setting; Differential Tax Rates
(LO 6, 7)

2. U.S. operation, income after tax: $24.00
3. German operation, income after tax: $36.00

Alpha Communications, Inc., which produces telecommunications equipment in the United States, has a very strong local market for its circuit board. The variable production cost is $130, and the company can sell its entire supply domestically for $170. The U.S. tax rate is 40 percent.

    Alternatively, Alpha can ship the circuit board to its division in Germany, to be used in a product that the German division will distribute throughout Europe. Information about the German product and the division's operating environment follows.

    Selling price of final product: $360

    Shipping fees to import circuit board: $20

    Labor, overhead, and additional material costs of final product: $115

    Import duties levied on circuit board (to be paid by the German division): 10% of transfer price

    German tax rate: 60%

Assume that U.S. and German tax authorities allow a transfer price for the circuit board set at either U.S. variable manufacturing cost or the U.S. market price. Alpha's management is in the process of exploring which transfer price is better for the firm as a whole.

Required:

1. Compute overall company profitability per unit if all units are transferred and U.S. variable manufacturing cost is used as the transfer price. Show separate calculations for the U.S. operation and the German division.

2. Repeat requirement (1), assuming the use of the U.S. market price as the transfer price. Which of the two transfer prices is better for the firm?

3. Assume that the German division can obtain the circuit board in Germany for $155.

    a. If you were the head of the German division, would you rather do business with your U.S. division or buy the circuit board locally? Why?

    b. Rather than proceed with the transfer, is it in the best interest of Alpha to sell its goods domestically and allow the German division to acquire the circuit board in Germany? Why? Show computations to support your answer.

4. Generally speaking, when tax rates differ between countries, what strategy should a company use in setting its transfer prices?

5. *Build a spreadsheet:* Construct an Excel spreadsheet to solve requirements (1) and (2) above. Show how the solution will change if the following information changes: the U.S. tax rate is 35 percent, the German tax rate is 55 percent, and the import duties are 8 percent of the transfer price.

■ **Problem 13–49**
Transfer Pricing; Management Behavior
(LO 6, 7, 8)

2. Total contribution margin, Mining Division: $19 million

Pretoria Consolidated Resources Company (PCRC) has several divisions. However, only two divisions transfer products to other divisions. The Mining Division refines toldine, which is then transferred to the Metals Division. The toldine is processed into an alloy by the Metals Division, and the alloy is sold to customers at a price of $150 per unit. The Mining division is currently required by PCRC to transfer its total yearly output of 500,000 units of toldine to the Metals Division at total actual manufacturing cost plus 10 percent. Unlimited quantities of toldine can be purchased and sold on the open market at $90 per unit. While the Mining Division could sell all the toldine it produces at $90 per unit on the open market, it would incur a variable selling cost of $5 per unit.

    Jacob Ncube, manager of the Mining Division, is unhappy with having to transfer the entire output of toldine to the Metals Division at 110 percent of cost. In a meeting with the management of PCRC, he said, "Why should my division be required to sell toldine to the Metals Division at less than market price? For the year just ended in May, Metals' contribution margin was $24 million on sales of 500,000 units, while Mining's contribution was only $7 million on the transfer of the same number of units. My division is subsidizing the profitability of the Metals Division. We should be allowed to charge the market price for toldine when transferring to the Metals Division."

    The following table shows the detailed unit cost structure for both the Mining and Metals divisions during the most recent year.

	Mining Division	Metals Division
Transfer price from Mining Division	—	$ 66
Direct material	$12	6
Direct labor	16	20
Manufacturing overhead	32*	25†
Total cost per unit	$60	$117

*Manufacturing-overhead cost in the Mining Division is 25 percent fixed and 75 percent variable.
†Manufacturing-overhead cost in the Metals Division is 60 percent fixed and 40 percent variable.

Required:

1. Explain why transfer prices based on total actual costs are not appropriate as the basis for divisional performance measurement.

2. Using the market price as the transfer price, determine the contribution margin for both the Mining Division and the Metals Division.

3. If Pretoria Consolidated Resources Company were to institute the use of negotiated transfer prices and allow divisions to buy and sell on the open market, determine the price range for toldine that would be acceptable to both the Mining Division and the Metals Division. Explain your answer.

4. Use the general transfer-pricing rule to compute the lowest transfer price that would be acceptable to the Mining Division. Is your answer consistent with your conclusion in requirement (3)? Explain.

5. Identify which one of the three types of transfer prices (cost-based, market-based, or negotiated) is most likely to elicit desirable management behavior at PCRC. Explain your answer.

(CMA, adapted)

Cases

Holiday Entertainment Corporation (HEC), a subsidiary of New Age Industries, manufactures go-carts and other recreational vehicles. Family recreational centers that feature not only go-cart tracks but miniature golf, batting cages, and arcade games as well have increased in popularity. As a result, HEC has been receiving some pressure from New Age's management to diversify into some of these other recreational areas. Recreational Leasing, Inc. (RLI), one of the largest firms that leases arcade games to family recreational centers, is looking for a friendly buyer. New Age's top management believes that RLI's assets could be acquired for an investment of $3.2 million and has strongly urged Bill Grieco, division manager of HEC, to consider acquiring RLI.

Grieco has reviewed RLI's financial statements with his controller, Marie Donnelly, and they believe the acquisition may not be in the best interest of HEC. "If we decide not to do this, the New Age people are not going to be happy," said Grieco. "If we could convince them to base our bonuses on something other than return on investment, maybe this acquisition would look more attractive. How would we do if the bonuses were based on residual income, using the company's 15 percent cost of capital?"

New Age Industries traditionally has evaluated all of its divisions on the basis of return on investment. The desired rate of return for each division is 20 percent. The management team of any division reporting an annual increase in the ROI is automatically eligible for a bonus. The management of divisions reporting a decline in the ROI must provide convincing explanations for the decline in order to be eligible for a bonus. Moreover, this bonus is limited to 50 percent of the bonus paid to divisions reporting an increase in ROI.

In the following table are condensed financial statements for both HEC and RLI for the most recent year.

	RLI	HEC
Sales revenue	—	$9,500,000
Leasing revenue	$3,100,000	—
Variable expenses	(1,300,000)	(6,000,000)
Fixed expenses	(1,200,000)	(1,500,000)
Operating income	$ 600,000	$2,000,000
Current assets	$1,900,000	$2,300,000
Long-lived assets	1,100,000	5,700,000
Total assets	$3,000,000	$8,000,000
Current liabilities	$ 850,000	$1,400,000
Long-term liabilities	1,200,000	3,800,000
Stockholders' equity	950,000	2,800,000
Total liabilities and stockholders' equity	$3,000,000	$8,000,000

Required:

1. If New Age Industries continues to use ROI as the sole measure of divisional performance, explain why Holiday Entertainment Corporation would be reluctant to acquire Recreational Leasing, Inc.

2. If New Age Industries could be persuaded to use residual income to measure the performance of HEC, explain why HEC would be more willing to acquire RLI.

3. Discuss how the behavior of division managers is likely to be affected by the use of the following performance measures: (*a*) return on investment and (*b*) residual income.

(CMA, adapted)

InterGlobal Industries is a diversified corporation with separate operating divisions. Each division's performance is evaluated on the basis of profit and return on investment.

The Air Comfort Division manufactures and sells air-conditioner units. The coming year's budgeted income statement, which follows, is based upon a sales volume of 15,000 units.

■ **Case 13–50**
ROI versus Residual Income;
Incentive Effects
(LO 1, 2, 4, 8)

2. Residual income, RLI:
$120,000

■ **Case 13–51**
Interdivisional Transfers;
IPricing the Final Product
(LO 6, 7, 8)

1. Increase in net income
before taxes: $132,000
3. Increase in net income
before taxes for InterGlobal
Industries: $312,500

AIR COMFORT DIVISION
Budgeted Income Statement
(In thousands)

	Per Unit	Total
Sales revenue	$400	$6,000
Manufacturing costs:		
Compressor	$ 70	$1,050
Other direct material	37	555
Direct labor	30	450
Variable overhead	45	675
Fixed overhead	32	480
Total manufacturing costs	$214	$3,210
Gross margin	$186	$2,790
Operating expenses:		
Variable selling	$ 18	$270
Fixed selling	19	285
Fixed administrative	38	570
Total operating expenses	$ 75	$1,125
Net income before taxes	$111	$1,665

Air Comfort's division manager believes sales can be increased if the price of the air-conditioners is reduced. A market research study by an independent firm indicates that a 5 percent reduction in the selling price would increase sales volume 16 percent, or 2,400 units. The division has sufficient production capacity to manage this increased volume with no increase in fixed costs.

The Air Comfort Division uses a compressor in its units, which it purchases from an outside supplier at a cost of $70 per compressor. The Air Comfort Division manager has asked the manager of the Compressor Division about selling compressor units to Air Comfort. The Compressor Division currently manufactures and sells a unit to outside firms that is similar to the unit used by the Air Comfort Division. The specifications of the Air Comfort Division compressor are slightly different, which would reduce the Compressor Division's direct material cost by $1.50 per unit. In addition, the Compressor Division would not incur any variable selling costs in the units sold to the Air Comfort Division. The manager of the Air Comfort Division wants all of the compressors it uses to come from one supplier and has offered to pay $50 for each compressor unit.

The Compressor Division has the capacity to produce 75,000 units. Its budgeted income statement for the coming year, which follows, is based on a sales volume of 64,000 units without considering Air Comfort's proposal.

COMPRESSOR DIVISION
Budgeted Income Statement
(In thousands)

	Per Unit	Total
Sales revenue	$100	$6,400
Manufacturing costs:		
Direct material	$ 12	$ 768
Direct labor	8	512
Variable overhead	10	640
Fixed overhead	11	704
Total manufacturing costs	$ 41	$2,624
Gross margin	$ 59	$3,776
Operating expenses:		
Variable selling	$ 6	$ 384
Fixed selling	4	256
Fixed administrative	7	448
Total operating expenses	$ 17	$1,088
Net income before taxes	$ 42	$2,688

Required:

1. Should the Air Comfort Division institute the 5 percent price reduction on its air-conditioner units even if it cannot acquire the compressors internally for $50 each? Support your conclusion with appropriate calculations.

2. Independently of your answer to requirement (1), assume the Air Comfort Division needs 17,400 units. Should the Compressor Division be willing to supply the compressor units for $50 each? Support your conclusions with appropriate calculations.

3. Independently of your answer to requirement (1), assume Air Comfort needs 17,400 units. Suppose InterGlobal's top management has specified a transfer price of $50. Would it be in the best interest of *InterGlobal Industries* for the Compressor Division to supply the compressor units at $50 each to the Air Comfort Division? Support your conclusions with appropriate calculations.

4. Is $50 a goal-congruent transfer price? [Refer to your answers for requirements (2) and (3).]

(CMA, adapted)

General Instrumentation Company manufactures dashboard instruments for heavy construction equipment. The firm is based in Stockholm and operates several divisions in the Americas, Asia, and Europe. The Vietnam Division manufactures complex electrical panels that are used in a variety of the firm's instruments. There are two basic types of panels. The high-density panel (HDP) is capable of many functions and is used in the most sophisticated instruments, such as tachometers and pressure gauges. The low-density panel (LDP) is much simpler and is used in less-complicated instruments. Although there are minor differences among the different high-density panels, the basic manufacturing process and production costs are the same. The high-density panels require considerably more skilled labor than the low-density panels, but the unskilled labor needs are about the same. Moreover, the direct materials in the high-density panel run substantially more than the cost of materials in the low-density panels. Production costs are summarized as follows:

■ **Case 13–52**
Minimum and Maximum Acceptable Transfer Prices; Multinational
(LO 6, 7, 8)

2. Unit contribution margin, LDP: $6

5. Net savings if TCH-320 is produced using an HDP: $112.00

	LDP	HDP
Unskilled labor (.5 hour @ $10)	$ 5	$ 5
Skilled labor:		
LDP (.25 hour @ $20)	5	
HDP (1.5 hours @ $20)		30
Raw material	3	8
Purchased components	4	12
Variable overhead	5	15
Total variable cost	$22	$70

The annual fixed overhead in the Vietnam Division is $1,000,000. There is a limited supply of skilled labor available in the area, and the division must constrain its production to 40,000 hours of skilled labor each year. This has been a troublesome problem for Thuy Anh Tran, the division manager. Tran has successfully increased demand for the LDP line to the point where it is essentially unlimited. Each LDP sells for $28. Business also has increased in recent years for the HDP, and Tran estimates the division could now sell anywhere up to 6,000 units per year at a price of $115.

General Instrumentation operates its Volkmar Tachometer Division in Berlin. A recent acquisition of General Instrumentation, the division was formerly a German company known as Volkmar Construction Instruments. The division's main product is a sophisticated tachometer used in heavy-duty cranes, bulldozers, and backhoes. The instrument, designated as a TCH–320, has the following production costs.

TCH–320

Unskilled labor (.5 hour @ $9)	$ 4.50
Skilled labor (3 hours @ $17)	51.00
Raw material	11.50
Purchased components	150.00
Variable overhead	11.00
Total variable cost	$228.00

The cost of purchased components includes a $145 control pack currently imported from Turkey. Fixed overhead in the Volkmar Tachometer Division runs about $800,000 per year. Both skilled and unskilled labor are in abundant supply. The TCH–320 sells for $270.

Bertram Mueller, the division manager of the Volkmar Tachometer Division, recently participated in a high-level global production teleconference. In a conversation with Thuy Anh Tran, it was apparent that Vietnam Division's high-density panel might be a viable substitute for the control pack currently imported from Turkey and used in Volkmar's TCH–320. Upon returning to Berlin, Mueller asked his chief engineer to look into the matter. Hans Schmidt obtained several HDP units from Vietnam Division, and a minor R&D project was mounted to determine if the HDP could replace the Turkish control pack. Several weeks later, the following conversation occurred in Mueller's office:

Schmidt: There's no question that Vietnam Division's HDP unit will work in our TCH–320. In fact, it could save us some money.

Mueller: That's good news. If we can buy our components within the company, we'll help General Instrumentation's bottom line without hurting ours. Also, it will look good to corporate management if they see us working hard to integrate our division into General Instrumentation's overall production program.

Schmidt: I've also been worried about the reliability of supply of the control pack. I don't like being dependent on such a critical supplier that way.

Mueller: I agree. Let's look at your figures on the HDP replacement.

Schmidt: I got together with the controller's people, and we worked up some numbers. If we replace the control pack with the HDP from Vietnam, we'll avoid the $145 control pack cost we're now incurring. In addition, I figure we'll save $5.50 on the basic raw materials. There is one catch, though. The HDP will require some adjustments in order to use it in the TCH–320. We can make the adjustments here in Berlin. I'm guessing it will require an additional two hours of skilled labor to make the necessary modifications. I don't think variable overhead would be any different. Then there is the cost of transporting the HDPs to Berlin. Let's figure on $4.50 per unit.

Mueller: Sounds good. I'll give Thuy Anh Tran a call and talk this over. We can use up to 10,000 of the HDP units per year given the demand for the TCH–320. I wonder what kind of a transfer price Vietnam Division will want.

Required:

1. Draw a simple diagram depicting the two divisions and their products. Also show the two alternatives that the Volkmar Tachometer Division has in the production of its TCH–320.

2. From the perspective of General Instrumentation's top management, should any of the TCH–320 units be produced using the high-density panel? If so, how many?

3. Suppose Vietnam Division transfers 10,000 HDP units per year to Volkmar. From the perspective of General Instrumentation's top management, what effect will the transfer price have on the company's income?

4. What is the minimum transfer price that the Vietnam Division would find acceptable for the HDP?

5. What is the maximum transfer price that the Volkmar Tachometer Division would find acceptable for the HDP?

6. As the corporate controller for General Instrumentation, recommend a transfer price.

THIS CHAPTER'S FOCUS COMPANY is Worldwide Airways, an international airline based in London, England. Using this service-industry company for our illustration, we will explore a variety of decisions that managers make routinely. Examples of such decisions are accepting or rejecting a special offer for the

company's services, outsourcing a service, and adding or dropping a service or department. We will find in this chapter that different kinds of cost information are relevant, depending on the type of decision to be made.

14 Decision Making: Relevant Costs and Benefits

In contrast to the transportation-services setting of Worldwide Airways, we will explore certain types of decisions that most often arise in a manufacturing setting. Our illustration will be based on International Chocolate Company, which produces a variety of chocolate products in Brussels, Belgium. In addition to producing gourmet chocolates, the company processes cocoa beans into cocoa powder and cocoa butter. The cocoa powder can then be processed further into instant cocoa mix. We will explore a variety of decisions faced by International Chocolate Company's management.

1 Describe seven steps in the decision-making process and the managerial accountant's role in that process.

2 Explain the relationship between quantitative and qualitative analyses in decision making.

3 List and explain two criteria that must be satisfied by relevant information.

4 Identify relevant costs and benefits, giving proper treatment to sunk costs, opportunity costs, and unit costs.

5 Prepare analyses of various special decisions, properly identifying the relevant costs and benefits.

6 Analyze manufacturing decisions involving joint products and limited resources.

7 Explain the impact of an advanced manufacturing environment and activity-based costing on a relevant-cost analysis.

8 Formulate a linear program to solve a product-mix problem with multiple constraints (appendix).

Decision making is a fundamental part of management. Decisions about the acquisition of equipment, mix of products, methods of production, and pricing of products and services confront managers in all types of organizations. This chapter covers the role of managerial accounting information in a variety of common decisions. The next chapter examines pricing decisions.

The Managerial Accountant's Role in Decision Making

Managerial accountants are increasingly playing important roles as full-fledged members of cross-functional management teams. These management teams face a broad array of decisions, including production, marketing, financial, and other decisions. All managers and management teams need information pertinent to their decisions. In support of the decision-making process, managerial accountants play a specific role in providing relevant information. Thus, the managerial accountant must have a good understanding of the decisions faced by managers throughout the organization.

Steps in the Decision-Making Process

Seven steps characterize the decision-making process:

1. *Clarify the decision problem.* Sometimes the decision to be made is clear. For example, if a company receives a special order for its product at a price below the usual price, the decision problem is to accept or reject the order. But the decision problem is seldom so clear and unambiguous. Perhaps demand for a company's most popular product is declining. What exactly is causing this problem? Increasing competition? Declining quality control? A new alternative product on the market? Before a decision can be made, the problem needs to be clarified and defined in more specific terms. Considerable managerial skill is required to define a decision problem in terms that can be addressed effectively.

2. *Specify the criterion.* Once a decision problem has been clarified, the manager should specify the criterion upon which a decision will be made. Is the objective to maximize profit, increase market share, minimize cost, or improve public service? Sometimes the objectives are in conflict, as in a decision problem where production cost is to be minimized but product quality must be maintained. In such cases, one objective is specified as the decision criterion—for example, cost minimization. The other objective is established as a constraint—for example, product quality must not be worse than one defective part in 1,000 manufactured units.

3. *Identify the alternatives.* A decision involves selecting between two or more alternatives. If a machine breaks down, what are the alternative courses of action? The machine can be repaired or replaced, or a replacement can be leased. But perhaps repair will turn out to be more costly than replacement. Determining the possible alternatives is a critical step in the decision process.

4. *Develop a decision model.* A *decision model* is a simplified representation of the choice problem. Unnecessary details are stripped away, and the most important elements of the problem are highlighted. Thus, the decision model brings together the elements listed above: the criterion, the constraints, and the alternatives.

5. *Collect the data.* Although the managerial accountant often is involved in steps 1 through 4, he or she is chiefly responsible for step 5. Selecting data pertinent to decisions is one of the managerial accountant's most important roles in an organization.

6. *Select an alternative.* Once the decision model is formulated and the pertinent data are collected, the appropriate manager makes a decision.

7. *Evaluate decision effectiveness.* After a decision has been implemented, the results of the decision are evaluated with the objective of improving future decisions.

> **Learning Objective 1**
>
> Describe seven steps in the decision-making process and the managerial accountant's role in that process.

> "We are looked upon as more business advisors than just accountants, and that has a lot to do with the additional analysis and the forward looking goals we are setting." (14a)
>
> **Caterpillar**

Quantitative versus Qualitative Analysis

Decision problems involving accounting data typically are specified in quantitative terms. The criteria in such problems usually include objectives such as profit maximization or cost minimization. When a manager makes a final decision, however, the qualitative characteristics of the alternatives can be just as important as the quantitative measures. **Qualitative characteristics** are the factors in a decision problem that cannot be expressed effectively in numerical terms. To illustrate, suppose Worldwide Airways' top management is considering the elimination of its hub operation in Frankfurt. Airlines establish hubs at airports where many of their routes intersect. Hub operations include facilities for in-flight food preparation, aircraft maintenance and storage, and administrative offices. A careful quantitative analysis indicates that Worldwide Airways' profit-maximizing alternative is to eliminate the Frankfurt hub. In making its decision, however, the company's managers will consider such qualitative issues as the effect of the closing on its Frankfurt employees and on the morale of its remaining employees in the airline's London, Atlanta, and Hong Kong hubs.

> **Learning Objective 2**
>
> Explain the relationship between quantitative and qualitative analyses in decision making.

To clarify what is at stake in such qualitative analyses, quantitative analysis can allow the decision maker to put a "price" on the sum total of the qualitative characteristics. For example, suppose Worldwide Airways' controller gives top management a quantitative analysis showing that elimination of the Frankfurt hub will increase annual profits by $2,000,000. However, the qualitative considerations favor the option of continuing the Frankfurt operation. How important are these qualitative considerations to the top managers? If they decide to continue the Frankfurt operation, the qualitative considerations must be worth at least $2,000,000 to them. Weighing the quantitative and qualitative considerations in making decisions is the essence of management. The skill, experience, judgment, and ethical standards of managers all come to bear on such difficult choices.

Exhibit 14–1 depicts the seven steps in the decision process, and the relationship between quantitative and qualitative analysis.

Obtaining Information: Relevance, Accuracy, and Timeliness

What criteria should the managerial accountant use in designing the accounting information system that supplies data for decision making? Three characteristics of information determine its usefulness.

Relevance   Information is **relevant** if it is *pertinent* to a decision problem. Different decisions typically will require different data. The primary theme of this chapter is how to decide what information is relevant to various common decision problems.

Accuracy   Information that is pertinent to a decision problem also must be **accurate,** or it will be of little use. This means the information must be precise. For example, the cost incurred by Worldwide Airways to rent facilities at Flughafen Frankfurt am Main is

Exhibit 14–1
The Decision-Making Process

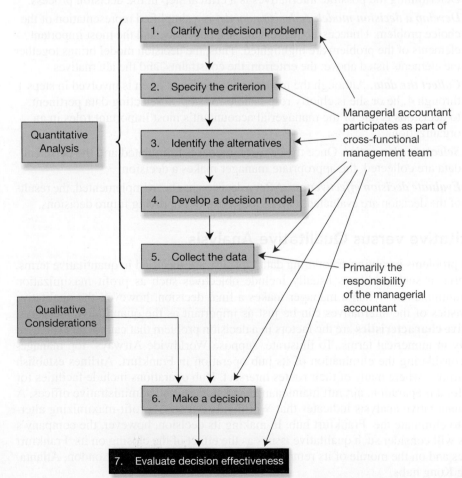

relevant to a decision about eliminating the airline's Frankfurt hub. However, if the rental cost data are imprecise, due to incomplete or misplaced records, the usefulness of the information will be diminished.

Conversely, highly accurate but irrelevant data are of no value to a decision maker. Suppose Worldwide Airways will continue its daily round-trip flight between Hong Kong and Frankfurt regardless of its decision about eliminating the Frankfurt hub. Precise data about fuel consumption on the Hong Kong-Frankfurt route are irrelevant to the decision about closing down the Frankfurt hub.

Timeliness   Relevant and accurate data are of value only if they are **timely,** that is, available in time for a decision. Thus, timeliness is the third important criterion for determining the usefulness of information. Some situations involve a trade-off between the accuracy and the timeliness of information. More accurate information may take longer to produce. Therefore, as accuracy improves, timeliness suffers, and vice versa. For example, a company may test-market a potential new product in a particular city. The longer the test-marketing program runs, the more accurate will be the marketing data generated. However, a long wait for the accurate marketing report may unduly delay management's decision to launch the new product nationally.

To summarize, the managerial accountant's primary role in the decision-making process is twofold:

1. Decide what information is *relevant* to each decision problem.
2. Provide *accurate* and *timely* data, keeping in mind the proper balance between these often-conflicting criteria.

Relevant Information

What makes information relevant to a decision problem? Two criteria are important.

Bearing on the Future   The consequences of decisions are borne in the future, not the past. To be relevant to a decision, cost or benefit information must involve a future event. The cost information relevant to Worldwide Airways' decision concerning its Frankfurt operations involves the costs that *will be incurred in the future* under the airline's two alternatives. Costs incurred in the past in the airline's Frankfurt operations will not change regardless of management's decision, and they are irrelevant to the decision at hand.

Since relevant information involves future events, the managerial accountant must predict the amounts of the relevant costs and benefits. In making these predictions, the accountant often will use estimates of cost behavior based on historical data. There is an important and subtle issue here. *Relevant* information must involve costs and benefits to be realized in the *future*. However, the accountant's *predictions* of those costs and benefits often are based on data from the *past*.

Different under Competing Alternatives   Relevant information must involve costs or benefits that *differ among the alternatives*. Costs or benefits that are the same across all the available alternatives have no bearing on the decision. For example, suppose Worldwide Airways' management decides to keep its reservations and ticketing office in Frankfurt regardless of whether its Frankfurt hub is eliminated. Then the costs of the reservations and ticketing office will not differ between the two alternatives regarding elimination of the Frankfurt hub. Hence, those costs are irrelevant to that decision.

Unique versus Repetitive Decisions

Unique decisions arise infrequently or only once. Worldwide Airways' decision regarding its Frankfurt hub is an example. Compiling data for unique decisions usually

> **Learning Objective 3**
>
> List and explain two criteria that must be satisfied by relevant information.

> "You have to try to summarize numbers. You can't just give numbers. People in marketing are going to make decisions based on your numbers. They have to understand what those numbers mean." (14b)
>
> **Abbott Laboratories**

requires a special analysis by the managerial accountant. The relevant information often will be found in many diverse places in the organization's overall information system.

In contrast, *repetitive decisions* are made over and over again, at either regular or irregular intervals. For example, Worldwide Airways makes route-scheduling decisions every six months. Such a routine decision makes it worthwhile for the managerial accountant to keep a special file of the information relevant to the scheduling decision.

Cost predictions relevant to repetitive decisions typically can draw on a large amount of historical data. Since the decisions have been made repeatedly in the past, the data from those decisions should be readily available. Information relevant to unique decisions is harder to generate. The managerial accountant typically will have to give more thought to deciding which data are relevant, and will have less historical data available upon which to base predictions.

Importance of Identifying Relevant Costs and Benefits

Why is it important for the managerial accountant to isolate the relevant costs and benefits in a decision analysis? The reasons are twofold. First, generating information is a costly process. The relevant data must be sought, and this requires time and effort. By focusing on only the relevant information, the managerial accountant can simplify and shorten the data-gathering process.

Second, people can effectively use only a limited amount of information. Beyond this, they experience **information overload,** and their decision-making effectiveness declines. By routinely providing only information about relevant costs and benefits, the managerial accountant can reduce the likelihood of information overload.

Identifying Relevant Costs and Benefits

Learning Objective 4

Identify relevant costs and benefits, giving proper treatment to sunk costs, opportunity costs, and unit costs.

To illustrate how managerial accountants determine relevant costs and benefits, we will consider several decisions faced by the management of Worldwide Airways. Based in London, the airline flies routes between Europe and the United States, between various cities in Europe, and between Europe and several Asian and African cities.

Sunk Costs

Sunk costs are costs that have already been incurred. They do not affect any future cost and cannot be changed by any current or future action. Sunk costs are irrelevant to decisions, as the following two examples show.

Book Value of Equipment

At Heathrow Airport in London, Worldwide Airways has a three-year-old loader truck used to load in-flight meals onto airplanes. The box on the truck can be lifted hydraulically to the level of a jumbo jet's side doors. The *book value* of this loader, defined as the asset's acquisition cost less the accumulated depreciation to date, is computed as follows:

Acquisition cost of old loader	$100,000
Less: Accumulated depreciation	75,000
Book value	$ 25,000

The loader has one year of useful life remaining, after which its salvage value will be zero. However, it could be sold now for $5,000. In addition to the annual depreciation of $25,000, Worldwide Airways annually incurs $80,000 in variable costs to operate the loader. These include the costs of operator labor, gasoline, and maintenance.

John Orville, Worldwide Airways' ramp manager at Heathrow Airport, faces a decision about replacement of the loader. A new kind of loader uses a conveyor belt to move meals into an airplane. The new loader is much cheaper than the old hydraulic loader and costs less to operate. However, the new loader would be operable for only one year before it would need to be replaced. Pertinent data about the new loader are as follows:

Acquisition cost of new loader	$15,000
Useful life	1 year
Salvage value after one year	0
Annual depreciation	$15,000
Annual operating costs	$45,000

Orville's initial inclination is to continue using the old loader for another year. He exclaims, "We can't dump that equipment now. We paid $100,000 for it, and we've only used it three years. If we get rid of that loader now, we'll lose $20,000 on the disposal." Orville reasons that the old loader's book value of $25,000, less its current salvage value of $5,000, amounts to a loss of $20,000.

Fortunately, Orville's comment is overheard by Joan Wilbur, the managerial accountant in the company's Heathrow Airport administrative offices. Wilbur points out to Orville that the book value of the old loader is a *sunk cost.* It cannot affect any future cost the company might incur. To convince Orville that she is right, Wilbur prepares the analysis shown in Exhibit 14–2.

Regardless of which alternative is selected, the $25,000 book value of the old loader will be an expense or loss in the next year. If the old loader is kept in service, the $25,000 will be recognized as depreciation expense; otherwise, the $25,000 cost will be incurred by the company as a write-off of the asset's book value. Thus, the current book value of the old loader is a *sunk cost* and irrelevant to the replacement decision.

Notice that the *relevant* data in the equipment replacement decision are items (3), (4), and (5). Each of these items meets the two tests of relevant information:

1. The costs or benefits relate to the future.
2. The costs or benefits differ between the alternatives.

The proceeds from selling the old loader, item (3), will be received in the future only under the "replace" alternative. Similarly, the acquisition cost (depreciation) of the new loader,

> "[We are continually moving] from being the scorekeeper to being an active, involved participant in crafting business solutions." (14c)
> **Boeing**

Costs of Two Alternatives

		(a) Do Not Replace Old Loader*	(b) Replace Old Loader*	(c) Differential Cost: (a) − (b)
Sunk cost	(1) Depreciation of old loader	$ 25,000		
	OR			–0–
	(2) Write-off of old loader's book value		$25,000	
Relevant data	(3) Proceeds from disposal of old loader	–0–	(5,000)†	$ 5,000
	(4) Depreciation (cost) of new loader	–0–	15,000	(15,000)
	(5) Operating costs	80,000	45,000	35,000
	Total cost	$105,000	$80,000	$25,000

*Since costs are the focus of the analysis in this exhibit, costs are shown in columns (a) and (b) without parentheses.

†Parentheses denote a cash inflow in this case.

Exhibit 14–2

Equipment Replacement Decision: Worldwide Airways

item (4), is a future cost incurred only under the "replace" alternative. The operating cost, item (5), is also a future cost that differs between the two alternatives.

Differential Costs

Exhibit 14–2 includes a column entitled *Differential Cost*. A **differential cost** is the difference in a cost item under two decision alternatives. The computation of differential costs is a convenient way of summarizing the relative advantage of one alternative over the other. John Orville can make a correct equipment-replacement decision in either of two ways: (1) by comparing the total cost of the two alternatives, shown in columns (a) and (b); or (2) by focusing on the total differential cost, shown in column (c), which favors the "replacement" option.

Cost of Inventory on Hand

Never having studied managerial accounting, John Orville is slow to learn how to identify sunk costs. The next week he makes another mistake.

The inventory of spare aircraft parts held by Worldwide Airways at Heathrow Airport includes some obsolete parts originally costing $20,000. The company no longer uses the planes for which the parts were purchased. The obsolete parts include spare passenger seats, luggage racks, and galley equipment. The spare parts could be sold to another airline for $17,000. However, with some modifications, the obsolete parts could still be used in the company's current fleet of aircraft. Using the modified parts would save Worldwide Airways the cost of purchasing new parts for its airplanes.

John Orville decides not to dispose of the obsolete parts, because doing so would entail a loss of $3,000. Orville reasons that the $20,000 book value of the parts, less the $17,000 proceeds from disposal, would result in a $3,000 loss on disposal. Joan Wilbur, the managerial accountant, comes to the rescue again, demonstrating that the right decision is to dispose of the parts. Wilbur's analysis is shown in Exhibit 14–3.

Notice that the book value of the obsolete inventory is a sunk cost. If the parts are modified, the $20,000 book value will be an expense during the period when the parts are used. Otherwise, the $20,000 book value of the asset will be written off when the parts are sold. As a sunk cost, the book value of the obsolete inventory will not affect any future cash flow of the company.

As the managerial accountant's analysis reveals, the relevant data include the $17,000 proceeds from disposal, the $12,000 cost to modify the parts, and the $26,000 cost to buy new parts. All of these data meet the two tests of relevance: they affect future cash flows and they differ between the two alternatives. As Joan Wilbur's analysis shows, Worldwide Airways' cost will be $3,000 less if the obsolete parts are sold and new parts are purchased.

Exhibit 14–3
Obsolete Inventory Decision:
Worldwide Airways

		Costs of Two Alternatives		
		(a) Modify and Use Parts*	(b) Dispose of Parts*	(c) Differential Cost: (a) − (b)
Sunk cost	Book value of parts inventory: asset value written off whether parts are used or not	$20,000	$20,000	$ –0–
Relevant data	Proceeds from disposal of parts	–0–	(17,000)†	17,000
	Cost to modify parts	12,000	–0–	12,000
	Cost incurred to buy new parts for current aircraft fleet	–0–	26,000	(26,000)
	Total cost	$32,000	$29,000	$ 3,000

*Since costs are the focus of the analysis in this exhibit, costs are shown in columns (a) and (b) without parentheses.
†Parentheses denote a cash inflow in this case.

		Revenues and Costs under Two Alternatives		
Relevant or Irrelevant		(a) Nonstop Route*	(b) With Stop in Delhi*	(c) Differential Amount†: (a) – (b)
Relevant	(1) Passenger revenue	$240,000	$258,000	$(18,000)
Irrelevant	(2) Cargo revenue	80,000	80,000	–0–
Relevant	(3) Landing fee in Delhi	–0–	(5,000)	5,000
Relevant	(4) Use of airport gate facilities	–0–	(3,000)	3,000
Relevant	(5) Flight crew cost	(2,000)	(2,500)	500
Relevant	(6) Fuel	(21,000)	(24,000)	3,000
Relevant	(7) Meals and services	(4,000)	(4,600)	600
Irrelevant	(8) Aircraft maintenance	(1,000)	(1,000)	–0–
	Total revenue less costs	$292,000	$297,900	$ (5,900)

*In columns (a) and (b), parentheses denote costs and numbers without parentheses are revenues.

†In column (c), parentheses denote differential items favoring option (b).

Exhibit 14–4
Flight-Route Decision:
Worldwide Airways

Irrelevant Future Costs and Benefits

At Worldwide Airways' headquarters in London, Emma Rees, manager of flight scheduling, is in the midst of making a decision about the London-to-Hong Kong route. The flight is currently nonstop, but she is considering a stop in Delhi. She feels that the route would attract additional passengers if the stop is made, but there also would be additional variable costs. Her analysis appears in Exhibit 14–4.

The analysis indicates that the preferable alternative is the route that includes a stop in Delhi. Notice that the cargo revenue [item (2)] and the aircraft maintenance cost [item (8)] are irrelevant to the flight-route decision. Although these data do affect future cash flows, they *do not differ between the two alternatives.* All of the other data in Exhibit 14–4 are relevant to the decision, because they do differ between the two alternatives. The analysis in Exhibit 14–4 could have ignored the irrelevant data; the same decision would have been reached. (Exercise 14–30, at the end of the chapter, will ask you to prove this assertion by redoing the analysis without the irrelevant data.)

Opportunity Costs

Another decision confronting Emma Rees is whether to add two daily round-trip flights between London and Toronto. Her initial analysis of the relevant costs and benefits indicates that the additional revenue from the flights will exceed their costs by $30,000 per month. Hence, she is ready to add the flights to the schedule. However, Rex Ifans, Worldwide Airways' hangar manager in London, points out that Rees has overlooked an important consideration.

Worldwide Airways currently has excess space in its hangar. A commuter airline has offered to rent the hangar space for $40,000 per month. However, if the London-to-Toronto flights are added to the schedule, the additional aircraft needed in London will require the excess hangar space.

If Worldwide Airways adds the London-to-Toronto flights, it will forgo the opportunity to rent the excess hangar space for $40,000 per month. Thus, the $40,000 in rent forgone is an *opportunity cost* of the alternative to add the new flights. An **opportunity cost** is the potential benefit given up when the choice of one action precludes a different action. Although people tend to overlook or underestimate the importance of opportunity costs, they are just as relevant as out-of-pocket costs in evaluating decision alternatives. In Worldwide Airways' case, the best action is to rent the excess warehouse space to the commuter airline, rather than adding the new flights. The analysis in Exhibit 14–5 supports this conclusion.

Exhibit 14–5
Decision to Add Flights:
Worldwide Airways

	(a) Add Flights	(b) Do Not Add Flights	(c) Differential Amount: (a) − (b)
Additional revenue from new flights less additional costs	$30,000	–0–	$ 30,000
Rental of excess hangar space	–0–	$40,000	(40,000)*
Total	$30,000	$40,000	$(10,000)

*Parentheses denote that differential benefit favors option (b).

It is a common mistake for people to overlook or underweigh opportunity costs. The $40,000 hangar rental, which will be forgone if the new flights are added, is an *opportunity cost* of the option to add the flights. It is a *relevant cost* of the decision, and it is just as important as any out-of-pocket expenditure.

Summary

Relevant costs and benefits satisfy the following two criteria:

1. They affect the future.
2. They differ between alternatives.

Sunk costs are *not* relevant costs, because they do not affect the future. An example of a sunk cost is the book value of an asset, either equipment or inventory. *Future costs or benefits that are identical across all decision alternatives are not relevant.* They can be ignored when making a decision. *Opportunity costs are relevant costs.* Such costs deserve particular attention because many people tend to overlook them when making decisions.

> "I would say that they [line managers] view us as business partners." (14d)
>
> **Boeing**

Analysis of Special Decisions

Learning Objective 5

Prepare analyses of various special decisions, properly identifying the relevant costs and benefits.

What are the relevant costs and benefits when a manager must decide whether to add or drop a product or service? What data are relevant when deciding whether to produce or buy a service or component? These decisions and certain other nonroutine decisions merit special attention in our discussion of relevant costs and benefits.

Accept or Reject a Special Offer

Jim Wright, Worldwide Airways' vice president for operations, has been approached by a Chinese tourist agency about flying chartered tourist flights from Hong Kong to London. The tourist agency has offered Worldwide Airways $150,000 per round-trip flight on a jumbo jet. Given the airline's usual occupancy rate and air fares, a round-trip jumbo-jet flight between Hong Kong and London typically brings in revenue of $250,000. Thus, the tourist agency's specially priced offer requires a special analysis by Jim Wright.

Wright knows that Worldwide Airways has two jumbo jets that are not currently in use. The airline has just eliminated several unprofitable routes, freeing these aircraft for other uses. The airline was not currently planning to add any new routes, and therefore the two jets were idle. To help make his decision, Wright asks for cost data from the controller's office. The controller provides the information in Exhibit 14–6, which pertains to a typical round-trip jumbo-jet flight between Hong Kong and London.

The variable costs cover aircraft fuel and maintenance, flight-crew costs, in-flight meals and services, and landing fees. The fixed costs allocated to each flight cover Worldwide Airways' fixed costs, such as aircraft depreciation, maintenance and depreciation of facilities, and fixed administrative costs.

Revenue:		
Passenger	$250,000	
Cargo	30,000	
Total revenue		$280,000
Expenses:		
Variable expenses of flight	$ 90,000	
Fixed expenses allocated to each flight	100,000	
Total expenses		190,000
Profit		$ 90,000

Exhibit 14–6

Data for Typical Flight Between Hong Kong and London: Worldwide Airways

If Jim Wright had not understood managerial accounting, he might have done the following *incorrect analysis.*

Special price for charter	$150,000
Total cost per flight	190,000
Loss on charter flight	$ (40,000)

This calculation suggests that the special charter offer should be rejected. What is the error in this analysis? The mistake is the inclusion of allocated fixed costs in the cost per flight. This is an error, because the *fixed costs will not increase in total* if the charter flight is added. Since the fixed costs will not change under either of the alternate choices, they are irrelevant.

Fortunately, Jim Wright does not make this mistake. He knows that only the variable costs of the proposed charter are relevant. Moreover, Wright determines that the variable cost of the charter would be less than that of a typical flight, because Worldwide Airways would not incur the variable costs of reservations and ticketing. These variable expenses amount to $5,000 for a scheduled flight. Thus, Wright's analysis of the charter offer is as shown below.

Assumes excess capacity (idle aircraft)	Special price for charter		$150,000
	Variable cost per routine flight	$90,000	
	Less: Savings on reservations and ticketing	5,000	
	Variable cost of charter		85,000
	Contribution from charter		$ 65,000

Wright's analysis shows that the special charter flight will contribute $65,000 toward covering the airline's fixed costs and profit. Since the airline has excess flight capacity, due to the existence of idle aircraft, the optimal decision is to accept the special charter offer.

No Excess Capacity

Now let's consider how Wright's analysis would appear if Worldwide Airways had no idle aircraft. Suppose that in order to fly the charter between Hong Kong and London, the airline would have to cancel its least profitable route, which is between Tokyo and Hong Kong. This route contributes $80,000 toward covering the airline's fixed costs and profit. Thus, if the charter offer is accepted, the airline will incur an opportunity cost of $80,000 from the forgone contribution of the Tokyo-Hong Kong route. Now Wright's analysis should appear as shown below.

Assumes no excess capacity (no idle aircraft)	Special price for charter		$150,000
	Variable cost per routine flight	$90,000	
	Less: Savings on reservations and ticketing	5,000	
	Variable cost of charter	$85,000	
	Add: Opportunity cost, forgone contribution on canceled Tokyo-Hong Kong route	80,000	165,000
	Loss from charter		$ (15,000)

Thus, if Worldwide Airways has no excess flight capacity, Jim Wright should reject the special charter offer.

Summary   The decision to accept or reject a specially priced order is common in both service-industry and manufacturing firms. Manufacturers often are faced with decisions about selling products in a special order at less than full price. The correct analysis of such decisions focuses on the relevant costs and benefits. Fixed costs, which often are allocated to individual units of product or service, are usually irrelevant. Fixed costs typically will not change in total, whether the order is accepted or rejected.

When excess capacity exists, the only relevant costs usually will be the variable costs associated with the special order. When there is no excess capacity, the opportunity cost of using the firm's facilities for the special order is also relevant to the decision.

Outsource a Product or Service

Ellie Rickenbacker is Worldwide Airways' manager of in-flight services. She supervises the airline's flight attendants and all of the firm's food and beverage operations. Rickenbacker currently faces a decision regarding the preparation of in-flight dinners at the airline's Atlanta hub. In the Atlanta flight kitchen, full-course dinners are prepared and packaged for long flights that pass through Atlanta. In the past, all of the desserts were baked and packaged in the flight kitchen. However, Rickenbacker has received an offer from an Atlanta bakery to bake the airline's desserts. Thus, her decision is whether to *outsource* the dessert portion of the in-flight dinners. An **outsourcing decision,** also called a **make-or-buy decision,** entails a choice between producing a product or service in-house and purchasing it from an outside supplier. To help guide her decision, Rickenbacker has assembled the cost information in Exhibit 14–7, which shows a total cost per dessert of 25 cents.

The Atlanta bakery has offered to supply the desserts for 21 cents each. Rickenbacker's initial inclination is to accept the bakery's offer, since it appears that the airline would save 4 cents per dessert. However, the controller reminds Rickenbacker that not all of the costs listed in Exhibit 14–7 are relevant to the outsourcing decision. The controller modifies Rickenbacker's analysis as shown in Exhibit 14–8.

If Worldwide Airways stops making desserts, it will save all of the variable costs but only 1 cent of fixed costs. The 1-cent saving in supervisory salaries would result because the airline could get along with two fewer kitchen supervisors. The remainder of the fixed costs would be incurred even if the desserts were purchased. These remaining fixed costs of supervision and depreciation would have to be reallocated to the flight kitchen's other products. In light of the controller's revised analysis, Rickenbacker realizes that the airline should continue to make its own desserts. To outsource the desserts would require an expenditure of 21 cents per dessert, but only 15 cents per dessert would be saved.

Exhibit 14–7
Cost of In-Flight Desserts:
Worldwide Airways

	Cost per Dessert
Variable costs:	
Direct material (food and packaging)	$.06
Direct labor	.04
Variable overhead	.04
Fixed costs (allocated to products):	
Supervisory salaries	.04
Depreciation of flight-kitchen equipment	.07
Total cost per dessert	$.25

Management
Accounting
Practice

Northwest, JetBlue,
America West,
British Airways,
Emirates Airways,
Mercator, and Infosys

GLOBAL AIRLINE OUTSOURCING

Outsourcing is widely used in a variety of businesses and airlines are no exception. The management at Northwest Airlines, for example, has decided to outsource some of its flight attendants in order to reduce the cost of filling the most expensive of these positions. According to *The Wall Street Journal*, it's a sign "that Northwest, which has filed for bankruptcy protection, wants to become a 'virtual airline,' with all sorts of jobs previously claimed by organized labor outsourced to cheaper workers, some overseas."

Other airlines are outsourcing key maintenance operations. JetBlue Airways "will fly at least 17 of its 68 Airbus A320 jets to" El Salvador. "There, over six days, local mechanics working for an aircraft-overhaul shop under contract to JetBlue will inspect each plane nose to tail." After any required maintenance is performed, the jets will fly back to the U.S. America West Airlines also is flying its planes to El Salvador for inspections required by the FAA. "Northwest Airlines flies its wide-body jets to Singapore and Hong Kong for service by outside contractors."

Back-office operations are outsourced as well. British Airways partners with outsource providers for significant parts of their information technology services, including processing of reservations and frequent-flyer program transactions.

Emirates Airways sees outsourcing of airline services as a business opportunity. They created a technology division called Mercator that partners with Indian outsourcing giant Infosys to provide their own technology support and to sell those services to other companies.[1]

To clarify her decision further, Rickenbacker asks the controller to prepare an analysis of the *total costs* per month of making or buying desserts. The controller's report, displayed in Exhibit 14–9, shows the total cost of producing 1,000,000 desserts, the flight kitchen's average monthly volume.

The total-cost analysis confirmed Rickenbacker's decision to continue making desserts in the airline's flight kitchen.

	Cost per Dessert	Costs Saved by Purchasing Desserts
Variable costs:		
Direct material	$ .06	$ .06
Direct labor	.04	.04
Variable overhead	.04	.04
Fixed costs (allocated to products):		
Supervisory salaries	.04	.01
Depreciation of flight-kitchen equipment	.07	–0–
Total cost per dessert	$ .25	$ .15
Cost of purchasing desserts (per dessert)		$ .21
Loss per dessert if desserts are purchased (savings per dessert minus purchase cost per dessert, or $.15 − $.21)		$(.06)

Exhibit 14–8

Cost Savings from Buying In-Flight Desserts: Worldwide Airways

[1]The sources for these anecdotes are S. Carey, "Northwest Targets Flight Attendants for Outsourcing," *The Wall Street Journal,* October, 26, 2005, pp. A1, A8; S. Carey and A. Frangos, "Airlines, Facing Cost Pressure, Outsource Crucial Safety Tasks," *The Wall Street Journal,* January 21, 2005, pp. A1, A5; and G. Jenner, "Airlines Deepen Ties with Outsourcing Partners," *Airline Business,* April 24, 2009.

In today's global economy, more and more companies are outsourcing significant products and services. Gallo Winery, for example, buys a significant portion of its grapes from other vintners. Kodak outsources its entire data processing operation. Cummins Engine outsources many of its pistons, and Intel Corporation buys microchips. Chase Bank outsources its cafeteria and legal services. Many pharmaceutical companies, such as Japan's Yamanouchi Pharmaceutical, have outsourced much of their production to cut costs.[2] Pictured here are wine and pharmaceutical production.

Beware of Unit-Cost Data   Fixed costs often are allocated to individual units of product or service for product-costing purposes. For decision-making purposes, however, unitized fixed costs can be misleading. As the total-cost analysis in Exhibit 14–9 shows, only $10,000 in fixed monthly cost will be saved if the desserts are purchased. The remaining $100,000 in monthly fixed cost will continue whether the desserts are made or

Exhibit 14–9
Total-Cost Analysis of
Outsourcing Decision:
Worldwide Airways

	Cost per Month	Costs Saved by Purchasing Desserts
Variable costs:		
Direct material	$ 60,000	$ 60,000
Direct labor	40,000	40,000
Variable overhead	40,000	40,000
Fixed costs (allocated to products):		
Supervisory salaries	40,000	10,000*
Depreciation of flight-kitchen equipment	70,000	–0–
Total cost per month	$250,000	$150,000
Cost of purchasing desserts (per month)		$210,000
Total loss if desserts are purchased (total savings minus total cost of purchasing, or $150,000 − $210,000)		$ (60,000)

*Cost of monthly compensation for two kitchen supervisors, who will not be needed if desserts are purchased.

---

[2]Peter Landers, "Japan's Local Drug Makers to Outsource to Suppliers," *The Wall Street Journal,* March 26, 2002, p. A20.

purchased. Rickenbacker's initial cost analysis in Exhibit 14–7 implies that each dessert costs the airline 25 cents, but that 25-cent cost includes 11 cents of unitized fixed costs. Most of these costs will remain unchanged regardless of the outsourcing decision. By allocating fixed costs to individual products or services, they are made to appear variable even though they are not.

Add or Drop a Service, Product, or Department

Worldwide Airways offers its passengers the opportunity to join its World Express Club. Club membership entitles a traveler to use the club facilities at the airport in London. Club privileges include a private lounge and restaurant, discounts on meals and beverages, and use of a small health spa.

Jayne Wing, the president of Worldwide Airways, is worried that the World Express Club might not be profitable. Her concern is caused by the statement of monthly operating income shown in the Excel spreadsheet in Exhibit 14–10.

In her weekly staff meeting, Wing states her concern about the World Express Club's profitability. The controller responds by pointing out that not all of the costs on the club's income statement would be eliminated if the club were discontinued. The vice president for sales adds that the club helps Worldwide Airways attract passengers who it might otherwise lose to a competitor. As the meeting adjourns, Wing asks the controller to prepare an analysis of the relevant costs and benefits associated with the World Express Club. The controller's analysis is displayed in Exhibit 14–11.

The controller's analysis in Exhibit 14–11 contains two parts. Part I focuses on the relevant costs and benefits of the World Express Club only, while ignoring any impact of the club on other airline operations. In column (a), the controller has listed the club's revenues and expenses from the income statement presented in Exhibit 14–10. Column (b) in Exhibit 14–11 lists the expenses that will continue if the club is eliminated. These expenses are called **unavoidable expenses.** In contrast, the expenses appearing in column (a) but not column (b) are **avoidable expenses.** The airline will no longer incur these expenses if the club is eliminated.

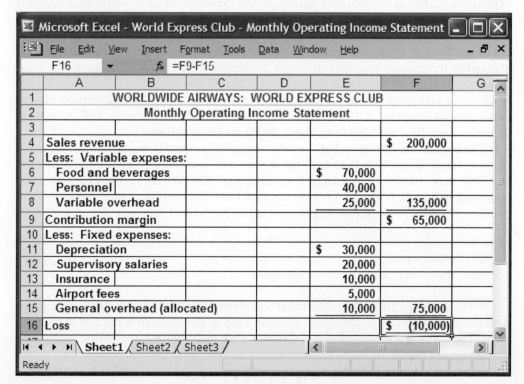

Exhibit 14–10
World Express Club Monthly Operating Income Statement: Worldwide Airways

Exhibit 14–11
Relevant Costs and Benefits
of World Express Club:
Worldwide Airways

	(a) Keep Club	(b) Eliminate Club	(c) Differential Amount: (a) − (b)
Part I:			
Sales revenue	$200,000	–0–	$200,000
Less: Variable expenses:			
Food and beverages	(70,000)	–0–	(70,000)
Personnel	(40,000)	–0–	(40,000)
Variable overhead	(25,000)	–0–	(25,000)
Contribution margin	$ 65,000	–0–	$ 65,000
Less: Fixed expenses:			
Depreciation	$ (30,000)	$(30,000)	$ –0–
Supervisory salaries	(20,000)	–0–	(20,000)
Insurance	(10,000)	(10,000)	–0–
Airport fees	(5,000)	–0–	(5,000)
General overhead (allocated)	(10,000)	(10,000)	–0–
Total fixed expenses	$ (75,000)	$(50,000)	$ (25,000)
Profit (loss)	$ (10,000)	$(50,000)	$ 40,000*
		Expenses in the column above are **unavoidable** expenses	Expenses in the column above are **avoidable** expenses
Part II:			
Contribution margin from general airline operations that will be forgone if club is eliminated	$ 60,000	–0–	$ 60,000

*The *positive* $40,000 differential amount reflects the fact that the company is $40,000 *better off* by keeping the club.

Notice that all of the club's variable expenses are avoidable. The depreciation expense, $30,000, is an allocated portion of the depreciation on a Worldwide Airways building, part of which is used by the World Express Club. If the Club is discontinued, the airline will continue to own and use the building, and the depreciation expense will continue. Thus, it is an unavoidable expense. The fixed supervisory salaries are avoidable, since these employees will no longer be needed if the club is eliminated. The fixed insurance expense of $10,000 is not avoidable; the $5,000 fee paid to the airport for the privilege of operating the club is avoidable. Finally, the club's allocated portion of general overhead expenses, $10,000, is not avoidable. Worldwide Airways will incur these expenses regardless of its decision about the World Express Club.

The conclusion shown by Part I of the controller's report is that the club should not be eliminated. If the club is closed, the airline will lose more in contribution margin, $65,000, than it saves in avoidable fixed expenses, $25,000. Thus, the club's $65,000 contribution margin is enough to cover the avoidable fixed expenses of $25,000 and still contribute $40,000 toward covering the overall airline's fixed expenses.

World Express Club's contribution margin	$65,000
Avoidable fixed expenses	25,000
Contribution of club toward covering overall airline's fixed expenses	$40,000

Now consider Part II of the controller's analysis in Exhibit 14–11. As the vice president for sales pointed out, the World Express Club is an attractive feature to many travelers. The controller estimates that if the club were discontinued, the airline would lose $60,000 each month in forgone contribution margin from general airline operations.

ADDING A SERVICE

Changing business conditions can cause a company to rethink its business model and add new services. Federal Express, for example, found that a sizable portion of its over-night letter delivery business was eliminated by e-mail. Customers no longer needed to ship a hard-copy document overnight, when the same document could be sent instanta-neously via e-mail. FedEx also found a decline in the need for overnight repair parts ship-ments. Many customers' improved supply chain systems resulted in better spare parts preparedness and less need for last-minute overnight shipments. FedEx responded by adding slower ground shipment services to compete more directly with UPS and other ground-based delivery services. While FedEx still excels when an overnight shipment is needed, its ground transport business is becoming an increasing part of its operations. FedEx also is adding new technology-based services that give customers greater ability to track shipments in transit.

 Caterpillar has added heavy equipment overhaul services to its already successful manufacturing operations. The company uses available capacity in its manufacturing plants to disassemble and rebuild heavy diesel engines, after cleaning, inspecting, and repairing them. This new service component of Caterpillar's operations has become the company's fastest-growing business unit, with annual revenue topping $1 billion.[3]

This loss in contribution margin would result from losing to a competing airline current passengers who are attracted to Worldwide Airways by its World Express Club. This $60,000 in forgone contribution margin is an *opportunity cost* of the option to close down the club.

 Considering both Parts I and II of the controller's analysis, Worldwide Airways' monthly profit will be greater by $100,000 if the club is kept open. Recognition of two issues is key to this conclusion:

1. Only the avoidable expenses of the club will be saved if it is discontinued.
2. Closing the club will adversely affect the airline's other operations.

Special Decisions in Manufacturing Firms

Some types of decisions are more likely to arise in manufacturing companies than in service-industry firms. We will examine two of these decisions.

Joint Products: Sell or Process Further

A **joint production process** results in two or more products, called *joint products*. An example is the processing of cocoa beans into cocoa powder and cocoa butter. Cocoa beans constitute the input to the joint production process, and the two joint products are cocoa powder and cocoa butter. The point in the production process where the joint

> **Learning Objective 6**
>
> Analyze manufacturing decisions involving joint products and limited resources.

---

[3]"Delivering the Goods at FedEx," *BusinessWeek,* June 13, 2005, pp. 60–62; D. Foust, "The Ground War at FedEx," *BusinessWeek,* November 28, 2005, pp. 42, 43; "Overnight, Everything Changed for FedEx; Can It Reinvent Itself?" *The Wall Street Journal,* November 4, 1999, p. A1; and M. Arndt, "Cat Sinks Its Claws into Services," *BusinessWeek,* December 5, 2005, pp. 56–59.

products are identifiable as separate products is called the **split-off point.** Other examples of joint production processes include the slaughtering of animals for various cuts of meat and the processing of petroleum into various products, such as kerosene and gasoline.

Manufacturers with joint production processes sometimes must decide whether a product should be sold at the split-off point or processed further before being sold. Such a decision recently confronted Bernard Semal, the president of Brussels-based International Chocolate Company. Semal's firm imports cocoa beans and processes them into cocoa powder and cocoa butter. Only a portion of the cocoa powder is used by International Chocolate Company in the production of chocolates. The remainder of the cocoa powder is sold to an ice cream producer. Semal is considering the possibility of processing his remaining cocoa powder into an instant cocoa mix. Data pertaining to Semal's decision are displayed in Exhibit 14–12.

Notice from the diagram that cocoa beans are processed in one-tonne (1,000-kilogram) batches. The total cost of the cocoa beans and the joint processing is $1,100. This is called the **joint cost.** The output of the joint process is 750 kilograms of cocoa butter and 250 kilograms of cocoa powder.

How should Bernard Semal approach the decision about processing the cocoa powder into instant cocoa mix? What are the relevant costs and benefits? First, let's consider the joint cost of $1,100. Is this a relevant cost in the decision at hand? *The joint cost is not a relevant cost,* because it will not change regardless of the decision Semal makes.

Suppose the $1,100 joint cost had been allocated to the two joint products for product-costing purposes. A common method of allocating a joint cost is the **relative-sales-value method,** in which the joint cost is allocated between the joint products in proportion to their sales value at the split-off point.[4] International Chocolate Company would make the following joint cost allocation.

Joint Cost	Joint Products	Sales Value at Split-Off Point	Relative Proportion	Allocation of Joint Cost
	Cocoa butter	$750	.60	$ 660
$1,100	Cocoa powder	500	.40	440
	Total joint cost allocated			$1,100

Exhibit 14–12

Joint Processing of Cocoa Beans: International Chocolate Company

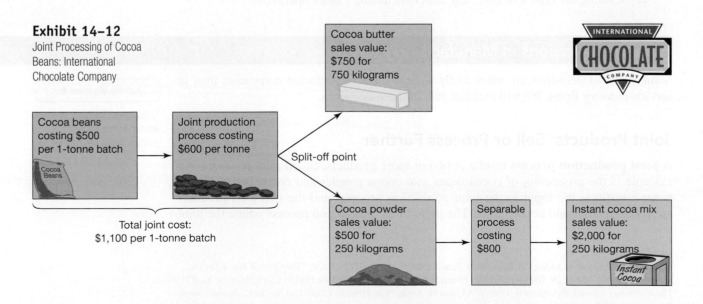

[4]Other methods of allocating joint costs are covered in Chapter 17.

Relevant or Irrelevant		(a) Process Cocoa Powder into Instant Cocoa Mix	(b) Sell Cocoa Powder at Split-Off Point	(c) Differential Amount: (a) − (b)
	Sales revenue:			
Irrelevant	Cocoa butter	$ 750	$ 750	–0–
Relevant	Instant cocoa mix	2,000		} → $1,500
Relevant	Cocoa powder		500	
	Less: Costs:			
Irrelevant	Joint cost	(1,100)	(1,100)	–0–
Relevant	Separable cost of processing cocoa powder into instant cocoa mix	(800)	–0–	(800)
	Total	$ 850	$ 150	$ 700

Exhibit 14–13
Decision to Sell or Process Further: International Chocolate Company

Does this allocation of the $1,100 joint cost make it relevant to the decision about processing cocoa powder into instant cocoa mix? The answer is no. *The $1,100 joint cost still does not change in total,* whether the cocoa powder is processed further or not. The joint cost is irrelevant to the decision at hand.

The only costs and benefits relevant to Semal's decision are those that differ between the two alternatives. The proper analysis is shown in Exhibit 14–13.

There is a shortcut method that arrives at the same conclusion as Exhibit 14–13. In this approach, the incremental revenue from the further processing of cocoa powder is compared with the **separable processing cost,** which is the cost incurred after the split-off point, as follows:

Sales value of instant cocoa mix	$2,000
Sales value of cocoa powder	500
Incremental revenue from further processing	$1,500
Less: Separable processing cost	(800)
Net benefit from further processing	$ 700

Both analyses indicate that Bernard Semal should process his excess cocoa powder into instant cocoa mix. The same conclusion is reached if the analysis is done on a per-unit basis rather than a total basis:

Sales value of instant cocoa mix ($2,000 ÷ 250 kilograms)	$8.00 per kilogram
Sales value of cocoa powder ($500 ÷ 250 kilograms)	2.00 per kilogram
Incremental revenue from further processing	$6.00 per kilogram
Less: Separable processing cost ($800 ÷ 250 kilograms)	(3.20) per kilogram
Net benefit from further processing	$2.80 per kilogram

Once again, the analysis shows that Bernard Semal should decide to process the cocoa powder into instant cocoa mix.

Decisions Involving Limited Resources

Organizations typically have limited resources. Limitations on floor space, machine time, labor hours, or raw materials are common. Operating with limited resources, a firm often must choose between sales orders, deciding which orders to fill and which ones to decline. In making such decisions, managers must decide which product or service is the most profitable.

Exhibit 14–14
Contribution Margin per
Case: International Chocolate
Company

	Bars	Truffles
Sales price	$10.00	$14.00
Less: Variable costs:		
Direct material	$ 3.00	$ 3.75
Direct labor	2.00	2.50
Variable overhead	3.00	3.75
Variable selling and administrative costs	1.00	2.00
Total variable costs	$ 9.00	$12.00
Contribution margin per case	$ 1.00	$ 2.00

Exhibit 14–15
Contribution Margin per
Machine Hour: International
Chocolate Company

		Bars	Truffles
(a)	Contribution margin per case	$1.00	$2.00
(b)	Machine hours required per case	.02	.05
(a) ÷ (b)	Contribution margin per machine hour	$50	$40

To illustrate, suppose International Chocolate Company's Bruges plant makes two specialty products, Truffles and Bars. The contribution margin for a case of each of these products is computed in Exhibit 14–14.

A glance at the contribution-margin data suggests that Truffles are more profitable than Bars. It is true that a case of Truffles contributes more toward covering the company's fixed cost and profit. However, an important consideration has been ignored in the analysis so far. The Bruges plant's capacity is limited by its available machine time. Only 700 machine hours are available in the plant each month. International Chocolate Company can sell as many cases of either specialty chocolate as it can produce, so production is limited only by the constraint on machine time.

To maximize the plant's total contribution toward covering fixed cost and profit, management should strive to use each machine hour as effectively as possible. This realization alters the analysis of product profitability. The relevant question is *not,* Which specialty chocolate has the highest contribution margin *per case?* The pertinent question is, Which product has the highest contribution margin *per machine hour?* This question is answered with the calculation in Exhibit 14–15.

A machine hour spent in the production of Bars will contribute $50 toward covering fixed cost and profit, while a machine hour devoted to Truffles contributes only $40. Hence, the Bruges plant's most profitable product is Bars, when the plant's scarce resource is taken into account.

Suppose International Chocolate Company's Bruges plant manager, Christine Belleflamme, is faced with a choice between two sales orders, only one of which can be accepted. Only 100 hours of unscheduled machine time remains in the month, and it can be used to produce either Truffles or Bars. The analysis in Exhibit 14–16 shows that Belleflamme should devote the 100-hour block of machine time to filling the order for Bars.

As Exhibit 14–16 demonstrates, a decision about the best use of a limited resource should be made on the basis of the *contribution margin per unit of the scarce resource.*

Multiple Scarce Resources Suppose the Bruges plant had a limited amount of *both* machine hours *and* labor hours. Now the analysis of product profitability is more complicated. The choice as to which product is most profitable typically will involve a trade-off between the two scarce resources. Solving such a problem requires a powerful mathematical tool called *linear programming,* which is covered in the appendix to this chapter.

	Bars	Truffles
Contribution margin per case	$1.00	$2.00
Number of cases produced in 100 hours of machine time	× 5,000*	× 2,000†
Total contribution toward covering fixed cost and profit	$5,000	$4,000

*Bars: 100 hours ÷ .02 hour per case = 5,000 cases
†Truffles: 100 hours ÷ .05 hour per case = 2,000 cases

Exhibit 14–16
Total Contribution from 100 Machine Hours: International Chocolate Company

Theory of Constraints As the previous analysis suggests, a binding constraint can limit a company's profitability. For example, a manufacturing company may have a *bottleneck operation,* through which every unit of a product must pass before moving on to other operations. The *theory of constraints (TOC)* calls for identifying such limiting constraints and seeking ways to relax them. Also referred to as *managing constraints,* this management approach can significantly improve an organization's level of goal attainment. Among the ways that management can relax a constraint by expanding the capacity of a bottleneck operation are the following:

- *Outsourcing* (subcontracting) all or part of the bottleneck operation.
- Investing in additional production equipment and employing *parallel processing,* in which multiple product units undergo the same production operation simultaneously.
- Working *overtime* at the bottleneck operation.
- *Retraining* employees and shifting them to the bottleneck.
- Eliminating any *non-value-added activities* at the bottleneck operation.

Uncertainty

Our analyses of the decisions in this chapter assumed that all relevant data were known with certainty. In practice, of course, decision makers are rarely so fortunate. One common technique for addressing the impact of uncertainty is *sensitivity analysis.* **Sensitivity analysis** is a technique for determining what would happen in a decision analysis if a key prediction or assumption proved to be wrong.

To illustrate, let's return to Christine Belleflamme's decision about how to use the remaining 100 hours of machine time in International Chocolate Company's Bruges plant. The calculation in Exhibit 14–15 showed that Bars have the higher contribution margin per machine hour. Suppose Belleflamme is uncertain about the contribution margin per case of Bars. A sensitivity analysis shows how sensitive her decision is to the value of this uncertain parameter. As Exhibit 14–17 shows, the Bars contribution margin could decline to $.80 per case before Belleflamme's decision would change. As long as

		Bars	Truffles
Original Analysis			
(a)	Contribution margin per case predicted	$1.00	$2.00
(b)	Machine hours required per case	.02	.05
(a) ÷ (b)	Contribution per machine hour	$50.00	$40.00
Sensitivity Analysis			
(c)	Contribution margin per case hypothesized in sensitivity analysis	$.80	
(d)	Machine hours required per case	.02	same
(c) ÷ (d)	Contribution per machine hour	$40.00 ←	

Exhibit 14–17
Sensitivity Analysis: International Chocolate Company

Exhibit 14–18

Use of Expected Values: International Chocolate Company

Bars			Truffles		
Possible Values of Contribution Margin		**Probability**	**Possible Values of Contribution Margin**		**Probability**
$ .75		.5	$1.50		.3
1.25		.5	2.00		.4
			2.50		.3
Expected value	(.5)($.75) + (.5)($1.25) = $1.00		(.3)($1.50) + (.4)($2.00) + (.3)($2.50) = $2.00		
Machine hours required per case		.02			.05
Expected value of contribution per machine hour		$50	>		$40

the contribution margin per case of Bars exceeds $.80 per case, the 100 hours of available machine time should be devoted to Bars.

Sensitivity analysis can help the managerial accountant decide which parameters in an analysis are most critical to estimate accurately. In this case, the managerial accountant knows that the contribution margin per case of Bars could be as much as 20 percent lower than the original $1.00 prediction without changing the outcome of the analysis.

Expected Values   Another approach to dealing explicitly with uncertainty is to base the decision on expected values. The **expected value** of a random variable is equal to the sum of the possible values for the variable, each weighted by its probability. To illustrate, suppose the contribution margins per case for Truffles and Bars are uncertain, as shown in Exhibit 14–18. As the exhibit shows, the choice as to which product to produce with excess machine time may be based on the *expected value* of the contribution per machine hour. Statisticians have developed many other methods for dealing with uncertainty in decision making. These techniques are covered in statistics and decision analysis courses.

Activity-Based Costing and Today's Advanced Manufacturing Environment

Learning Objective 7

Explain the impact of an advanced manufacturing environment and activity-based costing on a relevant-cost analysis.

In this chapter we have explored how to identify the relevant costs and benefits in various types of decisions. How will the relevant-costing approach change in the new manufacturing environment, characterized by just-in-time (JIT) production methods and flexible manufacturing systems (FMS)? How would a relevant-costing analysis change if a company uses an activity-based costing (ABC) system?[5]

The *concepts* underlying a relevant-costing analysis continue to be completely valid in an advanced manufacturing setting and in a situation where activity-based costing is used. The objective of the decision analysis is to determine the costs and benefits that are relevant to the decision. As we found earlier in this chapter, relevant costs and benefits *have a bearing on the future and differ among the decision alternatives.*

What *will* be different in a setting where activity-based costing is used is the decision maker's ability to determine what costs are relevant to a decision. Under ABC, the decision maker typically can associate costs with the activities that drive them much more accurately than under a conventional product-costing system. Let's explore these issues with an illustration.

---

[5]Activity-based costing (ABC), which was introduced conceptually in Chapter 3, is thoroughly explored in Chapter 5. This section can be studied most effectively after completing Chapter 5.

Conventional Outsourcing (Make-or-Buy) Analysis

International Chocolate Company makes filled chocolates in its Brussels plant. The chocolates are packaged in one-kilogram and two-kilogram gift boxes. The company also manufactures the gift boxes in the Brussels plant. The plant manager, Sonia Candotti, was approached recently by a packaging company with an offer to supply the gift boxes at a price of $.45 each. Candotti concluded that the offer should be rejected on the basis of the relevant-costing analysis in Exhibit 14–19. International Chocolate Company's traditional, volume-based product-costing system showed a unit product cost of $.80 per box. However, Candotti realized that not all of the costs would be avoided. She reasoned that all of the direct material, direct labor, and variable overhead would be avoided, but only a small part of the assigned fixed overhead would be saved. She concluded that $60,000 of supervisory salaries and $20,000 of machinery depreciation could be traced directly to gift package production. These costs would be avoided, she felt, but the remaining fixed

A. Manufacturing Overhead Budget for Brussels Plant

Variable overhead:

Electricity	$ 700,000
Oil and lubricants	120,000
Equipment maintenance	180,000
Total variable overhead	$1,000,000

Variable overhead rate: $1,000,000 ÷ 100,000 direct-labor hours = $10 per hour

Fixed overhead:

Plant depreciation	$1,650,000
Product development	300,000
Supervisory salaries	600,000
Material handling	800,000
Purchasing	250,000
Inspection	300,000
Setup	400,000
Machinery depreciation	200,000
Total fixed overhead	$4,500,000

Fixed overhead rate: $4,500,000 ÷ 100,000 direct-labor hours = $45 per hour

B. Conventional Product-Costing Data: Gift Boxes

Direct material	$ 100,000
Direct labor (10,000 hr. at $15 per hr.)	150,000
Variable overhead ($10 per direct-labor hr.)	100,000
Fixed overhead ($45 per direct-labor hr.)	450,000
Total cost	$ 800,000

Unit cost: $800,000 ÷ 1,000,000 boxes = $.80 per box

C. Conventional Outsourcing Analysis: Gift Boxes

Relevant costs (costs that will be avoided if the gift boxes are purchased):

Direct material	$ 100,000
Direct labor	150,000
Variable overhead	100,000

Fixed overhead:

Supervision	60,000
Machinery depreciation	20,000
Total costs to be avoided by purchasing	$ 430,000
Total cost of purchasing (1,000,000 boxes × $.45 per box)	$ 450,000

Exhibit 14–19

Conventional Product-Costing Data and Outsourcing Analysis: International Chocolate Company costs would not. Candotti concluded that only $430,000 of costs would be avoided by purchasing, while $450,000 would be spent to buy the boxes. The decision was clear; the supplier's offer should be rejected.

Activity-Based Costing Analysis of the Outsourcing Decision

At a staff meeting, Candotti mentioned her tentative decision to Johan Iversen, the plant controller. Iversen then explained to Candotti that he was completing a pilot project using activity-based costing. Iversen offered to analyze the outsourcing decision using the new ABC database. Candotti agreed, and Iversen proceeded to do the ABC analysis shown in Exhibit 14–20.

In stage one of the ABC analysis, Iversen designated 11 activity cost pools corresponding to the major items in the Brussels plant's overhead budget. These activity cost pools were categorized as facility-level, product-sustaining level, batch-level, or unit-level activities. In stage two of the ABC project, cost drivers were identified and pool rates were computed. The ABC analysis showed that $243,000 of overhead should be assigned to the gift boxes, rather than $550,000 as the conventional product-costing system had indicated.

Using the ABC database, Iversen completed a new relevant-costing analysis of the outsourcing decision. Iversen felt that all of the overhead costs assigned to the gift

Exhibit 14–20
Activity-Based Costing Analysis of Outsourcing Decision: International Chocolate Company

A. Activity Cost Pools and Pool Rates

Activity Cost Pools	Budgeted Cost	Pool Rate and Cost Driver	Cost Assigned to Gift Boxes
Facility level:			
Plant depreciation	$1,650,000	—	
Product-sustaining level:			
Product development	300,000	$600 per product spec	$600 × 5* = $ 3,000
Supervisory salaries	600,000	$40 per supervisory hour	$40 × 1,500 = 60,000
Batch level:			
Material handling	800,000	$8 per material-handling hour	$8 × 5,000 = 40,000
Purchasing	250,000	$250 per purchase order	$250 × 40 = 10,000
Inspection	300,000	$300 per inspection	$300 × 20 = 6,000
Setup	400,000	$400 per setup	$400 × 10 = 4,000
Unit level:			
Electricity	700,000	$1.40 per machine hour	$1.40 × 50,000 = 70,000
Oil and lubrication	120,000	$.24 per machine hour	$.24 × 50,000 = 12,000
Equipment maintenance	180,000	$.36 per machine hour	$.36 × 50,000 = 18,000
Machinery depreciation	200,000	$.40 per machine hour	$.40 × 50,000 = 20,000
Total overhead for Brussels plant	$5,500,000		
Total overhead assigned to gift box production			$243,000

*The numbers in this column are the quantities of each cost driver required for gift box production.

B. ABC Outsourcing Analysis: Gift Boxes

Relevant costs (costs that will be avoided if the gift boxes are purchased):	
Direct material	$100,000
Direct labor	150,000
Overhead (from ABC analysis in panel A, above)	243,000
Total costs to be avoided by purchasing	$493,000
Total cost of purchasing (1,000,000 boxes × $.45 per box)	$450,000

box operation could be avoided if the boxes were purchased. Notice that none of the facility-level costs are relevant to the analysis. They will not be avoided by purchasing the gift boxes. Iversen's ABC analysis showed that a total of $493,000 of costs could be avoided by purchasing the boxes at a cost of $450,000. This would result in a net saving of $43,000.

Iversen showed the ABC relevant-costing analysis to Candotti. After some discussion, they agreed that various qualitative issues needed to be explored before a final decision was made. For example, would the new supplier be reliable, and would the gift boxes be of good quality? Nevertheless, Candotti and Iversen agreed that the ABC data cast an entirely different light on the decision.

The Key Point   What has happened here? Why did the conventional and ABC analyses of this decision reach different conclusions? Is the relevant-costing concept faulty?

The answer is no; the relevant-costing idea is alive and well. Both analyses sought to identify the relevant costs as those that would be avoided by purchasing the gift boxes. That approach is valid. The difference in the analyses lies in the superior ability of the ABC data to properly identify what the avoidable costs are. This is the key point. The conventional analysis relied on a traditional, volume-based product-costing system. That system lumps all of the fixed overhead costs together and assigns them using a single, unit-based cost driver (i.e., direct-labor hours). That analysis simply failed to note that many of the so-called fixed costs are *not* really fixed with respect to the appropriate cost driver. The more accurate ABC system correctly showed this fact, and identified additional costs that could be avoided by purchasing.

To summarize, under activity-based costing, the concepts underlying relevant-costing analysis remain valid. However, the ABC system does enable the decision maker to apply the relevant-costing decision model more accurately.

Other Issues in Decision Making

Incentives for Decision Makers

In this chapter, we studied how managers should make decisions by focusing on the relevant costs and benefits. In previous chapters, we covered accounting procedures for evaluating managerial performance. There is an important link between *decision making* and *managerial performance evaluation*. Managers typically will make decisions that maximize their perceived performance evaluations and rewards. This is human nature. If we want managers to make optimal decisions by properly evaluating the relevant costs and benefits, then the performance evaluation system and reward structure had better be consistent with that perspective.

The proper treatment of sunk costs in decision making illustrates this issue. Earlier in this chapter, we saw that sunk costs should be ignored as irrelevant. For example, the book value of an outdated machine is irrelevant in making an equipment-replacement decision. Suppose, however, that a manager correctly ignores an old machine's book value and decides on early replacement of the machine he purchased a few years ago. Now suppose the hapless manager is criticized by his superior for "taking a loss" on the old machine, or for "buying a piece of junk" in the first place. What is our manager likely to do the next time he faces a similar decision? If he is like many people, he will tend to keep the old machine in order to justify his prior decision to purchase it. In so doing, he will be compounding his error. However, he also may be avoiding criticism from a superior who does not understand the importance of goal congruence.

The point is simply that if we want managers to make optimal decisions, we must give them incentives to do so. This requires that managerial performance be judged on the same factors that should be considered in making correct decisions.

Short-Run versus Long-Run Decisions

The decisions we have examined in this chapter were treated as short-run decisions. *Short-run decisions* affect only a short time period, typically a year or less. In reality, many of these decisions would have longer-term implications. For example, managers usually make a decision involving the addition or deletion of a product or service with a relatively long time frame in mind. The process of identifying relevant costs and benefits is largely the same whether the decision is viewed from a short-run or long-run perspective. One important factor that does change in a long-run analysis, however, is the *time value of money.* When several time periods are involved in a decision, the analyst should account for the fact that a $1.00 cash flow today is different from a $1.00 cash flow in five years. A dollar received today can be invested to earn interest, while the dollar received in five years cannot be invested over the intervening time period. The analysis of long-run decisions requires a tool called *capital budgeting,* which is covered in Chapter 16.

Pitfalls to Avoid

Identification of the relevant costs and benefits is an important step in making any economic decision. Nonetheless, analysts often overlook relevant costs or incorrectly include irrelevant data. In this section, we review four common mistakes to avoid in decision making.

1. *Sunk costs.* The book value of an asset, defined as its acquisition cost less the accumulated depreciation, is a sunk cost. Sunk costs cannot be changed by any current or future course of action, so they are irrelevant in decision making. Nevertheless, a common behavioral tendency is to give undue importance to book values in decisions that involve replacing an asset or disposing of obsolete inventory. People often seek to justify their past decisions by refusing to dispose of an asset, even if a better alternative has been identified. *The moral: Ignore sunk costs.*

2. *Unitized fixed costs.* For product-costing purposes, fixed costs often are divided by some activity measure and assigned to individual units of product. The result is to make a fixed cost appear variable. While there are legitimate reasons for this practice from a *product-costing* perspective, it can create havoc in *decision making.* Therefore, in a decision analysis, it is usually wise to include a fixed cost in its total amount, rather than as a per-unit cost. *The moral: Beware of unitized fixed costs in decision making.*

3. *Allocated fixed costs.* It is also common to allocate fixed costs across divisions, departments, or product lines. A possible result is that a product or department may appear unprofitable when in reality it does make a contribution toward covering fixed costs and profit. Before deciding to eliminate a department, be sure to ask which costs will be *avoided* if a particular alternative is selected. A fixed cost that has been allocated to a department may continue, in total or in part, even after the department has been eliminated. *The moral: Beware of allocated fixed costs; identify the avoidable costs.*

4. *Opportunity costs.* People tend to overlook opportunity costs, or to treat such costs as less important than out-of-pocket costs. Yet opportunity costs are just as real and important to making a correct decision as are out-of-pocket costs. *The moral: Pay special attention to identifying and including opportunity costs in a decision analysis.*

Focus on Ethics

EFFECTS OF DECISION TO CLOSE A DEPARTMENT AND OUTSOURCE

Outsourcing has become a common way of reducing costs in many organizations. Such decisions, though, often have repercussions that may not be captured "by the numbers." Employee morale, product quality, and vendor reliability are some of the issues that should be considered. Let's revisit the scenario described earlier at the International Chocolate Company. Recall that the Brussels plant manager, Sonia Candotti (M), was considering outsourcing the production of gift boxes for the company's fine chocolates. A conventional analysis of the decision pointed toward keeping the production operation in-house. Now let's change the scenario a bit, and consider the following conversation between Johan Iversen, plant controller (C), and Jack Edgeworth, supervisor of the gift box production department (SG). The conversation takes place after the two friends' weekly tennis game.

> **Iversen (C):** "Well, you beat me again, Jack. I'm starting to feel old."
>
> **Edgeworth (SG):** "It was a close match, Johan. Always is. Fortunately, it looks like we'll be able to keep our matches up, too."
>
> **Iversen (C):** "What do you mean?"
>
> **Edgeworth (SG):** "I'm talking about the outsourcing decision Sonia was considering. Fortunately, the analysis showed her that we should keep making our own gift boxes. So my department stays in business. And I won't have to consider a transfer. My wife's very happy about that, with the kids in school and all."
>
> **Iversen (C):** "Uh, Jack, I think there's something you need to know about."
>
> **Edgeworth (SG):** "What's that?"
>
> **Iversen (C):** "I've been doing some preliminary studies using a technique called activity-based costing. I think it could improve our decision making in a lot of areas."
>
> **Edgeworth (SG):** "So?"
>
> **Iversen (C):** "That outsourcing decision is one of the areas where I tried out the new ABC approach. I just finished the analysis yesterday. I was going

to schedule an appointment with Sonia and you next week to discuss it."
>
> **Edgeworth (SG):** "I'm getting queasy about where this is going, Johan. What did your analysis show?"
>
> **Iversen (C):** "It changes the conclusion—pretty dramatically, in fact. The ABC study shows that we'd save over $40,000 each year by outsourcing."
>
> **Edgeworth (SG):** "That's not really all that much, of a savings, is it, Johan? Between friends, I mean?"
>
> **Iversen (C):** "It's not a trivial amount, Jack."
>
> **Edgeworth (SG):** "Look, Johan, I don't think I've ever asked anything of you before. But can't you bury this one for me? Our family really doesn't need another move. And I've got people working for me who will probably lose their jobs. We've done a good job for the company. Our product is top notch. Nobody's ever complained about a thing."
>
> **Iversen (C):** "I don't see how I can withhold the analysis from Sonia, Jack. She has a right to all the information I have."
>
> **Edgeworth (SG):** "But you said you were just doing preliminary studies, Johan. Sonia doesn't know anything about this one, does she?"
>
> **Iversen (C):** "Not yet, Jack, but I've got a professional obligation to show it to her."
>
> **Edgeworth (SG):** "You're opening a Pandora's box, Johan. What about employee morale if you close my department? And what about product quality, and reliability of the supply?"
>
> **Iversen (C):** "Those are valid issues, Jack. But they need to be addressed on their own merits, in a full and open discussion."
>
> **Edgeworth (SG):** "Could you at least share this so-called ABC study with me before you show it to Sonia? Maybe I'll see something you've missed."
>
> **Iversen (C):** "I don't see why not, Jack. Come by my office tomorrow morning—say about 10:00."

Identify any ethical issues you see in this scenario. How would you resolve them? What should the controller do?

Chapter Summary

LO1 Describe seven steps in the decision-making process and the managerial accountant's role in that process. The decision-making steps are: (1) clarify the decision problem; (2) specify the criterion; (3) identify the alternatives; (4) develop a decision model; (5) collect the data; (6) select an alternative; and (7) evaluate decision effectiveness.

LO2 Explain the relationship between quantitative and qualitative analyses in decision making. The managerial accountant's key role in the decision-making process is to provide data relevant to the decision. Managers can then use these data in preparing a quantitative analysis of the decision. Qualitative factors also are considered in making the final decision.

LO3 List and explain two criteria that must be satisfied by relevant information. In order to be relevant to a decision, a cost or benefit must (1) bear on the future and (2) differ under the various decision alternatives.

LO4 Identify relevant costs and benefits, giving proper treatment to sunk costs, opportunity costs, and unit costs. Sunk costs, such as the book value of equipment or inventory, are not relevant to decisions. Such costs do not have any bearing on the future. Opportunity costs frequently are relevant to decisions, but they often are overlooked by decision makers. Unit costs bear particular scrutiny in decision-making situations. Fixed costs often are unitized and assigned to products or services for product-costing purposes. For decision-making purposes, however, unit costs can be misleading, since the total fixed cost will not increase as the total number of units produced increases.

LO5 Prepare analyses of various special decisions, properly identifying the relevant costs and benefits. To analyze any special decision, the proper approach is to determine all of the costs and benefits that will differ among the alternatives. Common decisions include the following: (1) accept or reject a special offer; (2) outsource a product or service; and (3) add or drop a service, product, or department.

LO6 Analyze manufacturing decisions involving joint products and limited resources. A common decision that arises in a joint-product environment is whether to sell a joint product at the split-off point or process it further. This decision should be based on the incremental costs and benefits occurring after the split-off point. A common decision involving limited resources is which of several products to produce. The correct decision is to produce the product with the highest contribution margin per unit of the scarce resource.

LO7 Explain the impact of an advanced manufacturing environment and activity-based costing on a relevant-cost analysis. The concepts underlying a relevant-cost analysis remain valid in an advanced manufacturing environment and in situations where activity-based costing is used. However, an ABC system typically enables a decision maker to estimate the relevant costs in a decision problem more accurately.

LO8 Formulate a linear program to solve a product-mix problem with multiple constraints (appendix). A linear program can be used to solve a firm's product-mix problem when the production process is constrained by scarce resources. A linear program consists of a linear objective function and a set of linear constraints. The solution to the optimization problem consists of finding the optimal solution point within the feasible region, as determined by the constraints.

Review Problem on Relevant Costs

Guangzhou Camera Company has received a special order for photographic equipment it does not normally produce. The company has excess capacity, and the order could be manufactured without reducing production of the firm's regular products. Discuss the relevance of each of the following items in computing the cost of the special order.

1. Equipment to be used in producing the order has a book value of $2,000. The equipment has no other use for Guangzhou Camera Company. If the order is not accepted, the equipment will be sold for $1,500. If the equipment is used in producing the order, it can be sold in three months for $800.

2. If the special order is accepted, the operation will require some of the storage space in the company's plant. If the space is used for this purpose, the company will rent storage space temporarily in a nearby warehouse at a cost of $18,000. The building depreciation allocated to the storage space to be used in producing the special order is $12,000.

3. If the special order is accepted, it will require a subassembly. Guangzhou Camera Company can purchase the subassembly for $24 per unit from an outside supplier or make it for $30 per unit. The $30 cost per unit was determined as follows:

Direct material	$10.00
Direct labor	6.00
Variable overhead	6.00
Allocated fixed overhead	8.00
Total unit cost of subassembly	$30.00

Solution to Review Problem

1. The book value of the equipment is a sunk cost, irrelevant to the decision. The relevant cost of the equipment is $700, determined as follows:

Sales value of equipment now	$1,500
Sales value after producing special order	800
Differential cost	$ 700

2. The $12,000 portion of building depreciation allocated to the storage space to be used for the special order is irrelevant. First, it is a sunk cost. Second, any costs relating to the company's factory building will continue whether the special order is accepted or not. The relevant cost is the $18,000 rent that will be incurred only if the special order is accepted.

3. Guangzhou Camera Company should make the subassembly. The subassembly's relevant cost is $22 per unit.

Relevant Cost of Making Subassembly (per unit)		Relevant Cost of Purchasing Subassembly (per unit)	
Direct material	$10.00	Purchase price	$24.00
Direct labor	6.00		
Variable overhead	6.00		
Total	$22.00		

Notice that the unitized fixed overhead, $8, is not a relevant cost of the subassembly. Guangzhou Camera Company's *total* fixed cost will not change, whether the special order is accepted or not.

Key Terms

For each term's definition refer to the indicated page, or turn to the glossary at the end of the text.

accurate information, 628
avoidable expenses, 639
constraints,* 654
decision variables,* 654
differential cost, 632
expected value, 646
feasible region,* 654

information overload, 630
joint cost, 642
joint production process, 641
make-or-buy decision, 636
objective function,* 654
opportunity cost, 633
outsourcing decision, 636

qualitative characteristics, 627
relative-sales-value method, 642
relevant information, 628
sensitivity analysis, 645

separable processing cost, 643
split-off point, 642
sunk costs, 630
timely information, 629
unavoidable expenses, 639

---

*Term appears in the appendix.

APPENDIX TO CHAPTER 14

Linear Programming

Learning Objective 8

Formulate a linear program to solve a product-mix problem with multiple constraints (appendix).

When a firm produces multiple products, management must decide how much of each output to produce. In most cases, the firm is limited in the total amount it can produce, due to constraints on resources such as machine time, direct labor, or raw materials. This situation is known as a *product-mix problem.*

To illustrate, we will use International Chocolate Company's Bruges plant, which produces Truffles and Bars. Exhibit 14–21 provides data pertinent to the problem.

Linear programming is a powerful mathematical tool, well suited to solving International Chocolate Company's product-mix problem. The steps in constructing the linear program are as follows:

1. Identify the **decision variables,** which are the variables about which a decision must be made. International Chocolate's decision variables are as follows:

   Decision X = Number of cases of Bars to produce each month
   variables Y = Number of cases of Truffles to produce each month

2. Write the **objective function,** which is an algebraic expression of the firm's goal. International Chocolate's goal is to *maximize its total contribution margin.* Since Bars bring a contribution margin of $1 per case, and Truffles result in a contribution margin of $2 per case, the firm's objective function is the following:

   Objective function   Maximize $Z = X + 2Y$

3. Write the **constraints,** which are algebraic expressions of the limitations faced by the firm, such as those limiting its productive resources. International Chocolate has a constraint for machine time and a constraint for direct labor.

   Machine-time constraint $.02X + .05Y \leq 700$
   Labor-time constraint $.20X + .25Y \leq 5,000$

Suppose, for example, that management decided to produce 20,000 cases of Bars and 6,000 cases of Truffles. The machine-time constraint would appear as follows:

   $(.02)(20,000) + (.05)(6,000) = 700$

Thus, at these production levels, the machine-time constraint would just be satisfied, with no machine hours to spare.

Graphical Solution

To understand how the linear program described above will help International Chocolate's management solve its product-mix problem, examine the graphs in Exhibit 14–22. The two colored lines in panel A represent the constraints. The colored arrows indicate that the production quantities, X and Y, must lie on or below these lines. Since the production quantities must be nonnegative, colored arrows also appear on the graphs' axes. Together, the axes and constraints form an area called the **feasible region,** in which the solution to the linear program must lie.

The black slanted line in panel A represents the objective function. Rearrange the objective function equation as follows:

   $$Z = X + 2Y \longrightarrow Y = \frac{Z}{2} - \frac{1}{2}X$$

Exhibit 14–21
Data for Product-Mix Problem: International Chocolate Company

	Bars	Truffles
Contribution margin per case	$1.00	$2.00
Machine hours per case	.02	.05
Direct-labor hours per case	.20	.25
	Machine Hours	**Direct-Labor Hours**
Limited resources: hours available per month	700	5,000

A. Constraints, Feasible Region, and Objective Function

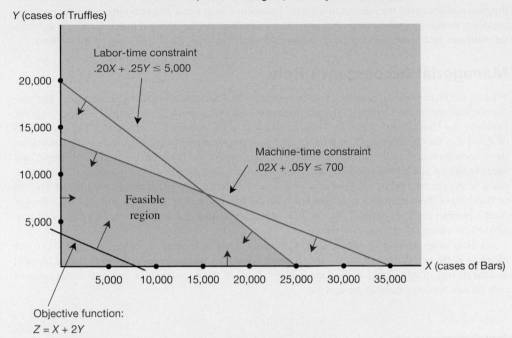

Exhibit 14–22
Product-Mix Problem
Expressed as Linear Program:
International Chocolate
Company

B. Solution of Linear Program

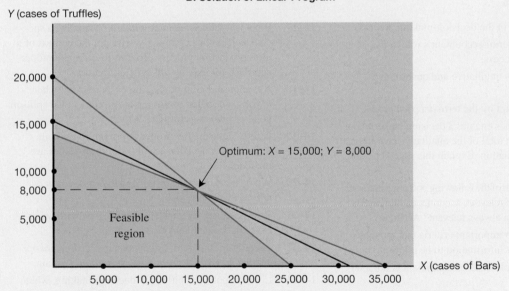

This form of the objective function shows that the slope of the equation is $-\frac{1}{2}$, which is the slope of the objective-function line in the exhibit. Management's goal is to maximize total contribution margin, denoted by Z. To achieve the maximum, the objective-function line must be moved as far outward and upward in the feasible region as possible, while maintaining the same slope. This goal is represented in panel A by the arrow that points outward from the objective-function line.

Solution   The result of moving the objective-function line as far as possible in the indicated direction is shown in panel B of the exhibit. The objective-function line intersects the feasible region at exactly one point, where X equals 15,000 and Y equals 8,000. Thus, International Chocolate's optimal product mix is 15,000 cases of Bars and 8,000 cases of Truffles per month. The total contribution margin is calculated as shown below.

$$\text{Total contribution margin} = (15,000)(\$1) + (8,000)(\$2) = \$31,000$$

Simplex Method and Sensitivity Analysis   Although the graphical method is instructive, it is a cumbersome technique for solving a linear program. Fortunately, mathematicians have developed a more efficient solution method called the *simplex algorithm*. A computer can apply the algorithm to a complex linear program and determine the solution in seconds. In addition, most linear programming computer packages provide a sensitivity analysis of the problem. This analysis shows the decision maker the extent to which the estimates used in the objective function and constraints can change without changing the solution.

Managerial Accountant's Role

What is the managerial accountant's role in International Chocolate's product-mix decision? The production manager in the company's Bruges plant makes this decision, with the help of a linear program. However, the linear program uses *information supplied by the managerial accountant*. The coefficients of X and Y in the objective function are unit contribution margins. Exhibit 14–14 shows that calculating these contribution margins requires estimates of direct-material, direct-labor, variable-overhead, and variable selling and administrative costs. These estimates were provided by a managerial accountant, along with estimates of the machine time and direct-labor time required to produce a case of Truffles or Bars. All of these estimates were obtained from the standard-costing system, upon which the Bruges plant's product costs are based. Thus, the managerial accountant makes the product-mix decision possible by providing the relevant cost data.

Linear programming is widely used in business decision making. Among the applications are blending in the petroleum and chemical industries; scheduling of personnel, railroad cars, and aircraft; and the mixing of ingredients in the food industry. In all of these applications, managerial accountants provide information crucial to the analysis.

Review Questions

14–1. List the seven steps in the decision-making process.

14–2. Describe the managerial accountant's role in the decision-making process.

14–3. Distinguish between qualitative and quantitative decision analyses.

14–4. Explain what is meant by the term *decision model.*

14–5. A quantitative analysis enables a decision maker to put a "price" on the sum total of the qualitative characteristics in a decision situation. Explain this statement, and give an example.

14–6. What is meant by each of the following potential characteristics of information: relevant, accurate, and timely? Is objective information always relevant? Accurate?

14–7. List and explain two important criteria that must be satisfied in order for information to be relevant.

14–8. Explain why the book value of equipment is not a relevant cost.

14–9. Is the book value of inventory on hand a relevant cost? Why?

14–10. Why might a manager exhibit a behavioral tendency to inappropriately consider sunk costs in making a decision?

14–11. Give an example of an irrelevant future cost. Why is it irrelevant?

14–12. Define the term *opportunity cost*, and give an example of one.

14–13. What behavioral tendency do people often exhibit with regard to opportunity costs?

14–14. How does the existence of excess production capacity affect the decision to accept or reject a special order?

14–15. What is meant by the term *differential cost analysis?*

14–16. Briefly describe the proper approach for making a decision about adding or dropping a product line.

14–17. What is a *joint production process?* Describe a special decision that commonly arises in the context of a joint production process. Briefly describe the proper approach for making this type of decision.

14–18. Are allocated joint processing costs relevant when making a decision to sell a joint product at the split-off point or process it further? Why?

14–19. Briefly describe the proper approach to making a production decision when limited resources are involved.

14–20. What is meant by the term *contribution margin per unit of scarce resource?*

14–21. How is sensitivity analysis used to cope with uncertainty in decision making?

14–22. There is an important link between *decision making* and *managerial performance evaluation*. Explain.

14–23. List four potential pitfalls in decision making, which represent common errors.

14–24. Why can unitized fixed costs cause errors in decision making?

14–25. Give two examples of sunk costs, and explain why they are irrelevant in decision making.

14–26. "Accounting systems should produce only relevant data and forget about the irrelevant data. Then I'd know what was relevant and what wasn't!" Comment on this remark by a company president.

14–27. Are the concepts underlying a relevant-cost analysis still valid in an advanced manufacturing environment? Are these concepts valid when activity-based costing is used? Explain.

14–28. List five ways that management can seek to relax a constraint by expanding the capacity of a bottleneck operation.

Exercises

Choose an organization and a particular decision situation. Then give examples, using that decision context, of each step illustrated in Exhibit 14–1. For example, you could choose a decision that would be made by a retailer, such as H & M or Virgin Megastores. Or you could focus on a service provider, such as Hertz rent-a-car or Iberostar Hotels. Alternatively, select a manufacturer, such as Nike or Nokia. Or consider a decision to be made by your college or home city.

■ **Exercise 14–29**
Steps in Decision-Making Process
(LO 1)

Redo Exhibit 14–4 without the irrelevant data.

■ **Exercise 14–30**
Irrelevant Future Costs and Benefits
(LO 3, 4)

Vernazza Pizza's owner bought his current pizza oven four years ago for $10,000, and it has one more year of life remaining. He is using straight-line depreciation for the oven. He could purchase a new oven for $1,400, but it would last only one year. The owner figures the new oven would save him $1,500 in annual operating expenses compared to operating the old one. Consequently, he has decided against buying the new oven, since doing so would result in a "loss" of $500 over the next year.

■ **Exercise 14–31**
Machine Replacement
(LO 4, 5)

Required:

1. How do you suppose the owner came up with $500 as the loss for the next year if the new pizza oven were purchased? Explain.
2. Criticize the owner's analysis and decision.
3. Prepare a correct analysis of the owner's decision.

Lamont Industries produces chemicals for the swimming pool industry. In one joint process, 10,000 liters of GSX are processed into 7,000 liters of xenolite and 3,000 liters of banolide. The cost of the joint process, including the GSX, is $19,000. The firm allocates $13,300 of the joint cost to the xenolite and $5,700 of the cost to the banolide. The 3,000 liters of banolide can be sold at the split-off point for $2,500, or be processed further into a product called kitrocide. The sales value of 3,000 liters of kitrocide is $10,000, and the additional processing cost is $8,100.

■ **Exercise 14–32**
Joint Products
(LO 4, 5, 6)

Required: Lamont's president has asked your consulting firm to make a recommendation as to whether the banolide should be sold at the split-off point or processed further. Write a letter providing an analysis and a recommendation.

Day Street Deli's owner is disturbed by the poor profit performance of his ice cream counter. He has prepared the following profit analysis for the year just ended.

■ **Exercise 14–33**
Drop Product Line
(LO 4, 5)

Sales		$45,000
Less: Cost of food		20,000
Gross profit		$25,000
Less: Operating expenses:		
Wages of counter personnel	$12,000	
Paper products (e.g., napkins)	4,000	
Utilities (allocated)	2,900	
Depreciation of counter equipment and furnishings	2,500	
Depreciation of building (allocated)	4,000	
Deli manager's salary (allocated)	3,000	
Total		28,400
Loss on ice cream counter		$ (3,400)

Required: Criticize and correct the owner's analysis.

■ Exercise 14–34
Outsourcing Decision; Use of
Internet
(LO 1, 2, 5)

Visit the Web site of one of the following companies, or a different company of your choosing.

Hauwei Technologies	www.hauwei.com
Novartis	www.novartis.com
Corning	www.corning.com
Gucci	www.gucci.com
Unilever	www.unilever.com
BBC	www.bbc.co.uk

Required: Read about the company's activities and operations. Choose an activity that is necessary for the company's operations, and then discuss the pros and cons of outsourcing that activity.

■ Exercise 14–35
Obsolete Inventory
(LO 4, 5)

Tourmalet Corporation manufactures bicycle parts. The company currently has an $18,000 inventory of parts that have become obsolete due to changes in design specifications. The parts could be sold for $10,000, or modified for $12,000 and sold for $23,400.

Required:

1. Which of the data above are relevant to the decision about the obsolete parts?
2. Prepare an analysis of the decision.

■ Exercise 14–36
Special Order
(LO 4, 5)

Intercontinental Chemical Company, located in Buenos Aires, Argentina, recently received an order for a product it does not normally produce. Since the company has excess production capacity, management is considering accepting the order. In analyzing the decision, the assistant controller is compiling the relevant costs of producing the order. Production of the special order would require 8,000 kilograms of theolite. Intercontinental does not use theolite for its regular product, but the firm has 8,000 kilograms of the chemical on hand from the days when it used theolite regularly. The theolite could be sold to a chemical wholesaler for $14,500. The book value of the theolite is $2.00 per kilogram. Intercontinental could buy theolite for $2.40 per kilogram.

Required:

1. What is the relevant cost of theolite for the purpose of analyzing the special-order decision?
2. Discuss each of the numbers given in the exercise with regard to its relevance in making the decision.

■ Exercise 14–37
Continuation of Preceding
Exercise
(LO 4, 5)

Intercontinental's special order also requires 1,000 kilograms of genatope, a solid chemical regularly used in the company's products. The current stock of genatope is 8,000 kilograms at a book value of $8.10 per kilogram. If the special order is accepted, the firm will be forced to restock genatope earlier than expected, at a predicted cost of $8.70 per kilogram. Without the special order, the purchasing manager predicts that the price will be $8.30 when normal restocking takes place. Any order of genatope must be in the amount of 5,000 kilograms.

Required:

1. What is the relevant cost of genatope?
2. Discuss each of the figures in the exercise in terms of its relevance to the decision.

■ Exercise 14–38
Closing a Department
(LO 4, 5)

Fusion Metals Company is considering the elimination of its Packaging Department. Management has received an offer from an outside firm to supply all Fusion's packaging needs. To help her in making the decision, Fusion's president has asked the controller for an analysis of the cost of running Fusion's Packaging Department. Included in that analysis is $9,100 of rent, which represents the Packaging Department's allocation of the rent on Fusion's factory building. If the Packaging Department is eliminated, the space it used will be converted to storage space. Currently Fusion rents storage space in a nearby warehouse for $11,000 per year. The warehouse rental would no longer be necessary if the Packaging Department were eliminated.

Required:

1. Discuss each of the figures given in the exercise with regard to its relevance in the department-closing decision.
2. What type of cost is the $11,000 warehouse rental, from the viewpoint of the costs of the Packaging Department?

If Fusion Metals Company closes its Packaging Department, the department manager will be appointed manager of the Cutting Department. The Packaging Department manager makes $45,000 per year. To hire a new Cutting Department manager will cost Fusion $60,000 per year.

Required: Discuss the relevance of each of these salary figures to the department-closing decision.

■ **Exercise 14–39**
Continuation of Preceding
Exercise
(LO 4, 5)

Zytel Corporation produces cleaning compounds and solutions for industrial and household use. While most of its products are processed independently, a few are related. Grit 337, a coarse cleaning powder with many industrial uses, costs $1.60 per kilogram to make and sells for $2.00 a per kilogram. A small portion of the annual production of this product is retained for further processing in the Mixing Department, where it is combined with several other ingredients to form a paste, which is marketed as a silver polish selling for $4.00 per jar. This further processing requires 250 grams of Grit 337 per jar. Costs of other ingredients, labor, and variable overhead associated with this further processing amount to $2.50 per jar. Variable selling costs are $.30 per jar. If the decision were made to cease production of the silver polish, $5,600 of Mixing Department fixed costs could be avoided. Zytel has limited production capacity for Grit 337, but unlimited demand for the cleaning powder.

Required: Calculate the minimum number of jars of silver polish that would have to be sold to justify further processing of Grit 337.

(CMA, adapted)

■ **Exercise 14–40**
Joint Products; Relevant
Costs; Cost-Volume-Profit
Analysis
(LO 4, 6)

Duo Company manufactures two products, Uno and Dos. Contribution margin data follow.

■ **Exercise 14–41**
Limited Resource
(LO 6)

	Uno	Dos
Unit sales price	$13.00	$31.00
Less variable cost:		
Direct material	$ 7.00	$ 5.00
Direct labor	1.00	6.00
Variable overhead	1.25	7.50
Variable selling and administrative cost	.75	.50
Total variable cost	$10.00	$19.00
Unit contribution margin	$ 3.00	$12.00

Duo company's production process uses highly skilled labor, which is in short supply. The same employees work on both products and earn the same wage rate.

Required: Which of Duo Company's products is more profitable? Explain.

Refer to the data given in the preceding exercise for Duo Company. Assume that the direct-labor rate is $24 per hour, and 10,000 labor hours are available per year. In addition, the company has a short supply of machine time. Only 8,000 hours are available each year. Uno requires 1 machine hour per unit, and Dos requires 2 machine hours per unit.

Required: Formulate the production planning problem as a linear program. Specifically identify (1) the decision variables, (2) the objective function, and (3) the constraints.

■ **Exercise 14–42**
Linear Programming
(Appendix)
(LO 6, 8)

■ **Exercise 14–43**
Linear Programming;
Formulate and Solve
wvwwGraphically (Appendix)
(LO 8)

Chennai Chemical Company manufactures two industrial chemical products, called kreolite-red and kreolite-blue. Two machines are used in the process, and each machine has 24 hours of capacity per day. The following data are available:

	Kreolite-Red	Kreolite-Blue
Selling price per drum	$36	$42
Variable cost per drum	$28	$28
Hours required per drum on machine I	2 hr	2 hr
Hours required per drum on machine II	1 hr	3 hr

The company can produce and sell partially full drums of each chemical. For example, a half drum of kreolite-red sells for $18.

Required:

1. Formulate the product-mix problem as a linear program.
2. Solve the problem graphically.

Problems

All applicable Problems are available with McGraw-Hill's *Connect Accounting™*. ■ **connect** |ACCOUNTING

■ **Problem 14–44**
Production Decisions;
Limited Capacity
(LO 5, 6)

Kitchen Magician, Inc. has assembled the following data pertaining to its two most popular products.

	Blender	Electric Mixer
Direct material	$ 6	$11
Direct labor	4	9
Manufacturing overhead @ $16 per machine hour	16	32
Cost if purchased from an outside supplier	20	38
Annual demand (units)	20,000	28,000

Past experience has shown that the fixed manufacturing overhead component included in the cost per machine hour averages $10. Kitchen Magician's management has a policy of filling all sales orders, even if it means purchasing units from outside suppliers.

Required:

1. If 50,000 machine hours are available, and management desires to follow an optimal strategy, how many units of each product should the firm manufacture? How many units of each product should be purchased?
2. With all other things constant, if management is able to reduce the direct material for an electric mixer to $6 per unit, how many units of each product should be manufactured? Purchased?
3. *Build a spreadsheet:* Construct an Excel spreadsheet to solve requirement (1) above. Show how the solution will change if the following information changes: the unit cost if purchased from an outside supplier is $22 for the blender and $40 for the electric mixer.

(CMA, adapted)

■ **Problem 14–45**
Special Order; Financial and
Production Considerations
(LO 4, 5)

1. Net contribution to profit:
$34,050

Jupiter Corporation manufactures skateboards. Several weeks ago, the firm received a special-order inquiry from Venus, Inc. Venus desires to market a skateboard similar to one of Jupiter's and has offered to purchase 11,000 units if the order can be completed in three months. The cost data for Jupiter's model no. 43 skateboard follow.

Direct material	$ 8.20
Direct labor: .25 hour at $9.00	2.25
Total manufacturing overhead:	
.5 hour at $20	10.00
Total	$20.45

Additional data:

- The normal selling price of model no. 43 is $26.50; however, Venus has offered Jupiter only $15.75 because of the large quantity it is willing to purchase.

- Venus requires a modification of the design that will allow a $2.10 reduction in direct-material cost.

- Jupiter's production supervisor notes that the company will incur $3,700 in additional setup costs and will have to purchase a $2,400 special device to manufacture these units. The device will be discarded once the special order is completed.

- Total manufacturing overhead costs are applied to production at the rate of $20 per machine hour. This figure is based, in part, on budgeted yearly fixed overhead of $750,000 and planned production activity of 60,000 machine hours (5,000 per month).

- Jupiter will allocate $1,800 of existing fixed administrative costs to the order as ". . . part of the cost of doing business."

Required:

1. Assume that present sales will not be affected. Should the order be accepted from a financial point of view (i.e., is it profitable)? Why? Show calculations.

2. Assume that Jupiter's current production activity consumes 70 percent of planned machine-hour activity. Can the company accept the order and meet Venus' deadline?

3. What options might Jupiter consider if management truly wanted to do business with Venus in hopes of building a long-term relationship with the firm?

■ **Problem 14–46**
Introducing a New Product
(LO 4, 5)

1. Unit contribution margin, Enhanced Model, $218

Johnson and Gomez, Inc. is a small firm involved in the production and sale of electronic business products. The company is well known for its attention to quality and innovation.

During the past 15 months, a new product has been under development that allows users handheld access to e-mail and video images. Johnson and Gomez code named the product the Wireless Wizard and has been quietly designing two models: Basic and Enhanced. Development costs have amounted to $121,000 and $175,000, respectively. The total market demand for each model is expected to be 40,000 units, and management anticipates being able to obtain the following market shares: Basic, 25 percent; Enhanced, 20 percent. Forecasted data follow.

	Basic	Enhanced
Projected selling price	$ 270	$ 350
Per-unit production costs:		
Direct material	28	45
Direct labor	15	20
Variable overhead	24	32
Marketing and advertising	130,000	200,000
Sales salaries	57,000	57,000
Sales commissions*	10%	10%

*Computed on the basis of sales dollars.

Since the start of development work on the Wireless Wizard, advances in technology have altered the market somewhat, and management now believes that the company can introduce only one of the two models. Consultants confirmed this fact not too long ago, with Johnson and Gomez paying $23,000 for an in-depth market study. The total fixed overhead is expected to be the same, regardless of which product is manufactured.

Required:

1. Compute the per-unit contribution margin for both models.
2. Which of the data in the table above should be ignored in making the product-introduction decision? For what reason?
3. Prepare a financial analysis and determine which of the two models should be introduced.
4. What other factors should Johnson and Gomez, Inc. consider before a final decision is made?

■ **Problem 14–47**

Closing an Unprofitable
Department
(LO 4, 5)

1. Income (loss) from closure:
$(12,800)

Tipton One-Stop Decorating sells paint and paint supplies, carpet, and wallpaper at a single-store location. Although the company has been very profitable over the years, management has seen a significant decline in wallpaper sales and earnings. Much of this decline is attributable to the Internet and to companies that advertise deeply discounted prices in magazines and offer customers free shipping. Recent figures follow.

	Paint and Supplies	Carpeting	Wallpaper
Sales	$380,000	$460,000	$140,000
Variable costs	$228,000	$322,000	$112,000
Fixed costs	56,000	75,000	45,000
Total costs	$284,000	$397,000	$157,000
Operating income (loss)	$ 96,000	$ 63,000	$ (17,000)

Tipton is studying whether to drop wallpaper because of the changing market and accompanying loss. If the line is dropped, the following changes are expected to occur:

- The vacated space will be remodeled at a cost of $12,400 and will be devoted to an expanded line of high-end carpet. Sales of carpet are expected to increase by $120,000, and the line's overall contribution margin ratio will rise by five percentage points.
- Tipton can cut wallpaper's fixed costs by 40 percent. Remaining fixed costs will continue to be incurred.
- Customers who purchased wallpaper often bought paint and paint supplies. Sales of paint and paint supplies are expected to fall by 20 percent.
- The firm will increase advertising expenditures by $25,000 to promote the expanded carpet line.

Required:

1. Should Tipton close its wallpaper operation? Show computations to support your answer.

2. Assume that Tipton's wallpaper inventory at the time of the closure decision amounted to $23,700. How would you have treated this additional information in making the decision?

3. What advantages might Internet- and magazine-based firms have over Tipton that would allow these organizations to offer deeply discounted prices—prices far below what Tipton can offer?

4. *Build a spreadsheet:* Construct an Excel spreadsheet to solve requirement (1) above. Show how the solution will change if the following information changes: sales were $400,000, $450,000, and $130,000, for paint and supplies, carpeting, and wallpaper, respectively.

■ **Problem 14–48**

Excess Production Capacity
(LO 5, 6)

2. Contribution margin per
direct-labor hour, Deluxe
Model: $12

Carpenter's Mate, Inc. manufactures electric carpentry tools. The Production Department has met all production requirements for the current month and has an opportunity to produce additional units of product with its excess capacity. Unit selling prices and unit costs for three different drill models are as follows:

	Home Model	Deluxe Model	Pro Model
Selling price	$58	$65	$80
Direct material	16	20	19
Direct labor ($10 per hour)	10	15	20
Variable overhead	8	12	16
Fixed overhead	16	5	15

Variable overhead is applied on the basis of direct-labor dollars, while fixed overhead is applied on the basis of machine hours. There is sufficient demand for the additional production of any model in the product line.

Required:

1. If Carpenter's Mate, Inc. has excess machine capacity and can add more labor as needed (i.e., neither machine capacity nor labor is a constraint), the excess production capacity should be

devoted to producing which product? (Assume that the excess capacity will be used for a single product line.)

2. If Carpenter's Mate has excess machine capacity but a limited amount of labor time, the excess production capacity should be devoted to producing which product or products?

(CMA, adapted)

■ Problem 14–49
Make or Buy
(LO 4, 5)

Casting Technology Resources (CTR) has purchased 10,000 pumps annually from Kobec, Inc. Because the price keeps increasing and reached $68.00 per unit last year, CTR's management is developing an estimate of the cost of manufacturing the pump in CTR's facilities. CTR makes stampings and castings and has little experience with products requiring assembly.

The engineering, manufacturing, and accounting departments have prepared a report for management that includes the following estimate for an assembly run of 10,000 pumps. Additional production employees would be hired to manufacture the pumps but no additional equipment, space, or supervision would be needed.

The report states that total costs for 10,000 units are estimated at $903,000, or $90.30 per unit. The current purchase price is $68.00 per unit, so the report recommends continued purchase of the product.

Components (outside purchases)	$110,000
Assembly labor*	300,000
Manufacturing overhead†	450,000
General and administrative overhead‡	43,000
Total costs	$903,000

*Assembly labor consists of hourly production workers.

†Manufacturing overhead is applied to products on a direct-labor-dollar basis. Variable-overhead costs vary closely with direct-labor dollars.

Fixed overhead	50% of direct-labor dollars
Variable overhead	100% of direct-labor dollars
Manufacturing-overhead rate	150% of direct-labor dollars

‡General and administrative overhead is applied at 5 percent of the total cost of material (or components), assembly labor, and manufacturing overhead.

Required: Was the analysis prepared by Casting Technology Resources' engineering, manufacturing, and accounting departments and their recommendation to continue purchasing the pumps correct? Explain your answer and include any supporting calculations you consider necessary.

(CMA, adapted)

■ Problem 14–50
Outsourcing Decision;
Relevant Costs; Ethics
(LO 3, 4, 5)

1(a). Savings if purchased from Izmir Manufacturing: $(5,840)

The Aegean Division of the Paibec Corporation manufactures subassemblies that are used in the corporation's final products. Osman Arikan of Aegean's Profit Planning Department has been assigned the task of determining whether a component, MTR–2000, should continue to be manufactured by Aegean or purchased from Izmir Manufacturing, an outside supplier. MTR–2000 is part of a subassembly manufactured by Aegean.

Izmir Manufacturing has submitted a bid to manufacture and supply the 32,000 units of MTR–2000 that Paibec will need for 20x1 at a unit price of $17.50. Izmir Manufacturing has assured Paibec that the units will be delivered according to Paibec's production specifications and needs. While the contract price of $17.30 is only applicable in 20x1, Izmir Manufacturing is interested in entering into a long-term arrangement beyond 20x1.

Arikan has gathered the following information regarding Aegean's cost to manufacture MTR–2000 in 20x0. These annual costs will be incurred to manufacture 30,000 units.

Direct material	$195,000
Direct labor	120,000
Factory space rental	84,000
Equipment leasing costs	36,000
Other manufacturing overhead	225,000
Total manufacturing costs	$660,000

Arikan has collected the following additional information related to manufacturing MTR–2000.

- Direct materials used in the production of MTR–2000 are expected to increase 8 percent in 20x1.

- Aegean's direct-labor contract calls for a 2.5 percent increase in 20x1.

- The facilities used to manufacture MTR–2000 are rented under a month-to-month rental agreement. Thus, Aegean can withdraw from the rental agreement without any penalty. Aegean will have no need for this space if MTR–2000 is not manufactured.

- Equipment leasing costs represent special equipment that is used in the manufacture of MTR–2000. This lease can be terminated by paying the equivalent of one month's lease payment for each year left on the lease agreement. Aegean has two years left on the lease agreement, through the end of the year 20x2.

- Forty percent of the other manufacturing overhead is considered variable. Variable overhead changes with the number of units produced, and this rate per unit is not expected to change in 20x1. The fixed manufacturing overhead costs are not expected to change regardless of whether MTR–2000 is manufactured. Equipment other than the leased equipment can be used in Aegean's other manufacturing operations.

Huseyin Kaya, divisional manager of Aegean, stopped by Arikan's office to voice his concern regarding the outsourcing of MTR–2000. Kaya commented, "I am really concerned about outsourcing MTR–2000. I have a son-in-law and a nephew who work on MTR–2000. They could lose their jobs if we buy that component from Izmir Manufacturing. I really would appreciate anything you can do to make sure the cost analysis comes out right to show we should continue making MTR–2000. Corporate is not aware of the material increases and maybe you can leave out some of those fixed costs. I just think we should continue making MTR–2000!"

Required:

1. *a.* Prepare an analysis of relevant costs that shows whether or not the Aegean Division of Paibec Corporation should make MTR–2000 or purchase it from Izmir Manufacturing for 20x1.

   b. Based solely on the financial results, recommend whether the 32,000 units of MTR–2000 for 20x1 should be made by Aegean or purchased from Izmir Manufacturing.

2. Identify and briefly discuss three qualitative factors that the Aegean Division and Paibec Corporation should consider before agreeing to purchase MTR–2000 from Izmir Manufacturing.

3. By referring to the standards of ethical conduct for managerial accountants given in Chapter 1, explain why Osman Arikan would consider the request of Huseyin Kaya to be unethical.

(CMA, adapted)

■ **Problem 14–51**
Joint Products; Sell or
Process Further
(LO 6)

Total revenue from further
processing $460,000

China West Chemical Company is a diversified chemical processing company. The firm manufactures swimming pool chemicals, chemicals for metal processing, specialized chemical compounds, and pesticides.

Currently, the Noorwood plant is producing two derivatives, RNA–1 and RNA–2, from the chemical compound VDB developed by the company's research labs. Each week, 1,200,000 pounds of VDB are processed at a cost of $246,000 into 800,000 pounds of RNA–1 and 400,000 pounds of RNA–2. The proportion of these two outputs cannot be altered, because this is a joint process. RNA–1 has no market value until it is converted into a pesticide with the trade name Fastkil. Processing RNA–1 into Fastkil costs $240,000. Fastkil wholesales at $50 per 100 pounds.

RNA–2 is sold as is for $80 per hundred pounds. However, management has discovered that RNA–2 can be converted into two new products by adding 400,000 pounds of compound LST to the 400,000 pounds of RNA–2. This joint process would yield 400,000 pounds each of DMZ–3 and Pestrol, the two new products. The additional direct-material and related processing costs of this joint process would be $120,000. DMZ–3 and Pestrol would each be sold for $57.50 per 100 pounds. The company's management has decided not to process RNA–2 further based on the analysis presented in the following schedule.

| | Process Further | | | |
	RNA–2	DMZ–3	Pestrol	Total
Production in pounds	400,000	400,000	400,000	
Revenue	$320,000	$230,000	$230,000	$ 460,000
Costs:				
VDB costs	$ 82,000*	$ 61,500	$ 61,500	$ 123,000†
Additional direct materials (LST) and processing of RNA–2	—	60,000	60,000	120,000
Total costs	$ 82,000	$121,500	$121,500	$ 243,000
Weekly gross profit	$238,000	$108,500	$108,500	$ 217,000

*$82,000 is one-third of the $246,000 cost of processing VDB. When RNA–2 is not processed further, one-third of the final output is RNA–2 (400,000 out of a total of 1,200,000 pounds).

†$123,000 is one-half of the $246,000 cost of processing VDB. When RNA–2 is processed further, one-half of the final output consists of DMZ–3 and Pestrol. The final products then are: 800,000 pounds of RNA–1; 400,000 pounds of DMZ–3; and 400,000 pounds of Pestrol.

Required: Evaluate China West Chemical Company's analysis, and make any revisions that are necessary. Your critique and analysis should indicate:

a. Whether management made the correct decision.

b. The gross savings or loss per week resulting from the decision not to process RNA–2 further, if different from management's analysis.

(CMA, adapted)

■ **Problem 14–52**
Add a Product Line
(LO 4, 5)

1. Incremental contribution margin: $42,945

Milan Fashions Limited, a high-fashion dress manufacturer, is planning to market a new cocktail dress for the coming season. Milan Fashions supplies retailers worldwide.

Four yards of material are required to lay out the dress pattern. Some material remains after cutting, which can be sold as remnants. The leftover material also could be used to manufacture a matching cape and handbag. However, if the leftover material is to be used for the cape and handbag, more care will be required in the cutting operation, which will increase the cutting costs.

The company expects to sell 1,250 dresses. Market research reveals that dress sales will be 20 percent higher if a matching cape and handbag are available. The market research indicates that the cape and handbag will be salable only as accessories with the dress. The combination of dresses, capes, and handbags expected to be sold by retailers are as follows:

	Percent of Total
Complete sets of dress, cape, and handbag	70%
Dress and cape	6
Dress and handbag	15
Dress only	9
Total	100%

The material used in the dress costs $12.50 per meter, or $50.00 for each dress. The cost of cutting the dress if the cape and handbag are not manufactured is estimated at $20.00 a dress, and the resulting remnants can be sold for $5.00 per dress. If the cape and handbag are manufactured, the cutting costs will be increased by $9.00 per dress and there will be no salable remnants. The selling prices and the costs to complete the three items once they are cut are as follows:

	Selling Price per Unit	Unit Cost to Complete (excludes costs of material and cutting operation)
Dress	$200.00	$80.00
Cape	27.50	19.50
Handbag	9.50	6.50

Required:

1. Calculate Milan Fashions' incremental profit or loss from manufacturing the capes and handbags in conjunction with the dresses.

2. Identify any qualitative factors that could influence the company's management in its decision to manufacture capes and handbags to match the dresses.

(CMA, adapted)

■ **Problem 14–53**
Outsourcing Decision
(LO 4, 5)

1. Total variable cost per unit:
$10.50
2. Quantity of component B81
to be purchased: 4,000 units

Uppsala Mechanical has been producing two bearings, components T79 and B81, for use in production. Data regarding these two components follow.

	T79	B81
Machine hours required per unit	2.5	3.0
Standard cost per unit:		
Direct material	$ 2.25	$ 3.75
Direct labor	4.00	4.50
Manufacturing overhead		
Variable*	2.00	2.25
Fixed[†]	3.75	4.50
Total	$12.00	$15.00

*Variable manufacturing overhead is applied on the basis of direct-labor hours.

[†]Fixed manufacturing overhead is applied on the basis of machine hours.

Uppsala Mechanical's annual requirement for these components is 8,000 units of T79 and 11,000 units of B81. Recently, management decided to devote additional machine time to other product lines, leaving only 41,000 machine hours per year for producing the bearings. An outside company has offered to sell Uppsala Mechanical its annual supply of bearings at prices of $11.25 for T79 and $13.50 for B81. Management wants to schedule the otherwise idle 41,000 machine hours to produce bearings so that the firm can minimize costs (maximize net benefits).

Required:

1. Compute the net benefit (loss) per machine hour that would result if Uppsala Mechanical accepts the supplier's offer of $13.50 per unit for component B81.

2. Choose the correct answer. Uppsala Mechanical will maximize its net benefits by:

   a. purchasing 4,800 units of T79 and manufacturing the remaining bearings.

   b. purchasing 8,000 units of T79 and manufacturing 11,000 units of B81.

   c. purchasing 11,000 units of B81 and manufacturing 8,000 units of T79.

   d. purchasing 4,000 units of B81 and manufacturing the remaining bearings.

   e. purchasing and manufacturing some amounts other than those given above.

3. Suppose management has decided to drop product T79. Independently of requirements (1) and (2), assume that the company's idle capacity of 41,000 machine hours has a traceable, avoidable annual fixed cost of $44,000, which will be incurred only if the capacity is used. Calculate the maximum price Uppsala Mechanical should pay a supplier for component B81.

(CMA, adapted)

■ **Problem 14–54**
Outsource a Component;
Relevant Costs, Opportunity
Costs, and Quality Control
(LO 3, 4, 5)

2. Increase in monthly cost:
$23,000

Chenango Industries uses 10 units of part JR63 each month in the production of radar equipment. The cost of manufacturing one unit of JR63 is the following:

Direct material	$ 1,000
Material handling (20% of direct-material cost)	200
Direct labor	8,000
Manufacturing overhead (150% of direct labor)	12,000
Total manufacturing cost	$21,200

Material handling represents the direct variable costs of the Receiving Department that are applied to direct materials and purchased components on the basis of their cost. This is a separate charge in addition to manufacturing overhead. Chenango Industries' annual manufacturing overhead budget is one-third variable and two-thirds fixed. Scott Supply, one of Chenango Industries' reliable vendors, has offered to supply part number JR63 at a unit price of $15,000.

Required:

1. If Chenango Industries purchases the JR63 units from Scott, the capacity Chenango Industries used to manufacture these parts would be idle. Should Chenango Industries decide to purchase the parts from Scott, the unit cost of JR63 would increase (or decrease) by what amount?

2. Assume Chenango Industries is able to rent out all its idle capacity for $25,000 per month. If Chenango Industries decides to purchase the 10 units from Scott Supply, Chenango's monthly cost for JR63 would increase (or decrease) by what amount?

3. Assume that Chenango Industries does not wish to commit to a rental agreement but could use its idle capacity to manufacture another product that would contribute $52,000 per month. If Chenango's management elects to manufacture JR63 in order to maintain quality control, what is the net amount of Chenango's cost from using the space to manufacture part JR63?

(CMA, adapted)

■ Problem 14–55
Analysis of Special Order
(LO 4, 5)

2. Contribution from sale to Kaytell: $53,848

Miami Industries received an order for a piece of special machinery from Jay Company. Just as Miami completed the machine, Jay Company declared bankruptcy, defaulted on the order, and forfeited the 10 percent deposit paid on the selling price of $72,500.

Miami's manufacturing manager identified the costs already incurred in the production of the special machinery for Jay Company as follows:

Direct material		$16,600
Direct labor		21,400
Manufacturing overhead applied:		
Variable	$10,700	
Fixed	5,350	16,050
Fixed selling and administrative costs		5,405
Total		$59,455

Another company, Kaytell Corporation, will buy the special machinery if it is reworked to Kaytell's specifications. Miami Industries offered to sell the reworked machinery to Kaytell as a special order for $68,400. Kaytell agreed to pay the price when it takes delivery in two months. The additional identifiable costs to rework the machinery to Kaytell's specifications are as follows:

Direct material	$ 6,200
Direct labor	4,200
Total	$10,400

A second alternative available to Miami's management is to convert the special machinery to the standard model, which sells for $62,500. The additional identifiable costs for this conversion are as follows:

Direct material	$2,850
Direct labor	3,300
Total	$6,150

A third alternative for Miami Industries is to sell the machine as is for a price of $52,000. However, the potential buyer of the unmodified machine does not want it for 60 days. This buyer has offered a $7,000 down payment, with the remainder due upon delivery.

The following additional information is available regarding Miami's operations.

- The sales commission rate on sales of standard models is 2 percent, while the rate on special orders is 3 percent.

- Normal credit terms for sales of standard models are 2/10, net/30. This means that a customer receives a 2 percent discount if payment is made within 10 days, and payment is due no later than 30 days after billing. Most customers take the 2 percent discount. Credit terms for a special order are negotiated with the customer.

- The allocation rates for manufacturing overhead and fixed selling and administrative costs are as follows:

Manufacturing costs:	
Variable	50% of direct-labor cost
Fixed	25% of direct-labor cost
Fixed selling and administrative costs	10% of the total of direct-material, direct-labor, and manufacturing-overhead costs

- Normal time required for rework is one month.

Required:

1. Determine the dollar contribution each of the three alternatives will add to Miami Industries' before-tax profit.
2. If Kaytell makes Miami Industries a counteroffer, what is the lowest price Miami should accept for the reworked machinery from Kaytell? Explain your answer.
3. Discuss the influence fixed manufacturing-overhead cost should have on the sales price quoted by Miami Industries for special orders.

(CMA, adapted)

■ **Problem 14–56**
Special Order; Ethics
(LO 3, 4, 5)

2. Accepting the special order will result in a total additional contribution margin of $37,500

Winner's Circle, Inc. manufactures medals for winners of athletic events and other contests. Its manufacturing plant has the capacity to produce 10,000 medals each month. Current monthly production is 7,500 medals. The company normally charges $175 per medal. Variable costs and fixed costs for the current activity level of 75 percent of capacity are as follows:

Production Costs

Variable costs:	
Manufacturing:	
Direct labor	$ 375,000
Direct material	262,500
Marketing	187,500
Total variable costs	$ 825,000
Fixed costs:	
Manufacturing	$ 275,000
Marketing	175,000
Total fixed costs	$ 450,000
Total costs	$1,275,000
Variable cost per unit	$110
Fixed cost per unit	60
Average unit cost	$170

Winner's Circle has just received a special one-time order for 2,500 medals at $100 per medal. For this particular order, no variable marketing costs will be incurred. Cathy Donato, a management accountant with Winner's Circle, has been assigned the task of analyzing this order and recommending whether the company should accept or reject it. After examining the costs, Donato suggested to her supervisor, Gerard LePenn, who is the controller, that they request competitive bids from vendors for the raw material as the current quote seems high. LePenn insisted that the prices are in line with other vendors and told her that she was not to discuss her observations with anyone else. Donato later discovered that LePenn is a brother-in-law of the owner of the current raw-material supply vendor.

Required:

1. Identify and explain the costs that will be relevant to Cathy Donato's analysis of the special order being considered by Winner's Circle, Inc.
2. Determine if Winner's Circle should accept the special order. In explaining your answer, compute both the new average unit cost and the incremental unit cost for the special order.
3. Discuss any other considerations that Donato should include in her analysis of the special order.

4.   What steps could Donato take to resolve the ethical conflict arising out of the controller's insistence that the company avoid competitive bidding?

5.   ***Build a spreadsheet:*** Construct an Excel spreadsheet to solve requirement (2). Show how the solution will change if the sales price is $170 per medal.

(CMA, adapted)

■ **Problem 14–57**
Production Planning
(LO 5, 6)

2. Contribution margin, product M07: $93

2. Total contribution margin: $123,250

Osten Industries manufactures and sells three products, which are manufactured in a factory with four departments. Both labor and machine time are applied to the products as they pass through each department. The machines and labor skills required in each department are so specialized that neither machines nor labor can be switched from one department to another.

Osten Industries' management is planning its production schedule for the next few months. The planning is complicated, because there are labor shortages in the community and some machines will be down several months for repairs.

Management has assembled the following information regarding available machine and labor time by department and the machine hours and direct-labor hours required per unit of product. These data should be valid for the next six months.

	Department			
Monthly Capacity Availability	**1**	**2**	**3**	**4**
Normal machine capacity in machine hours	3,500	3,500	3,000	3,500
Capacity of machines being repaired in machine hours	(500)	(400)	(300)	(200)
Available machine capacity in machine hours	3,000	3,100	2,700	3,300
Available labor in direct-labor hours	3,700	4,500	2,750	2,600

Labor and Machine Specifications per Unit of Product					
Product	**Labor and Machine Time**				
M07	Direct-labor hours	2	3	3	1
	Machine hours	1	1	2	2
T28	Direct-labor hours	1	2	—	2
	Machine hours	1	1	—	2
B19	Direct-labor hours	2	2	2	1
	Machine hours	2	2	1	1

The sales department believes that the monthly demand for the next six months will be as follows:

Product	**Monthly Unit Sales**
M07	500
T28	400
B19	1,000

Inventory levels are satisfactory and need not be increased or decreased during the next six months. Unit price and cost data that will be valid for the next six months are as follows:

	Product		
	M07	**T28**	**B19**
Unit costs:			
Direct material	$ 7	$ 13	$ 7
Direct labor:			
Department 1	12	6	12
Department 2	21	14	14
Department 3	24	—	16
Department 4	9	18	9
Variable overhead	27	20	25
Fixed overhead	15	10	30
Variable selling expenses	3	2	4
Unit selling price	196	123	167

Required:

1. Calculate the monthly requirement for machine hours and direct-labor hours for the production of products M07, T28, and B19 to determine whether the monthly sales demand for the three products can be met by the factory.

2. What monthly production schedule should Osten Industries select in order to maximize its dollar profits? Explain how you selected this production schedule, and present a schedule of the contribution to profit that would be generated by your production schedule.

3. Identify the alternatives Osten Industries might consider so it can supply its customers with all the product they demand.

(CMA, adapted)

■ **Problem 14–58**
Conventional versus
Activity-Based-Costing
Analyses; Relevant Costs
(LO 5, 7)

2. Costs to be avoided by
purchasing (ABC analysis),
total: $810,750

In addition to fine chocolate, International Chocolate Company also produces chocolate-covered pretzels in its Brussels plant. This product is sold in two-kilogram metal canisters, which also are manufactured at the Brussels facility. The plant manager, Sonia Candotti, was recently approached by Catawba Canister Company with an offer to supply the canisters at a price of $1.00 each. International Chocolate's traditional product-costing system assigns the following costs to canister production.

Direct material	$ 300,000
Direct labor (12,000 hrs. at $15 per hr.)	180,000
Variable overhead ($10 per direct-labor hr.)	120,000
Fixed overhead ($45 per direct-labor hr.)	540,000
Total cost	$1,140,000

Unit costs: $1,140,000 ÷ 760,000 canisters = $1.50 per canister

Candotti's conventional make-or-buy analysis indicated that Catawba's offer should be rejected, since only $708,000 of costs would be avoided (including $80,000 of supervisory salaries and $28,000 of machinery depreciation). In contrast, the firm would spend $760,000 buying the canisters. The controller, Johan Iversen, came to the rescue with an activity-based costing analysis of the decision. Iversen concluded that the cost driver levels associated with canister production are as follows:

10 product specs	30 inspections
2,000 supervisory hours	15 setups
6,000 material-handling hours	70,000 machine hours
55 purchase orders	

Additional conventional and ABC data from the Brussels plant are given in Exhibits 14–19 and 14–20.

Required:

1. Show how Candotti arrived at the $708,000 of cost savings in her conventional make-or-buy analysis.

2. Determine the costs that will be saved by purchasing canisters, using Iversen's ABC data.

3. Complete the ABC relevant-costing analysis of the make-or-buy decision. Should the firm buy from Catawba?

4. If the conventional and ABC analyses yield different conclusions, briefly explain why.

■ **Problem 14–59**
Linear Programming;
Formulate and Solve
Graphically (Appendix)
(LO 8)

3. Total contribution margin:
$55,000

Deru Chocolate Company manufactures two popular candy bars, the Venus bar and the Comet bar. Both candy bars go through a mixing operation where the various ingredients are combined, and the Coating Department where the bars from the Mixing Department are coated with chocolate. The Venus bar is coated with both white and dark chocolate to produce a swirled effect. A material shortage of an ingredient in the Comet bar limits production to 300 batches per day. Production and sales data are presented in the following table. Both candy bars are produced in batches of 200 bars.

		Use of Capacity in Hours per Batch of Product	
Department	**Available Daily Capacity in Hours**	**Venus**	**Comet**
Mixing	525	1.5	1.5
Coating	500	2.0	1.0

Management believes that Deru Chocolate can sell all of its daily production of both the Venus and Comet bars. Other data follow.

	Venus	Comet
Selling price per batch	$ 300	$ 350
Variable cost per batch	100	225
Monthly fixed costs (allocated evenly between both products)	375,000	375,000

Required:

1. Formulate the objective function and all of the constraints in order to maximize contribution margin. Be sure to define the variables.
2. How many batches of each type of candy bar (Venus and Comet) should be produced to maximize the total contribution margin?
3. Calculate the contribution margin at the optimal solution.

(CMA, adapted)

■ **Problem 14–60**
Linear Programming
(Appendix)
(LO 8)

4. Contribution margin at the optimal solution: $4,500

Meals for Professionals, Inc. offers monthly service plans providing prepared meals that are delivered to the customers' homes. The target market for these meal plans includes double-income families with no children and retired couples in upper income brackets. The firm offers two monthly plans: Premier Cuisine and Haute Cuisine. The Premier Cuisine plan provides frozen meals that are delivered twice each month; this plan generates a contribution margin of $120 for each monthly plan sold. The Haute Cuisine plan provides freshly prepared meals delivered on a daily basis and generates a contribution margin of $90 for each monthly plan sold. The company's reputation provides a market that will purchase all the meals that can be prepared. All meals go through food preparation and cooking steps in the company's kitchens. After these steps, the Premier Cuisine meals are flash frozen. The time requirements per monthly meal plan and hours available per month are as follows:

	Preparation	Cooking	Freezing
Hours required:			
Premier Cuisine	2	2	1
Haute Cuisine	1	3	0
Hours available	60	120	45

For planning purposes, Meals for Professionals, Inc. uses linear programming to determine the most profitable number of Premier Cuisine and Haute Cuisine monthly meal plans to produce.

Required:

1. Using the notation P for Premier Cuisine and H for Haute Cuisine, state the objective function and the constraints that management should use to maximize the total contribution margin generated by the monthly meal plans.
2. Graph the constraints on the meal preparation process. Be sure to clearly label the graph.
3. Using the graph prepared in requirement (2), determine the optimal solution to the company's production planning problem in terms of the number of each type of meal plan to produce.
4. Calculate the value of the objective function at the optimal solution.
5. If the constraint on preparation time could be eliminated, determine the revised optimal solution.

(CMA, adapted)

■ **Problem 14–61**
Linear Programming; Formulate
and Discuss (Appendix)
(LO 8)

2(a). Contribution margin,
R_L: $10.30

Aztec Corporation manufactures two types of electric coffeemakers, Regular and Deluxe. The major difference between the two appliances is capacity. Both are considered top-quality units and sell for premium prices. Both coffeemakers pass through two manufacturing departments: Plating and Assembly. Aztec has two assembly operations, one automated and one manual. The Automated Assembly Department has been in operation for one year and was intended to replace the Labor Assembly Department. However, Aztec's business has expanded rapidly in recent months, and both assembly operations are still being used. Workers have been trained for both operations and can be used in either department. The only difference between the two departments is the proportion of machine time versus direct labor used. Data regarding the two coffeemakers are presented in the following schedule.

Sales Data

	Regular Model	Deluxe Model
Selling price per unit	$ 45.00	$ 60.00
Variable selling cost per unit	3.00	3.00
Annual allocated fixed overhead	900,000	900,000

Unit Variable Manufacturing Costs

	Plating Department		Labor Assembly	Automated Assembly
	Regular	Deluxe		
Raw material:				
Casing	$7.75	$14.50	—	—
Heating element	6.00	6.00	—	—
Other	8.25	8.25	—	—
Direct labor:				
At $12.50 per hour	2.50	2.50	—	—
At $15 per hour	—	—	$3.75	$0.75
Manufacturing overhead:				
Supplies	1.25	1.25	1.50	1.50
Power	1.20	1.20	.75	1.80

Machine Hour Data

	Plating	Labor Assembly	Automated Assembly
Machine hours required per unit	.18	.03	.05
Machine hours available per month	25,000	1,500	5,000
Annual machine hours available	300,000	18,000	60,000

Aztec produced and sold 600,000 Deluxe coffeemakers and 900,000 Regular coffeemakers last year. Management estimates that total unit sales could increase by 20 percent or more if the units can be produced. Aztec already has contracts to produce and sell 35,000 units of each model each month. Aztec has a monthly maximum labor capacity of 30,000 direct-labor hours in the Plating Department and 40,000 direct-labor hours for the assembly operation (Automated Assembly and Labor Assembly, combined). Sales, production, and costs occur uniformly throughout the year.

Required:

1. Aztec Corporation's management believes that linear programming could be used to determine the optimum mix of Regular and Deluxe coffeemakers to produce and sell. Explain why linear programming is appropriate to use in this situation.

2. Management has decided to use linear programming to determine the optimal product mix. Formulate and label the following:

   a. Objective function

   b. Constraints

   Be sure to define your variables.

(CMA, adapted)

Cases

Bo Vonderweidt, the production manager for Sportway Corporation, had requested to have lunch with the company president. Vonderweidt wanted to put forward his suggestion to add a new product line. As they finished lunch, Meg Thomas, the company president, said, "I'll give your proposal some serious thought, Bo. I think you're right about the increasing demand for skateboards. What I'm not sure about is whether the skateboard line will be better for us than our tackle boxes. Those have been our bread and butter the past few years."

Vonderweidt responded with, "Let me get together with one of the controller's people. We'll run a few numbers on this skateboard idea that I think will demonstrate the line's potential."

Sportway is a wholesale distributor supplying a wide range of moderately priced sports equipment to large chain stores. About 60 percent of Sportway's products are purchased from other companies while the remainder of the products are manufactured by Sportway. The company has a Plastics Department that is currently manufacturing molded fishing tackle boxes. Sportway is able to manufacture and sell 8,000 tackle boxes annually, making full use of its direct-labor capacity at available work stations. The selling price and costs associated with Sportway's tackle boxes are as follows:

■ **Case 14–62**
Adding a Product Line
(LO 4, 5)

1. Contribution per hour, tackle boxes: $26.40
2. Improvement in contribution margin: $236,250

Selling price per box		$86.00
Costs per box:		
Molded plastic	$ 8.00	
Hinges, latches, handle	9.00	
Direct labor ($15.00 per hour)	18.75	
Manufacturing overhead	12.50	
Selling and administrative cost	17.00	65.25
Profit per box		$20.75

Because Sportway's sales manager believes the firm could sell 12,000 tackle boxes if it had sufficient manufacturing capacity, the company has looked into the possibility of purchasing the tackle boxes for distribution. Maple Products, a steady supplier of quality products, would be able to provide up to 9,000 tackle boxes per year at a price of $68.00 per box delivered to Sportway's facility.

Bo Vonderweidt, Sportway's production manager, has come to the conclusion that the company could make better use of its Plastics Department by manufacturing skateboards. Vonderweidt has a market study that indicates an expanding market for skateboards and a need for additional suppliers. Vonderweidt believes that Sportway could expect to sell 17,500 skateboards annually at a price of $45.00 per skateboard.

After his lunch with the company president, Vonderweidt worked out the following estimates with the assistant controller.

Selling price per skateboard		$45.00
Costs per skateboard:		
Molded plastic	$5.50	
Wheels, hardware	7.00	
Direct labor ($15.00 per hour)	7.50	
Manufacturing overhead	5.00	
Selling and administrative cost	9.00	34.00
Profit per skateboard		$11.00

In the Plastics Department, Sportway uses direct-labor hours as the application base for manufacturing overhead. Included in the manufacturing overhead for the current year is $50,000 of factorywide, fixed manufacturing overhead that has been allocated to the Plastics Department. For each unit of product that Sportway sells, regardless of whether the product has been purchased or is manufactured by Sportway, there is an allocated $6.00 fixed overhead cost per unit for distribution that is included in the selling and administrative cost for all products. Total selling and administrative costs for the purchased tackle boxes would be $10.00 per unit.

Required: In order to maximize the company's profitability, prepare an analysis that will show which product or products Sportway Corporation should manufacture or purchase.

1. First determine which of Sportway's options makes the best use of its scarce resources. How many skateboards and tackle boxes should be manufactured? How many tackle boxes should be purchased?
2. Calculate the improvement in Sportway's total contribution margin if it adopts the optimal strategy rather than continuing with the status quo.

(CMA, adapted)

■ **Case 14–63**
Drop a Product Line
(LO 4, 5)

Unit contribution, E-gauge:
$19.00

Alberta Gauge Company, Ltd., a small manufacturing company in Calgary, Alberta, manufactures three types of electrical gauges used in a variety of machinery. For many years the company has been profitable and has operated at capacity. However, in the last two years, prices on all gauges were reduced and selling expenses increased to meet competition and keep the plant operating at capacity. Second-quarter results for the current year, which follow, typify recent experience.

ALBERTA GAUGE COMPANY, LTD.
Income Statement
Second Quarter
(in thousands)

	Q-Gauge	E-Gauge	R-Gauge	Total
Sales	$1,600	$900	$ 900	$3,400
Cost of goods sold	1,048	770	950	2,768
Gross margin	$ 552	$130	$ (50)	$ 632
Selling and administrative expenses	370	185	135	690
Income before taxes	$ 182	$ (55)	$(185)	$ (58)

Alice Carlo, the company's president, is concerned about the results of the pricing, selling, and production prices. After reviewing the second-quarter results, she asked her management staff to consider the following three suggestions:

• Discontinue the R-gauge line immediately. R-gauges would not be returned to the product line unless the problems with the gauge can be identified and resolved.

• Increase quarterly sales promotion by $100,000 on the Q-gauge product line in order to increase sales volume by 15 percent.

• Cut production on the E-gauge line by 50 percent, and cut the traceable advertising and promotion for this line to $20,000 each quarter.

Jason Sperry, the controller, suggested a more careful study of the financial relationships to determine the possible effects on the company's operating results of the president's proposed course of action. The president agreed and assigned JoAnn Brower, the assistant controller, to prepare an analysis. Brower has gathered the following information.

• All three gauges are manufactured with common equipment and facilities.

• The selling and administrative expense is allocated to the three gauge lines based on average sales volume over the past three years.

• Special selling expenses (primarily advertising, promotion, and shipping) are incurred for each gauge as follows:

	Quarterly Advertising and Promotion	Shipping Expenses
Q-gauge	$210,000	$10 per unit
E-gauge	100,000	4 per unit
R-gauge	40,000	10 per unit

- The unit manufacturing costs for the three products are as follows:

	Q-Gauge	E-Gauge	R-Gauge
Direct material	$ 31	$17	$ 50
Direct labor	40	20	60
Variable manufacturing overhead	45	30	60
Fixed manufacturing overhead	15	10	20
Total	$131	$77	$190

- The unit sales prices for the three products are as follows:

Q-gauge	$200
E-gauge	90
R-gauge	180

- The company is manufacturing at capacity and is selling all the gauges it produces.

Required:

1. JoAnn Brower says that Alberta Gauge Company's product-line income statement for the second quarter is not suitable for analyzing proposals and making decisions such as the ones suggested by Alice Carlo. Write a memo to Alberta Gauge's president that addresses the following points.

   a. Explain why the product-line income statement as presented is not suitable for analysis and decision making.

   b. Describe an alternative income-statement format that would be more suitable for analysis and decision making, and explain why it is better.

2. Use the operating data presented for Alberta Gauge Company and assume that the president's proposed course of action had been implemented at the beginning of the second quarter. Then evaluate the president's proposal by specifically responding to the following points.

   a. Are each of the three suggestions cost-effective? Support your discussion with an analysis that shows the net impact on income before taxes for each of the three suggestions.

   b. Was the president correct in proposing that the R-gauge line be eliminated? Explain your answer.

   c. Was the president correct in promoting the Q-gauge line rather than the E-gauge line? Explain your answer.

   d. Does the proposed course of action make effective use of the company's capacity? Explain your answer.

3. Are there any qualitative factors that Alberta Gauge Company's management should consider before it drops the R-gauge line? Explain your answer.

(CMA, adapted)

THIS CHAPTER'S FOCUS COMPANY is Sydney Sailing Supplies, a manufacturer of sailing supplies and equipment in Sydney, Australia. One of the company's most popular products is the Wave Darter, a two-person sailboat. In this chapter, we will explore a variety of issues surrounding how Sydney Sailing Supplies' management could set a price for the Wave Darter. We also will study a pricing method called target costing. Under this approach, management determines what consumers are willing to pay for a particular product. Then management must find a way to produce that product at a low enough cost to justify the price the consumers are willing to pay.

SYDNEY
SAILING SUPPLIES

15 Target Costing and Cost Analysis for Pricing Decisions

In contrast to the product-pricing setting explored in the first part of the chapter, we turn our attention to competitive bidding on projects, services, or products. In a competitive-bidding situation, two or more companies submit sealed bids for a job, and the buyer selects from among the bids. We will explore competitive bidding in the context of Sydney Sailing Supplies' Marine Services Division. The company's Marine Services Division specializes in marina maintenance and construction, and its management is preparing a bid to build a new marina in Sydney harbor.

SYDNEY
SAILING SUPPLIES

1 List and describe the four major influences on pricing decisions.

2 Explain and use the economic, profit-maximizing pricing model.

3 Set prices using cost-plus pricing formulas.

4 Discuss the issues involved in the strategic pricing of new products.

5 List and discuss the key principles of target costing.

6 Explain the role of activity-based costing in setting a target cost.

7 Explain how product-cost distortion can undermine a firm's pricing strategy.

8 Explain the process of value engineering and its role in target costing.

9 Determine prices using the time and material pricing approach.

10 Set prices in special-order or competitive-bidding situations by analyzing the relevant costs.

11 Describe the legal restrictions on setting prices.

Setting the price for an organization's product or service is one of the most important decisions a manager faces. It is also one of the most difficult, due to the number and variety of factors that must be considered. The pricing decision arises in virtually all types of organizations. Manufacturers set prices for the products they manufacture; merchandising companies set prices for their goods; service firms set prices for such services as insurance policies, train tickets, theme park admissions, and bank loans. Nonprofit organizations often set prices also. For example, governmental units price vehicle registrations, park-use fees, and utility services. The optimal approach to pricing often depends on the situation. Pricing a mature product or service that a firm has sold for a long time may be quite different from pricing a new product or service. Public utilities and TV cable companies face political considerations in pricing their products and services, since their prices often must be approved by a governmental commission.

In this chapter, we will study pricing decisions, with an emphasis on the role of managerial accounting information. The setting for our discussion is Sydney Sailing Supplies, a manufacturer of sailing supplies and equipment located in Sydney, Australia.

Major Influences on Pricing Decisions

Four major influences govern the prices set by Sydney Sailing Supplies:

1. Customer demand.
2. Actions of competitors.
3. Costs.
4. Political, legal, and image-related issues.

Customer Demand

The demands of customers are of paramount importance in all phases of business operations, from the design of a product to the setting of its price. Product-design issues and pricing considerations are interrelated, so they must be examined simultaneously. For example, if customers want a high-quality sailboat, this will entail greater production time and more expensive raw materials. The result almost certainly will be a higher price. On the other hand, management must be careful not to price its product out of the market. Discerning customer demand is a critically important and continuous process. Companies routinely obtain information from market research, such as customer surveys and test-marketing campaigns, and through feedback from sales personnel. To be successful, Sydney Sailing Supplies must provide the products its customers want at a price they perceive to be appropriate.

> **Learning Objective 1**
>
> List and describe the four major influences on pricing decisions.

Actions of Competitors

Although Sydney Sailing Supplies' managers would like the company to have the sailing market to itself, they are not so fortunate. Domestic and foreign competitors are striving to sell their products to the same customers. Thus, as Sydney Sailing Supplies' management designs products and sets prices, it must keep a watchful eye on the firm's competitors. If a competitor reduces its price on sailboats of a particular type, Sydney Sailing Supplies may have to follow suit to avoid losing its market share. Yet the company cannot follow its competitors blindly either. Predicting competitive reactions to its product-design and pricing strategy is a difficult but important task for Sydney Sailing Supplies' management.

In considering the reactions of customers and competitors, management must be careful to properly define its product. Should Sydney Sailing Supplies' management define its product narrowly as sailing supplies, or more broadly as boating supplies? For example, if the company raises the price of its two-person sailboat, will this encourage potential customers to switch to canoes, rowboats, and small motorboats? Or will most potential sailboat customers react to a price increase only by price-shopping among competing sailboat manufacturers? The way in which Sydney Sailing Supplies' management answers these questions can profoundly affect its marketing and pricing strategies.

Costs

The role of costs in price setting varies widely among industries. In some industries, prices are determined almost entirely by market forces. An example is the agricultural industry, where grain and meat prices are market-driven. Farmers must meet the market price. To make a profit, they must produce at a cost below the market price. This is not always possible, so some periods of loss inevitably result. In other industries, managers set prices at least partially on the basis of production costs. For example, cost-based pricing is used in the aircraft, household appliance, and gasoline industries. Prices are set by adding a markup to production costs. Managers have some latitude in determining the markup, so market forces influence prices as well. In public utilities, such as electricity and natural gas companies, prices generally are set by a regulatory agency of the state government. Production costs are of prime importance in justifying utility rates. Typically, a public utility will make a request to a Public Utility Commission for a rate increase on the basis of its current and projected production costs.

Balance of Market Forces and Cost-Based Pricing   In most industries, both market forces and cost considerations heavily influence prices. No organization or

industry can price its products below their production costs indefinitely. And no company's management can set prices blindly at cost plus a markup without keeping an eye on the market. In most cases, pricing can be viewed in either of the following ways.

How Are Prices Set?

Prices are determined by the market, subject to the constraint that costs must be covered in the long run.

Costs ⟷ Market forces

Prices are based on costs, subject to the constraint that the reactions of customers and competitors must be heeded.

In our illustration of Sydney Sailing Supplies' pricing policies, we will assume the company responds to both market forces and costs.

Political, Legal, and Image-Related Issues

Setting prices requires a balance between cost considerations and market forces. A good example is provided by the airlines, which keep a close eye on the fares of their competitors, while striving to cover operating costs. The large airlines, like Continental, British Airways, and Singapore Airlines, are increasingly finding it necessary to cut fares to compete with discounters like Southwest, easyJet, and AirAsia.

Beyond the important effects on prices of market forces and costs are a range of environmental considerations. In the *legal* area, managers must adhere to certain laws. The law generally prohibits companies from discriminating among their customers in setting prices. Also prohibited is collusion in price setting, where the major firms in an industry all agree to set their prices at high levels.

Political considerations also can be relevant. For example, if the firms in an industry are *perceived* by the public as reaping unfairly large profits, there may be political pressure on legislators to tax those profits differentially or to intervene in some way to regulate prices.

Companies also consider their *public image* in the price-setting process. A firm with a reputation for very-high-quality products may set the price of a new product high to be consistent with its image. As we have all discovered, the same brand-name product may be available in a discount store at half the price charged in a more exclusive store.

Economic Profit-Maximizing Pricing

Learning Objective 2

Explain and use the economic, profit-maximizing pricing model.

Companies are sometimes **price takers,** which means their products' prices are determined totally by the market. Some agricultural commodities and precious metals are examples of such products. In most cases, however, firms have some flexibility in setting prices. Generally speaking, as the price of a product or service is increased, the quantity demanded declines, and vice versa.

Total Revenue, Demand, and Marginal Revenue Curves

The trade-off between a higher price and a higher sales quantity can be shown in the shape of the firm's **total revenue curve,** which graphs the relationship between total sales revenue and quantity sold. Sydney Sailing Supplies' total revenue curve for its two-person sailboat, the Wave Darter, is displayed in Exhibit 15–1, panel A. The total revenue

Exhibit 15–1
Total Revenue, Demand, and
Marginal Revenue Curves

SYDNEY
SAILING SUPPLIES

A. Total Revenue Curve

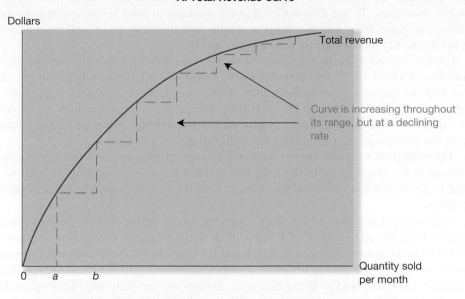

Dollars

Total revenue

Curve is increasing throughout its range, but at a declining rate

0   a   b   Quantity sold per month

B. Demand (or Average Revenue) Curve and Marginal Revenue Curve

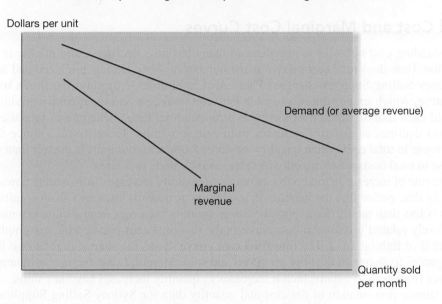

Dollars per unit

Demand (or average revenue)

Marginal revenue

Quantity sold per month

C. Tabulated Price, Quantity, and Revenue Data

Quantity Sold per Month	Unit Sales Price	Total Revenue per Month	Changes in Total Revenue
10	$1,000	$10,000	
			$9,500
20	975	19,500	
			9,000
30	950	28,500	
			8,500
40	925	37,000	
			8,000
50	900	45,000	
			7,500
60	875	52,500	

Related to demand curve   Related to total revenue curve   Related to marginal revenue curve

curve increases throughout its range, but the rate of increase declines as monthly sales quantity increases. To see this, notice that the increase in total revenue when the sales quantity increases from zero to a units is greater than the increase in total revenue when the sales quantity increases from a units to b units.

Closely related to the total revenue curve are two other curves, which are graphed in panel B of Exhibit 15–1. The **demand curve** shows the relationship between the sales price and the quantity of units demanded. The demand curve decreases throughout its range, because any decrease in the sales price brings about an increase in the monthly sales quantity. The demand curve is also called the **average revenue curve,** since it shows the average price at which any particular quantity can be sold.

The **marginal revenue curve** shows the *change* in total revenue that accompanies a *change* in the quantity sold. The marginal revenue curve is decreasing throughout its range to show that total revenue increases at a declining rate as monthly sales quantity increases.

A tabular presentation of the price, quantity, and revenue data for Sydney Sailing Supplies is displayed in panel C of Exhibit 15–1. Study this table carefully to see how the data relate to the graphs shown in panels A and B of the exhibit. No matter what approach a manager takes to the pricing decision, a good understanding of the relationships shown in Exhibit 15–1 will lead to better decisions. Before we can fully use the revenue data, however, we must examine the cost side of Sydney Sailing Supplies' business.

Total Cost and Marginal Cost Curves

Understanding cost behavior is important in many business decisions, and pricing is no exception. How does total cost behave as the number of Wave Darters produced and sold by Sydney Sailing Supplies changes? Panel A of Exhibit 15–2 displays the firm's **total cost curve,** which graphs the relationship between total cost and the quantity produced and sold each month.[1] Total cost increases throughout its range. The rate of increase in total cost declines as quantity increases from zero to c units. To verify this, notice that the increase in total costs when quantity increases from zero to a units is greater than the increase in total costs when quantity increases from a units to b units.

The rate of increase in total costs increases as quantity increases from c units upward. To verify this, notice that the increase in total costs as quantity increases from c units to d units is less than the increase in total costs as quantity increases from d units to e units.

Closely related to the total cost curve is the marginal cost curve, which is graphed in panel B of Exhibit 15–2. The **marginal cost curve** shows the change in total cost that accompanies a change in quantity produced and sold. Marginal cost declines as quantity increases from zero to c units; then it increases as quantity increases beyond c units.

A tabular presentation of the cost and quantity data for Sydney Sailing Supplies is displayed in panel C of Exhibit 15–2. Examine this table carefully, and trace the relationships between the data and the graphs shown in panels A and B of the exhibit.

Profit-Maximizing Price and Quantity

Now we have the tools we need to determine the profit-maximizing price and quantity. In Exhibit 15–3, we combine the revenue and cost data presented in Exhibits 15–1 and 15–2. Sydney Sailing Supplies' profit-maximizing sales quantity for the Wave Darter is determined by the intersection of the marginal cost and marginal revenue curves. (See panel B of Exhibit 15–3.) This optimal quantity is denoted by q^* on the graph. The profit-maximizing price, denoted by p^*, is determined from the demand curve for the quantity, q^*.

---

[1]Notice that the demand and revenue curves are based on the quantity sold, while the cost curves are based on the quantity produced. We will assume for simplicity that Sydney Sailing Supplies' monthly sales and production quantities are the same. This assumption tends to be true in the pleasure boat industry.

Exhibit 15–2
Total Cost and Marginal
Cost Curves

A. Total Cost Curve

Dollars

Total cost

Quantity sold
per month

a   *b*   *c*   *d*   *e*

Total cost increases
at a declining rate
in this range

Total cost increases
at an increasing rate
in this range

B. Marginal Cost Curve

Dollars per unit   Marginal cost

Quantity sold
per month
c

C. Tabulated Cost and Quantity Data

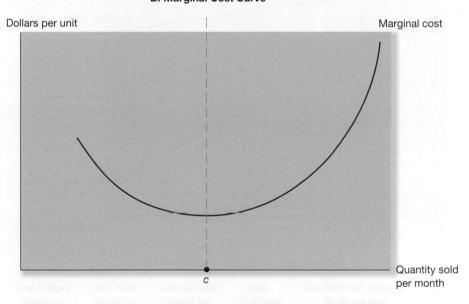

Quantity Produced and Sold per Month	Average Cost per Unit	Total Cost per Month	Changes in Total Cost
10	$1,920	$19,200	
			$ 5,600
20	1,240	24,800	
			4,300
30	970	29,100	
			2,900
40	800	32,000	
			9,000
50	820	41,000	
			15,400
60	940	56,400	

Related to total cost curve   Related to marginal cost curve

Exhibit 15–3
Determining the Profit-
Maximizing Price and Quantity

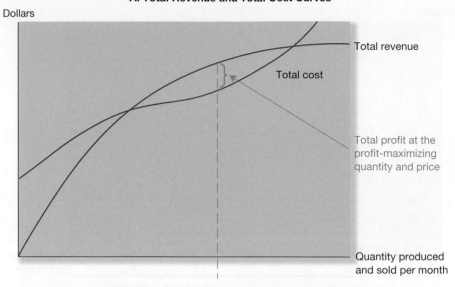

A. Total Revenue and Total Cost Curves

Dollars

Total revenue

Total cost

Total profit at the
profit-maximizing
quantity and price

Quantity produced
and sold per month

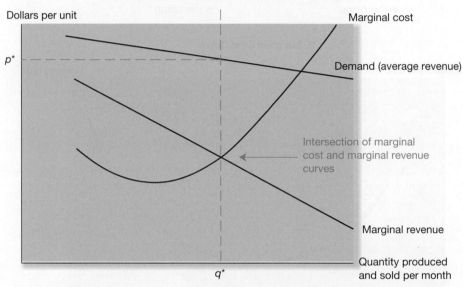

B. Marginal Revenue and Marginal Cost Curves

Dollars per unit

Marginal cost

$p^\star$

Demand (average revenue)

Intersection of marginal
cost and marginal revenue
curves

Marginal revenue

Quantity produced
and sold per month

$q^\star$

C. Tabulated Revenue, Cost, and Profit Data

	Quantity Produced and Sold per Month	Unit Sales Price	Total Revenue per Month	Total Cost per Month	Profit (Loss) per Month
	10	$1,000	$10,000	$19,200	$(9,200)
	20	975	19,500	24,800	(5,300)
Profit-maximizing quantity and price {	30	950	28,500	29,100	(600)
	40	925	37,000	32,000	5,000
	50	900	45,000	41,000	4,000
	60	875	52,500	56,400	(3,900)

Examine the total revenue and total cost curves in panel A of Exhibit 15–3. At the profit-maximizing quantity (and price), the distance between these curves, which is equal to total profit, is maximized.

A tabular presentation of the revenue, cost, and profit data is shown in panel C of Exhibit 15–3. Notice that monthly profit is maximized when the price is set at $925 and 40 Wave Darters are produced and sold each month.

Price Elasticity

The impact of price changes on sales volume is called the **price elasticity.** Demand is *elastic* if a price increase has a large negative impact on sales volume, and vice versa. Demand is *inelastic* if price changes have little or no impact on sales quantity. **Cross-elasticity** refers to the extent to which a change in a product's price affects the demand for other *substitute products.* For example, if Sydney Sailing Supplies raises the price of its two-person sailboat, there may be an increase in demand for substitute recreational craft, such as small powerboats, canoes, or windsurfers.

Measuring price elasticity and cross-elasticity is an important objective of market research. Having a good understanding of these economic concepts helps managers to determine the profit-maximizing price.

Limitations of the Profit-Maximizing Model

The economic model of the pricing decision serves as a useful framework for approaching a pricing problem. However, it does have several limitations. First, the firm's demand and marginal revenue curves are difficult to discern with precision. Although market research is designed to gather data about product demand, it rarely enables management to predict completely the effects of price changes on the quantity demanded. Many other factors affect product demand in addition to price. Product design and quality, advertising and promotion, and company reputation also significantly influence consumer demand for a product.

Second, the marginal-revenue, marginal-cost paradigm is not valid for all forms of market organization. In an **oligopolistic market,** where a small number of sellers compete among themselves, the simple economic pricing model is no longer appropriate. In an *oligopoly,* such as the automobile industry, the reactions of competitors to a firm's pricing policies must be taken into account. While economists have studied oligopolistic pricing, the state of the theory is not sufficient to provide a thorough understanding of the impact of prices on demand.

The third limitation of the economic pricing model involves the difficulty of measuring marginal cost. Cost accounting systems are not designed to measure the marginal changes in cost incurred as production and sales increase unit by unit. To measure marginal costs would entail a very costly information system. Most managers believe that any improvements in pricing decisions made possible by marginal-cost data would not be sufficient to defray the cost of obtaining the information.

Costs and Benefits of Information

Managerial accountants always face a cost-benefit trade-off in the production of cost information for pricing and other decisions. As Exhibit 15–4 shows, only a sophisticated information system can collect marginal-cost data. However, such information is more costly to obtain. The result is that the optimal approach to pricing and other decisions is likely to lie in between the extremes shown in Exhibit 15–4. For this reason, most managers make pricing decisions based on a combination of economic considerations and accounting product-cost information.

In spite of its limitations, the marginal-revenue, marginal-cost paradigm of pricing serves as a useful conceptual framework for the pricing decision. Within this overall framework, managers typically rely heavily on a cost-based pricing approach, as we shall see next.

Exhibit 15–4
Cost-Benefit Trade-Off in
Information Production

Optimal Decisions		Suboptimal Decisions
Economic model of pricing		Cost-based approach to pricing

Sophisticated decision model and information requirements —— Simplified decision model and information requirements

Marginal-cost and marginal-revenue data   Accounting product-cost data

More Costly Approach   Less Costly Approach

Best approach, in terms of costs and benefits, typically lies between the extremes.

Role of Accounting Product Costs in Pricing

> "Today we spend more of our time analyzing and understanding . . . our margins, understanding our prices, understanding the markets in which we do business." (15b)
>
> **Caterpillar**

Most managers base prices on accounting product costs, at least to some extent. There are several reasons for this. First, most companies sell many products or services. There simply is not enough time to do a thorough demand and marginal-cost analysis for every product or service. Managers must rely on a quick and straightforward method for setting prices, and cost-based pricing formulas provide it. Second, even though market considerations ultimately may determine the final product price, a cost-based pricing formula gives the manager a place to start. Finally, and most importantly, the cost of a product or service provides a floor below which the price cannot be set in the long run. Although a product may be "given away" initially, at a price below cost, a product's price ultimately must cover its costs in order for the firm to remain in business. Even a nonprofit organization, unless it is heavily subsidized, cannot forever price products or services below their costs.

Cost-Plus Pricing

Learning Objective 3

Set prices using cost-plus pricing formulas.

Cost-based pricing formulas typically have the following general form.

$$\text{Price} = \text{Cost} + (\text{Markup percentage} \times \text{Cost})$$

Such a pricing approach often is called **cost-plus pricing,** because the price is equal to *cost plus a markup.* Depending on how cost is defined, the markup percentage may differ. Several different definitions of cost, each combined with a different markup percentage, can result in the same price for a product or service.

Exhibit 15–5 illustrates how Sydney Sailing Supplies' management could use several different cost-plus pricing formulas and arrive at a price of $925 for the Wave Darter. Cost-plus formula (1) is based on variable manufacturing cost. Formula (2) is based on absorption (or full) manufacturing cost, which includes an allocated portion of fixed manufacturing costs. Formula (3) is based on all costs: both variable and fixed costs of the manufacturing, selling, and administrative functions. Formula (4) is based on all variable costs, including variable manufacturing, selling, and administrative costs. Notice that all four pricing formulas are based on a linear representation of the cost function, in which all costs are categorized as fixed or variable.

As Sydney Sailing Supplies includes more costs in the cost base of the pricing formula, the required markup percentage declines. This reflects the fact that, one way or another, the price must cover all costs as well as a normal profit margin. If only variable manufacturing costs are included explicitly in the cost base, as in formula (1), then all of the other costs (and the firm's profit) must be covered by the markup. However, if the cost base used in the pricing formula includes all costs, as in formula (3), the markup can be much lower, since it need cover only the firm's normal profit margin.

Each of the following cost-plus pricing formulas yields the same $925 price for the Wave Darter.

Price and Cost Data			Cost-Plus Pricing Formulas
Variable manufacturing cost	$400	1	$925 = \$400 + (131.25\% \times \$400) = \text{Variable manufacturing cost} + \left(\text{Markup percentage} \times \text{Variable manufacturing cost} \right)$
Applied fixed manufacturing cost	250*		
Absorption manufacturing cost	650	2	$925 = \$650 + (42.3\%^\dagger \times \$650) = \text{Absorption manufacturing cost} + \left(\text{Markup percentage} \times \text{Absorption manufacturing cost} \right)$
Variable selling and administrative cost	50		
Allocated fixed selling and administrative cost	100*		
Total cost	$800	3	$925 = \$800 + (15.63\%^\dagger \times \$800) = \text{Total cost} + \left(\text{Markup percentage} \times \text{Total cost} \right)$
Variable manufacturing cost	$400		
Variable selling and administrative cost	50		
Total variable cost	$450	4	$925 = \$450 + (105.56\%^\dagger \times \$450) = \text{Total variable cost} + \left(\text{Markup percentage} \times \text{Total variable cost} \right)$

* Based on planned monthly production of 40 units (or 480 units per year).

† Rounded.

Exhibit 15–5
Alternative Cost-Plus Pricing Formulas

SYDNEY
SAILING SUPPLIES

A company typically uses only one of the four cost-plus pricing formulas illustrated in Exhibit 15–5. Which formula is best? Let's examine the advantages and disadvantages of each approach.

Absorption-Cost Pricing Formulas

Most companies that use cost-plus pricing use either absorption manufacturing cost or total cost as the basis for pricing products or services. [See formulas (2) and (3) in Exhibit 15–5.] The reasons generally given for this tendency are as follows:

1. In the long run, the price must cover *all* costs and a normal profit margin. Basing the cost-plus formula on only variable costs could encourage managers to set too low a price in order to boost sales. This will not happen if managers understand that a variable cost-plus pricing formula requires a higher markup to cover fixed costs and profit. Nevertheless, many managers argue that people tend to view the cost base in a cost-plus pricing formula as the floor for setting prices. If prices are set too close to variable manufacturing cost, the firm will fail to cover its fixed costs. Ultimately, such a practice could result in the failure of the business.

2. Absorption-cost or total-cost pricing formulas provide a justifiable price that tends to be perceived as equitable by all parties. Consumers generally understand that a company must make a profit on its product or service in order to remain in business. Justifying a price as the total cost of production, sales, and administrative activities, plus a reasonable profit margin, seems reasonable to buyers.

3. When a company's competitors have similar operations and cost structures, cost-plus pricing based on full costs gives management an idea of how competitors may set prices.

4. Absorption-cost information is provided by a firm's cost accounting system, because it is required for external financial reporting under generally accepted

accounting principles. Since absorption-cost information already exists, it is cost-effective to use it for pricing. The alternative would involve preparing special product-cost data specifically for the pricing decision. In a firm with hundreds of products, such data could be expensive to produce.

The primary disadvantage of absorption-cost or total-cost pricing formulas is that they obscure the cost behavior pattern of the firm. Since absorption-cost and total-cost data include allocated fixed costs, it is not clear from these data how the firm's total costs will change as volume changes. Another way of stating this criticism is that absorption-cost data are not consistent with cost-volume-profit analysis. CVP analysis emphasizes the distinction between fixed and variable costs. This approach enables managers to predict the effects of changes in prices and sales volume on profit. Absorption-cost and total-cost information obscures the distinction between variable and fixed costs.

Variable-Cost Pricing Formulas

To avoid blurring the effects of cost behavior on profit, some managers prefer to use cost-plus pricing formulas based on either variable manufacturing costs or total variable costs. [See formulas (1) and (4) in Exhibit 15–5.] Three advantages are attributed to this pricing approach:

1. Variable-cost data do not obscure the cost behavior pattern by unitizing fixed costs and making them appear variable. Thus, variable-cost information is more consistent with cost-volume-profit analysis often used by managers to see the profit implications of changes in price and volume.

2. Variable-cost data do not require allocation of common fixed costs to individual product lines. For example, the annual salary of Sydney Sailing Supplies' vice president of sales is a cost that must be borne by all of the company's product lines. Arbitrarily allocating a portion of her salary to the Wave Darter product line is not meaningful.

3. Variable-cost data are exactly the type of information managers need when facing certain decisions, such as whether to accept a special order. This decision, examined in detail in the preceding chapter, often requires an analysis that separates fixed and variable costs.

The primary disadvantage of the variable-cost pricing formula was described earlier. If managers perceive the variable cost of a product or service as the floor for the price, they may tend to set the price too low for the firm to cover its fixed costs. Eventually this can spell disaster. Therefore, if variable-cost data are used as the basis for cost-plus pricing, managers must understand the need for higher markups to ensure that all costs are covered.

Determining the Markup

Regardless of which cost-plus formula is used, Sydney Sailing Supplies must determine its markup on the Wave Darter. If management uses a variable-cost pricing formula, the markup must cover all fixed costs and a reasonable profit. If management uses an absorption-costing formula, the markup still must be sufficient to cover the firm's profit on the Wave Darter product line. What constitutes a reasonable or normal profit margin?

Return-on-Investment Pricing   A common approach to determining the profit margin in cost-plus pricing is to base profit on the firm's target return on investment (ROI). To illustrate **return-on-investment pricing,** suppose Sydney Sailing Supplies' production plan calls for 480 Wave Darters to be manufactured during the year. Based on the cost data shown in Exhibit 15–5, this production plan will result in the following total costs.

Variable costs:		
Manufacturing	$192,000	
Selling and administrative	24,000	
Total variable costs		$216,000
Fixed costs:		
Manufacturing	$120,000	
Selling and administrative	48,000	
Total fixed costs		168,000
Total costs		$384,000

Suppose the year's average amount of capital invested in the Wave Darter product line is $300,000. If Sydney Sailing Supplies' target return on investment for the Wave Darter line is 20 percent, the required annual profit is computed as follows:

$$\text{Average invested capital} \times \text{Target ROI} = \text{Target profit}$$
$$\$300,000 \times 20\% = \$60,000$$

The markup percentage required to earn Sydney Sailing Supplies a $60,000 profit on the Wave Darter line depends on the cost-plus formula used. We will compute the markup percentage for two cost-plus formulas.

1. *Cost-plus pricing based on total costs.* The total cost of a Wave Darter is $800 per unit (Exhibit 15–5). To earn a profit of $60,000 on annual sales of 480 sailboats, the company must make a profit of $125 per boat ($125 = $60,000 ÷ 480). This entails a markup percentage of 15.63 percent *above* total cost of $800.

$$15.63\% = \frac{\$925}{\$800} - 100\%$$

A shortcut to the same conclusion uses the following formula.

$$\frac{\text{Markup percentage}}{\text{on total cost}} = \frac{\text{Target profit}}{\text{Annual volume} \times \text{Total cost per unit}}$$

$$15.63\% = \frac{\$60,000}{480 \times \$800}$$

2. *Cost-plus pricing based on total variable costs.* The total variable cost of a Wave Darter is $450 per unit (Exhibit 15–5). The markup percentage applied to variable cost must be sufficient to cover *both* annual profit of $60,000 *and* total annual fixed costs of $168,000. The required markup percentage is computed as follows:

$$\frac{\text{Markup percentage}}{\text{on total variable cost}} = \frac{\text{Target profit} + \text{Total annual fixed cost}}{\text{Annual volume} \times \text{Total variable cost per unit}}$$

$$105.56\% = \frac{\$60,000 + \$168,000}{480 \times \$450}$$

General Formula The general formula for computing the markup percentage in cost-plus pricing to achieve a target ROI is as follows:

$$\frac{\begin{array}{c}\text{Markup percentage}\\ \text{applied to cost base in}\\ \text{cost-plus pricing formula}\end{array}}{} = \frac{\begin{array}{c}\text{Profit required to}\\ \text{achieve target ROI}\end{array} + \begin{array}{c}\text{Total annual costs } not\\ \text{included in cost base}\end{array}}{\begin{array}{c}\text{Annual}\\ \text{volume}\end{array} \times \begin{array}{c}\text{Cost base per unit}\\ \text{used in cost-plus}\\ \text{pricing formula}\end{array}}$$

Exercise 15–34 at the end of the chapter gives you an opportunity to employ this formula to compute the markup percentage for the other two cost-plus pricing formulas in Exhibit 15–5.

Management
Accounting
Practice

Bharti Airtel, Iliad SA,
France Telecom, China
Telecom, China Unicom,
IPTV

PRICE COMPETITION AND COST MANAGEMENT

Intense price competition, sometimes referred to as a *price war*, can occur in just about any industry, and the competition can be regional, national, or international in scope. In telecommunications, where national regulation tends to limit cross-border competition, pricing competition can nevertheless be fierce within a country. In India, leading telecom company **Bharti Airtel** has been forced to alter its business strategy in response to pricing competition: "A price war in India has driven call rates down to less than 1 cent a minute, forcing Bharti, India's largest telecom, to look overseas for growth."[2]

As the number of competitors in an industry increases, price pressure grows, often because one of the companies adopts low pricing as a strategy for differentiating itself in the market. France has added a fourth telecom competitor, awarding a license to **Iliad SA**. Iliad has previously followed a low-price strategy in Internet pricing, and even though Iliad has less than 3% of the revenues of market leader **France Telecom**, its presence in the market is widely expected to drive price reductions. "If [Iliad] can do what they do on the Internet side, we should see prices fall and service get a lot better very quickly."[3] Enhanced service delivery will increase costs at a time of declining revenues, emphasizing the importance of cost control.

Price competition can also develop around a market shift, frequently when advances in technology drive strategic mergers between companies or products and services. For example, as a service like voice calling based in over-the-air telecom becomes available in broadband cable as VOIP, price competition with newfound competitors can develop. In China, telecom providers **China Telecom** and **China Unicom** are fighting for customers with the country's cable providers like **IPTV**. "Cable-telecom convergence may be new to China, but it's brought back the bad old days, with excessive price competition . . . With cable operators winning over their customers with low prices, China Telecom and Unicom are responding with their own discounts."[4]

Companies facing lower prices and increased discounting have to reduce costs if they want to maintain their profitability. Meeting competitive prices and effectively managing costs go hand-in-hand in any business.

Cost-Plus Pricing: Summary and Evaluation

We have examined two different approaches to setting prices: (1) the economic, profit-maximizing approach and (2) cost-plus pricing. Although the techniques involved in these methods are quite different, the methods complement each other. In setting prices, managers cannot ignore the market, nor can they ignore costs. Cost-plus pricing is used widely in practice to establish a starting point in the process of determining a price. Cost-plus formulas are simple; they can be applied mechanically without taking the time of top management. They make it possible for a company with hundreds of products or services to cope with the tasks of updating prices for existing products and setting initial prices for new products.

Cost-plus pricing formulas can be used effectively with a variety of cost definitions, but the markup percentage must be appropriate for the type of cost used. It is imperative that price-setting managers understand that ultimately the price must cover all costs and a normal profit margin. Absorption-cost-plus or total-cost-plus pricing has the advantage of keeping the manager's attention focused on covering total costs. The variable-cost-plus formulas have the advantage of not obscuring important information about cost behavior.

---

[2]"Bharti Airtel Profit Down on Price War, Forex Loss," *The Times of India*, August 11, 2010.

[3]Taylor Reynolds, OECD economist, quoted in Matthew Campbell, "France Telecom, Vivendi May Face Price War from Iliad," *Bloomberg*, December 18, 2009.

[4]Robert Clark, "Cable, Telecom Price War in China," *TelecomAsia.net*, September 21, 2010.

Cost-plus pricing formulas establish a starting point in setting prices. Then the price setter must weigh market conditions, likely actions of competitors, and general business conditions. Thus, effective price setting requires a constant interplay of market considerations and cost awareness.

Strategic Pricing of New Products

Pricing a new product is an especially challenging decision problem. The newer the concept of the product, the more difficult the pricing decision is. For example, if Sydney Sailing Supplies comes out with a new two-person sailboat, its pricing problem is far easier than the pricing problem of a company that first markets products using a radically new technology. Genetic engineering, superconductivity, nanotechnology, and solar photovoltaics are all examples of such frontier technologies.

Learning Objective 4

Discuss the issues involved in the strategic pricing of new products.

Pricing a new product is harder than pricing a mature product because of the magnitude of the uncertainties involved. New products entail many uncertainties. For example, what obstacles will be encountered in manufacturing the product, and what will be the costs of production? Moreover, after the product is available, will anyone want to buy it, and at what price? If Sydney Sailing Supplies decides to market a new two-person sailboat, management can make a good estimate of both the production costs and the potential market for the product. The uncertainties here are far smaller than the uncertainties facing a company developing artificial hearts.

In addition to the production and demand uncertainties, new products pose another sort of challenge. There are two widely differing strategies that a manufacturer of a new product can adopt. One strategy is called **skimming pricing,** in which the initial product price is set high, and short-term profits are reaped on the new product. The initial market will be small, due in part to the high initial price. This pricing approach often is used for unique products, where there are people who "must have it" whatever the price. As the product gains acceptance and its appeal broadens, the price is lowered gradually. Eventually the product is priced in a range that appeals to several kinds of buyers. An example of a product for which skimming pricing was used is the high-definition television. Initially HDTVs were priced quite high and were affordable by only a few buyers. Eventually the price was lowered, and HDTVs were purchased by a wide range of consumers.

"... Our prices reflect a conscious choice to create high-quality, environmentally conscious clothing for the outdoor and lifestyle fashion markets ... We recognize, and regret, that for some customers our products will be too expensive ... " (15d)
Nau, Inc.

An alternative initial pricing strategy is called **penetration pricing,** in which the initial price is set relatively low. By setting a low price for a new product, management hopes to penetrate a new market deeply, quickly gaining a large market share. This pricing approach often is used for products that are of good quality, but do not stand out as vastly better than competing products.

The decision between skimming and penetration pricing depends on the type of product and involves trade-offs of price versus volume. Skimming pricing results in much slower acceptance of a new product, but higher unit profits. Penetration pricing results in greater initial sales volume, but lower unit profits.

Regardless of the pricing strategy used, companies must closely monitor and manage costs in order to remain price competitive.

Target Costing

Earlier in this chapter, we described product pricing as a process whereby the cost of the product is determined, and then an appropriate price is chosen. Increasingly, the opposite approach is being taken. The company first uses market research to determine the price at which a new product can be sold. Given the likely sales price, management computes the cost for which the product must be manufactured in order to provide the firm with an acceptable profit margin. Finally, engineers and cost analysts work together to design a product that can be manufactured for the allowable cost. This process, called **target costing,** is used widely by companies in the development stages of new products. A new

Learning Objective 5

List and discuss the key principles of target costing.

PRICING ON THE INTERNET BY "E-TAILERS"

One of the most difficult issues in building an online retail business has proven to be pricing. "Many Internet merchants are still struggling to find ways to set prices to attract as many customers as possible, while fattening up their razor-thin profit margins. What these retailers do know is what *hasn't* worked."

As the dot-com industry struggles, flawed pricing strategies have taken much of the blame. "Too many merchants raced for the bottom with deep discounts that made profits all but impossible to achieve—especially when the stock market bottomed out and funding for dot-coms froze. Others have felt the consumer backlash to so-called price discrimination, as the Internet has given shoppers the ability to better detect price discrepancies and bargains. The survivors must now figure out if it is even possible to take advantage of the Internet's unique capabilities to set dynamic prices, which would better reflect a customer's willingness to pay more under different circumstances. 'Before the Internet existed, retail was a very competitive, difficult, low-margin business,' says economist Austan Goolsbee. 'With the advent of Internet retailers, there was a brief moment in which they and others believed they had broken the iron chain of low margins and high competition in retail by introducing the Internet. Now, retail online is starting to look like retail offline—very competitive, with squeezed profit margins. In all, a very tough place to be.'

Pricing on the Internet "was expected to offer retailers a number of advantages." First, "it would be far easier to raise or lower prices in response to demand, without the need of a clerk running through a store with a pricing gun. Online prices could be changed in far smaller increments—even by just a penny or two—as frequently as a merchant desired, making it possible to fine-tune pricing strategies."

The real payoff, though, "was supposed to be better information on exactly how price-conscious customers are. For instance, knowing that customer A doesn't care whether the 'Gladiator' DVD in her shopping basket costs $21.95 or $25.95 would leave an enterprising merchant free to charge the higher price on the spot. By contrast, knowing that customer B is going to put author John Le Carre's latest thriller back on the shelf unless it's priced at $20, instead of $28, would open an opportunity for a bookseller to make the sale by cutting the price in real time." However, putting this concept "into practice online has turned out to be exceptionally difficult, in part because the Internet also has empowered consumers to compare prices to find out if other merchants are offering a better deal or if other consumers are getting a bigger break." It has also made it easier for consumers to register a complaint. For example, "Amazon.com raised a furor . . . when customers learned they were paying different prices for the same DVD movies, the result of a marketing test in which the retailer varied prices to gauge the effect on demand." After receiving many complaints from irate consumers, "Amazon announced it would refund the difference between the highest and lowest prices in the test."[5]

product's **target cost** is the projected long-run cost that will enable a firm to enter and remain in the market for the product and compete successfully with the firm's competitors.

A Strategic Profit and Cost Management Process

Target costing can be a critical tool for management as it seeks to strategically manage the company's costs and profits. By ensuring that products are designed so that they can be produced at a low enough cost to be priced competitively, management can achieve and maintain a sustainable competitive position in the market.

---

[5]David P. Hamilton, "The Price Isn't Right: Internet Pricing Has Turned Out to Be a Lot Trickier Than Retailers Expected," *The Wall Street Journal,* February 12, 2001, p. R8.

Key Principles of Target Costing   Target costing involves seven key principles.[6]

- *Price-led costing.* Target costing sets the target cost by *first* determining the price at which a product can be sold in the marketplace. Subtracting the *target profit margin* from this *target price* yields the *target cost,* that is, the cost at which the product must be manufactured. This simple, but strategically important, relationship can be expressed in the following equation.

$$\text{Target cost} = \text{Target price} - \text{Target profit}$$

  Notice that in a target costing approach, the price is set *first,* and *then* the target product cost is determined. This is opposite from the order in which the product cost and selling price are determined under traditional cost-plus pricing.

- *Focus on the customer.* To be successful at target costing, management must listen to the company's customers. What products do they want? What features are important? How much are they willing to pay for a certain level of product quality? Management needs to aggressively seek customer feedback, and then products must be designed to satisfy customer demand and be sold at a price they are willing to pay. In short, the target costing approach is market driven.

- *Focus on product design.* Design engineering is a key element in target costing. Engineers must design a product from the ground up so that it can be produced at its target cost. This design activity includes specifying the raw materials and components to be used as well as the labor, machinery, and other elements of the production process. In short, a product must be designed for manufacturability.

- *Focus on process design.* As indicated in the preceding point, every aspect of the production *process* must be examined to make sure that the product is produced as efficiently as possible. The use of touch labor, technology, global sourcing in procurement, and every aspect of the production process must be designed with the product's target cost in mind.

- *Cross-functional teams.* Manufacturing a product at or below its target cost requires the involvement of people from many different functions in an organization: market research, sales, design engineering, procurement, production engineering, production scheduling, material handling, and cost management. Individuals from all these diverse areas of expertise can make key contributions to the target costing process. Moreover, "a cross-functional team is not a set of specialists who contribute their expertise and then leave; they are responsible for the entire product."[7]

- *Life-cycle costs.* In specifying a product's target cost, analysts must be careful to incorporate all of the product's *life-cycle costs.* These include the costs of product planning and concept design, preliminary design, detailed design and testing, production, distribution, and customer service. Traditional cost-accounting systems have tended to focus only on the production phase and have not paid enough attention to the product's other life-cycle costs.[8]

- *Value-chain orientation.* Sometimes the projected cost of a new product is above the target cost. Then efforts are made to eliminate *non-value-added costs* to bring the projected cost down.[9] In some cases, a close look at the company's entire *value chain* can help managers identify opportunities for cost reduction. For

> "Target costing is neither easily nor quickly done." (15e)
> **U.S. Navy Acquisition Center**

> "Target costing with suppliers involves developing detailed cost models of both existing products and those in development. This necessitates the open sharing of cost information in an ethical and professional manner." (15f)
> **Eastman Kodak Company**

---

[6]This section is based on Shahid L. Ansari, Jan E. Bell, and the CAM-I Target Cost Core Group, *Target Costing: The Next Frontier in Strategic Cost Management* (Burr Ridge, IL: Irwin, 1997).

[7]Ibid., p. 15.

[8]See Chapter 9 for further discussion of product life-cycle costing.

[9]The elimination of non-value-added costs is covered in Chapter 5 as part of the discussion of activity-based management.

Price-led costing
Customer focus
Product design
Process design
Cross-functional teams
Life-cycle costing
Value-chain orientation

example, Procter & Gamble placed order-entry computers in Walmart stores. This resulted in substantial savings in order-processing costs for both companies.[10]

Activity-Based Costing and Target Costing

An activity-based costing (ABC) system can be particularly helpful as product design engineers try to achieve a product's target cost. ABC enables designers to break down the production process for a new product into its component activities. Then designers can attempt cost improvement in particular activities to bring a new product's projected cost in line with its target cost.

To illustrate, Sydney Sailing Supplies' Marine Instruments Division, located in Perth, Australia, wants to introduce a new depth finder. Target costing studies indicate that a target cost of $340 must be met in order to successfully compete in this market. Exhibit 15–6 shows how ABC was used to bring the depth finder's initial cost estimate of $399 down to $337, just below the target cost. The company's design engineers were able to focus on key activities in the production process, such as material handling and inspection, and reduce the projected costs.

Computer-Integrated Manufacturing   When a computer-integrated manufacturing (CIM) system is used, the process of target costing sometimes is computerized. A manufacturer's computer-aided design and cost-accounting software are interconnected. An engineer can try out many different design features and immediately see the product-cost implications, without ever leaving the computer terminal.

Product-Cost Distortion and Pricing: The Role of Activity-Based Costing

Use of a traditional, volume-based product-costing system may result in significant cost distortion among product lines. In many cases, high-volume and relatively simple products are overcosted while low-volume and complex products are undercosted. This results from the fact that high-volume and relatively simple products require proportionately less activity per unit for various manufacturing-support activities than do low-volume and complex products. Yet a traditional product-costing system, in which all overhead is assigned on the basis of a single unit-level activity like direct-labor hours, fails to capture the cost implications of product diversity. In contrast, an activity-based costing (ABC) system does measure the extent to which each product line drives costs in the key production-support activities.

---

[10]J. Shank and V. Govindarajan, "Strategic Cost Management and the Value Chain," *Journal of Cost Management* 5, no. 4 (Winter 1992), p. 10. See also T. Tanaka, "Target Costing at Toyota," *Journal of Cost Management* 7, no. 1 (Spring 1993), pp. 4–12.

A. Activity-Based Costing System

Activity Cost Pool	Cost Driver	Pool Rate
Purchasing	Number of parts	$1 per part
Material handling	Dollar value of parts	$.20 per direct-material dollar
Inspection	Inspection hours	$28 per inspection hour

This is a highly simplified example of activity-based costing. ABC systems, which were introduced conceptually in Chapter 3, are covered in detail in Chapter 5.

B. Cost Projections for a New Product: Depth Finder

	Original Cost Projection	Improved Cost Projection
Direct material	$200	$190
Direct labor	100	70
Purchasing:		
$1 per part (45 parts)	45	
$1 per part (32 parts)		32
Material handling:		
$.20 per direct-material dollar ($200)	40	
$.20 per direct-material dollar ($190)		38
Inspection:		
$28 per inspection hour (.5 hour)	14	
$28 per inspection hour (.25 hour)		7
Total projected cost	$399	$337
Target cost	$340	

Exhibit 15–6
Target Costing and Cost Improvement for a New Product

SYDNEY SAILING SUPPLIES

Managers should be aware that cost distortion can result in overpricing high-volume and relatively simple products, while low-volume and complex products are undercosted. This can undermine any effort to set prices competitively, even under the target-costing approach. The competitive implications of such strategic pricing errors can be disastrous.[11]

Value Engineering and Target Costing

Target costing is an outgrowth of the concept of **value engineering,** which is a cost-reduction and process-improvement technique that utilizes information collected about a product's design and production processes and then examines various attributes of the design and processes to identify candidates for improvement efforts.

Learning Objective 8

Explain the process of value engineering and its role in target costing.

Much of the historical development of the target-costing approach has taken place in Japanese industry, where "more than 80 percent of all assembly industries in Japan use target costing. Some of the best practitioners of target costing are leading Japanese companies."[12] In recent years, however, many other companies, including Caterpillar, Chrysler, Boeing, and Kodak, have made significant contributions to target costing theory and practice.

Isuzu Motors, Ltd. is a leading Japanese manufacturer of automobiles, buses, and both light- and heavy-duty trucks. "At Isuzu, value engineering (VE) has been developed

---

[11]This whole issue of cost distortion and the role of ABC in product pricing is covered extensively in Chapter 5.

[12]Shahid L. Ansari, Jan E. Bell, and the CAM-I Target Cost Core Group, *Target Costing: The Next Frontier in Strategic Cost Management* (Burr Ridge, IL: Irwin, 1997). See also Y. Kato, "Target Costing Support Systems: Lessons from Leading Japanese Companies," *Management Accounting Research* 4 (1992), pp. 33–47; and T. Tani, H. Okano, N. Shimizu, Y. Iwabuchi, J. Fukuda, and S. Cooray, "Target Cost Management in Japanese Companies: Current State of the Art," *Management Accounting Research* 6 (1994), pp. 67–81.

to cover all stages of product design and manufacture. Indeed, three different stages of VE—zeroth, first, and second 'looks'—are used in the design phase to increase the functionality of new products."[13]

- *Zeroth look VE* is applied at the earliest stages of new product design—"the concept proposal stage, when the basic concept of the product is developed and its preliminary quality, cost, and investment targets are established."
- *First look VE* is applied during the last half of the concept proposal stage and throughout the product planning phase. During this stage, a product's quality, functionality, and selling price are determined; a design plan is submitted; and target costs are determined for each of the new vehicle's major functions (e.g., engine and transmission). Also, the degree of component commonality is set. "First look VE is used at this stage to increase the value of the product by increasing its functionality without increasing its cost."
- *Second look VE* is applied during the last half of the product planning stage and the first half of the product development and preparation stage. "The components of the vehicle's major functions are identified, and hand-made prototypes are assembled. At this stage, VE works to improve the value and functionality of existing components, not to create new ones."

In addition, various *tear-down methods* are used by Isuzu, and many other companies, "to analyze competitive products in terms of materials they contain, parts they use, ways they function, and ways they are manufactured." At Isuzu, for example, *dynamic tear-down* focuses on reducing the number of vehicle assembly operations or the time required to perform them. *Cost tear-down* examines ways to reduce the cost of the components used in a vehicle. *Material tear-down* compares the materials and surface treatments of the components used by Isuzu with those of its competitors. *Static tear-down* disassembles a competitor's product into its components to enable Isuzu's engineers to compare Isuzu's components with those used in the competitor's product.

Although the Isuzu approach is illustrative of target costing methods, many different approaches are used by the thousands of companies now engaged in target costing programs. However, the Isuzu target costing and value-engineering process is indicative of the seriousness with which companies approach the problem of reducing costs in order to meet a product's target cost and remain competitive in an ever more difficult market.

> "An old Japanese saying states that 'there are many ways to the top of a mountain.' Analogously, there is no one right way to do target costing." (15h)
>
> **Honda of America Manufacturing, Inc.**

Time and Material Pricing

Learning Objective 9

Determine prices using the time and material pricing approach.

Another cost-based approach to pricing is called **time and material pricing.** Under this approach, the company determines one charge for the labor used on a job and another charge for the materials. The labor typically includes the direct cost of the employee's time and a charge to cover various overhead costs. The material charge generally includes the direct cost of the materials used in a job plus a charge for material handling and storage. Time and material pricing is used widely by construction companies, printers, repair shops, and professional firms, such as engineering, law, and public accounting firms.

To illustrate, we will examine a special job undertaken by Sydney Sailing Supplies. The company's vice president for sales, Richard Moby, was approached by a successful local physician about refurbishing her yacht. She wanted an engine overhaul, complete refurbishment and redecoration of the cabin facilities, and stripping and repainting of the hull and deck. The work would be done in the Repair Department of the company's Yacht Division, located in Melbourne, Australia.

---

[13]This description of Isuzu's target costing and value-engineering methods is drawn from Robin Cooper, *When Lean Enterprises Collide* (Boston, MA: Harvard Business School Press, 1995), pp. 165–83.

Data regarding the operations of the Repair Department are as follows:

Labor rate, including fringe benefits	$18.00 per hour
Hourly charge to cover profit margin	$7.00 per hour
Annual labor hours	10,000 hours
Annual overhead costs:	
Material handling and storage	$40,000
Other overhead costs (supervision, utilities, insurance, and depreciation)	$200,000
Annual cost of materials used in Repair Department	$1,000,000

Based on these data, the Repair Department computed its time and material prices as follows:

Time Charges

$$\text{Hourly labor cost} + \frac{\text{Annual overhead (excluding material handling and storage)}}{\text{Annual labor hours}} + \text{Hourly charge to cover profit margin}$$

$$\$18 \text{ per hour} + \frac{\$200,000}{10,000 \text{ hours}} + \$7 \text{ per hour} = \frac{\$45 \text{ per}}{\text{labor hour}}$$

Material Charges

$$\text{Material cost incurred on job} + \left(\text{Material cost incurred on job} \times \frac{\text{Material handling and storage costs}}{\text{Annual cost of materials used in Repair Department}} \right)$$

$$\text{Material cost incurred on job} + \left(\text{Material cost incurred on job} \times \frac{\$40,000}{\$1,000,000} \right)$$

$.04 per dollar of material cost

The effect of the material-charge formula is to include a charge for the costs incurred in the handling and storage of materials.

Richard Moby estimates that the yacht refurbishment job will require 200 hours of labor and $8,000 in materials. Moby's price quotation for the job is shown in the Excel spreadsheet in Exhibit 15–7.

Included in the $17,320 price quotation for the yacht refurbishment are charges for labor costs, overhead, material costs, material handling and storage costs, and a normal profit margin. Some companies also charge an additional markup on the materials used in a job in order to earn a profit on that component of their services. Sydney Sailing Supplies' practice is to charge a high enough profit charge on its labor to earn an appropriate profit for the Repair Department.

Competitive Bidding

In a **competitive bidding** situation, two or more companies submit sealed bids (or prices) for a project, service, or product to a potential buyer. The buyer selects one of the companies for the job on the basis of the bid price and the design specifications for the job. Competitive bidding complicates a manager's pricing problem, because now the manager

Learning Objective **10**

Set prices in special-order or competitive-bidding situations by analyzing the relevant costs.

Exhibit 15–7
Time and Material Pricing

	A	B	C	D	E	F	G	H
	G15	▼	fx	=G13+G14				
1			SYDNEY SAILING SUPPLIES					
2			Price Quotation					
3			Yacht Division: Repair Department					
4								
5	Time charges	Labor time					200	hours
6		x Rate				x	$ 45	per hour
7		Total					$ 9,000	
8								
9	Material charges	Cost of materials for job					$ 8,000	
10		+ Charge for material handling and storage*					320	
11		Total					$ 8,320	
12								
13	Total price of job	Time					$ 9,000	
14		Material					8,320	
15		Total					$ 17,320	
16								
17	*Charge for material handling and storage:							
18	($8,000 material cost) x ($.04 per dollar of material cost) = $320							

Microsoft Excel - Time and Material Pricing

File   Edit   View   Insert   Format   Tools   Data   Window   Help

Sheet1 / Sheet2 / Sheet3 /

Ready

is in direct competition with one or more competitors. If all of the companies submitting bids offer a roughly equivalent product or service, the bid price becomes the sole criterion for selecting the contractor. The higher the price that is bid, the greater will be the profit on the job, *if* the firm gets the contract. However, a higher price also lowers the probability of obtaining the contract to perform the job. Thus, there is a trade-off between bidding high, to make a good profit, and bidding low, to land the contract. Some say there is a "winner's curse" in competitive bidding, meaning that the company bidding low enough to beat out its competitors probably bid too low to make an acceptable profit on the job. Despite the winner's curse, competitive bidding is a common form of selecting contractors in many types of business.

Richard Moby was approached recently by the city of Sydney about building a new marina for moderate-sized sailing vessels. Moby decided that his company's Marine Services Division should submit a bid on the job. The Marine Services Division specializes in marina maintenance and construction. The city announced that three other firms also would be submitting bids. Since all four companies were equally capable of building the marina to the city's specifications, Moby assumed that the bid price would be the deciding factor in selecting the contractor.

Moby consulted with the controller and chief engineer of the Marine Services Division, and the following data were compiled.

Estimated direct-labor requirements, 1,500 hours at $12.00 per hour	$18,000
Estimated direct-material requirements	30,000
Estimated variable overhead (allocated on the basis of direct labor), 1,500 direct-labor hours at $5.00 per hour	7,500
Total estimated variable costs	$55,500
Estimated fixed overhead (allocated on the basis of direct labor), 1,500 direct-labor hours at $8.00 per hour	12,000
Estimated total cost	$67,500

The Marine Services Division allocates variable-overhead costs to jobs on the basis of direct-labor hours. These costs consist of indirect-labor costs, such as the wages of equipment-repair personnel, gasoline and lubricants, and incidental supplies such as rope, chains, and drill bits. Fixed-overhead costs, also allocated to jobs on the basis of direct-labor hours, include such costs as workers'compensation insurance, depreciation on vehicles and construction equipment, depreciation of the division's buildings, and supervisory salaries.

It was up to Richard Moby to decide on the bid price for the marina. In his meeting with the divisional controller and the chief engineer, Moby argued that the marina job was important to the company for two reasons. First, the Marine Services Division had been operating well below capacity for several months. The marina job would not preclude the firm from taking on any other construction work, so it would not entail an opportunity cost. Second, the marina job would be good advertising for Sydney Sailing Supplies. City residents would see the firm's name on the project, and this would promote sales of the company's boats and sailing supplies.

Based on these arguments, Moby pressed for a bid price that just covered the firm's variable costs and allowed for a modest contribution margin. The chief engineer was obstinate, however, and argued for a higher bid price that would give the division a good profit on the job. "My employees work hard to do an outstanding job, and their work is worth a premium to the city," was the engineer's final comment on the issue. After the threesome tossed the problem around all morning, the controller agreed with Moby. A bid price of $60,000 was finally agreed upon.

This is a typical approach to setting prices for special jobs and competitively bid contracts. When a firm has excess capacity, a price that covers the incremental costs incurred because of the job will contribute toward covering the company's fixed cost and profit. None of the Marine Services Division's fixed costs will increase as a result of taking on the marina job. Thus, a bid price of $60,000 will cover the $55,500 of variable costs on the job and contribute $4,500 toward covering the division's fixed costs.

Bid price	$60,000
Variable costs of marina job (incremental costs incurred only if job is done)	55,500
Contribution from marina job (contribution to covering the division's fixed costs)	$ 4,500

Naturally, Sydney Sailing Supplies' management would like to make a larger profit on the marina job, but bidding a higher price means running a substantial risk of losing the job to a competitor.

No Excess Capacity   What if the Marine Services Division has no excess capacity? If management expects to have enough work to fully occupy the division, a different approach is appropriate in setting the bid price. The fixed costs of the division are capacity-producing costs, which are costs incurred in order to create productive capacity. Depreciation of buildings and equipment, supervisory salaries, insurance, and property taxes are examples of fixed costs incurred to give a company the capacity to carry on its operations. When such costs are allocated to individual jobs, the cost of each job reflects an estimate of the opportunity cost of using limited capacity to do that particular job. For this reasoning to be valid, however, the organization must be at full capacity. If there is excess capacity, there is no opportunity cost in using that excess capacity.

If the Marine Services Division has no excess capacity, it would be appropriate to focus on the estimated full cost of the marina job, $67,500, which includes an allocation of the division's fixed capacity-producing costs. Now Richard Moby might legitimately argue for a bid price in excess of $67,500. If the division is awarded the marina contract by the city, a price above $67,500 will cover all the costs of the job and make a contribution toward the division's profit.

However, as Richard Moby pointed out, there will be valuable promotional benefits to Sydney Sailing Supplies if its Marine Services Division builds the marina. This is a qualitative factor, because these potential benefits are difficult to quantify. Moby will have to make a judgment regarding just how important the marina job is to the company.

The greater the perceived qualitative benefits, the lower the bid price should be set to maximize the likelihood that the company will be awarded the contract.

Summary of Competitive-Bidding Analysis   The Marine Services Division's pricing problem is summarized in Exhibit 15–8. As you can see, the final pricing decision requires managerial judgment to fully consider the quantitative cost data, the qualitative promotional benefits, and the trade-off between a higher profit and a greater likelihood of getting the marina contract.

Accept or Reject a Special Order   In the preceding chapter, we examined in detail the decision as to whether a special order should be accepted or rejected. The analysis focused on identifying the relevant costs of the special order. The existence of excess capacity was an important factor in that analysis. Accepting a special order when excess capacity exists entails no opportunity cost. But when there is no excess capacity, one relevant cost of accepting a special order is the opportunity cost incurred by using the firm's limited capacity for the special order instead of some other job. After all relevant costs of the order have been identified, the decision maker compares the total relevant cost of the order with the price offered. If the price exceeds the relevant cost, the order generally should be accepted.

The decision is conceptually very similar to the bid-pricing problem discussed in this chapter. Setting a price for a special order or competitive bid also entails an analysis of the relevant costs of the job. Whether the decision maker is setting a price or has been offered a price, he or she must identify the relevant costs of providing the product or service requested.

Effect of Antitrust Laws on Pricing

Learning Objective 11

Describe the legal restrictions on setting prices.

Companies are not free to set any price they wish for their products or services. Competition laws, also called antitrust laws, have been adopted in most industrialized countries. The purpose of these laws is to promote competitive behavior in markets for the benefit of consumers, and one of the ways they do so is by restricting pricing practices. These laws generally prohibit **price discrimination,** which means quoting different prices to different customers for the same product or service. Such price differences are unlawful unless they can be clearly justified by differences in the costs incurred to produce, sell, or deliver the product or service. Managers should keep careful records justifying such cost differences when they exist, because the records may be vital to a legal defense if price differences are challenged in court.

Another pricing practice prohibited by law is **predatory pricing.** This practice involves temporarily cutting a price to broaden demand for a product with the intention of later restricting the supply and raising the price again. In determining whether a price is predatory, the courts examine a business's cost records. If the product is sold below cost, the pricing is deemed to be predatory. The laws and court cases are ambiguous as to the appropriate definition of cost. However, various court decisions make it harder to prove predatory pricing. Nevertheless, this is one area where a price-setting decision maker is well advised to have an accountant on the left and a lawyer on the right before setting prices that could be deemed predatory.

Competition law is even more complex in an international context. The laws discussed above are specific to the nation in which the law was enacted and do not apply to cross-border trade. However, pricing is addressed in international trade agreements and there is great political interest in issues such as predatory pricing, whether through "dumping" of products below cost to gain access to a market in another country or via government subsidies that are perceived as unfair or anti-competitive. The topic will continue to be discussed in international negotiations, both in conjunction with specific trade agreements and more broadly through the trade talks sponsored by the World Trade Organization.

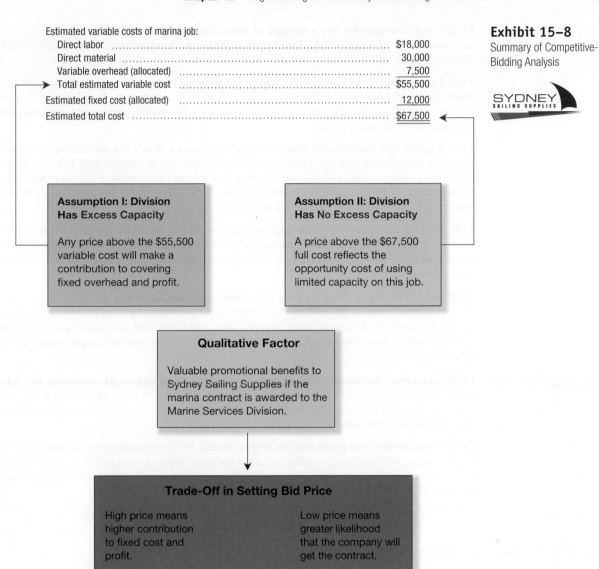

Estimated variable costs of marina job:

Direct labor	$18,000
Direct material	30,000
Variable overhead (allocated)	7,500
Total estimated variable cost	$55,500
Estimated fixed cost (allocated)	12,000
Estimated total cost	$67,500

Exhibit 15–8

Summary of Competitive-Bidding Analysis

SYDNEY SAILING SUPPLIES

Assumption I: Division Has Excess Capacity

Any price above the $55,500 variable cost will make a contribution to covering fixed overhead and profit.

Assumption II: Division Has No Excess Capacity

A price above the $67,500 full cost reflects the opportunity cost of using limited capacity on this job.

Qualitative Factor

Valuable promotional benefits to Sydney Sailing Supplies if the marina contract is awarded to the Marine Services Division.

Trade-Off in Setting Bid Price

High price means higher contribution to fixed cost and profit.

Low price means greater likelihood that the company will get the contract.

Chapter Summary

LO1 List and describe the four major influences on pricing decisions. Many influences affect pricing decisions. Chief among these are: customer demand; the actions of competitors; the costs of the products or services; and political, legal, and image-related issues.

LO2 Explain and use the economic, profit-maximizing pricing model. Under this approach to pricing, the profit-maximizing quantity is determined by the intersection of the marginal revenue and marginal cost curves. At this optimal sales quantity level, the profit-maximizing price is determined from the demand (or average-revenue) curve.

LO3 Set prices using cost-plus pricing formulas. Cost-plus pricing formulas are commonly based on four product-cost measures: (1) variable manufacturing cost; (2) absorption manufacturing cost; (3) total cost; and (4) total variable cost. Markups often are set to earn the company a target profit on its products, based on a target rate of return on investment.

LO4 Discuss the issues involved in the strategic pricing of new products. Strategic pricing of new products is an especially challenging problem for management. Various pricing approaches, such as skimming pricing or penetration pricing, may be appropriate depending on the product.

LO5 List and discuss the key principles of target costing. Target costing often is used to design a new product that can be produced at a cost that will enable the firm to sell it at a competitive price. Value engineering and activity-based costing are valuable tools used in the target costing process.

LO6 Explain the role of activity-based costing in setting a target cost. Activity-based costing helps to avoid product cost distortion, in which relatively high-volume and relatively simple products tend to be overcosted by traditional product-costing systems, and relatively low-volume and relatively complex products tend to be undercosted.

LO7 Explain how product-cost distortion can undermine a firm's pricing strategy. Product-cost distortion occurs when relatively high-volume and relatively simple products tend to be overcosted by traditional product-costing systems, and relatively low-volume and relatively complex products tend to be undercosted. This phenomenon can lead a company to lose sales by overpricing certain products and lose profit by selling other products at too low a price.

LO8 Explain the process of value engineering and its role in target costing. Value engineering analyzes a product's design and production process to identify areas for cost reduction and process improvement. By reducing a product's cost, management can bring a product's production cost down to meet its target cost.

LO9 Determine prices using the time and material pricing approach. In industries such as construction, repair, printing, and professional services, time and material pricing often is used. Under this approach, the price is determined as the sum of a labor-cost component and a material-cost component. Either or both of these components may include a markup to ensure that the company earns a profit on its services.

LO10 Set prices in special-order or competitive-bidding situations by analyzing the relevant costs. Pricing special orders and determining competitive bid prices entail an analysis of the relevant costs to be incurred in completing the job. The relevant-cost analysis should incorporate the existence of excess capacity or the lack of it.

LO11 Describe the legal restrictions on setting prices. The law prohibits price discrimination, which means quoting different prices to different customers for the same product or service. Also outlawed is predatory pricing, which involves temporarily cutting a price to broaden demand for a product with the intention of later restricting the supply and raising the price again.

Review Problem on Cost-Plus Pricing

Kitchenware Corporation manufactures high-quality copper pots and pans. Greta Cooke, one of the company's price analysts, is involved in setting a price for the company's new Starter Set. This set consists of seven of the most commonly used pots and pans. During the next year, the company plans to produce 10,000 Starter Sets, and the controller has provided Cooke with the following cost data.

Predicted Costs of 10,000 Starter Sets

Direct material per set	$60
Direct labor per set, 2 hours at $10.00 per hr	20
Variable selling cost per set	5
Total	$85
Variable-overhead rate	$ 8.00 per direct-labor hour
Fixed-overhead rate	$12.00 per direct-labor hour

In addition, the controller indicated that the Accounting Department would allocate $20,000 of fixed administrative expenses to the Starter Set product line.

Required:

1. Compute the cost of a Starter Set using each of the four cost definitions commonly used in cost-plus pricing formulas.

2. Determine the markup percentage required for the Starter Set product line to earn a target profit of $317,500 before taxes during the next year. Use the total cost as the cost definition in the cost-plus formula.

Solution to Review Problem

1.

Variable manufacturing cost*	$ 96	①
Applied fixed-overhead cost†	24	
Absorption manufacturing cost	$120	②
Variable selling cost	5	
Allocated fixed administrative cost‡	2	
Total cost	$127	③
Variable manufacturing cost	$ 96	
Variable selling cost	5	
Total variable cost	$101	④
*Direct material	$ 60	
Direct labor	20	
Variable overhead	16	(2 × $8.00 per hour)
Total variable manufacturing cost	$ 96	
†Applied fixed overhead cost	$ 24	(2 × $12 per hour)
‡Allocated fixed administrative cost	$ 2	($20,000 ÷ 10,000 sets)

2. Markup percentage on total cost $= \dfrac{\$317,500}{10,000 \times \$127} = 25\%$

Proof: Price = Total cost + (.25 × Total cost) = $127 + (.25)($127) = $158.75

Income Statement

Sales revenue (10,000 × $158.75)		$1,587,500
Less: Variable costs:		
Direct material	$600,000	
Direct labor	200,000	
Variable overhead	160,000	
Variable selling cost	50,000	
Total variable costs		1,010,000
Contribution margin		$ 577,500
Less: Fixed costs:		
Manufacturing overhead	$240,000	
Administrative cost	20,000	
Total fixed costs		260,000
Profit		$ 317,500

Key Terms

For each term's definition refer to the indicated page, or turn to the glossary at the end of the text.

competitive bidding, 697

cost-plus pricing, 686

cross-elasticity, 685

demand curve (average revenue curve), 682

marginal cost curve, 682

marginal revenue curve, 682

oligopolistic market, 685

penetration pricing, 691

predatory pricing, 700

price discrimination, 700

price elasticity, 685

price taker, 680

return-on-investment pricing, 688

skimming pricing, 691

target cost, 692

target costing, 691

time and material pricing, 696

total cost curve, 682

total revenue curve, 680

value engineering, 695

Review Questions

15–1. Comment on the following remark made by a bank president: "The prices of our banking services are determined by the financial-services market. Costs are irrelevant."

15–2. "All this marginal revenue and marginal cost stuff is just theory. Prices are determined by production costs." Evaluate this assertion.

15–3. List and briefly describe four major influences on pricing decisions.

15–4. Explain what is meant by the following statement: "In considering the reactions of competitors, it is crucial to define your product."

15–5. Explain the following assertion: "Price setting generally requires a balance between market forces and cost considerations."

15–6. Briefly explain the concept of *economic, profit-maximizing pricing*. It may be helpful to use graphs in your explanation.

15–7. Define the following terms: *total revenue, marginal revenue, demand curve, price elasticity,* and *cross-elasticity.*

15–8. Briefly define *total cost* and *marginal cost.*

15–9. Describe three limitations of the economic, profit-maximizing model of pricing.

15–10. Determining the best approach to pricing requires a cost-benefit trade-off. Explain.

15–11. Write the general formula for cost-plus pricing, and briefly explain its use.

15–12. List the four common cost bases used in cost-plus pricing. How can they all result in the same price?

15–13. List four reasons often cited for the widespread use of absorption cost as the cost base in cost-plus pricing formulas.

15–14. What is the primary disadvantage of basing the cost-plus pricing formula on absorption cost?

15–15. List three advantages of pricing based on variable cost.

15–16. Explain the behavioral problem that can result when cost-plus prices are based on variable cost.

15–17. Briefly explain the concept of *return-on-investment pricing.*

15–18. Explain the phrase *price-led costing.*

15–19. Why is a focus on the customer such a key principle of target costing?

15–20. Explain the role of value engineering in target costing.

15–21. Could *tear-down* methods be used effectively for target pricing in a service-industry company, such as a hotel or an airline? Explain.

15–22. Briefly describe the *time-and-material pricing approach.*

15–23. Explain the importance of the excess-capacity issue in setting a competitive bid price.

15–24. The decision to accept or reject a special order and the selection of a price for a special order are very similar decisions. Explain.

15–25. Describe the following approaches to pricing new products: skimming pricing, penetration pricing, and target costing.

15–26. Explain what is meant by unlawful price discrimination and predatory pricing.

15–27. Briefly explain the potential negative consequences in pricing decisions from using a traditional, volume-based product-costing system.

Exercises

All applicable Exercises are available with McGraw-Hill's *Connect Accounting*™.

■ **Exercise 15–28**
Demand and Revenue Data
(LO 1, 2)

Spectrum Sound, Inc. manufactures compact disc players with unusual features in its Helsinki Division. The divisional sales manager has estimated the following demand-curve data.

Quantity Sold per Month	Unit Sales Price
10	$1,000
20	950
30	900
40	850
50	800

Required:

1. Prepare a table similar to panel C of Exhibit 15–1 summarizing Spectrum Sound's price, quantity, and revenue data.

2. Draw a graph similar to panel A of Exhibit 15–1 reflecting the data tabulated in requirement (1).

Refer to the preceding exercise. The divisional controller at Spectrum Sound's Helsinki Division has estimated the following cost data for the division's CD players. (Assume there are no fixed costs.)

■ **Exercise 15–29**
Continuation of Preceding Exercise; Cost Data
(LO 1, 2)

Quantity Produced and Sold per Month	Average Cost per Unit
10	$900
20	850
30	820
40	860
50	890

Required:

1. Prepare a table similar to panel C of Exhibit 15–2 summarizing Spectrum Sound's cost relationships.
2. Draw a graph similar to panel A of Exhibit 15–2 reflecting the data tabulated in requirement (1).

Refer to the data given in the preceding two exercises.

■ **Exercise 15–30**
Continuation of Preceding Two Exercises; Profit-Maximizing Price
(LO 1, 2)

Required:

1. Prepare a table of Spectrum Sound's revenue, cost, and profit relationships. For guidance, refer to panel C of Exhibit 15–3.
2. Draw a graph similar to panel A of Exhibit 15–3 reflecting the data tabulated in requirement (1).
3. To narrow down the pricing decision, the Helsinki Division's sales manager has decided to price the CD player at one of the following prices: $1,600, $1,700, $1,800, $1,900, or $2,000. Which price do you recommend? Why?

The marginal cost, marginal revenue, and demand curves for Houston Home and Garden's deluxe wheelbarrow are shown in the graph below.

■ **Exercise 15–31**
Marginal Revenue and Marginal Cost Curves
(LO 1, 2)

Required: Before completing any of the following requirements, read over the entire list.

1. Trace the graph onto a blank piece of paper, and label all parts of the graph.
2. Draw a companion graph directly above the traced graph. Use this graph to draw the firm's total revenue and total cost curves.
3. Show the company's profit-maximizing price on the lower graph and its profit-maximizing quantity on both graphs.

Dollars per unit

Quantity sold per month

■ **Exercise 15–32**
Pricing, Advertising, and
Special-Order Decisions
(LO 10)

Corrientes Company produces a single product in its Buenos Aires plant that currently sells for $5.00 per unit. Fixed costs are expected to amount to $60,000 for the year, and all variable manufacturing and administrative costs are expected to be incurred at a rate of $3.00 per unit. Corrientes has two salespeople who are paid strictly on a commission basis. Their commission is 10 percent of the sales revenue they generate. (Ignore income taxes.)

Required:

1. Suppose management alters its current plans by spending an additional amount of $5,000 on advertising and increases the selling price to $6.00 per unit. Calculate the profit on 60,000 units.

2. The Sorde Company has just approached Corrientes to make a special one-time purchase of 10,000 units. These units would not be sold by the sales personnel, and therefore, no commission would have to be paid. What is the price Corrientes would have to charge per unit on this special order to earn additional profit of $20,000?

(CMA, adapted)

■ **Exercise 15–33**
Target Costing for a New
Product; Use of Internet
(LO 5, 8)

Visit the Web site of one of the following companies, or a different company of your choosing.

Apple Computer	www.apple.com
Club Med	www.clubmed.com
Nedbank	www.nedbank.com
Ericsson	www.ericsson.com
Intel Corporation	www.intel.com
Nintendo	www.nintendo.com
Godrej	www.godrej.com

Required: Read about a new product or service to be offered by the company. Then explain how the firm could use target costing to price the new product or service.

■ **Exercise 15–34**
Determining Markup Percent-
age; Target ROI
(LO 1, 3)

Refer to the cost and production data for the Wave Darter in Exhibit 15–5. The target profit is $60,000.

Required: Use the general formula for determining a markup percentage to compute the required markup percentages with the following two cost-plus formulas:

1. Variable manufacturing costs [formula (1) in Exhibit 15–5].
2. Absorption manufacturing cost [formula (2) in Exhibit 15–5].

■ **Exercise 15–35**
Cost-Plus Pricing Formulas;
Missing Data
(LO 1, 3)

The following data pertain to Lawn Master Corporation's top-of-the-line lawn mower.

Variable manufacturing cost	$250
Applied fixed manufacturing cost	50
Variable selling and administrative cost	60
Allocated fixed selling and administrative cost	?

To achieve a target price of $450 per lawn mower, the markup percentage is 12.5 percent on total unit cost.

Required:

1. What is the fixed selling and administrative cost allocated to each unit of Lawn Master's top-of-the-line mower?

2. For each of the following cost bases, develop a cost-plus pricing formula that will result in a target price of $450 per mower: (*a*) variable manufacturing cost, (*b*) absorption manufacturing cost, and (*c*) total variable cost.

The following data pertain to Royal Lighting Company's oak-clad, contemporary chandelier.

■ **Exercise 15–36**
Cost-Plus Pricing Formulas
(LO 1, 3)

Variable manufacturing cost	$200
Applied fixed manufacturing cost	70
Variable selling and administrative cost	30
Allocated fixed selling and administrative cost	50

Required: For each of the following cost bases, develop a cost-plus pricing formula that will result in a price of $400 for the oak chandelier.

1.   Variable manufacturing cost.
2.   Absorption manufacturing cost.
3.   Total cost.
4.   Total variable cost.

Refer to Exhibit 15–7. Suppose the Repair Department of Sydney Sailing Supplies adds a markup of 5 percent on the material charges of a job (including the cost of material handling and storage).

■ **Exercise 15–37**
Time and Material Pricing
(LO 9)

Required:

1.   Rewrite the material component of the time and material pricing formula to reflect the markup on material cost.
2.   Compute the new price to be quoted on the yacht refurbishment described in Exhibit 15–7.

Problems

All applicable Problems are available with McGraw-Hill's *Connect Accounting*™.

Note: Several of the problems and cases in Chapter 5 relate to pricing and may be assigned with Chapter 15 as well. These problems emphasize the impact of cost distortion on pricing decisions. They stress the differences between traditional, volume-based costing systems and activity-based costing systems with respect to their role in pricing. These problems should be assigned only after Chapter 5 has been completed. The following problems are relevant: 5–46, 5–47, 5–49, 5–56, and 5–60.

Bangalore Valve and Fitting Company manufactures a variety of industrial valves and pipe fittings that are sold to customers in India. Currently, the company is operating at about 70 percent capacity and is earning a satisfactory return on investment. Management has been approached by Glasgow Industries Ltd. of Scotland with an offer to buy 120,000 units of a pressure valve. Glasgow Industries manufactures a valve that is almost identical to Bangalore Valve's pressure valve; however, a fire in Glasgow Industries' valve plant has shut down its manufacturing operations. Glasgow needs the 120,000 valves over the next four months to meet commitments to its regular customers in the United Kingdom. Glasgow is prepared to pay $20 each for the valves. Bangalore Valve's total product cost, based on current attainable standards, for the pressure valve is $22, calculated as follows:

■ **Problem 15–38**
Pricing a Special Order;
International
(LO 10)

2. Total incremental profit:
$432,000

Direct material	$ 7.00
Direct labor	6.00
Manufacturing overhead	9.00
Total product cost	$22.00

Manufacturing overhead is applied to production at the rate of $18 per standard direct-labor hour. This overhead rate is made up of the following components.

Variable manufacturing overhead	$ 6.00
Fixed manufacturing overhead (traceable)	8.00
Fixed manufacturing overhead (allocated)	4.00
Applied manufacturing overhead rate	$18.00

Additional costs incurred in connection with sales of the pressure valve include sales commissions of 5 percent and freight expense of $1.00 per unit. However, the company does not pay sales commissions on special orders that come directly to management. In determining selling prices, Bangalore Valve adds a 40 percent markup to total product cost. This provides a $30.80 suggested selling price for the pressure valve. The Marketing Department, however, has set the current selling price at $29 in order to maintain market share. Production management believes that it can handle the Glasgow Industries order without disrupting its scheduled production. The order would, however, require additional fixed factory overhead of $12,000 per month in the form of supervision and clerical costs. If management accepts the order, 30,000 pressure valves will be manufactured and shipped to Glasgow Industries each month for the next four months. Glasgow's management has agreed to pay the shipping charges for the valves.

Required:

1. Determine how many direct-labor hours would be required each month to fill the Glasgow Industries order.

2. Prepare an analysis showing the impact of accepting the Glasgow Industries order.

3. Calculate the minimum unit price that Bangalore Valve and Fitting Company's management could accept for the Glasgow Industries order without reducing net income.

4. Identify the factors, other than price, that Bangalore Valve's management should consider before accepting the Glasgow Industries order.

5. *Build a spreadsheet:* Construct an Excel spreadsheet to solve requirements (2) and (3) above. Show how the solution will change if the following information changes: the direct material and direct labor per unit are $6.90 and $6.10, respectively.

(CMA, adapted)

■ **Problem 15–39**
Cost-Plus Pricing; Bidding
(LO 3, 10)

2. Total bid price: $14,950

North American Pharmaceuticals, Inc. specializes in packaging bulk drugs in standard dosages for local hospitals. The company has been in business for seven years and has been profitable since its second year of operation. Don Greenway, Assistant Controller, installed a standard costing system after joining the company three years ago.

Wyant Memorial Hospital has asked North American Pharmaceuticals to bid on the packaging of one million doses of medication at total cost plus a return on total cost of no more than 15 percent. Wyant defines total cost as including all variable costs of performing the service, a reasonable amount of fixed overhead, and reasonable administrative costs. The hospital will supply all packaging materials and ingredients. Wyant has indicated that any bid over $.015 per dose will be rejected.

Greenway has accumulated the following information prior to the preparation of the bid.

Direct labor	$8.00 per direct-labor hour (DLH)
Variable overhead	$6.00 per DLH
Fixed overhead	$10.00 per DLH
Incremental administrative costs	$1,000 for the order
Production rate	2,000 doses per DLH

Required:

1. Calculate the minimum price per dose that North American Pharmaceuticals could bid for the Wyant Memorial Hospital job that would not reduce the pharmaceutical company's income.

2. Calculate the bid price per dose using total cost and the maximum allowable return specified by Wyant Memorial Hospital.

3. Independent of your answer to requirement (2), suppose that the price per dose that North American Pharmaceuticals, Inc. calculated using the cost-plus criterion specified by Wyant Memorial Hospital is greater than the maximum bid of $.015 per dose allowed by Wyant. Discuss the factors that the pharmaceutical company's management should consider before deciding whether or not to submit a bid at the maximum price of $.015 per dose that Wyant allows.

(CMA, adapted)

■ **Problem 15–40**
Target Costing
(LO 5, 6, 8)

4. Target profit: $2,520,000

MPE, Inc. will soon enter a very competitive marketplace in which it will have limited influence over the prices that are charged. Management and consultants are currently working to fine-tune the company's sole service, which hopefully will generate a 12 percent first-year return (profit) on the firm's $18,000,000 asset investment. Although the normal return in MPE's industry is 14 percent, executives are willing to accept the lower figure because of various start-up inefficiencies. The following information is available for first-year operations:

Hours of service to be provided: 25,000

Anticipated variable cost per service hour: $22

Anticipated fixed cost: $1,900,000 per year

Required:

1. Assume that management is contemplating what price to charge in the first year of operation. The company can take its cost and add a markup to achieve a 12 percent return; alternatively, it can use target costing. Given MPE's marketplace, which approach is probably more appropriate? Why?
2. How much profit must MPE generate in the first year to achieve a 12 percent return?
3. Calculate the revenue per hour that MPE must generate in the first year to achieve a 12 percent return.
4. Assume that prior to the start of business in year 1, management conducted a planning exercise to determine if MPE could attain a 14 percent return in year 2. Can the company achieve this return if (*a*) competitive pressures dictate a maximum selling price of $175 per hour and (*b*) service hours and the variable cost per service hour are the same as the amounts anticipated in year 1? Show calculations.
5. If your answer to requirement (4) is no, suggest and briefly describe a procedure that MPE might use to achieve the desired results.

For many years, Tianjin Products Ltd. has used a straightforward cost-plus pricing system, marking its goods up approximately 25 percent of total cost. The company has been profitable; however, it has recently lost considerable business to competitors that have become very aggressive in the marketplace. These firms appear to be using target costing.

An example of Tianjin's problem is typified by item no. 8976, which has the following unit-cost characteristics:

Direct material	$ 60
Direct labor	150
Manufacturing overhead	100
Selling and administrative expenses	50

Problem 15–41
Cost-Plus Pricing vs. Target Costing
(LO 3, 5, 6, 8)

3. Required cost reduction: $48

The going market price for an identical product of comparable quality is $390, which is significantly below what Tianjin is charging.

Required:

1. Contrast cost-plus pricing and target costing. Which of the two approaches could be aptly labeled price-led costing? Why?
2. What is Tianjin's current selling price of item no. 8976?
3. If Tianjin used target costing for item no. 8976, what must happen to costs if the company desires to meet the market price and maintain its current rate of profit *on sales?* By how much?
4. Would the identification of value-added and non-value-added costs assist Tianjin in this situation? Briefly explain.
5. Suppose that by previous cost-cutting drives, costs had already been "pared to the bone" on item no. 8976. What might Tianjin be forced to do with its markup on cost to remain competitive? By how much?
6. Early in this chapter, the text noted that in many industries, prices are the result of an interaction between market forces and costs. Explain what is meant by this statement.
7. *Build a spreadsheet:* Construct an Excel spreadsheet to solve requirements (2) and (3) above. Show how the solution will change if the following information changes: the direct material and direct labor per unit are $55 and $160, respectively.

Danish Furniture (DF) manufactures easy-to-assemble wooden furniture for home and office. The firm is considering modification of a table to make it more attractive to individuals and businesses that buy products through office supply discounters. The table is small, can be used to hold a computer printer or fax machine, and has several shelves for storage.

Problem 15–42
Target Costing; Selection of Product Features
(LO 5, 8)

3. Maximum allowable cost: $76.00

The company's marketing department surveyed potential buyers of the table regarding five proposed modifications. The 200 survey participants were asked to evaluate the modifications by using a five-point scale that ranged from 1 (strongly disagree) to 5 (strongly agree). Their responses, along with DF's related unit costs for the modifications, follow.

	1 Strongly Disagree	2 Disagree	3 Neutral	4 Agree	5 Strongly Agree
Add cabinet doors in storage area ($6.00)	10	20	30	60	80
Expand storage area ($2.50)	10	40	70	50	30
Add security lock to storage area ($1.65)	30	60	50	40	20
Give table top a more rich, marble appearance ($4.25)	10	20	50	60	60
Extend warranty to five years ($5.10)	40	70	30	35	25

The table currently costs $64 to produce and distribute, and DF's selling price for this unit averages $80. An analysis of competitive tables in the marketplace revealed a variety of features, with some models having all of the features that DF is considering and other models having only a few. The current manufacturers' selling prices for these tables averages $95.

Required:

1. Why is there a need in target costing to (*a*) focus on the customer and (*b*) have a marketing team become involved with product design?

2. DF's marketing team will evaluate the survey responses by computing a weighted-average rating of each of the modifications. This will be accomplished by weighting (multiplying) the point values (1, 2, etc.) by the frequency of responses, summing the results, and dividing by 200. Rank the popularity of the five modifications using this approach.

3. Management desires to earn approximately the same rate of profit on sales that is being earned with the current design.

   a. If DF uses target costing and desires to meet the current competitive selling price, what is the maximum cost of the modified table?

   b. Which of the modifications should DF consider?

4. Assume that DF wanted to add a modification or two that you excluded in your answer to requirement (3*b*). What process might management adopt to allow the company to make its target profit for the table? Briefly explain.

■ **Problem 15–43**
Pricing of Special Order
(LO 10)

1. The order will boost Graydon's net income by: $27,900

Graydon, Inc. manufactures food blending machinery according to customer specifications. The company operated at 75 percent of practical capacity during the year just ended, with the following results (in thousands):

Sales revenue	$25,000
Less: Sales commissions (10%)	2,500
Net sales	$22,500
Expenses:	
Direct material	$ 6,000
Direct labor	7,500
Manufacturing overhead—variable	2,250
Manufacturing overhead—fixed	1,500
Corporate administration—fixed	750
Total costs	$18,000
Income before taxes	$ 4,500
Income taxes (40%)	1,800
Net income	$ 2,700

Graydon, which expects continued operations at 75 percent of capacity, recently submitted a bid of $165,000 on some custom-designed machinery for Premier Foods, Inc. Graydon used a pricing formula in deriving the bid amount, the formula being based on last year's operating results. The formula follows.

Estimated direct material		$ 29,200
Estimated direct labor		56,000
Estimated manufacturing overhead at 50% of direct labor		28,000
Estimated corporate overhead at 10% of direct labor		5,600
Estimated total costs excluding sales commissions		$118,800
Add 25% for profit and taxes		29,700
Suggested price (with profit) before sales commissions		$148,500
Suggested total price: $148,500 ÷ 0.9 to adjust for 10% commission		$165,000

Required:

1. Calculate the impact the order would have on Graydon's net income if the $165,000 bid were accepted by Premier Foods, Inc.

2. Assume that Premier has rejected Graydon's bid but has stated it is willing to pay $127,000 for the machinery. Should Graydon manufacture the machinery for the counteroffer of $127,000? Explain your answer and show calculations.

3. At what bid price will Graydon break even on the order?

4. Explain how the profit performance in the coming year would be affected if Graydon accepted all of its work at prices similar to Premier's $127,000 counteroffer described in requirement (2).

5. *Build a spreadsheet:* Construct an Excel spreadsheet to solve requirements (1) and (2) above. Show how the solution will change if the following information changes: the direct material and direct labor for the year just ended were $5,900 and $7,800, respectively; and sales commissions were 8%.

(CMA, adapted)

■ **Problem 15–44**
Target Costing; Value
Engineering; ABC; JIT
(LO 5, 6, 8)

3. Pharsalia Electronics'
current profit on sales is 10
percent

Alexis Kunselman, president of Pharsalia Electronics (PE), is concerned about the prospects of one of its major products. The president has been reviewing a marketing report with Jeff Keller, marketing product manager, for their 10-disc car compact disc (CD) changer. The report indicates another price reduction is needed to meet anticipated competitors' reductions in sales prices. The current selling price for their 10-disc car CD changers is $350 per unit. It is expected that within three months PE's two major competitors will be selling their 10-disc car CD changers for $300 per unit. This concerns Kunselman because their current cost of producing the CD changers is $315, which yields a $35 profit on each unit sold.

The situation is especially disturbing because PE had implemented an activity-based costing (ABC) system about two years ago. The ABC system helped them better identify costs, cost pools, cost drivers, and cost reduction opportunities. Changes made when adopting ABC reduced costs on this product by approximately 15 percent during the last two years. Now it appears that costs will need to be reduced considerably more to remain competitive and to earn a profit on the 10-disc car CD changers. Total costs to produce, sell, and service the CD changer units are as follows:

10-Disc Car CD Changer

		Per Unit
Material	Purchased components	$110
	All other material	40
Labor	Manufacturing, direct	65
	Setups	9
	Material handling	18
	Inspection	23
Machining	Cutting, shaping, and drilling	21
	Bending and finishing	14
Other	Finished-goods warehousing	5
	Warranty	10
	Total unit cost	$315

Kunselman has decided to hire Donald Collins, a consultant, to help decide how to proceed. After two weeks of review, discussion, and value engineering analysis, Collins suggested that PE adopt a just-in-time (JIT) cell manufacturing process to help reduce costs. He also suggested that using target costing would help in meeting the new target price.

By changing to a JIT cell manufacturing system, PE expects that manufacturing direct labor will increase by $15 per finished unit. However, setup, material handling, inspection, and finished goods warehousing will all be eliminated. Machining costs will be reduced from $35 to $30 per unit, and warranty costs are expected to be reduced by 40 percent.

Required:

1. Define *target costing.*

2. Define *value engineering.*

3. Determine Pharsalia Electronics' unit target cost at the $300 competitive sales price while maintaining the same percentage of profit on sales as is earned on the current $350 sales price.

4. If the just-in-time cell manufacturing process is implemented with the changes in costs noted, will Pharsalia Electronics meet the unit target cost you determined in requirement (3)? Prepare a schedule detailing cost reductions and the unit cost under the proposed JIT cell manufacturing process.

(CMA, adapted)

■ **Problem 15–45**
Time and Material Pricing
(LO 9)

2. Total price of job: $69,500

Patagonia Heating, Ltda. installs heating systems in commercial construction built in Chile and Argentina. Jobs are priced using the time and materials method. The president of Patagonia Heating is pricing a job to provide the heating systems for a small office complex in Santiago. He has made the following estimates.

Material cost	$50,000
Labor hours	500

The following predictions pertain to the company's operations for the next year.

Labor rate, including fringe benefits	$16.00 per hour
Annual labor hours	12,000 hours
Annual overhead costs:	
Material handling and storage	$20,000
Other overhead costs	$132,000
Annual cost of materials used	$250,000

Required: Patagonia Heating adds a markup of $4.00 per hour on its time charges, but there is no markup on material costs.

1. Develop formulas for the company's (*a*) time charges and (*b*) material charges.

2. Compute the price for the job described above.

3. What would be the price of the job if Patagonia Heating also added a markup of 10 percent on all material charges (including material handling and storage costs)?

■ **Problem 15–46**
Bidding on a Special Order
(LO 10)

2. Bid price: $26.45

Ozman Synthetic Fibers Inc. specializes in the manufacture of synthetic fibers that the company uses in many products such as blankets, coats, and uniforms for police and firefighters. The company has been in business for 20 years and has been profitable each of the past 15 years. Ozman Synthetic Fibers uses a standard-costing system and applies overhead on the basis of direct-labor hours. Management has recently received a request to bid on the manufacture of 800,000 blankets scheduled for delivery to government emergency shelters. The bid must be stated at full cost per unit plus a return on full cost of no more than 15 percent before income taxes. Full cost has been defined as including all variable costs of manufacturing the product, a reasonable amount of fixed overhead, and reasonable incremental administrative costs associated with the manufacture and sale of the product. The contractor has indicated that bids in excess of $22 per blanket are not likely to be considered.

In order to prepare the bid for the 800,000 blankets, Ozman's controller has gathered the following information about the costs associated with the production of the blankets.

Direct material	$2.00 per kilogram of fibers
Direct labor	$7.00 per hour
Direct machine costs*	$10.00 per blanket
Variable overhead	$3.00 per direct-labor hour
Fixed overhead	$8.00 per direct-labor hour
Incremental administrative costs	$2,500 per 1,000 blankets
Special fee†	$.50 per blanket
Material usage	3 kilograms per blanket
Production rate	4 blankets per direct-labor hour

*Direct machine costs consist of items such as special lubricants, replacement of needles used in stitching, and maintenance costs. These costs are not included in the normal overhead rates.

†Ozman Synthetic Fibers recently developed a new blanket fiber at a cost of $750,000. In an effort to recover this cost, management has instituted a policy of adding a $.50 fee to the cost of each blanket using the new fiber. To date, the company has recovered $125,000. The controller knows that this fee does not fit within the definition of full cost as it is not a cost of manufacturing the product.

Required:

1. Calculate the minimum price per blanket that Ozman Synthetic Fibers Inc. could bid without reducing the company's net income.

2. Using the full cost criteria and the maximum allowable return specified, calculate Ozman Synthetic Fibers Inc.'s bid price per blanket.

3. Independent of your answer to requirement (2), assume that the price per blanket that Ozman Synthetic Fibers Inc. calculated using the cost-plus criteria specified is greater than the maximum bid of $22 per blanket allowed. Discuss the factors that management should consider before deciding whether to submit a bid at the maximum acceptable price of $22 per blanket.

(CMA, adapted)

■ **Problem 15–47**
Product Cost Distortion and
Product Pricing; Departmental
Overhead Rates
(LO 7)

1. Predetermined overhead
rate: $10 per direct-labor
hour
5. Price, Advanced Model:
$588.80

Sounds Fine, Inc. manufactures two models of stereo speakers. Cost estimates for the two models for the coming year are as follows:

	Basic Model	Advanced Model
Direct material	$160	$260
Direct labor (10 hours at $14 per hour)	140	140
Manufacturing overhead*	100	100
Total cost	$400	$500

*The predetermined overhead rate is $10 per direct-labor hour.

Each stereo speaker requires 10 hours of direct labor. Each Basic Model unit requires two hours in Department I and eight hours in Department II. Each unit of the Advanced Model requires eight hours in Department I and two hours in Department II. The manufacturing overhead costs expected during the coming year in Departments I and II are as follows:

	Department I	Department II
Variable overhead	$8 per direct-labor hour	$4 per direct-labor hour
Fixed overhead	$150,000	$150,000

The expected operating activity for the coming year is 37,500 direct-labor hours in each department.

Required:

1. Show how Sounds Fine, Inc. derived its predetermined overhead rate.

2. What will be the price of each model stereo speaker if the company prices its products at absorption manufacturing cost plus 15 percent?

3. Suppose Sounds Fine, Inc. were to use departmental overhead rates. Compute these rates for Departments I and II for the coming year.

4. Compute the absorption cost of each model stereo speaker using the departmental overhead rates computed in requirement (3).

5. Suppose management sticks with its policy of setting prices equal to absorption cost plus 15 percent. Compute the new price for each speaker model using the product costs developed in requirement (4).

6. Should Sounds Fine, Inc. use plantwide or departmental overhead rates? Explain your answer.

Cases

■ **Case 15–48**
Pricing in a Tight Market;
Possible Plant Closing
(LO 1, 10)

2(a). Contribution margin,
Standard: $350

Gargantuan Industries is a multiproduct company with several manufacturing plants. The Boise Plant manufactures and distributes two household cleaning and polishing compounds, standard and commercial, under the Super Clean label. The forecasted operating results for the first six months of the current year, when 100,000 cases of each compound are expected to be manufactured and sold, are presented in the following statement.

SUPER CLEAN COMPOUNDS—BOISE PLANT
Forecasted Results of Operations
For the Six-Month Period Ending June 30
(in Thousands)

	Standard	Commercial	Total
Sales	$2,000	$3,000	$5,000
Cost of goods sold	1,600	1,900	3,500
Gross profit	$ 400	$1,100	$1,500
Selling and administrative expenses:			
Variable	$ 400	$ 700	$1,100
Fixed*	240	360	600
Total selling and administrative expenses	$ 640	$1,060	$1,700
Income (loss) before taxes	$ (240)	$ 40	$ (200)

*The fixed selling and administrative expenses are allocated between the two products on the basis of dollar sales volume.

The standard compound sold for $20 a case and the commercial compound sold for $30 a case during the first six months of the year. The manufacturing costs, by case of product, are presented in the schedule below. Each product is manufactured on a separate production line. Annual normal manufacturing capacity is 200,000 cases of each product. However, the plant is capable of producing 250,000 cases of standard compound and 350,000 cases of commercial compound annually.

	Cost per Case	
	Standard	Commercial
Direct material	$ 7.00	$ 8.00
Direct labor	4.00	4.00
Variable manufacturing overhead	1.00	2.00
Fixed manufacturing overhead*	4.00	5.00
Total manufacturing cost	$16.00	$19.00
Variable selling and administrative costs	$ 4.00	$ 7.00

*Depreciation charges are 50 percent of the fixed manufacturing overhead of each line.

The following schedule reflects the consensus of top management regarding the price-volume alternatives for the Super Clean products for the last six months of the current year. These are essentially the same alternatives management had during the first six months of the year.

Standard Compound			Commercial Compound	
Alternative Prices (per case)	**Sales Volume (in cases)**		**Alternative Prices (per case)**	**Sales Volume (in cases)**
$18	120,000		$25	175,000
20	100,000		27	140,000
21	90,000		30	100,000
22	80,000		32	55,000
23	50,000		35	35,000

Gargantuan's top management believes the loss for the first six months reflects a tight profit margin caused by intense competition. Management also believes that many companies will leave this market by next year and profit should improve.

Required:

1. What unit selling price should Gargantuan Industries select for each of the Super Clean compounds for the remaining six months of the year? Support your selection with appropriate calculations.

2. Independently of your answer to requirement (1), assume the optimum alternatives for the last six months were as follows: a selling price of $23 and volume of 50,000 cases for the standard compound, and a selling price of $35 and volume of 35,000 cases for the commercial compound.

   a. Should Gargantuan Industries consider closing down its operations until January 1 of the next year in order to minimize its losses? Support your answer with appropriate calculations.

   b. Identify and discuss the qualitative factors that should be considered in deciding whether the Boise Plant should be closed down during the last six months of the current year.

(CMA, adapted)

■ Case 15–49
Bidding on a Special Order; Ethics
(LO 10)

2. Variable overhead rate: $5.40

Zylar Industries is a manufacturer of standard and custom-designed bottling equipment. Early in December 20x0, Lyan Company asked Zylar to quote a price for a custom-designed bottling machine to be delivered in April. Lyan intends to make a decision on the purchase of such a machine by January 1, so Zylar would have the entire first quarter of 20x1 to build the equipment.

Zylar's pricing policy for custom-designed equipment is 50 percent markup on absorption manufacturing cost. Lyan's specifications for the equipment have been reviewed by Zylar's Engineering and Cost Management Departments, which made the following estimates for direct material and direct labor.

Direct material	$256,000
Direct labor (11,000 hours at $15)	165,000

Manufacturing overhead is applied on the basis of direct-labor hours. Zylar normally plans to run its plant at a level of 15,000 direct-labor hours per month and assigns overhead on the basis of 180,000 direct-labor hours per year. The overhead application rate for 20x1 of $9.00 per hour is based on the following budgeted manufacturing overhead costs for 20x1.

Variable manufacturing overhead	$ 972,000
Fixed manufacturing overhead	648,000
Total manufacturing overhead	$1,620,000

Zylar's production schedule calls for 12,000 direct-labor hours per month during the first quarter. If Zylar is awarded the contract for the Lyan equipment, production of one of its standard products would have to be reduced. This is necessary because production levels can only be increased to 15,000 direct-labor hours each month on short notice. Furthermore, Zylar's employees are unwilling to work overtime.

Sales of the standard product equal to the reduced production would be lost, but there would be no permanent loss of future sales or customers. The standard product for which the production schedule would be reduced has a unit sales price of $12,000 and the following cost structure.

Direct material	$2,500
Direct labor (250 hours at $15)	3,750
Manufacturing overhead (250 hours at $9)	2,250
Total cost	$8,500

Lyan needs the custom-designed equipment to increase its bottle-making capacity so that it will not have to buy bottles from an outside supplier. Lyan Company requires 5,000,000 bottles annually. Its present equipment has a maximum capacity of 4,500,000 bottles with a directly traceable cash outlay cost of 15 cents per bottle. Thus, Lyan has had to purchase 500,000 bottles from a supplier at 40 cents each. The new equipment would allow Lyan to manufacture its entire annual demand for bottles at a direct-material cost savings of 1 cent per bottle. Zylar estimates that Lyan's annual bottle demand will continue to be 5,000,000 bottles over the next five years, the estimated life of the special-purpose equipment.

Required: Zylar Industries plans to submit a bid to Lyan Company for the manufacture of the special-purpose bottling equipment.

1.   Calculate the bid Zylar would submit if it follows its standard pricing policy for special-purpose equipment.

2.   Calculate the minimum bid Zylar would be willing to submit on the Lyan equipment that would result in the same total contribution margin as planned for the first quarter of 20x1.

3.   Suppose Zylar Industries has submitted a bid slightly above the minimum calculated in requirement (2). Upon receiving Zylar's bid, Lyan's assistant purchasing manager telephoned his friend at Tygar Corporation: "Hey Joe, we just got a bid from Zylar Industries on some customized equipment. I think Tygar would stand a good chance of beating it. Stop by the house this evening, and I'll show you the details of Zylar's bid and the specifications on the machine."
      Is Lyan Company's assistant purchasing manager acting ethically? Explain.

(CMA, adapted)

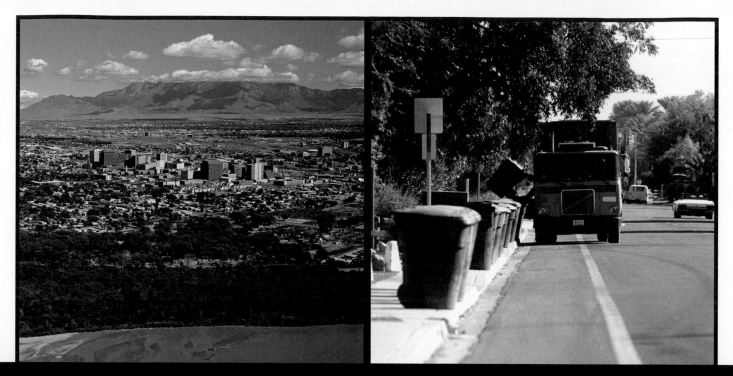

THIS CHAPTER'S FOCUS is on the City of Mountainview, New Mexico in the United States. As with many cities around the world, Mountainview is governed by a mayor and city council who face a variety of decisions that involve cash flows over several periods of time. The decision tool used in making such multiperiod decisions is called discounted-cash-flow analysis, because it takes account of the timing of cash flows that occur in different time periods. Among the decisions that Mountainview's lead-

CITY OF
MOUNTAINVIEW

ership makes is whether to purchase a new computer system for the city government. Since the City of Mountainview is not a profit-seeking enterprise, income taxes play no role in the decisions faced by the city's leadership.

16 Capital Expenditure Decisions

HIGH COUNTRY
DEPARTMENT STORES

In contrast to the Mountainview city government setting, in which income taxes play no role in decisions, we turn our attention to High Country Department Stores. This chain of retail department stores, located in Mountainview, also faces some significant decisions involving multiperiod cash flows. Since High Country is a profit-seeking enterprise, it does pay income taxes. Therefore, when the company's management uses discounted-cash-flow analysis, it must take taxes into account. Among the decisions faced by High Country's management is whether to purchase a new computerized checkout system.

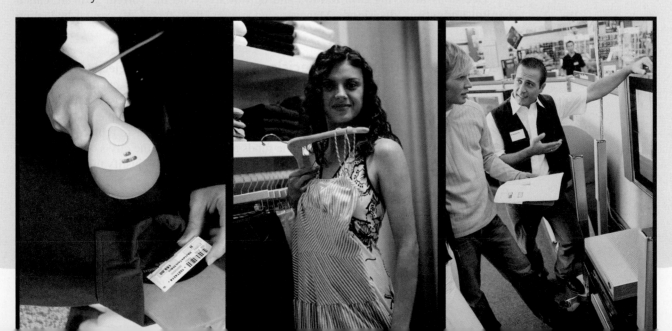

1 Use the net-present-value method and the internal-rate-of-return method to evaluate an investment proposal.

2 Compare the net-present-value and internal-rate-of-return methods, and state the assumptions underlying each method.

3 Use both the total-cost approach and the incremental-cost approach to evaluate an investment proposal.

4 Determine the after-tax cash flows in an investment analysis.

5 Use an accelerated tax depreciation system to determine an asset's depreciation schedule for tax purposes.

6 Evaluate an investment proposal using a discounted-cash-flow analysis, giving full consideration to income-tax issues.

7 Discuss the difficulty of ranking investment proposals, and use the profitability index.

8 Use the payback method and accounting-rate-of-return method to evaluate capital investment projects.

9 Describe the impact of activity-based costing and advanced manufacturing technology on capital-budgeting decisions.

10 Explain the impact of inflation on a capital-budgeting analysis (Appendix B).

Managers in all organizations periodically face major decisions that involve cash flows over several years. Decisions involving the acquisition of machinery, vehicles, buildings, or land are examples of such decisions. Other examples include decisions involving significant changes in a production process or adding a major new line of products or services to the organization's activities.

Decisions involving cash inflows and outflows beyond the current year are called **capital-budgeting decisions.** Managers encounter two types of capital-budgeting decisions.

Acceptance-or-Rejection Decisions In **acceptance-or-rejection decisions,** managers must decide whether they should undertake a particular capital investment project. In such a decision, the required funds are available or readily obtainable, and management must decide whether the project is worthwhile. For example, the controller for the city of Mountainview is faced with a decision as to whether to replace one of the city's oldest street-cleaning machines. The funds are available in the city's capital budget. The question is whether the cost savings with the new machine will justify the expenditure.

Capital-Rationing Decisions In **capital-rationing decisions,** managers must decide which of several worthwhile projects makes the best use of limited investment funds. To illustrate, suppose the voters in the city of Mountainview have recently passed a proposition mandating the city government to undertake a cost-reduction program to trim administrative expenses. The voters also passed a bond issue, which enables the city government to raise $100,000 through the sale of bonds, to provide capital to finance the cost-reduction program. The mayor has in mind three cost-reduction programs, each of which would reduce administrative costs significantly over the next five years. However, the city can afford only two of the programs with the $100,000 of investment capital available. The mayor's decision problem is to decide which projects to pursue.

Focus on Projects Capital-budgeting problems tend to focus on specific projects or programs. Is it best for Mountainview to purchase the new street cleaner or not? Which cost-reduction programs will provide the city with the greatest benefits? Should a university buy a new electron microscope? Should a manufacturing firm acquire a computer-integrated manufacturing system?

Over time, as managers make decisions about a variety of specific programs and projects, the organization as a whole becomes the sum total of its individual investments, activities, programs, and projects. The organization's performance in any particular year is the combined result of all the projects under way during that year.

Chapter Organization This chapter is divided into three modular sections, each of which explores a particular aspect of capital expenditure decisions. Section 1 should be studied first, after which either Section 2 or Section 3 may be studied.

- Section 1: Discounted-Cash-Flow Analysis
- Section 2: Income Taxes and Capital Budgeting
- Section 3: Alternative Methods for Making Investment Decisions

Section 1: Discounted-Cash-Flow Analysis

How do managers evaluate capital investment projects? Our discussion will be illustrated by several decisions made by the Mountainview city government. The controller of Mountainview routinely advises the mayor and city council on major capital-investment decisions.

Currently under consideration is the purchase of a new street cleaner. The controller has estimated that the city's old street-cleaning machine would last another five years. A new street cleaner, which also would last for five years, can be purchased for $50,470. It would cost the city $14,000 less each year to operate the new equipment than it costs to operate the old machine. The expected cost savings with the new machine are due to lower expected maintenance costs. Thus, the new street cleaner will cost $50,470 and save $70,000 over its five-year life ($70,000 = 5 × $14,000 savings per year). Since the $70,000 in cost savings exceeds the $50,470 acquisition cost, one might be tempted to conclude that the new machine should be purchased. However, *this analysis is flawed, since it does not account for the time value of money*. The $50,470 acquisition cost will occur now, but the cost savings are spread over a five-year period. It is a mistake to add cash flows occurring at different points in time. The proper approach is to use **discounted-cash-flow analysis**, which takes into account the timing of the cash flows. There are two widely used methods of discounted-cash-flow analysis: the net-present-value method and the internal-rate-of-return method. [Those who wish to review the basic concept of present value should read Appendix II (on pages 807–813) before continuing.]

C I T Y   O F

MOUNTAINVIEW

Learning Objective 1

Use the net-present-value method and the internal-rate-of-return method to evaluate an investment proposal.

Net-Present-Value Method

The following four steps constitute a net-present-value analysis of an investment proposal:

1. Prepare a table showing the cash flows during each year of the proposed investment.
2. Compute the present value of each cash flow, using a discount rate that reflects the cost of acquiring investment capital. This discount rate is often called the **hurdle rate** or **minimum desired rate of return.**
3. Compute the **net present value,** which is the sum of the present values of the cash flows.
4. If the net present value (NPV) is equal to or greater than zero, accept the investment proposal. Otherwise, reject it.

Exhibit 16–1 displays these four steps for the Mountainview controller's street-cleaner decision. In step (2) the controller used a discount rate of 10 percent. Notice that the cost savings are $14,000 in each of the years 1 through 5. Thus, the cash flows in those years comprise a five-year, $14,000 annuity. The controller used the annuity discount factor to compute the present value of the five years of cost savings. (The discount factors are found in Table IV in Appendix A at the end of this chapter.)

The net-present-value analysis indicates that the city should purchase the new street cleaner. The present value of the cost savings exceeds the new machine's acquisition cost.

"We're key members of the decision making team when it comes to significant capital expenditure decisions." (16a)

Ford Motor Company

Internal-Rate-of-Return Method

An alternative discounted-cash-flow method for analyzing investment proposals is the internal-rate-of-return method. An asset's **internal rate of return** (or **time-adjusted rate of return**) is the true economic return earned by the asset over its life. Another way of stating the definition is that an asset's *internal rate of return (IRR)* is the discount rate that would be required in a net-present-value analysis in order for the asset's net present value to be exactly *zero.*

What is the internal rate of return on Mountainview's proposed street-cleaner acquisition? Recall that the asset has a positive net present value, given that the city's cost of acquiring investment capital is 10 percent. Would you expect the asset's IRR to be higher or lower than 10 percent? Think about this question intuitively. The higher the discount rate used in a net-present-value analysis, the lower the present value of all future cash flows will be. This is true because a higher discount rate means that it is even more

Exhibit 16–1
Net-Present-Value Method

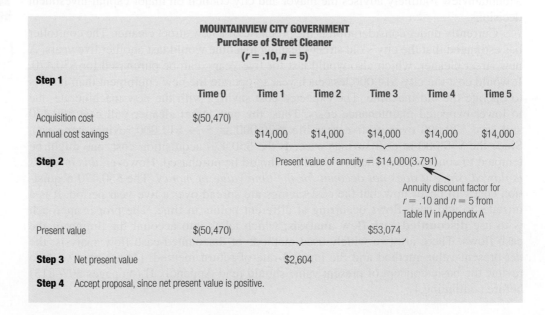

MOUNTAINVIEW CITY GOVERNMENT
Purchase of Street Cleaner
($r = .10, n = 5$)

Step 1	Time 0	Time 1	Time 2	Time 3	Time 4	Time 5
Acquisition cost	$(50,470)					
Annual cost savings		$14,000	$14,000	$14,000	$14,000	$14,000

Step 2   Present value of annuity = $14,000(3.791)

Annuity discount factor for $r = .10$ and $n = 5$ from Table IV in Appendix A

Present value	$(50,470)			$53,074		

Step 3   Net present value $2,604

Step 4   Accept proposal, since net present value is positive.

important to have the money earlier instead of later. Thus, a discount rate higher than 10 percent would be required to drive the new street cleaner's net present value down to zero.

Finding the Internal Rate of Return

How can we find this rate? One way is trial and error. We could experiment with different discount rates until we find the one that yields a zero net present value. We already know that a 10 percent discount rate yields a positive NPV. Let's try 14 percent. Discounting the five-year, $14,000 cost-savings annuity at 14 percent yields a negative NPV of $(2,408).

$$(3.433)(\$14,000) - \$50,470 = \$(2,408)$$

↑

Annuity discount factor for $r = .14$ and
$n = 5$ from Table IV in Appendix A.

What does this negative NPV at a 14 percent discount rate mean? We increased the discount rate too much. Therefore, the street cleaner's internal rate of return must lie between 10 percent and 14 percent. Let's try 12 percent:

$$(3.605)(\$14,000) - \$50,470 = 0$$

↑

Annuity discount factor for $r = .12$ and
$n = 5$ from Table IV in Appendix A.

That's it. The new street cleaner's internal rate of return is 12 percent. With a 12 percent discount rate, the investment proposal's net present value is zero, since the street cleaner's acquisition cost is equal to the present value of the cost savings.

We could have found the internal rate of return more easily in this case, because the street cleaner's cash flows exhibit a very special pattern. The cash inflows in years 1 through 5 are identical, as shown below.

Time	0	1	2	3	4	5
Cash flow	$(50,470)	$14,000	$14,000	$14,000	$14,000	$14,000

Initial cash outflow
(acquisition cost)

Equal cash inflows
(operating-cost savings)

When we have this special pattern of cash flows, the internal rate of return is determined in two steps, as follows:

1. Divide the initial cash outflow by the equivalent annual cash inflows:

$$\frac{\$50,470}{\$14,000} = 3.605 = \text{Annuity discount factor}$$

2. In Table IV, find the discount rate associated with the annuity discount factor computed in step (1), given the appropriate number of years in the annuity.

		r	
	10%	12%	14%
From Table IV of Appendix A			
$n = 5$	3.791	3.605	3.433

Decision Rule

Now that we have determined the investment proposal's internal rate of return to be 12 percent, how do we use this fact in making a decision? The decision rule in the internal-rate-of-return method is to accept an investment proposal if its internal rate of return is greater than the organization's cost of capital (or hurdle rate). Thus, Mountainview's controller should recommend that the new street cleaner be purchased. The internal rate of return on the proposal, 12 percent, exceeds the city's hurdle rate, 10 percent.

To summarize, the internal-rate-of-return method of discounted-cash-flow analysis includes the following three steps:

1. Prepare a table showing the cash flows during each year of the proposed investment. This table will be identical to the cash-flow table prepared under the net-present-value method. (See Exhibit 16–1.)

2. Compute the internal rate of return (IRR) for the proposed investment. This is accomplished by finding a discount rate that yields a zero net present value for the proposed investment.

3. If the IRR is equal to or greater than the hurdle rate (cost of acquiring investment capital), accept the investment proposal. Otherwise, reject it.

> "Our role is to be internal management consultants for the key decisions facing management." (16b)
> **Hewlett-Packard**

Recovery of Investment   The reason for purchasing an asset is an expectation that it will provide benefits in the future. Thus, Mountainview may purchase the new street cleaner because of expected future operating-cost savings. For a capital investment proposal to be accepted, the expected future benefits must be sufficient for the purchaser to recover the investment and earn a return on the investment equal to or greater than the cost of acquiring capital. We can illustrate this point with Mountainview's street-cleaner acquisition.

Exhibit 16–2 examines the investment proposal's cash flows from the perspective of recovering the investment and earning a return on the investment. Focus on the Year 1 column in the exhibit. The street cleaner costs $50,470, so this is the unrecovered investment at the beginning of year 1. The operating-cost savings in year 1 are $14,000. Since the asset's internal rate of return is 12 percent, it must earn $6,056 during the first year (12% × $50,470). Therefore, $6,056 of the $14,000 cost savings represents a *return on* the unrecovered investment. This leaves $7,944 as a *recovery of* the investment during year 1 ($14,000 − $6,056). Subtracting the year 1 recovery of investment from the unrecovered investment at the beginning of the year leaves an unrecovered investment of $42,526 at year-end ($50,470 − $7,944).

Exhibit 16–2
Recovery of Investment and Return on Investment

	Year 1	Year 2	Year 3	Year 4	Year 5
MOUNTAINVIEW CITY GOVERNMENT — Purchase of Street Cleaner ($r = .12, n = 5$)					
1. Unrecovered investment at beginning of year	$50,470	$42,526	$33,629	$23,664	$12,504
2. Cost savings during year	14,000	14,000	14,000	14,000	14,000
3. Return on unrecovered investment [12% × amount in row (1)]	6,056	5,103	4,035	2,840	1,500
4. Recovery of investment during year [row (2) amount minus row (3) amount]	7,944	8,897	9,965	11,160	12,500
5. Unrecovered investment at end of year [row (1) amount minus row (4) amount]	42,526	33,629	23,664	12,504	4*

* We are left with an unrecovered investment of $4 because of accumulated rounding errors in the table. If we had carried out each number to cents, the table would have finished up with an unrecovered investment of zero.

Uneven Cash Flows A complication that often arises in finding a project's internal rate of return is an uneven pattern of cash flows. In Mountainview's proposed street-cleaner acquisition, the cost savings are $14,000 per year for all five years of the machine's life. Suppose, instead, that the pattern of cost savings is as follows:

Such an uneven cost-savings pattern is quite plausible, since the maintenance costs could rise in the machine's latter years. When the cash-flow pattern is uneven, iteration must be used to find the internal rate of return. You can try various discount rates iteratively until you find the one that yields a zero net present value for the investment proposal. This sort of computationally intensive work is the kind of task for which computers are designed. Numerous computer software packages are available to find a project's IRR almost instantaneously.

Comparing the NPV and IRR Methods

The decision to accept or reject an investment proposal can be made using either the net-present-value method or the internal-rate-of-return method. The different approaches used in the methods are summarized as follows:

Net-Present-Value Method	Internal-Rate-of-Return Method
1. Compute the investment proposal's net present value, using the organization's hurdle rate as the discount rate.	1. Compute the investment proposal's internal rate of return, which is the discount rate that yields a zero net present value for the project.
2. Accept the investment proposal if its net present value is equal to or greater than zero; otherwise reject it.	2. Accept the investment proposal if its internal rate of return is equal to or greater than the organization's hurdle rate; otherwise reject it.

Notice that the hurdle rate is used in each of the two methods.

Advantages of Net-Present-Value Method

The net-present-value method exhibits two potential advantages over the internal-rate-of-return method. First, if the investment analysis is carried out by hand, it is easier to compute a project's NPV than its IRR. For example, if the cash flows are uneven across time, trial and error must be used to find the IRR. This advantage of the NPV approach is not as important, however, when a computer is used.

A second potential advantage of the NPV method is that the analyst can adjust for risk considerations. For some investment proposals, the further into the future that a cash flow occurs, the less certain the analyst can be about the amount of the cash flow. Thus, the later a projected cash flow occurs, the riskier it may be. It is possible to adjust a net-present-value analysis for such risk factors by using a higher discount rate for later cash flows than earlier cash flows. It is not possible to include such a risk adjustment in the internal-rate-of-return method, because the analysis solves for only a single discount rate, the project's IRR.

Assumptions Underlying Discounted-Cash-Flow Analysis

As is true of any decision model, discounted-cash-flow methods are based on assumptions. Four assumptions underlie the NPV and IRR methods of investment analysis.

1. In the present-value calculations used in the NPV and IRR methods, all cash flows are treated as though they occur at year-end. If the city of Mountainview were to acquire the new street cleaner, the $14,000 in annual operating-cost savings actually would occur uniformly throughout each year. The additional computational complexity that would be required to reflect the exact timing of all cash flows would complicate an investment analysis considerably. The error introduced by the year-end cash-flow assumption generally is not large enough to cause any concern.

2. Discounted-cash-flow analyses treat the cash flows associated with an investment project as though they were known with certainty. Although methods of capital budgeting under uncertainty have been developed, they are not used widely in practice. Most decision makers do not feel that the additional benefits in improved decisions are worth the additional complexity involved. As mentioned above, however, risk adjustments can be made in an NPV analysis to partially account for uncertainty about the cash flows.

3. Both the NPV and IRR methods assume that each cash inflow is immediately reinvested in another project that earns a return for the organization. In the NPV method, each cash inflow is assumed to be reinvested at the same rate used to compute the project's NPV, the organization's hurdle rate. In the IRR method, each cash inflow is assumed to be reinvested at the same rate as the project's internal rate of return.

   What does this reinvestment assumption mean in practice? In the case of Mountainview's proposed new street cleaner, the city must instantly reinvest the money saved each year either in some interest-bearing investment or in some other capital project.

4. A discounted-cash-flow analysis assumes a perfect capital market. This implies that money can be borrowed or lent at an interest rate equal to the hurdle rate used in the analysis.

In practice, these four assumptions rarely are satisfied. Nevertheless, discounted-cash-flow models provide an effective and widely used method of investment analysis. The improved decision making that would result from using more complicated models seldom is worth the additional cost of information and analysis.

Choosing the Hurdle Rate

The choice of a hurdle rate is a complex problem in finance. The hurdle rate is determined by management based on the **investment opportunity rate.** This is the rate of return the organization can earn on its best alternative investments of equivalent risk. In general, the greater a project's risk is, the higher the hurdle rate should be.

Investment versus Financing Decisions   In capital-expenditure decisions, the investment decision should be separated from the financing decision. The decision as to whether to invest in a project should be made first using a discounted-cash-flow approach with a hurdle rate based on the investment opportunity rate. If a project is accepted, then a separate analysis should be made as to the best way to finance the project.

Cost of Capital   How do organizations generate investment capital? Nonprofit organizations, such as local, city, and state governments and charitable organizations, often acquire capital through special bond issues or borrowing from financial institutions. In such cases, the cost of capital is based on the interest rate paid on the debt.

Another source of capital for both nonprofit and profit-oriented organizations is invested funds, such as a university's endowment fund. In this case, the cost of using the capital for an investment project is the interest rate forgone on the original investment. For example, suppose your university's endowment earns interest at the rate of 10 percent. If the university uses a portion of these funds to buy new laboratory equipment, the cost of capital is the 10 percent interest rate that is no longer earned on the funds removed from the endowment.

Profit-oriented enterprises fund capital projects by borrowing, by issuing stock, or by using invested funds. In most cases, capital projects are funded by all of these sources. Then the cost of capital should be a combination of the costs of obtaining money from each of these sources.

Depreciable Assets

When a long-lived asset is purchased, its acquisition cost is allocated to the time periods in the asset's life through depreciation charges. However, we did not include any depreciation charges in our discounted-cash-flow analysis. Both the NPV and IRR methods focus on cash flows, and *periodic depreciation charges are not cash flows.* Suppose that the controller for the city of Mountainview depreciates assets using the straight-line method. If the city purchases the new street cleaner for $50,470, the depreciation charges will be recorded as follows:

The only cash flow in the diagram above is the $50,470 cash outflow incurred to acquire the street cleaner. The $10,094 annual depreciation charges are not cash flows. Thus, the acquisition cost is recorded as a cash flow in our investment analysis (Exhibit 16–1), but the annual depreciation charges are not.

Nonprofit versus Profit-Oriented Organizations   Suppose our illustration had focused on a profit-seeking enterprise instead of the city of Mountainview. For example, if the street-cleaner acquisition is contemplated by the management of a private industrial park, would this change our treatment of the annual depreciation charges for the street cleaner? The depreciation charges still are not cash flows. However, in a profit-seeking enterprise, depreciation expense is deductible for income-tax purposes in most countries. Since tax payments *are* cash flows, the reduction in tax due to depreciation expense is a legitimate cash flow that should be included in an investment analysis. In Section 2 of this chapter, we will study the tax implications of depreciable assets in detail. For now, let's return to our focus on the city of Mountainview. As a governmental organization, the city pays no income tax. Therefore, depreciation is irrelevant in our discounted-cash-flow analysis.

Comparing Two Investment Projects

We have developed all of the tools and concepts required to use discounted-cash-flow analysis in an investment decision. Now we can expand on our discussion using an illustration that combines the net-present-value method of investment analysis with the concepts of relevant costs and benefits studied in Chapter 14. The first step in any investment analysis is to determine the cash flows that are relevant to the analysis.

Learning Objective 3

Use both the total-cost approach and the incremental-cost approach to evaluate an investment proposal.

The computing system used by the city of Mountainview is outdated. The city council has voted to purchase a new computing system to be funded through municipal bonds. The mayor has asked the city's controller to make a recommendation as to which of two computing systems should be purchased. The two systems are equivalent in their ability to meet the city's needs and in their ease of use. The *terminal system* consists of a blade enclosure and blade servers running a Unix-based terminal network, with remote terminals and printers located throughout the city offices. The *personal computer system* consists of a rack-mount network server, a few remote terminals, and a dozen personal computers, which will be networked to the server. Each system would last five years. The controller has decided to use a 12 percent hurdle rate for the analysis.

Exhibit 16–3 presents data pertinent to the decision. Examine these data carefully. Most of the items are self-explanatory. Item (9) is the annual cost of a data-link service. This service enables Mountainview to participate in a nationwide computer network, which allows cities to exchange information on such issues as crime rates, demographic data, and economic data. Item (10) is the revenue the city will receive from two time-sharing customers. The Mountainview City School District and the county legislature each has agreed to pay the city in return for a limited amount of time on the city's computer.

Before we begin the steps of the net-present-value method, let's examine the cash-flow data in Exhibit 16–3 to determine if any of the data can be ignored as irrelevant. Notice that items (1) and (9) do not differ between the two alternatives. Regardless of which new computing system is purchased, certain components of the old system can be sold now for $25,000. Moreover, the data-link service will cost $20,000 annually, regardless of which system is acquired. If the only purpose of the NPV analysis is to determine

Exhibit 16–3

Data for Extended Illustration of Net-Present-Value Analysis

CITY OF
MOUNTAINVIEW

Microsoft Excel - Data for Extended Illustration of Net-Present-Value Analysis

File   Edit   View   Insert   Format   Tools   Data   Window   Help

C20 f_x 20000

	A	B	C	D
1		MOUNTAINVIEW CITY GOVERNMENT		
2		Purchase of Computing System		
3				
4				Personal
5			Terminal	Computer
6			System	System
7				
8	(1)	Salvage value of city's old computer (time 0)*	$ 25,000	$ 25,000
9	(2)	Acquisition cost of new system (time 0)	(400,000)	(300,000)
10	(3)	Acquisition cost of software (time 0)	(40,000)	(75,000)
11	(4)	Cost of updating system (time 3)	(40,000)	(60,000)
12	(5)	Salvage value of new system (time 5)	50,000	30,000
13				
14				
15		Operating costs (times 1,2,3,4,5):		
16	(6)	Personnel	(300,000)	(220,000)
17	(7)	Maintenance	(25,000)	(10,000)
18	(8)	Other	(10,000)	(5,000)
19	(9)	Data-link service (times 1,2,3,4,5)	(20,000)	(20,000)
20	(10)	Revenue from time-share customers (times 1,2,3,4,5)	20,000	-
21				
22		*Time 0 denotes "immediately." Time 1 denotes the end of year 1, etc.		

Sheet1 / Sheet2 / Sheet3 /

Ready

which computer system is the least-cost alternative, items (1) and (9) can be ignored as irrelevant, since they will affect both alternatives' NPVs equally.

Total-Cost Approach Exhibit 16–4 displays a net-present-value analysis of the two alternative computing systems. The exhibit uses the *total-cost approach,* in which all of the relevant costs of each computing system are included in the analysis. Then the net present value of the cost of the terminal system is compared with that of the personal computer system. Since the NPV of the costs is lower with the personal computer system, that will be the controller's recommendation to the Mountainview City Council.

A decision such as Mountainview's computing-system choice, in which the objective is to select the alternative with the lowest cost, is called a *least-cost decision.* Rather than maximizing the NPV of cash inflows minus cash outflows, the objective is to *minimize the NPV of the costs to be incurred.*

Incremental-Cost Approach Exhibit 16–5 displays a different net-present-value analysis of the city's two alternative computing systems. This exhibit uses the *incremental-cost approach,* in which the difference in the cost of each relevant item under the two alternative systems is included in the analysis. For example, the incremental computer acquisition cost is shown in Exhibit 16–5 as $(100,000). This is the amount by which the acquisition cost of the terminal system exceeds that of the personal computer system.

Exhibit 16–4
Net-Present-Value Analysis:
Total-Cost Approach

MOUNTAINVIEW

Item Number (from Exhibit 16–3)	Time 0	Time 1	Time 2	Time 3	Time 4	Time 5
MOUNTAINVIEW CITY GOVERNMENT Purchase of Computing System ($r = .12, n = 5$)						
Terminal System						
(2) Acquisition cost: computer	$(400,000)					
(3) Acquisition cost: software	(40,000)					
(4) System update				$ (40,000)		
(5) Salvage value						$ 50,000
(6), (7), (8) Operating costs		$(335,000)	$(335,000)	(335,000)	$(335,000)	(335,000)
(10) Time-sharing revenue		20,000	20,000	20,000	20,000	20,000
Total cash flow	$(440,000)	$(315,000)	$(315,000)	$(355,000)	$(315,000)	$(265,000)
× Discount factor	× 1.000	× .893	× .797	× .712	× .636	× .567
Present value	$(440,000)	$(281,295)	$(251,055)	$(252,760)	$(200,340)	$(150,255)
Net present value of costs			Sum = $(1,575,705)			
Personal Computer System						
(2) Acquisition cost: computer	$(300,000)					
(3) Acquisition cost: software	(75,000)					
(4) System update				$ (60,000)		
(5) Salvage value						$ 30,000
(6), (7), (8) Operating costs		$(235,000)	$(235,000)	(235,000)	$(235,000)	(235,000)
(10) Time-sharing revenue		–0–	–0–	–0–	–0–	–0–
Total cash flow	$(375,000)	$(235,000)	$(235,000)	$(295,000)	$(235,000)	$(205,000)
× Discount factor	× 1.000	× .893	× .797	× .712	× .636	× .567
Present value	$(375,000)	$(209,855)	$(187,295)	$(210,040)	$(149,460)	$(116,235)
Net present value of costs			Sum = $(1,247,885)			
Difference in NPV of costs (favors personal computer system)			$ (327,820)			

MOUNTAINVIEW CITY GOVERNMENT
Purchase of Computing System
(r = .12, n = 5)

Item Number (from Exhibit 16–3)	Time 0	Time 1	Time 2	Time 3	Time 4	Time 5
Incremental Cost of Terminal System over Personal Computer System						
(2) Acquisition cost: computer	$(100,000)					
(3) Acquisition cost: software	35,000					
(4) System update				$ 20,000		
(5) Salvage value						$ 20,000
(6), (7), (8) Operating costs		$(100,000)	$(100,000)	(100,000)	$(100,000)	(100,000)
(10) Time-sharing revenue		20,000	20,000	20,000	20,000	20,000
Incremental cash flow	$ (65,000)	$ (80,000)	$ (80,000)	$ (60,000)	$ (80,000)	$ (60,000)
× Discount factor	× 1.000	× .893	× .797	× .712	× .636	× .567
Present value	$ (65,000)	$ (71,440)	$ (63,760)	$ (42,720)	$ (50,880)	$ (34,020)
Net present value of incremental costs (favors personal computer system)			Sum = $(327,820)			

Exhibit 16–5
Net-Present-Value Analysis:
Incremental-Cost Approach

The result of this analysis is that the NPV of the costs of the terminal system exceeds that of the personal computer system by $327,820. Notice that this is the same as the difference in NPVs shown at the bottom of Exhibit 16–4.

The total-cost and incremental-cost approaches always will yield equivalent conclusions. Choosing between them is a matter of personal preference.

Managerial Accountant's Role

To use discounted-cash-flow analysis in deciding about investment projects, managers need accurate cash-flow projections. This is where the managerial accountant plays a role. The accountant often is asked to predict cash flows related to operating-cost savings, additional working-capital requirements, or incremental costs and revenues. Such predictions are difficult in a world of uncertainty. The managerial accountant often draws upon historical accounting data to help in making cost predictions. Knowledge of market conditions, economic trends, and the likely reactions of competitors also can be important in projecting cash flows.

Postaudit

"Apple has forecast a 70 percent increase in capital expenditures . . . which one analyst has said could be a sign the Mac maker is investing in 'strategic new infrastructure.'" (16c)

Apple

The discounted-cash-flow approach to evaluating investment proposals requires cash-flow projections. The desirability of a proposal depends heavily on those projections. If they are highly inaccurate, they may lead the organization to accept undesirable projects or to reject projects that should be pursued. Because of the importance of the capital-budgeting process, most organizations systematically follow up on projects to see how they turn out. This procedure is called a **postaudit** (or **reappraisal**).

In a postaudit, the managerial accountant gathers information about the actual cash flows generated by a project. Then the project's actual net present value or internal rate of return is computed. Finally, the projections made for the project are compared with the actual results. If the project has not lived up to expectations, an investigation may be warranted to determine what went awry. Sometimes a postaudit will reveal shortcomings in the cash-flow projection process. In such cases, action may be taken to improve future cash-flow predictions. Two types of errors can occur in discounted-cash-flow analyses:

undesirable projects may be accepted, and desirable projects may be rejected. The post-audit is a tool for following up on accepted projects. Thus, a postaudit helps to detect only the first kind of error, not the second.

As in any performance-evaluation process, a postaudit should not be used punitively. The focus of a postaudit should provide information to the capital-budgeting staff, the project manager, and the management team.

Capital-investment decisions go through an elaborate capital-budgeting process. This computer-controlled injection-molding machine cost tens of millions of dollars, and the capital expenditure decision was carefully analyzed. For what types of decisions would capital budgeting be used by the administration of the college you attend?

Real Option Analysis

One way managerial accountants can assist the management team is by assessing the consequences of changes in an investment decision that may develop after the project has been approved. In long-term projects, there is often considerable uncertainty about the future cash flows, due to uncertainty about future economic, political, or cultural events. As a project unfolds, management may decide to alter the course of the project or even postpone it. Suppose, for example, that the city of Mountainview decides to build a new municipal water system that will take 5 years to build and is expected to last 75 years. The project involves collaboration with several private enterprises, other municipalities, and the state and national governments. As the project develops and various uncertainties are resolved, it may be desirable to make changes in the water system or postpone certain parts of it. A capital-budgeting tool called *real option analysis* can be used to quantify and analyze the merits of such changes. Real option analysis is covered in advanced cost management and finance courses.

Section 2: Income Taxes and Capital Budgeting

When a business makes a profit, it usually must pay income taxes, just as individuals do. Since many of the cash flows associated with an investment proposal affect the company's profit, they also affect the firm's income-tax liability. The following equation shows the four types of items that appear on an income statement.

> Income = Revenue − Expenses + Gains − Losses

Any aspect of an investment project that affects any of the items in this equation generally will affect the company's income-tax payments. These income-tax payments are cash flows, and they must be considered in any discounted-cash-flow analysis. In some cases, tax considerations are so crucial in a capital-investment decision that they dominate all other aspects of the analysis.

Learning Objective 4

Determine the after-tax cash flows in an investment analysis.

After-Tax Cash Flows

The first step in a discounted-cash-flow analysis for a profit-seeking enterprise is to determine the after-tax cash flows associated with the investment projects under consideration. An **after-tax cash flow** is the cash flow expected after all tax implications have been taken into account. Each financial aspect of a project must be examined carefully to determine its potential tax impact.

HIGH COUNTRY
DEPARTMENT STORES

To illustrate the tax implications of various types of financial items, we will focus on a retail business. High Country Department Stores, Inc. operates two department stores in the city of Mountainview. The firm has a large downtown store and a smaller branch store in the suburbs. The company is quite profitable, and management is considering several capital projects that will enhance the firm's future profit potential. Before analyzing these projects, let's pause to consider the tax issues the company is likely to face. For the purposes of our discussion, we will assume that High Country Department Stores' income tax rate is 40 percent. Thus, if the company's net income is $1,000,000, its income-tax payment will be $400,000 ($1,000,000 × 40%).

Cash Revenue   Suppose High Country's management is considering the purchase of an additional delivery truck. The sales manager estimates that a new truck will allow the company to increase annual sales revenue by $110,000. Further suppose that this incremental sales revenue will be received in cash during the year of sale. Any credit sales will be paid in cash within a short time period. High Country's additional annual sales revenue will result in an increase of $60,000 per year in cost of goods sold. Moreover, the additional merchandise sold will be paid for in cash during the same year as the related sales. Thus, the net incremental cash inflow resulting from the sales increase is $50,000 per year ($110,000 − $60,000).

What is High Country's *after-tax cash flow* from the incremental sales revenue, net of cost of goods sold? As the following calculation shows, the firm's incremental cash inflow from the additional sales is only $30,000.

Incremental sales revenue, net of cost of goods sold (cash inflow)	$50,000
Incremental income tax (cash outflow), $50,000 × 40%	(20,000)
After-tax cash flow (net inflow after taxes)	$30,000

Although the incremental sales amounted to an additional net cash inflow of $50,000, the cash outflow for income taxes also increased by $20,000. Thus, the after-tax cash inflow from the incremental sales, net of cost of goods sold, is $30,000.

A quick method for computing the after-tax cash inflow from incremental sales is the following:

$$\underset{\text{net of cost of goods sold}}{\text{Incremental sales revenue,}} \times (1 - \text{Tax rate}) = \underset{\text{cash inflow}}{\text{After-tax}}$$

$$\$50,000 \qquad \times \quad (1 - .40) \quad = \quad \$30,000$$

Cash Expenses   What are the tax implications of cash expenses? Suppose the addition of the delivery truck under consideration by High Country's management will involve hiring an additional employee, whose annual compensation and fringe benefits will amount to $30,000. As the following computation shows, the company's incremental cash outflow is only $18,000.

Incremental expense (cash outflow)	$(30,000)
Reduction in income tax (reduced cash outflow), $30,000 × 40%	12,000
After-tax cash flow (net outflow after taxes)	$(18,000)

Although the incremental employee compensation is $30,000, this expense is tax-deductible. Thus, the firm's income-tax payment will be reduced by $12,000. As a result, the after-tax cash outflow from the additional compensation is $18,000.

A quick method for computing the after-tax cash outflow from an incremental cash expense is given in the following equation:

$$\underset{\text{cash expense}}{\text{Incremental}} \times (1 - \text{Tax rate}) = \underset{\text{cash outflow}}{\text{After-tax}}$$

$$\$(30,000) \quad \times \quad (1 - .40) \quad = \quad \$(18,000)$$

Noncash Expenses

Not all expenses represent cash outflows. The most common example of a noncash expense is depreciation expense. Suppose High Country Department Stores' management is considering the purchase of a delivery truck that costs $40,000 and has no salvage value. We will discuss the specific methods of depreciation allowed under the tax law later in the chapter, but for now assume the truck will be depreciated as follows:

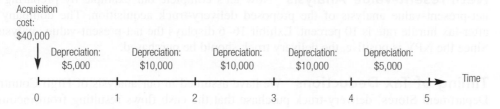

The only cash flow shown in the diagram above is the truck's acquisition cost of $40,000 at time zero. The depreciation expense in each of the next five years is *not a cash flow*. However, *depreciation is an expense* on the income statement, and it reduces the firm's income. For example, the $5,000 depreciation expense in year 1 will reduce High Country's income by $5,000. As a result, the company's year 1 income-tax payment will decline by $2,000 (40% × $5,000).

The annual depreciation expense associated with the truck provides a reduction in income-tax expense equal to the firm's tax rate times the depreciation deduction. This reduction in income taxes is called a **depreciation tax shield.**

To summarize, depreciation is a noncash expense. Although depreciation is not a cash flow, it does cause a reduced cash outflow through the depreciation tax shield.

$$\underset{\text{Is not a cash flow}}{\underbrace{\begin{matrix}\text{Depreciation or}\\\text{any other noncash expense}\end{matrix}}} \times \begin{matrix}\text{Tax}\\\text{rate}\end{matrix} = \underset{\text{Is a cash flow}}{\underbrace{\begin{matrix}\text{Reduced cash outflow}\\\text{for income taxes}\end{matrix}}}$$

$$\underset{\text{Is not a cash flow}}{\underbrace{\begin{matrix}\text{Year 1 depreciation}\\\text{of } \$5,000\end{matrix}}} \times 40\% = \underset{\text{Is a cash flow}}{\underbrace{\$2,000}}$$

The following schedule shows High Country Department Stores' depreciation tax shield over the depreciable life of the proposed delivery truck.

Year	Depreciation Expense	Tax Rate	Cash Flow: Reduced Tax Payment	
1	$ 5,000	40%	$2,000	⎫
2	10,000	40	4,000	⎪
3	10,000	40	4,000	⎬ Depreciation tax shield
4	10,000	40	4,000	⎪
5	5,000	40	2,000	⎭

The cash flows constituting the depreciation tax shield occur in five different years. Thus, in a discounted-cash-flow analysis, we still must discount these cash flows to find their present value.

Cash Flows Not on the Income Statement

Some cash flows do not appear on the income statement. They are not revenues, expenses, gains, or losses. A common example of such a cash flow is the purchase of an asset. If High Country Department Stores purchases the delivery truck, the $40,000 acquisition cost is a cash outflow but not an expense. A purchase is merely the exchange of one asset (cash) for another (a delivery truck). The expense associated with the truck's purchase is recognized through depreciation expense recorded throughout the asset's depreciable life. Thus, the cash flow resulting from the purchase of an asset does not affect income and has no direct tax consequences.

Net-Present-Value Analysis

Now let's complete our example by preparing a net-present-value analysis of the proposed delivery-truck acquisition. The company's after-tax hurdle rate is 10 percent. Exhibit 16–6 displays the net-present-value analysis. Since the NPV is positive, the delivery truck should be purchased.

Timing of Tax Deductions

We have assumed in our analysis of High Country Department Stores' delivery-truck purchase that the cash flows resulting from income taxes occur during the same year as the related before-tax cash flows. This assumption is realistic, as most businesses must make estimated tax payments throughout the tax year. They generally cannot wait until the following year and pay their prior year's taxes in one lump sum.

Inflation

Our discussion of discounted-cash-flow analysis has assumed no inflation. The additional complexity of inflation is discussed in Appendix B at the end of this chapter.

Accelerated Depreciation

Exhibit 16–6
Net-Present-Value Analysis
with After-Tax Cash Flows

HIGH COUNTRY
DEPARTMENT STORES

The main concept underlying discounted-cash-flow analysis is the time value of money. We discount each cash flow to find its present value. Since money has a time value, it is advantageous for a business to take tax deductions as early as allowable under the tax law.

Although national and state income tax laws are changed periodically by the appropriate governmental legislative bodies, income-tax laws often permit some form of accelerated depreciation for tax purposes. An *accelerated depreciation method* is any method

HIGH COUNTRY DEPARTMENT STORES, INC.
Purchase of Delivery Truck
($r = .10, n = 5$)

	Time 0	Time 1	Time 2	Time 3	Time 4	Time 5
Acquisition cost	$(40,000)					
After-tax cash flow from incremental sales revenue, net of cost of goods sold $50,000 × (1 − .40)		$30,000	$30,000	$30,000	$30,000	$30,000
After-tax cash flow from incremental compensation expense, $30,000 × (1 − .40)		(18,000)	(18,000)	(18,000)	(18,000)	(18,000)
After-tax cash flow from depreciation tax shield, depreciation expense × .40		2,000	4,000	4,000	4,000	2,000
Total cash flow	$(40,000)	$14,000	$16,000	$16,000	$16,000	$14,000
× Discount factor	× 1.000	× .909	× .826	× .751	× .683	× .621
Present value	$(40,000)	$12,726	$13,216	$12,016	$10,928	$ 8,694
Net present value......................................				Sum = $17,580		

under which an asset is depreciated more quickly in the early part of its life than it would be by using straight-line depreciation. For example, suppose High Country Department Stores purchased personal computers and peripheral devices for $10,000. The equipment's useful life is four years with no salvage value. Exhibit 16–7 shows the pattern of depreciation deductions, the associated after-tax cash flows, and the present value of the depreciation tax shield under three different depreciation methods. Notice that both the double-declining-balance method and the sum-of-the-years'-digits method result in a greater present value for the depreciation tax shield than the straight-line method does. Thus, it usually is desirable for a business to use accelerated depreciation for tax purposes whenever the tax law permits. The current tax law does not require that the same depreciation method be used for both the tax purpose and the external-reporting purpose. Thus, management could use straight-line depreciation when preparing published financial statements but use an accelerated method for tax purposes.

"It's clear that we have an important role to play in the decision-making process. we bring a perspective that is different from the other functions." (16d)
Boeing

Accelerated Depreciation in a National Tax Code

We will illustrate the effects of an accelerated tax depreciation system using the model in effect under United States tax law. Although your country's tax code probably differs in many ways, if it allows accelerated depreciation for tax purposes, this discussion should give you a good starting point for understanding how your country's tax code affects capital asset decisions

Under U.S. tax law's **Modified Accelerated Cost Recovery System, or MACRS,** every asset is placed in one of eight classes, depending on the asset's expected useful life. These eight classes, along with examples of the assets included, are shown in columns (a) and (b) of Exhibit 16–8. For each class, the tax law, known as the Internal Revenue Code, specifies the number of years over which the asset may be depreciated, and the depreciation method to be used. These specifications are shown in column (c) of Exhibit 16–8. Notice that the number of years of depreciation specified by the tax code is not the same as an asset's useful life. Thus, each asset's useful life is used only to place the asset in its appropriate MACRS class. Then the tax code specifies the appropriate number of years of depreciation.

Learning Objective 5

Use an accelerated tax depreciation system to determine an asset's depreciation schedule for tax purposes.

Depreciation Expense (Double-Declining-Balance*)	Depreciation Tax Shield (Depreciation × 40%)	Depreciation Expense (Sum-of-the-Years'-Digits)	Depreciation Tax Shield (Depreciation × 40%)	Depreciation Expense (Straight-Line)	Depreciation Tax Shield (Depreciation × 40%)
$5,000	$2,000	$4,000	$1,600	$2,500	$1,000
2,500	1,000	3,000	1,200	2,500	1,000
1,250	500	2,000	800	2,500	1,000
1,250	500	1,000	400	2,500	1,000
Present value of depreciation tax shield (10% discount rate)	$3,361		$3,320		$3,170

Exhibit 16–7
Present Value of Depreciation Tax Shield: Alternative Depreciation Methods

HIGH COUNTRY
DEPARTMENT STORES

* Steps in applying the double-declining-balance (DDB) method:

To apply the double-declining-balance depreciation method, use the following steps:

1. Divide 100% by the number of years of depreciation to be taken.

2. Multiply the answer obtained in step (1) by 200%.

3. Compute the asset's depreciation each year by applying the percentage obtained in step (2) to the asset's undepreciated cost at the beginning of the year.

4. Switch to straight-line depreciation during the first year in which the straight-line amount, computed for the asset's remaining life, is greater than the double-declining-balance amount.

(a) Asset's Useful Life*	(b) Types of Assets in MACRS Class	(c) MACRS Class and Depreciation Method
Up to 4 years	Industrial tools	3-year class; double-declining-balance
Between 4 and 10 years	Automobiles, trucks, office equipment, computers, research equipment	5-year class; double-declining-balance
Between 10 and 16 years	Most industrial equipment and machinery; office furniture	7-year class; double-declining-balance
Between 16 and 20 years	Equipment and machinery for specified purposes	10-year class; double-declining-balance
Between 20 and 25 years	Land improvements; some industrial machinery	15-year class; 150%-declining-balance
25 years or longer	Specified real property, such as farm buildings	20-year class; 150%-declining-balance
—	Residential rental property	27.5-year class; straight-line
—	Nonresidential real property	39-year class; straight-line

* In the tax law, an asset's useful life is referred to as the Asset Depreciation Range (ADR) Midpoint Life.

Exhibit 16–8
U.S. Tax Law's Modified Accelerated Cost Recovery System

Depreciation Methods

As Exhibit 16–8 indicates, assets in the 3-year, 5-year, 7-year, and 10-year MACRS property classes are depreciated using the double-declining-balance (DDB) method. Assets in the 15-year and 20-year MACRS property classes are depreciated using the 150%-declining-balance method. To apply this depreciation method, use the same steps as those listed in Exhibit 16–7 for the DDB method, except change 200% in step (2) to 150%. Assets in the 27.5-year and 39-year MACRS property classes are depreciated using the straight-line method.

The utility company that owns these trucks uses an accelerated method of depreciation for its utility equipment. The trucks are categorized in the five-year property class under the Modified Accelerated Cost Recovery System (MACRS).

Half-Year Convention

An asset may be purchased at any time during the tax year. MACRS assumes that, on average, assets will be placed in service halfway through the tax year. Thus, the tax code allows only a half-year's depreciation during the tax year in which an asset is placed in service. The other half of the first year's depreciation is picked up in the second tax year in which the asset is in service. The following diagram shows the pattern with which a five-year asset's depreciation is recorded, for tax purposes, under MACRS.

MACRS Depreciation Tables

To assist taxpayers, the U.S. taxing authority, known as the Internal Revenue Service (IRS), has published tables of the MACRS depreciation percentages for each MACRS property class. The IRS tables use the depreciation method specified in Exhibit 16–8 and incorporate the half-year convention. Exhibit 16–9 provides a convenient table of the MACRS percentages, as computed by the IRS, for selected property classes. In the 5-year column, we see 20 percent for year 1. This results from the half-year convention, since 20 percent is half of the double-declining balance rate of 40 percent.

No Salvage Values   Under MACRS, an asset's estimated salvage value is not subtracted in computing the asset's depreciation basis. Thus, for an asset costing $10,000 with an estimated salvage value of $1,000, the full $10,000 cost is depreciated over the asset's life.

Optional Straight-Line Depreciation   The tax law permits a business to depreciate any asset using the straight-line method instead of the method prescribed in Exhibit 16–8. A business with a loss might prefer this approach for tax reasons. If the straight-line method is used, the business may depreciate the asset over either the MACRS life or the asset's estimated useful life. Thus, businesses have considerable flexibility in choosing a depreciation schedule for tax purposes. Regardless of the depreciation method chosen, the half-year convention still must be followed.

Income-Tax Complexities   Every country's tax code is a complex document with a multitude of provisions. It is not possible to cover all of these provisions in this text, so it is wise to consult a tax expert regarding the complexities that may apply in your country and for a particular investment decision. Since the tax code is changed frequently, a tax rule that applied last year may not apply this year. For example, the *investment tax credit* is one important U.S. tax-code provision that has been switched on and off repeatedly. During periods when the investment tax credit has been in effect, a company has been allowed a substantial reduction in its income taxes when particular types of investments are made. The intent of the investment credit was to stimulate the economy by giving businesses an incentive to make new investments. The status of the investment tax credit is always subject to change. If there is a moral to the changing-tax-code story, it is this: When making an important investment decision, a manager should have a managerial accountant on one side and a tax accountant on the other.

> "The tax issues can often drive a client's business decision." (16e)
>
> **A. T. Kearney**

Gains and Losses on Disposal

When a business sells an asset, there often is a gain or loss on the sale. Since gains and losses are included in income, the business's income taxes generally are affected. Capital investment decisions frequently involve the disposal of assets, and sometimes gains or losses are recorded on those sales. Thus, the tax effects of gains and losses on disposal of assets can be an important feature of an investment decision.

The *book value* of an asset is defined as the asset's acquisition cost minus the accumulated depreciation on the asset. When an asset is sold for more than its current book

> **Learning Objective 6**
>
> Evaluate an investment proposal using a discounted-cash-flow analysis, giving full consideration to income-tax issues.

Year	MACRS Property Class			
	3-year	5-year	7-year	10-year
1	33.33%	20.00%	14.29%	10.00%
2	44.45	32.00	24.49	18.00
3	14.81*	19.20	17.49	14.40
4	7.41	11.52*	12.49	11.52
5		11.52	8.93*	9.22
6		5.76	8.92	7.37
7			8.93	6.55*
8			4.46	6.55
9				6.56
10				6.55
11				3.28

* Denotes the year during which the depreciation method switches to the straight-line method.

Source: IRS Publication 946, entitled "How to Depreciate Property."

Exhibit 16–9

Selected MACRS Depreciation Percentages as Computed by the IRS (incorporates half-year convention; also incorporates recent modifications in the tax laws) value, a *gain on disposal* is recorded. The *gain* is defined as the difference between the sales proceeds and the asset's book value. A *loss on disposal* is recorded when an asset is sold for less than its current book value. The *loss* is equal to the difference between the asset's current book value and the sales proceeds.

To illustrate, suppose High Country Department Stores owns a forklift, which cost $10,000 and currently has accumulated depreciation of $6,000. The forklift's book value is computed as follows:

Book value = Acquisition cost − Accumulated depreciation

$4,000 = 10,000 − $6,000

Scenario I: Gain on Disposal

Suppose High Country sells the forklift for $5,000. The gain on the sale is $1,000 ($5,000 proceeds minus $4,000 book value). If High Country's income-tax rate is 40 percent, the following cash flows will occur at the time of the sale.

Cash inflow: proceeds from sale	$5,000
Cash outflow: incremental income tax due to the gain, $1,000 × 40%	(400)
Net cash flow	$4,600

Although High Country sold the forklift for $5,000, the company's net cash benefit is only $4,600. The firm will have to pay the other $400 in increased income taxes on the $1,000 gain.

Scenario II: Loss on Disposal

Now assume instead that High Country Department Stores sells the forklift for $3,200. The *loss* on the sale is $800 ($3,200 proceeds minus $4,000 book value). If High Country's income-tax rate is 40 percent, the following cash flows will occur at the time of the sale.

Cash inflow: proceeds from sale	$3,200
Reduced cash outflow: reduction in income tax due to the loss, $800 × 40%	320
Total cash flow	$3,520

Although High Country sold the forklift for only $3,200, the company's total benefit from the sale is $3,520. The extra $320 comes in the form of a reduction in income taxes due to the loss on the sale.

Tax Rates on Gains and Losses

Another complexity of the tax code that changes from time to time is that capital gains and losses may be taxed at different rates than ordinary income (i.e., revenue minus expenses). Thus, before preparing an NPV analysis, it is wise to check with a tax expert to obtain the proper income-tax rate to apply to a gain or loss on disposal.

Investment in Working Capital

Some investment proposals require additional outlays for working capital. **Working capital,** defined as the excess of current assets over current liabilities, often increases as the result of higher balances in accounts receivable or inventory necessary to support a project. Such increases are uses of cash and should be included in a discounted-cash-flow analysis. To illustrate, suppose the city of Mountainview has offered High Country Department Stores a contract to sell special T-shirts and mementos commemorating the city's bicentennial. The contract covers the three-year period leading up to the bicentennial celebration. The cash flows associated with the proposal are displayed in panel A of Exhibit 16–10. Notice that the sales proposal would require a $2,000 outlay for additional working capital throughout the three-year period. The increased working capital is largely due to a higher balance in merchandise inventory. Panel B of Exhibit 16–10 analyzes the contract proposal. Notice that the time 0 cash investment in working capital is included as a $2,000 cash outflow. Since the increase in working capital is not released until the end of year 3, that $2,000 inflow is discounted. The city's proposal has a positive net present value, so it should be accepted.

Notice that the presentation format used for the analysis in Exhibit 16–10 is different from the format we used previously. Instead of listing the cash flows for each item by year and then adding the columns, we have computed the present value of each financial item pertinent to the decision. The one-time cash flows at time zero then are added to the present value of the cost-savings annuity to determine the net present value. This alternative presentation format will yield the same conclusion as the year-by-year, columnar approach. The choice of format is a matter of personal preference.

Extended Illustration of Income-Tax Effects in Capital Budgeting

Now we have covered all of the most important concepts for analyzing an investment proposal in a profit-seeking enterprise. A comprehensive illustration will help you solidify your understanding of these concepts. High Country Department Stores' management is considering the installation of a new checkout system for its suburban store. The new computerized system would include new cash registers at each checkout station. In

Exhibit 16–10
Investment In Working Capital

HIGH COUNTRY
DEPARTMENT STORES

HIGH COUNTRY DEPARTMENT STORES, INC.
Contract Proposal for the City's Bicentennial

A. Data for Illustration

Annual sales revenue from T-shirts and mementos	$25,000
Annual expenses	(12,000)
Annual contract fee to city	(3,000)
Investment in working capital (time 0)	(2,000)
Release of working capital (end of year 3)	2,000
Tax rate	40%
After-tax hurdle rate	10%

B. Discounted-Cash-Flow Analysis

Investment in working capital (time 0)		$ (2,000)
Release of working capital:		
Working capital released (end of year 3)	$ 2,000	
Discount factor ($n = 3, r = .10$)	× .751*	
Present value of working capital released		1,502
Annual revenue and expenses:		
Sales revenue	$25,000	
Expenses	(12,000)	
Contract fee	(3,000)	
Before-tax annual income	10,000	
× (1 − tax rate)	× .60	
After-tax annual income	6,000	
× Annuity discount factor	× 2.487†	
Present value of after-tax annual income		14,922
Net present value of contract proposal		$14,424

* From Table III of Appendix A.

† From Table IV of Appendix A.

Learning Objective **6**

Evaluate an investment proposal using a discounted-cash-flow analysis, giving full consideration to income-tax issues.

addition, the new checkout system would include an updated bar-code reading system. The new system will be faster and more accurate, and it will minimize the annoyance of the reader failing to recognize a product's bar code. Among the advantages of the new system are accuracy in the checkout process, automatic updating of computerized inventory records, and the ability to gather data about customers' buying patterns and trends.

Exhibit 16–11 presents the data pertinent to the decision. Notice that the old equipment has been fully depreciated already. However, its useful life can be extended to six more years if an overhaul is done in year 2. The new equipment also has an expected useful life of six years, so its MACRS classification is the 5-year property class.

Most of the data in Exhibit 16–11 are self-explanatory. The last two items in the exhibit under annual data relate to the new checkout system's ability to gather data about customer demand patterns. The extra data analysis will cost $4,500 annually, but it is expected to generate another $40,000 in annual sales, net of cost of goods sold.

A net-present-value analysis of the checkout equipment proposal is presented in Exhibit 16–12. A total-cost approach is used. The present value of each financial item is computed for both alternatives; then these present values are added to determine each alternative's net present value. An explanation of each line in the exhibit follows.

(1) Line (1) in Exhibit 16–12 records the acquisition cost of the new checkout equipment. This cash flow has no tax impact and does not need to be discounted since it occurs at time 0.

(2), (3) These one-time cash flows are required to retrain checkout personnel and retag merchandise to accommodate the new bar-code readers. Since these costs are expenses, we multiply by $(1 - .40)$.

(4), (5) Since the old equipment has a current book value of zero, there is a $1,200 gain on the sale. The $1,200 proceeds are not taxed [line (4)], but the $1,200 gain on the sale is taxed [line (5)].

(6) The cost of updating the software in year 3 is an expense, so we multiply by $(1 - .40)$.

Exhibit 16–11
Data for Extended Illustration

HIGH COUNTRY
DEPARTMENT STORES

HIGH COUNTRY DEPARTMENT STORES, INC.
Computerized Checkout Equipment Decision

Old checkout equipment:	
Remaining useful life, assuming overhaul in year 2	6 years
Cost of overhaul in year 2	$3,500
Current book value (fully depreciated)	–0–
Current salvage value	$1,200
Salvage value in six more years	–0–
New checkout equipment:	
Useful (ADR midpoint) life	6 years
MACRS property classification	5-year class
Acquisition cost of new equipment	$50,000
Update of software required in year 3	$4,000
Salvage value of new equipment in six years	$1,000
Cost to retrain checkout personnel	$5,000
Cost to retag merchandise	$3,000
Annual data:	
Annual operating-cost savings	$15,000
Annual cost of computer-system operator	$30,000
Annual cost of marketing-data analysis	$4,500
Annual incremental sales resulting from marketing analysis, net of cost of goods sold	$40,000
After-tax hurdle rate	10%
Tax rate	40%

(7), (8) The new equipment can be sold in year 6 for $1,000. Since it will be fully depreciated, there will be a $1,000 gain. The $1,000 proceeds are not taxed [line (7)], but the $1,000 gain is taxed [line (8)].

(9) The depreciation tax shield on the new equipment is computed using the MACRS depreciation schedule for the 5-year property class. The annual depreciation deductions are not cash flows, but they do cause a reduction in income taxes. Each cash flow is then discounted using the appropriate discount factor from Table III in Appendix A.

(10), (11), (12), (13) These items are annual cash flows. The flows are summed, and then the $20,500 annuity is multiplied by (1 − .40) because each of the cash flows

Exhibit 16–12
Net-Present-Value Analysis for Extended Illustration

HIGH COUNTRY
DEPARTMENT STORES

HIGH COUNTRY DEPARTMENT STORES, INC.
Computerized Checkout Equipment Decision

	Year	Amount	Income-Tax Impact	After-Tax Cash Flow	Discount Factor (10%)	Present Value of Cash Flow
Purchase New Equipment						
(1) Acquisition cost of new equipment	Time 0	$50,000	None	$(50,000)	1.000	$(50,000)
(2) Cost to retrain checkout personnel	Time 0	5,000	(1 − .40)*	(3,000)	1.000	(3,000)
(3) Cost to retag merchandise	Time 0	3,000	(1 − .40)	(1,800)	1.000	(1,800)
(4) Proceeds from sale of old equipment	Time 0	1,200	None	1,200	1.000	1,200
(5) Gain on sale of old equipment	Time 0	1,200	.40	(480)	1.000	(480)
(6) Update of software	Year 3	4,000	(1 − .40)	(2,400)	.751	(1,802)
(7) Salvage value of new equipment	Year 6	1,000	None	1,000	.564	564
(8) Gain on sale of new equipment	Year 6	1,000	.40	(400)	.564	(226)

(9) Depreciation tax shield:

Year	Cost	MACRS Percentage (rounded)	Depreciation Expense					
1	$50,000	20.0%	$10,000	10,000	.40	4,000	.909	3,636
2	50,000	32.0%	16,000	16,000	.40	6,400	.826	5,286
3	50,000	19.2%	9,600	9,600	.40	3,840	.751	2,884
4	50,000	11.5%	5,750	5,750	.40	2,300	.683	1,571
5	50,000	11.5%	5,750	5,750	.40	2,300	.621	1,428
6	50,000	5.8%	2,900	2,900	.40	1,160	.564	654
Total			$50,000					

Annual incremental costs and benefits (years 1 through 6):

(10) Annual operating cost savings	$15,000					
(11) Annual cost of computer operator	(30,000)				Annuity discount factor for $n = 6, r = .10$	
(12) Annual cost of marketing analysis	(4,500)					
(13) Annual incremental sales revenue, net of cost of goods sold	40,000				↓	
Total annual amount	$20,500	$20,500	(1 − .40)	$12,300	4.355	53,567
(14) Net present value						$13,482

Keep Old Equipment†

	Year	Amount	Income-Tax Impact	After-Tax Cash Flow	Discount Factor (10%)	Present Value of Cash Flow
(15) Cost of overhaul	Year 2	$3,500	(1 − .40)	$(2,100)	.826	$ (1,735)
(16) Net present value						$ (1,735)

* High Country Department Stores' tax rate is 40%.

† There is no depreciation tax shield if the old equipment is kept, since it has been depreciated fully already.

Pfizer and Merck

CAPITAL BUDGETING AT PHARMACEUTICAL FIRMS

Among the many large companies making extensive use of capital budgeting are the big pharmaceutical companies. It can take 10 years or more to develop a new drug. It takes huge outlays of cash to develop a drug, test it, and then shepherd it through the governmental approval process. Yet much of what the drug companies claim as the cost of a new drug is actually the opportunity cost of tying up these big dollar outlays for many years before any revenue stream begins.

"Overall, the average tab for developing a new drug is $500 million to $880 million, the industry says. But the amount actually spent on any one marketable product is roughly one-quarter of that. To understand why, just look at the drug-development process. In the past, scientists made many variations of existing chemicals and tested them to see which ones had the ability to fight a particular disease." Now, with the advent of genetic engineering and greatly expanded knowledge of biology, "the process has gotten more complicated—and oddly enough, more difficult. Researchers try to identify the best target in a particular disease—for instance, a damaged gene that causes cancer—then they make a drug to hit the target and cure the disease. Since that process can take 10 years or more, that means that about half of the calculated $500 million to $880 million total isn't actually spent at all. Instead, it's the opportunity cost—the measure of what the money tied up in the drug for so many years could have earned with alternative investments." This is where capital budgeting comes into play, since the NPV of a drug development project takes into account the opportunity cost associated with the time value of money.

Pharmaceutical companies "have upped research spending in recent years—Pfizer spends $4.9 billion annually; Merck, about $2.6 billion—but with no big payoff in productivity. Hefty up-front investments in genomics, in particular, have so far failed to yield a big crop of new compounds." The uncertainties big pharmaceutical companies confront are a large part of the problem. First, only a small percentage of drugs under development ever make it as far as human trials. And only 1 in 10 of those makes it through to wide-scale testing. Then there's the pricing uncertainty as well. How much will people pay for a new drug treatment? To take account of these uncertainties, many drug companies use simulation in conjunction with capital budgeting to decide whether to proceed with a drug's development. A discounted-cash-flow analysis is run many times with differing assumptions about the drug's success, its development costs, and its eventual pricing. Then a probability distribution is generated for the drug's NPV. Management can then make a decision about proceeding with development given the likelihood of a profitable drug.[1]

will be on the income statement. The after-tax cash-flow annuity of $12,300 is then discounted using the annuity discount factor for $n = 6$ and $r = .10$.

(14) The net present value of the new equipment is $13,482.

(15) The only specific cash flow related to the alternative of keeping the old equipment is the $3,500 overhaul in year 2. This will be an expense, so we multiply by $(1 - .40)$. Then the after-tax cash flow is discounted.

(16) The net present value of the alternative to keep the old equipment is $(1,735).

[1]Based on S. Hensley, R. Winslow, and W. Mathews, "FDA Approves Pfizer Drug for Two Cancers," *The Wall Street Journal,* January 27, 2006, pp. 31, 34; J. Carey and A. Barrett, "Drug Prices: What's Fair," *BusinessWeek,* December 10, 2001, pp. 61–70; and the author's discussions with pharmaceutical company personnel.

Decision Rule The analysis indicates that High Country Department Stores should purchase the new checkout equipment. The NPV of the new equipment exceeds that of the old equipment.

Ranking Investment Projects

Suppose a company has several potential investment projects, all of which have positive net present values. If a project has a positive net present value, this means that the return projected for the project exceeds the company's cost of capital. In this case, every project with a positive NPV should be accepted. In spite of the theoretical validity of this argument, practice often does not reflect this viewpoint. In practice, managers often attempt to rank investment projects with positive net present values. Then only a limited number of the higher-ranking proposals are accepted.

The reasons for this common practice are not clear. If a discount rate is used that accurately reflects the firm's cost of capital, then any project with a positive NPV will earn a return greater than the cost of obtaining capital to fund it. One possible explanation for the practice of ranking investment projects is a limited supply of scarce resources, such as managerial talent. Thus, a form of *capital rationing* takes place, not because of a limited supply of investment capital, but because of limitations on other resources. A manager may feel that he or she simply cannot devote sufficient attention to all of the desirable projects. The solution, then, is to select only some of the positive-NPV proposals, which implies a ranking.

Unfortunately, no valid method exists for ranking independent investment projects with positive net present values. To illustrate, suppose the management of High Country Department Stores has the following two investment opportunities:

Learning Objective **7**

Discuss the difficulty of ranking investment proposals, and use the profitability index.

1. Proposal A: Open a gift shop at the Mountainview Convention Center. High Country's management believes the benefits of this proposal would last only six years. High Country's management expects that after six years, the firm's competitors will move into the Convention Center and eliminate High Country's current advantageous position.

2. Proposal B: Open a small gift shop at the Mountainview Airport. The airport gift concession would belong to High Country Department Stores for 10 years under a contract with the city.

The predicted cash flows for these investment proposals are as follows:

Investment Proposal	Cash Outflow Time 0	After-Tax Cash Inflows Years 1–6	After-Tax Cash Inflows Years 7–10	Present Value of Inflows (10% Discount Rate)	Net Present Value	Internal Rate of Return
A (Convention Center)	$ (54,450)	$14,000	—	$ 60,970	$6,520	14%
B (Airport)	(101,700)	18,000	$18,000	110,610	8,910	12%

Both investment proposals have positive net present values. Suppose, however, that due to limited managerial time, High Country's management has decided to pursue only one of the projects. Which proposal should be ranked higher? This is a difficult question to answer. Proposal B has a higher net present value, but it also requires a much larger initial investment. Proposal A exhibits a higher internal rate of return. However, proposal A's return of 14 percent applies only to its six-year time horizon. If management accepts proposal A, what will happen in years 7 through 10? Will the facilities and equipment remain idle? Or could they be used profitably for some other purpose? These questions are left unanswered by the analysis above.

The main reason that the NPV and IRR methods of analysis yield different rankings for these two proposals is that the projects have different lives. Without making an assumption about what will happen in years 7 through 10 if proposal A is accepted, the

NPV and IRR methods simply are not capable of ranking the proposals in any sound manner. The only theoretically correct answer to the problem posed in this illustration is that both projects are desirable, and both should be accepted. Each proposal exhibits a positive NPV and an IRR greater than the hurdle rate of 10 percent.

Profitability Index One criterion that managers sometimes apply in ranking investment proposals is called the **profitability index** (or **excess present value index**), which is defined as follows:

$$\text{Profitability index} = \frac{\text{Present value of cash flows,}}{\text{Initial investment}}$$

The profitability indices for High Country's two investment proposals are computed as follows:

Investment Proposal	Calculation		Profitability Index	Net Present Value	Internal Rate of Return
A	$\dfrac{\text{Present value of inflows}}{\text{Initial investment}} = \dfrac{\$60,970}{\$54,450} =$		1.12	$6,520	14%
			∨	∧	∨
B	$\dfrac{\text{Present value of inflows}}{\text{Initial investment}} = \dfrac{\$110,610}{\$101,700} =$		1.09	$8,910	12%

Although proposal A has a lower NPV than proposal B, proposal A exhibits a higher profitability index. Proposal A's higher profitability index is due to its considerably lower initial investment than that required for proposal B. Is the profitability index a foolproof method for ranking investment proposals? Unfortunately, it too suffers from the same drawbacks as those associated with the NPV or IRR method. Both proposals exhibit a profitability index greater than 1.00, which merely reflects their positive NPVs. Thus, both projects are desirable. The unequal lives of the two proposals prevent the profitability index from indicating a theoretically correct ranking of the proposals. The relative desirability of proposals A and B simply depends on what will happen in years 7 through 10 if proposal A is selected.

In summary, the problem of ranking investment projects with positive NPVs has not been solved in a satisfactory manner. This lack of resolution is due to an inconsistency inherent to the problem. The inconsistency is that if several projects have positive NPVs, they all are desirable. They all will earn a return greater than the cost of capital. If a manager chooses not to accept all projects with positive NPVs, then the required ranking ultimately must be made on the basis of subjective criteria.

Section 3: Alternative Methods for Making Investment Decisions

Learning Objective 8

Use the payback method and accounting-rate-of-return method to evaluate capital investment projects.

HIGH COUNTRY
DEPARTMENT STORES

The best way to decide whether to accept an investment project is to use discounted-cash-flow analysis, as described in Sections 1 and 2 of this chapter. Both the net—present-value and the internal-rate-of-return methods will yield the correct accept-or-reject decision. The strength of these methods lies in the fact that they properly account for the time value of money. In spite of the conceptual superiority of discounted-cash-flow decision models, managers sometimes use other methods for making investment decisions. In some cases, these alternative methods are used in conjunction with a discounted-cash-flow analysis. Two of these alternative decision methods are described next.

Our discussion is based on decisions faced by the management of High Country Department Stores. The firm operates two department stores in the city of Mountainview.

Payback Method

The **payback period** of an investment proposal is the amount of time it will take for the after-tax cash inflows from the project to accumulate to an amount that covers the original investment. The following formula defines an investment project's payback period.

$$\text{Payback period} = \frac{\text{Initial investment}}{\text{Annual after-tax cash inflow}}$$

There is no adjustment in the payback method for the time value of money. A cash inflow in year 5 is treated the same as a cash inflow in year 1.

To illustrate the payback method, suppose High Country Department Stores' management is considering the purchase of a new conveyor system for its warehouse. The two alternative machines under consideration have the following projected cash flows.

Conveyor System	Initial Investment	After-Tax Cash Flows: Years 1 through 7	After-Tax Cash Flow When System Is Sold
I	$(20,000)	$4,000	–0–
II	(27,000)	4,500	$14,000

The payback period for each conveyor system is computed below. Notice that *after-tax cash flows are used* in the payback method, just as they are in discounted-cash-flow methods of analysis.

Conveyor System	Initial Investment / Annual After-Tax Cash Inflow	Payback Period
I	$\dfrac{\$20,000}{\$4,000}$	5 years
II	$\dfrac{\$27,000}{\$4,500}$	6 years

According to the payback method, system I is more desirable than system II. System I will "pay back" its initial investment in five years, while system II requires six years. This conclusion is too simplistic, however, because it ignores the large salvage value associated with system II. Indeed, the NPV of system I is negative, while the NPV of system II is positive, as shown in the following analysis.

After-Tax Cash Flows	Present Value of Cash Flows (10% Discount Factor)	
	System I	System II
Initial investment	$(20,000) × 1.000 = $(20,000)	$(27,000) × 1.000 = $(27,000)
Years 1–7	4,000 × 4.868 = 19,472	4,500 × 4.868 = 21,906
Cash inflow from sale	–0–	14,000 × .513 = 7,182
Net present value	$ (528)	$ 2,088

The net-present-value analysis demonstrates that only system II can generate cash flows sufficient to cover the company's cost of capital. The payback method makes it appear as though system I "pays back" its initial investment more quickly, but the method fails to consider the time value of money.

Another shortcoming of the payback method is that it fails to consider an investment project's profitability beyond the payback period. Suppose High Country Department Stores' management has a third alternative for its warehouse conveyor system. System III requires an initial investment of only $12,000 and will generate after-tax cash inflows of \$6,000 in years 1 and 2. Thus, System III's payback period is two years, as computed below.

$$\text{System III payback period} = \frac{\$12,000}{\$6,000} = 2 \text{ years}$$

Strict adherence to the payback method would rank system III above systems I and II, due to its shorter payback period. However, suppose we add another piece of information. System III's useful life is only two years, and it has no salvage value after two years. It is true that system III will "pay back" its initial investment in only two years if we ignore the time value of money. But then what? System III provides no further benefits beyond year 2. In spite of system III's short payback period, it is not a desirable investment proposal. The NPV of system III, \$(1,584), is negative [\$(1,584) = (1.736 × \$6,000) − \$12,000].

Payback Period with Uneven Cash Flows The simple payback formula given on page 711 will not work if a project exhibits an uneven pattern of cash flows. Instead, the after-tax cash flows must be accumulated on a year-to-year basis until the accumulation equals the initial investment. Suppose High Country Department Stores' management is considering the expansion of the downtown store's parking facilities. Management expects that the additional parking will result in much greater sales initially. However, this benefit will gradually taper off, due to the reactions of competitors. The projected after-tax cash flows are shown in Exhibit 16–13, which also presents the pay-back calculation for the parking lot proposal. The project's payback period is five years.

Payback: Pro and Con In summary, the payback method of evaluating invest-ment proposals has two serious drawbacks. First, the method fails to consider the time value of money. Second, it does not consider a project's cash flows beyond the pay-back period. Despite these shortcomings, the payback method is used widely in practice, for two legitimate reasons.

First, the payback method provides a tool for roughly screening investment propos-als. If a project does not meet some minimal criterion for the payback period, manage-ment may wish to reject the proposal regardless of potential large cash flows predicted well into the future. Second, a young firm may experience a shortage of cash. For such a company, it may be crucial to select investment projects that recoup their initial investment quickly. A cash-poor firm may not be able to wait for the big payoff of a project with a long payback period. Even in these cases, it is wise not to rely on the payback method alone. If the payback method is used, it should be in conjunction with a discounted-cash-flow analysis.

Accounting-Rate-of-Return Method

Discounted-cash-flow methods of investment analysis focus on *cash flows* and incorpo-rate the time value of money. The **accounting-rate-of-return method** focuses on the incremental *accounting income* that results from a project. Accounting income is based on accrual accounting procedures. Revenue is recognized during the period of sale, not necessarily when the cash is received; expenses are recognized during the period they are incurred, not necessarily when they are paid in cash. The following formula is used to compute the accounting rate of return on an investment project.

$$\text{Accounting rate of return} = \frac{\left(\begin{array}{c}\text{Average}\\\text{incremental}\\\text{revenue}\end{array}\right) - \left(\begin{array}{c}\text{Average incremental expenses}\\\text{(including depreciation}\\\text{and income taxes)}\end{array}\right)}{\text{Initial investment}}$$

To illustrate the accounting-rate-of-return method, suppose High Country Department Stores' management is considering the installation of a small lunch counter

HIGH COUNTRY DEPARTMENT STORES, INC.
Parking Lot Expansion

After-Tax Cash Flows

Year	Type of Cash Flow	Outflows	Inflows	Accumulated Cash Flows (excluding initial investment)	
0	Initial investment	$(200,000)		—	
1	Incremental sales*		$60,000	$ 60,000	
2	Incremental sales*		50,000	110,000	
3	Incremental sales*		45,000	155,000	
4	Incremental sales*		35,000	190,000	
4	Repave parking lot	(20,000)		170,000	Payback
5	Incremental sales*		30,000	200,000	← period:
6	Incremental sales*		30,000	230,000	5 years
7	Incremental sales*		30,000	260,000	
8	Incremental sales*		30,000	290,000	

* Incremental sales, net of cost of goods sold.

Exhibit 16–13
Payback Period with Uneven Cash Flows

HIGH COUNTRY
DEPARTMENT STORES

in its downtown store. The required equipment and furnishings cost $210,000 and are in the MACRS 7-year property class. The company has elected to use the optional straight-line depreciation method with the half-year convention. The Excel spreadsheet shown in Exhibit 16–14 displays management's revenue and expense projections for the lunch counter. The total income projected over the project's 10-year useful life is $174,000. Thus, the average annual income is $17,400. The accounting rate of return on the lunch-counter proposal is computed as follows:

$$\text{Accounting rate of return} = \frac{\$17,400}{\$210,000} = 8.3\% \text{ (rounded)}$$

To compute the lunch-counter project's internal rate of return, let's assume that each year's sales revenue, cost of goods sold, operating expenses, and income taxes are cash flows in the same year that they are recorded under accrual accounting. Recall that the depreciation expense is not a cash flow. These assumptions imply the following cash-flow pattern for the project.

Net After-Tax Cash Inflows

Year	Amount	Year	Amount
Initial investment	$(210,000)		
1	36,000	6	$42,000
2	42,000	7	42,000
3	42,000	8	36,000
4	42,000	9	30,000
5	42,000	10	30,000

The internal rate of return on the lunch-counter proposal is approximately 13.5 percent. That is, if we compute the present value of the cash flows using a discount rate of 13.5 percent, we obtain approximately a zero NPV.[2] Notice that the project's accounting rate of return, at 8.3 percent, is much lower than its IRR of 13.5 percent.

---

[2]You can verify the IRR of 13.5% using Table III in Appendix A. You will need to interpolate to find the discount factors for 13.5%, which lie between the 12% and 14% discount factors. For example, .881 is the approximate discount factor for 13.5% and $n = 1$ [.881 = .877 + (.25)(.893 − .877)]. Alternatively, you can calculate the discount factor for 13.5% using the formula given in Table III.

Exhibit 16–14

Accounting-Rate-of-Return
Method

HIGH COUNTRY
DEPARTMENT STORES

Microsoft Excel - Accounting-Rate-of-Return Method

H18   =SUM(H8:H17)

HIGH COUNTRY DEPARTMENT STORES, INC.

Lunch Counter for Downtown Store

Year	Sales Revenue	Cost of Goods Sold	Operating Expenses	MACRS Depreciation*	Income Before Taxes	Income Taxes 40%	Net Income
1	$ 200,000	$ 100,000	$ 50,000	$ 15,000	$ 35,000	$ 14,000	$ 21,000
2	200,000	100,000	50,000	30,000	20,000	8,000	12,000
3	200,000	100,000	50,000	30,000	20,000	8,000	12,000
4	200,000	100,000	50,000	30,000	20,000	8,000	12,000
5	200,000	100,000	50,000	30,000	20,000	8,000	12,000
6	200,000	100,000	50,000	30,000	20,000	8,000	12,000
7	200,000	100,000	50,000	30,000	20,000	8,000	12,000
8	200,000	100,000	50,000	15,000	35,000	14,000	21,000
9	200,000	100,000	50,000	-	50,000	20,000	30,000
10	200,000	100,000	50,000	-	50,000	20,000	30,000
Total				$ 210,000			$ 174,000

*Annual straight-line depreciation = ($210,000 / 7) = $30,000

Note: In accordance with the half-year convention, only half a year's depreciation is recorded in years 1 & 8

Sheet1 / Sheet2 / Sheet3 /

Ready

Use of the Average Investment

Some managers prefer to compute the
accounting rate of return using the average amount invested in a project for the denominator, rather than the project's full cost. The formula is modified as follows:

$$\text{Accounting rate of return (using average investment)} = \frac{\left(\begin{array}{c}\text{Average}\\\text{incremental}\\\text{revenue}\end{array}\right) - \left(\begin{array}{c}\text{Average incemental expenses}\\\text{(including depreciation}\\\text{and income taxes)}\end{array}\right)}{\text{Average investment}}$$

A project's average investment is the average accounting book value over the project's life.

Refer again to High Country Department Stores' lunch-counter data given in
Exhibit 16–14. The project's book value at the beginning of each year is tabulated as follows:

Year	(a) Book Value at Beginning of Year	MACRS Depreciation	(b) Book Value at End of Year	(a) + (b) / 2 Average Book Value During Year
1	$210,000	$15,000	$195,000	$202,500
2	195,000	30,000	165,000	180,000
3	165,000	30,000	135,000	150,000
4	135,000	30,000	105,000	120,000
5	105,000	30,000	75,000	90,000
6	75,000	30,000	45,000	60,000
7	45,000	30,000	15,000	30,000
8	15,000	15,000	–0–	7,500
9	–0–	–0–	–0–	–0–
10	–0–	–0–	–0–	–0–

The average investment over the project's useful life is the average of the amounts
in the right-hand column, which is $84,000. Thus, the modified version of the project's

accounting rate of return is 20.7 percent. (The average annual income of $17,400 divided by the average investment of $84,000 equals 20.7 percent, rounded.)

Notice that this modified version of the accounting rate of return yields a significantly higher return than the project's internal rate of return, which we computed as 13.5 percent. As a general rule of thumb, the following relationships will be observed.

$$\begin{array}{ccc} \text{Accounting rate of return} & < \text{Internal rate} & < \text{Accounting rate of return} \\ \text{(using initial investment)} & \text{of return} & \text{(using average investment)} \end{array}$$

Accounting Rate of Return: Pro and Con Like the payback method, the accounting-rate-of-return method is a simple way of screening investment proposals. Some managers use this method because they believe it parallels financial accounting statements, which also are based on accrual accounting. However, like the payback method, the accounting-rate-of-return method does not consider the time value of money.

Inconsistent Terminology Many different terms for the accounting rate of return are used in practice. Among these terms are *simple rate of return, rate of return on assets,* and the *unadjusted rate of return.*

Estimating Cash Flows: The Role of Activity-Based Costing

The validity of any discounted-cash-flow analysis is dependent on the accuracy of the cash-flow estimates. Activity-based-costing (ABC) systems generally improve the ability of an analyst to estimate the cash flows associated with a proposed project. By separating costs into activity cost pools and identifying a cost driver for each pool, the analyst can more accurately determine the levels of various costs that will be incurred if the project is implemented. Costs that are treated as fixed under a traditional, volume-based costing system often are seen to be variable, with respect to the appropriate cost driver, under an ABC system.[3]

Accuracy in estimating cash flows is particularly important in evaluating a proposed investment in advanced manufacturing equipment. These decisions are complex, involving many peripheral cash flows besides the actual purchase of the equipment. Flexible manufacturing systems (FMSs) generally require cash outlays for software, retraining of employees, realignment of the production line, and engineering. The benefits of such systems often are difficult to quantify also. Intangible benefits such as greater production flexibility are important considerations in making these investment decisions.

In today's manufacturing environment, it is crucial that companies make the best decisions possible regarding huge investments such as those in flexible manufacturing systems. Flawed decisions can spell disaster in today's globally competitive arenas.

> **Learning Objective 9**
>
> Describe the impact of activity-based costing and advanced manufacturing technology on capital-budgeting decisions.

Justification of Investments in Advanced Manufacturing Systems

The manufacturing industry is changing dramatically as firms adopt a just-in-time (JIT) inventory management approach and move toward computer-integrated-manufacturing (CIM) systems. Many firms have found that JIT and CIM, coupled with a revised managerial accounting system, have provided a competitive edge in the marketplace. In many cases, however, managers have been frustrated when an NPV analysis projects a negative net present value for a proposed investment in a CIM system. Managers often believe

> **Learning Objective 9**
>
> Describe the impact of activity-based costing and advanced manufacturing technology on capital-budgeting decisions.

---

[3] Activity-based-costing systems are covered extensively in Chapter 5.

Focus on Ethics

DYSFUNCTIONAL FOCUS ON EARLY CASH FLOWS

The timing of cash flows in investment decisions can sometimes create behavioral incentives to make dysfunctional decisions. The following hypothetical scenario presents such a situation.

The Institute for Environmental Studies (IES) is a privately funded, nonprofit scientific organization based in Montreal. The organization's director of field research is scheduled to retire in two years, and the assistant director, Marie Fenwar, is hoping to be appointed to the post at that time. In her current position, Fenwar has significant administrative responsibilities, including the approval of research proposals and equipment acquisitions. Fenwar has developed a reputation for carefully scrutinizing every proposed project and keeping the institute's field research branch within its budget. Fenwar has been so successful in her job that she has been quietly assured by several members of the IES board of directors that she is in line for her boss's job. She knows, however, that her prospects depend on her continued success in keeping the field research branch in solid financial shape.

IES recently signed a contract with the U.S. and Canadian governments to do a five-year study of the effects of global warming on the migration of water fowl. The contract fee is $500,000, payable in equal annual installments over the contract term. Fenwar is now considering two alternative proposals for carrying out the study. Each proposal entails the purchase of equipment and the incurrence of various operating costs throughout the term of the contract. Fenwar's normal procedure for project evaluation is to calculate each proposal's NPV, using an 8 percent hurdle rate. The projected costs follow:

Year	Type of Cost	Research Proposal I	Research Proposal II
Time 0	Equipment acquisition*	$ 40,000	$70,000
Year 1	Operating costs	150,000	75,000
Year 2	Operating costs	120,000	75,000
Year 3	Operating costs	75,000	95,000
Year 4	Operating costs	40,000	95,000
Year 5	Operating costs	40,000	95,000

* The equipment will be obsolete at the end of the contract term.

Fenwar calculated an NPV of $1,370 for Proposal I and $(14,375) for Proposal II. After completing her NPV analysis, however, Fenwar was tempted to ignore it. These thoughts ran through her mind as she drove to work: "If I approve Proposal I, the financial picture for the field research branch is going to pieces for the next two years. After a $40,000 initial investment in equipment, I'm going to show losses of $50,000 and $20,000 in the first two years. That's not going to look very good when the board considers my promotion." When she arrived at the office, Fenwar wrote a memo approving Proposal II.

Which research proposal should Fenwar have accepted? Why? Comment on the ethical issues in this scenario.

intuitively that such an investment is justified, but they are stymied when the NPV analysis points to rejection of the proposal.

What is the problem here? Are managers overly optimistic about the advantages of CIM? Or is the NPV approach inappropriate for such an investment decision? Most likely neither of these conjectures is true. Managers often are right when their intuition tells them that the company would benefit from advanced manufacturing technology. And it is difficult to find fault with the NPV investment decision model. It is economically and mathematically sound. The problem lies in the difficulties of applying the NPV approach in a CIM investment decision. Some of these difficulties are listed here.[4]

---

[4]This section is based on discussions in R. Kaplan, "Must CIM Be Justified by Faith Alone?" *Harvard Business Review* 64, no. 2 (March 1986), pp. 87–95; Callie Berliner and James A. Brimson, eds., *Cost Management for Today's Advanced Manufacturing* (Boston: Harvard Business School Press, 1988), pp. 16–18, 36–38, 150; and Jean L. Noble, "A New Approach for Justifying Computer-Integrated Manufacturing," *Journal of Cost Management* 3, no. 4 (Winter 1990), pp. 14–19.

1. *Hurdle rates that are too high.* Sometimes managers have a tendency to set hurdle rates that are too high in a CIM investment analysis. They tend to forget that the purpose of discounting in the NPV model is to account for the time value of money. The appropriate hurdle rate for any investment decision is the investment opportunity rate for alternative investment projects of equivalent risk. In many cases managers tend to overstate this rate.

2. *Time horizons that are too short.* Another common mistake is to evaluate a CIM investment proposal with too short a time horizon. The acquisition cost of a CIM system can be enormous, and the benefits may be realized over a lengthy period of time.

3. *Bias toward incremental projects.* Most firms require that large investments be authorized by managers at higher levels than are required for smaller investments. One result of this sensible practice is an incentive for lower-level managers to request relatively small, incremental improvements in the manufacturing process rather than a large, comprehensive improvement, such as a move to CIM. In many cases, a series of such incremental improvements will not bring about the benefits that could be attained with a full commitment to advanced manufacturing technology.

4. *Greater uncertainty about operating cash flows.* Managers often have greater uncertainty about the cash flows that will result when an advanced manufacturing system is implemented. This increased uncertainty is due to the complexity of the machinery and the firm's inexperience with such advanced technology.

5. *Exclusion of benefits that are difficult to quantify.* The benefits to the firm from JIT and CIM systems are extensive. Some are easy to estimate, such as lower inventory levels, less floor space, and improved product quality. Others that can be even more significant are often difficult to quantify. Some of these benefits are listed below.

   a. *Greater flexibility in the production process.* A flexible manufacturing system cell often can produce runs of several distinct products in the same day. Flexible manufacturing systems also allow engineering changes to be made more easily as products are adapted to changing customer preferences.

   b. *Shorter cycle times and reduced lead times* are possible with an FMS. This enables the firm to fill customer orders more quickly.

   c. *Reduction of non-value-added costs* often results when JIT and FMS systems are adopted. Part of the philosophy of these systems is to encourage employees to seek out activities that can be made more efficient or eliminated.

   d. *Reduced inventory levels* result in savings on working capital investment, less storage space, and reduced obsolescence.

   e. *Lower floor-space requirements* in a flexible manufacturing system require less space than several stand-alone machines.

   f. *Product quality* becomes higher and more constant because of advanced manufacturing systems.

Although it is difficult to quantify these benefits, few managers doubt their existence. Excluding them from an NPV analysis means they are being valued at zero. In many cases it would be preferable to make some estimate of these benefits, however crude it may be, than to ignore them. If a manager believes it is impossible to make such an estimate, then the investment criteria should be expanded to consider these intangible benefits along with a proposal's NPV.

Chapter Summary

LO1 Use the net-present-value method and the internal-rate-of-return method to evaluate an investment proposal. Under the net-present-value method, an investment proposal should be accepted if its net present value is zero or positive. A project's net present value is the present value of the project's future cash flows, less its initial acquisition cost. In computing the present value of the cash flows, the discount rate is the organization's cost of acquiring investment capital. Under the internal-rate-of-return method, an investment proposal should be accepted if its internal rate of return equals or exceeds the organization's hurdle rate. A project's internal rate of return is the discount rate required to make the project's net present value equal to zero.

LO2 Compare the net-present-value and internal-rate-of-return methods, and state the assumptions underlying each method. The net-present-value method is somewhat easier to apply. It also has the advantage of allowing the decision maker to adjust the discount rate upward for highly uncertain cash flows. Both the net-present-value method and the internal-rate-of-return method are based on important assumptions, including the following: (1) All cash flows are assumed to occur at year-end. (2) Cash flow amounts are assumed to be certain. (3) Cash flows are assumed to be reinvested immediately in another return-generating project. (4) A perfect capital market is assumed.

LO3 Use both the total-cost approach and the incremental-cost approach to evaluate an investment proposal. Under the total-cost approach, all projects' cash flows are included in the analysis at their total amounts. Under the incremental-cost approach, the differences in each cash flow, between alternatives, are included in the analysis.

LO4 Determine the after-tax cash flows in an investment analysis. For financial items that are both cash flows and on the income statement, the cash flow is multiplied by 1 minus the tax rate to compute the after-tax cash flow. For financial items that are not cash flows but are on the income statement, the cash flow is multiplied by the tax rate to compute the relevant after-tax cash flow. For financial items that are cash flows but are not on the income statement, the cash flow is multiplied by 1 to determine the after-tax cash flow. (In other words, for these items, the cash flow is already on an after-tax basis.)

LO5 Use an accelerated tax depreciation system to determine an asset's depreciation schedule for tax purposes. The U.S. tax-law-based depreciation schedule, known as MACRS, serves as an example. It places every asset in one of eight classes and then states the depreciation rate for each year in the asset's depreciable life.

LO6 Evaluate an investment proposal using a discounted-cash-flow analysis, giving full consideration to income-tax issues. For any organization subject to income taxes, the first step in a discounted-cash-flow analysis is to determine the after-tax cash flows related to the investment proposal under consideration. Then these after-tax cash flows are discounted in accordance with the net-present-value method or the internal-rate-of-return method.

LO7 Discuss the difficulty of ranking investment proposals, and use the profitability index. No valid method exists for ranking independent investment projects with positive net present values. In theory, *all* projects with positive net present values should be accepted, because the returns expected for the projects exceed the company's cost of capital. Nevertheless, in practice, managers often do attempt to rank investment projects. One commonly used criterion for such rankings is the profitability index, which is defined as follows: present value of a project's cash flows, exclusive of the initial investment, divided by the project's initial investment.

LO8 Use the payback method and accounting-rate-of-return method to evaluate capital investment projects. A project's payback period is its initial investment divided by the annual after-tax cash inflow. As explained in the chapter, for projects with uneven cash flows, the payback period requires a more complex calculation. A project's accounting rate of return is computed as follows: (the project's average incremental revenue minus its average incremental expenses, including depreciation and income taxes) divided by the project's initial investment. Since these methods do not account for the time value of money, they are conceptually inferior to discounted-cash-flow methods. However, many organizations use these methods in conjunction with the NPV or IRR method.

LO9 Describe the impact of activity-based costing and advanced manufacturing technology on capital-budgeting decisions. The validity of any discounted-cash-flow analysis depends on the accuracy of the cash-flow estimates. Activity-based costing systems generally improve the cost analyst's ability to accurately estimate projects' cash flows. Some observers argue that, for a variety of reasons, discounted-cash-flow analyses tend to underestimate the benefits of investing in advanced manufacturing technology.

LO10 Explain the impact of inflation on a capital-budgeting analysis (Appendix B). Inflation (a decline in the purchasing power of a monetary unit) can be incorporated in a discounted-cash-flow analysis in either of two ways: (1) The cash flows are measured in nominal dollars, and the nominal interest rate is used to compute the nominal discount rate. (2) The cash flows are measured in real dollars, and the real interest rate is used to compute the real discount rate.

Review Problems on Capital Expenditure Decisions

Problem 1

Bay City's Department of Public Works (DPW) is considering the replacement of some machinery. This machinery has zero book value but its current market value is $960. One possible alternative is to invest in new machinery, which has a cost of $46,800. This new machinery would produce estimated annual operating cash savings of $15,000. The estimated useful life of the new machinery is four years. The DPW uses straight-line depreciation. The new machinery has an estimated salvage value of $2,400 at the end of four years. The investment in the new machinery would require an additional investment in working capital of $3,600, which would be recovered after four years.

If the DPW accepts this investment proposal, disposal of the old machinery and investment in the new equipment will take place on December 31, 20x4. The cash flows from the investment will occur during the calendar years 20x5 through 20x8.

Required: Prepare a net-present-value analysis of the county DPW's machinery replacement decision. The city has a 10 percent hurdle rate.

Problem 2

River City Pool Company recently purchased a truck for $40,000. The first year's depreciation was $8,000. The truck driver's salary in the first year of operation was $42,000.

Required: Show how each of the amounts mentioned above should be converted to an after-tax amount. The company's tax rate is 35 percent.

Solutions to Review Problems
Problem 1

	Time 0	Time 1	Time 2	Time 3	Time 4
Acquisition cost	$(46,800)				
Investment in working capital	(3,600)				
Recovery of working capital					$ 3,600
Salvage value of old machinery	960				
Salvage value of new machinery					2,400
Annual operating cash savings		$15,000	$15,000	$15,000	15,000
Total cash flow	$(49,440)	$15,000	$15,000	$15,000	$21,000
Discount factor*	× 1.000	× .909	× .826	× .751	× .683
Present value	$(49,440)	$13,635	$12,390	$11,265	$14,343
Net present value			Sum = $2,193		

* The discount factors are from Table III in Appendix A (r = .10)

Conclusion: The DPW's proposed investment in new machinery has a positive net present value and should be accepted.

Problem 2

a. Acquisition cost = $40,000

After-tax cash outflow = $(40,000)

b. Depreciation expense = $8,000

After-tax cash flow = $8,000(.35) = $2,800 savings in cash outflow for taxes

c. Salary expense = $42,000

After-tax cash outflow = ($42,000)(1 − .35) = $(27,300)

Key Terms

For each term's definition refer to the indicated page, or turn to the glossary at the end of the text.

acceptance-or-rejection
  decision, 720
accounting-rate-of-
  return method, 746
after-tax cash flow, 731
capital-budgeting
  decision, 720
capital-rationing
  decision, 720

depreciation tax shield, 733
discounted-cash-flow
  analysis, 721
hurdle rate (or minimum
  desired rate of
  return), 722
internal rate of return (or
  time-adjusted rate of
  return), 722

investment opportunity
  rate, 726
Modified Accelerated
  Cost Recovery System
  (MACRS), 735
net present value, 722
nominal currency,* 757
nominal interest rate,* 756
payback period, 745

postaudit (or
  reappraisal), 730
profitability index (or excess
  present value index), 744
real currency,* 757
real interest rate,* 756
working capital, 738

*Terms appear in Appendix B.

APPENDIX A TO CHAPTER 16

Future Value and Present Value Tables

Table I
Future Value of $1.00
$(1 + r)^n$

Period	4%	6%	8%	10%	12%	14%	20%
1	1.040	1.060	1.080	1.100	1.120	1.140	1.200
2	1.082	1.124	1.166	1.210	1.254	1.300	1.440
3	1.125	1.191	1.260	1.331	1.405	1.482	1.728
4	1.170	1.263	1.361	1.464	1.574	1.689	2.074
5	1.217	1.338	1.469	1.611	1.762	1.925	2.488
6	1.265	1.419	1.587	1.772	1.974	2.195	2.986
7	1.316	1.504	1.714	1.949	2.211	2.502	3.583
8	1.369	1.594	1.851	2.144	2.476	2.853	4.300
9	1.423	1.690	1.999	2.359	2.773	3.252	5.160
10	1.480	1.791	2.159	2.594	3.106	3.707	6.192
11	1.540	1.898	2.332	2.853	3.479	4.226	7.430
12	1.601	2.012	2.518	3.139	3.896	4.818	8.916
13	1.665	2.133	2.720	3.452	4.364	5.492	10.699
14	1.732	2.261	2.937	3.798	4.887	6.261	12.839
15	1.801	2.397	3.172	4.177	5.474	7.138	15.407
20	2.191	3.207	4.661	6.728	9.646	13.743	38.338
30	3.243	5.744	10.063	17.450	29.960	50.950	237.380
40	4.801	10.286	21.725	45.260	93.051	188.880	1,469.800

Period	4%	6%	8%	10%	12%	14%	20%
1	1.000	1.000	1.000	1.000	1.000	1.000	1.000
2	2.040	2.060	2.080	2.100	2.120	2.140	2.220
3	3.122	3.184	3.246	3.310	3.374	3.440	3.640
4	4.247	4.375	4.506	4.641	4.779	4.921	5.368
5	5.416	5.637	5.867	6.105	6.353	6.610	7.442
6	6.633	6.975	7.336	7.716	8.115	8.536	9.930
7	7.898	8.394	8.923	9.487	10.089	10.730	12.916
8	9.214	9.898	10.637	11.436	12.300	13.233	16.499
9	10.583	11.491	12.488	13.580	14.776	16.085	20.799
10	12.006	13.181	14.487	15.938	17.549	19.337	25.959
11	13.486	14.972	16.646	18.531	20.655	23.045	32.150
12	15.026	16.870	18.977	21.385	24.133	27.271	39.580
13	16.627	18.882	21.495	24.523	28.029	32.089	48.497
14	18.292	21.015	24.215	27.976	32.393	37.581	59.196
15	20.024	23.276	27.152	31.773	37.280	43.842	72.035
20	29.778	36.778	45.762	57.276	75.052	91.025	186.690
30	56.085	79.058	113.283	164.496	241.330	356.790	1,181.900
40	95.026	154.762	259.057	442.597	767.090	1,342.000	7,343.900

Table II
Future Value of a Series of $1.00 Cash Flows (Ordinary Annuity)
$$\frac{(1 + r)^n - 1}{r}$$

Period	4%	6%	8%	10%	12%	14%	16%	18%	20%	22%	24%	26%	28%	30%	32%
1	.962	.943	.926	.909	.893	.877	.862	.847	.833	.820	.806	.794	.781	.769	.758
2	.925	.890	.857	.826	.797	.769	.743	.718	.694	.672	.650	.630	.610	.592	.574
3	.889	.840	.794	.751	.712	.675	.641	.609	.579	.551	.524	.500	.477	.455	.435
4	.855	.792	.735	.683	.636	.592	.552	.516	.482	.451	.423	.397	.373	.350	.329
5	.822	.747	.681	.621	.567	.519	.476	.437	.402	.370	.341	.315	.291	.269	.250
6	.790	.705	.630	.564	.507	.456	.410	.370	.335	.303	.275	.250	.227	.207	.189
7	.760	.665	.583	.513	.452	.400	.354	.314	.279	.249	.222	.198	.178	.159	.143
8	.731	.627	.540	.467	.404	.351	.305	.266	.233	.204	.179	.157	.139	.123	.108
9	.703	.592	.500	.424	.361	.308	.263	.225	.194	.167	.144	.125	.108	.094	.082
10	.676	.558	.463	.386	.322	.270	.227	.191	.162	.137	.116	.099	.085	.073	.062
11	.650	.527	.429	.350	.287	.237	.195	.162	.135	.112	.094	.079	.066	.056	.047
12	.625	.497	.397	.319	.257	.208	.168	.137	.112	.092	.076	.062	.052	.043	.036
13	.601	.469	.368	.290	.229	.182	.145	.116	.093	.075	.061	.050	.040	.033	.027
14	.577	.442	.340	.263	.205	.160	.125	.099	.078	.062	.049	.039	.032	.025	.021
15	.555	.417	.315	.239	.183	.140	.108	.084	.065	.051	.040	.031	.025	.020	.016
20	.456	.312	.215	.149	.104	.073	.051	.037	.026	.019	.014	.010	.007	.005	.004
30	.308	.174	.099	.057	.033	.020	.012	.007	.004	.003	.002	.001	.001	—	—
40	.208	.097	.046	.022	.011	.005	.003	.001	.001	—	—	—	—	—	—

Table III
Present Value of $1.00
$$\frac{1}{(1 + r)^n}$$

Period	4%	6%	8%	10%	12%	14%	16%	18%	20%	22%	24%	25%	26%	28%	30%
1	0.962	0.943	0.926	0.909	0.893	0.877	0.862	0.847	0.833	0.820	0.806	0.800	0.794	0.781	0.769
2	1.886	1.833	1.783	1.736	1.690	1.647	1.605	1.566	1.528	1.492	1.457	1.440	1.424	1.392	1.361
3	2.775	2.673	2.577	2.487	2.402	2.322	2.246	2.174	2.106	2.042	1.981	1.952	1.923	1.868	1.816
4	3.630	3.465	3.312	3.170	3.037	2.914	2.798	2.690	2.589	2.494	2.404	2.362	2.320	2.241	2.166
5	4.452	4.212	3.993	3.791	3.605	3.433	3.274	3.127	2.991	2.864	2.745	2.689	2.635	2.532	2.436
6	5.242	4.917	4.623	4.355	4.111	3.889	3.685	3.498	3.326	3.167	3.020	2.951	2.885	2.759	2.643
7	6.002	5.582	5.206	4.868	4.564	4.288	4.039	3.812	3.605	3.416	3.242	3.161	3.083	2.937	2.802
8	6.733	6.210	5.747	5.335	4.968	4.639	4.344	4.078	3.837	3.619	3.421	3.329	3.241	3.076	2.925
9	7.435	6.802	6.247	5.759	5.328	4.946	4.607	4.303	4.031	3.786	3.566	3.463	3.366	3.184	3.019
10	8.111	7.360	6.710	6.145	5.650	5.216	4.833	4.494	4.192	3.923	3.682	3.571	3.465	3.269	3.092
11	8.760	7.887	7.139	6.495	5.938	5.453	5.029	4.656	4.327	4.035	3.776	3.656	3.544	3.335	3.147
12	9.385	8.384	7.536	6.814	6.194	5.660	5.197	4.793	4.439	4.127	3.851	3.725	3.606	3.387	3.190
13	9.986	8.853	7.904	7.103	6.424	5.842	5.342	4.910	4.533	4.203	3.912	3.780	3.656	3.427	3.223
14	10.563	9.295	8.244	7.367	6.628	6.002	5.468	5.008	4.611	4.265	3.962	3.824	3.695	3.459	3.249
15	11.118	9.712	8.559	7.606	6.811	6.142	5.575	5.092	4.675	4.315	4.001	3.859	3.726	3.483	3.268
20	13.590	11.470	9.818	8.514	7.469	6.623	5.929	5.353	4.870	4.460	4.110	3.954	3.808	3.546	3.316
30	17.292	13.765	11.258	9.427	8.055	7.003	6.177	5.517	4.979	4.534	4.160	3.995	3.842	3.569	3.332
40	19.793	15.046	11.925	9.779	8.244	7.105	6.234	5.548	4.997	4.544	4.166	3.999	3.846	3.571	3.333

Table IV
Present Value of Series of
$1.00 Cash Flows
$$\frac{1}{r}\left(1 - \frac{1}{(1 + r^n)}\right)$$

APPENDIX B TO CHAPTER 16

Impact of Inflation

Most countries have experienced inflation to some degree over the past 30 years, and some countries have experienced severe inflation. *Inflation* is defined as a decline in the general purchasing power of a monetary unit, such as a dollar, across time. Since capital-budgeting decisions involve cash flows over several time periods, it is worthwhile to examine the impact of inflation in capital-budgeting analyses.

Inflation can be incorporated in a discounted-cash-flow analysis in either of two ways. Both approaches yield correct results, but the analyst must be careful to be consistent in applying either approach. The two approaches are distinguished by the use of either *nominal* or *real* interest rates and currencies. These terms are defined below.

Interest Rates: Real or Nominal   The **real interest rate** is the underlying interest rate, which includes compensation to investors for the *time value of money* and the *risk* of an investment. The **nominal interest rate** includes the real interest rate, plus an additional premium to compensate investors for inflation. Suppose the real interest rate is 10 percent, and inflation of 5 percent is projected. Then the nominal interest rate is determined as follows:[5]

Real interest rate	.10
Inflation rate	.05
Combined effect (.10 × .05)	.005
Nominal interest rate	.155

---

[5]An alternative way to compute the nominal interest rate is: $(1.10 \times 1.05) - 1.00 = .155$.

Currency: Real or Nominal A cash flow measured in **nominal currency** is the actual cash flow we observe. For example, a particular model of automobile cost $10,000 in year 1 but it cost $12,155 in year 5. Both the $10,000 cash flow in year 1 and $12,155 cash flow in year 5 are measured in *nominal currency*. A cash flow measured in **real currency** reflects an adjustment for the currency's purchasing power. The following table shows the relationship between nominal and real currency, assuming an inflation rate of 5 percent.

Year	(a) Cash Flow in Nominal Currency	(b) Price Index	(c) = (a) ÷ (b) Cash Flow in Real Currency
Year 1	$10,000	1.0000	$10,000
Year 2	10,500	$(1.05)^1 = 1.0500$	10,000
Year 3	11,025	$(1.05)^2 = 1.1025$	10,000
Year 4	11,576	$(1.05)^3 = 1.1576$	10,000
Year 5	12,155	$(1.05)^4 = 1.2155$	10,000

As the table shows, cash flows in nominal currency must be deflated, which means dividing by the price index, to convert them to cash flows in real currency. The real-currency cash flows are expressed in year 1 currency.

Two Capital-Budgeting Approaches under Inflation

A correct capital-budgeting analysis may be done using either of the following approaches.

1. Use cash flows measured in *nominal currency* and a nominal interest rate to determine the *nominal discount rate*.
2. Use cash flows measured in *real currency* and a real interest rate to determine the *real discount rate*.

To illustrate these two approaches, we will focus on an equipment-replacement decision faced by the management of High Country Department Stores. The company operates an appliance-repair service for the household appliances it sells. Management is considering the replacement of a sophisticated piece of testing equipment used in repairing TVs and VCRs. The new equipment costs $5,000 and will have no salvage value. Over its four-year life, the new equipment is expected to generate the cost savings and depreciation tax shield shown below. The cash flows in column (f) of the table are the total after-tax cash inflows, measured in *nominal currency*.

HIGH COUNTRY
DEPARTMENT STORES

Measured in Nominal Currency

Year	(a) Acquisition Cost	(b) Cost Savings	(c) After-Tax Cost Savings [(b) × (1 − .40)]	(d) MACRS Depreciation (3-year class)	(e) Depreciation Tax Shield [(d) × .40]	(f) Total After-Tax Cash Flow [(c) + (e)]
Year 1	$(5,000)					
Year 2		$1,900	$1,140	$1,667	$667	$1,807
Year 3		2,000	1,200	2,223	889	2,089
Year 4		2,100	1,260	740	296	1,556
Year 5		2,500	1,500	370	148	1,648

Approach 1: Nominal Currency and Nominal Discount Rate Under this capital-budgeting approach, we discount the nominal-currency cash flows in the preceding table using the nominal discount rate of 15.5 percent. The net-present-value analysis is as follows:

Year	(a) Cash Flow in Nominal Currency	(b) Discount Factor for Nominal Discount Rate of 15.5%	(c) = (a) × (b) Present Value
Year 1	$(5,000)	1.000	$(5,000)
Year 2	1,807	.8658 [1/(1.155)]*	1,564
Year 3	2,089	.7496 [1/(1.155)²]	1,565
Year 4	1,556	.6490 [1/(1.155)³]	1,009
Year 5	1,648	.5619 [1/(1.155)⁴]	926
Net present value			$ 64

* The 15.5% discount factors are computed using the formula in Table III of Appendix A.

High Country's management should purchase the new testing equipment, since its NPV is positive.

Approach 2: Real Currency and Real Discount Rate   Under this capital-budgeting approach, we first convert the cash flows measured in nominal currency to cash flows in real currency, as follows:

Year	(a) After-Tax Cash Flow in Nominal Currency	(b) Price Index	(c) = (a) ÷ (b) After-Tax Cash Flow in Real Currency*
Year 1	$(5,000)	1.0000	$(5,000)
Year 2	1,807	1.0500	1,721
Year 3	2,089	1.1025	1,895
Year 4	1,556	1.1576	1,344
Year 5	1,648	1.2155	1,356

* Real-currency cash flows expressed in terms of year 1 currency.

Now we discount the after-tax cash flows, measured in real currency, using the real discount rate of 10 percent. The net-present-value analysis is shown below.

Year	(a) Cash Flow in Real Currency	(b) Discount Factor for Real Discount Rate of 10%	(c) = (a) × (b) Present Value
Year 1	$(5,000)	1.000	$(5,000)
Year 2	1,721	.909	1,564
Year 3	1,895	.826	1,565
Year 4	1,344	.751	1,009
Year 5	1,356	.683	926
Net present value			$ 64

Notice that the new testing equipment's NPV is the same under both capital-budgeting approaches. Under both approaches, we conclude that High Country Department Stores should purchase the new equipment.

Consistency Is the Key   Either capital-budgeting approach will provide the correct conclusion, as long as it is applied consistently. Use either nominal currency and a nominal discount rate or real currency and a real discount rate. A common error in capital budgeting is to convert the after-tax cash flows to real currency, but then use the nominal discount rate. This faulty analysis creates a bias against acceptance of worthwhile projects.

To illustrate, suppose High Country's management had made this error in its testing-equipment analysis. The following *incorrect* analysis is the result.

Incorrect Analysis of Testing-Equipment Decision

Inconsistency

Year	(a) Cash Flow in Real Currency	(b) Discount Factor for Nominal Discount Rate of 15.5%	(c) = (a) × (b) Present Value
Year 1	$(5,000)	1.0000	$(5,000)
Year 2	1,721	.8658	1,490
Year 3	1,895	.7496	1,420
Year 4	1,344	.6490	872
Year 5	1,356	.5619	762
Net present value			$ (456)

This inconsistent and incorrect analysis will lead High Country's management to the wrong conclusion.

Review Questions

Note: Review questions 1 through 10 relate to Section 1 of the chapter. Questions 11 through 18 relate to Section 2, and questions 19 through 22 relate to Section 3. Question 23 relates to Appendix B.

16–1. "Time is money!" is an old saying. Relate this statement to the evaluation of capital-investment projects.

16–2. Distinguish between the following two types of capital-budgeting decisions: acceptance-or-rejection decisions and capital-rationing decisions.

16–3. "The greater the discount rate, the greater the present value of a future cash flow." True or false? Explain your answer.

16–4. Briefly explain the concept of *discounted-cash-flow analysis*. What are the two common methods of discounted-cash-flow analysis?

16–5. State the decision rule used to accept or reject an investment proposal under each of these methods of analysis: (1) net-present-value method and (2) internal-rate-of-return method.

16–6. Explain the following terms: *recovery of investment* versus *return on investment*.

16–7. List and briefly explain two advantages that the net-present-value method has over the internal-rate-of-return method.

16–8. List and briefly explain four assumptions underlying discounted-cash-flow analysis.

16–9. Distinguish between the following approaches to discounted-cash-flow analysis: total-cost approach versus incremental-cost approach.

16–10. What is meant by a *postaudit* of an investment project?

16–11. Give an example of a noncash expense. What impact does such an expense have in a capital-budgeting analysis? Explain how to compute the after-tax impact of a noncash expense.

16–12. Explain how to compute the after-tax amount of a cash revenue or expense.

16–13. What is a *depreciation tax shield?* Explain the effect of a depreciation tax shield in a capital-budgeting analysis.

16–14. Give an example of a cash flow that is not on the income statement. How do you determine the after-tax amount of such a cash flow?

16–15. Why is accelerated depreciation advantageous to a business?

16–16. Explain how a gain or loss on disposal is handled in a capital-budgeting analysis.

16–17. Why may the net-present-value and internal-rate-of-return methods yield different rankings for investments with different lives?

16–18. Define the term *profitability index*. How is it used in ranking investment proposals?

16–19. What is meant by the term *payback period?* How is this criterion sometimes used in capital budgeting?

16–20. What are the two main drawbacks of the payback method?

16–21. How is an investment project's *accounting rate of return* defined? Why do the accounting rate of return and internal rate of return on a capital project generally differ?

16–22. Discuss the pros and cons of the accounting rate of return as an investment criterion.

16–23. (Appendix B) Briefly describe two correct methods of net-present-value analysis in an inflationary period.

Exercises

All applicable Exercises are available with McGraw-Hill's *Connect Accounting*™.

Note: Several exercises on the basics of compound interest and the concept of present value are included in Appendix II, which appears at the end of the text. See pages 807–813.

Jack and Jill's Place is a nonprofit nursery school run by the parents of the enrolled children. Since the school is out of town, its water comes from a well rather than a city water supply. Lately, the well has become unreliable, and the school has had to bring in bottled drinking water. The school's governing board is considering drilling a new well (at the top of the hill, naturally). A new well would cost $3,687 and save the school $600 annually for 10 years. The school's hurdle rate is 8 percent.

■ **Exercise 16–24**
Net Present Value (Section 1)
(LO 1)

Required: Compute the new well's net present value. Should the governing board approve the new well?

Refer to the data given in the preceding exercise.

■ **Exercise 16–25**
Internal Rate of Return (Section 1)
(LO 1)

Required: Compute the internal rate of return on the new well. Should the governing board approve the new well?

■ **Exercise 16–26**
Internal Rate of Return;
Uneven Cash Flows
(Section 1)
(LO 1)

The trustees of the Danube School of Art and Music, located in Tuttlingen, Germany, are considering a major overhaul of the school's audio system. With or without the overhaul, the system will be replaced in two years. If an overhaul is done now, the trustees expect to save the following repair costs during the next two years: year 1, $3,000; year 2, $5,000. The overhaul will cost $6,664.

Required: Use trial and error to compute the internal rate of return on the proposed overhaul. (*Hint:* The NPV of the overhaul is positive if an 8 percent discount rate is used, but the NPV is negative if a 16 percent rate is used.)

■ **Exercise 16–27**
Use of Internet; City
Government; Capital
Projects (Section 1)
(LO 1)

Use the internet to access the home page for the City of Chicago, www.ci.chi.il.us. Use one of the links there to access the home page for one of Chicago's sister organizations, such as the following:

Chicago Housing Authority	www.thecha.org
Chicago Park District	www.chicagoparkdistrict.com
Chicago Public Schools	www.cps.k12.il.us
Chicago Transit Authority	www.transitchicago.com

Each of these linked pages contains information about the organization's budget and its capital projects. Read about one or more of these capital projects, and then discuss how the organization's managers should go about making significant decisions about expenditures for major capital projects like the one you have explored.

■ **Exercise 16–28**
New Present Value with
Different Discount Rates
(Section 1)
(LO 1)

Vancouver Shakespearean Theater's board of directors is considering the replacement of the theater's lighting system. The old system requires two people to operate it, but the new system would require only a single operator. The new lighting system will cost $129,750 and save the theater $27,000 annually for the next eight years.

Required:

1. Prepare a table showing the proposed lighting system's net present value for each of the following discount rates: 8 percent, 10 percent, 12 percent, 14 percent, and 16 percent. Use the following headings in your table. Comment on the pattern in the right-hand column.

Discount Rate	Annuity Discount Factor	Annual Savings	Present Value of Annual Savings	Acquisition Cost	Net Present Value

2. *Build a spreadsheet:* Construct an Excel spreadsheet to solve the preceding requirement. Show how the solution will change if the following information changes: the new lighting system will cost $131,000, and the annual savings amount to $27,500.

■ **Exercise 16–29**
Sensitivity Analysis; NPV
(Section 1)
(LO 1)

Refer to the data given in the preceding exercise. Suppose the Vancouver Shakespearean Theater's board is uncertain about the cost savings with the new lighting system.

Required: How low could the new lighting system's annual savings be and still justify acceptance of the proposal by the board of directors? Assume the theater's hurdle rate is 12 percent.

■ **Exercise 16–30**
After-Tax Cash Flows
(Section 2)
(LO 4)

Daly Publishing Corporation recently purchased a truck for $40,000. Under MACRS, the first year's depreciation was $8,000. The truck driver's salary in the first year of operation was $45,000.

Required: Show how each of the amounts mentioned above should be converted to an after-tax amount. The company's tax rate is 30 percent.

■ **Exercise 16–31**
Using an accelerated tax
depreciation system
(Section 2)
(LO 5)

For each of the following assets, indicate the property class and depreciation method under the U.S. tax code's MACRS depreciation system.

1. A pharmaceutical company bought a new microscope to use in its Research and Development Division.
2. A farmer constructed a new barn to house cattle.
3. A steel fabrication company bought a machine, which is expected to be useful for 18 years.

4. The president of an insurance company authorized the purchase of a new desk for her office.

5. A pizza restaurant purchased a new delivery car.

In December of 20x4, Atlas Chemical Corporation sold a forklift for $9,255. The machine was purchased in 20x1 for $50,000. Since then $38,845 in depreciation has been recorded on the forklift.

Required:

1. What was the forklift's book value at the time of sale?

2. Compute the gain or loss on the sale.

3. Determine the after-tax cash flow at the time the forklift was sold. The firm's tax rate is 45 percent.

Sharpe Machining Company purchased industrial tools costing $100,000, which fall in the 3-year property class under MACRS.

Required:

1. Prepare a schedule of depreciation deductions assuming:

   a. The firm uses the accelerated depreciation schedule specified by MACRS.

   b. The firm uses the optional straight-line depreciation method and the half-year convention.

2. Calculate the present value of the depreciation tax shield under each depreciation method listed in requirement (1). Sharpe Machining Company's after-tax hurdle rate is 12 percent, and the firm's tax rate is 30 percent.

The owner of Turkish Delight Confectionary is considering the purchase of a new semiautomatic candy machine. The machine will cost $24,000 and last 10 years. The machine is expected to have no salvage value at the end of its useful life. The owner projects that the new candy machine will generate $4,000 in after-tax savings each year during its life (including the depreciation tax shield).

Required: Compute the profitability index on the proposed candy machine, assuming an after-tax hurdle rate of: (*a*) 8 percent, (*b*) 10 percent, and (*c*) 12 percent.

The management of Niagra National Bank is considering an investment in additional automatic teller machines. The machines would cost $124,200 and have a useful life of seven years. The bank's controller has estimated that the automatic teller machines will save the bank $27,000 after taxes during each year of their life (including the depreciation tax shield). The machines will have no salvage value.

Required:

1. Compute the payback period for the proposed investment.

2. Compute the net present value of the proposed investment assuming an after-tax hurdle rate of: (*a*) 10 percent, (*b*) 12 percent, and (*c*) 14 percent.

3. What can you conclude from your answers to requirements (1) and (2) about the limitations of the payback method?

4. *Build a spreadsheet:* Construct an Excel spreadsheet to solve requirements (1) and (2) above. Show how the solution will change if the following information changes: the machines would cost $134,400, and the annual savings amount to $28,000.

Security Insurance Company's management is considering an advertising program that would require an initial expenditure of $165,500 and bring in additional sales over the next five years. The projected additional sales revenue in year 1 is $75,000, with associated expenses of $25,000. The additional sales revenue and expenses from the advertising program are projected to increase by 10 percent each year. Security's tax rate is 40 percent. (*Hint:* The $165,500 advertising cost is an expense.)

Required:

1. Compute the payback period for the advertising program.

2. Calculate the advertising program's net present value, assuming an after-tax hurdle rate of 10 percent.

Metro Car Washes, Inc. is reviewing an investment proposal. The initial cost as well as the estimate of the book value of the investment at the end of each year, the net after-tax cash flows for each year, and the net income for each year are presented in the following schedule. The salvage value of the investment at the end of each year is equal to its book value. There would be no salvage value at the end of the investment's life.

Year	Initial Cost and Book Value	Annual Net After-Tax Cash Flows	Annual Net Income
0	$105,000		
1	70,000	$50,000	$15,000
2	42,000	45,000	17,000
3	21,000	40,000	19,000
4	7,000	35,000	21,000
5	0	30,000	23,000

Management uses a 16 percent after-tax target rate of return for new investment proposals.

Required: For requirement (1) *only*, assume that the cash flows in years 1 through 5 occur uniformly throughout each year.

1. Compute the project's payback period.
2. Calculate the accounting rate of return on the investment proposal. Base your calculation on the initial cost of the investment.
3. Compute the proposal's net present value.

(CMA, adapted)

■ **Exercise 16–38**
Inflation and Capital Budgeting (Appendix B)
(LO 10)

The Ministry of Education is considering the purchase of a new computer system for $110,000. A cost study indicates that the new computer should save the Ministry $30,000, measured in real dollars, during each of the next eight years.

The real interest rate is 20 percent and the inflation rate is 10 percent. As a governmental agency, the Ministry of Education pays no taxes.

Required:

1. Prepare a schedule of cash flows measured in real dollars. Include the initial acquisition and the cost savings for each of the next eight years.
2. Using cash flows measured in real dollars, compute the net present value of the proposed computer. Use a real discount rate equal to the real interest rate.

■ **Exercise 16–39**
Inflation and Capital Budgeting (Appendix B)
(LO 10)

Refer to the data in the preceding exercise.

Required:

1. Compute the nominal interest rate.
2. Prepare a schedule of cash flows measured in nominal dollars.
3. Using cash flows measured in nominal dollars, compute the net present value of the proposed computer. Use a nominal discount rate equal to the nominal interest rate.

Problems

All applicable Problems are available with McGraw-Hill's *Connect Accounting*™.

■ **Problem 16–40**
County Government; Net-Present-Value Analysis (Section 1)
(LO 1, 3, 6)

Net present value: $5,829

The supervisor of the regional Department of Transportation (DOT) is considering the replacement of some machinery. This machinery has zero book value but its current market value is $800. One possible alternative is to invest in new machinery, which has a cost of $35,000. This new machinery would produce estimated annual operating cash savings of $12,500. The estimated useful life of the new machinery is four years. The DOT uses straight-line depreciation. The new machinery has an estimated salvage value of $2,000 at the end of four years. The investment in the new machinery would require an additional investment in working capital of $3,000, which would be recovered after four years.

If the DOT accepts this investment proposal, disposal of the old machinery and investment in the new equipment will take place on December 31, 20x1. The cash flows from the investment will occur during the calendar years 20x2 through 20x5.

Required: Prepare a net-present-value analysis of the county DOT's machinery replacement decision. The county has a 10 percent hurdle rate.

(CMA, adapted)

The chief ranger of the state's Department of Natural Resources is considering a new plan for fighting forest fires in the state's forest lands. The current plan uses eight fire-control stations, which are scattered throughout the interior of the state forest. Each station has a four-person staff, whose annual compensation totals $200,000. Other costs of operating each base amount to $100,000 per year. The equipment at each base has a current salvage value of $120,000. The buildings at these interior stations have no other use. To demolish them would cost $10,000 each.

The chief ranger is considering an alternative plan, which involves four fire-control stations located on the perimeter of the state forest. Each station would require a six-person staff, with annual compensation costs of $300,000. Other operating costs would be $110,000 per base. Building each perimeter station would cost $200,000. The perimeter bases would need helicopters and other equipment costing $500,000 per station. Half of the equipment from the interior stations could be used at the perimeter stations. Therefore, only half of the equipment at the interior stations would be sold if the perimeter stations were built.

The state uses a 10 percent hurdle rate for all capital projects.

Required:

1. Use the total-cost approach to prepare a net-present-value analysis of the chief ranger's two fire-control plans. Assume that the interior fire-control stations will be demolished if the perimeter plan is selected. The chief ranger has decided to use a 10-year time period for the analysis.
2. What qualitative factors would the chief ranger be likely to consider in making this decision?

Refer to the data in the preceding problem.

Required: Use the incremental-cost approach to prepare a net-present-value analysis of the chief ranger's decision between the interior fire-control plan and the perimeter fire-control plan.

Kagoshima Regional Hospital is a nonprofit hospital operated by the prefecture government. The hospital's administrator is considering a proposal to open a new outpatient clinic in the nearby city of Ibusuki. The administrator has made the following estimates pertinent to the proposal.

1. Construction of the Ibusuki clinic building will cost $780,000 in two equal installments of $440,000, to be paid at the end of 20x0 and 20x1. The clinic will open on January 2, 20x2. All staffing and operating costs begin in 20x2.
2. Equipment for the clinic will cost $150,000, to be paid in December of 20x1.
3. Staffing of the clinic will cost $800,000 per year.
4. Other operating costs at the clinic will be $200,000 per year.
5. Opening the clinic is expected to increase charitable contributions to the hospital by $250,000 per year.
6. The clinic is expected to reduce costs at Kagoshima Regional Hospital. Annual cost savings at the hospital are projected to be $1,000,000.
7. A major refurbishment of the clinic is expected to be necessary toward the end of 20x5. This work will cost $180,000.
8. Due to shifting medical needs in the county, the administrator doubts the clinic will be needed after 20x9.
9. The clinic building and equipment could be sold for $290,000 at the end of 20x9.
10. The hospital's hurdle rate is 12 percent.

Required:

1. Compute the cash flows for each year relevant to the analysis.
2. Prepare a table of cash flows, by year, similar to Exhibit 16–4.

■ Problem 16–41
Net Present Value; Total-Cost Approach (Section 1)
(LO 1, 3)

Difference in NPV of costs: $(2,270,200)

■ Problem 16–42
Net Present Value; Incremental-Cost Approach (Section 1)
(LO 1, 3)

Net present value of excess cash outflows with interior stations: $(2,270,200)

■ Problem 16–43
Net-Present-Value Analysis; Hospital (Section 1)
(LO 1, 3)

Net present value: $144,760

3. Compute the net present value of the proposed Ibusuki outpatient clinic.

4. Should the administrator recommend to the hospital's trustees that the clinic be built? Why?

5. ***Build a spreadsheet:*** Construct an Excel spreadsheet to solve requirements. (1), (2), and (3) above. Show how the solution will change if the following information changes: staffing will cost $790,000 per year, and the increased charitable contributions will be $265,000.

■ **Problem 16–44**
Net Present Value; Qualitative Issues (Section 1)
(LO 1, 3)

1. Old machine, net present value: $(494,605)

Special People Industries (SPI) is a nonprofit organization that employs only people with physical or mental disabilities. One of the organization's activities is to make cookies for its snack food store. Several years ago, Special People Industries purchased a special cookie-cutting machine. As of December 31, 20x0, this machine will have been used for three years. Management is considering the purchase of a newer, more efficient machine. If purchased, the new machine would be acquired on December 31, 20x0. Management expects to sell 300,000 dozen cookies in each of the next six years. The selling price of the cookies is expected to average $1.15 per dozen.

Special People Industries has two options: continue to operate the old machine or sell the old machine and purchase the new machine. No trade-in was offered by the seller of the new machine. The following information has been assembled to help management decide which option is more desirable.

	Old Machine	New Machine
Original cost of machine at acquisition	$80,000	$120,000
Remaining useful life as of December 31, 20x0	6 years	6 years
Expected annual cash operating expenses:		
Variable cost per dozen	$.38	$.29
Total fixed costs	$21,000	$ 11,000
Estimated cash value of machines:		
December 31, 20x0	$40,000	$120,000
December 31, 20x6	$ 7,000	$ 20,000

Assume that all operating revenues and expenses occur at the end of the year.

Required:

1. Use the net-present-value method to determine whether Special People Industries should retain the old machine or acquire the new machine. The organization's hurdle rate is 16 percent.

2. Independent of your answer to requirement (1), suppose the quantitative differences are so slight between the two alternatives that management is indifferent between the two proposals. Write a memo to the president of SPI that identifies and discusses any nonquantitative factors that management should consider.

(CMA, adapted)

■ **Problem 16–45**
Internal Rate of Return; Even Cash Flows (Section 1)
(LO 1, 3)

1. Initial cost of investment: $(429,440)

Wellington County's Board of Representatives is considering the construction of a longer runway at the county airport. Currently, the airport can handle only private aircraft and small commuter jets. A new, long runway would enable the airport to handle the midsize jets used on many domestic flights. Data pertinent to the board's decision appear below.

Cost of acquiring additional land for runway	$ 70,000
Cost of runway construction	200,000
Cost of extending perimeter fence	29,840
Cost of runway lights	39,600
Annual cost of maintaining new runway	28,000
Annual incremental revenue from landing fees	40,000

In addition to the preceding data, two other facts are relevant to the decision. First, a longer runway will require a new snowplow, which will cost $100,000. The old snowplow could be sold now for $10,000. The new, larger plow will cost $12,000 more in annual operating costs. Second, the County Board of Representatives believes that the proposed long runway, and the major jet service it will bring to the county, will increase economic activity in the community. The board projects that the increased economic activity will result in $64,000 per year in additional tax revenue for the county.

In analyzing the runway proposal, the board has decided to use a 10-year time horizon. The county's hurdle rate for capital projects is 12 percent.

Required:

1. Compute the initial cost of the investment in the long runway.
2. Compute the annual net cost or benefit from the runway.
3. Determine the IRR on the proposed long runway. Should it be built?

■ **Problem 16–46**
Net Present Value (Section 1)
(LO 1, 3)

1. Present value of annual benefits: $361,600

Refer to the data given in the preceding problem.

Required:

1. Prepare a net-present-value analysis of the proposed long runway.
2. Should the County Board of Representatives approve the runway?
3. Which of the data used in the analysis are likely to be most uncertain? Least uncertain? Why?

■ **Problem 16–47**
Internal Rate of Return;
Sensitivity Analysis (Section 1)
(LO 1, 3)

Initial cost of investment:
$429,440

Refer to the data given in Problem 16–45. The County Board of Representatives believes that if the county conducts a promotional effort costing $20,000 per year, the proposed long runway will result in substantially greater economic development than was projected originally. However, the board is uncertain about the actual increase in county tax revenue that will result.

Required: Suppose the board builds the long runway and conducts the promotional campaign. What would the increase in the county's annual tax revenue need to be in order for the proposed runway's internal rate of return to equal the county's hurdle rate of 12 percent?

■ **Problem 16–48**
MACRS Depreciation; Present
Value of Tax Shield (Section 2)
(LO 4, 5)

Computer-controlled printing press, present value of tax shield: $81,140

Mind Challenge, Inc. publishes innovative science textbooks for public schools. The company's management recently acquired the following two new pieces of equipment.

*   Computer-controlled printing press: cost, $250,000; expected useful life, 12 years.
*   Duplicating equipment to be used in the administrative offices: cost, $60,000; expected useful life, six years.

The company uses straight-line depreciation for book purposes and the MACRS accelerated depreciation schedule for tax purposes. The firm's tax rate is 45 percent; its after-tax hurdle rate is 10 percent. Neither machine has any salvage value.

Required: For each of the publishing company's new pieces of equipment:

1. Prepare a schedule of the annual depreciation expenses for book purposes.
2. Determine the appropriate MACRS property class.
3. Prepare a schedule of the annual depreciation expenses for tax purposes.
4. Compute the present value of the depreciation tax shield.

■ **Problem 16–49**
After-Tax Cash Flows; NPV
(Section 2)
(LO 3, 4, 5, 6)

1. Total initial cash outflow: $(312,000)

Philadelphia Fastener Corporation manufactures nails, screws, bolts, and other fasteners. Management is considering a proposal to acquire new material-handling equipment. The new equipment has the same capacity as the current equipment but will provide operating efficiencies in labor and power usage. The savings in operating costs are estimated at $150,000 annually.

The new equipment will cost $300,000 and will be purchased at the beginning of the year when the project is started. The equipment dealer is certain that the equipment will be operational during the second quarter of the year it is installed. Therefore, 60 percent of the estimated annual savings can be obtained in the first year. The company will incur a one-time expense of $30,000 to transfer production activities from the old equipment to the new equipment. No loss of sales will occur, however, because the processing facility is large enough to install the new equipment without interfering with the operations of the current equipment. The equipment is in the MACRS 7-year property class. The firm would depreciate the machinery in accordance with the MACRS depreciation schedule.

The current equipment has been fully depreciated. Management has reviewed its condition and has concluded that it can be used an additional eight years. The company would receive $10,000, net of removal costs, if it elected to buy the new equipment and dispose of its current equipment at this time. The new equipment will have no salvage value at the end of its life. The company is subject to a 40 percent income-tax rate and requires an after-tax return of at least 12 percent on any investment.

Required:

1. Calculate the annual incremental after-tax cash flows for Philadelphia Fastener Corporation's proposal to acquire the new equipment.

2. Calculate the net present value of the proposal to acquire the new equipment using the cash flows calculated in requirement (1), and indicate what action management should take. Assume all cash flows take place at the end of the year.

(CMA, adapted)

■ **Problem 16–50**
After-Tax Cash Flows; Robotic Equipment (Section 2)
(LO 4, 5, 6)

Computer expert's salary and fringe benefits (after-tax): $(56,000)
Tax effect of gain on sale: $(15,000)

Scientific Frontiers Corporation manufactures scientific equipment for use in elementary schools. In December of 20x0 the company's management is considering the acquisition of robotic equipment, which would radically change its manufacturing process. The controller has collected the following data pertinent to the decision.

1. The robotic equipment would cost $1,000,000, to be paid in December of 20x0. The equipment's useful life is projected to be eight years. The equipment is in the MACRS 5-year property class. The company will use the MACRS accelerated depreciation schedule.

2. The robotic equipment requires software, which will be developed over a two-year period in 20x1 and 20x2. Each software expenditure, which will amount to $25,000 per year, will be expensed during the year incurred.

3. A computer systems operator will be hired immediately to oversee the operation of the new robotic equipment. The computer expert's annual salary will be $60,000. Fringe benefits will cost $20,000 annually.

4. Maintenance technicians will be needed. The total cost of their wages and fringe benefits will be $150,000 per year.

5. The changeover of the manufacturing line will cost $90,000, to be expensed in 20x1.

6. Several employees will need retraining to operate the new robotic equipment. The training costs are projected as follows:

20x1	$35,000
20x2	25,000
20x3	10,000

7. An inventory of spare parts for the robotic equipment will be purchased immediately at a cost of $60,000. This investment in working capital will be maintained throughout the eight-year life of the equipment. At the end of 20x8, the parts will be sold for $60,000.

8. The robotic equipment's salvage value at the end of 20x8 is projected to be $50,000. It will be fully depreciated at that time.

9. Aside from the costs specifically mentioned above, management expects the robotic equipment to save $480,000 per year in manufacturing costs.

10. Switching to the robotic equipment will enable Scientific Frontiers Corporation to sell some of its manufacturing machinery over the next two years. The following sales schedule is projected.

	Acquisition Cost of Equipment Sold	Accumulated Depreciation at Time of Sale	Sales Proceeds
20x1	$150,000	$100,000	$ 20,000
20x2	305,000	215,000	140,000

11. Scientific Frontiers Corporation's tax rate is 30 percent.

12. The company's after-tax hurdle rate is 12 percent.

Required: Prepare a year-by-year columnar schedule including all of the after-tax cash flows associated with the robotic-equipment decision. Assume that each cash flow will occur at year-end.

■ **Problem 16–51**
Robotic Equipment; Taxes Net Present Value (Section 2)
(LO 3, 4, 6)

Net present value: $68,098

Refer to the data given in the preceding problem.

Required: Compute the net present value of Scientific Frontiers Corporation's proposed acquisition of robotic equipment.

The management of Metroplex Air Taxi is considering the replacement of an old machine used in its helicopter repair facility. It is fully depreciated but it can be used by the corporation through 20x5. If management decides to replace the old machine, James Transportation Company has offered to purchase it for $60,000 on the replacement date. The old machine would have no salvage value in 20x5. If the replacement occurs, a new machine would be acquired from Hillcrest Industries on December 31, 20x1. The purchase price of $1,000,000 for the new machine would be paid in cash at the time of replacement. Due to the increased efficiency of the new machine, estimated annual cash savings of $300,000 would be generated through 20x5, the end of its expected useful life. The new machine is not expected to have any salvage value at the end of 20x5. Metroplex management requires all investments to earn a 12 percent after-tax return. The company's tax rate is 42 percent. The new machine would be classified as three-year property for MACRS purposes.

Required:

1. Compute the net present value of the machine replacement investment.
2. Between which of the following two percentages is the internal rate of return on the machine replacement: 4 percent, 6 percent, 8 percent, 10 percent, 12 percent, and 14 percent?
3. Between what two whole numbers of years is the machine replacement's payback period?
4. How much would the salvage value of the new machine have to be on December 31, 20x5, in order to turn the machine replacement into an acceptable investment?

(CMA, adapted)

■ **Problem 16–52**
Net Present Value; Internal Rate of Return; Payback; Sensitivity Analysis; Taxes (Sections 2, 3)
(LO 3, 4, 6, 8)

Total after-tax cash flow, 20x1: $(965,200)
3. Total after-tax cash inflow (years 20x2, 20x3, 20x4): $910,878

The owner of Waco Waffle House is considering an expansion of the business. He has identified two alternatives, as follows:

- Build a new restaurant near the mall.
- Buy and renovate an old building downtown for the new restaurant.

The projected cash flows from these two alternatives are shown below. The owner of the restaurant uses a 10 percent after-tax discount rate.

■ **Problem 16–53**
Ranking Investment Proposals; NPV versus Profitability Index; Taxes (Section 2)
(LO 4, 6, 7)

1(a). Mall restaurant, net present value: $25,700
2(b). Downtown restaurant, profitability index: 1.10 (rounded)

Investment Proposal	Cash Outflow: Time 0	Net After-Tax Cash Inflows*	
		Years 1–10	Years 11–20
Mall restaurant	$400,000	$50,000	$50,000
Downtown restaurant	200,000	35,800	—

* Includes after-tax cash flows from all sources, including incremental revenue, incremental expenses, and depreciation tax shield.

Required:

1. Compute the net present value of each alternative restaurant site.
2. Compute the profitability index for each alternative.
3. How do the two sites rank in terms of (a) NPV and (b) the profitability index?
4. Comment on the difficulty of ranking the owner's two options for the new restaurant site.

Refer to the data given in the preceding problem. The owner of Waco Waffle House will consider capital projects only if they have a payback period of six years or less. The owner also favors projects that exhibit an accounting rate of return of at least 15 percent. The owner bases a project's accounting rate of return on the initial investment in the project.

■ **Problem 16–54**
Payback; Accounting Rate of Return (Section 3)
(LO 8)

1(a). Payback period, mall restaurant: 8 years

Required:

1. Compute the payback period for each of the proposed restaurant sites.
2. Compute the accounting rate of return for each proposed site. Assume the average annual incremental income is $50,000 for the mall restaurant and $35,800 for the downtown restaurant.
3. If the owner of the restaurant sticks to his criteria, which site will he choose?
4. Comment on the pros and cons of the restaurant owner's investment criteria.

■ **Problem 16–55**
Payback; Accounting Rate of
Return; Ethics (Section 3)
(LO 8)

2. Accounting rate of return
(ARR) using initial
investment: .108

Schuylkill TheaterWorks is a nonprofit enterprise in downtown Philadelphia. The board of directors is considering an expansion of the theater's seating capacity, which will entail significant renovations to the existing facilities. The board has been promised by the city government that in five years the city will build a new building for the theater, so the proposed expansion is only a temporary solution to the theater's strained seating capacity. The seating expansion project will cost $139,000. The following table lists the incremental ticket revenue, the incremental operating expenses, the depreciation expense, and the incremental operating income over the five-year life of the investment expected as a result of the theater expansion. The theater's revenue and operating expenses are in cash. Thus, depreciation is the only noncash expense. As a nonprofit enterprise, the theater company is not subject to income taxes.

Year	Incremental Revenue	Incremental Operating Expenses	Net Incremental Cash Flow	Annual Straight-Line Depreciation
1	$70,000	$30,000	$40,000	$24,000
2	72,000	32,000	40,000	24,000
3	74,000	34,000	40,000	24,000
4	76,000	38,000	38,000	24,000
5	78,000	41,000	37,000	24,000

Required:

1. Compute the payback period for the proposed expansion of the theater's seating capacity.

2. Compute the project's accounting rate of return using the project's initial investment.

3. Compute the project's accounting rate of return using the project's average investment.

4. Explain why many managerial accountants believe that discounted-cash-flow methods of evaluating investment proposals are superior to the payback and accounting-rate-of-return methods.

5. Suppose the chairperson of the theater's board, who was formerly a managerial accountant, has calculated the seating expansion project's internal rate of return to be lower than the project's accounting rate of return. Moreover, the theater's cost of acquiring expansion capital is above the expansion project's internal rate of return but below its accounting rate of return. As a champion of the theater, and a strong proponent of the expansion, the board chairperson has decided to present only the project's accounting rate of return to the board for its approval of the project. Is this ethical on the part of the board's chairperson? Explain.

■ **Problem 16–56**
Sensitivity Analysis; NPV with
Taxes (Section 2)
(LO 6)

The increase in annual
before-tax sales revenue
could fall to: $34,840

Refer to the data for High Country Department Stores' computerized checkout equipment decision given in Exhibit 16–11. Also refer to the net-present-value analysis presented in Exhibit 16–12.

Required: The annual incremental sales revenue resulting from the marketing analysis is estimated at $40,000. How low could this amount be and still result in a nonnegative net present value for the new equipment?

■ **Problem 16–57**
Inflation; NPV; Nominal
Dollars (Appendix B)
(LO 4, 6, 10)

1. Time 0 cash outflow:
$(188,000)
3. Net present value:
$56,204

Pensacola Cablevision Company provides television cable service to two counties in the Florida panhandle. The firm's management is considering the construction of a new satellite dish in December of 20x0. The new antenna would improve reception and the service provided to customers. The dish antenna and associated equipment will cost $200,000 to purchase and install. The company's old equipment, which is fully depreciated, can be sold now for $20,000. The company president expects the firm's improved capabilities to result in additional revenue of $80,000 per year during the dish's useful life of seven years. The incremental operating expenses associated with the new equipment are projected to be $10,000 per year. These incremental revenues and expenses are in real dollars.

The new satellite dish will be depreciated under the MACRS depreciation schedule for the 5-year property class. The company's tax rate is 40 percent.

Pensacola Cablevision's president expects the real rate of interest in the economy to remain stable at 10 percent. She expects the inflation rate, currently running at 20 percent, to remain unchanged.

Required:

1. Prepare a schedule of cash flows projected over the next eight years (20x0 through 20x7), measured in nominal dollars. The schedule should include the initial costs of purchase and installation,

the after-tax incremental revenue and expenses, and the depreciation tax shield. Remember to express the incremental revenues and expenses in nominal dollars.

2.   Compute the nominal interest rate.

3.   Prepare a net-present-value analysis of the proposed new satellite dish. Use cash flows measured in nominal dollars and a nominal discount rate equal to the nominal interest rate.

Refer to the data given in the preceding problem for Pensacola Cablevision Company.

Required:

1.   Compute the price index for each year from 20x1 through 20x7, using 1.0000 as the index for 20x0.

2.   Prepare a schedule of after-tax cash flows measured in real dollars.

3.   Compute the net present value of the proposed new satellite dish using cash flows measured in real dollars. Use a real discount rate equal to the real interest rate.

■ **Problem 16–58**
Inflation; NPV; Real Dollars
(Appendix B)
(LO 4, 6, 10)

Time 0 cash outflow:
$(188,000)

Cases

The board of education for the Warringah Central School is considering the acquisition of several minibuses for use in transporting students to school. Five of the school district's bus routes are under-populated, with the result that the full-size buses on those routes are not fully utilized. After a careful study, the board has decided that it is not feasible to consolidate these routes into fewer routes served by full-size buses. The area in which the students live is too large for that approach, since some students' bus ride to school would exceed the state maximum of 45 minutes.

The plan under consideration by the board is to replace five full-size buses with eight minibuses, each of which would cover a much shorter route than a full-size bus. The bus drivers in this rural school district are part-time employees whose compensation costs the school district $18,000 per year for each driver. In addition to the drivers' compensation, the annual costs of operating and maintaining a full-size bus amount to $50,000. In contrast, the board projects that a minibus will cost only $20,000 annually to operate and maintain. A minibus driver earns the same wages as a full-size bus driver. The school district controller has estimated that it will cost the district $15,250, initially, to redesign its bus routes, inform the public, install caution signs in certain hazardous locations, and retrain its drivers.

A minibus costs $27,000, whereas a full-size bus costs $90,000. The school district uses straight-line depreciation for all of its long-lived assets. The board has two options regarding the five full-size buses. First, the buses could be sold now for $15,000 each. Second, the buses could be kept in reserve to use for field trips and out-of-town athletic events and to use as backup vehicles when buses break down. Currently, the board charters buses from a private company for these purposes. The annual cost of chartering buses amounts to $30,000. The school district controller has estimated that this cost could be cut to $5,000 per year if the five buses were kept in reserve. The five full-size buses have five years of useful life remaining, either as regularly scheduled buses or as reserve buses. The useful life of a new minibus is projected to be five years also.

Warringah Central School uses a hurdle rate of 12 percent on all capital projects.

Required:

1.   Think about the decision problem faced by the board of education. What are the board's two main alternatives?

2.   One of these main alternatives has two options embedded within it. What are those two options?

3.   Before proceeding, check the hint given at the end of the chapter, which explains and diagrams the school board's alternatives. Suppose the board of education chooses to buy the minibuses. Prepare a net-present-value analysis of the two options for the five full-size buses. Should these buses be sold now or kept in reserve?

4.   From your answer to requirement (3), you know the best option for the board to choose regarding the full-size buses *if* the minibuses are purchased. Now you can ignore the other option. Prepare a net-present-value analysis of the school board's two *main alternatives: (a)* continue to use the full-size buses on regular routes or *(b)* purchase the minibuses. Should the minibuses be purchased?

5.   Compute the internal rate of return on the proposed minibus acquisition.

6.   What information given in this case was irrelevant to the school board's decision problem? Explain why the information was irrelevant.

■ **Case 16–59**
Decision Problem with
Suboptions; NPV; IRR; Ethics
(Section 1)
(LO 1, 2, 3)

4. Present value of
incremental annual cash
flows: $129,780
Acquisition cost of minibuses:
$(216,000)
5. Initial cost if the minibuses
are purchased: $(231,250)

7. Independent of requirements (1) through (6), suppose the NPV analysis favors keeping the full-size buses. George Lynagh, the business manager for the Warringah Central School, was prepared to recommend that the board not purchase the minibuses. Before doing so, however, Lynagh ran into a long-time friend at the racquet club. David Windon was the vice president for sales at a local automobile dealership from which the minibuses would have been purchased. Lynagh broke the bad news about his impending recommendation about the minibuses to his friend. The two talked for some time about the pros and cons of the minibus alternative. Finally, Windon said, "George, you and I have been mates for a long time. I know you're not paid all that well at the school district. Our top financial person is retiring next year. How would you like to come to work for the dealership?"

"That's pretty tempting, David. Let me think it over," was Lynagh's response.

"Sure, George, take all the time you want. In the meantime, how about rethinking that minibus decision? It's no big deal to you, and I could sure use the business."

"But David, I told you what the figures say about that," responded Lynagh.

"Come on, George. What are friends for?"

Discuss the ethical issues in this situation. What should George Lynagh do?

■ **Case 16–60**
Investment in Robotic
Manufacturing Equipment;
Net Present Value; Payback
(Sections 2, 3)
(LO 6, 8)

1. Net present value: $47,359

Office King Corporation manufactures three different models of paper shredders including the waste container that serves as the base. While the shredder heads are different for the three models, the waste container is the same. The number of waste containers that Office King will need during the next five years is estimated as follows:

20x1	50,000
20x2	50,000
20x3	52,000
20x4	55,000
20x5	55,000

The equipment used to manufacture the waste container must be replaced because it is broken and cannot be repaired. Management is considering the purchase of robotic equipment to replace the old machinery. The new equipment would have a purchase price of $945,000. There will be a 2 percent discount if payment is made within 10 days. Company policy is to take all purchase discounts. The freight on the equipment would be $11,000, and installation costs would total $22,900. Freight and installation costs will be included in the equipment's cost basis for MACRS depreciation purposes. The equipment would be purchased in December of the current year and placed into service on January 1, 20x1. It would have a five-year useful life but would be treated as three-year property under MACRS because of the nature of the equipment. This equipment is expected to have a salvage value of $12,000 at the end of its useful life in 20x5. The new equipment will result in a 25 percent reduction in both direct labor and variable overhead. There will be an additional one-time permanent decrease in working capital requirements of $2,500, resulting from a reduction in direct-material inventories. This working capital reduction would be recognized in the analysis at the time of equipment acquisition. The old equipment is fully depreciated, and it can be sold for a salvage amount of $1,500.

Rather than replace the equipment, one of Office King's production managers has suggested that the waste containers be purchased. Office King has no alternative use for the manufacturing space at this time, so if the waste containers are purchased, the old equipment would be left in place. One supplier has quoted a price of $27 per container. This price is $8 less than Office King's current manufacturing cost, which is as follows:

Direct material		$ 8.00
Direct labor		10.00
Variable overhead		6.00
Fixed overhead:		
Supervision	$2.00	
Facilities	5.00	
General	4.00	11.00
Total manufacturing cost per unit		$35.00

Office King employs a plantwide fixed overhead rate in its operations. If the waste containers are purchased outside, the salary and benefits of one supervisor, included in the fixed overhead budget at $45,000, would be eliminated. There would be no other changes in the other cash and noncash items included in fixed overhead, except depreciation on the new equipment. Office King is subject to a 40 percent income tax rate. Management assumes that all annual cash flows and tax payments occur at the end of the year and uses a 12 percent after-tax discount rate.

Required:

1. Office King must decide whether to purchase the waste containers from an outside supplier or purchase the equipment to manufacture the waste containers. Calculate the net present value of the estimated after-tax cash flows and determine which of these two options to pursue.

2. Explain why some companies calculate the payback period of an investment in addition to determining the net present value.

3. Between what two consecutive whole number amounts is the payback period for the new equipment?

(CMA, adapted)

Hint for Case 16–59

The school board's two main alternatives are as follows: (1) continue to use the five full-size buses on regular routes or (2) purchase eight minibuses to cover the regular bus routes. Under alternative (2), the board has two options. The full-size buses could be *(a)* sold now or *(b)* kept in reserve.

Thus, the board's decision problem can be diagrammed as follows:

Main Alternatives	**Secondary Options**
(1) Full-size buses on regular routes	
	(a) Sell full-size buses
(2) Minibuses on regular routes	
	(b) Keep full-size buses in reserve

THIS CHAPTER'S FOCUS COMPANY is Clínica Neruda, an outpatient medical facility in Santiago, Chile. The clinic has two direct-patient-care

CLÍNICA NERUDA

departments: Orthopedics and Internal Medicine. In these two departments, patients are treated by medical professionals. Clínica Neruda also has three service departments, which are not directly involved in patient care. The clinic's Patient Records, Human Resources, and Administration and Accounting departments are necessary for the clinic to function, but they operate in a support role to the two direct-patient-care departments. In this chapter, we explore several methods for allocating the costs of the clinic's service departments to the direct-patient-care departments.

17 Allocation of Support Activity Costs and Joint Costs

In contrast to the health-care services setting of Clínica Neruda, we explore a different type of allocation issue in the context of International Chocolate Company of Brussels, Belgium. This company, introduced in Chapter 14, uses a joint production process to turn cocoa beans into cocoa butter and cocoa powder. The cocoa powder can be processed further into instant cocoa mix. A joint production process results in two or more products, which are called joint products. We will discuss several different methods that International Chocolate Company could use to allocate the costs of its joint production process to its two joint products.

1 Allocate service department costs using the direct method and the step-down method.

2 Use the dual approach to service department cost allocation.

3 Explain the difference between two-stage cost allocation with departmental overhead rates and activity-based costing (ABC).

4 Allocate joint costs among joint products using each of the following techniques: physical-units method, relative-sales-value method, and net-realizable-value method.

5 Describe the purposes for which joint cost allocation is useful and those for which it is not.

6 Allocate service department costs using the reciprocal-services method (appendix).

In earlier chapters, we studied cost allocation and explored its role in an organization's overall managerial accounting system. We also examined several purposes of cost allocation. The goal of cost allocation is to ensure that all costs incurred by the organization ultimately are assigned to its products or services. This is important for several purposes, including cost-based pricing and bidding, cost reimbursements from outside parties such as insurance companies, valuation of inventory, and determination of cost of goods sold. In addition, the allocation of all costs to departments serves to make departmental managers aware of the costs incurred to produce services their departments use.

This chapter is divided into two sections, each of which explores a particular cost-allocation topic in greater detail. The two sections, which may be studied separately, cover the following topics:

- Service department cost allocation[1]
- Joint product cost allocation[2]

Section 1: Service Department Cost Allocation

Learning Objective 1

Allocate service department costs using the direct method and the step-down method.

A **service department** is a unit in an organization that is not involved *directly* in producing the organization's goods or services. However, a service department does provide a service that enables the organization's production process to take place. For example, the Maintenance Department in an automobile plant does not make automobiles, but if it did not exist, the production process would stop when the manufacturing machines broke down. Thus, the Maintenance Department is crucial to the production operation even though the repair personnel do not work directly on the plant's products.

---

[1]The section on service department cost allocation is written as a module, which can be studied separately from the rest of the chapter. This material may be studied after the completion of Chapter 3, which covers basic issues in product costing.

[2]The section on joint cost allocation is written as a module, which can be studied separately from the rest of the chapter. This material may be studied after the completion of Chapter 3.

Service departments are important in nonmanufacturing organizations also. For example, a hospital's Human Resources Department is responsible for staffing the hospital with physicians, nurses, lab technicians, and other employees. The Human Resources Department never serves the patients, yet without it the hospital would have no staff to provide medical care.

A service department such as the Maintenance Department or the Human Resources Department must exist in order for an organization to carry out its primary function. Therefore, the cost of running a service department is part of the cost incurred by the organization in producing goods or services. In order to determine the cost of those goods or services, all service department costs must be allocated to the production departments in which the goods or services are produced. For this reason, the costs incurred in an automobile plant's Maintenance Department are allocated to all of the production departments that have machinery. The costs incurred in a hospital's Human Resources Department are allocated to all of the departments that have personnel. Direct-patient-care departments, such as Surgery and Physical Therapy, are allocated their share of the Human Resources Department's costs.

To see how service department cost allocation fits into the overall picture of product and service costing, it may be helpful to review Exhibit 3–12 on page 139. The exhibit shows three types of allocation processes, as follows:

1. *Cost distribution.* Costs in various cost pools are distributed to all departments, including both service and production departments.

2. *Service department cost allocation.* Service department costs are allocated to production departments.

3. *Cost application.* Costs are assigned to the goods or services produced by the organization.

It is the second type of allocation process listed above that we are focusing on now. The context for our discussion is Clínica Neruda, an outpatient medical facility in Santiago, Chile.

The clinic is organized into three service departments and two direct-patient-care departments. Exhibit 17–1 displays a simple organization chart for Clínica Neruda. Since the clinic is not a manufacturing organization, we refer to *direct-patient-care departments* instead of *production departments*. These two departments, Orthopedics and Internal Medicine, directly provide the health care that is the clinic's primary objective. Thus, the clinic's direct-patient-care departments are like the production departments in a manufacturing firm.

> "Support, or service, department costs are becoming a greater and greater percentage of our cost structure."(17a)
>
> **Chrysler**

Notice that the Human Resources Department and the Administration and Accounting Department provide services to each other. When this situation occurs, the two service departments exhibit *reciprocal services*.

Exhibit 17–2 provides some of the details for our illustration of service department cost allocation. Panel A shows the proportion of each service department's output that is consumed by each of the departments using its services. Panel B shows the allocation

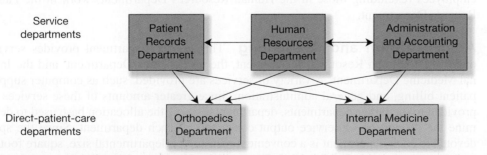

Exhibit 17–1
Organization Chart for Clínica Neruda*

*The arrows in the organization chart depict the provision of service by the three service departments. For example, the Human Resources Department serves the Patient Records Department, but not vice versa.

Exhibit 17–2
Provision of Services by
Service Departments in 20x1:
Clínica Neruda

CLÍNICA NERUDA

A. Percentage of Service Output Consumed by Using Departments

User of Service		Provider of Service		
		Patient Records	Human Resources	Administration and Accounting
Service departments	Patient Records	—	5%	—
	Human Resources	—	—	5%
	Administration and Accounting	—	20%	—
Direct-patient-care departments	Orthopedics	30%	25%	35%
	Internal Medicine	70%	50%	60%

B. Allocation Bases

Service Department	Allocation Base
Patient Records	Annual patient load
Human Resources	Number of employees
Administration and Accounting	Size of department (measured in square feet of space)

C. Service Department Costs

Service Department	Variable Cost	Fixed Cost	Total Cost to Be Allocated
Patient Records	$24,000	$ 76,000	$100,000
Human Resources	15,000	45,000	60,000
Administration and Accounting	47,500	142,500	190,000
Total	$86,500	$263,500	$350,000

bases, which are used to determine the proportions shown in panel A. Further explanation of the information in Exhibit 17–2 follows.

Patient Records   The service output of the Patient Records Department is consumed only by the Orthopedics and Internal Medicine Departments. *Annual patient load* is the *allocation base* used to determine that 30 percent of the Patient Records Department's services were consumed by Orthopedics and 70 percent by Internal Medicine.

Human Resources   The Human Resources Department serves each of the clinic's other departments, including the other two service departments and the two direct-patient-care departments. The *allocation base* used to determine the proportions of the Human Resources Department's output consumed by the four using departments is the *number of employees* in the using departments. For example, 5 percent of the clinic's employees (excluding those in the Human Resources Department) work in the Patient Records Department.

Administration and Accounting   This service department provides services only to the Human Resources Department, the Orthopedics Department, and the Internal Medicine Department. A variety of services are provided, such as computer support, patient billing, and general administration. Since greater amounts of these services are provided to the larger departments, departmental size is the allocation base used to determine the proportion of service output consumed by each department. Since the space devoted to each department is a convenient measure of departmental size, square footage is the measure used in Exhibit 17–2. For example, 5 percent of the clinic's space (excluding that occupied by Administration and Accounting and Patient Records) is devoted to the Human Resources Department.

Panel C of Exhibit 17–2 shows the total budgeted cost of each service department that is to be allocated among the using departments.

There are two widely used methods of service department cost allocation, the direct method and the step-down method. These methods are discussed and illustrated next, using the data for Clínica Neruda.

Direct Method

Under the **direct method,** each service department's costs are allocated among *only the direct-patient-care departments* that consume part of the service department's output. This method ignores the fact that some service departments provide services to other service departments. Thus, even though Clínica Neruda's Human Resources Department provides services to two other service departments, none of its costs are allocated to those departments. Exhibit 17–3 presents Clínica Neruda's service department cost allocations under the direct method.

Notice that the proportion of each service department's costs to be allocated to each direct-patient-care department is determined by the *relative proportion* of the service department's output consumed by each direct-patient-care department. For example, a glance at Exhibit 17–2 shows that the Human Resources Department provides 25 percent of its services to Orthopedics and 50 percent to Internal Medicine. Summing these two percentages yields 75 percent. Thus, 25/75 is the fraction of the Human Resources Department's cost allocated to Orthopedics and 50/75 is the fraction allocated to Internal Medicine.

Step-Down Method

As stated above, the direct method ignores the provision of services by one service department to another service department. This shortcoming is overcome partially by the **step-down method** of service department cost allocation. Under this method, the managerial accountant first chooses a sequence in which to allocate the service departments' costs. A common way to select the first service department in the sequence is to choose the one that serves the largest number of other service departments. The service departments are ordered in this manner, with the last service department being the one that serves the smallest number of other service departments.[3] Then the managerial accountant allocates each service department's costs among the direct-patient-care departments and all of the other service departments that follow it in the sequence. Note that the ultimate cost allocations assigned to the direct-patient-care departments will differ depending on the sequence chosen.

The step-down method is best explained by way of an illustration. Clínica Neruda's Human Resources Department serves two other service departments: Patient Records, and Administration and Accounting. The Administration and Accounting Department serves only one other service department: Human Resources. Finally, the Patient Records

Provider of Service	Cost to Be Allocated	Direct-Patient-Care Departments Using Services			
		Orthopedics		**Internal Medicine**	
		Proportion	Amount	Proportion	Amount
Patient Records	$100,000	3/10	$ 30,000	7/10	$ 70,000
Human Resources	60,000	25/75	20,000	50/75	40,000
Administration and Accounting	190,000	35/95	70,000	60/95	120,000
Total	$350,000		$120,000		$230,000

Grand total = $350,000

Exhibit 17–3
Direct Method of Service Department Cost Allocation: Clínica Neruda

CLÍNICA
NERUDA

---

[3]A tie occurs when two or more service departments serve the same number of other service departments. Then the sequence among the tied service departments usually is an arbitrary choice.

Department serves no other service departments. Thus, Clínica Neruda's service department sequence is as follows:

| (1) Human Resources | (2) Administration and Accounting | (3) Patient Records |

In accordance with this sequence, each service department's costs are allocated to the other departments as follows:

Cost Allocated from This Service Department ⟶	To These Departments
Human Resources	Administration and Accounting
	Patient Records
	Orthopedics
	Internal Medicine
Administration and Accounting	Orthopedics
	Internal Medicine
Patient Records	Orthopedics
	Internal Medicine

Notice that even though Administration and Accounting serves Human Resources, there is no cost allocation in that direction. This results from the placement of Human Resources before Administration and Accounting in the allocation sequence. Moreover, no costs are allocated from Patient Records to either of the other service departments, because Patient Records does not serve those departments.

Exhibit 17–4 presents the results of applying the step-down method at Clínica Neruda. First, the Human Resources Department's $60,000 in cost is allocated among the four departments using its services. Second, the cost of the Administration and Accounting Department is allocated. The total cost to be allocated is the department's original $190,000 *plus* the $12,000 allocated from the Human Resources Department. The new total of $202,000 is allocated to the Orthopedics and Internal Medicine Departments according to the *relative proportions* in which these two departments use the services of the Administration and Accounting Department. Finally, the Patient Records Department's cost is allocated.

Reciprocal-Services Method

The direct method and the step-down method both ignore the fact that the Administration and Accounting Department serves the Human Resources Department. Neither of these methods allocates any of the costs incurred in Administration and Accounting back to Human Resources.

Review the relationships between the service departments depicted in Exhibit 17–1. Notice that the Administration and Accounting Department and the Human Resources Department *serve each other.* This mutual provision of service is called reciprocal service. A more accurate method of service department cost allocation, called the **reciprocal-services method,** fully accounts for the mutual provision of services. This method, which is more complex than the direct and step-down methods, is covered in the appendix at the end of this chapter.

Fixed versus Variable Costs

In our allocation of Clínica Neruda's service department costs, we did not distinguish between fixed and variable costs. Under some circumstances, this simple approach can result in an unfair cost allocation among the using departments. To illustrate, we will use

	Service Department			Direct-Patient-Care Department	
	Human Resources	Administration and Accounting	Patient Records	Orthopedics	Internal Medicine
Costs prior to allocation	$60,000	$190,000	$100,000		
Allocation of Human Resources Department costs	$60,000 ⟶	12,000 (20/100)†	3,000 (5/100)	$ 15,000 (25/100)	$ 30,000 (50/100)
Allocation of Administration and Accounting Department costs		$202,000 ⟶		74,421* (35/95)	127,579* (60/95)
Allocation of Patient Records Department costs			$103,000 ⟶	30,900 (30/100)	72,100 (70/100)
Total cost allocated to each department				$120,321	$229,679
Total cost allocated to direct-patient-care departments				$350,000	

* Rounded.

† Fractions in parentheses are relative proportions of service department's output consumed by departments to which costs are allocated.

Exhibit 17–4

Step-Down Method of Service Department Cost Allocation: Clínica Neruda

CLÍNICA NERUDA

the data about Clínica Neruda's fixed and variable costs given in panel C of Exhibit 17–2. Consider the cost data for the Patient Records Department, which serves only the Orthopedics and Internal Medicine departments. Under the *direct method* of service department cost allocation, the Patient Records Department's costs were allocated as follows:

Cost Allocation for 20x1: Direct Method

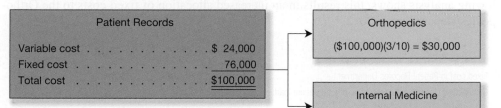

Patient Records	
Variable cost	$ 24,000
Fixed cost	76,000
Total cost	$100,000

Orthopedics

($100,000)(3/10) = $30,000

Internal Medicine

($100,000)(7/10) = $70,000

The allocation base used in this cost allocation is the annual patient load in the Orthopedics and Internal Medicine departments. Let's assume the following patient loads in 20x1, the year for which the cost allocation has been done.

Department	Patient Load	Proportion of Total
Orthopedics	30,000	(30,000/100,000) = 3/10
Internal Medicine	70,000	(70,000/100,000) = 7/10
Total	100,000	

Now suppose the projections for 20x2 are as follows:

Department	Projected Patient Load	Projected Proportion of Total
Orthopedics	30,000	(30,000/80,000) = 3/8
Internal Medicine	50,000	(50,000/80,000) = 5/8
Total	80,000	

Department	Budgeted Variable Cost	Budgeted Fixed Cost	Budgeted Total Cost
Patient Records	$19,200	$76,000	$95,200

The projections for 20x2 include a stable patient load in the Orthopedics Department but a decline in the patient load of the Internal Medicine Department. Since the projected total patient load is lower for 20x2, the projected variable cost in the Patient Records Department is lower also.

What will be the effect of these changes on the 20x2 allocation of the Patient Records Department's costs? Using the direct method, we obtain the following allocation.

Cost Allocation for 20x2: Direct Method

Patient Records		Orthopedics
Variable cost . . . . $ 19,200		($95,200)(3/8) = $35,700
Fixed cost 76,000		
Total cost . . . . $ 95,200		Internal Medicine
		($95,200)(5/8) = $59,500

Compare the costs allocated to the two direct-patient-care departments in 20x1 and 20x2. Notice that the cost allocated to the Orthopedics Department *increased by* $5,700 (from $30,000 to $35,700), even though Orthopedics' patient load is projected to remain constant. What has happened here? The projected decline in the Internal Medicine Department's volume resulted in lower budgeted variable costs for the Patient Records Department, but the budgeted *fixed costs* did not change. At the same time, the lower projected patient load in Internal Medicine resulted in a higher proportion of the total projected patient load for Orthopedics (from 3/10 in 20x1 up to 3/8 in 20x2). As the following analysis shows, this results in an increased allocation of fixed costs to the Orthopedics Department in 20x2.

	20x1	20x2
Fixed cost in Patient Records Department	$76,000	$76,000
Orthopedics Department's proportion of total patient load	3/10	3/8
Orthopedics Department's allocation of fixed cost	$22,800	$28,500

Difference = $5,700

This difference of $5,700 is equal to the increase in the Orthopedics Department's total cost allocation from the Patient Records Department in 20x2.

To summarize, the projected decline in Internal Medicine's 20x2 patient load will result in an increased cost allocation from the Patient Records Department to the Orthopedics Department in 20x2. The cause of this increased allocation is our failure to distinguish between fixed and variable costs in the allocation process.

Dual Cost Allocation

The problem illustrated in the preceding section can be resolved by allocating fixed and variable costs separately. This approach, called **dual cost allocation,** works with either the direct method or the step-down method of allocation. Under dual cost allocation, *variable costs* are allocated on the basis of *short-run usage* of the service department's output; *fixed costs* are allocated on the basis of *long-run average usage* of the service department's output. The rationale for this approach is that fixed costs are capacity-producing costs. When service departments are established, their size and scale usually are determined by the projected long-run needs of the using departments.

To illustrate dual cost allocation for Clínica Neruda, we need estimates of the long-run average usage of each service department's output by each using department. These estimates are given in Exhibit 17–5.

Management
Accounting
Practice

Medicare, National
Health Service,
Asian Healthcare,
Healthcare IT

COST MANAGEMENT IN THE WORLD'S HEALTH CARE

The cost of health care is a challenge to individuals, companies, and governments worldwide. As the sophistication of health and pharmaceutical treatments increases, so does the cost of providing those services. And, not unreasonably, everyone wants the best, most effective medical treatments available regardless of the cost.

All medical systems must deal with the problem of cost management, and a variety of approaches have been devised. In the United States, for instance, the Medicare system of medical care for those over the age of 65 uses a price-based system based on diagnosis-related groups (DRG). Under this system, a flat amount of fees is paid to a health care provider for a given category of illness (per case or DRG), transferring the challenge of cost control from the government to the medical provider (who in most cases is not employed by the national government). Providers have responded by using cost reduction approaches that "analyze and correct inefficiencies in the flow of care delivery."[4]

Similarly, in the United Kingdom, there are substantial efforts under way to maintain treatment effectiveness while reducing costs. In such an environment, financial management skills, including managerial accounting, play a critical role. "There is a lack of financial management expertise in the NHS [National Health Service], and a need to strengthen communication between those responsible for the finances and for the delivery of local health services. Measures to bring about financial balance need to . . . enhance both the efficiency and the effectiveness of healthcare."[5]

Finally, the cost-benefit trade-off of information technology (IT) is being examined. "Challenges such as rising healthcare costs . . . are making it imperative for health care organizations to integrate IT solutions in their administrative and clinical workflow."[6] In a study of 41 hospitals, researchers found that "a 10-point increase in the automation of notes and records was associated with a 15% decrease in the adjusted odds of fatal hospitalizations" and that improved processes for "test results, order entry, and decision support were associated with lower costs for all hospital admissions."[7]

"There is a need for economic evaluation in health care because it recognizes the reality of fixed resources and brings this to the attention of the public; exposes the opportunity cost of new interventions; enables consistency in investment—and disinvestment—decisions; and helps to direct innovation into those areas regarded as priorities by the health system."[8]

		Provider of Service		
User of Service		**Patient Records**	**Human Resources**	**Administration and Accounting**
Service departments	Patient Records	—	10%	—
	Human Resources	—	—	10%
	Administration and Accounting	—	10%	—
Direct-patient-care departments	Orthopedics	40%	20%	45%
	Internal Medicine	60%	60%	45%

Exhibit 17–5

Provision of Services by Service Departments: Long-Run Average Usage, Clínica Neruda

CLÍNICA NERUDA

[4]Jack Gottlieb et al., "Achieving Operational Efficiencies Using a DRG-Based Tracer Approach," *Healthcare Financial Management (HFM) Magazine,* June 2010.

[5]House of Commons Committee of Public Accounts, "Financial Management in the NHS," HC361, p. 5, March 20, 2007.

[6]Sourabh Kankhar, "Healthcare IT: Adoption in Asia Pacific," *Asian Hospital and Healthcare Management,* 2010.

[7]R. Amarasingham et al., "Clinical Information Technologies and Inpatient Outcomes: A Multiple Hospital Study," *Archives of Internal Medicine* 169(2), pp.108–114, January 26, 2009.

[8]Andrew Dillon, Director of the UK's National Institute for Health and Clinical Excellence, as quoted in "6th Annual China Health Care Forum Explores 'Better Management, Better Care'", www.ceibs.edu/media/archive/52950.shtml, June 6, 2010.

To combine the dual-allocation approach with either the direct method or the step-down method, we simply apply the allocation method twice, as follows:

Costs to Be Allocated	Basis for Allocation	Allocation Method	
Variable costs in 20x1	Short-run usage in 20x1	Direct	Step-down
(Exhibit 17–2, panel C)	(Exhibit 17–2, panel A)	method	method
		OR	
Fixed costs in 20x1	Long-run average usage	Direct	Step-down
(Exhibit 17–2, panel C)	(Exhibit 17–5)	method	method

After both of these allocation procedures have been completed, the resulting variable- and fixed-cost allocations for each direct-patient-care department are summed. Exhibit 17–6 presents the allocation computations when the dual approach is combined with the direct method. Compare the final direct allocations with those in Exhibit 17–3, where the dual approach was not used. Notice that the final allocations are different. Exhibit 17–7 presents the computations for the step-down method. Compare the final step-down allocations with those in Exhibit 17–4, where the dual approach was not used. Again, the final allocations are different.

A Behavioral Problem

Dual cost allocation prevents a change in the short-run activity of one using department from affecting the cost allocated to another using department. However, the approach sometimes presents a problem of its own. In order to implement the technique, we need accurate projections of the long-run average usage of each service department's output by each using department. This is the information in Exhibit 17–5. Typically, these estimates come from the managers of the departments that consume the services. The problem is that the higher a manager's estimate of the department's long-run average usage is, the greater will be the department's allocation of fixed service department costs. This creates an incentive for using-department managers to understate their expected long-run service needs. Ultimately, such understatements can result in building service facilities that are too small.

How can we prevent this behavioral problem? First, we can rely on the professionalism and integrity of the managers who provide the estimates. Second, we can reward managers through promotions and pay raises for making accurate estimates of their departments' service needs.

> "When cost reduction becomes a priority . . . the key is to understand which services should be reduced, redesigned or restructured . . . [which] can save about 10–30% of G&A costs." (17c)
>
> **Bain & Company India**

Exhibit 17–6
Dual Allocation Combined with Direct Method: Clínica Neruda

CLÍNICA NERUDA

		Direct-Patient-Care Department Using Services			
		Orthopedics		**Internal Medicine**	
Provider of Service	**Cost to Be Allocated**	**Proportion**	**Amount**	**Proportion**	**Amount**
I. Variable Costs					
Patient Records	$ 24,000	3/10	$ 7,200	7/10	$ 16,800
Human Resources	15,000	25/75	5,000	50/75	10,000
Administration and Accounting	47,500	35/95	17,500	60/95	30,000
Total variable cost	$ 86,500		$ 29,700		$ 56,800
II. Fixed Costs					
Patient Records	$ 76,000	4/10	$ 30,400	6/10	$ 45,600
Human Resources	45,000	20/80	11,250	60/80	33,750
Administration and Accounting	142,500	45/90	71,250	45/90	71,250
Total fixed cost	$263,500		$112,900		$150,600
Total cost (variable + fixed)	$350,000		$142,600		$207,400
				Grand total =	$350,000

	Service Department			Direct-Patient-Care Department	
	Human Resources	Administration and Accounting	Patient Records	Orthopedics	Internal Medicine
I. Variable Costs					
Variable cost prior to allocation	$15,000	$ 47,500	$24,000		
Allocation of Human Resources Department costs	$15,000	3,000 (20/100)†	750 (5/100)	$ 3,750 (25/100)	$ 7,500 (50/100)
Allocation of Administration and Accounting Department costs		$ 50,500		18,605* (35/95)	31,895* (60/95)
Allocation of Patient Records Department costs			$24,750	7,425 (30/100)	17,325 (70/100)
Total variable cost allocated to each department				$ 29,780	$ 56,720
II. Fixed Costs					
Fixed cost prior to allocation	$45,000	$142,500	$76,000		
Allocation of Human Resources Department costs	$45,000	4,500 (10/100)	4,500 (10/100)	$ 9,000 (20/100)	$ 27,000 (60/100)
Allocation of Administration and Accounting Department costs		$147,000		73,500 (45/90)	73,500 (45/90)
Allocation of Patient Records Department costs			$ 80,500	32,200 (40/100)	48,300 (60/100)
Total fixed cost allocated to each department				$ 114,700	$ 148,800
Total cost allocated to each department (variable + fixed)				$ 144,480	$ 205,520
				Grand total = $350,000	

* Rounded

† Fractions in parentheses are relative proportions of service department's output consumed by departments to which costs are allocated. Variable costs allocated on basis of short-run proportions. Fixed costs allocated on basis of long-run average proportions.

Allocate Budgeted Costs

Exhibit 17–7
Dual Allocation Combined with Step-Down Method: Clínica Neruda

CLÍNICA NERUDA

When service department costs are allocated to production departments, such as the direct-patient-care departments of Clínica Neruda, *budgeted* service department costs should be used. If actual costs are allocated instead, any operating inefficiencies in the service departments are passed along to the using departments. This reduces the incentive for service department managers to control the costs in their departments. The proper approach is as follows:

1. Compare budgeted and actual service department costs and compute any variances.
2. Use these variances to help control costs in the service departments.
3. Close out the service department cost variances against the period's income.
4. Allocate the service departments' budgeted costs to the departments that directly produce goods or services.

Today's Advanced Manufacturing Environment

In traditional manufacturing environments, service department costs are allocated to production departments to ensure that all manufacturing costs are assigned to products. For example, the costs incurred in a machine-maintenance department typically are allocated to the other service departments and the production departments that use maintenance services. Service department cost allocation continues to be used in the new manufacturing environment, characterized by JIT inventory management and CIM systems. However, the extent of such allocations is diminished in advanced manufacturing systems, because more costs are directly traceable to product lines. In a flexible manufacturing system, almost all operations are performed in the FMS cell. Even machine maintenance is done largely by the FMS cell operators rather than a separate maintenance department. Inspection often is performed by FMS cell operators, eliminating the need for a separate inspection department. In short, as more and more costs become directly traceable to products, the need for allocation of indirect costs declines.

The Rise of Activity-Based Costing

Learning Objective 3

Explain the difference between two-stage cost allocation with departmental overhead rates and activity-based costing (ABC).

Service department cost allocation is one type of allocation procedure used in two-stage allocation with departmental overhead rates. (See Exhibit 3–12 on page 139). Under this approach, costs first are distributed to *departments;* then they are allocated from service *departments* to production *departments.* Finally, they are assigned from production *departments* to products or services. *Departments* play a key role as intermediate cost objects under this approach.

In an activity-based costing (ABC) system, on the other hand, the key role is played by *activities,* not departments. (See Exhibit 5–4 on page 207). First, the costs of various *activities* are assigned to *activity* cost pools; then these costs are assigned to products or services.

The breakdown of costs by activity in an ABC system is much finer than a breakdown by departments. For example, under the service department cost allocation approach, the Purchasing Department might be one of the service departments identified. However, under ABC, the various activities engaged in by purchasing personnel would be separately identified. Activities such as part specification, vendor identification, vendor selection, price negotiation, ordering, expediting, receiving, inspection, and invoice paying might be identified separately under ABC. Then the costs of each of these activities would be assigned to products or services on the basis of the appropriate cost drivers. The ABC approach generally will provide a much more accurate cost for each of the organization's products or services.[9]

Section 2: Joint Product Cost Allocation

Learning Objective 4

Allocate joint costs among joint products using each of the following techniques: physical-units method, relative-sales-value method, and net-realizable-value method.

A **joint production process** results in two or more products, which are termed **joint products.** The cost of the input and the joint production process is called a *joint product cost.* The point in the production process where the individual products become separately identifiable is called the **split-off point.** To illustrate, International Chocolate Company produces cocoa powder and cocoa butter by processing cocoa beans in the joint production process depicted in Exhibit 17–8.

As the diagram shows, cocoa beans are processed in 1-tonne batches. The beans cost $500 and the joint process costs $600, for a total *joint cost* of $1,100. The process results

---

[9]Activity-based costing is covered extensively in Chapter 5.

Milk processing provides an example of joint product cost allocation in the agriculture industry. The cost of producing raw milk must be allocated among such joint products as heavy cream, light cream, whole milk, 2 percent milk, and skim milk.

in 750 kilograms of cocoa butter and 250 kilograms of cocoa powder. Each of these two joint products can be sold at the split-off point or processed further. Cocoa butter can be separately processed into a sunscreen, and cocoa powder can be separately processed into instant cocoa mix.

Exhibit 17–8
Joint Processing of Cocoa Beans: International Chocolate Company

Allocating Joint Costs

For product-costing purposes, a joint product cost usually is allocated to the joint products that result from the joint production process. Such allocation *is necessary* for inventory valuation and income determination, among other reasons.[10] As we discussed in Chapter 14, however, joint cost allocation is *not useful* for making substantive economic decisions about the joint process or the joint products. For example, Chapter 14 shows that joint cost allocation is not useful in deciding whether to process a joint product further. (See pages 641–643.) There are three commonly used methods for allocating joint product costs. Each of these is explained next.

Learning Objective 5

Describe the purposes for which joint cost allocation is useful and those for which it is not.

Physical-Units Method The **physical-units method** allocates joint product costs on the basis of some physical characteristic of the joint products at the split-off point. Panel A of Exhibit 17–9 illustrates this allocation method for International Chocolate Company using the *weight* of the joint products as the allocation basis.

Exhibit 17–9
Methods for Allocating Joint Product Costs

	A. Physical-Units Method			
Joint Cost	**Joint Products**	**Weight at Split-off Point**	**Relative Proportion**	**Allocation of Joint Cost**
$1,100	Cocoa butter	750 kilograms	3/4	$ 825
	Cocoa powder	250 kilograms	1/4	275
	Total joint cost allocated			$1,100
	B. Relative-Sales-Value Method			
Joint Cost	**Joint Products**	**Sales Value at Split-off Point**	**Relative Proportion**	**Allocation of Joint Cost**
$1,100	Cocoa butter	$750	3/5	$ 660
	Cocoa powder	500	2/5	440
	Total joint cost allocated			$1,100

(continued)

---

[10]The purposes of product costing are covered in Chapter 3.

Exhibit 17–9
Methods for Allocating Joint
Product Costs

(concluded)

C. Net-Realizable-Value Method

Joint Cost	Joint Products	Sales Value of Final Product	Separable Cost of Processing	Net Realizable Value	Relative Proportion	Allocation of Joint Cost
$1,100	Sunscreen	$3,000	$1,560	$1,440*	6/11[†]	$ 600
	Instant cocoa mix	2,000	800	1,200*	5/11[†]	500
	Total joint cost allocated					$1,100

*Sales value of final product	−	Separable cost of processing	=	Net realizable value	[†]Calculation of relative proportions:			
$3,000	−	$1,560	=	$1,440	$1,440	+	$1,200	= $2,640
2,000	−	800	=	1,200	1,440	÷	2,640	= 6/11
					1,200	÷	2,640	= 5/11

Relative-Sales-Value Method   The **relative-sales-value method** is based on the relative sales value of each joint product *at the split-off point.* In the International Chocolate Company illustration, these joint products are cocoa butter and cocoa powder. This method is illustrated in Exhibit 17–9 (panel B).

Net-Realizable-Value Method   Under the **net-realizable-value method,** the relative value of the final products is used to allocate the joint cost. International Chocolate Company's final products are sunscreen and instant cocoa mix.

M anagement
A ccounting
P ractice

Royal Dutch Shell

JOINT COST ALLOCATION IN THE PETROLEUM INDUSTRY

One of the most complicated problems in joint cost allocation routinely occurs in the petroleum industry. When an oil company, such as Royal Dutch Shell, drills a successful oil well, the well almost always produces natural gas in addition to crude oil. Moreover, the crude oil produced by a typical oil well is of various grades. Lighter crude oils suitable for production of such products as gasoline are generally near the top of an oil reservoir, while the heavier crudes are near the bottom. The heavier crude oils are used to make such products as fuel oil for heating homes and businesses and for the generation of electricity.

All of these products obtained from a successful oil well are joint products: the various grades of crude oil and the natural gas. Most of these products will require further processing before they will be salable products such as gasoline, diesel fuel, or home heating oil. Thus, substantial separable costs will be incurred in processing the joint products in addition to the joint costs incurred in the oil field operations. Millions of dollars of joint costs are incurred in the development of an off-shore oil field. The costs of locating the oil field, building the drilling platforms, and the drilling itself are all joint costs. Then there are the costs of crewing the oil rigs and the ongoing costs of bringing oil and natural gas to the surface.

Oil companies such as Royal Dutch Shell typically use the net realizable value of the products manufactured as the basis for allocating the joint production costs. The full costs of the company's various products then become the basis for pricing and product-mix decisions.

The next time you pump gas for your automobile, think about the salaries of the helicopter pilots who bring food and other supplies to the many off-shore oil platforms. Those costs comprise a part of the joint cost allocated to the gasoline you obtain from the pump.

The **net realizable value** of each final product is its sales value less any separable costs incurred *after* the split-off point. The joint cost is allocated according to the relative magnitudes of the final products' net realizable values. Panel C of Exhibit 17–9 illustrates this allocation method.

Notice how different the cost allocations are under the three methods, particularly the physical-units method. Since the physical-units approach is not based on the *economic* characteristics of the joint products, it is the least preferred of the three methods.

By-Products   A joint product with minimal value relative to the other joint products is termed a **by-product.** For example, whey is a by-product in the production of cheese. A common practice in accounting is to subtract a by-product's net realizable value from the cost of the joint process. Then the remaining joint cost is allocated among the major joint products.

An alternative procedure is to inventory the by-product at its sales value at the split-off point. Then the by-product's sales value is deducted from the production cost of the main products.

> "Joint costing problems crop up more often than you might think. They're among the thornier [cost management] issues our clients have to deal with." (17d)
>
> **A. T. Kearney**

Chapter Summary

LO1 Allocate service department costs using the direct method and the step-down method. Under the direct method, the costs of each service department are allocated directly to each production department in proportion to each production department's usage of each service department's output. Under the step-down method, the service departments are first ranked by the number of other service departments that each one serves. Then the costs of each service department in the ranked sequence are allocated among all of the remaining service departments in the sequence together with all of the production departments.

LO2 Use the dual approach to service department cost allocation. Either the direct or the step-down method may be combined with the dual-allocation approach, in which variable and fixed costs are allocated separately.

LO3 Explain the difference between two-stage cost allocation with departmental overhead rates and activity-based costing (ABC). Two-stage allocation with departmental overhead rates involves the following three steps: (1) All overhead costs are allocated among all service and production departments. (2) Service-department costs are allocated to production departments. (3) Production department costs are applied to products or services. In contrast, two-stage allocation under ABC involves the following two steps: (1) Resource costs are assigned to activity cost pools. (2) The costs in these activity cost pools are assigned to cost objects (e.g., products or services) using appropriate cost drivers.

LO4 Allocate joint costs among joint products using each of the following techniques: physical units method, relative-sales-value method, and net-realizable-value method. In the physical-units method, the joint cost is allocated to the joint products in proportion to some physical characteristic of the joint products, such as weight or volume. In the relative-sales-value method, the joint cost is allocated to the joint products in proportion to the joint products' sales values at the split-off point In the net-realizable-value method, the joint cost is allocated to the joint products in proportion to the joint products' net realizable values.

LO5 Describe the purposes for which joint cost allocation is useful and those for which it is not. Joint cost allocation is useful for product-costing purposes, but the allocated costs should not affect substantive economic decisions.

LO6 Allocate service department costs using the reciprocal-services method (appendix). Under the reciprocal-services method, simultaneous equations are specified to show how each service and production department uses the services of the various service departments. When these equations are solved simultaneously, the result is the amount of service department cost to be allocated to each production department. Unlike the direct and step-down methods, the reciprocal-services method fully accounts for all reciprocal services among service departments.

Review Problem on Service Department Cost Allocation

Renaissance School of Music and Art provides classes for school-age children. The students are enrolled in two departments: Music Education and Art Education. The school also has two service departments: Administration and Human Resources (A & HR) and Maintenance (M). The budgeted costs in the two service departments are as follows:

Administration and Human Resources $342,000
Maintenance 171,000

The usage of the service department's output for the year is as follows:

	Provider of Service	
User of Service	Administration & Human Resources	Maintenance
Administration & Human Resources	—	5%
Maintenance	10%	—
Music Education	40%	40%
Art Education	50%	55%

Required: Allocate the two services departments' costs to the Music Education and Art Education departments using each of the following allocation methods.

1. Direct method.
2. Step-down method (Since each service department serves one other service department, allocate the cost of A & HR first.)

Solution to Review Problem

1. Cost allocation using direct method:

		Departments Using Services			
		Music Education		Art Education	
Provider of Service	Cost to Be Allocated	Proportion	Amount	Proportion	Amount
A & HR	$342,000	(4/9)	$152,000	(5/9)	$190,000
M*	171,000	(8/19)	72,000	(11/19)	99,000
Total	$513,000		$224,000		$289,000

*(8/19) = [40/(40 + 55)]; (11/19) = [55/(40 + 55)].

2. Cost allocation using step-down method:

	Service Departments		Departments Using Services	
	A&HR	M	Music Education	Art Education
Costs prior to allocation	$342,000	$171,000		
Allocation of A & HR costs*	$342,000	34,200 (10%)	$136,800 (40%)	$171,000 (50%)
Allocation of M costs*		$205,200	86,400 (8/19)	118,800 (11/19)
Total costs allocated to each department			$223,200	$289,800
Total cost allocated to academic departments			$513,000	

*(8/19) = [40/(40 + 55)]; (11/19) = [55/(40 + 55)].

Key Terms

For each term's definition, refer to the indicated page or turn to the glossary at the end of the text.

by-product, 787

direct method, 777

dual cost allocation, 780

joint production process, 784

joint products, 784

net realizable value, 787

net-realizable-value
  method, 786

physical-units method, 785

reciprocal-services
  method, 778

relative-sales-value
  method, 786

service department, 774

split-off point, 784

step-down method, 777

APPENDIX TO CHAPTER 17

Reciprocal-Services Method

The reciprocal-services method of service department cost allocation fully accounts for the mutual provision of services among all the service departments. The relationships between Clínica Neruda's three service departments are portrayed in the following diagram.

Patient Records (Department R) ◄► Human Resources (Department H) ◄► Administration and Accounting (Department A)

CLÍNICA NERUDA

Learning Objective 6

Allocate service department costs using the reciprocal services method (appendix).

The first step in the technique is to specify a set of equations that express the relationships between the departments. The following equations, which express these relationships for Clínica Neruda, are based on the data in Exhibit 17–2 on page 776.

$$R = 100{,}000 + .05H \tag{1}$$

$$H = 60{,}000 + .05A \tag{2}$$

$$A = 190{,}000 + .20H \tag{3}$$

where R denotes the total cost of the Patient Records Department

H denotes the total cost of the Human Resources Department

A denotes the total cost of the Administration and Accounting Department

Equation (1) says that the *total cost* of operating the Patient Records Department (R) is $100,000 *plus* 5 percent of the total cost of operating the Human Resources Department (H). The $100,000 comes from Exhibit 17–2 (panel C) and is the total cost *traceable* to the Patient Records Department. We add to this amount 5 percent of the total cost of operating the Human Resources Department. Why? Because Exhibit 17–2 (panel A) tells us that the Patient Records Department used 5 percent of the Human Resources Department's services. Similar explanations underlie equations (2) and (3).

The second step in the reciprocal-services method is to solve the simultaneous equations.[11] Let's begin by substituting the expression for A from equation (3) into equation (2), and solving for H as follows:

$$H = 60{,}000 + .05(190{,}000 + .20H)$$

$$= 60{,}000 + 9{,}500 + .01H$$

$$.99H = 69{,}500$$

$$H = 70{,}202 \text{ (rounded)}$$

Then we substitute the value for H we just obtained into equation (3), and solve for A as follows:

$$A = 190{,}000 + .20H$$

$$= 190{,}000 + (.20)(70{,}202)$$

$$= 204{,}040 \text{ (rounded)}$$

---

[11]Simultaneous equations are more quickly solved by computers than by people. Numerous software packages are available for this purpose.

	Service Department			Direct-Patient-Care Department	
	Human Resources	**Administration and Accounting**	**Patient Records**	**Orthopedics**	**Internal Medicine**
Traceable costs	$60,000	$190,000	$100,000		
Allocation of Human Resources Department costs	(70,202)	14,040* (.20)	3,510* (.05)	$ 17,551*(.25)	$ 35,101 (.50)
Allocation of Administration and Accounting Department costs	10,202 (.05)†	(204,040)	–0– (0)	71,414 (.35)	122,424 (.60)
Allocation of Patient Records Department costs	–0– (0)	–0– (0)	(103,510)	31,053 (.30)	72,457 (.70)
Total cost allocated to each direct-patient-care department				$120,018	$229,982
Total costs allocated				$350,000	

*Rounded.

†Percentages in parentheses are relative proportions of a service department's output consumed by departments to which costs are allocated (from Exhibit 17–2, panel A).

Exhibit 17–10

Reciprocal-Services Method of Service Department Cost Allocation: Clínica Neruda

CLÍNICA
NERUDA

Now we can solve for R by substituting the value for H into equation (1) as follows:

$$R = 100,000 + .05H$$

$$= 100,000 + (.05)(70,202)$$

$$= 103,510 \text{ (rounded)}$$

Thus, we have determined that $H = 70,202$, $A = 204,040$, and $R = 103,510$.

The final step in the reciprocal-services method is to allocate the *total cost* of operating each service department (R, H, and A) to the various departments that use its services. For example, we will allocate the total cost of operating the Human Resources Department (H) among all four of Clínica Neruda's other departments, because they all use services from Human Resources. This allocation is made in proportion to the use of Human Resources's services by the other departments, as given in Exhibit 17–2 (panel A).

The allocations are shown in Exhibit 17–10. Focus on the second row of numbers, which refers to the Human Resources Department. The $70,202 shown in parentheses in the Human Resources column is that department's total cost, as computed using the simultaneous equations. This $70,202 total cost is allocated as follows:

- 20 percent (or $14,040) to Administration and Accounting, because that department uses 20 percent of the Human Resources Department's services

- 5 percent (or $3,510) to Patient Records, because that department uses 5 percent of the Human Resources Department's services

- 25 percent (or $17,551) to Orthopedics, because that department uses 25 percent of the Human Resources Department's services

- 50 percent (or $35,101) to Internal Medicine, because that department uses 50 percent of the Human Resources Department's services.

A similar explanation underlies the Administration and Accounting row and the Patient Records row in Exhibit 17–10.

The total costs allocated to Clínica Neruda's two direct-patient-care departments are as follows: $120,018 to Orthopedics and $229,982 to Internal Medicine. Notice that these two amounts add up to $350,000, which is the total of the original traceable costs for the three service departments. Thus, all service department costs have been fully allocated.

The reciprocal-services method is more accurate than the direct and step-down methods, because it fully accounts for reciprocal services. To make the reciprocal-services method even more accurate, it can be combined with the dual-allocation approach. In this approach, variable and fixed costs are allocated separately. This method is explored in Problem 17–34.

Review Questions

17–1. Distinguish between a service department and a production department. Give an example of the counterpart of a manufacturer's "production" department in a bank.

17–2. Define the term *reciprocal services.*

17–3. Explain briefly the main differences between the direct, step-down, and reciprocal-services methods of service department cost allocation.

17–4. How does the managerial accountant determine the department sequence in the step-down method? How are ties handled?

17–5. Why does the dual-allocation approach improve the resulting cost allocation?

17–6. What potential behavioral problem can result when the dual approach is used?

17–7. Should actual or budgeted service department costs be allocated? Why?

17–8. Explain the difference between two-stage allocation with departmental overhead rates and activity-based costing. Which approach generally results in more accurate product costs?

17–9. Define the following terms: joint production process, joint costs, joint products, split-off point, separable costs, and by-product.

17–10. Briefly explain how to use the physical-units method of joint cost allocation.

17–11. Describe the relative-sales-value method of joint cost allocation.

17–12. Define the term *net realizable value,* and explain how this concept can be used to allocate joint costs.

17–13. Are joint cost allocations useful? If they are, for what purpose?

17–14. For what purpose should the managerial accountant be careful to not use joint cost allocations?

Exercises

All applicable Exercises are available with McGraw-Hill's *Connect Accounting*™.

Perth Academy enrolls students in two departments, Liberal Arts and Sciences. The school also has two service departments, the Library and the Computing Services Department. The usage of these two service departments' output for the year is as follows:

■ **Exercise 17–15**
Direct Method of Service Department Cost Allocation; College
(LO 1)

	Provider of Service	
User of Service	**Library**	**Computing Services**
Library	—	20%
Computing Services	—	—
Liberal Arts	60%	30%
Sciences	40%	50%

The budgeted costs in the two service departments for the year are as follows:

Library	$750,000
Computing Services	320,000

Required:

1. Use the direct method to allocate the budgeted costs of the Library and Computing Services Department to the school's Liberal Arts and Sciences departments.

2. *Build a spreadsheet:* Construct an Excel spreadsheet to solve the preceding requirement. Show how the solution will change if the following information changes: the budgeted costs of the Library and Computing Services are $590,000 and $280,000, respectively.

Refer to the data given in the preceding exercise.

■ **Exercise 17–16**
Step-Down Method of Service Department Cost Allocation; College
(LO 1)

Required:

1. Use the step-down method to allocate Perth Academy's service department costs to the Liberal Arts and Sciences departments.

2. *Build a spreadsheet:* Construct an Excel spreadsheet to solve the preceding requirement. Show how the solution will change if the following information changes: the budgeted costs of the Library and Computing Services are $590,000 and $280,000, respectively.

■ **Exercise 17–17**
Direct Method of Service
Department Cost Allocation;
Bank
(LO 1)

Diaspora Bank has two service departments, the Human Resources (HR) Department and the Computing Department. The bank has two other departments that directly service customers, the Deposit Department and the Loan Department. The usage of the two service departments' output for the year is as follows:

	Provider of Service	
User of Service	**HR**	**Computing**
HR	—	15%
Computing	10%	—
Deposit	60%	50%
Loan	30%	35%

The budgeted costs in the two service departments for the year are as follows:

HR	$153,000
Computing	229,500

Required: Use the direct method to allocate the budgeted costs of the HR and Computing departments to the Deposit and Loan departments.

■ **Exercise 17–18**
Step-Down Method of Service
Department Cost Allocation;
Bank
(LO 1)

Refer to the data given in the preceding exercise.

Required: Use the step-down method to allocate the budgeted costs of the HR and Computing departments to the Deposit and Loan departments. Diaspora Bank allocates the costs of the HR Department first.

■ **Exercise 17–19**
Service Department Cost
Allocation; Use of Internet
(LO 1)

Visit the Web site of one of the following organizations, or a different organization of your choosing.

BNP Paribas Bank	www.bnpparibas.com
Penfolds Wines	www.penfolds.com.au
Mayo Clinic	www.mayo.edu
Rotana Hotels	www.rotana.com
Walt Disney Studios	www.disney.com

Required: Read about the organization's activities and operations. Then list three activities that you think the organization would need that would likely be established as service departments. For what purposes would it be relevant to allocate those service department costs to nonservice departments within the organization?

■ **Exercise 17–20**
Physical-Units Method; Joint
Cost Allocation
(LO 4)

Great Grains Company manufactures two oat products in a joint process. Cost and quantity information is as follows:

Joint Cost	Cereal	Quantity at Split-Off Point	Sales Price per Kilogram
$60,000	Oat bran	12,000 kilograms	$1.50
	Rolled oats	8,000 kilograms	3.00

Required: Use the physical-units method to allocate the company's joint production cost between oat bran and rolled oats.

■ **Exercise 17–21**
Relative-Sales-Value Method;
Joint Cost Allocation
(LO 4)

Refer to the data given in the preceding exercise.

Required: Use the relative-sales-value method to allocate Great Grains Company's joint production cost between oat bran and rolled oats.

■ **Exercise 17–22**
Net-Realizable-Value Method;
Joint Cost Allocation
(LO 4)

Refer to the data given in Exercise 17–20. Great Grains Company has an opportunity to process its rolled oats further into a powdered health drink enhancer. The additional processing operation costs $.50 per kilogram, and the health drink enhancer will sell for $4.50 per kilogram. The weight of the powdered health drink enhancer is the same as the weight of the rolled oats that are used to make it.

Required:

1. Should Great Grains' management process rolled oats into powdered health drink enhancer? Why?
2. Suppose the company does process rolled oats into health drink enhancer. Use the net-realizable-value method to allocate the joint production cost between health drink enhancer and the oat bran.

Refer to the data given in Exercise 17–17 for Diaspora Bank.

Required: Use the reciprocal-services method to allocate the budgeted costs of the HR and Computing departments to the Deposit and Loan departments.

■ **Exercise 17–23**
Reciprocal-Services Method;
Bank (Appendix)
(LO 6)

Problems

All applicable Problems are available with McGraw-Hill's *Connect Accounting*™.

Toluca Instrument Company manufactures gauges for construction machinery. The company has two production departments: Machining and Assembly. There are three service departments: Maintenance, Human Resources (HR), and Computer Aided Design (CAD). The usage of these service departments' output during the year just completed is as follows:

■ **Problem 17–24**
Direct and Step-Down
Methods of Service
Department Cost Allocation
(LO 1)

1. HR department cost
allocated to assembly:
$100,000
3. HR department cost
allocated to CAD: $9,000

Provision of Service Output (in hours of service)

User of Service	HR	Maintenance	CAD
		Provider of Service	
HR	—	—	—
Maintenance	500	—	—
CAD	500	500	—
Machining	4,000	3,500	4,500
Assembly	5,000	4,000	1,500
Total	10,000	8,000	6,000

The budgeted costs in Toluca Instrument Company's service departments during the year are as follows:

	HR	Maintenance	CAD
Variable	$ 50,000	$ 80,000	$ 50,000
Fixed	130,000	150,000	300,000
Total	$180,000	$230,000	$350,000

Required:

1. Use the direct method to allocate Toluca Instrument Company's service department costs to its production departments.
2. Determine the proper sequence to use in allocating the firm's service department costs by the step-down method.
3. Use the step-down method to allocate the company's service department costs.
4. *Build a spreadsheet:* Construct an Excel spreadsheet to solve requirements (1) and (3) above. Show how the solution will change if the following information changes: the budgeted variable costs in the three departments are $60,000, $70,000, and $55,000, for Human Resources, Maintenance, and CAD, respectively.

Refer to the data given in the preceding problem. When Toluca Instrument Company established its service departments, the following long-run needs were anticipated.

■ **Problem 17–25**
Dual Allocation of Service
Department Costs
(LO 1, 2)

1(a). Variable costs, CAD,
allocated to machining:
$37,500
1(b). Fixed costs, HR department, allocated to assembly:
$76,471

Long-Run Service Needs (in hours of service)			
	Provider of Service		
User of Service	**HR**	**Maintenance**	**CAD**
HR	—	—	—
Maintenance	500	—	—
CAD	1,000	800	—
Machining	3,500	4,800	4,800
Assembly	5,000	2,400	1,200
Total	10,000	8,000	6,000

Required: Use the dual approach in conjunction with each of the following methods to allocate Toluca Instrument Company's service department costs: (1) direct method and (2) step-down method.

■ **Problem 17–26**
Service Department Cost
Allocation
(LO 1)

1. Overhead rate per hour, etching: $10.602 (rounded)
2. Maintenance department costs allocated to finishing: $87,111

Celestial Artistry Company is developing departmental overhead rates based on direct-labor hours for its two production departments, Etching and Finishing. The Etching Department employs 20 people and the Finishing Department employs 80 people. Each person in these two departments works 2,000 hours per year. The production-related overhead costs for the Etching Department are budgeted at $200,000, and the Finishing Department costs are budgeted at $320,000. Two service departments, Maintenance and Computing, directly support the two production departments. These service departments have budgeted costs of $48,000 and $250,000, respectively. The production departments' overhead rates cannot be determined until the service departments' costs are allocated. The following schedule reflects the use of the Maintenance Department's and Computing Department's output by the various departments.

	Using Department			
Service Department	**Maintenance**	**Computing**	**Etching**	**Finishing**
Maintenance (maintenance hours)	0	1,000	1,000	8,000
Computing (minutes)	240,000	0	840,000	120,000

Required:

1. Use the direct method to allocate service department costs. Calculate the overhead rates per direct-labor hour for the Etching Department and the Finishing Department.

2. Use the step-down method to allocate service department costs. Allocate the Computing Department's costs first. Calculate the overhead rates per direct-labor hour for the Etching Department and the Finishing Department.

(CMA, adapted)

■ **Problem 17–27**
Joint Costs
(LO 4, 5)

2. CBL, allocation of joint cost: $225,000
3. MSB, net realizable value: $200,000

Snake River Sawmill manufactures two lumber products from a joint milling process. The two products developed are mine support braces (MSB) and unseasoned commercial building lumber (CBL). A standard production run incurs joint costs of $300,000 and results in 60,000 units of MSB and 90,000 units of CBL. Each MSB sells for $2, and each unit of CBL sells for $4.

Required:

1. Calculate the amount of joint cost allocated to commercial building lumber (CBL) on a physical-units basis.

2. Calculate the amount of joint cost allocated to the mine support braces (MSB) on a relative-sales-value basis.

3. Assume the commercial building lumber is not marketable at split-off but must be further planed and sized at a cost of $200,000 per production run. During this process, 10,000 units are unavoidably lost; these spoiled units have no value. The remaining units of commercial building lumber are saleable at $10 per unit. The mine support braces, although saleable immediately at the split-off point, are coated with a tarlike preservative that costs $100,000 per production run. The braces are then sold for $5 each. Using the net-realizable-value basis, compute the completed cost assigned to each unit of commercial building lumber.

4. If Snake River Sawmill chose not to process the mine support braces beyond the split-off point, the contribution from the joint milling process would increase or decrease by what amount?

5. Did you use the joint cost allocation results in answering requirement (4)? If so, how? Why did you use or not use the allocation results?

(CMA, adapted)

■ **Problem 17–28**
Service Department Cost Allocation; Plantwide versus Departmental Overhead Rates; Cost Drivers
(LO 3)

Travelcraft Company manufactures a complete line of fiberglass suitcases and attaché cases. The firm has three manufacturing departments: Molding, Component, and Assembly. There are also two service departments: Power and Maintenance.

The sides of the cases are manufactured in the Molding Department. The frames, hinges, and locks are manufactured in the Component Department. The cases are completed in the Assembly Department. Varying amounts of materials, time, and effort are required for each of the cases. The Power Department and Maintenance Department provide services to the three manufacturing departments.

Travelcraft has always used a plantwide overhead rate. Direct-labor hours are used to assign overhead to products. The predetermined overhead rate is calculated by dividing the company's total estimated overhead by the total estimated direct-labor hours to be worked in the three manufacturing departments.

Karen Mason, director of cost management, has recommended that Travelcraft use departmental overhead rates. The planned operating costs and expected levels of activity for the coming year have been developed by Mason and are presented by department in the following schedules. (All numbers are in thousands.)

1. Plantwide overhead rate: $20.55 per direct-labor hour
2(c). Rate, molding: $37.44 per MH

	Service Departments	
	Power	**Maintenance**
Departmental activity measures:		
Maximum capacity	1,000 kilowatt-hours	Adjustable
Estimated usage for the coming year	800 kilowatt-hours	125 hours
Departmental costs:		
Materials and supplies	$ 5,000	$1,500
Variable labor	1,400	2,250
Fixed overhead	12,000	250
Total service department costs	$18,400	$4,000

	Manufacturing Departments		
	Molding	**Component**	**Assembly**
Department activity measures:			
Direct-labor hours	500	2,000	1,500
Machine hours	875	125	–0–
Departmental costs:			
Direct material	$12,400	$30,000	$ 1,250
Direct labor	3,500	20,000	12,000
Variable overhead	3,500	10,000	16,500
Fixed overhead	17,500	6,200	6,100
Total departmental costs	$36,900	$66,200	$35,850
Use of service departments:			
Maintenance:			
Estimated usage in labor hours for the coming year	90	25	10
Power (in kilowatt-hours):			
Estimated usage for the coming year	360	320	120
Maximum allotted capacity	500	350 .	150

Required:

1. Calculate the plantwide overhead rate for Travelcraft Company for the coming year using the same method as used in the past.

2. Karen Mason has been asked to develop departmental overhead rates for comparison with the plantwide rate. The following steps are to be followed in developing the departmental rates.

a. The Maintenance Department costs should be allocated to the three manufacturing departments using the direct method.

b. The Power Department costs should be allocated to the three manufacturing departments using the dual method combined with the direct method. Fixed costs are to be allocated according to maximum allotted capacity, and variable costs are to be allocated according to planned usage for the coming year.

c. Calculate departmental overhead rates for the three manufacturing departments using a machine-hour cost driver for the Molding Department and a direct-labor-hour cost driver for the Component and Assembly departments.

3. As Karen Mason's assistant, draft a memo for her to send to Travelcraft's president recommending whether the company should use a plantwide rate or departmental rates to assign overhead to products.

(CMA, adapted)

■ Problem 17–29

Joint Costs; Allocation and Production Decisions
(LO 4, 5)

1. HTP-3, net realizable value: $1,926,000
2. HTP-3, cost per liter: $2.21 (rounded)

Biondi Industries is a manufacturer of chemicals for various purposes. One of the processes used by Biondi produces HTP–3, a chemical used in hot tubs and swimming pools; PST–4, a chemical used in pesticides; and RJ–5, a product that is sold to fertilizer manufacturers. Biondi uses the net-realizable-value method to allocate joint production costs. The ratio of output quantities to input quantities of direct material used in the joint process remains consistent from month to month. Biondi Industries uses FIFO (first-in, first-out) in valuing its finished-goods inventories.

Data regarding Biondi's operations for the month of October are as follows. During this month, Biondi incurred joint production costs of $1,400,000 in the manufacture of HTP–3, PST–4, and RJ–5.

	HTP–3	PST–4	RJ–5
Finished goods inventory in liters (October 1)	18,000	52,000	3,000
October sales in liters	650,000	325,000	150,000
October production in liters	700,000	350,000	170,000
Additional processing costs	$874,000	$816,000	$60,000
Final sales value per liter	$4.00	$6.00	$5.00

Required:

1. Determine Biondi Industries' allocation of joint production costs for the month of October. (Carry calculation of relative proportions to four decimal places.)

2. Determine the dollar values of the finished-goods inventories for HTP–3, PST–4, and RJ–5 as of October 31. (Round the cost per liter to the nearest cent.)

3. Suppose Biondi Industries has a new opportunity to sell PST–4 at the split-off point for $3.80 per liter. Prepare an analysis showing whether the company should sell PST–4 at the split-off point or continue to process this product further.

(CMA, adapted)

■ Problem 17–30

Joint Cost Allocation; Missing Data
(LO 1)

1. Omega, joint cost allocation: $9,000
3. Kappa, net realizable value: $20,000

Berger Company manufactures products Delta, Kappa, and Omega from a joint process. Production, sales, and cost data for July follow.

	Delta	Kappa	Omega	Total
Units produced	4,000	2,000	1,000	7,000
Joint cost allocation	$36,000	?	?	$60,000
Sales value at split-off	?	?	$15,000	$100,000
Additional costs if processed further	$7,000	$5,000	$3,000	$15,000
Sales value if processed further	$70,000	$25,000	$20,000	$115,000

Required:

1. Assuming that joint costs are allocated using the relative-sales-value method, what were the joint costs allocated to products Kappa and Omega?

2. Assuming that joint costs are allocated using the relative-sales-value method, what was the sales value at split-off for product Delta?

3. Use the net-realizable-value method to allocate the joint production costs to the three products.

(CPA, adapted)

Xi'an Chemicals uses a joint process to produce VX-4, a chemical used in the manufacture of paints and varnishes; HD-10, a chemical used in household cleaning products; and FT-5, a by-product that is sold to fertilizer manufacturers. Joint production costs are allocated to the main products on the basis of net realizable value. The by-product is inventoried at its net realizable value, and this value is used to reduce the joint production cost before allocation to the main products.

During the month of November, Xi'an Chemicals incurred joint production costs of $1,568,000. Data regarding Xi'an's November operations are as follows:

	VX-4	HD-10	FT-5
November production in liters	600,000	320,000	85,000
Sales value per liter at split-off	None	$3.00	$.90*
Separable processing cost	$720,000	$920,000	None
Final sales value per liter	$4.00	$6.375	None
Finished-goods inventory in liters on November 30 (all produced during November)	9,000	26,000	1,500

*Disposal costs of $.10 per liter will be incurred in order to sell the by-product.

Required:

1. Define the terms *joint costs* and *split-off point*.
2. Determine the dollar values of Xi'an Chemicals' finished-goods inventories on November 30 for VX-4 and HD-10.
3. Xi'an Chemicals has an opportunity to sell HD-10 for its sales value at the split-off point. Determine if Xi'an should sell HD-10 at the split-off point or continue to process it further.

(CPA, adapted)

Montpelier Cie. manufactures two products out of a joint process: Compod and Ultrasene. The joint costs incurred are $250,000 for a standard production run that generates 120,000 liters of Compod and 80,000 liters of Ultrasene. Compod sells for $2.00 per liter while Ultrasene sells for $3.25 per liter.

Required:

1. If there are no additional processing costs incurred after the split-off point, calculate the amount of joint cost of each production run allocated to Compod on a physical-units basis.
2. If there are no additional processing costs incurred after the split-off point, calculate the amount of joint cost of each production run allocated to Ultrasene on a relative-sales-value basis.
3. Suppose the following additional processing costs are required beyond the split-off point in order to obtain Compod and Ultrasene: $.10 per liter for Compod and $1.10 per liter for Ultrasene.
   a. Calculate the amount of joint cost of each production run allocated to Ultrasene on a physical-units basis.
   b. Calculate the amount of joint cost of each production run allocated to Compod on a net-realizable-value basis.
4. Assuming the same data as in requirement (3), suppose Compod can be processed further into a product called Compodalene, at an additional cost of $.40 per liter. Compodalene will be sold for $2.60 per liter by independent distributors. The distributors' commission will be 10% of the sales price. Should Montpelier Cie. sell Compod or Compodalene?
5. Independent of your answer to requirement (4), suppose Anne-Marie Guillotin, the assistant controller, has completed an analysis showing that Compod should not be processed further into Compodalene. Before presenting her analysis to top management, however, she got a visit from Charles LaMarque, Montpelier Cie.'s director of research. LaMarque was upset upon learning that Compodalene, a product he had personally developed, would not be manufactured.

   LaMarque: "The company's making a big mistake if it passes up this opportunity. Compodalene will be a big seller and get us into new markets."

   Guillotin: "But the analysis shows that we'd be losing money on every liter of Compod that we process further."

   LaMarque: "I know, Anne-Marie, but that's a temporary problem. Eventually, we'll bring down the cost of making Compodalene."

■ **Problem 17–31**
Joint Products; Sell or
Process Further
(LO 4, 5)

2. Joint cost allocation, VX-4: $900,000
3. Incremental revenue: $160,000

■ **Problem 17–32**
Joint Costs; Allocation and
Production Decisions; Ethics
(LO 4, 5)

1. Ultrasene, relative proportion: 40%
3(b). Ultrasene, separable cost of processing: $88,000

> **Guillotin:** "Can you find me some estimates on the cost reduction you expect?"
>
> **LaMarque:** "I don't have a crystal ball, Anne-Marie. Look, if you could adjust the numbers a little bit to help me get approval to produce some Compodalene, I can get this product off the ground. I know the cost reduction will come."

Comment on the ethical issues in this scenario. What should Anne-Marie Guillotin do?

6. Assume the same data as given in requirements (3) and (4). The industrial chemical industry has experienced a downturn, which has left Montpelier Cie. with idle capacity. Suppose Montpelier Cie. can sell only half of the Compod made in each production run, but the remainder could be sold as Compodalene. Should Montpelier Cie. process the remaining Compod into Compodalene?

(CMA, adapted)

■ **Problem 17–33**
Reciprocal-Service Method
(Appendix)
(LO 6)

M = $100,000, where *M* denotes the "total" cost of the Maintenance Department; Service Department costs allocated to Etching: $192,000

Refer to the data given in Problem 17–26 for Celestial Artistry Company.

Required:

1. Use the reciprocal-services method to allocate service department costs. Calculate the overhead rates per direct-labor hour for the Etching Department and the Finishing Department.

2. Which of the three methods of service department cost allocation results in the most accurate overhead rates? Why?

■ **Problem 17–34**
Reciprocal-Services Method;
Dual Allocation (Appendix)
(LO 2, 6)

1. Variable costs:
H = $17,551 (rounded), where *H* denotes the "total" cost of the HR Department; total variable cost allocated to Orthopedics: $29,705
2. *H* = $59,848 (rounded), where *H* denotes the "total" cost of the HR Department; total fixed cost allocated to Internal Medicine: $151,918

Refer to the data for Clínica Neruda given in Exhibits 17–2 and 17–5.

Required: Use the reciprocal-services method in combination with the dual-allocation approach to allocate Clínica Neruda's service department costs. *Hint:* You will need to apply the reciprocal-services method twice. First, allocate the three service departments' variable costs using the short-run usage proportions in Exhibit 17–2 (panel A). Second, allocate the three service departments' fixed costs using the long-run average usage proportions in Exhibit 17–5. Finally, add the variable costs and fixed costs allocated to each direct-patient-care department.

Cases

■ **Case 17–35**
Joint Cost Allocation;
By-Product
(LO 4)

2. Juice, net realizable value: $17,000
3. Allocation of joint cost, slices: $30,160

Top Quality Fruit Company, based in Costa Rica, grows, processes, cans, and sells three main pineapple products: sliced, crushed, and juice. The outside skin is cut off in the Cutting Department and processed as animal feed. The feed is treated as a by-product. The company's production process is as follows:

*   Pineapples first are processed in the Cutting Department. The pineapples are washed and the outside skin is cut away. Then the pineapples are cored and trimmed for slicing. The three main products (sliced, crushed, juice) and the by-product (animal feed) are recognizable after processing in the Cutting Department. Each product then is transferred to a separate department for final processing.

*   The trimmed pineapples are sent to the Slicing Department, where the pineapples are sliced and canned. Any juice generated during the slicing operation is packed in the cans with the slices.

*   The pieces of pineapple trimmed from the fruit are diced and canned in the Crushing Department. Again, the juice generated during this operation is packed in the can with the crushed pineapple.

- The core and surplus pineapple generated from the Cutting Department are pulverized into a liquid in the Juicing Department. There is an evaporation loss equal to 8 percent of the weight of the good output produced in this department that occurs as the juices are heated.
- The outside skin is chopped into animal feed in the Feed Department.

Top Quality Fruit Company uses the net-realizable-value method to assign the costs of the joint process to its main products. The net realizable value of the by-product is subtracted from the joint cost before the allocation.

A total of 270,000 kilograms were entered into the Cutting Department during June. The following schedule shows the costs incurred in each department, the proportion by weight transferred to the four final processing departments, and the selling price of each end product.

Processing Data and Costs for June

Department	Costs Incurred	Proportion of Product by Weight Transferred to Departments	Selling Price per Pound of Final Product
Cutting	$60,000	—	none
Slicing	4,700	35%	$.60
Crushing	10,580	28	.55
Juicing	3,250	27	.30
Animal feed	700	10	.10
Total	$79,230	100%	

Required: Compute each of the following amounts.

1. The number of kilograms of pineapple that result as output for pineapple slices, crushed pineapple, pineapple juice, and animal feed.
2. The net realizable value at the split-off point of the three main products.
3. The amount of the cost of the Cutting Department allocated to each of the three main products.

(CMA, adapted)

■ **Case 17–36**
Comprehensive Case on Joint Cost Allocation
(LO 4, 5)

1. Total joint cost: $210,000
2(b). Resoline, sales value at split-off point: $200,000

Valdosta Chemical Company manufactures two industrial chemical products in a joint process. In May, 10,000 liters of input costing $60,000 were processed at a cost of $150,000. The joint process resulted in 8,000 kilograms of Resoline and 2,000 kilograms of Krypto. Resoline sells for $25 per kilogram, and Krypto sells for $50 per kilogram. Management generally processes each of these chemicals further in separable processes to produce more refined chemical products. Resoline is processed separately at a cost of $5 per kilogram. The resulting product, Resolite, sells for $35 per kilogram. Krypto is processed separately at a cost of $15 per kilogram. The resulting product, Kryptite, sells for $95 per kilogram.

Required:

1. Draw a diagram similar to Exhibit 17–8 to depict Valdosta Chemical Company's joint production process.
2. Allocate the company's joint production costs for May using
   a. The physical-units method.
   b. The relative-sales-value method.
   c. The net-realizable-value method.
3. Valdosta's management is considering an opportunity to process Kryptite further into a new product called Omega. The separable processing will cost $40 per kilogram. Packaging costs for Omega are projected to be $6 per kilogram, and the anticipated sales price is $130 per kilogram. Should Kryptite be processed further into Omega? Why?
4. In answering requirement (3), did you use your joint cost allocation from requirement (2)? If so, how did you use it?
5. *Build a spreadsheet:* Construct an Excel spreadsheet to solve requirements (2) and (3) above. Show how the solution will change if the following information changes: the joint cost is $245,000, and the sales price of Omega is $125 per kilogram.

Appendix I

Internal Controls and the Global Effects of the Sarbanes-Oxley Act

AFTER COMPLETING THIS APPENDIX, YOU SHOULD BE ABLE TO:

1   Understand and discuss the concept of internal controls over financial reporting and financial management.

2   Understand and discuss the internal control requirements of the U.S. Sarbanes-Oxley Act and its effect on companies worldwide.

Management accountants play an integral part in the creation and monitoring of systems of internal control, which are the systems and processes by which companies worldwide ensure that their goals and objectives are accomplished.

In 2002, following a series of corporate accounting scandals, the Sarbanes-Oxley Act (often abbreviated as SOX) was enacted in the United States. Accounting problems, including failures in internal control systems, at Enron, WorldCom, and many other companies (most of them U.S. companies though ultimately including other companies worldwide such as Parmalat in Italy and Kanebo in Japan), resulted in a precipitous drop in the investing public's confidence in companies' published financial statements. SOX was enacted to bring about reform in companies' financial reporting processes, as well as the internal and external auditing of the financial reporting process. Under SOX, a company's top executives, including the CEO (chief executive officer) and the CFO (chief financial officer), can be held criminally responsible if their firm's financial statements prove to be fraudulent or materially misstate the firm's financial condition.

The Sarbanes-Oxley Act applies to all companies that offer shares for sale to the public on U.S. stock exchanges. So it applies not only to U.S. companies but to all companies worldwide that choose to participate in the main U.S. capital markets. In addition, the accounting scandals in the United States and the subsequent adoption of SOX have served as a wake-up call worldwide on the importance of adequate systems of internal controls, inspiring other efforts to require improved control performance. Comparable post-SOX legislation includes the Financial Security Law in France (2003), Australia's Corporate Law Economic Reform Program (2004), and the Financial Instruments and Exchange Law in Japan (2006). For this reason it is useful for management accountants everywhere to understand the content of SOX and especially its implications for internal controls.

The SOX Act runs 66 pages long and consists of 11 major parts (called titles), each of which is organized into several sections. SOX is a very complicated piece of legislation, and most of it relates primarily to corporate governance, financial accounting, auditing, and the penalties that the courts can invoke for violations of the law.[1] Three sections of SOX are germane to management accounting, because they address aspects of *internal controls* over financial reporting. Before covering these three sections of SOX, let's digress for a brief discussion of internal controls.

Internal Controls over Financial Reporting and Financial Management

Internal control may be "broadly defined as a process, established by an entity's board of directors, management, and other personnel, designed to provide reasonable assurance regarding the achievement of objectives in the following categories:

- Effectiveness and efficiency of operations.
- Reliability of financial reporting.
- Compliance with applicable laws and regulations."[2]

Bullets one and three above refer to *internal controls over financial management* and the second bullet point refers to *internal controls over financial reporting*. Together they refer to the broad set of policies, processes, and procedures that enable both the organization's management and interested outside parties to have confidence in the integrity of the organization's operations and the accuracy of its financial reports. These reports include the financial statements in the organization's annual report, the 10K filed with the SEC (U.S. Securities and Exchange Commission), tax returns filed with tax authorities, and other public financial disclosures. Even a moderately large company has thousands of procedures that can properly be viewed as internal controls. "They include a range of activities as diverse as approvals, authorizations, verifications, reconciliations, reviews of operating performance, security of assets, and separation of duties."[3] A few examples follow.

- Physical control over raw-material, work-in-process, and finished-goods inventories to prevent loss due to theft.
- Maintenance of adequate cost records to justify inventory valuations.
- Limitations on who is authorized to make purchases of various types and value.
- Requirement that two individuals sign checks to reduce the possibility of fraudulent expenditures.

This list could go on and on. Moreover, in the age of computerized accounting systems, many internal control procedures are automated. When you make a purchase from a major retailer, for example, the sale is entered into a computerized cash register by the salesperson. All sales are then accumulated across time by the retailer's accounting software system, and the result is a sales revenue figure on the firm's income statement. Suppose, though, that there was a glitch in the company's accounting software such that this sales accumulation process was not accurate. Among the retailer's internal controls

> **Learning Objective 1**
>
> Understand and discuss the concept of internal controls over financial reporting and financial management.

---

[1]The entire Sarbanes-Oxley Act is available at http://pcaobus.org/About/History/Documents/PDFs/Sarbanes_Oxley_Act_of_2002.pdf.

[2]*Internal Controls—Integrated Framework: Executive Summary* (New York: AICPA, Committee of Sponsoring Organizations of the Treadway Commission, or COSO, 2005), p. 1.

[3]Ibid., p. 2.

would be safeguards to ensure that the software is working properly and doing what it is supposed to do.[4] Other important software controls include limits on who in the organization has the authority to access computer programs and data.

To summarize, a large company's internal controls over financial reporting and financial management comprise a vast array of policies and procedures involving potentially hundreds of individuals. Since accounting information is used by both managers inside the company and interested parties outside the organization, internal controls are crucial to the integrity of both managerial and financial accounting. Now let's turn our attention to the three sections of the Sarbanes-Oxley Act that address internal controls.

Public Company Accounting Oversight Board

Learning Objective 2

Understand and discuss the internal control requirements of the U.S. Sarbanes-Oxley Act and similar legislation worldwide.

Any company whose registered shares are available for purchase by the general public, usually through trading on a stock exchange, is called a *public company*. Title I, Section 101 of SOX established the **Public Company Accounting Oversight Board (PCAOB)** in the United States. Similar oversight organizations were created by the post-SOX legislation adopted in other countries. With five full-time board members operating under the auspices of the SEC, the PCAOB's mission is to "oversee the auditors of companies in order to protect the interests of investors and further the public interest in the preparation of informative, fair and independent audit reports."[5] This mission applies to any company publicly traded in the United States, whether the company is based in the United States or elsewhere in the world.[6] The PCAOB's *Auditing Standard No. 2,* entitled *An Audit of Internal Control over Financial Reporting Performed in Conjunction with an Audit of Financial Statements,* details the board's requirements for auditors as they assess and attest to a client's internal control system.

SOX Sections 302 and 404

The SOX sections that have caused the most significant challenges for companies, and hence created the most controversy, are sections 302 and 404.

SOX 302 Entitled *Corporate Responsibility for Financial Reports,* SOX section 302 requires the signing officers of a company's financial reports to establish, maintain, and periodically evaluate the effectiveness of the company's internal controls over financial reporting. The following is an excerpt from SOX section 302, part (a).

> (4) The signing officers:
>> (A) are responsible for establishing and maintaining internal controls;
>> (B) have designed such internal controls to ensure that material information relating to the issuer [of the financial reports] and its consolidated subsidiaries is made known to such officers by others within those entities . . . ;
>> (C) have evaluated the effectiveness of the issuer's internal controls as of a date within 90 days prior to the report;
>> (D) have presented in the report their conclusions about the effectiveness of their internal controls based on their evaluation as of that date.[7]

Section 302 goes on to require that the signing officers must disclose to the company's auditors any material weaknesses or changes in the company's internal control system.

---

[4]There are many anecdotes of software glitches that resulted in flawed financial information or other mistakes. In one such incident, a company's billing software was incorrectly designed to express amounts in cents, rather than dollars, resulting in the company sending out bills for, say 10,000 dollars rather than the correct amount of 100 dollars (which is equivalent to 10,000 cents).

[5]PCAOB, "Mission, Structure & History," http://pcaobus.org/About/History/Pages/default.aspx.

[6]Specifically, SOX applies to non-U.S. companies whose securities, offered as stock-equivalents called American Depository Receipts or ADRs, are publicly traded on U.S. securities exchanges or are quoted on NASDAQ. These are referred to as Level II or Level III ADRs.

[7]Excerpt from the Sarbanes-Oxley Act, available at http://pcaobus.org/About/History/Documents/PDFs/ Sarbanes_Oxley_Act_of_2002.pdf [bracketed clarification added].

SOX 404 Entitled *Management Assessment of Internal Controls,* SOX section 404 requires a company to include in its annual report an internal control report. SOX section 404, part (a) states that the internal control report shall:

(1) state the responsibility of management for establishing and maintaining an adequate internal control structure and procedures for financial reporting; and

(2) contain an assessment, as of the end of the most recent fiscal year of the issuer, of the effectiveness of the internal control structure and procedures of the issuer for financial reporting.[8]

SOX section 404, part (b) addresses the role of the company's auditor, as the following excerpt shows:

(b) Internal Control Evaluation and Reporting: With respect to the internal control assessment required by subsection (a), each registered public accounting firm that prepares or issues the audit report for the issuer [of the financial reports] shall attest to and report on the assessment [of the internal controls] made by the management of the issuer.[9]

Implications of SOX Sections 302 and 404

SOX section 302(a)(4)(C), excerpted earlier in this appendix, is "one of the most serious and onerous requirements imposed by SOX. The CEO and CFO are expected to be able to demonstrate that there is a reliable process in place to evaluate, at least quarterly, the internal controls in place to ensure the reliability of the data being produced."[10] SOX section 404 then adds the requirement that the company's annual report include a report assessing the company's internal controls over financial reporting.

To summarize, SOX sections 302 and 404 go hand in hand. Section 302 essentially requires that management establish, maintain, and periodically assess the company's internal controls over financial reporting. Section 404 then requires that management include in the company's annual report a separate report that assesses those internal controls. Moreover, the company's auditors are required to attest as to the effectiveness of the internal controls.

In the relatively short time since its enactment, SOX sections 302 and 404 have caused a firestorm of controversy in business and accounting. Managers of many companies have complained about the onerous requirements imposed by sections 302 and 404 for detailed reporting on internal controls, as well as the extensive documentation required to back up the internal control reports. These requirements have been particularly burdensome for small businesses, which often lack the resources to comply with sections 302 and 404. Others defend sections 302 and 404 as necessary reforms in the wake of Enron and other corporate scandals. The SEC's chief accountant had this to say, "If you think [SOX section] 404 does nothing for fraud, you're doing it wrong." He went on to say that "companies may indeed be implementing 404 incorrectly by failing to focus on those controls that pose substantial risk." Nevertheless, the chief accountant admitted that the SEC was surprised by the cost of compliance with section 404. "Our estimates were way off," he said.[11]

The concept of controlling substantial risk exposure may well be the key to making SOX sections 302 and 404 work. It is probably not reasonable to require companies to report on the minutia of their internal controls over financial reporting. If management maintains, assesses, and reports on the internal control areas where the greatest risk of fraud or material misstatement occurs, that may be enough to achieve the objectives of SOX. Accordingly, the PCAOB has announced its intention to investigate whether auditors appropriately use a risk-based approach in determining where to focus their

---

[8]Ibid

[9]Ibid. [bracketed clarifications added].

[10]T. J. Leech, "Sarbanes-Oxley Sections 302 and 404: A White Paper Proposing Practical, Cost Effective Compliance Strategies," CARDdecisions, April 2003, p. 1, available at http://www.sec.gov/rules/proposed/s74002/card941503.pdf.

[11]"SEC Chief Defends 404," CFO.com, May 5, 2006, available at http://www.cfo.com/article.cfm/6899520?f=home_featured. See also Joann Lublin and Kara Scannell, "Critics See Some Good From Sarbanes-Oxley," *The Wall Street Journal,* July 30, 2007, p. B1.

evaluations of internal controls.[12] The PCAOB also issued a statement that it would be examining whether accountants "focused on those controls that pose the greatest risk to the company's financial statements."[13] For example, asks the SEC's chief accountant, "can the CFO go into the [accounting] system and make entries?"[14]

The controversy over SOX sections 302 and 404 is not going away any time soon. Several U.S. senators have called for the repeal of Sarbanes-Oxley altogether. Others in Congress believe the law needs modification. Still other lawmakers have suggested that small businesses should be exempt from SOX sections 302 and 404. A Google search of SOX section 404 yielded many current news articles. Among the headlines are the following:

- "Sarbanes-Oxley 404: The Section of Unintended Consequences"
- "Will the SEC Change the Sarbanes-Oxley Law?"
- "Sarbanes-Oxley Weighs on Small Companies"
- "SEC to Hear Complaints over Sarbanes-Oxley Law"
- "U.S. Supreme Court to Decide Corporate Reform Law"
- "Sarbanes-Oxley Audit Board Unconstitutional, Top Court Says"

SOX Section 301

One section of SOX that has been controversial internationally, especially in Europe, is Section 301. This section requires that companies establish "procedures for the receipt, retention, and treatment of complaints received by the issuer regarding accounting, internal accounting controls, or auditing matters" and that there be a way for employees to report such concerns confidentially and anonymously.[15] Commonly known as the "whistleblower hotline" provision, this requirement is not widely controversial in the United States but has run into problems with data privacy and labor law in other countries. Companies, therefore, must adapt their practices to try to be consistent with SOX but also comply with the laws of the countries in which they have operations. Most such laws are based on the guidance provided by the European Union's Article 29 Data Protection Working Party. An Opinion issued by this group provides that such procedures may exist but must be restricted largely to the accounting and internal control context of SOX and that anonymity, while allowed, is discouraged.[16]

The Uncertain Future

On June 28, 2010, as reported by *Bloomberg Business Week,* "The U.S. Supreme Court ruled that Congress violated the Constitution when it set up an auditing board after the Enron Corp. and WorldCom Inc. collapses, saying the panel was too insulated from presidential control. In a 5-4 decision that reinvigorates separation of powers principles, the court said the [U.S.] president must have more power to remove the members of the Public Company Accounting Oversight Board. . . . The ruling leaves it to Congress to re-establish the panel with tighter oversight, potentially setting up a new legislative fight that might sweep in other aspects of Sarbanes-Oxley."[17]

---

[12]PCAOB Release No. 104-2006-105, May 1, 2006, available at http://www.pcaobus.org/Inspections/2006-05-01_Release_104-2006-105.pdf.

[13]"SEC Chief Defends 404," CFO.com, May 5, 2006, available at http://www.cfo.com/article.cfm/6899520?f=home_featured.

[14]Ibid., p. 1.

[15]Excerpt from the Sarbanes-Oxley Act available at http://pcaobus.org/About/History/Documents/PDFs/Sarbanes_Oxley_Act_of_2002.pdf.

[16]European Union, ARTICLE 29 Data Protection Working Party, "Opinion 1/2006 on the application of EU data protection rules to internal whistleblowing schemes in the fields of accounting, internal accounting controls, auditing matters, fight against bribery, banking and financial crime," February 1, 2006.

[17]Greg Stohr, "Sarbanes-Oxley Audit Board Unconstitutional, Top Court Says" *Bloomberg Business Week* (online), June 28, 2010.

The high court did not strike down the key oversight authority of the PCAOB, but rather the procedures used to appoint or remove its members. Therefore, most of the key provisions of the Sarbanes-Oxley Act remain in force, at least for the foreseeable future.

Exactly where SOX will end up is anybody's guess, but it is likely to remain in some form. Moreover, the SEC is unlikely to eliminate the law's reforms on internal controls over financial reporting embodied in sections 302 and 404.

Key Terms

For each term's definition, refer to the indicated page or turn to the glossary at the end of the text.

internal control, 801	Public Company Accounting Oversight Board (PCAOB), 802	SOX 301, 804	SOX 302, 802 SOX 404, 803

Review Questions

I–1. Briefly describe the overall intent of the Sarbanes-Oxley Act of 2002.

I–2. Explain the nature and importance of internal controls over financial reporting.

I–3. Why is SOX important to companies outside of the United States?

I–4. Which non-U.S. companies must comply with SOX requirements?

I–5. What is the PCAOB? Describe its mission.

I–6. What does SOX section 302 require of management?

I–7. What does SOX section 404 require of management?

I–8. Why are SOX sections 302 and 404 controversial?

I–9. What does SOX section 301 require of management, and why is it controversial outside of the United States?

Exercises

All applicable Exercises are available with McGraw-Hill's *Connect Accounting*™.

Can you describe any internal controls you observed in a job you have held? Alternatively, what kinds of internal controls do you think are in place at your college or university?

■ **Exercise I–10**
Internal Controls
(LO 1)

Can the CEO of a large company really be expected to know what is going on at all levels in the organization? In various court cases, CEOs have argued that they could not be held accountable for the actions of others in their companies. As a group, stage an in-class debate about this issue.

■ **Exercise I–11**
Need for Internal Controls; Accountability
(LO 1)

Go online and use Google or another search engine to find several current news articles about SOX. Read and summarize three of these articles for your classmates.

■ **Exercise I–12**
Implications of Sarbanes-Oxley
(LO 2)

As a group, stage an in-class debate about the future of the Sarbanes-Oxley Act. At least four positions can be staked out: leave SOX as is, repeal SOX, modify SOX, and grant exemptions from SOX sections 302 and 404 for small businesses.

■ **Exercise I–13**
Implications of Sarbanes-Oxley
(LO 2)

■ **Exercise I–14**
Implications of
Sarbanes-Oxley
(LO 2)

What does it mean to say that the concept of risk exposure may be the key to making SOX sections 302 and 404 work?

■ **Exercise I–15**
Internal Controls and
Sarbanes-Oxley
(LO 1, 2)

Read Exercise 13–32 on page 612. Instead of answering the requirements listed in the exercise, discuss the implications of SOX sections 302 and 404 for the company's internal control issues.

■ **Exercise I–16**
Internal Controls and
Sarbanes-Oxley
(LO 1, 2)

Read Problem 9–44 on pages 428 and 429. Instead of answering the requirements listed in the problem, discuss the implications of SOX sections 302 and 404 regarding John Winslow's contemplated actions.

Appendix II
Compound Interest and the Concept of Present Value

AFTER COMPLETING THIS APPENDIX, YOU SHOULD BE ABLE TO:

1 Explain the importance of the time value of money in capital-budgeting decisions.

2 Compute the future value and present value of cash flows occurring over several time periods.

Before we can study the methods used to make capital-budgeting decisions, we must examine the basic tools used in those methods. The fundamental concept in a capital-budgeting decision analysis is the *time value* of money. Would you rather receive a $100 gift check from a relative today, or would you rather receive a letter promising the $100 in a year? Most of us would rather have the cash now. There are two possible reasons for this attitude. First, if we receive the money today, we can spend it on that new sweater now instead of waiting a year. Second, as an alternative strategy, we can invest the $100 received today at 10 percent interest. Then, at the end of one year, we will have $110. Thus, there is a time value associated with money. A $100 cash flow today is not the same as a $100 cash flow in 1 year, 2 years, or 10 years.

Learning Objective 1

Explain the importance of the time value of money in capital-budgeting decisions.

Compound Interest Suppose you invest $100 today (time 0) at 10 percent interest for one year. How much will you have after one year? The answer is $110, as the following analysis shows.

The $110 at time 1 (end of one year) is composed of two parts, as shown below.

Learning Objective 2

Compute the future value and present value of cash flows occurring over several time periods.

Principal, time 0 amount	$100
Interest earned during year 1 (.10 × $100)	10
Amount at time 1	$110

Thus, the $110 at time 1 consists of the $100 at time 0, called the **principal,** plus the $10 of interest earned during the year.

Now suppose you leave your $110 invested during the second year. How much will you have at the end of two years? As the following analysis shows, the answer is $121.

We can break down the $121 at time 2 into two parts as follows:

Amount at time 1	$110
Interest earned during year 2 (.10 × $110)	11
Amount at time 2	$121

Notice that you earned more interest in year 2 ($11) than you earned in year 1 ($10). Why? During year 2, you earned 10 percent interest on the original principal of $100 *and* you earned 10 percent interest on the year 1 interest of $10. Interest earned on prior periods' interest is called **compound interest.** Exhibit II–1 shows how your invested funds grow over the five-year period of the investment. As the exhibit shows, the **future value** of your initial $100 investment is $161.05 after five years.

As the number of years in an investment increases, it becomes more cumbersome to compute the future value of the investment using the method in Exhibit II–1.

Exhibit II–1
Compound Interest and Future Value

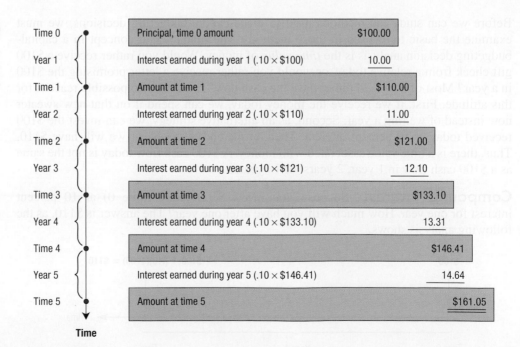

Fortunately, the simple formula shown below may be used to compute the future value of any investment.

$$F_n = P(1 + r)^n \tag{1}$$

where P denotes principal

r denotes interest rate per year

n denotes number of years

Using formula (1) to compute the future value after five years of your $100 investment, we have the following computation.

$$F_n = P(1 + r)^n$$

$$= \$100(1 + .10)^5$$

$$= \$100(1.6105) = \$161.05$$

The value of $(1 + r)^n$ is called the **accumulation factor.** The values of $(1 + r)^n$, for various combinations of r and n, are tabulated in Table I of Appendix A to Chapter 16, which appears on page 754.

Use formula (1) and the tabulated values in Table I to compute the future value after 10 years of an $800 investment that earns interest at the rate of 12 percent per year.[1]

Present Value   In the discussion above, we computed the future value of an investment when the original principal is known. Now consider a slightly different problem. Suppose you know how much money you want to accumulate at the end of a five-year investment. Your problem is to determine how much your initial investment needs to be in order to accumulate the desired amount in five years. To solve this problem, we start with formula (1):

$$F_n = P(1 + r)^n$$

Now divide each side of the preceding equation by $(1 + r)^n$

$$P = F_n \left(\frac{1}{(1 + r)^n} \right) \tag{2}$$

In formula (2), P denotes what is commonly referred to as the **present value** of the cash flow F_n, which occurs after n years when the interest rate is r.

Let's try out formula (2) on your investment problem, which we analyzed in Exhibit II–1. Suppose you did not know the value of the initial investment required if you want to accumulate $161.05 at the end of five years in an investment that earns 10 percent per year. We can determine the present value of the investment as follows:

$$P = F_n \left(\frac{1}{(1 + r)^n} \right)$$

$$= \$161.05 \left(\frac{1}{(1 + .10)^5} \right)$$

$$= \$161.05(.6209) = \$100$$

---

[1]Using formula (1): $F = \$800(1 + .12)^{10}$. From Table I, $(1 + .12)^{10} = 3.106$. (Note that the values in Table I are rounded.) Thus, the future value of the investment is $(\$800)(3.106) = \$2,484.80$. Compound interest will more than triple the original $800 investment in 10 years.

Thus, as we knew already, you must invest $100 now in order to accumulate $161.05 after five years in an investment earning 10 percent per year. The *present value* of $100 and the *future value* of $161.05 at time 5 are *economically equivalent,* given that the annual interest rate is 10 percent. If you are planning to invest the $100 received now, then you should be indifferent between receiving the present value of $100 now or receiving the future value of $161.05 at the end of five years.

When we used formula (2) to compute the present value of the $161.05 cash flow at time 5, we used a process called *discounting.* The interest rate used when we discount a future cash flow to compute its present value is called the **discount rate.** The value of $1/(1 + r)^n$, which appears in formula (2), is called the *discount factor.* Discount factors, for various combinations of r and n, are tabulated in Table III of Appendix A to Chapter 16.

Suppose you want to accumulate $18,000 to buy a car in four years, and you can earn interest at the rate of 8 percent per year on an investment you make now. How much do you need to invest now? Use formula (2) and the discount factors in Table III of Appendix A to Chapter 16 (p. 755) to compute the present value of the required $18,000 amount needed at the end of four years.[2]

Present Value of a Cash-Flow Series

The present-value problem we just solved involved only a single future cash flow. Now consider a slightly different problem. Suppose you just won $5,000 in the state lottery. You want to spend some of the cash now, but you have decided to save enough to rent a beach condominium during spring break of each of the next three years. You would like to deposit enough in a bank account now so that you can withdraw $1,000 from the account at the end of each of the next three years. The money in the bank account will earn 8 percent per year. The question, then, is how much do you need to deposit? Another way of asking the same question is, what is the *present value* of a series of three $1,000 cash flows at the end of each of the next three years, given that the discount rate is 8 percent?

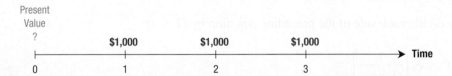

One way to figure out the answer to the question is to compute the present value of each of the three $1,000 cash flows and add the three present-value amounts. We can use formula (2) for these calculations, as shown in panel A of Exhibit II–2. Notice that the present value of each of the $1,000 cash flows is different, because the timing of the cash flows is different. The earlier the cash flow will occur, the higher is its present value.

Examine panel A of Exhibit II–2 carefully. We obtained the $2,577 total present value by adding three present-value amounts. Each of these amounts is the result of multiplying $1,000 by a discount factor. Notice that we can obtain the same final result by adding the three discount factors first, and then multiplying by $1,000. This approach is taken in panel B of Exhibit II–2. The sum of the three discount factors is called an *annuity discount factor,* because a series of equivalent cash flows is called an **annuity.** Annuity discount factors for various combinations of r and n are tabulated in Table IV of Appendix A to Chapter 16 (p. 756).

---

[2]Using formula (2): $P = \$18,000 \times [1/(1 + .08)^4]$. From Table III, $1/(1 + .08)^4 = .735$. (Note that the values in Table III are rounded.) Thus, the present value of the required $18,000 amount is ($18,000)(.735) = $13,230. An investment of $13,230 made now, earning annual interest at 8 percent, will accumulate to $18,000 at the end of four years.

A. Present Value of Cash-Flow Series Using Three Independent Present-Value Calculations

Present-value formula [formula (2)]: $P = F_n \left(\dfrac{1}{(1+r)^n} \right)$

Present value of time 1 cash flow: $\$1,000 \left(\dfrac{1}{(1+.08)^1} \right) = \$1,000\ (.9259) = \quad \$\ 925.90$

Present value of time 2 cash flow: $\$1,000 \left(\dfrac{1}{(1+.08)^2} \right) = \$1,000\ (.8573) = \quad \$\ 857.30$

Present value of time 3 cash flow: $\$1,000 \left(\dfrac{1}{(1+.08)^3} \right) = \$1,000\ (.7938) = \quad \underline{\$\ 793.80}$

Total: present value of series of three cash flows $\qquad\qquad$ $\$2,577.00$

Sum of Three Discount Factors
is the Annuity Discount Factor

B. Present Value of Cash-Flow Series Using the Annuity Discount Factor

Present value of series of three cash flows = $\$1,000\ (2.5770) = \qquad \underline{\$2,577.00}$

Exhibit II–2
Present Value of a Series of
Cash Flows

Now let's verify that $2,577 is the right amount to finance your three spring-break vacations. Exhibit II–3 shows how your bank account will change over the three-year period as you earn interest and then withdraw $1,000 each year.

Future Value of a Cash-Flow Series   To complete our discussion of present-value and future-value concepts, let's consider the series of $1,000 condo rental payments

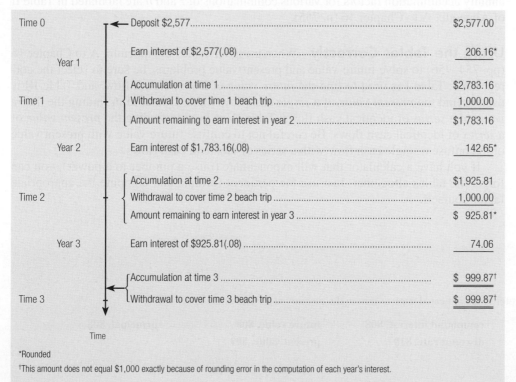

Time 0	Deposit $2,577	$2,577.00
Year 1	Earn interest of $2,577(.08)	206.16*
Time 1	Accumulation at time 1	$2,783.16
	Withdrawal to cover time 1 beach trip	1,000.00
	Amount remaining to earn interest in year 2	$1,783.16
Year 2	Earn interest of $1,783.16(.08)	142.65*
Time 2	Accumulation at time 2	$1,925.81
	Withdrawal to cover time 2 beach trip	1,000.00
	Amount remaining to earn interest in year 3	$ 925.81*
Year 3	Earn interest of $925.81(.08)	74.06
	Accumulation at time 3	$ 999.87†
Time 3	Withdrawal to cover time 3 beach trip	$ 999.87†

Time

*Rounded

†This amount does not equal $1,000 exactly because of rounding error in the computation of each year's interest.

Exhibit II–3
Verification of Present-Value
Calculation for Cash-Flow
Series

Exhibit II–4
Future Value of a Series of
Cash Flows

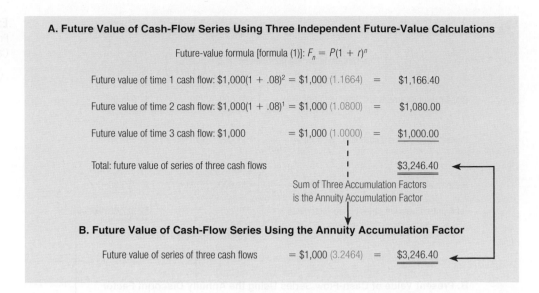

A. Future Value of Cash-Flow Series Using Three Independent Future-Value Calculations

Future-value formula [formula (1)]: $F_n = P(1 + r)^n$

Future value of time 1 cash flow: $1,000(1 + .08)^2 = $1,000 (1.1664)$ = $1,166.40

Future value of time 2 cash flow: $1,000(1 + .08)^1 = $1,000 (1.0800)$ = $1,080.00

Future value of time 3 cash flow: $1,000 = $1,000 (1.0000)$ = $1,000.00

Total: future value of series of three cash flows $3,246.40

Sum of Three Accumulation Factors
is the Annuity Accumulation Factor

B. Future Value of Cash-Flow Series Using the Annuity Accumulation Factor

Future value of series of three cash flows   = $1,000 (3.2464)$ = $3,246.40

from the condo owner's perspective. Suppose the owner invests each $1,000 rental payment in a bank account that pays 8 percent interest per year. How much will the condo owner accumulate at the end of the three-year period? An equivalent question is, What is the future value of the three-year series of $1,000 cash flows, given an annual interest rate of 8 percent? Exhibit II–4 answers the question in two ways. In panel A of the exhibit, three separate future-value calculations are made using formula (1). Notice that the $1,000 cash flow at time 1 is multiplied by $(1.08)^2$, since it has two years to earn interest. The $1,000 cash flow at time 2 has only one year to earn interest, and the time 3 cash flow has no time to earn interest.

In panel B of the exhibit, the three-year *annuity accumulation factor* is used. This factor is the sum of the three accumulation factors used in panel A of the exhibit. The annuity accumulation factors for various combinations of *r* and *n* are tabulated in Table II of Appendix A to Chapter 16 (p. 755).

Using the Tables Correctly

When using the tables in Appendix A to Chapter 16 (pp. 754–756) to solve future-value and present-value problems, be sure to select the correct table. Table I is used to find the *future value* of a *single* cash flow, and Table III is used to find the *present value* of a *single* cash flow. Table II is used in finding the *future value* of a *series* of identical cash flows; Table IV is used in finding the *present value* of a *series* of identical cash flows. Be careful not to confuse future value with present value or to confuse a single cash flow with a series of identical cash flows.

If you have a calculator that will exponentiate (raise a number to a power), you can forget the tables altogether. Just use the pertinent formula and compute the appropriate factor yourself.

Key Terms

For each term's definition, refer to the indicated page or turn to the glossary at the end of the text.

accumulation factor, 809	**compound interest, 808**	**future value, 808**	**principal, 808**
annuity, 810	**discount rate, 810**	**present value, 809**	

Review Questions

II–1.   What is meant by the term *compound interest?*

II–2.   Explain in words the following future-value formula:
$F_n = P(1 + r)^n$.

II–3.   Define the term *present value.*

II–4.   "The greater the discount rate, the greater the present value of a future cash flow." True or false? Explain your answer.

II–5.   "If the interest rate is 10 percent, a present value of $100 and a future value of $161.10 at the end of five years are *economically equivalent.*" Explain.

II–6.   What is an *annuity?*

Exercises

All applicable Exercises are available with McGraw-Hill's *Connect Accounting*™.

Answer each of the following independent questions. Ignore personal income taxes.

1. Suppose you invest $3,000 in an account bearing interest at the rate of 14 percent per year. What will be the future value of your investment in six years?

2. Your best friend won the state lottery and has offered to give you $12,000 in five years, after he has made his first million dollars. You figure that if you had the money today, you could invest it at 12 percent annual interest. What is the present value of your friend's future gift?

3. In four years, you would like to buy a small cabin in the mountains. You estimate that the property will cost you $91,875 when you are ready to buy. How much money would you need to invest each year in an account bearing interest at the rate of 6 percent per year in order to accumulate the $91,875 purchase price?

4. You have estimated that your educational expenses over the next three years will be $15,000 per year. How much money do you need in your account now in order to withdraw the required amount each year? Your account bears interest at 10 percent per year.

■ **Exercise II–7**
Future Value and Present Value
(LO 1, 2)

Refer to the answers given for the preceding exercise.

Required:

1. Refer to requirement (1) of the preceding exercise. Prepare a display similar to Exhibit II–1 to show how your accumulation grows each year to equal $6,585 after six years.

2. Refer to requirement (4) of the preceding exercise. Prepare a display similar to Exhibit II–3 to verify that $37,305 is the amount you need to fund your educational expenses.

■ **Exercise II–8**
Continuation of Preceding Exercise
(LO 1, 2)

You plan to retire at age 40 after a highly successful but short career. You would like to accumulate enough money by age 40 to withdraw $225,000 per year for 40 years. You plan to pay into your account 15 equal installments beginning when you are 25 and ending when you are 39. Your account bears interest of 12 percent per year.

Required:

1. How much do you need to accumulate in your account by the time you retire?

2. How much do you need to pay into your account in each of the 15 equal installments?

3. Is this a future-value problem or a present-value problem? Explain.

■ **Exercise II–9**
Future Value and Present Value
(LO 1, 2)

Appendix III

Inventory Management

Learning Objective 1

Calculate the economic order quantity (EOQ) using the EOQ decision model.

A key decision in manufacturing, retail, and some service industry firms is how much inventory to keep on hand. Once inventory levels are established, they become an important input to the budgeting system. Inventory decisions involve a delicate balance between three classes of costs: ordering costs, holding costs, and shortage costs. Examples of costs in each of these categories are given in Exhibit III–1.

The following illustration emphasizes the benefits of a sound inventory policy.

Economic Order Quantity

cozycamp.com

Cozycamp.com, a camping equipment manufacturer, has recently expanded its product line into winter sports equipment. The company's newest product is a fiberglass snowboard. One of the raw materials is a special resin used to bind the fiberglass in the molding phase of production. The production manager, Helmut Reichert, uses an **economic order quantity (EOQ)** decision model to determine the size and frequency with which resin is ordered. The EOQ model is a mathematical tool for determining the order quantity that minimizes the costs of ordering and holding inventory.

Resin is purchased in 250-liter drums, and 9,600 drums are used each year. Each drum costs $400. The controller estimates that the cost of placing and receiving a typical resin order is $225. The controller's estimate of the annual cost of carrying resin in inventory is $3 per drum.

Tabular Approach Suppose Reichert orders 800 drums of resin in each order placed during the year. The total annual cost of ordering and holding resin in inventory is calculated as follows:

Exhibit III–1
Inventory Ordering, Holding,
and Shortage Costs

Ordering Costs

Clerical costs of preparing purchase orders

Time spent finding suppliers and expediting orders

Transportation costs

Receiving costs (e.g., unloading and inspection)

Holding Costs

Costs of storage space (e.g., warehouse depreciation)

Security

Insurance

Forgone interest on working capital tied up in inventory

Deterioration, theft, spoilage, or obsolescence

Shortage Costs

Disrupted production when raw materials are unavailable:

Idle workers

Extra machinery setups

Lost sales resulting in dissatisfied customers

Loss of quantity discounts on purchases

$$\frac{\text{Annual requirement}}{\text{Quantity per order}} = \frac{9{,}600}{800} = 12 = \text{Number of orders}$$

$$\text{Annual ordering cost} = 12 \text{ orders} \times \$225 \text{ per order} = \$2{,}700$$

$$\text{Average quantity in inventory} = \frac{\text{Quantity per order}}{2} = \frac{800}{2} = 400 \text{ drums}$$

$$\text{Annual holding cost} = (\text{Average quantity in inventory}) \times (\text{Annual carrying cost per drum})$$

$$= 400 \times \$3 = \$1{,}200$$

$$\frac{\text{Total annual cost}}{\text{of inventory policy}} = \text{Ordering cost} + \text{Holding cost} = \$2{,}700 + \$1{,}200 = \$3{,}900$$

Notice that the $3,900 cost does not include the purchase cost of the resin at $400 per drum. We are focusing only on the costs of *ordering* and *holding* resin inventory.

Can Reichert do any better than $3,900 for the annual cost of his resin inventory policy? Exhibit III–2, which tabulates the inventory costs for various order quantities, indicates that Reichert can lower the costs of ordering and holding resin inventory. Of the five order quantities listed, the 1,200-drum order quantity yields the lowest total annual cost. Unfortunately, this tabular method for finding the least-cost order quantity is cumbersome. Moreover, it does not necessarily result in the optimal order quantity. It is possible that some order quantity other than those listed in Exhibit III–2 is the least-cost order quantity.

Equation Approach The total annual cost of ordering and holding inventory is given by the following equation.

$$\text{Total annual cost} = \left(\frac{\text{Annual requirement}}{\text{Order quantity}}\right)\left(\begin{array}{c}\text{Cost per}\\\text{order}\end{array}\right)$$

$$+ \left(\frac{\text{Order quantity}}{2}\right)\left(\begin{array}{c}\text{Annual holding}\\\text{cost per unit}\end{array}\right)$$

Exhibit III–2
Tabulation of Inventory Ordering and Holding Costs

cozycamp.com

Order size (drums)	800	960	1,200	1,600	2,400
Number of orders (9,600 ÷ order size)	12	10	8	6	4
Ordering costs ($225 × number of orders)	$2,700	$2,250	$1,800	$1,350	$ 900
Average inventory (order size ÷ 2)	400	480	600	800	1,200
Holding costs ($3 × average inventory)	$1,200	$1,440	$1,800	$2,400	$3,600
Total annual cost (ordering cost + holding cost)	$3,900	$3,690	$3,600	$3,750	$4,500

Minimum

The following formula for the least-cost order quantity, called the economic order quantity (or EOQ), has been developed using calculus.

$$\text{Economic order quantity} = \sqrt{\frac{(2)(\text{Annual requirement})(\text{Cost per order})}{(\text{Annual holding cost per unit})}}$$

The EOQ formula in Cozycamp.com's problem yields the following EOQ for resin.

$$\text{EOQ} = \sqrt{\frac{(2)(9,600)(225)}{3}} = 1,200 \text{ drums per order}$$

Graphical Approach
Another method for solving the EOQ problem is the graphical method, which is presented in Exhibit III–3. Notice that the ordering-cost line slants down to the right. This indicates a decline in these costs as the order size increases and the order frequency decreases. However, as the order size increases, so does the average inventory on hand. This results in an increase in holding costs, as indicated by the positive slope of the holding-cost line. The EOQ falls at 1,200 drums, where the best balance is struck between these two costs. Total costs are minimized at $3,600.

Timing of Orders

The EOQ model helps management decide how much to order at a time. Another important decision is when to order. This decision depends on the **lead time,** which is the length of time it takes for the material to be received after an order is placed. Suppose the lead time for resin is one month. Since Cozycamp.com uses 9,600 drums of resin per year, and the production rate is constant throughout the year, this implies that 800 drums are used each month. Production manager Reichert should order resin, in the economic order quantity of 1,200 drums, when the inventory falls to 800 drums. By the time the new order arrives, one month later, the 800 drums in inventory will have been used in production. Exhibit III–4 depicts this pattern of ordering and using inventory. By placing an order early enough to avoid a stockout, management takes into account the potential costs of shortages.

Safety Stock
Our example assumed that the usage of resin is constant at 800 drums per month. Suppose instead that monthly usage fluctuates between 600 and 1,000 drums. Although average monthly usage still is 800 drums, there is the potential for an excess usage of 200 drums in any particular month. In light of this uncertainty, management may wish to keep a safety stock of resin equal to the potential excess monthly usage of 200 drums. With a safety stock of 200 drums, the reorder point is 1,000 drums. Thus, Reichert should order the EOQ of 1,200 drums whenever resin inventory falls to 1,000 drums. During the one-month lead time, another 600 to 1,000 drums of resin will be consumed in production. Although a safety stock will increase inventory holding costs, it will minimize the potential costs caused by shortages.

Exhibit III–3
Graphical Solution to
Economic Order Quantity
Decision

cozycamp.com

Exhibit III–4
Ordering, Lead Time, and
Usage of inventory

cozycamp.com

JIT Inventory Management: Implications for EOQ

The EOQ model minimizes the total cost of ordering and holding purchased inventory. Thus, this inventory management approach seeks to balance the cost of ordering against the cost of storing inventory. Under the JIT philosophy, the goal is to keep *all* inventories as low as possible. *Any* inventory holding costs are seen as inefficient and wasteful. Moreover, under JIT purchasing, ordering costs are minimized by reducing the number of vendors, negotiating long-term supply agreements, making less frequent payments, and eliminating inspections. The implication of the JIT philosophy is that inventories should be minimized by more frequent deliveries in smaller quantities. This result can be demonstrated using the EOQ formula, as shown in Exhibit III–5. As the

Learning Objective 2

Understand the differences between the economic-order-quantity and just-in-time approaches to inventory management.

Exhibit III–5

Economic Order Quantity with Different Ordering and Holding Costs

cozycamp.com

Holding Costs per Unit	Ordering Costs per Order				
	$225	$150	$100	$50	
$3	1,200*	980	800	566	EOQ declines
4	1,039	849	693	490	
5	930	759	620	438	
6	849	693	566	400	
	EOQ declines				

*The annual requirement is assumed to be 9,600 units for each case in this table. This was the annual requirement for drums of resin in the Cozycamp.com illustration. (Several of the EOQs in the table are rounded.)

cost of holding inventory increases, the EOQ decreases. Moreover, as the cost of placing an order declines, the EOQ decreases.

The economics underlying the EOQ model support the JIT viewpoint that inventory should be purchased or produced in small quantities, and inventories should be kept to the absolute minimum. However, the basic philosophies of JIT and EOQ are quite different. The EOQ approach takes the view that some inventory is necessary, and the goal is to optimize the order quantity in order to balance the cost of ordering against the cost of holding inventory. In contrast, the JIT philosophy argues that holding costs tend to be higher than may be apparent because of the inefficiency and waste of storing inventory. Thus, inventory should be minimized, or even eliminated completely if possible. Moreover, under the JIT approach, orders typically will vary in size, depending on needs. The EOQ model, in contrast, results in a constant order quantity.

Key Terms

For each term's definition refer to the indicated page, or turn to the glossary at the end of the text.

economic order quantity   **lead time, 816**
(EOQ), 814

Review Questions

III–1. Define and give examples of *inventory ordering,* *holding,* and *shortage costs.*

III–2. Explain the differences in the basic philosophies underlying the JIT and EOQ approaches to inventory management.

Exercises

All applicable Exercises are available with McGraw-Hill's *Connect Accounting*™.

■ **Exercise III–3**
Economic Order Quantity
(LO 1)

For each of the following independent cases, use the equation method to compute the economic order quantity.

	Case A	Case B	Case C
Annual requirement (in units)	11,664	34,445	29,160
Cost per order	$300	$200	$15
Annual holding cost per unit	6	5	3

Andrew and Fulton, Ltd. uses 840 tonnes of a chemical bonding agent each year. Monthly demand fluctuates between 50 and 80 tonnes. The lead time for each order is one month, and the economic order quantity is 130 tonnes.

■ **Exercise III–4**
Lead Time and Safety Stock
(LO 1)

Required:

1. Determine the safety stock appropriate for the chemical bonding agent.
2. At what order point, in terms of tonnes remaining in inventory, should Andrew and Fulton, Ltd. order the bonding agent?

Fiber Technology, Inc. manufactures glass fibers used in the communications industry. The company's materials and parts manager is currently revising the inventory policy for XL-20, one of the chemicals used in the production process. The chemical is purchased in 10-kilogram canisters for $95 each. The firm uses 4,800 canisters per year. The controller estimates that it costs $150 to place and receive a typical order of XL-20. The annual cost of storing XL-20 is $4 per canister.

■ **Exercise III–5**
Economic Order Quantity
Equation Approach; JIT
Purchasing
(LO 1, 2)

Required:

1. Write the formula for the total annual cost of ordering and storing XL-20.
2. Use the EOQ formula to determine the optimal order quantity.
3. What is the total annual cost of ordering and storing XL-20 at the economic order quantity?
4. How many orders will be placed per year?
5. Fiber Technology's controller, Jay Turnbull, recently attended a seminar on JIT purchasing. Afterward he analyzed the cost of storing XL-20, including the costs of wasted space and inefficiency. He was shocked when he concluded that the real annual holding cost was $19.20 per canister. Turnbull then met with Doug Kaplan, Fiber Technology's purchasing manager. Together they contacted Reno Industries, the supplier of XL-20, about a JIT purchasing arrangement. After some discussion and negotiation, Kaplan concluded that the cost of placing an order for XL-20 could be reduced to just $20. Using these new cost estimates, Turnbull computed the new EOQ for XL-20.
   a. Use the equation approach to compute the new EOQ.
   b. How many orders will be placed per year?

Refer to the *original* data given in the preceding exercise for Fiber Technology, Inc.

■ **Exercise III–6**
Economic Order Quantity;
Tabular Approach
(LO 1)

Required:

1. Prepare a table showing the total annual cost of ordering and storing XL-20 for each of the following order quantities: 400, 600, and 800 canisters.
2. What are the weaknesses in the tabular approach?

Refer to the *original* data given in Exercise III–5 for Fiber Technology, Inc.

■ **Exercise III–7**
Economic Order Quantity;
Graphical Approach
(LO 1)

Required: Prepare a graphical analysis of the economic order quantity decision for XL-20.

Refer to the *original* data given in Exercise III–5 for Fiber Technology, Inc. The lead time required to receive an order of XL-20 is one month.

■ **Exercise III–8**
Economic Order Quantity;
Lead Time and Safety Stock
(LO 1)

Required:

1. Assuming stable usage of XL-20 each month, determine the reorder point for XL-20.
2. Draw a graph showing the usage, lead time, and reorder point for XL-20.
3. Suppose that monthly usage of XL-20 fluctuates between 300 and 500 canisters, although annual demand remains constant at 4,800 canisters. What level of safety stock should the materials and parts manager keep on hand for XL-20? What is the new reorder point for the chemical?

Chapter One

(1a)* Gary Siegel and James E. Sorensen, principal investigators for the Gary Siegel Organization, *Counting More, Counting Less: Transformations in the Management Accounting Profession* (Montvale, NJ: Institute of Management Accountants, 1999).

(1b) Ibid.

(1c) Ibid.

(1d) Ibid.

(1e) Ibid.

(1f) CUBUS AG, "Balanced Scorecard for the Controlling of the Manufacturing Network," http://www.cubus.eu/_en/assets/downloads/Case-Study-sri_E.pdf

(1g) Gary Siegel and James E. Sorensen, principal investigators for the Gary Siegel Organization, *Counting More, Counting Less: Transformations in the Management Accounting Profession* (Montvale, NJ: Institute of Management Accountants, 1999).

(1h) Ibid.

(1i) Ibid.

(1j) Ibid.

(1k) Ibid.

Chapter Two

(2a) Gary Siegel and James E. Sorensen, principal investigators for the Gary Siegel Organization, *Counting More, Counting Less: Transformations in the Management Accounting Profession* (Montvale, NJ: Institute of Management Accountants, 1999).

(2b) Gary Siegel, project director, *The Practice Analysis of Management Accounting* (Montvale, NJ: Institute of Management Accountants, 1996) pp. 17, 18.

(2c) Ibid., p. 14.

(2d) Ibid., p. 19.

(2e) *Activity-Based Management: Part I,* a management education video (Boston: President and Fellows of Harvard College, 1993).

(2f) Gary Siegel, project director, *The Practice Analysis of Management Accounting* (Montvale, NJ: Institute of Management Accountants, 1996), p. 18.

(2g) Interview with a Delta Air Lines accountant conducted during research by the author.

(2h) Gary Siegel and James E. Sorensen, principal investigators for the Gary Siegel Organization, *Counting More, Counting Less: Transformations in the Management Accounting Profession* (Montvale, NJ: Institute of Management Accountants, 1999).

Chapter Three

(3a) *The Management Accounting Video,* a management education video (New York: McGraw-Hill, 1997). *Note:* Since this video was made, MiCRUS was sold to Philips.

(3b) Gary Siegel and James E. Sorensen, principal investigators for the Gary Siegel Organization, *Counting More, Counting Less: Transformations in the Management Accounting Profession* (Montvale, NJ: Institute of Management Accountants, 1999).

(3c) *The Management Accounting Video,* a management education video (New York: McGraw-Hill, 1997). *Note:* Since this video was made, MiCRUS was sold to Philips.

(3d) Interview with a Chrysler accountant conducted during research by the author.

(3e) Interview with an accountant for The Walt Disney Company conducted during research by the author.

(3f) Interview with a Chrysler accountant conducted during research by the author.

(3g) Gary Siegel, project director, *The Practice Analysis of Management Accounting* (Montvale, NJ: Institute of Management Accountants, 1996), p. 17.

(3h) Interview with a Cornell University accountant conducted during research by the author.

(3i) *The Management Accounting Video,* a management education video (New York: McGraw-Hill, 1997).

Chapter Four

(4a) Steve Player and Carol Cobble, *Cornerstones of Decision Making: Profiles of Enterprise ABM* (Greensboro, NC: Oakhill Press, 1999), p. 161.

(4b) Ibid., p. 12.

(4c) Ibid., p. 168.

Chapter Five

(5a) *Activity-Based Management: Part I,* a management education video (Boston: The President and Fellows of Harvard College, 1993).

(5b) Joyce R. Ochs and Kenneth L. Parkinson, "Moving to Activity-Based Cost Analysis," *Business Finance* 5, no. 11 (November 1999), p. 101.

(5c) Steve Player and Carol Cobble, *Cornerstones of Decision Making: Profiles of Enterprise ABM* (Greensboro, NC: Oakhill Press, 1999), p. 167.

(5d) Steve Player and Carol Cobble, *Cornerstones of Decision Making: Profiles of Enterprise ABM* (Greensboro, NC: Oakhill Press, 1999), p. 119.

(5e) Tad Leahy, "The A to Z of ABC Dictionaries," *Business Finance* 5, no. 12 (December 1999), p. 82.

(5f) Steve Player and Carol Cobble, *Cornerstones of Decision Making: Profiles of Enterprise ABM* (Greensboro, NC: Oakhill Press, 1999), p. 151.

(5g) Ibid., p. 226.

(5h) Scott Smith, in Steve Player and Carol Cobble, *Cornerstones of Decision Making: Profiles of Enterprise ABM* (Greensboro, NC: Oakhill Press, 1999), p. 187.

(5i) *The Management Accounting Video,* a management education video (New York: McGraw-Hill, 1997).

Chapter Six

(6a) Paulo Salgado, Margarida Bajanca, and Nuno Belo, in Steve Player and Carol Cobble, *Cornerstones of Decision Making: Profiles of Enterprise ABM* (Greensboro, NC: Oakhill Press, 1999), p. 172.

*The references are organized by chapter. Thus, reference (1a) relates to the first quote in Chapter 1, and so forth.

(6b) Steve Player and Carol Cobble, *Cornerstones of Decision Making: Profiles of Enterprise ABM* (Greensboro, NC: Oakhill Press, 1999), p. 214.

(6c) Interview with a Ford Motor Company accountant conducted during research by the author.

(6d) Company Web site, http://www.nau.com/about/think/true-cost.html (August 2010).

(6e) Richard McDonell, "Do you know your true cost of test?," *Test and Measurement World*, (November 2, 2009).

(6f) Walden Rhines, "Semiconductor Input Costs vs. Output Prices— Managing the Squeeze," *EE Times* (July 15, 2010).

Chapter Seven

(7a) Gary Siegel and James E. Sorensen, principal investigators for the Gary Siegel Organization, *Counting More, Counting Less: Transformations in the Management Accounting Profession* (Montvale, NJ: Institute of Management Accountants, 1999).

(7b) Victor Muller, "Spyker Cars N.V. Reports 2009 Full Year Results," http://www.spykercars.com/download/investor/Spyker_Cars_N_V_reports_2009_full_year_results.pdf (March 26, 2010).

(7c) Nick Reilly, "Personal Message from Nick Reilly to the Opel/Vauxhall employees," http://media.opel.com/content/media/intl/en/news/news_detail.brand_opel.html/content/Pages/news/intl/en/2010/OPEL/01_15_message_reilly (January 19, 2010).

(7d) Gary Siegel and James E. Sorensen, principal investigators for the Gary Siegel Organization, *Counting More, Counting Less: Transformations in the Management Accounting Profession* (Montvale, NJ: Institute of Management Accountants, 1999).

(7e) Steve Player and Carol Cobble, *Cornerstones of Decision Making: Profiles of Enterprise ABM* (Greensboro, NC: Oakhill Press, 1999), p. 78.

Chapter Eight

(8a) Timothy Aeppel, "Firms Race to Regain Control Over Inventories," *The Wall Street Journal* (February 9, 2009).

Chapter Nine

(9a) *The Management Accounting Video,* a management education video (New York: McGraw-Hill, 1997). Best Foods introduced several well-known brands, such as Skippy peanut butter, Hellman's mayonnaise, and Thomas' English Muffins. Best Foods was acquired by Unilever in 2000.

(9b) Anne Stuart, "The Importance of Accurate Forecasting: A CFO's Perspective," *Sales Performance Journal* (March 2006).

(9c) Gary Siegel and James E. Sorensen, principal investigators for the Gary Siegel Organization, *Counting More, Counting Less: Transformations in the Management Accounting Profession* (Montvale, NJ: Institute of Management Accountants, 1999).

(9d) Jay Collins, "Advanced Use of ABM: Using ABC for Target Costing, Activity-Based Budgeting, and Benchmarking," in *Activity-Based Management: Arthur Andersen's Lessons from the ABM Battlefield,* ed. Steve Player and David E. Keys (New York: John Wiley & Sons, 1999), p. 153.

(9e) James A. Brimson and John Antos, *Driving Value Using Activity-Based Budgeting* (New York: John Wiley & Sons, 1999), p. 10.

(9f) Steve Hornyak, "Budgeting Made Easy," *Management Accounting* 80, no. 4 (October 1998), pp. 18–23.

Chapter Ten

(10a) *The Management Accounting Video,* a management education video (New York: McGraw-Hill, 1997).

(10b) African Performance Specialists, "Purchasing Efficiency Improvement Project," *APS NewsLetter* (October 2008).

(10c) *The Management Accounting Video,* a management education video (New York: McGraw-Hill, 1997).

(10d) Rockwell Collins, "*Engineer of the Year* Awards," *Horizons Online* 15, Issue 2 (2010).

(10e) David Johnsen and Parvez Sopariwala, "Standard Costing Is Alive and Well at Parker Brass," *Management Accounting Quarterly* 1, no. 2 (Winter 2000), p. 13.

(10f) *The Management Accounting Video,* a management education video (New York: McGraw-Hill, 1997).

(10g) *The Balanced Scorecard,* a management education video (Boston: The President and Fellows of Harvard College, 1993).

(10h) Mark Green, Jeanine Garrity, Andra Gumbus, and Bridget Lyons, "Pitney Bowes Calls for New Metrics," *Strategic Finance* 83, no. 11 (May 2002), p. 34.

Chapter Eleven

(11a) Gary Siegel and James E. Sorensen, principal investigators for the Gary Siegel Organization, *Counting More, Counting Less: Transformations in the Management Accounting Profession* (Montvale, NJ: Institute of Management Accountants, 1999).

(11b) Interview with an A. T. Kearney consultant conducted during research by the author.

(11c) Hugh Waters et al., "Application of Activity-Based Costing (ABC) in a Peruvian NGO Healthcare System," *Operations Research Results* 1(3, Revised) (Bethesda, MD: Quality Assurance Project (QAP), 2003), p. ii.

(11d) Cynthia Beier Greeson and Mehmet C. Kocakulah, "Implementing an ABC Pilot at Whirlpool," *Journal of Cost Management* 11, no. 2 (March/April 1997), pp. 16–21.

(11e) Interview with an A. T. Kearney consultant conducted during research by the author.

Chapter Twelve

(12a) Interview with Chrysler accountant conducted during research by the author.

(12b) Gary Siegel and James E. Sorensen, principal investigators for the Gary Siegel Organization, *Counting More, Counting Less: Transformations in the Management Accounting Profession* (Montvale, NJ: Institute of Management Accountants, 1999).

(12c) Ibid.

(12d) Company presentation at www.univarcorp.com/040506/UKUnivarAGM-1.ppt (May 2004).

(12e) Gary Siegel and James E. Sorensen, principal investigators for the Gary Siegel Organization, *Counting More, Counting Less: Transformations in the Management Accounting Profession* (Montvale, NJ: Institute of Management Accountants, 1999).

(12f) GE company Web site www.ge.com/en/company/companyinfo/quality/whatis.htm (2010).

Chapter Thirteen

(13a) Gary Siegel and James E. Sorensen, principal investigators for the Gary Siegel Organization, *Counting More, Counting Less: Transformations in the Management Accounting Profession* (Montvale, NJ: Institute of Management Accountants, 1999).

(13b) Thomas P. Kunes, "Environmental Cost Management," *Strategic Finance,* February 2001, p. 83.

(13c) *Current Practices, Perceptions and Trends: Transfer Pricing— 1997 Global Survey* (Chicago: Ernst & Young, 1997), p. 1.

(13d) Ibid., p. 4.

(13e) Ibid., p. 11.

(13f) Ibid., p. 11.

Chapter Fourteen

(14a) Gary Siegel and James E. Sorensen, principal investigators for the Gary Siegel Organization, *Counting More, Counting Less: Transformations in the Management Accounting Profession* (Montvale, NJ: Institute of Management Accountants, 1999).

(14b) Gary Siegel and James E. Sorensen, principal investigators for the Gary Siegel Organization, *Counting More, Counting Less: Transformations in the Management Accounting Profession* (Montvale, NJ: Institute of Management Accountants, 1999).

(14c) Ibid.

(14d) Ibid.

(14e) Ibid.

Chapter Fifteen

(15a) Gary Siegel and James E. Sorensen, principal investigators for the Gary Siegel Organization, *Counting More, Counting Less: Transformations in the Management Accounting Profession* (Montvale, NJ: Institute of Management Accountants, 1999).

(15b) Ibid.

(15c) Walter L. Baker, Michael V. Marn, and Craig C. Zawada, "The Payoff from Investing in Pricing Capabilities," *IndustryWeek* (September 8, 2010).

(15d) From Nau, Inc. company Web site at www.nau.com/about/think/true-cost.html (September 2010).

(15e) Presentation by U.S. Navy Acquisition Center, *The Second Annual International Conference on Target Costing,* sponsored by the Consortium for Advanced Manufacturing—International, Arthur Andersen, Ernst & Young, and the University of Akron (Washington, DC: CAM-I, 1998).

(15f) Presentation by Eastman Kodak Company, *The Second Annual International Conference on Target Costing,* sponsored by the Consortium for Advanced Manufacturing—International, Arthur Andersen, Ernst & Young, and the University of Akron (Washington, DC: CAM-I, 1998).

(15g) Presentation by Honda of America, *The Second Annual International Conference on Target Costing,* sponsored by the Consortium for Advanced Manufacturing—International, Arthur Andersen, Ernst & Young, and the University of Akron (Washington, DC: CAM-I, 1998).

(15h) Ibid.

Chapter Sixteen

(16a) Interview with a Ford Motor Company accountant conducted during research by the author.

(16b) Interview with a Hewlett-Packard accountant conducted during research by the author.

(16c) Neil Hughes, "Apple's 2010 Capital Expenditures Could Signal Major Investments," *AppleInsider.com* (November 2, 2009).

(16d) Interview with a Boeing Company accountant conducted during research by the author.

(16e) Interview with an A. T. Kearney consultant conducted during research by the author.

Chapter Seventeen

(17a) Interview with a Chrysler accountant conducted during research by the author.

(17b) Interview with a Cornell University accountant conducted during research by the author.

(17c) David Mountain, "For Cost Reduction, Streamline Support Services," *Mint,* April 2, 2009.

(17d) Interview with an A. T. Kearney consultant conducted during research by the author.

absorption costing (or **full costing**) A method of product costing in which both variable and fixed manufacturing overhead are included in the product costs that flow through the manufacturing accounts (i.e., Work-in-Process Inventory, Finished-Goods Inventory, and Cost of Goods Sold). 361

acceptance-or-rejection decision A decision as to whether or not a particular capital investment proposal should be accepted. 720

account-classification method (also called **account analysis**) A cost-estimation method involving a careful examination of the ledger accounts for the purpose of classifying each cost as variable, fixed, or semivariable. 279

accounting-rate-of-return method A percentage formed by taking a project's average incremental revenue minus its average incremental expenses (including depreciation and income taxes) and dividing by the project's initial investment. 746

accumulation factor The value of $(1 + r)^n$, in a future value calculation, where r denotes the interest rate per year and n denotes the number of years. 809

accurate information Precise and correct data. 628

activity A measure of an organization's output of goods or services. 84

activity accounting The collection of financial or operational performance information about significant activities in an enterprise. 59

activity analysis The detailed identification and description of the activities conducted in an enterprise. 220

activity base (or **cost driver**) A measure of an organization's activity that is used as a basis for specifying cost behavior. The activity base also is used to compute a predetermined overhead rate. The current trend is to refer to the activity base as a volume-based cost driver. 123

activity-based budgeting (ABB) The process of developing a master budget using information obtained from an activity-based costing (ABC) analysis. 387

activity-based costing (ABC) system A two-stage procedure used to assign overhead costs to products or services produced. In the first stage, significant activities are identified, and overhead costs are assigned to activity cost pools in accordance with the way resources are consumed by the activities. In the second stage, the overhead costs are allocated from each activity cost pool to each product line in proportion to the amount of the cost driver consumed by the product line. 59, 206

activity-based flexible budget A flexible budget based on several cost drivers rather than on a single, volume-based cost driver. 508

activity-based management (ABM) Using an activity-based costing system to improve the operations of an organization. 59, 220

activity-based responsibility accounting A system for measuring the performance of an organization's people and subunits, which focuses not only on the cost of performing activities but on the activities themselves. 548

activity cost pool A grouping of overhead costs assigned to various similar activities identified in an activity-based costing system. 206

activity dictionary A complete listing of the activities included in an organization's ABC analysis. 219

actual costing A product-costing system in which actual direct-material, direct-labor, and *actual* manufacturing-overhead costs are added to Work-in-Process Inventory. 136

actual manufacturing overhead The actual costs incurred during an accounting period for manufacturing overhead. Includes actual indirect material, indirect labor, and other manufacturing costs. 130

actual overhead rate The rate at which overhead costs are actually incurred during an accounting period. Calculated as follows: actual manufacturing overhead ÷ actual cost driver (or activity base). Supp

after-tax cash flow The cash flow expected after all tax implications have been taken into account. 731

after-tax net income An organization's net income after its income-tax expense is subtracted. 338

aggregate (or **total**) **productivity** Total output divided by total input. 460

allocation base A measure of activity, physical characteristic, or economic characteristic that is associated with the responsibility centers that are the cost objects in an allocation process. 546, Supp*

annuity A series of equivalent cash flows. 810

applied manufacturing overhead The amount of manufacturing-overhead costs added to Work-in-Process Inventory during an accounting period. 129

appraisal costs Costs of determining whether defective products exist. 553

attention-directing function The function of managerial accounting information in pointing out to managers issues that need their attention. 41

average cost per unit The total cost of producing a particular quantity of product divided by the number of units produced. 92

average revenue curve *See* **demand curve.**

avoidable expenses Expenses that will no longer be incurred if a particular action is taken. 639

balanced scorecard A model of business performance evaluation that balances measures of financial performance, internal operations, innovation and learning, and customer satisfaction. 43

batch-level activity An activity that must be accomplished for each batch of products rather than for each unit. 207

batch manufacturing High-volume production of several product lines that differ in some important ways but are nearly identical in others. 182

benchmarking (or **competitive benchmarking**) The continual search for the most effective method of accomplishing a task, by

---

*Supp refers to Supplement. Several terms defined in this glossary appear in the various supplements to the text, rather than in the text itself. See page 17 for a list of supplements to this textbook.

comparing existing methods and performance levels with those of other organizations or with other subunits within the same organization.   461

best practices   The most effective methods of accomplishing various tasks in a particular industry, often discovered through benchmarking.   Supp

bill of activities (for a product or service)   A complete listing of the activities required for that product or service to be produced.   219

bill of materials   A list of all the materials needed to manufacture a product or product component.   122

break-even point   The volume of activity at which an organization's revenues and expenses are equal. May be measured either in units or in sales dollars.   311

budget   A detailed plan, expressed in quantitative terms, that specifies how resources will be acquired and used during a specified period of time.   380

budget administration   The procedures used to prepare a budget, secure its approval, and disseminate it to the people who need to know its contents.   Supp

budget committee   A group of top-management personnel who advise the budget director during the preparation of the budget.   406

budget director (or **chief budget officer**)   The individual designated to be in charge of preparing an organization's budget.   406

budget manual   A set of written instructions that specify who will provide budgetary data, when and in what form the data will be provided, how the master budget will be prepared and approved, and who should receive the various schedules constituting the budget.   406

budget period   The time period covered by a budget.   Supp

budgetary slack   The difference between the budgetary projection provided by an individual and his or her best estimate of the item being projected. (For example, the difference between a supervisor's expected departmental utility cost and his or her budgetary projection for utilities.)   409

budgeted balance sheet   Shows the expected end-of-period balances for the company's assets, liabilities, and owners' equity.   402

budgeted financial statements (or **pro forma financial statements**)   A set of planned financial statements showing what an organization's overall financial condition is expected to be at the end of the budget period if planned operations are carried out.   383

budgeted income statement   Shows the expected revenue and expenses for a budget period, assuming that planned operations are carried out.   400

budgeted schedule of cost of goods manufactured and sold   Details the direct material, direct labor, and manufacturing overhead costs to be incurred and shows the cost of the goods to be sold during a budget period.   399

budgeted statement of cash flows   A budget schedule providing information about the expected sources and uses of cash for operating activities, investing activities, and financing activities during a particular period of time.   401

budgeting system   The set of procedures used to develop a budget.   382

by-product   A joint product with very little value relative to the other joint products.   787

CAD/CAM system   *See* **computer-aided design** and **computer-aided manufacturing.**

capacity   The upper limit on the amount of goods or services that an organization can produce in a specified period of time.   52

capital budget   A long-term budget that shows planned acquisition and disposal of capital assets, such as land, buildings, and equipment.   383

capital-budgeting decision   A decision involving cash flows beyond the current year.   720

capital-intensive   A production process accomplished largely by machinery.   Supp

capital-rationing decision   A decision in which management chooses which of several investment proposals to accept to make the best use of limited investment funds.   720

capital turnover   Sales revenue divided by invested capital.   585

cash bonus   *See* **pay for performance.**

cash budget   Details the expected cash receipts and disbursements during a budget period.   398

cash disbursements budget   A schedule detailing expected cash payments during a budget period.   397

cash receipts budget   A schedule detailing the expected cash collections during the budget period.   396

cellular manufacturing   The organization of a production facility into FMS cells.   Supp

Certified Management Accountant (CMA)   An accountant who has earned professional certification in managerial accounting.   63

chief financial officer (CFO)   An organization's top managerial and financial accountant. (*See also* **controller.**)   48

coefficient of determination   A statistical measure of goodness of fit; a measure of how closely a regression line fits the data on which it is based.   291

committed cost   A cost that results from an organization's ownership or use of facilities and its basic organization structure.   277

common costs   Costs incurred to benefit more than one organizational segment.   549

competitive benchmarking   *See* **benchmarking.**

competitive bidding   A situation where two or more companies submit bids (prices) for a product, service, or project to a potential buyer.   697

compound interest   The interest earned on prior periods' interest.   808

comptroller   *See* **controller.**

computer-aided design (CAD) system   Computer software used by engineers in the design of a product.   Supp

computer-integrated manufacturing (CIM) system   The most advanced form of automated manufacturing, in which virtually all parts of the production process are accomplished by computer-controlled machines and automated material-handling equipment.   Supp

computer-numerically-controlled (CNC) machines   Standalone machines controlled by a computer via a numerical, machine-readable code.   Supp

constraints   Algebraic expressions of limitations faced by a firm, such as those limiting its productive resources.   654

consumption ratio The proportion of an activity consumed by a particular product. 215

continuous improvement The constant effort to eliminate waste, reduce response time, simplify the design of both products and processes, and improve quality and customer service. 58

contribution income statement An income statement on which fixed and variable expenses are separated. 328

contribution margin Sales revenue minus variable expenses. The amount of sales revenue, which is left to cover fixed expenses and profit after paying variable expenses. Supp

contribution margin per unit The difference between the unit sales price and the unit variable expense. The amount that each unit contributes to covering fixed expenses and profit. Supp

contribution-margin ratio The unit contribution margin divided by the sales price per unit. Also may be expressed in percentage form; then it is called the contribution-margin percentage. 313

controllability The extent to which managers are able to control or influence a cost or cost variance. 451

controllable cost A cost that is subject to the control or substantial influence of a particular individual. 89

controller (or **comptroller**) The top managerial and financial accountant in an organization. Supervises the accounting department and assists management at all levels in interpreting and using managerial-accounting information. (*See also* **chief financial officer.**) 48

controlling Ensuring that an organization operates in the intended manner and achieves its goals. Supp

conversion costs Direct-labor cost plus manufacturing-overhead cost. 81

cost The sacrifice made, usually measured by the resources given up, to achieve a particular purpose. 72

cost accounting system Part of the basic accounting system that accumulates cost for use in both managerial and financial accounting. 45

cost allocation The process of assigning costs in a cost pool to the appropriate cost objects. *See also* **cost distribution.** 546

cost behavior The relationship between cost and activity. 268

cost center A responsibility center whose manager is accountable for its costs. 540

cost distribution (sometimes called **cost allocation**) The first step in assigning manufacturing-overhead costs. Overhead costs are assigned to all departmental overhead centers. 138

cost driver A characteristic of an activity or event that results in the incurrence of costs by that activity or event. 61, 84, 217

cost estimation The process of determining how a particular cost behaves. 268

cost hierarchy The classification of activities into levels, such as unit-level, batch-level, product-sustaining level, and facility-level activities. 207

cost management system (CMS) A management planning and controlling system that measures the cost of significant activities, identifies non-value-added costs, and identifies activities that will improve organizational performance. 59

cost objects Responsibility centers, products, or services to which costs are assigned. 86, 546

cost of capital The cost of acquiring resources for an organization, either through debt or through the issuance of stock. Supp

cost of goods manufactured The total cost of direct material, direct labor, and manufacturing overhead transferred from Work-in-Process Inventory to Finished-Goods Inventory during an accounting period. 81, 133

cost of goods sold The expense measured by the cost of the finished goods sold during a period of time. 73

cost-plus pricing A pricing approach in which the price is equal to cost plus a markup. 686

cost pool A collection of costs to be assigned to a set of cost objects. 546

cost prediction Forecast of cost at a particular level of activity. 268

cost structure The relative proportions of an organization's fixed and variable costs. 329

cost variance The difference between actual and standard cost. 441

cost-volume-profit (CVP) analysis A study of the relationships between sales volume, expenses, revenue, and profit. 310

cost-volume-profit (CVP) graph A graphical expression of the relationships between sales volume, expenses, revenue, and profit. 314

cross-elasticity The extent to which a change in a product's price affects the demand for substitute products. 685

curvilinear cost A cost with a curved line for its graph. 274

customer-acceptance measures The extent to which a firm's customers perceive its product to be of high quality. 460

customer-profitability analysis Using the concepts of activity-based costing to determine the activities, costs, and profit associated with serving particular customers. 223, 551

customer-profitability profile A graphical portrayal of a company's customer profitability analysis. 226

cycle time *See* **throughput time.** 137

decentralization A form of organization in which subunit managers are given authority to make substantive decisions. Supp

decision making Choosing between alternatives. Supp

decision variables The variables in a linear program about which a decision is made. 654

delivery cycle time The average time between the receipt of a customer order and delivery of the goods. 460

demand curve A graph of the relationship between sales price and the quantity of units sold. 682

departmental overhead center Any department to which overhead costs are assigned via overhead cost distribution. 138

departmental overhead rate An overhead rate calculated for a single production department. 138

departmental production report The key document in a process-costing system. This report summarizes the physical flow of units, equivalent units of production, cost per equivalent unit, and analysis of total departmental costs. 174

dependent variable A variable whose value depends on other variables, called *independent variables.* 283

depreciation tax shield The reduction in a firm's income-tax expense due to the depreciation expense associated with a depreciable asset. 733

differential cost The difference in a cost item under two decision alternatives. 91, 632

direct cost A cost that can be traced to a particular department or other subunit of an organization. 86

direct-labor budget A schedule showing the number of hours and cost of direct labor to be used in production of services or goods during a budget period. 392

direct-labor cost The cost of salaries, wages, and fringe benefits for personnel when they are working directly on the manufactured products. 79

direct-labor efficiency variance The difference between actual and standard hours of direct labor multiplied by the standard hourly labor rate. 447

direct-labor rate variance The difference between actual and standard hourly labor rate multiplied by the actual hours of direct labor used. 447

direct material Raw material that is physically incorporated in the finished product. 79

direct-material budget A schedule showing the number of units and the cost of material to be purchased during a budget period. 390

direct-material price variance (or **purchase price variance**) The difference between actual and standard price multiplied by the actual quantity of material purchased. 445

direct-material quantity variance The difference between actual and standard quantity of materials allowed, given actual output, multiplied by the standard price. 445

direct method (of service department cost allocation) A method of service department cost allocation in which service department costs are allocated directly to the production departments. 777

discount rate The interest rate used in computing the present value of a cash flow. 810

discounted-cash-flow analysis An analysis of an investment proposal that takes into account the time value of money. 721

discretionary cost A cost that results from a discretionary management decision to spend a particular amount of money. 277

distribution cost The cost of storing and transporting finished goods for sale. Supp

dual cost allocation An approach to service department cost allocation in which variable costs are allocated in proportion to short-term usage and fixed costs are allocated in proportion to long-term usage. 780

e-budgeting An electronic and enterprisewide budgeting process in which employees throughout the organization can submit and retrieve budget information electronically via the Internet. 406

economic order quantity (EOQ) The order size that minimizes inventory ordering and holding costs. 814

economic value added (EVA) An investment center's after-tax operating income minus the investment center's total assets (net of its current liabilities) times the company's weighted-average cost of capital. 589

electronic data interchange (EDI) The direct exchange between organizations of data via a computer-to-computer interface. Supp

empowerment The concept of encouraging and authorizing workers to take the initiative to improve operations, reduce costs, and improve product quality and customer service. 42

engineered cost A cost that results from a definitive physical relationship with the activity measure. 277

engineering method A cost-estimation method in which a detailed study is made of the process that results in cost incurrence. 285

environmental cost management Strategies for reducing, eliminating, or otherwise controlling environmental costs. 559

environmental costs Costs incurred in dealing with environmental issues. 558

equivalent unit A measure of the amount of production effort applied to a physical unit of production. For example, a physical unit that is 50 percent completed represents one-half of an equivalent unit. 173

estimated manufacturing overhead The amount of manufacturing-overhead cost expected for a specified period of time. Used as the numerator in computing the predetermined overhead rate. Supp

expected value The sum of the possible values for a random variable, each weighted by its probability. 646

expense The consumption of assets for the purpose of generating revenue. 73

experience curve A graph (or other mathematical representation) that shows how a broad set of costs decline as cumulative production output increases. 286

external failure costs Costs incurred because defective products have been sold. 553

facility- (or general-operations-) level activity An activity that is required for an entire production process to occur. 207

feasible region The possible values for decision variables that are not ruled out by constraints. 654

FIFO (first-in, first-out) method A method of process costing in which the cost assigned to the beginning work-in-process inventory is not added to current-period production costs. The cost per equivalent unit calculated under FIFO relates to the current period only. Supp

financial accounting The use of accounting information for reporting to parties outside the organization. 45

financial budget A schedule that outlines how an organization will acquire financial resources during the budget period (for example, through borrowing or sale of capital stock). 383

financial leverage The concept that a relatively small increase in income can provide a proportionately much larger increase in return to the common stockholders. Supp

financial planning model A set of mathematical relationships that express the interactions among the various operational, financial, and environmental events that determine the overall results of an organization's activities. 405

financing activities Transactions involving a company's debt or equity capital. Supp

finished goods Completed products awaiting sale. 77

fixed cost A cost that does not change in total as activity changes. 86, 271

fixed-overhead budget variance The difference between actual and budgeted fixed overhead. 505

fixed-overhead volume variance   The difference between budgeted and applied fixed overhead.   505

flexible budget   A budget that is valid for a range of activity.   495

flexible manufacturing system (FMS)   A series of manufacturing machines, controlled and integrated by a computer, which is designed to perform a series of manufacturing operations automatically.   Supp

FMS cell   A group of machines and personnel within a flexible manufacturing system (FMS).   Supp

full (or absorption) cost   A product's variable cost plus an allocated portion of fixed overhead.   603

future value   The amount to which invested funds accumulate over a specified period of time.   808

gain-sharing plan   An incentive system that specifies a formula by which the cost savings from productivity gains achieved by a company are shared with the workers who helped accomplish the improvements.   461

goal congruence   A meshing of objectives, where managers throughout an organization strive to achieve the goals set by top management.   540, 583

goodness of fit   The closeness with which a regression line fits the data upon which it is based.   284

grade   The extent of a product's capability in performing its intended purpose, viewed in relation to other products with the same functional use.   552

high-low method   A cost estimation method in which a cost line is fit using exactly two data points—the high and low activity levels.   281

homogeneous cost pool   A grouping of overhead costs in which each cost component is consumed in roughly the same proportion by each product line.   Supp

hurdle rate   The minimum desired rate of return used in a discounted-cash-flow analysis.   722

hybrid product-costing system   A system that incorporates features from two or more alternative product-costing systems, such as job-order and process costing.   182

idle time   Unproductive time spent by employees due to factors beyond their control, such as power outages and machine breakdowns.   80

imperfect competition   A market in which a single producer or group of producers can affect the market price.   601

incentive compensation   *See* **pay for performance.**

incremental cost   The increase in cost from one alternative to another.   91

independent variable   The variable upon which an estimate is based in least-squares regression analysis.   283

indirect cost   A cost that cannot be traced to a particular department.   86

indirect labor   All costs of compensating employees who do not work directly on the firm's product but who are necessary for production to occur.   80

indirect-labor budget   A schedule showing the amount and cost of indirect labor to be used during a budget period.   Supp

indirect materials   Materials that either are required for the production process to occur but do not become an integral part of the finished product, or are consumed in production but are insignificant in cost.   80

information overload   The provision of so much information that, due to human limitations in processing information, managers cannot effectively use it.   630

in-process quality controls   Procedures designed to assess product quality before production is completed.   460

inspection time   The time spent on quality inspections of raw materials, partially completed products, or finished goods.   Supp

internal auditor   An accountant who reviews the accounting procedures, records, and reports in both the controller's and treasurer's areas of responsibility.   49

internal control system   A process designed to provide reasonable assurance regarding the achievement of objectives in the following categories: effectiveness and efficiency of operations, reliability of financial reporting, and compliance with applicable laws and regulations.   607, 801

internal failure costs   Costs of correcting defects found prior to product sale.   553

internal rate of return   The discount rate required for an investment's net present value to be zero; also known as the *time-adjusted rate of return.*   722

inventoriable cost   Cost incurred to purchase or manufacture goods. *See also* **product cost.**   74

inventoriable goods   Goods that can be stored before sale, such as durable goods, mining products, and some agricultural products.   Supp

inventory budgets   Schedules that detail the amount and cost of finished-goods, work-in-process, and direct-material inventories expected at the end of a budget period.   Supp

investment center   A responsibility center whose manager is accountable for its profit and for the capital invested to generate that profit.   541, 582

investment opportunity rate   The rate of return an organization can earn on its best alternative investments that are of equivalent risk.   726

job-cost record   A document that records the costs of direct material, direct labor, and manufacturing overhead for a particular production job or batch. The job-cost record is a subsidiary ledger account for the Work-in-Process Inventory account in the general ledger.   120

job-order costing   A product-costing system in which costs are assigned to batches or job orders of production. Used by firms that produce relatively small numbers of dissimilar products.   119

joint cost   The cost incurred in a joint production process before the joint products become identifiable as separate products.   642

joint production process   A production process that results in two or more joint products.   641, 784

joint products   The outputs of a joint production process.   784

just-in-time (JIT) inventory and production management system   A comprehensive inventory and manufacturing control system in which no materials are purchased and no products are manufactured until they are needed.   57, 235

just-in-time (JIT) purchasing   An approach to purchasing management in which materials and parts are purchased only as they are needed.   236

kaizen costing The process of cost reduction during the manufacturing phase of a product. Refers to continual and gradual improvement through small betterment activities. 59

labor-intensive A production process accomplished largely by manual labor. Supp

lag indicators Measures of the final outcomes of earlier management decisions. Supp

lead indicators Performance measures that identify future nonfinancial and financial outcomes to guide management decision making. Supp

lead time The time required to receive inventory after it has been ordered. 816

learning curve A graphical expression of the decline in the average labor time required per unit as cumulative output increases. 286

least-squares regression method A cost estimation method in which the cost line is fit to the data by statistical analysis. The method minimizes the sum of the squared deviations between the cost line and the data points. 282

line positions Positions held by managers who are directly involved in providing the goods or services that constitute an organization's primary goals. 47

make-or-buy (or **outsourcing**) **decision** A decision as to whether a product or service should be produced in-house or purchased from an outside supplier. 636

management by exception A managerial technique in which only significant deviations from expected performance are investigated. 441

management by objectives (MBO) The process of designating the objectives of each subunit in an organization and planning for the achievement of these objectives. Managers at all levels participate in setting goals, which they then will strive to achieve. 583

managerial accounting The process of identifying, measuring, analyzing, interpreting, and communicating information in pursuit of an organization's goals. 38

manufacturing The process of converting raw materials into finished products. Supp

manufacturing costs Costs incurred in a manufacturing process, which consist of direct material, direct labor, and manufacturing overhead. Supp

manufacturing cycle efficiency (MCE) The ratio of process time to the sum of processing time, inspection time, waiting time, and move time. 460

manufacturing cycle time The total amount of production time (or throughput time) required per unit. 460

manufacturing overhead All manufacturing costs other than direct-material and direct-labor costs. 80

manufacturing-overhead budget Shows the cost of overhead expected to be incurred in the production process during the budget period. 393

manufacturing-overhead variance The difference between actual overhead cost and the amount specified in the flexible budget. Supp

marginal cost The extra cost incurred in producing one additional unit of output. 92

marginal cost curve A graph of the relationship between the change in total cost and the quantity produced and sold. 682

marginal revenue curve A graph of the relationship between the change in total revenue and the quantity sold. 682

marketing cost The cost incurred in selling goods or services. Includes order-getting costs and order-filling or distribution costs. Supp

mass-customization A manufacturing environment in which many standardized components are combined to produce custommade products to customer order. 78

master budget (or **profit plan**) A comprehensive set of budgets that covers all phases of an organization's operations for a specified period of time. 383

material-requirements planning (MRP) An operations-management tool that assists managers in scheduling production in each stage of a complex manufacturing process. Supp

material requisition form A document used by the production department supervisor to request the release of raw materials for production. 121

merchandise cost The cost of acquiring goods for resale. Includes purchasing and transportation costs. Supp

merchandising The business of acquiring finished goods for resale, either in a wholesale or a retail operation. Supp

merit pay *See* **pay for performance.**

mixed cost *See* **semivariable cost.**

Modified Accelerated Cost Recovery System (MACRS) The depreciation schedule specified by the United States tax code. 735

multiple regression A statistical method in which a linear (straight-line) relationship is estimated between a dependent variable and two or more independent variables. 284

multistage cost allocation The three-step process in which costs are assigned to products or services: (1) cost distribution (or allocation), (2) service department cost allocation, and (3) cost application. Supp

net present value The present value of a project's future cash flows less the cost of the initial investment. 722

net realizable value A joint product's final sales value less any separable costs incurred after the split-off point. 787

net-realizable-value method A method in which joint costs are allocated to the joint products in proportion to the net realizable value of each joint product. 786

nominal currency The measure used for an actual cash flow that is observed. 757

nominal interest rate The real interest rate plus an additional premium to compensate investors for inflation. 756

non-value-added activities Operations that are either (1) unnecessary and dispensable or (2) necessary, but inefficient and improvable. 220

non-value-added costs The costs of activities that can be eliminated without deterioration of product quality, performance, or perceived value. 59, 220

normal costing A product-costing system in which actual direct-materials, actual direct-labor, and applied manufacturing-overhead costs are added to Work-in-Process Inventory. 134

normalized overhead rate An overhead rate calculated over a relatively long time period. Supp

objective function An algebraic expression of the firm's goal. 654

off-line quality control Activities during the product design and engineering phases that will improve the manufacturability of the product, reduce production costs, and ensure high quality. Supp

oligopolistic market (or **oligopoly**) A market with a small number of sellers competing among themselves. 685

operating activities All activities that are not investing or financing activities. Generally speaking, operating activities include all cash transactions that are involved in the determination of net income. Supp

operating expenses The costs incurred to produce and sell services, such as transportation, repair, financial, or medical services. 76

operating income Profits from operations, excluding nonoperating profits such as interest income as well as interest expense and taxes. 327

operating leverage The extent to which an organization uses fixed costs in its cost structure. The greater the proportion of fixed costs, the greater the operating leverage. 330

operating leverage factor A measure of operating leverage at a particular sales volume. Computed by dividing an organization's total contribution margin by its net income. 330

operation costing A hybrid of job-order and process costing. Direct material is accumulated by batch of products using job-order costing methods. Conversion costs are accumulated by department and assigned to product units by process-costing methods. 182

operational budgets A set of budgets that specify how operations will be carried out to produce an organization's services or goods. 385

opportunity cost The potential benefit given up when the choice of one action precludes selection of a different action. 90, 633

outlier A data point that falls far away from the other points in a scatter diagram and is not representative of the data. 280

out-of-pocket costs Costs incurred that require the expenditure of cash or other assets. 90

outsourcing (or **make-or-buy**) **decision** A decision as to whether a product or service should be produced in-house or purchased from an outside supplier. 636

overapplied overhead The amount by which the period's applied manufacturing overhead exceeds actual manufacturing overhead. 131

overhead application (or **absorption**) The third step in assigning manufacturing-overhead costs. All costs associated with each production department are assigned to the product units on which a department has worked. 123

overhead budget A schedule showing the cost of overhead expected to be incurred in the production of services or goods during a budget period. Supp

overhead cost performance report A report showing the actual and flexible-budget cost levels for each overhead item, together with variable-overhead spending and efficiency variances and fixed-overhead budget variances. 507

overtime premium The extra compensation paid to an employee who works beyond the normal period of time. 80

padding the budget The process of building budgetary slack into a budget by overestimating expenses and underestimating revenue. 409

partial (or **component**) **productivity** Total output (in dollars) divided by the cost of a particular input. 461

participative budgeting The process of involving people throughout an organization in the budgeting process. 410

pay for performance A one-time cash payment to an investment-center manager as a reward for meeting a predetermined criterion on a specified performance measure. 594

payback period The amount of time required for a project's after-tax cash inflows to accumulate to an amount that covers the initial investment. 745

penetration pricing Setting a low initial price for a new product in order to penetrate the market deeply and gain a large and broad market share. 691

percentage of completion The extent to which a physical unit of production has been finished with respect to direct material or conversion activity. Supp

perfect competition A market in which the price does not depend on the quantity sold by any one producer. 601

perfection (or **ideal**) **standard** The cost expected under perfect or ideal operating conditions. 442

performance report A report showing the budgeted and actual amounts, and the variances between these amounts, of key financial results for a person or subunit. 544

period costs Costs that are expensed during the time period in which they are incurred. 74

physical unit An actual item of production, fully or partially completed. Supp

physical-units method A method in which joint costs are allocated to the joint products in proportion to their physical quantities. 785

planning Developing a detailed financial and operational description of anticipated operations. Supp

plantwide overhead rate An overhead rate calculated by averaging manufacturing-overhead costs for the entire production facility. 138

pool rate The cost per unit of the cost driver for a particular activity cost pool. 209

postaudit (or **reappraisal**) A systematic follow-up of a capital-budgeting decision to see how the project turned out. 730

practical capacity The upper limit on the amount of goods or services that an organization can produce in a specified period of time, allowing for normal occurrences such as machine downtime and employee fatigue or illness. 52

practical (or **attainable**) **standard** The cost expected under normal operating conditions. 443

predatory pricing An illegal practice in which the price of a product is set low temporarily to broaden demand. Then the product's supply is restricted and the price is raised. 700

predetermined overhead rate The rate used to apply manufacturing overhead to Work-in-Process Inventory, calculated as: estimated manufacturing overhead cost ÷ estimated amount of cost driver (or activity base). 124

present value The economic value now of a cash flow that will occur in the future. 809

prevention costs Costs of preventing defective products. 553

pre-tax income An organization's income before its income tax expense is subtracted. 338

price discrimination The illegal practice of quoting different prices for the same product or service to different buyers, when the price differences are not justified by cost differences. 700

price elasticity The impact of price changes on sales volume. 685

price takers Firms whose products or services are determined totally by the market. 680

prime costs The costs of direct material and direct labor. 81

principal The amount originally invested, not including any interest earned. 808

process A set of linked activities. 222

process-costing system A product-costing system in which production costs are averaged over a large number of product units. Used by firms that produce large numbers of nearly identical products. 120, 170

process time The amount of time during which a product is actually undergoing conversion activity. Supp

process value analysis (PVA) Another term for *activity analysis,* which is the detailed identification and description of the activities conducted in an enterprise. 222

product cost Cost associated with goods for sale until the time period during which the products are sold, at which time the costs become expenses. See also **inventoriable cost.** 73

product-costing system The process of accumulating the costs of a production process and assigning them to the products that constitute the organization's output. 116

production budget A schedule showing the number of units of services or goods that are to be produced during a budget period. 390

production department A department in which work is done directly on a firm's products. Supp

production Kanban A card specifying the number of parts to be manufactured in a particular work center. 235

product-sustaining-level activity An activity that is needed to support an entire product line but is not always performed every time a new unit or batch of products is produced. 207

profit center A responsibility center whose manager is accountable for its profit. 540

profit plan (or **master budget**) A comprehensive set of budgets that cover all phases of an organization's operations during a specified period of time. 383

profit-volume graph A graphical expression of the relationship between profit and sales volume. 317

profitability index (or **excess present value index**) The present value of a project's future cash flows (exclusive of the initial investment), divided by the initial investment. 744

project costing The process of assigning costs to projects, cases, contracts, programs, or missions in nonmanufacturing organizations. Supp

proration The process of allocating underapplied or overapplied overhead to Work-in-Process Inventory, Finished-Goods Inventory, and Cost of Goods Sold. 132

Public Company Accounting Oversight Board (PCAOB) An organization operating under the auspices of the SEC, whose mission is to oversee and investigate the audits and auditors of public companies, and sanction both firms and individuals for violations of laws, rules, and regulations. 802

pull method A method of coordinating stages in a production process. Goods are produced in each stage of manufacturing only as they are needed in the next stage. 235

qualitative characteristics Factors in a decision analysis that cannot be expressed easily in numerical terms. 627

quality of conformance The extent to which a product meets the specifications of its design. 552

quality of design The extent to which a product is designed to perform well in its intended use. 552

raw material Material entered into a manufacturing process. 77

real currency A measure that reflects an adjustment for the purchasing power of a monetary unit. 757

real interest rate The underlying interest rate in the economy, which includes compensation to an investor for the time value of money and the risk of an investment. 756

reciprocal-services method A method of service department cost allocation that accounts for the mutual provision of reciprocal services among all service departments. 778

regression line A line fit to a set of data points using least-squares regression. 282

relative-sales-value method A method in which joint costs are allocated to the joint products in proportion to their total sales values at the split-off point. 642, 786

relevant information Data that are pertinent to a decision. 628

relevant range The range of activity within which management expects the organization to operate. 275

repetitive production The manufacture of large numbers of identical or very similar products in a continuous flow. 170

research and development (R&D) costs Costs incurred to develop and test new products or services. Supp

residual income Profit minus an imputed interest charge, which is equal to the invested capital times an imputed interest rate. 587

responsibility accounting Tools and concepts used by managerial accountants to measure the performance of an organization's people and subunits. 540

responsibility center A subunit in an organization whose manager is held accountable for specified financial results of its activities. 540

return on investment (ROI) Income divided by invested capital. 584

return-on-investment pricing A cost-plus pricing method in which the markup is determined by the amount necessary for the company to earn a target rate of return on investment. 688

revenue center A responsibility center whose manager is accountable for its revenue. 540

rolling budget (also **revolving** or **continuous budget**) A budget that is continually updated by adding another incremental time period and dropping the most recently completed period. 383

safety margin Difference between budgeted sales revenue and break-even sales revenue. 319

safety stock Extra inventory consumed during periods of above-average usage in a setting with fluctuating demand. Supp

sales budget A schedule that shows the expected sales of services or goods during a budget period, expressed in both monetary terms and units. 389

sales forecasting The process of predicting sales of services or goods. The initial step in preparing a master budget. 384

sales margin Income divided by sales revenue. 585

sales mix Relative proportion of sales of each of an organization's multiple products. 324

sales-price variance The difference between actual and expected unit sales price multiplied by the actual quantity of units sold. 518

sales-volume variance The difference between actual sales volume and budgeted sales volume multiplied by the budgeted unit contribution margin. 518

scatter diagram A set of plotted cost observations at various activity levels. 279

schedule of cost of goods manufactured A detailed schedule showing the manufacturing costs incurred during an accounting period and the change in work-in-process inventory. 81, 133

schedule of cost of goods sold A detailed schedule showing the cost of goods sold and the change in finished-goods inventory during an accounting period. 81, 133

segmented income statement A financial statement showing the income for an organization and its major segments (subunits). 549

selling costs Costs of obtaining and filling sales orders, such as advertising costs, compensation of sales personnel, and product promotion costs. Supp

selling, general, and administrative (SG&A) expense budget A schedule showing the planned amounts of selling, general, and administrative expenses during a budget period. 394

semivariable (or mixed) cost A cost with both a fixed and a variable component. 273

sensitivity analysis A technique for determining what would happen in a decision analysis if a key prediction or assumption proves to be wrong. 326, 645

separable processing cost Cost incurred on a joint product after the split-off point of a joint production process. 643

service department cost allocation The second step in assigning manufacturing-overhead costs. All costs associated with a service department are assigned to the departments that use the services it produces. 138

service (or support) departments Subunits in an organization that are not involved directly in producing the organization's output of goods or services. 80, 138, 774

service-industry firm A firm engaged in production of a service that is consumed as it is produced, such as air transportation service or medical service. Supp

shareholder value analysis Calculation of the residual income associated with a major product line, with the objective of determining how the product line affects a firm's value to its shareholders. 589

simple regression A regression analysis based on a single independent variable. 284

Six Sigma An analytical method that aims at achieving near perfect results in a production process. 555

skimming pricing Setting a high initial price for a new product in order to reap short-run profits. Over time, the price is reduced gradually. 691

source document A document that is used as the basis for an accounting entry. Examples include material requisition forms and direct-labor time tickets. 122

SOX 301 A section of the Sarbanes-Oxley Act that requires companies to establish procedures for handling complaints about accounting and internal controls. Controversial internationally due to its requirement to establish a "whistleblower hotline." 804

SOX 302 A section of the Sarbanes-Oxley Act that requires the signing officers of a company's financial reports to establish, maintain, and periodically evaluate the effectiveness of the company's internal controls over financial reporting. 802

SOX 404 A section of the Sarbanes-Oxley Act that requires a company to include in its annual report an internal control report. 803

split-off point The point in a joint production process at which the joint products become identifiable as separate products. 642, 784

staff positions Positions held by managers who are only indirectly involved in producing an organization's product or service. 48

standard cost A predetermined cost for the production of goods or services that serves as a benchmark against which to compare the actual cost. 440

standard-costing system A cost-control and product-costing system in which cost variances are computed and production costs are entered into work-in-process inventory at their standard amounts. 455

standard direct-labor quantity The number of labor hours normally needed to manufacture one unit of product. 445

standard direct-labor rate Total hourly cost of compensation, including fringe benefits. 445

standard direct-material price The total delivered cost, after subtracting any purchase discounts taken. 444

standard direct-material quantity The total amount of material normally required to produce a finished product, including allowances for normal waste and inefficiency. 444

standard quantity allowed The standard quantity per unit of output multiplied by the number of units of actual output. Supp

statement of cash flows A major financial statement that shows the change in an organization's total cash and cash equivalents and explains that change in terms of the organization's operating, investing, and financing activities during a period. Supp

static budget A budget that is valid for only one planned activity level. 495

statistical control chart A plot of cost variances across time, with a comparison to a statistically determined critical value. 452

step-down method A method of service department cost allocation in which service department costs are allocated first to service departments and then to production departments. 777

step-fixed cost A cost that remains fixed over wide ranges of activity, but jumps to a different amount for activity levels outside that range. 271

step-variable cost A cost that is nearly variable, but increases in small steps instead of continuously. 270

storyboarding   A procedure used to develop a detailed process flowchart, which visually represents activities and the relationships among the activities.   218

strategic cost analysis   A broad-based managerial-accounting analysis that supports strategic management decisions.   Supp

strategic cost management   Overall recognition of the cost relationships among the activities in the value chain, and the process of managing those cost relationships to a firm's advantage.   61

summary cash budget   A combination of the cash receipts and cash disbursements budgets.   Supp

sunk costs   Costs that were incurred in the past and cannot be altered by any current or future decision.   90, 630

supply chain   The flow of all goods, services, and information into and out of an organization.   122

sustainable development   Business activity that produces the goods and services needed in the present without limiting the ability of future generations to meet their needs.   558

target cost   The projected long-run product cost that will enable a firm to enter and remain in the market for the product and compete successfully with the firm's competitors.   692

target costing   The design of a product, and the processes used to produce it, so that ultimately the product can be manufactured at a cost that will enable a firm to make a profit when the product is sold at an estimated market-driven price. This estimated price is called the *target price,* the desired profit margin is called the *target profit,* and the cost at which the product must be manufactured is called the *target cost.*   691

target profit (or **income**)   The profit level set as management's objective.   317

task analysis   Setting standards by analyzing the production process.   442

theoretical capacity   The upper limit on production of goods or services, during a specified period of time, if everything works perfectly (i.e., no employees miss time for illness, no machines break down, there are no unexpected interruptions such as power outages or severe storms, and so forth).   Supp

theory of constraints   A management approach that focuses on identifying and relaxing the constraints that limit an organization's ability to reach a higher level of goal attainment.   61, 460

throughput costing   A product-costing system that assigns only the unit-level spending for direct costs as the cost of products or services.   367

throughput time   The average amount of time required to convert raw materials into finished goods ready to be shipped to customers.   137

time and material pricing   A cost-plus pricing approach that includes components for labor cost and material cost, plus markups on either or both of these cost components.   696

time record   A document that records the amount of time an employee spends on each production job.   123

timely information   Data that are available in time for use in a decision analysis.   629

total contribution margin   Total sales revenue less total variable expenses.   312, 517

total cost curve   Graphs the relationship between total cost and total quantity produced and sold.   682

total quality control (TQC)   A product-quality program in which the objective is complete elimination of product defects.   236

total quality management (TQM)   The broad set of management and control processes designed to focus an entire organization and all of its employees on providing products or services that do the best possible job of satisfying the customer.   58, 555

total revenue curve   Graphs the relationship between total sales revenue and quantity sold.   680

transfer price   The price at which products or services are transferred between two divisions in an organization.   582

transferred-in costs   Costs assigned to partially completed products that are transferred into one production department from a prior department.   172

treasurer   An accountant in a staff position who is responsible for managing an organization's relationships with investors and creditors and maintaining custody of the organization's cash, investments, and other assets.   49

trend analysis   A comparison across time of three or more observations of a particular financial item, such as net income.   Supp

two-dimensional ABC model   A combination of the cost assignment view of the role of activity-based costing with its process analysis and evaluation role. Two-dimensional ABC is one way of depicting activity-based management.   220

two-stage cost allocation   A two-step procedure for assigning overhead costs to products or services produced. In the first stage, all production costs are assigned to the production departments. In the second stage, the costs that have been assigned to each production department are applied to the products or services produced in those departments.   138

unavoidable expenses   Expenses that will continue to be incurred even if a subunit or activity is eliminated.   639

underapplied overhead   The amount by which the period's actual manufacturing overhead exceeds applied manufacturing overhead.   131

unit contribution margin   Sales price minus the unit variable cost.   313, 517

unit-level activity   An activity that must be done for each unit of production.   207

value analysis   *See* **value engineering.**

value chain   An organization's set of linked, value-creating activities, ranging from securing basic raw materials and energy to the ultimate delivery of products and services.   59

value engineering (or **value analysis**)   A cost-reduction and process improvement technique that utilizes information collected about a product's design and production processes and then examines various attributes of the design and processes to identify candidates for improvement efforts.   695

variable cost   A cost that changes in total in direct proportion to a change in an organization's activity.   85, 269

variable costing (or **direct costing**)   A method of product costing in which only variable manufacturing overhead is included as a product cost that flows through the manufacturing accounts (i.e., Work-in-Process Inventory, Finished-Goods Inventory, and

Cost of Goods Sold). Fixed manufacturing overhead is treated as a period cost. 361

variable-overhead efficiency variance The difference between actual and standard hours of an activity base (e.g., machine hours) multiplied by the standard variable-overhead rate. 502

variable-overhead spending variance The difference between actual variable-overhead cost and the product of the standard variable-overhead rate and actual hours of an activity base (e.g., machine hours). 502

velocity The number of units produced in a given time period. 460

vertical analysis An analysis of the relationships among various financial items on a particular financial statement. Generally presented in terms of common-size financial statements. Supp

visual-fit method A method of cost estimation in which a cost line is drawn through a scatter diagram according to the visual perception of the analyst. 279

volume-based cost driver (or **activity base**) A cost driver that is closely associated with production volume, such as direct-labor hours or machine hours. 123

volume-based (or **throughput-based**) **costing system** A product-costing system in which costs are assigned to products on the basis of a single activity base related to volume (e.g., direct-labor hours or machine hours). 205

waiting time The time during which partially completed products wait for the next phase of production. Supp

weighted-average cost of capital (WACC) A weighted average of the after-tax cost of debt capital and the cost of equity capital. 589

weighted-average method A method of process costing in which the cost assigned to beginning work-in-process inventory is added to the current-period production costs. The cost per equivalent unit calculated under this process-costing method is a weighted average of the costs in the beginning work in process and the costs of the current period. 175

weighted-average unit contribution margin Average of a firm's several products' unit contribution margins, weighted by the relative sales proportion of each product. 324

withdrawal Kanban A card sent to the preceding work center indicating the number and type of parts requested from that work center by the next work center. 235

work in process Partially completed products that are not yet ready for sale. 77

working capital Current assets minus current liabilities. 738

Photo Credits

Front Matter

Page 23 left: © HSBC Holdings plc 2010. All rights reserved; 23 right: © PhotoLink/Getty Images/DAL; 24: © Alaska Stock LLC/DAL; 25 left: © Orlin Wagner/AP Images; 25 right: © Patti McConville/Photographer's Choice/Getty Images; 26 left: © Burke/Triolo Productions/Getty Images; 26 right: © Royalty-Free/Corbis; 27 left: © photostock 1/Alamy/DAL; 27 right: © Comstock Images/Alamy/DAL; 28 bottom: © Roulier/Turiot/photocuisine/Corbis; 29 left: © Kike Calvo via AP Images; 29 right: © Ingram Publishing/SuperStock; 30: © Luca Tettoni/Robert Harding World Imagery/Corbis; 31 left: © Marcus Donner/Reuters/Corbis; 31 right: © PhotoLink/Getty Images; 32 left: © Comstock/PunchStock/DAL; 32 right: © Theo van Pelt/Imageshop/DAL.

Chapter One

Page 36 top left: © HSBC Holdings plc 2010. All rights reserved; 36 top right: © HSBC Holdings plc 2010. All rights reserved; 36 bottom: © HSBC Holdings plc 2010. All rights reserved; 37 left: © Castello-Ferbos/Godong/Corbis; 37 middle: © Pawel Liberia/Corbis; 37 right: © Manan Vatsyayana/AFP/Getty Images; 46 left: © PhotoLink/Getty Images; 46 right: © Susan Van Etten/PhotoEdit; 51 top left: © Digital Vision/Getty Images; 51 top right: © Matt Stroshane/Bloomberg/Getty Images; 51 bottom left: © Stockbyte/Getty Images; 51 bottom right: © AP Photo/Jacques Brinon; 60 top left: © Kent Knudson/PhotoLink/Getty Images; 60 top middle: © Royalty-Free/Corbis; 60 bottom left: © JG Photography/Alamy; 60 bottom center: © Lars A Niki/DAL; 60 bottom right: © Lars A Niki/DAL.

Chapter Two

Page 70 top left: © 2009 Jupiterimages Corporation/DAL; 70 top right: © Bananastock/age fotostock; 70 bottom: © PhotoLink/Getty Images/DAL; 71 left: © Collin Young Wolff/PhotoEdit; 71 middle: © ColorBlind Images/Getty Images/DAL; 71 right: © BananaStock/PunchStock; 77 top: © 20th Century Fox. All rights reserved/Courtesy Everett Collection; 77 top middle: © Michael Abramson/Woodfin Camp & Associates; 77 middle: © Royalty-Free/Corbis; 77 bottom middle: © The McGraw-Hill Companies, Inc./Jill Braaten, photographer; 77 bottom: © Malcolm Fife/Getty Images; 84: © Digital Vision/Getty Images.

Chapter Three

Page 114 top left: © Royalty-Free/Corbis/DAL; 114 top right: © Vanderlei Almeida/AFP/Getty Images; 114 bottom: © Alaska Stock LLC/DAL; 115 left: © Spike Mafford/Getty Images/DAL; 115 middle: © image100/PunchStock; 115 right: © Lourens Smak/Alamy/DAL; 119 left: © Creatas Images/DAL; 119 middle: © Chris Kerrigan/DAL; 119 right: © Radius Images/Getty Images; 128: © Gideon Mendel/Corbis.

Chapter Four

Page 168 top left: © AP Photo/Shizuo Kambayashi; 168 top right: © AP Photo/Kyodo News; 168 bottom: © Orlin Wagner/AP Images; 169 left: © Brand X Pictures/PunchStock/DAL; 169 middle: © Stockdisc/PunchStock/DAL; 169 right: © Brand X Pictures/PunchStock/DAL; 174 left: © Royalty-Free/Corbis 174 right: © Eric Martin, photographer/Iconotec.

Chapter Five

Page 202 top left: © Purestock/PunchStock; 202 top right: © BananaStock/PunchStock; 202 bottom: © Patti McConville/Photographer's Choice/Getty Images; 203 left: © Masterfile Royalty-Free; 203 middle: © Dennis MacDonald/Alamy/DAL; 203 right: © Ryan McVay/Getty Images; 212 left: © Royalty-Free/Corbis; 212 right: © Monty Rakusen/Getty Images;

219 left: © Flying Colours Ltd/Getty Images; 219 right: © Ronald W. Hilton; 227: © The McGraw-Hill Companies, Inc./Andrew Resek, photographer.

Chapter Six

Page 266 top left: © Chris Kasson/AP Images; 266 top right: © Roy Ooms/All Canada Photos/Corbis; 266 bottom: © Burke/Triolo Productions/Getty Images; 267 left: © John Raoux/AP Images; 267 middle: © Ingram Publishing/SuperStock; 267 right: © Photodisc/Getty Images; 277: © Bloomberg/Getty Images.

Chapter Seven

Page 308 top left: © Siri Stafford/Getty Images; 308 top right: © Jeff Greenberg/The Image Works; 308 bottom: © Royalty-Free/Corbis; 309 left: © Nick Koudis/Getty Images; 309 middle: © TRB foto/Getty Images/DAL; 309 right: © JupiterImages/Brand X/Corbis; 312 left: © Cultura RF/Getty Images; 312 right: © The McGraw-Hill Companies, Inc./Jill Braaten, photographer; 324: © George Hall/Corbis; 334: © Lonnie Duka/Getty Images.

Chapter Eight

Page 358 top left: © PhotoAlto/Frederic Cirou/Getty Images; 358 top right: © John A. Rizzo/Getty Images/DAL; 358 bottom: © photostock 1/Alamy/DAL; 359 left: © AP Photo/Eric F.Marti; 359 middle: © Stockbyte/PunchStock; 359 right: © Greatstock Photographic Library/Alamy/DAL; 362: © Ryan Pyle/Corbis.

Chapter Nine

Page 380 top left: © Corbis/DAL; 380 top right: © Royalty-Free/Corbis/DAL; 380 bottom: © Comstock Images/Alamy/DAL; 381 left: © Royalty-Free/Corbis; 381 middle: © Photodisc/Getty; 381 right: © Jupiterimages/DAL; 383: © Karen Bleier/AFP/Getty Images; 385: © Jack Kurtz/The Image Works; 407: © The McGraw-Hill Companies, Inc./Barry Barker, photographer.

Chapter Ten

Page 438 top left: © Photodisc/Getty Images; 438 top left: © Brand X Pictures/PunchStock; 438 bottom: © Roulier/Turiot/photocuisine/Corbis; 439 left: © Photodisc/SuperStock; 439 middle: © Ariel Skelley/Getty Images; 439 right: © Royalty-Free/Corbis; 443: © Press Association/AP Images; 457: Courtesy of Texas Instruments; 464: © Digital Vision/PunchStock.

Chapter Eleven

Page 492 top left: © Stockbyte/Getty Images; 492 top right: © AP Photo/Laurent Cipriani; 492 bottom: © Kike Calvo via AP Images; 493 left: © Darren McCollester/Getty Images; 493 middle: © Royalty-Free/Corbis; 493 right: © AP Photo/Michael Sohn; 500 left: © Elmer Martinez/AFP/Getty Images; 500 right: © Andreas Rentz/Getty Images; 511: © Digital Vision/Getty Images.

Chapter Twelve

Page 538 top left: © AP Photo/Kamran Jebrelli; 538 top right: © AP Photo/Kamran Jebrelli; 538 bottom: © Ingram Publishing/SuperStock; 539 left: © AP Photo/Vahid Salemi; 539 middle: © AP Photo/Mississippi Department of Corrections/Kent Crocker; 539 right: © Kaveh Kazemi/Getty Images; 541 top left: © Jim West/The Image Images; 541 top right: © Image Source/Getty Images/DAL; 541 bottom left: © Brand X Pictures/PunchStock; 541 bottom right: © Patrick Baz/AFP/Getty Images.

Chapter Thirteen

Page 580 top left: © Imaginechina via AP Images; 580 top right: © Jon Feingersh/Getty Images; 580 bottom: © Luca Tettoni/Robert Harding World Imagery/Corbis; 581 left: © Sylvain Grandadam/Getty Images; 581 middle: © AP Photo/Wong Maya_E; 581 right: © Royalty-Free/Corbis; 587: © Royalty-Free/Corbis; 597: © Ali Haider/epa/Corbis; 606: © D. & I. MacDonald/Photolibrary.

Chapter Fourteen

Page 624 top left: © Inti St. Clair/Getty Images/DAL; 624 top right: © Steve Allen/Getty Images; 624 bottom: © Marcus Donner/Reuters/Corbis; 625 left: © Bloomberg/Getty Images; 625 middle: © Maximilian Stock Ltd/Getty Images; 625 right: © Royalty-Free/Corbis/DAL; 638 left: © Digital Vision/PunchStock/DAL; 638 right: © vario images GmbH & Co.KG/Alamy.

Chapter Fifteen

Page 676 top left: © Wiesenhofer/PhotoLink/Getty Images; 676 top right: © AP Photo/Greg Wood; 676 bottom: © PhotoLink/Getty Images; 677 left: © Daniel Munoz/Reuters/Landov; 677 middle: © Dennis MacDonald/PhotoEdit; 677 right: © Kelly-Mooney Photography/Corbis; 680: © AP Photo/Vincent Thian.

Chapter Sixteen

Page 718 top left: © Scenics of America/PhotoLink/Getty Images; 718 top right: © James Hardy/PaloAlto/DAL; 718 bottom: © Comstock/PunchStock/DAL; 719 left: © Junior Gonzalez/Getty Images/DAL; 719 middle: © Brand X Pictures/Getty Images; 719 right: © Digital Vision/SuperStock; 731: © Maximilian Stock Ltd/Getty Images; 736: © Bob Pool/ Getty Images.

Chapter Seventeen

Page 772 top left: © Flying Colours Ltd/Getty Images/DAL; 772 top right: © Photodisc Collection/Getty Images/DAL; 772 bottom: © Theo van Pelt/Imageshop/DAL; 773 left: © L. Hobbs/PhotoLink/Getty Images; 773 middle: © Iconotec/Alamy; 773 right: © PhotoAlto/PunchStock; 784: © Lester Lefkowitz/Corbis.

Page numbers followed by n refer to notes.

Index of Subjects

Page numbers followed by n refer to notes.